The Sage Handbook of
Brand Management

The Sage Handbook of
Brand Management

Edited by

Lia Zarantonello and
Daniela Andreini

Sage

Sage

1 Oliver's Yard
55 City Road
London EC1Y 1SP

2455 Teller Road
Thousand Oaks, California 91320

10th Floor, Emaar Capital Tower 2
MG Road, Sikanderpur, Sector 26
Gurugram, Haryana – 122002
India

8 Marina View Suite 43-053
Asia Square Tower 1
Singapore 018960

Editor: Rhoda Toweh
Editorial Assistant: Benedict Hegarty
Production Editor: Gourav Kumar
Copyeditor: Mahalakshmi Nagarajan
Proofreader: Shirley Hridayadas
Indexer: Nova Techset Private Limited
Marketing Manager: Danielle Nemeth
Cover Design: Siam Ginkhan
Typeset by Nova Techset Private Limited
Printed in the UK

Library of Congress Control Number: 2025947482

British Library Cataloguing in Publication data

A catalogue record for this book is available from the British Library

ISBN 978-1-5296-9295-2

Contents

Notes on Editors and Contributors viii

Introduction xxi
Lia Zarantonello and Daniela Andreini

PART 1 INTRODUCTION TO BRAND MANAGEMENT

1 The Resilience of the Brand Management System: Historical Perspective and Current Challenges 3
Isabelle Aimé, Fabienne Berger-Remy, and Marie-Eve Laporte

2 Perspectives on Brand Management 18
Tilde Heding

3 Corporate Brand Management: Formation and Evolution Since the 1990s 33
John M. T. Balmer

4 Global Branding: Past, Present and Future 50
Ayşegül Özsomer and Selin Altaras

5 Brand Management Across Countries and Cultures: The Challenges and Opportunities 68
Laurence Minsky and Ilan Geva

PART 2 FOUNDATIONS OF BRAND MANAGEMENT

6 Visual Brand Identity: The Role of Logos in Brand Management 83
Minjung Kim and Joon Ho Lim

7 Brand Identity, Brand Reputation and Brand Image in the B2B Context 98
Sheena Leek

8 B2C and B2B Brand Personality in a Digital World 118
Mijka Ghorbani

9 Brand Authenticity: Conceptualization and Future Directions 133
Filipa Rosado-Pinto and Sandra Maria Correia Loureiro

10 Unraveling Brand Equity: A Theoretical Review and Directions for Future Research 146
Salvador del Barrio-García, Juan Miguel Alcántara-Pilar, María Eugenia Rodríguez-López, Álvaro J. Rojas-Lamorena, and Beatriz García-Carrión

11 Employee-Based Brand Equity 162
Irina Gorea and Jenna Jacobson

PART 3 STRATEGIC BRAND MANAGEMENT

12 Principles of Corporate Brand Management 177
John M. T. Balmer

13 Brand Portfolio Auditing and Brand Architecture Strategy 197
Clarinda Jansberg

14 'What's in a Name?' A Discourse on Brand Naming 212
Sunny Vijay Arora, Arti D. Kalro, and Dinesh Sharma

15 Co-Branding Strategy: Theoretical Perspectives, Contemporary Practices and Research Directions 229
Ceyda Paydas Turan

16 Brand Relationships 245
Cleopatra Veloutsou, Asli Tolunay, Sergio Andrés Osuna-Ramírez, and Hui Chen

17 Brand Management in Times of Crisis 259
Robert Karaszewski

18 Managing Luxury Brands: Strategies in Brand Management 274
Gabriele Murtas and George Christodoulides

19 Business-to-Business Brand Management: Insights for Entrepreneurship 289
Susan M. Mudambi and Jessica Keech

PART 4 BRAND MANAGEMENT PERFORMANCE

20 Positive Brand-Related Constructs: Antecedents, Outcomes and Moderators 309
Faheem Gul Gilal, Jian Zhang, Zhiyong Yang, and Shadma Shahid

21 Negative Emotions Towards Brands: Theoretical Perspectives, Measurement and Future Research 323
Daniela Andreini and Lia Zarantonello

22 Enhancing Brand Experience in the Digital Transformation Age: Insights from Qualitative and Quantitative Research Methodologies 338
Michela Addis and Giulia Miniero

23 Brand Engagement Overview: Definitions, Measurements and Strategies 355
Valentina Mazzoli

24 The Role of Consumption Communities in Brand Value Co-Creation and Co-Destruction 373
Daniele Dalli

25 Internal Branding for Practice and Research: Guidance for Its Definition, Implementation and Outcomes Measurement 390
David Barros-Arrieta

26 Unraveling the Complexity of Brand Performance: Holistic Framework and Practical Guidelines 403
M. Berk Ataman, Koen Pauwels, and Burcu Sezen

27 An Overview of Brand Metrics: Monitoring Brand's Competitive Standing 429
Jacek Kall

PART 5 CONTEMPORARY ISSUES IN BRAND MANAGEMENT

28 Brand Morality: A Critical Review and Contemporary Challenges 447
Yunyi Wei, Kokho (Jason) Sit, and Yuksel Ekinci

29 Brand Social Responsibility 467
Bianca Grohmann

30 Diversity, Equity and Inclusion in Branding 482
Zoe Lee, Rossella C. Gambetti, and Sharifah Faridah Syed Alwi

31 Brands in the Firing Line: Unveiling the Cultural Controversies of Contemporary Brand Activism 495
Angela A. Beccanulli, Silvia Biraghi, and Rossella C. Gambetti

32 Branding for Impact in Nonprofit Organizations: Understanding the Strategies 508
Lara Mendes Christ Bonella Sepulcri and Emerson Wagner Mainardes

33 Brand Happiness as a Promising Brand Asset: Important Empirical Insights 521
Manfred Bruhn, Stefanie Stilz, and Anja Zimmermann

34 Technology-Augmented Brand Management 537
Saleh Bazi

35 The Influencer Effect: Mapping Influencer Marketing in Brand Management 556
Martina Quadri and Liselot Hudders

36 Play Smart, Win Big: How Game Elements Can Benefit Brands 571
Laurence Dessart and Lisa Baiwir

PART 6 FUTURE DIRECTIONS IN BRAND MANAGEMENT

37 Augmenting Brands: Harnessing Artificial Intelligence for Brand Management 589
Yang Cheng, Mengge Yang, and Chen Lin

38 Branding and Ageing Consumers: Breaking the Stereotype 605
Carolyn Wilson-Nash

39 Becoming Conscientious: How Brands Can Shape a Better World 619
Nicholas Ind, Michela Mingione, and Oriol Iglesias

Index 633

Notes on Editors and Contributors

EDITORS

Lia Zarantonello is a Professor of Marketing at Roehampton University in London. Previously, she has held academic positions at prestigious universities in the UK, France and Italy and has been a visiting scholar at renowned institutions worldwide. Her research expertise lies in brand management and consumer psychology, with a particular focus on consumer experiences, well-being, scale development and brand communications. Her work has been published in leading journals, including the *Annual Review of Psychology*, the *Journal of Consumer Psychology* and the *Journal of Marketing*. She currently serves as an Associate Editor for both the *Journal of Business Research* and the *Italian Journal of Marketing* and is an active member of several editorial boards, including the *Journal of Brand Management* and the *Journal of Product & Brand Management*. She is recognized as one of the world's top scientists in the Stanford/Elsevier Top 2% Scientist Rankings and has won various awards for her research on brands and consumers.

Daniela Andreini, PhD is a Professor of Marketing and the Head of the Department of Management at the University of Bergamo in Italy. She has been a Visiting Professor at the University of Washinton Bothell for several years. Her research focus on brand management, digital marketing and business model innovation, and her research contributions have been published in numerous prestigious journals such as the *Journal of Advertising*, the *Journal of Business Research, Industrial Marketing Management, Organization Studies*, the *Journal of Advertising Research, Family Business Review*, and the *Journal of Business Ethics*. She is also actively involved in editorial roles for journals such as the Journal of Product and Brand Management and the *International Journal of Management Reviews*. Additionally, she is a member of various scientific committees, including the Special Interest Group (SIG) Brand, Identity & Corporate Reputation of the Academy of Marketing.

CONTRIBUTORS

Michela Addis is a Full Professor of Marketing at the University of Roma Tre and the Director of the Center for Market and Industrial Relations Studies (CeSMeR). She holds a PhD in Management from Bocconi University. Her research explores customer experience, brand management, consumer well-being and cultural marketing. She has authored seminal contributions on experiential consumption and transformative brand experiences, and her work bridges marketing theory with managerial practice. She has published widely in leading journals including the *Journal of Consumer Research*, the *European Journal of Marketing*, the *Journal of Service Research* and *Psychology & Marketing*. She serves as an Associate Editor for the *International Journal of Arts Management* and is actively engaged in international research collaborations and funded projects on innovation, customer centricity and cultural branding. She is also the author of *Engaging Brands* (Routledge, 2020).

Isabelle Aimé, PhD, is a Full Professor of Marketing at KEDGE Business School, France, leading Marketing MSc at the Paris campus, following 12 years as a Marketing Executive in FMCG companies such as Unilever and Yoplait. Her research focuses primarily on brand management and the impact of datafication on marketing organization. She has published in the *Journal of Business Research*, the *European Journal of Marketing*, the *Journal of Historical Research in Marketing*, the *Journal of Strategic Marketing, Décisions Marketing, Revue Française du Marketing* and *Management et Avenir*. She is also the author of the book *La Marque* (Dunod, 2016). She is a reviewer in multiple journals and conferences.

Juan Miguel Alcántara-Pilar is an Associate Professor of Marketing in the Department of Marketing and Market Research at the Faculty of Education, Economy and Technology of Ceuta, University of Granada (Spain). His research focuses on Cross-Cultural Marketing and Communication, Language Effect on Consumer Behavior and Tourism Marketing. He has published extensively in high-impact journals indexed in the *Journal Citation Reports (JCR)*, including the *Journal of Business Research*, *Cross Cultural Management: An International Journal*, *Tourism Management*, *Computers in Human Behavior* and the *Journal of Marketing Communications*, among others. His academic activity includes participation in several competitive research projects, as well as active involvement in national and international scientific conferences.

Selin Altaras is a Doctoral Candidate in Marketing at Koç University, Istanbul, Türkiye. She has extensive experience in consumer and market insights in the consumer packaged goods (CPG) industry. She is the author of an influential article on global branding published in the *Journal of International Marketing*. Her research areas include global branding and consumer behavior in the context of prosocial-oriented marketing strategies, particularly purpose-driven branding and meaning-oriented consumption.

Sunny Vijay Arora is an Associate Professor of Marketing at S. P. Jain Institute of Management and Research in Mumbai, India. With 19 years of total experience, he has spent 15 years in academics. He has to his credit articles and case studies published in top international journals such as the *Journal of Brand Management*, the *Journal of Product & Brand Management*, the *Journal of Global Fashion Marketing*, *Emerald Emerging Markets Case Studies*, *The Case Journal* and *Ivey Publishing*. He has presented his research at various international conferences, such as the American Marketing Association (AMA) Winter Academic Conference, ANZMAC and the Association for Consumer Research Latin America Conference, among others. His research interests include brand naming, pricing and consumer psychology.

M. Berk Ataman is an Associate Professor of Marketing at the Faculty of Business, Özyeğin University. His research focuses on developing quantitative models to support marketing decision-making, with an emphasis on long-term brand and firm performance in dynamic market environments. His work has appeared in leading journals such as the *Journal of Marketing Research*, *Marketing Science* and *International Journal of Research in Marketing*. He has also served on the Editorial Review Board of the *International Journal of Research in Marketing*.

Lisa Baiwir is a PhD Candidate and Teaching Assistant in Marketing at HEC Liège, Management School of the University of Liège in Belgium. Her research centers on the intersection of consumer psychology, technology interactions and transformative services, with a focus on how digital experiences drive engagement and well-being. She has published in journals including the *Journal of Consumer Affairs* and the *Journal of Service Theory and Practice*.

John M. T. Balmer is an Emeritus Professor at Brunel Business School, University of London (UK), and is a Quondam Professor of Corporate Brand/Identity Management at Bradford University. After a first degree from the University of Reading, and two periods of postgraduate study at Durham University, he took his PhD at the University of Strathclyde. Known as the 'father' of the corporate brand and corporate marketing fields, he is a co-originator of the corporate heritage brand concept. He is internationally renowned for his scholarship of corporate identity, recognised as one of the world's top 2% of scholars in a study by Stanford University and celebrated for holding the world's first (full) professorships in Corporate Brand/Identity Management, Corporate Identity and Corporate Marketing. He is the Chairman of the Board of Senior Consultant Editors of the *Journal of Brand Management* and sits as a Senior Advisory Board Member of the *Journal of Product and Brand Management*.

Salvador del Barrio-García is a Full Professor in the Department of Marketing and Market Research at the University of Granada. His areas of expertise include integrated marketing communications (IMC), cross-cultural communication, brand management, consumer behaviour and tourism marketing. He has published over 70 peer-reviewed papers in prestigious journals in these fields. He has produced 10 books and 21 book chapters published by prestigious international publishers such as Springer, SAGE, Wiley, Edward Elgar Publishing, IGI-Global and Pearson.

He has also directed research projects with businesses and the public administration and has taught master's and doctoral studies at various universities. He has carried out research and teaching stays at the University of Texas at Austin (USA), Burgundy School of Business (Dijon, France), Austral University of Chile and University of San Andrés (Argentina), among others.

David Barros-Arrieta is a Full-Time Professor, Director of the Specialization in Strategic Marketing and the Master's in Marketing Management at Universidad de la Costa (Barranquilla, Colombia). He is a PhD Candidate in Business Administration, MBA, and a Specialist in Strategic Marketing, and a Professor, Researcher and Consultant in marketing. His research work and consultancy work are on the following topics: strategic marketing, market research, internal marketing, internal branding, customer experience management, service logic and value facilitation.

Saleh Bazi is an Associate Professor of Digital Marketing at Yarmouk University, Jordan. His research interests include social commerce, luxury brand, artificial intelligence and Metaverse. His research has appeared in *Information Technology and People Journal,* the *Journal of Business Research* and Industrial Marketing Management. He has presented his research at several top global conferences. He is a reviewer at the *Journal of Business Research*, *Industrial Marketing Management*, *Computers in Human Behavior*, *Information Technology & People*, *Technological Forecast & Social Change*, the *Journal of Strategic Marketing* and the *International Journal of Information Management.*

Angela A. Beccanulli, PhD, is a Postdoctoral Researcher at Università Cattolica del Sacro Cuore in Milan and a Research Fellow at LABCOM (Research Lab on Business Communication) since 2018. With a professional background in both international and national communication agencies, her current research adopts an interpretative approach, specializing in netnography. Her work explores the intersections between consumers and objects, with a particular focus on technology and tourism, and cultural branding. A former visiting scholar at Università della Svizzera Italiana (USI), she also collaborates on projects promoted by UNESCO. At Università Cattolica, she teaches courses in consumer behavior, corporate communication and brand communication in art and tourism.

Fabienne Berger-Remy is an Associate Professor of Marketing at Université Paris Dauphine – PSL, accredited to supervise research. She holds a PhD in Management Sciences and has a professional background in marketing, brand management and consulting within the consumer goods sector. Since transitioning to academia in 2014, she has taught and conducted research at the Sorbonne Business School and, since 2023, at Université Paris Dauphine – PSL. Her multidisciplinary research focuses on the transformation of marketing professions and organizations, the relationship between work, brands and consumption, and the creation of value through intangible capital. Her work has been published in journals such as *M@n@gement*, the *Journal of Business Research*, the *Journal of Marketing Management*, the *Psychology & Marketing*, the *Journal of Historical Research in Marketing*, *Recherche et Applications en Marketing*, and *Revue Française de Gestion.*

Silvia Biraghi, PhD, is an Associate Professor at Università Cattolica del Sacro Cuore and Research Associate at LABCOM (Research Lab on Business Communication), where she explores the intersections of consumer culture, communication, branding and technosociality. Her academic journey has taken her to the Boston University Department of Mass Communication, Advertising and PR, as well as the Medill School at Northwestern University, where she was a visiting scholar. A specialist in qualitative and interpretive research methodologies, she has a deep expertise in netnography, consumer collectives and consumer-brand interactions. As an educator, Silvia teaches Corporate Communication and Branding, Brand Management and Innovation, and Omnichannel Management, and she also coordinates postgraduate programs in Markets and Corporate Strategies and Corporate Communication and Branding. Her work has been published in leading academic journals, including *Marketing Theory*, the *Journal of Business Research*, the *Journal of Marketing Management*, the *Journal of Product and Brand Management*, and *Futures*, where she has explored topics ranging from brand activism, digital consumer cultures and technosocial dynamics.

Manfred Bruhn spent his academic training at the University of Münster (Germany). He held his first professorship for marketing and commerce from 1983 to 1995 at the EBS University of Business and Law, a private university in Germany. Various calls to the universities in Cologne, Jena and Munich were turned down. Since 1995, he has held the Chair of Marketing and Corporate Management at the University of Basel and has been an honorary professor at the Technical University of Munich. Honorary doctorates from the Universities of Hohenheim and Rostock. He is the Founder and a partner of the strategy and marketing consultancy Professor Bruhn & Partner AG (Basel). His research and consultancy work focuses on strategic management, service marketing, relationship marketing, integrated communication, sponsoring, quality management and non-profit marketing.

Hui Chen is a PhD researcher at the Adam Smith Business School of the University of Glasgow (UK). Her research interests are in the areas of consumer–brand relationship, country of origin and self-brand congruity.

Yang Cheng (PhD, MBA) is a tenured professor in the Department of Communication at North Carolina State University, University Faculty Scholar and an Adjunct Professor in the Poole College of Management. Recognized among Stanford University's top 2% most-cited scholars, her research focuses on artificial intelligence, crisis communication, relationship management and global public relations. She has published over 75 journal articles in top journals such as *New Media & Society* and *Public Relations Review*. She has secured over $2 million in research funding from agencies including the NSF and NEH. She has received numerous international awards and lectures globally. She teaches courses in strategic management, crisis communication and research methods. With extensive experience in marketing and social science research, she is widely respected for advancing the intersection of AI, communication and public relations.

George Christodoulides is Associate Dean of Research and Innovation and the Chalhoub Group Professor of Luxury Brand Management at the American University of Sharjah in the United Arab Emirates. His research focuses on the areas of brand management and luxury marketing. He is a frequent presenter and keynote speaker at international conferences, and his work has been supported by external funding bodies such as the Economic and Social Research Council and the British Academy. His research has been published in leading peer-reviewed journals. He has guest edited several special issues and is currently Associate Editor of International Marketing Review.

Daniele Dalli is a Professor of Marketing at the University of Pisa, where he teaches Consumer Behavior and Marketing Management. His research explores the intersection between consumption practices, consumer culture and market dynamics, focusing on consumer identity, resistance and prosumption. He has published in the *Journal of Business Research, Marketing Theory,* the *International Journal of Research in Marketing,* the *Annals of Tourism Research, Organization Studies*, and the *Journal of The Academy of Marketing Science*. He also serves on the editorial boards of various international journals. Over the years, he has coordinated several national and international research projects and regularly collaborates with companies and institutions on marketing strategy and consumer insight initiatives.

Laurence Dessart is a Professor of Marketing at HEC Liège, Management School of the University of Liège in Belgium. She holds a PhD from the University of Glasgow in the UK and previously taught at KEDGE Business School in France. Her research explores brand management, consumer engagement and digital marketing. She published in top-tier marketing journals, including the *International Journal of Research in Marketing*, the *Journal of Business Research* and *Psychology & Marketing*, among others. She has received several awards for her work and sits on the editorial boards of the *Journal of Product and Brand Management* and of the *Journal of Business Research.*

Yuksel Ekinci joined the University of Portsmouth as a Professor of Marketing in 2017, following his role as a Professor and the Director of Postgraduate Research at Henley Business School. His research on consumer behaviour, business methods and brand management in services has been cited over 17,000 times and published in leading journals. With a background in the hotel and tourism industry, he combines academic insight with practical expertise, having led marketing and brand strategy projects for organisations across the UK and Europe, including IBM, Ogilvy and BSkyB.

Sharifah Faridah Syed Alwi is a Reader of Corporate Branding at the Cranfield School of Management, Cranfield University, UK, where she is the Director of MSc Strategic Marketing. Her main research focus is corporate branding, with special interest in responsible branding, corporate brand image and corporate brand equity. Her research works have appeared in the *British Journal of Management*, *Business Ethics Quarterly*, the *Journal of Business Research*, *International Marketing Review*, *Industrial Marketing Management*, *Information Technology & People* and the *European Journal of Marketing*.

Rossella C. Gambetti, PhD, is a Professor of Branding and Consumer Culture at the Università Cattolica del Sacro Cuore in Milan, where she is the Director of LABCOM (Research Lab on Business Communication). She is also a research fellow of the Jayne and Hans Hufschmid Chair of Strategic Public Relations and Business Communication at the Annenberg School for Communication and Journalism, University of Southern California (LA). She is an interpretive scholar whose research is focused on the interplays between consumer culture, branding and technology and how these are shaping consumption, communication and society. She has been a visiting scholar at universities in the USA and in Japan and has published her works in journals such as *Marketing Theory*, the *Journal of Business Research*, *California Management Review*, *Business Ethics Quarterly*, *Futures* and *Management Decision*.

Beatriz García-Carrión is an Assistant Professor in the Department of Personality, Assessment, and Psychological Treatment at the Faculty of Education, Economy and Technology of Ceuta, University of Granada (Spain). She holds a PhD in Marketing from the University of Granada, a degree in Psychology from the University Jaume I of Castellón and two master's degrees: one in Cognitive and Behavioral Neuroscience and the other in Marketing and Consumer Behaviour. Her main research area focuses on consumer behaviour and consumer neuroscience. She has published several articles in high-impact journals, including *Tourism Management*, *Hospitality and Tourism Management*, *Journal of Destination Marketing and Management*, *Psychological Research* and *Psychophysiology*. She has participated in numerous national and international scientific conferences, where she has received two research awards.

Ilan Geva is an Author, Speaker, Trainer and Adjunct Professor as well as a Seasoned International Branding Expert, having lived and worked in four continents, visited over 60 countries and served clients around the globe. Among his clients were many multinationals such as Citibank, Shell, McDonald's, Nestle, VW Audi, Fiat and United Airlines. He co-authored the book *Global Brand Management* and has had articles published on medical tourism and international healthcare publications. Among his recent clients are ministries of health, trade and commerce, chambers of commerce, medical travel clusters, city councils, hospital organizations and private clinics. And he has received over 100 industry awards for his work. In addition to his training workshops, Ilan has taught at The University of Chicago, Columbia College Chicago and DePaul University and currently teaches at Loyola University Chicago and the Center for Medical Tourism Research – UIW in San Antonio. Ilan is a member of the editorial board at the *Healthcare Standards Institute Journal*.

Mijka Ghorbani, PhD, has recently completed her doctoral studies on the topic of digital brand personality in the Department of Marketing of the Strathclyde Business School (SBS) at the University of Strathclyde in Glasgow (UK). Besides her academic work, she works as a consultant in a full-service marketing and advertising agency. Her research interests focus on branding, consumer–brand relationships and digital marketing. Her research has been published in the *International Journal of Consumer Studies* and the *Journal of Product & Brand Management*.

Irina Gorea is a Research Assistant at the Retail Leadership Institute, Toronto Metropolitan University. Irina has extensive marketing experience, including teaching at Humber College and managing various social media campaigns as a marketing manager. Irina brings a blend of academic research and hands-on digital marketing experience to her work. She earned her Master's degree from Toronto Metropolitan University, where her research on influencers sponsorship disclosure in tourism was nominated for the Distinguished Thesis Award.

Bianca Grohmann, MBA, PhD, is a Professor of Marketing and Concordia University Research Chair in the Consumer Psychology of Gender at the John Molson School of Business (Concordia University) in Montreal, Canada. Her research explores branding, social responsibility and gender-related topics from a mostly experimental consumer psychology perspective. She has also contributed to the development of scales that are now widely used in the marketing literature. Over the years, her research has appeared in leading marketing journals and was presented at many international conferences. She is also the Founder of Concordia University's Laboratory for Sensory Research and is a Member of the John Molson Climate Business Institute.

Faheem Gul Gilal is an Associate Professor of Marketing in the Department of Business Administration at Sukkur IBA University, Sindh, Pakistan. His research primarily focuses on consumer motivation and emotion, with a particular emphasis on brand passion, product design techniques, consumer behavior change strategies and self-determination theory. He has an impressive publication record, with over 60 research papers published in SSCI-, ABDC- and SCOPUS-listed journals, including the *International Journal of Hospitality Management, Psychology & Marketing,* the *Journal of Business Research, Business Strategy and the Environment,* the *Journal of Brand Management* and the *Journal of Consumer Behaviour*, among others. He serves as the Editor-in-Chief of the *Sukkur IBA Journal of Management and Business*, a guest editor for *Frontiers in Psychology* and a member of the Editorial Review Boards of several journals, including the *Journal of Consumer Marketing*, the *Journal of Research in Interactive Marketing* and the *Italian Journal of Marketing*.

Tilde Heding is a Teaching Associate Professor at Copenhagen Business School, as well as an author and advisor. She holds a Master of Science degree from Copenhagen Business School and has extensive experience as a brand consultant, particularly within the fields of art, design, and culture. Her textbook *Brand Management – Mastering Research, Theory and Practice* (co-authored with Charlotte Knudtzen and Mogens Bjerre) will be published in its fourth edition in 2026. Tilde has also contributed to several Danish and international publications.

Liselot Hudders is a Full Professor of persuasive communication and marketing ethics at Ghent University, Belgium, and the Director of the Center for Persuasive Communication. Her research examines the impact of digital media on children and the importance of digital empowerment, with a focus on influencer marketing and kidfluencing. In 2024, she has been awarded an ERC consolidator grant to further study the kidfluencer phenomenon. She has published in leading advertising and communication journals, earning several awards for her research and valorisation initiatives. She is also a Board Member of the *European Advertising Academy* and serves as associate editor for the *International Journal of Advertising* and the *Journal of Interactive Advertising*.

Nicholas Ind is a Professor at Kristiania University of Applied Sciences and a Visiting Professor at ESADE-Universitat Ramon Llull and Edinburgh Napier University. He is a Member of the Editorial Board of the *Journal of Brand Management*, the Editorial Review Board of the *Journal of Product and Brand Management* and the Scientific Committee of the Global Brand Conference. He is the author of fourteen books, which have been published in nine languages, and he has published articles in the *Journal of Brand Management, California Management Review, Business Horizons* and *Industrial Marketing Management*.

Oriol Iglesias is a Professor at ESADE-Universitat Ramon Llull. He is a Member of the Editorial Board of the *Journal of Brand Management*, the Editorial Review Board of the *Journal of Product and Brand Management* and the Scientific Committee of the Global Brand Conference. His research has been published in academic outlets such as the *Journal of Business Ethics, California Management Review, Business and Society*, the *Journal of Business Research* and the *European Journal of Marketing*.

Jenna Jacobson is an Associate Professor and Eaton Chair of Retailing at Toronto Metropolitan University's Ted Rogers School of Management. She is also the Director of the Retail Leadership Institute in Toronto, Canada. Her research analyzes the consumer and producer perspectives of digital technologies with a focus on digital retailing, social media and user behaviour. She received her PhD from the University of Toronto, Faculty of Information.

Clarinda Jansberg is an Associate Professor in Marketing at the School of Business and Economics at Linnaeus University in Sweden. Her research focuses on strategic brand management, more specifically on the interplay between brand experiences, consumer–brand relationships and socially responsible brand building. Her work has been published in the *Journal of Brand Management,* the *Journal of Product and Brand Management,* the *International Review of Retail, Distribution and Consumer Research, European*

Business Review and the *Journal of Marketing Communications*, among others. She serves as the Associate Editor of the *International Review of Retail, Distribution and Consumer Research* and is a regular reviewer of many reputed journals and international conferences. Jansberg has a wide experience as a practitioner in brand management and international marketing prior to joining academia in 2015.

Jacek Kall is a Marketing Expert specializing in brand management. He serves as a Professor of Marketing at the WSB Merito University in Poznań. His academic contribution include several books on branding and brand communication (his recent publication, 'Brand Metrics: Measuring Brand Efficacy along the Customer Journey' was published in 2021 by Routledge). Beyond academia, he has been working as a marketing consultant and researcher. He co-founded the marketing research agency Presto in Poznań. For the past 10 years, he has been a strategic consultant for the brand design agency Soul&Mind.

Arti D. Kalro is a Professor of Marketing at the Shailesh J. Mehta School of Management, Indian Institute of Technology Bombay India. Her research interests include consumer psychology, consumer neuroscience and consumer behavior, branding and marketing communications. She has published papers in journals such as the *European Journal of Marketing*, the *Journal of Interactive Marketing*, the *Journal of Product & Brand Management*, the *Journal of Retailing and Consumer Services*, the *Journal of Brand Management*, the *Marketing Intelligence and Planning*, the *Journal of Consumer Behaviour* and the *International Journal of Retail* and *Distribution Management* and presented numerous papers in various international conferences such as American Marketing Association (AMA) Winter Academic Conference, Asia Pacific Association of Consumer Research (ACR) Conference and others. She is currently serving as an Editorial Review Board Member for the *Journal of Consumer Behavior*, an International Research Review, since July 2020, and the *Journal of Global Marketing* since March 2024.

Robert Karaszewski is a distinguished academic and executive education expert with over 25 years of experience spanning Europe, the Middle East and the USA. He currently serves as a Professor and Thought Leader in business strategy, leadership and innovation, with a particular focus on the practical application of emotional intelligence, complexity leadership theory and strategic transformation. He is full professor in Management and Leadership at Abu Dhabi School of Management (ADSM), Abu Dhabi, UAE and Faculty of Management, Politechnika Bydgoska, Bydgoszcz Poland. His academic and consulting career includes collaborations with leading business institutions and government entities. https://orcid.org/0000-0002-8980-4392

Karaszewski is the Creator of multiple executive education courses across platforms such as Udemy and Kajabi, empowering professionals worldwide in areas such as corporate finance, talent management and inclusive leadership. A champion of interdisciplinary and intercultural learning, he actively bridges academic theory with real-world business practice. His research and teaching emphasize ethics, long-term stakeholder value and adaptive leadership in rapidly changing environments.

Jessica Keech is an Associate Professor of Marketing in the Department of Business, Organizations and Society at Franklin and Marshall College. Her research examines consumer behavior with an emphasis on branding, technology and sustainability. She received her PhD from Temple University. She has published in *Psychology and Marketing,* the *Journal of Consumer Marketing,* the *Journal of International Consumer Marketing* and *Management Decision,* among others.

Minjung Kim is an Associate Professor of Marketing at Manhattan University. She received her PhD in Business Administration (Marketing) from Texas A&M University. She teaches courses in consumer behavior and consumer analytics. Her research interests encompass personal financial decision-making, logo design/redesign and the influence of cultural factors on consumer responses to marketing strategies.

Marie-Eve Laporte is a Professor at Université Paris-Saclay, where she holds the 'Innovation Management & Future of Healthcare' chair within the 'RITM' research center in Economics & Management. A graduate of ESSEC Business School, she holds a PhD and a habilitation to direct research (HDR) in management sciences. She previously worked as a marketing and quality director in the agri-food industry. Her teaching focuses on behavior, research methods, marketing and communication. Her research areas include health management, health-related behaviors, food and health marketing, brand management and digital transformation. Her work has been published in books and in peer-reviewed academic journals such as the *Journal of Business Research, Psychology & Marketing,* the *Journal of Consumer Affairs,* the *Journal of Historical Research in Marketing* and *Recherche et Applications en Marketing*. Her publications are available at www.ritm.universite-paris-saclay.fr/profil/marie-eve.laporte.

Zoe Lee is a Reader (Associate Professor) in Marketing at Cardiff Business School, Cardiff University, UK. She is an Associate Editor of the *Journal of Strategic Marketing* and a member of the Editorial Review Board for the *Journal of Business Research,* the *Journal of Product and Brand Management,* the *Journal of Philanthropy and Marketing and* the *International Journal of Advertising*. She has published in top ranked peer-reviewed academic journals including the *Journal of Business Research, Industrial Marketing Management*, the *Journal of Business Ethics*, the *European Journal of Marketing* and the *Journal of Brand Management*. Her research focuses on contemporary branding issues (including corporate brand activism and rebranding), sustainability (including communication strategies in fashion and disability inclusion) and nonprofit marketing strategy.

Sheena Leek is an Associate Professor at the University of Birmingham. Her research interests include business-to-business branding, networking and the initiation of business relationships and development of networks, and the communication process within business-to-business relationships. She has published in a range of publications such as the *Journal of Management Studies, Industrial Marketing Management*, the *Journal of Marketing Management* and the *Journal of Product and Brand Management*.

Joon Ho Lim is an Associate Professor of Marketing at Illinois State University. He teaches in the Marketing Analytics area. He earned his PhD in Business Administration (major – Marketing) from Texas A&M University. He is interested in the empirical modeling of consumer behavior and firm decision-making. His research focuses on marketing and public policy, nutrition labeling, data breach, retailing and branding.

Chen Lin is a student of Zhejiang University majoring in International Journalism. She integrates academic rigor with a passion for emerging technologies. Having delved deeply into courses such as AI for Strategic Communication and Public Relations, she cultivates a deep understanding of AI's transformative potential in brand management and focuses on exploring the intersection of emerging technologies and strategic brand communication. Passionate about the evolving role of technology in global markets, she wants to bridge theoretical frameworks with practical applications in brand management in the context of evolving AI technology. At the same time, she seeks to explore how artificial intelligence can reshape strategic narratives based on the interplay of technology, communication theory and social impact.

Sandra Maria Correia Loureiro (full professor) Sandra Loureiro, a Full Professor, is recognized among the top 2% of scientists globally by Stanford University, in collaboration with Elsevier and SciTech Strategies. She is the coordinator of marketing for the PhD in Management and the coordinator of the marketing group at Business Research Unit (BRU). Her current research interests include Marktech and tourism marketing. Her papers have been published in a variety of peer-reviewed journals that include the *Journal of Marketing*, the *Journal of Retailing*, the *Journal of Business Research, Tourism Management*, the *Journal of Travel Research*, the *International Journal of Hospitality Management* or the *Journal of Sustainable Tourism*. She serves as a reviewer for several international journals and conferences and has participated in several research projects funded by the EU and FCT (Foundation for Science and Technology).

Emerson Wagner Mainardes is Professor of Marketing at FEA-USP. Visiting Professor at the Turku School of Economics, University of Turku, Pori Unit (Finland). He holds a PhD in Business Administration from the University of Beira Interior (UBI – Covilhã, Portugal – 2010). His research focuses on nonprofit marketing, retail marketing, bank marketing, brand management, and related topics. He has published over 200 articles and two books. He coordinates the Center for Studies in Marketing for Social Organizations (www.cemos.com.br). He is a visiting researcher at NECE (Center for Studies in Business Sciences), a research center at UBI. He is a research associate at the International Association on Public and Nonprofit Marketing (IAPNM). He is an associate editor of the Brazilian Business Review (BBR). He is a director of the Brazilian Association of Scientific Editors (ABEC). He is a research follow in CNPq, FAPES, and NECE/FCT.

Valentina Mazzoli, PhD, is an Assistant Professor of Marketing at the University of Verona (Italy), Department of Management. She previously held academic positions at the University of Florence (Italy), the University of Pisa (Italy) and the University of Roehampton (UK), reflecting her international academic experience. Her research interests lie in brand management and communication, with a particular focus on emotions, social media and retail communication, ethicality and corporate social responsibility. Her work seeks to bridge academic insight and managerial practice, offering valuable contributions to both scholarly research and marketing strategy. She has published in leading international peer-reviewed journals such as the *Journal of Retailing*, *Industrial Marketing Management*, *Psychology and Marketing*, the *International Journal of Advertising*, the *Journal of Brand Management*, the *Journal of Product and Brand Management* and *Business Strategy and the Environment*. She is also actively involved in teaching marketing and branding courses at both undergraduate and postgraduate levels.

Michela Mingione is Postdoctoral Research Fellow in the Department for the Promotion of Human Science and Quality of Life, University of San Raffaele Roma. She is a member of the Editorial Review Board of the *Journal of Product and Brand Management*. Her work has been published in international journals, such as *Industrial Marketing Management*, the *Journal of Business Research*, the *Journal of Brand Management*, the *Journal of Product & Brand Management*, the *Journal of Marketing Management*, the *Journal of Consumer Behaviour* and the *Journal of Marketing Communications*.

Giulia Miniero is an Associate Professor of Marketing at the Università Statale di Milano, Italy. Prior to this position, she was an Associate Professor at Franklin University Switzerland, where she also served as Chair of the Business and Economics Division and Director of the Master of Science in International Management. Giulia earned her PhD in Business Administration and Management from Bocconi University, where she continues to teach in both master's and executive programs. Following her PhD, she was awarded a postdoctoral research fellowship for excellence in research at the Università della Svizzera italiana in Lugano. Her research interests focus on consumer behavior, particularly customer experience and sustainability, with an emphasis on cultural contexts and the consumer–brand relationship. Her work has been published in leading international marketing journals, including the *International Journal of Research in Marketing*, *Psychology and Marketing*, the *International Journal of Consumer Studies* and the *Journal of Consumer Marketing*.

Laurence Minsky is a Full Professor in the School of Business and Entrepreneurship at Columbia College Chicago, a best-selling author and a strategic branding and marketing consultant for ad agencies, design firms, corporations (from the Fortune 5 and more in the Fortune 500 to fast-growing startups), nonprofits and governmental organizations worldwide. His books include *Voice Marketing: Harnessing the Power of Conversational AI to Drive Customer Engagement*; *Global Brand Management: A Guide to Developing, Building & Managing an International Brand; Audio Branding: Using Sound to Build Your Brand; The Activation Imperative: How to Build Brands and Business by Inspiring Action; How to Succeed in Advertising When All You Have Is Talent Second Edition*; and *The Get A Job Workshop: How to Find Your Way to a Creative Career*. He has also published articles in *The Harvard Business Review* (11 times to date), the *Journal of Healthcare Management Standards, Advertising & Society Quarterly* and elsewhere. As a recognized industry thought leader, Laurence has been quoted in major media outlets throughout the globe. And as a consultant helping his clients achieve their branding, behavioral marketing and revenue goals, he has received more than 125 industry accolades to date.

Susan M. Mudambi is a Professor Emeritus of Marketing at the Fox School of Business, Temple University. Her research examines marketing and international business, with special attention to branding, information technology and supply chain relationships. She received her PhD from Warwick University (UK). She has published in *MIS Quarterly*, the *Journal of Management Studies,* the *Journal of Product Innovation Management, Industrial Marketing Management*, the *Journal of Product and Brand Management*, the *Journal of International Management* and *Computers in Human Behavior*, among others.

Gabriele Murtas is a postdoctoral research fellow in Marketing at the Department of Management, University of Bergamo (Italy). He served as a visiting PhD student at the School of Business Administration, American University of Sharjah (UAE). His research focuses on the evolution of the luxury industry and the implementation of innovative marketing strategies in luxury brands. Early outputs of his research have been published in outlets such as the *Journal of Strategic Marketing*, *AMS Review*, the *Journal of Global Fashion Marketing* and the *Journal of Consumer Behaviour*.

Sergio Andrés Osuna-Ramírez is an Associate Professor of Marketing at Universidad EIA (Colombia). He received his PhD from the Adam Smith Business School at the University of Glasgow (UK). His research interests are in Brand Management and Consumer Behaviour. His work has been published in academic journals such as the *Journal of Business* Research and the *Journal of Product and Brand Management* and presented at various international academic conferences.

Ayşegül Özsomer is a Professor of Marketing at Koç University, Istanbul, Türkiye. Her research focuses on global marketing, branding and marketing strategy. She investigates how firms navigate dynamic and volatile environments and build strong brands across diverse international contexts. Her work has been published in leading journals, including the *Journal of Marketing*, the *Journal of Marketing Research*, the *International Journal of Research in Marketing* and the *Journal of International Marketing*. Her co-authored book, *The New Emerging Market Multinationals: Four Strategies for Disrupting Markets and the Competition*, was selected as the best strategy book by Business+Strategy. She has received several prestigious awards, such as the Gerald Hills Best Paper Award for long-term impact in entrepreneurship research, two times the American Marketing Association S. Tamer Cavusgil Award for advancing international marketing practice and the 2025 Significant Contributions to Global Marketing Award. She currently serves as the Editor-in-Chief of the *Journal of International Marketing*.

Koen Pauwels is a Distinguished Professor of Marketing at Northeastern University, Boston, and the Associate Dean of Research at its D'Amore-McKim School of Business. In the NIM Research Advisory Board, he contributes his expertise in the fields of marketing analytics, data-driven decision making and business model innovation. He is the Editor-in-Chief of the *International Journal of Research in Marketing* and an Associate Editor for the *Journal of Marketing*, the *Journal of Consumer Research* and the *Journal of Interactive Marketing*. His books include *Modeling Markets* and *Advanced Methods for Modeling Markets* for analysts and *Break the Wall: Why and How to Democratize Digital in Your Business* and *It's Not the Size of the Data – It's How You Use It: Smarter Marketing with Analytics and Dashboards* for managers. In 2004, he founded the Annual Marketing Dynamics Conference to connect researchers focused on dynamic marketing challenges. With extensive experience consulting for companies across three continents – including Amazon, Heinz, Kayak, Kraft, Marks & Spencer, Microsoft, Nissan, Sony, Tetrapak and Unilever – he specializes in evaluating and optimizing marketing effectiveness, designing and interpreting field experiments, integrating marketing attribution with mix modeling, aligning online and offline marketing metrics, enhancing long-term brand equity and innovating business models. He frequently shares insights into marketing return on investment through his LinkedIn Newsletter 'Pauwels on Marketing' and into retail media through his Substack 'Amazon Days'.

Martina Quadri is a PhD Candidate in Business and Law at the Department of Management, University of Bergamo, Italy. Her research focuses on the impact of innovative technologies on online consumer behavior and brand management, with particular attention to influencer marketing and live streaming. She has received two beginner research awards and recently published in the *Journal of Marketing Management*. During her doctoral studies, she was a visiting PhD student at the Center for Persuasive Communication at Ghent University, Belgium.

María Eugenia Rodríguez-López is an Associate Professor in the Department of Marketing and Market Research at the Faculty of Education, Economy and Technology of Ceuta, University of Granada (Spain). Her main research interests focus on Cross-Cultural Marketing, and Hospitality and Tourism Marketing, with a particular emphasis on customer satisfaction and customer experience. She has published more than 15 scientific articles in journals indexed in the Web of Science (WOS) and SCOPUS databases, many of which appear in high-impact journals. Additionally, she has authored over 11 book chapters, some of them published by prestigious international publishers such as IGI Global, Thomson Reuters and Dykinson. Her research activity includes participation in more than 40 scientific conferences – primarily at the international level – where she has received five research awards.

Álvaro J. Rojas-Lamorena holds a PhD in Business Administration from the University of Granada, (Spain) and is currently an Assistant Professor in the Department of Business Administration at the Faculty of Education, Economy and Technology of Ceuta, University of Granada (Spain). His main research interests include brand management, cross-cultural studies, media marketing and tourism marketing. He has published several peer-reviewed articles in internationally recognized journals such as the *Journal of Business Research*, the *Journal of Marketing Communications* and *Technological Forecasting and Social Change*. In 2023, he received the award for Best Doctoral Thesis in Marketing from the Spanish Association of Academic and Professional Marketing (AEMARK). Additionally, he has participated in various international scientific conferences, contributing to the dissemination of his research work.

Filipa Rosado-Pinto is an Adjunct Assistant Professor at Iscte – Instituto Universitário de Lisboa. She is also currently an Adjunct Assistant Professor at NOVA SBE. Filipa obtained her PhD in Management (Marketing specialization) at Iscte, in 2022. She also holds an MBA from IE Business School and a bachelor's degree in management from NOVA SBE. Following 10 years of experience in marketing, in multinational companies, from Fast Moving Consumer Goods and the Pharmaceutical Industry, she moved into Academia in 2016.

Her current research interests include consumer–brand relationships, brand management and services marketing. Her research has been published in international scientific journals, such as the *EuroMed Journal of Business*, the *Journal of Promotion Management* and the *International Journal of Hospitality Management*. Her work has also been presented at reputable international scientific conferences such as European Marketing Academy Conference (EMAC), Global Marketing Conference (GAMMA-GMC) and the EuroMed Academy of Business Conference.

Lara Mendes Christ Bonella Sepulcri is an Associate Professor at FUCAPE Business School (Brazil), where she also earned her Ph.D. in Accounting and Administration. Her research focuses on marketing, consumer behavior, and nonprofit organizations. Dr. Sepulcri is a Researcher at the Center for Studies in Marketing for Social Organizations (CEMOS) and an Associate Fellow of the Higher Education Academy (AFHEA) in the United Kingdom. She has also served as a Visiting Researcher at Bournemouth University (UK). Her academic work explores the intersection of marketing, social value, and organizational performance, with publications in leading international journals.

Burcu Sezen is an Associate Professor of Marketing at the Universidad de los Andes, in the School of Management in Bogota, Colombia. Her research focuses on branding and global branding. She has previously published in the *Journal of Business Research* and the *Journal of Marketing Analytics*, among others. She has presented her research at Marketing Science, Marketing Dynamics, AMA and AMA Global Marketing Sig conferences.

Shadma Shahid is currently an Assistant Professor at the Ted Rogers School of Management, Canada. She completed her postdoctoral research in the Department of Marketing, International Business, and Strategy at Brock University, Canada. She holds a PhD in Marketing from Jamia Millia Islamia University, India. Her research interests include technology, luxury consumption, customer experience and consumer behavior. Her work has been published in reputed journals, including *Psychology & Marketing*, the *Journal of Business Research*, *Technological Forecasting and Social Change*, the *Journal of Marketing Management* and *Journal of Retailing and Consumer Services*, among others.

Dinesh Sharma comes with diverse experience in marketing as a practitioner, researcher and teacher. His areas of interest in teaching are marketing strategy, marketing research, brand management, sales and distribution management. His areas of interest in research are marketing strategy, consumer value, and brands. He has published papers in many peer-reviewed international journals and has written case studies.

Kokho (Jason) Sit is a Senior Lecturer in Marketing at the University of Portsmouth, specialising in shopper behaviour, experiential marketing and retail branding. His research is published in top journals and featured in outlets such as *The Conversation*, with media coverage for projects on the fear of social crowds and shopping in a cashless society. Before academia, he worked as a marketing assistant at a community shopping centre in Australia.

Stefanie Stilz (formerly Schnebelen) is the Manager of Branding, Communication and Marketing at the Gesundheitszentrum Fricktal AG in Switzerland. She holds a doctorate from the University of Basel, where she completed her PhD in 2015. Following her PhD, she pursued postdoctoral research at the University of Basel, focusing on brand happiness, branding strategies and integrated marketing communication. Afterward, she worked as a Brand Consultant at a branding agency in Zurich, advising clients on brand strategy and positioning. At Medgate AG in Basel, a leading provider of telemedicine services, she held various roles in branding, product management and business development, gaining extensive experience in shaping strategic communication and expanding business opportunities. In her current role at the Gesundheitszentrum Fricktal AG in Rheinfelden, she focuses on developing and implementing strategic brand initiatives, sharpening brand positioning and strengthening employer branding efforts in the healthcare sector.

Asli Tolunay is an Associate Professor of Marketing at the Business Administration Department of Yeditepe University (Turkey). She holds a PhD in Marketing from Bogazici University, Turkey. Her primary research interests are in the areas of brand management and digital consumer behaviour. She has published in the *Journal of Business Research* and other peer-reviewed journals and has presented at various national and international conferences on these topics including the Academy of Marketing Science conference, the Academy of Marketing conference, the Academy of Marketing Science World Marketing Congress and the European Marketing Academy Conference. At the Academy of Marketing Conference in 2020, she received the Best Paper Award in the Consumer Behaviour track.

Ceyda Paydas Turan is the Deputy Director of the BRAINS Lab and Senior Lecturer in Marketing at Kingston University London, conducting research on brand strategy, consumer behaviour and human–AI decision-making. Prior to academia, she held senior leadership and marketing roles in international organisations across both emerging and developed markets. Her academic research is deeply informed by this extensive industry background. She has published in leading journals such as the *Journal of Business Research*, the *International Journal of Hospitality Management*, the *International Journal of Consumer Studies*, the *Journal of Retailing and Consumer Services* and *Computers in Human Behavior*. Her research has been presented at esteemed conferences including the Academy of Management (AOM), American Marketing Association (AMA) and European Group for Organizational Studies (EGOS). She is a member of Kingston University's Faculty Research, Business & Innovation Committee and chairs the Customer Insights Hub Research Seminars. Dr. Paydas Turan actively collaborates with industry partners through research, knowledge exchange and consultancy projects.

Cleopatra Veloutsou is a Professor of Brand Management in the Adam Smith Business School at the University of Glasgow (UK), a Visiting Professor at the Aristotle University of Thessaloniki (Greece), University of Coimbra (Portugal), University of West of Attica (Greece) and the Head of the Marketing Research Unit of the Athens Institute of Education and Research (ATINER) (Greece). Her primary research is Brand Management, and she has published over 60 articles in international academic journals and featured on the top world's 2% of the most cited researchers across disciplines Stanford University's analysis since 2020 (SCOPUS database based). She has been editing the *Journal of Product and Brand Management* since 2014 and has acted as an Associate Editor of the *Journal of Business Research* since 2019 and the *Spanish Journal of Marketing* since 2024, and she is a Member of the editorial board of various international academic journals and has been the Conference Chair and a Member of the organising committee for numerous international academics conferences.

Yunyi Wei Yunyi is an Associate Professor and Associate Dean at the School of Economics and Management, Yantai Institute of Technology. His research interests focus on brand morality and consumer behavior. His work has appeared in prestigious marketing journals, including the *Journal of Retailing and Consumer Services* and *Psychology & Marketing*. Prior to his academic career, he gained industry experience as a sales training specialist at two leading insurance companies in China.

Carolyn Wilson-Nash is a Senior Lecturer in Marketing and Retail at the University of Stirling, where she teaches Consumer Behaviour and Research Methods. Her overarching research focus is on technology consumption by older people. She investigates the usage of everyday digital devices and digital health services by older people, care home residents, patients with long-term conditions and in palliative care. Recently, she has been on a project funded by the Scottish Funding Council and the Digital Health & Care Innovation Centre, evaluating the Scottish Government's initiative to provide iPads to care homes during the pandemic.

Her publications explore how technology creates paradoxes conquered by older consumers' coping strategies, how older consumers engage with social media and generate electronic word-of-mouth. Her work has been published in high-impact ABS three-star journals, including the *Journal of Interactive Marketing*, the *Journal of Business Research*, the *European Journal of Marketing* and *Psychology & Marketing*.

Mengge Yang, a postgraduate student in Journalism and Communication at Nanjing Normal University, demonstrates exceptional academic rigor. She has published four papers in domestic peer-reviewed journals and presented her findings at multiple academic conferences in communication studies. Bridging theoretical and practical dimensions, she has interned at university-affiliated media platforms and Jiangsu Broadcasting Corporation, where she honed skills in news editing, multimedia content production and cross-platform storytelling. Her current research focuses on emerging media ecosystems, media-society governance paradigms and historical journalism studies, with particular emphasis on analyzing the co-evolutionary relationship between communication technologies and social transformation. Her interdisciplinary approach underscores her commitment to advancing media scholarship through empirical investigation and critical discourse analysis.

Zhiyong Yang is a Professor of Marketing at the Farmer School of Business, Miami University, USA. His research primarily focuses on family decision-making and cultural psychology, with an emphasis on two key areas: (1) how parenting strategies exert long-lasting effects on children's consumption patterns and (2) how situationally activated cultural identities (e.g., self-construal, sense of power and local-global identity) influence consumer decision-making. His work has been published in leading scholarly journals, including the *Journal of Marketing,* the *Journal of Marketing Research,* the *Journal of Consumer Research, MIS Quarterly* and the *Journal of Experimental Social Psychology.* He serves as an Associate Editor for the *Journal of Business Research,* a guest editor for *Industrial Marketing Management* and a member of the Editorial Review Boards of several other journals, including *the Journal of the Academy of Marketing Science.*

Jian Zhang is a Professor of Management and Psychology at the School of Economics and Management, University of Science and Technology Beijing, China. She earned her MS in Psychology from Beijing Normal University and her PhD in Psychology from Capital Normal University, China. Her research interests primarily focus on motivation and emotion in the workplace, consumer behavior and motivation in tourism management. Her work has been published in leading scholarly journals, including the *Journal of Consumer Behaviour*, the *Journal of Retailing and Consumer Services*, *European Management Journal* and the *Review of Managerial Science*, among others.

Anja Zimmermann works at the Lucerne University of Applied Sciences and Art as the Head of the Competence Center of Service and Operations Management and is a Member of the Management Board of the Institute of Management and Economics (IBR), Lucerne School of Business. She is engaged as a Lecturer and Project Manager in training and further executive education as well as in research. She runs several executive education programs in Lucerne in the field of Strategic Management & Leadership, Services Management, Crisis Management and Resilience and advises profit, non-profit and public institutions on strategy and marketing issues. As an executive coach and organizational developer, she supports individual and organizational transformation and development processes.

Introduction

Lia Zarantonello and Daniela Andreini

'The only constant in life is change'
Heraclitus

This famous quote from Heraclitus resonates deeply with the field of brand management, where change is the only certainty. As consumer behaviours evolve, technological advancements progress and societal values shift, brands must continuously adapt to maintain their relevance in an ever-changing environment. The *SAGE Handbook of Brand Management* reflects this ongoing transformation by offering a comprehensive examination of the discipline, covering its past, present and future. The handbook not only frames the historical development and foundational theories of brand management but also explores current strategic practices, along with concepts and metrics for assessing brand performance. It further addresses the most pressing contemporary issues in brand management, such as ethics and social responsibility, psychological and societal well-being, and the impact of new technologies.

Through this lens, the *SAGE Handbook of Brand Management* presents a broad, multi-perspective view, evolving from traditional functional models of brand management to more socially constructed and technology-mediated understandings of brands. Covering diverse brand targets and industries across global, international and local contexts, the handbook underscores the complexity of managing brands in a rapidly changing world. It serves as an essential resource for scholars and practitioners seeking to navigate and understand the ever-evolving landscape of brand management.

This book is meticulously designed to serve as an indispensable resource for a wide audience: bachelor, master and PhD students seeking a comprehensive and theoretically grounded understanding of brand management. Scholars and professors look for an authoritative overview of current research and best practices, and managers aim to find neutral and scientific-based studies to enhance their strategic decision-making in the dynamic world of branding.

The *SAGE Handbook of Brand Management* bridges the gap between theory and practice, empowering readers to navigate the complexities of brand management and build brands that resonate in our rapidly transforming world.

STRUCTURE AND CONTENTS OF THE HANDBOOK

The handbook begins with *Part 1: Introduction to Brand Management*. This part is dedicated to exploring the history and evolution of brand management as a discipline, establishing its significance in the modern global economy. The first part of the handbook looks at how brand management originated at the end of the nineteenth century and evolved over the subsequent decades. It discusses how, in the second half of the twentieth century, the concept of brand management expanded further alongside the development of a more complex, post-modern society, leading to the development of a brand management system (*Isabelle Aimé, Fabienne Berger-Remy and Marie-Eve Laporte*). While a positivistic paradigm dominated brand management during this time, a constructivist paradigm surfaced and gained momentum during the 1990s. Both paradigms are now established and are viewed as essential for understanding the complex and multi-faceted nature of brands and branding. The various approaches that have emerged in the study of brand management over the years are presented and discussed, each focusing on distinct aspects and factors of brands and branding (*Tilde Heding*). The evolution of corporate brand management is also covered, examining how the strategic importance of corporate brands has grown over time in response to shifting market conditions and consumer trends (*John M. T. Balmer*). Moreover, the first part of the handbook discusses the role of brand management as a discipline in the current, technology-intensive and globalised society, emphasising the significance and role of global brand management (*Ayşegül Özsomer and Selin Altaras*). Given its focus on the evolution of brand management and its role across countries in today's multicultural society, this first part is essential for understanding the contemporary relevance of concepts such as brand, branding and brand management in a global and cross-cultural context. It highlights how brand strategies must adapt to diverse cultural contexts, balancing global consistency with local relevance to meet the expectations of a multicultural audience (*Laurence Minsky and Ilan Geva*).

The second part of the handbook, *Part 2: Foundations of Brand Management*, focuses on the core concepts of brand management, specifically brand identity, brand image, brand reputation and brand equity. These concepts are explored in light of the current challenges faced by companies, highlighting their role in developing and maintaining brand competitiveness in increasingly dynamic markets. Of the foundational concepts considered, visual elements are explored for their role in shaping both brand identity and brand image, highlighting their influence on consumer perceptions (*Minjung Kim* and *Joon Ho Lim*). Furthermore, this part of the handbook not only provides an account of traditional models of brand identity but also discusses the subsequent evolutions of the concept, such as brand personality (*Mijka Ghorbani*) and brand authenticity (*Filipa Rosado-Pinto and Sandra Maria Correia Loureiro*). Finally, this part covers the fundamental concepts of brand reputation and brand equity, which represent an evolution of the brand image construct. While brand reputation is a well-established concept in the corporate brand management literature (*Sheena Leek*), brand equity is more prominent in the general brand management literature and is examined by both consumer (*Salvador del Barrio-García, Juan Miguel Alcántara-Pilar, María Eugenia Rodríguez-López, Álvaro J. Rojas-Lamorena and Beatriz García-Carrión*) and employee perspectives (*Irina Gorea and Jenna Jacobson*). This part of the handbook reviews the relevant models and examines their applicability across both B2B (*Sheena Leek*) and B2C sectors (*Mijka Ghorbani*).

The part that follows, titled *Part 3: Strategic Brand Management*, views brand management as a dynamic and strategic process, exploring the different levels at which this process operates within contemporary organisations. The chapters in this part offer a comprehensive overview of brand management, beginning with a foundational exploration of the principles of corporate brand management (*John M. T. Balmer*) and progressing through a range of more specialised topics. These include brand portfolio management (*Clarinda Jansberg*), brand naming (*Sunny Vijay Arora, Arti D. Kalro and Dinesh Sharma*), co-branding strategies (*Ceyda Paydas Turan*), the development of brand relationships (*Cleopatra Veloutsou, Asli Tolunay, Sergio Andrés Osuna-Ramírez and Hui Chen*) and brand crisis management (*Robert Karaszewski*), concluding with sector-specific strategies for luxury brands (*Gabriele Murtas and George Christodoulides*) and B2B brands (*Susan M. Mudambi and Jessica Keech*). Each chapter in this part contributes a critical element to the broader understanding of strategic brand management, offering both theoretical frameworks and actionable insights. The interplay of these concepts allows organisations to gain a deeper understanding of how to strategically align their brand portfolios, build meaningful consumer relationships and implement effective branding strategies across diverse sectors. In examining these areas, this part of the handbook not only highlights the importance of aligning strategic decisions with overarching corporate goals but also emphasises the need for adaptability and responsiveness in a rapidly changing, competitive environment.

The fourth part of the handbook, *Part 4: Brand Management Performance*, focuses on the measurement, metrics and evaluation of branding strategies, which are central to the practice of brand management. These aspects are examined from both consumer-based and non-consumer-based perspectives. From the consumer-based perspective, the focus is on understanding consumers' positive responses to the brand, including emotional, cognitive and behavioural reactions to brands (*Faheem Gul Gilal, Jian Zhang, Zhiyong Yang and Shadma Shahid*), the quality and intensity of experiences consumers have with the brand across different touchpoints (*Michela Addis and Giulia Miniero*), the level of consumer engagement with the brand in both online and offline contexts (*Valentina Mazzoli*) and consumer participation in brand communities (*Daniele Dalli*). Due to important outcomes such as the dissolution of brand relationships, negative word of mouth and boycotting, there has been a growing focus in recent years on the negative aspects of consumer responses, including negative emotions, which are also analysed (*Daniela Andreini and Lia Zarantonello*). From a non-consumer-based perspective, the handbook includes an examination of positive, proactive and supportive behaviours exhibited by employees (*David Barros-Arrieta*), as well as an assessment of brand performance in terms of product-market outcomes, such as market share, and financial outcomes, like financial brand equity (*M. Berk Ataman, Koen Pauwels and Burcu Sezen*). This part of the handbook explores the applicability of these metrics across different product categories and countries, providing a comprehensive view of how brand performance is measured from multiple angles (*Jacek Kall*).

The fifth part of the handbook, entitled *Part 5: Contemporary Issues in Brand Management*, addresses the key issues in brand management that are currently being debated in both the academic and managerial literature. The contemporary issues explored in this part include ethics and social responsibility, psychological and societal well-being, and the intersection of brands and new technologies. As societal expectations evolve, brands in general, and particularly global brands, are expected to behave morally (*Yunyi Wei, Kokho [Jason] Sit and Yuksel Ekinci*) and contribute positively to society (*Bianca Grohmann*). Socio-cultural issues have also become increasingly prominent, with brands sometimes taking a stance on various socio-cultural matters, incorporating diversity, equity and inclusion into their strategies (*Zoe Lee, Rossella C. Gambetti and Sharifah Faridah Syed Alwi*), while also making brand communication more divisive and controversial (*Angela A. Beccanulli, Silvia Biraghi and Rossella C. Gambetti*). Moreover, brands are increasingly focusing on fostering psychological well-being, with some brands leveraging the concept of brand happiness as a valuable asset (*Manfred Bruhn, Stefanie Stilz and Anja Zimmermann*) and nonprofit organizations using branding strategies to create positive societal impact (*Lara Mendes Christ Bonella Sepulcri and Emerson Wagner Mainardes*). Finally, digital technologies have transformed brand management practices across digital, physical and hybrid contexts. The rapid pace of technological adoption in brand management has led to the emergence of technology-augmented brand management (*Saleh Bazi*), influenced relationships with consumers through new intermediaries, such as influencers (*Martina Quadri and Liselot Hudders*), and new engagement channels, such as gaming platforms (*Laurence Dessart and Lisa Baiwir*). Overall, this part of the handbook reflects the growing complexity of brand management and its evolving role in contemporary society. It explores the opportunities and challenges presented by these contemporary issues, encouraging readers to reflect on the ethical and societal implications of brand management.

The handbook concludes with *Part 6: Future Directions in Brand Management*, which explores prospective areas that require new research and innovation in the field. It anticipates the evolving landscape of brand management over the coming decades and highlights future avenues for academic exploration. In particular, brands are examined in relation to several key factors, including further technological advancements, particularly in artificial intelligence (*Yang Cheng, Mengge Yang and Chen Lin*), the changing dynamics of future consumer generations, including aging populations (*Carolyn Wilson-Nash*) and the impact of social conflicts and inequalities in an era marked by unstable social, economic and political environments (*Nicholas Ind, Michela Mingione and Oriol Iglesias*). It examines how brands can maintain their relevance and meaning for a diverse range of consumer groups, both current and future, and considers how brands can navigate and thrive in an increasingly unequal and volatile global landscape. This part encourages readers to reflect on the broader implications of these factors for the ongoing evolution of brand management theory and practice.

WORDS OF THANKS

This handbook would not have been possible without the incredible contributions of many dedicated scholars from around the world, to whom we are deeply grateful. These scholars are experts in their respective fields, bringing diverse perspectives and knowledge from various regions, industries and sectors. Their insights have been instrumental in shaping this handbook and reflecting the current state of brand management across these fields. We are thankful to them for sharing their expertise, which has also highlighted the key directions for future research in this domain. We would also like to extend our sincere gratitude to Michael and Ben at Sage for inviting us to undertake this project and for their ongoing support throughout. Lastly, we express our deep appreciation to you, dear readers. We hope this handbook proves useful in your studies and professional journey. With Heraclitus' wisdom in mind, we trust that this work will provide a solid foundation for students, scholars and managers to navigate the ever-evolving landscape of brand management, fostering both reflection and growth in the field. Enjoy!

PART 1

Introduction to Brand Management

1

The Resilience of the Brand Management System: Historical Perspective and Current Challenges

Isabelle Aimé, Fabienne Berger-Remy, and Marie-Eve Laporte

INTRODUCTION

Branding, as we know it in the Western world, began in the late 19th century when manufacturers started putting their names on products to differentiate them from their competitors. Many brands were named after their founders, such as King Camp Gillette in the USA, Joseph Rowntree in the UK, Victor Auguste Poulain in France and Werner von Siemens in Germany. At that time, brand management was not a formalized process. Since the brand carried the founder's name, company owners managed it intuitively and made most decisions themselves (Low & Fullerton, 1994). They retained near-total control, as exemplified by Henry Ford and his Model T (Tedlow, 1990). Before 1914, an integrated approach to marketing, including product development, sales organization, branding and advertising to meet consumer needs, did not exist (Fitzgerald, 1995). Brand management was not yet a serious concern (Tedlow, 1990).

At the turn of the 20th century, brand management became increasingly professionalized (Fitzgerald, 1995). This shift was driven by several interrelated changes: 1) Companies began using fantasy brand names, distancing brands from their founders; 2) the first generation of skilled marketing executives graduated from business schools and 3) advertising became more sophisticated. As a result, brand management responsibilities shifted from top management to specialized departments (Low & Fullerton, 1994). These departments could be either internal or external to the company, with advertising agencies and market research institutes often handling tasks like copywriting, art and market research. These external partners wielded significant influence over brand decisions and, in some cases, acted as the true architects of brand strategy.

In the late 1920s, a new organizational structure emerged in which a single individual was responsible for planning, organizing, directing and controlling the marketing program for each product line or brand within a company (Fulmer & Brunner, 1968). This structure, known as the Brand Management System, featured a hierarchy of roles: assistant brand managers, who handled operational tasks; brand managers and brand-group supervisors, who oversaw multiple brand managers and reported to the chief marketing officer (CMO) (Fulmer, 1965). Credited to N. H. McElroy at Procter & Gamble, the Brand Management System became the organizational standard for most Western companies. Brand managers became the central coordinators of all marketing activities for their brands, responsible

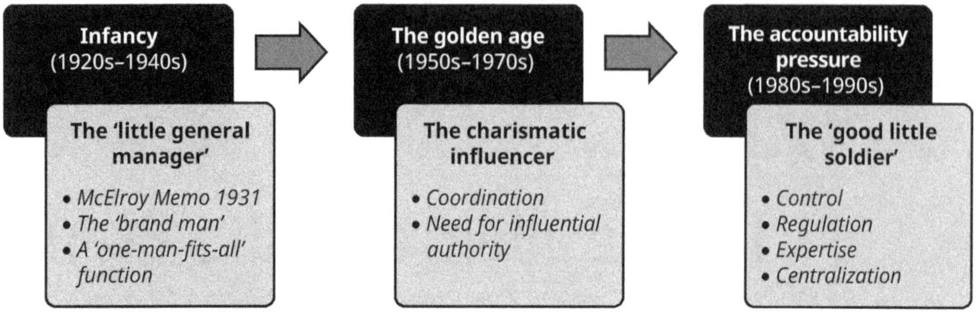

Figure 1.1 Development of the brand management system

Source: Adapted from Aimé et al. (2018).

for developing and implementing marketing plans (Low & Fullerton, 1994). Despite criticisms, the Brand Management System has proved resilient by adapting to various companies and environments. However, alternative forms of brand management, such as founder-led management and functional management, continue to exist, particularly in startups and small and medium-sized enterprises (SMEs) (Aimé et al., 2018).[1]

Since the mid-2000s, digitalization and the explosion of data have intensified critiques of the Brand Management System and prompted discussions on rethinking marketing organizations (Joshi & Giménez, 2014) and developing new competencies for brand managers (De Swaan et al., 2014). The emergence of specialized roles, such as data analysts and content creators, has further challenged the role of brand managers (Brinker & McLellan, 2014). Because of the complexity of mastering big data analysis and the nuances of social media algorithms, brand managers, who were once generalists, have been overshadowed by specialized functions. Many scholars and practitioners have predicted or advocated for significant changes to the Brand Management System, and major fast-moving consumer goods (FMCG) companies like Danone and PepsiCo have implemented substantial modifications (De Swaan et al., 2014). However, while the digital revolution initially required greater technical expertise, the rise of generative artificial intelligence (GenAI; particularly since 2015 and accelerating in recent years) has the potential to strengthen brand managers' influence and restore their strategic role.

This chapter explores the origins and development of the Brand Management System, examines the forces driving its transformation and analyzes its current status for both managers and scholars. It is divided into two sections. The first section traces the historical evolution of the Brand Management System's organizational structure, from its emergence in FMCG companies in the USA to its adoption across various Western industries and countries (Figure 1.1). The second section describes the current developments of the Brand Management System, particularly since the mid-2000s, in response to technological advancements in digitalization, data analytics and AI. It explains how the rise of the internet and social networks, along with increasing data-driven decision-making, has transformed the system by expanding required skill sets and returning some power to the consumer. Finally, it assesses how the advent of GenAI, first emerging in the mid-2010s and accelerating dramatically in recent years, may once again redefine the role of brand managers. The chapter concludes with key historical lessons and a forward-looking discussion on the role of the Brand Management System and the evolving function of brand managers in the AI era.

ORIGIN AND DEVELOPMENT OF THE BRAND MANAGEMENT SYSTEM

The Infancy (1920s–1940s)

Early forms of the Brand Management System

Procter & Gamble (P&G) is often credited with creating the Brand Management System in 1931, having formalized it through the famous McElroy

[1] Part of this chapter draws on the findings of the article 'Lessons from nearly a century of the brand management system', published by the authors in *Journal of Historical Research in Marketing* (Aimé et al., 2018).

memo (Dyer et al., 2004; Fulmer, 1965). However, early forms of the system had already appeared in the late 19th century. The idea of a single person being responsible for a group of products may have originated in department stores, although the tasks and roles were not entirely comparable to those of a product manager in industry or FMCG (Fulmer, 1965, p. 65). The term 'product manager' was already in use at General Electric by 1894, and a rudimentary version of the Brand Management System was present at Libby, McNeil and Libby (Fulmer & Brunner, 1968, p. 25). In the 1910s and 1920s, companies increasingly needed better coordination across their various functions or divisions, whether they were unitary forms (U-forms) or multidivisional forms (M-forms), according to Chandler's terminology (1977). This need was initially met by creating committees. For example, Rowntree set up a sales committee in 1911. After a trip to the USA, Seebohm Rowntree adopted a functional structure in 1921 and created a marketing committee in 1923 to forecast product needs (Fitzgerald, 1995, p. 208). In 1931, Rowntree integrated marketing and distribution into a single marketing department based on U.S. practices observed by director George Harris. This department coordinated the products of all manufacturing units, a practice that was uncommon in the UK at the time (Fitzgerald, 1995, p. 279). However, this did not constitute a Brand Management System, and Rowntree did not adopt a divisional structure until 1962. At General Motors, one of the first multidivisional firms, an institutional advertising committee was formed in 1922 to unify the divisions and create a cohesive internal and external corporate image for the 'soulless corporation' (Marchand, 1991).

The McElroy memo (1931): The official birth of the Brand Management System

To address the need for a more integrated brand management approach, Procter & Gamble developed what would become the industry norm. Brand management had gradually emerged in the 1910s and 1920s as new managers took on senior roles and decentralized brand promotion responsibilities. This approach was already evident in the launch of Crisco in 1911 (Dyer et al., 2004, p. 60). The Brand Management System evolved into a unified brand-building process, crucial for connecting advanced R&D with the market research department, established in 1924, and for coordinating marketing campaigns, distribution and production. In January 1928, C. C. Uhling became P&G's first brand manager, overseeing Lava soap (Fulmer, 1965, p. 65). However, the formalization of the system came on 13 May 1931, with the McElroy memo (Gupta, 2003). Neil McElroy, a junior manager in P&G's advertising department, realized during a Camay soap campaign that the brand was struggling to compete with Lever, Palmolive and P&G's own Ivory soap (McCraw, 2001). Responding to his president's call for innovation during the Great Depression, McElroy wrote a three-page memo advocating for dedicated teams for each brand. He argued that brands should be managed as separate businesses, each with a defined target group and strategy, to avoid internal competition (see the Appendix). McElroy proposed the creation of a 'brand man' position, with full responsibility for all marketing aspects, likening the role to a 'little general manager' (Buell, 1975, p. 6). According to the memo, brand managers should analyze brand sales by units and territories, review sales patterns, examine past advertising and promotional history and develop necessary sales materials. The memo quickly established the Brand Management System as a foundational principle at P&G (Dyer et al., 2004, p. 61) and contributed to the successful launch of brands such as Tide in 1946. McElroy later rose to become P&G's president and, subsequently, U.S. Secretary of Defense under President Dwight Eisenhower.

Slow spread of the Brand Management System in the Western world after World War II

Initially, the Brand Management System spread slowly beyond P&G. For about two decades, most companies retained functional management structures, with only a few exceptions in the USA (Fulmer & Brunner, 1968; Low & Fullerton, 1994). Johnson & Johnson adopted the system in 1935, Monsanto in 1940 and Merck in 1946. It was not until the 1950s that the Brand Management System gained widespread adoption (Buell, 1975, p. 4). The terminology used for this organizational structure varied, with some referring to it as the 'product management system' (Buell, 1975, p. 3). Despite differences in titles (brand manager, product manager or business manager), the core responsibilities and structure of the marketing department remained consistent, and the organization could still be classified under the Brand Management System (Luck, 1969, p. 32).

Why did the Brand Management System take so long to spread despite P&G's success? Rogers's theory of diffusion of innovation offers one explanation (Low & Fullerton, 1994). It suggests that new ideas take time to spread from early adopters to the majority (Rogers, 1962). Moreover, World War II likely slowed the expansion of the Brand Management

System, as branding became less of a priority during the war (Low & Fullerton, 1994). In the USA, many companies were content with their existing functional management structures. Some, like Sears & Roebuck and Standard Oil, organized operations around geographic regions, while General Motors relied on interdivisional committees for coordination (Dyer et al., 2004; Marchand, 1991). In Europe, several factors contributed to the delayed adoption of the Brand Management System. The persistence of family-run businesses and the relatively smaller market sizes reduced the urgency for such organizational changes. In both the UK and France, family businesses were resistant to allowing salaried managers to become directors, maintaining conservative management structures (Fitzgerald, 1995, p. 191). In addition, the smaller scale of European companies made the need for cross-functional coordination less pressing. Despite these barriers, the Brand Management System gained significant traction from the 1950s to the 1970s, first in the USA and later in Europe (Buell, 1975; Low & Fullerton, 1994).

The Golden Age (1950s–1970s)

Professionalization of consumer knowledge and market research

Following World War II, global population growth and economic expansion fueled mass production, widespread distribution and increased consumer spending. During this period, aspirations for an improved lifestyle, often epitomized by the phrase 'keeping up with the Joneses', became widespread. The 1950s marked a pivotal decade for marketing, as it was the first time a significant proportion of the population had the means to participate in mass consumption (Fitzgerald, 1995, p. 32). Tedlow (1990, p. 6) described this period as 'the third phase of American marketing', characterized by more detailed market segmentation based on demographics and psychographics. This shift allowed marketers to target specific groups more effectively, creating a demand for sophisticated marketing intelligence. In Europe, too, 'mass manufacturing had made the intuition of the individual entrepreneurs less reliable and inappropriate' (Fitzgerald, 1995, p. 31). As Fullerton (1988) observed, analyzing consumer needs has long been a part of marketing. Many large American companies had established internal market analysis departments as early as the 1920s. Procter & Gamble (P&G) was at the forefront of this movement, thanks to one of its executives, 'Doc' Smelser. Around 1924 or 1925, Smelser set up what was then considered the most advanced internal marketing research department, which he led until 1959 (Dyer et al., 2004; McCraw, 2001). However, he later acknowledged that the methods used at the time were quite primitive (Dyer et al., 2004). His team of door-to-door interviewers collected consumer data, enabling brand managers to refine their marketing strategies. The first brand to use market research systematically was Camay (Dyer et al., 2004, p. 58), and this approach became a key part of P&G's product development and improvement process (McCraw, 2001).

In the UK, companies like Unilever and Rowntree imported market research methods from the USA during the 1920s and 1930s to guide their product development and marketing strategies (Fitzgerald, 1995, p. 32). However, such practices were rare. Despite the growing need for specialized marketing services and more professional approaches in firms, most companies in the USA and the UK did not adopt market research until the 1950s and 1960s (Fitzgerald, 1995, p. 32). After World War II, more companies began to recognize the value of their internal data for market assessment and started establishing their own market research departments. Moreover, advances in techniques, such as consumer panels and focus groups, facilitated more extensive data collection and analysis (Wedel & Kannan, 2016). Large market research firms emerged in North America and Europe to support businesses in this endeavor. For example, Nielsen (1923), Burke (1931), and Gallup (1935) were founded in the USA, while GfK (1934) and IFOP (1938) were established in Germany and France, respectively. These companies developed innovative tools to analyze sales data using household panels (following Nielsen's introduction of the first panel, the Nielsen Drug Index, in 1933), measure advertising effectiveness (first introduced by Nielsen for radio in 1936) and study consumer attitudes and behaviors through field experiments. They also began conducting telephone surveys as household telephone access expanded. As mass media like television and radio grew in influence, advertising costs increased, making it even more important for companies to understand and manage their consumer base effectively.

Extension and standardization of the Brand Management System

The growing use of consumer data and market research required new internal organizational structures. Companies were also becoming more complex, with expanded product lines and larger brand portfolios, which demanded greater efficiency in their multidivisional structures (Low & Fullerton, 1994). Between 1950 and 1970, the position of brand manager became standard in the USA and the UK, coinciding with broader shifts in management practices and the widespread adoption of divisional structures in large companies. For example, a 1958 job advertisement in the *Financial Times* for a product manager stated: 'He will need drive, enthusiasm, and the ability to get things done, taking full responsibility for promoting the 3-In-One and Teal products'. The Brand Management System gained popularity as a solution to marketing and organizational challenges. 'The product manager system evolved out of necessity due to the increased complexity of marketing lines and programs' (Fulmer & Brunner, 1968, p. 29). During the 1950s and 1960s, the system became a trend among American companies, leading to rushed and, at times, poorly executed implementations. 'In the United States, the product manager system is widely accepted. At least two-thirds of consumer companies with multiple products now use product managers, including eighty-four percent of the largest 500 American corporations. Some companies adopted it just because their competitors did' (Fulmer & Brunner, 1968, p. 26). By 1974, the Association of National Advertisers found that 85% of U.S. packaged goods companies (93% of those with annual advertising expenditures over $10 million) had implemented the Brand Management System, along with 55% of industrial goods producers (Buell, 1975, p. 4).

The Brand Management System was later introduced to subsidiaries outside the USA. 'As a management technology, product management was exported from the USA to Europe, especially through multinational corporations, to adapt to changing competitive environments' (Venkatesh & Wilemon, 1980, p. 68). In Germany, the Brand Management System was first introduced by a British/Dutch consumer goods subsidiary from North America. For more than a decade, German product managers were primarily employed in foreign subsidiaries, mainly from the USA. The first German company to adopt the system did so in 1963. By the late 1960s, 75% of German companies using the Brand Management System were American subsidiaries. As the system was still viewed as an American innovation, it sparked some nationalistic resentment and skepticism, particularly in a country with smaller companies and fewer product lines. A similar pattern emerged in other European countries, contributing to the broader adoption of the Brand Management System across the Western world. For example, a 1964 job advertisement for Fisons Limited in the *Financial Times* stated that the recruited brand managers would be trained at the headquarters before being sent overseas.

In its early decades, academic research largely overlooked the Brand Management System (Luck, 1969). The system evolved out of practical necessity, and only after decades of demonstrated success did scholars start to take notice. The first academic article on the Brand Management System was published in 1960 by marketing practitioner Robert Keith, who described the 'marketing revolution' it had brought to Pillsbury (Keith, 1960). However, some scholars questioned the reliability of his account and whether Pillsbury's experience was representative. Fullerton (1988) noted that Keith failed to provide evidence that other firms had undergone similar transformations and neglected external economic and social factors (e.g., the Great Depression of the 1930s) that had contributed to the decline of the Production Era. Despite these criticisms, Keith's account remains valuable as a firsthand testimony of early Brand Management System implementation. Academic interest in the system increased in the 1970s and 1980s, with studies focusing on the roles and responsibilities of brand managers (Buell, 1975, Luck, 1969). Research highlighted that while brand managers bore significant responsibilities, including profit and advertising, they lacked formal authority. At best, they relied on influence, legitimacy from expertise and personal charisma, shifting from the '*little general manager*' concept to *charismatic influencers*. However, this absence of formal authority, combined with managerial inexperience, often caused problems and weakened the Brand Management System. Critics argued that the system fostered brand bureaucracy, stifled creativity and hindered customer orientation.

The Accountability Pressure (1980s–1990s)

Globalization of brands

In the 1980s, the global balance of power, previously structured around three main blocs (the Western allies, the Soviet bloc and the Third World), began to shift. With the end of the Cold War and the collapse of the Eastern Bloc, symbolized by the fall of the Berlin Wall on 9 November 1989, neoliberal globalization gained momentum. This change, driven by market liberalization, lower transport costs and increased human mobility, made consumer goods more widely available across the world. During this period, the number of global organizations grew significantly. T. Levitt, an economics professor at Harvard Business School, highlighted this trend in his influential article 'The Globalization of Markets', published in the *Harvard Business Review* (May–June 1983). He argued that companies should operate as if the world were a single large market, driven by a convergence of consumer needs and desires, while disregarding regional and national differences. In this environment, the ability to create strong brands that could win consumer preference worldwide became a key skill. Global brands became cultural icons, exemplified by the success of McDonald's in Paris and Tokyo, Coca-Cola in Bahrain, Pepsi in Moscow and the widespread popularity of rock music, Greek salad, Hollywood movies, Revlon cosmetics, Sony TVs and Levi's jeans (Levitt, 1983). Beyond the commercial opportunities of a global market, companies sought to leverage economies of scale in manufacturing, promotion, advertising and sales. To achieve this, many multinational companies streamlined their brand portfolios, reducing the number of brands to focus on a few large, global brands. As these global brands grew in size and reach, they came to be viewed as financial assets. The emergence of brand valuation metrics reflected this shift, with Rupert Murdoch including his newspaper brands on balance sheets in 1984 and Interbrand valuing the UK's Rank Hovis McDougall brands in 1988. Since then, Interbrand has published annual rankings of the world's most valuable brands. At this time, brands evolved from mere names on products to sources of competitive advantage by becoming valuable, rare, inimitable and non-substitutable. The growing recognition of financial brand equity elevated brand management to a key strategic function for companies. This shift led to a division of responsibilities within organizations: Strategic branding decisions were made at higher corporate levels by senior executives, while execution tasks were handled locally by brand managers. For example, in the early 1980s, Nestlé centralized strategic decisions related to advertising campaigns, package design and new product development. General Motors followed a similar model, with strategic roles outlined in a study by Townsend et al. (2010). P&G implemented 'Euro Brand Teams to leverage capabilities and scale across the region, coordinate new product and marketing initiatives and avoid costly duplication of effort' (Dyer et al., 2004, p. 203). Meanwhile, more tactical tasks like sales promotions were managed at the country level.

To unlock their financial value, brands required significant investment, particularly in advertising. This era saw the professionalization and standardization of the brand manager role, with more formalized processes and increased accountability (John & Martin, 1984). The rise of computing in the workplace played a crucial role in this transformation. Brand managers started using personal computers and software, especially spreadsheets like Lotus (1983) and Excel (1985). These tools enhanced control and monitoring systems, both internally (through dashboards and scorecards) and externally (via market data analysis). This shift had two major effects on brand managers: 1) Their responsibilities expanded to include more reporting, sometimes resembling management accounting and 2) they devoted more time to analyzing market data. Major market research companies began using retail panel data powered by scanner technology, such as Nielsen's point-of-sale scanner data in 1980 and IRI's in-home barcode scanning service in 1995. While these methods improved data accuracy, they also increased the frequency of reported issues and the sheer volume of data collected.

Category management: A threat to the Brand Management System

In the 1980s and 1990s, intense competition among retailers for market share, driven by end-user prices, led to a more concentrated retail sector and increased the bargaining power of retailers' buyers. In response, manufacturers reorganized and created category management departments (Zenor, 1994). In 1987, P&G pioneered this approach, which was considered the company's most significant reorganization in 30 years (Dyer et al., 2004). This restructuring addressed internal competition among brand managers, which had previously hindered collaboration and knowledge sharing. The Brand Management System was criticized for its inability to coordinate strategy across product categories, as no single individual was responsible for identifying new market segments or opportunities for line extensions and new brands. The new Category Manager role sought to redirect internal competition outward, toward external competitors (Dyer et al., 2004), and initially competed with the Brand Management System. Some scholars, such as Lindblom and Olkkonen (2006), even predicted the system's gradual disappearance. However, P&G integrated these changes without adding a new management layer. Instead, it pushed decision-making closer to the operational level and trade customers. Category Business Unit managers oversaw brand managers and representatives from sales, finance and product development. Ultimately, both organizational models coexisted, creating a new interface for brand managers while also diluting their influence, as they found themselves caught between the demands of sales functions and management controllers. During this period, brand managers lost authority over the sales department and shifted their focus to internal planning and coordination without a strategic orientation (Cossé & Swan, 1983). As accountability increased, they became more like management accountants, detached from the market – '*good little soldiers*' (Figure 1.1). This transformation led them away from their original role, and they were even accused of undermining brand assets (Shocker et al., 1994).

CURRENT ERA: THE ADAPTATION OF THE BRAND MANAGEMENT SYSTEM TO DIGITALIZATION AND DATAFICATION

The Transformations Brought by Digitalization and Datafication

Digitalization refers to 'the adoption or increase in use of digital or computer technology by an organization, industry, country, etc.' (Brennen & Kreiss, 2016). Datafication, meanwhile, is defined as the conversion of processes or activities into actionable data (Leonardi & Treem, 2020). Since the beginning of the 21st century, technological advancements driven by digitalization and datafication have profoundly transformed marketing in three main ways: the volume and granularity of available data, the heightened focus on consumer centricity and the growing complexity and diversification of required expertise.

The rise of data and data analytics (2000s)

Starting in 1995, the widespread adoption of the World Wide Web led to the development of clickstream data, which fueled the emergence of Customer Relationship Management (CRM) systems such as Salesforce's cloud computing platform, launched in 1999. The founding of Google in 1998 and the rise of keyword searches significantly expanded the volume and variety of data, including user-generated content like blogs and product reviews. The proliferation of social media platforms such as Facebook (2004), YouTube (2005), Twitter and Flickr (2006), Tumblr (2007), Instagram (2010) and Snapchat (2011) further accelerated this data explosion by generating vast amounts of text and video content. The advent of smartphones with GPS capabilities, starting with the Apple iPhone in 2007, also enabled marketers to capture consumer location data, thus further transforming marketing practices. While consumer data were once scarce, digital advancements since the 2000s have generated massive volumes of data that marketers can now leverage. Marketing organizations that invest in big data resources have enhanced their market-oriented capabilities and thereby improved their differentiation strategy to achieve superior performance (Suoniemi et al., 2020).

Algorithms, defined as a series of operations and rules applied iteratively through a systematic method, represent the early stages of AI use in marketing (Kumar et al., 2024). This type of AI, known as analytical AI, primarily relies on structured data to predict outcomes and optimize large-scale operations (Grewal et al., 2024; Huang & Rust, 2021). Analytical AI can automate routine tasks, which Huang and Rust call *mechanical AI* (2018, p. 156). It can also conduct complex data analysis more efficiently than human brand managers or market research managers – referred to as *thinking AI* in Huang and Rust's terminology. While *mechanical AI* is well-established, *thinking AI* is rapidly advancing (Huang & Rust, 2018).

Analytical AI has allowed marketing organizations to compete by using existing models rather than depending on proprietary algorithms. This technology enables the personalization of marketing strategies through big data analysis, creating unprecedented opportunities for customer targeting. It facilitates 'the process of searching and analyzing data (quantitative or qualitative) to find implicit, but potentially useful information' (Manis & Madhavaram, 2023, p. 12). Throughout the 2000s, it transformed marketing approaches by leveraging real-time data from consumer interactions with products and services. Key marketing applications include geofencing, search marketing, retargeting, A/B testing, programmatic advertising and chatbots (Kopalle et al., 2020; Kumar et al., 2024). Analytical AI is expected to replace humans in most data analysis tasks as they perform them more efficiently and accurately. While this development may threaten market research roles, brand managers remain essential for interpreting and contextualizing the data.

Toward more consumer- and customer-centric organizations (2000–present)

At the turn of the 21st century, research and case studies increasingly highlighted the need for marketing organizations to adopt a more customer-centric approach in order to better adapt to the digital and technological environment. An in-depth study of 50 managers by Homburg et al. (2000) found that many firms, traditionally structured around the Brand Management System and organized by geographical areas (e.g., U.S. regions or countries in Europe), were shifting toward a more customer-centric model. While the Brand Management System was not completely abandoned, its prominence declined. For example, in P&G's marketing organization restructured in 2000, Gupta (2003) described the emergence of a 'cohort management strategy', which targeted groups of consumers with similar attitudes and needs. Similarly, a Harvard Business School case study (Shapiro, 2002) recommended establishing customer-centric teams by integrating sales and marketing through a CRM program as a best practice. Some major companies, such as Nike and PepsiCo, quickly made significant changes to their Brand Management System (De Swaan et al., 2014). However, many marketing departments continued to follow the same structure they had used for the past 40 years, with product or brand managers working in silos and CMOs struggling to design more efficient organizations (De Swaan et al., 2014). Implementing customer-centric approaches often proved too complex. Some companies introduced a Chief Customer Officer (CCO) to gain a comprehensive view of each customer through various data sets and to involve customers in the creative process. In addition, as the sales department oversees the customer journey more and more, the brand manager's power has diminished. Therefore, some authors argued that the Brand Management System was losing influence in favor of the sales department (Homburg et al., 2015).

Moreover, datafication has disrupted traditional brand–consumer relationships, leading to new intermediation processes that have empowered consumers (Gielens & Steenkamp, 2019). Social media has fundamentally changed how consumers interact with brands, both online and offline, through social conversations, co-creation, brand communities and mobile communication (Muninger et al., 2019). The traditional top-down conversations have shifted to multilayered debates involving multiple stakeholders (Kornum et al., 2017). Brand meaning is increasingly co-created through brand–consumer relationships and is reinterpreted at each touchpoint, whether through brand interfaces, employees or external stakeholders. Among these stakeholders, marketing influencers have become essential in industries such as fashion, beauty, travel and beverages to effectively reach target groups like millennials (Haenlein et al., 2020). Consequently, this shift is transforming how marketers manage brands, as they have partially lost control over brand meaning. Power has shifted toward consumers through brand communities and co-creation, fostering greater creativity. To better describe this evolving landscape, Quinton (2013) suggested moving from a relational paradigm to a community paradigm. Iglesias and Bonet (2012) described this transformation as 'persuasive brand management', in which brand managers no longer fully control brand meaning but instead become co-producers of stories and narratives to influence brand perception. For all these reasons, the Brand Management System, which was once a fairly generalist structure in which the brand manager orchestrated all aspects of brand strategy, now requires greater coordination. Brand managers must collaborate with both external and internal experts, such as data scientists, digital privacy analysts and content editors, all of whom challenge the brand manager's traditional role (Aimé et al., 2022; Brinker & McLellan, 2014). Researchers have highlighted the evolving role of brand managers as facilitators. De Swaan et al. (2014) described them as 'orchestrators', while Brexendorf and Daecke (2012) noted that brand managers now handle a wider range of tasks due to the complexity of the digital ecosystem, which includes numerous touchpoints and customer journey management. To navigate this landscape, brand managers must integrate market and brand research insights with creative, entrepreneurial and practical thinking (Brexendorf & Daecke, 2012; Cluley et al., 2020). While these changes have not eliminated the role of the brand manager, they have reshaped it by broadening the required skill set.

Facilitators and data experts: The dual expertise of brand managers

Datafication presents major challenges, as data-driven decision-making requires expertise spanning marketing, statistics, econometrics and IT (Cluley et al., 2020; Joshi & Giménez, 2014). Ideally, brand managers should possess dual expertise: a combination of strategic and management skills alongside a broad and deep understanding of data and analytics (Aimé et al., 2022; Wedel & Kannan, 2016). This makes them 'two-headed' – on the one hand, acting as facilitators who unite teams around the brand mission; on the other hand, mastering digital and analytical skills. Brand managers must be strategists, allocating resources to align with company priorities and maximize ROI, while also being technologists who leverage the latest advancements in their field. Over the past decade, companies such as Danone and L'Oréal have significantly restructured their organizations, creating digital activation units distinct from the classic brand manager function, which now primarily focuses on brand strategy, product development and innovation. These activation units consist of digital experts recruited from the digital ecosystem, specializing in areas like automation marketing, SEO and SEA, to activate all offline and online sales and communication levers. These units have gained more and more influence and now manage substantial budgets at the expense of brand managers. As a result, in these companies, the brand manager has effectively been split into two distinct teams that have to work hand in hand. In parallel, some companies have introduced more specialized marketing roles, such as the Chief Marketing Technologist (CMT), who acts as a liaison between the CMO and other departments like IT (Brinker & McLellan, 2014).

Moreover, in terms of soft skills, brand managers must work efficiently in cross-functional teams and adopt a test-and-learn approach through experimentation (Aimé et al., 2022; Joshi & Giménez, 2014). Collaboration and networking are now central to the Brand Management System. Brand managers are expected to 'cross organizational boundaries' and 'make and execute shared decisions' (Joshi & Giménez, 2014, pp. 66–67). Companies like Target and Nordstrom have revamped their decision-making processes, thereby fostering greater collaboration between brand management and other functions across planning, strategy, execution and operations. Altogether, this evolution challenges marketing education and training, as knowledge must be continuously updated in a rapidly changing environment (Iyer & Bright, 2024).

A Prospective Outlook on GenAI

Following digitalization and datafication at the turn of the century, a new technological shift could once again disrupt the Brand Management System: GenAI. GenAI refers to a class of advanced AI capable of producing new content, including text, images and videos, using deep-learning models trained on existing data (Cillo & Rubera, 2025; Grewal et al., 2024; Huang & Rust, 2024). This transformation is exemplified by the creation of OpenAI in 2015, which launched ChatGPT in 2022, a chat-based interface built on a large language model first introduced in 2018. OpenAI also launched DALL·E in 2021, integrating it into ChatGPT in 2023.[2] GenAI constitutes 'a quantum leap in marketing's ability to target individual customers' (Huang & Rust, 2021, p. 47). The emergence of foundation models (i.e., large pre-trained models that serve as the basis for specialized, task-specific applications) has further enhanced GenAI's capabilities (Bommasani et al., 2022). These models enable content generation, exemplified by large language models (LLMs) like ChatGPT, and allow organizations to compete by leveraging existing models rather than developing proprietary algorithms. This shift emphasizes the strategic importance of fully harnessing the potential of these technologies.

GenAI is expected to significantly influence most business functions, particularly marketing (Cillo & Rubera, 2025; Manis & Madhavaram, 2023). According to a report by McKinsey (Harkness et al., 2023), marketing productivity could increase by up to 15% of total marketing expenditure. Sullivan and Fosso Wamba (2024) show that AI-powered capabilities bring value to marketing organizations by enhancing their ability to adapt to market changes. GenAI not only generates new data based on learned patterns (*mechanical AI* and *thinking AI*, as defined by Huang & Rust, 2018, 2024) but also creates emotional interactions (*feeling AI*), as demonstrated by ChatGPT. GenAI produces textual predictions and generates original content, thereby marking a distinct evolution in AI applications. Unlike traditional supervised AI models, GenAI demonstrates superior adaptability to novel settings, which enhances its applicability in dynamic environments and fosters serendipity and creativity. GenAI's content-generation capabilities enable marketers to produce contextually relevant and innovative materials. This has led to various marketing applications, including generating insights and innovative ideas for products and services, as well as producing effective communication content. In addition, GenAI is emerging as a critical tool for enhancing customer relationships (Peltier et al., 2023). It enables machines to understand and respond to human emotions, which is pivotal for establishing emotional connections between firms and customers (Huang & Rust, 2018, 2021).

However, aligning GenAI with strategic marketing goals remains a challenge. To address this, scholars advocate for developing self-aware AI systems capable of distinguishing between customer, firm and AI perspectives to ensure strategic alignment and foster meaningful relationships (Huang & Rust, 2024).

In summary, GenAI represents a paradigm shift in marketing, offering unprecedented opportunities for personalization, creativity and customer engagement by generating outputs that closely resemble human-created content. Analytical and GenAI are complementary: Analytical AI helps companies make informed decisions, while GenAI enhances creativity and automation. This places them in direct competition with the dual expertise of brand managers described above and positions the Brand Management System at another crossroads. To date, no research has examined how GenAI will impact marketing organizations and

[2] A history of AI and ChatGPT is available on the blog of Eddy Malik, www.officetimeline.com/blog/artificial-intelligence-ai-and-chatgpt-history-and-timelines (retrieved January 14, 2025), as cited by Grewal et al. (2024).

the Brand Management System. Moreover, it is unclear how to maximize GenAI's potential while addressing challenges related to emotional intelligence and alignment with organizational goals, especially in a context of high expectations, as well as fear and resistance from teams (Iyer & Bright, 2024; Sullivan & Fosso Wamba, 2024).

Companies remain uncertain about the new roles needed in response to the rise of specialized digital and AI skills. They face the dilemma of whether to hire specialists for each emerging area of expertise (such as AI) or to work with consultants and external agencies that excel in these fields. Another possibility could restore some power to brand managers. AI may facilitate the reintegration of certain design and creative functions that were previously outsourced to advertising or other external agencies. Similarly, AI could replace data scientists in performing key consumer and sales analyses, which would allow brand managers to reclaim these capabilities and regain their central role in the organization.

CONCLUSION

This chapter has examined why and how the Brand Management System established itself as a dominant organizational form in Western countries throughout the 20th century and the first two decades of the 21st century while adapting to a constantly evolving environment. The Brand Management System outpaced alternative structures like functional brand management (i.e., where responsibilities are divided across internal departments) and top-level brand management (i.e., managed by the founder) in the USA. After becoming the predominant method of brand management in the USA, it spread to Europe through American multinational companies. Over time, it has undergone significant transformations and demonstrated remarkable resilience to changes in consumer behavior, media, data and technology.

Once again, the Brand Management System seems to be at a crossroads. Just as advertising evolved in the late 19th century, brand managers may now be replaced by specialized roles, such as digital and AI experts, who work across multiple brands within a company. Alternatively, brand management could revert to a model in which visionary founders oversee branding themselves, as seen in many startups where founders personify their brands. However, the Brand Management System has faced and adapted to many disruptions before. Taking a historical perspective enables us to put into perspective the current transformations driven by data and AI. From a managerial standpoint, companies must carefully evaluate the role of brand management before restructuring their organizations. It is crucial to avoid being overly influenced by the prevailing discourse on digital transformation and AI. Creating parallel digital and AI functions alongside existing structures can reinforce silos, whereas a comprehensive re-engineering of brand management is needed to enhance networking and agility. Datafication and AI blur the boundaries between brand management, internal functions like IT, sales and finance, and external suppliers including communication agencies, market research institutes and data providers. Therefore, while the Brand Management System is likely to persist, the contours of this organizational form and the nature of both internal and external interfaces will need to be redefined.

In summary, the Brand Management System has demonstrated remarkable adaptability. It originally emerged out of practical necessity, offering an integrated approach over fragmented functional management and providing specific expertise instead of relying on intuitive management by founders or top executives. These fundamental needs remain relevant today, as strategic thinking and coordination will always be essential. While alternative brand management models have gained renewed interest during this period of change, the Brand Management System may once again prove to be the prevailing organization structure.

REFERENCES

Aimé, I., Berger-Remy, F., & Laporte, M.-E. (2018). Lessons from nearly a century of the brand management system. *Journal of Historical Research in Marketing*, *10*(4), 420–450. https://doi.org/10.1108/JHRM-06-2017-0026

Aimé, I., Berger-Remy, F., & Laporte, M.-E. (2022). The brand, the persona and the algorithm: How datafication is reconfiguring marketing work. *Journal of Business Research*, *145*, 814–827. https://doi.org/10.1016/j.jbusres.2022.03.047

Bommasani et al. (2022). On the opportunities and risks of foundation models. Center for research on foundation models (CRFM) Stanford institute for Human-Centered Artificial Intelligence (HAI) Stanford University. https://doi.org/10.48550/arXiv.2108.07258

Brennen, J. S., & Kreiss, D. (2016). Digitalization. In K. B. Jensen & R. T. Craig (Eds.), *The international encyclopedia of communication theory and philosophy* (pp. 1–11). Wiley. https://doi.org/10.1002/9781118766804.wbiect111

Brexendorf, T. O., & Daecke, N. (2012). The brand manager—Current tasks and skill requirements in FMCG companies. *Marketing Review St. Gallen, 29*(6), 32–37. https://doi.org/10.1365/s11621-012-0175-9

Brinker, S., & McLellan, L. (2014). The rise of the chief marketing technologist. *Harvard Business Review, 92*(7/8), 82–85.

Buell, V. P. (1975). The changing role of the product manager in consumer goods companies. *Journal of Marketing, 39*(3), 3–11. https://doi.org/10.1177/002224297503900303

Chandler, A. D. (1977). *The visible hand: The managerial revolution in American business*. Harvard University Press.

Cillo, P., & Rubera, G. (2025). Generative AI in innovation and marketing processes: A roadmap of research opportunities. *Journal of the Academy Marketing Science, 53*, 684–701. https://doi.org/10.1007/s11747-024-01044-7

Cluley, R., Green, W., & Owen, R. (2020). The changing role of the marketing researcher in the age of digital technology: Practitioner perspectives on the digitization of marketing research. *International Journal of Market Research, 62*(1), 27–42. https://doi.org/10.1177/1470785319865129

Cossé, T. J., & Swan, J. E. (1983). Strategic marketing planning by product managers: Room for improvement? *Journal of Marketing, 47*(3), 92–102. https://doi.org/10.1177/002224298304700310

De Swaan A. M., van den Driest, F., & Weed, K. (2014). The ultimate marketing machine. *Harvard Business Review, 92*(7/8), 54–63.

Dyer, D., Dalzell, F., & Olegario, R. (2004). *Rising tide: Lessons from 165 years of brand building at Procter & Gamble*. Harvard Business Review Press.

Fitzgerald, R. (1995). *Rowntree and the marketing revolution, 1862–1969*. Cambridge University Press.

Fullerton, R. A. (1988). How modern is modern marketing? Marketing's evolution and the myth of the 'production era'. *Journal of Marketing, 52*(1), 108–125. https://doi.org/10.2307/1251689

Fulmer, R. M. (1965). Product management: Panacea or Pandora's box? *California Management Review, 7*(4), 63–74. https://doi.org/10.2307/41165648

Fulmer, R. M., & Brunner, L. (1968). An analysis of US and German practices of product management. *Management International Review, 8*(2/3), 25–36. www.jstor.org/stable/40226826

Gielens, K., & Steenkamp, J.-B. E. M. (2019). Branding in the era of digital (dis)intermediation. *International Journal of Research in Marketing, 36*(3), 367–384. https://doi.org/10.1016/j.ijresmar.2019.01.005

Grewal, D., Satornino, C. B., Davenport, T., & Guha, A. (2024). How generative AI is shaping the future of marketing. *Journal of the Academy of Marketing Science, 53*, 1–21. https://doi.org/10.1007/s11747-024-01064-3

Gupta, V. (2003). *P&G's Brand Management System*. IBS Center for Management Research.

Haenlein, M., Anadol, E., Farnsworth, T., Hugo, H., Hunichen, J., & Welte, D. (2020). Navigating the new era of influencer marketing: How to be successful on instagram, TikTok, & Co. *California Management Review, 63*(1), 5–25. https://doi.org/10.1177/0008125620958166

Harkness, L., Robinson, K., Stein, E., & Wu, W. (2023). *The power of generative AI for marketing*. McKinsey & Company. www.mckinsey.com/capabilities/growth-marketing-and-sales/our-insights/how-generative-ai-can-boost-consumer-marketing

Homburg, C., Vomberg, A., Enke, M., & Grimm, P. (2015). The loss of the marketing department's influence: Is it really happening? And why worry? *Journal of the Academy of Marketing Science, 43*(1), 1–13. https://doi.org/10.1007/s11747-014-0416-3

Homburg, C., Workman, J. P., Jr., & Jensen, O. (2000). Fundamental changes in marketing organization: The movement toward a customer-focused organizational structure. *Journal of the Academy of Marketing Science, 28*(4), 459–478. https://doi.org/10.1177/0092070300284001

Huang, M.-H., & Rust, R. T. (2018). Artificial intelligence in service. *Journal of Service Research, 21*(2), 155–172. https://doi.org/10.1177/1094670517752459

Huang, M.-H., & Rust, R. T. (2021). A strategic framework for artificial intelligence in marketing. *Journal of the Academy of Marketing Science, 49*(1), 30–50. https://doi.org/10.1007/s11747-020-00749-9

Huang, M.-H., & Rust, R. T. (2024). The caring machine: Feeling AI for customer care. *Journal of Marketing, 88*(5), 1–23. https://doi.org/10.1177/00222429231224748

Iglesias, O., & Bonet, E. (2012). Persuasive brand management: How managers can influence brand meaning when they are losing control over it. *Journal of Organizational Change Management, 25*(2), 251–264. https://doi.org/10.1108/09534811211213937

Iyer, P., & Bright, L. F. (2024). Navigating a paradigm shift: Technology and user acceptance of big data and artificial intelligence among advertising and marketing practitioners. *Journal of Business Research, 180*, 114699. https://doi.org/10.1016/j.jbusres.2024.114699

John, G., & Martin, J. (1984). Effects of organizational structure of marketing planning on credibility and utilization of plan output. *Journal of Marketing Research (JMR), 21*(2), 170–183. https://doi.org/10.1177/002224378402100205

Joshi, A., & Giménez, E. (2014). Decision-driven marketing. *Harvard Business Review*, *92*(7/8), 64–71.

Keith, R. J. (1960). The marketing revolution. *Journal of Marketing*, *24*(3), 35–38. https://doi.org/10.1177/002224296002400306

Kopalle, P. K., Kumar, V., & Subramaniam, M. (2020). How legacy firms can embrace the digital ecosystem via digital customer orientation. *Journal of the Academy of Marketing Science*, *48*(1), 114–131. https://doi.org/10.1007/s11747-019-00694-2

Kornum, N., Gyrd-Jones, R., Al Zagir, N., & Brandis, K. A. (2017). Interplay between intended brand identity and identities in a Nike related brand community: Co-existing synergies and tensions in a nested system. *Journal of Business Research*, *70*, 432–440. https://doi.org/10.1016/j.jbusres.2016.06.019

Kumar, V., Ashraf, A. R., & Nadeem, W. (2024). AI-powered marketing: What, where, and how? *International Journal of Information Management*, *77*(August), 102783. https://doi.org/10.1016/j.ijinfomgt.2024.102783

Leonardi, P. M., & Treem, J. W. (2020). Behavioral visibility: A new paradigm for organization studies in the age of digitization, digitalization, and datafication. *Organization Studies*, *41*(12), 1601–1625. https://doi.org/10.1177/0170840620970728

Levitt, T. (1983). The globalization of markets. *Harvard Business Review*, *61*(3), 92–102.

Lindblom, A., & Olkkonen, R. (2006). Category management tactics: An analysis of manufacturers' control. *International Journal of Retail & Distribution Management*, *34*(6), 482–496. https://doi.org/10.1108/09590550610667065

Low, G. S., & Fullerton, R. A. (1994). Brands, brand management, and the brand manager system: A critical-historical evaluation. *Journal of Marketing Research*, *31*(2), 173–190. https://doi.org/10.1177/002224379403100203

Luck, D. J. (1969). Interfaces of a product manager. *Journal of Marketing*, *33*(4), 32–36. https://doi.org/10.1177/002224296903300406

Manis, K. T., & Madhavaram, S. (2023). AI-enabled marketing capabilities and the hierarchy of capabilities: Conceptualization, proposition development, and research avenues. *Journal of Business Research*, *157*, 113485. https://doi.org/10.1016/j.jbusres.2022.113485

Marchand, R. (1991). The corporation nobody knew: Bruce Barton, Alfred Sloan, and the founding of General Motors. *Business History Review*, *65*(4), 825. https://doi.org/10.2307/3117266

McCraw, T. K. (2001). *American business since 1920: How it worked* (2nd ed.). Wiley-Blackwell.

Muninger, M.-I., Hammedi, W., & Mahr, D. (2019). The value of social media for innovation: A capability perspective. *Journal of Business Research*, *95*, 116–127. https://doi.org/10.1016/j.jbusres.2018.10.012

Peltier, J. W., Dahl, A. J., & Schibrowsky, J. A. (2023). Artificial intelligence in interactive marketing: A conceptual framework and research agenda. *Journal of Research in Interactive Marketing*, *18*(1), 54–90. https://doi.org/10.1108/JRIM-01-2023-0030

Quinton, S. (2013). The community brand paradigm: A response to brand management's dilemma in the digital era. *Journal of Marketing Management*, *29*(7/8), 912–932. https://doi.org/10.1080/0267257X.2012.729072

Rogers, E. M. (1962). *Diffusion of innovations* (5th ed. in 2023). Free Press.

Shapiro, B. P. (2002). *Creating the customer-centric team: Coordinating sales and marketing (Harvard Business School Case No. 9-999-006).* Harvard Business School Publishing.

Shocker, A. D., Srivastava, R. K., & Ruekert, R. W. (1994). Challenges and opportunities facing brand management: An introduction to the special issue. *Journal of Marketing Research*, *31*(2), 149–158. https://doi.org/10.1177/002224379403100201

Sullivan, Y., & Fosso Wamba, S. (2024). Artificial intelligence and adaptive response to market changes: A strategy to enhance firm performance and innovation. *Journal of Business Research*, *174*, 114500. https://doi.org/10.1016/j.jbusres.2024.114500

Suoniemi, S., Meyer-Waarden, L., Munzel, A., Zablah, A. R., & Straub, D. (2020). Big data and firm performance: The roles of market-directed capabilities and business strategy. *Information & Management*, *57*(7), 103365. https://doi.org/10.1016/j.im.2020.103365

Tedlow, R. S. (1990). *New and improved: The story of mass marketing in America*. Basic Books.

Townsend, J. D., Cavusgil, S. T., & Baba, M. L. (2010). Global integration of brands and new product development at General Motors. *Journal of Product Innovation Management*, *27*(1), 49–65. https://doi.org/10.1111/j.1540-5885.2009.00699.x

Venkatesh, A., & Wilemon, D. (1980). American and European product managers: A comparison. *Columbia Journal of World Business*, *15*(3), 67–74.

Wedel, M., & Kannan, P. K. (2016). Marketing analytics for data-rich environments. *Journal of Marketing*, *80*(6), 97–121. https://doi.org/10.1509/jm.15.0413

Zenor, M. J. (1994). The profit benefits of category management. *Journal of Marketing Research*, *31*(2), 202–213. https://doi.org/10.1177/002224379403100205

APPENDIX: THE MCELROY MEMO

C
O
P
Y

MARKETING
- Brand Teams, 1931

cc: Mr. W. G. Werner

Mr. N. H. McElroy May 13, 1931

Mr. R. F. Rogan

ADV**N. H. MCELROY

Because I think it may be of some help to you in putting through our recommendation for additional men for the Promotion Department, I am outlining briefly below the duties and responsibilities of the brand men.

This outline does not represent the situation as it is but as we will have it when we have sufficient man power. In past years the brand men have been forced to do work that should have been passed on to assistant brand men, if they had been available and equal to the job.

Brand Man

(1) Study carefully shipments of his brands by units:

(2) Where brand development is heavy and where it is progressing, examine carefully the combination of effort that seems to be clicking and try to apply this same treatment to other territories that are comparable.

(3) Where brand development is light

(a) Study the past advertising and promotional history of the brand; study the territory personally at first hand - both dealers and consumers - in order to find out the trouble.

(b) After uncovering our weakness, develop a plan that can be applied to this local sore spot. It is necessary, of course, not simply to work out the plan but also to be sure that the amount of money proposed can be expected to produce results at a reasonable cost per case.

(c) Outline this plan in detail to the Division Manager under whose jurisdiction the weak territory is, obtain his authority and support for the corrective action.

C
O
P
Y

cc: Mr. W. G. Werner

Mr. N. H. McElroy May 13, 1931

Mr. R. F. Rogan

- 2 -

(d) Prepare sales helps and all other necessary material for carrying out the plan. Pass it on to the districts. Work with the salesmen while they are getting started. Follow through to the very finish to be sure that there is no let-down in sales operation of the plan.

(e) Keep whatever records are necessary, and make whatever field studies are necessary to determine whether the plan has produced the expected results.

(4) Take full responsibility, not simply for criticizing individual pieces of printed word copy, but also for the general printed word plans for his brands.

(5) Take full responsibility for all other advertising expenditures - Field, D.C.A. etc. - on his brands.

(6) Experiment with and recommend wrapper revisions.

(7) See each District Manager a number of times a year to discuss with him any possible faults in our promotion plans for that territory.

In short, when the brand men have approached their fullest responsibilities, they should be able to take from the shoulders of the Division Managers and of the District Managers a very heavy share of individual brand responsibility. This would leave the sales heads in a much freer position to administer the sales policies of the Company and apply general volume pressure without having to give such a large proportion of their time to thought on how to bring up volume on a certain brand in a certain part of the territory.

Assistant Brand Man

(1) Take care of the office work which will have been laid out by the brand man, which must be followed through, checked and edited.

(2) Make field studies as directed by the brand man.

C
O
P
Y

Mr. N. H. McElroy May 13, 1931

Mr. R. F. Rogan

- 3 -

(3) Keep in touch with all printed word, field and D.C.A. plans.

(4) Finally, be able to step into the shoes of his superior at a moment's notice.

****

With the above outline of responsibilities it is not hard to understand that one man should not have to work on more than two brands at the very most. I am sure that the need for a Group Products brand man, part of whose responsibility will be chain and voluntary chain promotion, will be equally obvious.

Group Products Check-Up Men

The brand men in the past have unfortunately been tied up too closely to their office work because their assistants have had to be out of the office on field check-ups a large share of the time. A great majority of these checking jobs could be handled by less responsible men than assistant brand men.

We believe that we can relieve the entire situation by adding to our organization two men - and perhaps more as their need is felt - whose duties would be field checking on all products. These men would relieve the assistant brand men of a good share of their traveling. This, in turn, would allow the brand men to pass over to their assistants office work which is keeping them from their more important field studies.

With these two men our organization would be lined up as shown on the attached chart headed "Division of Brand Responsibilities in 6-Man Organization."

N. H. McELROY

N

2

Perspectives on Brand Management[1]

Tilde Heding

THE HISTORY OF BRAND MANAGEMENT

Like other interesting commercial and pop-cultural phenomena, brands move through time, seem to absorb and express the zeitgeist of a given time, and can be understood from many different perspectives and change as time, culture and consumers do: 'As markets change, marketing theories must also change to accommodate them' (Kozinets et al. 2010, p. 71). Often, the most innovative brands seem to be condensates of complex changes in time and culture.

Corporations spend millions on planning and implementing brand activities. A new research study is published, and frameworks are developed on a daily basis in an attempt to find the holy grail of brand management. Since the mid-80s, in particular, researchers and practitioners alike have explored the domain, scope and potential of the brand. Many different concepts, theoretical frameworks and ideas have seen the light of day, and as a result, a wide spectrum of different perspectives on how a brand ought to be conceptualized and managed is in play today. Therefore, to obtain an overview of the field of brand management is an overwhelming task.

This chapter provides a complete overview of brand management understood as a product of the research environment (expressed through research published in high-ranking journals) focused on marketing and consumer behavior. Combining the research articles provided by these research communities has provided us with eight brand approaches (by 2020). More approaches will keep

[1] This chapter is based on the textbook *Brand Management—Mastering Theory, Research and Practice* (Heding et al., 2020). The book was first published in 2008, revised in 2016, and went through a third revision in 2020. In the time of writing, the three authors are in the process of preparing the 4th edition for publication in 2026/27. What started out in the early 00's with a joint wish to 'tidy up' the discipline of brand management. Over the years, following the development in brand managements has given us fascinating insights into how scientific knowledge develops over time. Therefore, we owe a world of gratitude to the late philosopher of science, Thomas Kuhn, as we have based our methodology on his thoughts on scientific revolutions (Berthon & Money, 2003; Bjerre et al., 2008; Kuhn, 1964). This chapter is an introduction to the taxonomy of the textbook, and it is based on the work by the three of us and is an invitation to catch up with the latest development in brand management when the 4th edition is published (by Routledge).

developing as scientific knowledge evolves at all times. These eight 'schools of thought' or 'clusters of literature' represent fundamentally different perceptions of the brand, the nature of the brand–consumer exchange and how brand equity is created and managed. Understanding the eight brand approaches separately provides us a deep insight into the strengths and weaknesses of each approach and, hence, the potential of brand management as a whole. The approaches are presented in a chronological order. This comprehensive understanding will enable the reader to create customized brand strategies matching the unique challenges and possibilities facing a brand at any time.

The background of the proposed taxonomy is a systematic analysis of 650+ brand management research articles spanning the period of 1985–2020. The analysis has been executed in accordance with the logic of the methodology *The Dynamic Paradigm Funnel* (Berthon et al., 2003; Bjerre et al., 2008). *The Dynamic Paradigm Funnel* is based on theory about how science evolves: The philosophy of science developed by Thomas Kuhn (1996). As mentioned briefly in Chapter 1, this proposed taxonomy of 35 years of brand management is based on an analysis of 650+ articles from the most influential marketing journals (*Journal of Marketing*, *Journal of Marketing Research*, *Journal of Consumer Research*, *Harvard Business Review* and *European Journal of Marketing*). The journals are selected due to their academic influence (Hult et al., 1997) (the first four), and the last one is to add a European perspective to the dataset.

TAXONOMY OF BRAND MANAGEMENT 1985–2020

In Figure 2.1, the most significant traits of each approach are presented side by side. By going through the characteristics of each approach, a clear overview of the eight brand approaches is gained. It is important to notice that each approach is presented as an 'ideal type'. It must be emphasized that the taxonomy highlights an ideal type of each approach rather than eventual nuances and similarities because it enables you to understand the differences between the mindsets underlying each approach.

The time of origin (or academic conceptualization) of each brand approach is more or less precise. Some of the approaches are born from a specific, groundbreaking article introducing a whole new brand perspective. These approaches can be dated to a specific publication. Others emerge incrementally, and from the hands of several researchers, they can only be dated approximately. The eight approaches are presented in a chronological order reflecting when the approaches were conceptualized in the context of brand management. In the cases of the easy-to-date approaches, the groundbreaking articles are identified as *key readings*. In the other approaches, key readings are research articles central to and representative of the approach, written by the most important and influential researchers constituting the approach.

Keywords are the main concerns of the approach. The *brand perspective* describes the overall 'take' on the brand in the given approach. We have focused not only on clarifying the different brand perspectives but also on the different *consumer perspectives* associated with the different brand perspectives.

Each brand approach can be traced to a specific *scientific tradition*. The clarification of the respective traditions implies differences in consumer perceptions and methods and also hints toward differences in philosophical standpoints. These aspects of the proposed taxonomy might seem difficult and over the top, but in our experience, it actually facilitates the understanding of the discipline to add the assumed, 'taken for granted' stuff, as it guides the overall concerns of each approach: What is investigated, which methods are presumed valid, view of man (as consumer) and so on. When it comes to *methods*, the model makes it very clear that the methods formally applied to the brand management research have developed from a focus on quantitative methods to the use of a wide variety of methods and that they are primarily qualitative in the later approaches.

The *managerial keywords* evolve from reflecting the control with the process of brand value creation to keywords reflecting a perception of the brand manager having to acknowledge the influence of other forces on the brand value creation. In the theoretical building blocks of each approach, we have presented core theories and supporting theories. The *supporting theories* form the backdrop of the main theory of the approach, and reflecting upon them should facilitate the understanding of each approach.

The aim of this model is also to contribute to an overview of how it is assumed that the brand management can endow brands with value. The two first approaches (economic and identity) assumed that the brand value is created in the domain of the marketer. This brand value creation shifted in the third approach (consumer-based approach), where it is a thorough understanding of the consumer that is presumed to be at the heart of superior brand value creation. In the personality approach and the relational approach, the creation of brand value is presumed to be dialogue-based and takes place in

	The economic approach	**The identity approach**	**The consumer-based approach**	**The personality approach**	**The relational approach**	**The community approach**	**The cultural approach**	**The sensory approach**
Time of origin	Before 1985	Mid – 1990's	1993	1997	1998	2001	Around 2000	Around 2015
Key reading	McCarthy, E. J. (1964), Basic marketing, a managerial approach, Richard, D. Irwin, Inc. Borden, N. (1964), The Concept of the Marketing Mix, in G. Schwatz (ed.) Science in Marketing	Hatch, M. J. and Schultz, M. (1997), 'Relations between organizational culture, identity and image', *European Journal of Marketing*	Keller, K. L. (1993), 'Conceptualizing, measuring and managing customer-based brand equity', *Journal of Marketing*	Aaker, J. L. (1997), 'Dimensions of brand personality', *Journal of Marketing Research*. Plummer, J. (1985) 'How personality makes a difference', *Journal of Advertising Research*	Fournier, S. (1998), 'Consumers and their brands: Developing relationship theory in consumer research', *Journal of Consumer Research*	Muñiz, A. M. Jr, and O'Guinn, T. C. (2001), 'Brand community', *Journal of Consumer Research*	Holt, D. B. (2002), 'Why do brands cause trouble? A dialectical theory of consumer culture and branding', *Journal of Consumer Research*	Fajardo et al. (2016), 'The contingent nature of the symbolic associations of visual design elements: The case of brand logo frames', *Journal of Consumer Research*
Keywords	The economic man, transaction theory, marketing mix (four P's)	Corporate branding, identity, organizational culture, vision, image	Customer-based brand equity, brand image, brand associations	Personality, self, congruity, archetypes	Dyadic brand – consumer relationship, brand relationship quality	Brand communities, brandfests, the brand triad, web 2.0	Globalization, popular culture, brand icons, ideology	Sensory branding, priming, grounded cognition, sensory identities, brand experiences
Brand perspective	Functional	Corporate	Cognitive construal	Human	Human	Social	Cultural	Sensory
Consumer perspective	Economic man	Stakeholder	Computer	Psychological	Existential being	Tribe member, homo connectus	Homo mercans	Homo sapiens
Scientific tradition	Positivism, empiricism	Socio-economic constructivism/ interpretivism	Cognitive psychology	Human personality, psychology	Existentialism, phenomenology	Anthropology, micro-perspective	Cultural studies	Grounded cognition
Methods	Scanner panel data, laboratory setting, quantitative data	Organizational culture studies and organizational values, heuristic methods and storytelling	Cognitively based association maps, interviews, projective techniques	A mix of quantitative and qualitative methods, scaling techniques	Depth interviews, life story method	Ethnography, netnography	Macro-level analysis on micro-level data	Self-reporting, laboratory setting, biological response, neurophysiology
Managerial keyword	Control	Linear communication	Programming	Symbolic exchange	Friendship	Discretion	Bird perspective	Physical. Manifestations of the brand
Supporting theories	The economic man, marketing mix	Organizational identity, corporate identity, image, reputation	Cognitive psychology, the information processing consumer	Personality, consumer self, brand self congruity	Animism, relationship theory	Community theory, subcultures of consumption	Cultural consumption, dobbelgänger brands, anti-branding discourse, CSR, global ideoscapes	The five senses, brand experiences

Figure 2.1 An taxonomy of brand management

Source: Heding et al. (2020).

dyadic exchange between the consumer and the marketer. The community approach adds the triadic brand–consumer relationship to the assumptions of what drives brand value creation: Creating a whole new value-creating dynamic:real brand value is assumed to be created not so much in the interaction between the marketer and the consumer, as was the case in the previous approaches, but in the interaction between the consumers. In the cultural approach, the addition of macro-level culture makes the assumed brand value creation very complicated because the marketer is assumed to be dependent on macro and consumer culture more than on the exchange with one or more consumers. In the sensory approach, the value is created through exposing the consumer to carefully designed sensory inputs. The literature is somewhat ambiguous when it comes to the exchange between the marketer and the consumer: In some important sources, it is assumed that the consumer can be 'primed' (meaning that he or she is rather predictable and, thus, a manipulable object), while the consumer is referred to as a 'prosumer' (hence an active subject in the meaning making and value creation) in most literature about brand experiences.

EIGHT BRAND APPROACHES

As described in the Introduction, we have identified eight brand approaches forming the backbone of this book.

The eight approaches can be seen as links in a continuous evolution that slowly but surely has changed the field of brand management. It is important to stress that the birth of one approach does not imply the end of the 'previous' one(s); rather, they complement each other. All approaches have evolved and continue to do so. Claiming that an approach becomes important in a given period of time does not necessarily mean that it becomes dominant but rather that it is novel and that the research behind it is strong enough to constitute a new school of thought. Some of the older approaches are easy to criticize because much effort has been put into creating new and more suitable methods to explain consumption phenomena since their day. Still, valuable things can be learned from all eight approaches.

What Is an Approach?

The eight 'schools of thought' are 'clusters' of literature sharing distinct brand perceptions. In each cluster, there is coherence between assumptions, theories and methods/data. The three 'scientific layers' (assumptions, theories and methods/data) add up to managerial implications. The structure of the eight approach chapters is guided by this coherence between assumptions, theories, methods/data and managerial implications.

Traditionally, brand management textbooks offer an introduction to main concepts and the wide array of theories but often fail to discriminate between how different approaches result in very different outcomes and why. It is important for us to stress that the aim of this work is to *deconstruct* brand management to enhance understanding and reflection on the differences. The different approaches to brand management draw on many different scientific traditions such as economics, strategic management, organizational behavior, consumer research, psychology and anthropology, just to mention a few, understanding these and the consequences, we believe, will better equip students and practitioners with a reflected brand management understanding and toolbox.

A complete overview of the brand management, hence, requires multidimensional thinking. Most textbooks take on this multidimensionality through the integration of several perspectives in all-encompassing frameworks. If you look at the list of brand approaches, you will most likely recognize many of the brand elements (e.g., personality, relation and consumer) that are encompassed in the classical textbook models (e.g., see Aaker's brand identity model [2012], Kapferer's brand prism [2012]) and Keller's customer-based brand equity pyramid (1993, 2003). The integrated frameworks are, however, not necessarily ideal when it comes to understanding and getting an overview of the field of brand management. Integration tends to blur the differences and similarities between different approaches in brand management and perhaps leave the reader somewhat confused. Still, the integrated frameworks have the advantage that a strategist can take into consideration all relevant aspects without losing oneself in detail.

The textbook behind the brand approaches (Heding et al., 2020 [fourth edition will be published in 2026]) can be read in two ways: Either as a standalone textbook or as a supplement to the textbooks by the abovementioned authors. Read as a supplement, the book offers the inquiring reader the opportunity to understand the components of the traditional models in depth. Read alone, the book offers the opportunity to evaluate the most important schools of thought in brand management and create his or her brand management model featuring the components that are most relevant for the challenge at hand. Furthermore, it provides a chronological account of 35 years of brand management and marketing theory.

Resting on a comprehensive analysis of brand management as a scientific discipline, *Brand Management: Mastering Research, Theory and Practice* offers the reader a scientifically grounded overview of the main schools/approaches in brand management and of their managerial implications. *Brand Management: Mastering Research, Theory and Practice* presents each approach separately and as an 'ideal type' based on the conviction that understanding the exact content of each approach and its origin will better equip the reader to combine different approaches, being in an educational or a managerial setting.

True to its objective, the proposed taxonomy does not provide one 'how to' solution meaning that we sustain from being normative when it comes to the overall management of a brand. Still, we are normative *within* each approach and leave it to the reader to reflect upon how different situations and circumstances require different means of action. It is the authors' hope that this book will equip readers with an overview and a deeper understanding that will enable them to create splendid, customized brand management strategies and that this somewhat different approach to the communication of brand management will provide a sound platform for anyone interested in the field.

The eight approaches are as follows:

- *The economic approach:* The brand as a product of the traditional marketing mix.
- *The identity approach:* The brand as linked to corporate identity.
- *The consumer-based approach:* The brand as linked to consumer associations.
- *The personality approach:* The brand as a human-like character.
- *The relational approach:* The brand as a viable relationship partner.
- *The community approach:* The brand as the pivotal point of social interaction.
- *The cultural approach:* The brand as part of the broader cultural fabric.
- *The sensory approach*: The brand as experienced through our senses.

The Economic Approach: The Brand as Part of the Traditional Marketing Mix

The point of departure for brand management is that it is a breakaway discipline from the broad scope of marketing. Hence, the discipline starts out with a research environment marked by traditional marketing mix theory (Borden 1964) and later the four Ps. The creation of brand value is investigated as influenced by changes in, for example, distribution channels, price modifications and promotions. A functionalistic brand perspective applies, as does a consumer perspective based on the notion of the 'economic man'. The economic consumer bases consumption decisions on rational considerations and the exchange between the brand and the consumer is assumed to be isolated tangible transactions. Laboratory settings and scanner data are illustrative of the methodologies and (always quantitative) data. The marketer is in charge of brand value creation, and hence, consumers are believed to 'receive' and understand the messages 'sent' to them from the marketer exactly as intended.

The assumptions and premises of the economic approach have their origin in the ideas of exchange from micro-economic theory. The model of exchange in microeconomics is purely theoretical, which means that the assumptions and key models are the result of theorizing rather than empirical research. In *The Wealth of Nations*, Adam Smith (1776) argued that if one would let market forces govern the allocation of resources and the exchange of goods, then an 'invisible hand' would allocate resources in a way that optimizes both the individual and societal beneficial use of available resources. In this perception of market forces lies an assumption that individuals pursue self-interest and attempt to maximize own revenue or functional utility.

The principle of the 'invisible hand' assumes that resources are allocated according to where they will give the highest possible functional outcome or revenue because efficient methods of production will be adopted by manufacturers in order to accommodate the utility-maximizing behavior displayed by the individual. Marketing is an academic discipline stemming from microeconomics, just like brand management stems from marketing. Thereby, it is very logical that these assumptions govern the first brand management approach.

The *economic man* is a key concept in this line of thinking. The logic is hence applicable both at the level of the market and the individual. In a consumption and brand management context, this means that a consumer will always go for the deal that provides the best functional utility related to the price of the product.

'Perfect information' is another keyword in this approach. The economic man is assumed not only able to oversee all available choices but also able to evaluate all of them and choose the best functional deal. Thereby, we are dealing with a consumer able and willing to take in 'perfect information' to make the most rational choice in any situation.

In the economic approach understanding of the brand, it operates in a market, where the consumer is assumed to make primarily rational consumption decisions, interactions with consumers are linear and standalone isolated events rather than an ongoing relationship. Consumers evaluate brands on their functional utility against its price, and the four Ps are the mix of marketing actions that make the transaction with consumers possible; getting to the right mix is essential for whether a brand will be successful.

The economic approach rests upon a positivist research ideal. This line of thought is very much in opposition to the stream of qualitative research methods that have become more and more dominant in marketing research in recent decades. In the quantitative methods, objectiveness is important, and phenomena are presumed to be measurable. The objectivity of data is important for validity, and closeness to the subject of research is not essential.

The Identity Approach: The Brand as Linked to Corporate Identity

The economic approach lays the foundation for brand management as an independent scientific discipline, but one more stream of research is also influential during the first decades of this inquiry. The identity approach behind the notion of corporate branding is still very influential and under constant theoretical development. Especially in the European research environment, the brand as linked with corporate identity is a very influential school of thought. Focusing on corporate identity, the brand is also primarily perceived as an entity 'owned' by the marketer (even though that perception has changed to encompass multiple stakeholders as the approach has evolved). Integration of the brand on all levels within and outside the organization is key in the management of the brand. The marketer (as corporation) is in charge of brand value creation. Processes of organizational culture and corporate construction of identity are key processes.

In 1907, Allgemeine Elektricitäts-Gesellschaft (AEG) appointed Peter Behrens to be, what at the time was called, an 'Artistic Consultant'. His job turned out to be the first corporate engagement in the conscious management of identity. Peter Behrens's philosophy was simple – the products, design and communication should express one unified identity. To accomplish this, he created products, logos, advertising material and company publications with a consistent, unified design. This unified design and visual expression of identity made Peter Behrens and AEG the founders of the rationale behind the corporate identity concept and corporate identity management programs in practice.

Originally based on the assumption that a strong brand is created through consistent and reliable communication of the corporation behind the brand, it *was* based on a sender perspective on the brand–consumer exchange and in that sense comparable to the economic approach. However, this approach is a much more all-encompassing idea of how to manage the brand since it involves the whole organization (in terms of incorporating the organization, it can be argued that it is the most far-reaching brand approach of this taxonomy).

In the late 1980s and early 1990s, the line of thought originating with AEG and the design school began to take shape in brand management academia, laying the ground for the identity approach. Shee & Abratt (1989) elaborated on the conceptual development of the approach by adding an in-depth study of the dimensions that link the interior processes (corporate identity) with the exterior-focused activities (corporate image). A new stream of research (especially in a European context) has led to a conceptualization of brand identity during the 1990s, where the interplay between corporate identity, organizational identity, image and reputation provides the elements to explore and create a strong brand within this approach.

After the millennium, the theoretical constructs, frameworks and methodologies have been evaluated, altered and refined, and the scope was further expanded to entail larger networks of stakeholders and additional sources of identity. Recently, the impact of social media and open source developments on brand identity is a trending topic, exploring the ambiguity of organizing brand identity versus the volatile dynamics of social media.

We will refrain from listing the complete selection but mention two collections that in particular have set the scene in the recent perspectives on brand identity. *The Expressive Organization* by Schultz et al. (2000) is a selection of articles exploring the identity domain from multiple academic fields, with the aim of discussing the relational differences between identity, image and culture in organizations with the aim of clarifying and articulating the theoretical domain of identity (Schultz et al., 2000). *Revealing the Corporation: Perspectives on Identity, Image, Reputation, Corporate Branding, and Corporate-level Marketing* (Balmer & Greyser, 2003) is another important collection guiding the reader through influential classics and contemporary academic articles shedding light on different perspectives on identity, image, reputation and corporate branding.

The identity approach brings into focus the creation of a unified, visual and behavioral identity (Hatch & Schultz, 1997). It is assumed that consumers attribute identity characteristics to *companies* and that people form images of companies based on the *total experience of the company*. This places the corporation and its employees at the center of brand equity creation and, hence, adds the corporate brand identity to the domain of brand management.

In a brand management context, the key assumption of the identity approach is that all marketing and communication activities should be integrated, aligned and elevated from a product-focused and tactical level to a strategic, corporate level. Only in that way will it be possible to create a coherent company experience for consumers. It is from that assumption that the idea of corporate branding and integrated market communication stems. The notion of identity is applicable to the individual brand level, but corporate-level branding plays a vital role in the identity approach because the alignment of all communication in one unified identity and the management of the total customer experience across all touchpoints require strategic-level brand management. Identity is something that is initiated from inside the company. Some of the questions corporations need to ask themselves are in the identity approach. Who are we? What do we stand for? What do we want to become? Brand value creation is, hence, dependent on finding the right answers to these questions and implementing them in every aspect of the business. Only then will the corporation be able to develop and get a coherent total experience across to the consumers.

The idea of corporate branding is the assumption that creating one unified (at corporate level) message across all functions will elevate brand management from a tactical operational discipline involving only the marketing and sales department to a strategic, corporate level involving the whole organization. Creating one unified message across functions, hence, requires one unified corporate identity. Corporate branding implies deserting product branding with its marketing-driven focus on tactical and functional processes. Product branding has been criticized for having a too narrow, external perspective, detached from the organization behind the products. Corporate branding is an attempt to accommodate these weaknesses. Product branding is based on short-term advertising ideas, while corporate branding is based on a long-term brand idea. Corporate branding also expands the parameters of differentiation by enabling companies to use their rich heritage actively to create strong brands.

Corporate branding involves the whole organization and emphasizes the pivotal role employees play in the creation of a strong corporate brand. Values and beliefs held by employees are key elements in the differentiation strategy. Corporate branding is a 'move towards conceiving more integrated relationships between internal and external stakeholders linking top management, employees, customers and other stakeholders' (Schultz et al., 2005, p. 24).

The identity approach assumes that a strong and coherent brand identity is pivotal for brand value creation and acknowledges that balancing multiple identities is key (due to its fragmented nature). The corporate brand identity is the result of a continuous journey exploring and answering 'who we are' as an organization to facilitate the expression of one coherent identity to all stakeholders. Attention has shifted from a focus on the visual representation of product brands to a focus on how organizational behavior affects identity and ultimately image and reputation. The perception of the consumer in the identity approach has also evolved. Scope and perception of the brand consumer exchange have shifted from the idea that brand identity could be managed and controlled by the corporation and a linear perception of the exchange between the brand and the consumer. To a much broader perception, where it is acknowledged that identity is not enduring but context-dependent and it can, hence, not be communicated linearly but is the result of negotiation between internal and external shareholders.

The Consumer-Based Approach: The Brand as Linked With Consumer Associations

In 1993, Kevin Lane Keller founded a completely new approach to brand management. The brand is perceived as a cognitive construal in the mind of the consumer. It is assumed that a strong brand holds strong, unique and favorable associations in the minds of consumers. In this fashion, attention shifts from the sender toward the receiving end of brand communication. The consumer is the 'owner' of the brand in this approach, but still an assumption of linear communication applies. The consumer perspective of this approach is rooted in cognitive psychology, and in this tradition, the computer is the main metaphor for man as a consumer. This consumer perspective implies linear communication because the marketer is perceived to be able to 'program' the consumer into intended action. This school of thought has since become very dominant in brand management especially in the USA.

In the early years of brand management, the focus was on the 'sender end' of brand communication (the economic approach and the identity approach). Still, in the accompanying scientific discipline of consumer research, a new view of the consumer was being thoroughly investigated in the 1980s. The idea of the information-processing consumer (Bettman, 1979) as well as the ideas about positioning (Ries & Trout, 1983, 2001) paved the way for a radically new brand perspective. In the year of 1993, brand management was profoundly shaken by one research article in particular. Kevin Lane Keller published the article 'Conceptualizing, measuring, and managing customer-based brand equity' in the *Journal of Marketing* and thereby instigated a major change in the field of brand management. Customer-based brand equity is based on the premise that the brand resides in the minds of consumers as a cognitive construal, which is why we have chosen to name it the consumer-based approach. Consumer research was, at this point in time, very much influenced by cognitive psychology and the related information-processing theory of consumer choice. Insights from these veins of literature were adapted to brand management theory with the birth of the consumer-based approach.

This brand perspective has been tremendously influential in the shaping of brand management and is still considering a pivotal point in the discipline. The publication of research-based literature exploring this brand perspective is still significant; the more recent research tries to understand and explain how *context* is influencing our memory processes, brand evaluations and consumption choices. Hence, the new research tries to understand one of the basic premises of this brand perspective that we are living in an over-communicated society.

The consumer has, thus, become the main point of interest in this approach. He or she is considered the 'owner' of the brand. Where the two prior approaches stressed an inside–out perspective on brand value creation, the consumer-based approach introduces an outside–in approach to brand management. The consumer-based approach, hence, embraces external strategy formation, as opposed to the internal strategy formation focus of the two prior approaches and requires a more adaptive mindset (Louro & Cunha, 2001).

Brand value creation takes place by molding the brand associations held in the consumers' minds. Understanding the consumer is, hence, central in this take on brand value creation; but it is important to notice that the approach implies a specific view on the consumer. The consumer is analyzed by means of theories adopted from cognitive psychology and the information-processing theory of consumer choice.

In cognitive psychology, an 'if–then' logic applies. *If* the marketer feeds the 'consumer computer' with the most appropriate information, *then* the consumer will do as intended and choose the brand. One is able to program a computer into doing the same thing every time, and this is the logic that applies to the brand–consumer exchange. In other words, the consumer is the focal point, but the marketer is still assumed to control the brand in the consumer-based approach. A linear response to sensory input → consumer → brand choice is, hence, assumed.

At a first glance, the consumer appears to be all-powerful in the brand–consumer exchange, but the consumer 'ownership' of the approach is paradoxical; even though the consumer 'owns' the brand, he or she is still treated as a generic entity that the skilled communicator is able to 'program' into intended action. The chaotic, unpredictable and 'autonomous' aspects of consumer behavior that are taken into consideration in the later approaches (the relational, the community and the cultural approaches) are not considered in this consumer perspective.

The consumer-based approach assumes that the brand is a cognitive construal residing in the mind of the consumer.

This assumption indicates that the consumer is very much in control of the brand–consumer exchange. This is, however, not entirely the case. The consumer is seen through a lens borrowed from cognitive psychology and the main metaphor for man in this perspective is that of the computer.

And just like a skilled computer programmer is able to program the computer into doing as intended, the marketer who is willing to map out the brand construal in the mind of the consumer will be able to choose exactly the right brand elements and communicate them to a consumer who will respond accordingly. These, seemingly contradictory, assumptions are what lie behind the consumer-based approach.

The Personality Approach: The Brand as a Human-Like Character

Another mountaintop in brand management was established in 1997, when a research study into brand personality was published (Aaker 1997). This study shows that consumers have a tendency to endow brands with human-like personalities. It is the 'human' brand perspective and the symbol-consuming consumer that are in the spotlight in this approach. Consumers endow brands with personalities and use these personalities in a dialogue-based exchange of symbolic value for their individual identity construction and expression. The personality approach is rooted in human personality psychology and uses quantitative scaling techniques in a combination with more explorative methods to identify and measure brand personality. The personality approach is a prerequisite for and very much associated with the relational approach.

Creating a so-called brand personality has been a well-known trick in the advertising industry for decades. In 1997, one article stirred the pot and set a new agenda in brand management. The validated theoretical construct of the brand personality entered brand management academia by Jennifer Aaker's article 'Dimensions of Brand Personality', which presented a whole new theoretical framework and method.

The publication of this research introduced a new brand perspective in brand management, inspired by human personality psychology and with a new dialogue-based brand–consumer exchange as a major implication.

Consumers automatically ascribe personality to brands. This process is a central aspect of consumers' symbolic consumption and construction of self. The personality approach in brand management explains how and why people choose brands with certain personalities and how imbuing brands with personality can be a powerful tool to create and enhance brand equity. The assumptions, theories and methods of the personality approach borrow from related academic fields like human psychology, sociology, personality research and consumer behavior.

Understanding consumers' attraction to brand personalities has for long been an area of interest in consumer behavior, where research has focused on how brand personality enables consumers to express 'self' through the symbolic use of brand personality. This focus has been prevalent in an advertising context until mid-1990s. Since the publication of 'Dimensions of Brand Personality', the personality contrast has also been immersed in a brand management context academically. Practitioners have viewed brand personality primarily as a way to position and differentiate the brand from other brands in the same product category, as a driver of consumer preference and as a common denominator that can be used across national cultures.

Research into how personality affects consumer choice of brands and how personality can lead to stronger brands began in the field of consumer and advertising research. Adjunct Professor Joseph Plummer was one of the first to undertake substantial research into how personality plays a role in advertising and affects consumer behavior. His studies were based on conceptual models and mechanisms from human psychology (Plummer, 2000). These early studies of personality primarily focused on the product-related personality.

Several research articles have expanded the applicability of the Aaker framework and empirically tested the structure of personality dimensions across, for example, national cultures, firm stereotypes and gender, and also the importance of category versus product-level personality has been a subject to empirical testing (Batra et al., 2010; Grohman, 2009; Sung & Tinkham, 2005).

The Relational Approach: The Brand as a Viable Relationship Partner

The idea of a dyadic relationship between brand and consumer profoundly changed the academic discipline of brand management. The notion of the brand being a viable relationship partner builds on the same human brand metaphor as the personality approach. The approach extends the dialogue-based approach to brand management as instigated in the personality approach. The relational approach is rooted in the philosophical tradition of existentialism, and the methods are of a phenomenological nature. These roots imply that a paradigm shift is taking place because they are so fundamentally different from the roots of research methods used in the first approaches to brand management.

Brand relationship theory reached a wide brand management audience when 'Consumers and their brands: developing relationship theory in consumer research' by Susan Fournier was published in the *Journal of Consumer Research* (March of 1998). Drawing on theories about human relationships and the idea of brand personality, the study investigated one of the 'buzz words' of the 1990s, relationship marketing.

It also turned the whole idea of the brand upside down, which is why brand management never became the same after the introduction of this approach. The research focused on understanding the three respondents' life worlds fully and in that process understanding which roles brands play in their lives. Previous research had focused more on respondents as consumers – not the holistic perceptions of the entire human beings in this research. The research also took place in the homes of respondents, not in either an artificial, neutral setting or in a situation of consumption. This primary and holistic focus on the *lives* of the consumers is still a challenge in the (practical as well as academic) world of brand management: '…our metrics suffer from firm-centricity, focusing on evaluation of the person's satisfaction with or depth of commitment to the brand relationship that is formed. But relationships that resonate have a different focal goal: they are engaged to make people's lives easier, better, or happier' (Fournier, 2012, p. 9).

The brand is understood as a phenomenon. Vicki, Jean and Karen (the three respondents of the original research) experience relationships with certain brands, and these relationships are closely linked to their life situations and values. Interesting and compelling! The challenge is that it does not necessarily make us cleverer when we have to market brand X.

Brand relationship theory did not only shift its focus from the B2B relationship to a B2C setting but also offer new insights into brand loyalty (refer to Chapter 12 for an elaboration and additional literature on brand loyalty). Loyalty is often closely linked with the sensation of a relationship. Loyal consumers are valuable consumers. Creating brand loyalty is all about managing the brand–consumer exchange long-term instead of a short-term exchange focusing on the transaction. But while brand loyalty is an expression of *if* a consumer chooses the brand on a continuous basis, applying the brand relationship theory offers explanations of *how* and *why* brands are consumed by loyal consumers.

The Community Approach: The Brand as the Pivotal Point of Social Interaction

The community approach is based on anthropological research into so-called brand communities. Brand value is created in these communities where a brand serves as the pivotal point of social interaction among consumers (Muniz & O'Guinn 2001). This approach, thus, adds an understanding of the social context of consumption to the overall picture of brand management. This understanding has become a prerequisite for managing many brands, especially after the Internet has profoundly changed the market place. In the community approach, the marketer deals with 'autonomous' groups of consumers who are able to collectively influence marketing actions and potentially 'take over' the brand and take it into a direction not at all intended by the marketer. The field of brand management has come a long way from the assumptions of linear communication behind the earlier approaches to accepting the chaotic autonomous consumer forces in this approach.

In 2001, a seminal new brand perspective was presented by two American researchers instigating a new take on the conceptual understanding of the brand but also on the meaning creation *among* consumers. The idea of the brand community was inspired by subcultures of consumption, was immediately compelling, and soon gathered its own research community and thereby established a new school of thought within brand management. Despite the immediate interest spurred by die-hard fans of Ford Broncos and their brand-related behavior, the ideas seemed only applicable to a good handful of high-involvement brands at the time.

The rest is history; it must have been impossible for the founding fathers of this approach to imagine how influential their idea of the 'brand community' would later become. The birth and the wildfire-like influence of web 2.0 and social media made the idea of the 'community' and 'triangular communication' into something revolutionizing the world of brand management. In brand management academia, the community approach has developed with studies into the transparency of communities, value-creating practices, communities' impact on product adoption, and the importance of online word-of-mouth.

The Cultural Approach: The Brand as Part of the Broader Cultural Fabric

Just like the community approach, the cultural approach emanates around the millennium. The brand is seen as a cultural artifact in this approach and has a theory of how to build an iconic brand as its backbone. The approach borrows from the scientific tradition of cultural studies and makes use of a wide variety of qualitative methods. The attention has shifted from the transaction between a marketer and a consumer (or groups of consumers) to a macro-perspective. The approach both explains how embedding the brand in cultural forces can be used strategically to build an iconic brand as well as take ideological issues into account.

The cultural approach has since evolved into two very different streams of literature. The theory of how to deliberately use cultural sources to build iconic brands is managerial by nature, while the ideological stream definitely is not. In the cultural approach, we find managerial, ethical, political and philosophical discussions more than in the other approaches. We also find research into, to what extent consumers can or cannot liberate themselves from consumer culture.

Still, the two streams of literature have the same point of departure, the same brand perspective and consumer perspective, and thereby, they adhere to the same paradigmatic assumptions about the brand–consumer exchange – hence the same approach. However, for pedagogical reasons, we will present the two streams of literature separately; therefore, this chapter will feature two sub-chapters reflecting the two streams of research literature activated to explore: 'iconic brands' and 'ideological issues'.

The theory about how to build an iconic brand is very much the doing of the researcher and author Douglas B. Holt. The managerial aspects of the cultural brand perspective articulated in the seminal 2002 article *Why do brands cause trouble? A dialectical theory of consumer culture and branding*, are elaborated greatly in *How to Build an Iconic Brand* (2004) and *Cultural Strategy* (2010).

The ideological discourse has very much developed through the publication of several academic articles. The most recent literature deals with global, ideological issues with both positive and negative stances toward global, Western brands. Though critical and ideological by nature, these articles (or their subject of analysis; critical consumers) have led to new managerial practices, namely, that corporate social responsibility has become a must in the toolbox of any contemporary brand manager. Corporate social responsibility is also investigated in the research, and concrete managerial implications are deducted.

These two streams of literature are in many respects opposing, still the founding 2002 article presents the most logical bridge between the two with the concept of the citizen-artist brand; a brand *both* communicating relevant cultural meaning and acting as a responsible citizen. Hence, this article both establishes the approach and bridges the contained dilemmas of it.

The Sensory Approach: The Brand as Experienced Through Our Senses

This new approach is all about bodily perceptions of brands – how we experience brands on a sensory level – and how these biological sensory experiences lead to the mental constructs we have thoroughly described in the previous approaches (Fajardo et al., 2016). Working on this chapter, it struck us that the previous approaches have been all about mental constructs – associations, emotions, abstract ideas and notions. Now, we take a huge jump back logic-wise to the channels through which consumers experience something physically before they can process it mentally.

FOUR PERIODS OF TIME

These eight brand approaches represent four different main periods. The periods are distinctively different and form the backdrop of the eight approaches. Understanding the dynamic movement from one period to another provides insight into the development of the body of research literature constituting the academic discipline of brand management. Holding on to underlying principles is always beneficial when it comes to understanding the elusive nature of the brand.

The first period of time is 1985–1992, the second one is 1993–1999, the third one begins around 2000, while the last one begins around 2010. These three periods of time follow a logical path, from a sender to a receiver to a societal/cultural perspective (a little bit simplified). The fourth period of time (with the most recent approach of the eight ones) begins to take shape from around 2010. From a paradigmatic perspective, the addition of the sensory approach does not follow the abovementioned logical development. The sensory approach is in many cases a return to an older paradigm with its fundamental ideas of 'priming' and a consumer perspective linked to a biological consumer perspective. Who would have thought that Homo Sapiens would be the new big thing in brand management? But hey – we are open to anything, and the sensory approach is a welcome addition to the more and more varied, nuanced and colorful discipline that is academic brand management.

In the first period, the brand management focused on the company behind the brand and the actions the company would take to influence the consumer. In the next period, the receiver of brand communication is the main point of interest, and brand management adopts a human and psychological perspective on the nature of the brand. In the third period, it is the contextual and cultural force behind consumption choices and brand loyalty that are investigated in the groundbreaking articles and new literature. The fourth one sheds light on the sensory experiences of any brand.

1985–1992: Company/Sender Focus

In the infancy of brand management, the research focuses on the company as a sender of brand communication. This focus forms the background of the two first approaches in brand management: The economic approach and the identity approach.

The research of the economic approach is centered on the possibilities of the company to manage the brand via the marketing mix elements: Product, placement, price and promotion, and how these factors can be manipulated to affect consumer brand choice. Quantitative data are the principal rule in this period. Researchers often use either data from supermarket scanner systems or laboratory experiments as the empirical basis of data. In the identity approach, research focuses on how the identity of the company as a whole can shape a coherent brand message that is communicated to all shareholders.

It is assumed that the brand is 'owned' by the company but influenced by multiple stakeholders and that the brand is communicated in a linear fashion from the company to the consumer.

1993–1999: Human/Receiver Focus

The shift in attention toward the receiver of brand communication instigates a new period of time entirely different from the period 1985–1993. New and groundbreaking research articles investigate the receiver of communication, and knowledge from different veins of human psychology is adapted to brand management theory. The human perspective is two-sided: The consumer is investigated closely *and* different human brand perspectives are coming into play. The humanistic and individualistic approaches – namely, the consumer-based approach, the personality approach and the relational approach – see the light of day in these years.

During 1993–1999, data collection becomes "softer'; quantitative, qualitative as well as mixed research designs are applied to the studies of the brand–consumer exchange. The relational approach is the first approach founded on an entirely qualitative study.

2000–2015: Cultural/Context Focus

Profound theoretical changes emerge both from academic discussions and from significant environmental changes affecting how humans consume brands. Environmental changes often imply a development of our theoretical frameworks because new phenomena arise that cannot be explained by means of the existing theories. A need for new theoretical tools to explain new phenomena is very much the driver behind the two newest approaches. Technological and cultural changes have profoundly changed the rules of the game in brand management in the last period of time.

The new phenomena calling for new theories are phenomena like autonomous consumers, brand icons, anti-branding movements and Internet-based brand communities. The most novel and innovative research looks at these new consumption patterns through new lenses trying to explain the context of brand consumption.

Two approaches can be identified in this period of time: The community approach and the cultural approach. The community approach brings influences from anthropological consumption studies, socio-cultural influences and consumer empowerment. The cultural approach explores how brands are an inherent part of our culture and explains how playing an active role in mainstream culture can turn a brand into an icon. Hence, cultural and contextual influences add new perspectives to the discipline of brand management from 2000 to 2015.

From Around 2015: A Sensory/ Biological Perspective

In the years around 2015, quite a few articles about sensory branding was published in the top academic journals, which are the basis of our data set (read more in Chapter 3). The research focuses on our senses, how they work and how we as brand managers can impact them. There is an attention on humans' physiologies and a biological consumer perspective. The managerial implications bring attention to brand identities, brand experiences and branded touchpoints. With assumptions leaning on the possibility of priming the receivers of our branded messages, we find ourselves in a more positivistic paradigm than has been the case up until now. The sensory approach is a welcome addition to the academic discipline of brand management – one usually found in designers' materials.

TWO BRAND MANAGEMENT PARADIGMS

Perhaps due to the elusive nature of the brand, the term 'brand paradigm' is often used at random in the branding discipline. The analysis of brand management that has provided the eight approaches' framework or categorization of brand management presented in this chapter is based on the philosophy of science by Thomas Kuhn, who is one of the most influential contributors to knowledge about 'paradigms'. Without going into too much detail with the paradigm concept, this chapter will touch briefly on the paradigmatic development of brand management. From 1985 to 2020, two overriding paradigms have been present in the academic world of brand management: One with a positivistic point of departure and one of a constructivist or interpretive nature. The positivistic stance implies a notion of the brand being 'owned' by the marketer, who controls the communication to a passive recipient/consumer. Brand equity is perceived to be something created by the marketer, and the brand is seen as: 'A manipulable lifeless artefact (product plus that is created by its owners/managers and that can be positioned, segmented and used to create an image)' (Hanby, 1999, p. 12).

The interpretive paradigm reflects on the nature of the brand and the value of brand equity as something created in the interaction between the marketer and an active consumer: 'As holistic entities with many of the characteristics of living beings' (Hanby, 1999, p. 10) and 'As a living entity (with a personality with which we can form a relationship and that can change and evolve over time)' (Hanby, 1999, p. 12).

A paradigm shift takes place in brand management over the course of the 1990s. It does not happen overnight but is an incremental process changing the discipline. The birth of the relational approach is an important indicator of the shift from a positivist paradigm with a more functionalistic brand perspective to an interpretive paradigm with a constructivist perspective on the brand and how it should be managed. The relational approach is grounded in phenomenology. Phenomenology is a qualitative, constructionist research tradition emphasizing the accessing of an 'inner reality' and, consequently, the validity of 'lived experience'. The relational approach also is the first approach relying on purely qualitative research. Brand consumption is understood only through a deep and holistic understanding of the personal context in which the brand is consumed.

The relational approach implies a major paradigmatic shift in brand management and can be identified as the one approach leading brand management into the 21st century.

This distinction is based on a literature analysis: 'The received view on branding is squarely grounded in the disciplines of psychology and information economics' (Allen et al., 2008, p. 783) – hence related to the dominant consumer-based approach. 'The emergent paradigm' encapsulates the relational, community and cultural approaches (in our terminology) and the development toward the interpretive paradigm: 'By all counts we are living in a different branding world. Co-creation, collaborations, complexity, ambiguity, dynamism, loss of control, multivocality: such are the tenets of the new marketing world to which our brands must be held responsible' (Allen et al., 2008, p. 814).

SUMMARY

In marketing research, eight brand management approaches have been identified during 1985–2020: The economic approach, the identity approach, the consumer-based approach, the personality approach, the relational approach, the community approach, the cultural approach and the sensory approach. These approaches reflect a development where the focus has shifted from the sending end of brand communications in the first period, have then turned their attention to the receiving end in the second period and have addressed contextual and cultural influences on the brand to the global understanding of brand consumption. Lastly, sensory branding – with priming and brand experiences as keywords of the sensory approach – has added a physical aspect to the overall picture.

It is important to stress that none of the approaches are obsolete and only of a historical interest. At the time of writing, there is academic activity in all the eight approaches. In other words, each approach is its own little microcosmos (within the larger cosmos of brand management) with scientific knowledge developing with each new published study.

Somewhere around the birth of the relational approach in 1998, a paradigm shift is instigated in brand management (see the above distinction between the received view and the emergent paradigm), with an implied shift from quantitative to qualitative methods, an acknowledgment of consumers' ownership of the brand and an embrace of the more chaotic forces in consumer culture.

The interconnected web of assumptions, brand perspective, consumer perspective, theories and methods of each approach is explained further in Heding et al. (2020) (and upcoming 2026/2027 edition). Looking into the material for the upcoming edition, interesting new perspectives on brand management are emerging. The impact of *diversity and social justice* on brands is a developing area (Davis et al., 2025; Rodas et al., 2021) carving out new responsibilities of and societal expectations toward brands. As explained above, the idea of the *brand relationship* has been an important theoretical area since 1998 (see overview in Noel & Thomson 2024). In recent research articles, several interesting new angles on the concept are presented, such as the role of anger (Buffy et al., 2024) and faith (Vo et al., 2025). Changes in consumer–brand relationships are investigated in Alvarez et al. (2021), while the experience of relationships with an artificial intelligence (AI) is explored in Bergner et al. (2023). Furthermore, there seems to be an extended interest in the craft of brand management – the *language, design and concrete communication* of the brand. Good examples are how to navigate narratives in transmedia (Feiereisen et al., 2021), the impact of logo design on different cultures (Gupta & Hagtvedt, 2021), size cues in brand names (Zhang et al., 2022) and the influence of perceptual structure on brand performance (Affonso & Janiszewski, 2023), while Costello et al. (2023) investigated the best spelling of brand names. Pogacar et al. (2021) asked whether Nestlé is a Lady? in an also interesting study of brand names' masculine and feminine associations.

We expect to see a boom in *AI-related branding research* soon. Already now, we find several studies into the human experiences in AI-driven encounters. Interesting examples are Bergner et al. (2023) and an investigation of consumer responses to crises caused by algorithm errors (Srinivasan & Sarial-Abi, 2021). Also, Wichmann et al. (2021) investigated the role of the brand in new business models in The Platformization of Brands. Completely new types of brands are, thus, also conceptualized.

The abovementioned examples of new research points toward an increase in the expectations of the cultural brand when it comes to diversity and social justice. There are many studies of brand relationships, and it seems likely that the deep understanding of brand–consumer relationships will be an important vehicle when understanding future AI-driven commercial encounters. The quite extended focus on the craft behind branding (language and design) is also likely to merge with AI studies soon.

REFERENCES

Aaker, D. A., & Joachimsthaler, E. (2012). *Brand leadership. Simon & Schuster.*

Aaker, J. (1997). Dimensions of brand personality. *Journal of Marketing Research*, *34*(August), 347–56. https://doi.org/10.1177/002224379703400304

Affonso, F. M., & Janiszewski, C. (2023). Marketing by design: The influence of perceptual structure on brand performance. *Journal of Marketing*, *87*(5), 736–54. https://doi.org/10.1177/00222429221142281

Allen, C. T., Fournier, S., & Miller, F. (2008). Brands and their meaning makers. In C. P. Haugtvedt, P. M. Herr, & F. R. Kardes (Eds.), *Handbook of consumer psychology*. Lawrence Erlbaum Associates.

Alvarez, C., Brick, D., & Fournier, S. (2021). Doing relationship work: A theory of change in consumer-brand relationships. *Journal of Consumer Research*, *48*(4), 610–32. https://doi.org/10.1093/jcr/ucab022

Balmer, J. M. T., & Greyser, S. E. (2003). *Revealing the corporation: Perspectives on identity, image, reputation, corporate branding, and corporate-level marketing*. Routledge.

Batra, R., Lenk, P., & Wedel, M. (2010). Brand extension strategy planning: Empirical estimation of brand-category personality fit and atypicality. *Journal of Marketing Research*, *47*(2), 335–47. https://doi.org/10.1509/jmkr.47.2.335

Bergner, A., Hildebrand, C., & Häubl, G. (2023). Machine talk: How verbal embodiment in conversational AI shapes consumer–brand relationships. *Journal of Consumer Research*, *50*(4), 742–64. https://doi.org/10.1093/jcr/ucad014

Berthon, P., Nairn, A., & Money, A. (2003). Through the paradigm funnel: Conceptual tool for literature analysis. *Marketing Education Review*, *13*(2), 55–66. https://doi.org/10.1080/10528008.2003.11488830

Bettman, J. R. (1979) *An Information Processing Theory of Consumer Choice*, Reading. Addison-Wesley.

Bjerre, M., Heding, T., & Knudtzen, C. (2008). Using the dynamic paradigm funnel to analyse brand management. In K. Tollin & A. Caru (Eds.), *Strategic market creation: A new perspective on marketing and innovation management*. Wiley.

Borden, N. (1964). The concept of the marketing mix. In G. Schwartz (Ed.), *Science in marketing*. Wiley.

Buffy, M., Schweidel, D. A., & Zhang, K. (2024). When connection turns to anger: How consumer-brand relationships and crisis type moderate language on social media. *Journal of Consumer Research*, *50*(5), 907–22. https://doi.org/10.1093/jcr/ucad027

Costello, J. P., Walker, J., & Reczek, R. W. (2023). 'Choozing' the best spelling: Consumer response to unconventionally spelled brand names. *Journal of Marketing*, *87*(6), 889–905. https://doi.org/10.1177/00222429231162367

Davis, N., Smith, R., & Sevilla, J. (2025). Mixed couples, mixed attitudes: How interracial couples in marketing appeals influence brand outcomes. *Journal of Consumer Research*, *51*(6), 1144–66. https://doi.org/10.1093/jcr/ucae047

Fajardo, T. M., Zhang, J., & Tsiros, M. (2016). The contingent nature of the symbolic associations of visual design elements: The case of brand logo frames. *Journal of Consumer Research*, *43*(2), 549–66. https://doi.org/10.1093/jcr/ucw048

Feiereisen, S., Rasolofoarison, D., & Russell, C. A. (2021). One brand, many trajectories: Narrative navigation in transmedia. *Journal of Consumer Research*, *48*(4), 651–81. https://doi.org/10.1093/jcr/ucaa046

Fournier, S. (1998). Consumers and their brands: Developing relationship theory in consumer research. *Journal of Consumer Research*, *24*(4), 343–73. https://doi.org/10.1086/209515

Fournier, S. (2012). Lessons learned about consumers' relationships with their brands. In Priester, MacInnis, & Park (Eds.), *Handbook of brand relationships*. M.E. Sharpe.

Grohmann, B. (2009). Gender dimensions of brand personality. *Journal of Marketing Research*, *46*(1), 105–19.

Gupta, T., & Hagtvedt, H. (2021). Safe together, vulnerable apart: How Interstitial space in text logos impacts brand attitudes in tight versus loose cultures. *Journal of Consumer Research*, *48*(3), 474–91. https://doi.org/10.1093/jcr/ucab006

Hanby, T. (1999). Brands dead or alive. *Journal of Market Research Society*, *41*(1), 7–19. https://doi.org/10.1177/147078539904100107

Hatch, M. J., & Schultz, M. (1997). Relations between organizational culture, identity and image. *European Journal of Marketing*, *31*(5/6): 356–65. https://doi.org/10.1108/eb060636

Heding, T., Knudtzen, C., & Bjerre, M. (2020). *Brand management – mastering research, theory and practice*. Routledge.

Holt, D. B. (2002). Why do brands cause trouble? A dialectical theory of consumer culture and branding. *Journal of Consumer Research*, *29*(1), 70–90. https://doi.org/10.1086/339922

Holt, D. B. (2004). *How brands become icons: The principles of cultural branding*. Harvard Business School Press.

Holt, D. B., & Cameron, D. (2010). *Cultural strategy: Using innovative ideologies to build breakthrough brands*. Oxford University Press.

Hult, G. T. M., Neese, W. T., & Bashaw, E. R. (1997). Faculty perceptions of marketing journals. *Journal of Marketing Education*, *19*(1), 37–52. https://doi.org/10.1177/027347539701900105

Kapferer, J.-N. (2012). *The new strategic brand management: Advanced insights and strategic thinking*. Kogan Page.

Keller, K. L. (1993). Conceptualizing, measuring, and managing customer-based brand equity. *Journal of Marketing*, *57*(January), 1–22. https://doi.org/10.1177/002224299305700101

Keller, K. L. (2003). *Strategic brand management: Building, measuring, and managing brand equity*. Prentice Hall.

Kozinets, R. V., de Valck, K., Wojnicki, A. C., & Wilner, S. J. S. (2010). Networked narratives: Understanding word-of-mouth marketing in online communities. *Journal of Marketing*, *74*(2), 71–89.

Kuhn, T. S. (1996). *The structure of scientific revolutions*. University of Chicago Press.

Louro, M. J., & Cunha, P. V. (2001). Brand management paradigms. *Journal of Marketing Management*, *17*, 849–75. https://doi.org/10.1362/026725701323366845

Muniz, Jr., A. M., & O'Guinn, T. C. (2001). Brand community. *Journal of Consumer Research*, *27*(4), 412–32. https://doi.org/10.1086/319618

Noel, A., & Thomson, M. (2024). Epistemological Jangle and Jingle fallacies in the consumer-brand relationship subfield: A call to action. *Journal of Consumer Research*, *51*(2), 383–407. https://doi.org/10.1093/jcr/ucad064

Plummer, J. T. (2000). How personality makes a difference. *Journal of Advertising Research*, *40*(6), 79–83. https://doi.org/10.2501/jar-40-6-79-83

Pogacar, R., Angle, J., & Lowrey, T. M. (2021). Is Nestlé a lady? The feminine brand name advantage. *Journal of Marketing*, *85*(6), 101–17. https://doi.org/10.1177/0022242921993060

Ries, A., & Trout, J. (1983, 2001). *Positioning: The battle for your mind*. McGraw-Hill.

Rodas, M. A., John, D. B., & Torelli, C. J. (2021). Building brands for the emerging bicultural market: The appeal of paradox brands. *Journal of Consumer Research*, *48*(4), 633–50. https://doi.org/10.1093/jcr/ucab037

Schultz, M., Antorini, Y. M., & Csaba, F. F. (2005). *Corporate branding: Purpose, people, process*. Copenhagen Business School Press.

Schultz, M., Hatch, M. J., & Larsen, M. H. (Eds.). (2000). *The expressive organization: Linking identity, reputation and the corporate brand*. Oxford University Press.

Shee, P. S. B., & Abratt, R. (1989). A new approach to the corporate image management process. *Journal of Marketing Management*, *5*(1), 63–76. https://doi.org/10.1080/0267257X.1989.9964088

Smith, A. (1776). *The wealth of nations*. W. Strahan and T. Cadell.

Srinivasan, R., & Sarial-Abi, G. (2021). When algorithms fail: Consumers' responses to brand harm crises caused by algorithm errors. *Journal of Marketing*, *85*(5). https://doi.org/10.1177/0022242921997082

Sung, Y., & Tinkham, S. F. (2005). Brand personality structures in the United States and Korea: Common and culture-specific factors. *Journal of Consumer Psychology*, *15*(4), 334–50. https://doi.org/10.1207/s15327663jcp1504_8

Vo, K., Choe, Y., Manoj, T., Senkar, S., & Goenka, S. (2025). Fate, forgiveness, and brands: How karmic beliefs impact consumer responses toward transgressing brands. *Journal of the Association for Consumer Research*, *10*(1), 24–35. https://doi.org/10.1086/733043

Wichmann, J. R. K., Wiegand, N., & Reinartz, W. J. (2021). The platformization of brands. *Journal of Marketing*, *86*(1), 109–31. https://doi.org/10.1177/00222429211054073

Zhang, K., Li, S., & Ng, S. (2022). Sizes are gendered: The effect of size cues in brand names on brand stereotyping. *Journal of Consumer Research*, *49*(2), 252–67. https://doi.org/10.1093/jcr/ucab058At

3

Corporate Brand Management: Formation and Evolution Since the 1990s

John M. T. Balmer

INTRODUCTION

Since time immemorial, there have been corporate brands. Just as products and services can be brands, so can corporate entities of whatever shape and form. Organisations, institutions, family businesses, cities, countries, etc., can all be corporate brands.

Although corporate branding, for some, can mean turning the company into a brand (Morsing, 2002), it would be wrong to regard the corporate brand as merely a synonym for the organisation or, indeed, as an equivalent notion for corporate reputation. Things are more complicated and nuanced than this. Invariably, corporate brands are redolent with values and meaning. Sometimes, a corporate brand can have considerable heft and power. Corporate brands can be viewed as unique, portable and highly valuable corporate assets, which are often sought by customers and stakeholders (Balmer, 2012a). Of course, they can be coveted by other organisations that might seek to acquire a particular corporate brand.

More particularly, corporate brands represent a distinct, and often highly valuable and meaningful, identity type. It is an identity mode that augments the organisation's identity (Balmer & Greyser, 2003). It is also an identity type, which is underpinned by a corporate brand covenant. The corporate brand covenant represents a distillation of a finite set of certain corporate identity characteristics. Characteristics that are found to be valuable for both the organisation and its customers/stakeholders.

For the organisation, this represents a type of guarantee given to customers and other stakeholders. For customers/stakeholders, the corporate brand covenant represents their understandings and expectations associated with the corporate brand name and/or marque. Increasingly, contemporary corporations need to be understood and managed not only as organisations but, crucially, as corporate brands in addition. Progressively, for many entities, it is incumbent for senior managers to scrutinise their organisation through a corporate brand lens on an ongoing basis whilst not disregarding more traditional means of evaluation. Additionally, and importantly, the corporate brand covenant can be efficacious for customers/stakeholders. This enables them to discriminate between corporate brands and to identify those which they find to be attractive and valuable.

What is clear, however, is that now, as in the past, corporate brands are of pivotal importance for both organisations and individuals alike. Reviews of corporate brand scholarship (Abratt & Mingione, 2002; Balmer, 2010a, 2010b; Balmer et al., 2017; Burghausen, 2024) are testimony to the exponential growth of interest and importance attached to the territory since the 1990s when the corporate brand notion was introduced.

Moreover, the standing and significance of the corporate branding field continues unabated as recent corporate brand scholarship attests (Boukis et al., 2021; de Villartay et al., 2023; Einwiller & Will, 2002; Greyser & Urde, 2019; Iglesias & Ind, 2020; Kristal et al., 2020; Mingione & Leoni, 2020; Porto et al., 2024; Sarasvuo et al., 2023; Törmälä & Saraniemi, 2018).

Thus, whilst the corporate landscape has become a brand-scape (Sherry, 1998), this brand-scape has metamorphosed into a more pronounced *corporate* brand-scape (Balmer, 2006). Arguably, corporate brands are the most prominent, meaningful, valuable, well known and ubiquitous of branding modes. Certainly, many corporate brands are adored, venerated and coveted by customers/stakeholders and organisations alike (Balmer & Gray, 2003). They can also be the least understood.

Corporate brands are wide in scope. Not only do they encapsulate a single organisation but often embody multiple organisations (Balmer & Gray, 2003; Balmer & Thomson, 2009). This is something that is frequently overlooked. Consider the Mitsubishi, Rolls-Royce, Virgin and Yamaha corporate brands in this regard. The aforementioned brands function as umbrella brands for two or more entities. Furthermore, corporate brands can be found in subsidiaries, business units as well as inter-organisational bodies.

Consequently, corporate brands represent a principal (and sometimes, the principal) mode of mutually profitable exchange relationships between an organisation and its customers and other key stakeholders. As such, corporate brands often serve as powerful conduits that engender trust and confidence between organisations and stakeholders. This explains the logic of organisations seeking to leverage the latent power of their corporate brands (cf. Aaker, 2004).

Moreover, given their importance, corporate brand management is a board-level responsibility, and the *de facto* corporate brand manager is an organisation's CEO (Balmer, 1995). However, everyone within an organisation has a responsibility for upholding and delivering the corporate brand covenant to customers/stakeholders.

Progressively, since the formal introduction of the corporate brand concept in the mid-1990s (Balmer, 1995), the acquisition of a strong and meaningful corporate brand is increasingly regarded, by scholars and practitioners alike, to be a strategic imperative. This is because a corporate brand can serve as a luminous lodestar. For an organisation, it is a powerful, centripetal force that can guide an entity. This is especially the case when there is an organisational-wide corporate brand orientation (Balmer, 2013).

Additionally, it can assist senior managers in achieving organisational-wide alignment with the corporate brand apropos The ACID Test of Corporate Brand Management (Balmer, 2005, 2012a, 2012b).

Traditionally, an understanding of the corporate brand covenant notion has been central to understanding corporate brands. This covenant equates to a powerful bilateral compact between an organisation and its customers and other stakeholders. Importantly, this covenant takes time to develop and emerges from numerous organisational/stakeholder interactions. Both organisations and their stakeholders, albeit in different ways, can lay claim to having corporate brand ownership. Thus, a key dimension of corporate brands is to appreciate, and differentiate, between two forms of corporate brand ownership: *legal* and *emotional* (Balmer, 2006, 2010a, 2010b, 2012a).

Legal ownership of a corporate brand is vested in an organisation. A corporate brand can be regarded as one of an organisation's most important, if not the most important, of its strategic assets. *Emotional ownership* of a strong corporate brand belongs to customers/stakeholders. Importantly, emotional ownership of a corporate brand by customers/stakeholders is where the real power and strength of a corporate brand resides. For individuals, a corporate brand can not only be seen to be meaningful, credible and valuable for them in meeting their wants, needs and desires but can often form part of an individual's social identity.

Whilst the corporate brand notion shares certain characteristics with other brand types, the corporate brand is *sui generis* (one-of-a-kind). Thus, corporate brands need to be understood as a singular branding type. It is a branding type that, in comparison to product brands, is distinct in terms of its nature, formation, characteristics, foci, management and importance. In terms of service, brand things are a little more complicated since some service brands are also corporate brands but not all are; the categories of passenger service categories on international air travel are illustrative of this. For instance, consider the first, business, business class, premium economy and economy service brand classes of British Airways. Each is a service brand, but they are qualitatively different from the British Airways services brand and which, arguably, is better categorised as a corporate brand.

For a considerable period of time, many marketing/brand scholars were oblivious to the existence of corporate brands. Even those who recognised their existence were often indifferent to their importance. Sadly, even those who write on corporate brands are sometimes unschooled in the roots of the area. Those who do sometimes fail to appreciate the nuance that characterises the foundational literature. Sometimes, the eschewal of the pre-2000 literature can give the impression that the foundation of the field is a post-2000 phenomenon. For some authors, the avoidance of reference to the foundational marketing literature can erroneously infer that the roots of corporate brand scholarship are to be found in management studies and organisational behaviour rather than in marketing.

Within marketing, whilst some authors acknowledge the links to diverse areas of marketing apropos corporate brands, others studiously ignore these connections or downplay them. Yet, there are strong overlaps between the corporate branding domain and other marketing areas such as brand orientation (Gromark, 2020); corporate marketing (Balmer & Greyser 2006); employer brand (Ambler & Barrow, 1996; Näppä et al., 2023); internal branding (Punjaisri et al., 2009); services branding (Endo et al., 2019); stakeholder marketing (Hult et al., 2011), and the theory of the marketing firm (Foxall, 2021), among others.

HISTORICAL ORIGINS

Ostensibly, the very roots of branding are to be found in corporate brands (Balmer, 2010). Notably, for the greater part of human history, corporate, rather than product, brands have predominated.

Whilst it has been asserted that brands are as old as civilisation (Moore & Reid, 2008), there is a growing body of evidence to show that it is a particular genus of brand that is as old as civilisation, namely, the corporate brand.

At this juncture, it should be noted that, in business history, the earlier conceptualisations of the corporate brand seemingly differ somewhat from contemporary corporate brand scholarship (Balmer & Greyser, 2003). This is because historical evidence invariably focuses on artefacts which reveal the existence and use of brand marques. However, such evidence does not necessarily preclude individuals from conceiving corporate brands as a corporate brand covenant with customers, and others, having an emotional bond with a corporate brand. Indeed, the existence of corporate heritage brands would suggest this to be the case (Balmer & Burghausen, 2015). The example of the British Monarchy is a case in point (Balmer, 2011). Tellingly, it was asserted in 1910 that trademarks played almost the same role in Ancient Roman culture as they do in recent times (Rogers, 1910).

This being noted, it is reasonable to conclude that over the arc of time the corporate brand can be categorised as a protean notion. Thus, although this section will refer to corporate brands, in many instances, it may be more accurate to designate them as proto-corporate brands.

Historically, there seems to be a link between burning a mark on something and the notion of branding. Sometimes, the branding literature emphasises that the origins of branding are to be found in family-owned farming businesses that burnt identifying marks on livestock, as well as on human slaves, to denote ownership. This was certainly the case in ancient Egypt, Greece and Rome (Bastos & Levey, 2012).

In truth, the historiography of corporate branding is richer, broader and more subtle than is typically realised. For instance, it was not only farming enterprises but, seemingly, other family-owned enterprises such as bakers, blacksmiths, builders, carpenters, inn-keepers and potters who recognised the importance, and perhaps necessity, of having an identifying name and/or corporate marque. Historical evidence would suggest this has been the case since time immemorial.

Since the mists of time, (corporate) brands' marques had two immutable features in that they communicated both product origin and product quality (Moore & Reid, 2008).

Moreover, these proto-corporate brands were meaningful for both customers and other stakeholders. The use of corporate brand marques for these purposes can be viewed as important precursors to our contemporary understanding of the territory.

More specifically, the earliest known example of branding is to be found in Asia, circa 2250–2000 BC, in 'India's' Harappan Civilisation (Moore & Reid, 2008). During this era, Indian craftsmen used seals (corporate brand marques) to communicate not only product origins and quality but also image power and information logistics (Moore & Reid, 2008). Similarly, in China during the Shang Dynasty (2000–1500 BC), artisanal brand marques were deployed to convey product origins and quality. Later on, in Cyprus (1500–1000 BC), in Tyre/Phoenicia (1000–500 BC) and in Greece (825–336 BC), visual brand devices were imprinted on goods by business entities to convey information on far broader spectrum that encompassed brand origin, quality, brand image-power and brand image-value.

During the Middle Ages, European craftsmen, and their industry guilds, used brand marks (both collectively and singularly) as a means of protecting intellectual property. As with much earlier periods, they were also used to communicate product quality to customers. Furthermore, these corporate marques served as a guarantee that guild standards had been met (Belfanti, 2020; Mainoni, 1984). Several centuries on, the same was also true for Sheffield's cutlery makers in the 17th century (Belfanti, 2020; Higgins & Tweedale, 1995) as it was for the Wedgwood ceramics company in the 18th century (Koehn, 2001).

The rationale for the use of corporate trademarks in past times continues today. Whilst corporate brand marques are superfluous when trading face to face, when a company is held in esteem outside its immediate locality, the trademark is not only a point of differentiation but a marque that visualises and perpetuates a company's reputation (Rogers, 1910).

It is noticeable, for instance, that the world's first multinational organisation, The British East India Company (est. 1600) and the world's oldest surviving multinational, The Hudson Bay Company (est. 1670), had distinguishing coats of arms. Today, as in centuries past, corporate heraldry – often seen as an epitome of quality – is used by organisations as their corporate brand marque (Balmer, 2023a, 2023b). Heraldry, the favoured mode of brand marque of Ivy League Universities in the USA, is widely used in Great Britain and favoured by many Universities in the Commonwealth.

Furthermore, a heraldic motto can be shorthand for an organisation's corporate brand covenant: The University of Strathclyde's motto, 'Useful Learning' is a case in point (Balmer, 2023b). Importantly, heraldic courts of law, such as those in Scotland, are an integral part of that country's legal system. Coats of arms are granted by the Crown and once granted allow legal redress for their improper use by others in Scotland's Court of the Lord Lyon.

In 1876, a red triangle marque, was registered in England as the first trademark in the world by the brewers Bass & Co. Notably, this was a corporate brand marque. This corporate brand logo became immortalised owing to its appearance in Manet's painting, 'A bar at the Folies-Bergere'. From the late 19th century onward, trademark law/corporate branding practices grew in their significance. It has been asserted that the ability to register corporate brand marques was pivotal to the rise of the modern corporation in the 20th century (Wilkins, 1992). Additionally, they were meaningful in boosting economic efficiency (Landes & Posner, 1987). Moreover, they were consequential in counteracting quality uncertainty in markets and, furthermore, provided valuable informational conduits for consumers (Akerlof, 1970; Sáiz & Castro, 2020). Mercer (2010) noted that, for brands, a trademark represents an intangible item of intellectual property but also noted the significance of brand intangibles such as identity, associations and personality. However, a brand trademark not only denotes but also connotes (Baston & Levey, 2012). Thus, a corporate brand visual symbol along with a corporate name is redolent with meanings. Seemingly, by the end of the 19th century, in certain markets, individuals could discriminate between competing corporate brands. Many railway passengers in Great Britain, for instance, would be aware of the distinguishing corporate brand covenants of railway companies and, therefore, would be able to distinguish between them. As noted by Sir John Betjamin (1972), the Midland Railway corporate brand was associated with comfort, attuned design values and superlative neo-Gothic architecture. It was *not* noted for its speed. In contrast, the Great Northern Railway embraced homeliness rather than beauty. Its primary emphasis was on its fine engineering and, importantly, speed of conveyance. Most distinctive of all was the Great Western Railway (GWR). GWR's highly distinctive corporate brand covenant was greatly shaped by two individuals: the celebrated civil engineer Isambard Kingdom Brunel and, to a lesser degree, the locomotive engineer Daniel Gooch. Notably, GWR was renowned for its leading-edge engineering prowess including its broad gauge track, distinctive engine design and meticulously-maintained rolling stock.

Although the 20th century can often be viewed as the century where product brands predominated, this overlooks the abiding importance of corporate brands. For instance, in the celebrated article on corporate image in the 1970s (Kennedy, 1977, p. 130), reference was made to a company report by Philips which stated

> In this age of technology and competition, the buying public is being increasingly faced with a wide choice of similar designs and features within each price range for all kinds of products. It is clear that when there are no obvious differences in price, quality, design and features, the purchase decision may increasingly be influenced by a positive reputation of the brand and of the manufacturer.

In considering the development of the corporate brand, sight should not be lost that great institutions utilise corporate brand marques in powerful ways. Examples include the golden dragon of Imperial China (Balmer & Chen, 2015); the crucifix of the catholic church (McBrien, 1995) and the crown of Western monarchies, such as the British (Balmer, 2023a). Notably, the swastika enjoys wide currency as a sacred symbol in Hinduism, Jainism and Buddhism. However, in the 20th century, it was adopted as the defining corporate marque of Hitler's Third Reich (Olins, 1978). This being noted, whilst the swastika is regarded as a mark of malevolence, particularly in Europe, it remains a sacred symbol in India, for example.

CORPORATE BRAND SCHOLARSHIP: THE FOUNDATIONS

Although the very roots of branding, as evidenced above, are to be found in corporate brands, for most of the 20th century, brand scholarship primarily focused on product brands and, latterly, accorded recognition to the importance of service brands.

However, organisational-level brands went unrecognised, or were eschewed, other than fleeting references to corporate brands. Thus, a distorted mirror characterised the broad brand scholarship domain.

By means of context, the modern, scholarly notion of a brand and of brand management – which primarily focused on product brands – grew out of the growth of FMCGs (Fast Moving Consumer Goods) in the late 19th/early 20th centuries (Burghausen, 2024). It was only in the concluding decade of the 20th century that a distinct literature on corporate brands emerged. The initial work on the territory was undertaken in the UK by marketing scholars (Balmer, 1995, 2001a, 2001b, 2001c; Balmer & Greyser, 2003; Knox & Bickerton, 2003) and by marketing practitioners (Ind, 1998; King, 1991).

Two articles are of note with regard to the above: King (1991) and (Balmer, 1995).

King's (1991) article, which focused on the broad branding territory, is notable in that it makes reference to what he called *company brands*. Although King's article primarily concentrates on organisational-level services brands, it does, all the same, represents an important progenitor article apropos the corporate brand domain, which developed from the mid-1990s, as noted by Balmer and Greyser (2003). Writing from a practitioner perspective, King (1991) opined that increased attention should be accorded to the company brand in the future (in the 1990s).

Balmer's (1995) article, arguably, is noteworthy since it represents the formal introduction of the corporate brand concept. His article not only makes explicit reference to the corporate brand in its title but also makes it the main focus of the article. Balmer's article had an overtly management focus and sought to explain how corporate brands differed from product brands.

The formal introduction of the corporate brand concept by Balmer (1995) rectified a glaring omission in the nascent corporate marketing domain. This is because it recognised that entities – and not just products and services – could be brands. It was as if corporate brands did not exist. Yet, logic dictated they did.

Moreover, this formal introduction of the corporate brand concept occurred at a time when some corporate levels had achieved prominence and others were beginning to do so (viz., corporate communication, corporate identity, corporate image, corporate reputation, etc.). Given this, the absence of a corporate-level branding designation was a clear oversight.

Whilst it might be deemed that the company brand and corporate brand are equivalents in terms of meaning this is not the case. Whereas a company refers to a specific type of organisation in law, the 'corporate' appellation is broader in scope and encompasses a far wider range of entities. Notably, the word 'corporate': it is derived from the latin word corpus, which refers to a body of people. This is significant in that one of the characteristics of a corporate brand. As such, a corporate brand is a brand category where a group of people within an entity support (or 'work' for) the corporate brand.

From these early foundations, interest in the corporate brand category among scholars gradually burgeoned. Slowly, a distinct strand of scholarship focusing on the corporate brand transpired (Balmer, 1998, 2001a, 2001b, 2001c; Balmer & Gray, 2003; Balmer & Greyser, 2003; Bickerton, 2000; Harris & De Chernatony, 2001; Hatch & Schultz, 2001; Ind, 1997, 1998; Kapferer, 2002; Knox, 2004; Knox & Bickerton, 2003; Schultz & Hatch, 2003).

Furthermore, the nascent corporate brand literature led to a gradual discernment by marketing scholars and others, that corporate brands constituted a new branding mode. Moreover, and importantly, it came with a realisation that a corporate brand represented a significant platform on which companies and stakeholders could have mutually enduring and profitable interactions and relationships (Balmer, 2012a).

Since these beginnings, the corporate brand territory has undergone different stages of development, although there is not always unanimity in this regard (cf. Balmer, 2010a, 2010b; Balmer & Gray, 2003; Balmer & Greyser, 2003; Schultz et al., 2005).

CORPORATE BRANDS: WHAT ARE THEY?

The corporate brand is a protean notion. Today, as over the passage of time, corporate brands have been viewed in a variety of different ways. As we have seen, in centuries past – and even in ancient times – they have been employed by entities to communicate product origin and quality.

For instance, a corporate brand can be equated with a promise on the part of the organisation (Aaker, 2004), Balmer (2001a) states corporate identity is a distinct identity type that is inextricably linked to an organisation's traits (its corporate identity) and is grounded in a bilateral organisational-stakeholder (corporate brand) covenant based on an organisational guarantee and stakeholders understanding and expectations of activities associated with the corporate name/marque; Kapferer, 2002). In contrast, Hatch and Schultz (2001) argue that it is constituted in the alignment between vision, culture and image. They also argue that at its core is organisational identity (Hatch & Schultz, 2008). As such, at its core are organisational members' perceptions of an organisation rather than its actual traits, or corporate identity, Knox and Bickerton (2003) contending that it is the visual, verbal and behavioural expression of an organisation's business model.

An early analysis of the corporate brand opus canon uncovered that corporate brand were viewed as having a number of uses including: a means communicating ownership; a device for image-building device; a means of encapsulating key corporate values; a basis on which individual identities can constructed and a platform on which pleasurable experiences can be consumed (Balmer & Gray, 2003).

In terms of the distinguishing attributes of a corporate brand scholars have noted, it is a distinct identity type (Balmer, 2001a). It is inextricably linked to corporate identity, however, it can have a life of its own and, therefore, can be separable and divisible from a corporate identity from which it emerged (Balmer, 2005). As such, corporate brands can be bought, sold and borrowed (Balmer, 2005). It is multidisciplinary in scope (Balmer, 1995, 2001a, 2001b, 2001c; Hatch & Schultz, 2001; King, 1991). It is an important management/senior management concern (Balmer, 1995, 2001a, 2001b, 2001c; Einwiller & Will, 2002; Hatch & Schultz, 2001; King, 1991). Moreover, corporate brand management is an ongoing management concern (Balmer, 2012a) and requires an abiding commitment on the part of managers, a permanent ongoing management commitment (van Riel & van Bruggen, 2002). It necessitates the engagement of all staff (Balmer, 1995, 2001a, 2001b; King, 1991).

THE CORPORATE BRAND COVENANT

Seemingly, the dominant, quasi-canonical, corporate brand perspective views the corporate brand from the prism of the corporate band covenant. According to this perspective, the kernel of a corporate brand is grounded in a corporate brand covenant. As such, the corporate brand covenant provides an important platform on which customer–stakeholders relationships are forged (Balmer, 2001b). Within the corporate brand canon, the corporate brand covenant receives a good deal of attention within the literature (Abratt & Mingione, 2002; Ashworth & Kavaratzis, 2009; Balmer, 1995, 2001b; Balmer & Gray, 2003; Boukis et al., 2021; Burghausen, 2024; Hamzah et al., 2014; He & Balmer, 2007; Kavaratzis, 2009; Lawer & Knox, 2007; Leitch & Daveonport, 2007; Mingione & Abratt, 2020; Mukherjee & Balmer, 2007; Muzellec & Lambkin, 2006, 2009; Otubanjo et al., 2010; Stuart, 2011, 2012, 2013; Tarnovskaya, 2015; Urde et al., 2007).

The general meaning of the corporate brand covenant is that it denotes a bilateral agreement between an organisation and its stakeholders (Balmer, 2012a). It is an affirmative, morally binding covenant that encompasses assurances (or promises) from the organisation and expectations on the part of customers/stakeholders. Whilst not non-legally binding, the corporate brand covenant is often powerful and highly meaningful. Furthermore, although non-legally binding corporate brand covenants should be seen as morally binding.

Although 'covenant' and 'promise' are sometimes used interchangeably, they can have different meanings. In general terms, a promise denotes a commitment made by one party to another. The same can be true for a covenant but, importantly, it can also represent a two-way compact. Both Balmer (1995) and Kapferer (2002) make reference to a corporate brand promise, and this represents the organisation's side of the contract between an organisation and its customers/stakeholders. Increasingly, however, the term covenant is used with greater frequency and has been popularised by Balmer. In prosaic terms, a corporate brand covenant represents an ongoing bilateral compact between an organisation and its customers/stakeholders. Thus, it needs to be beneficial to both the organisation and to its customers/stakeholders (Balmer, 2012a). It needs to be stressed that for a corporate brand covenant to be meaningful, it needs to be long-lasting. However, this is not to say it is immutable. The nature of a corporate brand covenant can be modified both in subtle and not-so-subtle ways.

Significantly, the term 'covenant' is an important legal and theological notion. Although it can have different meanings, it is a central notion in both Christian theology and law and can have distinct meanings (cf. Biraghi & Gambetti, 2013; McBrien, 1995; Otubanjo et al., 2010; Tarnovskaya, 2015).

In law, it can entail a requirement to do, or not to do, something. In religious thought, there are various covenants. In both the Hebrew Bible and Christian Bibles, for instance, it variously relates to an agreement, commitment or promise between God and Man (Otubanjo et al., 2010). Mindful of the aforementioned, some scholars have averred that the corporate brand covenant can be deemed to be a social contract (McMurran & Washburn, 2008; Noack et al., 2023; Tarnovskaya, 2015).

Perceiving the corporate brand covenant as a social covenant means that norms are shared by organisations and their customers/stakeholders which engender bonds of trust and which for customers/stakeholders can result in satisfaction and loyalty (McMurran & Washburn, 2008). The corporate brand covenant result has affirmed that it is viewed as a bilateral organisational–stakeholder contract (Tarnovskaya, 2015).

However, Tarnovskaya (2015) found that there were in fact two types of contracts in operation. The first type of contract was underpinned by an unconditional organisation pledge. This, perhaps, equates to the notion of the organisation-side corporate brand promise. The second type of contract is pragmatic in character. This contract involved a negotiation of benefits between the organisation and customers/stakeholders. Whilst the unconditional contract typically preceded the pragmatic contract, the latter served to inform the former (Tarnovskaya, 2015).

By means of context, a corporate brand according to this doctrine means that the corporate brand is far removed from merely being a distinguishing name/marque but, moreover, is emblematic of a corporate guarantee directed at customers and stakeholders in terms of meeting wants, needs and desires. Thus, it provides them with surety. Importantly, as with any contract or covenant, it only becomes actualised. Thus, this requires a response from customers/stakeholders. Thus, customers/stakeholders can positively respond by engaging in a form of corporate brand relationship/commitment, as a customer, employee, business partner, etc. Only then will the corporate brand covenant be actualised and materialise as a reality for customers/stakeholders along with the organisation.

When a corporate brand has real value for individuals, it can sometimes translate into an individual having a positive, meaningful and often durable relationship being formed with the organisation. At its most powerful state, such organisational/stakeholder relationships can be ongoing: in the case of corporate heritage brands, they are multigenerational (Balmer, 2017).

Whilst some customer/stakeholder relationships can be enduring and immutable (He & Balmer, 2007), others can involve infrequent, or even a single, 'one-off' relationship (Yang et al., 2020).

CORPORATE BRANDS AND PRODUCT BRANDS DIFFERENCES

Although corporate brands share certain similarities with other branding types, there are also fundamental differences. This can be seen in terms of their nature, formation and maintenance and management (Balmer, 2001a; Balmer & Gray, 2003; King, 1991).

Words, along with concepts, can be defined by their relationship with other words (Saussure, 1966; Schultz et al., 2000). Consequently, comparing corporate brands and product brands can be purposeful in understanding and advancing the corporate brand domain. Such an approach was followed in the earliest works on corporate brands where the differences between corporate and product brands were articulated (King, 1991). By the early 2000s, a more comprehensive list of the differences between the corporate brand and product brand concepts emerged (Balmer, 2001a, 2001b, 2001c).

Table 3.1 illustrates how corporate brands differ from product brands. It represents an updated version of the earlier list (cf. Balmer, 2001a, 2001b, 2001c) and incorporates some more recent insights and reflection on corporate and product brand differences. These are evidenced in new sets of differences and also include a more expansive explanation of some of the original differences.

CORPORATE BRAND FORMATION AND THE SIGNIFICANCE OF CORPORATE IDENTITY, TOTAL CORPORATE BRAND COMMUNICATION AND CORPORATE BRAND IMAGE

Brand formation has been defined as a dialectic process. Traditionally, this has involved the marketer and the consumer (Holt, 2002). For corporate brands, this dialectic process is broader; it is also more convoluted. This is because the interplay is not between a marketer and the consumer but, rather, involves an organisation and its customers/stakeholders. To emphasise this point, the foundational literature on corporate brands not only asserts that corporate brands are complex (Balmer, 1995; Kapferer, 2002; King, 1991) but also that corporate brand formation is protracted (Balmer, 1995, 2001b).

Table 3.1 Differences between corporate and product brands

	Corporate Brands	*Product Brands*
Foci	The brand notion as applied to organisations and other corporate-level entities. *Includes individual entities, subsidiaries, business units and groups of organisations. It should be remembered that a corporate brand will have managers and staff who are de facto corporate brand employees*	The brand notion as applied to products *Includes individual products and product category brands.* *Product brands typically have only a few individuals who specifically 'work' for the product brand such as the product brand manager*
Formation*	Corporate brand formation is over a *medium to long time scale* *Develops from a dialectic process involving the organisation's corporate identity and resultant customer/stakeholders corporate image/reputation.*	Product brand formation is over a *short time-scale* *Develops from a product's communication/ identity and customers product image/ reputation*
Management*	Chief Executive and Senior Management. *The CEO is, de facto, the corporate brand manager. The corporate brand requires commitment from all managers.* *Where there is a franchise arrangement, or where certain corporate brand functions are outsourced, this will also include managers in these organisations as well*	Product brand manager
General Responsibility*	*All Employees* within an organisation have responsibility for the corporate brand. *Where there is a franchise arrangement, or where certain corporate brand functions are outsourced, this will also include employees in these organisations as well*	A few people within an organisation but, primarily, the product brand manager
Disciplinary/Functional Responsibility within the organisation*	Multidisciplinary/All Departments	Marketing department
Foci: customers or stakeholders?*	Customers/Stakeholders	Consumers/customers
Brand Values*	Corporate brand values are manifest in and delivered via an organisation's corporate identity. Thus, there is little scope for creativity. The corporate brand values need to be real.	Product brand values, whilst they can be grounded in a product's identity but, sometimes, are the result of creative license and, therefore, can be contrived. Thus, there is significant scope for creativity
Communication*	'Total Corporate Brand Communications' Promissory Communication: *(corporate brand-based communication)* .... Primary Communication *(corporate identity-based communication)* .... Secondary Communication *(controlled corporate communication-based communication)* .... Tertiary Communication *(word-of-mouth and third-party based communication)* .... Quaternary Communication *(digital and artificial intelligence-based communication)* .... Responsory Communication *(customer/stakeholder feedback based communication)*	Marketing communication

(Continued)

Table 3.1 (Continued)

	Corporate Brands	*Product Brands*
Dimensions requiring alignment**	All organisation's should be dynamically aligned with the corporate brand. *(However, this is not to say that the corporate brand itself is immutable: it too may change over time)* .... **Corporate Brand** in terms of the corporate brand covenant *(Covenanted Identity)* .... **Corporate Identity** (*Actual Identity*) .... **Corporate Communication** *(Communicated Identity)* .... **Corporate Images/Reputations** *vis-a-vis customers/stakeholders* *(Conceived Identity)* .... **Corporate Strategy** *(Ideal Identity)* .... **Management Vision** *(Desired Identity)* .... **The Organisation's Culture** *(Cultural Identity)*	The marketing mix should be in alignment with the product brand promise
Legal ownership of the brand**	The legal ownership of a corporate brand (including trademarks/patents apropos the corporate name, marque, colours, etc.) resides with an organisation	The legal ownership of a product brand (including trademarks/patents, etc.) resides with an organisation
Emotional ownership of the brand**	The real value of a corporate brand comes from the emotional ownership of a corporate brand on the part of customers and other stakeholders.	The real value of a product brand comes from the emotional ownership of a corporate brand on the part of customers.
Type of Brand Orientation (co)**	Corporate Brand Orientation *The corporate brand acts a key cornerstone for an organisation's activities, behaviours.*	Brand Orientation based on product/services brands *The organisation's brands serves as key foundations for an organisation's activities*
Type of Marketing Orientation/ Philosophy**	Corporate Marketing and Philosophy. (Corporate Brand/Organisational-Focused Philosophy) *Corporate marketing philosophy/management serves as one of the foundations for an organisation's activities, behaviours.* *As such, the corporate brand/the organisation is viewed as a highly meaningful platform on which mutually profitable exchange relationships exist between the corporate/brand/the organisation with customers/ other stakeholders.*	Traditional marketing philosophy (product/ product brand-focused) philosophy. *(Traditional) marketing philosophy/ management serves as one of the foundations for an organisation 's activities and behaviours* *As such, products/services*[†] *are viewed as highly meaningful platforms on which mutually profitable exchange relationships exist between product brands/products and customers*

Source: Adapted from Balmer (2001a)

* Mentioned in the original list of corporate and product brand differences.

** Supplemental to the original list of corporate and product brand differences.

[†] It should be noted that serving products/brands can have roles similar to traditional marketing as well as to corporate marketing.

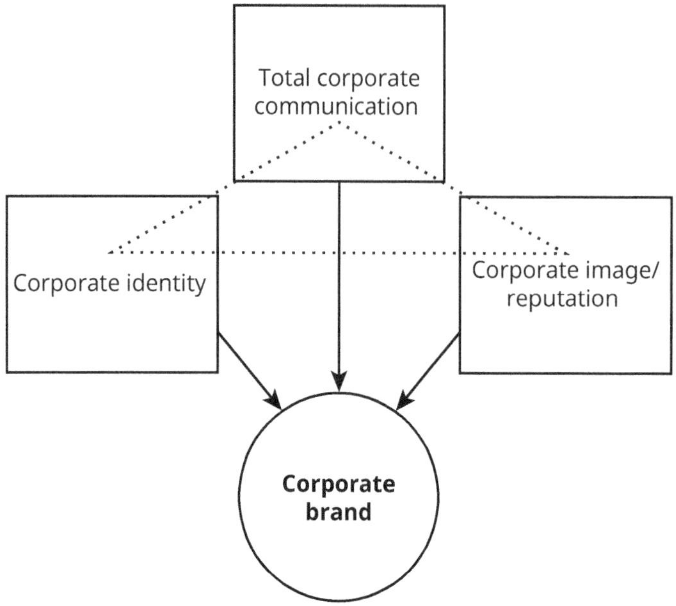

Figure 3.1 Corporate Brand Formation: The corporate identity, total corporate communication and corporate image/reputation dynamic

In comprehending corporate brand formation, reference, necessarily, needs to be made to four corporate-level concepts: corporate brand, corporate identity, total corporate communication, corporate image and corporate reputation (see Figure 3.1).

Corporate Identity

Corporate identity is of pivotal importance to an understanding of corporate brands (Balmer, 1995). In short, a corporate identity provides the grit around which the pearl of a corporate brand is formed (Balmer, 2001a). Thus, the formation of a corporate brand represents a mode of corporate biogenesis (Balmer, 2005). This is when one form of identity (corporate identity) gives being to another (the corporate brand). Consequently, a corporate brand, in part, emerges from an organisation's corporate identity and is transmitted via total corporate communications from which an individual will form perceptions (corporate images and corporate reputations) of an entity.

Moreover, an organisation's corporate identity is not only meaningful apropos corporate brand formation but also necessary for the ongoing delivery, and saliency, of the corporate brand covenant. Thus, a corporate brand/corporate brand covenant on its own would represent an agreement that has not been actualised or is in abeyance. Ergo, it is the corporate identity (an organisation's traits as manifest in what organisation's activities, behaviours, values, standards, etc.) which delivers the corporate brand so that it is palpable to customers and other stakeholders. Corporate identities provide materiality to corporate brand covenants.

At this juncture, it should be emphasised that corporate identity is sometimes viewed as being analogous to visual identity. This is not the case here. Corporate identity refers to the distinguishing and differentiating traits of an entity company. An organisation's corporate identity characteristics give it specificity, stability and coherence (Larçon & Reitter, 1979). Albert and Whetten (1985), albeit referring to the related concept of organisational identity but sharing commonalities with the explanation by Larçon and Reitter (1979), stated that organisational identity characteristics are central, distinctive and enduring. However, it has been argued that an organisation's corporate identity characteristics are best characterised as central, distinctive and evolving (Balmer, 2001a, 2001b, 2001c, 2008). Thus, according to the latter explanation, corporate identities are not immutable; rather, they are mutable.

Elaborating on the above, a more recent explanation argued that an organisation's corporate identity confers an organisation with distinctiveness, differentiation, cohesiveness, representativeness, effectiveness and competitive advantage (Balmer & Podnar, 2021).

Corporate identity encompasses a wide range of traits including what an organisation does, makes, behaves and can incorporate the values of an establishment's founder/s along with its business purpose (Balmer, 2008).

Total Corporate Communications

Total corporate communications provide the essential bridge linking an organisation's corporate identity and stakeholders' corporate images and corporate reputation. It is grounded in the notion that everything an organisation, says, makes and does will communicate (Balmer, 1995), whilst recognising that word-of-mouth, media commentary and competitor commentary are equally significant (Balmer & Gray, 1999).

Traditionally, total corporate communications consisted of Primary Communication (this represents the communication effects of an organisation's activities, behaviours, products/services, etc., and can be characterised, therefore, as corporate identity-based communication); Secondary Communication (this represents formal corporate communications and Tertiary Communication this encompasses word of mouth, third party communications, media commentary, etc.).

More recently, Quaternary Communication (Balmer & Yen, 2016) and Responsory Communication have also been added (Balmer, 2023c, 2024a, 2024b). Quaternary Communication embraces digital and artificial intelligence-based communication, whilst Responsory Communication takes into account communication feedback from customers/stakeholders.

Total corporate communications (Balmer, 1995, 1998, 2017; Balmer & Gray, 1999) is a broader notion than corporate communication (cf. van Riel, 1995). However, both represent a nexus that bridges an organisation's corporate identity with stakeholders' perceptions of an organisation's corporate identity (Gray & Balmer, 1998). It is of special significance since it both shapes corporate image and corporate reputation (Cornelissen, 2008; Gray & Balmer, 1998). Traditionally, corporate communication subsumed managerial, marketing and organisational communication (van Riel, 1995). Total corporate communication is a broader notion.

Corporate Image and Corporate Reputation

Positive images held of an organisation over time can result in positive corporate reputation. Thus, it can be argued that the existence of positive corporate reputations by customers/stakeholders leads to trust. It also leads to the emergence of a corporate brand in the mindset of customers and other stakeholders. Customer/stakeholder trust is manifested in terms of what the corporate brand name/marque connotes in terms of what they can expect from a corporate brand in meeting their wants and needs and the benefits they can derive from the corporate brand. One critical task of senior managers is to regularly appraise customers'/stakeholders' perceptions.

Both corporate image and corporate reputation relate to an individual's perceptions of an entity. However, they are qualitatively different from each other (Gray & Balmer, 1998). Corporate image denotes an individual's immediate mental picture of an organisation at one point in time. Corporate reputation, in contrast, occurs over time as a result of consistent corporate images apropos corporate performance and communication. It constitutes a value judgement apropos an organisation's attributes (Gray & Balmer, 1998). A corporate reputation can relate to an individual's cumulative cognitions of an organisation's corporate identity traits. Of course, such reputations can be positive, negative or ambivalent. Such conceptualisation of corporate identity traits can be broad in scope. Significantly, given that individuals will have different perceptions, it is important to recognise that we are talking about corporate images and corporate reputations. (However, a stereotype image/reputation is, potentially, one that can be held in common.)

The divide between corporate reputation and resultant corporate brand image/reputation may at first appear to be problematical, incomprehensible and inconsequential. Thus, it is important to appreciate that corporate identity and the corporate brand, although linked, are distinct identity types. As such, whereas corporate image and corporate reputation relate to customer/stakeholder perceptions of an organisation, corporate brand image and corporate brand reputation, plainly, refer to customer/perceptions of the corporate brand. Thus, they are intrinsically different. However, as emphasised here, corporate images/reputations, along with total corporate communications, had significantly underpinned the emergence of a corporate brand. Consequently, parallel to individuals forming perceptions of the corporate identity, they, along with senior managers, are likely to focus on a finite and narrower set of the organisation's characteristics. The latter begins to explain the difference between corporate identity and the corporate brand.

The above being noted, not everyone will be enamoured with a corporate brand. Thus, just as some can be ardent supporters of a corporate brand, 'corporate brand evangelists', there can be corporate brand detractors (Balmer, 2006). In extreme cases, corporate brand detractors can become quasi 'corporate brand terrorists' who seek to undermine a particular corporate brand. In the UK, some of the most popular corporate brands can also be the most hated and, in the past, have included Manchester United FC, McDonald's and the supermarket chain Lidl (Balmer, 2006).

EMERGENCE OF THE CORPORATE BRAND

From the above logic, it will be apparent that corporate brands take time to emerge and establish (Balmer, 1995, 2001b). Consequently, the corporate name/marque, over time increasingly becomes associated with particular characteristics.

Thus, over the passage of time, a defined set of corporate identity traits, which are perceived to be distinguishing, attractive, meaningful and valuable for customers/stakeholders, can be crystallised in the minds of customers/other stakeholders. Similarly, senior managers should have identified which corporate identity traits are valuable, meaningful and 'profitable' for the organisation, in the widest sense of the word. Additionally, and importantly, senior managers will need to be fully cognisant of customer/stakeholder perceptions of the corporate brand.

Of course, and to reiterate, they will also need to ensure that such corporate brand traits are firmly grounded in an organisation's corporate identity so that they can continually deliver the, *de facto*, guarantee that is inherent in the organisation's corporate brand.

From such foundations, imperceptibly, a corporate brand takes shape and gently starts to emerge as a stand-alone perceptual identity type. It is an identity type that is grounded in a bilateral corporate covenant between an organisation and customers/stakeholders. Once firmly established, a corporate brand can be separable and divisible from the corporate identity and can have a life of its own (Balmer, 2006). At this juncture, it can be a highly valuable corporate asset.

When such a crystallisation has occurred by the organisation as well as in the minds of customers/stakeholders, senior managers should formulate this in a corporate brand covenant's ideals. Moreover, they should articulate their organisation's commitment to these ideals and, importantly, communicate them both internally and externally. At this point, a corporate brand-oriented organisational approach may be deemed to be efficacious.

This should come with a realisation, on the part of senior managers, that the corporate brand covenant represents a commitment, and guarantee, on the part of an organisation. Moreover, the covenant, for customers and stakeholders, represents their conceptualisations and expectations of the corporate brand. Furthermore, senior managers need to constantly remind themselves that whereas legal ownership of the corporate brand is vested with an organisation, the emotional ownership of the corporate brand resides with customers and stakeholders; that is where the real power of a corporate brand resides (Balmer, 2006, 2012a).

However, when such a crystallisation occurs, this is far from the end of the story. This is because, if a corporate brand covenant is to be continually realised on the part of an organisation (and concomitantly trusted on the part of customers/stakeholders), there needs to be an ongoing bilateral and dynamic dovetailing between the corporate identity and the corporate brand.

The centrality of the corporate identity/corporate brand dynamic cannot be overstated. To recapitulate, it is an organisation's corporate identity that actualises and delivers an organisation's side of the corporate brand covenant. In short, it brings, from the organisation's perspective, the corporate brand covenant to life (Balmer, 2012a, 2012b). The logic for the aforementioned is because the corporate brand is a distinct, often powerful, identity type, albeit, an identity type that is largely perceptual and psychological.

Consequently, it is the corporate identity that ensures an organisation's corporate brand delivery is vital, viable and sustainable. It is by this means that the conceptualisations, expectations and benefits associated with the corporate brand name/marque by customers/stakeholders are met.

Furthermore, senior managers – in addition to focusing on the corporate brand/corporate brand covenant – need to embrace new corporate brand-related concerns relating to total corporate brand communication, corporate brand image and corporate brand reputation.

Thus, corporate brand image relates to the immediate mental picture an individual has of a corporate brand, whereas a corporate brand reputation is derived from a synthesis of consistent corporate brand images held over time (Balmer et al., 2020). This follows on a similar logic apropos corporate image and corporate reputation (cf. Gray & Balmer, 1998), For some, the acquisition of a positive corporate brand image is an ultimate corporate brand management goal (Abratt & Kleyn, 2023, with positive corporate brand images engendering positive behavioural responses by customers (Alwi & Kitchen, 2014).

Significantly, the total corporate brand communication notion (Balmer, 2023c) now comes to the fore. Markedly different from Total Corporate Communication, it comprises promissory, primary, secondary, tertiary, quaternary and responsory communication (see Table 3.1).

As such, this provides an arch that connects corporate brand delivery from the organisation side and corporate brand perceptions from the customer/stakeholder side.

CONCLUSION

Although largely overlooked in the branding canon until comparatively recently, the corporate brand concept has emerged as one of the fundamental facets of brand management and scholarship.

The corporate brand historiography has not only revealed that the roots of corporate brand go back to the mists of time but that, seemingly, the very roots of branding are to be found in corporate brands. Moreover, since time immemorial, not only have corporate brands been important but also, for an increasing number of organisations, they are indispensable. Corporate brands often provide the principal platform on which organisational–customer/stakeholder relationships are forged. Moreover, for individuals (customers/stakeholders), they are an indispensable means of navigating the modern world with all its complexities.

However, as we have seen, corporate brands are broader and more complicated than product brands, and their management is a senior management concern.

Finally, the recent upsurge in interest in corporate brands can be seen as a corrective to a clear reality that corporate brands have been present and substantial since time immemorial. Seemingly, they are going to remain so.

REFERENCES

Aaker, D. A. (2004). Levering the corporate brand. *California Management Review*, *46*(3), 6–18. https://doi.org/10.1177/000812560404600301

Abratt, R., & Kleyn, N. (2023). The conscientious corporate brand: Definition, operationalization and application in a B2B context. *Journal of Business & Industrial Marketing*, *38*(10), 2122–2133. https://doi.org/10.1108/JBIM-10-2021-0468

Abratt, R., & Mingione, N. (2002). Demarcating the field of corporate brand management. In O. Iglesias, N. Ind, & M. Schultz (Eds.), *The Routledge companion to corporate branding* (pp. 24–41). Routledge.

Akerlof, G. A. (1970). The market for lemons: Quality uncertainty and the market mechanism. *The Quarterly Journal of Economics*, *84*(3), 488–500. https://doi.org/10.2307/1879431

Albert, A., & Whetten, D. A. (1985). Organizational identity. In B. M. Staw, & L. L. Cummings (Eds.), *Research in organizational behavior* (pp. 263–295). JAI Press.

Alwi, S. F. S., & Kitchen, P. J. (2014). Projecting corporate brand image and behavioral response in business schools: Cognitive or affective brand attributes? *Journal of Business Research*, *6*(11), 2324–2336. https://doi.org/10.1016/j.jbusres.2014.06.020

Ambler, T., & Barrow, S. (1996). The employer brand. *Journal of Brand Management*, *4*(3), 185–206. https://doi.org/10.1057/bm.1996.42

Ashworth, G., & Kavaratzis, M. (2009). Beyond the logo: Brand management for cities. *Journal of Brand Management*, *16*, 520–531. https://doi.org/10.1057/palgrave.bm.2550133

Balmer, J. M. T. (1995). Corporate branding and connoisseurship. *Journal of General Management*, *21*(1), 24–46. https://doi.org/10.1177/030630709502100102

Balmer, J. M. T. (1998). Corporate identity and the advent of corporate marketing. *Journal of Marketing Management*, *14*(8), 963–996. https://doi.org/10.1362/026725798784867536

Balmer, J. M. T. (2001a). Corporate identity, corporate branding, and corporate marketing: Seeing through the fog. *European Journal of Marketing*, *35*(3/4), 248–291. https://doi.org/10.1108/03090560110694763

Balmer, J. M. T. (2001b). The three virtues and seven deadly sins of corporate brand management. *Journal of General Management*, *27*(1), 1–17. https://doi.org/10.1177/030630700102700101

Balmer, J. M. T. (2001c). From the Pentagon: A new identity framework. *Corporate Reputation Review*, *4*(1), 11–22. https://doi.org/10.1057/palgrave.crr.1540129

Balmer, J. M. T. (2005). Corporate brands: A strategic management framework. *Bradford School of Management Working Paper Series*, *5*(3), 1–15.

Balmer, J. M. T. (2006). Corporate brand cultures and communities. In J. E. Schroeder & M. Salzer Morling (Eds.), *Brand culture* (pp. 34–49). Routledge.

Balmer, J. M. T. (2008). Identity based views of the corporation: Insights from corporate identity, organisational identity, social identity, visual identity, corporate brand identity and corporate image. *European Journal of Marketing*, *42*(9/10), 879–906. https://doi.org/10.1108/03090560810891055

Balmer, J. M. T. (2010a). Explicating corporate brands and their management: Reflections, and directions from 1995 to the present. *Journal of Brand Management, 18*(3), 180–196. https://doi.org/10.1057/bm.2010.46

Balmer, J. M. T. (2010b). The BP Deepwater Horizon débâcle and corporate brand exuberance. *Journal of Brand Management, 18*, 97–104. https://doi.org/10.1057/bm.2010.33

Balmer, J. M. T. (2011). Corporate heritage identities, corporate heritage brands and the multiple heritage identities of the British Monarchy. *European Journal of Marketing, 45*(9/10), 1380–1398. https://doi.org/10.1108/03090561111151817

Balmer, J. M. T. (2012a). Corporate brand management imperatives: Custodianship, credibility, and calibration. *California Management Review, 54*(3), 6–33. https://doi.org/10.1525/cmr.2012.54.3.6

Balmer, J. M. T. (2012b). Strategic corporate brand alignment: Perspectives from identity-based views of corporate brands. *European Journal of Marketing, 46*(7/8), 1064–1092. https://doi.org/10.1108/03090561211230205

Balmer, J. M. T. (2013). Corporate brand orientation: What is it? What of it? *Journal of Brand Management, 20*(9), 723–741. https://doi.org/10.1057/bm.2013.15

Balmer, J. M. T. (2017). *Foundations of corporate heritage*. Routledge.

Balmer, J. M. T. (2023a). Design, corporate brand design, and corporate heritage brand design: What are they? What of them? *Journal of Brand Management, 30*(2), 97–115. https://doi.org/10.1057/s41262-023-00314-z

Balmer, J. M. T. (2023b). Heraldry, mottos, and corporate heritage discovery at the University of Strathclyde: A case of useful learning. *Journal of Brand Management, 30*(2), 170–183. https://doi.org/10.1057/s41262-023-00316-x

Balmer, J. M. T. (2023c). Digital corporate communication and brand communication. In M. Bedlam (Ed.), *Handbook of corporate communication* (pp. 34–50). Cheltenham: Edward Elgar.

Balmer, J. M. T. (2024a). Corporate brand communication. In K. Podnar (Ed.), *Elgar encyclopedia of corporate communication* (pp. 176–180). Cheltenham: Edward Elgar.

Balmer, J. M. T. (2024b). Corporate brand architecture. In K. Podnar (Ed.), *Elgar encyclopedia of corporate communication* (pp. 143–148). Cheltenham: Edward Elgar.

Balmer, J. M. T., & Burghausen, M. (2015). Explicating corporate heritage, corporate heritage brands and organisational heritage. *Journal of Brand Management, 22*(5), 364–384. https://doi.org/10.1057/bm.2015.26

Balmer, J. M. T., & Chen, W. (2015). Corporate heritage brands in China. Consumer engagement with China's most celebrated corporate heritage brand–Tong Ren Tang: 同仁堂. *Journal of Brand Management, 22*(1), 194–210. https://doi.org/10.1057/bm.2015.14

Balmer, J. M. T., & Gray, E. R. (1999). Corporate identity and corporate communications: Creating a competitive advantage. *Corporate Communications: An International Journal, 4*(4), 171–176. https://doi.org/10.1108/EUM0000000007299

Balmer, J. M. T., & Gray, E. R. (2003). Corporate brands: What are they? What of them*? European Journal of Marketing, 37*(7/8), 972–997. https://doi.org/10.1108/03090560310477627

Balmer, J. M. T., & Greyser, S. A. (2003). *Revealing the corporation. Perspectives on identity, image, reputation, corporate branding and corporate-level marketing*. Routledge.

Balmer, J. M. T., & Greyser, S. A. (2006). Corporate marketing: Integrating corporate identity, corporate branding, corporate communications, corporate image and corporate reputation. *European Journal of Marketing, 40*(7–8), 730–741. https://doi.org/10.1108/03090560610669964

Balmer, J. M. T., & Podnar, K. (2021). Corporate brand orientation: Identity, internal images, and corporate identification matters. *Journal of Business Research, 134*, 729–737. https://doi.org/10.1016/j.jbusres.2021.06.016

Balmer, J. M. T., & Thomson, I. (2009). The shared management and ownership of corporate brands: The case of Hilton. *Journal of General Management, 34*(4), 15–37. https://doi.org/10.1177/030630700903400402

Balmer, J. M. T., & Yen, D. A. (2016). The internet of total corporate communications, quaternary corporate communications and the corporate marketing internet revolution. *Journal of Marketing Management, 33*(1–2), 131–144. https://doi.org/10.1080/0267257X.2016.1255440

Balmer, J. M. T., Lin, Z., Chen, W., & He, X. (2020). The role of corporate brand image for B2B relationships of logistics service providers in China. *Journal of Business Research, 117*, 850–861. https://doi.org/10.1016/j.jbusres.2020.03.043

Balmer, J. M. T., Powell, S. M., Kernstock, J., & Brexendorf, T. O. (2017). Introduction. Current state and future directions for research on corporate brand management. In J. M. T. Balmer, S. M. Powell, J. Kernstock, & T. O. Brexendorf (Eds.), *Advances in corporate branding. Journal of brand management advanced collections* (pp. 1–21). Palgrave Macmillan.

Bastos, W., & Levey, S. J. (2012). A history of the concept of branding: Practice and theory. *Journal of Historical Research in Marketing, 4*(3), 347–368. https://doi.org/10.1108/17557501211252934

Belfanti, C. M. (2020). Branding before the brands: Marks, imitations and counterfeits in pre-modern

Europe. In R. Castro & P. Saiz (Eds.), *The brand and its history* (pp. 23–34). Routledge.

Betjeman, J. (1972). *London's historic railway stations*. John Murray (Publishers) Ltd.

Bickerton, D. (2000). Corporate reputation versus corporate branding: The realist debate. *Corporate Communications: An International Journal*, *5*(1), 42–48. https://doi.org/10.1108/13563280010317578

Biraghi, S., & Gambetti, R. C. (2013). Corporate branding: Where are we? A systematic communication-based inquiry. *Journal of Marketing Communications*, *21*(4), 260–283. https://doi.org/10.1080/13527266.2013.768535

Boukis, A., Punjaisri, K., Balmer, J. M. T., Kaminakis, K., & Papastathopoulos, A. (2021). Unveiling front-line employees' brand construal types during corporate brand promise delivery: A multi-study analysis. *Journal of Business Research*, *131*, 673–685. https://doi.org/10.1016/j.jbusres.2020.12.068

Burghausen, M. (2024). Corporate brand. In K. Podnar (Ed.), *Elgar encyclopedia of corporate communication* (pp. 122–131). Edward Elgar.

Cornelissen, J. P. (2008). *Corporate communication*. Sage.

de Villartay, S., Abid-Dupont, M. A., & Berger-Remy, F. (2023). The dynamic of employees' trust in their organisation in a corporate brand crisis: The bounce-back effect of organisational identification. *Journal of Marketing Management*, *40*(3–4), 260–288.

Einwiller, S., & Will, M. (2002). Towards an integrated approach to corporate branding – an empirical study. *Corporate Communications: An International Journal*, *7*(2), 100–109. https://doi.org/10.1108/13563280210426160

Endo, A. C. B., de Farias, L. A., & Coelho, P. S. (2019). Service branding from the perspective of higher education administrators. *Marketing Intelligence & Planning*, *37*(4), 401–416. https://doi.org/10.1108/MIP-06-2018-0237

Foxall, G. (2021). The theory of the marketing firm. *Management and Decision Economics*, *41*(2), 164–184. https://doi.org/10.1002/mde.3047

Gray, E. R., & Balmer, J. M. T. (1998). Managing corporate image and corporate reputation. *Long Range Planning*, *31*(5), 695–702. https://doi.org/10.1016/S0024-6301(98)00074-0

Greyser, S. A., & Urde, M. (2019). What does your corporate brand stand for? *Harvard Business Review*, *97*(1), 80–88.

Gromark, J. (2020). Brand orientation in action-a transformational learning intervention. *Journal of Business Research*, *119*(2), 412–422. https://doi.org/10.1016/j.jbusres.2019.10.058

Hamzah, Z. L., Alwi, S. F. S., & Othman, M. N. (2014). Designing corporate brand experience in an online context: A qualitative insight. *Journal of Business Research*, *67*(11), 2299–2310. https://doi.org/10.1016/j.jbusres.2014.06.018

Harris, F., & De Chernatony, L. (2001). Corporate branding and corporate brand performance. *European Journal of Marketing*, *5*(3/4), 441–456. https://doi.org/10.1108/03090560110382101

Hatch, M. J., & Schultz, M. (2001). Are the strategic stars aligned for your corporate brand? *Harvard Business Review*, *79*(2), 129–134.

Hatch, M. J., & Schultz, M. (2008). *Taking brand initiative*. Jossey-Bass.

He, H., & Balmer, J. M. T. (2007). Identity studies: Multiple perspectives and implications for corporate-level marketing. *European Journal of Marketing*, *41*(7–8), 65–785.

Higgins, D., & Tweedale, G. (1995). Asset or liability? Trademarks in the Sheffield cutlery and tool trades. *Business History*, *37*, 1–27. https://doi.org/10.1080/00076799500000088

Holt, D. B. (2002). Why do brands cause trouble? A dialectical theory of consumer culture and branding. *Journal of Consumer Research*, *2*(1), 70–90.

Hult, G. T. M., Mena, J. A., Ferrell, O. C., & Ferrell, L. (2011). Stakeholder marketing: A definition and conceptual framework. *Academy of Marketing Review*, *1*(1), 44–65. https://doi.org/10.1007/s13162-011-0002-5

Iglesias, O., & Ind, N. (2020). Towards a theory of conscientious corporate brand co-creation: The next key challenge in brand management. *Journal of Brand Management*, *27*, 710–720. https://doi.org/10.1057/s41262-020-00205-7

Ind, N. (1997). *The corporate brand*. Macmillan.

Ind, N. (1998). An integrated approach to corporate branding. *Journal of Brand Management*, *5*, 323–329. https://doi.org/10.1057/bm.1998.20

Kapferer, J.-N. (2002). Corporate brand and organizational identity. In B. Moingeon, & G. Soenen (Eds.), *Corporate and organizational identities* (pp. 175–194). Routledge.

Kavaratzis, M. (2009). Cities and their brands: Lessons from corporate branding. *Place Branding & Public Diplomancy*, *5*, 26–37. https://doi.org/10.1057/pb.2008.3

Kennedy, S. H. (1977). Nurturing corporate images. *European Journal of Marketing*, *11*(3), 119–164. https://doi.org/10.1108/EUM0000000005007

King, S. (1991). Brand-building in the 1990s. *Journal of Marketing Management*, *7*, 3–13. https://doi.org/10.1080/0267257X.1991.9964136

Knox, S. (2004). Positioning and branding your organisation. *Journal of Product & Brand Management*, *13*(2), 105–115. https://doi.org/10.1108/10610420410529735

Knox, S., & Bickerton, D. (2003). The six conventions of corporate branding. *European Journal of Marketing*, *37*(7/8), 998–1016. https://doi.org/10.1108/03090560310477636

Koehn, N. F. (2001). *Brand new: How entrepreneurs earned consumers' trust from Wedgewood to Dell*. Harvard University Press.

Kristal, S., Baumgarth, C., & Henseler, J. (2020). Performative corporate brand identity in industrial markets: The case of German prosthetics manufacturer Ottobock. *Journal of Business Research, 114*, 240–253. https://doi.org/10.1016/j.jbusres.2020.04.026

Landes, W. M., & Posner, R. A. (1987). Trademark law: An economic perspective. *Journal of Law and Economics, 30*(2), 265–309. https://doi.org/10.1086/467138

Larçon, J. P., & Reitter, R. (1979). *Structures de pouvoir et identité de l'entreprise*. Nathan.

Lawer, C., & Knox, S. (2007). Reverse-market orientation and corporate brand development. *International Studies of Management & Organization, 37*(4), 64–83. https://doi.org/10.2753/IMO0020-8825370403

Leitch, S., & Davenport, S. (2007). Corporate brands and social brands: Co-branding GM-free and UK supermarkets. *International Studies of Management & Organization, 37*(4), 45–63. https://doi.org/10.2753/IMO0020-8825370402

Mainoni, P. (1984). Il mercato della lana a Milano dal XIV al XV secolo. *Archivo Storico Lombardo*, 20–43.

McBrien, R. P. (Ed.). (1995). *Encyclopedia of catholicism*. Harper Collins.

McMurran, R., & Washburn, J. H. (2008). Branding: a social contract between a business and its customer. In T. C. Melewar, & E. Karaosmanoglu (Eds.), *Contemporary thoughts on corporate branding and corporate identity management* (pp. 5–22). Palgrave Macmillan.

Mercer, J. (2010). A mark of distinction: Branding and trade mark law in the UK from the 1960s. *Business History, 22*(1), 17–42. https://doi.org/10.1080/00076790903281033

Mingione, M., & Abratt, R. (2020). Building a corporate brand in the digital age: Imperatives for transforming born-digital startups into successful corporate brands. *Journal of Marketing Management, 36*(11–12), 981–1008. https://doi.org/10.1080/0267257X.2020.1750453

Mingione, M., & Leoni, L. (2020). Blurring B2C and B2C boundaries: Corporate brand value co-creation in B2BB2C markets. *Journal of Marketing Management, 361*(1–2), 72–99. https://doi.org/10.1080/0267257X.2019.1694566

Moore, K., & Reid, S. (2008). The birth of brand: 4000 years of branding. *Business History, 50*(4), 419–432. https://doi.org/10.1080/00076790802106299

Morsing, M. (2002). Corporate branding basics. *Design DK, 1*(April), 33–44. @article{15a031d0c02311db9769000ea68e967b

Mukherjee, A., & Balmer, J. M. T. (2007). Preface: New frontiers and perspectives in corporate brand management: In search of a theory. *International Studies of Management & Organization, 37*(4), 3–19. www.jstor.org/stable/40397711

Muzellec, L., & Lambkin, M. (2006). Corporate rebranding: Destroying, transferring or creating brand equity? *European Journal of Marketing, 40*(7/8), 803–824. https://doi.org/10.1108/03090560610670007

Muzellec, L., & Lambkin, M. C. (2009). Corporate branding and brand architecture: A conceptual framework. *Marketing Theory, 9*(1), 31–54. https://doi.org/10.1177/1470593108100060

Näppä, A., Ek Styvén, M., & Foster, T. (2023). I just work here! Employees as co-creators of the employer brand. *Scandinavian Journal of Hospitality and Tourism, 23*(1), 73–93. https://doi.org/10.1080/15022250.2023.2190934

Noack, S., Bordiyanu, I., Zirkler, B., & Brauweller, C. (2023). Sustainability covenants as a financial measure to enhance the efficiency of companies. *Eurasian Journal of Economic and Business Studies, 67*(3), 104–121. https://doi.org/10.47703/ejebs.v3i67.294

Olins, W. (1978). *The corporate personality*. Design Council.

Otubanjo, O., Abimbola, T., & Amujo, O. (2010). Conceptualising the notion of corporate brand covenant. *Journal of Product & Brand Management, 19*(6), 410–422. https://doi.org/10.1108/10610421011085721

Porto, R. B., Foxall, G. R., Limongi, R., & Barbosa, D. L. (2024). Unraveling corporate brand equity: A measurement model based on consumer perception of corporate brands. *Journal of Modelling in Management, 19*(4), 1237–1261. https://doi.org/10.1108/JM2-04-2023-0067

Punjaisri, K., Evanschitzky, H., & Wilson, A. (2009). Internal branding: An enabler of employees' brand-supporting behaviours. *Journal of Service Management, 20*(2), 209–226. https://doi.org/10.1108/09564230910952780

Rogers, E. S. (1910). Historical matter concerning trade-marks. *Michigan Law Review, 9*(1), 29–43. https://doi.org/10.2307/1276308

Sáiz, P., & Castro, R. (2020). Trademarks in branding: Legal issues and commercial practices. In R. Castro, & P. Sáiz (Eds.), *The brand and its history*. Routledge.

Sarasvuo, S., Liljander, V., & Haahtela, K. (2023). Buyer perceptions of corporate brand extension attractiveness and fit in B2B services. *Industrial Marketing Management, 115*, 69–85. https://doi.org/10.1016/j.indmarman.2023.09.006

Saussure, F. (1966). *Course in general linguistics*. McGraw Hill.

Schultz, M., & Hatch, M. J. (2003). The cycles of corporate branding: The case of the LEGO company. *California Management Review*, *46*(1), 6–26. https://doi.org/10.2307/41166229

Schultz, M., Antorini, Y.-M., & Csaba, F. F. (2005). *Corporate branding*. Copenhagen Business School Press.

Schultz, M., Hatch, M. J., & Larsen, M. H. (Eds.) (2000). *The expressive organization: Linking identity, reputation, and the corporate brand*. Oxford: Oxford University Press. https://doi.org/10.1093/oso/9780198297789.001.0001

Sherry, J. F., Jr. (Ed.) (1998). *Servicescapes: The concept of place in contemporary markets*. American Marketing Association.

Stuart, H. (2012). Living the corporate rebrand: The employee perspective. *Corporate Reputation Review*, *15*, 158–168. https://doi.org/10.1057/crr.2012.9

Stuart, H. J. (2011). An identity-based approach to the sustainable corporate brand. *Corporate Communications: An International Journal*, *16*(2), 139–149. https://doi.org/10.1108/13563281111141660

Stuart, J. H. (2013). Positioning the corporate brand as sustainable: Leadership de rigueur. *Journal of Brand Management*, *20*, 793–799. https://doi.org/10.1057/bm.2013.17

Tarnovskaya, V. (2015). Corporate brand as a contract with stakeholders – Theology or pragmatism? *Marketing Intelligence & Planning*, *33*(6), 865–886. https://doi.org/10.1108/MIP-06-2014-0111

Törmälä, M., & Saraniemi, S. (2018). The role of business partners in corporate brand image co-creation. *Journal of Product & Brand Management*, *27*(1), 29–40. https://doi.org/10.1108/JPBM-01-2016-1089

Urde, M., Greyser, S. A., & Balmer, J. M. T. (2007). Corporate brands with a heritage. *Journal of Brand Management*, *15*, 4–19. https://doi.org/10.1057/palgrave.bm.2550106

van Riel, C. B. M. (1995). *Principles of corporate communication*. Routledge.

van Riel, C. B. M., & van Bruggen, G. H. (2002). Incorporating business unit managers' perspectives in corporate-branding strategy decision making. *Corporate Reputation Review*, *5*(2/3), 241–252. https://doi.org/10.1057/palgrave.crr.1540177

Wilkins, M. (1992). The neglected intangible asset: The influence of the trade mark on the rise of the modern corporation. *Business History*, *34*(1), 66–95. https://doi.org/10.1080/00076799200000004

Yang, H.-P., Yen, D., & Balmer, J. M. T. (2020). Higher education: A once-in-a-lifetime purchase. *Qualitative Market Research*, *23*(4), 865–890. https://doi.org/10.1108/QMR-12-2017-0169

4

Global Branding: Past, Present and Future

Ayşegül Özsomer and Selin Altaras

INTRODUCTION

With the onset of globalization, global brands have gained importance in both advanced and emerging markets. Research on global branding has also blossomed over the past 25 years. From a practitioner's perspective, many multi-nationals, such as P&G, Unilever and Henkel, have streamlined their portfolios, focusing on fewer, more powerful global brands. Global brands offered significant advantages to these companies, including economies of scale and scope in R&D, marketing and production (Özsomer & Simonin, 2004). During these phases of globalization, global brands were positioned rather uniformly around the world, targeting similar segments across the market based on the premise of a single global consumer culture (GCC) and leveraging consumers with homogenized needs and desires across the markets (Alden et al., 2006). There was general consensus that global brands offered significant functional and psychological benefits over local brands (e.g., Steenkamp, 2017; Xie et al., 2015).

However, recent trends of deglobalization (e.g., USA–China trade tensions, 'America First,' Eurozone crisis), shifts in global trade and supply chains such as nearshoring and reshoring, and growing demand for local brands have prompted scholars to investigate implications for global branding. Furthermore, the global brand landscape is highly dynamic. The Interbrand Best Global Brands report (2024) highlights that, since 2000, 185 brands have appeared in the rankings, but 85 have disappeared, including once-powerful brands like Kodak, Heinz and Nokia. Only 35 brands have consistently remained in the top 100, and only two – Microsoft and Coca-Cola – have consistently held top 10 positions. Over the past 25 years, these top global brands collectively missed out on approximately $3.5 trillion in potential earnings due to myopic marketing investments prioritizing short-term performance over long-term brand building. Given this changing context, understanding factors that differentiate these enduring global brands from others is timely and informative.

In this chapter, we synthesize extant literature to identify the central and emerging debates, issues, and theoretical frameworks on global branding against the changing landscape. We delve into the key drivers of global branding from consumer, category and brand strategy perspectives. We also explore the definition and conceptualization of global brands, reviewing relevant theoretical frameworks. Consumer- and category-level constructs conditioning global brand effects are discussed. We provide an overview of compensatory

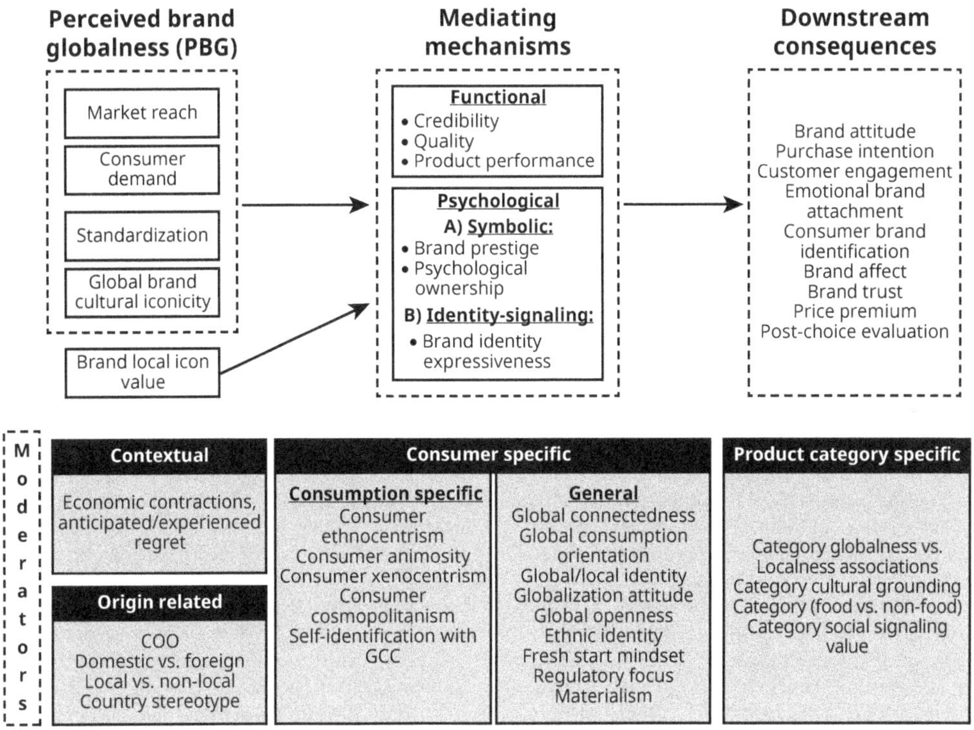

Figure 4.1 Global brand preference framework

Source: The authors.

and hybrid branding strategies. The chapter also reviews emerging trends such as rising anti-global sentiments, stalling globalization and introducing emerging debates regarding the future of global brands such as the decreasing relevance of 'globalness' positioning in an era of deglobalization. Finally, we conclude by identifying promising avenues for future research. We also summarize the current knowledge base in a Global Brand Preference Framework presented in Figure 4.1.

DEFINITION AND CONCEPTUALIZATION OF GLOBAL BRANDS

There is no universally accepted definition of 'global brands' (Mandler, 2019; Samiee, 2019). Two schools of thought seem prevalent when defining the concept. The first, the supply-side perspective, is concerned about the brand, packaging, communications and distribution strategies, mostly under the control of managers. The second, the demand-side perspective, is focused more on consumer perceptions regarding a brand's globalness and its downstream implications. Research from the demand side places more weight on how the brand is perceived regardless of the brand's actual state (Samiee, 2019). Perceptions of brand globalness, not the objective reality, determine whether a particular brand is considered as global or not. Due to these differing perspectives, various definitions have emerged in the literature (cf. Mandler, 2019; Özsomer & Altaras, 2008). Despite these definitional and conceptual variations, a common consensus exists: Global brands are characterized by their widespread availability, highlighting a brand's market reach and widespread global acceptance, in terms of distribution, awareness and preference.

One of the most widely accepted conceptualizations from the demand side is that of Steenkamp et al. (2003). These authors were the first to coin the term Perceived Brand Globalness (PBG) to reflect consumer perceptions of a brand as global (i.e., as widely available and accepted across the world). PBG is formally defined as consumers' beliefs that a brand 'is marketed in multiple countries and is generally recognized as global in these countries' (p. 54). Consumers may form such beliefs through media exposure, word-of-mouth, or travel experiences (Steenkamp et al., 2003). Since the introduction of the PBG concept, research on global branding has significantly advanced the understanding of consumer perceptions, beliefs and behavioral intentions toward global brands.

Reconciling the supply and demand perspectives, Özsomer and Altaras (2008) defined global brands as those 'that have global awareness, availability, acceptance and desirability and are often found under the same name with consistent positioning, image, personality, look and feel in major markets enabled by standardized and centrally coordinated marketing strategies and programs' (p. 1). It is worthwhile to note that Özsomer and Altaras's definition is the most comprehensive, incorporating the global market reach with consistent marketing mix elements (brand name, positioning, personality, image and look/feel) captured in standardized marketing programs and coordination as supply-side dimensions. This definition was also utilized by Özsomer et al. (2012) in an influential paper. A closer examination of all definitions reveals that global brands are defined by four specific characteristics: (1) Wide market reach, (2) Widespread demand, (3) Standardization of marketing mix elements across countries and (4) Global symbolism.

While the first two components are well captured by Steenkamp et al.'s (2003) PBG scale, the remaining two components are not explicitly measured by the PBG scale (Liu et al., 2021; Mandler, 2019) although they are implicitly assumed. Indeed, building on Özsomer and Altaras (2008), Mandler (2019) proposed an extended conceptualization of PBG that incorporates standardization and GCC as additional facets of brand globalness. Similarly, in their review of the global branding literature, Liu et al. (2021) recommend adding global symbolism to the PBG conceptualization. Hsieh (2002) also proposed to measure a brand's degree of globalness (i.e., brand globalization) based on its level of standardization, more specifically how consistently a brand's image is perceived across markets. According to Hsieh (2002), a higher degree of perceptual similarity indicates greater brand globalness.

While we agree with Mandler (2019), Liu et al. (2021) and Hsieh (2002), we believe that these constructs would be better captured if conceptualized differently. Regarding the standardization component, we propose a different operationalization. Mandler (2019) operationalized standardization with two bipolar items capturing the opposite of (good) local adaptation, specifically, 'This brand adapts very well (not at all) to the needs and wants of local consumers. This brand cares very much (does not care at all) about the needs and wants of local consumers' (p. 660). The wording for the standardization end of the seven-point bipolar scale is loaded with negative connotations (e.g., does not care at all). Hence, it is not surprising to find a strong negative association with both brand evaluations and attitudes, cognitive and affective downstream consequences. A more 'neutral' conceptualization of standardization builds upon the perceived similarity or consistency of a brand's marketing mix elements (e.g., product, packaging, positioning and communications) across different countries (Özsomer & Simonin, 2004). The standardization facet of PBG can be better captured by measuring it as the degree to which consumers perceive similarity across markets in terms of marketing mix variables, particularly regarding the product, positioning and advertising dimensions for which they can form impressions through travel, on-line and offline media exposure, and overall brand communication (Güzel et al., 2025; Steenkamp et al., 2003). Conceptualizing standardization as a facet rather than as the opposite end of adaptation would also enable capturing hybrid or glocal brands that standardize some while simultaneously adapting other elements of the mix.

Regarding the global symbolism aspect of PBG, we agree with Liu et al. (2021) and Mandler (2019) that it should be explicitly included in conceptualizing PBG. However, building on Özsomer and Altaras (2008), we recommend approaching this construct from a cultural perspective, as captured by their concept of global brand cultural capital (GBCC). GBCC refers to the degree to which a global brand is imbued with mythic or cultural values shared by members of a society. The referred society can be defined either geographically (local, foreign or global) or based on interest groups, such as consumption communities, which transcend geographical boundaries. In other words, GBCC is the story behind the brand. Indeed, the cultural capital construct is conceptually similar to the cultural symbolism and iconicity construct (Torelli et al., 2010) or the global myth construct (Holt, 2004) in the cultural branding literature. Building on this literature, we propose that future research on global branding should explore in detail the facets of 'global brand cultural iconicity' and 'brands as icon of global culture' in addition to worldwide reach, widespread demand and standardization facets of global brands. We believe GBCC to be an important facet that cannot be overlooked as it has the potential to capture global brand effects above and beyond those captured by the other three facets.

In the global branding literature, cultural iconicity has been primarily approached from a local perspective, captured under the concept of 'brands as icons of local culture' or local iconicity (e.g., Steenkamp et al., 2003). Local iconness as a widely researched and influential construct has been recognized as a critical competitive edge for both domestic and global brands to differentiate themselves from the competition. Surely, one way for brands to cope with the challenges of globalization and global brands is to become 'icons of the local culture' (e.g., Özsomer, 2012; Steenkamp et al., 2003). While becoming an 'icon of local culture' can help global brands navigate the challenges of globalization, we suggest that a brand's cultural capital and symbolism can extend beyond local associations, transcending national borders. Global brands can build cultural capital by tapping into the needs, values, aspirations, myths, metaphors or narratives of specific global cultural groups that are not confined to a particular nation or country (Torelli et al., 2010), such as rock or pop fans, soccer fans (football), fast food, fashion, home décor (e.g., scandi), TV series and global cuisines (sushi, pizza, kebab, etc.). As such, global brands can build global brand cultural iconicity (GBCI).

Building on the cultural psychology literature, we define GBCI as the degree to which a brand is consensually perceived to symbolize the values, needs and aspirations held dear by members of a global cultural segment, transcending specific national or cultural boundaries. A globally culturally iconic brand becomes a symbol of the shared beliefs, stories and values of a specific global cultural group. The cultural group could either be a truly global group or a specific cultural group that is not confined to a single national border. It is also important to note that although global consumer culture is often treated as a singular entity, there are multiple global consumer cultures that global brands can tap into (Özsomer, 2019; Steenkamp, 2019). For example, the Korean Wave (Hallyu or K-Pop culture) has emerged as a significant global cultural phenomenon, driven by the global dissemination of South Korean culture, including music, TV dramas, films, food, language and beauty trends. Many brands are now targeting the global K-pop fan base. Other examples of global subcultures include Gen Z, millennials, gamers and followers of minimalism and the quiet luxury trend, characterized by understated elegance and refined consumption, emphasizing exclusivity and discerning taste without overt displays of wealth. Global consumer culture positioning (GCCP) and GBCI are distinct concepts. While GCCP is a tool for building global brand cultural iconicity, it is an antecedent, or a precursor, to PBG (e.g., De Meulenaer et al., 2015; Iversen & Hem, 2011; Steenkamp, 2019).

In summary, aside from wide market reach, demand and availability, we recommend future research to explore standardization and global cultural iconicity as part of the extended conceptualization of PBG. Only 35 out of 100 global brands have consistently remained in the top 100 Interbrand list over the past 25 years (Interbrand, 2024). Poor strategic management of marketing standardization and GBCI across markets could help explain why some global brands with high reach and demand still fail to endure over time. We next focus on consumer-level drivers of global brand preference.

WHY DO CONSUMERS PREFER GLOBAL BRANDS? PATHWAYS TO GLOBAL BRAND PREFERENCE

As global brands expanded rapidly into both advanced and emerging markets throughout the 1990s and 2000s, competition between global brands and their local counterparts intensified. Consequently, a significant body of research examined the competition between global brands and their local counterparts (e.g., Holt et al., 2004; Özsomer, 2012; Steenkamp et al., 2003; Strizhakova et al., 2011). This literature documents that consumers prefer global brands mainly because of the 1) functional and 2) psychological values they provide to them as shown in Figure 4.2 (Swoboda et al.,

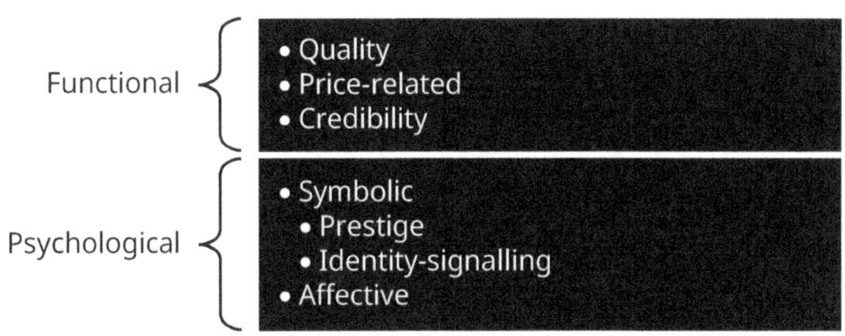

Figure 4.2 Functional and psychological benefits of global brands

Source: The authors.

2012; Swoboda & Hirschmann, 2016). Functional value is related to the price and quality-related brand characteristics. Indeed, quality has been touted as one of the key underlying mechanisms of how PBG drives preference (Özsomer, 2012; Steenkamp et al., 2003; Swoboda et al., 2012). Since PBG entails wide availability and acceptance across markets, consumers may infer high quality from such widely available and demanded brands. Additionally, related to its standardized facet, PBG also evokes credibility perceptions among consumers, which subsequently reduce consumers' perceived risk (Mandler et al., 2021; Özsomer & Altaras, 2008). Lastly, previous research cites price-related reasons as a key functional value global brands provide to consumers. In other words, it is about whether the brand is reasonably priced or offering good value for money (Swoboda & Hirschmann, 2016; Swoboda et al., 2012) that enhances the functional value associated with a global brand.

Global brands also provide strong psychological benefits to consumers. One of the most researched psychological pathways is the prestige aspect of global brands. Research finds that because of the higher price and the greater scarcity of global brands in some markets (e.g., Debat, 2009; Guo & Hong, 2018; Güzel et al., 2025; Steenkamp et al., 2003), they are seen as sources of high prestige for consumers. Prior literature has documented that higher quality and prestige are key advantages of global brands (Batra et al., 2000; Steenkamp et al., 2003). However, recent studies have shifted their attention to possible alternative psychological benefits for positive global brand effects. One such benefit is the strong identity cues or signals evoked by global brands. Global brands can provide consumers with a desired identity. In fact, Strizhakova et al. (2008) refer to global brands as 'identity currency' and argue that (some) consumers prefer global brands to appear cosmopolitan in the eyes of other consumers. Similarly, Davvetas and Diamantopoulos (2016) find that global brands hold an advantage over their local counterparts in product categories where social signaling is a primary consumer motivation, while Xie et al. (2015) identify brand-identity expressiveness as an additional mediating mechanism explaining favorable behavioral intentions toward global brands. Prior literature also cites affective reasons (e.g., Dimofte et al., 2008; Swoboda et al., 2012; Xie et al., 2015) which help explain global brand preference. For example, Xie et al. (2015) find brand affect as an important additional mediator for global brand preference

It is also important to note that while these functional and psychological processes have been identified as the main mechanisms driving global brand preference, some scholars question their stability as robust processes due to inconsistent findings (Liu et al., 2021). Inconsistencies are mainly spotted between developed and developing countries, or due to methodological issues (e.g., using real brand names instead of fictitious ones).

THEORETICAL FOUNDATIONS OF GLOBAL BRAND PREFERENCE

Majority of studies in the global branding literature heavily rely on cognitive-based theories with signaling theory used most frequently to explain global brand preference mechanisms (Table 4.1). Signaling theory (Erdem & Swait, 2004) suggests that information asymmetry and imperfection exist in the marketplace. Brands use their marketing mix strategies (e.g., high prices signaling high quality) to signal quality and reduce consumer uncertainty and risk. For instance, a strong global brand signals high quality due to its widespread availability and acceptance, as consumers associate it with premiumness (Steenkamp et al., 2003). On the other hand, a powerful local brand signals quality in culturally specific product categories, as it demonstrates a deep understanding of local needs and preferences (Özsomer, 2012). Other cognitive-based theories such as social identity theory and social categorization theory have also been frequently implemented in the literature. For instance, categorization theory has been used to understand how consumers engage in stereotypical assessments about brands based on consumer–brand relationship theory (Fournier, 1998).

Overall, we recommend that future research consider theories beyond cognitive-based ones as these theories may have reached their explanatory limits (Davvetas et al., 2020). For example, in line with the calls of Gürhan-Canli et al., 2018 and Liu et al., 2021, we believe there is room to apply theories that explain consumer affective responses, as observed in the recent literature (e.g., Davvetas et al., 2020).

IS GLOBAL BRAND ADVANTAGE STILL STRONG?

With the onset of globalization, global brands have emerged as powerful players, exerting significant pressure on local brands. The general consensus in the global branding literature was that global brands benefited from the so-called 'global brand halo effect' or the 'global equals better' heuristic

Table 4.1 Theories used in the global branding literature[a]

Study	*Theory*
Schuetz & Swoboda (2025)	Institutional economics Isomorphism
Sayin et al. (2024)	Shifting standards theory
Hu et al. (2023)	Signaling theory
Bhattacharjee et al. (2023)	Self-congruity theory
Azzari et al. (2023)	Signaling theory
Baršytė et al. (2023)	International marketing theory
Davvetas et al. (2023)	Equity theory
Mandler et al. (2023)	Associative network memory theory
Mandler et al. (2021)	Signaling theory
Bourdin et al. (2021)	Stereotype theory
Davvetas et al. (2020)	Regret theory
	Decision justification theory
Davvetas and Halkias (2019)	Stereotype theory
Mandler (2019)	Signaling theory
Kolbl et al. (2019)	Stereotype theory
Guo et al. (2019)	Social categorization theory
Sichtmann et al. (2019)	Consumer culture theory
	Social identity theory
Davvetas and Diamantopoulos (2018)	Regret theory
Mohan et al. (2018)	Signaling theory
Bartsch et al. (2016)	Attitude theory
	Social identity theory
Davvetas and Diamantopoulos (2016)	Schema theory
Halkias et al. (2016)	Stereotype theory
Swoboda and Hirschmann (2016)	Accessibility–diagnosticity theory
	Self-concept theory
Xie et al. (2015)	Social Identity Theory
Davvetas et al. (2015)	International marketing literature
Strizhakova and Coulter (2015)	Dual drivers theory
	Global consumer culture theory
Westjohn et al. (2015)	Attitude theory
Guo (2013)	Identity theory
Sichtmann and Diamantopoulos (2013)	Signaling theory
	Categorization theory
Özsomer (2012)	Signaling theory
	Associative network memory model
Riefler (2012)	Categorization theory
	Consumer culture theory
Swoboda et al. (2012)	Accessibility–diagnositicity theory
Strizhakova et al. (2011)	Signaling theory
	Social identity theory
Steenkamp and De Jong (2010)	Consumer culture theory
	Social adaptation theory
	Value theory
Dimofte et al. (2008)	International marketing theory
Steenkamp et al. (2003)	International marketing theory
Batra et al. (2000)	COO literature

[a]This table is an updated version of Davvetas et al. (2020) created by the authors, ordered based on recency.

(Davvetas et al., 2023; Dimofte et al., 2008), which implies that a brand's perceived globalness creates a favorable bias in consumers' minds, and as a result, the consumers link a brand's worldwide availability with superior brand perceptions such as quality, prestige, status, credibility and performance (Davvetas & Diamantopoulos, 2018; Dimofte et al., 2008).

Although the use of such 'global equals better' heuristics is well documented, recent developments such as rising anti-global sentiments, weakening of global economic integration initiatives (e.g., USA–China and EU–China trade frictions), and the ongoing climate crisis have led consumers and consequently scholars to question the positive influence of brand globalness on consumer choice. Some research even highlighted the growing segment of consumers who simply do not care about the globalness or localness of the products they purchase (Steenkamp & De Jong, 2010) and are against brands or even shy away from consuming well-known brands supporting smaller, local, niche brands.

Considering these challenges, extant literature indicates that global brands face specific vulnerabilities, particularly in developed countries in competing with local brands. While they may still maintain appeal in developing or globalizing countries (Xie et al., 2015), there is evidence that developed market consumers are getting more and more skeptical of market globalization and are re-embracing local values and products (Özsomer, 2012; Steenkamp & De Jong, 2010; Xie et al., 2015). Consequently, brand globalness has come to symbolize globalization's negative sides, such as inequalities and cultural homogenization (Beverland & Farrelly, 2010) in developed countries. Recent research also shows increasing mistrust and skepticism toward global brands, with some consumer segments in emerging markets are feeling that they get cheated by receiving the worst unstandardized versions (or older verions) of global products and that mid-market products are marketed as premium and expensive in such markets.

Furthermore, consumers in developed markets perceive their local brands of equal quality to global brands and better tailored to local tastes (Özsomer, 2012), whereas emerging-market consumers prefer global brands as they believe they outperform local alternatives (Batra et al., 2000). Emerging-market consumers also associate global brands with increased status and prefer them for identity-signaling reasons (Laforet & Chen, 2012; Wong & Ahuvia, 1998). The opposite trend is observed in developed markets.

Additionally, Özsomer (2012) finds that PBG enhances iconness only in emerging markets, whereas it lowers iconness in developed markets. Similarly, Mandler et al. (2021) found that though PBG is a much weaker signal of brand credibility than PBL in the globalized German market, it is equivalent in strength to PBL in the globalizing Korean market. To understand whether PBG is still relevant or has been trivialized to the benefit of other attributes, Davvetas et al. (2023), using conjoint, found that consumers in developed markets often prioritize other attributes (e.g., price) over globalness or localness, allocating only half the importance. However, in the developing market, consumers heavily considered the global or local origin of a product (top two attributes driving preference), accounting for about 27% of their purchase decision. In terms of preference, emerging-market consumers preferred global products, while developed market consumers preferred local products more. In summary, the study suggests that a brand's globalness versus localness might have lost its relevance and local brands are preferred more in developed markets (Davvetas et al., 2023). Similarly, Mandler et al. (2021) found that brand globalness continues to enhance brand credibility in globalizing developed markets, while localness is a stronger credibility signal for consumers in already globalized markets.

Even though global brands still seem to maintain their elevated status in emerging markets, in a recent study, Sayin et al. (2024) identified that this elevated status might be a double-edged sword in the context of product failures and that emerging-market consumers can react even more negatively in such situations because of their higher initial expectations from global brands. That is, consumers shift their standards when evaluating global relative to local brands, and they expect more from global brands. Extant research identifies another vulnerability of global brands: Their stereotypical associations. Because of their size and worldwide demand/availability, the global brands are perceived to possess significant power in terms of financial resources, increased competitive capabilities and advanced capacity to make investments across markets (Özsomer & Altaras, 2008). As a result, the consumers tend to stereotype global brands as competent, while local brands are primarily stereotyped as warm (Davvetas & Halkias, 2019). Interestingly, brand competence can evoke both admiration, which increases purchase intention, and contempt, which can lead to brand switching (Davvetas & Halkias, 2019). Hence, from the stereotype perspective, global brands' competence associations can act as a double-edged sword since competent global brands can also be perceived as greedy and devious, thus generating a negative affect (Davvetas & Halkias, 2019).

Lastly, research suggests that global brands might face challenges especially in foods' categories.

For example, Baršytė et al. (2023) found that globally (vs. locally) positioned brands evoke lower freshness perceptions, which, in turn, lead to lower purchase intentions. Research generally finds that consumers display a preference for local (vs. global brands) brands in cultural-bound categories (including food) (Mandler et al., 2021; Özsomer, 2012).

BOUNDARY CONDITIONS

In the next section, we review the extant literature on how consumer-specific dispositions and product-/category-level characteristics interact with PBG in forming consumer preference for global brands.

CONSUMER DISPOSITIONS

The global branding literature has proposed and tested various consumer dispositions to explain the consumer preference for global versus local brands. In this section, we provide a broad overview of these constructs with a focus on common findings and issues, which could be addressed in future research. For an exhaustive list and review, please refer to Bartsch et al. (2016).

As shown in Table 4.2, consumer dispositions related to global brand preference can be categorized based on two dimensions: Consumption-specific versus domain-general and in-group versus out-group orientation. Among these, consumer ethnocentrism, cosmopolitanism, global/local identity and globalization attitude are the most frequently studied dispositions (in bold in Table 4.2).

As highlighted in recent reviews by Diamantopoulos et al. (2019) and Bartsch et al. (2016), the literature on consumer dispositions suffers from several issues: First, a multitude of conceptually overlapping constructs are used. There is a clear need to verify whether these constructs are indeed different from each other, and if so, what are overlapping versus unique facets. Large-scale studies for establishing construct and discriminant validity as well as articulate and affirm their positions in distinct nomological networks (Diamantopoulos et al., 2019) are needed. For example, consumer ethnocentrism is treated as a moderator in some and as a mediator in others. Second, many of these constructs seem to suffer from a lack of robust theoretical base and are challenged by rival theories (Diamantopoulos et al., 2019). Third, despite being widely studied, there are inconsistent findings with respect to the predictive power of constructs such as global/local identities, cosmopolitanism and ethnocentrism in explaining global brand preference. In terms of consumer ethnocentrism, defined as 'beliefs held by consumers about the appropriateness, indeed morality, of purchasing foreign-made products' (Shimp & Sharma, 1987, p. 280), while some scholars find a negative relationship to PBG and associated outcomes (Akram et al., 2011; Steenkamp et al., 2003; Swoboda & Hirschmann, 2016), other researchers find no significant relationship (Davvetas et al., 2015).

A meta-analytic review by Diamantopoulos et al. (2019) reveals that although the predictive power of consumer dispositions such as ethnocentrism, cosmopolitanism and global/local identities is statistically significant, their effect sizes are rather low, casting doubt on their practical significance. The authors find that moderation is the most intuitively appealing approach for modelling the effects of consumer dispositions

Table 4.2 Consumer dispositions used in the global branding literature

	Consumption Specific	*General*
In-group orientation	**Consumer ethnocentrism**	**Local identity**
	Consumer economic nationalism	Ethnic identity
	Consumer patriotism	Country-level animosity
	Global brand animosity	Susceptibility to normative influence?
Out-group orientation	Global connectedness	**Global identity**
	Consumer cosmopolitanism	Consumer xenocentrism
	Global consumption orientation	**Global connectedness**
	Identification with global consumer culture	World-mindedness
	Susceptibility to global consumer culture	Globalization attitude
	Cultural openness	
	Global openness	
	Global citizenship (through global brands)	

Source: Adapted from Bartsch et al. (2016).

Note: Those in bold are the most frequently used.

(e.g., Steenkamp et al., 2003), yet only a minority (about 10%) of the tested models support a moderation effect. Echoing suggestions of previous studies, we recommend future research to establish the discriminant validity of consumer dispositions proposed by extant literature and develop a robust theoretical foundation that improves model specification to explain global brand preference.

Due to high expected conceptual overlap of such dispositions, we recommend future research to explore other individual-specific variables that approach brand preference from a behavioral perspective. For instance, exploring the influence of relevant psychological mindsets will be a valuable addition. Strizhakova et al. (2021) find that the fresh start mindset is an important consumer characteristic in the context of environmentally friendly global brands. Similarly, future research can explore how scarcity mindset (Shah et al., 2012), a highly relevant phenomenon in the context of economic recessions and global pandemics, as well as how fixed versus growth mindsets (Murphy & Dweck, 2016) interact with preference for global brands. Alternatively, scholars can focus on consumers' construal level (Trope & Liberman, 2010) and specifically how the abstract versus concrete mindsets condition PBG effects on consumer preferences.

In line with repeated calls (Hussein & Hassan, 2018; Sichtmann et al., 2019), we recommend future research to investigate cultural variables at the individual level. We recommend exploring not only Hofstede's cultural dimensions but also Schwartz's universal values because of the latter's suitability to capture higher level brand concepts generally leveraged by the global brands such as achievement and self-direction (e.g., Nike). Utilizing Schwartz's values, Torelli et al. (2012) introduced a generalizable and robust structure of abstract brand concepts as representations of human values, which can be used by the global brands in conveying brand concepts that not only are consistent across borders but also resonate with consumers of different cultures. Finally, thinking styles (analytic vs. holistic), tightness versus looseness and vertical versus horizontal cultural aspects are fruitful consumer-level constructs to generate deeper insights into global and local brand preference.

PRODUCT-/CATEGORY-LEVEL CHARACTERISTICS

Product category characteristics can shape preference for global brands (e.g., Davvetas & Diamantopoulos, 2016; Özsomer, 2012). Based on schema theory, Davvetas and Diamantopoulos (2016) conceptualized how the product category influences the consumer preferences for global or local brands. The authors found that category's global or local nature depends on the perceived globalness or localness of its most dominant brands. When global brands are dominating a product category, globalness becomes a more important attribute in shaping preferences, whereas when local brands are dominating a product category, localness becomes an important assessment criterion. Thus, product category schemas have an influence on whether a global or a local brand will be preferred in that category. For example, Davvetas and Diamantopoulos (2016) showed that the global brands are perceived as superior to local brands in technology categories but inferior to local brands in food categories. Relatedly, Sayin et al. (2024) showed that negative consumer reactions to global brands in the context of product failures are attenuated in categories associated with localness, such as foods.

Similarly, Özsomer (2012) found that category cultural grounding has an important effect on global versus local brand preference. Food categories have much stronger cultural grounding because they are strongly shaped by unique cultural and local preferences. Özsomer finds that local iconness is positively related to the local brand quality perceptions in culturally grounded categories of food in an emerging market, whereas in non-food categories, the local iconness has no connection to quality. Mandler et al. (2021) corroborated the results in culturally non-grounded categories. In culturally mixed symbolic products (CMPSs, which blend local symbols with global ones), Guo et al. (2019) also showed that, even though consumers form exclusionary reactions toward global brands, these negative reactions are attenuated in food categories.

When consumers anticipate regret in deciding on a product (high likelihood of dissonance), consumers rely more on the global brand heuristic (i.e., global equals better) if there is a congruency with the product schema, as in a category dominated by superior global brands (Davvetas et al., 2020). If the product category is not dominated by superior global brands, then consumers are less likely to rely on the global brand heuristic.

CATEGORY SOCIAL SIGNALING

The social signaling value of a category refers to the extent to which certain products signal a person's social status (Batra et al., 2000). Extant literature offers ample evidence that consumers use brands as status symbols, a behavior deeply rooted in human psychology (Arnould & Thompson, 2005; Belk, 1988; Strizhakova & Coulter, 2013). Global brands are particularly suitable in such a context as they signal prestige, sophistication and modernity to consumers (Holt et al., 2004; Steenkamp et al., 2003). Indeed, Mandler et al. (2021) found that brand globalness enhances brand credibility only in product categories of high social signaling value (e.g., cars and clothing). Similarly, Strizhakova and Coulter (2015) provide evidence that consumers prefer global brands in product categories high in social symbolism. Clearly, these studies provide valuable insights, but the different mechanisms, types and contexts of social signaling by different types of global brands remain a wide open area.

STRATEGIES EMPLOYED BY GLOBAL BRANDS

Origin-Based Strategies

A significant body of research has focused on how brand globalness interacts with perceived brand origin (e.g., Riefler, 2012, Westjohn et al., 2015; Winit et al., 2014). Perceived brand origin refers to the country of association (Josiassen & Harzing, 2008) and is defined as 'the country a brand is associated with or the headquarters of where the brand's owner is perceived to be located, regardless of where it is manufactured' (Samiee et al., 2005, p. 382). Various studies showed that the picture of how consumers respond to global and local brands cannot be fully captured unless the brand origin effects are simultaneously considered. These studies suggest that the effect of brand globalness/localness on brand preference is contingent on the brand's perceived origin (e.g., Riefler, 2012).

Mainly drawing from categorization theory, studies have suggested three distinct ways in which brand origin is perceived and processed by consumers. The first approach of categorization is implemented (1) at the individual country level, referred to as the country of origin (COO), while other approaches reduce complexity such that (2) consumers can categorize COO as either domestic or foreign or (3) based on countries' stereotypical perceptions of competence or warmth, based on the Stereotype Content Model (Halkias & Diamantopoulos, 2020).

While early literature focused on COO to explain the interplay between brand globalness versus localness and brand origin, several scholars argue that COO has lost its importance in a globalized marketplace (i.e., Usunier, 2006). As a result, many more recent studies embrace the second (domestic vs. foreign) or the third categorizations (stereotype-based categorizations). However, recent developments such as buy local campaigns, trade frictions, deglobalization and de-coupling may increase the relevance of the COO categorization. Covering more nuanced approaches, we focus on two key strategies that global brands implement in terms of brand origin: Compensatory and hybrid strategies.

Compensatory Strategies Based on Country Stereotypes

Global brands can strategically leverage their COO to mitigate negative connotations associated with their global image. In other words, country stereotypes and brand globalness can operate in a compensatory manner. Specifically, Halkias et al. (2016) and Bourdin et al. (2021) found that consumers' stereotypical beliefs about a global brand's origin can compensate for the unfavorable aspects of brand globalness, ultimately strengthening the effect of brand globalness on consumers' attitudes and preferences (Bourdin et al., 2021; Halkias et al., 2016). According to the Stereotype Content Model (SCM; Fiske et al., 2002), individuals tend to perceive social groups, including nations and countries, based on two fundamental dimensions: Competence and warmth (Cuddy et al., 2009; Kervyn et al., 2008). Competence is reflected in capability, efficiency and intelligence, and warmth in friendliness, kindness, good-naturedness, and good intent. Since global brands are generally associated with high quality and credibility and wide market reach (Johansson & Ronkainen, 2005; Özsomer, 2012; Steenkamp et al., 2003; Swoboda et al., 2012), they are more likely to be perceived as higher on competence than warmth. However, as a direct consequence of their size and worldwide presence, the global brands are also perceived to have access to or own significant financial resources and increased competitive capabilities (Özsomer & Altaras, 2008). These competency associations can be a liability in the sense that global brands might also be viewed as highly greedy, profit seeking, aggressive, insincere (Davvetas & Halkias, 2019) and providing lower quality or older models to emerging country customers, in a way short-changing them (Güzel et al., 2025).

The warm image of the global brand's origin (country high on warmth) can mitigate the negative perceptions associated with brand globalness (Bourdin et al., 2021). This is because when an origin country is perceived as warm and well-intentioned, consumers are more likely to trust its products to be harmless and, therefore, more likely to buy them (Xu et al., 2013). Therefore, a strong association between a brand's origin and warmth can help mitigate the negative connotations associated with brand globalness. Specifically, global brands originating from countries with warm stereotypes can benefit from this positive association.

HYBRID/HYBRIDIZATION STRATEGIES

Hybridization strategies involve integrating strong elements of both global and local symbolism in brand positioning (Sichtmann et al., 2019). To identify these specific elements, Schmidt-Devlin et al. (2022), using an interpretive analysis of interviews with executives, developed an 'omnibrand' orientation framework, which consists of two main pillars: Local authenticity and global acceptance. According to their framework, the building blocks of local authenticity are brand image, local connection, local iconness, local insights and originality, while those of global acceptance are perceived brand globalness, innovation, product performance quality and global brand power. As evidence of the effectiveness of hybrid approaches, recently, Hu et al. (2023) found that a combination of local and foreign appeals leads to more favorable brand and product evaluations, compared with either local or foreign appeals alone, due to a heightened level of perceived brand globalness, a phenomenon the authors call 'the coalescence effect.'

The extant literature suggests two primary approaches for global brands to implement hybrid strategies. The first approach involves domestic brands (that originate from the consumers' home country) implementing a global-focused strategy (global reach). For instance, Winit et al. (2014) found that the positive effects of perceived globalness on brand attitudes and purchase intent are stronger for domestic than foreign brands. Similarly, Özsomer (2012) found that local brands in emerging markets can benefit from a combination of globalness and local iconness, as these seemingly contradictory perceptions can reinforce each other positively. Recently, Spielmann et al. (2024) proposed the concept of terroir branding, which in fact is a special example of how 'local icon' brands adopt internationalizing strategies.

The second path involves foreign/global brands nurturing 'local iconness' perceptions by developing close connections with the local culture. While the literature is relatively scant regarding evidence for this approach, Guo et al. (2019) provided evidence that foreign global brands, which normally have difficulty tapping into local cultural capital, find success with 'culturally mixed symbolic products' (CMSPs) that evoke feelings of cultural respect among consumers. Starbucks' moon cake is a good example of this approach, which combines iconic aspect globalness with local symbols.

There are broadly two explanatory mechanisms as to why and how such hybrid strategies work. The first explanation approaches the topic from an identity perspective (Sichtmann et al., 2019). The authors propose that consumers have the need to satisfy both their global and local identity needs. Hence, these authors view global and local identity values as complementary. In the case of brands with foreign origins, consumers tend to value more a brand's local connectedness, whereas for brands originating from their home countries, a brand's globalness creates higher relevance for such consumers. Put differently, consumers tend to 'engage in compensatory identity mechanisms whereby domestic origin of a brand compensates for the lack of localness associations while foreign origin compensates for the lack of globalness associations' (p. 601).

The second explanation revolves around the stereotypical perceptions of global versus local brands. As mentioned previously, brand globalness/foreignness evokes competency and quality associations among consumers, whereas brand localness evokes warmth or good intent (Davvetas & Halkias, 2019). Brands implementing hybrid strategies, rather than a focused strategy, signal to consumers not only their positive intentions but also information about their quality. In essence, hybrid brands offer the best of both worlds to consumers.

Despite strong evidence for the benefits of a hybrid strategy, it is important to acknowledge that there are also contradictory results in the literature. While strong evidence points toward some form of combination of global and local elements, a few papers point to a different direction. For example, Swoboda et al. (2012) found that retailer origin is a 'diagnosticity multiplier' for consumers in the sense that foreign retailers benefit more from globalness associations; on the other hand, domestic retailers benefit more from localness associations. Similarly, Mandler et al. (2021) provided evidence of the synergy between PBG and foreignness in globalizing markets, as well as between localness and domestic perceptions in both globalized and globalizing markets. Hence, we recommend future research to explore when and why such combinations create synergies for consumers.

We also encourage future research to approach hybridization from a cultural psychology perspective. Currently, despite calls by Gürhan-Canli et al. (2018) and Steenkamp (2017), there is scant research that tackles consumer responses to hybridization from a culture mixing perspective except for the study conducted by Guo et al. (2019) regarding culturally mixed symbolic products. Culture mixing literature identifies two types of consumer reactions toward culture mixing: Integrative versus exclusionary responses. For example, in the cultural psychology literature, Hao et al. (2016) identified that the extent of culture mixing whether it is only juxtaposition of different cultural elements of intersection versus overlap versus superimposition or fusion drives different consumer reactions. Or Yang et al. (2016) provided evidence that people are more likely to exhibit exclusionary reactions in response to the mixing of foreign and local icons when the contrastive symbols overlap in space than when placed side by side separately. Cheon et al. (2016) found that blending or the fusion of the two stimuli evokes more 'disgust' emotions compared to side-by-side presentation. Another factor is the extent of cultural symbolism. The co-presence of symbols/icons of local culture with those of a foreign culture may lead to cultural contamination, which, in turn, can lead to negative responses (Yang et al., 2016). In future research, scholars can explore the contextual factors that drive consumers' integrative versus exclusionary responses to culture mixing employed by global brands.

METHODOLOGICAL APPROACHES USED IN THE GLOBAL BRANDING LITERATURE

A diversification of research methodologies is crucial, as the current literature heavily relies on survey-based designs (Liu et al., 2021). To establish stronger causal relationships, future research should adopt experiments, as used in recent studies (e.g., Davvetas & Diamantopoulos, 2018; Davvetas et al., 2020; Hu et al., 2023; Sayin et al., 2024) and quasi experimental methods. To enhance external validity, experimental methods can be complemented with correlational, real-world data and field studies. Additionally, qualitative methods (e.g., Schmidt-Devlin et al., 2022) can be employed to uncover novel insights and new constructs for future quantitative investigation. Given the substantial body of research on global brand preference, meta-analyses could provide valuable insights by synthesizing existing findings. With all these methods, artificial intelligence (AI) can be used in all stages of the research including design, data collection, analysis and reporting/presenting results.

To mitigate the confounding effects of brand strength, future research can use fictitious brands in experimental designs and validate the results with real brands. Cross-cultural research can provide deeper insights into the impact of cultural differences on global brand preference (e.g., Torelli et al., 2012). To ensure generalizability, it is essential to diversify samples across demographics, including age and country. For example, to represent a developed country setting, future research should aim to diversify away from the ones heavily used in the literature (e.g., Austria, the USA and Türkiye).

FUTURE RESEARCH AGENDA

Significant progress has been made in understanding global branding over the past two decades. The changing global competitive landscape suggests several areas in need of further research. We present key research areas and suggest research questions in Table 4.3. To advance the field of global branding, we propose extending the PBG conceptualization by incorporating standardization and global brand cultural iconicity. Standardization can be operationalized as the perceived similarity or consistency of a brand's marketing mix elements (product, packaging and communications) across different markets (e.g., Özsomer & Simonin, 2004). Furthermore, while cognitive-based theories, particularly signaling theory, have been influential in global branding research, their explanatory power may have reached their limit to explain different consequences. Future research could benefit from exploring alternative theoretical frameworks that can better account for affective responses to global brands such as stereotype theory and shifting standards theory. Institutional economics and isomorphism can also provide useful theoretical lenses to understand influences on strategic global branding decisions particularly in online settings such as e-commerce firms (Schuetz & Swoboda, 2025).

Another promising avenue for future research is to investigate strategies as to how global brands can maintain their appeal amidst growing skepticism, anti-globalization sentiments and the resurgence of local brand preference, in both advanced and emerging markets. Tariffs imposed by the USA on imports from Canada, China, the EU and Mexico and and potential trade wars can also enhance consumer animosity to countries and eventually to global brands associated with those countries (e.g., Tesla cars originating from the USA). Can global brands cultivate cultural iconicity to shield themselves from such vulnerabilities? Future research could also explore strategies to maintain the relevance, differentiation and contemporary appeal of global brands. The potential effectiveness of brand

Table 4.3 Future research agenda

Extend PBG conceptualization

- Develop a more 'neutral' conceptualization of standardization, one that builds upon the perceived similarity or consistency of a brand's marketing mix elements (e.g., product, packaging, positioning, and communications) across different countries
- Incorporate GBCI as a facet of global brand conceptualization

Mechanisms

- Explore alternative pathways beyond functional and psychological processes

Theoretical approaches

- Consider theories beyond cognitive-based ones – e.g., apply theories that explain consumer affective responses to global brands

Moderators – Consumer dispositions

- Establish discriminant validity of consumer dispositions proposed by the literature and develop a robust theoretical foundation to explain global brand preference.
- Explore other individual-specific variables that approach brand preference from a behavioral perspective (e.g., psychological mindsets and construal level)
- Investigate cultural variables at the individual level – explore both Hofstede's cultural and Schwartz's universal values, thinking styles (analytic vs. holistic), tightness vs. looseness, and vertical vs. horizontal cultural dimensions

Moderators – Country level

- Resolve inconsistent findings regarding developing (emerging) vs. developed country settings – use multifaceted approaches to classify countries (e.g., level of globalization, culture, economic integration, affluence)

Methodological approaches

- Adopt mixed methods, reduce reliance on survey methods.
- Blend experimental designs with real-world data to establish causality and ecological validity
- Use fictitious brands to mitigate the confounding effects of brand strength
- Diversify samples across demographics, including age and country

Strategies employed by global brands

- Glocal/Hybrid Strategies: When, why, and how different combinations (e.g., domestic and global vs. domestic and local) create synergies?
- Approach hybridization from a cultural psychology perspective – explore contextual factors that drive consumers' integrative versus exclusionary responses to culture mixing employed by global brands
- What are positioning options/strategies for global brands in an increasingly polarized world?
- What are implications of supply chain changes such as nearshoring and reshoring on global brands?
- How to maintain appeal/the secrets of enduring global brands and ways to overcome the vulnerabilities of a global brands particularly in developed countries?
- How can global brands maintain their appeal amidst growing skepticism, anti-globalization sentiments particularly in developed markets? Can cultural iconicity be a way for global brands to shield themselves from such vulnerabilities?
- What are strategies for maintaining relevance, freshness, and contemporary appeal for global brands (e.g., brand purpose activation, brand activism, and AI)
- What are the essentials of long-term brand building strategy for global brands?
- How can global brands contribute to consumer well-being?
- What are supply and demand side effects of AI and use of AI on global brands?

Source: The authors.

purpose activation and brand activism as strategies to achieve this goal warrants further investigation.

Consumer well-being is another important emerging topic in the consumer behavior literature. Future research could investigate how global brands can contribute to consumer well-being. Can global brands have an advantage when competing with local competitors in this context? Identifying contexts in which global brands can help consumers increase their well-being are interesting avenues for future research.

We call for further research on combining global and local elements in hybridized (Schmidt-Devlin et al., 2022) and agile brand strategies (Özsomer et al., 2023). Exploring contextual factors that drive consumers' integrative versus exclusionary responses to culture mixing (hybrid strategies) employed by global brands remains a critical area for future investigation. From a methods perspective, we encourage the use of mixed methods (e.g., field experiments), reducing reliance on survey methods. Blending experimental designs with real-world data can enhance both internal and external validity.

While numerous consumer dispositions have been explored to explain consumers' preference of global versus local brands, future research could delve into individual-level variables that approach global brand preference from a behavioral perspective (e.g., psychological mindsets and construal level). Furthermore, by measuring cultural variables at the individual level, researchers can gain deeper insights into cross-cultural differences in brand preference. This could involve exploring not only Hofstede's cultural dimensions but also Schwartz's universal values, thinking styles and tightness-looseness and vertical-horizontal cultural dimensions.

Disruptions during the COVID-19 pandemic, followed by geopolitical tensions and trade conflicts, have led to shifts in supply chains such as the increase in nearshoring and reshoring. Companies are looking for ways to reduce geopolitical risk in product development and manufacturing. 'Unilever, for example, is doing less customization for markets, and relying instead on industry standard specifications, to be able to move products quickly from one market to another as the political environment changes' (Foroohar, 2025, p. 15). This means less local adaptation and responsiveness by global brands. The implications of this move to more standardized products and less customization can present challenges, limiting the strategic and tactical flexibility of global brands in local markets and presenting opportunities for local brands in local customer segments with unmet needs. This new context presents very interesting research opportunities.

Finally, AI is influencing global brands from both the supply and demand sides. Global brands are using AI in both their customer-facing as well as non-facing, back-stage operations. Global brands are using AI, for example, to generate advertising material, to conduct market research, to simulate demand and to increase the effectiveness and efficiency of customer interactions along the customer journey in different local markets. AI is also used to predict where new trade disruptions might occur and to manage supply chains swiftly (Foroohar, 2025). The use of AI in global branding presents many interesting research questions.

CONCLUSION

Research on global branding has blossomed over the past 25 years. This chapter has provided a comprehensive overview of global branding in a dynamic and evolving landscape. By synthesizing existing literature, we have illuminated central debates, persistent issues and relevant theoretical frameworks, while also highlighting key drivers from consumer, category and brand strategy perspectives. Our discussion of compensatory, hybrid and omnibrand strategies, alongside emerging trends like rising anti-global sentiments, trade disruptions and the potential decline of the allure of 'global' positioning, highlights shifting paradigms in the literature. Building upon this foundation, this chapter has identified several promising avenues for future research and developed research questions, to further advance our understanding of global branding in an increasingly interconnected yet fragmented world. Given increasing geopolitical conflicts and geopolitical fragmentation, global brands are facing new challenges and opportunities. The impact of nationalistic rhetoric in media on consumer perceptions of global brands, the effect of trade policies on brand loyalty among consumers in protectionist economies, strategies for global brands to mitigate risks associated with geopolitical tensions, managing global brand reputation amidst international conflicts, the (changing) perceptions of consumers in politically polarized countries of global and foreign brands, and the impact of diplomatic relations on country-of-origin effects (e.g., perceptions of US goods by Canadian or Mexican consumers and vice versa) all present opportunities for global branding management and research.

REFERENCES

Akram, A., Merunka, D., & Shakaib Akram, M. (2011). Perceived brand globalness in emerging markets and the moderating role of consumer ethnocentrism. *International Journal of Emerging Markets*, *6*(4), 291–303. https://doi.org/10.1108/17468801111170329

Alden, D. L., Steenkamp, J. B. E., & Batra, R. (2006). Consumer attitudes toward marketplace globalization: Structure, antecedents and consequences. *International Journal of Research in Marketing*, *23*(3), 227–239. https://doi.org/10.1016/j.ijresmar.2006.01.010

Arnould, E. J., & Thompson, C. J. (2005). Consumer culture theory (CCT): Twenty years of research. *Journal of Consumer Research*, *31*(4), 868–882. https://doi.org/10.1086/426626

Azzari, V., Zambaldi, F., Guissoni, L. A., Rodrigues, J. M., & Scornavacca, E. (2023). Brand origin effects during economic declines: Evidence from an emerging market. *Journal of International Marketing*, *31*(2), 25–42. https://doi.org/10.1177/1069031X231154483

Baršytė, J., Ruzeviciute, R., Neciunskas, P., & Schlegelmilch, B. B. (2023). When 'Global' becomes a challenge: The role of freshness in food brand preference formation. *Journal of International Marketing*, *31*(4), 23–35. https://doi.org/10.1177/1069031X231179149

Bartsch, F., Riefler, P., & Diamantopoulos, A. (2016). A taxonomy and review of positive consumer dispositions toward foreign countries and globalization. *Journal of International Marketing*, *24*(1), 82–110. https://doi.org/10.1509/jim.15.0021

Batra, R., Ramaswamy, V., Alden, D. L., Steenkamp, J. B. E., & Ramachander, S. (2000). Effects of brand local and nonlocal origin on consumer attitudes in developing countries. *Journal of Consumer Psychology*, *9*(2), 83–95. https://doi.org/10.1207/S15327663JCP0902_3

Belk, R. W. (1988). Possessions and the extended self. *Journal of Consumer Research*, *15*(2), 139–168. https://doi.org/10.1086/209154

Beverland, M. B., & Farrelly, F. J. (2010). The quest for authenticity in consumption: Consumers' purposive choice of authentic cues to shape experienced outcomes. *Journal of Consumer Research*, *36*(5), 838–856. https://doi.org/10.1086/615047

Bhattacharjee, D. R., Kuanr, A., Malhotra, N., Pradhan, D., & Moharana, T. R. (2023). How does self-congruity foster customer engagement with global brands? Examining the roles of psychological ownership and global connectedness. *International Marketing Review*, *40*(6), 1480–1508. https://doi.org/10.1108/IMR-09-2022-0206

Bourdin, D., Halkias, G., & Makri, K. (2021). The compensatory influences of country stereotypes and the global/local nature of brands: An extended framework. *Journal of Business Research*, *137*, 28–38. https://doi.org/10.1016/j.jbusres.2021.08.020

Cheon, B. K., Christopoulos, G. I., & Hong, Y. Y. (2016). Disgust associated with culture mixing: Why and who? *Journal of Cross-Cultural Psychology*, *47*(10), 1268–1285. https://doi.org/10.1177/0022022116667845

Cuddy, A. J., Fiske, S. T., Kwan, V. S., Glick, P., Demoulin, S., Leyens, J. P., & Ziegler, R. (2009). Stereotype content model across cultures: Towards universal similarities and some differences. *British Journal of Social Psychology*, *48*(1), 1–33. https://doi.org/10.1348/014466608X314935

Davvetas, V., & Diamantopoulos, A. (2016). How product category shapes preferences toward global and local brands: A schema theory perspective. *Journal of International Marketing*, *24*(4), 61–81. https://doi.org/10.1509/jim.15.0110

Davvetas, V., & Diamantopoulos, A. (2018). 'Should have I bought the other one?' experiencing regret in global versus local brand purchase decisions. *Journal of International Marketing*, *26*(2), 1–21. https://doi.org/10.1509/jim.17.0040

Davvetas, V., & Halkias, G. (2019). Global and local brand stereotypes: Formation, content transfer, and impact. *International Marketing Review*, *36*(5), 675–701. https://doi.org/10.1108/IMR-01-2018-0017

Davvetas, V., Diamantopoulos, A., & Liu, L. (2020). Lit up or dimmed down? Why, when, and how regret anticipation affects consumers' use of the global brand halo. *Journal of International Marketing*, *28*(3), 40–63. https://doi.org/10.1177/1069031X20910112

Davvetas, V., Sichtmann, C., & Diamantopoulos, A. (2015). The impact of perceived brand globalness on consumers' willingness to pay. *International Journal of Research in Marketing*, *32*(4), 431–434. https://doi.org/10.1016/j.ijresmar.2015.05.004

Davvetas, V., Sichtmann, C., Saridakis, C., & Diamantopoulos, A. (2023). The global/local product attribute: Decomposition, trivialization, and price trade-offs in emerging and developed markets. *Journal of International Marketing*, *31*(3), 19–40. https://doi.org/10.1177/1069031X221143095

Debat, M. (2009). The effects of perceived brand globalness on brand trust. In J.-M. Aurifeille, C. J. Medlin, & C. Tisdell (Eds.), *Trust, globalisation and market expansion* (pp. 1175–1192). Nova Science Publishers.

De Meulenaer, S., Dens, N., & De Pelsmacker, P. (2015). Which cues cause consumers to perceive brands as more global? A conjoint analysis. *International Marketing Review*, *32*(6), 606–626. https://doi.org/10.1108/IMR-04-2014-0144

Diamantopoulos, A., Davvetas, V., Bartsch, F., Mandler, T., Arslanagic-Kalajdzic, M., & Eisend, M. (2019). On the interplay between consumer dispositions and perceived brand globalness: Alternative theoretical perspectives and empirical assessment.

Journal of International Marketing, *27*(4), 39–57. https://doi.org/10.1177/1069031X19865527

Dimofte, C. V., Johansson, J. K., & Ronkainen, I. A. (2008). Cognitive and affective reactions of US consumers to global brands. *Journal of International Marketing*, *16*(4), 113–135. https://doi.org/10.1509/jimk.16.4.113

Erdem, T., & Swait, J. (2004). Brand credibility, brand consideration, and choice. *Journal of Consumer Research*, *31*(1), 191–198. https://doi.org/10.1086/383434

Fiske, S. T., Cuddy, A. J. C., Glick, P., & Xu, J. (2002). A model of stereotype content as often mixed: Separate dimensions of competence and warmth respectively follow from status and competition. *Journal of Personality and Social Psychology*, *82*(6), 878–902. https://doi.org/10.1037/0022-3514.82.6.878

Fournier, S. (1998). Consumers and their brands: Developing relationship theory in consumer research. *Journal of Consumer Research*, *24*(4), 343–373. https://doi.org/10.1086/209515

Foroohar, R. (2025, February 17). Global trade isn't all about Trump. *Financial Times*, 15.

Guo, X. (2013). Living in a global world: Influence of consumer global orientation on attitudes toward global brands from developed versus emerging countries. *Journal of International Marketing*, *21*(1), 1–22. https://doi.org/10.1509/jim.12.0065

Guo, X., & Hong, Y. Y. (2018). How do consumers from developed regions evaluate global brands from emerging countries? An investigation from the perspective of global–local identity. *Journal of Contemporary Marketing Science*, *1*(1), 2–21. https://doi.org/10.1108/JCMARS-08-2018-0008

Guo, X., Heinberg, M., & Zou, S. (2019). Enhancing consumer attitude toward culturally mixed symbolic products from foreign global brands in an emerging-market setting: the role of cultural respect. *Journal of International Marketing*, *27*(3), 79–97. https://doi.org/10.1177/1069031X19843912

Gürhan-Canli, Z., Sarial-Abi, G., & Hayran, C. (2018). Consumers and brands across the globe: Research synthesis and new directions. *Journal of International Marketing*, *26*(1), 96–117. https://doi.org/10.1509/jim.17.0063

Güzel, Z. M., Özsomer, A., & Sezen, B. (2025). Mind the standardization gap: An emerging market phenomenon. *Journal of Business Research*, *191*, 115249. https://doi.org/10.1016/j.jbusres.2025.115249

Halkias, G., Davvetas, V., & Diamantopoulos, A. (2016). The interplay between country stereotypes and perceived brand globalness/localness as drivers of brand preference. *Journal of Business Research*, *69*(9), 3621–3628. https://doi.org/10.1016/j.jbusres.2016.03.022

Halkias, G., & Diamantopoulos, A. (2020). Universal dimensions of individuals' perception: Revisiting the operationalization of warmth and competence with a mixed-method approach. *International Journal of Research in Marketing*, *37*(4), 714–736. https://doi.org/10.1016/j.ijresmar.2020.02.004

Hao, J., Li, D., Peng, L., Peng, S., & Torelli, C. J. (2016). Advancing our understanding of culture mixing. *Journal of Cross-Cultural Psychology*, *47*(10), 1257–1267. https://doi.org/10.1177/0022022116670514

Holt, D. B. (2004). *How brands become icons: The principles of cultural branding*. Harvard Business Review Press.

Holt, D. B., Quelch, J. A., & Taylor, E. L. (2004). How global brands compete. *Harvard Business Review*, *82*(9), 68–75.

Hsieh, M. H. (2002). Identifying brand image dimensionality and measuring the degree of brand globalization: A cross-national study. *Journal of International Marketing*, *10*(2), 46–67. https://doi.org/10.1509/jimk.10.2.46.19538

Hu, M., Chen, J., Alden, D. L., & Chen, Q. (2023). The coalescence effect: How a combination of foreign and local appeals enhances customer engagement through perceived brand globalness. *Journal of International Marketing*, *31*(1), 49–68. https://doi.org/10.1177/1069031X221134495

Hussein, R., & Hassan, S. (2018). Antecedents of global brand purchase likelihood: Exploring the mediating effect of quality, prestige and familiarity. *Journal of International Consumer Marketing*, *30*(5), 288–303. https://doi.org/10.1080/08961530.2018.1455549

Interbrand. (2024, January 20). Best global brands. [Report] Retrieved from www.thebrandingjournal.com/2024/10/interbrands-2024-best-global-brands-report/

Iversen, N. M., & Hem, L. E. (2011). Reciprocal transfer effects for brand extensions of global or local origin: Evidence from Norway. *International Marketing Review*, *28*(4), 365–411. https://doi.org/10.1108/02651331111149949

Johansson, J. K., & Ronkainen, I. A. (2005). The esteem of global brands. *Journal of Brand Management*, *12*, 339–354. https://doi.org/10.1057/palgrave.bm.2540230

Josiassen, A., & Harzing, A. W. (2008). Comment: Descending from the ivory tower: reflections on the relevance and future of country-of-origin research. *European Management Review*, *5*(4), 264–270. https://doi.org/10.1057/emr.2008.19

Kervyn, N., Yzerbyt, V. Y., Demoulin, S., & Judd, C. M. (2008). Competence and warmth in context: The compensatory nature of stereotypic views of national groups. *European Journal of Social Psychology*, *38*(7), 1175–1183. https://doi.org/10.1002/ejsp.526

Kolbl, Ž., Arslanagic-Kalajdzic, M., & Diamantopoulos, A. (2019). Stereotyping global brands: is warmth more important than competence? *Journal of Business Research*, *104*, 614–621. https://doi.org/10.1016/j.jbusres.2018.12.060

Laforet, S., & Chen, J. (2012). Chinese and British consumers' evaluation of Chinese and international brands and factors affecting their choice. *Journal of World Business*, *47*(1), 54–63. https://doi.org/10.1016/j.jwb.2010.10.020

Liu, H., Schoefer, K., Fastoso, F., & Tzemou, E. (2021). Perceived brand globalness/localness: A systematic review of the literature and directions for further research. *Journal of International Marketing*, *29*(1), 77–94. https://doi.org/10.1177/1069031X20973184

Mandler, T. (2019). Beyond reach: An extended model of global brand effects. *International Marketing Review*, *36*(5), 647–674. https://doi.org/10.1108/IMR-01-2018-0032

Mandler, T., Bartsch, F., & Han, C. M. (2021). Brand credibility and marketplace globalization: The role of perceived brand globalness and localness. *Journal of International Business Studies*, *52*, 1559–1590. https://doi.org/10.1057/s41267-020-00312-2

Mandler, T., Bartsch, F., Krüger, T., Kim, K., & Han, C. M. (2023). Consumer animosity: the mitigating effect of perceived brand globalness. *International Marketing Review*, *40*(2), 365–384. https://doi.org/10.1108/IMR-08-2022-0186

Mohan, M., Brown, B. P., Sichtmann, C., & Schoefer, K. (2018). Perceived globalness and localness in B2B brands: A co-branding perspective. *Industrial Marketing Management*, *72*, 59–70. https://doi.org/10.1016/j.indmarman.2018.03.014

Murphy, M. C., & Dweck, C. S. (2016). Mindsets shape consumer behavior. *Journal of Consumer Psychology*, *26*(1), 127–136 https://doi.org/10.1016/j.jcps.2015.06.005

Özsomer, A. (2012). The interplay between global and local brands: A closer look at perceived brand globalness and local iconness. *Journal of International Marketing*, *20*(2), 72–95. https://doi.org/10.1509/jim.11.0105

Özsomer, A., & Altaras, S. (2008). Global brand purchase likelihood: A critical synthesis and an integrated conceptual framework. *Journal of International Marketing*, *16*(4), 1–28. https://doi.org/10.1509/jimk.16.4.1

Özsomer, A., Batra, R., Chattopadhyay, A., & ter Hofstede, F. (2012). A global brand management roadmap. *International Journal of Research in Marketing*, *29*(1), 1–4. https://doi.org/10.1016/j.ijresmar.2012.01.001

Özsomer, A., & Simonin, B. L. (2004). Marketing program standardization: A cross-country exploration. *International Journal of Research in Marketing*, *21*(4), 397–419. https://doi.org/10.1016/j.ijresmar.2004.06.003

Özsomer, A. (2019). Some recent influences on global consumer culture: Digital networked technologies, emerging market brands and bottom of the pyramid consumers. *International Marketing Review*, *36*(4), 548–552. https://doi.org/10.1108/IMR-11-2018-0315

Özsomer, A., Simonin, B. L., & Mandler, T. (2023). Marketing agility in subsidiaries: Market orientation and marketing program standardization as the 'Twin Engines' of performance. *Journal of International Marketing*, *31*(2), 6–24. https://doi.org/10.1177/1069031X221130740

Riefler, P. (2012). Why consumers do (not) like global brands: The role of globalization attitude, GCO and global brand origin. *International Journal of Research in Marketing*, *29*(1), 25–34. https://doi.org/10.1016/j.ijresmar.2011.11.001

Samiee, S. (2019). Reflections on global brands, global consumer culture and globalization. *International Marketing Review*, *36*(4), 536–544. https://doi.org/10.1108/IMR-11-2018-0342

Samiee, S., Shimp, T. A., & Sharma, S. (2005). Brand origin recognition accuracy: Its antecedents and consumers' cognitive limitations. *Journal of International Business Studies*, *36*, 379–397. https://doi.org/10.1057/palgrave.jibs.8400145

Sayin, E., Aydınoğlu, N. Z., Özsomer, A., & Gürhan-Canlı, Z. (2024). Shifting standards in consumer evaluations of Global and Local Brands after product-harm crises. *Journal of International Marketing*, *32*(3), 83–100. https://doi.org/10.1177/1069031X231222865

Schmidt-Devlin, E., Özsomer, A., & Newmeyer, C. E. (2022). How to go glocal: Omni-brand orientation framework. *Journal of International Marketing*, *30*(4), 1–20. https://doi.org/10.1177/1069031X211070607

Schuetz, A., & Swoboda, B. (2025). Institutional Distances and International E-CommerceFirms' Standardization of Online Offers and Services. *Journal of International Marketing*, forthcoming. https://doi.org/10.1177/1069031X211070607

Shah, A. K., Mullainathan, S., & Shafir, E. (2012). Some consequences of having too little. *Science*, *338*(6107), 682–685. https://doi.org/10.1126/science.1222426

Shimp, T. A., & Sharma, S. (1987). Consumer ethnocentrism: Construction and validation of the CETSCALE. *Journal of Marketing Research*, *24*(3), 280–289.

Sichtmann, C., & Diamantopoulos, A. (2013). The impact of perceived brand globalness, brand origin image, and brand origin–extension fit on brand extension success. *Journal of the Academy of Marketing Science*, *41*(5), 567–585. https://doi.org/10.1007/s11747-013-0328-7

Sichtmann, C., Davvetas, V., & Diamantopoulos, A. (2019). The relational value of perceived brand globalness and localness. *Journal of Business Research*, *104*, 597–613. https://doi.org/10.1016/j.jbusres.2018.10.025

Spielmann, N., Williams, C., & Kohli, A. K. (2024). Local roots and global responsibility: Terroir brands and their responsible engagement. *Journal of International Marketing*, *32*(3), 65–82. https://doi.org/10.1177/1069031X231205255

Steenkamp, J. B. (2017). *Global brand strategy: World-wise marketing in the age of branding*. Springer.

Steenkamp, J. B. E. (2019). Global versus local consumer culture: Theory, measurement, and future research directions. *Journal of International Marketing*, *27*(1), 1–19. https://doi.org/10.1177/1069031X18811289

Steenkamp, J. B. E., Batra, R., & Alden, D. L. (2003). How perceived brand globalness creates brand value. *Journal of International Business Studies*, *34*, 53–65. https://doi.org/10.1057/palgrave.jibs.8400002

Steenkamp, J. B. E., & De Jong, M. G. (2010). A global investigation into the constellation of consumer attitudes toward global and local products. *Journal of Marketing*, *74*(6), 18–40. https://doi.org/10.1509/jmkg.74.6.18

Strizhakova, Y., & Coulter, R. A. (2013). The 'green' side of materialism in emerging BRIC and developed markets: The moderating role of global cultural identity. *International Journal of Research in Marketing*, *30*(1), 69–82. https://doi.org/10.1016/j.ijresmar.2012.08.003

Strizhakova, Y., & Coulter, R. A. (2015). Drivers of local relative to global brand purchases: A contingency approach. *Journal of International Marketing*, *23*(1), 1–22. https://doi.org/10.1509/jim.14.0037

Strizhakova, Y., Coulter, R. A., & Price, L. L. (2008). Branded products as a passport to global citizenship: Perspectives from developed and developing countries. *Journal of International Marketing*, *16*(4), 57–85. https://doi.org/10.1509/jimk.16.4.57

Strizhakova, Y., Coulter, R. A., & Price, L. L. (2011). Branding in a global marketplace: The mediating effects of quality and self-identity brand signals. *International Journal of Research in Marketing*, *28*(4), 342–351. https://doi.org/10.1016/j.ijresmar.2011.05.007

Strizhakova, Y., Coulter, R. A., & Price, L. L. (2021). The fresh start mindset: a cross-national investigation and implications for environmentally friendly global brands. *Journal of International Marketing*, *29*(4), 45–61. https://doi.org/10.1177/1069031X211021822

Swoboda, B., & Hirschmann, J. (2016). Does being perceived as global pay off? An analysis of leading foreign and domestic multinational corporations in India, Japan, and the United States. *Journal of International Marketing*, *24*(3), 1–30. https://doi.org/10.1509/jim.15.0088

Swoboda, B., Pennemann, K., & Taube, M. (2012). The effects of perceived brand globalness and perceived brand localness in China: Empirical evidence on Western. *Asian, and Domestic Retailers. Journal of International Marketing*, *20*(4), 72–95. https://doi.org/10.1509/jim.12.0105

Torelli, C. J., Keh, H. T., & Chiu, C. Y. (2010). Cultural symbolism of brands. In *Brands and brand management* (pp. 113–132). Psychology Press. https://doi.org/10.4324/9781003421320

Torelli, C. J., Özsomer, A., Carvalho, S., Keh, H. T., & Mæhle, N. (2012). Brand concepts as representations of human values: Do cultural congruity and compatibility between values matter? *Journal of Marketing*, *76*(4), 92–108. https://doi.org/10.1509/jm.10.0400

Trope, Y., & Liberman, N. (2010). Construal-level theory of psychological distance. *Psychological Review*, *117*(2), 440. https://doi.org/10.1037/a0018963

Usunier, J. C. (2006). Relevance in business research: The case of country-of-origin research in marketing. *European Management Review*, *3*(1), 60–73. https://doi.org/10.1057/palgrave.emr.1500049

Westjohn, S. A., Magnusson, P., & Zhou, J. X. (2015). Does the value of global brands apply to both foreign and domestic-based global brands?. In: Shaoming Zou, Hui Xu, & Linda Hui Shil (Eds.), *Entrepreneurship in international marketing* (pp. 267–286). Emerald Group Publishing Limited.

Winit, W., Gregory, G., Cleveland, M., & Verlegh, P. (2014). Global vs local brands: How home country bias and price differences impact brand evaluations. *International Marketing Review*, *31*(2), 102–128. https://doi.org/10.1108/IMR-01-2012-0001

Wong, N. Y., & Ahuvia, A. C. (1998). Personal taste and family face: Luxury consumption in Confucian and Western societies. *Psychology & Marketing*, *15*(5), 423–441. https://doi.org/10.1002/(SICI)1520-6793(199808)15:5<423::AID-MAR2>3.0.CO;2-9

Xie, Y., Batra, R., & Peng, S. (2015). An extended model of preference formation between global and local brands: The roles of identity expressiveness, trust, and affect. *Journal of International Marketing*, *23*(1), 50–71. https://doi.org/10.1509/jim.14.0009

Xu, H., Leung, A., & Yan, R. N. (2013). It is nice to be important, but it is more important to be nice: Country-of-origin's perceived warmth in product failures. *Journal of Consumer Behaviour*, *12*(4), 285–292. https://doi.org/10.1002/cb.1419

Yang, D. Y. J., Chen, X., Xu, J., Preston, J. L., & Chiu, C. Y. (2016). Cultural symbolism and spatial separation: Some ways to deactivate exclusionary responses to culture mixing. *Journal of Cross-Cultural Psychology*, *47*(10), 1286–1293. https://doi.org/10.1177/0022022116665169

5

Brand Management Across Countries and Cultures: The Challenges and Opportunities

Laurence Minsky and Ilan Geva

A central premise of our book *Global Brand Management: A Guide to Developing, Building & Managing an International Brand* (Minsky & Geva, 2019, p. xxii) was that every brand is inherently global, thanks to the internet. It is not just the brand's websites that can be accessed simply by entering the complete web address – or by using a Virtual Private Network (VPN) should the website be blocked to people from outside of the target country – that makes it global, but also mentions on social media and other outlets by people followed across the world. The mention might not be about the merits of the product, service or other entity. Rather, it could be about their brand's advertising, packaging, distribution strategy, employment policies, management actions, customer in-store experience or other random topics. The sentiment of the post can be either positive or negative. The mention in combination with all the other brand exposures contributes to the overall perceptions of the brand, good or bad, which in turn, can influence consideration, transaction frequency and brand loyalty in the countries where the product, service or other entity is available.

While what makes a global brand allows for the simple answer above – people hold views about the product, service or other entity in more than one country – the answer to what enables the brand to be successful in more than one country is not as straightforward.

Recognizing the various definitions of the terms 'brand' and 'branding' and what constitutes a brand that other contributors to this handbook are exploring, we need to keep in mind one basic truism with any branding effort: The marketer's goal is to have all the brand signals convey the essence and promise – what is at the core of the brand – and that they are aligned and conveyed across all the touchpoints to ensure that the interpretation of the signals is as the brand marketer intended. These signals need to remain clear, constant and unwavering, particularly for those in the target audiences. Otherwise, the brand can come across as disjointed and confusing and be seen as contrary to the intentions of the brand marketer.

Of course, the marketer would like the signals the brand touchpoints convey to be perceived as (mostly) positive to the key prospects as well. Additionally, the experience of using the brand – or the results of using it – should fulfill the brand's promise. This holds true at local, national, international and global levels.

THE BENEFITS OF BECOMING A GLOBAL BRAND

Becoming a global brand can bring many opportunities, including increased revenue, economies of scale and greater stability in case one market enters a recession. And it is becoming easier to be a monetized global brand, thanks to worldwide digital distribution outlets like Amazon and such placement sites as Fiverr for services. But that does not mean that becoming one is easy. All too often, brand marketers apply the tactics and strategic templates from their home country where their success is fueling its expansion to a host country. These templates, however, do not always play the same way in the new country – and can lead to massive failures.

Sean Duffy, for instance, in his 2021 book *International Brand Strategy: A Guide to Achieving Global Brand Strategy,* pointed out Target's cross-border failure when they first tried expanding beyond the USA. In 2013, the company opened four stores in Canada within a 3-week period, with the goal of opening an additional 120 stores in Canada during the next nine months (Duffy, 2021, p. 1).

This large-scale retail 'invasion' into the neighboring country did not go as planned. Within 14 months, the CEO of Target and the CEO of Target Canada was fired and then about 24 months later, the company announced that they would be exiting Canada, closing all of the stores there – 133 locations at this point – resulting in 17,600 employees losing their jobs and costing them 5.5 billion USD (Duffy, 2021, p. 2). It has since become a case study of what not to do (Shaw, 2015).

What went wrong? Duffy (2021, pp. 4–8) pointed out a few factors: (1) Purchasing the 'overpriced' leases of a failing Canadian retailer, so that the retailer could enter the market 'with a "national presence;"' (2) technical difficulties, because their proprietary purchasing and logistics software was not set up to work internationally, so it couldn't translate the currencies; and (3) the pricing was higher than the US stores, noticed by cross-border shoppers.

Duffy (2021, p. 9) summed it up with the statement: 'Target seemed to enter Canada determined to change the market rather than adapt to it.' This point is a key to developing an effective global brand management – that brands need to maintain their core while adapting to each market.

It is important to note that Target was simply trying to operate in more than one country, which we define as an international brand – a product, service or other entity where the home and host countries either share a border, are on the same continent, or share common historical roots. A global brand, on the other hand, is one that is widely available across the globe.

KEY INTERNATIONAL ISSUES TO EXPLORE

We offer this key distinction between international and global brands because the issues are often greater and more varied for global brands, although many issues experienced by an international brand and how they approach their cross-border brand management can be the same. So, what are some of the other issues that global (and some international) brands experience? They include:

- **Brand Ownership**: What consumers think of the brand's owner or founder can affect the perception of the brand itself. In 2023, Forbes conducted an analysis of the mentions and reputations of 50 of the world's leading CEOs and they found that Elon Musk dominated coverage, but that the conversation was mostly negative. What's more, 'data show that Musk's reputation, shaped by his multiple controversies (Klawans, 2024; Levison, 2023), including the promotion of false conspiracy theories (Valle, 2024), is harming the reputations of the brands he helms. As Biglione (2023) wrote, 'Tesla and Twitter, in particular, are each seeing their reputational trendlines dipping.' In addition, in an article published in *The Verge*, UK-based news reporter Jess Weatherbed (2024) wrote that Musk's controversial behavior is 'very likely' contributing to Tesla's declining sales. The impact is not just limited to the home country, especially if the company is not using advertising, but is allowing the personality of its CEO to be the sole face of the brand. What is more, since the concerns in the host country might not be the same as the home country, an action that was not seen as controversial in the country where the action occurred can hurt the brand in one or more of its other outposts.
- **Cultural Differences**: On a macro level, Avery et al., in their book *Consumer Behavior: Human Pursuit of Happiness in The World of Goods, 5th Edition* (2021), argued that the world is divided into two major cultural groups: Eastern and Western. The Western values they identified are Accomplishment, Change, Competitiveness, Individualism, Equality of Opportunity, Freedom,

Materialism, Merit, and Progress and the Eastern Values they listed include Collective Identity, Inner Harmony, Respect for Tradition, Respect for Hierarchy and Humanism (Avery et al., 2021, pp. 188–189). These differences alone suggest that not every brand would appeal to all consumers wherever they live. In addition, on a micro level, even within a continent, the different countries often embrace their own origin stories, legends, heroes, tastes and more. Pasta consumption in France or Germany, for instance, is much lower than pasta consumption in Italy: 8.3, 7.9, and 23 kg, respectively, of pasta annually in 2022 (Ozbun, 2024). Likewise, some countries maintain the tradition of siestas and some do not. While space limits us from providing additional examples, the bottom line is that cultural differences can affect the acceptance of a brand from another country, and, if accepted, the volume, of sales for the brand's products.

- **Global Developments**: What happens in one part of the globe can affect a brand sold in another part. Colgate-Palmolive in partnership with Hawley & Hazel long maintained a brand with a clearly racist name and imagery in China, Indonesia, Malaysia, Singapore, Taiwan The Republic of China (ROC), Thailand and Vietnam, as well as other countries in Asia, until the Black Lives Matter movement put pressure on U.S. brands with racist legacies to change their names (Grundy, 2020). Known in English as Darlie since 1989 (Grundy, 2020) – we will not mention the original racist English-language or Chinese names for it – the brand's name change in Chinese did not take place until 2021 and did not roll out until 2022 (Hazel, 2021). We think this forced name change was appropriate and long overdue, and it demonstrates the power of events in one country affecting – for good or bad – brands marketed in other parts of the globe – just one more factor global marketers need to think about and have on their radars.
- **Language and Pronunciation Differences:** The same word can have different shades and meanings across the globe, important because the brand name could have a negative connotation in the new country even though it has a positive connotation in the brand's home country. Likewise, the same considerations are for the positioning statements or the taglines – the brand needs to find ways of conveying the same essence in an appropriate way. Finally, marketers need to be sensitive to the fact that people in countries beyond the home country might have difficulty pronouncing certain words or letters from other languages. Some brands, however, intentionally embrace the words or letters that a target segment might mispronounce. For instance, the founder of the retailer Lululemon, Chip Wilson, selected the brand's name 'because he thought the difficulty Japanese people had pronouncing the letter 'L' was an extra marketing tool for the product' (Encinas, 2024). Here's how he described his thinking process:

> The reason the Japanese liked [my former skateboard brand, 'Homeless'] was because it had an L in it and a Japanese marketing firm wouldn't come up with a brand name with an L in it. L is not in their vocabulary. It is a tough pronunciation for them. So, I thought, next time I have a company, I'll make a name with three Ls and see if I can get three times the money. It is kind of exotic for them. I was playing with Ls, and I came up with Lululemon. It is funny to watch them try to say it. (Shaw, 2013)

As marketers, the chapter authors would not have taken Wilson's approach and even caution against it – but it seems to have worked for him.

- **Localized Brand Performance**: Some brands that are successful for a time, start to fade away and even go out of business. But as we had mentioned in our book *Global Brand Management* (Minsky & Geva, 2019, p. 104) the 'brand may also decline at different rates within different countries.' It may even go out of business in its home country but leave behind outposts across the globe. For instance, Borders went out of business in 2011, but we 'spotted a Borders store still in operation in a hospital shopping mall in Malaysia and there might well be other pockets in the world where a store or two exists.' (Minsky & Geva, 2019, p. 104). The same can be said for Toys 'R' Us. Despite filing for bankruptcy in the USA in 2017 and closing all its domestic stores, the brand persists through various ownership structures and partnerships and can still be found in a range of countries, including: Canada, China, India, Japan and South Africa, Southeast Asia and United Arab Emirates as well as in several Western and Eastern European nations. As a result, the Toys 'R' Us and Borders brands would still need to be maintained and managed with coordinated branding activities across all the places where it operates. Conversely, a brand might be quickly growing in some pockets of the globe while in other parts, struggling to grow and the brand stewards would need to figure out where to spend their time. Do the marketers focus on the countries where it is growing or on fixing the problems in the countries where it is struggling? In other words, priority setting is one of the key tasks of a marketer of a global brand, just like it is for a local one, but the list of what needs to be prioritized seems to multiply exponentially.

- **Perceptions Regarding the Country (or City) of Origin**: Which would you rather buy: Spaghetti made in Mexico or spaghetti made in Italy? To most in most Western countries, a spaghetti brand from Italy would feel more 'authentic' and, thus, better than one from Mexico even if the one from Italy was seen as a low-end discount brand back home. (The same example would work in the opposite direction if the product were tortilla chips, and the countries were reversed.) That is because the attributes associated with the brand's country of origin reflect on products, services and other entities, for good or bad. It is important to note, it is not just food or ingredient products. The enhanced (or reduced) image can be for automotive design, engineering, fashion, manufacturing quality or price, and more. As a result, understanding the perceptions regarding their country of origin (and addressing them) becomes a key action for marketers looking to expand beyond their home borders.
- **Pricing**: While the costs and exchange rates may change from one country to another, the perception of pricing needs to align with the positioning of the brand. It is rare for a brand to display 'luxury' pricing in one country and be seen as a 'discount' brand in another. If the marketer creates a 'disconnect' between consumer expectations and the actual prices, it can hurt the brand in countries beyond its home. For example, let us go back to Target. As mentioned earlier, the prices at Target Canada were higher than those in the USA. This could have been acceptable – the prices were lower than other Canadian chains – except for one issue: 'From the start, Canadian consumers were not comparing Target's prices to other local discount retailers,' wrote Duffy (2021, p. 11). 'They were comparing Target's prices to Target's own prices across the border.' This turned out to be one of the core reasons that Target Canada failed. After all, pricing is one of the key signals of 'value' – whether that value comes from the money being saved, the luxury experience it implies or from what it says about the user.
- **Product Education**: The new markets might not be familiar with the product category or the usage occasions. Consumers in the new countries might not know when or how to use it. One example is the introduction of the kiwifruit to Europe. It was originally known as Chinese gooseberry, but was rebranded when it was first cultivated in the USA and New Zealand back in 1905. But it still took years for the product adoption. 'France and Italy were pioneers in adopting this delicious fruit in 1967 and 1971, respectively,' according to the plant nutrition company Cultifort (2024). The lag was because consumers needed to become educated about this fruit before they would adopt it. For another example, let us look at coffee consumption in Japan. Coffee was first introduced to the country by Dutch traders based in Nagasaki during the 17th Century (Team, 2023). And, inspired by the French coffeehouses, the first Japanese coffee shop opened in Ueno, Tokyo during the late 19th Century (*For the Love of Coffee*, 2024). But coffee sales were still essentially 'nonexistent in 1970' (Rapaille, 2006, p. 9). Nestle wanted to change all that, particularly so they could more successfully market their instant coffee. The problem: People were emotionally attached to tea. The solution: Focus on imprinting the flavor of coffee on Japanese children through desserts (but without the caffeine). Their strategy – while ethically questionable – was a success, and coffee obtained a 'beachhead in Japan (Rapaille, 2006, p. 9). Starbucks then advanced the coffee battle in Japan. They first introduced their stores to Japan in 1996, and by 2023, they had 1,733 coffee shops operating in Japan (Arba, 2024). To enter the market, they adapted their products to be in conformance with the preferences of the consumers in the country. First, they made the drinks to taste less sugary. They also adjusted the serving sizes to be smaller (no Trenta size and instead offered a 'Short,' which is smaller than a 'Tall.' And they include tea-based options on their menu (Jackson, 2023). Today, according to the Japan House article *For the Love of Coffee* (2024), 'Japan is considered one of the global hubs of coffee culture.' It is important to note that today's overall Japanese coffee culture adheres to Eastern core values more than those in the West (Goldstein-Gidoni, 2001). While these

obvious examples are food related, the issue we discussed extends to other types of products, other services and other entities. The bottom line: Consumers need to understand when to use the new brand, where to use it, how to use it, how often to use it, and, intuitively, how it will fit into their lives and cultural practices.

We also need to point out that marketers have additional issues to explore when expanding into a new country, but these are too numerous to fall within one chapter of a handbook.

And while all these points can be perceived as issues, a smart marketer can often convert many of them to be opportunities as well. Therefore, be careful when initially applying any positive or negative valence to what you find; each one can be either. As a chapter co-author Laurence Minsky and Dave Aaron suggested in their 2021 *Harvard Business Review* article, 'Are You Doing the SWOT Backwards,' 'these environmental conditions exist not only for your firm but for all competitors.' It is, 'in effect, the external factors create the arena in which the competition takes place' (Minsky & Aron, 2021). To respond to these factors, 'managers must adjust their strategies to reflect it, even as this environment changes' (Minsky & Aron, 2021).

KEY MISTAKES MARKETERS MAKE

In addition to the inclination to immediately label a factor to be either an issue or an opportunity before fully assessing the situation and thinking about how to best 'position' it for the brand's benefit, there are other key mistakes that marketers make with their global brands. One of them is seeking a 'magic bullet' that covers every country rather than executing against the situation in each market, and that a single marketing tactic or campaign will have a direct, powerful and immediate impact on very large audiences. This outdated theory suggests that media messages are like 'bullets' that penetrate the minds of consumers, instantly influencing their thoughts and behaviors without any resistance, so that the consumers will 'act in ways that are useful to the propagandist' (Baran & Davis, 2012), the earlier name used to define Mass Communication. We should point out that the Magic Bullet Theory is closely linked to the Hypodermic Needle Theory, which employs the analogy of a long medical needle inserting the ideas into the brain to convey essentially the same concept. Both theories emerged during the early 20th century when mass media was a relatively new phenomenon.

But we have seen marketers turn to it even today. One magic-bullet marketers often use today is to apply Maslow's Hierarchy of Needs as a guiding light. The basic human needs of hunger, thirst and shelter reassured many brands that all humans will use them if sold for an affordable price at a convenient location. But in most countries that are advanced enough to support the marketing of competitive brands, there is an abundance of options that solve the same problem, with most available in convenient locations. As a result, promoting that a brand satisfies a basic need is not enough because it doesn't differentiate itself enough from the other products that offer the same benefits.

Similar thinking led to media buyer's adoption of the rule of three: 'That consumers simply need to be exposed to a message three or more times for it to be effective' (Rosen & Minsky, 2018, p. 43). But this so-called 'rule' was never based on research. And 'in fact, research indicates that wear-in is almost immediate – and wear-out happens quickly thereafter' (Rosen & Minsky, 2018, p. 43). Another mistake that marketers often make is using the 'matching suite of luggage' approach to brand messaging: They create one piece of core communication – the same headline and the same visual – and then apply it to every shape and size and platform. This approach became popular during the start of digital marketing when platforms were proliferating. With both, the 'bullet' was essentially the same, but multiple shots were needed for the brand message to penetrate.

Modern marketing has largely rejected the Magic Bullet and Hypodermic Needle Theories, the rule of three and the 'matching suite of luggage' branding approach, although these still pop up from time to time with various marketers. We now understand that people are more complex and influenced by a variety of factors beyond media messages, including their personal experiences, social interactions and individual values.

Rather than relying on a 'magic bullet,' a product, service or other entity must provide value with every touchpoint in each market where it is available to stand out from its competition. 'To create value beyond the monetary, marketers can deliver shoppers and consumers real functional utility, entertainment content and/or opportunities to participate in something of interest – such as games, contests, photo/video sharing or how-to information – versus merely sending marketing messages and perhaps a coupon' (Rosen & Minsky, 2018, p. 68). Then every 'signal' that is conveyed by the brand needs to align, but they should not be the same exact message merely repeated in different shapes and sizes and on different media platforms. The tone, wording and imagery for each touchpoint can vary, must be appropriate to the situation and must align with the brand essence and positioning. In other words, while there is no 'magic bullet' for marketing success; rather, the combination of well-executed strategies, audience understanding, data-driven insights and a consistency in the tone and execution of the marketing communication elements is more likely to yield positive results.

If the brand does not provide that value in one market; however, there is a chance that it will not be noticed in other markets and, thus, it will not globally hurt the brand. On the other hand, if a brand makes a branding mistake in one market, there is a strong chance that it will be noticed in other markets as well.

That is exactly what happened to the German brand Adidas. During the summer of 2024, Adidas decided to market and promote a retro 1972 Summer Olympic Games sneaker. The brand campaign coincided with the 52nd anniversary of the Munich Olympic Games, where members of the Black September Organization, a Palestinian terrorist organization, stormed the Olympic Village, took 12 Israeli coaches and athletes hostage and then were eventually massacred. The issue: Adidas picked a vocal anti-Israel model, Bella Hadid, to promote the sneakers and it immediately backfired on them (Vlessing, 2024). This leads to two questions:

1. Why did Adidas create a nostalgic shoe based on an incredibly gruesome occurrence?
2. Why did Adidas pick a model known as spokesperson and influencer for antisemitic and anti-Israeli policies?

It did not take long for Adidas to apologize, following the international outrage. This case is a clear demonstration of a critical rule in global marketing today: Do not insult ANY ethnic, religious or national group (despite Lululemon's success story). Marketers, unfortunately, do not always follow this basic tenet, and they fail to carry out due diligence in all markets when launching a product or marketing campaign. A complaint both chapter authors heard during our advertising agencies' days is that the client (and/or the agency) is 'overthinking' the creative, but this is better than launching a campaign that backfires on them.

It also does not have to be a global product or campaign that requires global due diligence. A local social and political event in one market can impact the global brand in other markets. A unique example of the social and political changes in one country affecting its international standing as a global brand is the Kingdom of Saudi Arabia. The ability of the Kingdom to accomplish its vision and goals in a relatively short time and position itself as a global brand is due to three points:

1. Commitment of top management (Royal family),
2. Complete participation of all participants (Government offices, private sector, citizens) and
3. Virtually unlimited financial support.

But the ultimate reason is the leadership of Crown Prince Muhammad Bin Salman. Appointed a deputy crown prince and defense minister after his father became king in 2015, then promoted to crown prince in 2017, and prime minister in 2022. Since 2017, he has introduced a series of social and economic reforms under Saudi Arabia's strategic framework titled, 'Vision 2030' that aims to diversify the country's economy, society and culture, and to create a more innovative, world-leading nation. The country has opened itself up to the global markets – and it worked! In fact, Saudi Arabia's World Travel & Tourism Council's (WTTC) 2024 Economic Impact Research (EIR) study revealed a record-breaking year for Travel & Tourism, with new records in GDP contribution, sector jobs and visitor spend. This sector is now soaring past all previous records, a testament to the country's commitment to becoming a global tourism hotspot (World, 2019), welcoming over 100MN tourists in 2023. Said Julia Simpson, WTTC President & CEO, 'Saudi Arabia's Travel & Tourism sector's extraordinary achievements last year mark a pivotal moment in its journey towards becoming a global tourism leader' (World, 2019).

LOCATION, LOCATION, LOCATION

Another trend increasing the importance of global branding efforts was described in *Proximity: How Coming Breakthroughs in Just-in-Time Transform Business, Society, and Daily Life* (2024). The authors of this book, Wolcott and Krippendorff, show that digital technologies and other technological advancements are enabling the move of physical production and product delivery closer in time and location to the point 'of demand' – that is, when the consumer or business-to-business (B2B) product is purchased and needs to be delivered. Imagine a car not getting assembled until you order it with your unique specifications; then image the assembly and delivery of the car taking place immediately. Now imagine the same with medicine, even with low volume, long-tail type prescriptions (after real-time diagnosis because of 24/7 medical monitoring), foods (lab-grown meats, anyone?), replacement parts and more. The authors define this trend as 'proximity' and sum it up with the line, 'Proximity is about anticipating, sensing and responding with greater precision' (2024). The job of the product manager is to figure out how to take advantage of this trend and new technologies to update their product delivery.

Fulfilling the need for proximity is easy for undifferentiated commodity products, where there is only one option such as a generic prescription medicine. The key challenge for brand marketers – often a different position and skill set than product managers within the marketing organization – is that proximity diffuses the delivery of the brand experience. In other words, the strategy of micro localization and the overall concept of proximity puts even more importance and pressure on the need for building a stronger brand image, because that would be the only constant across all its markets.

So, what are some of the constant brands marketers can use that can work across languages and borders? The first area to examine is sensory branding – the use of scenting, sounds, flavoring and textures to contribute to the brand experience. Of course, sight is a sense, but visual branding is what marketers automatically use. We are not saying that brand marketers should stay away from defining the brand colors, imagery style, fonts, design structures, language choices, personality and tone, and brand essence – these foundational branding elements all remain vitally important and should remain consistent across borders – but to expand the foundational library of the brand elements to address the other senses as well.

In fact, perhaps the most important sense beyond vision for marketing purposes is sound. That is because the meaning of composed sounds translates across borders and languages and they help the receiver spot the ad, billboard, sign, product, display, booth associated with the sound more quickly than without this added sensory input. In other words, as Paddock reported in *Medical News Today*, 'Processing auditory information enables the human visual system to predict incoming information, thus giving us a survival advantage' (2014). As a result, 'adding an audio logo can infuse layers of meaning into a visual logo' (Minsky & Fahey, 2014). We should also remind readers that most people use their smartphone to access news and entertainment, followed by their desktop computer, limiting available senses that can be activated for digital communications are only two, sight and sound (Shearer, 2021). The other three senses – touch, taste and smell – are not (yet) activated by technology, so they tend to get overlooked. However, touch and smell are very important for physical environments and, of course, taste is important for food items, and they should be considered when creating the core of the brand.

Once the marketer has solidified the core foundation, they can start exploring which components can and should be localized, called glocalization. As we had mentioned earlier, Starbucks localized its product mix in Japan to better appeal to local consumers. McDonald's also localized its menu options throughout the world. In India, for instance, McDonald's does not sell its beef or pork items, and, instead, the brand offers a range of chicken, paneer and egg options. In Israel, some of their restaurants are fully Kosher. They also practice Halal traditions in predominantly Muslim populated countries. And they offer a range of other food products that appeal to local palates, all delivered under a consistent global brand foundation.

In other words, local religious practices become a key consideration for global food brands, as local 'forbidden foods' cannot be included in their global menus (Ritzer, 2010) and that the local taste preferences, which are formed during childhood imprinting (Rapaille, 2006, pp. 21–24), need to be considered as well.

But the practice of glocalization is not restricted to global restaurant brands. A retailer brand that is inherently 'glocalized,' because different branches are not managed by the same company, is 7-Eleven. This American company was formed in 1927 but was not branded 7-Eleven until 1946. As a pioneer in offering 24-hour operations, self-serve soda fountains, coffee to-go and more, it was seen as a leader in the convenience store category. Expanding globally, the brand launched 7-Eleven in Japan in 1974 through a partnership with Japanese retailer Ito-Yokado, and the brand introduced a wider range of products into their Japanese stores, including fresh food, hot meals and payment services. Under the same brand name, both companies delivered to consumers the same core emotional promise of convenience. Then, in a twist of fate, the parent company of 7-Eleven experienced financial difficulties and Ito-Yokado bought the brand, bringing the separate entities closer together. We just learned, as we go to press, that 7-Elevan is considering adopting the Japanese model for the US market, a potential change to watch.

IT IS THE CORE THAT COUNTS: GLOCALIZED BRAND CAMPAIGN EXAMPLES

Another brand that has a strong glocalization program is Oreo. The brand was introduced by the National Biscuit Company (Nabisco) in 1912, now part of Mondelez International (i.e., formally known as Kraft), and the Oreo cookie was inspired by the Hydrox cookie, which was introduced in 1908 by Sunshine Biscuits (Rosenberg, 2019) and were discontinued in 2003 (Dent, 2024). Today, Oreo is the world's top-selling cookie brand and is sold in more than 100 countries (Mondelēz International, 2023).

For the localization, Oreo comes in flavors and forms that are only available specific countries to appeal to their preferences, including the dulce de leche Oreo in Argentina (Mondelēz International, 2023), the Cadbury Coated Oreo in Australia, the Chocolate Creme Oreo in the Australia, Canada, New Zealand, the UK and the USA, the Strawberry Creme Oreo in Asia and Australia (Kirk, 2024), the Green Tea Oreo in China and Japan, the Blueberry Ice Cream Oreo in China, Indonesia, Malaysia, Singapore, Thailand and Vietnam, the Orange Ice Cream Oreo in Indonesia, Malaysia, Singapore and Thailand (Bokksu, 2023), and the Maple Syrup Oreo in the USA (Mondelēz International, 2023). Exclusively in China, there is also a Hot Chicken Wing Oreo, Orange Mango Oreo and Wasabi Oreo (Bokksu, 2023). The forms and shapes beyond the traditional round version include wafer sticks, wafer rolls and soft cakes (Bokksu, 2023) as well as thins, double-stuffed, ice cream cones and consumable straws (Broderick, 2023). It is important to note that this list is just a beginning, as there are additional flavors, forms and shapes available. But for Oreo's essence of its brand, there is one thing that remains the same across the globe: The iconic experience of the 'twist, lick, dunk' ritual (Mondelēz International, 2023) and the playfulness it conveys.

'China is now the world's largest Oreo market outside the USA,' according to the article *How Kraft Won in China*, which was published in *Forbes* (2009). The brand, however, was not immediately adopted in that country. It lingered for approximately 20 years after it had first entered the Chinese market. Why? Research indicated that the consumers in China thought that a package of it was too expensive and that the traditional Oreo cream filling was considered too sweet for the Chinese palate (*How Kraft Won in China*, Forbes, 2009). In addition, its outer cookie shell was too bitter for the local preferences as well (Smith, 2012).

Also, according to *How Kraft Won in China* (2009), Oreo's parent company, then known as Kraft, changed from their 'original belief that what was good for one market would also be good for every market' to the current strategy, which they called 'Winning Through Focus' when they launched it (2009). The brand managers then strategically tailored Oreo's products, marketing strategies and distribution channels to resonate with local preferences and cultural nuances. For instance, the brand leaders asked themselves, 'why does an Oreo have to be black and white?' as well as 'why should an Oreo be round?' (Smith, 2012). As a result, the brand departed from its 'Western strategy' in a variety of ways, including:

- **Flavor Innovation:** As we mentioned above, Oreo introduced novel flavor combinations that appealed to the Chinese palate.
- **Reimagined Packaging:** It was redesigned to incorporate traditional Chinese elements and symbols, making it more attractive to Chinese consumers.
- **Package Size:** The brand introduced smaller portion sizes to cater to their preference for individual snacking. This, according to the Forbes' article *'How Kraft Won in China'* (2009) enabled the Oreo brand to go from 'the original price at 5 yuan [73 cents] for 14 cookies' to 'a smaller size at 2 yuan [29 cents] for seven cookies.'
- **Celebrity Endorsements:** The brand partners with popular Chinese celebrities to help it increase its brand awareness and appeal. For example, Oreo partnered with Jay Chou, a popular singer in China, to be their brand ambassador for Alibaba's Tmall 2020 'Super Brand Day.' The brand used the occasion to celebrate the 20th anniversary of Chou's first album by offering 'Jay Chou milk teacups and fashion merchandise' on their storefront, among other marketing activities with Chou, including an ad campaign and an art exhibit made from expired Oreo cookies in a busy train station. The result: Oreo increased their transaction volume by 20% and followers by over 100,000 on their storefront (Team, D., 2020).
- **Social Media Engagement:** Oreo has leveraged popular Chinese social media platforms such as WeChat and YouTube to engage with local consumers and create a strong online presence. The messaging is localized. For instance, their 'YouTube channel features videos dubbed in Mandarin that highlight Chinese cultural references' (Bhargava, 2023).
- **Cultural Integration:** Oreo participates in local events, festivals and traditions to foster a stronger sense of connection with consumers. They, of course, extend this integration to their promotions. It is what inspired them to offer four-pack and six-pack Oreo mooncakes for the Mid-Autumn Festival, a holiday in China celebrating the harvest (Jie, 2024).

EXPORTING THE AMERICAN EXPRESS BRAND TO SOUTH AFRICA

Finally, glocalization can work for service brands as well. One example: American Express, also known as AmEx. One of the members of this authorship team, Ilan Geva, worked on the AmEx account for Ogilvy in South Africa in the early Eighties. Back then, there were only two AmEx cards: Green and Gold, with the Gold Card being a significant status symbol. Marketing was also limited, but well targeted via direct mail, promotions and other common marketing activities of the time. Today, American Express leverages a combination of traditional and digital channels to reach its target audiences. Some of their key strategies in South Africa, and elsewhere, include:

- **Partnerships:** American Express partners with airlines, hotels and other businesses to offer exclusive benefits and promotions to its cardholders, helping to increase the brand's visibility and loyalty as well as attract new customers who want the benefits.
- **Digital Marketing:** The brand employs email marketing, online advertising and social media to reach consumers. The brand's digital campaigns often highlight the benefits of the cards, such as travel rewards, purchase protection and concierge services.
- **Events and Experiences:** They arrange and secure exclusive events and experiences for their cardholders, such as concerts, sporting events and travel packages. These events help to strengthen the brand's connection with its customers and create a sense of exclusivity.
- **Television and Print Advertising:** Traditional media advertising and streaming services enable American Express to reach a wide audience as well as showcase the benefits of its cards. These campaigns often feature well-known celebrities or influencers who align with the brand's values. 'It is a brand that exists through advertising,' said Steve Hayden, Vice Chairman (now retired) of Ogilvy, summing up the importance of using advertising for service brands. What's more, AmEx advertising is used for more than reaching and influencing prospects; rather, as a worldwide brand, it also 'reminded employees, first of all, of the important global scale and quality of the company' (Minsky, 2007, p. 70).
- **In-Branch Promotions:** Finally, the company works with its partner banks to promote its cards through in-branch promotions and cross-selling initiatives.

The last point is important because the expansion of any financial product to become a global brand comes with one big hurdle: The laws and regulations are different in each country. To be able to operate in certain countries, American Express needs to partner with the local banks and fintechs in Africa to have them issue cards and convince and enable merchants to accept them.

One of American Express' longest-running partnerships is with Nedbank, a South African-based bank, which started in 1968 and enabled the AmEx-branded credit card to be offered in South Africa through the bank (American Express, 2025). In addition to helping American Express expand its worldwide reach, the partnership also allowed Nedbank to leverage the recognition and prestige of the American Express brand and provide its customers with access to a wide range of benefits and services via the credit cards. In return, Nedbank ensures that its marketing and customer service align with the American Express brand values and standards and maintains a consistent brand experience for cardholders, ensuring that its customer service team is fully trained to effectively handle any cardholder inquiries and issues at a high level of service. Finally, Nedbank actively promotes the AmEx brand in South Africa, highlighting the benefits and prestige associated with the cards, which in turn, increases the prestige of their overall brand as well.

In other words, the marketing strategy for the American Express brand in South Africa is focused on highlighting the premium benefits and exclusive experiences it offers to customers. Then, by targeting specific customer segments through the marketing channels the prospects use, Nedbank maintains a strong presence for AmEx in the South African market. And to ensure consistency, the American Express brand team in its corporate headquarters works to ensure that Nedbank – and its other financial partners throughout their global network – follow their brand guidelines and accurately implement the brand standards.

The result: Nedbank's partnership with American Express has been successful in providing South African consumers with access to premium credit card products and services. And by effectively managing the American Express brand, Nedbank has strengthened its position in the market and enhanced its reputation as a provider of high-quality financial solutions. What's more, this approach allows American Express to profitably expand its network through these partnerships without investing additional costs.

MarTech ENABLING A BRAND'S GLOBAL CONSISTENCY

While technology cannot (perhaps yet) replace human thought and oversight, some tools can help manage the branding elements across borders and cultures, enabling effective and consistent brand management across the globe. The types of MarTech tools available range from platforms automating the delivery of the brand's paid and owned marketing communications – everything from advertising to social placements – to data management and more.

One of the best utilizations of MarTech in global branding is the control it gives brands for them to maintain their graphic standards as they are being implemented around the world. After all, to state the obvious, ensuring consistent graphic standards across the globe is truly challenging. It is common to see out-of-date logos and other branding elements in use among brands – even the top ones such as Pepsi, HP, Coke and others – in the continents beyond their home countries. Some strategies brands employ to maintain control that MarTech tools can enhance include:

- **Comprehensive, Centralized Style Guides:** These should detail the brand colors, logo usage typography, imagery, tone and language and more. And these guides should be easily accessible to all brand team members and external partners. Of course, the style guides should be regularly audited to ensure that they are up to date.
- **Centralized Digital Asset Management (DAM) System:** Brand managers should store all brand assets (such as logos, imagery, branded fonts, design files, audio files and video elements) in a centralized system that all brand team members and external partners can access. Brand managers should also track changes to all your brand elements and ensure only approved assets are used. They should also set up controls on who can access the various files to ensure the correct assets are used in each country.
- **Template Libraries:** Brands can create templates for their marketing materials (such as websites, social media posts, emails) that adhere to their brand standards, so they can ensure consistency from their marketing professionals and agencies across the globe. To be effective, the brand manager should provide clear instructions on how to customize the templates to ensure they help maintain brand consistency.
- **Online Collaboration Tools:** In addition to storing brand assets in a Centralized Digital Asset Management System and creating branded templates, brands should use such tools as Figma and Adobe XD to enable real-time collaboration and feedback on designs across the globe. However, be sure to track changes and ensure everyone is working with the latest approved versions.
- **Automation of Checks and Validations:** Brand Marketers can integrate their guidelines into the design software such as Adobe Creative Suite and Sketch to automatically check for compliance. There are also production platforms where brands can keep their design files, so if something like a logo, font, or other design element is updated, the change is implemented across all the design files, so everything automatically remains up to date. However, even with this production tool, be sure to conduct regular audits of your online properties to identify and rectify any deviations from the most recent brand standards.

This short overview is just the beginning, but we have one caveat: these technology-based tools and platforms are just enablers. They will not replace hard work, commitment, diligence, consistency, oversight and the implementation of the basic brand management practices. Marketers still need to ensure that their content and elements are correct for each country; these tools are available for one simple reason: To make the process a little easier. As a result, brand marketers will still need to identify internally their 'Brand Police' in each region of the globe to ensure that brand guidelines are adapted to local cultural nuances while maintaining the overall consistency of the message and execution. Be sure to leverage their knowledge, having them provide guidance on local marketing practices and preferences as well as to have them check brand and promotional campaigns being developed in other parts of the globe to ensure they do not reflect negatively on the brand in their locality.

By implementing these strategies, brands can effectively control their graphic standards and other brand foundational elements globally online, ensuring a consistent and recognizable brand identity across all channels. Corporations and their local brand managers should also monitor their online channels (website and social media) for compliance with brand standards. And do not be afraid to implement consequences for any non-compliance to reinforce the importance of adhering to brand guidelines.

Finally, when selecting the MarTech stack, brand marketers should also seek capabilities for the delivery of training sessions about the brand, including internal podcasts, webinars and online asynchronous courses, to their network across the globe. But even if the training is conducted the old school way of face to face, be sure to conduct them regularly, so the brand's internal teams and external partners know how to apply brand guidelines in different contexts, and they maintain standards.

LET US GET SMART ON MARKETING ARTIFICIAL INTELLIGENCE FOR GLOBAL BRAND MANAGEMENT

Another emerging area that can expand the audience reach for a global brand and facilitate the marketing of brands is the use of artificial intelligence (AI). But while most recent discussions about marketing AI have centered around one type of AI – generative – there are many different types and levels of sophistication; they include:

- **Generative AI**: This type of AI creates images, text, videos and other content, so it can be used for writing branded content for social posts, emails, ads or even radio and television commercials. It can also be used for generating your imagery for one of these messages. Skyrocketing into popular discussion by the commercial launch of ChatGPT in 2022, generative AI is the type that most people in marketing are currently referring to when they talk about AI, and it can help brands produce productivity gains in the development of their materials. However, it comes with many issues for brand marketers. For instance, the imagery is not copyrightable, and the content generation can produce what is called hallucinations, so the resulting content sounds assuredly accurate, but it is not true at all or has errors embedded in it. As of this writing, the best recommendation from this authorship team is to use generative AI as a brainstorming tool, but the output should not be used as the final content. If the prompts are good, it can help lead to insights and new, culturally appropriate ideas, but it still takes a human to turn the output into usable, highly effective branded marketing content.
- **Conversational AI**: Think Siri, Alexa, Jasper and other popular voice apps, but it could also be the audio prompts and the more templated verbal responses customers give when filing a prescription or leaving a message (Minsky et al., 2023, p. 2). This powerful interface can not only enable low literacy, visually impaired, physically constrained and other individuals access the brand, it can also expand the accessibility of the brand, translating marketing messages languages not covered by the brand, so the brand can 'be' in more places at more times and is a very promising technology for marketers. Conversational AI is also the interface that enables the conversations with chatbot while generative AI develops the responses. The one caveat: Brand managers will need to apply the voice technology to be in the voice of the brand, within its personality, and conveyed within the brand essence. The emergence of conversational AI is one of the factors driving the need for audio or sonic branding, which we mentioned earlier. After all, on a voice app, the brand must live and be recognizable without the presence of a visual logo.
- **Predictive AI**: While generative AI is currently receiving the bulk of the media attention, it is predictive AI that promises the most benefits for product managers and is receiving the bulk of the investments in AI development. With Predictive AI, algorithms can help analyze data – that is, a series of previous events – to find patterns and trends that enable the system to forecast future outcomes or events. For instance, it can be employed to forecast the weather and an increase in umbrella purchases as a result to determine the distribution or the pricing of umbrellas on certain days. We should also note that predictive AI comes with the potential for bias and other ethical concerns, because of the quality of the data being analyzed and the assumptions used when developing the algorithms. We see predictive AI becoming an even more powerful tool for media planning, distribution, pricing and other targeting activities associated with the product management side of marketing, but the authors of this chapter have not yet identified predictive AI's eventual application to the management of a brand on a global scale. Perhaps the role of predictive AI in global brand management is an area ripe for future research. In the meantime, media planning, distribution, pricing and other targeting activities are all executed on a local level. The core through all the local executions – the brand's essence – needs to stay the same and be consistent for a product, service, or other entity to become a truly powerful global brand.

As you can see, much of the theory of what makes a strong global brand stays the same, but the technology fueling global brands is changing and advancing, which brings us to where we started: That brands need to be managed and aligned – and provide value – in all markets they serve. Whether the product, services, or entity is in a single market, a single country, several countries or available across the globe, it is not all the 'fancy stuff' that matters. Those tactics are the lucky extras to enable and extend what you are doing. Rather, it is the consistent execution of the basics that matters most. Any time the brand does not fulfill its core brand promise, it negatively impacts the trust in the brand. And that negative impact can go global. After all, while every brand is inherently global, people respond to it locally. And while the tools have changed, the basic principles have stayed the same. Whether it is local or global, a strong brand requires commitment, consistency and tenacity. You have the current thinking on the state of global brand management. Now it is your turn to execute.

REFERENCES

American Express Expands Footprint in Africa. (2025). *Americanexpress.com*. Retrieved November 24, 2024, from www.americanexpress.com/en-us/newsroom/articles/amex-for-business/american-express-expands-footprint-in-africa.html

Arba, A. (2024, April 3). *Starbucks: Number of stores in Japan 2021*. Statista. Retrieved September 27, 2024, from www.statista.com/statistics/1305935/starbucks-store-number-japan/

Avery, J., Kozinets, R., Mittal, B., Raghubir, P., & Woodside, A. G. (2021). *Consumer behavior, consumer psychology – How humans think, feel, and act in the marketplace* (5th ed.). Open Mentis Publishers.

Baran, S. J., & Davis, D. K. (2012). *Mass communication theory: Founders, ferment, and future*. Wadsworth.

Bhargava, V. (2023, June 19). *Unlocking the secrets of Oreo's social media marketing strategy*. Radarr. Retrieved October 28, 2024, from www.radarr.com/blog/oreos-social-media-marketing-strategy-breakdown/

Biglione, S. (2023, February 1). *Houston, Elon Musk has a reputation problem*. Forbes. Retrieved September 24, 2024, from www.forbes.com/sites/shannbiglione/2023/02/01/houston-elon-musk-has-a-reputation-problem/

Bokksu, S. (2023). *Oreo: A world of Asian flavors to savor*. Bokksu Market. Retrieved October 23, 2024, from www.bokksumarket.com/blogs/magazine/oreo-a-world-of-asian-flavors-to-savor

Broderick, N. (2023, November 5). *Whatever happened to Oreo sippers?* Tasting Table. Retrieved October 28, 2024, from www.tastingtable.com/1438152/whatever-happened-oreo-sippers/

Cultifort. (2024, February 5). *Kiwi in Spain, trends and challenges in cultivation: From…* Cultifort. Retrieved March 19, 2025, from www.cultifort.com/en/trends-and-challenges-of-kiwi-cultivation-en/

Dent, M. (2024, January 8). *The curious case of the disappearing Hydrox cookies*. Thehustle.co; HubSpot. Retrieved October 23, 2024, from https://thehustle.co/the-curious-case-of-the-disappearing-hydrox-cookies

Duffy, S. (2021). *International brand strategy: A guide to achieving global brand growth*. Kogan Page.

Encinas, A. (2024, January 4). *Lululemon founder says brand isn't for everyone: 'You don't want certain customers coming in.'* USA TODAY. Retrieved September 21, 2024, from www.usatoday.com/story/money/business/2024/01/04/chip-wilson-lululemon-comments/72109070007/#

Forbes. (2009, December 8; Updated: 2012, July 11). *How kraft won in China*. Forbes. Retrieved October 23, 2024, from www.forbes.com/2009/12/08/china-oreo-tang-cmo-network-kraft.html

Goldstein-Gidoni, O. (2001). The making and marking of the 'Japanese' and the 'Western' in Japanese contemporary material culture. *Journal of Material Culture*, 6(1), 67–90. https://doi.org/10.1177/135918350100600104

Grundy, T. (2020, November 27). *Darlie toothpaste remains on shelves five months after Colgate vowed to rethink 'racist' brand*. Hong Kong Free Press HKFP. Retrieved September 25, 2024, from https://hongkongfp.com/2020/11/27/darlie-toothpaste-remains-on-shelves-five-months-after-colgate-vowed-to-rethink-racist-brand/

Hazel, H. (2021, December 14). *Hawley & Hazel introduces new brand initiative to uplift brand value and capture new growth opportunities in the oral care category*. www.prnewswire.com. Retrieved September 25, 2024, from www.prnewswire.com/news-releases/hawley–hazel-introduces-new-brand-initiative-to-uplift-brand-value-and-capture-new-growth-opportunities-in-the-oral-care-category-301443829.html

Jackson, N. (2023, May 12). *Starbucks' localization success story in Japan*. Medusa. Retrieved September 27, 2024, from https://medusajapan.com/starbucks-localization-success-story-in-japan-strategies-for-global-expansion/

Japan House (Los Angeles). (n.d.). *For the love of coffee*. Japan House Los Angeles. Retrieved September 27, 2024, from www.japanhousela.com/articles/for-the-love-of-coffee/

Jie, J. (2024). *OREO to compete in the mooncake sales for China's Mid-Autumn Festival – People's Daily Online*. People.cn. Retrieved October 28, 2024, from http://en.people.cn/n3/2017/0823/c90000-9259244.html

Kirk, D. (2024, June 17). *The definitive ranking of Oreo flavours around the world*. Six-Two by Contiki. Retrieved October 28, 2024, from www.contiki.com/six-two/article/definitive-ranking-oreo-flavours/

Klawans, J. (2024, January 16). *Elon Musk's most controversial moments*. The Week. Retrieved September 24, 2024, from https://theweek.com/elon-musk/1022182/elon-musks-most-controversial-moments

Levison, J. (2023, November 30). *Elon Musk: A timeline of his most recent controversial moments*. Sky News. Retrieved September 24, 2024, from https://news.sky.com/story/elon-musk-what-are-his-most-recent-controversial-moments-13019651

Minsky, L. (2007). *How to succeed in advertising when all you have is talent* (2nd ed.). The Copy Workshop.

Minsky, L., & Aron, D. (2021, February 23). *Are you doing the SWOT analysis backwards?* Harvard Business Review. Retrieved September 25, 2024, from https://hbr.org/2021/02/are-you-doing-the-swot-analysis-backwards

Minsky, L., & Fahey, C. (2014, August 6). *Sounds speeds sight*. Data-Driven Marketing Network. Archive.ph. Retrieved September 24, 2024, from https://archive.ph/20140806090417/http://www.data-driven-marketing.net/articles/organization/sounds-speeds-sight

Minsky, L., Fahey, C., Westwater, S., & Westwater, S. (2023). *Voice marketing: Harnessing the power of conversational AI to drive customer engagement*. Rowman & Littlefield.

Minsky, L., & Geva, I. (2019). *Global brand management: A guide to developing, building & managing an international brand*. Kogan Page.

Mondelēz International. (2023). *Oreo*. Mondelēz International, Inc. www.mondelezinternational.com. Retrieved October 28, 2024, from www.mondelezinternational.com/Our-Brands/Oreo/

Ozbun, T. (2024). *Leading countries in pasta consumption per capita in 2022*. Statista. Retrieved September 24, 2024, from www.statista.com/statistics/1379424/per-capita-consumption-pasta-by-country/

Paddock, C. (2014, May 27). *Brain's visual system also processes sound*. Medicalnewstoday.com. Medical News Today. Retrieved September 24, 2024, from www.medicalnewstoday.com/articles/277325

Rapaille, C. (2006). *The culture code: An ingenious way to understand why people around the world live and buy as they do*. Crown Currency.

Ritzer, G. (2010). An introduction to McDonaldization. In G. Ritzer (Ed.), *McDonaldization: The reader*. Pine Forge Press, an imprint of Sage.

Rosen, W., & Minsky, L. (2018). *The activation imperative: How to build brands and business by inspiring action*. Rowman & Littlefield Publishers.

Rosenberg, J. (2019, September 13). *How did the Oreo get its name?* ThoughtCo. Retrieved October 31, 2024, from www.thoughtco.com/history-of-the-oreo-cookie-1779206

Shaw, H. (2013, December 10). *Lululemon founder Chip Wilson's 5 most controversial quotes*. Financial Post. Retrieved March 19, 2025, from https://financialpost.com/news/retail-marketing/lululemon-athletica-chip-wilson-controversy

Shaw, H. (2015, January 15). *Target Corp's spectacular Canada flop: A gold standard case study for what retailers shouldn't do*. Financial Post. Retrieved March 19, 2025, from https://financialpost.com/news/retail-marketing/target-corps-spectacular-canada-flop-a-gold-standard-case-study-for-what-retailers-shouldnt-do

Shearer, E. (2021, January 12). *More than eight-in-ten Americans get news from digital devices*. Pew Research Center. Retrieved November 3, 2024, from www.pewresearch.org/short-reads/2021/01/12/more-than-eight-in-ten-americans-get-news-from-digital-devices/

Smith, R. (2012, January 27). *Rethinking the Oreo for Chinese consumers, NPR Choice page*. Npr.org. Retrieved November 3, 2024, from www.npr.org/sections/money/2012/01/27/145918343/rethinking-the-oreo-for-chinese-consumers

Team, C. E. (2023, February 14). *A look at coffee culture in Japan*. CoffeeBI | Coffee Business Intelligence. Retrieved September 27, 2024, from https://coffeebi.com/2023/02/14/a-look-at-coffee-culture-in-japan/

Team, D. (2020, October 27). *Oreo works with singer Jay Chou for super brand day*. Dao Insights. Retrieved October 28, 2024, from https://daoinsights.com/works/oreo-works-with-famous-singer-jay-chou-for-super-brand-day/

Valle, G. D. (2024, March 25). *Elon Musk has fully bought into the 'great replacement.'* The Verge. Retrieved September 24, 2024, from www.theverge.com/2024/3/25/24111405/elon-musk-great-replacement-conspiracy-immigration-don-lemon

Vlessing, E. (2024, July 18). *Bella hadid adidas ad faces backlash for 1972 olympics sneakers*. The Hollywood Reporter. Retrieved July 18, 2024, from www.hollywoodreporter.com/news/general-news/bella-hadid-adidas-ad-backlash-1972-olympics-sneakers-1235952510/

Weatherbed, J. (2024, April 3). *Elon Musk's reputation is falling – and it's taking Tesla with it*. The Verge. Retrieved September 24, 2024, from www.theverge.com/2024/4/3/24119918/elon-musk-reputation-impact-tesla-falling-sales

Wolcott, R. C., & Krippendorff, K. (2024). *Proximity: How coming breakthroughs in just-in-time transform business, society, and daily life*. Columbia University Press.

World. (2019, December 19). *News-article: 'Saudi Arabia's travel & tourism breaks all records.'* Wttc.org; World Travel & Tourism Council. Retrieved September 27, 2024, from wttc.org/news-article/saudi-arabias-travel-tourism-breaks-all-records

PART 2

Foundations of Brand Management

6

Visual Brand Identity: The Role of Logos in Brand Management

Minjung Kim and Joon Ho Lim

Early in 2024, Apple Inc. announced the end of its practice of including iconic Apple logo stickers in product boxes, a tradition spanning nearly 47 years. Apple cited this change as a part of its broader environmental commitment, aiming for carbon neutrality by reducing waste and minimizing packaging materials by 2030 (Apple, 2024). However, some loyal consumers voiced their disappointment on social media, sparking discussions about the nostalgic and symbolic value of the stickers (Rossignol, 2024). For Apple, the iconic logo sticker has served as a tangible expression of brand loyalty, demonstrating how symbolic values can be conveyed through visual brand elements such as logos. This example, illustrating the consumers' attachment to a brand's logo as a symbol of their loyalty, highlights the crucial role a logo can play in brand management (Aaker, 1996; Keller, 2013).

Logos are defined as 'the graphic design that a company uses, with or without its name, to identify itself or its products' (Henderson & Cote, 1998, p. 14). Effective logos help brands differentiate themselves from their competitors and, in turn, contribute to enhancing brand recognition and brand recall, forming positive brand attitudes and building strong brand equity (Aaker, 1991; Keller, 2013). That is, logos can help reinforce a brand's presence and emotional connection with its consumers (Park et al., 2013). Accordingly, logos are essential for successful brand management, calling for attention from both academics and practitioners (Foroudi et al., 2017; Henderson & Cote, 1998; Kim & Lim, 2019).

This chapter aims to provide a review of the existing logo literature to discuss the role of logos in successful brand management. To this end, we first review the influence of logo elements – such as color, shape and typeface – on conveying brand identity to consumers. Next, we delve into logo executions by highlighting the importance of developing a strategy to cohesively present logos at every consumer touchpoint. We then discuss the potential impacts of an evolving business landscape on logo design and logo execution. Lastly, we discuss future research directions by suggesting potential research questions and methodologies. In doing so, this chapter aims to provide valuable insights into and guidelines for logo design/redesign as well as effective logo execution to facilitate the visual communication of brand identity and, thus, to build strong brands.

THE ROLE OF LOGO ELEMENTS IN COMMUNICATING BRAND IDENTITY

Brand identity refers to the unique set of visual, verbal and experiential elements that define and distinguish a brand in the market (Kapferer, 2012).

It serves as an integral part of the brand's communication strategy, conveying its values and strategic direction to consumers and supporting the brand's positioning strategy (Aaker, 1996; Kapferer, 2012). Prior literature has well documented that a brand's logo, as a visual element, plays an important role in communicating brand identity to consumers (Colman et al., 1995; Janiszewski & Meyvis, 2001; Park et al., 2013).

It is important to note that brand identity (i.e., the message) is carefully planned and crafted by brand managers (i.e., the message senders) and then communicated to consumers (i.e., the message receivers), who perceive the brand and form the associated brand images based on their understanding of the conveyed brand identity (Kapferer, 2012). In other words, consumers may interpret brand identity in ways that differ from the brand managers' intentions, potentially resulting in an unintended brand position in the market. This highlights the importance of understanding the consumers' perceptions of the logo elements – such as color, shape and typeface – in delivering brand identity and guiding brands to incorporate the most effective visual representation in their logo design/redesign to deliver their intended brand identity (Foroudi et al., 2017; Kim & Lim, 2019). Accordingly, the previous logo research focuses on how consumers perceive various logo elements and associate these perceptions with the brand. By leveraging prior findings, practitioners can design or redesign logo elements to convey their intended brand identity more effectively by minimizing the risk of miscommunication.

In the following sections, we present a brief review of the existing literature on three major logo elements – color, shape and typeface – to provide guidelines for an effective communication of the brand identity to consumers. Next, we further discuss the importance of harmonizing logo elements to create a cohesive and consistent brand identity that resonates with consumers, thereby building strong brand equity. Figure 6.1 illustrates a conceptual framework, showing how logo elements and their sub-dimensions influence brand perceptions and contribute to brand equity.

Logo Color

A body of literature suggests that colors evoke emotions and associations, influencing consumer perception and behavior (Labrecque, 2020; Sutton

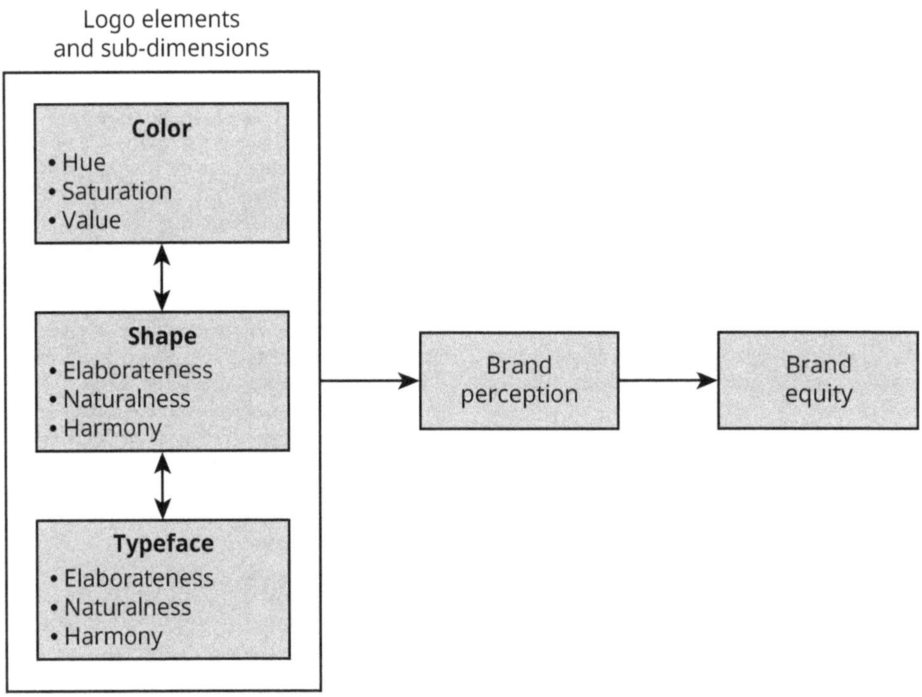

Figure 6.1 A conceptual framework in the logo literature

Source: The authors.

& Altarriba, 2016). For instance, red is frequently associated with excitement and urgency, often used in retail to attract attention and stimulate appetite (Labrecque & Milne, 2012). On the other hand, blue tends to evoke feelings of trust and reliability, making it popular in the finance industry where trustworthiness is essential (Bottomley & Doyle, 2006). Building on this stream of research, the logo literature has shown that colors used in logos can evoke certain brand perceptions. For instance, green is often associated with sustainability (Labrecque & Milne, 2012), and thus, consumers tend to evaluate a brand more ethically when green is used in its logo (Sundar & Kellaris, 2017).

Labrecque (2020) further explained that the people's perceptions of color can vary based on the differences in color sub-dimensions, such as hue (i.e., the actual color or spectral wavelength composition), saturation (i.e., the purity and intensity or vividness of the color) and value (i.e., the relative lightness or darkness of the color). The associations elicited by colors can, in turn, be strengthened or weakened by adjusting these color sub-dimensions. For instance, highly saturated logos can enhance brand intimacy perception, resulting in a closer connection between brands and consumers (Xiao et al., 2021). Similarly, recent research on color saturation indicates that consumers often associate lower saturation with a stronger perception of sustainability (Pichierri & Pino, 2023). According to these findings, if a brand aims to communicate a more sustainable brand identity, using a less vivid shade of green in its logo could be an effective choice. In short, this line of research underscores the importance of selecting logo colors that align with brand identity and highlights the potential benefits of adjusting color sub-dimensions to help these perceptions.

Furthermore, the impact of the logo color on brand perceptions can vary based on contextual factors, such as logo background color and logo colorfulness. Celhay and Luffarelli (2024) suggested that the impact of a logo's color hue on brand perceptions can vary significantly based on the background color. For instance, a blue logo on a white background might convey a sense of competence, while the same logo on a black background may evoke sadness. Therefore, brand managers should carefully consider the background color used with their logo, as it may influence consumer responses in unexpected ways. Also, it is very common to use multiple colors (i.e., logo colorfulness) in designing a brand's logo. Bottomley and Doyle (2006) suggested that varied color schemes evoke perceptions of diversity and flexibility. Similarly, recent research shows that using a combination of multiple colors in logos can lead consumers to perceive the brand as offering a wider range of options, positively influencing their attitudes toward the brand (Song et al., 2022). Thus, independent of the specific brand perceptions evoked by individual colors, a logo featuring multiple colors can create additional positive brand perceptions such as diversity and product variety. By considering these contextual factors, the brand managers can more precisely communicate their intended brand identity to consumers with their choice of logo color.

It is worth noting that competitive dynamics also play a role in shaping consumers' brand perceptions influenced by the logo color. Labrecque and Milne (2013) found that differentiating a brand's logo color from that of a major competitor (i.e., the market leader) does not always result in distinct brand perceptions. When a dominant market leader exists, its logo color often establishes a visual norm in the consumers' minds. As a result, deviating from this norm may inadvertently signal inferiority, potentially leading to lower brand equity evaluations. This finding further supports the notion that a brand's logo color is a crucial element in communicating its values to consumers, thereby impacting its positioning in the marketplace.

Logo Shape

Logo shape refers to the graphic design of a logo, which can be understood through three universal design dimensions: Elaborateness (i.e., the concept of design richness and the ability to use simple lines to capture the essence of something), naturalness (i.e., the design depicts the commonly experienced objects) and harmony (i.e., a congruent pattern or arrangement of parts that combines symmetry and balance) (Henderson & Cote, 1998; Kim & Lim, 2019). A few further research findings confirm that these three design dimensions are universal across different cultures and countries (Henderson et al., 2003; van der Lans et al., 2009).

While this body of research offers general design guidelines for the logo shape, extensive studies mostly focus on how specific logo shapes influence the consumers' brand perceptions and consequently downstream business outcomes. For example, prior findings show that rounded (vs. angular) logos are often associated with softness (vs. rigidness) (Jiang et al., 2016), femininity (vs. masculinity) (Lieven et al., 2015), more (vs. less) sustainability (Meiting & Hua, 2021) and less (vs. more) brand premiumness (Li et al., 2023). Such different brand perceptions, in turn, produce varying downstream outcomes, such as brand preferences and purchase intentions. For instance, asymmetric (vs. symmetric) logos evoke more exciting brand images (Luffarelli et al., 2019) and are, thus, more preferred by consumers who view themselves in the consistent manner (Bettels & Wiedmann, 2019) or those with more liberal (vs. conservative) political ideologies (Northey & Chan, 2020). These findings suggest that careful selection of the logo shape is essential, as it serves as a powerful tool for conveying brand identity.

A substantial body of research has also examined how other factors related to the logo shape influence brand perceptions. For instance, a logo frame (i.e., the physical boundary of a logo) may influence consumers' purchase risk perceptions (Fajardo et al., 2016). That is, consumers with high (vs. low) purchase risk perception may view the logo frame as a signal of protection (vs. confinement), leading to increased (vs. decreased) purchase intention. A logo frame can also affect the perceived brand breadth, potentially impacting the consumer's acceptance of the brand's expansion into new categories (Chen & Bei, 2020). Furthermore, logo orientation (i.e., the direction in which a brand's logo is displayed) is found to influence brand perceptions. Specifically, the logos placed on an upward (vs. downward) diagonal are associated with perceptions of greater activity and effort, which can lead to stronger beliefs in product efficacy (Schlosser et al., 2016). These findings highlight the importance of employing holistic design approaches to selecting logo shape along with its related design factors, as recommended by Henderson and Cote (1998).

It is worth noting that any visual stimulus can be further understood based on its sub-dimensions such as simplicity, symmetry or self-similarity (Berga et al., 2019; Iigaya et al., 2021; Mayer & Landwehr, 2018). Hence, similar to the logo color, academics and practitioners can benefit from studying the sub-dimensions of the logo shape. As previously discussed, a few logo research studies explored the effect of logo symmetry on consumer attitudes and evaluations (e.g., Luffarelli et al., 2019), and such a symmetric feature contributes to forming the harmony (Henderson & Cote, 1998). Furthermore, logo simplicity, as discussed as a sub-dimension of elaborateness (Henderson & Cote, 1998), is well-aligned with an emerging logo design trend – the growing popularity of minimalism in logo design (Entheos, 2024; Kim & Lim, 2019). Preliminary finding shows that logo simplicity (vs. complexity) certainly influences brand perceptions; a simple (vs. complex) logo design is associated with perceptions of approachability (vs. prestige) (Tang et al., 2022). In turn, logo simplicity can influence downstream outcomes, such as food consumption (Bossel et al., 2019). Given the preliminary evidence documenting the role of such sub-dimensions in influencing brand perceptions and evaluations, we call for further academic attention to better inform brand managers' logo design decisions.

Logo Typeface

Certainly, overall logo design dimensions – such as elaborateness, naturalness and harmony – also apply to a logo typeface (Grohmann et al., 2013; Henderson et al., 2004). However, extensive research has been more interested in how a specific logo typeface elicits certain emotions and associations, thereby influencing consumers' brand perceptions. For example, using a serif typeface can lead people to perceive the associated brand as innovative (Henderson et al., 2004). An innovative brand image can also be evoked using an incomplete typeface (Hagtvedt, 2011). Also, when a typeface is easy to read or remember, it aids marketers in delivering consistent communication across various mediums, thereby enhancing the brand perception (Childers & Jass, 2002). These findings suggest that the choice of the logo typeface plays a pivotal role in shaping how the consumers perceive a brand. A well-chosen typeface not only enhances the aesthetic appeal of the logo but also reinforces brand perceptions.

Related to the logo typeface, one of the underexplored areas that deserve academic attention is wordmark logos, which prominently display brand names with minimal design elements (Henderson & Cote, 1998). Accordingly, wordmark logos may be more dependent on typeface selection in communicating the desired brand identity, potentially limiting the brand's ability to stand out in the market. However, brands can utilize typeface-related factors, such as uppercase vs. lowercase letters and letter-spacing, to evoke specific associations even within the constraints of wordmark logos. Research has shown that uppercase (vs. lowercase) letters in wordmark logos elicit various associations such as brand authority (Xu et al., 2017), competence (vs. warmth) (Teng et al., 2021), femininity (vs. masculinity) (Kim & Maglio, 2021; Wen & Lurie, 2018) and premiumness (Yu et al., 2022). Also, prior research finds that increased spacing between letters may negatively impact the perceptions of product safety, resulting in less favorable brand attitudes (Gupta & Hagtvedt, 2021). Hence, despite their minimalistic design, the wordmark logos can offer a distinctive opportunity for brands to communicate their brand identity solely through their choice of typeface. Moreover, prior literature suggests the benefit of using the wordmark logos when the brands lack familiarity; text-based logos, as opposed to image-based logos, are more effective for less familiar brands by making it easier for consumers to recognize and process the brand, which, in turn, fosters more positive brand attitudes (Morgan et al., 2021). According to this research, new brands can strategically opt for wordmark logos to enhance their brand recognition. Hence, more research in this area can help the introduction of new brands to the market.

Interplay Among Logo Elements

In previous sections, we reviewed the existing literature on how each of the three major logo elements – color, shape and typeface – influences the consumers' brand perceptions and ultimately contributes to building a strong brand equity.

While each logo element plays a critical role in shaping brand perceptions and ultimately building brand equity, it is also important to consider the interactions among these elements. Prior research suggests that while the logo color may play a dominant role in conveying brand personality, the logo shape can also help enhance this process (Labrecque & Milne, 2012). Similarly, the interplay between logo shape and typeface in affecting the brand attitude and evaluation has also been documented (Salgado-Montejo et al., 2014). Given that the congruency between the color and typeface in packaging design leads to more favorable consumer evaluations (Tian & Huang, 2025), we can also anticipate a similar interaction effect in the context of logos. Despite its importance, there are few research studies that delve into exploring the interplay among logo elements in shaping brand perceptions and evaluations (Kim & Lim, 2019). Furthermore, other logo elements, such as the inclusion of brand names (Melewar, 2003) or slogans in logos (Li & Ma, 2023), can contribute to shaping brand associations and perceptions. Notably, the literature on visual perception highlights that people tend to process visual elements simultaneously rather than independently (Buetti et al., 2019; Garg et al., 2019; Mayer & Landwehr, 2018). Hence, to advance the understanding and application of logos in brand management, we urge academics and practitioners to further explore the interplay among logo elements and their combined effects on brand equity.

LOGO EXECUTION FOR EFFECTIVE BRAND IDENTITY COMMUNICATION

Once a brand's logo is introduced, consumers are likely to encounter it across various touchpoints and in multiple contexts (Bottomley & Doyle, 2006; Henderson & Cote, 1998; Kim & Lim, 2019). Each encounter contributes to consumers' impressions and interpretations of the brand, making it crucial for brands to strategically plan how and where to present their logos seamlessly. We define *logo execution* as a process in which a brand's logo is strategically presented across various consumer touchpoints to communicate the brand's desired identity to consumers. By thoughtfully orchestrating the logo execution, brands can create an integrated brand experience that enhances brand recognition, fosters positive brand perceptions and ultimately cultivates everlasting brand equity.

In the following sections, we examine the underlying mechanism in which the consumers visually process logos as information and how such processing shapes brand attitudes and evaluations. We then discuss strategies for effectively presenting logos across various consumer touchpoints to ensure a consistent communication of brand identity.

Processing Fluency Theory

Extensive research on logos has demonstrated their positive impact on brand attitudes and business outcomes based on processing fluency theory (Janiszewski & Meyvis, 2001; Kim & Lim, 2019). Processing fluency theory posits that when people find it easier to process information, this sense of ease – or *fluency* – results in more favorable attitudes and evaluations toward the information (Alter & Oppenheimer, 2009; Schwarz et al., 2021). Previous literature identifies two distinct types of processing fluency: Perceptual fluency and conceptual fluency (Janiszewski & Meyvis, 2001; Whittlesea, 1993). Perceptual fluency is rooted in feature-based memory representations, where the sense of ease is driven by how easily a stimulus's physical characteristics are processed. In contrast, conceptual fluency comes from meaning-based memory representations, where the sense of ease arises from the associative meaning of the stimulus (Kim & Lim, 2019; Vogel et al., 2020; Zhang et al., 2022).

Building on the processing fluency literature, research on logos argues that the enhanced processing fluency facilitated by the visual characteristics of logo elements plays a pivotal role in shaping brand attitudes and evaluations. For example, logos that are visually simple, symmetrical or incorporate familiar shapes and colors are generally easier to process, which enhances both brand recognition and brand attitudes (e.g., van Grinsven & Das, 2014). This stream of research suggests that any visual characteristics that facilitate easier visual processing should be considered when designing logos. Another stream of research suggests that processing fluency extends to meaningful associations with brands. For instance, the alignment between a brand name and its logo in describing real-world objects (i.e., figurativeness) enhances brand attitudes and evaluations, as such a congruency helps in cognitive interpretation (de Lencastre et al., 2023). Similarly, some design characteristics of a brand's logo, such as the thickness (Eyni et al., 2023) and the perceived stability of a logo's design (Huang et al., 2021), can help the consumers build semantic associations with the brand, thereby enhancing their understanding of brand identity. These findings emphasize the importance of designing logos that not only help visual processing but also align with any meaningful associations with the brand.

While brands can enhance processing fluency by carefully considering the design aspects of their logos, it is also important to note that both types of processing fluency emphasize a key pathway to achieving the ease in processing: repeated exposure to a stimulus. Repeated exposure enhances familiarity, which, in turn, reduces cognitive effort, resulting in positive evaluations: the mere exposure effect (Zajonc, 1968). In other words, when consumers repeatedly encounter a logo, they become familiar with it. Over time, this familiarity leads to positive evaluations of the logo, contributing to brand equity (DelVecchio et al., 2024; Ingendahl et al., 2021; Lee & Labroo, 2004; Nunes et al., 2015). Indeed, a brand's logo can be presented to consumers repeatedly across various touchpoints (Kim & Lim, 2019). Hence, if brands strategically plan the presentation of their logos across various consumer touchpoints aiming for such a positive effect of repeated exposure, it will certainly help them achieve the increased brand familiarity, leading to stronger brand equity. In the following section, we discuss a strategic approach to planning logo execution across various consumer touchpoints.

Logo Execution Across Various Consumer Touchpoints

To ensure consumers' best experiences with the brand, prior research underscores the importance of understanding the consumer journey – that is, the process a consumer goes through at every touchpoint with the brand (Hamilton & Price, 2019; Lemon & Verhoef, 2016). A consumer touchpoint refers to 'an episode of direct or indirect interactions with the brand' (Baxendale et al., 2015, p. 236). Consumers' direct interactions include, but not limited to, advertising from the brand or retailers and through in-store communications. Their indirect interactions include observing others' consumption and word-of-mouth (Baxendale et al., 2015). Recently, digital touchpoints (e.g., websites, search engines and social media) have also increasingly drawn attention from researchers and practitioners (Hallikainen et al., 2019). More importantly, researchers have emphasized that designing and managing successful interactions at any touchpoints is crucial in building long-term relationships with consumers (Maechler et al., 2016; Verhoef et al., 2009) and, thus, plays a significant role in brand management (Kuehnl et al., 2019). Furthermore, Batra and Keller (2016) argued that the integrated marketing communication through all touchpoints is key to achieving the brand's strategic goals.

Logos can help consumers identify and differentiate the brand in a competitive marketplace (MacInnis et al., 1999). To best utilize the role of logos, brands strive to effectively present them across all consumer touchpoints to shape brand perceptions, attitudes and evaluations (Wedel & Pieters, 2008). Indeed, a brand's logo can be displayed at every consumer touchpoint. Whether watching TV commercials, walking into retail stores, examining packaging designs, or scrolling through brand-generated social media posts, consumers likely encounter the brand's logo and may form the basis of their brand experiences. As discussed previously, logo elements can elicit certain emotions and associations, thereby influencing brand perceptions while interacting with other contextual factors (Foroudi et al., 2017; Henderson & Cote, 1998; Kim & Lim, 2019). Although slight modifications to a brand's existing logo may not undermine its efforts to maintain a consistent brand identity (Sääksjärvi et al., 2015), prior literature has well documented that changes to the logo can often lead to negative backlash from consumers (Walsh et al., 2010). These findings further suggest that brand managers should carefully consider how the nature of various consumer touchpoints may influence brand perceptions, as these touchpoints can significantly affect how the logo is presented to consumers, thereby affecting brand perceptions. For example, placing a brand's logo in the top-left corner of its website is recommended to enhance brand recall without disrupting consumers' browsing experience (Whitenton, 2017). On a different note, the placement of a brand's logo on the top of its packaging may elicit additional association (e.g., power) and, thus, extend brand perceptions, resulting in different consumer preferences (Sundar & Noseworthy, 2014). As these examples illustrate, understanding the characteristics of various consumer touchpoints is crucial for effective logo execution. However, despite its importance, this area remains underexplored. Therefore, we urge researchers to focus on the benefits and challenges in each of consumer touchpoints when presenting a brand's logo to provide deeper insights and advance the field.

As mentioned earlier, thoughtful consideration of the characteristics of each consumer touchpoint is crucial when strategically presenting a brand's logo. Furthermore, these considerations should be incorporated into a comprehensive and cohesive logo execution strategy across multiple touchpoints, as it can help achieve a successful communication of brand identity (Gregersen & Johansen, 2018; Kohli et al., 2002; Kuehnl et al., 2019). Hence, we suggest that brand managers should consider developing a harmonized presentation of logos during the early stages of logo design/redesign. A recent study supports this notion showing that, when a new logo is introduced with logo presentation examples in various contexts (e.g., a new logo on the package or a new logo included in marketing materials such as pamphlets), consumers tend to evaluate the new logo more positively (Wertz, 2023). In other words, logo design/redesign that accounts for the potential integration of logos across various consumer touchpoints is more likely to capture attention, enhance recognition and ultimately build strong brand equity. To develop a cohesive presentation strategy of logos across various consumer touchpoints, brand managers must put an emphasis on the adaptability of their logos to various consumer touchpoints (Airey, 2009). For instance, if a brand's logo features a complex shape, multiple colors and an overly stylized typeface, it may face significant challenges when adapting the logo to digital platforms with display constraints. The characteristics of digital platforms may, in turn, drive the simpler logo design trend (Reddit, 2022). This example further highlights the importance of brand managers considering potential changes in the business landscape that may affect consumer touchpoints and incorporating such analyses into logo design and execution strategies. In the following section, we delve into the current business challenges the brands are likely to face and discuss their potential impact on brand management strategies, particularly related to logos.

LOGOS IN EVOLVING BUSINESS LANDSCAPES

The history of a brand's visual identity spans from the industrial revolution to the present, evolving alongside business landscape changes related to technological advancements. Foroudi et al. (2017) examined the history of corporate logos to understand their impact on a company's image and reputation. In the period of the early development of brand logos between 1760 and 1949, a corporate visual identity became more important due to advancements in printing technologies and color lithography. From 1950 to 1979, a logo evolved to a marketing tool (e.g., packaging) that helps attract customers and signal a brand's size, scale and strategic directions (Capitman, 1976; Foroudi et al., 2017; Napoles, 1988). In the 1980s, mass marketing, primarily due to the development of mass production techniques and new mass media channels, significantly enhanced the value of the logo by showcasing how it conveyed its identity, value, reliability and origins (Foroudi et al., 2017). During this period, the visual designers gained legitimacy as businesses recognized the positive effect of good design on sales (Murphy & Rowe, 1988). Since then, the brand logos, a vital component of visual identity, have adapted to new technologies and are expected to continue evolving to meet the demands of the rapidly changing business landscapes. Consequently, the effective development and strategic management of a brand's visual identity necessitates careful consideration of the evolving role, function and design elements of its logo in light of current and anticipated future changes. In the following sections, we further discuss the evolution of logos as a key visual identity element, considering the influence of technological innovations such as digital media platforms and artificial intelligence (AI).

Adaptation to New Digital Media Platforms

The rise of digital media platforms, particularly screen-based media and mobile devices like smartphones and tablets, has profoundly impacted our lives. These devices have become critical customer touchpoints, making it essential for brands to effectively leverage such a new format for branding, including logo design/redesign for both small and high-resolution screens (Guido et al., 2016; Kim & Lim, 2019).

In particular, the interactivity of digital media platforms enables dynamic logo displays. Existing research suggests that the animated logos can be an effective marketing tool for capturing the consumer attention and fostering more distinctive and memorable brand identities (Brasel & Hagtvedt, 2016; Guido et al., 2016; Rapp et al., 2013). For instance, Guido et al. (2016) found that the consumers prefer animated logos with upward motion, especially upright and convex trajectories, particularly for innovative companies. This highlights the importance of strategically designing animated logos to align with brand identity. Therefore, adapting logos for digital media allows brands to leverage the unique characteristics of these platforms to enhance brand identity communication.

Furthermore, different presentation environments across digital media platforms may necessitate logo design modifications. Just as digital platforms allow for dynamic logos, the emergence of digital platforms requires brand managers to evaluate the logo modifications for these new environments without compromising the established brand identity across traditional touchpoints such as retail stores and print advertising. Prior literature has documented how to incorporate digital platform characteristics into mobile app icon design; for instance, Wang and Li (2017) found that slightly asymmetrical mobile app designs are perceived as more dynamic and appealing, thereby increasing downloads. Similarly, the brand managers can consider modifying logos for digital platforms, including mobile apps, to leverage platform characteristics and attract consumer attention. On a related note, a notable logo design trend, specifically influenced by screen-based media and mobile devices, is minimalism. Brands increasingly use clean lines, simple shapes and negative space to create impactful, memorable and adaptable logos (Vazofsky, 2024). The rise of simple and minimal logo designs has been significantly shaped by the need for clarity and functionality on social media platforms and mobile devices (Gumber, 2023). For instance, Mastercard redesigned its logo in 2019 by removing the brand name and focusing solely on the iconic interlocking red and yellow circles, creating a modern and minimalist identity. Driven by the digital environment and a desire to become a 'symbol brand', the redesign reflects a focus on 'modern simplicity', as stated by Mastercard's CMO (Stalzer, 2019). This minimalist trend is likely to continue with advancements in digital devices such as smart watches and smart glasses. However, it remains unclear how brands adapt logos to the evolving digital environment, how consumers perceive minimalist designs and how these changes affect brand value. Therefore, we advocate for further research in this area.

Adaptation to AI

AI technologies are revolutionizing the process of creating a new logo and redesigning an existing logo. According to Deloitte (2024), 25% of enterprises utilizing generative AI are expected to deploy AI agents by 2025, which are software solutions designed to complete tasks with minimal human intervention, and this number is projected to reach 50% by 2027. Statista has also highlighted that AI-driven design tools have cut logo design turnaround times by as much as 50%, boosting productivity and delivering significant cost savings for businesses (EMB Global, 2024). Gartner projects that by 2026, over 80% of enterprises will have either utilized generative AI application programming interfaces (APIs) or implemented generative AI-enabled applications, and by 2025, 30% of outbound marketing messages from large organizations are expected to be generated using synthetic methods, leveraging AI technologies to enhance efficiency and personalization (Gartner, 2023a, 2023b).

Platforms like Tailor Brands (www.tailorbrands.com) and Segmind (www.segmind.com) utilize cutting-edge AI technologies to quickly and efficiently generate professional logos. These tools accommodate a wide range of needs by integrating essential design elements, including color schemes, typeface and brand-specific symbols, ensuring that the resulting logos align closely with the brand's identity. This ability to customize logos based on specific brand requirements enhances both creativity and efficiency in the design process (Sujitha, 2023). In addition, originally inspired by Deloitte Digital's internal rebranding efforts on its iconic green dot logo, Deloitte Digital developed a generative AI-based tool, Orb Foundry, designed to enable personalization-at-scale in marketing asset creation (Forbes, 2024). The Orb Foundry, powered by Adobe's Firefly generative AI platform, features a prompt-driven interface that allows users to input descriptions and create three-dimensional orbs. These orbs seamlessly combine elements from the inputs while ensuring compliance with brand guidelines and regulatory requirements (Forbes, 2024). A generative AI has been successfully used in the field of product packaging as well. For instance, based on a database of a variety of patterns and colors, Nutella used algorithms to create seven millions of different unique packaging designs for its Nutella jars, and the products with the AI-based packaging were sold out in just 1 month (Dezeen, 2017; Forbes, 2024).

Although the use of generative AI has been notable and important tremendously these days, there is dearth of research in the logo literature on this topic. As one exceptional case, Dew et al. (2022) examined how AI, specifically a multi-view representation learning, can improve the logo design and rebranding process. By linking a brand's logo design features and consumers' perceptions of its brand personality, the authors provided insights into creating or modifying a logo that better communicates a brand's identity and desired brand associations. This research emphasized the potential of AI and machine learning in implementing a data-driven logo design process and enhancing creativity in logo design, leading to an optimal integration between logo design features and a brand's targeted brand perception.

The evolution of visual brand identity underscores the enduring relationship between technological advancements and branding strategies. As brands navigate a rapidly evolving business landscape shaped by digital innovations and AI advancements, strategically managing visual brand identity has become essential than ever before. Future research should continue to examine how a brand's logo can evolve successfully by harmonizing technological advancements, visual appeal and brand authenticity to maintain relevance and impact.

FUTURE RESEARCH DIRECTIONS

Although the field of research in logo and visual brand identity has continued to evolve and offer invaluable insights, there are still promising areas that remain unexplored. In this section, building on the review of the existing literature on the role of logos in brand management and the key themes discussed earlier in this chapter, we provide researchers with a set of potential research questions that can significantly contribute to our current understanding of visual brand identity. Additionally, we propose methodologies and discuss potential implications of the research questions.

Future studies could not only further examine the role of each logo design element in a successful establishment of brand identity but also investigate how different logo design elements interact with each other to affect consumers' brand perceptions and brand equity. Moreover, further research is needed to assess the effects of logo execution across various consumer touchpoints on consumers' brand perceptions, attitudes and evaluations, and how logo execution can be effectively designed and implemented as intended. Given the rapidly changing business landscape due to the development of new digital media platforms and AI, another promising area of research involves assessing the impacts of the dynamic and interactive logos in digital media and investigating the role of AI in logo design process and consumers' responses toward logos designed by AI. Additionally, it could be important to examine how brands can successfully adapt the fast-changing logo design trends (e.g., minimalism) to enhance consumer engagement and ultimately increase their brand equity. In Table 6.1, we present a list of potential research topics and questions that can offer valuable insights for academics and brand managers.

To address the research questions listed in Table 6.1, researchers can use a variety of methodological approaches. While the most prior literature on logo and brand visual identity has relied on a controlled lab experiment where subjects are asked to provide their own subjective experiences and opinions about a logo through self-reported surveys or questionnaires, there has still been a dearth of research utilizing biometric tools to understand consumers' responses toward a brand visual identity. The biometric tools, such as eye-tracking, facial expression recognition, galvanic skin response, electroencephalogram and functional magnetic resonance imaging (fMRI), can capture consumers' subconscious reactions, real-time physiological and neurological responses, attention patterns and emotional engagement rather than relying on their conscious recall and subjective interpretation. Combining these tools with traditional lab experiments, we can better understand how consumers perceive and respond to logos and gain deeper insights into design effectiveness and consumers' cognitive processing that previous studies may overlook. Furthermore, since most brands keep updating their logos, more longitudinal studies that can monitor the effects of logo changes on consumer responses and brand equity over time are needed. Machine learning and AI-driven sentiment analysis can also be employed to evaluate consumer reactions to logo redesigns and forecast brand performance outcomes. Lastly, we suggest future researchers to implement a large-scale, cross-cultural or cross-industrial study, employing an in-depth interview with a variety of practitioners and consumers to obtain qualitative insights and deeper understanding of the effect of brand visual identity for a broader and more complete picture of this research field. This is because critical factors for logo effectiveness such as aesthetic preferences, symbolic interpretations, consumer expectations and brand associations can vary across different cultural contexts and industries.

The findings from the proposed future research directions have several theoretical and practical implications. From a theoretical perspective, future research can advance branding and consumer perception theories by exploring how consumer responses toward a brand visual identity differ across industries, customer segments, digital platforms and touchpoints. It can also provide insights into the underlying mechanisms driving logo effectiveness, including interaction among logo design elements and potential synergies between AI and human designers in logo creation. The proposed research questions can also broaden our understanding of cultural and industrial differences in logo evaluation, shedding light on how multi-national brands can adapt to evolving digital trends. Practically, future research can help brands refine their logo adaptation strategies to enhance consumer engagement and recognition in the fast-evolving digital environments. Additionally, insights into AI-generated logos guide companies in balancing automation with human creativity, ensuring alignment with brand positioning and industry expectations. Future research can also

Table 6.1 Future research directions

Research Area	*Future Research Directions*
Logo elements	• Is there a hierarchy among logo elements in terms of their influence on brand perception and evaluation? How do these elements interact to create an overall brand image? • How do the sub-dimensions of each logo element contribute to brand perception? How crucial is a detailed analysis of these micro-level elements for fully understanding their effect on brand perceptions? • How do marketers strategically design logo elements to achieve effective brand differentiation? What are the advantages and disadvantages of aligning with versus deviating from the industry norm in logo design?
Logo execution	• What role does each consumer touchpoint play in shaping consistent brand perceptions of a logo? What guidelines can inform the strategic prioritization of touchpoints for effective logo presentation? • What types of logo modifications do marketers consider or implement for various consumer touchpoints (e.g., color, shape, animation and simplification)? What specific logo modifications are recommended for each consumer touchpoint? • What strategic considerations should guide marketers in deciding when and how to adapt their logos for various consumer touchpoints? How can these adaptations balance brand consistency with the unique demands of each platform?
Logos in evolving business landscapes	• What is the impact of various digital platforms (e.g., smartphones, smartwatches and augmented reality (AR)/virtual reality (VR) devices) on how consumers perceive and evaluate logos? Do these platforms shape brand perceptions differently? • How do consumers perceive and evaluate the AI-generated logos compared to the traditionally designed logos (created by human designers)? How do AI-generated logos perform (in terms of brand perception and equity) across different industries and brands? • What is the optimal level of human designer involvement in the AI-driven logo design process? How can organizations select appropriate algorithms and ensure quality in AI-driven logo design?

Source: The authors.

highlight potential consumer backlash to AI-driven logo redesigns, helping brands develop strategies to mitigate consumers' negative reactions, particularly among high-loyal customers. Finally, understanding the role of training data quality, algorithms and designer inputs enables brands to optimize AI-driven logo design processes and allocate resources effectively.

CONCLUSION

This chapter reviewed the existing logo literature, discussing the role of logos in successful brand management. Given that each logo element (i.e., color, shape and typeface) contributes to brand identity, we encourage future research exploring the interplay of these elements in shaping overall brand image. Furthermore, since consistent logo presentation across touchpoints fosters brand familiarity and builds brand equity, we emphasized the importance of a cohesive cross-touchpoint logo execution strategy. We also discussed the emergence of digital media platforms, which may necessitate new logo presentation methods or design adaptations, and the increasing use of AI in logo design. Therefore, we call for future research investigating the role of AI in logo design and consumer responses to AI-generated logos. Ultimately, a deeper understanding of these evolving dynamics is crucial for effective brand management in the changing business landscape.

REFERENCES

Aaker, D. A. (1991). *Managing brand equity*. The Free Press, New York.

Aaker, D. A. (1996). Measuring brand equity across products and markets. *California Management Review*, *38*(3), 102–120. https://doi.org/10.2307/41165845

Airey, D. (2009). *Logo design love: A guide to creating iconic brand identities*. Pearson Education.

Alter, A. L., & Oppenheimer, D. M. (2009). Uniting the tribes of fluency to form a metacognitive nation. *Personality and Social Psychology Review*, *13*(3), 219–235. https://doi.org/10.1177/1088868309341564

Apple. (2024). Apple 2030: A plan as innovative as our products. Retrieved November 30, 2024, from www.apple.com/environment/

Batra, R., & Keller, K. L. (2016). Integrating marketing communications: New findings, new lessons, and new ideas. *Journal of Marketing*, *80*(6), 122–145. https://doi.org/10.1509/jm.15.0419

Baxendale, S., Macdonald, E. K., & Wilson, H. N. (2015). The impact of different touchpoints on brand consideration. *Journal of Retailing*, *9*(2), 235–253. https://doi.org/10.1016/j.jretai.2014.12.008

Berga, D., Fdez-Vidal, X. R., Otazu, X., Leborán, V., & Pardo, X. M. (2019). Psychophysical evaluation of individual low-level feature influences on visual attention. *Vision Research*, *154*, 60–79. https://doi.org/10.1016/j.visres.2018.10.006

Bettels, J., & Wiedmann, K.-P. (2019). Brand logo symmetry and product design: The spillover effects on consumer inferences. *Journal of Business Research*, *97*, 1–9. https://doi.org/10.1016/j.jbusres.2018.12.039

Bossel, V., Geyskens, K., & Goukens, C. (2019). Facing a trend of brand logo simplicity: The impact of brand logo design on consumption. *Food Quality and Preference*, *71*, 129–135. https://doi.org/10.1016/j.foodqual.2018.06.009

Bottomley, P. A., & Doyle, J. R. (2006). The interactive effects of colors and products on perceptions of brand logo appropriateness. *Marketing Theory*, *6*(1), 63–83. https://doi.org/10.1177/1470593106061263

Brasel, S. A., & Hagtvedt, H. (2016). Living brands: Consumer responses to animated brand logos. *Journal of the Academy of Marketing Science*, *44*(5), 639–653. https://doi.org/10.1007/s11747-015-0449-2

Buetti, S., Xu, J., & Lleras, A. (2019). Predicting how color and shape combine in the human visual system to direct attention. *Scientific Reports*, *9*, 20258. https://doi.org/10.1038/s41598-019-56238-9

Capitman, B. B. (1976). *American trademark designs: A survey of seven hundred and thirty two marks logos and corporate identity symbols*. Peter Smith Publisher Inc.

Celhay, F., & Luffarelli, J. (2024). Competent or sad blue? Lively or aggressive red? Why, how, and when background color shapes the meanings of logo hues. *Journal of Consumer Research*, *51*(4), 820–844. https://doi.org/10.1093/jcr/ucae019

Chen, Y.-S. A., & Bei, L.-T. (2020). The effects of logo frame design on brand extensions. *Journal of Product & Brand Management*, *29*(1), 97–113. https://doi.org/10.1108/JPBM-12-2017-1698

Childers, T. L., & Jass, J. (2002). All dressed up with something to say: Effects of typeface semantic associations on brand perceptions and consumer memory. *Journal of Consumer Psychology*, *12*(2), 93–106. https://doi.org/10.1207/S15327663JCP1202_03

Colman, A. M., Wober, J. M., & Norris, C. E. (1995). Sight bites: A study of viewers' impressions of corporate logos in the communications industry. *Journal of the Market Research Society*, *37*(4), 405–415. https://doi.org/10.1177/1470785395037004

de Lencastre, P., Machado, J. C., & Costa, P. (2023). The effect of brand names and logos' figurativeness on memory: An experimental approach. *Journal of Business Research*, *164*, 113944. https://doi.org/10.1016/j.jbusres.2023.113944

Deloitte. (2024). Deloitte 2025 predictions report 'Generative AI: Paving the way for a transformative future in technology, media and telecommunications.' Retrieved November 23, 2024, from www2.deloitte.com/us/en/pages/about-deloitte/articles/press-releases/deloitte-technology-media-telecom-2025-predictions.html

DelVecchio, D., Jones, W. J., & Baugh, L. (2024). From easy to known: How fluent brand processing fosters self-brand connection. *Psychology & Marketing*, *41*(4), 754–773. https://doi.org/10.1002/mar.21951

Dew, R., Ansari, A., & Toubia, O. (2022). Letting logos speak: Leveraging multiview representation learning for data-driven branding and logo design. *Marketing Science*, *41*(2), 401–425. https://doi.org/10.1287/mksc.2021.1326

Dezeen. (2017). Algorithm designs seven million different jars of Nutella. Retrieved November 23, 2024, from www.dezeen.com/2017/06/01/algorithm-seven-million-different-jars-nutella-packaging-design/

EMB Global. (2024). The role of AI in logo design: Future trends and current practices. Retrieved November 23, 2024, from https://blog.emb.global/role-of-ai-in-logo-design/

Entheos. (2024). The power of simplicity: Logo trends for a modern world. Retrieved November 30, 2024 from www.entheosweb.com/the-power-of-simplicity-logo-trends-for-a-modern-world/

Eyni, A., Thongpapanl, N., Ashraf, A. R., & Wang, K.-Y. (2023). The logo 'visual thickness effect': When and why it boosts brand personality. *Journal of Consumer Behavior*, *22*(2), 343–364. https://doi.org/10.1002/cb.2133

Fajardo, T. M., Zhang, J., & Tsiros, M. (2016). The contingent nature of the symbolic associations of visual design elements: The case of brand logo frames. *Journal of Consumer Research*, *43*(4), 549–566. https://doi.org/10.1093/jcr/ucw048

Forbes. (2024). Deloitte Digital using Adobe to bring personalization-at-scale to life. Retrieved November 23, 2024, from www.forbes.com/sites/tiriasresearch/2024/04/03/deloitte-digital-using-adobe-to-bring-personalization-at-scale-to-life/

Foroudi, P., Melewar, T. C., & Gupta, S. (2017). Corporate logo: History, definition, and components. *International Studies of Management & Organization*, *47*, 176–196. https://doi.org/10.1080/00208825.2017.1256166

Garg, A. K., Li, P., Rashid, M. S., & Callaway, E. M. (2019). Color and orientation are jointly coded and spatially organized in primate primary visual cortex. *Science*, 34(6447), 1275-1279. https://doi.org/10.1126/science.aaw5868

Gartner. (2023a). *Gartner says more than 80% of enterprises will have used generative AI APIs or deployed generative AI-enabled applications by 2026*. Gartner Newsroom. Retrieved November 23, 2024, from www.gartner.com/en/newsroom/press-releases/2023-10-11-gartner-says-more-than-80-percent-of-enterprises-will-have-used-generative-ai-apis-or-deployed-generative-ai-enabled-applications-by-2026

Gartner. (2023b). *How tech marketing teams are capitalizing on generative AI to improve content marketing*. Gartner Research. Retrieved November 23, 2024, from www.gartner.com/en/doc/785385-how-tech-marketing-teams-are-capitalizing-on-generative-ai-to-improve-content-marketing

Gregersen, M. K., & Johansen, T. S. (2018). Corporate visual identity: Exploring the dogma of consistency. *Corporate Communications: An International Journal*, *23*(3), 342–356. https://doi.org/10.1108/ccij-10-2017-0088

Grohmann, B., Giese, J. L., Parkman, I. D. (2013). Using type font characteristics to communicate brand personality of new brands. *Journal of Brand Management*, *20*, 389–403. https://doi.org/10.1057/bm.2012.23

Guido, G., Pichierri, M., Nataraajan, R., & Pino, G. (2016). Animated logos in mobile marketing communications: The roles of logo movement directions and trajectories. *Journal of Business Research*, *69*(12), 6048–6057. https://doi.org/10.1016/j.jbusres.2016.06.003

Gumber, S. (2023). Minimalism in design: A trend of simplicity in complexity. *ShodhKosh: Journal of Visual and Performing Arts*, *4*(2), 357–365. https://doi.org/10.29121/shodhkosh.v4.i2.2023.539

Gupta, T., & Hagtvedt, H. (2021). Safe together, vulnerable apart: How interstitial space in text logos impacts brand attitudes in tight versus loose cultures. *Journal of Consumer Research*, *48*(3), 474–491. https://doi.org/10.1093/jcr/ucab006

Hagtvedt, H. (2011). The impact of incomplete typeface logos on perceptions of the firm. *Journal of Marketing*, *75*(4), 86–93. https://doi.org/10.1509/jmkg.75.4.86

Hallikainen, H., Alamäki, A., & Laukkanen, T. (2019). Individual preferences of digital touchpoints: A latent class analysis. *Journal of Retailing and Consumer Services*, *50*, 386–393. https://doi.org/10.1016/j.jretconser.2018.07.014

Hamilton, R., & Price, L. L. (2019). Consumer journeys: Developing consumer-based strategy. *Journal of the Academy of Marketing Science*, *47*, 187–191. https://doi.org/10.1007/s11747-019-00636-y

Henderson, P. W., & Cote, J. A. (1998). Guidelines for selecting or modifying logos. *Journal of Marketing*, *62*(2), 14–30. https://doi.org/10.1177/002224299806200202

Henderson, P. W., Cote, J. A., Leong, S. M., & Schmitt, B. (2003). Building strong brands in Asia: Selecting the visual components of image to maximize brand strength. *International Journal of Research in Marketing*, *20*(4), 297–313. https://doi.org/10.1016/j.ijresmar.2003.03.001

Henderson, P. W., Giese, J. L., & Cote, J. A. (2004). Impression management using typeface design. *Journal of Marketing*, *68*(4), 60–72. https://doi.org/10.1509/jmkg.68.4.60.42736

Huang, H., Cai, Y., & Xu, L. (2021). Stability or instability: The impact of brand concepts on logo design preferences. *Journal of Brand Management*, *28*, 465–480. https://doi.org/10.1057/s41262-021-00238-6

Iigaya, K., Yi, S., Wahle, I. A., Tanwisuth, K., & O'Doherty, J. P. (2021). Aesthetic preference for art can be predicted from a mixture of low- and high-level visual features. *Nature Human Behavior*, *5*, 743–755. https://doi.org/10.1038/s41562-021-01124-6

Ingendahl, M., Schöne, T., Wänke, M., & Vogel, T. (2021). Fluency in the in-out effect: The role of structural mere exposure effects. *Journal of Experimental Social Psychology*, *92*, 104079. https://doi.org/10.1016/j.jesp.2020.104079

Janiszewski, C., & Meyvis, T. (2001). Effects of brand logo complexity, repetition, and spacing on processing fluency and judgment. *Journal of Consumer Research*, *28*(1), 18–32. https://doi.org/10.1086/321945

Jiang, Y., Gorn, G. J., Galli, M., & Chattopadhyay A. (2016). Does your company have the right logo? How and why circular- and angular-logo shapes influence brand attribute judgments. *Journal of Consumer Research*, *42*(5), 709–726. https://doi.org/10.1093/jcr/ucv049

Kapferer, J.-N. (2012). *The new strategic brand management: Advanced insights and strategic thinking*. Kogan Page.

Keller, K. L. (2013). *Strategic brand management: Building measuring, and managing brand equity*. Pearson Education.

Kim, A., & Maglio, S. J. (2021). Text is gendered: The role of letter case. *Marketing Letters: A Journal of Research in Marketing*, *32*(2), 179–190. https://doi.org/10.1007/s11002-021-09556-w

Kim, M. J., & Lim, J. H. (2019). A comprehensive review on logo literature: Research topics, findings, and future directions. *Journal of Marketing Management*, *35*(13–14), 1291–1365. https://doi.org/10.1080/0267257X.2019.1604563

Kohli, C., Suri, R., & Thakor, M. (2002). Creating effective logos: Insights from theory and Practice. *Business Horizons*, *45*(3), 58–64. https://doi.org/10.1016/s0007-6813(02)00203-3

Kuehnl, C., Jozic, D. & Homburg, C. (2019). Effective customer journey design: Consumers' conception, measurement, and consequences. *Journal of the Academy of Marketing Science*, *47*, 551–568. https://doi.org/10.1007/s11747-018-00625-7

Labrecque, L. I. (2020). Color research in marketing: Theoretical and technical considerations for conducting rigorous and impactful color research. *Psychology & Marketing*, *37*(7), 855–863. https://doi.org/10.1002/mar.21359

Labrecque, L. I., & Milne, G. R. (2012). Exciting red and competent blue: The importance of color in marketing. *Journal of the Academy of Marketing Science*, *40*(5), 711–727. https://doi.org/10.1007/s11747-010-0245-y

Labrecque, L. I., & Milne, G. R. (2013). To be or not to be different: Exploration of norms and benefits of color differentiation in the marketplace. *Marketing Letter*, *24*(2), 165–176. https://doi.org/10.1007/s11002-012-9210-5

Lee, A. Y., & Labroo, A. A. (2004). The effect of conceptual and perceptual fluency on brand evaluation. *Journal of Marketing Research*, *41*(2), 151–165. https://doi.org/10.1509/jmkr.41.2.151.28665

Lemon, K. N., & Verhoef, P. C. (2016). Understanding customer experience throughout the customer journey. *Journal of Marketing*, *80*(6), 69–96. https://doi.org/10.1509/jm.15.0420

Li, F. (Sam), & Ma, J. (2023). The effectiveness of the destination logo: Congruity effect between logo typeface and destination stereotypes. *Tourism Management*, *98*, 104772. https://doi.org/10.1016/j.tourman.2023.104772

Li, R., Wang, Y., & Zhang, H. (2023). The shape of premiumness: Logo shape's effects on perceived brand premiumness and brand preference. *Journal of Retailing and Consumer Services*, *75*, 103516. https://doi.org/10.1016/j.jretconser.2023.103516

Lieven, T., Grohmann, B., Herrmann, A., Landwehr, J. R., & van Tilburg, M. (2015). The effect of brand design on brand gender perceptions and brand preference. *European Journal of Marketing*, *49*(1/2), 146–169. https://doi.org/10.1108/EJM-08-2012-0456

Luffarelli, J., Stamatogiannakis, A., & Yang, H. (2019). The visual asymmetry effect: An interplay of logo design and brand personality on brand equity. *Journal of Marketing Research*, *56*(1), 89–103. https://doi.org/10.1177/0022243718820548

MacInnis, D. J., Shapiro, S., & Mani, G. (1999). Enhancing brand awareness through brand symbols. In E. J. Arnould, & L. M. Scott (Eds.), *Advances in consumer research* (Vol. *26*, p. 601). Association for Consumer Research.

Maechler, N., Neher, K., & Park, R. (2016). *From touchpoints to journeys: Seeing the world as customers do*. McKinsey & Company. Retrieved November 30, 2024, from www.mckinsey.com/capabilities/growth-marketing-and-sales/our-insights/from-touchpoints-to-journeys-seeing-the-world-as-customers-do#/

Mayer, S., & Landwehr, J. R. (2018). Quantifying visual aesthetics based on processing fluency theory: Four algorithmic measures for antecedents of aesthetic preferences. *Psychology of Aesthetics, Creativity, and the Arts*, *12*(4), 399–431. https://doi.org/10.1037/aca0000187

Meiting, L., & Hua, W. (2021). Angular or rounded? The effect of the shape of green brand logos on consumer perception. *Journal of Cleaner Production*, *279*, 123801. https://doi.org/10.1016/j.jclepro.2020.123801

Melewar, T. C. (2003). Determinants of the corporate identity construct: A review of the literature. *Journal of Marketing Communications*, *9*(4), 195–220. https://doi.org/10.1080/1352726032000119161

Morgan, C., Fajardo, T. M., & Townsend, C. (2021). Show it or say it: How brand familiarity influences the effectiveness of image-based versus text-based logos. *Journal of the Academy of Marketing Science*, *49*(3), 566–583. https://doi.org/10.1007/s11747-020-00760-0

Murphy, J. M., & Rowe, M. (1988). *How to design trademarks and logos*. Phaidon Press.

Napoles, V. (1988). *Corporate identity design*. Van Nostrand Reinhold.

Northey, G., & Chan, E. Y. (2020). Political conservatism and preference for (a)symmetric brand logos. *Journal of Business Research*, *115*, 149–159. https://doi.org/10.1016/j.jbusres.2020.04.049

Nunes, J. C., Ordanini, A., & Valsesia, F. (2015). The power of repetition: Repetitive lyrics in a song increase processing fluency and drive market success. *Journal of Consumer Psychology*, *25*(2), 187–199. https://doi.org/10.1016/j.jcps.2014.12.004

Park, C. W., Eisingerich, A. B., Pol, G., & Park, J. W. (2013). The role of brand logos in firm performance. *Journal of Business Research*, *66*(2), 180–187. https://doi.org/10.1016/j.jbusres.2012.07.011

Pichierri, M., & Pino, G. (2023). Less saturated, more eco-friendly: Color saturation and consumer perception of product sustainability. *Psychology & Marketing*, *40*(9), 1830–1849. https://doi.org/10.1002/mar.21858

Rapp, J. T., Swanson, G., Sheridan, S. M., Enloe, K. A., Maltese, D., Sennott, L. A., Shrader, L., Carroll, R. A., Richling, S. M., Long, E. S., & Lanovaz, M. J. (2013). Immediate and subsequent effects of matched and unmatched stimuli on targeted vocal stereotypy and untargeted motor stereotypy. *Behavior Modification*, *37*(4), 543–567. https://doi.org/10.1177/0145445512461650

Reddit. (2022). What is the mindset behind company's oversimplifying their logos? Retrieved November 30, 2024, from www.reddit.com/r/graphic_design/comments/10of6ym/what_is_the_mindset_behind_companys/

Rossignol, J. (2024). *RIP, Apple stickers (kind of)*. MacRumors. Retrieved November 30, 2024, from www.macrumors.com/2024/11/07/rip-apple-stickers-kind-of/

Sääksjärvi, M., van den Hende, E., Mugge, R., & van Peursem, N. (2015). How exposure to logos and logo varieties fosters brand prominence and freshness. *Journal of Product & Brand Management*, *24*(7), 736–744. https://doi.org/10.1108/jpbm-06-2014-0648

Salgado-Montejo, A., Velasco, C., Olier, J., Alvarado, J., & Spence, C. (2014). Love for logos: Evaluating the congruency between brand symbols and typefaces and their relation to emotional words. *Journal of Brand Management*, *21*(7–8), 635–649. https://doi.org/10.1057/bm.2014.29

Schlosser, A. E., Rikhi, R. R., & Dagogo-Jack, S. W. (2016). The ups and downs of visual orientation: The effects of diagonal orientation on product judgment. *Journal of Consumer Psychology*, *26*(4), 496–509. https://doi.org/10.1016/j.jcps.2016.01.003

Schwarz, N., Jalbert, M., Noah, T., & Zhang, L. (2021). Metacognitive experiences as information: Processing fluency in consumer judgment and decision making. *Consumer Psychology Review*, *4*(1), 4–25. https://doi.org/10.1002/arcp.1067

Song, J. (Flora), Xu, F. (Katie), & Jiang, Y. (2022). The colorful company: Effects of brand logo colorfulness on consumer judgments. *Psychology & Marketing*, *39*(8), 1610–1620. https://doi.org/10.1002/mar.21674

Stalzer, J. (2019). *Mastercard evolves its brand mark by dropping its name*. Mastercard Newsroom. Retrieved November 22, 2024, from newsroom.mastercard.com/news/press/2019/january/mastercard-evolves-its-brand-mark-by-dropping-its-name/

Sujitha, G. (2023). *Empowering logo design with Segmind's generative AI*. Analytics Vidhya. Retrieved November 23, 2024, from www.analyticsvidhya.com/blog/2023/10/empowering-logo-design-with-segminds-generative-ai/

Sundar, A., & Kellaris, J. J. (2017). How logo colors influence shoppers' judgments of retailer ethicality: The mediating role of perceived eco-friendliness. *Journal of Business Ethics*, *146*(3), 685–701. https://doi.org/10.1007/s10551-015-2918-4

Sundar, A., & Noseworthy, T. (2014). Place the logo high or low? Using conceptual metaphors of power in packaging design. *Journal of Marketing*, *78*(5), 138–151. https://doi.org/10.1509/jm.13.0253

Sutton, T. M., & Altarriba, J. (2016). Color associations to emotion and emotion-laden words: A collection of norms for stimulus construction and selection. *Behavior Research Methods*, *48*, 686–728. https://doi.org/10.3758/s13428-015-0598-8

Tang, Q., Huang, X. (Irene), & Zhang, K. (2022). Simple or complex logos? The impact of logo complexity on the brand perception. *Advances in Consumer Research*, 50, 222.

Teng, L., Xie, C., Liu, T., Wang, F., & Foti, L. (2021). The effects of uppercase vs. lowercase letters on consumers' perceptions and brand attitudes. *Journal of Business Research*, *136*, 164–175. https://doi.org/10.1016/j.jbusres.2021.07.013

Tian, Z., & Huang, C.-H. (2025). Effects of color-typeface congruence on product evaluation. *Journal of Retailing and Consumer Services*, *82*, 104104. https://doi.org/10.1016/j.jretconser.2024.104104

van der Lans, R., Cote, J. A., Cole, C. A., Leong, S. M., Smidts, A., Henderson, P. W., Bluemelhuber C., Bottomley, P. A., Doyle, J. R., Fedorikhin, A., & Moorthy, J. (2009). Cross-national logo evaluation analysis: An individual-level approach. *Marketing Science*, *28*(5), 968–985. https://doi.org/10.1287/mksc.1080.0462

van Grinsven, B., & Das, E. (2014). Logo design in marketing communications: Brand logo complexity moderates exposure effects on brand recognition and brand attitude. *Journal of Marketing Communications*, *22*(3), 256–270. https://doi.org/10.1080/13527266.2013.866593

Vazofsky, M. (2024). Visual identity trends: The latest in logo design and brand aesthetics. Aspect Journal. Retrieved November 22, 2024, from https://aspectusjournal.com/2024/09/17/visual-identity-trends-the-latest-in-logo-design-and-brand-aesthetics/

Verhoef, P. C., Lemon, K. N., Parasuraman, A., Roggeveen, A., Tsiros, M., & Schlesinger, L. A. (2009). Customer experience creation: Determinants, dynamics and management strategies. *Journal of Retailing*, *85*(1), 31–41. https://doi.org/10.1016/j.jretai.2008.11.001

Vogel, T., Silva, R. R., Thomas, A., & Wänke, M. (2020). Truth is in the mind, but beauty is in the eye: Fluency effects are moderated by a match between fluency source and judgment dimension. *Journal of Experimental Psychology: General*, *149*(8), 1587–1596. https://doi.org/10.1037/xge0000731

Walsh, M. F., Winterich, K. P., & Mittal, V. (2010). Do logo redesigns help or hurt your brand? The role of brand commitment. *Journal of Product & Brand Management*, *19*(2), 76–84. https://doi.org/10.1108/10610421011033421

Wang, M., & Li, X. (2017). Effects of the aesthetic design of icons on app downloads: Evidence from an android market. *Electronic Commerce Research*, *17*(1), 83–102. https://doi.org/10.1007/s10660-016-9245-4

Wedel, M., & Pieters, R. (Eds.). (2008). *Visual marketing: From attention to action*. Taylor & Francis Group/Lawrence Erlbaum Associates.

Wen, N., & Lurie, N. H. (2018). The case for compatibility: Product attitudes and purchase intentions for upper versus lowercase brand names. *Journal of Retailing*, *94*(4), 393–407. https://doi.org/10.1016/j.jretai.2018.10.002

Wertz, R. A. (2023). Brand new: How visual context shapes initial response to logos and corporate visual identity systems. *Journal of Product & Brand Management*, *32(8)*, 1388–1398. https://doi.org/10.1108/JPBM-08-2022-4124

Whitenton, K. (2017, December 19). *Website logo placement for maximum brand recall*. Nielsen Norman Group. www.nngroup.com/articles/logo-placement-brand-recall/

Whittlesea, B. W. A. (1993). Illusions of familiarity. *Journal of Experimental Psychology: Learning, Memory, and Cognition*, *19*(6), 1235–1253. https://doi.org/10.1037/0278-7393.19.6.1235

Xiao, C., Zhu, H., Wang, X., & Wu, L. (2021). Vividly warm: The color saturation of logos on brands' customer sensitivity judgment. *Color Research and Application*, *46*(6), 147–1359. https://doi.org/10.1002/col.22682

Xu, X., Chen, R., & Liu, M. W. (2017). The effects of uppercase and lowercase wordmarks on brand perceptions. *Marketing Letters: A Journal of Research in Marketing*, *28*(3), 449–460. https://doi.org/10.1007/s11002-016-9415-0

Yu, Y., Zhou, X., Wang, L., & Wang, Q. (2022). Uppercase premium effect: The role of brand letter case in brand premiumness. *Journal of Retailing*, *98*(2), 335–355. https://doi.org/10.1016/j.jretai.2021.03.002

Zajonc, R. B. (1968). Attitudinal effects of mere exposure. *Journal of Personality and Social Psychology*, *9*(2 Pt. 2), 1–27. https://doi.org/10.1037/h0025848

Zhang, L., Atari, M., Schwarz, N., Newman, E. J., & Afhami, R. (2022). Conceptual metaphors, processing fluency, and aesthetic preference. *Journal of Experimental Social Psychology*, *98*, 104247. https://doi.org/10.1016/j.jesp.2021.104247

7

Brand Identity, Brand Reputation and Brand Image in the B2B Context

Sheena Leek

INTRODUCTION

In the past, branding in business-to-business (B2B) marketing was often perceived as irrelevant or gimmicky and as a tool for business-to-consumer (B2C) companies (McDowell Mudambi et al., 1997). However, this perception has been changing, as B2B branding has been found to convey a number of advantages. It can improve perceptions of the quality (Balmer, 2010; Cretu & Brodie, 2007), technology used, after-sales service (Leek & Christodoulides, 2012), it provides the basis for differentiation (Kapferer, 2008; Törmälä & Saraniemi, 2018), confers uniqueness (Marvi et al., 2024; Michell et al., 2001; Shankar et al., 2024) and enables a premium price to be charged (Low & Blois, 2002; Marvi et al., 2024; Ohnemus, 2009). It helps to maintain financial performance (Marvi et al., 2024). A brand raises the barriers to entry for other companies (Michell et al., 2001) and helps reduce counterfeiting (Iglesias et al., 2020). Companies with a brand can communicate more effectively with their buyers (Brown et al., 2012) and their communications will be more readily accepted (Low & Blois, 2002; Michell et al., 2001; Ohnemus, 2009). Brands are also more likely to receive referrals (Bendixen et al., 2004).

From the buyers' perspective, their confidence in and satisfaction with their purchase can be increased by a brand (Low & Blois, 2002; Michell et al., 2001; Ohnemus, 2009). Brands can provide buyers with reassurance and a feel-good factor (Leek & Christodoulides, 2012; Mudambi, 2002) and reduce the level of uncertainty and perceived risk associated with a purchase (Balmer, 2010; Bengtsson & Servais, 2005; Brown et al., 2012; Leek & Christodoulides, 2012; Mudambi, 2002; Ohnemus, 2009). In addition, buyers may be more loyal to a brand (McQuiston, 2004; Marvi et al., 2024), which can lead to the rejection of competitors (Low & Blois, 2002; Ohnemus, 2009).

The aforementioned advantages have led to branding in the B2B context becoming increasingly important. In 2024 for example, Microsoft was the second best global brand with an estimated value of $352.5 m (US dollars), and Cisco was ranked 13th with an estimated value of $45.5 m (US dollars) (Interbrand, n.d.). This chapter examines how, in order to reap the benefits, companies need to understand what brand identity is whilst acknowledging how it contributes to brand reputation. It investigates how buyers construct their suppliers' brand image and also determines how brand identity is co-created by both suppliers and buyers.

BRAND IDENTITY

In order to capitalize on the advantages of a brand, it is necessary for a company to develop a brand identity. A brand identity is the company's perception of the brand (Kapferer, 2012) that has been determined by the managers (Rode & Vallaster, 2005). Within the B2C context, a considerable amount of research has been carried out to determine what brand identity is resulting in the theoretical development of brand identity models, for example, de Chernatony's (2003) brand identity model and Kapferer's (2012) brand identity prism. These B2C models are examined in more detail below before looking at two B2B models, that is, Rode and Vallaster's (2004) corporate identity and Coleman et al.'s (2011) service brand identity network to determine their similarities and differences both within and across the contexts.

de Chernatony's (2003) Brand Identity Model

de Chernatony's (2003) brand identity model is captured in Figure 7.1. He states that the brand vision is central to brand identity and encapsulates the purpose of the brand, its values and the direction of the brand for the future. Culture reflects that of the organization and consists of the visible artefacts, for example, office layout, the organization's values and its basic assumptions (Schein, 1984). The brand vision and culture contribute to the construction of the personality of the brand, that is, its anthropomorphization. These elements contribute to determining the positioning of the brand in the market and where it will lie in comparison to its competitors.

Relationships play a role in influencing the various elements of brand identity. The employees' willingness to take on board the brand identity is influenced by their relationships with managers. This, in turn, affects how the employees enact brand values with customers and other stakeholders. A unified understanding of the brand vision, culture, personality and positioning facilitates a strong presentation of the brand identity. The interactions between the various elements are two-way, for example, the staff–customer relationship simultaneously influences and is influenced by the personality of the brand.

Kapferer's (2012) Brand Prism

Kapferer's (2012) brand prism like de Chernatony's (2003) brand identity model was also developed for the B2C context. Kapferer's (2012) brand prism perceives brand identity as being made up of six facets – physique, personality, culture, relationship, reflection and self-image – all of which are interrelated (see Figure 7.2).

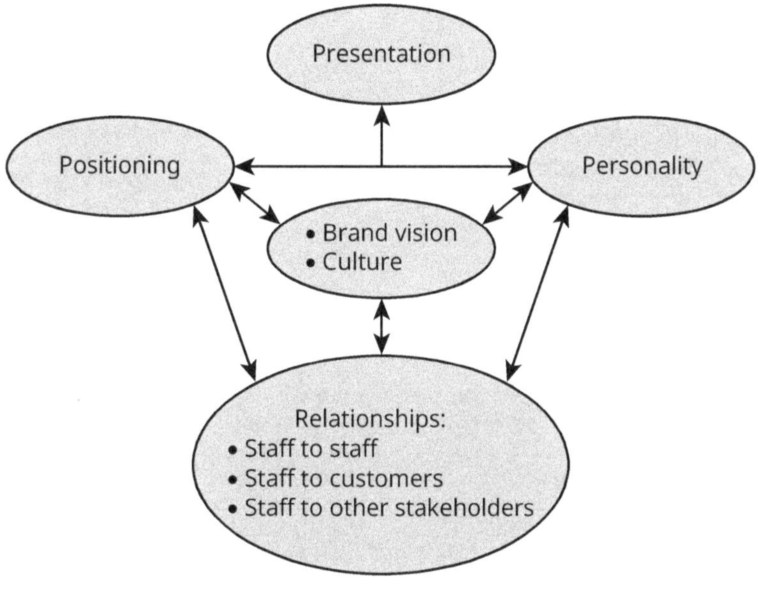

Figure 7.1 de Chernatony's (2003) components of brand identity

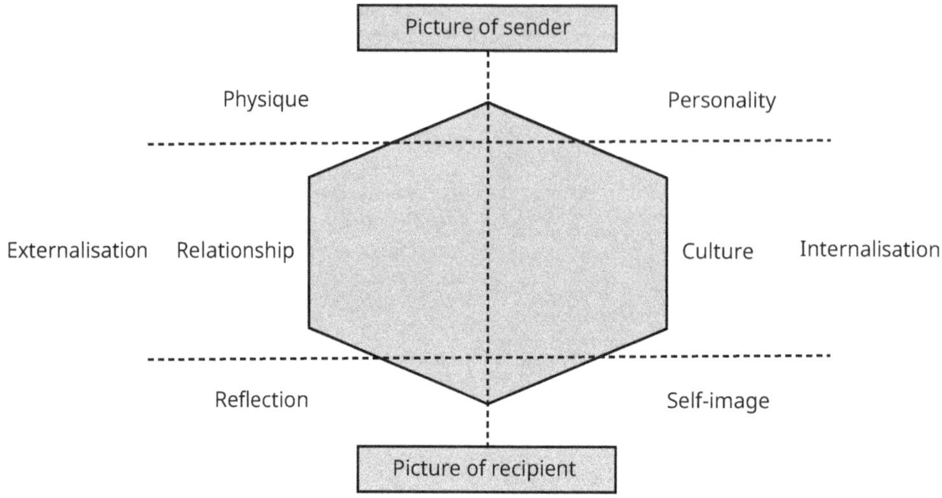

Figure 7.2 Kapferer's brand identity prism

- Physique – The physique refers to the tangible, physical features of the brand.
- Personality – A brand has a character or personality which has been developed and communicated over time. This brand personality enables the customer to identify with the brand.
- Culture – Brands are both driven by culture and convey the organization's culture, both of which are encapsulated in this facet.
- Relationships – Brands can represent different kinds of relationships, for example, love, friendship. They are also represented in service interactions.
- Customer reflection – Brands through communications will build a reflection of the customer of the brand (they are). It indicates how the customer wishes to be perceived.
- Self-image – Customers develop an inner relationship with a brand (I am).

The prism is based on the idea that brands 'speak' so there is a sender of communications conveyed by the physique and personality and there is a receiver of communications captured by both the customer reflection and the self-image. There is a vertical line on the prism; the social facets to the left – physique, relationship and reflection – convey the brand's external/outward expression and the facets to the right – personality, culture, self-image – are those incorporated in the brand itself.

There are commonalities between de Chernatony's (2003) and Kapferer's (2012) B2C models. Both models recognize the importance of brand personality. Common to both models is the culture of the organization, but Kapferer (2012) additionally acknowledges the contribution of societal culture. Whilst relationships are also mentioned in both models they are interpreted differently; Kapferer (2012) identifies the nature of the relationship encapsulated by the brand and also recognizes the importance of staff relationships with the customers, while de Chernatony (2003) recognizes not only the influence of relationships between the staff and customers but also those between staff and other stakeholders. There are also more substantial differences between the models. Kapferer (2012) in physique acknowledges the physical qualities of the brand; however, these are not explicitly included in de Chernatony's (2003) model, which instead concentrates on the vision. Kapferer's (2012) model includes reflection and self-image, neither of which is included in de Chernatony's (2003) model.

There has not been a widespread acceptance or integration of either de Chernatony's (2003) or Kapferer's (2012) models into B2B research. Research applying these models to B2B contexts is limited, for example, the brand prism has been applied to South African B2B banks (Zwakala & Steenkamp, 2021). Within the B2B context, research has led to the development of brand identity models; Rode and Vallaster (2005) discussed the concept of corporate brand identity and Coleman et al. (2011) developed a brand identity scale for B2B service contexts. As in the B2C context, the purpose of B2B brand identity is to convey the brand to the outside world (Koporcic & Halinen, 2018), demonstrate that the brand is unique and relevant (Iglesias et al., 2020; Kapferer, 2008; Shankar et al., 2024) and differentiate it from its competitors (de Chernatony, 1999). Brand identity is traditionally perceived as being created internally and as stable over time (Essamri et al., 2019; Koporcic & Halinen, 2018). Consequently, the B2B models have many components in common with both de Chernatony's (2003) and Kapferer's (2012) B2C models and with each other. There are differences between the B2C and B2B models and the B2B models themselves, which are discussed in more detail below after describing the B2B models.

Rode and Vallaster's (2005) Corporate Identity Model

Rode and Vallaster (2005) perceived corporate brand identity as being composed of corporate culture/personality, corporate design, corporate behavior and corporate communications, all of which are interrelated and influence each other (see Figure 7.3). Central to corporate culture is the mission statement, which encompasses the core values and philosophy of the company. Corporate design relates to the visual elements of the corporate brand, which includes logos, symbols, jingles and characters. Corporate behavior refers to the recruitment of employees and empowering and supporting them. Corporate communication consists of both internal and external communications and how these stakeholders are reached. Corporate identity is the sum of these components within the company. It is conveyed externally through communication channels to the various targeted stakeholder groups who use this information to construct their corporate brand image.

Coleman et al. (2011) Brand Identity Model

Coleman et al.'s (2011) model focuses on brand identity for B2B services and in contrast to Rode and Vallaster's (2005) approach does not include brand image. Coleman et al.'s (2011) brand identity encompasses five facets: human resource initiatives, employee and client focus, brand personality, corporate visual identity and consistent communications (see Figure 7.4). The human resource initiatives refer to the importance of employees both within the organization and in responding to clients. Employee and client focus considers the training and performance of employees. Brand personality, as with de Chernatony (2003) and Kapferer's (2012) B2C models, is the attribution of human characteristics to the brand. Corporate visual identity encompasses the logos, symbols, etc., which are used to communicate the brand, and consistent communications refers to the necessity for companies to convey the same message through various channels. These dimensions have synergies, which are integrated to reflect brand identity holistically as shown in Figure 7.4.

Coleman et al. (2011) and Rode and Vallaster (2005) applied elements of the B2C models to the

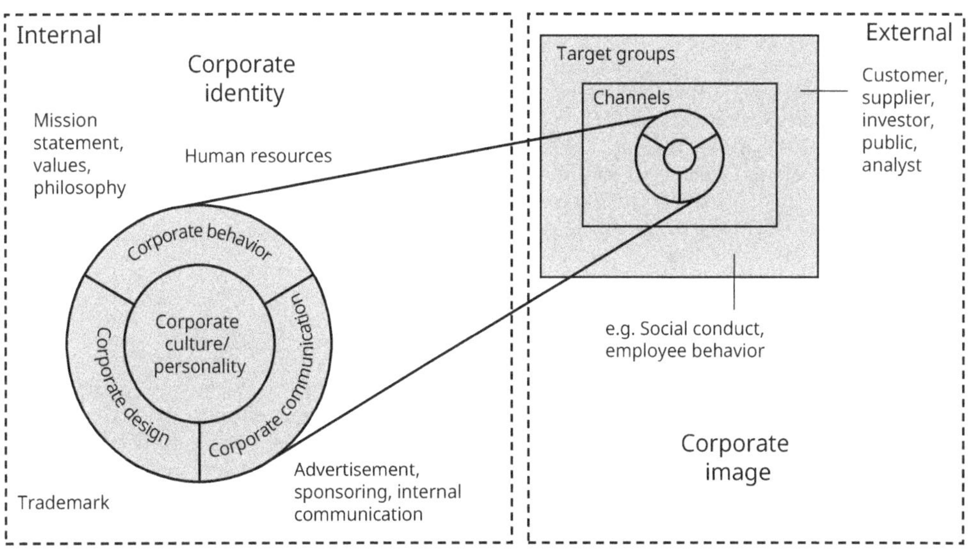

Figure 7.3 A holistic approach to corporate branding (Rode, 2004 in Rode & Vallaster, 2005)

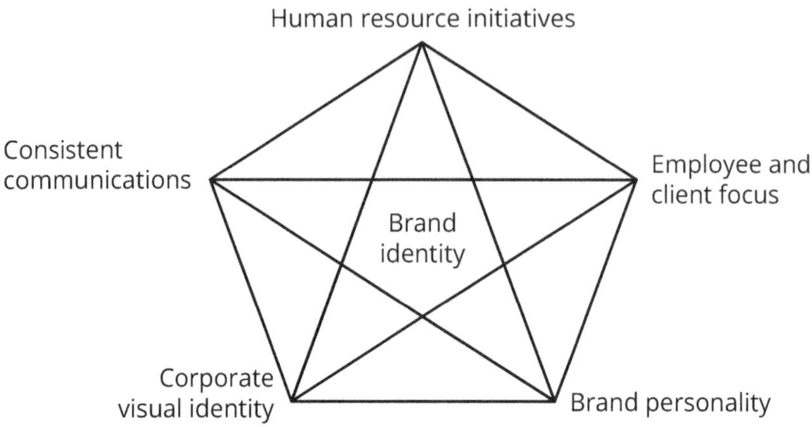

Figure 7.4 The B2B service brand identity network (Coleman et al., 2011)

B2B context, that is, visual identity, personality, relationships and culture. B2C facets of brand identity have been adapted to reflect the specific demands of the B2B context. Both Coleman et al.'s (2011) and Rode and Vallaster (2005) models have included the corporate visual identity encompassing logos, symbols, etc. Interestingly, both B2B models have included brand personality in their B2B contexts. Keller (2003) perceived personality to be less important in B2B marketing as customers have fewer psychological needs. Relationships are considered in both the B2C and the B2B models with all of them considering the relationship with the customer. Coleman et al.'s (2011), de Chernatony (2003) and Rode and Vallaster (2005) all consider other stakeholders besides the customer, such as investors, suppliers, etc. Employee-related elements have a greater emphasis in both B2B models; in Rode and Vallaster's (2005) model, there is corporate behavior, and in Coleman et al.'s (2011) model, there are two components, employee and client focus and human resources issues. In de Chernatony (2003) and Kapferer's (2012) B2C models, communication is not considered as a facet of brand identity but as an activity to be done to mobilize brand identity. In contrast, communications are common to both B2B models but refer to different aspects of communications, with Rode and Vallaster (2005) including communications with both internal and external parties and Coleman et al. (2011) focusing more on the consistency of messaging. Culture was incorporated in both B2C models. It is also present in Rode and Vallaster's (2005) B2B model, which explicitly identifies corporate culture as encompassing the mission, values and philosophy of the organization, whereas this aspect is not included in Coleman et al.'s (2011) model. Both of the B2B models are operating at the corporate level of B2B branding. With Rode and Vallaster's (2005) model, there may be difficulties applying it to a house of brands or individual brand due to the need to reconcile the corporate facets, for example, mission, values, with those of the brand(s). Whilst Rode and Vallaster's (2005) model does not specifically state whether it was developed for a product or a service context, Coleman et al.'s (2011) model was developed specifically for the B2B service context and may need to be adapted to a product context.

Although there is development of brand identity models in both the B2C and B2B context with similarities and differences occurring, currently, there is no widely accepted model of B2B brand identity and the lack of theory development generally in B2B marketing is a problem (Keränen et al., 2012). Past application of B2C models to the B2B context is limited and may not be wholly appropriate (Keränen et al., 2012). In transferring B2C constructs to B2B, there may be problems with the conceptualization of constructs, the equivalency of constructs and the measurement scales used.

B2B Brand Architecture

Brand identity development will depend on the brand architecture utilized. The B2C and B2B brand identity models take a corporate perspective of brand identity, with regard to the B2B models, Rode and Vallaster (2005) focus on corporate brand identity, and similarly, Coleman et al. (2011) focus on the service context, seemingly at the corporate level. Different brand architectures may require the elements of the brand identity models to be adapted accordingly. The different brand architectures, that is, corporate brand, house of brands and mixed branding that may be used in both the B2C and the B2B context are discussed in more detail below.

The corporate brand strategy entails the company name being dominant in endorsing its products or services. The company name is an integral part of the product name, and it is used by subsidiaries and at all company levels, for example, Hewlett Packard (Rao et al., 2004). Hewlett Packard abbreviated as HP is an integral part of the vast majority of its products' names, and its subsidiaries, for example, HP Teradici (Teradici, 2024). This approach facilitates the further introduction of products and services at a lower financial cost as the company is using and building on the current brand equity and will not need to spend as much on advertising and promotion as would be necessary with a new brand. It enables economies of scale when marketing its products, and it also costs less when introducing new products (Rao et al., 2004).

A house of brands strategy does not utilize the corporate name or the name of subsidiaries instead using individual product names (Rao et al., 2004), for example, Novartis (Novartis, 2024). This approach is less common in the B2B context because it is costly, there are no economies of scale when advertising or promoting, and it is necessary to build a new brand for the new product (Rao et al., 2004). This approach demands more shelf space in retailers, but this is not always applicable in the B2B context, where buyers may be dealing directly with the company.

The mixed brand strategy includes using a set of house brand names and using the corporate name for specific products (Rao et al., 2004), for example, Brembo, FedEx, General Electric, Microsoft. General Electric is composed of GE Aerospace, GE Vernova and GE Healthcare (General Electric, 2024). Brembo's brands include Brembo, Brembo Racing, AP Racing, SBS Friction, J. Juan, Marchesini, Bybre (Brembo, 2024).

Each strategy has advantages and disadvantages for the supplier and the customer, which are depicted in Table 7.1 (Rao et al., 2004). The mixed brand strategy combines both the advantages and the disadvantages of both the corporate brand and the house brand strategies.

It may be difficult for B2B companies to determine what branding strategy they should be utilizing. Richter (2007) quoted in Baumgarth (2010) found that 31% of B2B companies concentrated on a corporate brand strategy and 47% utilized both corporate branding with another type of brand architecture. However, this research is somewhat dated and it is difficult to say whether it reflects B2B companies' current brand strategies. Baumgarth (2010) suggested the dominance of the mixed approach to branding may be due to issues including short product life cycles, the number of product variations, and customization and these issues continue to be pertinent for many B2B companies. The fact that there are multiple approaches to brand architecture may be contributing to the lack of B2B brand identity theory development. Further research is required to investigate companies' reasons for their brand architecture and to determine how B2B brand identity models might vary with different brand architectures with the aim of facilitating effective brand management.

Table 7.1 Supply- and demand-side advantages and disadvantages of different branding strategies (Rao et al., 2004)

	Supply-Side Advantages (+) and Disadvantages (–)	*Demand-Side Advantages (+) and Disadvantages (–)*
Corporate branding	Economies of scale in marketing (+)	Easier extension of brands (+)
	Total costs of advertising/promotion can be lower (+)	Limits firm's ability to expand into some categories (–)
	Lower costs of creating brand equity (+)	Higher cannibalization among firm's brands likely (–)
	Lower costs of new product introductions (+)	Efficient means to communicate to various stakeholders (+)
House of brands	No identifiable economies of scale in marketing (–)	Distinctly customized brands can be offered (+)
	Higher costs of advertising (–)	Lower cannibalization (+)
	Can command larger retail shelf space (+)	
	Significantly higher costs of new product introductions (–)	
Mixed branding	Combination of advantages and disadvantages of corporate branding and house of brands	Combination of advantages and disadvantages of corporate branding and house of brands

REPUTATION

Reputation encompasses how stakeholders think, feel and talk about the brand/company (Rust et al., 2021) and corporate reputation is the overall appraisal of the company by its stakeholders. Reputation has been distinguished from brand identity. It is suggested reputation is the image of the brand/company perceived by all of its stakeholders (Abratt & Kleyn, 2012; Fombrun et al., 2000; Mudambi, 2002), which includes not just the customers, but suppliers, investors, shareholders, the general public, etc. This is in contrast to brand identity, which is the construction of the company. Reputation can be perceived as the collective stakeholders' assessment as to whether the company is meeting the expectations and commitments stated by the brand identity (Cretu & Brodie, 2007). As with brand identity, reputation can be discussed at the corporate level or the brand level. Brand reputation is potentially similar to corporate reputation when the company uses a corporate brand strategy, for example, Hewlett Packard (Rust et al., 2021). Brand reputation can be perceived as a component of corporate reputation when a house of brands strategy is used, for example, Novartis (Rust et al., 2021).

A positive reputation is a valuable asset and has been linked to the performance of the company (Rust et al., 2021), including share performance (Kapferer, 2012). It is linked to the ability of the company to create and deliver value (Harvey et al., 2017; Iglesias et al., 2020; Pfarrer et al., 2017). Customers perceive a brand/company with a positive reputation as more reliable (Brady et al., 2008) and more trustworthy (Ahmadi & Ataei, 2024). It attracts more customers (Fombrun, 2012; Milewicz & Herbig, 1994) and positively influences customer loyalty (Iglesias et al., 2020).

Although there is not a universally accepted definition of brand or corporate reputation (Baruah & Panda, 2020), a number of common characteristics of corporate reputation have emerged. Brand and corporate reputation can be either positive or negative (Rust et al., 2021). It has a temporal aspect in that a good reputation is developed and established over time through consistent positive evaluations (Caviggioli et al., 2020; Petkova, 2012). Although the aim of a company is to maintain a positive, stable reputation, it is dynamic. Changes in brand reputation are influenced by brand/corporate events; these may be controlled events, for example, marketing events such as product launches or they may be uncontrollable events (Rust et al., 2021), for example, product failure. Crowdstrike's software failure adversely affected airports, GPs, pharmacies and banking and its reputation (Edser et al., 2024; Washkuch, 2024). Changing reputation takes time, and there is often a lag between the action taken and the outcome (Shapiro, 1983).

Baruah and Panda (2020) developed their definition of corporate reputation which encompasses these characteristics; they state that '*Corporate reputation is a dynamic intangible asset built through a consistent assessment and value judgement of the cumulative behavior and characteristics of a company in order to influence the cognitive structure of the decision-makers in every value creating process of the company*' (p. 142). This definition of reputation does not specifically identify the company characteristics and behaviors which are being evaluated by the stakeholders. A number of scales have been developed for companies to measure their reputation. Fombrun et al. (2000) examined a number of measures of reputation including the Fortune AMAC, Fortune GAC, Manager Magazine, Asian Business, Far Eastern Economic Review, Financial Times and Industry Review. Similarly, Baruah and Panda (2020) examined Fortune, Management Today, Financial Times, Capital, Spanish Monitor of Corporate Reputation, Business World, Harris-Fombrun, Schwaiger, Reputation Institute, the Brady model, Trotto and Cavallaro measures of reputation. Both of these studies examined the similarities and differences of the qualities used to capture and measure reputation. Fombrun et al.'s (2000) study found the scales had a number of similar qualities in common, including qualities of products and services, quality of management, long-term investment value, financial soundness, the ability to attract and retain talent, responsibility to the environment and the community. There were some qualities only a few of the measures had in common; these included innovativeness, wise use of corporate assets, communication ability, overall admiration, successful change management, robust and human corporate culture and globalization of business and markets (Fombrun et al., 2000). There were a series of unique qualities included across the various measurement scales including maximizing customer satisfaction and loyalty, being a company others try to emulate, and company awareness (Fombrun et al., 2000). Baruah and Panda (2020) found the measures of reputation included in their research captured 10 dimensions, quality of management, quality of products and services, innovation, long-term investment value, financial soundness, people practices and talent management, global competitiveness, use of corporate assets, quality of marketing, and ethics and transparency. Corporate social responsibility (CSR) including environmental practices has become increasingly important (Noor Rashidah Mohd Sofia et al., 2023). While the majority of Baruah and Panda's (2020) qualities overlap with Fombrun et al.'s (2000), they included a new quality, ethics and transparency. Fombrun et al. (2000) criticized the measures, stating they lacked content validity. Baruah and Panda (2020) agree, claiming the concept of reputation and its measurement in the past was rather vague and abstract. Whilst many of the measures examine the concept of overall reputation, it has been argued that it is important to study the dimensions to understand how they function and interact with other variables (Walsh & Beatty, 2007). It is also necessary for companies to see how they are performing on each of the dimensions so that actions can be taken by them to address any issues (Walsh & Beatty, 2007). In the past, research has often focused on obtaining the perceptions of financial analysts and executives rather than multiple stakeholders (Fombrun et al., 2000). However, it has been suggested that stakeholders' perceptions of a company's reputation will vary depending on their background, economic, social situation (Fombrun, 1996) and their relationship to the company (Dowling, 2001). Consequently, a company's reputation may vary depending on the stakeholder group (Wartick, 2002). Wartick (2002) suggests that customers have the most influence on reputation, as through their interactions, they will have experienced whether the company delivers its brand identity.

Reputation as a concept is evolving in what it means for both companies and their stakeholders. It is dynamic as stakeholders assess the company's performance on the various reputation dimensions over time. As a positive reputation influences the company's performance, that is, it attracts customers (Fombrun, 2012), enhances perceptions of reliability (Brady et al., 2008), improves share performance (Kapferer, 2012) and loyalty (Iglesias et al., 2020), the company needs to monitor how its stakeholders perceive their reputation so they can address any negative issues.

BRAND IMAGE

Brand image resides in the minds of the company's external stakeholders and other audiences (Hatch & Schultz, 2003). It is the overall perception of how external stakeholders and other audiences perceive the brand (de Chernatony, 2003; Dobni & Zinkhan, 1990; Veloutsou & Mouthino, 2009). If a company is using a corporate branding strategy, then the corporate reputation may overlap significantly with the corporate brand image. In contrast, if a company is using a house of brands strategy, then there will be less overlap between the products' brand image and corporate reputation.

This section firstly examines how brand image, as developed by management, is formed in customers' minds in the B2C and B2B contexts. Corporate brand identity is linked to corporate brand image, as illustrated in Figure 7.3 (Rode, 2004 in Rode & Vallaster, 2005). Corporate identity is conveyed by the company through various communication channels to its stakeholders in the outside world. These communications convey the culture, the personality, the visual identification of the corporate brand or the product/service brand. Various channels are used to communicate with stakeholders including the logo, advertisements, websites, social media, sponsorship, trade shows and sales representatives (Higgins & Bannister, 1992; Keller & Swaminathan, 2020). In order to form the brand image, stakeholders take the communications about brand identity, break them down to decode them and interpret them to extract meaning (Kapferer, 2012) and encode them to develop their interpretation of the brand image. Sources of information external to the company include competitors, investors, regulatory bodies, the media and stakeholders' experience with the products and interactions with the company, all of which contribute to the establishment and maintenance of brand image (Keller & Swaminathan, 2020). Ideally, companies want their customers to perceive the company or the brand in the way they intended, so that the brand identity and brand image are the same or very similar. However, the development of brand image is not entirely in the company's control (Hatch & Schultz, 2003), and consequently, there may be a difference between the brand identity and brand image (de Chernatony, 2003). The brand image held by stakeholders is subjective and can be discussed, negotiated and contested (Iglesias & Bonet, 2012; Iglesias et al., 2020). Companies need to maintain an up-to-date understanding of stakeholders' brand image to ensure that the positive associations are being understood in the intended way and that any negative, unintended associations are eliminated.

In the B2C context, the brand image has been said to be based upon the functional and emotional associations that consumers develop about the brand (Bruhn et al., 2012; Schivinski et al., 2020). The functional associations are related to the tangible, utilitarian qualities of the brand (e.g., quality) whereas the emotional aspects are related to the intangible aspects of the brand – such as how the brand contributes to self-image (Aaker, 1996; Keller & Swaminathan, 2020; Schivinski et al., 2020). These associations are formed in relation to the attributes of the brand and the benefits they convey to the consumer (Park et al., 1986). The importance of the emotional elements in purchase decisions has long been acknowledged in the B2C context. In contrast, in the B2B context, for a long time, branding was considered irrelevant as B2B buyers were perceived as rational and as relying more on functional attributes when considering their purchase decisions (Bendixen et al., 2004; Leek & Christodoulides, 2012). Research into buying criteria highlighted the importance of tangible elements, with quality, price and delivery most frequently being found to be the most important attributes (Abratt, 1986; Billesbach et al., 1991; Lehmann & O'Shaughnessy, 1974; Perreault & Russ, 1976; Wind et al., 1968). The brand in itself was not mentioned as a supplier selection criterion in these studies. There is increasing recognition that businesses need to establish brands which connect emotionally with buyers, enabling trust within relationships to be established (Lynch & de Chernatony, 2007). The importance of relationships in the B2B context has long been emphasized (Håkansson, 1982) and is discussed in more detail below.

The Role of Brand Image and Reputation in B2B Buying

Much of the theorizing of and research into brand identity, brand reputation and brand image has been done in the B2C context, which differs from the B2B context. Within the B2C context, there is limited interaction between the suppliers and the customers and consequently customers are relying on the brand image they have formed via official company mass media communications, for example, adverts, social media posts, sponsorship and through communications from various other stakeholders including friends and family, unofficial social media groups, social media influencers, etc. The B2B context, while requiring the use of mass media, may rely more heavily on face-to-face interactions, which leads to the development of personal relationships. This section specifically examines the various types of buying situations to determine when and how brand image and reputation might be influential factors.

Interestingly, past research has found that brand did not figure in buyers' selection criteria for suppliers when questioned (Abratt, 1986; Billesbach et al., 1991; Lehmann & O'Shaughnessy, 1974; Perreault & Russ, 1976; Wind et al., 1968). Buyers' selection criteria tended to focus on the functional attributes of the product/service such as quality, technical specifications, maintenance and after sales support. Intangible criteria were also used including previous experience with and confidence in the salesman, past experience with the company and reputation. Although brand image is not explicitly mentioned, these attributes will be utilized to varying degrees to construct the brand image from the communications received from both the company and other sources and through interactions with the company. Reputation was mentioned as a criterion for evaluating suppliers (Abratt, 1986; Lehmann & O'Shaughnessy, 1974; Wind et al., 1968), which encompasses the consideration of brand image to varying degrees depending on the brand architecture used.

Within the B2B context, there are many variables, which may affect the purchase decision and the role of brand within it.

B2B market buyers may deal with a variety of purchasing situations from straight rebuys to modified rebuys to new purchases. New purchases often have a high transaction value and are complex (Brennan et al., 2024), and in these situations, there is often a greater degree of risk due to uncertainties around the characteristics of the need, the market and/or the transaction. Need uncertainty occurs when the buyer has difficulty identifying the exact nature of the component, service, etc. that is required by the company. Market uncertainty occurs when the buyer is struggling to discern the differences between potential suppliers regarding attributes such as product quality, after-sales service, etc. Transaction uncertainty relates to potential issues conveying the product to the buyer such as trading procedures, language differences, etc. The greater the uncertainties the greater the degree of risk involved in the purchase, which in turn increases the number of people involved in the purchase decision, that is, the size of the decision-making unit increases. Additionally, the length of the buying process, and the number of choice criteria increase when there is a greater risk. Buying decisions become longer as the people involved discuss the details of the purchase and the ability of the suppliers to meet the company's needs when there is a greater risk. The number of choice criteria discussed increases when there is greater risk as less is known about the product. When uncertainty is present in a purchase the financial aspect becomes increasingly important as buyers do not want to make a poor decision which costs the company money. The risk and uncertainty will be experienced by the buyers as, anxiety, discomfort and/or concern (Dowling & Staelin, 1994). Brand image may be more important for buyers when dealing with uncertainty (McDowell Mudambi et al., 1997) and risk (Bengtsson & Servais, 2005). In dealing with risk in purchase situations buying the same brand or buying a popular brand can increase the certainty of the purchase outcome. Remaining loyal to a brand reduces risk as the buyer knows what to expect from the brand. Buying a popular brand is a safe strategy and reduces the risk to a greater degree than buying a less well-known brand. Similarly, buying less of the same brand or buying a cheaper brand can reduce the consequences of product failure. Buying a less popular brand may require the buyer to lower expectations of the product. In these situations, brand image itself may not be one of the main criteria, as previous research found, many functional attributes took a higher priority. These functional attributes contribute to the core of the supplier's brand identity. In these situations, reputation, which encompasses brand image to varying degrees, was found to be influential in evaluating suppliers (Abratt, 1986; Lehmann & O'Shaughnessy, 1974; Wind et al., 1968).

In a modified rebuy, there may be a lower level of uncertainty and risk around the purchase in contrast to a new buy. This may lead to a certain amount of consideration of the functional elements of the product, but in order to reduce the decision-making time, brand image and reputation may also be considered as relatively important criteria. In this purchase situation, fewer people may be involved than in a new buy, which may contribute to a reduced decision-making time.

When purchases are straight rebuys, such as a standard product and/or have a lower purchase value, the buying process may be carried out by a single buyer. In these situations, there is a lower level of risk, which may lead to brand image being used as a main criterion. The buyer may buy the same brand or a popular brand to both reduce any risk and to save time, that is, brand image is used as a heuristic. Reputation may also be considered.

In addition to the nature of the purchase situation affecting when a brand may be influential, the stage of the relationship between the supplier and buyer might be influential (Leek & Christodoulides, 2011; Ozdemir et al., 2020; Webster & Keller, 2004). When the two parties do not know each other, brand image and reputation may be key factors in leading buyers to initiate an interaction with a view to developing a relationship. The supplier, therefore, needs to have developed a strong brand identity and reputation, which will subsequently facilitate initial interactions.

Whilst there is little actual research in the role of brand image and reputation in buyers' decision-making, it is clear that they will be influencing stakeholders depending on the purchase situation and the stage of the relationship between the supplier and buyer.

The Co-Creation of Brand Identity/ Image and Corporate Reputation

Previously, it has been suggested that companies create a brand identity that is long term and stable. This is communicated to customers and other stakeholders who interpret the information received to construct the brand image (Csaba & Bengtsson, 2006). However, this perception is being questioned in B2B marketing, and it is suggested that customers and various other stakeholders are also responsible for shaping the brand identity and consequently the brand image. The research discussed below has examined how co-creation of brand identity occurs when a company is being set up and how it occurs within smaller companies. It considers Törmälä and Gyrd-Jones (2017) research on the development of corporate brand in a new venture, it then goes on to examine how brand identity is co-created firstly looking at Mäläskä et al.'s (2011) relational network approach and then Koporcic and Halinen's (2018) individual approach. This is followed by examining research which identifies the activities (Mäläskä et al., 2011) and roles (Törmälä & Saraniemi, 2018) involved in co-creation.

Törmälä and Gyrd-Jones (2017) investigated how the corporate brand developed in a new B2B venture. Their framework demonstrates how brand identity was the result of interactions between the company and its stakeholders within the ecosystem (see Figure 7.5).

It can be seen from Figure 7.5 that the development of corporate identity was a process consisting of a number of stages involving consideration of the internal and external contextual factors and the activities that occurred and how they influenced brand identity meanings. The stages are discussed further below.

Latent Corporate Brand Identity – At this stage, the brand identity was not formed but characterized by elements such as the founders' personal identities, expertise and values, the core product/service and external investors. Internally, at this stage, the founders lacked a strategic direction and vision due to a lack of understanding of their offerings. Externally, there were a number of market opportunities which could have been exploited, but potential customers lacked knowledge of the company's reputation. Activities at this stage were focused on developing prototypes, establishing the visual identity and obtaining the first investor.

Emergent Corporate Brand Identity – At this stage, the corporate brand identity began to emerge. The company, having gained their first reference customer, learned more about its customers' needs and its target market. They refined the product and the marketing communications. Internal operations were altered as they gained this knowledge. Any incompatibilities between the supplier and customer were identified.

Clarified Corporate Vision and Values – At this stage, as the company interacted with more customers, the corporate vision and values became

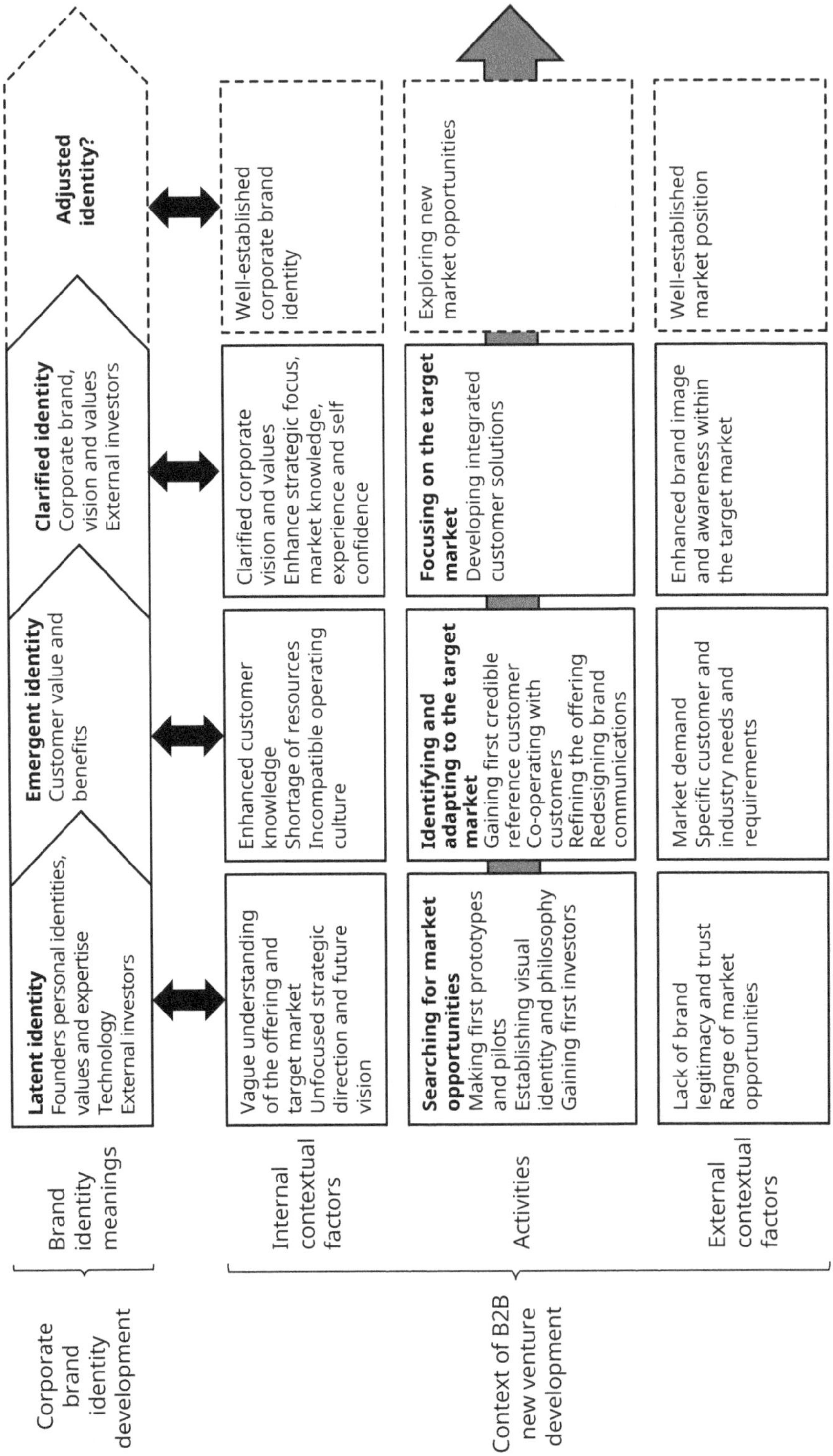

Figure 7.5 The development of corporate brand identity in a new B2B venture (Törmälä & Gyrd-Jones, 2017)

increasingly clear and better defined. This assisted in developing the company's vision for the future, enabling employees to prioritize areas and allocate resources more efficiently. The brand image was refined and built further within the target market. The company's external actors, through the interactions, were felt to have contributed to building the corporate brand identity.

Adjusted Corporate Brand Identity – At this stage, the company's corporate brand had become well established in the market. This was a period of stabilization but it was recognized that there were opportunities to explore other markets.

This model illustrates that building a corporate brand identity is a dynamic process and has a temporal dimension. It illustrates how a company needs to be open to its ecosystem as the development of corporate brand identity involves not only the company itself but also other stakeholders and the market, which influence each other. Intensive reciprocal learning occurs at the beginning as the company is developing its corporate brand identity. The interactions enable the company to incorporate external stakeholders', particularly important customers', values and ideas. As the corporate brand becomes more established, it becomes less susceptible to outside influences. The stabilization of corporate brand identity may only be temporary before its ongoing interactions change.

While Törmälä and Gyrd-Jones (2017) are looking at the creation of a new corporate identity, research has looked at how the co-creation of branding occurs in SMEs (e.g., Mäläskä et al., 2011; Koporcic & Halinen, 2018). This research acknowledges that SMEs have limited resources and they need to access and utilize the resources and expertise of a wide variety of other actors in their network to help them develop their brand.

Mäläskä et al. (2011) take a relational network approach to corporate brand identity with internal and external actors contributing to its development (see Figure 7.6). Interactions between managers and between managers and employees in the company lead to the creation of the brand identity. Employees in managing their relationships with external stakeholders further contribute to branding (de Chernatony & Harris, 2000; Mäläskä et al., 2011). The focal company interacts externally with customers, suppliers, partners, service providers, channel members, who may all make contributions to the functional performance of the product/service and consequently to the brand identity. Building relationships with specific reputable stakeholders in the network to obtain information, reduce

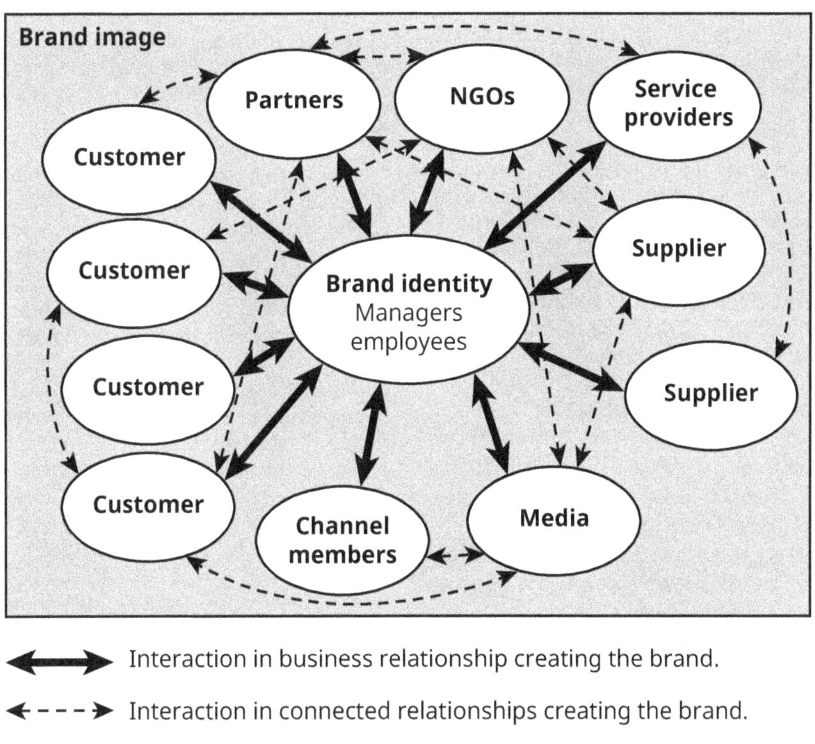

Figure 7.6 Network of actors in B2B branding (Mäläskä et al., 2011)

risk, generate positive WOM and repeat business enhances the brand identity of the company (Ojasalo et al., 2008). Companies interact with non-governmental organizations and the media. Consultancies and advertising agencies may be hired to help support the development of brand identity but this may only be for a short time due to the SMEs' limited resources (Ojasalo et al., 2008). Interactions also occur between external actors, for example, between customers or between suppliers and the media (Mäläskä et al., 2011). This network of interactions contributes to the development of the focal company's brand identity. The network is not controlled by the focal company or any other company and similarly the outcomes of the relationships are not controlled by one actor (Håkansson & Ford, 2002), instead the actors in the network influence and are influenced by each other (Håkansson & Snehota, 2006; Ritter & Gemünden, 2003). Consequently, the brand is not fully controlled by the company. Whilst the interactions are considered to be positively influencing brand image, there is also the danger that they will have a negative influence, for example, employees may sabotage the brand, media outlets may reveal scandals about the brand (Christopher & Gaudenzi, 2009). Mäläskä et al. (2011) define the stakeholders that have a direct effect on the brand identity as the branding pool.

Rather than taking an actor-focused approach, Koporcic and Halinen (2018) adopt an individual approach, which they refer to as interactive network branding. They state that individuals are the ones who are acting on behalf of companies in business relationships and networks to create corporate identity and reputation which are socially constructed. These individuals bring their own knowledge and understanding upon which they act (Håkansson & Snehota, 1995). Koporcic and Halinen (2018) identify three types of interactions that influence corporate identity and reputation: (1) internal interactions, (2) external interactions and (3) boundary spanning interactions.

1. Internal interactions – These interactions occur between individuals within the focal company from different departments and hierarchical levels. Corporate identity is created through internal interactions.
2. External interactions – These interactions occur between individuals who are not within the focal company but who represent other stakeholders. These individuals may be connected directly or indirectly with individuals in the focal company. The interactions may be references, word of mouth or other perceptions of the focal company. These communications contribute to the development of a reputation.
3. Boundary spanning interactions – These interactions are between individuals within the focal company and individuals in external parties. For example, sales reps are individuals acting on behalf of the focal organization, who interact with a variety of individuals across different organizations and markets. The corporate identity of the company can be challenged or strengthened through these interactions, and reputation can be grounded more through the experience.

These three types of interactions are simultaneously occurring (see Figure 7.7).

Although Koporcic and Halinen (2018) focus on the individual level, they believe that the individual can act at the organizational level and that these two levels are enmeshed.

There are some criticisms of these models. In Mäläskä et al. (2011) and Koporcic and Halinen's (2018) research, there is little consideration of the temporal dimension, that is, the time it takes for corporate brand identity to change, which is acknowledged in Törmälä and Gyrd-Jones's (2017) research. SMEs and individuals in SMES are the respective objects of Mäläskä et al. (2011) and Koporcic and Halinen's (2018) research, but there is a lack of research available conducted with large companies to determine whether these models would be applicable. Further studies need to consider whether a large B2B company's brand can equally be shaped by external actors/individuals, either directly or indirectly or whether it is less malleable.

Co-creation occurs through various activities, which are examined below. Mäläskä et al. (2011) state that the branding pool – that is, the independent group of network actors involved in branding – engages through both direct and indirect actions (see Figure 7.8). The direct actions are discussed first. There are a number of stakeholders, for example, suppliers, distributors who contribute to determining the functional value of the brand and the subsequent satisfaction of customers. The branding pool can contribute to the brand by providing references. A reference from a trusted, reputable company, for example, a partner, or a customer provides the focal company with status and can be used to strengthen their brand image. Positive word of mouth may be provided by the actors in the branding pool after satisfactory interactions, which enhances brand identity. Of course, negative word of mouth may also occur and have a detrimental effect on the brand. Media channels can create positive publicity for the company, for example, through announcing product launches, the creation of jobs. They can also have an adverse effect on brands by running stories on

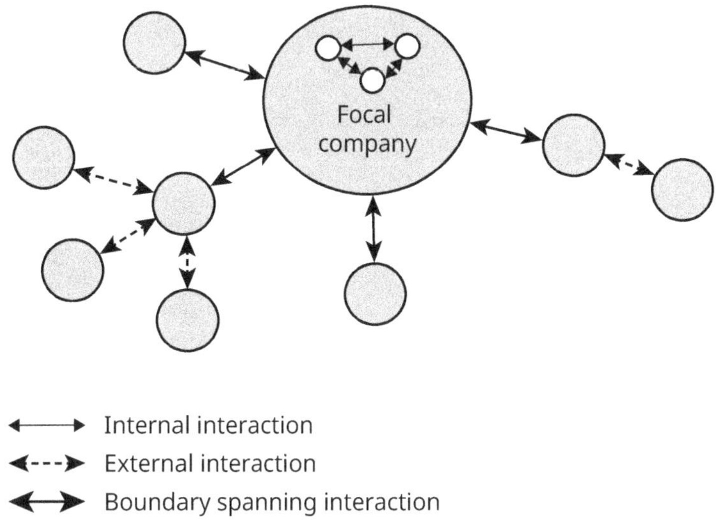

Figure 7.7 Interactive network branding's three types of interactions (Koporcic & Halinen, 2018)

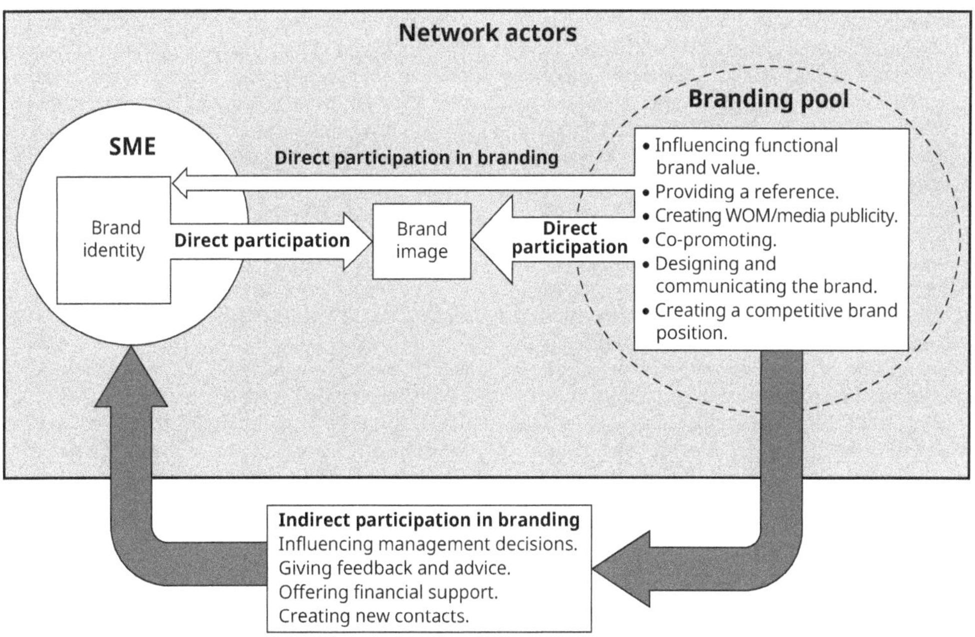

Figure 7.8 Network actors' participation in SME B2B branding (Mäläskä et al., 2011)

issues such as poor performance and irresponsible behavior. Companies may copromote each other, for example, a company may present at an industrial event on a product they have co-produced, which would result in publicity and interest for both parties, and a company may use the logos of its partners on marketing material. If a company lacks expertise, the marketing may be outsourced to agencies that will contribute to the development of the brand identity. A competitive position will be created by the company in relation to its competitors (Mäläskä et al., 2011). These direct actions between the company and various stakeholders contribute to the development of the brand identity. They also contribute directly to the creation and development of the brand image.

There are also a number of activities which contribute to the company's internal operations and indirectly influence the brand. Powerful customers may influence managers' decisions, for example, a company may co-brand with a larger customer they are dependent on over a long period during which time the brand co-evolves. External actors can provide formal or informal feedback on the functional aspects of the products, which can influence the brand identity/image. Financial support may be obtained from stakeholders, which tends to be used for Research and Development, but can indirectly influence the brand identity. Through a network of actors, there can be further introductions which broadens access to resources and can contribute to strengthening the brand (Mäläskä et al., 2011).

The branding pool is specific to the company and may vary by industry (Mäläskä et al., 2011). Both interorganizational and interpersonal connections need to be considered as they will both have an effect on the activities undertaken (Mäläskä et al., 2011).

While Mäläskä et al. (2011) have looked at the direct and indirect activities of a wide range of stakeholders, Törmälä and Saraniemi's (2018) research took a different perspective and identified brand co-creator roles amongst a company's partners using a single case study. They used two dimensions to create a 2 by 2 matrix to categorize the roles (see Figure 7.9). The first dimension is concerned with whether the action takes place with the company itself (relationship-level roles) or other actors in the value-creating ecosystem (ecosystem-level roles). The second dimension determined whether the brand co-creation activities were assigned by the company or were proactively adopted by the partner. These roles are examined more closely below.

In the *company assigned/relationship level* roles category, there are three roles, such as Co-innovator, Co-marketer and Brand Specialist. There is the Co-innovator who participates in developing and producing innovative new products. The company communicates their expectations clearly to the other party. The relationship needs to be transparent and the Co-innovator needs to be trusted in dealing with confidential information. There also needs to be benefits for both parties. The Co-marketer is asked to become involved in marketing activities. Together, they may cut marketing expenditure and exploit each other's networks, for example, through sharing an exhibition stand, running joint marketing campaigns, developing promotional videos together and sharing press releases. These activities are performed due to having mutual interests and may be done without a formal contract. Brand specialists can be hired to help a company develop their branding if they lack the specialist knowledge (Törmälä & Saraniemi, 2018).

In the *proactively adopted, relationship-level* roles category, there are Knowledge providers. These partners were found to have technical, market or customer knowledge. They often provide the company with ideas on how to improve operations, performance or products. They contribute to developing the brand through these innovations (Törmälä & Saraniemi, 2018).

In the *ecosystem-level/company assigned* category, there are Referees and Intermediaries. Referees convince others of the company's competence and trustworthiness. They may improve confidence in a potential or a new customer, increasing perceptions of the company's credibility, thus influencing the brand (Törmälä & Saraniemi, 2018). In the same category are Intermediaries, who deliver the company's product to customers. Customers

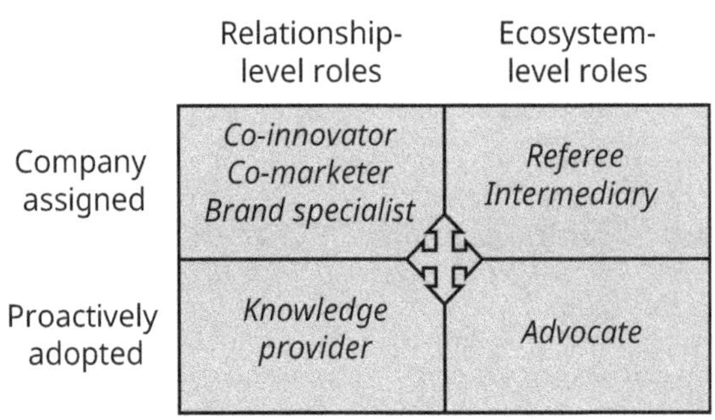

Figure 7.9 Partners' roles in co-creating corporate brand image (Törmälä & Saraniemi, 2018)

do not necessarily distinguish Intermediaries from the company itself; therefore, the Intermediaries are responsible for maintaining the brand through their interactions, their installation of the product, etc. They need to be aware of the brand identity and ideally have received training enabling them to enact the brand (Törmälä & Saraniemi, 2018).

Finally, in the *ecosystem-level/proactively adopted* category, there is the role of Advocates who choose to promote the corporate brand through positive WOM to other actors in their network. This has a positive influence on brand particularly if their network is relevant to the company's (Törmälä & Saraniemi, 2018).

This research (Mäläskä et al., 2011; Törmälä & Saraniemi, 2018) provides helpful insights into how companies can engage companies in brand co-creation. A company needs to consider which stakeholders it would actively want to be involved in their brand co-creation from their network of relationships (Mäläskä et al., 2011). It needs to consider the stakeholders' brand image and reputation. The choice of who to consider will be influenced by the company's tactics and strategy for their brand identity, for example, whether it needs to raise awareness, improve their brand image or introduce an innovative improvement to the brand. In addition, the individuals in the stakeholder relationships who are spanning the boundaries of the organizations (Koporcic & Halinen, 2018) and whether the relationship between the company and the individual is trusting, committed, co-operative, reliable and the nature of any power differential between them will need to be taken into account. The company needs to consider what activities it wants the stakeholders to be involved in, for example, feedback on the product, collaboration to develop a product, co-promotion, etc. and ascertain what value they in turn might offer to the stakeholders. The parties may need to negotiate to determine each other's requirements and expectations. These stages and the nature of the requirements and expectations will be affected by the stage of the company's development, the size of the company, which will determine the resources that they have available, the nature of the activities that need to be performed and the size of the network upon which they can draw (Koporcic & Halinen, 2018; Mäläskä et al., 2011; Törmälä & Saraniemi, 2018). Further research is needed to determine the exact nature of this process.

Both Mäläskä et al.'s (2011) and Törmälä and Saraniemi's (2018) research determine that there are different actors performing various tasks which lead to co-creation of the brand image, and there are criticisms of both. Mäläskä et al. (2011) state that tasks may directly or indirectly influence the brand but the distinction between the two routes of influence is not entirely clear, for example, whilst influencing management decisions and giving feedback and advice are depicted in Figure 7.1 as indirect participation in branding they may be perceived as direct ways of influencing the brand and similarly WOM depicted as direct might be perceived as indirect. They also have the direct activities influencing both brand identity and brand image, and the indirect activities only influencing the brand image, which needs further consideration. In contrast, Törmälä and Saraniemi (2018) take a more structured approach, explicitly distinguishing between whether the focal company has either asked the actors to do an activity or whether the actors have proactively decided to undertake activities themselves. They also differentiate between actors that are in a relationship with the company and actors within the ecosystem of the company which may need further examination as they put an intermediary in the ecosystem-level category. Both Mäläskä et al. (2011) and Törmälä and Saraniemi's (2018) research was carried out with SMEs. There is a lack of research examining brand co-creation in large organizations or multinational corporations. Research needs to be carried out in these organizations to investigate whether brand co-creation occurs and to determine whether the influence of the branding pool has a larger or smaller influence on brand identity, whether the roles and tasks performed are the same or whether there are fewer or more roles. These studies have also tended to focus on corporate brand with little attention to how B2B co-creation works with other branding strategies, for example, individually branded products or house of brands.

In summary, there has been a substantial amount of research conducted on brand identity, reputation and brand image in the B2C context and while this has been applied to the B2B context to some extent, it has hindered the development of theory specifically for industrial markets. While there are some broadly accepted definitions of brand identity, reputation and brand image, further research could examine how they relate to each other and how they vary across different brand architectures. It is also acknowledged that the role of brand varies in different purchase situations and at different stages of a relationship, and this could be examined further as the role of the emotional attributes of a brand has become increasingly important over recent years. B2B relationships have facilitated companies and their stakeholders co-creating the brand leading to a shift from brand identity, reputation and brand image as relatively static concepts to becoming ones which are dynamic and evolving.

There are also a number of broader ways in which the co-creation of brand identity and image needs to be investigated. B2B companies are often operating across multinational boundaries and research needs to determine how companies can best utilize their multicultural branding pool to co-create an appropriate brand image(s) to maximize its appeal. The extent and nature of brand co-creation that companies are prepared to be involved in and the reciprocal value expected may be culturally dependent. Technology can be used to gather data from various sources, including social media, websites, interactions with artificial intelligence, traditional media and analyze it to identify and monitor the nature of the brand being created and determine the influential stakeholders in the process. This will enable companies to utilize and develop any positive aspects of brand co-creation and address any potential miscommunications of stakeholders to some degree; the co-created brand is dynamic and not fully under the company's control. Specific technological aspects could be examined. Research could, for example, investigate how artificial intelligence is used in company interactions and how it affects perceptions of brand identity and co-creation in a B2B context where relationships can be extremely important. Online B2B communities could be investigated to examine how they co-create companies' brands within the group, the degree of input from the companies themselves within these communities and the degree to which the communities' influence extends beyond their immediate membership.

REFERENCES

Aaker, D. A. (1996). Measuring brand equity across products and markets. *California Management Review*, *38*(3), 102–120. www.proquest.com/scholarly-journals/measuring-brand-equity-across-products-markets/docview/216148797/se-2?accountid=8630

Abratt, R. (1986). Industrial buying in high tech markets. *Industrial Marketing Management*, *15*(4), 293–298. https://doi.org/10.1016/0019-8501(86)90021-0

Abratt, R., & Kleyn, N. (2012). Corporate identity, corporate branding and corporate reputations: Reconciliation and integration. *European Journal of Marketing*, *46*(7/8), 1048–1063. https://doi.org/10.1108/03090561211230197

Ahmadi, A., & Ataei, A. (2024). Emotional attachment: A bridge between brand reputation and brand advocacy. *Asia-Pacific Journal of Business Administration*, *16*(1), 1–20. https://doi.org/10.1108/APJBA-11-2021-0579

Balmer, J. M. T. (2010). Explicating corporate brands and their management: Reflections and directions from 1995. *Journal of Brand Management*, *18*(3), 180–196. https://doi.org/10.1057/bm.2010.46

Baruah, L., & Panda, N. M. (2020). Measuring corporate reputation: A comprehensive model with enhanced objectivity. *Asia-Pacific Journal of Business*, *12*(2), 139–161. https://doi.org/10.1108/APJBA-10-2019-0215

Baumgarth, C. (2010). 'Living the brand': Brand orientation in the business-to-business sector. *European Journal of Marketing*, *44*(5), 653–671. https://doi.org/10.1108/03090561011032315

Bendixen, M., Bukasa, K. A., & Abratt, R. (2004). Brand equity in the business-to-business market. *Industrial Marketing Management*, *33*, 371–380. https://doi.org/10.1016/j.indmarman.2003.10.001

Bengtsson, A., & Servais, P. (2005). Co-branding on industrial markets. *Industrial Marketing Management*, *34*, 706–713. https://doi.org/10.1016/j.indmarman.2005.06.004

Billesbach, T. J., Harrison, A., & Croom-Morgan, S. (1991). Supplier performance measures in JIT companies in the U. S. and U.K. *Journal of Supply Chain Management*, *27*(4), 24–28. https://doi.org/10.1111/j.1745-493X.1991.tb00545.x

Brady, M. K., Cronin, J. J., Jr., Fox, G. L., & Roehm, M. L. (2008). Strategies to offset performance failures: The role of brand equity. *Journal of Retailing*, *84*(2), 151–164. https://doi.org/10.1016/j.jretai.2008.04.002

Brembo. (2024). *The group brands*. Brembo. Retrieved August 27, 2024.

Brennan, R., Canning, L., & McGrath, H. (2024). *Business to business marketing* (6th ed.). Sage.

Brown, B. P., Zablah, A. R., Bellenger, D. N., & Donthu, N. (2012). What factors influence buying center brand sensitivity? *Industrial Marketing Management*, *41*(3), 508–520. https://doi.org/10.1016/j.indmarman.2011.06.008

Bruhn, M., Schoenmueller, V., & Schäfer, D. B. (2012). Are social media replacing traditional media in terms of brand equity creation? *Management Research Review*, *35*(9), 770–790. https://doi.org/10.1108/01409171211255948

Caviggioli, F., Lamberti, L., Landoni, P., & Meola, P. (2020). Technology adoption news and corporate reputation: Sentiment analysis about the introduction of bitcoin. *Journal of Product and Brand Management*, *29*(7), 877–897. https://doi.org/10.1108/JPBM-03-2018-1774

Christopher, M., & Gaudenzi, B. (2009). Exploiting knowledge across networks through reputation management. *Industrial Marketing Management*, *38*(2), 191–197. https://doi.org/10.1016/j.indmarman.2008.12.014

Coleman, D., de Chernatony, L., & Christodoulides, G. (2011). B2B service brand identity: Scale development and validation. *Industrial Marketing

Management, *40*, 1063–1071. https://doi.org/10.1016/j.indmarman.2011.09.010

Cretu, A. E., & Brodie, R. J. (2007). The influence of brand image and company reputation where manufacturers market to small firms: A customer value perspective. *Industrial Marketing Management*, *36*, 230–240. https://doi.org/10.1016/j.indmarman.2005.08.013

Csaba, F. F., & Bengtsson, A. (2006). Rethinking identity in brand management. In J. Schroeder, & M. S. Morling (Eds.), *Corporate brand cultures and communities*. Routledge.

de Chernatony, L. (1999). Brand management through narrowing the gap between brand identity and reputation. *Journal of Marketing Management*, *15*(1–3), 157–179. https://doi.org/10.1362/026725799784870432

de Chernatony, L. (2003). Brand building. In M. J. Baker (Ed.), *The marketing book* (5th ed.). Butterworth Heinemann.

de Chernatony, L., & Harris, F. (2000). Developing corporate brands through considering internal and external stakeholders. *Corporate Reputation Review*, *3*(3), 268–274. https://doi.org/10.1057/palgrave.crr.1540119

Dobni, D., & Zinkhan, G. M. (1990). In search of brand image: A foundation analysis. *Advances in Consumer Research*, *17*, 110–119.

Dowling, G. (2001). *Creating corporate reputations: Identity, image and performance*. Oxford University Press.

Dowling, G. R., & Staelin, R. (1994). A model of perceived risk and intended risk handling activity. *Journal of Consumer Research*, *21*(1), 119–134. https://doi.org/10.1086/209386

Edser, N., Armstrong, K., & Phillips, A. (2024). *GPs, Airports and banks in UK hit by IT outage. GPs, pharmacies and airports in UK affected by IT outage*. BBC News. Retrieved November 1, 2024.

Essamri, A., McKechnie, S., & Winkelhofer, H. (2019). Co-creating brand identity with online brand communities: A managerial perspective. *Journal of Business Research*, *96*, 366–375. https://doi.org/10.1016/j.jbusres.2018.07.015

Fombrun, C. J. (1996). *Reputation: Realizing value from the corporate image*. Harvard Business School Press.

Fombrun, C. J. (2012). The building blocks of corporate reputation: Definitions, antecedents, consequences. In T. G. Pollock, & M. L. Barnett (Eds.), *The Oxford handbook of corporate reputation*. Oxford University Press. https://doi.org/10.1093/oxfordhb/9780199596706.001.0001

Fombrun, C. J., Gardbergh, N. A., & Sever, J. M. (2000). The reputation quotient: A multi stakeholder measure of corporate reputation. *The Journal of Brand Management*, *7*(4), 241–255. https://doi.org/10.1057/bm.2000.10

General Electric. (2024). *About us; empowering the next generation. About: GE Today, GE History*. General Electric. Retrieved August 27, 2024.

Håkansson, H. (ed.). (1982). *International marketing and purchasing of industrial goods – An interaction approach*. Wiley.

Håkansson, H., & Snehota, I. (1995). *Developing relationships in business networks*. International Thomson.

Håkansson, H., & Snehota, I. (2006). No business is an island: The network concept of business strategy. *Scandinavian Journal of Management*, *22*(3), 256–270. https://doi.org/10.1016/j.scaman.2006.10.005

Håkansson, H., & Ford, D. (2002). How should companies interact in business networks? *Journal of Business Research*, *55*(2), 133–139. https://doi.org/10.1016/S0148-2963(00)00148-X

Hatch, M. J., & Schultz, M. (2003). Bringing the corporation into corporate branding. *European Journal of Marketing*, *37*(7/8), 1041–1064. 10.1108/03090560310477654

Harvey, W. S., Morris, T., & Santos, M. S. (2017). Reputation and identity conflict in management consulting. *Human Relations*, *70*(1), 92–118. https://doi.org/10.1177/0018726716641747

Higgins, R. B., & Bannister, B. D. (1992). How corporate communication of strategy affects share price. *Long Range Planning*, *25*, 27–35. https://doi.org/10.1016/0024-6301(92)90366-A

Iglesias, O., & Bonet, E. (2012). Persuasive brand management how managers can influence brand meaning when they are losing control over it. *Journal of Organizational Change Management*, *25*(2), 251–264. https://doi.org/10.1108/09534811211213937

Iglesias, O., Landgraf, P., Ind, N., Markovic, S., & Koporcic, N. (2020). Corporate brand identity co-creation in B2B contexts. *Industrial Marketing Management*, *85*, 32–43. https://doi.org/10.1016/j.indmarman.2019.09.008

Interbrand. (n.d.). *Best global brands top 100 2024*. BGB – Interbrand. Retrieved November 6, 2024.

Kapferer, J. N. (2008). *The new strategic brand management: Creating and sustaining brand equity long term* (4th ed.). Kogan Page.

Kapferer, J. N. (2012). *The new strategic brand management: Advanced insights and strategic thinking* (5th ed.). Kogan Page.

Keller, K. L. (2003). *Strategic brand management: Building, measuring and managing brand equity*. Prentice Hall.

Keller, K. L., & Swaminathan, V. (2020). *Strategic brand management building, measuring and managing brand equity* (5th ed.). Pearson.

Keränen, J., Piirainen, K. A., & Salminen, R. T. (2012). Systematic review on B2B branding: Research issues and avenues for research. *Journal of*

Product & Brand Management, *21*(6), 404–417. https://doi.org/10.1108/10610421211264892

Koporcic, N., & Halinen, A. (2018). Interactive network branding, creating corporate identity and reputation through interpersonal interaction. *IMP Journal*, *12*(2), 392–408. https://doi.org/10.1108/IMP-05-2017-0026

Leek, S., & Christodoulides, G. (2011). A literature review and future agenda for B2B branding: Challenges of branding in a B2B Context. *Industrial Marketing Management*, *40*(6), 830–837. https://doi.org/10.1016/j.indmarman.2011.06.006

Leek, S., & Christodoulides, G. (2012). A framework for generating brand value in B2B markets: The contributing role of functional and emotional components. *Industrial Marketing Management*, *41*(1), 106–114. https://doi.org/10.1016/j.indmarman.2011.11.009

Lehmann, D. R., & O'Shaughnessy, J. (1974). Difference in attribute importance for different industrial products. *Journal of Marketing*, *38*(2), 36–42. https://doi.org/10.2307/1250195

Low, J., & Blois, K. (2002). The evolution of generic brands in industrial markets: The challenges to owners of brand equity. *Industrial Marketing Management*, *31*, 385–392. https://doi.org/10.1016/S0019-8501(00)00131-0

Lynch, J., & de Chernatony, L. (2007). Winning hearts and minds: Business to business branding and the role of the salesperson. *Journal of Marketing Management*, *23*(1), 123–135. https://doi.org/10.1362/026725707X178594

Mäläskä, M., Saraniemi, S., & Tähtinen, J. (2011). Network actors' participation in B2B SME branding. *Industrial Marketing Management*, *40*, 1144–1152. https://doi.org/10.1016/j.indmarman.2011.09.005

Marvi, R., Zha, D., & Foroudi, P. (2024). Elevating B2B branding in a global context: Integrating existing literature and proposing a forward thinking conceptual framework. *Industrial Marketing Management*, *120*, 247–272. https://doi.org/10.1016/j.indmarman.2024.06.006

McDowell Mudambi, S., Doyle, P., & Wong, V. (1997). An exploration of branding in industrial markets. *Industrial Marketing Management*, *26*, 433–446. https://doi.org/10.1016/S0019-8501(96)00151-4

McQuiston, D. H. (2004). Successful branding of a commodity product: The case of RAEX laser steel. *Industrial Marketing Management*, *33*, 345–354. https://doi.org/10.1016/j.indmarman.2003.07.001

Michell, P., King, J., & Reast, J. (2001). Brand values related to industrial products. *Industrial Marketing Management*, *30*, 415–425. https://doi.org/10.1016/S0019-8501(99)00097-8

Milewicz, J., & Herbig, P. (1994). Evaluating the brand extension decision using a model of reputation building. *Journal of Product & Brand Management*, *3*(1), 39–47. https://doi.org/10.1108/10610429410053077

Mudambi, S. (2002). Branding importance in business-to-business markets three buyer clusters. *Industrial Marketing Management*, *31*, 525–533. https://doi.org/10.1016/S0019-8501(02)00184-0

Noor Rashidah Mohd Sofia, F., Hafezad Abdullah, K., & Modh-Sabrun, I. (2023). Research on Corporate Reputation: A bibliometric review of 43 years (1977–2020). *International Journal of Information Science and Management*, *21*(2), 31–54. https://doi.org/10.22034/ijism.2023.1977558.0

Novartis. (2024). *Products*. Novartis. Retrieved October 31, 2024.

Ohnemus, L. (2009). B2B branding: A financial burden for shareholders? *Business Horizons*, *52*, 159–166. https://doi.org/10.1016/j.bushor.2008.10.004

Ojasalo, J., Nätti, S., & Olkkenen, R. (2008). Brand building in software SMEs: An empirical study. *Journal of Product & Brand Management*, *17*(2), 92–107. https://doi.org/10.1108/10610420810864702

Ozdemir, S., Gupta, S., Foroudi, P., Wright, L.-T., & Eng, T.-Y. (2020). Corporate branding and value creation for initiating and managing relationships in B2B markets. *Qualitative Market Research: An International Journal*, *23*(4), 627–661. https://doi.org/10.1108/QMR-12-2017-0168

Park, C. W., Jaworski, B. J., & MacInnis, D. J. (1986). Strategic brand concept-image management. *Journal of Maerketing*, *50*(4),135–145. https://doi.org/10.2307/1251291

Perreault, W. D., Jr., & Russ, F. A. (1976). Physical distribution service in industrial purchase decisions. *Journal of Marketing*, *40*(2), 3–10. https://doi.org/10.2307/1251000

Petkova, A. (2012). From the ground up: Building young firms' reputation. In M. L. Barnett, & T. G. Pollock (Eds.), *The Oxford handbook of corporate reputation* (pp. 383–401). Oxford University Press.

Pfarrer, M. D., Pollock, T. G., & Rindova, V. P. (2017). A tale of two assets: The effects of firm reputation and celebrity on earnings surprises and investors' reactions. *Academy of Management Journal*, *53*(5), 1131–1152. https://doi.org/10.5465/amj.2010.54533222

Rao, V. R., Agarwal, M. K., & Dahlhoff, D. (2004). How is manifest branding strategy related to the intangible value of a corporation? *Journal of Marketing*, *68*(October), 126–141. https://doi.org/10.1509/jmkg.68.4.126.42735

Richter, M. (2007). *Markenbedeutung und -management im Industriegüterbereich*. DUV. Quoted in Baumgarth, C. (2010). 'Living the brand': Brand orientation in the business-to-business sector. *European Journal of Marketing*, *44*(5), 653–671. https://doi.org/10.1108/03090561011032315

Ritter, T., & Gemünden, H. G. (2003). Interorganizational relationships and networks: An overview. *Journal of Business Research*, *56*(9), 691–697. https://doi.org/10.1016/S0148-2963(01)00254-5

Rode, V., & Vallaster, C. (2005). Corporate branding for start-ups: The crucial role for entrepreneurs. *Corporate Reputation Review*, *8*(2), 121–135. https://doi.org/10.1057/palgrave.crr.1540244

Rust, R. T., Rand, W., Huang, M.-H., Stephen, A. T., Brooks, G., & Chabuk, T. (2021). Real-time brand reputation tracking using social media. *Journal of Marketing*, *85*(4), 21–43. https://doi.org/10.1177/0022242921995173

Schein, E. (1984). Culture as an environment context for careers. *Journal of Occupational Behaviour*, *5*(1), 71–81. www.jstor.org/stable/3000310

Schivinski, B., Langaro, D., Fernandes, T., & Guzman, F. (2020). Social media brand engagement in the context of collaborative consumption: The case of AIRBNB. *Journal of Brand Management*, *27*, 645–661. https://doi.org/10.1057/s41262-020-00207-5

Shankar, A., Kumar, A., Behl, A., Pereira, V., & Budhwar, P. (2024). You or an imposter? how to protect brand identity in a business-to-business context. *Industrial Marketing Management*, *116*, 93–105. https://doi.org/10.1016/j.indmarman.2023.12.001

Shapiro, C. (1983). Premiums for high quality products as returns to reputations. *The Quarterly Journal of Economics*, *98*(4), 659–680. https://doi.org/10.2307/1881782

Teradici. (2024). *The future is bright for Teradici customers as the world shifts to hybrid working. The Future Is Bright For Teradici Customers And Partners As The World Shifts To Hybrid Working*. Retrieved November 11, 2024.

Törmälä, M., & Gyrd-Jones, R. I. (2017). Development of new B2B corporate brand identity: A narrative performance approach. *Industrial Marketing Management*, *65*, 76–85. https://doi.org/10.1016/j.indmarman.2017.05.002

Törmälä, M., & Saraniemi, S. (2018). The role of business partners in corporate brand image co-creation. *Journal of Product and Brand Management*, *27*(1), 29–40. 10.1108/JPBM-01-2016-1089

Veloutsou, C., & Mouthino, L. (2009). Brand relationships through brand reputation and brand tribalism. *Journal of Business Research*, *62*, 314–322. https://doi.org/10.1016/j.jbusres.2008.05.010

Walsh, G., & Beatty, S. E. (2007). Customer-based corporate reputation of a service firm: Scale development and validation. *Journal of the Academy of Management Science*, *35*, 127–143. https://doi.org/10.1007/s11747-007-0015-7

Washkuch, F. (2024, July 25). *A B2B problem to a B2C disaster: why the Crowdstrike outage is a wake-up call for all brands*. PR Week 2024. Retrieved November 8, 2024.

Wartick, S. L. (2002). Measuring corporate reputation: Definition and data. *Business and Society*, *41*(4), 393–414. https://doi.org/10.1177/0007650302238774

Webster, F. E., Jr., & Keller, K. L. (2004). A roadmap for branding industrial markets. *Journal of Brand Management*, *11*(5), 388–402. https://doi.org/10.1057/palgrave.bm.2540184

Wind, Y., Green, P. E., & Robinson, P. J. (1968). The determinants of vendor selection: The evaluation function approach. *Journal of Purchasing*, *4*(3), 29–41. https://doi.org/10.1111/j.1745-493X.1968.tb00592.x

Zwakala, K. M., & Steenkamp, P. (2021). Brand identity-image congruence: A framework for business-to-business banks in South Africa. *Journal of Business and Industrial Marketing*, *28*(3), 283–305. https://doi.org/10.1080/1051

8

B2C and B2B Brand Personality in a Digital World

Mijka Ghorbani

INTRODUCTION

In an increasingly digital world, consumers encounter brands at a variety of touchpoints and platforms. Brands attempt to differentiate themselves by humanizing their brands, for example, through their social media content strategy or the use of virtual brand agents like chatbots (Chang et al., 2019; Youn & Jin, 2021). For both business-to-consumer (B2C) and business-to-business (B2B) companies, a strong brand personality can be a powerful marketing instrument to set a brand apart from competitors and to connect with customers on a more personal level (Aaker, 1997; Keller & Richey, 2006; Veloutsou & Taylor, 2012). Brand personality is defined as the humanlike characteristics and traits that are ascribed to brands (Aaker, 1997; Azoulay & Kapferer, 2003). The rise of digital and in particular social media has opened new avenues to personify brands and imbue them with humanlike attributes. There is a growing stream of research that has studied how a brand can adopt a humanlike personality through digital instruments and the consequent impact on digital consumer–brand interactions, which is crucial for both brand researchers and practitioners to understand (Garanti & Kissi, 2019; Torres & Augusto, 2019). Researchers have begun to examine how consumers perceive brands as persons in different digital settings, including websites (Poddar et al., 2009; Shobeiri et al., 2015), social media (Machado et al., 2019; Pentina et al., 2013; Walsh et al., 2013), apps (Fang, 2019) and interactions with virtual brand agents (Jin & Sung, 2010; Youn & Jin, 2021). However, the majority of research remains isolated as the different digital contexts have been studied independently. This chapter aims to provide a contemporary, integrative overview of the emerging scholarly literature on B2C and B2B brand personality in a digital world, synthesizing the main theories, contexts and methods used for investigation and highlighting gaps in current knowledge and opportunities for further research.[1]

[1] This book chapter emerged from the author's doctoral research and builds in part on the insights into a systematic literature review on digital brand personality perceptions, which was published in the International Journal of Consumer Studies (Ghorbani et al., 2022), to offer a novel integrative review of the literature on the subject of B2C and B2B brand personality in a digital world.

B2C AND B2B BRAND PERSONALITY

In brand management, brand personality has been recognized as a key element in building long-term, emotional relationships with consumers as it helps them to identify with brands (Aaker, 1997; Fournier, 1998). In branding research, numerous studies have shown how a strong, recognizable brand personality affects consumer responses as it strengthens brand affect (Sung & Kim, 2010), brand trust (Louis & Lombart, 2010), brand loyalty (Freling & Forbes, 2005) and even brand equity (Valette-Florence et al., 2011). While the construct of brand personality has traditionally been more strongly associated with consumer product brands (Saeed et al., 2022), it has also been adapted to other industries and branded entities, including destination branding (Hassan et al., 2024; Kim & Lehto, 2013), university branding (Opoku et al., 2006) and corporate and institution branding (Keller & Richey, 2006; Venable et al., 2005). More recently, researchers have begun to specifically explore the characteristics of B2B brand personality with regard to how it is built by companies through their products and interactions with customers, and how it is perceived by different stakeholders, including manufacturers, buyers and (potential) employees (Aagerup et al., 2022; Coleman et al., 2011; Herbst & Merz, 2011; Kovalchuk et al., 2023; Veloutsou & Taylor, 2012).

Brand personality theory has its roots in anthropomorphism and human personality (Aaker, 1997). The underlying mechanism of anthropomorphism describes the human 'tendency to imbue the real or imagined behavior of nonhuman agents with humanlike characteristics, motivations, intentions, or emotions' (Epley et al., 2007, p. 864). In the branding context, this implies that consumers endow brands or brand representations with human features, minds and personality traits (MacInnis & Folkes, 2017). Brand personality researchers have mainly drawn on trait theories of personality psychology to capture how consumers perceive brands as if they were persons (Aaker, 1997; Davies et al., 2018; Geuens et al., 2009). Trait theories view human personality as made up of personality traits, which have become encoded in language over time (lexical hypothesis) and can be grouped into higher-order factors (Goldberg, 1992; John, 2021). Personality traits refer to internal personality characteristics, which differentiate individuals from one another and relate to patterns of how people think, feel and act (American Psychological Association, 2022). Today, the five factors of extraversion, agreeableness, conscientiousness, emotional stability/neuroticism and openness to experience are widely regarded as the universal human personality structure (John, 2021; McCrae & Costa, 1997). Accordingly, brand personality is a psychological and metaphorical construct that is typically conceptualized as a factorial, multi-faceted structure (Aaker, 1997; Geuens et al., 2009).

However, brand personality theory and research are divided into two schools of thought that differ in how they conceptualize and measure brand personality (Geuens et al., 2009; Ghorbani et al., 2022; Oklevik et al., 2020). On the one hand, Aaker (1997) conceptualized brand personality as the total set of human characteristics associated with a brand, including gender, profession, status and traits. Her seminal study proposed a distinct 'Big Five' structure comprising excitement, sincerity, competence, sophistication and ruggedness as the overarching brand personality dimensions. This brand-as-a-person metaphor assumed that brand personality and human personality are analogous, but not the same, since they are constructed through different antecedents (Aaker, 1997; Aaker et al., 2001). Consequently, numerous studies have developed novel personality frameworks and trait inventories to capture consumers' perceptions of the brand as a person for particular national or industry contexts (Aaker et al., 2001; d'Astous & Lévesque, 2003; Sung & Tinkham, 2005) as well as for corporate and industrial brands (Davies et al., 2004; Herbst & Merz, 2011). On the other hand, scholars have argued for a narrower definition of brand personality, whereby the metaphor should be restricted to include human personality factors and traits only (Azoulay & Kapferer, 2003; Geuens et al., 2009). This definition, which views brands as personalities, assumes they are like humans and can be assessed using the same frameworks, in both B2B and B2C settings (Aagerup et al., 2022; Huang et al., 2012). To conclude, there is no consensus in general brand personality theory about what dimensions and traits constitute brand personality and whether they are generalizable across contexts.

THEORIES AND CHARACTERISTICS OF DIGITAL BRAND PERSONALITY

There is a growing stream of research that has studied brand personality in the digital world (Garanti & Kissi, 2019; Torres & Augusto, 2019). In the mid-2000s, researchers began to explore how consumers perceive brands as persons in interactions with online websites (Okazaki, 2006). Since then, research that studied both B2C and B2B brand personality in various digital settings has significantly increased (Ghorbani et al., 2022). However, various labels have been applied rather interchangeably to describe a brand's 'digital', 'online', 'virtual' or 'social media' brand personality (Garanti & Kissi, 2019; Okazaki, 2006; Ong et al., 2017; Wood & Solomon, 2008). It is argued that brands may have a distinct digital-based personality that is different from the general or offline-based personality because digital consumer–brand interactions operate according to new rules and are mediated by digital technologies such as social media, leading to different brand personalities (Kim et al., 2018; Yun et al., 2019). Researchers have adopted different perspectives to conceptualize how brands become personified online in different ways, relating to different senders projecting brand personality messages or digital instruments used to influence perceived digital brand personality. Table 8.1 provides an overview of the different conceptualizations that have been used in the scholarly literature.

Notably, extant conceptual approaches are limited and fragmented as they are restricted either to one facet of brand personality (e.g., communicated vs. perceived), to one specific digital setting (e.g., social media) or to one type of brand (e.g., online-only brands). Yet, in today's digital world, almost every brand is represented or talked about online and therefore has the potential to become humanized digitally. This chapter proposes a definition of digital brand personality that applies to all types of brands with a digital presence: *Digital brand personality is defined as the human personality attributes that are ascribed to brands in digital consumer–brand interactions*. Hence, this definition integrates several viewpoints of digital brand personality as it acknowledges how digital brand personality becomes encoded in the digital content communicated by different senders and how consumers' digital brand personality perceptions are inferred from a wide range of interactions with brands, technologies and online content. This definition also emphasizes that it is necessary to conceptualize a brand's digital personality as distinct from its overall brand personality as it is bound to and shaped by the respective digital environment.

Regarding the theoretical underpinnings of digital brand personality research, extant literature has heavily drawn on traditional brand personality theory and related theories, such as consumer–brand relationships theory or self-congruity theory (Bernritter et al., 2016; Ranfagni et al., 2016; Yun et al., 2019). Most studies have extended these theoretical frameworks and their assumptions to the digital world to argue for how a strong, recognizable brand personality would positively affect consumer behavior in digital brand interactions. In online banking, for example, Torres and Augusto (2019) highlighted the significance of brand personality (Aaker, 1997) as a marketing concept in a digital setting by demonstrating how it had a direct effect on brand attitude and electronic word-of-mouth of social media users, which strengthened resilience to negative information and purchase intention. Furthermore, several studies showed that building a strong brand personality through digital interactions can contribute to forming emotional brand relationships online (Machado et al., 2019; Roy et al., 2016). Taken together, this shows how extant research has assumed that digital consumer–brand interactions mostly resemble interpersonal interactions or analog consumer–brand interactions, which is why the same models have been applied. However, there is a lack of novel theorization that accounts for the potential influence and changed conditions of a digital environment, in particular, regarding alternative forms of interactions enabled by new technologies.

Extant research has mainly followed the trait-based conceptualizations of brand personality as a multi-dimensional construct – drawing parallels

Table 8.1 Different perspectives and angles taken to conceptualize digital brand personality

	Conceptualization	*Exemplary References*
1	The brand personality put forth by brand managers and communicated through brand website content	Okazaki (2006); Opoku et al. (2006)
2	The brand personality perceived by online consumers and/or social media users/followers of the brand	Garanti and Kissi (2019); Ong et al. (2017); Torres and Augusto (2019)
3	The brand personality perceptions expressed by consumers in user-generated social media content	Paschen et al. (2017); Ranfagni et al. (2016)
4	The brand personality perceptions elicited by interactions with new technologies and digital media	Anselmsson and Tunca (2019); De Gauquier et al. (2018)
5	The brand personality represented through digital non-human agents (e.g., avatars and chatbots)	Wood and Solomon (2008)
6	The brand personality of online-only brands (e.g., online retailers)	Syed Alwi and Da Silva (2007)

Source: The author.

to the factorial structure of human personality. The two schools of thought of brand personality theory discussed above have been carried over into the digital world as the main models and measurements have been applied to assess how consumers view brands as persons or personalities online, thus further replicating the conceptual confusion about what factors make up brand personality (Ghorbani et al., 2022; Radler, 2018). First, several studies have applied the Big Five of Aaker (1997): excitement, sincerity, competence, sophistication and ruggedness (Béal & Grégoire, 2022; Priporas et al., 2020; Youn & Jin, 2021). Similar to traditional brand personality research, studies subscribing to this definition have also developed new idiographic scales to measure digital brand personality perceptions, for example, for digital-based entities such as internet media brands using dimensions like intelligent or sociable (Ham & Lee, 2015).

Second, another stream of research has applied brand-as-a-personality or even human personality models to measure consumers' digital brand personality perceptions, including the New Brand Personality Scale by Geuens et al. (2009) encompassing activity, responsibility, aggressiveness, simplicity and emotionality (Garanti & Kissi, 2019; He et al., 2021), the Brands-as-Intentional-Agents-Framework (Aaker et al., 2010; Kervyn et al., 2012) capturing warmth and competence (Carpentier et al., 2019; Chang et al., 2019; Eigenraam et al., 2021; Fang, 2019; Wu et al., 2017) or human personality's five-factor model (Rojas-Méndez & Hine, 2017; Wang et al., 2021). Importantly, this second stream of research has opened a debate revolving around the central question of whether brands become more humanlike in the digital world.

Research has argued in favor of the claim that brands may be perceived as more humanlike in digital interactions and especially in social media conversations that resemble interpersonal interactions, as brands adopt a human voice (Beukeboom et al., 2015; Kim et al., 2018; Wang et al., 2021). The notion of the human voice assumes that consumer–brand interactions online, for example, in social media, more closely resemble interpersonal interactions than traditional offline-based interactions (e.g., TV, radio, out-of-home advertising). Some contend brands assume a conversational human voice so that social media users feel like they are talking to brands like they would talk to other human users, as brand communication via social media is more personal, interactive and sociable (Harrison & Kwon, 2023; Kim et al., 2018). Indeed, Beukeboom et al. (2015) showed that brand followers on social media develop more positive brand evaluations over time, which were attributed to the conversational human voice.

As a result, researchers have discussed whether and to what extent a brand's digital personality may be more similar in structure to human personality (Kim et al., 2018; Wang et al., 2021; Yun et al., 2019). To illustrate, Kim et al. (2018) discovered that the brand personality perceptions of brand followers on social networking sites could be assessed through a scale that resembled more closely the five human personality factors, whereas the brand personality scale constructed from the survey data of non-followers appeared to be more similar to the brand personality scale of Aaker (1997). Drawing on the self-congruity premise, Yun et al. (2019) also argued for the applicability of the five-factor model to brands in social media brand communications. They offered additional arguments for why brands acquire a more humanlike presence on social media, either that it could be attributed to the influence of the personalities of social media managers or that it could be the case that social media require a new, more humanlike conceptualization of the brand personality construct (Yun et al., 2019).

To summarize, digital brand personality research has replicated or transferred the two schools of thought of brand personality research to the online world. Following the brand-as-a-person metaphor has allowed some researchers to adapt Aaker's (1997) model and add dimensions suitable for digital brands or settings, whereas others have followed the brand-as-a-personality definition and argued that brands may become more humanlike in digital interactions.

BRAND PERSONALITY RESEARCH ACROSS DIGITAL CONTEXTS

Digital media and new technologies have significantly changed the ways in which brands communicate with consumers as well as patterns of consumer behavior and communication between consumers (Hoyer et al., 2020; Swaminathan et al., 2020). Consumers now encounter brands across a variety of touchpoints, that is, any direct or indirect contact with a brand, which can be digital like social media and websites, physical like retail stores or out-of-home advertising or hybrid like apps with augmented reality (AR) applications or retail stores with smart mirrors (Sestino, 2024). Consequently, research into B2C and B2B personality has begun to explore how brands become imbued with humanlike personalities through digital media and new technologies. Regarding the research contexts, the majority of studies explored B2C settings, in particular, product brands (Youn & Jin, 2021), service brands (Shi & Shan, 2019) and tourism brands (Hassan et al., 2024). Nonetheless, there is burgeoning research interest in the digital personalities of B2B brands, also termed organizational brands or industrial brands (Carpentier et al., 2019; Mora Cortez & Ghosh Dastidar, 2022; Robertson et al., 2019); this trend reflects the generally growing interest in B2B brand personality as a marketing construct (Aagerup et al., 2022; Kovalchuk et al., 2023).

Regarding the digital contexts, researchers have initially focused on brand websites and e-stores as the first online touchpoints to create brand personality (Merrilees & Miller, 2005; Okazaki, 2006; Syed Alwi & Da Silva, 2007). With the introduction of social media in the mid-2000s (Facebook was founded in 2004 and YouTube in 2005), these new platforms have gained massive research interest as studies have explored how both brands and consumers turned to social media to either position themselves with humanlike attributes or to talk about a brand as if it were a person (Paschen et al., 2017; Peco-Torres et al., 2021). More recently, research has broadened its scope to include more varied digital environments and new technologies based on artificial intelligence (AI), Internet of Things (IoT) or extended reality (Plotkina et al., 2022; Sestino, 2024). In the following, research streams that have focused upon one particular type of digital touchpoint are reviewed with regard to how they examined digital brand personality, its antecedents and consequences in the context of (i) websites, e-stores and apps; (ii) social media platforms; and (iii) new technologies.

Websites, e-Stores and Apps

A vast body of research has examined digital brand personality in the context of websites,[2] e-stores and apps as primarily brand-owned touchpoints used to communicate and sell to consumers, including brand websites (e.g., adidas.com), website brands (e.g., amazon.com) or internet media brands (e.g., YouTube.com) (Ham & Lee, 2015; Okazaki, 2006; Poddar et al., 2009). Branded apps can also be seen as a similar channel that enables consumers to experience a brand digitally (Fang, 2019).

The research considered how brands may design their websites and e-stores to build specific digital brand personality impressions, which would affect consumer responses. To illustrate, Shobeiri et al. (2015) showed the differentiated impact of website personality dimensions on site involvement and site attitudes, respectively. For example, impressions of website personality's enthusiasm and genuineness positively affected the site attitude. In a similar vein, Fang (2019) showed how affordances of branded apps such as visibility or interactivity shaped value-in-use, which strengthened consumers' digital brand personality perceptions along the dimensions of warmth and competence. These studies highlight the importance of online experiential values in shaping consumers' digital brand personality perceptions, thus extending the brand experience-brand personality link (Brakus et al., 2009) from the offline to the online world.

Branded websites have emerged as a central instrument for brand managers to put forth their digital brand personality (Hassan et al., 2024; Okazaki, 2006). In one of the earliest works of the discipline, Okazaki (2006) explored the sender-side of brand personality as communicated online through functional and expressive advertising stimuli. The website analysis revealed five underlying dimensions of intended brand personalities of American multinational corporations (MNCs), namely, excitement, sophistication, affection, popularity and competence. Along similar lines, numerous studies have investigated brand website communication, analyzing either the entire online presence or specific pages (like 'about us'), to understand how the digital brand personality is conveyed through chosen adjectives, which are linked to established brand or human personality scales (Opoku et al., 2006; Rojas-Méndez & Hine, 2017; Shi & Shan, 2019). Since then, a growing body of research has taken to study digital contents to extract the digital brand personality, using not only brand websites but also social media platforms.

Social Media Platforms

Social media platforms are among the most widely researched touchpoints in extant digital brand personality research (Ghorbani et al., 2022). According to Gretzel (2017, p. 1), social media are '[w]eb-based communication platforms or applications that take advantage of Web 2.0 technologies, which make it possible for users without technical expertise to easily produce and publish contents on the Internet'. In view of the proliferation of social media applications, digital brand personality researchers have studied consumer–brand

[2] Researchers sometimes used the term 'website personality' or 'e-store personality' to conceptualize the digital personalities of online stores (Chang & Kwon, 2022; Poddar et al., 2009). Yet, those efforts can be understood as specific applications of the brand personality concept, in the same manner that researchers talked about destination brand personality or university brand personality, and these are likewise included in the new digital brand personality definition proposed above.

interactions across a number of social media platforms, including social networking sites like Facebook (Machado et al., 2019), review sites like TripAdvisor (Borges-Tiago et al., 2021), instant messaging applications like X (formerly Twitter) (Yun et al., 2019) and video and photo sharing sites like Instagram or YouTube (Gretzel, 2017; Priporas et al., 2020; Wen & Song, 2017).

In general, research has shown that a brand's use of social media communication can enhance anthropomorphic beliefs, strengthen consumers' brand personality perceptions and improve brand relationship quality (Hudson et al., 2016; Peco-Torres et al., 2021; Walsh et al., 2013). Hence, a number of studies explored how brands may utilize their social media content strategies to position themselves with humanlike attributes, which in turn would affect consumer responses (Harrison & Kwon, 2023; He et al., 2021; Wen & Song, 2017). In particular, research has shown how digital brand personality encoded in social media posts increases consumer brand engagement (Lee et al., 2018; Mora Cortez & Ghosh Dastidar, 2022). In a widely cited study, Lee et al. (2018) discovered a positive link between brand personality-related appeals like humor or emotion in Facebook messages and increased consumer engagement (i.e., message interactions). In a similar study using B2B brands only, Mora Cortez and Ghosh Dastidar (2022) found that brand personality dimensions present in brand posts on LinkedIn had positive effects on various customer engagement behaviors. More specifically, the brand's excitement (Aaker, 1997) led to an increase in impressions and likes, competence increased clicks and ruggedness increased new followers. These studies show that, for both B2C and B2B brands, social media platforms offer opportunities to position their digital brand personality and strengthen relationships with their customers.

However, it is also important for brands to adapt their social media strategies to their digital brand personality positioning (Béal & Grégoire, 2022; Eigenraam et al., 2021). To illustrate, Béal and Grégoire (2022) examined how observers react to brand responses to consumer complaints in social media using humor. In the context of service recovery, the authors found different results for different brand personalities: To increase purchase intentions in observers through social media responses to public complaints, affiliative humor is more effective for sincere brands due to the emphasis on the inferred intentions, whereas aggressive humor is more suitable for exciting brands, thanks to appropriate humor appreciation and overall fit with the brand personality traits (Béal & Grégoire, 2022). Another example stems from Eigenraam et al. (2021) who found interaction effects between social media engagement strategies and brand types. Most importantly, they provided evidence that entertaining initiatives are perceived as more authentic for warm brands (vs. competent brands), whereas informative initiatives were regarded as authentic for both warm and competent brands. This highlights the need for research that focuses on the individual dimensions of digital brand personality and explores their suitability and interaction effects with different online platforms.

Another emerging trend in branding theory and research is the notion of co-creation, which can be applied to brand experiences, brand meaning and brand personality (Rosenthal & Brito, 2017). In a digitalized world, consumers are enabled to directly interact with brand messages, to talk to each other about a brand and to produce brand-related content (Swaminathan et al., 2020). Because of the hyperconnected environment, brand experiences and brand meanings become increasingly co-created, and managers may have to rethink their approach from single to shared ownership of a brand (Swaminathan et al., 2020). Many recent studies acknowledged that brand personality also becomes co-created by multiple actors (i.e., senders) in a digital environment and especially on social media platforms (Borges-Tiago et al., 2019, 2021; Rosenthal & Brito, 2017). More specifically, studies on digital brand personality showed that brand content, user-generated content and employee-generated content may be used to derive brand personality perceptions (Borges-Tiago et al., 2021; Hu et al., 2019). To illustrate, Borges-Tiago et al. (2021) compared brand-generated and user-generated content on touristic review platforms to measure the brand personality factors (Aaker, 1997) expressed, hence identifying misalignments between how brands seek to position themselves and how users evaluate brands publicly. Another example stems from Masiello et al. (2020) who contrasted sender and receiver perspectives and found various types of brand personality misalignments throughout the whole communication process as some brand personality items were intended but not properly communicated, communicated but not intended, communicated but not properly perceived or perceived but not communicated. These examples show how social media transferred power over how a brand's personality is portrayed digitally to senders and sources outside of the brand's control.

New Technologies

Apart from websites and social media, a growing stream of research has explored how new technologies pose challenges but also offer opportunities to imbue a brand with a humanlike personality (Hoyer et al., 2020; MacInnis & Folkes, 2017). Research in this field has mainly focused either on new technologies like extended reality applications that may enhance digital brand personality perceptions or on the emergence of non-human agents, as brands become represented through smart objects, virtual avatars, robots in retail and through text- or voice-based chatbots, which refers back to the notion of anthropomorphism and its fundamental relations to brand personality.

In the context of extended reality technologies, including AR, virtual reality (VR) and mixed reality (MR) (Hoyer et al., 2020), research has shown that brand experiences through such tools can strengthen consumers' brand personality perceptions (De Gauquier et al., 2018; Plotkina et al., 2022). To illustrate, De Gauquier et al. (2018) demonstrated that advertising using VR formats can significantly enhance brand personality perceptions compared to 2D advertising because of the more substantial brand experience. Similarly, Plotkina et al. (2022) found that consumers' attitude toward an AR app positively affected their brand personality perceptions. These studies show how new technologies have enriched digital brand personality, as they offer novel forms of brand experiences characterized by immersion that bring brands to life for consumers.

Other researchers have explored specific digital instruments like smart objects or AI-driven chatbots as new ways to manifest digital brand personality (Wu et al., 2017; Yang & Hu, 2022; Youn & Jin, 2021) via anthropomorphized brand agents that interact with consumers instead of human brand representatives. In an experimental study, Wu et al. (2017) showed that the interaction style of smart objects (IoT) influenced the warmth and competence perceptions of the brand and these influenced the brand attachments. Their findings confirmed the effectiveness of a friend-like interaction style, associated with a friendly, interactive approach, as it more strongly affected brand warmth and equally affected brand competence compared to the more professional engineer-style. This underscores the importance of taking a relationship-oriented approach to the design of consumer technology. In a similar vein, Youn and Jin (2021) examined the effects of the relationship style of an AI-powered chatbot as a brand's conversational agent on brand personality perceptions. Their findings showed a chatbot framed as an assistant led to higher competence perceptions, yet a chatbot framed as a friend did not yield higher sincerity perceptions. Drawing a comparison to human brand representatives, Yang and Hu (2022) further reinforced the link between chatbots and perceived competence as they confirmed the positive effects for matching a sincere brand personality with human-staffed service provision and a competent brand personality with AI-enabled service provision. Taken together, these studies suggest that, at the moment, anthropomorphized non-human brand agents are particularly suited to convey brand competence, with first attempts also illuminating implications for brand warmth.

DIGITAL-BASED METHODS TO STUDY BRAND PERSONALITY

The rise of digital technologies has not only shifted research attention to new phenomena regarding consumer behavior but also changed how these new phenomena can be studied. For digital brand personality research, new research methods have been developed to infer personality from online content. Hence, it is worth comparing and contrasting new digital-based methods to study digital brand personality with more traditional research and measurement approaches. However, it is critical to keep in mind that both offline-based and online-based brand personality research studies are dominated by positivist-quantitative approaches, whereas qualitative works are scarce (Ghorbani et al., 2022; Saeed et al., 2022).

There are two main ways in which extant research has studied digital brand personality online, either through survey-based or content-based approaches, which are juxtaposed in Table 8.2 (Ghorbani et al., 2022). On the one hand, a number of studies followed traditional brand personality and human personality research and applied psychometric scales to measure personality (Machado et al., 2019; Ong et al., 2017). Some of these studies utilized existing brand personality frameworks and scales, such as the well-known models of Aaker (1997) or Geuens et al. (2009), to assess consumers' brand personality perceptions in diverse digital contexts (Garanti & Kissi, 2019; Shobeiri et al., 2015; Torres & Augusto, 2019). Other studies in this domain have adopted the scale development procedure proposed by Aaker (1997) to develop their own brand personality frameworks with items deemed more applicable to a specific type of brand like internet media brands (Ham & Lee, 2015). Altogether, these studies have further perpetuated the traditional understanding of brand personality as a perceptual construct in the minds of consumers (Aaker, 1997).

On the other hand, there is a growing body of research that used new content-based approaches to extract digital brand personality from online content by means of documentary analysis, content

Table 8.2 Comparison of survey-based and content-based research approaches to studying digital brand personality

Research Approach	*Survey-Based*	*Content-Based*
Rationale based on human personality psychology	Brand personality metaphor enables peer-rating of brands in a similar manner as real people	Lexical hypothesis (i.e., relevant traits are encoded in language) enables extracting personality from written content
Research design	Quantitative survey-based designs (surveys; experiments)	Quantitative documentary/content analysis designs
Data collection and types of data collected	Self-completion questionnaires using psychometric rating scales (primary data)	Digital content, for example, reviews, social media postings and conversations in forums (secondary data)
Data analysis techniques	Exploratory and/or confirmatory factor analysis	Documentary analysis, dictionary analysis, text mining and linguistic analysis

Source: The author.

analysis or text mining (Masiello et al., 2020; Paschen et al., 2017; Ranfagni et al., 2016). These procedures are based on the shared premise that consumers' brand personality perceptions surface in how they discuss brands online and thus become encoded in user-generated content (Liu et al., 2020; Paschen et al., 2017). This is in line with the lexical hypothesis underpinning trait theories, claiming that most relevant traits become encoded in language. Likewise, the intended digital brand personality as communicated by brands has been inferred from their official online communications via websites or social media (Opoku et al., 2006; Wang et al., 2021). Thereby, digital brand personality research once again mirrors human personality research, as modern psychology has turned to study personality through digital footprints and self-disclosing information that people leave online (Hu et al., 2019; Kim, 2022).

Content-based studies have approached digital brand personality and how it is projected digitally from multiple angles (Ghorbani et al., 2022). First, researchers focused on the digital brand personality as communicated by the brand mainly through their website content (Okazaki, 2006; Opoku et al., 2006). Building on the personality theory of Hogan (1991), these studies sought to examine the intrinsic brand personality, which describes 'what the brand says about itself' (Pitt et al., 2007). Later on, this approach was extended to examine the brand's social media communications, for example, on platforms like X (formerly Twitter) (Baştuğ et al., 2020; Wang et al., 2021). Second, other researchers have focused on the extrinsic brand personality (Hogan, 1991), which refers to 'what others say about the brand' (Paschen et al., 2017). The foundation of this approach is the belief that consumers' perceptions of a brand's personality are naturally revealed in online conversations and social media posts related to the brand. Therefore, these posts are analyzed to extract and examine the traits and attributes used within them (Paschen et al., 2017). Third, other researchers have adopted a dyadic understanding of brand personality (Malär et al., 2012) as something that is both communicated and perceived (Ranfagni et al., 2016). Some studies combined methods to address the notion of alignment by applying content analysis to assess the brand personality digitally communicated by brands and survey-based measurements to assess consumers' brand personality perceptions (George & Anandkumar, 2014; Kim & Lehto, 2013). Other studies explored the alignment between digital brand personality as projected through the content from both brands and consumers, thus further contributing to the trend toward digital brand personality co-creation (Borges-Tiago et al., 2021; Hassan et al., 2024; Masiello et al., 2020).

Since the first content-based studies exploring brand website communication (Okazaki, 2006; Opoku et al., 2006), the digital-based measurement approaches have become more advanced as researchers embraced more sophisticated techniques such as text mining and sentiment analysis to infer digital brand personality from online contents (Lopez et al., 2020; Pamuksuz et al., 2021; Ranfagni et al., 2016). Initially, the very first content-based studies introduced a dictionary approach, building on existing brand personality inventories (Aaker, 1997) to match synonymous words communicated on brand websites (Opoku et al., 2006) and later also social media communications (Borges-Tiago et al., 2019; Robertson et al., 2019). More recently, researchers have further developed this approach using instruments of text mining and corpus linguistics, such as part-of-speech tagging software and co-occurrence analysis (Ranfagni et al., 2016), or machine learning tools (Pamuksuz et al., 2021). To illustrate, Ranfagni et al. (2016) collected and compared textual data on fashion brands from a multi-authored fashion blog and official brand communications (websites/ Facebook). In their data analysis, they drew on linguistic analysis to identify adjectives that reflected brand personality items, as defined by Aaker (1997). Finally, most recent studies also utilized supervised and unsupervised machine learning tools, thus taking advantage of natural language processing (Hassan et al., 2024; Hu et al., 2019; Pamuksuz et al., 2021; Yun et al., 2019). However, these studies have focused on measuring digital brand personality using textual content, with only a few studies considering how digital brand personality may also be conveyed through visual content (Liu et al., 2020; Taecharungroj, 2019).

Compared to traditional survey-based measurement approaches, there are both advantages and disadvantages to this new digital-based way of measuring brand personality. Content-based approaches and linguistic analysis can be automated and provide a cheap, quick and repeatable way of capturing brand personality at a specific point in time. Likewise, this approach allows to draw direct comparisons to competitors whose brand personalities can be accessed in a similar manner using publicly available data (Hu et al., 2019; Pamuksuz et al., 2021; Paschen et al., 2017; Yun et al., 2019). Researchers have argued for content-based approaches to be unobtrusive and providing 'real-world evidence' (Hu et al., 2019, p. 923) as they draw on naturalistic data and investigate consumer behavior in natural environments like social media or online forums (Crawford Camiciottoli et al., 2014). Indeed, digital-based research has shown that consumers naturally use personality terms when discussing brands (Paschen et al., 2017) highlighting the authentic expression of brand personality perceptions (Ranfagni et al., 2016). This observation significantly contributes to the argument that brand personality is an actual phenomenon, not just a manufactured research tool, as previously suggested by critics (Oklevik et al., 2020).

However, content-based approaches also fall short if compared to traditional survey-based measures as they may suffer from selection bias regarding the sources that can be chosen to measure digital brand personality, since extant research has gravitated to text-based and publicly accessible data sites like review platforms (Borges-Tiago et al., 2021). Like survey-based approaches, there is no established standard for how to define and measure brand personality in content-based approaches, which hinders the selection of relevant brand personality dimensions and appropriate social media analytics tools. While some argue that content-based approaches provide more realistic accounts of digital brand personality as they draw on secondary data, it may likewise be argued that this approach neglects consumers' unconscious brand personality associations. In contrast, survey-based approaches generate primary data that elicit brand personality perceptions that may not have been articulated otherwise, as they prompt consumers to think about a particular brand as if it were a person (Aaker, 1997).

Taken together, either approach offers near reverse advantages and disadvantages to the other. Therefore, digital-based measurement techniques should not be viewed as a substitute for traditional surveys but are considered a complementary way of studying digital brand personality. Moreover, both approaches have in common that they are currently dominated by quantitative-deductive studies and exploratory work remains the exception. Nevertheless, some alternative approaches have been proposed, for example, for new scales measuring brand personality not with traditional items like traits but with emojis (Moussa, 2021). Another example of an innovative method that combines digital tools with visual methods is Dzyabura and Peres' (2021) Brand Visual Elicitation Platform, where consumers create collages representing their brand associations, through which researchers then extract attributions and link them to, for example, brand personality dimensions (Aaker, 1997). While these efforts show the opportunities brought in by digital-based or digital-inspired research approaches, there is still room for broadening the methodological scope of the field of digital brand personality.

THE FUTURE OF DIGITAL BRAND PERSONALITY RESEARCH

This chapter has reviewed research on B2C and B2B brand personality in a digital world, focusing upon its theoretical underpinnings and conceptualizations, the digital contexts explored so far and the integration of digital-based methods to study the phenomenon. The previous sections have shown how digital brand personality is an important marketing instrument for both B2C and B2B brands that increasingly rely on digital technologies and online media to position themselves and seek to strengthen relationships with their customers through digital interactions. Moreover, this chapter has highlighted central debates driving the research with respect to the questions of what digital brand personality is, whether brands may gain a more humanlike personality in the digital world and how different digital contexts offer new instruments to build digital brand personality perceptions. Furthermore, this chapter has revealed how digital brand personality is increasingly co-created on social media platforms and how new digital-based research approaches can shed light on how digital brand personality becomes encoded in the digital content published by different senders. Now, this chapter turns to look ahead to where the discipline of digital brand personality is going in terms of its theoretical development, research contexts and methodological approaches.

First, there is room to broaden the conceptual and theoretical foundations of digital brand personality research. To overcome conceptual confusion, this chapter has proposed a novel definition of digital brand personality as an entity in its own right that is distinct from a brand's overall personality. This definition may provide a starting point for future research to consider digital brand personality as a multi-faceted construct that can be both projected and perceived (Jun & Lee, 2024; Masiello et al., 2020). Moreover, the majority of studies have transferred theoretical frameworks and models from the offline world to the online world without accounting for the differences in consumer–brand interactions. Thus, there is room for introducing theories that go beyond traditional brand personality, brand relationships and self-congruity theories and integrate digital technologies. On the one hand, future studies may continue exploring how co-creation and signaling theory may help to understand how digital brand personality is shaped by communications of different senders online (Borges-Tiago et al., 2019; Davies et al., 2018). On the other hand, future research is encouraged to direct more attention to exploring the digital world with its different spheres and their respective rules and conditions. Some researchers have already used notions of affordances and online experiential values to help understand how consumers experience and perceive digital brand personality in a particular context, like branded apps (e.g., Fang, 2019). Likewise, research drawing on human–machine interaction or human–computer interaction theories to better understand how consumers interact with technologies and the resulting implications for brand perceptions is limited (Jin & Sung, 2010; Pentina et al., 2013). Yet, these theoretical frameworks may help to understand the increasingly diversified new technologies introduced to the field and especially the role of anthropomorphized non-human brand agents.

Second, extant research has explored only a part of today's digital world. Since the first attempts at studying digital brand personality, research on websites and especially social media like Facebook and X (formerly Twitter) has proliferated. Although this chapter has revealed that digital-based studies have begun to explore brand personality in more diverse settings, there remain a number of digital contexts that are currently under-explored. Existing research into avatars and digital representations of human agents, for example, has heavily focused on brand agents communicating with potential consumers (Jin & Sung, 2010; Youn & Jin, 2021). Yet, in digital spheres like online games or the metaverse, consumers themselves may become digitally represented and it may be interesting to explore how they relate to brands through their own digital personalities. In addition, generative AI applications are becoming more popular for everyday usage and are increasingly integrated into brand services. Hence, future studies should be carried out, tracing the different personality constellations among brands, users and AI providers. What is more, as the review has shown, the different digital contexts studied have mainly remained isolated from one another. While some researchers have studied online–offline comparisons and illuminated differences in brand personality perceptions (Anselmsson & Tunca, 2019; Syed Alwi & Da Silva, 2007), no similar research has considered online–online comparisons. In a similar vein, while B2C settings have been the focus of most studies, future work is needed to fully understand the importance of brand personality as a marketing tool for B2B brands that connect with customers through digital platforms and social media (Aagerup et al., 2022; Robertson et al., 2019).

Third, the rise of digital technologies has also given rise to the use of digital-based methods to study brand personality. Thus far, these approaches have mainly utilized quantitative content analysis procedures to extract digital brand personality from texts published on social media and websites. Yet, digital conversations, especially on social media, are increasingly dominated by image and video content formats. Therefore, there is room to broaden the methodological scope and further integrate digital methods and visual methods to study digital brand personality as it is projected and perceived digitally.

In today's digital world, B2C and B2B brand personalities are increasingly shaped online by multiple actors and technologies. While extant research has widely argued for the positive effects of digital brand personality projections and perceptions, future research may explore how digital brand personalities are formed across different digital touchpoints. Future research can also address the increasingly diversified digital spheres and new technological instruments that mediate consumer–brand interactions. This chapter encourages future studies to recognize digital brand personality as a distinct entity, to broaden their theoretical frameworks and to experiment with digital-based methodologies.

REFERENCES

Aagerup, U., Andersson, S., & Awuah, G. B. (2022). Building a warm and competent B2B brand personality. *European Journal of Marketing*, *56*(13), 167–193. https://doi.org/10.1108/EJM-06-2019-0528

Aaker, J. L. (1997). Dimensions of brand personality. *Journal of Marketing Research*, *34*(3), 347–356. https://doi.org/10.2307/3151897

Aaker, J. L., Benet-Martínez, V., & Garolera, J. (2001). Consumption symbols as carriers of culture: A study of Japanese and Spanish brand personality constructs. *Journal of Personality and Social Psychology*, *81*(3), 492–508. https://doi.org/10.1037/0022-3514.81.3.492

Aaker, J. L., Vohs, K. D., & Mogilner, C. (2010). Nonprofits are seen as warm and for-profits as competent: Firm stereotypes matter. *Journal of Consumer Research*, *37*(2), 224–237. https://doi.org/10.1086/651566

American Psychological Association. (2022). *APA dictionary of psychology*. https://dictionary.apa.org/

Anselmsson, J., & Tunca, B. (2019). Exciting on Facebook or competent in the newspaper? Media effects on consumers' perceptions of brands in the fashion category. *Journal of Marketing Communications*, *25*(7), 720–737. https://doi.org/10.1080/13527266.2017.1392337

Azoulay, A., & Kapferer, J. N. (2003). Do brand personality scales really measure brand personality? *Journal of Brand Management*, *11*(2), 143–155. https://doi.org/10.1057/palgrave.bm.2540162

Baştuğ, S., Şakar, G. D., & Gülmez, S. (2020). An application of brand personality dimensions to container ports: A place branding perspective. *Journal of Transport Geography*, *82*, 1–13. https://doi.org/10.1016/j.jtrangeo.2019.102552

Béal, M., & Grégoire, Y. (2022). How do observers react to companies' humorous responses to online public complaints? *Journal of Service Research*, *25*(2), 242–259. https://doi.org/10.1177/10946705219894

Bernritter, S. F., Verlegh, P. W., & Smit, E. G. (2016). Why nonprofits are easier to endorse on social media: The roles of warmth and brand symbolism. *Journal of Interactive Marketing*, *33*(1), 27–42. https://doi.org/10.1016/j.intmar.2015.10.002

Beukeboom, C. J., Kerkhof, P., & de Vries, M. (2015). Does a virtual like cause actual liking? How following a brand's Facebook updates enhances brand evaluations and purchase intention. *Journal of Interactive Marketing*, *32*(1), 26–36. https://doi.org/10.1016/j.intmar.2015.09.003

Borges-Tiago, M. T., Tiago, F., Veríssimo, J. M., & Silva, T. (2019). A brand-new world: Brand-endorsers-users fit on social media. *Academia Revista Latinoamericana De Administración*, *32*(4), 472–486. https://doi.org/10.1108/ARLA-02-2019-0047

Borges-Tiago, M. T., Arruda, C., Tiago, F., & Rita, P. (2021). Differences between TripAdvisor and Booking.com in branding co-creation. *Journal of Business Research*, *123*, 380–388. https://doi.org/10.1016/j.jbusres.2020.09.050

Brakus, J. J., Schmitt, B. H., & Zarantonello, L. (2009). Brand experience: What is it? How is it measured? Does it affect loyalty? *Journal of Marketing*, *73*(3), 52–68. https://doi.org/10.1509/jmkg.73.3.52

Carpentier, M., van Hoye, G., & Weijters, B. (2019). Attracting applicants through the organization's social media page: Signaling employer brand personality. *Journal of Vocational Behavior*, *115*, 1–14. https://doi.org/10.1016/j.jvb.2019.103326

Chang, J. Y., & Kwon, W. S. (2022). E-store brand personality congruence for multichannel apparel retail brands. *Journal of Fashion Marketing and Management*, *26*(1), 159–178. https://doi.org/10.1108/JFMM-08-2019-0167

Chang, Y., Li, Y., Yan, J., & Kumar, V. (2019). Getting more likes: The impact of narrative person and brand image on customer-brand interactions. *Journal of the Academy of Marketing Science*, *47*(6), 1027–1045. https://doi.org/10.1007/s11747-019-00632-2

Coleman, D., de Chernatony, L., & Christodoulides, G. (2011). B2B service brand identity: Scale development and validation. *Industrial Marketing Management*, *40*(7), 1063–1071. https://doi.org/10.1016/j.indmarman.2011.09.010

Crawford Camiciottoli, B., Ranfagni, S., & Guercini, S. (2014). Exploring brand associations: An innovative methodological approach. *European Journal of Marketing*, *48*(5/6), 1092–1112. https://doi.org/10.1108/EJM-12-2011-0770

d'Astous, A., & Lévesque, M. (2003). A scale for measuring store personality. *Psychology & Marketing*, *20*(5), 455–469. https://doi.org/10.1002/mar.10081

Davies, G., Chun, R., Da Silva, R. V., & Roper, S. (2004). A corporate character scale to assess employee and customer views of organization reputation. *Corporate Reputation Review*, *7*(2), 125–146. https://doi.org/10.1057/palgrave.crr.1540216

Davies, G., Rojas-Méndez, J. I., Whelan, S., Mete, M., & Loo, T. (2018). Brand personality: Theory and dimensionality. *Journal of Product and Brand Management*, *27*(2), 115–127. https://doi.org/10.1108/JPBM-06-2017-1499

De Gauquier, L., Brengman, M., Willems, K., & van Kerrebroeck, H. (2018). Leveraging advertising to a higher dimension: Experimental research on the impact of virtual reality on brand personality impressions. *Virtual Reality*, *23*(3), 235–253. https://doi.org/10.1007/s10055-018-0344-5

Dzyabura, D., & Peres, R. (2021). Visual elicitation of brand perception. *Journal of Marketing, 85*(4), 44–66. https://doi.org/10.1177/002224292199 6661

Eigenraam, A. W., Eelen, J., & Verlegh, P. W. (2021). Let me entertain you? *The Importance of Authenticity in Online Customer Engagement. Journal of Interactive Marketing, 54*, 53–68. https://doi.org/10.1016/j.intmar.2020.11.001

Epley, N., Waytz, A., & Cacioppo, J. T. (2007). On seeing human: A three-factor theory of anthropomorphism. *Psychological Review, 114*(4), 864–886. https://doi.org/10.1037/0033-295X.114.4.864

Fang, Y. H. (2019). An app a day keeps a customer connected: Explicating loyalty to brands and branded applications through the lens of affordance and service-dominant logic. *Information and Management, 56*(3), 377–391. https://doi.org/10.1016/j.im.2018.07.011

Fournier, S. (1998). Consumers and their brands: Developing relationship theory in consumer research. *Journal of Consumer Research, 24*(4), 343–373. https://doi.org/10.1086/209515

Freling, T. H., & Forbes, L. P. (2005). An examination of brand personality through methodological triangulation. *Journal of Brand Management, 13*(2), 148–162. https://doi.org/10.1057/palgrave.bm.2540254

Garanti, Z., & Kissi, P. S. (2019). The effects of social media brand personality on brand loyalty in the Latvian banking industry. *International Journal of Bank Marketing, 37*(6), 1480–1503. https://doi.org/10.1108/IJBM-09-2018-0257

George, J., & Anandkumar, S. V. (2014). Portrayed and perceived online destination personality of select island destinations. *Anatolia: An International Journal of Tourism and Hospitality Research, 25*(2), 280–289. https://doi.org/10.1080/1303 2917.2014.894480

Geuens, M., Weijters, B., & de Wulf, K. (2009). A new measure of brand personality. *International Journal of Research in Marketing, 26*(2), 97–107. https://doi.org/10.1016/j.ijresmar.2008.12.002

Ghorbani, M., Karampela, M., & Tonner, A. (2022). Consumers' brand personality perceptions in a digital world: A systematic literature review and research agenda. *International Journal of Consumer Studies, 46*(5), 1960–1991. https://doi.org/10.1111/ijcs.12791

Goldberg, L. R. (1992). The development of markers for the big-five factor structure. *Psychological Assessment, 4*(1), 26–42. https://doi.org/10.1037/1040-3590.4.1.26

Gretzel, U. (2017). Social media activism in tourism. *Journal of Hospitality and Tourism, 15*(2), 1–14. www.researchgate.net/publication/322971829_Social_Media_Activism_in_Tourism/link/5b19fa000f7e9b68b428bd5e/download

Ham, C. D., & Lee, H. S. (2015). Internet media personality: Scale development and advertising implications. *International Journal of Advertising, 34*(2), 327–349. https://doi.org/10.1080/02650487.2014.996195

Harrison, E. N. B., & Kwon, W. S. (2023). Brands talking on events? Brand personification in real-time marketing tweets to drive consumer engagement. *Journal of Product & Brand Management, 32*(8), 1319–1337. https://doi.org/10.1108/JPBM-10-2022-4180

Hassan, M. A. E., Zerva, K., & Aulet, S. (2024). A model for brand personality word embedding: Identifying UNESCO world heritage personality categories. *Journal of Travel Research, 63*(1), 44–63. https://doi.org/10.1177/00472875221147142

He, A. Z., Cai, Y., Cai, L., & Zhang, Y. (2021). Conversation, storytelling, or consumer interaction and participation? The impact of brand-owned social media content marketing on consumers' brand perceptions and attitudes. *Journal of Research in Interactive Marketing, 15*(3), 419–440. https://doi.org/10.1108/JRIM-08-2019-0128

Herbst, U., & Merz, M. A. (2011). The industrial brand personality scale: Building strong business-to-business brands. *Industrial Marketing Management, 40*(7), 1072–1081. https://doi.org/10.1016/j.indmarman.2011.09.003

Hogan, R. (1991). Personality and personality measurement. In M. D. Dunnette, & L. M. Hough (Eds.), *Handbook of industrial and organizational psychology* (2nd ed., pp. 873–919). Consulting Psychologists Press.

Hoyer, W. D., Kroschke, M., Schmitt, B. H., Kraume, K., & Shankar, V. (2020). Transforming the customer experience through new technologies. *Journal of Interactive Marketing, 51*(1), 57–71. https://doi.org/10.1016/j.intmar.2020.04.001

Hu, Y., Xu, A., Hong, Y., Gal, D., Sinha, V., & Akkiraju, R. (2019). Generating business intelligence through social media analytics: Measuring brand personality with consumer-, employee-, and firm-generated content. *Journal of Management Information Systems, 36*(3), 893–930. https://doi.org/10.1080/07421222.2019.1628908

Huang, H. H., Mitchell, V. W., & Rosenaum-Elliott, R. (2012). Are consumer and brand personalities the same? *Psychology & Marketing, 29*(5), 334–349. https://doi.org/10.1002/mar.20525

Hudson, S., Huang, L., Roth, M. S., & Madden, T. J. (2016). The influence of social media interactions on consumer-brand relationships: A three-country study of brand perceptions and marketing behaviors. *International Journal of Research in Marketing, 33*(1), 27–41. https://doi.org/10.1016/j.ijresmar.2015.06.004

Jin, S. A. A., & Sung, Y. (2010). The roles of spokes-avatars' personalities in brand communication in

3D virtual environments. *Journal of Brand Management*, *17*(5), 317–327. https://doi.org/10.1057/bm.2009.18

John, O. P. (2021). History, measurement, and conceptual elaboration of the big-five trait taxonomy: The paradigm matures. In O. P. John, & R. W. Robins (Eds.), *Handbook of personality: Theory and research* (4th ed., pp. 35–82). The Guilford Press.

Jun, Y., & Lee, H. (2024). Measuring brand personality in the digital age: A review, theoretical reconceptualization, and research agenda. *Journal of Marketing Communications*, 1–34. https://doi.org/10.1080/13527266.2024.2345101

Keller, K. L., & Richey, K. (2006). The importance of corporate brand personality traits to a successful 21st century business. *Journal of Brand Management*, *14*(1-2), 74–81. https://doi.org/10.1057/palgrave.bm.2550055

Kervyn, N., Fiske, S. T., & Malone, C. (2012). Brands as intentional agents framework: How perceived intentions and ability can map brand perception. *Journal of Consumer Psychology*, *22*(2), 166–176. https://doi.org/10.1016/j.jcps.2011.09.006

Kim, J., Kwon, E. S., & Kim, B. (2018). Personality structure of brands on social networking sites and its effects on brand affect and trust: Evidence of brand anthropomorphization. *Asian Journal of Communication*, *28*(1), 93–113. https://doi.org/10.1080/01292986.2017.1363794

Kim, S., & Lehto, X. Y. (2013). Projected and perceived destination brand personalities. *Journal of Travel Research*, *52*(1), 117–130. https://doi.org/10.1177/0047287512457259

Kim, Y. (2022). Personality of nonprofit organizations' Instagram accounts and its relationship with their photos' characteristics at content and pixel levels. *Frontiers in Psychology*, *13*, 923305. https://doi.org/10.3389/fpsyg.2022.923305

Kovalchuk, M., Gabrielsson, M., & Rollins, M. (2023). Industrial BRAND-personality formation in a B2B stakeholder network: A service-dominant logic approach. *Industrial Marketing Management*, *114*, 313–330. https://doi.org/10.1016/j.indmarman.2023.05.006

Lee, D., Hosanagar, K., & Nair, H. S. (2018). Advertising content and consumer engagement on social media: Evidence from Facebook. *Management Science*, *64*(11), 5105–5131. https://doi.org/10.1287/mnsc.2017.2902

Liu, L., Dzyabura, D., & Mizik, N. (2020). Visual listening in: Extracting brand image portrayed on social media. *Marketing Science*, *39*(4), 669–686. https://doi.org/10.1287/mksc.2020.1226

Lopez, A., Guerra, E., Gonzalez, B., & Madero, S. (2020). Consumer sentiments toward brands: The interaction effect between brand personality and sentiments on electronic word of mouth. *Journal of Marketing Analytics*, *8*(4), 203–223. https://doi.org/10.1057/s41270-020-00085-5

Louis, D., & Lombart, C. (2010). Impact of brand personality on three major relational consequences (trust, attachment, and commitment to the brand). *Journal of Product and Brand Management*, *19*(2), 114–130. https://doi.org/10.1108/10610421011033467

Machado, J. C., Vacas-de-Carvalho, L., Azar, S. L., André, A. R., & Dos Santos, B. P. (2019). Brand gender and consumer-based brand equity on Facebook: The mediating role of consumer-brand engagement and brand love. *Journal of Business Research*, *96*, 376–385. https://doi.org/10.1016/j.jbusres.2018.07.016

MacInnis, D. J., & Folkes, V. S. (2017). Humanizing brands: When brands seem to be like me, part of me, and in a relationship with me. *Journal of Consumer Psychology*, *27*(3), 355–374. https://doi.org/10.1016/j.jcps.2016.12.003

Malär, L., Nyffenegger, B., Krohmer, H., & Hoyer, W. D. (2012). Implementing an intended brand personality: A dyadic perspective. *Journal of the Academy of Marketing Science*, *40*(5), 728–744. https://doi.org/10.1007/s11747-011-0251-8

Masiello, B., Bonetti, E., & Izzo, F. (2020). Multiple identities of a festival: Intended, communicated and perceived brand personality in the social media environment. *International Journal of Contemporary Hospitality Management*, *32*(2), 749–768. https://doi.org/10.1108/IJCHM-11-2018-0937

McCrae, R. R., & Costa, P. T., Jr. (1997). Personality trait structure as a human universal. *American Psychologist*, *52*(5), 509–516. https://doi.org/10.1037/0003-066X.52.5.509

Merrilees, B., & Miller, D. (2005). Emotional brand associations: A new KPI for e-retailers. *International Journal of Internet Marketing and Advertising*, *2*(3), 206–218. https://doi.org/10.1504/IJIMA.2005.007747

Mora Cortez, R., & Ghosh Dastidar, A. (2022). A longitudinal study of B2B customer engagement in LinkedIn: The role of brand personality. *Journal of Business Research*, *145*, 92–105. https://doi.org/10.1016/j.jbusres.2022.02.086

Moussa, S. (2021). Measuring brand personality using emoji: Findings from Mokken scaling. *Journal of Brand Management*, *28*(2), 116–132. https://doi.org/10.1057/s41262-020-00220-8

Okazaki, S. (2006). Excitement or sophistication? A preliminary exploration of online brand personality. *International Marketing Review*, *23*(3), 279–303. https://doi.org/10.1108/02651330610670451

Oklevik, O., Supphellen, M., & Maehle, N. (2020). Time to retire the concept of brand personality? Extending the critique and introducing a new framework. *Journal of Consumer Behaviour*, *19*(3), 211–218. https://doi.org/10.1002/cb.1805

Ong, K. S., Nguyen, B., & Syed Alwi, S. F. (2017). Consumer-based virtual brand personality (CBVBP), customer satisfaction and brand loyalty in the online banking industry. *International Journal of Bank Marketing*, *35*(3), 370–390. https://doi.org/10.1108/IJBM-04-2016-0054

Opoku, R. A., Abratt, R., & Pitt, L. (2006). Communicating brand personality: Are the websites doing the talking for the top South African business schools? *Journal of Brand Management*, *14*(1–2), 20–39. https://doi.org/10.1057/palgrave.bm.2550052

Pamuksuz, U., Yun, J. T., & Humphreys, A. (2021). A brand-new look at you: Predicting brand personality in social media networks with machine learning. *Journal of Interactive Marketing*, *56*(1), 55–69. https://doi.org/10.1016/j.intmar.2021.05.001

Paschen, J., Pitt, L., Kietzmann, J., Dabirian, A., & Farshid, M. (2017). The brand personalities of brand communities: An analysis of online communication. *Online Information Review*, *41*(7), 1064–1075. https://doi.org/10.1108/OIR-08-2016-0235

Peco-Torres, F., Polo-Peña, A. I., & Frías-Jamilena, D. M. (2021). Brand personality in cultural tourism through social media. *Tourism Review*, *76*(1), 164–183. https://doi.org/10.1108/TR-02-2019-0050

Pentina, I., Zhang, L., & Basmanova, O. (2013). Antecedents and consequences of trust in a social media brand: A cross-cultural study of Twitter. *Computers in Human Behavior*, *29*(4), 1546–1555. https://doi.org/10.1016/j.chb.2013.01.045

Pitt, L. F., Opoku, R. A., Hultman, M., Abratt, R., & Spyropoulou, S. (2007). What I say about myself: Communication of brand personality by African countries. *Tourism Management*, *28*(3), 835–844. https://doi.org/10.1016/j.tourman.2006.06.003

Plotkina, D., Dinsmore, J., & Racat, M. (2022). Improving service brand personality with augmented reality marketing. *Journal of Services Marketing*, *36*(6), 781–799. https://doi.org/10.1108/JSM-12-2020-0519

Poddar, A., Donthu, N., & Wei, Y. (2009). Web site customer orientations, web site quality, and purchase intentions: The role of web site personality. *Journal of Business Research*, *62*(4), 441–450. https://doi.org/10.1016/j.jbusres.2008.01.036

Priporas, C. V., Stylos, N., & Kamenidou, I. (2020). City image, city brand personality and generation Z residents' life satisfaction under economic crisis: Predictors of city-related social media engagement. *Journal of Business Research*, *119*, 453–463. https://doi.org/10.1016/j.jbusres.2019.05.019

Radler, V. M. (2018). 20 Years of brand personality: A bibliometric review and research agenda. *Journal of Brand Management*, *25*(4), 370–383. https://doi.org/10.1057/s41262-017-0083-z

Ranfagni, S., Crawford Camiciottoli, B., & Faraoni, M. (2016). How to measure alignment in perceptions of brand personality within online communities: Interdisciplinary insights. *Journal of Interactive Marketing*, *35*(1), 70–85. https://doi.org/10.1016/j.intmar.2015.12.004

Robertson, J., Ferguson, S., Eriksson, T., & Näppä, A. (2019). The brand personality dimensions of business-to-business firms: A content analysis of employer reviews on social media. *Journal of Business-to-Business Marketing*, *26*(2), 109–124. https://doi.org/10.1080/1051712X.2019.1603354

Rojas-Méndez, J. I., & Hine, M. J. (2017). Countries' positioning on personality traits: Analysis of 10 south American national tourism websites. *Journal of Vacation Marketing*, *23*(3), 233–247. https://doi.org/10.1177/1356766716649227

Rosenthal, B., & Brito, E. P. Z. (2017). The brand meaning co-creation process on Facebook. *Marketing Intelligence and Planning*, *35*(7), 923–936. https://doi.org/10.1108/MIP-09-2016-0171

Roy, P., Khandeparkar, K., & Motiani, M. (2016). A lovable personality: The effect of brand personality on brand love. *Journal of Brand Management*, *23*(5), 97–113. https://doi.org/10.1057/s41262-016-0005-5

Saeed, M. R., Burki, U., Ali, R., Dahlstrom, R., & Zameer, H. (2022). The antecedents and consequences of brand personality: A systematic review. *EuroMed Journal of Business*, *17*(4), 448–476. https://doi.org/10.1108/EMJB-12-2020-0136

Sestino, A. (2024). The challenge of integrating 'intelligent' technologies in luxury shopping contexts: The role of brand personality appeal and consumers' status consumption orientation. *Journal of Retailing and Consumer Services*, *76*, 103488. https://doi.org/10.1016/j.jretconser.2023.103488

Shi, X., & Shan, X. (2019). Cross-cultural impact on financial companies' online brand personality. *Marketing Intelligence and Planning*, *37*(5), 482–496. https://doi.org/10.1108/MIP-06-2018-0233

Shobeiri, S., Mazaheri, E., & Laroche, M. (2015). How would the E-retailer's website personality impact customers' attitudes toward the site? *Journal of Marketing Theory and Practice*, *23*(4), 388–401. https://doi.org/10.1080/10696679.2015.1049682

Sung, Y., & Kim, J. (2010). Effects of brand personality on brand trust and brand affect. *Psychology & Marketing*, *27*(7), 639–661. https://doi.org/10.1002/mar.20349

Sung, Y., & Tinkham, S. F. (2005). Brand personality structures in the United States and Korea: Common and culture-specific factors. *Journal of*

Consumer Psychology, *15*(4), 334–350. https://doi.org/10.1207/s15327663jcp1504_8

Swaminathan, V., Sorescu, A., Steenkamp, J. B. E., O'Guinn, T. C. G., & Schmitt, B. H. (2020). Branding in a hyperconnected world: Refocusing theories and rethinking boundaries. *Journal of Marketing*, *84*(2), 24–46. https://doi.org/10.1177/0022242919899905

Syed Alwi, S. F., & Da Silva, R. V. (2007). Online and offline corporate brand images: Do they differ? *Corporate Reputation Review*, *10*(4), 217–244. https://doi.org/10.1057/palgrave.crr.1550056

Taecharungroj, V. (2019). User-generated place brand identity: Harnessing the power of content on social media platforms. *Journal of Place Management and Development*, *12*(1), 39–70. https://doi.org/10.1108/JPMD-11-2017-0117

Torres, P., & Augusto, M. (2019). Building resilience to negative information and increasing purchase intentions in a digital environment. *Journal of Business Research*, *101*, 528–535. https://doi.org/10.1016/j.jbusres.2018.11.045

Valette-Florence, P., Guizani, H., & Merunka, D. (2011). The impact of brand personality and sales promotions on brand equity. *Journal of Business Research*, *64*(1), 24–28. https://doi.org/10.1016/j.jbusres.2009.09.015

Veloutsou, C., & Taylor, C. S. (2012). The role of the brand as a person in business to business brands. *Industrial Marketing Management*, *41*(6), 898–907. https://doi.org/10.1016/j.indmarman.2012.02.004

Venable, B., Rose, G., Bush, V., & Gilbert, F. (2005). The role of brand personality in charitable giving: An assessment and validation. *Journal of the Academy of Marketing Science*, *33*(3), 295–312. https://doi.org/10.1177/0092070305276147

Walsh, P., Clavio, G., Lovell, M. D., & Blaszka, M. (2013). Differences in event brand personality between social media users and non-users. *Sport Marketing Quarterly*, *22*(4), 214–223.

Wang, X., Cheng, M., Wong, I. A., Teah, M., & Lee, S. (2021). Big-five personality traits in P2P accommodation platforms: Similar or different to hotel brands? *Current Issues in Tourism*, *24*(23), 3407–3419. https://doi.org/10.1080/13683500.2021.1884205

Wen, J., & Song, B. (2017). Corporate ethical branding on YouTube: CSR communication strategies and brand anthropomorphism. *Journal of Interactive Advertising*, *17*(1), 28–40. https://doi.org/10.1080/15252019.2017.1295291

Wood, N. T., & Solomon, M. R. (2008). Digital brand personality: Does the matchup hypothesis extend to online environments? In A. Y. Lee, & D. Soman (Eds.), *Advances in consumer research* (Vol. *35*, pp. 84–85). Assoc Consumer Research.

Wu, J., Chen, J., & Dou, W. (2017). The Internet of Things and interaction style: The effect of smart interaction on brand attachment. *Journal of Marketing Management*, *33*(1–2), 61–75. https://doi.org/10.1080/0267257X.2016.1233132

Yang, C., & Hu, J. (2022). When do consumers prefer AI-enabled customer service? The interaction effect of brand personality and service provision type on brand attitudes and purchase intentions. *Journal of Brand Management*, *29*(2), 167–189. https://doi.org/10.1057/s41262-021-00261-7

Youn, S., & Jin, S. V. (2021). 'In A.I. we trust?' The effects of parasocial interaction and Technopian versus Luddite ideological views on chatbot-based customer relationship management in the emerging 'feeling economy'. *Computers in Human Behavior*, *119*, 106721. https://doi.org/10.1016/j.chb.2021.106721

Yun, J. T., Pamuksuz, U., & Duff, B. R. L. (2019). Are we who we follow? Computationally analyzing human personality and brand following on Twitter. *International Journal of Advertising*, *38*(5), 776–795. https://doi.org/10.1080/02650487.2019.1575106

9

Brand Authenticity: Conceptualization and Future Directions

Filipa Rosado-Pinto and
Sandra Maria Correia Loureiro

INTRODUCTION

Authenticity plays a critical role in the 21st century (Lehman et al., 2019). In the last 20 years, academic research about the topic has grown significantly both in marketing and in related fields (Campagna et al., 2023; Nunes et al., 2021), as people value authentic products, services and experiences (Fritz et al., 2017). The study of authenticity is common across various fields of research, namely, management, anthropology, philosophy, sociology, psychology or marketing (Bruhn et al., 2012; Fritz et al., 2017; Kovács, 2019; Lehman et al., 2019; Nunes et al., 2021). According to Fritz et al. (2017), in philosophy, authenticity is linked to moral behavior and, within sociology, the concept is mainly perceived as a social construction. In anthropology, authenticity is related to the preservation of beliefs, values and cultural norms and in psychology, 'authenticity is rooted in subjective internal experiences that have implications for one's self-knowledge, understanding and relationship behavior' (Fritz et al., 2017, p. 326).

In the marketing field, authenticity is perceived as a core asset. Indeed, there has been a 'steady increase in the discourse on what constitutes authenticity in consumption, not only through popular culture, media coverage and political debate but also through marketing praxis and scholarship' (Södergren, 2021, p. 645). Different brand authenticity indexes emerged (e.g., Authenticity 500 Index, UK FTSE 50* Index, Cohn & Wolfe's Authentic 100 Index), mirroring authentic brand's importance in consumers' lives and brand management. In marketing research, consumers' quest for authenticity has been considered 'one of the cornerstones of contemporary marketing' (Brown et al., 2003, p. 21), being essential for companies to understand, manage and outperform in delivering authenticity (Gilmore & Pine, 2007; Murshed et al., 2023; Nunes et al., 2021). Gilmore and Pine (2007) recognize the importance of authenticity in the consumption context stating that consumers not only look for memorable experiences, but they also 'choose to buy or not to buy based on how real they perceive an offering to be' (Gilmore & Pine, 2007, p. 1). Although in literature different meanings can be found and different approaches are employed to explain the concept, some attributes are transversally accepted to describe the term in the consumption context, as authenticity is often associated with being genuine, real and/or true (Beverland & Farrelly, 2010). According to Fritz et al. (2017), two streams of research can be identified: authenticity as an attribute of a subject (for instance, employees' emotional authenticity) and authenticity as an attribute of an object (e.g., brand authenticity). When authenticity is applied in a brand context, the concept of brand authenticity emerges. The growing competition among brands has increased the consumer quest for brand authenticity and 'it has become a precondition for successful businesses' (Hyun et al., 2024, p. 1). Brand authenticity is an essential element of brand differentiation (Morhart et al., 2015; Napoli et al., 2014) and leads to important outcomes, such as purchase intentions, brand loyalty, brand trust, expected quality, brand equity or brand love.

Considering the role of brand authenticity in brand management, this chapter's main objectives are to explain the concept and to highlight its theoretical foundations, its meanings, dimensions and its evolution. Finally, this chapter presents a research agenda that can be useful for future studies on the topic.

BRAND AUTHENTICITY

Theoretical Foundations

Different theoretical approaches emerge from literature related to authenticity – objective authenticity, constructive authenticity and existential authenticity (see Figure 9.1). Objective authenticity assumes that the authenticity of objects or experiences can be judged based on an objective criterion. In contrast, constructive authenticity adopts a more subjective perspective as it is presented as 'a quality perceived by individuals that emerges from their own personal experiences' (Leigh et al., 2006, p. 483), leading to different interpretations of reality. The constructivist perspective aligns with the idea that authenticity is a socially constructed conception (Cohen, 1988), and the perception of authenticity is based on beliefs, perspectives and points of view (Wang, 1999). In a branding context, the objectivist perspective assumes that brand authenticity perceptions come from an 'evidence-based reality' that can be verified based on information about the brand – for example, labels of origin, ingredients or performance (Morhart et al., 2015).

Grayson and Martinec (2004) suggest two perspectives of authenticity applied to a market offering: indexical and iconic. Indexical authenticity refers to identifying the 'real thing' and its distinction from imitations. This differentiation relies on cues that have a factual and spatio-temporal connection with the claimed authenticity, such as certifications or a trustworthy context (indexical cues). Yet, iconic authenticity pertains to market offerings that are 'perceived as being similar to something else' (Grayson & Martinec, 2004, p. 298). In this sense, iconic authenticity emerges when an object is recognized as an 'authentic reproduction' or 'authentic recreation' of the original. Similar to indexical cues, iconic cues play a critical role in helping consumers identify an offering as authentic. According to Leigh et al. (2006) and Morhart et al. (2015), indexical authenticity presented by Grayson and Martinec (2004) is associated with

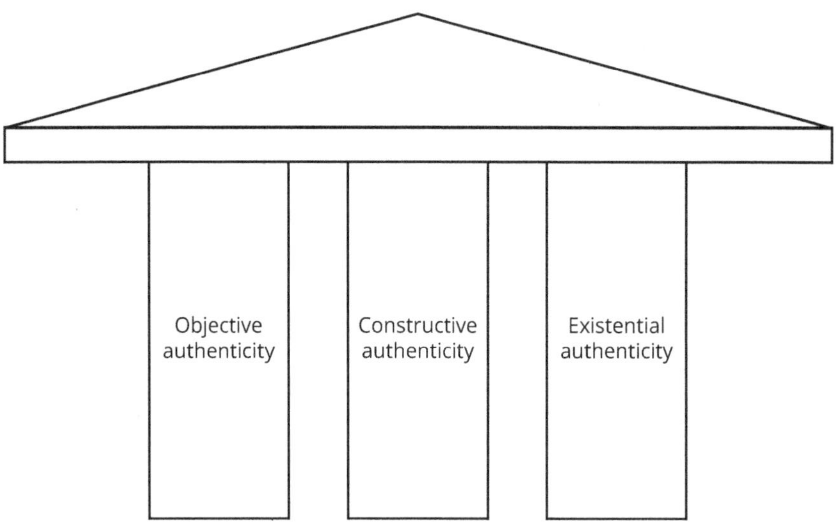

Figure 9.1 Theoretical foundations

Source: The authors.

objective authenticity and iconic authenticity is associated with the constructivist perspective.

Finally, the existentialist perspective perceives authenticity as related to one's identity. In a brand context, 'existential authenticity refers to a brand's ability to serve as a resource for consumers to reveal their true selves or to allow consumers to feel that they are true to themselves by consuming the brand' (Morhart et al., 2015, p. 202). Wang (1999) states that this is the perspective that best explains authenticity in the tourism context, arguing that existential authenticity has two main dimensions: interpersonal and intrapersonal authenticity. Intrapersonal authenticity is centered on the individual self. It involves feelings such as relaxation, entertainment or self-realization and interpersonal authenticity pertains to sharing and communicating the pleasure of tourism experiences with others. For many academics, authenticity in the marketplace appears to encompass a subjective element tied to consumers' perceptions of what is authentic (e.g., Le et al., 2019; Yuan et al., 2014).

Definitions and Dimensions

Different authenticity and brand authenticity definitions are presented in the literature, leading to a 'lack of clarity concerning the meaning(s) of brand authenticity' (Moulard et al., 2021, p. 97). According to Nunes et al. (2021) and Rosado-Pinto and Loureiro (2024), literature on the topic provides a fragmented picture of what it means to be authentic in the context of consumption. Despite the fragmented nature of the concept, a common thread among various authors is the association of authenticity with being genuine, real and true, which aligns closely with what is stated by Beverland and Farrelly (2010). The definitions presented by Fine (2003), who links authenticity to sincerity, innocence, originality and genuineness, and by Grayson and Martinec (2004), who use the term 'authentic' to describe something that is genuine and true, defining an authentic object as 'the original' or 'the real thing', are widely referenced in the literature.

Researchers often define authenticity by identifying the elements or attributes that a subject, object or experience must possess to be deemed authentic. For example, quality commitments, heritage and pedigree, relationship to place, method of production, stylistic consistency and downplaying commercial motives are key characteristics associated with authenticity (Beverland, 2006). In this vein, Bruhn et al. (2012) argue that brand authenticity is applied to objects and services, based on the individuals' perceptions and different attributes. Morhart et al. (2015) state that brand authenticity relates to the consumer's perception that a brand is faithful and true to consumers and itself, helping consumers to be true to themselves. Another widely referred definition is presented by Napoli et al. (2014) who state that brand authenticity is based on the consumer's subjective evaluation of the genuineness of a brand. Fritz et al. (2017) consider that a brand is authentic when its behaviors are consistent and reflect the core values, the essence and the norms of the brand. The perspective of Dwivedi and McDonald (2018) is very similar to the one of Fritz et al. (2017), assuming that an authentic brand is true to itself, knows what it stands for and keeps its promise. More recently, Nunes et al. (2021) identified six major components to define authenticity in the consumption context: accuracy, connectedness, integrity, legitimacy, originality and proficiency. Campagna et al. (2023) focus on the genuineness, uniqueness, openness and honesty of the brand to define the term, while Rosado-Pinto and Loureiro (2024) – based on a systematic literature review performed – conclude that 'in sum, considering the different definitions and dimensions of the construct, we claim that brand authenticity means a brand being genuine, real, true to itself and its consumers, and with consistent behavior, reflecting its values' (Rosado-Pinto & Loureiro, 2024, p. 555). Table 9.1 presents several definitions of brand authenticity in the literature.

Academics recognize that brand authenticity is a multidimensional construct. Based on several studies about the topic and on different measurement scales – for example, Akbar and Wymer (2017), Bruhn et al. (2012), Morhart et al. (2015) and Napoli et al. (2014) – that serve as reference for many studies about brand authenticity, Rosado-Pinto and Loureiro (2024) conclude that some transversal dimensions and attributes are referred by different scholars when analyzing the authenticity of a brand. These attributes and dimensions are 'genuineness (Akbar & Wymer, 2017; Beverland & Farrelly, 2010), continuity (Bruhn et al., 2012; Morhart et al., 2015), originality (Akbar & Wymer, 2017; Bruhn et al., 2012; Fine, 2003; Gundlach & Neville, 2012; Mody et al., 2019), reliability (Bruhn et al., 2012; Dwivedi & McDonald, 2018), quality commitment (Beverland, 2006; Napoli et al., 2014) and heritage (Beverland, 2006; Choi et al., 2015; Gundlach & Neville, 2012; Napoli et al., 2014; Spiggle et al., 2012)' (Rosado-Pinto & Loureiro, 2024, p. 555). These conclusions build on the findings of Fritz et al. (2017) who state that different scales to measure brand authenticity cover similar dimensions, as they all 'cover the aspects of consistency (i.e., continuity, heritage), honesty (i.e., reliability, quality commitment, credibility)

Table 9.1 Brand authenticity definitions

Authors	*Definition*
Beverland and Farrelly (2010, p. 839)	'Significantly, despite the multiplicity of terms and interpretations applied to authenticity, ultimately what is consistent across the literature is that authenticity encapsulates what is genuine, real and/or true'
Bruhn et al. (2012, p. 567)	'(1) Authenticity in the context of brands deals with the authenticity of market offerings (objects and services) in contrast to the authenticity of human beings; (2) Brand authenticity is based on the evaluations of individuals rather than being solely related to the inherent attributes of the brand (for references on this topic, cf. Beverland & Farrelly, 2010); (3) Brand authenticity corresponds to a variety of attributes since there is no unique definition of the authenticity concept, particularly in the branding context'
Napoli et al. (2014, p. 1091)	'In this study brand authenticity is defined as a subjective evaluation of genuineness ascribed to a brand by consumers'
Morhart et al. (2015, p. 203)	'We define PBA as the extent to which consumers perceive a brand to be faithful toward itself (continuity), true to its consumers (credibility), motivated by caring and responsibility (integrity) and able to support consumers in being true to themselves (symbolism)'
Fritz et al. (2017, p. 327)	'In summary, brand authenticity can be defined as the perceived consistency of a brand's behavior that reflects its core values and norms, according to which it is perceived as being true to itself, not undermining its brand essence or substantive nature, whereby the perceptual process involves two types of authenticity (i.e., indexical and iconic authenticity)'
Dwivedi and McDonald (2018, p. 1391)	'We define an authentic brand as one that is perceived by consumers as having a clear philosophy it lives by; one with a sense of what it stands for; a brand that lives up to its promise'
Nunes et al. (2021, p. 2)	'We define authenticity as it pertains to consumption as follows: a holistic consumer assessment determined by six component judgments (accuracy, connectedness, integrity, legitimacy, originality and proficiency) whereby the role of each component can change according to the consumption context'
Campagna et al. (2023, p. 138)	'A genuine brand with a unique style that cares about being open and honest with consumers and will survive times and trends'
Rosado-Pinto and Loureiro (2024, p. 555)	'In sum, considering the different definitions and dimensions of the construct, we claim that brand authenticity means a brand being genuine, real, true to itself and its consumers, and with consistent behavior, reflecting its values'

Source: The authors.

and genuineness (i.e., naturalness, sincerity, integrity)' (Fritz et al., 2017, p. 327).

Other forms of authenticity explored in the literature and applied to brands are, for instance, the concept of co-branding authenticity – when a consumer perceives the genuineness of a co-branding partnership (Ilicic et al., 2019) and the concept of brand extension authenticity that represents a consumer's perception that a brand extension is legitimate and consistent with the parent brand (Spiggle et al., 2012). In the context of Integrated Marketing Communications, it is considered crucial that the message being conveyed is grounded in attributes associated with authenticity and reflected in the product's performance (Beverland & Luxton, 2005). An authentic advertisement is defined as being genuine, real and true, considering executional elements or dimensions (Becker et al., 2019). Still in the brand context, when authenticity is applied to people, namely, when celebrities are perceived as brands, scholars refer to the term of celebrity brand authenticity. This is usually associated with the perception that the celebrity is being true to himself/herself (Ilicic & Webster, 2016), which means that the celebrity behaves according to his/her true self (Moulard et al., 2015).

Evolution

Rosado-Pinto and Loureiro (2024) identify various contexts where brand authenticity has been studied, from food and beverages and food services such as coffee shops, restaurants and catering (e.g., Lu et al., 2015; Rodrigues et al., 2021; Zhang et al., 2021), to fashion and apparel (e.g., Choi et al., 2015; Oh et al., 2019), luxury goods (e.g., Beverland & Luxton, 2005; Manthiou et al., 2018) or tourism (e.g., Grayson & Martinec, 2004; Kolar & Zabkar, 2010; Rather et al., 2019).

Figure 9.2 Evolution of brand authenticity-related themes

Source: The authors.

Over the years, various topics have been explored within the realm of brand authenticity research (see Figure 9.2). Seminal works, such as the ones of Cohen (1988), Wang (1999), and Grayson and Martinec (2004) explore the theoretical foundations of authenticity, paving the way for other studies to build on. Rosado-Pinto and Loureiro (2024) state that from 2005 to 2012, the discussion evolved around the characteristics and the attributes that market offerings need to have to be considered authentic (e.g., Beverland, 2005, 2006), as well as on how to project authenticity in marketing communications (e.g., Huang, 2010). Since 2012, different brand authenticity scales (e.g., Akbar & Wymer, 2017; Bruhn et al., 2012; Morhart et al., 2015; Napoli et al., 2014) with different dimensions have emerged, and studies have also been prolific in identifying how other constructs relate with brand authenticity, focusing on the antecedents and outcomes of brand authenticity in different industries (Rosado-Pinto & Loureiro, 2024). Some examples of constructs that have been studied as antecedents of authenticity are the perception of iconicity and indexicality, rarity (a brand being perceived as uncommon) and stability (having constant behavior over time) (Rosado-Pinto & Loureiro, 2024). Academics also demonstrate that manufacturing factors, such as manufacturing location, brand marketing communications, brand consistency, brand continuity and brand individuality enhance the perception of authenticity (Rosado-Pinto & Loureiro, 2024). Brand experiences and constructs linked to a brand's past, such as brand nostalgia and brand heritage, have been identified as key drivers of brand authenticity. Marketing literature also shows that perceptions of authenticity lead to purchase intentions, brand loyalty, brand trust, expected quality, perceived brand value, brand love, brand attachment and brand equity. These outcomes have been widely explored in the literature (Rosado-Pinto & Loureiro, 2024).

Besides the established relationships between brand authenticity and other related constructs, additional topics of interest emerged between 2012 and 2017 and after 2017 (Rosado-Pinto & Loureiro, 2024). Specifically, some researchers focus on the role of territory/country of origin, or provenance in creating authenticity perceptions (e.g., Collins & Weiss, 2015; Zhang & Merunka, 2015). Zhang and Merunka (2015) study the territory of origin as an antecedent of authenticity and confirm the positive impact of the territory of origin associations on perceived product authenticity and, consequently, on consumer/brand relationships. Collins and Weiss (2015) argue that 'it is widely accepted that authenticity, or the perception of authenticity, is critical to the successful formation of brand provenance' (Collins & Weiss, 2015, p. 1033). Other researchers address the specific case of celebrity brand authenticity (e.g., Moulard et al., 2015) defining the concept of authenticity applied to 'human brands' and identifying its antecedents. Brand extension authenticity (Spiggle et al., 2012) and co-branding authenticity (e.g.,

Ilicic et al., 2019) have also been topics that caught the attention of researchers. Brand extensions are, in fact, quite popular as most new products introduced in the market are brand extensions (Kotler et al., 2019). According to Spiggle et al. (2012), brand extension authenticity is related to the cultural link between the extension and the parent brand and its connection potential to consumers. They define the concept of brand extension authenticity as 'a consumer's sense that a brand extension is a legitimate, culturally consistent extension of the parent brand', develop a scale to measure it, and identify four dimensions for the construct: '(1) maintaining brand styles and standards, (2) honoring brand heritage, (3) preserving brand essence and (4) avoiding brand exploitation' (Spiggle et al., 2012, p. 969). Authentic brands present consistency in their style and aesthetics through elements, such as design and sensory aspects. Consistency of brand standards can be manifested, for example, in the production process, features or ingredients. Presenting inconsistency in any of these components can compromise the brand extension as it can be perceived as inauthentic. Brand extensions that preserve the brand heritage through cultural associations, such as the location of production or keeping traditional styles and design, tend to be perceived as more authentic, as well as the ones that preserve the brand essence – the fundamental values of the brand, what it stands for and what makes it unique. Finally, avoiding brand exploitation is key as consumers tend to perceive as more authentic brand extensions that are not exclusively driven by profit.

In the context of celebrity endorsement of cause-related products, Ilicic et al. (2019) introduce the concept of co-branding authenticity defined as the 'consumer perceptions of the genuineness of a co-branding partnership' (Ilicic et al., 2019, p. 50) and conclude that celebrity social responsibility enhances co-branding authenticity which, in turn, enhances purchase intentions.

Another theme of interest has been the role of authenticity as a specific brand attribute in the case of local and global brands (e.g., Riefler, 2020; Srivastava et al., 2020; Zebal & Jackson, 2019) and how local and global brands might differ in the perception of authenticity. Zebal and Jackson (2019) recognize the role of product authenticity as a cue to shape the purchase of local retail apparel brands, while Riefler (2020) concludes that the perceptions of authenticity lead to a higher brand value independently of brand globalness. Srivastava et al. (2020) analyze the effects of perceived brand globalness, perceived local iconness and brand authenticity on brand credibility and their impacts on purchase intentions, for both global and domestic brands. Findings show that brand authenticity positively impacts brand credibility in the case of global and domestic brands and that brand credibility is positively associated with purchase intentions.

In the service context, employee authenticity has also been found to have a key role in enhancing customer outcomes such as purchase intentions (Matthews et al., 2020). In services, employees, specifically frontline service employees, are an essential touchpoint between the company and consumers and are very important in conveying authenticity cues to consumers.

Since 2019, the study of authenticity in the online context has gained emphasis as scholars state that while authenticity has been extensively debated and explored in the marketing literature, 'there is little work on an online context that conceptualizes and measures the authentic experience and its sub-constructs' (Davis et al., 2019, p. 17). Studies have addressed this gap by analyzing, for instance, how a brand's social media can induce brand authenticity perceptions (e.g., Pink et al., 2023; Yang et al., 2021). For example, Yang et al. (2021) examine how visual cues on Instagram influence consumer perceptions of genuineness and trustworthiness and how these perceptions influence brand perceptions in concrete, brand authenticity. Findings show that a smile and snapshot photography result in a higher perceived source of genuineness, enhancing the brand's perceived authenticity. Pink et al. (2023) in a study applied to family brands conclude that social media posts with specific characteristics – creativity, information, persuasion and inspiration – can positively change or enhance brand perceptions (brand authenticity), leading to purchase intentions. Still in the social media context, how social media influencers induce authenticity has also been a topic of interest in Academia (e.g., Jun & Yi, 2020; Park et al., 2021). Jun and Yi (2020) reinforce that authenticity is an essential feature of influencer brands together with interactivity. They conclude that influencer interactivity is positively associated with influencer authenticity and emotional attachment, while influencer authenticity drives emotional attachment and brand trust.

The recent proliferation of artificial intelligence (AI) usage has raised attention to the relationship between AI usage and authenticity perceptions. In 2024, some studies focused on different angles of the topic, pointing out an emerging trend. For instance, Bui et al. (2024) argue that AI can challenge traditional views of authenticity and present the term 'AI-thenticity' to enhance the knowledge about authenticity in tourism. AI-thenticity is 'defined indexically as the originality of artificial intelligence-generated content and iconically as how accurately and faithfully artificial intelligence-generated content reproduces the original' (Bui et al., 2024, p. 1). While AI can enhance personalization and offer valuable experiences to tourists, it can also make AI-driven experiences seem less authentic leading to feelings of deception and negatively affecting consumer behavior. In this vein, academics study the perceived authenticity of AI-generated images to attract visitors, arguing that this perceived authenticity positively impacts trust and patronage intentions. Additionally, when comparing the perceived authenticity of AI and human-generated photos, results show that if the authorship of the stimuli is shown, tourists tend to perceive human-generated images as more authentic (Bui et al., 2024).

Although still in the initial stage, discussion has also begun around the disclosure (or not) of AI usage in a brand context, for example, in the 'brand voice' (Kirkby et al., 2023). In the study of Kirkby et al. (2023), it is analyzed if consumers' perception of 'brand voice' authenticity, brand authenticity and brand attitude are impacted when the source of the text is disclosed as being (AI)-generated or human-written. Findings point out that text disclosed as AI-generated is not perceived as less authentic when compared with human-written text. These findings contrast with mixed results found in the literature about human and AI sources, reinforcing the need to increase knowledge about the topic. For instance, the study of Brüns and Meißner (2024) takes a different approach by exploring followers' perceptions of brands that use GenAI to create content in social media. Results indicate that brand GenAI adoption leads to negative attitudinal and behavioral follower reactions as followers perceive brands that use GenAI for content creation as less authentic than those brands that do not use GenAI (Brüns & Meißner, 2024).

Research on how social media influencers induce brand authenticity has deepened with the study of virtual influencers. Scholars have started to explore the relationship between virtual endorsers and brand authenticity perceptions, revealing that consumers view brands using virtual endorsers as less authentic than those using human endorsers (Lv et al., 2023; Song et al., 2024). At the same time, aesthetic imperfection and multiple brand endorsements have a moderating role, which means that when endorsers are designed to be aesthetically imperfect and when they cover multiple brands, the negative effect on brand authenticity is diminished (Song et al., 2024). These conclusions are aligned with the study of Lv et al. (2023) who claim that 'aesthetic imperfection of avatar endorsers is one method of enhancing brand authenticity' (Lv et al., 2023, p. 2).

Another emerging trend relating brand authenticity with sustainability can also be identified. Understanding brand authenticity from the eco-friendly perspective is key and needs to be further explored, as it is very important for brand managers to understand how consumers perceive green brands as authentic (Chua et al., 2024; Moon et al., 2023). In the tourism context, green brand authenticity is defined as 'the extent to which consumers perceive a brand to be faithful toward its value for green, true to its consumers, motivated by caring and responsible for green, supportive for consumers in pursuing their value for green' (Moon et al., 2023, p. 329). Another related emerging theme is the phenomenon of brand authenticity in the context of brand activism (Ahmad et al., 2024; Bulmer et al., 2024) as brands are increasingly used as a marketing tool to drive societal change. Academics regard authentic brand sustainability activism as 'The extent to which a brand is consistently true towards its sustainability ethos and values and is willing to take a stance on sustainability issues for the greater good of society and the planet, while enabling consumers being true to themselves' (Bulmer et al., 2024, p. 10).

Finally, the exploration of drivers and outcomes of brand authenticity has continued over time, with recent studies continuing to build on the understanding of what drives authenticity and its outcomes. For example, brand experience continues to be an important antecedent (e.g., Murshed et al., 2023; Park et al., 2023), and outcomes such as purchase intentions, brand forgiveness, brand love and well-being are studied as relevant outcomes in recent studies (e.g., Papadopoulou et al., 2023; Rodrigues et al., 2024).

FUTURE RESEARCH AGENDA

Although brand authenticity is highly relevant in society and has garnered increasing academic interest, there are still research gaps that need to be addressed. These gaps could be explored by scholars to guide future studies. Table 9.2 presents suggestions of topics for future research, as well as suggested research questions that could pave the way for future studies to build on. First, from the literature, different theoretical foundations emerge associated with authenticity and brand authenticity. Thus, a theoretical perspective focusing exclusively on brand authenticity could be useful to stabilize the number of definitions and dimensions of the construct, delimiting the theoretical support of the concept (Rosado-Pinto & Loureiro, 2024). Moreover, the proliferation of research about authenticity and

Table 9.2 Future research

Topics	*Suggested Research Questions*
Theoretical foundation	What would be the main components of a unifying theory of brand authenticity?
Brand authenticity definition	What would be the dimensions of an integrated definition of brand authenticity, able to be applied in different contexts?
Context	How can specific product characteristics (e.g., utilitarian vs. hedonic products) impact the perceptions of authenticity? What are the most important cues to convey brand authenticity in the offline context and the online context? What are the most important cues driving authenticity perceptions in a physical store, in an online store and in an omnichannel strategy? How can omnichannel experiences impact brand authenticity? How can perceptions of authenticity be impacted along the customer journey?
Antecedents and consequences	How can brand authenticity be associated with other relevant marketing constructs such as brand forgiveness, customer well-being or brand coolness? Is the link to the past more important for specific product categories? What could be the possible negative consequences of brand authenticity? What are the main consumer outcomes when a brand is perceived as inauthentic?
Consumers' characteristics	How can specific consumer characteristics impact brand authenticity perceptions?
Brand extension authenticity	How is brand extension authenticity perceived in different product categories? How can different brand architecture strategies impact brand authenticity perceptions?
Authenticity and sustainability	What is green brand authenticity? What are the main drivers and outcomes of the concept? How does it relate to specific concepts such as environmental consciousness, greenwashing and green skepticism? How is the concept applied in different industries? What is brand authenticity for activist brands focused on sustainability?
Authenticity and AI	How will the theoretical perspectives of authenticity be impacted by the widespread use of AI? How do various brand stimuli (visual, audio, text), created by AI or humans, influence authenticity perceptions? What are the main differences? How do brand authenticity perceptions evolve with the proliferation and usage of AI in business practices? In a service context, how is the perception of authenticity impacted when a task is performed by a robot or an AI agent instead of being performed by an employee?

Source: The authors.

brand authenticity, especially in the most recent years, has led to a fragmentation of the knowledge around the topic. Researchers have developed several definitions applied to the different contexts, industries and product categories under investigation, which has created a 'fragmented picture of what it means for consumption to be authentic' (Nunes et al., 2021, p. 2) and a lack of clarity regarding the meaning of brand authenticity (Moulard et al., 2021). Despite the efforts to organize the existing knowledge around the topic (e.g., Campagna et al., 2023; Nunes et al., 2021; Rosado-Pinto & Loureiro, 2024; Södergren, 2021) and find common ground among researchers, scholars should continue working on an integrated definition of brand authenticity to be applied in different contexts.

A better understanding of the specificities of the context under study would help to foster a holistic understanding of brand authenticity. Although this construct has been studied in different industries, such as food and beverages, tourism, luxury products, fashion and restaurants, it would be important, for instance, to better understand how hedonic and utilitarian product types can influence consumers' evaluation of brand authenticity (Rosado-Pinto & Loureiro, 2024; Södergren, 2021). Moreover, despite the growing number of studies focusing on authenticity in the online context (e.g., in social media) in the most recent years, it would also be necessary to clearly distinguish the main drivers fostering brand authenticity perceptions in the online context and the offline context, not only concerning communication tools but also related with different distribution channels (physical stores and online stores). In terms of distribution strategies, there is a research gap concerning consumer behaviors and consumer perceptions associated with an omnichannel strategy, namely, how omnichannel experiences impact brand authenticity perceptions (Massi et al., 2023). Additionally, Rosado-Pinto and Loureiro (2024) suggest analyzing how brand authenticity perceptions evolve throughout the customer journey, as another path for future research.

The relationship between brand authenticity and other related constructs should continue to be fostered. Scholars have widely focused on the antecedents and outcomes of brand authenticity. Yet, academics could explore the relationship between brand authenticity and other marketing constructs that have not been so widely studied, such as brand forgiveness, customer well-being or brand coolness. Another research gap is related to the role of antecedents linked to the past (e.g., brand nostalgia and brand heritage) as it would be relevant to understand for which product categories these antecedents have a higher impact on brand authenticity perceptions (Södergren, 2021). Another interesting future direction for research is related to outcomes as scholars recognize that 'extant literature primarily focuses on positive outcomes of authentication' (Södergren, 2021, p. 657), neglecting its potential negative consequences. Thus, it would be important to have more research focused on the possible negative consequences of brand authenticity. Another angle to explore is potential consumer responses to brands that are perceived as inauthentic (Södergren, 2021).

Emerging from the constructivist perspective of authenticity, many scholars recognize that authenticity applied to market offerings appears to have a subjective component as it is linked to consumers' perceptions of what is authentic. Thus, another path of research could focus on conducting further research to explore potential factors related to consumers' characteristics driving differences in how individuals interpret authenticity (Kovács, 2019; Rodriguez-Lopez et al., 2020).

A further gap emerging from current research on the topic is associated with brand extension authenticity, which is regarded as a determinant of brand extension success (Spiggle et al., 2012). Although brand extension authenticity has been studied in different contexts, namely, celebrities (e.g., Osorio et al., 2021, 2022), tourism (e.g., del Barrio-García & Prados-Peña, 2019), education (e.g., Yuan et al., 2016) and luxury (e.g., Boisvert & Ashill, 2018, 2022), with findings revealing that it is an essential antecedent of brand extension success, research on the topic is still scant, considering the role that brand extensions have in portfolio strategies. Scholars call for more research on brand extension authenticity in specific contexts, for example, in tourism destinations (del Barrio-García & Prados-Peña, 2019). Additionally, exploring how different brand architecture strategies (e.g., branded house, house of brands, endorsed brands and sub-brands) impact authenticity perceptions would also enhance knowledge about the topic.

As brands play a key role in positively impacting society and the world, a clear understanding of what makes a green brand authentic is also needed (Chua et al., 2024). According to Moon et al. (2023), the 'understanding of brand authenticity is limited from the eco-friendly perspective' (Moon et al., 2023, p. 326). Thus, addressing this research gap is important not only to clarify what green brand authenticity stands for but also to understand what the main drives and outcomes of this construct are. Chua et al. (2024) suggest academics focus on specific relationships between brand authenticity and other relevant constructs, namely, environmental consciousness, greenwashing and green skepticism. An additional suggestion for future research is to expand research on the topic across different industries. Another research gap, still related to this topic, is the study of brand authenticity for activist brands with sustainability at their core as activism may lead to both negative and positive responses from consumers and brand followers. Scholars recognize that existing research falls short of capturing the full complexity of the topic (Bulmer et al., 2024).

Finally, the rapid and widespread usage of AI by individuals and companies makes it urgent to increase the knowledge about the relationship between consumers' perception of AI usage and brand authenticity perceptions. Although recent studies have focused on different angles of the topic, research on this is still in an initial stage. Academics claim that traditional theoretical perspectives of authenticity, such as objective, constructive and existential perspectives, do not reflect the emergence of AI and its potential to shape authenticity (Bui et al., 2024). Studies also present mixed results, indicating that more clarity is needed. Specifically, understanding how different brand stimuli (visual, audio, written) created by AI can impact consumers' behavior and disclosing (vs. not disclosing) the use of AI in marketing communications are areas where research should be fostered. Moreover, using a mixed-methods approach (qualitative and quantitative methods) would be useful in increasing knowledge about this complex phenomenon. Longitudinal studies would also be beneficial in capturing how consumers' reactions change with the proliferation and usage of AI in business practices. This applies to both goods and services, as service brands would also benefit from having a deeper understanding of how the perception of authenticity is impacted by specific tasks being performed by an AI agent (Rosado-Pinto & Loureiro, 2024).

CONCLUSION AND IMPLICATIONS

Authenticity plays a critical role in society and consumers' lives. Research on authenticity has increased since its seminal studies on the theoretical foundations of the term and has evolved over time. In the brand context, brand authenticity has been studied in different industries and geographies. Despite the proliferation of different definitions of the topic in the literature, common attributes and dimensions are identified among researchers. Brand authenticity leads to important marketing outcomes, and its relationship with other marketing constructs has been deeply studied. Although the role of authenticity in brand management has been widely recognized and the depth of discussion around the topic has grown, there are still research gaps that can be identified and that could be addressed in future studies of the topic. Future research could delve into the theoretical foundations of brand authenticity to delimit its theoretical support, continue building on an integrated definition of the term, explore the specificities of particular contexts, continue building on the relationships between brand authenticity and its antecedents and consequences or explore areas that need further investigation, such as consumer's characteristics or its application in a brand extension. Finally, emerging trends calling for additional clarification, such as the balance between authenticity and AI or the interplay between authenticity and sustainability also present avenues for future research.

For practitioners, acknowledging the role of authenticity and including it in their brand strategy is vital. Brand managers need to reflect upon what it means to be genuine, real and true for their brands in the product categories they serve and make decisions that enhance consistent behavior, reflecting the brand values. This will guide operational decisions related to marketing mix variables, such as product attributes or marketing communication elements that enhance brand authenticity perceptions. Finally, using tested scales to measure brand authenticity and being aware of the main antecedents that enhance authenticity will also be useful when selecting the most suited cues to drive authenticity perceptions in different touchpoints.

REFERENCES

Ahmad, F., Guzmán, F., & Al-Emran, M. (2024). Brand activism and the consequence of woke washing. *Journal of Business Research, 170,* 114362. https://doi.org/10.1016/j.jbusres.2023.114362

Akbar, M. M., & Wymer, W. (2017). Refining the conceptualization of brand authenticity. *Journal of Brand Management, 24*(1), 14–32. https://doi.org/10.1057/s41262-016-0023-3

Becker, M., Wiegand, N., & Reinartz, W. J. (2019). Does it pay to be real? Understanding authenticity in TV advertising. *Journal of Marketing, 83*(1), 24–50. https://doi.org/10.1177/0022242918815880

Beverland, M. (2006). The 'real thing': Branding authenticity in the luxury wine trade. *Journal of Business Research, 59*(2), 251–258. https://doi.org/10.1016/j.jbusres.2005.04.007

Beverland, M. B. (2005). Crafting brand authenticity: The case of luxury wines. *Journal of Management Studies, 42*(5), 1003–1029. https://doi.org/10.1111/j.1467-6486.2005.00530.x

Beverland, M. B., & Farrelly, F. J. (2010). The quest for authenticity in consumption: Consumers' purposive choice of authentic cues to shape experienced outcomes. *Journal of Consumer Research, 36*(5), 838–856. https://doi.org/10.1086/615047

Beverland, M., & Luxton, S. (2005). Managing integrated marketing communication (IMC) through strategic decoupling: How luxury wine firms retain brand leadership while appearing to be wedded to the past. *Journal of Advertising, 34*(4), 103–116. https://doi.org/10.1080/00913367.2005.10639207

Boisvert, J., & Ashill, N. J. (2018). The spillover effect of downward line extensions on U.S. consumers' evaluation of a French luxury parent brand: The role of branding strategies, authenticity, and fit. *Psychology and Marketing, 35*(10), 740–751. https://doi.org/10.1002/mar.21131

Boisvert, J., & Ashill, N. J. (2022). The impact of luxury brand status signaling, extension authenticity and fit on luxury line extension evaluation: A cross-national study. *International Marketing Review, 39*(2), 395–422. https://doi.org/10.1108/IMR-02-2021-0058

Brown, S., Kozinets, R. V., & Sherry, J. F. (2003). Teaching old brands new tricks: Retro branding and the revival of brand meaning. *Journal of Marketing, 67*(3), 19–33. https://doi.org/10.1509/jmkg.67.3.19.18657

Bruhn, M., Schoenmüller, V., Schäfer, D., & Heinrich, D. (2012). Brand authenticity: Towards a deeper understanding of its conceptualization and measurement. *Advances in Consumer Research, 40,* 567–576.

Brüns, J. D., & Meißner, M. (2024). Do you create your content yourself? Using generative artificial intelligence for social media content creation diminishes perceived brand authenticity. *Journal of Retailing and Consumer Services, 79,* 103790. https://doi.org/10.1016/j.jretconser.2024.103790

Bui, H. T., Filimonau, V., & Sezerel, H. (2024). AI-thenticity: Exploring the effect of perceived authenticity of AI-generated visual content on tourist patronage intentions. *Journal of Destination Marketing and Management*, *34*, 100956. https://doi.org/10.1016/j.jdmm.2024.100956

Bulmer, S., Palakshappa, N., Dodds, S., & Harper, S. (2024). Sustainability, brand authenticity and Instagram messaging. *Journal of Business Research*, *175*, 114547. https://doi.org/10.1016/j.jbusres.2024.114547

Campagna, C. L., Donthu, N., & Yoo, B. (2023). Brand authenticity: Literature review, comprehensive definition, and an amalgamated scale. *Journal of Marketing Theory and Practice*, *31*(2), 129–145. https://doi.org/10.1080/10696679.2021.2018937

Choi, H., Ko, E., Kim, E. Y., & Mattila, P. (2015). The role of fashion brand authenticity in product management: A holistic marketing approach. *Journal of Product Innovation Management*, *32*(2), 233–242. https://doi.org/10.1111/jpim.12175

Chua, B.-L., Kim, S., Baah, N. G., Moon, H., Yu, J., & Han, H. (2024). When hospitality brands go green: The role of authenticity and stereotypes in building customer-green brand relationships. *Journal of Sustainable Tourism*, *32*(6), 1118–1141. https://doi.org/10.1080/09669582.2023.2203406

Cohen, E. (1988). Authenticity and commoditization in tourism. *Annals of Tourism Research*, *15*(3), 371–386. https://doi.org/10.1016/0160-7383(88)90028-X

Collins, M., & Weiss, M. (2015). The role of provenance in luxury textile brands. *International Journal of Retail and Distribution Management*, *43*(10/11), 1030–1050. https://doi.org/10.1108/IJRDM-07-2014-0091

Davis, R., Sheriff, K., & Owen, K. (2019). Conceptualising and measuring consumer authenticity online. *Journal of Retailing and Consumer Services*, *47*, 17–31. https://doi.org/10.1016/j.jretconser.2018.10.002

del Barrio-García, S., & Prados-Peña, M. B. (2019). Do brand authenticity and brand credibility facilitate brand equity? The case of heritage destination brand extension. *Journal of Destination Marketing and Management*, *13*, 10–23. https://doi.org/10.1016/j.jdmm.2019.05.002

Dwivedi, A., & McDonald, R. (2018). Building brand authenticity in fast-moving consumer goods via consumer perceptions of brand marketing communications. *European Journal of Marketing*, *52*(7/8), 1387–1411. https://doi.org/10.1108/EJM-11-2016-0665

Fine, G. A. (2003). Crafting authenticity: The validation of identity in self-taught art. *Theory and Society*, *32*(2), 153–180. https://doi.org/10.1023/A:1023943503531

Fritz, K., Schoenmueller, V., & Bruhn, M. (2017). Authenticity in branding – Exploring antecedents and consequences of brand authenticity. *European Journal of Marketing*, *51*(2), 324–348. https://doi.org/10.1108/EJM-10-2014-0633

Gilmore, J. H., & Pine, B. J. (2007). *Authenticity: What consumers really want*. Harvard Business School Press.

Grayson, K., & Martinec, R. (2004). Consumer perceptions of iconicity and indexicality and their influence on assessments of authentic market offerings. *Journal of Consumer Research*, *31*(2), 296–312. https://doi.org/10.1086/422109

Gundlach, H., & Neville, B. (2012). Authenticity: Further theoretical and practical development. *Journal of Brand Management*, *19*(6), 484–499. https://doi.org/10.1057/bm.2011.51

Huang, W. (2010). Brand story and perceived brand image: Evidence from Taiwan. *Journal of Family and Economic Issues*, *31*(3), 307–317. https://doi.org/10.1007/s10834-010-9203-6

Hyun, H., Park, J., & Hong, E. (2024). Enhancing brand equity through multidimensional brand authenticity in the fashion retailing. *Journal of Retailing and Consumer Services*, *78*, 103712. https://doi.org/10.1016/j.jretconser.2024.103712

Ilicic, J., & Webster, C. M. (2016). Being true to oneself: Investigating celebrity brand authenticity. *Psychology and Marketing*, *33*(6), 410–420. https://doi.org/10.1002/mar.20887

Ilicic, J., Baxter, S. M., & Kulczynski, A. (2019). Keeping it real: Examining the influence of co-branding authenticity in cause-related marketing. *Journal of Brand Management*, *26*(1), 49–59. https://doi.org/10.1057/s41262-018-0109-1

Jun, S., & Yi, J. (2020). What makes followers loyal? The role of influencer interactivity in building influencer brand equity. *Journal of Product and Brand Management*, *29*(6), 803–814. https://doi.org/10.1108/JPBM-02-2019-2280

Kirkby, A., Baumgarth, C., & Henseler, J. (2023). To disclose or not disclose, is no longer the question – Effect of AI-disclosed brand voice on brand authenticity and attitude. *Journal of Product and Brand Management*, *32*(7), 1108–1122. https://doi.org/10.1108/JPBM-02-2022-3864

Kolar, T., & Zabkar, V. (2010). A consumer-based model of authenticity: An oxymoron or the foundation of cultural heritage marketing? *Tourism Management*, *31*(5), 652–664. https://doi.org/10.1016/j.tourman.2009.07.010

Kotler, P., Keller, K. L., Brady, M., Goodman, M., & Hansen, T. (2019). *Marketing management* (4th European ed.). Pearson Education.

Kovács, B. (2019). Authenticity is in the eye of the beholder: The exploration of audiences' lay associations to authenticity across five domains.

Review of General Psychology, *23*(1), 32–59. https://doi.org/10.1177/1089268019829469

Le, T. H., Arcodia, C., Novais, M. A., & Kralj, A. (2019). What we know and do not know about authenticity in dining experiences: A systematic literature review. *Tourism Management*, *74*, 258–275. https://doi.org/10.1016/j.tourman.2019.02.012

Lehman, D. W., O'Connor, K., Kovács, B., & Newman, G. E. (2019). Authenticity. *Academy of Management Annals*, *13*(1), 1–42. https://doi.org/10.5465/annals.2017.0047

Leigh, T. W., Peters, C., & Shelton, J. (2006). The consumer quest for authenticity: The multiplicity of meanings within the MG subculture of consumption. *Journal of the Academy of Marketing Science*, *34*(4), 481–493. https://doi.org/10.1177/0092070306288403

Lu, A. C. C., Gursoy, D., & Lu, C. Y. (2015). Authenticity perceptions, brand equity and brand choice intention: The case of ethnic restaurants. *International Journal of Hospitality Management*, *50*, 36–45. https://doi.org/10.1016/j.ijhm.2015.07.008

Lv, L., Huang, M., Guan, D., & Yang, K. (2023). Minor flaws are better: The positive effect of aesthetic imperfection about avatar endorsers on brand authenticity. *Journal of Business Research*, *166*, 114125. https://doi.org/10.1016/j.jbusres.2023.114125

Manthiou, A., Kang, J., Hyun, S. S., & Fu, X. X. (2018). The impact of brand authenticity on building brand love: An investigation of impression in memory and lifestyle-congruence. *International Journal of Hospitality Management*, *75*, 38–47. https://doi.org/10.1016/j.ijhm.2018.03.005

Massi, M., Piancatelli, C., & Vocino, A. (2023). Authentic omnichannel: Providing consumers with a seamless brand experience through authenticity. *Psychology and Marketing*, *40*(7), 1280–1298. https://doi.org/10.1002/mar.21815

Matthews, L., Eilert, M., Carlson, L., & Gentry, J. (2020). When and how frontline service employee authenticity influences purchase intentions. *Journal of Business Research*, *114*, 111–123. https://doi.org/10.1016/j.jbusres.2020.04.002

Mody, M., Hanks, L., & Dogru, T. (2019). Parallel pathways to brand loyalty: Mapping the consequences of authentic consumption experiences for hotels and Airbnb. *Tourism Management*, *74*, 65–80. https://doi.org/10.1016/j.tourman.2019.02.013

Moon, H., Yu, J., Chua, B.-L., & Han, H. (2023). Impact of green brand authenticity on warm glow, green satisfaction, and willingness to pay more. *Journal of Travel and Tourism Marketing*, *40*(4), 326–344. https://doi.org/10.1080/10548408.2023.2245446

Morhart, F., Malär, L., Guèvremont, A., Girardin, F., & Grohmann, B. (2015). Brand authenticity: An integrative framework and measurement scale. *Journal of Consumer Psychology*, *25*(2), 200–218. https://doi.org/10.1016/j.jcps.2014.11.006

Moulard, J. G., Garrity, C. P., & Rice, D. H. (2015). What makes a human brand authentic? Identifying the antecedents of celebrity authenticity. *Psychology and Marketing*, *32*(2), 173–186. https://doi.org/10.1002/mar.20771

Moulard, J. G., Raggio, R. D., & Folse, J. A. G. (2021). Disentangling the meanings of brand authenticity: The entity-referent correspondence framework of authenticity. *Journal of the Academy of Marketing Science*, *49*(1), 96–118. https://doi.org/10.1007/S11747-020-00735-1

Murshed, F., Dwivedi, A., & Nayeem, T. (2023). Brand authenticity building effect of brand experience and downstream effects. *Journal of Product and Brand Management*, *32*(7), 1032–1045. https://doi.org/10.1108/JPBM-02-2021-3377

Napoli, J., Dickinson, S. J., Beverland, M. B., & Farrelly, F. (2014). Measuring consumer-based brand authenticity. *Journal of Business Research*, *67*(6), 1090–1098. https://doi.org/10.1016/j.jbusres.2013.06.001

Nunes, J. C., Ordanini, A., & Giambastiani, G. (2021). The concept of authenticity: What it means to consumers. *Journal of Marketing*, *85*(4), 1–20. https://doi.org/10.1177/0022242921997081

Oh, H., Prado, P. H. M., Korelo, J. C., & Frizzo, F. (2019). The effect of brand authenticity on consumer–brand relationships. *Journal of Product and Brand Management*, *28*(2), 231–241. https://doi.org/10.1108/JPBM-09-2017-1567

Osorio, M. L., Centeno-Velázquez, E., López-Pérez, M. E., & del Castillo, E. (2021). Authenticity, fit and product type: Testing a celebrity brand extension model cross-culturally. *Journal of Retailing and Consumer Services*, *63*, 102736. https://doi.org/10.1016/j.jretconser.2021.102736

Osorio, M. L., Centeno, E., Cambra-Fierro, J., & del Castillo, E. (2022). In search of fit or authenticity? A product-type consumer decision in celebrity brand extensions. *Journal of Product and Brand Management*, *31*(6), 841–853. https://doi.org/10.1108/JPBM-04-2021-3437

Papadopoulou, C., Vardarsuyu, M., & Oghazi, P. (2023). Examining the relationships between brand authenticity, perceived value, and brand forgiveness: The role of cross-cultural happiness. *Journal of Business Research*, *167*, 114154. https://doi.org/10.1016/j.jbusres.2023.114154

Park, J., Lee, J. M., Xiong, V. Y., Septianto, F., & Seo, Y. (2021). David and Goliath: When and why micro-influencers are more persuasive than mega-influencers. *Journal of Advertising*, *50*(5), 584–602. https://doi.org/10.1080/00913367.2021.1980470

Park, J., Hong, E., & Park, Y.-N. (2023). Toward a new business model of retail industry: The role of brand experience and brand authenticity. *Journal of Retailing and Consumer Services*, *74*, 103426. https://doi.org/10.1016/j.jretconser.2023.103426

Pink, C., Wilkie, D., & Graves, C. (2023). The impact of brand perceptions on the post-to-purchase journey: A family branding perspective. *Journal of Product and Brand Management*, *32*(5), 737–751. https://doi.org/10.1108/JPBM-11-2021-3752

Rather, R. A., Hollebeek, L. D., & Islam, J. U. (2019). Tourism-based customer engagement: The construct, antecedents, and consequences. *The Service Industries Journal*, *39*(7–8), 519–540. https://doi.org/10.1080/02642069.2019.1570154

Riefler, P. (2020). Local versus global food consumption: The role of brand authenticity. *Journal of Consumer Marketing*, *37*(3), 317–327. https://doi.org/10.1108/JCM-02-2019-3086

Rodrigues, C., Brandão, A., Billore, S., & Oda, T. (2024). The mediating role of perceived brand authenticity between brand experience and brand love: A cross-cultural perspective. *Journal of Brand Management*, *31*(3), 293–309. https://doi.org/10.1057/s41262-023-00342-9

Rodrigues, P., Pinto Borges, A., & Sousa, A. (2021). Authenticity as an antecedent of brand image in a positive emotional consumer relationship: The case of craft beer brands. *EuroMed Journal of Business*, *17*, 634–651. https://doi.org/10.1108/EMJB-03-2021-0041

Rodriguez-Lopez, M., del Barrio-García, S., & Alcantara-Pilar, J. (2020). Formation of customer-based brand equity via authenticity the mediating role of satisfaction and the moderating role of restaurant type. *International Journal of Contemporary Hospitality Management*, *32*(2), 815–834. https://doi.org/10.1108/IJCHM-05-2019-0473

Rosado-Pinto, F., & Loureiro, S. M. C. (2024). Authenticity: Shedding light on the branding context. *EuroMed Journal of Business*, *19*(3), 544–570. https://doi.org/10.1108/EMJB-08-2021-0115

Södergren, J. (2021). Brand authenticity: 25 years of research. *International Journal of Consumer Studies*, *45*(4), 645–663. https://doi.org/10.1111/ijcs.12651

Song, X., Lu, Y., & Yang, Q. (2024). The negative effect of virtual endorsers on brand authenticity and potential remedies. *Journal of Business Research*, *185*, 114898. https://doi.org/10.1016/j.jbusres.2024.114898

Spiggle, S., Nguyen, H. T., & Caravella, M. (2012). More than fit: Brand extension authenticity. *Journal of Marketing Research*, *49*(6), 967–983. https://doi.org/10.1509/jmr.11.0015

Srivastava, A., Dey, D. K., & Balaji, M. S. (2020). Drivers of brand credibility in consumer evaluation of global brands and domestic brands in an emerging market context. *Journal of Product and Brand Management*, *29*(7), 849–861. https://doi.org/10.1108/JPBM-03-2018-1782

Wang, N. (1999). Rethinking authenticity in tourism experience. *Annals of Tourism Research*, *26*(2), 349–370. https://doi.org/10.1016/S0160-7383(98)00103-0

Yang, J., Teran, C., Battocchio, A. F., Bertellotti, E., & Wrzesinski, S. (2021). Building brand authenticity on social media: The impact of Instagram ad model genuineness and trustworthiness on perceived brand authenticity and consumer responses. *Journal of Interactive Advertising*, *21*(1), 34–48. https://doi.org/10.1080/15252019.2020.1860168

Yuan, R., Liu, M. J., Luo, J., Nguyen, B., & Yang, F. (2014). A critical review of the literature on authenticity: Evolution and future research agenda. *International Journal of Services, Economics and Management*, *6*(4), 339–356. https://doi.org/10.1504/IJSEM.2014.068270

Yuan, R., Liu, M. J., Luo, J., & Yen, D. A. (2016). Reciprocal transfer of brand identity and image associations arising from higher education brand extensions. *Journal of Business Research*, *69*(8), 3069–3076. https://doi.org/10.1016/j.jbusres.2016.01.022

Zebal, M. A., & Jackson, F. H. (2019). Cues for shaping purchase of local retail apparel clothing brands in an emerging economy. *International Journal of Retail and Distribution Management*, *47*(10), 1013–1028. https://doi.org/10.1108/IJRDM-11-2018-0241

Zhang, M., & Merunka, D. (2015). The impact of territory of origin on product authenticity perceptions: An empirical analysis in China. *Asia Pacific Journal of Marketing and Logistics*, *27*(3), 385–405. https://doi.org/10.1108/APJML-12-2014-0180

Zhang, S. N., Li, Y. Q., Liu, C. H., & Ruan, W. Q. (2021). A study on China's time-honored catering brands: Achieving new inheritance of traditional brands. *Journal of Retailing and Consumer Services*, *58*, 102290. https://doi.org/10.1016/J.JRETCONSER.2020.102290

10

Unraveling Brand Equity: A Theoretical Review and Directions for Future Research

Salvador del Barrio-García, Juan Miguel Alcántara-Pilar, María Eugenia Rodríguez-López, Álvaro J. Rojas-Lamorena, and Beatriz García-Carrión

INTRODUCTION

In today's highly competitive market environment, it is essential for companies to focus on securing competitive advantage. An effective strategy to achieve this is the cultivation of strong brands (Castañeda-García et al., 2020). Brands are widely recognized as key identifiers and primary assets for organizations, often regarded as a company's most valuable asset. They facilitate consumer decision-making by differentiating products associated with different brands, thereby stimulating the purchase process (Sasmita & Mohd Suki, 2015). In addition, brands play an important role in fostering long-term consumer commitment and loyalty (Aaker & Joachimsthaler, 2000). However, the true power of brands lies in consumer perceptions. Therefore, marketers must strive to develop strategies that effectively elicit positive perceptions, emotions, beliefs and opinions about the brand among consumers (Hoeffler & Keller, 2002).

A brand is an evolving mental collection of actual (offer-related) and emotional (human-like) characteristics and associations that convey the benefits of an offer, identified by a symbol or a collection of symbols, and differentiate that offer from the rest of the market (Veloutsou & Delgado-Ballester, 2018). Based on this definition, it is logical for companies to strive for strong brand establishment among their target audiences, given the benefits such brands offer in terms of effective marketing communications, enhanced consumer loyalty and increased resilience in crises.

From this perspective, business managers must plan brand management meticulously, as both overinvesting and underinvesting in the brand can lead to failure. Proper management of all strategic aspects of the brand is therefore critical to building brand equity. The brand management literature suggests that the brand equity models proposed by Aaker (1991) and Keller (1993) serve as valuable tools for marketing managers to assess and measure overall consumer perceptions of brands. Ultimately, brand equity plays a pivotal role in helping firms achieve competitive advantage by enhancing business performance and increasing firm value (Ahmad & Thyagaraj, 2014).

This chapter provides a theoretical and contemporary perspective on the functioning of brand equity and its critical role in brand management. We explore the conceptual boundaries of the construct, tracing its evolution from the seminal works of Aaker (1991) and Keller (1993) to subsequent notable contributions (Yoo & Donthu, 2001) and the most up-to-date research on the topic (Rojas-Lamorena et al., 2022). Particular emphasis is placed on examining the measurement of brand equity, including its dimensions and academic efforts to develop measurement scales. In addition, a significant part of the chapter is devoted to discussing ongoing research challenges related to brand equity, ranging from consumer-based measurement approaches to identifying its primary antecedents.

Future research efforts should prioritize the investigation of key antecedents of brand equity. Despite considerable progress in the academic literature, many aspects still require further clarification. An increasing number of studies aim to identify the variables that facilitate the formation of consumer-based brand equity (CBBE). However, these studies mainly focus on variables derived from *subjective evaluations* – such as self-congruence, satisfaction, value co-creation, credibility, behavioral intentions, experiences and motivations – and are mainly concentrated in the tourism industry (Castañeda-García et al., 2020; Frías et al., 2020; Frías-Jamilena et al., 2017; Prados-Peña & Del Barrio-García, 2021; Rodríguez-López et al., 2020).

When studying consumer behavior, it is crucial to recognize that behavior is influenced not only by the subjective judgements of consumers but also by various external and situational factors. These elements should not be ignored. According to the service-dominant logic (SDL), the context in which the consumer operates plays a crucial role in marketing and consumer behavior studies (Vargo & Lusch, 2011). Therefore, future research should also focus on contextual factors that significantly influence the formation of CBBE. We will briefly outline some of these factors that seem most promising for future investigation.

BRAND EQUITY CONCEPTUAL FRAMEWORK

Brand equity has been defined in many different ways depending on the perspective taken on the brand. Thus, the most basic is that which distinguishes between the financial approach and the consumer approach. Early studies on brand equity focused on financial indicators such as cost savings, cash flow, sales, prices and profits (Tasci, 2021). In general, the literature indicates that well-positioned products generate better consumer perceptions and a competitive advantage in the long run, which ultimately manifests itself in price premiums, higher market shares, higher revenues, higher profits and, ultimately, higher value. Consequently in the 1990s, indicators based on consumer perceptions began to receive greater attention. The measurement of non-financial brand effectiveness from the consumer's point of view is based on the understanding of how marketing actions affect consumer learning and recall.

Brand equity has long captured the attention of researchers in both academic and professional fields (Buil et al., 2008). Despite its importance as a cornerstone of brand management, there is still no clear agreement on its precise definition, the dimensions it entails, or the most effective methods for its measurement (Keller, 2014).

This construct has been studied through three main perspectives: financial-based brand equity, perception-based brand equity and combined approaches (Del Barrio-García et al., 2023; Tasci, 2021). The financial perspective focuses on analyzing brand equity from the standpoint of financial markets, cash flow or value-added contributions, emphasizing the value of the brand to the firm (Kamakura & Russell, 1993). This relates to the firm's market share and positioning based on intangible assets that are a source of strategic competitive advantage and increased economic value (O'Neill & Mattila, 2006). Estimating the financial value of the brand is a common need for companies and should highlight that knowledge of brand equity will help determine investment in brand building and brand changes through the evaluation of marketing activities (Aaker, 1996). However, critics argue that it falls short in informing marketing strategies because it overlooks the cognitive and behavioral dimensions of consumers (Keller, 1993). This limitation spurred growing interest in the early 1990s toward understanding brand equity from the consumer's perspective.

The perception-based perspective is also assessed through diverse perspectives, such as general consumers (Netemeyer et al., 2004) and employees of the company (Erkmen, 2018). While some researchers use consumer-based and CBBE as synonymous (Keller, 1993), CBBE focuses on actual brand users, whereas CBBE involves a broader audience, including individuals with or without direct experience with the brand. As a result, consumer-based studies frequently include constructs like satisfaction (Lee & Back, 2010), while consumer-based studies may emphasize perceptions regardless of prior interaction. The fundamental premise of this approach is that brands create value for firms only when they first create value for consumers (Yoo & Donthu, 2001). Researchers in this domain evaluate how consumers, employees or stakeholders respond to a brand based on the notion that strong brands are those that occupy a prominent place in people's minds (Christodoulides et al., 2015). Consequently, this perspective highlights how perceptions, attitudes and behaviors associated with a brand contribute to its equity.

Recognizing the limitations of examining brand equity solely through financial or consumer-focused lenses, scholars proposed the combined financial-consumer perspective, which integrates elements from both approaches (Kim & Kim, 2005). This holistic approach aims to overcome the weaknesses of using a single framework in isolation. For instance, Dyson et al. (1996) conducted surveys to measure the financial value linked to brand associations and consumer perceptions, bridging the gap between brand image and monetary worth. Similarly, Motameni and Shahrokhi (1998) proposed a global model for brand valuation that incorporates both financial metrics and consumer responses, enabling a more comprehensive understanding of brand equity. This combined perspective continues to evolve, offering firms tools to assess and manage their brands more effectively in today's complex markets.

Different approaches to defining brand equity have emerged, shaped by the financial and consumer-based perspectives. From a financial perspective, one notable definition is provided by Kapferer (2004), who describes brand equity as 'the net cash flow attributable to the brand after paying the cost of capital invested to produce and run the business and the cost of marketing'. This definition underscores the economic value a brand contributes directly to a firm's profitability.

In contrast, the perception-based perspective has inspired a far greater variety of definitions in the literature, reflecting its broader scope. Aaker (1991) emphasizes the value that brand equity creates for the consumer, highlighting its role in enhancing brand understanding, facilitating information processing, boosting confidence in decision-making, and increasing satisfaction. Aaker (1991, 1996) conceptualizes brand equity as a set of assets that add or subtract value and develops the Brand Equity Ten Scale, a tool adaptable to different brands and markets. Brand equity from this consumer perspective includes four main dimensions: brand loyalty, perceived quality, association and brand awareness. These elements are differentiated from the fifth dimension, market behavior, which is more focused on financial metrics.

Keller (1993) defines brand equity as 'the differential effect of brand knowledge on consumer response to the marketing activity for that brand', focusing on the influence of consumer perceptions and attitudes. Keller (1993, 2003) formulated the CBBE model, which is based on brand awareness, composed of brand awareness and brand image. This pyramid-structured model places the brand as its base, which supports performance and image, ultimately culminating in 'brand resonance with the consumer'. However, as Tasci (2021) points out, this model does not clearly specify the directions of the relationships between its components.

Yoo and Donthu (2001) broaden the perspective by highlighting the efficiency of CBBE in enhancing marketing effectiveness and gaining a competitive advantage. They emphasize that this advantage stems from the perceived difference between branded and unbranded products, even when both share identical characteristics. Furthermore, they argue that CBBE, by concentrating on cognitive and behavioral evaluations of the brand, should exclude the market dimension proposed by Aaker. In line with this reasoning, Yoo and Donthu (2001) define brand equity as 'the difference in consumer preference between a branded product and an otherwise identical unbranded product'. In conclusion, these authors propose a CBBE framework based on four dimensions: loyalty, perceived quality, associations and awareness, while merging awareness and associations into a three-dimensional approach.

Other researchers expanded the CBBE framework by incorporating components that were not originally proposed by Aaker or Keller. These additions include management trust and brand reliability (Hsu et al., 2012), quality of experience (Xu & Chan, 2010), personnel behavior (Sürücü et al., 2019) and brand engagement (Huerta-Álvarez et al., 2020), among others.

In summary, brand equity can be understood as the incremental value a brand name adds to a product, whether through financial returns for the firm or through perceptions and preferences that influence consumer behavior.

THE EVOLUTION OF ACADEMIC RESEARCH ON BRAND EQUITY

The study of brand equity, recognized as both a pivotal marketing concept and a critical asset for firms, has experienced significant growth since its emergence in the late 1980s. Due to the importance of this construct, alongside the extensive theoretical and methodological contributions addressing its conceptualization, measurement and management across various fields of knowledge, there is a clear need for a more comprehensive analysis than what previous studies have offered. Adopting a bibliometric perspective allows for deeper exploration, shedding light on the current state of the art in this area of research. In this section, we employ a bibliometric approach to examine the scientific output related to the brand equity construct over the period 1990–2023.

An examination of the evolution of scientific articles published on this topic shows that the number of papers published since the beginning of the 1990s has not stopped growing, especially since 2000. In the period from 2010 to 2023, annual publications on the term brand equity have grown almost exponentially (see Figure 10.1). This growth highlights the enormous interest stimulated by academia in this construct in recent years. The increase in the number of papers published has also led to a notable growth in the number of citations received, reaching 123,953 citations in Web of Science – Clarivate (WoS) and 133,783 citations in Scopus, the two bibliographic databases of global reference in the field of academic research.

It is worth noting the increase in the number of citations in 1993 due to the publication of Keller's seminal work, which, as mentioned above, is one of the reference works in the conceptual definition and subsequent measurement of brand equity. In this evolution, it is necessary to mention that the drop observed in the number of citations since 2021 reflects the recent publication of the articles analyzed, which need a minimum time of several years to begin to be incorporated by the authors in their academic works and thus generate citations.

Nevertheless, it is possible to anticipate the interest that the work on brand equity continues to generate among academics, given that the articles published in 2022 already have 2436 citations in WoS and 2745 in Scopus, and those published in 2023 are close to 1000 citations in WoS (963 citations), and exceed this number in Scopus (1288 citations).

Table 10.1 lists the five scientific articles that have received the most citations from the scientific community to date. The seminal papers by Keller (1993) and Aaker (1996) stand out as the most cited, which is not surprising given that their proposals for approaching the concept and measurement laid the foundations for the consumer-based perspective. Similarly, the works of Yoo et al. (2000) and Yoo and Donthu (2001) stand out as they further elaborate on Aaker and Keller's conceptual definition and propose a measurement scale for the construct from a multidimensional and global perspective. Finally, the work of Tax et al. (1998) provides an interesting conceptual framework for understanding brand equity from a relational perspective, particularly in complaint management contexts. This paper suggests a more dynamic approach to this construct by exploring how prior experiences and satisfaction in specific interactions, such as complaint handling, can influence key elements of brand equity, such as trust and commitment. In summary, this paper

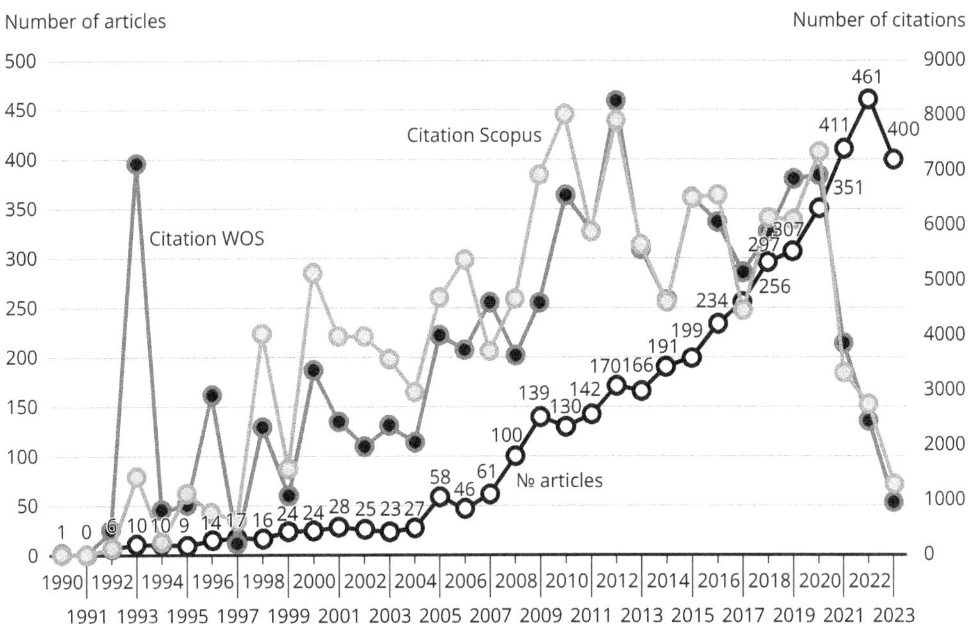

Figure 10.1 Evolution in the number of scientific articles about brand equity and citation (1990–2023)

Source: The authors.

Table 10.1 Top five articles by citations in WoS and Scopus

Authors	*Title*	*Journal*	*Year*	*Number of Citations (WoS)*	*Number of Citations (Scopus)*
Keller, K.L.	Conceptualizing, measuring and managing consumer-based brand equity (CBBE)	*Journal of Marketing*	1993	6604	N/A
Aaker, D.A.	Measuring brand equity across products and markets	*California Management Review*	1996	2653	1962
Yoo, B., Donthu, N. and Lee, S.	An examination of selected marketing mix elements and brand equity	*Journal of the Academy of Marketing Science*	2000	1515	1849
Yoo, B. and Donthu, N.	Developing and validating a multidimensional CBBE scale	*Journal of Business Research*	2001	1466	1778
Tax, S.S., Brown, S.W. and Chandrashekaran, M.	Consumer evaluations of service complaint experiences: Implications for relationship marketing	*Journal of Marketing*	1998	1370	1617

Source: The authors.

extends traditional approaches to brand equity by integrating a 'fairness' perspective into the handling of critical consumer interactions, such as complaints, and by positioning cumulative experience as a key moderator of brand equity perception.

With regard to the scientific journals that have paid the most attention to research on Brand Equity (see Table 10.2), it is worth highlighting journals in the field of business, such as the *Journal of Product and Brand Management* (157 articles) and the *Journal of Business Research* (151 articles), which together account for more than 3% of the publications on this topic indexed in WoS and Scopus. However, it was the *Journal of Business Research* that achieved the greatest impact of its publications, doubling the number of citations in WoS and surpassing those of the *Journal of Product and Brand Management* in Scopus. Another journal with more than 100 publications related to Brand Equity is the *Journal of Brand Management* (104 articles). It is also noteworthy that the set of journals included in the top five represent 12.38% of the indexed publications on Brand Equity.

Finally, in order to gain a better understanding of the state of the art on Brand Equity, we have highlighted the most prolific authors on this topic (see Table 10.3). In this regard, we find in first and second position in terms of the total number of publications, Professor Gil-Saura (41 articles) and Professor Šerić (24 articles), respectively, from the University of Valencia (Spain). Both authors have focused their work on the application of brand equity to areas such as environmental practices and the hotel sector. They are followed in third place by Keller with 23 articles, although the scientific impact of the latter author is much higher in terms of number of citations received.

Table 10.2 Top five journals by number of articles

Journal	*Ranking by Number of Articles*	*% of Total Sample*	*Number of Citations in WoS*	*Number of Citations in Scopus*
Journal of Product and Brand Management	157	3.33%	5531	9818
Journal of Business Research	151	3.20%	11,191	12,576
Journal of Brand Management	104	2.20%	2910	2473
Sustainability	97	2.06%	991	952
European Journal of Marketing	75	1.59%	3541	4815

Source: The authors.

Table 10.3 Top five authors by number of indexed articles

Authors	*Current Affiliation*	*Number of Articles in WoS*	*Number of Citations in WoS*	*Number of Articles in Scopus*	*Number of Citations in Scopus*
Gil-Saura, I.	University of Valencia (Spain)	40	694	26	666
Seric, M.	University of Valencia (Spain)	25	478	14	437
Keller, K.L.	Dartmouth College (USA)	18	9155	17	4894
Ruiz-Molina, M.E.	University of Valencia (Spain)	20	379	13	272
Pike, S.	Queensland University of Technology (Australia)	19	1054	11	1044
Liu, C.H.	National Kaohsiung University of Science and Technology (Taiwan)	20	648	14	635

Source: The authors.

CBBE MODELLING AND MEASUREMENT

As discussed in previous paragraphs, apart from the measurement of brand equity in financial terms, which represents brand performance, there is an alternative way to measure brand effectiveness: CBBE, which is based on the understanding of how marketing initiatives impact consumer learning and recall. This theory is based on the seminal works of Aaker (1991, 1996) and Keller (1993), and later on Yoo and Donthu (2001), which we will develop in more detail below.

Determining the key dimensions that constitute brand equity is a fundamental challenge for both academics and marketing practitioners (Buil et al., 2008). Although CBBE is widely recognized in both academic and practical spheres, there remains no complete consensus on how to determine its principal component dimensions (Oliveira et al., 2023).

Aaker's Model

In his book *Managing Brand Equity: Capitalizing on the Value of a Brand Name*, Aaker (1991) has stated that, while the assets and liabilities that constitute the foundation of brand equity can differ depending on the context, they can be grouped into five broad dimensions: (1) brand loyalty, (2) perceived quality, (3) brand associations, (4) brand awareness and (5) market behavior measures.

In 1996, Aaker operationalized these components through what he called the Brand Equity Ten Scale, which emerged as a starting point in the creation of a set of brand equity measures that can be applied in different markets and for different products. Aaker's model (1991, 1996), grounded in a consumer-based perspective, includes the first four elements mentioned above: brand loyalty, perceived quality, brand associations and brand awareness. This is because the fifth dimension – linked to company metrics such as market share or distribution and price indices – is not directly tied to the consumer. Consequently, many studies choose to exclude this dimension (Tasci, 2021) in order to concentrate solely on the aspects that pertain to the consumer experience.

Aaker's seminal framework remains highly influential in the academic literature on brand equity, as evidenced by numerous studies that adopt its component-based structure. Within higher education, for example, several papers have explored the importance of university branding and its value (Mourad et al., 2020), while others have empirically investigated the consumer-driven factors that shape brand equity in this sector. Some studies even use Aaker's original Brand Equity Ten Scale. In this regard, Sarwar and Siddiqui (2021) analyzed how loyalty, awareness, perceived quality and brand associations affect brand equity across multiple toothpaste categories, confirming the impact of each dimension. Their conclusions are consistent with earlier findings by Sasmita and Mohd Suki (2015), who conducted a similar study for various sports brands.

Additionally, Ekinci et al. (2023) selected Aaker's model for their study of tourist destinations, finding it to be the most frequently applied framework in tourism research. However, they also identified notable limitations in assessing tourist destinations when compared with a more expansive model that includes dimensions such as service interaction quality and brand self-congruence.

Keller's Model

Keller explored the concept of brand equity through the lens of cognitive psychology (Christodoulides et al., 2015), describing it as the distinct impact that brand knowledge has on how consumers respond to brand marketing efforts (Keller, 1993). As Keller (2014) highlights, the knowledge that marketers build around a brand over time plays a crucial role in shaping its future development. This accumulated knowledge serves as the foundation upon which consumers base their decisions regarding the brand's trajectory. Keller's model emphasizes that brand knowledge is the cornerstone of brand equity, with brand awareness and brand image forming its primary components. Brand awareness reflects the strength of a brand's presence in a consumer's memory, enabling recognition in different situations. Conversely, brand image pertains to the consumer's perceptions of the brand, represented through the associations stored in their memory.

In more recent works, Keller (2014) suggests that the development of CBBE unfolds progressively over time through four distinct and incremental stages: (1) Who are you? (brand identity); (2) What are you? (brand meaning); (3) What about you? (brand response); (4) What about you and me? (brand relationships). These four stages are, in turn, reflected in what Keller terms the Brand Resonance Pyramid, which comprises six building blocks that contribute to brand-building, starting with identity (salience) at the base. Only those brands that reach the top of the pyramid achieve significant brand equity.

Keller's (1993) CBBE model has not achieved the same level of widespread acceptance as Aaker's framework in the academic literature. Nevertheless, recent research has indeed adopted Keller's approach. For example, Bandyopadhyay et al. (2024) support and extend Keller's (1993) model by illustrating how rational and emotional pathways converge to shape brand equity in the context of wine regions, empirically demonstrating a cross-over effect between brand judgments and brand feelings. This interdependence reinforces Keller's central premise that strong, resonant brand equity arises from the holistic integration of cognitive assessments (e.g., performance, credibility) and affective responses (e.g., feelings, experiences), ultimately fostering more profound and enduring consumer-brand relationships.

Likewise, Keller's brand equity pyramid has been adapted to sports leagues in the work of Yağız and Özer (2023), who examined the relationship among brand awareness, brand responses and brand resonance. Their findings highlight, among other factors, that brand associations play a pivotal role in eliciting positive consumer responses and achieving 'resonance' within a league's audience.

Rajavi et al. (2023) extend Keller's (1993) CBBE model by analyzing how macroeconomic fluctuations influence brand equity. Using 17 years of data on 325 brands in the UK, they identify distribution breadth as the most crucial factor in both expansions and contractions, reinforcing Keller's emphasis on brand salience and resonance.

The Yoo and Donthu Model

Yoo and Donthu (2001) conceptualize brand equity in a way that aligns closely with the perspectives of Aaker (1991) and Keller (1993), defining it as the difference in consumer preference between a branded product and an identical unbranded product, assuming both share the same marketing efforts and product attributes. To test the brand equity models proposed by Aaker and Keller and establish a connection between brand equity and brand performance, the authors developed a multidimensional measure of CBBE that is easy to implement among consumers. Their approach relied on an etic methodology, which allows the scale to be universally applicable across cultures, facilitating cross-contextual comparisons. This is in contrast to the more traditional (emic) approach, which is based on developing scales for one culture and subsequently validating them in others.

To generate the scale, Yoo and Donthu (2001) drew on the component dimensions proposed by Aaker (1991) and Keller (1993): brand loyalty, perceived quality, brand awareness and brand associations. Following the results of a field study among consumers from three cultures, however, they opted to merge the 'awareness' and 'associations' dimensions, ultimately proposing a rather parsimonious three-dimensional CBBE measurement model: (1) brand loyalty measurement, (2) perceived quality measurement and (3) brand awareness/associations measurement.

An additional noteworthy contribution by these authors to the academic literature on CBBE measurement is the unidimensional scale they created for assessing overall brand equity (OBE), which is composed of four items:

1. It makes sense to buy X instead of any other brand, even if they are the same.
2. Even if another brand has the same features as X, I would prefer to buy X.
3. If there is another brand as good as X, I prefer to buy X.
4. If another brand is not different from X in any way, it seems smarter to purchase X.

Frías-Jamilena et al. (2017) examined this measure and confirmed that its psychometric properties were equivalent to those of the multidimensional measure. Due to its simplicity, it has been widely employed by various researchers in recent years

(Rodríguez-Molina et al., 2019; Rodríguez-López et al., 2020; Zollo et al., 2020).

Key Components of Perceptual Brand Equity

Empirical research conducted in international contexts (Zarantonello et al., 2020) confirms the continued relevance of Aaker's (1991) four classic dimensions of brand equity – brand loyalty, perceived quality, brand associations and brand awareness – while noting the frequent addition of a fifth dimension related to perceived value. Although perceived value was not part of the initial conceptual frameworks (Aaker, 1991; Keller, 1993), it consistently appears in subsequent studies (Boo et al., 2009; Buil et al., 2008; Rodríguez-Molina et al., 2019, among others) as a key factor in explaining the utility or benefits that consumers perceive in relation to the costs or sacrifices involved in acquiring a brand.

Brand loyalty

Several studies identify loyalty as a core dimension of brand equity (Buil et al., 2008; Christodoulides et al., 2015; Yoo & Donthu, 2001). Academic interest in brand loyalty emerged roughly five decades before the development of the CBBE framework. Academic literature suggests that loyalty determines how connected the consumer is to the brand, which is a factor that determines CBBE (Hsu et al., 2012). Achieving brand loyalty is highly beneficial for companies, as retaining a loyal consumer is less costly than acquiring new consumers, and loyal consumers are less price-sensitive.

Brand loyalty is a foundational dimension of brand equity that, unlike the other dimensions, requires prior purchase experience and use on the part of the consumer. However, some authors consider this construct as an outcome of CBBE (Netemeyer et al., 2004). Keller's (1993) CBBE framework did not include brand loyalty as a separate component. While Aaker's (1991) framework recognized brand loyalty as a distinct element, his original conceptualization fell short of encompassing both the behavioral and attitudinal dimensions of loyalty. In multicultural contexts, loyalty appears to be strongly influenced by consumers' perceived affinity with the brand, how well the brand aligns with local culture or by the brand's perceived prestige (Krautz, 2017).

Perceived quality

Much of the academic literature on CBBE includes perceived quality as a fundamental dimension of brand equity (Buil et al., 2008; Christodoulides et al., 2015). Aaker (1991) defines perceived quality as the consumer's judgement about a product's excellence or superiority regarding the function or purpose to be fulfilled compared with possible substitutes. It is based, therefore, on consumers' perceptions of the brand in relation to what matters to them. Consequently, perceived quality is not the objective quality of the product in terms of the absence of errors but, rather, a subjective assessment made by consumers (Su, 2016).

Under this framework, perceived quality is not only associated with premium pricing, price elasticity, brand usage, brand awareness and stock returns, but it also exerts a positive influence on purchase intention, consumer trust and – within international contexts – on the acceptance of global brands (Oliveira-Castro et al., 2008).

Brand associations

Brand associations refer to the knowledge about a given brand that is stored in the minds of consumers and can thus be both positive and negative. Such associations can deliver value to consumers that prompts them to purchase a given brand over its rivals due to the positive feelings it generates in them (Su, 2016). In the literature, these measures of association are often referred to as 'image', following Keller's (1993) suggestion. However, the extensive review by Zarantonello et al. (2020) underscores a broader perspective on brand associations, encompassing diverse meanings, images and emotions linked to the brand. In some instances, 'brand image' is employed as an equivalent term (Boo et al., 2009).

Brand association can be understood through three perspectives. First, brand as a product, focuses on perceived value, which goes beyond functional benefits to assess whether the brand offers good value for money and stands out from competitors. Perceived quality strongly influences perceived value, explaining 80% of its variance (Aaker, 1996). The second perspective, brand as a person, highlights brand personality, which creates emotional connections, supports self-expression and aids differentiation. Traits like trustworthiness (for banks) or ruggedness (for sports vehicles) are used to define its character and relationship with consumers. Finally, the brand as an organization considers the brand's associations with its people, values, and activities. This dimension distinguishes between product innovation and an enduring commitment to innovation, shaping trust and credibility. These three perspectives collectively offer a comprehensive view of how brands build value and differentiation.

Brand awareness

Brand awareness is the ability of a potential consumer to recognize or remember that a brand belongs to a certain product category (Aaker, 1991). This element is a determinant of brand choice and subsequent loyalty. It measures the prominence of the brand in the consumer's mind through three levels that would be represented in measurement scales under questions such as: 'Have you heard of brand X' (brand recognition); 'Which car brand can you remember' (immediate recall); 'Say the name of the first brand that comes to mind' (top-of-mind or first place in the consumer's mind). Both Aaker (1991, 1996) and Keller (1993) identify brand awareness as a determining dimension within brand equity. In cross-cultural studies (Christodoulides et al., 2015; Jung & Sung, 2008), awareness may exert varying degrees of impact depending on consumers' familiarity with the product category and on the brand's global prestige.

Perceived value

The concept of value, along with its derivatives – such as perceived value and consumer value – predates the development of the CBBE framework (Zeithaml, 1988). This author defines perceived value as the balance between the benefits and costs associated with purchasing and using a product or brand. In broader terms, perceived value captures consumers' assessments of a brand's benefit–cost ratio, and has been shown to influence both loyalty and the willingness to pay a premium (Heinberg et al., 2020).

Although Aaker (1991) and Keller (1993) did not formally include perceived value as a separate dimension, numerous investigations (e.g., Boo et al., 2009; Buil et al., 2008; Pike & Bianchi, 2016) highlight its significance in explaining purchase behavior in sectors such as tourism, hospitality, and fast-moving consumer goods.

In addition to the five core dimensions of CBBE, several other noteworthy dimensions emerge from the academic literature (Zarantonello et al., 2020). Although these dimensions are not universally integrated into every CBBE model, they broaden the conceptual scope by capturing a range of contextual, experiential and symbolic factors that can influence consumer perceptions and behaviors:

- Brand personality explores 'brand as a person', encompassing symbolic traits (e.g., sincerity, excitement and ruggedness) that help consumers differentiate brands and form emotional attachments (Buil et al., 2008).
- Brand trust focuses on the credibility and reliability a consumer attributes to a brand. It often mediates the relationship between brand associations and loyalty, highlighting that trust can have effects independent of loyalty (Broyles et al., 2010).
- Brand satisfaction emphasizes how well a brand meets or exceeds consumer expectations. In sectors such as hospitality or high-involvement goods, satisfaction may directly shape both attitudinal and behavioral loyalty (Çifci et al., 2016).
- Self-congruence assesses how closely the brand's imagery or values align with a consumer's self-concept or ideal self. Strong brand identification can, in turn, drive deeper emotional connections and encourage repeat purchases (Çifci et al., 2016).
- Broyles et al. (2010) introduce additional dimensions that capture how consistently the brand meets consumer expectations (brand reliability), the depth of consumers' emotional engagement (brand resonance) and the sensory or affective elements of interacting with the brand (brand experience).

In summary, extensive literature on the conceptualization and dimensionality of brand equity over the past decades (Tasci, 2021) has highlighted the evolution of the CBBE construct, which now encompasses approximately 40 components. Aaker (1996) anticipated such variations, recognizing that different brands and market segments may emphasize distinct components.

RESEARCH CHALLENGES AND OPPORTUNITIES IN BRAND EQUITY

This section shifts the focus to the key challenges confronting researchers in this field and the major research opportunities anticipated in the coming years.

Challenges in Measuring the Brand Equity

Based on the review of the literature, it becomes evident that the primary focus of researchers in the field of brand equity has revolved around the measurement of this concept and its main dimensions.

As previously discussed in this chapter, Yoo and Donthu (2001) proposed one of the most noteworthy approaches for developing and validating a multidimensional scale for CBBE. Drawing upon the seminal works of Aaker (1991) and Keller (1993) and employing an emic perspective, the authors introduced a dual measure of CBBE. This included: (1) a multidimensional 10-item scale capturing the dimensions of brand loyalty, perceived quality, and brand awareness/associations, and (2) a one-dimensional four-item OBE scale, which is highly correlated with the previous one. The introduction of the unidimensional OBE scale represents a notable contribution to marketing scholarship, particularly as it was designed to facilitate the use of complex analytical models in exploring the antecedents and outcomes of CBBE. Nonetheless, despite its substantial impact, several questions remain regarding the measurement of CBBE, which future research must endeavor to resolve.

The first issue concerns the dimensions that constitute CBBE. While subsequent researchers have introduced additional dimensions, such as perceived value (Boo et al., 2009; Pike & Bianchi, 2016), future studies should focus on identifying the most appropriate configuration for measuring CBBE, balancing parsimony with content validity. The second question that demands greater scholarly attention pertains to the true validity of the OBE scale in capturing the multiple facets of a concept as intricate as brand equity. Although Yoo and Donthu (2001) reported strong psychometric properties, and later studies by Im et al. (2012) and Frías-Jamilena et al. (2017) supported these findings, further research is needed to validate this measure across diverse product categories, including services and industrial goods. Additionally, extending these validation efforts to different cultural and linguistic contexts, as well as across various sectors, is essential to confirm the universal applicability of this CBBE scale.

Contextual Factors and Their Impact on Brand Equity

Beyond the conceptualization and measurement of brand equity, future research should prioritize exploring the primary drivers that influence the formation of this construct. Although the academic literature has made significant progress in this area, numerous questions remain unresolved. Many studies have focused on identifying antecedent variables that facilitate the development of CBBE. However, the majority of this research has concentrated on variables derived from consumers' personal assessments – such as self-congruity, satisfaction, value co-creation, credibility, experience, and motivations – while primarily targeting the tourism industry (e.g., Castañeda-García et al., 2020; Frías-Jamilena et al., 2017; Frías et al., 2020; Prados-Peña & Del Barrio-García, 2021; Rodríguez-López et al., 2020).

When investigating consumer behavior, it is crucial to recognize that such behavior is shaped not only by subjective antecedent variables but also by external and contextual factors, which must equally be considered. From the perspective of SDL (Vargo & Lusch, 2011), the consumer's context is pivotal in marketing and consumer behavior studies. Therefore, future research should give greater attention to contextual factors that influence the development of CBBE. Below, we outline several factors with significant potential for further investigation.

The geographical factor, as emphasized by Vargo and Lusch (2016), plays a pivotal role in facilitating value co-creation. Examining the influence of consumers' geographical environment on the formation of brand equity presents a promising avenue for future research. Such studies could explore the extent to which individuals within the same geographical area impact the development of CBBE. Conducting this type of research would necessitate the creation of a spatial econometric model, incorporating a range of explanatory variables linked to the consumer's personal experience – such as self-congruity, motivations, and credibility – thereby evaluating how changes in these variables in one location affect the dependent variable (CBBE) in neighboring areas.

Another external factor that can significantly impact brand equity, yet remains underexplored in the literature, is the marketing investment made by brands. Future research should delve deeper into the influence of companies' implementation of pricing, distribution, and communication initiatives – particularly those tied to digital marketing – on the development of CBBE.

Similarly, the impact of a brand's corporate reputation on the development of CBBE remains insufficiently explored in the existing literature (Davcik, 2013). A strong corporate reputation may serve as a signal to consumers, enhancing their perceptions of quality and value, which in turn contributes to strengthening brand equity. Conversely, some scholars have argued that one of the key advantages of robust brand equity is the superior corporate reputation it can confer upon a company. Further research is needed to clarify the circumstances under which corporate reputation influences brand equity, as well as the conditions in which this relationship operates reciprocally.

Among the external factors that have gained prominence in marketing in recent years, authenticity – whether related to the product or the service offered to consumers – stands out as particularly significant (Kovács et al., 2017). The greater the perceived authenticity of a product or service, the more likely consumers are to advocate for it, resulting in a higher level of brand equity compared to competing brands (Beverland, 2009). While prior studies have explored the antecedent role of authenticity in specific dimensions of CBBE, future investigations should examine this mechanism across varying levels of authenticity, different types of products and services and diverse research contexts.

Future research should examine how the current social and economic environment, supply chain disruptions and inflation impact CBBE, especially in services. Changing consumer priorities, supply chain issues, and pricing strategies may affect brand loyalty, perceived quality and brand associations, requiring firms to adapt to sustain brand equity amid instability.

New Contexts for Research: Digitalization and Sustainability

The consolidation of Web 2.0 has fundamentally transformed how consumers interact with brands, amplifying the prevalence of user-generated content (UGC) on digital platforms, which lies beyond the direct control of companies. This raises the question of how such consumer-generated content on social media influences the formation of CBBE. In this regard, Wei et al. (2023) concluded that while UGC provides consumers with more informational value and inspires greater trust, its effect on CBBE is not statistically significant. Other studies, however, suggest that UGC has a notable influence on perceived quality and brand loyalty, and therefore on CBBE, particularly when the brand operates on an international scale. Conversely, brand-generated content exerts a greater impact on CBBE in cases where the brand operates in local or national markets (Morra et al., 2017).

This distinction between consumer-generated and brand-generated content becomes even more relevant when considering the integration of emerging technologies like digital payment platforms and immersive technologies, such as augmented reality (AR) and virtual reality (VR). Recent research highlights how these technologies intersect with CBBE formation. For instance, Bapat and Hollebeek (2023) examined the relationship between perceived quality, hedonic value, social value, price value, and CBBE in the context of digital payment applications, confirming the mediating role of consumer engagement. Similarly, Sankaran and Chakraborty (2023) explored the drivers of mobile payment systems, their influence on satisfaction and their subsequent impact on brand equity.

The adoption of immersive technologies, accelerated by the COVID-19 pandemic, further underscores the need to explore how attributes of AR and VR applications influence consumer behavior. While limited research connects immersive experiences to CBBE, emerging studies reveal the potential for significant contributions. For example, Jiang and Lyu (2024) proposed that in the context of luxury brands, CBBE acts as a stimulus influencing consumer attitudes toward AR applications, reinforcing Keller's (1993) assertion that CBBE is a key determinant of consumer behavior. Conversely, Wu et al. (2024) focused on the impact of AR features – such as perceived augmentation, simulated physical control, and response time – on brand value. They found that AR attributes enhance cognitive fluency in information processing, thereby strengthening cognitive and affective brand associations, with affective associations exerting an even greater influence on brand equity.

In light of these findings, the integration of UGC, brand-generated content, and advanced technologies offers a fertile ground for future research into their interconnected effects on CBBE. Investigating these dynamics could provide deeper insights into how digital ecosystems shape the relationships between consumers and brands across diverse contexts.

In addition to digitalization, corporate social responsibility (CSR) in terms of sustainability is undoubtedly another factor that is significantly impacting – and will continue to impact – the performance of companies. This concept refers to organizational practices aimed at minimizing energy consumption and efficiently managing waste to reduce the adverse effects of corporate activities on climate change and, consequently, on society (Eltayeb et al., 2011). Since the onset of globalization, organizations have increasingly incorporated sustainability into their CSR programs (Carroll & Shabana, 2010) to achieve beneficial outcomes in terms of brand equity.

Tourism and Hospitality Applications

It is worth delving into the academic research on brand equity within the tourism and hospitality sectors, given the extensive volume of studies conducted in this field. Over the years, various studies have extended the application of the CBBE framework to emerging tourism segments. For instance, El-Adly and ELSamen (2018) developed and validated a novel scale called Guest-Based Hotel Equity (GBHE), incorporating perceived consumer value as a multidimensional construct in the hotel industry. Similarly, Roy et al. (2023) proposed a CBBE scale specific to medical tourism in emerging economies. Rahman et al. (2022) analyzed how the brand equity of health tourism destinations affects travelers' intention to revisit. Additionally, Bianchi et al. (2014) evaluated the validity of the CBBE model in three South American countries, highlighting its usefulness for exploring tourist attitudes in long-distance travel contexts.

Another extensively studied, but still promising research area, involves the influence of consumer engagement, consumer co-creation and consumer experience on the CBBE of tourism service brands. For example, Xie et al. (2024) explored how the features of online communities and their offline activities influence destination brand equity. Sahaf and Fazili (2024) propose that brand equity plays a crucial role in helping service companies within the tourism ecosystem mitigate the adverse effects of service failures. This finding opens new avenues for future research, particularly in exploring how brand equity can enhance resilience and consumer trust in service recovery processes.

Brand Equity in Luxury Tourism: Future Challenges

Academic literature has increasingly focused on the luxury segment within the tourism industry, particularly since 2011 (Liu et al., 2017). The rise of luxury travel and the proliferation of online sales channels offering discounts and flash sales have highlighted the need to adapt brand equity models to non-conventional products and services. In this context, research has shown that price promotions through online platforms can negatively impact consumers with a high need for status (Yang et al., 2016), reinforcing the importance of updating the CBBE model to better capture the specific characteristics of the luxury experience.

A significant step toward this adaptation was the incorporation of complementary variables into the traditional CBBE model, such as trust in management and brand reliability, as applied to luxury hotels in China (Hsu et al., 2012). The findings revealed that these factors had a stronger impact on brand loyalty than perceived quality or brand awareness. Based on these insights, it is suggested that luxury companies reinforce reliable management practices and enhance their ability to consistently deliver high-quality products and services.

The luxury sector is distinguished by its strong brand equity, which provides several advantages, including increased cash flow, future profitability, product diversification, lower operational risks and higher consumer loyalty (Sürücü et al., 2019). In response to evolving consumer expectations, luxury brands have begun integrating 'phygital marketing' (Hyun et al., 2024), a concept that seamlessly blends physical and digital experiences to enhance the customer journey. This shift necessitates a reassessment of service flows within physical retail spaces and a closer examination of how luxury brand websites are structured and perceived (Hyun et al., 2024). Key factors such as website design and online customer service have emerged as critical determinants of brand value, while digital marketing strategies, such as social media engagement, entertainment, interactivity, trendiness, customization and word of mouth, play an increasingly important role in shaping brand perceptions (Godey et al., 2016; Kim & Ko, 2012).

The rise of new luxury (Kumar et al., 2020), which emphasizes affordability and mass-market availability, has led to the emergence of the masstige (mass prestige) phenomenon. This shift has driven luxury brands to adopt masstige marketing strategies targeting the middle class, an area that remains underexplored in academic research (Al-Issa et al., 2024). This emerging trend presents a significant research opportunity to further understand how brand equity is developed within this segment. Future studies should explore how luxury brands can balance their exclusive positioning with mass-market commercialization while maintaining their high brand value in an increasingly competitive and evolving landscape.

Integrated Marketing Communication and Its Impact on Brand Equity

An emerging area of interest in recent years is the impact of integrated marketing communication (IMC) strategies on brand equity, a topic that has been primarily examined within the tourism sector. Decades ago, Keller's seminal work (2003) emphasized the critical role of marketing communication in building brand equity, particularly through brand awareness and brand image. Consistent messaging across communication channels is widely recognized as a key factor in creating CBBE (Castañeda-García et al., 2020; Rodríguez-Molina et al., 2019). Similarly, Madhavaram et al. (2005) argued that synergies achieved through consistent brand imagery positively influence the awareness and image dimensions of brand equity, while Anantachart (2004) highlighted that IMC strategies based on systematic message and media consistency enhance consumer evaluations and attitudes. Future research on IMC and CBBE could explore several promising directions. One key area involves examining brand equity perceptions among consumers from various countries to enhance the generalizability of findings.

Additionally, incorporating the moderating role of national culture in analyses could provide valuable insights into how cultural differences influence the formation of brand equity. Another important aspect to consider is the distinction between inexperienced and experienced consumers. Current findings on message consistency between external information sources apply solely to inexperienced consumers, as experienced consumers tend to rely more on internal information sources, such as personal knowledge or past experiences.

REFERENCES

Aaker, D. A. (1991). *Managing brand equity: Capitalizing on the value of a brand name*. The Free Press.

Aaker, D. A. (1996). Measuring brand equity across products and markets. *California Management Review*, *38*(3), 102–120.

Aaker, D. A., & Joachimsthaler, E. (2000). The brand relationship spectrum: The key to the brand architecture challenge. *California Management Review*, *42*(4), 8–23.

Ahmad, A., & Thyagaraj, K. S. (2014). Brand personality and brand equity research: Past developments and future directions. *The IUP Journal of Brand Management*, *11*(3), 19–56.

Al-Issa, N., Kwiatek, P., & Dens, N. (2024). Masstige buyers: Profile, perceived luxury values and purchase intentions. *International Journal of Consumer Studies*, *48*(1), e13005. https://doi.org/10.1111/ijcs.13005

Anantachart, S. (2004). Integrated marketing communications and market planning: Their implications to brand equity building. *Journal of Promotion Management*, *11*(1), 101–125. https://doi.org/10.1300/J057v11n01_07

Bandyopadhyay, A., Hall, J., Wong, H. Y., Lockshin, L., Zhang, Y., & Thaichon, P. (2024). 'Regions' as brands: An empirical validation of consumer-based brand equity framework and demonstration of cross-over effect. *Asia Pacific Journal of Marketing and Logistics*, *36*(2), 457–479. https://doi.org/10.1108/APJML-03-2023-0196

Bapat, D., & Hollebeek, L. D. (2023). Customer value, customer engagement, and customer-based brand equity in the context of a digital payment app. *Marketing Intelligence & Planning*, *41*(7), 837–853. https://doi.org/10.1108/MIP-09-2022-0417

Beverland, M. B. (2009). *Building brand authenticity: 7 habits of iconic brands*. Palgrave Macmillan.

Bianchi, C., Pike, S., & Lings, I. (2014). Investigating attitudes towards three South American destinations in an emerging long haul market using a model of consumer-based brand equity (CBBE). *Tourism Management*, *42*, 215–223. https://doi.org/10.1016/j.tourman.2013.11.014

Boo, S., Busser, J., & Baloglu, S. (2009). A model of customer-based brand equity and its application to multiple destinations. *Tourism Management*, *30*(2), 219–231. https://doi.org/10.1016/j.tourman.2008.06.003

Broyles, S. A., Leingpibul, T., Ross, R. H., & Foster, B. M. (2010). Brand equity's antecedent/consequence relationships in cross-cultural settings. *Journal of Product & Brand Management*, *19*(3), 159–169. https://doi.org/10.1108/10610421011046148

Buil, I., de Chernatony, L., & Martínez, E. (2008). A cross-national validation of the consumer-based brand equity scale. *Journal of Product & Brand Management*, *17*(6), 384–392. https://doi.org/10.1108/10610420810904121

Carroll, A. B., & Shabana, K. M. (2010). The business case for corporate social responsibility: A review of concepts, research and practice. *International Journal of Management Reviews*, *12*(1), 85–105. https://doi.org/10.1111/j.1468-2370.2009.00275.x

Castañeda-García, J. A., Frías-Jamilena, D. M., Del Barrio-García, S., & Rodríguez-Molina, M. A. (2020). The effect of message consistency and destination-positioning brand strategy type on consumer-based destination brand equity. *Journal of Travel Research*, *59*(8), 1447–1463. https://doi.org/10.1177/0047287519881506

Christodoulides, D., Cadogan, J. W., & Veloutsou, C. (2015). Consumer-based brand equity measurement: Lessons learned from an international study. *International Marketing Review*, *32*(3/4), 307–328. https://doi.org/10.1108/IMR-10-2013-0242

Çifci, S., Ekinci, Y., Whyatt, G., Japutra, A., Molinillo, S., & Siala, H. (2016). A cross validation of consumer-based brand equity models: Driving customer equity in retail brands. *Journal of Business Research*, *69*(9), 3740–3747. https://doi.org/10.1016/j.jbusres.2015.12.066

Davcik, N. (2013). An empirical investigation of brand equity: Drivers and their consequences. *British Food Journal*, *115*(9), 1342–1360. https://doi.org/10.1108/BFJ-01-2012-0005

Del Barrio-García, S., Rojas-Lamorena, Á. J., & Rodríguez-López, M. E. (2023). How does brand equity work? A review of theory and a research agenda. In C. King, & E. Murillo (Eds.), *A research agenda for brand management in a new era of consumerism* (pp. 77–88). Edward Elgar Publishing.

Dyson, P., Farr, A., & Hollis, N. S. (1996). Understanding, measuring, and using brand equity. *Journal of Advertising Research*, *36*(6), 9–22. https://doi.org/10.1080/00218499.1996.12466633

Ekinci, Y., Japutra, A., Molinillo, S., & Uysal, M. (2023). Extension and validation of a novel destination brand equity model. *Journal of Travel Research*, *62*(6), 1257–1276. https://doi.org/10.1177/00472875221125

El-Adly, M. I., & ELSamen, A. A. (2018). Guest-based hotel equity: Scale development and validation. *Journal of Product & Brand Management*, *27*(6), 615–633. https://doi.org/10.1108/JPBM-09-2017-1570

Eltayeb, T. K., Zailani, S., & Ramayah, T. (2011). Green supply chain initiatives among certified companies in Malaysia and environmental sustainability: Investigating the outcomes. *Resources, Conservation and Recycling*, *55*(5), 495–506. https://doi.org/10.1016/j.resconrec.2010.09.003

Erkmen, E. (2018). Managing your brand for employees: Understanding the role of organizational processes in cultivating employee brand equity. *Administrative Sciences*, *8*(3), 52. https://doi.org/10.3390/admsci8030052

Frías, D. M., Castaneda, J. A., del Barrio-Garcia, S., & Lopez-Moreno, L. (2020). The effect of self-congruity and motivation on consumer-based destination brand equity. *Journal of Vacation Marketing*, *26*(3), 287–304. https://doi.org/10.1177/1356766719886888

Frías-Jamilena, D. M., Polo-Peña, A. I., & Rodríguez-Molina, M. Á. (2017). The effect of value-creation on consumer-based destination brand equity. *Journal of Travel Research*, *56*(8), 1011–1031. https://doi.org/10.1177/0047287516663650

Godey, B., Manthiou, A., Pederzoli, D., Rokka, J., Aiello, G., Donvito, R., & Singh, R. (2016). Social media marketing efforts of luxury brands: Influence on brand equity and consumer behavior. *Journal of Business Research*, *69*(12), 5833–5841. https://doi.org/10.1016/j.jbusres.2016.04.181

Heinberg, M., Katsikeas, C. S., Ozkaya, H. E., & Taube, M. (2020). How nostalgic brand positioning shapes brand equity: Differences between emerging and developed markets. *Journal of the Academy of Marketing Science*, *48*, 869–890. https://doi.org/10.1007/s11747-019-00637-x

Hoeffler, S., & Keller, K. L. (2002). Building brand equity through corporate societal marketing. *Journal of Public Policy & Marketing*, *21*(1), 78–89. https://doi.org/10.1509/jppm.21.1.78.17600

Hsu, C. H., Oh, H., & Assaf, A. G. (2012). A customer-based brand equity model for upscale hotels. *Journal of Travel Research*, *51*(1), 81–93. https://doi.org/10.1177/0047287510394195

Huerta-Álvarez, R., Cambra-Fierro, J. J., & Fuentes-Blasco, M. (2020). The interplay between social media communication, brand equity and brand engagement in tourist destinations: An analysis in an emerging economy. *Journal of Destination Marketing & Management*, *16*, 100413. https://doi.org/10.1016/j.jdmm.2020.100413

Hyun, H., Park, J., & Hong, E. (2024). Enhancing brand equity through multidimensional brand authenticity in the fashion retailing. *Journal of Retailing and Consumer Services*, *78*, 103712. https://doi.org/10.1016/j.jretconser.2024.103712

Im, H. H., Kim, S. S., Elliot, S., & Han, H. (2012). Conceptualizing destination brand equity dimensions from a consumer-based brand equity perspective. *Journal of Travel & Tourism Marketing*, *29*(4), 385–403. https://doi.org/10.1080/10548408.2012.674884

Jiang, Z., & Lyu, J. (2024). The role of augmented reality app attributes and customer-based brand equity on consumer behavioral responses: An SOR framework perspective. *Journal of Product & Brand Management*, *33*(6), 702–716. https://doi.org/10.1108/JPBM-09-2023-4706

Jung, J., & Sung, E. (2008). Consumer-based brand equity: Comparisons among Americans and South Koreans in the USA and South Koreans in Korea. *Journal of Fashion Marketing and Management: An International Journal*, *12*(1), 24–35. https://doi.org/10.1108/13612020810857925

Kamakura, W. A., & Russell, G. J. (1993). Measuring brand value with scanner data. *International Journal of Research in Marketing*, *10*(1), 9–22. https://doi.org/10.1016/0167-8116(93)90030-3

Kapferer, J. N. (2004). *The new strategic brand management: Creating and sustaining brand equity long term*. Kogan Page.

Keller, K. L. (1993). Conceptualizing, measuring, and managing customer-based brand equity. *Journal of Marketing*, *57*(1), 1–22. https://doi.org/10.1177/002224299305700101

Keller, K. L. (2003). Brand synthesis: The multidimensionality of brand knowledge. *Journal of Consumer Research*, *29*(4), 595–600.

Keller, K. L. (2014). *Strategic brand management: Building, measuring, and managing brand equity* (4th ed.). Prentice Hall.

Kim, A. J., & Ko, E. (2012). Do social media marketing activities enhance customer equity? An empirical study of luxury fashion brand. *Journal of Business Research*, *65*(10), 1480–1486. https://doi.org/10.1016/j.jbusres.2011.10.014

Kim, H. B., & Kim, W. G. (2005). The relationship between brand equity and firms' performance in luxury hotels and chain restaurants. *Tourism Management*, *26*(4), 549–560. https://doi.org/10.1016/j.tourman.2004.03.010

Kovács, B., Carroll, G. R., & Lehman, D. W. (2017). The perils of proclaiming an authentic organizational identity. *Sociological Science*, *4*, 80–106.

Krautz, C. (2017). A cross-cultural study of collective brand perceptions within the brand equity framework. *Journal of Marketing Theory and Practice*, *25*(3), 274–290. https://doi.org/10.1080/10696679.2017.1311218

Kumar, A., Paul, J., & Unnithan, A. B. (2020). 'Masstige'marketing: A review, synthesis and research agenda. *Journal of Business Research*, *113*, 384–398. https://doi.org/10.1016/j.jbusres.2019.09.030

Lee, J. S., & Back, K. J. (2010). Reexamination of attendee-based brand equity. *Tourism Management*, *31*(3), 395–401. https://doi.org/10.1016/j.tourman.2009.04.006

Liu, M. T., Wong, I. A., Tseng, T. H., Chang, A. W. Y., & Phau, I. (2017). Applying consumer-based brand equity in luxury hotel branding. *Journal of Business Research*, *81*, 192–202. https://doi.org/10.1016/j.jbusres.2017.06.014

Madhavaram, S., Badrinarayanan, V., & McDonald, R. E. (2005). Integrated marketing communication (IMC) and brand identity as critical components of brand equity strategy: A conceptual framework and research propositions. *Journal of Advertising*, *34*(4), 69–80. https://doi.org/10.1080/00913367.2005.10639213

Morra, M. C., Ceruti, F., Chierici, R., & Di Gregorio, A. (2017). Social vs traditional media communication: Brand origin associations strike a chord. *Journal of Research in Interactive Marketing*, *12*(1), 2–21. https://doi.org/10.1108/JRIM-12-2016-0116

Motameni, R., & Shahrokhi, M. (1998). Brand equity valuation: A global perspective. *Journal of Product & Brand Management*, *7*(4), 275–290. https://doi.org/10.1108/10610429810229799

Mourad, M., Meshreki, H., & Sarofim, S. (2020). Brand equity in higher education: Comparative analysis. *Studies in Higher Education*, *45*(1), 209–231. https://doi.org/10.1080/03075079.2019.1582012

Netemeyer, R. G., Krishnan, B., Pullig, C., Wang, G., Yagci, M., Dean, D., Ricks, J., & Wirth, F. (2004). Developing and validating measures of facets of customer-based brand equity. *Journal of Business Research*, *57*(2), 209–224. https://doi.org/10.1016/S0148-2963(01)00303-4

O'Neill, J. W., & Mattila, A. S. (2006). Strategic hotel development and positioning: The effects of revenue drivers on profitability. *Cornell Hotel and Restaurant Administration Quarterly*, *47*(2), 146–154. https://doi.org/10.1177/0010880405281519

Oliveira, M. O. R. D., Heldt, R., Silveira, C. S., & Luce, F. B. (2023). Brand equity chain and brand equity measurement approaches. *Marketing Intelligence & Planning*, *41*(4), 442–456. https://doi.org/10.1108/MIP-06-2022-0222

Oliveira-Castro, J. M., Foxall, G. R., & James, V. K. (2008). Individual differences in price responsiveness within and across food brands. *The Service Industries Journal*, *28*(6), 733–753. https://doi.org/10.1080/02642060801988605

Pike, S., & Bianchi, C. (2016). Destination brand equity for Australia: Testing a model of CBBE in short-haul and long-haul markets. *Journal of Hospitality and Tourism Research*, *40*(1), 114–134. https://doi.org/10.1177/1096348013491604

Prados-Peña, M. B., & Del Barrio-García, S. (2021). Key antecedents of brand equity in heritage brand extensions: The moderating role of tourist heritage experience. *European Research on Management and Business Economics*, *27*(3), 100153. https://doi.org/10.1016/j.iedeen.2021.100153

Rahman, M. S., Bag, S., Hassan, H., Hossain, M. A., & Singh, R. K. (2022). Destination brand equity and tourist's revisit intention towards health tourism: An empirical study. *Benchmarking: An International Journal*, *29*(4), 1306–1331. https://doi.org/10.1108/BIJ-03-2021-0173

Rajavi, K., Kushwaha, T., & Steenkamp, J. B. E. (2023). Brand equity in good and bad times: What distinguishes winners from losers in consumer packaged goods industries? *Journal of Marketing*, *87*(3), 472–489. https://doi.org/10.1177/00222429221122698

Rodríguez-López, M. E., Del Barrio-García, S., & Alcántara-Pilar, J. M. (2020). Formation of customer-based brand equity via authenticity. *International Journal of Contemporary Hospitality Management*, *32*(2), 815–834. https://doi.org/10.1108/IJCHM-05-2019-0473

Rodríguez-Molina, M. A., Frías-Jamilena, D. M., Del Barrio-García, S., & Castañeda-García, J. A. (2019). Destination brand equity-formation: Positioning by tourism type and message consistency. *Journal of Destination Marketing & Management*, *12*, 114–124. https://doi.org/10.1016/j.jdmm.2019.03.010

Rojas-Lamorena, ÁJ, Del Barrio-García, S., & Alcántara-Pilar, J. M. (2022). A review of three decades of academic research on brand equity: A bibliometric approach using co-word analysis and bibliographic coupling. *Journal of Business Research*, *139*, 1067–1083. https://doi.org/10.1016/j.jbusres.2021.10.025

Roy, S. K., Singh, G., Hatton, C., Dey, B., Ameen, N., & Kumar, S. (2023). Customers' motives to co-create in smart services interactions. *Electronic Commerce Research*, *23*, 1367–1400. https://doi.org/10.1007/s10660-022-09633-w

Sahaf, T. M., & Fazili, A. I. (2024). Service failure and service recovery: A hybrid review and research agenda. *International Journal of Consumer Studies*, *48*(1), e12974. https://doi.org/10.1111/ijcs.12974

Sankaran, R., & Chakraborty, S. (2023). Measuring consumer perception of overall brand equity drivers for m-payments. *International Journal of Bank Marketing*, *41*(1), 130–157. https://doi.org/10.1108/IJBM-03-2022-0113

Sarwar, M., & Siddiqui, D. A. (2021). Exploring the brand equity of low and high involvement purchases in Pakistan: An application of Aaker's brand equity ten model. https://doi.org/10.2139/ssrn.3943863

Sasmita, J., & Mohd Suki, N. (2015). Young consumers' insights on brand equity. *International Journal of Retail & Distribution Management*, *43*(3), 276–292. https://doi.org/10.1108/IJRDM-02-2014-0024

Su, J. (2016). Examining the relationships among the brand equity dimensions: Empirical evidence from fast fashion. *Asia Pacific Journal of Marketing and Logistics*, *28*(3), 464–480. https://doi.org/10.1108/APJML-01-2015-0004

Sürücü, Ö, Öztürk, Y., Okumus, F., & Bilgihan, A. (2019). Brand awareness, image, physical quality and employee behavior as building blocks of customer-based brand equity: Consequences in the hotel context. *Journal of Hospitality and Tourism Management*, *40*, 114–124. https://doi.org/10.1016/j.jhtm.2019.07.002

Tasci, A. D. A. (2021). A critical review and reconstruction of perceptual brand equity. *International Journal of Contemporary Hospitality Management*, *33*(1), 166–198. https://doi.org/10.1108/IJCHM-03-2020-0186

Tax, S. S., Brown, S. W., & Chandrashekaran, M. (1998). Customer evaluations of service complaint experiences: Implications for relationship marketing. *Journal of Marketing*, *62*(2), 60–76. https://doi.org/10.1177/002224299806200205

Vargo, S. L., & Lusch, R. F. (2011). It's all B2B… and beyond: Toward a systems perspective of the market. *Industrial Marketing Management*, *40*(2), 181–187. https://doi.org/10.1016/j.indmarman.2010.06.026

Vargo, S. L., & Lusch, R. F. (2016). Institutions and axioms: An extension and update of service-dominant logic. *Journal of the Academy of Marketing Science*, *44*(1), 5–23. https://doi.org/10.1007/s11747-015-0456-3

Veloutsou, C., & Delgado-Ballester, E. D. (2018). New challenges in brand management. *Spanish Journal of Marketing-ESIC*, *22*(3), 254–271. https://doi.org/10.1108/SJME-12-2018-036

Wei, L., Gong, J., Xu, J., Abidin, N. E. Z., & Apuke, O. D. (2023). Do social media literacy skills help in combating fake news spread? Modelling the moderating role of social media literacy skills in the relationship between rational choice factors and fake news sharing behavior. *Telematics and Informatics*, *76*, 101910. https://doi.org/10.1016/j.tele.2022.101910

Wu, J. F., Dong, J., Wu, Y., & Chang, Y. P. (2024). Shopping through mobile augmented reality: The impacts of AR embedding and embodiment attributes on consumer-based brand equity. *Information & Management*, *61*(6), 103999. https://doi.org/10.1016/j.im.2024.103999

Xie, L., Guan, X., Yeh, S. S., & Huan, T. C. (2024). Using value co-creation behavior as a mediator to explore the influence of virtual tourism community characteristics on destination brand equity. *Journal of Brand Management*, *32*, 1–16. https://doi.org/10.1057/s41262-024-00365-w

Xu, J. B., & Chan, A. (2010). A conceptual framework of hotel experience and customer-based brand equity: Some research questions and implications. *International Journal of Contemporary Hospitality Management*, *22*(2), 174–193. https://doi.org/10.1108/09596111011018179

Yağız, K., & Özer, L. (2023). Examining the relationships between brand knowledge, brand responses and brand resonance in sports leagues within the scope of consumer-based brand equity. *European Sport Management Quarterly*, *23*(5), 1567–1586. https://doi.org/10.1080/16184742.2022.2047087

Yang, W., Zhang, L., & Mattila, A. S. (2016). Luxe for less: How do consumers react to luxury hotel price promotions? The moderating role of consumers' need for status. *Cornell Hospitality Quarterly*, *57*(1), 82–92. https://doi.org/10.1177/1938965515580

Yoo, B., & Donthu, N. (2001). Developing and validating a multidimensional consumer-based brand equity scale. *Journal of Business Research*, *52*(1), 1–14. https://doi.org/10.1016/S0148-2963(99)00098-3

Yoo, B., Donthu, N., & Lee, S. (2000). An examination of selected marketing mix elements and brand equity. *Journal of the Academy of Marketing Science*, *28*, 195–211. https://doi.org/10.1177/0092070300282002

Zarantonello, L., Grappi, S., Formisano, M., & Brakus, J. (2020). How consumer-based brand equity relates to market share of global and local brands in developed and emerging countries. *International Marketing Review*, *37*(2), 345–375. https://doi.org/10.1108/IMR-05-2018-0176

Zeithaml, V. A. (1988). Consumer perceptions of price, quality, and value: A means-end model and synthesis of evidence. *Journal of Marketing*, *52*(3), 2–22. https://doi.org/10.1177/00222429880520030

Zollo, L., Filieri, R., Rialti, R., & Yoon, S. (2020). Unpacking the relationship between social media marketing and brand equity: The mediating role of consumers' benefits and experience. *Journal of Business Research*, *117*, 256–267. https://doi.org/10.1016/j.jbusres.2020.05.001

11

Employee-Based Brand Equity

Irina Gorea and Jenna Jacobson

INTRODUCTION

Branding practices are important managerial concern as brands are among the most valuable intangible assets owned by an organization (Keller, 2020; Keller & Lehmann, 2006; Oh et al., 2020). A foundational definition of brand equity was introduced by David A. Aaker in 1991. Aaker (1992) defines brand equity as 'a set of brand assets and liabilities linked to a brand, its name, and symbol, that add to or subtract from the value provided by a product or service to a firm and/or to that firm's customers' (p. 15). Aaker's model identifies four key dimensions of brand equity: brand awareness, brand associations, perceived quality and brand loyalty. When considering brand equity, existing literature has extensively studied the consumer perspective and its significance on the brand (Erdem & Swait, 2001; Kocak et al., 2007; Machado et al., 2019). Brand equity has been dubbed an 'elusive construct' as inconsistent conceptualizations and measurements (Mikul & Mittal, 2023, p. 166). Typically, brand equity has been analyzed from a financial perspective or a consumer perspective.

Consumer-based brand equity (CBBE) focuses on consumers' brand perceptions and is the focus of most scholarly research. Research, applications and analysis on brand equity have increased significantly over the past decades, which indicates the growing scholarly interest and importance of brand equity in academic scholarship (Mikul & Mittal, 2023). CBBE is defined by Keller (1993) as 'the differential effect of brand knowledge on consumer response to the marketing of the brand' (p. 2), which speaks to the value of a brand as perceived by consumers. CBBE has been extensively conceptualized and measured, with numerous models and scales developed and adapted to the retail context. Keller and Lehmann (2006) laid the foundation for CBBE models. Subsequent CBBE models by Yoo and Donthu (2001), Christodoulides et al. (2006, 2015) and Nam et al. (2011) further expanded this research area. Several studies – particularly the work by Aaker (1991) and Keller (1993) – demonstrate that well-established, reputable brands generate greater consumer loyalty, allowing these brands to command premium prices. This is because consumers perceive strong brands as offering higher quality, reliability and emotional value. FBBE focuses on the financial market value of a brand as represented on a balance sheet (Simon & Sullivan, 1993; Sousa & Ferreira, 2024).

More recently, there has been interest in a different perspective on brand equity that analyzes brand equity from *within* the organization. Literature points to a niche, but growing, focus on employee-based brand equity (EBBE) as a novel approach to comprehending the impact of employees on brand value. Unlike CBBE, which focuses on stakeholders that are external to an organization, EBBE focuses on the role of employees from within the organization itself. King and Grace (2009) suggest that EBBE is a relatively new area of study, with researchers more recently beginning to systematically analyze employees' viewpoints. Miles and Mangold (2004) define EBBE as '…the process by which employees internalize the desired brand image and are motivated to project the image to customers and other organizational constituents' (p. 68). Importantly, EBBE differs from CBBE by offering a distinct, insider viewpoint of the brand, one that is uniquely held by employees themselves. EBBE recognizes the role and value of employees in sustaining and promoting the brand values from within the organization they work for.

Despite the growing interest, conceptualization and measurement of employee-brand equity remain an underexplored area of research (Jacobson et al., 2023; Poulis & Wisker, 2016; Rudkowski, 2024; Smith et al., 2021). This chapter analyzes EBBE as a pivotal aspect of brand management by identifying influential work in the area and highlighting different conceptualizations of EBBE as well as measurements and scales that have been used. With the retail industry being one of the largest employment sectors in Canada (Statistics Canada, 2015) and the USA (National Retail Federation, 2024), we provide context from this industry and consider the dual role of employee–consumers and their significance in EBBE. We further identify the changing nature of EBBE in a social media context. The chapter concludes by identifying gaps in existing research and providing suggestions for future research. By bridging this gap, researchers can gain a more holistic understanding of brand equity from an employee perspective and inform more effective brand management strategies.

EMPLOYEE-BASED BRAND EQUITY (EBBE): CONCEPTUALIZATIONS AND IMPLICATIONS

The concept of EBBE first appeared in an article by King and Grace when it was introduced as a new perspective on brand equity (King & Grace, 2009). King and Grace (2009) define EBBE as 'the differential effect that brand knowledge has on an employee's response to their work environment' (p. 130). EBBE plays a pivotal role across various industries, including retail (Smith et al., 2021), banking (Altaf et al., 2017; Kaur et al., 2024), consumer goods (Poulis & Wisker, 2016) and hospitality (Xiong & King, 2015). Drawing theoretical foundations from branding, human resource management and organizational behavior, the scholarly interest in EBBE is recent, and the body of literature has steadily increased over the past few years. Research suggests that EBBE is important in strengthening overall branding strategy and contributing to organizational success.

EBBE occurs when employees develop strong brand knowledge, leading to behaviors that align with the company's brand identity (Brexendorf & Kernstock, 2007). This alignment leads to brand consistent actions, reinforcing the brand's positioning internally and externally. EBBE represents the added value employees gain from a company's brand-building initiatives, influencing their attitudes, engagement and overall perception of their employer (Baumgarth & Schmidt, 2020). This added value extends beyond financial compensation or corporate reputation, shaping how employees interact with the brand and their level of commitment to it. As such, according to EBBE, employees themselves are brand stakeholders who internalize and deliver on an organization's brand values.

A key aspect of EBBE is internalizing the brand values, which manifests in employees' behavior, communication and long-term commitment to the organization (Lee et al., 2020). Employees who have a strong connection with the brand are more likely to demonstrate brand advocacy, actively endorsing and promoting the brand to external audiences. This process enhances customer perceptions and strengthens organizational culture by fostering a shared sense of purpose among employees. Furthermore, EBBE reflects the significance that employees derive from the brand beyond its external reputation, which can result in positive or negative behaviors toward the organization (Berger-Remy & Michel, 2015).

The concept of EBBE continues to evolve, with research exploring its various dimensions and implications. Studies highlight its role in shaping employee attitudes and behaviors by influencing how employees experience the brand and engage with its values (Tavassoli et al., 2014). The relationship between branding efforts and employee perceptions underscores the need for organizations to invest in internal branding strategies that effectively communicate and reinforce brand values. By fostering a strong sense of EBBE, organizations can cultivate a workforce that actively contributes to brand success through endorsement, loyalty and value co-creation. Table 11.1 in Appendix provides a summary of key scholarly definitions and perspectives on EBBE, organized in chronological order to evidence how the concept has evolved over time.

THE IMPLICATIONS OF EMPLOYEE-BASED BRAND EQUITY (EBBE) IN ORGANIZATIONAL BRANDING

Research has shown that EBBE has a significant positive impact on various aspects of managerial success. At an individual employee level, high levels of EBBE foster a stronger organizational identity and sense of purpose (King et al., 2012). As a result, EBBE impacts employees' compensation expectations; studies suggest that individuals are willing to accept lower salaries to work for stronger brands. For example, Tavassoli et al. (2014) found that executives place high value on being associated with reputable brands and may accept reduced compensation in exchange for that affiliation. This highlights EBBE's role in not only attracting and retaining top talent but also in reducing recruitment and compensation costs for organizations.

EBBE has been linked to brand loyalty and advocacy. Employees with a strong sense of EBBE are more likely to endorse their brand and act as internal brand ambassadors, actively promoting the brand to others (King & Grace, 2010). Additionally, EBBE has been shown to contribute to job satisfaction, which impacts talent attraction and retention. Employees who feel a strong connection to their organization's brand tend to experience greater job fulfillment, as they align with the company's values and mission (King & Grace, 2009). Companies with strong EBBE are able to attract and retain employees by creating a supportive workplace culture. This sense of belonging fosters workplace pride, reduces turnover rates and enhances overall organizational morale.

When companies foster strong EBBE, the internal alignment between brands and employees often translates into improved customer experiences, as employees' positive perceptions of the brand influence customer interactions, ultimately strengthening customer loyalty (Tavassoli et al., 2014). Overall, EBBE serves as a critical driver of both internal and external brand strength. By fostering strong EBBE, organizations can enhance their reputation, create a more committed workforce and establish a competitive advantage in the marketplace.

CROSS-CULTURAL AND INDUSTRY APPLICATIONS OF EBBE

With growing interest, researchers have sought to measure EBBE in various ways. King and Grace introduced the EBBE scale, which empirically tested EBBE (King & Grace, 2010). Expanding on this concept, King et al. (2012) identify three key dimensions of EBBE: (1) brand consistent behavior, which reflects what employees do; (2) brand endorsement, which captures what employees say and (3) brand allegiance, which represents employees' intentions for future actions. These dimensions collectively offer a comprehensive framework for understanding how brand knowledge influences employee behavior and attitudes and is widely recognized as the leading approach for measuring EBBE. Other researchers have grown, adapted and evolved this model over time. It has been thoroughly tested, validated and applied across various contexts such as banking (Altaf et al., 2017; Kaur et al., 2024), consumer goods (Poulis & Wisker, 2016), hospitality (Xiong & King, 2015) and retail (Rudkowski, 2024; Smith et al., 2021).

The model of EBBE developed by King and Grace (2010) has been tested in various cultural and industry-specific settings, providing insights into how different factors influence employees' perceptions of the organization's brand. Findings from these studies highlight key drivers of EBBE, including openness, knowledge sharing, role clarity and brand commitment, all of which shape how employees internalize and engage with brand values. For example, studies conducted in China demonstrate that these factors significantly impact EBBE both directly and indirectly, emphasizing the importance of fostering a transparent and supportive workplace culture (Awan et al., 2018).

Employer branding has also been identified as a critical factor in strengthening EBBE. In the private banking sector, employer branding positively influences brand consistent behavior, brand endorsement and brand allegiance, reinforcing its role in shaping employees' brand perceptions and actions (Kaur et al., 2024). By effectively communicating an organization's values and culture, employer branding enhances employees' identification with the brand, leading to stronger alignment between their behavior and the company's brand identity.

In the financial sector, particularly in Islamic and conventional banking, brand confidence has been found to play a crucial role in shaping EBBE. Employees who trust and believe in their organization's brand are more likely to exhibit brand consistent behaviors and develop stronger brand allegiance (Altaf et al., 2017). Additionally, the understanding of brand values and employees' psychological ownership of the brand mediate the relationship between brand empowerment and EBBE, further reinforcing the need for organizations to cultivate a sense of brand belonging among employees (Mohd Mokhtar et al., 2018).

By examining EBBE across different cultural and industry settings, research shows the importance of internal branding strategies that focus on fostering employee trust, commitment, and brand advocacy. Strengthening these elements enhances employee engagement and contributes to the organization's overall brand success and competitive advantage. Overall, testing the model of EBBE by King and Grace (2010) in diverse environments highlights the need for broader replication to establish a more comprehensive understanding of EBBE and its dynamics across global markets.

EXPANDING THE EMPLOYEE-BASED BRAND EQUITY (EBBE) MODEL: NEW FRAMEWORKS AND PERSPECTIVES

King and Grace's (2010) model for EBBE has served as a foundational framework for the development of new models that further explore the factors influencing EBBE (i.e., the antecedents of EBBE) and its broader implications (i.e., the outcomes of EBBE). Researchers have sought to extend the original model by incorporating additional dimensions and providing a more nuanced understanding of EBBE and its role in shaping organizational success.

One notable extension of the EBBE model is the integrated framework introduced by Boukis and Christodoulides (2020), which identifies two distinct pathways through which EBBE develops: a cognitive route, based on brand knowledge and an affective route, driven by brand identification. This model emphasizes the role of leadership in shaping employees' brand perceptions, highlighting that leadership involvement in branding efforts strengthens both cognitive and emotional connections between employees and the brand. The findings suggest that employees' understanding of brand values (i.e., brand knowledge) is a key predictor of EBBE, reinforcing the need for organizations to strategically prioritize internal branding initiatives. Additionally, fostering emotional engagement is equally crucial, as it enhances employees' identification with the brand and motivates them to actively promote it. Beyond individual alignment with the brand, the research also demonstrates how EBBE influences internal brand communication among colleagues and significantly enhances customer orientation, reinforcing its role in driving both employee and consumer experiences (Boukis & Christodoulides, 2020).

Rudkowski (2024) expands the conceptualization of EBBE by integrating both internal and external brand perceptions. Using the scale developed by King et al. (2012), the study introduces the concept of Integrated Retailer Brand Equity (IRBE) within the context of fashion retail. This model incorporates seven employee dimensions and four consumer dimensions, reflecting the dual role of frontline employees as both brand representatives and consumers. This multidimensional approach acknowledges the importance of considering diverse stakeholder perspectives when assessing EBBE. By recognizing employees as internal stakeholders who experience the brand from multiple vantage points, organizations can gain a more comprehensive understanding of how employee perceptions and behaviors contribute to brand equity.

Aligned with the customer experience, Kwon (2013) proposes a three-dimensional EBBE model: brand knowledge, role clarity and brand commitment. The model builds on King and Grace's (2009, 2010) work and is the first to measure brand knowledge in EBBE. While Kwon's work was published in a doctoral thesis, the model has been used by other scholars.

Moreover, the increasing visibility of employees as brand ambassadors on social media further underscores the relevance of this integrated approach. As employees actively engage with their employer's brand on platforms such as LinkedIn, Instagram and TikTok, their public interactions influence both internal and external perceptions of the brand. The dual-perspective approach introduced by Rudkowski (2024) offers a framework for examining how employees' online brand engagement translates into real-world behaviors, influencing their commitment, advocacy and customer interactions. This shift in perspective is particularly relevant in today's digital landscape, where social media plays an increasingly central role in shaping brand identity and reputation.

These advancements in EBBE research highlight the importance of integrating cognitive and affective processes, leadership influence and external brand perceptions into existing models. By adopting a more holistic view of EBBE, organizations can develop more effective internal branding strategies, foster stronger brand advocacy among employees and enhance overall brand performance.

Traditionally, most studies assessing EBBE have relied on survey-based methodologies, often utilizing the scale developed by King et al. (2012). While these approaches provide valuable insights, recent research has begun to adopt innovative methods to analyze EBBE, incorporating publicly available data sources and case study methodology. Notably, the role of social media in shaping and reflecting EBBE has emerged as a promising area of study, offering a new perspective on how employees engage with and communicate brand values. We now examine how EBBE has been specifically explored in the context of social media.

EBBE on Social Media

As digital communication continues to reshape brand management, social media has emerged as a critical avenue for understanding and measuring EBBE. The abundance of user-generated content – including posts, comments and multimedia shared by employees – provides rich data for researchers to analyze. This wealth of publicly available information enables researchers to observe how employees engage, endorse and co-create brand narratives. This adds deeper insights into the dynamics of EBBE in a social media context. Traditional approaches to EBBE measurement have relied heavily on survey-based methodologies, where employees self-report their perceptions of brand alignment, commitment and advocacy (King et al., 2012). However, recent research has shifted toward analyzing manifest employee behavior on social media platforms, which evidences what employees actually do on public-facing social media. This emerging research offers new insights into how employees contribute to brand equity through their online engagement.

One of the key advancements in this area is the exploration of employees as social media influencers within their organizations. Rather than relying solely on survey data, which has been the standard in EBBE scholarship, Smith et al. (2021) examine how employees actively co-create EBBE by analyzing their public social media content. Using a case study methodology, the study categorizes employee social media activity based on King et al.'s (2012) three dimensions of EBBE: brand consistent behavior, brand endorsement and brand allegiance. The findings reveal that brand consistent behavior, or what employees do online, is the most significant factor in shaping EBBE. This study demonstrates the potential of using publicly available social media data to measure EBBE in a 'real-world' applied practice, providing organizations with an alternative approach to understanding employee-brand engagement. Importantly, it also raises ethical considerations regarding the use of employee-generated content for research and brand monitoring, emphasizing the need for clear ethical guidelines in data collection and analysis.

Beyond individual employee influencers, social media platforms serve as spaces where employees collectively shape brand perceptions. Pitt et al. (2019) extend the discussion by examining employee engagement on employer review sites such as Glassdoor. Through a content analysis approach in a business-to-business (B2B) context, the study finds that employee engagement on these platforms significantly contributes to brand equity. Importantly, the research highlights differences in engagement between employees of highly rated employers and those of lower-rated ones. Employees from top-ranked B2B brands demonstrate more frequent and positive brand interactions on social media compared to employees from lesser-rated companies. These findings underscore the role of employer reputation in influencing employee advocacy and engagement, further reinforcing the link between EBBE and organizational success.

Additionally, LinkedIn has become a focal point for studying EBBE in professional settings. LinkedIn is a professional and employment-focused social media platform where individuals create a professional identity and foster a professional network. Unlike other social media platforms, such as Facebook, Instagram or TikTok that tend to focus on more personal networks, LinkedIn's professional focus makes the platform ideal for analyzing EBBE behavior. Hesse et al. (2022) analyzed corporate LinkedIn profiles and employee interactions, emphasizing the role of employees in brand co-creation. The study highlights how employee engagement on LinkedIn – through activities such as sharing company content, endorsing brand messages and participating in discussions – can strengthen overall brand equity. These insights demonstrate that actively managing and leveraging EBBE on professional networking platforms can enhance both internal brand alignment and external brand perception.

Collectively, these studies demonstrate the evolving nature of EBBE measurement, shifting from traditional survey methods to more dynamic analyses of social media behavior. By examining how employees interact with and represent their brands in digital spaces, organizations can gain a deeper understanding of EBBE's real-world impact. As social media continues to play a crucial role in brand building, integrating behavioral data from these platforms into EBBE research will provide more comprehensive insights into employee-brand advocacy and engagement.

However, the exploration of EBBE on social media is in its early stages. Researchers are beginning to leverage the potential of publicly available data to develop this area of study. The innovative methodological approaches highlighted in recent studies demonstrate the opportunities for expanding EBBE research beyond traditional survey approaches. By utilizing social media platforms and employee-generated content, researchers can gain insights into the dynamic ways employees contribute to brand equity. Even if the social media data are publicly available, importantly, researchers need to carefully consider the ethical implications of such research and consider best practices to protect users' privacy. Social media users still have expectations of privacy even if their data are publicly available. Furthermore, employees may feel pressure to post about their companies, which may represent a form of unpaid, extra-work labor. Further research is needed in this area to understand the challenges and opportunities of employee-generated content on social media as it relates to EBBE. Table 11.2 in Appendix summarizes various approaches to measuring EBBE, highlighting traditional and innovative methodologies across different sectors and contexts.

Employee-Generated Content on Social Media

Over the past decade, social media has significantly transformed branding practices. Popular platforms Instagram and TikTok boast 1.4 billion and 900 million active users, respectively, as of 2024 (Instagram Users Worldwide 2025, n.d.; Number of Global TikTok Users 2025, n.d.). The rise of social media also saw the rise of networked influence (Jacobson et al., 2019) and social media influencers. Influencers can play an important role in building brand equity. Freberg et al. (2011) define social media influencers as '…a new type of independent third-party endorsers who shape audience attitudes through blogs, tweets and the use of other social media' (p. 90). Typically external to the organization, the significance of social media influencers on branding has been demonstrated in various studies (Carter, 2016; Jiménez-Castillo & Sánchez-Fernández, 2019). Social media influencers play an important role in building brand equity.

Recently, a new type of social media influencer has emerged, one that is not an independent third-party endorser but rather internal to the brand. With the rise of workplace-related social media platforms, such as Glassdoor or Ratemyemployer, employees are increasingly empowered to voice their opinions through online channels, which further highlights the importance of understanding employee perspectives of brand equity. As noted by Smith et al. (2021), certain employees who have an influential presence on social media may be regarded as opinion leaders by their peers and therefore take on the role of an 'employee influencer' in order to voice their opinions about the workplace and brand.

Jacobson et al. (2023) define employee influencers as 'content creators who post about their employer to impact, persuade and influence internal and/or external audiences' (p. 33). Employee influencers have emerged as a unique category of social media influencers and play a crucial role in building brand equity in that they influence consumers' perceptions, other employees' perceptions of the brand, co-create value (Roncha & Radclyffe-Thomas, 2016) and champion the brand (Morhart et al., 2009). Prior to the emergence of social media, employees influenced others by expressing their opinions and ideas about their workplaces through verbal and direct communication channels, typically offline and in face-to-face interactions (Jacobson et al., 2023). Employees are increasingly empowered to voice their opinions through online channels, such as social media platforms and employer review sites.

In the retail sector, employees often double as loyal customers, embodying a powerful fusion of both consumers as well as brand advocates. This dual role affords employees a unique perspective of the brand. With 52,000 employees and 3000 retail locations worldwide (Sephora, n.d.), Sephora leverages the power of its own employees to showcase its brand values. A holiday campaign features a diverse range of employees coming together to promote the retailer's commitment to community-building and celebrating unique perspectives (Sephora Americas Casts Its Own Store Employees in New Campaign, 2017). The print and social media campaign highlights the importance of EBBE by giving employees a platform to act as brand ambassadors while showcasing the brand from an internal perspective.

At Starbucks, employees are referred to as 'partners', emphasizing their role as brand ambassadors and offering a wide range of career benefits (Starbucks Partner Benefits, n.d.). The retailer often features partnerships with employees to share their stories and experiences on social media. For example, Starbucks uses its Instagram page to showcase partner experiences across different departments of the organization. The content highlights the company culture through candid photos and videos of employees, creating an approachable brand identity. Posts include insights into day-to-day roles, which promote a sense of inclusivity to attract potential hires and foster a sense of community among current employees (Rise, 2016).

Yelp, a company that crowdsources reviews of companies, similarly leverages employee-generated content. Yelp's Instagram career page showcases employees' posts, which depict the work-life balance and company culture. For example, their social media page includes photos of employees at team-building events and corporate gatherings, which offer a behind-the-scenes glimpse into the workplace (Rise, 2016). This strategy may serve as an effective recruitment and engagement tool. By sharing authentic employee-generated content, Yelp fosters a transparent and appealing employer brand that can attract potential candidates and highlight opportunities for employees' personal and professional growth. The career page also creates a virtual community that strengthens bonds among current employees, promoting internal brand advocacy and ultimately contributing to retaining top talent.

Despite the multitude of benefits of leveraging employee-generated content, legal and compliance challenges, particularly regarding advertising disclosures, must be carefully considered. Advertising laws, such as the FTC guidelines in the USA and the Competition Act in Canada, emphasize the need for transparent disclosure of material connections between employees and their companies when content might influence consumer decisions (Musiyiwa & Jacobson, 2023). An employment relationship constitutes a material connection as an employee is paid by an employer. The guidelines call for clear and transparent disclosures on social media platforms. Employees endorsing a brand could clearly disclose their affiliation with the company, using simple and clear indicators such as 'ad' or 'sponsored' in their posts. Ambiguous terms such as '#sp' are discouraged as they may confuse viewers about the content's promotional nature. Failure to comply with these disclosure norms could lead to legal risks, including fines and penalties for deceptive advertising. However, employee-generated content tends not to include disclosures, which raises questions about best practices for individuals and companies.

For organizations leveraging employee-based content on social media, creating and implementing a comprehensive social media compliance policy is critical. Policies should include mandatory training for employees on advertising regulations, periodic updates to align with evolving legal standards and mechanisms for monitoring and correcting non-compliant posts. By doing so, companies can maintain transparency, build trust with their audiences and protect themselves legally while effectively harnessing employee contributions to their brand.

CONCLUSION AND DIRECTIONS FOR FUTURE RESEARCH

This chapter outlines the growing importance of EBBE in brand management. As organizations increasingly recognize the role of employees in shaping brand perceptions, further research is needed to refine and expand existing EBBE models across different industries and cultural contexts. In the following section, we highlight several key areas for future research. King et al.'s (2012) scale remains the foundational model for measuring EBBE, but its application in diverse sectors, particularly retail, is a promising area for future studies. Given the retail sector's unique reliance on front-line employees who frequently interact with customers, studying how brand consistent behavior, endorsement and allegiance manifest in these roles can provide researchers with valuable insights.

Expanding EBBE Across Cultural and Industry Contexts

A systematic review of EBBE literature by Sousa and Ferreira (2024) identifies a crucial gap in the empirical testing of EBBE across diverse cultural and industry contexts. Although studies have examined EBBE in banking (Altaf et al., 2017; Kaur et al., 2024), consumer goods (Poulis & Wisker, 2016), hospitality (Xiong & King, 2015) and retail (Rudkowski, 2024), much of this research has been concentrated in specific countries. Cross-cultural studies, such as those by Awan et al. (2018) in China and Sanuri and Mokhtar (2018) in Islamic banking, suggest that EBBE is influenced by cultural factors such as organizational hierarchy, workplace norms and employer–employee relationships. Future research should expand upon these findings by testing the EBBE model in additional global markets, in order to ensure its applicability in various business environments. Comparative studies may be particularly useful to understand the influence of culture on employee activities.

Leveraging Qualitative Approaches and Social Media Data for EBBE Research

Additionally, while most EBBE studies rely on survey-based methodologies, alternative research approaches can provide deeper insights into how employees engage with brand values. Sousa and Ferreira (2024) suggest that incorporating qualitative methods, such as interviews, ethnographic research and content analysis, could enhance understanding of EBBE's impact on workplace dynamics and employee-brand alignment. This may, therefore, lead to unexplored antecedents, dimensions of EBBE and outcomes. Certainly, more diverse methodological approaches to researching and measuring EBBE would lead to an enriched understanding of the area.

A particularly promising avenue for future research is the use of publicly available social media data to analyze EBBE in manifest digital posts and interactions. Unlike traditional survey methods, which capture self-reported perceptions, social media analysis allows researchers to observe employees' actual brand engagement behaviors in an organic setting. Content analysis and case studies of employee interactions on platforms such as LinkedIn, Instagram and Glassdoor have already provided valuable insights into EBBE's role in brand advocacy and reputation management (Hesse et al., 2022; Pitt et al., 2019; Smith et al., 2021).

However, as organizations increasingly monitor employee social media engagement, ethical considerations regarding data privacy must be carefully addressed. Future research should explore best practices for analyzing employee-generated content while ensuring transparency, employee privacy and ethical compliance. Establishing clear guidelines for ethical social media research, particularly regarding informed consent and data anonymization, is essential for maintaining trust between employees and organizations.

Integrating EBBE With Consumer-Based and Financial-Based Brand Equity

Another critical research direction involves examining the relationship between financial-based brand equity (FBBE) and other forms of brand equity, such as CBBE and FBBE. Sousa and Ferreira (2024) emphasize the need for an integrated approach to EBBE research, recognizing that employees play a pivotal role in shaping consumer perceptions and driving financial outcomes. Studies by Boukis and Christodoulides (2020) and Tavassoli et al. (2014) suggest that strong EBBE can enhance customer experiences, leading to increased customer loyalty and brand profitability. Building on this, further research is needed to quantify the financial impact of EBBE on brand performance. For example, investigating how employee advocacy influences customer purchase behavior or how internal brand alignment affects employee retention and productivity could provide tangible metrics for measuring the business value of EBBE.

The introduction of the IRBE scale by Rudkowski (2024) offers a multidimensional framework that integrates both employee and consumer perspectives. Future research could focus on validating and adapting this model in different industries to better understand the dual roles employees play as both internal stakeholders and external brand representatives. Additionally, scholars could explore whether this model can be extended to account for emerging trends, such as hybrid work environments, gig economy employment and influencer marketing.

The Future of EBBE in the Context of Artificial Intelligence

As organizations increasingly adopt artificial intelligence (AI) tools for employee engagement, new opportunities and challenges arise for EBBE research. Future studies can examine how AI technologies influence employee-brand interactions, particularly in terms of automated brand messaging, virtual employee communities and AI-driven training programs. Furthermore, AI-driven platforms, such as sentiment analysis tools, provide researchers with new ways to measure EBBE. Problematically, many of the algorithms driving AI tools are blackboxed, which means that researchers will need to critically assess the applicability, use and validity of AI in research. Moving forward, understanding the intersection between AI and EBBE will be important for brands in order to strengthen their internal branding strategy in the context of digital transformation.

Conclusions

While scholarly research on EBBE has grown significantly over the years, there is still much to explore. Expanding the scope of EBBE research across cultures, industries and digital platforms will provide a more holistic understanding of the antecedents, dimensions and outcomes of EBBE. Additionally, integrating EBBE with other brand equity dimensions and leveraging emerging technologies may further enhance its relevance in organizational branding. As businesses continue to navigate evolving work environments and the social media landscape, future research on EBBE will play a crucial role in shaping effective brand management strategies, supporting employee well-being and driving long-term organizational success.

REFERENCES

Aaker, D. A. (1991). *Managing brand equity*. Free Press. https://books.google.ca/books?id=FkO5AAAAIAAJ

Aaker, D. A. (1992). The value of brand equity. *Journal of Business Strategy*, *13*(4), 27–32. https://doi.org/10.1108/eb039503

Altaf, M., Mokhtar, S. S. M., & Ghani, N. (2017). Employee critical psychological states as determinants of employee brand equity in banking: A multi-group analysis. *Banks & Bank Systems*, *12*(3), 61–73. https://doi.org/10.21511/bbs.12(3).2017.05

Awan, T. M., Li, X., & Haizhong, W. (2018). Factors affecting employee-based brand equity: Evidence from China. *International Journal of Management Studies*, *25*(1), 1–20. https://doi.org/10.32890/ijms.25.1.2018.10482

Baumgarth, C., & Schmidt, M. (2020). Internal communicators' understanding of the definition and importance of employee advocacy. *Public Relations Review*, *46*(4), 101946. https://doi.org/10.1016/j.pubrev.2020.101946

Berger-Remy, F., & Michel, G. (2015). How brand gives employees meaning: Towards an extended view of brand equity. *Recherche et Applications En Marketing*, *30*(2), 30–54. https://doi.org/10.1177/0767370114565765

Boukis, A., & Christodoulides, G. (2020). Investigating key antecedents and outcomes of employee-based brand equity. *European Management Review*, *17*(1), 41–55.

Brexendorf, T. O., & Kernstock, J. (2007). Corporate behaviour vs brand behaviour: Towards an integrated view? *Journal of Brand Management*, *15*(1), 32–40. https://doi.org/10.1057/palgrave.bm.2550108

Carter, D. (2016). Hustle and brand: The sociotechnical shaping of influence. *Social Media+Society*, *2*(3), 2056305116666305.

Christodoulides, G., De Chernatony, L., Furrer, O., Shiu, E., & Abimbola, T. (2006). Conceptualising and measuring the equity of online brands. *Journal of Marketing Management*, *22*(7–8), 799–825. https://doi.org/10.1362/026725706778612149

Christodoulides, G., Cadogan, J. W., & Veloutsou, C. (2015). Consumer-based brand equity measurement: Lessons learned from an international study. *International Marketing Review*, *32*(3/4), 307–328. https://doi.org/10.1108/IMR-10-2013-0242

Erdem, T., & Swait, J. (2001). Brand equity as a signaling. *Journal of Consumer Psychology*, *7*(2), 131–157. https://doi.org/10.1207/s15327663jcp0702_02

Freberg, K., Graham, K., McGaughey, K., & Freberg, L. A. (2011). Who are the social media influencers? A study of public perceptions of personality. *Public Relations Review*, *37*(1), 90–92.

Hesse, A., Schmidt, H. J., Bosslet, R., Häusler, M., & Schneider, A. (2022). How posting in social networks affects employee-based brand equity. *European Journal of Marketing*, *56*(7), 1907–1925.

Instagram Users Worldwide 2025. (n.d.). *Statista*. www.statista.com/statistics/183585/instagram-number-of-global-users/

Jacobson, J., Gruzd, A., Kumar, P., & Mai, P. (2019). Networked influence: An introduction. *Social Media + Society*, *5*(3), 1–5. https://doi.org/10.1177/2056305119865473

Jacobson, J., Gomes Rinaldi, A., & Rudkowski, J. (2023). Decoding the employee influencer on social media: Applying Taylor's six segment message strategy wheel. *European Journal of Marketing*, *57*(1), 29–59. https://doi.org/10.1108/EJM-06-2021-0418

Jiménez-Castillo, D., & Sánchez-Fernández, R. (2019). The role of digital influencers in brand recommendation: Examining their impact on engagement, expected value and purchase intention. *International Journal of Information Management*, *49*, 366–376. https://doi.org/10.1016/j.ijinfomgt.2019.07.009

Kaur, R., Pingle, S., & Jaiswal, A. K. (2024). Effect of organisational culture on employer branding and resultant employee brand equity in the private banking sector. *International Journal of Bank Marketing*, *42*(1), 258–300. https://doi.org/10.1108/IJBM-11-2022-0517

Keller, K. L. (1993). Conceptualizing, measuring, and managing customer-based brand equity. *Journal of Marketing*, *57*(1), 1–22. https://doi.org/10.1177/002224299305700101

Keller, K. L. (2020). Consumer research insights on brands and branding: A JCR curation. *Journal of Consumer Research*, *46*(5), 995–1001. https://doi.org/10.1093/jcr/ucz058

Keller, K. L., & Lehmann, D. R. (2006). Brands and branding: Research findings and future priorities. *Marketing Science*, *25*(6), 740–759. https://doi.org/10.1287/mksc.1050.0153

King, C., & Grace, D. (2009). Employee based brand equity: A third perspective. *Services Marketing Quarterly*, *30*(2), 122–147. https://doi.org/10.1080/15332960802619082

King, C., & Grace, D. (2010). Building and measuring employee-based brand equity. *European Journal of Marketing*, *44*(7/8), 938–971. https://doi.org/10.1108/03090561011047472

King, C., Grace, D., & Funk, D. C. (2012). Employee brand equity: Scale development and validation. *Journal of Brand Management*, *19*(4), 268–288. https://doi.org/10.1057/bm.2011.44

Kocak, A., Abimbola, T., & Özer, A. (2007). Consumer brand equity in a cross-cultural replication: An evaluation of a scale. *Journal of Marketing Management*, *23*(1–2), 157–173. https://doi.org/10.1362/026725707X178611

Kwon, Y. (2013). *The influence of employee-based brand equity on the health supportive environment and culture-organizational citizenship behavior relation* [*Doctoral dissertation*]. University of Michigan.

Lee, Y.-H., Hsiao, C., Chan, H.-Y., & Lee, I.-C. (2020). Explorations of employee-based brand equity in the banking industry from a perceived-leadership perspective. *International Journal of Bank Marketing*, *38*(2), 425–455. https://doi.org/10.1108/IJBM-05-2019-0166

Machado, J. C., Vacas-de-Carvalho, L., Azar, S. L., André, A. R., & Dos Santos, B. P. (2019). Brand gender and consumer-based brand equity on Facebook: The mediating role of consumer-brand engagement and brand love. *Journal of Business Research*, *96*, 376–385. https://doi.org/10.1016/j.jbusres.2018.07.016

Mikul, & Mittal, I. (2023). The saga of brand equity: A comprehensive bibliometric analysis. *NMIMS Management Review*, *31*(3), 165–177. https://doi.org/10.1177/0974150X231205447

Miles, S. J., & Mangold, G. (2004). A conceptualization of the employee branding process. *Journal of Relationship Marketing*, *3*(2–3), 65–87. https://doi.org/10.1300/J366v03n02_05

Mohd Mokhtar, S. S., Altaf, M., & Abd Ghani, N. H. (2018). Employee brand equity and brand empowerment in islamic banking: Mediating role of brand psychological ownership. *Academy of Accounting & Financial Studies Journal*, *22*.

Morhart, F. M., Herzog, W., & Tomczak, T. (2009). Brand-specific leadership: Turning employees into brand champions. *Journal of Marketing*, *73*(5), 122–142. https://doi.org/10.1509/jmkg.73.5.122

Musiyiwa, R., & Jacobson, J. (2023). Sponsorship disclosure in social media influencer marketing: The algorithmic and non-algorithmic barriers. *Social Media + Society*, *9*(3), 1–19. https://doi.org/10.1177/20563051231196870

Nam, J., Ekinci, Y., & Whyatt, G. (2011). Brand equity, brand loyalty and consumer satisfaction. *Annals of Tourism Research*, *38*(3), 1009–1030. https://doi.org/10.1016/j.annals.2011.01.015

National Retail Federation. (2024). *Retail industry continues to be largest private-sector employer, according to new report*. https://nrf.com/media-center/press-releases/retail-industry-continues-be-largest-private-sector-employer-according

Number of Global TikTok Users 2025. (n.d.). *Statista*. www.statista.com/statistics/1327116/number-of-global-tiktok-users/

Oh, T. T., Keller, K. L., Neslin, S. A., Reibstein, D. J., & Lehmann, D. R. (2020). The past, present, and future of brand research. *Marketing Letters*, *31*(2–3), 151–162. https://doi.org/10.1007/s11002-020-09524-w

Pitt, C. S., Plangger, K. A., Botha, E., Kietzmann, J., & Pitt, L. (2019). How employees engage with B2B brands on social media: Word choice and verbal tone. *Industrial Marketing Management*, *81*, 130–137.

Poulis, A., & Wisker, Z. (2016). Modeling employee-based brand equity (EBBE) and perceived environmental uncertainty (PEU) on a firm's performance. *Journal of Product & Brand Management*, *25*(5), 490–503. https://doi.org/10.1108/JPBM-04-2015-0852

Rise. (2016, June 29). *9 Companies who've mastered employer branding on Instagram*. Rise. https://risepeople.com/blog/employer-branding-instagram/

Roncha, A., & Radclyffe-Thomas, N. (2016). How TOMS' "one day without shoes" campaign brings stakeholders together and co-creates value for the brand using Instagram as a platform. *Journal of Fashion Marketing and Management*, *20*(3), 300–321. https://doi.org/10.1108/JFMM-10-2015-0082

Rudkowski, J. (2024). Measuring employee-consumer integrated retailer brand equity. *Journal of Retailing and Consumer Services*, *76*, 103590. https://doi.org/10.1016/j.jretconser.2023.103590

Sephora. (n.d.). *Sephora: About | LinkedIn*. www.linkedin.com/company/sephora/about/

Sephora Americas Casts Its Own Store Employees in New Campaign. (2017, December 20). *LVMH*. www.lvmh.com/news-documents/news/sephora-americas-casts-its-own-store-employees-in-new-campaign/

Simon, C. J., & Sullivan, M. W. (1993). The measurement and determinants of brand equity: A financial approach. *Marketing Science*, *12*(1), 28–52. https://doi.org/10.1287/mksc.12.1.28

Smith, D., Jacobson, J., & Rudkowski, J. L. (2021). Employees as influencers: Measuring employee brand equity in a social media age. *Journal of Product & Brand Management*, *30*(6), 834–853. https://doi.org/10.1108/JPBM-03-2020-2821

Sousa, B., & Ferreira, P. (2024). Employee based brand equity: A systematic review of literature, framework development, and implications for future research. *Journal of Management History*, *30*(3), 475–492. https://doi.org/10.1108/JMH-07-2023-0069

Starbucks Partner Benefits. (n.d.). www.starbucks-benefits.com/en/home-ca-en/

Statistics Canada. (2015). *Employment, by industry*. www.150.statcan.gc.ca/n1/pub/71-222-x/2008001/sectione/e-employment-emploi-eng.htm

Tavassoli, N. T., Sorescu, A., & Chandy, R. (2014). Employee-based brand equity: Why firms with strong brands pay their executives less. *Journal of Marketing Research*, *51*(6), 676–690. https://doi.org/10.1509/jmr.13.0435

Xiong, L., & King, C. (2015). Motivational drivers that fuel employees to champion the hospitality brand. *International Journal of Hospitality Management*, *44*, 58–69. https://doi.org/10.1016/j.ijhm.2014.10.009

Yoo, B., & Donthu, N. (2001). Developing and validating a multidimensional consumer-based brand equity scale. *Journal of Business Research*, *52*(1), 1–14. https://doi.org/10.1016/S0148-2963(99)00098-3

APPENDIX

Table 11.1 Key conceptualizations of employee-based brand equity (EBBE)

Author(s)	*Definition*	*Year*
Brexendorf & Kernstock	EBBE arises when employees possess extensive brand knowledge, fostering behaviors that align with the organization's brand identity.	2007
King & Grace	'The differential effect that brand knowledge has on an employee's response to their work environment'.	2009
Tavassoli et al.	EBBE represents the value a brand imparts to a company by shaping employee attitudes and behaviors.	2014
Berger-Remy & Michel	EBBE reflects the additional significance employees derive from the brand, beyond the company's reputation, influencing either positive or negative behaviors.	2015
Baumgarth & Schmidt	EBBE is the perceived added value employees receive from a company's brand-building efforts, which influences their behaviors incrementally.	2020
Lee et al.	EBBE is the internalization of a brand's core values among employees, expressed through consistent brand behavior, endorsement and allegiance.	2020

Source: The authors.

Table 11.2 Use of EBBE

Author	*Year*	*Methodology*	*Key Findings*
King & Grace	2010	Survey-based (scale development)	• Developed the foundational employee-based brand equity (EBBE) scale. These dimensions offer a comprehensive framework for understanding how brand knowledge influences employee behavior and attitudes
King et al.	2012	Survey-based (scale validation)	• Expanded on King and Grace's (2010) model by empirically validating and testing the three dimensions of EBBE brand consistent behaviour, brand endorsement, and brand allegiance
Altaf et al.	2017	Survey-based (banking sector)	• Studied the role of brand confidence in EBBE within the banking sector, finding that employees who trust their organization's brand exhibit stronger brand consistent behavior and greater brand allegiance
Awan et al.	2018	Survey-based (contextual study in China)	• Examined how factors such as openness, knowledge sharing, role clarity and brand commitment influence EBBE in a Chinese cultural context. Findings highlight the importance of a transparent and supportive workplace culture for fostering strong EBBE
Sanuri & Mokhtar	2018	Survey-based (Islamic banking sector)	• Investigated how brand empowerment affects EBBE in the Islamic banking sector, identifying brand knowledge and psychological ownership as key mediators between empowerment and EBBE
Pitt et al.	2019	Content analysis (B2B context)	• Analyzed employee engagement on Glassdoor to assess its impact on EBBE. Found significant differences between employees of top-ranked and lower-ranked B2B companies in their social media engagement, influencing brand perceptions
Boukis & Christodoulides	2020	Integrated model (conceptual study)	• Introduced an integrated model of antecedents and consequences of EBBE, distinguishing between cognitive and affective pathways • Emphasized leadership involvement as a key driver in strengthening both cognitive and emotional connections to the brand

(*Continued*)

Table 11.2 (Continued)

Author	*Year*	*Methodology*	*Key Findings*
Smith et al.	2021	Case study (social media content analysis)	• Analyzed employee social media content (Instagram) rather than survey data to measure EBBE. Found that brand consistent behavior was the most important factor in shaping EBBE • Highlighted the importance and value of publicly available data in adding new depth to EBBE knowledge
Hesse et al.	2022	Case study (LinkedIn)	• Explored EBBE on LinkedIn, emphasizing the role of employee engagement in brand co-creation. Found that LinkedIn interactions, including sharing content and endorsing brand messages, strengthen overall brand equity
Rudkowski	2024	Survey-based (fashion retail sector)	• Developed a multidimensional model for Integrated Retailer Brand Equity (IRBE), incorporating employee and consumer perspectives • Validated the model across fashion retail, highlighting the dual role of employees as brand ambassadors and consumers
Kaur et al.	2024	Survey-based (private banking sector)	• Explored the relationship between employer branding and EBBE in India's private banking sector. Found that employer branding positively impacts brand consistent behavior, endorsement and allegiance, further strengthening EBBE

Source: The authors.

PART 3

Strategic Brand Management

12

Principles of Corporate Brand Management

John M. T. Balmer

WHY CORPORATE BRANDS ARE VALUABLE

Corporate brands are powerful manifestations of the soft power of organisations. For many entities, they can be regarded as their principal corporate asset. Given the above, many consider corporate brands to be the most powerful, durable, consequential and treasured of all branding modalities. Thus, it can be a corporate asset that is beyond comparison. Consequently, numerous scholars have enumerated the diverse ways by which corporate brands impart value to organisations, customers/stakeholders and to partner organisations and affiliate corporate brands (Abratt & Kleyn, 2012; Balmer, 2006; Balmer & Gray, 2003; Balmer & Greyser, 2002; Balmer & Podnar, 2021; Einwiller & Will, 2002; Greyser & Urde, 2019; Haigh, 2003; Kay, 2006; Knox & Bickerton, 2003; Leitch & Richardson, 2003; Morsing & Kristensen, 2001; Muzellec & Lambkin, 2009; Schultz & Hatch, 2003; Srivastava & Sharma, 2013; Tarnovskaya, 2015; Uggla, 2006). A key reason why corporate brands can be valuable is that they can be incomparable marques. As such, they are symbols of assurance for customers/stakeholders. This stakeholder trust is based on a corporate brand's strong track record in delivering the corporate brand covenant.

As a peerless corporate asset, a corporate brand can confer considerable esteem on an organisation. Furthermore, the corporate brand can be of considerable financial value for them. Corporate brands can be of strategic value too. For instance, the leasing/franchising of a corporate brand can be at the core of an organisation's business model. Cases in point are Coca-Cola, Subway and the International Hotel Group, which lease/franchise their corporate brands. It should not be forgotten that corporate brands are portable in that they can be bought, sought and borrowed by firms (Balmer, 2006).

Additionally, corporate brands can be invested with considerable emotional value for their customers and other stakeholders. A person can define themselves in relation to a corporate brand. Thus, an individual's association with a corporate brand may represent a profound sense of who they are as a person. Cases in point are supporters of sports teams. Thus, a corporate brand can provide identity for individuals.

Within the corporate brand canon, it has been asserted that corporate brands are an important strategic resource (Knox & Bickerton, 2003); can have considerable economic value (Balmer & Gray, 2003); can enhance corporate profitability (Keller, 2003); can drive corporate value (Haigh, 2003); can improve the standing of products (Greyser & Urde, 2019; Muzellec & Lambkin,

2009); can be meaningful apropos staff recruitment and retention (Balmer, 2006; Einwiller & Will, 2002); can be an imperative for customer satisfaction (Srivastava & Sharma, 2013; Tarnovskaya, 2015); can attract customers, investor, business partner, or an outright owner, etc. (Balmer, 2006); can provide a means of creating corporate messages and corporate meaning (Leitch & Richardson, 2003); can provide organisational coherence and guide those within an organisation (Balmer, 2013; Morsing & Kristensen, 2001); can provide a vital criterion against which management decisions and stratagems, corporate actions and the behaviour of organisational members can be evaluated (Balmer, 2013); can be important for market driving (Tarnovskaya et al., 2008), can provide a handrail for managers (Balmer, 2022) and can burnish the standing of affiliate brands owing to their associations with a corporate brand (Balmer, 2006; Kay, 2006; Uggla, 2006).

Often, attention is focused on the considerable, stand-alone, financial value of corporate brands. Historically, it was reasoned that the capitalisations of major corporations included a very high percentage attributable to the worth of their corporate brands. In the past, this accounted for 59% of the value of the Coca-Cola Company; 61% of the value of the Walt Disney Company and 64% of the capitalisation of McDonald's Corporation (Barwise et al., 2000). Corporate brand valuations are commonly determined by renowned brand consultancies such as Interbrand (Silk, 2006). A scrutiny of the 100 top global brands on Interbrand's list in 2024, for example, includes corporate brands. Furthermore, these corporate brand valuations are highly significant when companies merge or are acquired (Silk, 2006). Consider, for example, the $12.6bn buyout of Kraft by Philip Morris (six times Kraft's book value), which was directly attributed to financial worth 'goodwill' associated with the Kraft corporate brand (Newman, 2001). Of course, the real value – and the source of corporate brand value – resides in the customer/stakeholder loyalty and attractiveness toward the corporate brand. Importantly, whilst legal ownership of a corporate brand resides with an organisation, its emotional ownership resides with customers/stakeholders; that is where real corporate brand value resides (Balmer, 2006, 2012a).

In broad terms, therefore, corporate brands can impart value as (a) a currency, (b) a language and (c) as a navigational tool (Balmer, 2006, 2010a, 2010b, 2012a). As a currency, they can be endowed with economic, monetary and psychological value. As a language, they are languages that are redolent with meaning. Some are a worldwide *lingua franca* such as Coca-Cola, others are a local language which are known in specific regions, towns, or villages. Others are patois, which are known in particular professions or industries. As a navigational tool, they enable individuals to navigate a world of competing corporate brands. Therefore, they can be an indispensable mode of differentiation and positioning for diverse stakeholder groups.

Given that many organisations have hollowed out key corporate functions (e.g., outsourcing key aspects of their work so that they are increasingly reliant on other entities), the corporate brand has increasingly acquired a central role not only for the organisation itself but for partner organisations where the corporate brand serves as a guide. For such organisations, their corporate brand is their primary asset. As was noted in the early 20th century:

> The good will of a business is often of greater value than all the tangible property, and a trade mark is nothing but good will symbolised. (Rogers, 1910, p. 43)

THE IMPORTANCE OF A CORPORATE BRAND ORIENTATION AND CORPORATE MARKETING ORIENTATION

The orientation notion now enjoys wide acceptance in marketing and includes, among others, marketing orientation, relationship marketing orientation, services marketing orientation, corporate identity orientation and brand orientation (Balmer & Podnar, 2021). Several orientations can co-exist within an organisation. Thus, a corporate brand orientation can co-exist with a corporate marketing orientation (Balmer, 2013).

Corporate Marketing Orientation

Corporate marketing is informed by the perspective that organisations and, their corporate brands in particular, are principal conduits by which profitable exchange between entities and their customers/stakeholders (Balmer, 1998, 2001a). This is a logical development of traditional marketing, which aims to meet the wants, needs and desires of customers and, primarily, has a focus on products and product brands. Of course, services marketing will have a focus on its attendant services brands. Whereas a central tenet of marketing is to create value for customers (Dolan, 2006), corporate marketing meets the wants, needs and desires of not only customers, but stakeholders. Therefore, it seeks to create value for them (Balmer, 1998,

2001a). Corporate marketing is manifest in an organisational-wide philosophy and culture (Balmer & Greyser, 2006; Illia & Balmer, 2012). Its management is, unquestionably, strategic (Balmer, 2017). In contrast to mainstream marketing, corporate marketing accords importance to stakeholders, to corporate social responsibility. Significantly, it is enlightened by a trans-temporal perspective where the past/an entity's inheritance is accorded importance: Traditional marketing approaches typically accord importance to the present and to the future. Importantly, corporate-level concepts also inform corporate marketing (corporate brand, corporate identity, corporate image, corporate reputation, total corporate communication/corporate communication).

Concomitant with the introduction of the corporate marketing notion has been the rise of the stakeholder marketing perspective (Bhattacharya & Korschun, 2008). Although sharing certain similarities with corporate marketing, the stakeholder marketing perspective is narrower in scope. As with corporate marketing, stakeholder marketing notes the importance of maintaining value through exchange relationships with multiple stakeholders (Hult et al., 2011). The perspective that customer relationships can be influenced by relationships with other stakeholders/stakeholder networks (Gummesson, 2008).

Corporate Brand Orientation

Corporate brand orientation is where there is an organisational-wide culture and philosophy that is focused on the corporate brand/corporate brand covenant (Balmer, 2013).

A central tenet of corporate branding is the requirement for total organisational commitment (Balmer, 2001b). Accordingly, it is the responsibility of all organisational members to attune their actions, behaviours and communications so that they are calibrated with the corporate brand covenant. This is more likely to occur when employees have a strong sense of identification with the corporate brand's values. This helps to explain the importance of corporate brand orientation.

Initially, brand orientation was based on the premise that organisations should be orientated around their product brands (Urde, 1994). While a distinct literature on brand orientation emerged, from the mid-1990s onwards, the notion that the corporate brand represents a distinct form of brand orientation has largely been ignored although oblique references to the corporate brand can be made within the literature on brands (cf. Balmer, 2013).

Arguably, corporate brand orientation is the most profound form of brand orientation and represents the logical dénouement and apogee of the brand orientation perspective (Balmer, 2013). The reasoning behind this is that a brand-based organisational-wide culture and philosophy is decidedly more intelligible at the level of the corporate, rather than at the product brand level (Balmer, 2013). A sine qua non of corporate brand orientation is the requirement for the actions and behaviours of organisational members to be calibrated with the corporate brand covenant.

Notably, both corporate marketing/corporate brand orientation emphasise the importance of corporate brands and both have explicit organisational, stakeholder, CSR and trans-temporal foci which are complementary to a corporate brand orientation (Balmer, 2013).

Corporate Brand Identification Provides the Foundation for Corporate Brand Orientation

It has been argued that a key basis for an organisational-wide corporate brand orientation is corporate brand identification (Balmer, 2013, 2022; Balmer & Podnar, 2021).

Corporate brand identification is where individuals within an organisation, as well as customers and other stakeholders outside the organisation, can have a strong sense of affinity with the corporate brand/corporate brand covenant (Balmer, 2013, 2022).

Organisational members are of particular significance since they represent a group through which a corporate brand covenant is actualised and, thereby, experienced by customers/stakeholders.

Where employees understand, internalise and act on the corporate brand covenant – in short, are orientated towards the corporate brand – they are likely to have a strong sense of corporate brand identification with the corporate brand. Therefore, the corporate brand covenant provides them with a clearly understood benchmark, which guides and synchronises their actions, behaviours and communications.

Both social identity/self-categorisation theory are two mainstream theoretical lenses by which corporate brand orientation/corporate brand identification can be comprehended. These theories explain the conditions by which organisational members can have similar perceptions and, moreover, behaviours. From a theoretical perspective, corporate brand identification can be regarded as a branch application of social identity theory.

In marshalling social identity and self-categorisation theories in corporate brand contexts, it is apparent that an individual can have a sense of corporate brand identification where the corporate brand becomes self-defining (Balmer & Podnar, 2021).

According to social identity/self-categorisation theory, an individual can go beyond their personal identity in terms of engaging with a social identity (Tajfel & Turner, 1979). Thus, they can derive psychological meaning, worth and a sense of personal identity from their membership of a social group (Tajfel, 1972; Tajfel & Turner, 1979). Shared understanding within a social group serves as a cognitive mechanism that manifests itself in a unified group behaviour (Turner, 1982, 1987) and this accounts for coordinated group cognitions and behaviours (Cornilissen et al., 2007). The related *self-categorisation theory* (Turner, 1987) explains how social identities can be highly salient for individuals, and this theory reveals the requirements and conditions by which social identities become significant for them. Significantly, organisations can be important in providing a social identity to an employee so they have a sense of belonging and oneness, with an entity (Ashforth & Mael, 1989). The same is true for corporate brands.

Whilst a good deal of the above scholarship has focused on social identity in the context of organisations, corporate marketing scholarship has emphasised that social identity theory can be applicable to corporate brands per se (Balmer & Podnar, 2021). As such, this has generated interest in the corporate brand identification notion (Balmer & Liao, 2007; Balmer et al., 2010).

Moreover, corporate brand identification is not only relevant for employees and managers but other groups as well (Balmer & Liao, 2007; Balmer et al., 2010).

Furthermore, the corporate brand orientations of such groups may burnish an organisation's corporate brand orientation in ways that might not readily be appreciated.

Within the literature, the importance of consumer–company identification (Bhattacharya & Sen, 2003) and stakeholder–company identification (Hillebrand et al., 2015) has been established. Arguably, many of the same precepts can be applied to consumer as well as stakeholder–corporate brand identification generally. Ab initio, for identification to occur, a person's self-definitional needs should be met and this should be active, selective and volitional (Bhattacharya & Sen, 2003; Dutton et al., 1994; Pratt, 1998). Where there is a strong sense of identification it can mean that employees work harder (Hillebrand et al., 2015); customers can be willing to pay premium prices and, moreover, can be company advocates, champions and enthusiasts (Bhattacharya & Sen, 2003); non-government agencies can provide endorsements, and business suppliers may provide useful input and knowledge that can materially benefit the organisation (Hillebrand et al., 2015). Again, it would seem logical to infer that this would be similar in the context of corporate brands.

Consequently, just as organisations should foster a social identity which can result in deep, committed and meaningful consumer–company relationships (Bhattacharya & Sen, 2003), the same should be true for corporate brands. In particular, the nurturing by the entity of strong corporate brand identification among employees, managers, customers and other meaningful stakeholders should be an imperative for senior managers. As noted by Bhattacharya & Sen, 2003, these are significant psychological substrates. Therefore, they merit frequent scrutiny on the part of senior managers.

CORPORATE BRAND MANAGEMENT

What of senior managers? Given the centrality and strategic importance of corporate brands, and the fact that successful corporate brands can create customer/shareholder and stakeholder value, a primary task of the CEO (and the senior management team) is to comprehend, build, nurture, and sustain a strong, and attractive, corporate brand (Balmer, 2012a). Thus, the CEO/senior managers must have a profound sense of their custodial role apropos the corporate brand (Balmer, 1995; King, 1991).

However, the strategic management of a corporate brand is a critical, challenging and ceaseless senior management concern (Balmer, 2012a, 2012b). It is also complex (Balmer, 1995, 2001b; Gyrd-Jones et al., 2013; King, 1991). It requires managerial cognisance of the multi-faceted and multi-disciplinary, nature of corporate brands (Balmer, 1995, 2001a, 2001b). The complexity of corporate brand management can be gleaned from various corporate brand models and frameworks (Balmer, 2003, 2005, 2012a; Greyser & Urde, 2019; Hatch & Schultz, 2001, 2008).

Thus, managers should have a strong sense of 'managerial corporate brand identification' (Balmer, 2022). That is, they should have a strong affinity with the corporate brand and its underlying covenant. Senior managers have a pivotal custodial role apropos the corporate brand. This is important given that the corporate brand can be an organisation's principal asset and that the corporate brand can be the most important interface that connects an organisation with its customers and other stakeholders. This explains the need for a purposeful sense of 'managerial corporate brand orientation' (Balmer, 2022). This is where the corporate brand serves as an important navigation tool for senior managers. The absence of an authentic and purposeful managerial corporate brand orientation, will likely, militate against the establishment of a robust, and bona-fide, organisational-wide corporate brand orientation.

There are three management imperatives that require attention: *custodianship, credibility and calibration* (Balmer, 2012a).

The Corporate Brand Custodianship Imperative requires managers not only to guard but also to manage and, moreover, be mindful of the corporate brand covenant (Balmer, 2012a). Corporate brand management is a senior management concern, but a crucially important one at that. The underlying corporate brand management precept is *semper fidelis* (always faithful). In short, this comes with a realisation that senior managers should have ongoing fidelity to the corporate brand and, in common with the corporate marketing precept, need to ensure that the corporate brand is of value to both customers/stakeholders as well as the organisation. To reiterate an earlier point, while the organisation has legal ownership of a corporate brand, customers and other stakeholders have emotional ownership of the corporate brand (Balmer, 2006, 2012a).

This is where the real value of a corporate brand subsists, and senior managers need to be mindful of this. Where there is customer/stakeholder loyalty towards a corporate brand, the corporate brand is likely to emerge as a significant corporate asset.

The Corporate Brand Credibility Imperative requires managers to enact the corporate brand covenant via an organisation's values, behaviours, activities, purposes, products and services (Balmer, 2012a). In short, the whole organisation should 'live the corporate brand'. For this to be achieved, the corporate brand should be tightly coupled with an organisation's corporate identity. The organisation's promise and customer/stakeholder expectations inherent in the corporate brand covenant need to be realised in the organisations' activities and behaviour. In short, it is corporate identity. This imperative can be characterised by the *modus vivendi* precept: 'a way of living'. In order for a corporate brand to be credible, five criteria should be met (Balmer, 2012a).

Consequently, the corporate brand needs to be:

a. Authentic: The corporate brand needs to be closely dovetailed with the organisation's corporate identity.
b. Believable: the corporate brand, demonstrably, should reflect the firm's values and culture.
c. Durable: The corporate brand should be sustainable; in other words, long-lasting. This requires senior managers adopting a long-term perspective the corporate brand's ability to deliver benefits to stakeholders and to the firm for mutual benefit. Attendant corporate brand strategies should be in place to achieve this.
d. profitable: The corporate brand needs to be of value to customers/stakeholders. It, necessarily, should be of value for the organisation in addition.
e. Responsible: The corporate brand should be mindful of the corporate marketing philosophy-meet the firm's CSR and ethical responsibilities.

The Corporate Brand Calibration Imperative requires managers to ensure there is a dynamic alignment between the corporate brand covenant and other identity types. Sometimes, this might even require a change to the corporate brand covenant. Thus, the approach represents a habitual way of working/managing , a 'modus operandi' (Balmer, 2012a).

CORPORATE BRAND MANAGEMENT BENCHMARKS

Notably, the AC⁴ID Test of corporate brand management framework provides a way of ensuring the corporate brand retains its saliency as a benchmark that guides an organisation (Balmer, 2005, 2012a, 2012b). It provides a guide for both the present and the future. This is achieved through the dynamic calibrating the corporate brand covenant with other important identities. Furthermore, it is achieved by taking account of the time frames of the present and future.

The following includes many of the corporate brand responsibilities of senior managers

a. Understand that whereas the organisation has legal ownership of the corporate brand, emotional ownership of the corporate brand resides with customers/stakeholders.
b. Undertake ongoing monitoring of corporate brand perceptions of customers/stakeholders in order to show the degree to which the corporate brand covenant needs to be changed or finessed.
c. Internally, ensure that the corporate brand covenant is realised so that the organisation's corporate identity substantively delivers the corporate brand covenant.
d. Undertake periodic assessments to ensure that corporate identity, corporate communication, corporate image/reputation, corporate culture, corporate strategy and management vision are dynamically aligned with the corporate brand covenant. Where necessary, make changes to affect alignment (and where necessary, alter the corporate brand guarantee as part of the corporate brand covenant). The AC⁴ID test of corporate brand management is a key means through which this can be achieved.

e. Appointment of staff who are amenable to supporting the corporate brand covenant when recruiting.
f. Foster an organisational-wide corporate brand orientation.
g. Forster an organisational-wide marketing orientation.
h. Periodically appraise the corporate brand architecture to see whether it can be improved/strengthened.
i. Regularly appraise the corporate brand's financial/emotional equity.

CORPORATE BRANDS THROUGH THE VECTOR OF CORPORATE BRAND COMMUNICATION

A potentially efficacious way of comprehending corporate brands is via a communications lens. This represents one means of resolving what has been viewed as a corporate branding conundrum (Biraghi & Gambetti, 2013). For the main, communications in management/organisation have a variety of foci. It can have a product focus as in marketing communication (Eagle et al., 2020); a corporate focus as in corporate communication (van Riel, 1995); or a hybrid of the two (Syed-Alwi et al., 2022). The integrated marketing perspective. 'IMC' (Kitchen & Schultz, 1998), has been offered as one means of all-embracing solutions to the above divides (Biraghi & Gambetti, 2013).

A bespoke corporate brand approach is the Total Corporate Brand Communications perspective (Balmer, 2012a, 2023, 2024a). The latter is sexpartite in nature, its dimensions comprise promissory, primary, secondary, tertiary, quaternary and responsory communications. Although each dimension has its merits there, sometimes, is an overlap between the dimensions.

The six dimensions can be enumerated as follows:

Promissory Communication: A key notion that a corporate brand covenant equates to represent a bilateral organisational-customer/stakeholder agreement. According to this compact, an organisation commits to a corporate brand promise. Thus, this corporate brand covenant dimension recognises that the corporate brand promise not only needs to be known but stresses that it should be continually communicated.

Primary Communication: This takes account of the notion that what an organisation does, behaves, produces, etc., is a primary mode of communication. As such, an organisation's identity (an organisation's activities and behaviours) is the means by which a corporate brand is realised. Primary communication is important since it delivers the organisation's-side of the corporate brand covenant: the corporate brand promise. Significantly, the corporate brand promise needs to be in dynamic alignment with promissory communication.

Secondary Communication: Formal and controlled corporate communication directed at customers and other stakeholders, and which encompasses corporate advertising, corporate public relations, etc., transmits messages concerning an entity's corporate identity (an organisation's traits, mission, purpose, activities, quality levels and behaviours).

Tertiary Communication: Some dimensions of corporate brand communication are not controlled by the organisation and this is the case of tertiary communication. This primarily focuses on word-of-mouth, and third party corporate communication. This dimension recognises that customers, employees and other stakeholders along with the media and even other organisations-communicate with each other through their networks. As such, just as an organisation's promissory and primary communication can shape corporate brand image/reputation, so can tertiary communication.

Quaternary Communication: Increasingly important is quaternary communications. This encompasses the digital corporate communication and Artificial Intelligence 'AI' spheres (Balmer, 2023, 2024a; Balmer & Yen, 2016). As an information resource, this communication vector allows organisations to better understand their customers whilst assisting stakeholders in their understanding of the corporate brand. However, digital and AI platforms are controlled by intermediary digital/AI organisations (internet platforms).

Potentially, these organisational intermediaries can have powerful roles as significant adjudicators/censors of communication.

Responsory Communication: A critically important dimension of communication is feedback. Consequently, responsory-based corporate communication fully embraces the notion that customer/stakeholder feedback regarding the perception, experiences and usage of a corporate brand/corporate brand covenant can be highly meaningful. Responsory communication can be elicited by the organisation and could also include the observation of customers/stakeholders. Additionally, it can be initiated by customers and stakeholders. For adherents of the corporate brand co-creation perspective, responsory communication is of primary importance (Balmer, 2023, 2024a).

CORPORATE BRAND ALIGNMENT: THE CORPORATE BRAND AS AN ORGANISATION'S LODESTAR

The importance of corporate brand alignment has emerged as a conspicuous strand of corporate brand scholarship as the literature attests (Anisimova, 2010; Anisimova & Mavondo, 2010, 2014; Balmer in Balmer & Greyser, 2003, p. 251; Balmer, 2005, 2012a, 2012b; Hatch & Schultz, 2001, 2008; Lahtinen & Närvänen, 2020; Mingione, 2015; Mingione & Abratt, 2022; Morsing, 2006; Pranjal & Sarkar, 2020).

To date, two distinct approaches dominate the literature. One is informed by a corporate marketing/multi-disciplinary in character. The other is informed by management/organisational behaviour.

The Corporate Marketing/Multi-Disciplinary Approach: Balmer's AC^{3}ID Test/AC^{4}IDTest of Corporate Brand Management

According to this approach, corporate brand management alignment is based on the premise that key areas of an organisation's activities can be regarded as distinct identity types (Balmer, 2005, 2012a, 2012b). For corporate brand alignment, therefore, these identity types need to be dynamically aligned with the corporate brand/covenant, which itself is viewed as an identity type. These identity types comprise the organisation's corporate identity, corporate culture, corporate communication, corporate communication, customer/stakeholders' perceptions, corporate strategy (apropos the future shape of the organisation), management vision (apropos the future shape of the organisation). At the fulcrum of the framework, it should be remembered, is the corporate brand/corporate brand covenant.

Each of these key organisational areas has been identified in two ways. The first is by designating which organisational dimension it relates to, for example, corporate identity, management vision, etc. The second is to designate each area as an identity type. This helps to articulate the distinctiveness of each identity mode. In terms of the latter, the different area types result in the acronym acid (with the C part having four identity dimensions). The label AC^{4}ID Test is an appropriate label given that an acid test, according to the Oxford English Dictionary, denotes, 'a conclusive test of the success, truth, or value of something' (Soanes & Hawker, 2005, p. 9).

Thus, the corporate brand covenant (Covenanted Identity) needs to be *dynamically* aligned with. an organisation's:

a. corporate *identity* (Actual Identity)
b. corporate *culture* (Cultural Identity)
c. corporate *communications* (Communicated Identity)
d. customer/stakeholders corporate *images/reputations* (Conceived Identity)
e. corporate *strategy* apropos the future shape of the organisation (Ideal Identity)
f. senior management *vision* apropos the future of the organisation (Desired Identity)

An important characteristic of the AC^{4}ID Test of corporate brand management is that it considers alignment from the present as well as the future (Balmer, 2012a). This is because corporate strategy and senior management vision are future-oriented identity modes. Indeed, the model allows for simplified analyses which, respectively, focus on (a) the current time frame and (b) the future time frame (cf. Balmer, 2012a).

It should be noted that original versions of the ACID model were primarily concerned with *corporate identity alignment* (Balmer, 2001c; Balmer & Soenen, 1999). Thus, the central point of alignment was an organisation's corporate identity, which encompasses an organisation's key traits.

Notably, these early models, based on extant approaches adopted by consultancies and organisations, found that undue reliance was given to management vision within organisations and by consultancies and concluded that management vision should be in alignment with a considered, and well-grounded, corporate strategy.

Indeed, there have been prominent instances where management vision has resulted in corporate identities/corporate brands which were unsustainable and had to be changed. There are a number of well-documented examples of where an organisation's CEO and management board have championed a vision-driven approach that was sorely misaligned with the organisation's reality (its corporate identity/actual identity).

Examples include British Airways attempts to reposition itself as an international, rather than a quintessentially British, airline (Balmer et al., 2009), and the attempts of BP (the multinational oil giant) to reposition itself as a 'green' organisation rather than one that was fundamentally concerned with oil and gas extraction and distribution (Balmer, 2010b; Balmer et al., 2011; Balmer & Greyser, 2002).

Subsequently, these corporate identity-focused frameworks were further adapted so that the focus was on *corporate brand alignment*.

Thus, the central point of alignment was the organisation's corporate brand/corporate brand covenant. However, the corporate identity remained an important identity mode that should be in dynamic alignment with the corporate brand. As with earlier models, the importance of achieving dynamic alignment between all the identity types was emphasised.

Consequently, the revised framework was broadened to include the corporate brand as a distinct identity type. The model by Balmer appeared in the book 'Revealing the Corporation' (Balmer, 2003, p. 251) (see Figure 12.1).

As can be seen from this model, the corporate brand covenant is shown as an encompassing identity type. This model is known as the AC^{3}ID Test of Corporate Brand Management.

Later on, a simplified model of corporate brand alignment was introduced based on a hub-and-spoke representation with the corporate brand (Covenanted Identity) being placed in the centre (Balmer, 2005, 2012a, 2012b). Of course, this is not to ignore the importance of achieving dynamic alignment between all the identity types, which, as noted above, was a characteristic of earlier models.

Another difference is that an additional identity type, corporate culture (Cultural Identity) was incorporated into the model. As such, this framework became known as the AC^{4}ID Test of Corporate Brand Management (see Figure 12.2).

Furthermore, in using the framework a five-stage diagnostic process, The REDS^2 Diagnostic Process. Although originally advocated for the original corporate identity alignment framework (Balmer, 2001c), it is equally apposite for the corporate brand alignment frameworks (Balmer, 2003, 2005, 2012a).

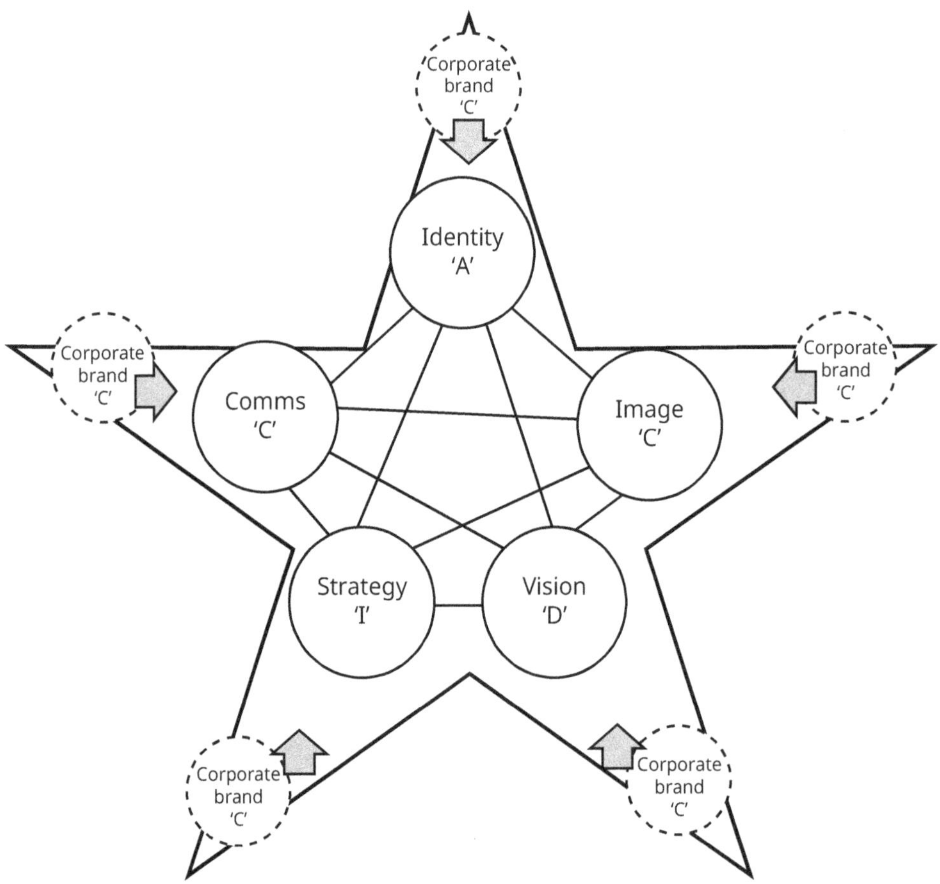

Figure 12.1 The first corporate brand alignment model by Balmer

Source: Adapted from Balmer (2003) in Balmer & Greyser (2003, p. 251).

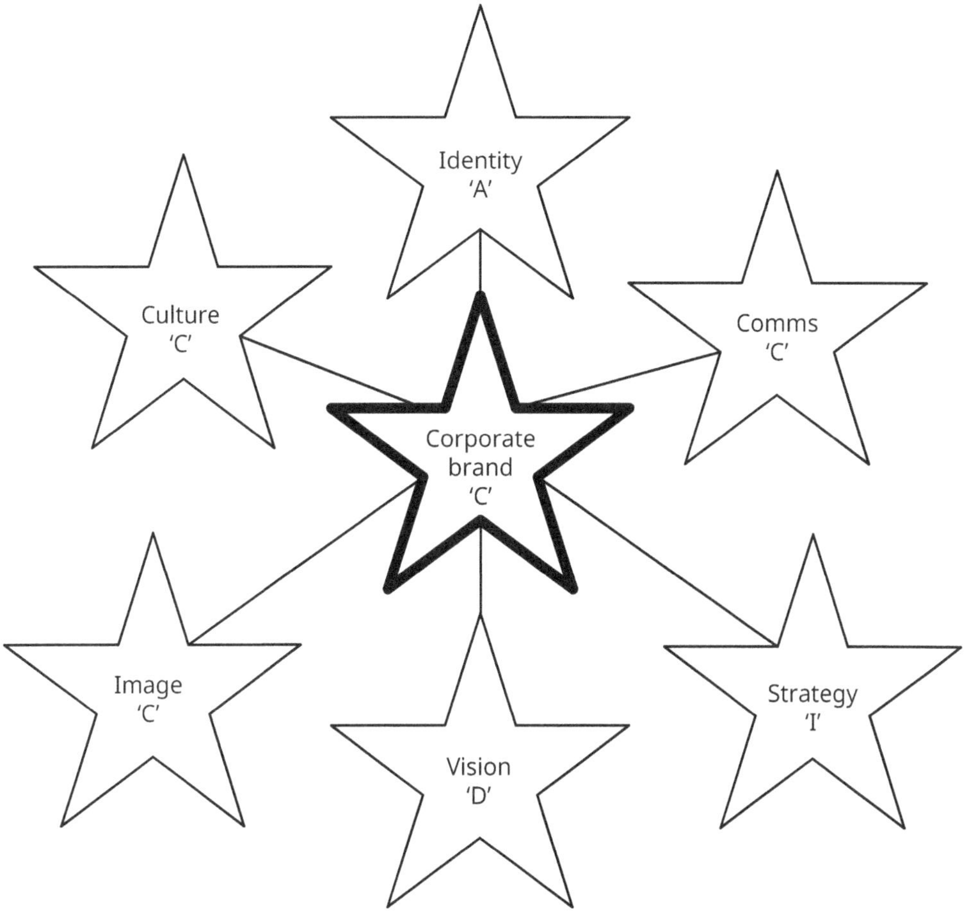

Figure 12.2 The second corporate brand alignment model by Balmer

Source: Adapted from Balmer (2005, 2012a).

The REDS² acronym aims to capture this five-stage diagnostic process, which can be detailed as follows:

a. Reveal: the *identity characteristics* of each identity type
b. Examine: the *interfaces* between the corporate brand (covenanted identity) and the other identity types
c. Diagnose: any *misalignments* between the corporate brand (covenanted identity) and other identity types
d. Select: those corporate brand misalignments by *prioritising* which ones require attention
e. Strategy: devise plans for *action/strategy* to ensure that individual misalignments are dynamically aligned.

Management/Organisational Behaviour Approach of Hatch & Schultz

The second stream of scholarship takes a pronounced management/organisational behaviour approach. The first iteration of this management/organisational perspective was in the early 2000s (Hatch & Schultz, 2001). This standpoint designated that a corporate brand required three organisational dimensions to be calibrated: management vision, organisational culture and stakeholders' images. Thus, this would suggest that the corporate brand is a sum of the above parts. However, in a later iteration of the Vision, Culture and Image approach, it is asserted that organisational identity is at the heart of their corporate brand approach (Hatch & Schultz, 2008). Hatch and Schultz (2008) explain that organisational identity relates to the claims made about the company.

There are some similarities with the early corporate identity approaches of Balmer in that both vision and image are accorded importance (Balmer, 2001c; Balmer & Soenen, 1999). Equally, Balmer's (2005) and (2012a), (2012b) model includes culture (Balmer, 2005, 2012a), which appeared in Hatch & Schultz model (2001).

However, Hatch and Schultz (2001, 2008) model of corporate brand alignment does not include the corporate brand covenant, communication, corporate strategy and the organisation's actual identity.

Moreover, Hatch and Schultz (2001, 2008) accord particular importance to management vision. In the Balmer models (Balmer, 2005, 2012a, 2012b), primary importance is accorded to the corporate brand covenant in providing the principal cornerstone by which to achieve corporate brand alignment.

For some, the Hatch and Schultz (2001, 2008) model may appear to be a framework that is primarily concerned with key alignments for an organisation rather than the corporate brand. The corporate brand per se is completely absent from their model.

Thus, the Hatch & Schultz models appear to be identity-based models rather than a corporate brand-based model (cf. Hatch & Schultz, 2001, 2008) owing to their focus on the organisation rather than on the corporate brand. As such, it has something in common with earlier corporate identity models (Balmer, 2001c; Balmer & Soenen, 1999).

Both models are likely to have their supporters, adherents, and detractors. Given the differences in their breadth, scope and foci, organisations will need to reflect on the nature, and efficacy, of these two frameworks in evaluating their organisation's corporate brand.

CORPORATE BRAND ARCHITECTURE

Corporate brand architecture is an important dimension of corporate brand management (Balmer, 2012a, 2024b; Balmer & Gray, 2003). This includes the way an organisation's corporate brand relates to its subsidiaries/business units, etc., as well as certain inter-organisational corporate brand relationships. The latter is important since it is possible for the same corporate brand to be used across organisations: consider Misuibishi, Rolls Royce, Volvo, Virgin and Yamaha.

Traditionally, brand architecture relates to the relationships between a corporate brand and its product and service brands. For the most part, brand architecture tended to limit itself to how visual identification/company names were used.

Corporate brand architecture is of strategic importance because it encompasses the corporate brand relationships inside organisations. Moreover, to emphasise an earlier point, these brand architecture relationships can occur between and across entities. Sometimes, they can operate in the same industry, as was formerly the case with Hilton (Balmer & Thomson, 2009). In other instances, the same corporate brand can be shared by organisations working in different sectors such as Rolls Royce (Balmer, 2012a).

Notably, an organisation can have several, sometimes many, corporate brands. Thus, each of these corporate brands will have a distinct corporate brand covenant, which is manifest in a distinct corporate identity. This fact is a reminder that corporate brands are not only *externally facing* but, importantly, can be *internally facing* too. As such, each corporate brand, typically, will have a distinct management structure, its own employees and, significantly, distinctive corporate brand values which encapsulate an entity's culture, ethos and purpose. These will, most likely, inform the corporate brand covenant.

A key strategic corporate brand management activity is to apprise an organisation's corporate brands and to examine whether they should be folded into the organisation's mother brand (have the same corporate brand); be linked to the mother corporate brand (by means of endorsement, or similar); or be categorised as a stand-alone corporate brand (where no reference is made to the mother corporate brand) among other options. Such analyses can be part of an organisation's strategic planning activities. Often such deliberations occur when there is a major change brought about by an organisational merger or business acquisition.

Given the above, corporate brand architecture can be viewed as a critical dimension of corporate brand management. Furthermore, the existence of multiple corporate brands within an entity with distinct corporate brand covenants and distinct corporate identity and values means that this is an important, but often complicated, task.

Brand Architecture Approaches: Olins, Aaker & Joachimsthaler, & Balmer

To date, two (largely product-based) brand architecture modes are common. This includes the well-known tripartite approach of Olins (1978) and a broadly similar approach by Aaker and Joachimsthaler (2000). Often, these product-brand approaches are discussed only in terms of communication and/or visual identification. A third approach by Balmer (Balmer, 2012a; Balmer & Gray, 2003) – with an explicit focus on corporate brands – is also evident.

The tripartite brand architecture approach of Olins (1978) delineated three broad brand relationships modes. The *monolithic* approach is where a single corporate brand name is used throughout the organisation with all products and services using the corporate brand. The *endorsed* approach, which represents a dual branding approach, is where a product/service brand makes reference to the corporate brand marque/name. Finally, the *branded approach is* where a stand-alone branding approach is adopted. This only focuses on the product/service brand. Unlike the other two approaches, the brand approach makes no reference to the corporate brand.

For their part, Aaker and Joachimsthaler (2000) identify four modalities apropos brand architecture. Three of them are similar to Olins, except that the taxonomy is different. For example, their *branded house* equates to Olins' monolithic approach; their endorsed brands category is identical to Olins' endorsed brands; and their *house of brands* modality equates to Olins' branded category. Their fourth dimension *sub-brands*, seemingly, is a variant of the endorsed brand category articulated by Olins. This is where a product brand includes the corporate brand name as part of its company/service brand name.

Although, primarily focusing on company-product brand architecture, Olins brand can be repurposed so that they have a utility apropos corporate brand architecture. This can be seen apropos Balmer's corporate brand architecture (cf. Balmer & Gray, 2003).

In terms of Balmer's corporate brand architecture classification, nine categories have been identified (Balmer, 2012a, 2024b; Balmer & Gray, 2003). It should be noted that whilst some of these categories are relatively common whilst others are comparatively infrequent.

It is important to note that organisations might adopt a flexible corporate brand architecture that includes two or more corporate brand types,

The following list details Balmer's different corporate brand types. It should be noted that a distinction can be made between intra-organisational corporate brands (corporate brands subsisting *within* the same corporate structure), and inter-organisational corporate brands (corporate brands subsisting *across* entities and which have distinct corporate structures).

The various corporate brand architecture modes can be classified as follows:

a. Monolithic (*intra-organisational in character*). This where a single, 'mother' corporate brand is deployed across an organisation's subsidiaries, business units, endeavors and activities such as the BBC.
b. Endorsed (*intra-organisational in character*). This is where a subsidiary has its own corporate brand. However, this corporate brand is endorsed by the mother corporate brand such as the constituent parts of London University (Brunel, London University).
c. Branded (*intra-organisational in character*). This is where a subsidiary's corporate brand name is a stand-alone corporate brand and makes no reference to the 'mother' corporate brand. An example is Bentley Motors, which makes no reference to its parent Volkswagen.
d. Familial (*inter-organisational in character*). This is where two or more organisations, *operating in an identical industry sector*, use the same corporate brand. In many cases, this was the case with Hilton (cf. Balmer & Thomson, 2009).
e. Shared (*inter-organisational in character*). This is where two or more organisations, *not operating in the same industry sector*, utilise the same corporate brand. Rolls Royce is an example of this, with the corporate brand being used by the aero-engine company and also, by the luxury automotive manufacturer.
f. Surrogate (*inter-organisation in character*). This where multiple organisations, operating under a franchise arrangement/license or similar, have recourse to the same corporate brand. Examples include Coca-Cola, Subway. Also common in the hotel sector.
g. Federal (*inter-organisational in character*). This is where several organisations cooperate to establish a common corporate brand and share responsibility for it. The Eurofighter air-defense company is owned by Airbus Defence & Space (France/Germany/Spain); BAE Systems (UK); and Leonardo (Italy).
h. Supra *(inter-organisational in character*). This characterises a corporate brand architecture type where a supra-organisational corporate brand ratifies member corporate brands. Thus, it acts as a quasi supra level endorsement. An example is the OneWorld Airline alliance.
i. *Multiplex* (intra-organisational and inter-organisational, this is where a multi-faceted corporate brand that is found in diverse sectors share the same brand. Sometimes such brands have multiple ownership too. An example is the Virgin corporate brand.

CO-CREATION OF CORPORATE BRANDS: A HERMENEUTIC OF DISRUPTION OR A HERMENEUTIC OF CONTINUITY?

One sign of an area's growing importance, prominence and saliency is when scholars demur from extant scholarship on a territory and the premises that underpin it. This has occurred within corporate brand scholarship where some scholars have embraced the co-creation perspective. Popularised by Ramaswamy and Goillart (2010), the co-creation standpoint is informed by the view that consumers, and not only managers, are integral to the development of products and services.

Thus, a number of articles taking this co-creation stance has started to permeate corporate brand scholarship (Essamri et al., 2019; Iglesias & Ind, 2020; Iglesias et al., 2013, 2020, 2022; Ind et al., 2013; Kristal et al., 2020; Lahtinen & Närvänen, 2020; Mingione & Leoni, 2020; Siano et al., 2022; Törmälä & Saraniemi, 2018). For some, corporate brand creation involves an eschewal of some of the underlying principles of the foundational corporate brand scholarship (Iglesias et al., 2022).

Corporate brand co-creation has been described as a dynamic process where stakeholders are engaged in four activities: communicating, internalising, contesting and elucidating (Iglesias et al., 2020).

In one sense, orthodox marketing scholars can regard the co-creation approach as a development of the famous dictum that the primary purpose of a business is to create customers and this can be accomplished by organisations resorting to marketing and innovation (Drucker, 1954). As such, an organisation's marketing philosophy is underpinned by the notion that organisations need to create value for customers (Dolan, 2006). Therefore, an organisation's corporate goals are achieved not only by meeting, but exceeding, customer needs and expectations better than the competition (Jobber & Ellis-Chadwick, 2020). Thus, customers need to always be at the forefront of the thoughts of managers/organisational members. For instance, it has been asserted that voice needs to be given to customers during a product/service development process (Elberse, 2006).

More broadly, traditional marketing precepts have emphasised that customers continually need to be in the consciousness of managers. As such, customers' perceptions are a vital concern. Within traditional marketing, the advent of relationship marketing has been identified as one of the developments in marketing thought with customers being viewed as an organisation's partners (Balmer & Greyser, 2006).

In the previously articulated corporate brand alignment frameworks (Balmer, 2003, 2012a; Hatch & Schultz, 2001, 2008) the importance of organisations having regard for customer/stakeholder images have been emphasised and this can also be seen in earlier corporate identity alignment models as well (Balmer, 2001c; Balmer & Greyser, 2002; Balmer & Soenen, 1999). Similarly, from corporate marketing/corporate branding perspectives customers and other stakeholders are critical concerns and must be taken into account (cf. Balmer, 1998; Balmer & Greyser, 2006). After all, in corporate marketing, one guiding maxim is that organisations need to understand customers/stakeholders before they, as companies, are understood by them.

Significantly, for those familiar with the foundational literature on the territory, the debate about who, and to what degree, managers or customers/stakeholders have agency over a corporate brand has characterised scholarship for some considerable time, as the literature attests (Balmer et al., 2017; Bickerton, 2000; Lawer & Knox, 2007; Pitt et al., 2006; Rindell & Strandvik, 2010). All of the aforementioned perspectives emphasise that greater emphasis should be accorded to customers/stakeholders' viewpoints apropos the nature, management, maintenance and development of corporate brands.

Thus, the co-creation perspective – which accords importance to both managers and stakeholders, apropos corporate brands, can be viewed as an accentuated part of this tradition of scholarly discourse.

Taking a panoptic perspective, the corporate brand co-creation perspective can even be characterised as a via media standpoint. Thus, it sits at the intersection between those who argue that managers have primary agency in contrast to the perspective and those who posit that consumers, and not managers, are brand-builders (Grönroos, 2007).

It has been argued that co-creation represents a paradigm shift (Iglesias et al., 2022), with these authors censoring the foundational literature for emphasising the role of the CEO/senior managers in corporate brand formation/development whilst downplaying the role of customers/stakeholders (Iglesias et al., 2022; Iglesias & Ind, 2020). Certainly, the foundational literature has variously highlighted the importance of senior managers in corporate brand formation and management (Balmer, 1995; Hatch & Schultz, 2001; Ind, 1997; King, 1991). For Hatch and Schultz (2001, 2008), it is management vision that is the driver for a corporate brand. In contrast, it has been argued that management vision can be problematic (Balmer & Soenen, 1999; Balmer et al., 2009, 2011).

From the outset, as evidenced in the formative literature, an enduring theme is the importance of senior managers taking account of customer/stakeholder perceptions (Balmer, 1995, 2001b; Hatch & Schultz, 2001).

Indeed a failure to take account of customer/stakeholder perceptions was identified as one of the 'deadly sins' of corporate brand management (Balmer, 2001b) and this is, of course, a key element of the corporate brand acid test (Balmer, 2003, 2005, 2012a, 2012b). Moreover, it has been emphasised that whereas organisations have legal ownership of the corporate brand, *the emotional ownership of the corporate brand-and thereby its real value-resides with customers/stakeholders* (Balmer, 2006, 2010a, 2010b, 2012a).

Importantly, new corporate brand perspectives/insights – such as the co-creation perspective – do not necessarily mean earlier discernments, practices and benefits are necessarily, or inevitably, vitiated. Certainly, if the corporate brand co-creation perspective accentuates the importance of listening to customers/stakeholders apropos the management and maintenance of corporate brands few in marketing would demure from this stance.

Given the above, it is debatable whether co-creation represents a paradigm shift. Rather than representing a 'hermeneutic of discontinuity', arguably, the corporate brand co-creation perspective, represents the 'hermeneutic of continuity'. Time will tell what the consequences of the co-create stance will take and whether this will result in a reformation in thought which, in turn, might engender a counter reformation.

It should be noted that the co-creation perspective has its detractors, however. It has been argued that there is a dark-side of corporate brand creation: this can have disruptive consequences (Bartsch & Claus, 2022). For instance, it has been surmised that co-creation activities can damage the brand. This is because stakeholders hijacking initiatives to elucidate customers and stakeholder feedback (Verhoef et al., 2013).

Certainly, even with a co-creation perspective, it is hard to see how managers will not have a central role. After all, it is they, not customers/stakeholders, who have responsibility for the corporate brand. At the end of the day, senior managers not only have to sign off any change to the corporate brand. Managers, rather than customers/stakeholders, are the ones who, 'carry the can', if there are problems with the corporate brand or if the corporate brand founders because of customer/stakeholder involvement.

There are also some practical difficulties to contemplate. Consider, for instance, the number of corporate brands that an individual engages with on a daily or weekly basis. There are numerous. As such, on a practical level, there are too many for a person to engage with as a co-creator. Seemingly, many individuals will not engage with any form of co-creation corporate brand activities. At this juncture, the reader might reflect on the corporate brands that are meaningful to them not only as a customer but as a stakeholder too. They then might reflect on which, if any, of these corporate brands the reader has engaged in a co-creation capacity.

Those individuals who do embark on such activities are likely to have an unusually heightened sense of personal identification with a particular corporate brand. However, there is the danger that such individuals will not be representative of rank and file customers/stakeholders. As such, senior managers would be unwise to abandon traditional forms of corporate marketing research methods of data collection for customers and other stakeholders in order to be apprised of their understandings, feelings and benefits/values, etc., apropos the corporate brand.

Another issue is the primary focus/foci of corporate brand co-creation. Is it in relation to the dimensions of the corporate brand covenant? Is it in relation to product/service innovation and development? If it is in relation to the latter is this activity occasional or is it an ongoing, and permanent, concern?

Given the above, three modes of corporate brand co-creation can be identified.

a. Substantive corporate brand co-creation. This would entail customers/other stakeholders having ongoing input to the content, and scope, of the corporate brand covenant.
b. Co-innovation corporate brand co-creation. This would entail customer/other stakeholder *ongoing* involvement in a corporate brand's product/service innovation. Consequently, and importantly, this would represent a significant, additional, dimension of the corporate brand covenant. As such, the organisation would need to provide a cast-iron assurance that customers/others stakeholders inputs are critical apropos to product/service innovation. Thus, customers/other stakeholders would need to be viewed as permanent co-innovators. For customers/other stakeholders such ongoing involvements would need to be established as part of the understandings, meanings, and expectations associated with a corporate brand/covenant.
c. Co-innovation corporate brand co-creation sojourners. This is similar to the above, *except*, it would entail customer/others stakeholder *occasional* involvement in a corporate brand's product/service innovation. At best, this would constitute a secondary order characteristic of the corporate brand covenant as guaranteed by an organisation. Similarly, for customers/other stakeholders this would constitute an occasional attribute of their understandings, meanings and expectation of the corporate brand/covenant.

WEAKNESSES AND STRENGTHS

In the past, a number of weaknesses in the territory were identified. As noted by Mukherjee and Balmer (2007), some time ago, they observed that many articles were conceptual and prescriptive; contingency scenarios were not always explored (e.g., how is the corporate brand literature affected by new trends and practices in business?); and insufficient emphasis is accorded to not for profit, and public organisations. However, the situation has markedly improved since then.

Moreover, it was noted that there was a lack of progress in theory development and the corporate brand domain fell short of fulfilling the requirement of a theory in management (Mukherjee & Balmer, 2007). Again, the situation has improved, but more attention could clearly be accorded to the development of theory.

Others have observed that whilst corporate brand scholarship is of considerable importance, it is also highly fragmented and complex (Biraghi & Gambetti, 2013; Järventie-Thesleff et al., 2011; Kay, 2006); and this is evidenced in the variety of research paradigms within the domain (Pillai, 2012). This has been exacerbated by differences between the practitioner and academic literatures (Biraghi & Gambetti, 2013).

Furthermore, and also different disciplinary lenses have different emphases including communications perspectives (Schultz & Kitchen, 2004); and even organisational behaviour (Hatch & Schultz, 2008).

Certainly, some of the contributing factors responsible for the 'fog' surrounding corporate brand and corporate marketing scholarship – already evident in the early 2000s – are still prevalent today (cf. Balmer, 2001a).

Strengths

However, divergence and disagreement can be a sign, also of richness. Certainly, since the first article on corporate brand management (Balmer, 1995), there has been an exponential growth in interest in corporate brands by scholars and practitioners alike. Moreover, the importance of corporate brands has increasingly been recognised. As noted by Burghausen (2024), developments within the field include categorising the literature into functionalist (Mingione & Abratt, 2022) or 'orthodox' (Balmer et al., 2017) standpoints. The functionalist perspective stresses the efficacy of an integrated and controlled approach to corporate brand management and different positions can also be discerned (Burghausen, 2024). This can be contrasted with the 'heterodox' (Balmer et al., 2016) and interpretivist (Mingione & Abratt, 2022) positions. Burghausen (2024) notes how the heterodox standpoint (Balmer et al., 2017) emphasises the significance of stakeholder involvements and interactions in corporate brand creation. It is possible for authors to recognise and comment on different perspectives of course.

Another sign of the richness and strengths of the territory are the industry sectors covered in the literature. Thus, corporate brands have been studied in the context of the airlines (Balmer et al., 2009); automotive sector (Essamri et al., 2019); children (Balmer et al. 202's educational toys (Schultz & Hatch, 2003); higher education (Balmer & Liao, 2007; Balmer et al., 2020b; Curtis et al., 2009); hospitality (Balmer & Thomson, 2009) and sports/Olympic Games (Motion et al., 2003; Seguin et al., 2008).

Additionally, the literature focuses on a wide range of corporate brand related themes/areas which include: business-to-business branding (Balmer et al., 2020a; Kristal et al., 2020; Kuenzel et al., 2019; Mingione & Leoni, 2020; Vallaster & Lindgreen, 2011); conscientious corporate brands (Abratt & Kleyn, 2023; Rindell et al., 2011); consumer relationships and loyalty (Ozdemir et al., 2020); corporate social responsibility (Kucharska, 2020; Maon et al., 2021); crises (de Villartay et al., 2023); dealers (Anisimova & Mavondo, 2014); digital/digital start-ups (Mingione & Abratt, 2020); equity impacts (Muzellec & Lambkin, 2006; Porto et al., 2024); corporate brand extensions (Sarasvuo et al., 2023); front-line employees (Boukis et al., 2021; Glanfield et al., 2018; Morsing, 2006); green products impact/innovation (Rahman, 2024); image formation (Törmälä & Saraniemi, 2018); managers and the corporate brand (Goland, 2012); international business (Melewar & Walker, 2003); leverage (Brexendorf & Keller, 2017); performance (Harris & de Chernanatony, 2001); moral branding and employees (Morsing, 2006); place impacts (Balmer et al., 2020b) positioning (Knox & Bickerton, 2003; Kuenzel et al., 2019); rebranding and renaming (Cassell & Juntunen, 2014; Gotsi & Andriopoulos, 2007; Lomax & Mador, 2006; Tarnovskaya & Biedenbach, 2018); salespersons (Anisimova & Mavondo, 2010); social media influencers impacts (Singh et al., 2020); stakeholders (Roper & Davies, 2007); Morsing & Kristensen, 2001); strategy formation (Vallaster & Lindgreen, 2011); sustainability (Lahtinen & Närvänen, 2020) and values (Urde, 2009).

CONCLUSIONS

In this chapter, the value of corporate brands, and the strategic importance of corporate brand management, have been articulated. Corporate brand management is an ongoing, complex and critically important management task. It involves many dimensions. It demands management time and effort. Significantly, corporate brands are highly meaningful for customers and other stakeholders. It is they who have emotional ownership of corporate brands. Their emotional ownership helps explain why corporate brands are often an organisation's principal asset. In a prescient observation made in 1910, it was noted,

> A well known brand, trade mark or label is now-a-days the most valuable asset a trader can possess. (Rogers, 1910, p. 430)

Unquestionably, the soft power that is often manifest in an organisation's corporate brand is as true now as it was in the early 20th century. It is likely to remain so for the foreseeable future.

REFERENCES

Aaker, D. A., & Joachimsthaler, E. (2000). The brand relationship spectrum: The key to the brand architecture challenge. *California Management Review*, *42*(4), 8–23. https://doi.org/10.1177/000812560004200401

Abratt, R., & Kleyn, N. (2012). Corporate identity, corporate branding and corporate reputations: Reconciliation and integration. *European Journal of Marketing*, *46*(7/8), 1048–1063. https://doi.org/10.1108/03090561211230197

Abratt, R., & Kleyn, N. (2023). The conscientious corporate brand: Definition, operationalization and application in a B2B context. *Journal of Business and Industrial Marketing*, *38*(10), 2122–2133. https://doi.org/10.1108/JBIM-10-2021-0468

Anisimova, T. A. (2010). Corporate brand: The company-customer misalignment and its performance implications. *Journal of Brand Management*, *17*(7), 488–501. https://doi.org/10.1057/bm.2010.7

Anisimova, T. A., & Mavondo, F. (2010). The performance implications of company-salesman corporate brand misalignment. *European Journal of Marketing*, *44*(6), 771–795. https://doi.org/10.1108/03090561011032711

Anisimova, T.., & Mavondo, F. (2014). Aligning company and dealer perspectives in corporate branding: Implications for dealer satisfaction and commitment. *Journal of Business-to-Business Marketing*, *21*(1), 35–56. https://doi.org/10.1080/1051712X.2014.857501

Ashforth, B., & Mael, F. (1989). Social identity theory and the organization. *Academy of Management Review*, *14*(1), 20–39. https://doi.org/10.2307/258189

Balmer, J. M. T. (1995). Corporate branding and connoisseurship. *Journal of General Management*, *21*(1), 24–46. https://doi.org/10.1177/030630709502100102

Balmer, J. M. T. (1998). Corporate identity and the advent of corporate marketing. *Journal of Marketing Management*, *14*(8), 963–996. https://doi.org/10.1362/026725798784867536

Balmer, J. M. T. (2001a). Corporate identity, corporate branding, and corporate marketing: Seeing through the fog. *European Journal of Marketing*, *35*(3/4), 248–291. https://doi.org/10.1108/03090560110694763

Balmer, J. M. T. (2001b). The three virtues and seven deadly sins of corporate brand management. *Journal of General Management*, *27*(1), 1–17. https://doi.org/10.1177/030630700102700101

Balmer, J. M. T. (2001c). From the pentagon. *Corporate Reputation Review*, *4*(1), 11–22. https://doi.org/10.1057/palgrave.crr.1540129

Balmer, J. M. T. (2003). Balmer's first corporate brand alignment model (The AC³ID Test. In J. M. T. Balmer, & S. A. Gresyer (Eds.), *Revealing the corporation* (pp. 251). Routledge.

Balmer, J. M. T. (2005). *Corporate brands: A strategic management framework* (Vol. 5, No. 3, pp. 1–15). Bradford School of Management Working Paper Series.

Balmer, J. M. T. (2006). Corporate brand cultures and communities. In J. E. Schroeder, & M. Salzer Morling (Eds.), *Brand culture* (pp. 34–49). Routledge.

Balmer, J. M. T. (2010a). Explicating corporate brands and their management: Reflections, and directions from 1995 to the present. *Journal of Brand Management*, *18*(3), 180–196. https://doi.org/10.1057/bm.2010.46

Balmer, J. M. T. (2010b). The BP deepwater horizon débâcle and corporate brand exuberance. *Journal of Brand Management*, *18*(2), 97–104. https://doi.org/10.1057/bm.2010.33

Balmer, J. M. T. (2012a). Corporate brand management imperatives: Custodianship, credibility, and calibration. *California Management Review*, *54*(3), 6–33. https://doi.org/10.1525/cmr.2012.54.3.6

Balmer, J. M. T. (2012b). Strategic corporate brand alignment: Perspectives from identity-based views of corporate brands. *European Journal of Marketing*, *46*(7/8), 1064–1092. https://doi.org/10.1108/03090561211230205

Balmer, J. M. T. (2013). Corporate brand orientation: What is it? What of it? *Journal of Brand Management*, *20*(9), 723–741. https://doi.org/10.1057/bm.2013.15

Balmer, J. M. T. (2017). Advances in corporate brand, corporate heritage, corporate identity, and corporate marketing scholarship. *European Journal of*

Marketing, *51*(9/10), 1462–1471. https://doi.org/10.1108/EJM-07-2017-0447

Balmer, J. M. T. (2022). Managerial corporate brand orientation: Explication, significance, and antecedents. *Journal of Brand Management*, *29*(3), 1–12. https://doi.org/10.1057/s41262-021-00265-3

Balmer, J. M. T. (2023). Digital corporate communication and brand communication. In M. Bedlam (Ed.), *Handbook of corporate communication* (pp. 34–50). Edward Elgar Publishing, Cheltenham.

Balmer, J. M. T. (2024a). Corporate brand communication. In K. Podnar (Ed.), *Elgar encyclopedia of corporate communication* (pp. 175–178). Edward Elgar Publishing, Cheltenham.

Balmer, J. M. T. (2024b). Corporate brand architecture. In K. Podnar (Ed.), *Elgar encyclopedia of corporate communication* (pp. 142–147). Edward Elgar Publishing, Cheltenham.

Balmer, J. M. T., & Gray, E. R. (2003). Corporate brands: What are they? What of them? *European Journal of Marketing*, *37*(7-8), 972–997. https://doi.org/10.1108/03090560310477627

Balmer, J. M. T., & Greyser, S. A. (2002). Managing the multiple identities of the corporation. *California Management Review*, *44*(3), 72–86. https://doi.org/10.2307/41166133

Balmer, J. M. T., & Greyser, S. A. (2003). *Revealing the corporation. Perspectives on identity, image, reputation, corporate branding and corporate-level marketing*. Routledge.

Balmer, J. M. T., & Greyser, S. A. (2006). Corporate marketing: Integrating corporate identity, corporate branding, corporate communications, corporate image and corporate reputation. *European Journal of Marketing*, *40*(7-8), 730–741. https://doi.org/10.1108/03090560610669964

Balmer, J. M. T., & Liao, M. N. (2007). Student corporate brand identification: An exploratory case study. *Corporate Communications: An International Journal*, *12*(4), 356–375. https://doi.org/10.1108/13563280710832515

Balmer, J. M. T., & Podnar, K. (2021). Corporate brand orientation: Identity, internal images, and corporate identification matters. *Journal of Business Research*, *134*, 729–737. https://doi.org/10.1016/j.jbusres.2021.06.016

Balmer, J. M. T., & Soenen, G. B. (1999). The Acid Test of corporate identity management™. *Journal of Marketing Management*, *15*(1-3), 69–92. https://doi.org/10.1362/026725799784870441

Balmer, J. M. T., & Thomson, I. (2009). The shared management and ownership of corporate brands: The case of Hilton. *Journal of General Management*, *34*(4), 15–37. https://doi.org/10.1177/030630700903400402

Balmer, J. M. T., & Yen, D. A. (2016). The Internet of total corporate communications, quaternary corporate communications and the corporate marketing internet revolution. *Journal of Marketing Management*, *33*(1-2), 131–144. https://doi.org/10.1080/0267257X.2016.1255440

Balmer, J. M. T., Stuart, H., & Greyser, S. A. (2009). Aligning identity and strategy: Corporate branding at British airways in the late 20th century. *California Management Review*, *51*(3), 6–23. https://doi.org/10.2307/41166491

Balmer, J. M. T., Liao, M. N., & Wang, W. Y. (2010). Corporate brand identification and corporate brand management: How top business schools do it. *Journal of General Management*, *35*(4), 77–102. https://doi.org/10.1177/030630701003500404

Balmer, J. M. T., Powell, S. M., & Greyser, S. A. (2011). Explicating ethical corporate marketing. Insights from the BP deepwater horizon catastrophe: The ethical brand that exploded and then imploded. *Journal of Business Ethics*, *102*(1), 1–14. https://doi.org/10.1007/s10551-011-0902-1

Balmer, J. M. T., Johansen, T. S., & Nielsen, A. N. (2016). Scrutinizing stakeholder thinking: Orthodoxy or heterodoxy? *International Studies of Management and Organization*, *46*(4), 205–215. https://doi.org/10.1080/00208825.2016.1140517

Balmer, J. M. T., Powell, S. M., Kernstock, J., & Brexendorf, T. O. (2017). Introduction: Current state and future directions for research on corporate brand management. In J. M. T. Balmer, S. M. Powell, J. Kernstock, & T. O. Brexendorf (Eds.), *Advances in corporate branding. Journal of brand management advanced collections* (pp. 1–21). Palgrave Macmillan.

Balmer, J. M. T., Lin, Z., Chen, W., & He, X. (2020a). The role of corporate brand image for B2B relationships of logistics service providers in China. *Journal of Business Research*, *117*, 850–861. https://doi.org/10.1016/j.jbusres.2020.03.043

Balmer, J. M. T., Mahmoud, R., & Chen, W. (2020b). Impact of multilateral place dimensions on corporate brand attractiveness and identification in higher education: Business school insights. *Journal of Business Research*, *116*, 628–641. https://doi.org/10.1016/j.jbusres.2019.03.015

Bartsch, F., & Claus, B. (2022). The dark side of brand co-creation: A psychological ownership perspective. In S. Markovic, R. Gyrd-Jones, S. von Wallpach, & A. Lindgreen (Eds.), *Research handbook on brand co-creation* (pp. 218–239). Edward Elgar.

Barwise, P., Dunham, A., & Ritson, M. (2000). Ties that bind; brands, consumers, and business. In J. Pavitt (Ed.), *Brand new* (pp. 70–96). V&A Publications.

Bhattacharya, C. B., & Korschun, D. (2008). Stakeholder marketing: Beyond the 4ps and the customer. *Journal of Public Policy and Marketing*, *27*(1), 113–116. https://doi.org/10.1509/jppm.27.1.113

Bhattacharya, C. B., & Sen, S. (2003). Consumer-company identification: A framework for understanding consumers' relationships with companies. *Journal of Marketing*, *67*(2), 76–88. https://doi.org/10.1509/jmkg.67.2.76.18609

Bickerton, D. (2000). Corporate reputation versus corporate branding: The realist debate. *Corporate Communications: An International Journal*, *5*(1), 42–48. https://doi.org/10.1108/13563280010317578

Biraghi, S., & Gambetti, R. C. (2013). Corporate branding: Where are we? A systematic communication-based inquiry. *Journal of Marketing Communications*, *21*(4), 260–283. https://doi.org/10.1080/13527266.2013.768535

Boukis, A., Punjaisri, K., Balmer, J. M. T., Kaminakis, K., & Papastathopoulos, A. (2021). Unveiling front-line employees' brand construal types during corporate brand promise delivery: A multi-study analysis. *Journal of Business Research*, *131*, 673–685. https://doi.org/10.1016/j.jbusres.2020.12.068. (www.sciencedirect.com/science/article/pii/S0148296320308961)

Brexendorf, T. O., & Keller, K. L. (2017). Leveraging the corporate brand: The importance of corporate brand innovativeness and brand architecture. *European Journal of Marketing*, *51*(9-10), 1530–1551. https://doi.org/10.1108/EJM-07-2017-04

Burghausen, M. (2024). Corporate brand. In K. Podnar (Ed.), *Elgar encyclopedia of corporate communication* (pp. 122–131). Edward Elgar.

Cassell, C., & Juntunen, G. S. M. (2014). Time-based modifications to process theory illustrations through a corporate rebranding case study. *Baltic Journal of Management*, *10*(2), 222–242. https://doi.org/10.1108/BJM-01-2014-0014

Cornilissen, J. P., Haslam, S. A., & Balmer, J. M. T. (2007). Social identity, organizational identity, and corporate identity: Towards an integrated understanding of processes, patternings, and products. *British Journal of Management*, *18*(S1), 1–16.

Curtis, T., Abratt, R., & Minor, W. (2009). Corporate brand management in higher education: The case of ERAU. *Journal of Product & Brand Management*, *18*(6), 404–413. https://doi.org/10.1108/10610420910989721

de Villartay, S., Abid-Dupont, M. A., & Berger-Remy, F. (2023). The dynamic of employees' trust in their organisation in a corporate brand crisis: The bounce-back effect of organisational identification. *Journal of Marketing Management*, *40*(3-4), 260–288. https://doi.org/10.1080/0267257X.2023.2276867

Dolan, R. J. (2006). Marketing strategy. In A. Silk (Ed.), *What is marketing?* (pp. 3–48). Harvard Business School Press.

Drucker, P. F. (1954). *The practice of management*. Harper-Collins.

Dutton, J. E., Dukerich, J. M., & Harquail, C. V. (1994). Organizational images and member identification. *Administrative Science Quarterly*, *39*(34), 239–263. https://doi.org/10.2307/2393235

Eagle, L., Czarnecka, B., Dahl, S., & Lloyd, J. (2020). *Marketing communications*. Routledge.

Einwiller, S., & Will, M. (2002). Towards an integrated approach to corporate branding-an integrated study. *Corporate Communications: An International Journal*, *7*(2), 100–109. https://doi.org/10.1108/13563280210426160

Elberse, A. (2006). Product policy. In A. Silk (Ed.), *What is marketing?* (pp. 97–110). Harvard Business School Press.

Essamri, A., McKechnie, S., & Winklhofer, H. (2019). Co-creating corporate brand identity with online brand communities: A managerial perspective. *Journal of Business Research*, *96*, 366–375. https://doi.org/10.1016/j.jbusres.2018.07.015

Glanfield, K., Ackfeldt, A.-L., & Melewar, T. (2018). Corporate branding's influence on front-line employee and consumer value co-creation in UK household consumer markets. *Journal of General Management*, *43*(2), 63–69. https://doi.org/10.1177/0306307017740184 (Original work published 2018).

Golant, B. (2012). Bringing the corporate brand to life: The brand manager as practical author. *Journal of Brand Management*, *20*, 115–127. https://doi.org/10.1057/bm.2012.44

Gotsi, M., & Andriopoulos, C. (2007). Understanding the pitfalls in the corporate rebranding process. *Corporate Communications: An International Journal*, *12*(4), 341–355. https://doi.org/10.1108/13563280710832506

Greyser, S. A., & Urde, M. (2019). What does your corporate brand stand for? *Harvard Business Review*, *97*(1), 80–88.

Grönroos, C. (2007). *Service management and marketing: Customer management in service competition* (2nd ed.). Wiley.

Gummesson, E. (2008). Extending the service-dominant logia: From customers centricity to balanced centricity. *Journal of the Academy of Marketing Science*, *36*(1), 15–17. https://doi.org/10.1007/s11747-007-0065-x

Gyrd-Jones, R. I., Merriless, B., & Miller, D. (2013). Revisiting the complexities of corporate branding: Issues, paradoxes, solutions. *Journal of Brand Management*, *20*(7), 1–19. https://doi.org/10.1057/bm.2013.1

Haigh, D. (2003). An introduction to brand equity-how to understand and appreciate brand value and the economic impact of brand investment. *Interactive Marketing*, *5*(1), 21–32. https://doi.org/10.1057/palgrave.im.4340214

Harris, F., & de Chernatony, L. (2001). Corporate branding and corporate brand performance.

European Journal of Marketing, 35(3-4), 441–456. https://doi.org/10.1108/03090560110382101

Hatch, M. J., & Schultz, M. (2001). Are the strategic stars aligned for your corporate brand? *Harvard Business Review, 79*(2), 129–134.

Hatch, M. J., & Schultz, M. (2008). *Taking brand initiative: How companies can align strategy, culture, and identity through corporate branding*. Jossey-Bass. ISBN 9780787998301

Hillebrand, B., Driessen, P. H., & Koll, O. (2015). Stakeholder marketing: Theoretical foundations and required capabilities. *Journal of the Academy of Marketing Science, 43*(4), 411–428. https://doi.org/10.1007/s11747-015-0424-y

Hult, G. T. M., Mena, J. A., Ferrell, O. C., & Ferrell, L. (2011). Stakeholder marketing: A definition and conceptual framework. *Academy of Marketing Review, 1*(1), 44–65. https://doi.org/10.1007/s13162-011-0002-5

Iglesias, O., Ind, N., & Alfaro, M. (2013). The organic view of the brand: A brand value co-creation model. *Journal of Brand Management, 20*, 670–688. https://doi.org/10.1057/bm.2013.8

Iglesias, O., & Ind, N. (2020). Towards a theory of conscientious corporate brand co-creation: the next key challenge in brand management. *Journal of Brand Management, 27*(6), 710–720. https://doi.org/10.1057/s41262-020-00205-7

Iglesias, O., Landgraf, P., Ind, N., Markovic, S., & Koporcic, N. (2020). Corporate brand identity co-creation in business-to-business contexts. *Industrial Marketing Management, 85*, 32–43. https://doi.org/10.1016/j.indmarman.2019.09.008

Iglesias, O., Ind, N., & Shultz, M. (2022). Towards a paradigm shift in corporate branding. In O. Iglesias, N. Ind, & M. Shultz (Eds.), *The Routledge companion to corporate branding* (pp. 3–23). Routledge.

Illia, L., & Balmer, J. M. T. (2012). Corporate communication and corporate marketing: Their nature, histories, differences and similarities. *Corporate Communications: An International Journal, 17*(4), 415–433. https://doi.org/10.1108/13563281211274121

Ind, N. (1997). *The corporate brand*. Macmillan.

Ind, N., Iglesias, O., & Schultz, M. (2013). Building brands together: Emergence and outcomes of co-creation. *California Management Review, 55*(3), 5–26. https://doi.org/10.1525/cmr.2013.55.3.5

Järventie-Thesleff, R., Moisander, J., & Laine, P.-M. (2011). Organizational dynamics and complexities of corporate brand building-a practice perspective. *Scandinavian Journal of Management, 27*(2), 196–204. https://doi.org/10.1016/j.scaman.2010.07.001

Jobber, D., & Ellis-Chadwick, F. (2020). *Principles and practice of marketing* (9th ed.). McGraw Hill.

Kay, M. J. (2006). Strong brands and corporate brands. *European Journal of Marketing, 40*(7/8), 742–760. https://doi.org/10.1108/03090560610669973

Keller, K. L. (2003). *Strategic brand management. Building, measuring and managing brand equity*. Prentice Hall.

King, S. (1991). Brand-building in the 1990s. *Journal of Marketing Management, 7*(1), 3–13. https://doi.org/10.1080/0267257X.1991.9964136

Kitchen, P. J., & Schultz, D. E. (1998). IMC – A UK Ad' agency perspective. *Journal of Marketing Management, 14*(5), 465–485. https://doi.org/10.1362/026725798784867806

Knox, S., & Bickerton, D. (2003). The six conventions of corporate branding. *European Journal of Marketing, 37*(7/8), 998–1016. https://doi.org/10.1108/03090560310477636

Kristal, S., Baumgarth, C., & Henseler, J. (2020). Performative corporate brand identity in industrial markets: The case of German prosthetics manufacturer Ottobock. *Journal of Business Research, 114*, 240–253. https://doi.org/10.1016/j.jbusres.2020.04.026

Kucharska, W. (2020). Employee commitment matters for CSR practice, Reputation and corporate brand performance—European model. *Sustainability, 12*(3), 940–946. https://doi.org/10.3390/su12030940

Kuenzel, S., Koch, C. H., Richard, I., & Gyrd-Jones, R. I. (2019). Corporate brand positioning in complex industrial firms: Introducing a dynamic, process approach to positioning. *Industrial Marketing Management, 81*, 40–53. https://doi.org/10.1016/j.indmarman.2019.03.011

Lahtinen, S., & Närvänen, E. (2020). Co-creating sustainable corporate brands: A consumer framing approach. *Corporate Communications: An International Journal, 24*(3), 447–461. https://doi.org/10.1108/CCIJ-11-2019-0121

Lawer, C., & Knox, S. (2007). Reverse-market orientation and corporate brand development. *International Studies of Management and Organization, 37*(4), 64–83. https://doi.org/10.2753/IMO0020-8825370403

Leitch, S., & Richardson, N. (2003). Corporate branding and the new economy. *European Journal of Marketing, 37*(7–8), 1065–1079. https://doi.org/10.1108/03090560310477663

Lomax, W., & Mador, M. (2006). Corporate rebranding: From normative models to knowledge management. *Journal of Brand Management, 14*, 82–95. https://doi.org/10.1057/palgrave.bm.2550029

Maon, F., Swaen, V., & De Roeck, K. (2021). Corporate branding and corporate social responsibility: Toward a multi-stakeholder interpretive perspective. *Journal of Business Research, 126*, 64–77. https://doi.org/10.1016/j.jbusres.2020.12.057.

(www.sciencedirect.com/science/article/pii/S0148296320308869)

Melewar, T., & Walker, C. (2003). Global corporate brand building: Guidelines and case studies. *Journal of Brand Management*, *11*, 157–170. https://doi.org/10.1057/palgrave.bm.2540163

Mingione, M. (2015). Inquiry into corporate brand alignment: A dialectical analysis and directions for its future research. *Journal of Product and Brand Management*, *24*(5), 518–536. https://doi.org/10.1108/JPBM-05-2014-0617

Mingione, M., & Abratt, A. (2022). In search of corporate brand alignment: Philosophical foundations and emerging trends. In O. Iglesias, N. Ind, & M. Schultz (Eds.), *The Routledge companion to corporate branding* (pp. 149–168). Routledge.

Mingione, M., & Abratt, R. (2020). Building a corporate brand in the digital age: Imperatives for transforming born-digital startups into successful corporate brands. *Journal of Marketing Management*, *36*(11-12), 981–1008. https://doi.org/10.1080/0267257X.2020.1750453

Mingione, M., & Leoni, L. (2020). Blurring B2C and B2C boundaries: Corporate brand value co-creation in B2BB2C markets. *Journal of Marketing Management*, *361*(1–2), 72–99. https://doi.org/10.1080/0267257X.2019.1694566

Morsing, M. (2006). Corporate moral branding: Limits to aligning employees. *Corporate Communications: An International Journal*, *11*(2), 97–108. https://doi.org/10.1108/13563280610661642

Morsing, M., & Kristensen, J. (2001). The question of coherency in corporate branding-over time and across stakeholders. *Journal of Communication Management*, *6*(1), 24–240. https://doi.org/10.1108/13632540210806919

Motion, J., Leitch, S., & Brodie, R. J. (2003). Equity in corporate co-branding: The case of Adidas and the All Blacks. *European Journal of Marketing*, *37*(7-8), 1080–1094. https://doi.org/10.1108/03090560310477672

Mukherjee, A., & Balmer, J. M. T. (2007). Preface: New Frontiers and perspectives in corporate brand management: In search of a theory. *International Studies of Management and Organization*, *37*(4), 3–19. https://doi.org/10.2753/IMO0020-8825370400

Muzellec, L., & Lambkin, M. C. (2009). Corporate branding and brand architecture: A conceptual framework. *Marketing Theory*, *9*(1), 31–54. https://doi.org/10.1177/1470593108100060

Muzellec, L., & Lambkin, M. (2006). Corporate rebranding: Destroying, transferring or creating brand equity? *European Journal of Marketing*, *40*(7-8), 803–824. https://doi.org/10.1108/03090560610670007

Newman, K. (2001). The sorcerer's apprentice? Alchemy, seduction and confusion in modern marketing. *International Journal of Advertising*, *20*(4), 409–429. https://doi.org/10.1080/02650487.2001.11104904

Olins, W. (1978). *The Corporate Personality*. Design Council, London.

Ozdemir, S., Zhang, S., Gupta, S., & Bebek, G. (2020). The effects of trust and peer influence on corporate brand—Consumer relationships and consumer loyalty. *Journal of Business Research*, *117*, 791–805. https://doi.org/10.1016/j.jbusres.2020.02.027. (www.sciencedirect.com/science/article/pii/S0148296320301338)

Pillai, A. (2012). Corporate branding literature: A research paradigm review. *Journal of Brand Management*, *19*, 331–343. https://doi.org/10.1057/bm.2011.43

Pitt, L. F., Watson, R., Berthon, T. P., Wynn, D., & Zinkhan, G. (2006). The Penguin's window: Corporate brands from an open-source perspective. *Journal of Academy of Marketing Science*, *34*(2), 115–27. https://doi.org/10.1177/0092070305284972

Porto, R. B., Foxall, G. R., Limongi, R., & Barbosa, D. B. (2024). Unraveling corporate brand equity: A measurement model based on consumer perception of corporate brands. *Journal of Modelling in Management*, *19*(4), 1237–1261. https://doi.org/10.1108/JM2-04-2023-0067

Pranjal, P., & Sarkar, S. (2020). Corporate brand alignment in business markets: A practice perspective. *Marketing Intelligence and Planning*, *38*(7), 907–920. https://doi.org/10.1108/MIP-10-2019-0539

Pratt, M. G. (1998). To be or not to be central questions in organizational identification. In D. Whetten, & P. C. Godfrey (Eds.), *Identity in organizations: Building theory through conversations* (pp. 171–207). Sage.

Rahman, M. (2024). The virtuous circle between green product innovation and performance: The role of financial constraint and corporate brand. *Journal of Business Research*, *15* (in press). https://doi.org/10.1016/j.jbusres.2022.09.001. (www.sciencedirect.com/science/article/pii/S0148296322007512)

Ramaswamy, V., & Goillart, F. (2010). *The power of co-creation*. Free Press.

Rindell, A., & Strandvik, T. (2010). Corporate brand evolution: Corporate brand images evolving in consumers' everyday life. *European Business Review*, *22*(3), 276–286. https://doi.org/10.1108/09555341011040976

Rindell, A., Svensson, G., Mysen, T., Billström, A., & Wilen, K. (2011). Towards a conceptual foundation of conscientious corporate brands. *Journal of Brand Management*, *18*, 709–719. https://doi.org/10.1057/bm.2011.38

Rogers, E. S. (1910). Historical matter concerning trade-marks. *Michigan Law Review*, *9*(1), 29–43. https://doi.org/10.2307/1276308

Roper, S., & Davies, G. (2007). The corporate brand: Dealing with multiple stakeholders. *Journal of Marketing Management*, *23*(1-2), 75–90. https://doi.org/10.1362/026725707X178567

Sarasvuo, S., Liljander, V., & Haahtela, K. (2023). Buyer perceptions of corporate brand extension attractiveness and fit in B2B services. *Industrial Marketing Management*, *115*, 69–85. https://doi.org/10.1016/j.indmarman.2023.09.006. (www.sciencedirect.com/science/article/pii/S0019850123001657)

Schultz, D., & Kitchen, P. J. (2004). Managing the changes in corporate branding and communication: Closing and reopening the corporate umbrella. *Corporate Reputation Review*, *6*(4), 347–366. https://doi.org/10.1057/palgrave.crr.1540004

Schultz, M., & Hatch, M. J. (2003). The cycles of corporate branding: The case of the LEGO company. *California Management Review*, *46*(1), 6–26. https://doi.org/10.2307/41166229

Seguin, B., Richelieu, A., & O'Reilly, N. (2008). Leveraging the Olympic brand through the reconciliation of corporate and consumers' brand perceptions. *Sport Management and Marketing*, *3*(1-2), 3–22. https://doi.org/10.1504/IJSMM.2008.015958

Siano, A., Vollero, A., & Bertolini, A. (2022). From brand control to brand co-creation: An integrated framework of brand paradigms and emerging brand perspectives. *Journal of Business Research*, *152*, 372–386. https://doi.org/10.1016/j.jbusres.2022.08.001

Silk, A. (2006). Brand valuation. In A. Silk (Ed.), *What is marketing?* (pp. 111–114). Harvard Business School Press.

Singh, J., Crisafulli, B., La Toya, Q., & Tao Xue, M. (2020). 'To trust or not to trust': The impact of social media influencers on the reputation of corporate brands in crisis. *Journal of Business Research*, *119*, 464–480. https://doi.org/10.1016/j.jbusres.2020.03.039. (www.sciencedirect.com/science/article/pii/S0148296320302034)

Soanes, C., & Hawker, S. (2005). *Compact Oxford English dictionary*. Oxford University Press.

Srivastava, K., & Sharma, N. K. (2013). Service quality, corporate brand image, and switching behavior: The mediating role of customer satisfaction and repurchase intention. *Services Marketing Quarterly*, *34*(4), 274–291. https://doi.org/10.1080/15332969.2013.827020

Syed-Alwi, S. F., Balmer, J. M. T., Stoian, M.-C., & Kitchen, P. J. (2022). Introducing integrated hybrid communication: The nexus linking marketing communication and corporate communication. *Qualitative Market Research*, *25*(4), 405–432. https://doi.org/10.1108/QMR-09-2021-0123

Tajfel, H. (1972). La catégorization sociale. In S. Moscovici (Ed.), *Introduction à la Psychologie sociale, 1* (pp. 272–302). Larousse.

Tajfel, H., & Turner, J. C. (1979). An integrative theory of intergroup conflict'. In W. G. Austin, & S. Worchel (Eds.), *The social psychology of intergroup relations* (pp. 7–24). Brooks/Cole.

Tarnovskaya, V. (2015). Corporate brand as a contract with stakeholders – theology or pragmatism? *Marketing Intelligence and Planning*, *33*(6), 865–886. https://doi.org/10.1108/MIP-06-2014-0111

Tarnovskaya, V., & Biedenbach, G. (2018). Corporate rebranding failure and brand meanings in the digital environment. *Marketing Intelligence & Planning*, *36*(1), 455–469. https://doi.org/10.1108/MIP-09-2017-0192

Tarnovskaya, V., Elg, U., & Burt, S. (2008). The role of corporate branding in a market driving strategy. *International Journal of Retail and Distribution Management*, *36*(11), 941–965. https://doi.org/10.1108/09590550810911692

Törmälä, M., & Saraniemi, S. (2018). The role of business partners in corporate brand image co-creation. *Journal of Product and Brand Management*, *27*(1), 29–40. https://doi.org/10.1108/JPBM-01-2016-1089

Turner, J. C. (1982). Towards a cognitive redefinition of the social group. In H. Tajfel (Ed.), *Social identity and intergroup relations* (pp. 15–40). Cambridge University Press.

Turner, J. C. (1987). *Rediscovering the social group: A self-categorization theory*. Blackwell.

Uggla, H. (2006). The corporate brand association base: A conceptual model for the creation of inclusive brand architecture. *European Journal of Marketing*, *40*(7/8), 785–802. https://doi.org/10.1108/03090560610669991

Urde, M. (1994). Brand orientation – a strategy for survival. *Journal of Consumer Marketing*, *11*(3), 18–32. https://doi.org/10.1108/07363769410065445

Urde, U. (2009). Uncovering the corporate brand's core values. *Management Decision*, *47*(4), 616–638. https://doi.org/10.1108/00251740910959459

Vallaster, C., & Lindgreen, A. (2011). Corporate brand strategy formation: Brand actors and the situational context for a business-to-business brand. *Industrial Marketing Management*, *40*(7), 1133–1143. https://doi.org/10.1016/j.indmarman.2011.09.008. (www.sciencedirect.com/science/article/pii/S0019850111001362)

van Riel, C. B. M. (1995). *Principles of Corporate Communication*, Routledge, London.

Verhoef, P. C., Beckers, S. F. M., & van Doom, J. (2013). Understand the perils of co-creation. *Harvard Business Review*, *91*(9), 1–18.

13

Brand Portfolio Auditing and Brand Architecture Strategy

Clarinda Jansberg

INTRODUCTION

Brands are striving to remain relevant and agile in today's competitive business arena in which a set of acquisitions and mergers are taking place (Brandão et al., 2020). During company growth phases, the tendency is to add new brands, products and services to their portfolios to meet new market demands or new distribution challenges (Fang & Wang, 2018; Kapferer, 2008). Empirical evidence shows that some companies get lost in large brand portfolios, either creating confusion in the marketplace or leaving some brands unprotected from competition (Hill et al., 2005). In fact, extensive brand portfolios can lead to unclarity, fragmented marketing resources and low economies of scale (Hill et al., 2005). The challenge facing companies is how to manage and leverage complex brand portfolios (Laforet & Saunders, 2005; Uggla & Filipsson, 2009), while creating strong brands and staying competitive in the marketplace. In the same line of thought, concerns arise on how to design effective brand architecture strategies as roadmaps for sustaining brands over the long term (Keller, 2013; Sarabia-Sanchez & Cerda-Bertomeu, 2017). Nguyen et al. (2018) argue that companies should strive for brand portfolio coherence so that (sub) brands share a common set of features reflecting their personality, design and status. This assumption is relevant, considering that the number of products affiliated to a particular brand and its quality variance plays an important role in brand reliability (DelVecchio, 2000). In this context, continuous brand audits are suggested as a holistic management exercise, which allows marketers to gain a better understanding of brand performance (Aaker, 2004a; Hill et al., 2005), inform long-term brand strategies (Brandão et al., 2020) and create opportunities for improvement (Kumar, 2003).

Departing from the main theories of brand portfolios and brand architecture, this chapter presents and discusses the examples of B2B and B2C companies. Additionally, it introduces the reader to the relevance of auditing brands on a regular basis and describes a dynamic and holistic framework that combines the brand portfolio audit with brand architecture redesign. This eight-step brand audit framework developed by Brandão et al. (2020) includes four steps of the brand portfolio audit (relevant brand set, assessment criteria, brand evaluation and brand prioritization) and four steps in the brand architecture redesign process (brand portfolio, portfolio roles, brand architecture strategy and portfolio structure).

BRAND PORTFOLIO MANAGEMENT

Brand portfolio management implies that companies not only create and acquire brands, but also modify and leverage them strategically over time (Uggla & Filipsson, 2009). This assumption is especially relevant, considering the constant pressure on brands to create value for their stakeholders, the growing number of mergers and acquisitions (Strebinger, 2004), market fragmentation and evolving channel dynamics (Aaker & Joachimsthaler, 2000), proliferation of products, services and (sub)brands (Petromilli et al., 2002), shorter product and services life cycles (Louro & Cunha, 2001), brand extensions and complex sub-brand structures (Laforet & Saunders, 2005). Hence, the main challenge is to decide whether to retain or discard weak brands, especially when brands with poor financial performance are of strategic importance to the company (Shah, 2015). Sometimes, brand deletions can also be perceived favorably by employees if it frees up talent and time that could be used to support brands with the potential to become market leaders (Varadarajan, 2006).

The marketing literature suggests that a brand portfolio strategy should accomplish business and marketing objectives harmoniously (Uggla, 2015) and align with consumer 'perceptions' (Nguyen et al., 2018). Effective brand portfolio management will allow companies to reach and target different market segments while also reaching a critical size more easily and rapidly (Brandão et al., 2020). Hence, companies should aim for coherence in their brand portfolio (Nguyen et al., 2018) by continuously accessing the scope, roles and interrelationships of their portfolio brands (Brandão et al., 2020). As noted by Laforet (2017), brand portfolio management facilitates greater brand focus, corporate shared vision and long-term orientation (Laforet & Saunders, 2005). This view is demonstrated by a recent empirical study on pharmaceutical companies, which shows that a specialized brand portfolio strengthens the connection with physicians and patients, which in turn enhances corporate brand reputation (Katsanis et al., 2023).

According to Chailan (2009, p. 258), a balanced portfolio should be 'conceived like a brand network made up of mature brands and brands in development, highly profitable brands and brands in an investment phase and finally brands that are either potentially or already global'. It should be noted, however, that there is no consensus among scholars on the optimal brand portfolio size. Some argue that wider brand portfolios allow companies to meet market demands more effectively and deter the entry of competitor brands, while others suggest that companies should rationalize their brand portfolios in order to consolidate their market share and manage their overall resources more effectively (e.g., Brandão et al., 2020). Nevertheless, an overbranded portfolio can damage strategic brands, create diseconomies of scale and inefficiency, misdirected resources and poor brand equity (e.g., Aaker, 2004b).

'The changes we are making to our US portfolio are not easy, but we know we are taking the right steps to return Kellogg's to growth' (Kris Bahner, senior vice-president of global corporate affairs at Kellogg)

In 2019, Kellogg sold its biscuit business, including Keebler and Amos, to Ferrero for $1.3 billion to be able to focus on its cereals and snacks. According to the senior vice-president of global corporate affairs at Kellogg, this decision enabled the company to increase its financial flexibility through a better margin mix as well as a debt reduction. In Bahner's opinion, it is crucial to continually review Kellogg's portfolio for growth opportunities while focusing their attention on their iconic and beloved brands. For example, the company anticipated a growth potential in the snacking category such as RXBar protein bars, whose brand was acquired in October 2017 for a reported $600 million. Nevertheless, most important is that the portfolios are fit for purpose (Rogers, 2019).

BRAND ARCHITECTURE

Brand architecture is conceptualized as an 'organized structure of brand portfolio that specifies brand roles and the nature of relationships between brands' (Aaker & Joachimsthaler, 2000, p. 8). This theoretical construct has been investigated in different fields, ranging from the public sector (Leijerholt et al., 2019) to place branding (Freire, 2016; Zelenskaya & Elkanova, 2021), fashion (Rashid et al., 2024), tourism (Brandão et al., 2020), higher education (Spry et al., 2020; Zinkan, 2018), retailing (Esbjerg & Bech-Larsen, 2009), beverages (Muzellec & Lambkin, 2009) and financial services (Devlin et al., 2008). Scholars argue that a well-defined brand architecture strategy can provide an efficient roadmap for sustaining brands, by clarifying where they can go and how they can get there (Keller, 2013, 2015; Sarabia-Sanchez & Cerda-Bertomeu, 2017).

It should be stressed the choice of brand architecture typology entails different risks that should be accessed thoroughly (Hsu et al., 2016). Furthermore, Freire (2016) highlighted that the brand architecture should be accessed and readjusted continuously, since brands are living entities that are dynamic and face different challenges over time. This is especially relevant when the expansion of distribution channels has driven the acquisition of subsidiaries, resulting in the proliferation of brands under the same company umbrella (Rashid et al., 2024). For instance, UK fashion companies are currently leveraging multiple channels and engaging in rapid takeovers, creating significant challenges for managers. More specifically, the transition from brick-and-mortar stores to online channels can lead to a misalignment with the corporate brand identity. This often occurs when sub-brands, each with distinct brand identities, are created to target different market segments (Rashid et al., 2024). Recent studies also emphasize the importance of ensuring that corporate identity is deeply rooted in heritage and history, particularly through collaboration with internal stakeholders (Rashid et al., 2024). For example, when a wholesale brand with a premium identity adopts a branded house strategy, the retailer's products and services are unified under a common identity. This approach fosters the communication of strong core values (e.g., heritage, innovation and invention), making them visible and understandable to both internal and external stakeholders. Zelenskaya and Elkanova (2021) also investigated the brand architecture in the context of place branding, using St. Petersburg (Russia) as a case study. Their findings show that place brand architecture facilitates the design of a distinct system of sub-brands that are customer-oriented. Creating sub-brands increases the credibility of the place brand, but it is also associated with some challenges such as higher promotion expenditure and communication risks, as well as stakeholder misalignment (Zelenskaya & Elkanova, 2021).

'You can't scale when you have that many brands telling different stories' (Amie Stankiste, LSEG)

From 2021 to 2024, The London Stock Exchange Group (LSEG) has expanded rapidly, driven by acquisitions, especially through the purchase of financial market data provider Refinitiv in 2021. Shortly after, the management team realized that its business should be refined to strengthen its brand identity. According to the CMO Amie Stankiste, the new acquisitions 'became a completely new business' for the LSEG, creating confusion for both internal and external stakeholders, especially in relation to the make-up of their business. The problem became so complex that senior managers would have to spend the first half of stakeholder meetings clarifying the group composition. Internally, the LSEG experienced a lack of cohesion and unity among their brands, and many employees questioned the overall brand identity. Moreover, many brands were perceived as a barrier to growing consistently. When Amie Sankiste joined as CMO, the LSEG had over 20 brands 'telling different stories'. The main challenge was to redesign the brand architecture and ensure that the LSEG as a strong parent brand with six sub-brands beneath it would represent the specialist areas, which added the most value to their customers and stakeholders. After simplifying the brand architecture, the next step consisted of rebranding the entire organization from sales to marketing materials, as well as product interfaces and all the operational documents (Rashbass, 2024).

BRAND AUDIT METHODOLOGIES

Brand auditing is defined as 'a comprehensive, systematic, independent, and periodic examination of the brand. The purpose of a brand audit is to detect problem areas and opportunities, and to recommend a plan of action for the improvement of brand performance' (Baumgarth et al., 2016, p. 55).

Whereas the focus of brand audits is on the analysis and evaluation of brands, the brand portfolio audit accesses the contribution of each brand to the overall portfolio of brands owned or shared by a company (Brandão et al., 2020). As such, this strategic tool can be used by companies to prioritize some brands in their portfolio, to reallocate resources to areas of greater growth (Hill et al., 2005; Serota & Bhargava, 2010) and to merge, sell, milk or eliminate brands (Kumar, 2003).

Brand Portfolio Frameworks

Several brand portfolio frameworks have been proposed in the last three decades according to various definitions, but its application has not been tested in a business context (Brandão et al., 2020). Table 13.1 summarizes those brand audit methodologies, which mainly focus on the brand portfolio rationalization rather than its extension, and lack an analysis of brand interrelationships (Brandão et al., 2020).

Brand Architecture Frameworks

Scholars have proposed different brand architecture frameworks, which are summarized in Table 13.2. These frameworks are similar in their approach to relationships between brands and the (dis)advantages of each brand architecture strategy but differ in their terminology (Brandão et al., 2020). Despite these frameworks enabling structuring the brand portfolio in an organized manner, they lack detail in terms of how to redesign brands in a particular context.

Table 13.1 Brand portfolio frameworks between 2001 and 2008

Framework/Authors	*Description/Aim*	*Steps*
Brand portfolio molecule (Lederer and Hill, 2001)	Graphical representation of brand portfolios, in which brands are visually as atoms and clustered according to customer 'perceptions'	1. Inventory of brands (determine which brands should or should not be included in the portfolio, using market research, brainstorming and managers' knowledge); 2. Classification of brands (group brands as lead, strategic, support and measure its relative importance to purchase, influence on purchase, positioning, connections and degrees of control and 3. Mapping the portfolio molecule according to the current structure and organization of the brand portfolio.
Brand audit sheet (Kumar, 2003)	Includes financial dimensions to measure brand performance	1. List all the brands in the company's portfolio, their global market shares, annual sales and profits, and market positioning; 2. Evaluation of each brand's market position (dominant, strong, weak and not present); 3. Classification of the brand positioning (value, upscale, fun) and 4. Debate each brand cash status (cash generator, cash neutral and cash user).
Strategic brand consolidation process (Aaker, 2004a, 2004b)	Create a comprehensive and objective method to review systematically the strength and utility of brands in the portfolio to rationalize their composition	1. Identification of the relevant brand set (all brands and sub-brands); 2. Establishment of assessment criteria (brand equity, business strength, strategic fit and branding options); 3. Evaluation of brands, using the defined criteria and scores based on the market knowledge briefed by the marketing team; 4. Prioritization of the brands (strategic, power, flanker, silver bullet or cash cow); 5. Development of a revised brand portfolio strategy including the brand architecture strategy definition and 6. Migration of the strategy (abruptly or gradually to the targeted strategy).
Brand portfolio renewal framework (Hill et al., 2005)	Captures all the brand equity dimensions and prioritizes brands, thus allowing for corrective actions. Also includes a migration step of the brand portfolio strategy excluded from previous frameworks	1. Understanding the brand portfolio composition (owned and partner brands); 2. Assessment of brand contribution (annual revenues, direct marketing expenses and other benefits and costs) and ranking each brand (top third, middle third and bottom third); 3. Assessment of the market brand position of each brand including current market performance (brand traction) and future prospects (brand momentum); 4. Identification of problems and opportunities, forwarded by classification of brands (power, sleeper, slider, soldier, black hole, rocket, wallflower or discard brands) and 5. Development of the brand portfolio renewal plan (strategic options and recommendations for each brand and for the overall brand portfolio).
Five A's of brand metrics (Rajagopal, 2008)	Focuses on the evolution of individual brands within the brand portfolio. It includes a brand scorecard to make an overall analysis of brands	It includes the following: 1. Perception metrics (awareness and acquaintance such as customer preference, customer value and loyalty); 2. Financial metrics (market share, share trend, market demand, aggregate demand and demand elasticity) and 3. Performance metrics (association and allegiance such as brand revenue and investments on brands).

Source: Adapted from Brandão et al. (2020).

Table 13.2 Brand architecture frameworks between 1989 and 2000

Framework/Authors	*Description/Aim*	*Typology*
Corporate identity structure (Olins, 1989)	It introduces an identity visual system that is divided into three levels. This framework was criticized for its oversimplicity	1. Monolithic (one single name and visual identity); 2. Endorsed (corporate identity in visual association with subsidiary names) and 3. Branded (different names and appearance).
Brand architecture (Kapferer, 1992, 2008)	It introduces the concept of brand architecture based on six main strategies. Criticism was raised due to the subtle distinction between the proposed strategies	1. Umbrella brand (flexible umbrella: single brand that covers several product categories or Masterbrand: single brand with sub-brands with descriptive names); 2. Range brand (one brand for each brand and competence area); 3. Line brand (one brand for each line of products); 4. Source brand (products have their own name instead of generic names as in the umbrella brand); 5. Endorsing brand (acts as a guarantor of the endorsed one for example the maker's mark facilitating the producer recognition) and 6. Product brand (one brand and positioning for each product).
Brand hierarchy (Laforet & Saunders, 1994)	This framework was developed to capture the way brands organize their portfolio in a clearer manner. It includes three main levels	1. Corporate dominant such as corporate brands (corporate name) and house of brands (subsidiary's name); 2. Mixed brands including dual brands (two or more names given equal prominence) and endorsed brands (brands endorsed by corporate or house identity) and 3. Brand dominant including mono brands (single brand name) and furtive brands (single brand name and corporate identity undisclosed).
Brand relationship spectrum (Aaker & Joachimsthaler, 2000)	This framework adds the brand driver's role as a new concept in the brand architecture literature	It consists of four main strategic options to organize brand portfolios and is one of the most cited frameworks in the literature due to its holistic approach, clarity and applicability.

Source: Adapted from Brandão et al. (2020).

Overall, the above-mentioned frameworks lack detail, are considered excessively complex and have never been tested in a business context, which has hindered their application by brand auditors (Brandão et al., 2020).

Eight-step brand audit framework combining brand portfolio and brand architecture

Drawing on previous frameworks, Brandão et al. (2020) proposed a dynamic and holistic framework that combines the brand portfolio audit with brand architecture redesign. This eight-step framework was developed and tested in Douro Azul between September 2024 and March 2015. Douro Azul is a Portuguese company that, at the time of the audit, comprised a portfolio of nine service trademarks and other services such as river cruises, river and city sightseeing tours, helicopter tours, a restaurant, a theme park and other tourism-related services (Table 13.3). Between 2016 and 2017, this framework was tested in two other Portuguese service companies, namely, OneBiz (the biggest Portuguese service franchising group with 18 brands in different market segments) and Valente Lopes (a Portuguese industrial company with nine brands in different market segments).

The framework presents a dynamic approach to brand portfolio and architecture in competitive markets and is divided into two sections: the brand portfolio audit and brand architecture as described in Figure 13.1. It should be noted that the brand portfolio audit is designed to assess the entire brand portfolio of a specific company. Consequently, each brand is not evaluated individually but in a holistic manner. In other words, the main aim is to assess brands within a specific portfolio and make comparisons between those brands.

The first section of the proposed framework – brand portfolio audit – contains four steps that will be described in detail in the following paragraphs:

Table 13.3 DouroAzul brand portfolio at the time of brand audit

Brands	*Business Segment*
DouroAzul	Luxury river cruises in hotel-ships and yacht
Helitours	Helicopter tours
Caminho das Estrelas	Space tourism
Mystic Cruises	International luxury river cruises in hotel-ships
Welcome Tourism Center	
BlueBus	Bus sightseeing tours
BlueBoats	River sightseeing tours
DouroAzul – Agencia de Viagens	Travel agency – to be launched
World of Discoveries	Interactive museum and theme park
Mundo dos Sabores	Theme restaurant of World of Discoveries
Trafaria Praia	Artwork and river sightseeing tours
Monumental Palace Hotel	Luxury Hotel – to be launched
Douro Marina Hotel	Heath tourism hotel – to be launched

Source: Adapted from Brandão et al. (2020).

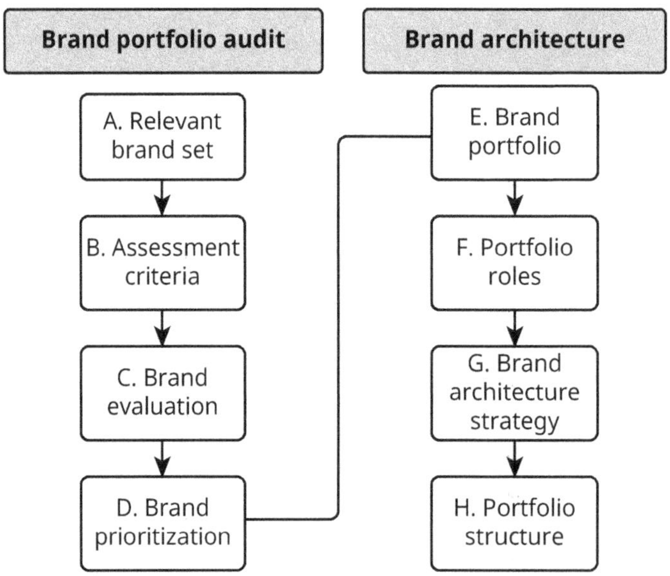

Figure 13.1 Theoretical framework

Source: Brandão et al. (2020).

1. relevant brand set,
2. assessment criteria,
3. brand evaluation and
4. brand prioritization.

According to Brandão et al. (2020), practitioners should start by evaluating the relevant brand set. After defining the selection criteria (e.g., sales contribution to the portfolio, launch year or number of employees working with a specific brand), the auditor should list all the company's brands, as well as sub-brands and co-brands. It is suggested that the auditor should start by meeting with the legal department followed by an analysis of how brands are promoted (e.g., website, reports and advertisements, among others). This first step should be concluded by determining which brands respect and conform to the predefined criteria before deciding on the relevant brand set. More precisely, the relevant brand set could include the following:

a. brands that are owned or managed by company itself;
b. brands currently in operation or communicated by the company to the market and
c. brands with recorded sales in the last year.

A brand audit scorecard should be used to conduct the brand portfolio audit (Figure 13.2). As stated by Brandão et al. (2020), the scorecard is a practical and simple tool that helps brand managers

	Assessment criteria	Weight	Brand score (1–7)						
			DouroAzul	World of discoveries	BlueBoats	BlueBus	Helitours	Trafaria praia	Caminho das Estrelas
Brand equity		**25**							
	Awareness	7							
	Reputation	5							
	Differentiation	4							
	Relevance	5							
	Loyalty	4							
Brand contribution		**60**							
Business strength	Sales contribution	10							
Business strength	Profit contribution	9							
Business strength	Current growth	7							
Business strength	Projected growth	6							
Business strength	Current market position	5							
Business strength	Projected market position	3							
Hidden costs	Senior management time sink	2							
Hidden costs	Number of employees	5							
Hidden costs	Customer complaints	3							
Hidden benefits	Network/partnerships	2							
Hidden benefits	Current cross-selling options	3							
Hidden benefits	Potential cross-selling options	5							
Strategic options		**15**							
	Extendibility	5							
	Business fit	5							
	Band equity transferability	2							
	Potential to merge	3							
Total sum		**100**							
Brand prioritization		**-**							

Figure 13.2 Brand audit scorecard

Source: Brandão et al. (2020).

to record and score the assessment criteria during the brand portfolio audit. This data-collection instrument includes both supply and demand-side measures and facilitates the measurement of brand prioritization in the overall context of brand portfolio audit.

Based on the predefined brand audit criteria, the auditor should select the brands that are part of the relevant brand set according to the size of the company and the segment in which they operate. For example, for small tech startups, auditors might select brands that are innovative and have a strong social media presence. In mid-sized retail companies, the focus could be on brands with high customer loyalty and consistent sales performance. For financial institutions, auditors might select brands with a strong reputation and high compliance standards. Lastly, in multinational companies, the selection could include brands with significant global presence and strong sustainability initiatives. By using these criteria, auditors can ensure that they focus on the most relevant and impactful brands for each company's unique market position.

The second step of the brand portfolio audit consists of defining the criteria that the auditor should analyze in order to compare the brands listed in the relevant brand set. This step is called assessment criteria.

It is proposed that the auditor should start by defining the specific criteria within three dimensions:

a. brand equity (measuring the brands from a market perspective);
b. brand contribution to the overall portfolio and
c. the strategic options for each brand.

In this process, the auditor should consider the available data and the audit goals. Secondly, during the criteria evaluation, the auditor should weight each criterion by considering its relative importance to the analysis, as well as the data accuracy. An important aspect to consider is that the criterion weights are case-dependent and there is no ideal distribution. Preferably, the weights' total should equal 100 points to facilitate the result comparisons. To operationalize this second step, the auditor can conduct interviews with mid- and top-level managers so as to identify the criteria for inclusion in the relevant brand set. Additionally, the auditor should distribute, for each brand, 100 points among brand equity, brand contribution to the overall portfolio and strategic options. This distribution should consider the analysis of the brand portfolio, supported by the interviews with managers and the market information on the chosen brands. For example, 25 points might be attributed to the brand equity dimension, whereas 60 points might be given to the brand contribution dimension and 15 points to the strategic options (see the Douro Azul case study for more details).

It worth noting that the brand equity dimension is linked to the level of demand and market assessment of brands. Therefore, the auditor should identify the key criteria for each brand and weight them in relation to the informants' intents and the brand portfolio specifications:

a. brand awareness: if the audited brand is well known in the marketplace;
b. brand reputation: if the audited brand is highly regarded and has high perceived quality in the marketplace;
c. brand differentiation: if the audited brand has a particular personality and points of differentiation in the marketplace;
d. brand relevance: if the audited brand is relevant in the marketplace and
e. brand loyalty: if the customers exhibit loyalty to the audited brand.

For example, when auditing the Douro Azul brand, the auditor considered the contribution of the brand to the overall portfolio as the most relevant part of the brand audit. Hence, 60 points were divided as follows:

a. business strength (40 points): financial and business performance of the audited brands;
b. hidden costs (10 points): costs that do not impact explicitly on the business performance but might negatively influence the overall brand portfolio and
c. hidden benefits (10 points): costs that do not impact explicitly on business performance but might positively influence the overall brand portfolio.

It should be noted that in this example, six different criteria were defined by the auditor so as to access the brand strength. More specifically, the auditor selected sales contribution, profit contribution, current growth, projected growth, market position and projected market position. Nevertheless, the weighting choice was dependent on the accuracy of the data collected by the auditor and its relative importance to the overall analysis. In the Douro Azul example, the auditor attributed the highest score to the sales contribution instead of the projected market position. As far as the hidden costs category is concerned, the auditor selected three criteria, namely, senior management time sink, number of employees and customer complaints. Lastly, three criteria were chosen for the hidden benefits, that is, network/partnerships, current cross-selling options and potential cross-selling options. All the chosen weights were calculated from the relative importance of each criterion within its specific category. Regarding the strategic options' dimension of the brand audit scorecard, the auditor of Douro Azul defined four criteria:

a. extendibility: if the audited brand stretches to other products/services (master brand or endorser);
b. business fit: if the audited brand is part of a business that conforms to the company's strategic orientation;
c. brand equity transferability: if the brand equity of the audited brand could be transferred to another brand within the portfolio (as a sub-brand or by developing a descriptor) and
d. potential to merge: if the audited brand could be aggregated with other brands in the portfolio to create one unified brand.

In the DouroAzul example, the auditor distributed the strategic options' weights based on the company's strategy at the time of the audit, with the highest weights allocated to extendibility and business fit. However, each company's strategic options' weights should be tailored to its specific industry and strategic goals. For instance, technology companies may prioritize extendibility to new tech products and services, while retailers may focus on new product lines. Additionally, each company ensures business fits with their specific strategy, leverages brand equity transferability differently and considers merging brands for a unified presence according to their overall strategy. Therefore, the auditor's challenge is to weight these strategic options by considering each company's characteristics within specific segments. This approach ensures that the audit aligns with the company's unique strategic priorities and industry context.

After completing the scoring of the assessment criteria, the auditor should evaluate the relative importance that informants place on the demand-side perspective (brand awareness) versus the supply-side perspective (sales). This involves understanding how much value participants assign to each perspective. For example, in the health and wellness sector, brand awareness may be seen as more important than sales, since consumers make decisions based on recognition and trust, whereas in the fast-moving consumer goods (FMCG) sector, sales are often prioritized over brand awareness because the focus is on driving high-volume transactions. Following this internal analysis, the auditor should assign higher scores to the perspective that is valued most by the participants. Specifically, if brand awareness is deemed more critical than sales, it should receive a higher weighting. In some cases, brand loyalty might be a less significant source of equity than brand awareness. Therefore, more points should be attributed to brand awareness if it is identified as a key driver of brand equity. This approach ensures that the audit reflects the true perceptions of the informants, leading to a more accurate and relevant assessment of criteria.

Lastly, a comprehensive analysis of the brand audit scorecard reveals the ranking of each brand within the portfolio across three key dimensions: brand equity, contribution to the overall portfolio and strategic options. This ranking provides a clear picture of how each brand performs in terms of its market strength, its value to the company's portfolio and its strategic potential. By evaluating these dimensions, the audit helps identifying which brands are leading, which need improvement and how they align with the company's strategic goals.

The third step of the brand portfolio audit relates to the brand evaluation. To operationalize this step, it is advisable to use diversified sources such as group annual reports, internal financial databases, organizational charts, corporate and brand brochures, corporate presentations, business press, websites and social media. Firstly, the auditor can survey a sample of employees from various management levels. The questionnaires can be distributed by the auditor within a specific timeframe, and a standardized scale can be used to assess the brand equity dimension to ensure consistency in the brand audit scorecard. Secondly, the auditor can use annual reports, internal financial databases, organizational charts, brochures, presentations, business press, websites and social media to measure business strength. This primary data ensure both validity and accuracy. Moreover, to analyze sales contribution, the auditor can use the average share of sales for each brand over the past 3 years. EBITDA can be used instead of sales volume to differentiate profit contribution from sales contribution. The auditor can also analyze current growth using the sales compound annual growth rate (CAGR) for a specific period and projected future growth using the same metric for the upcoming years. Finally, the current market position can be measured using the relative market share of each brand for a given period, while the projected market position can be estimated on the basis of expected relative market share for a future period. The sales data can be collected directly from the relevant department and converted using a standardized scale for the business strength section of the brand audit scorecard. The highest contributing brand should receive the maximum points, whereas other brands will score relative to their contribution. Additionally, custom score scales can be created for the remaining business strength criteria.

Overall, it is recommended that the data collected from multiple sources be converted to a seven-point scale (or any other suitable scale) to quantify the data and compare the audited brands. Moreover, auditors are advised to use market research to access brand equity, given that the aim is to capture the marketing perspective. If this is not possible, auditors should send surveys to the brand team and other staff members. Lastly, the brand contribution dimension can be assessed through archives and company databases to capture the internal dimension of the audited brands.

The fourth and final step of the brand portfolio audit relates to brand prioritization. This step consists of weighting the scores of each audited brand by using each criterion weight and the score of the given brand. Hence, the brand with the highest weight is the top brand in the prioritization category, whereas the lowest weight will identify the bottom brand. In most cases, the brand with the highest score is the portfolio anchor brand. This top position might be justified by factors such as brand heritage (being the oldest brand in the portfolio), market leadership in its segment, sales leadership (contributing a significant portion of overall sales revenue) and positive brand associations with well-known celebrities.

A detailed analysis of the brand equity and brand contribution dimensions might reveal that brand equity scores are similar for several brands. Additionally, some brands have higher brand contribution scores than their brand equity rankings. The audit might also show that brands with lower brand equity scores may show higher contributions to the portfolio, suggesting greater brand potential. Conversely, some brands may score high in brand equity but low in brand contributions. This might indicate that investments in these brands have not translated into proportional contributions to the overall portfolio, as shown by their lower scores in the strategic options' dimension.

Another relevant aspect to analyze is the relationship between business fit, brand awareness, brand contribution and the final ranking of audited brands. Research findings indicate that brands with the highest business fit scores also score high in the awareness dimension. This can be attributed to the greater allocation of financial and marketing resources by top managers to brands that have a stronger business fit within the portfolio. Consequently, these brands are likely to achieve higher levels of brand awareness, which may lead to higher brand contribution and prioritization scores in the brand audit scorecard. It is worth noting that sometimes top- and mid-level managers may underestimate the potential of some brands, despite their being well classified in the brand audit scorecard. This misperception could negatively impact the allocation of financial and marketing resources for cross-selling and communication efforts for that brand.

After concluding the brand portfolio audit, Brandão et al. (2020) suggest revising the brand architecture strategy, which includes four main steps:

a. brand portfolio;
b. portfolio roles;
c. brand architecture strategy and
d. portfolio structure.

The first step in the brand architecture redesign relates to the Brand Portfolio. Contrary to the brand audit phase, which focuses on a relevant set of brands using specific evaluation criteria, the brand architecture analysis and its redesign are based on the overall brand portfolio. Hence, the brand portfolio should include those brands that are owned or just managed (e.g., external or co-brands) by the audited company and are important for the consumer-buying decision process. For example, Coca-Cola's portfolio includes brands such as Fanta, Innocent and Vitaminwater, as well as co-brands like Diet Coke or acquired brands, such as Costa Coffee. In this regard, it is advisable that the auditor designates a shared principle (e.g., industry or sector where the company operates) to select the brands to include its overall portfolio. To facilitate easier identification, each segment is assigned a different color.

The second step in the brand architecture redesign relates to portfolio roles. It is argued that the definition of those roles is crucial to planning the allocation of resources by the management teams, as well as to understanding the brand portfolio's composition. There are two potential approaches to defining the roles in the brand portfolio: one consists of classifying the portfolio brands as strategic, branded energizer, silver bullet brand, flanker brand or cash cow brand (Aaker, 2004a, 2004b; cited by Brandão et al., 2020); and the other one relates to the Boston Consulting Group (BCG) matrix methodology that classifies brands as question mark, star, cash cow or dog, depending on the brands' relative market share and growth rate (Johnson et al., 2008; cited by Brandão et al., 2020). For instance, Apple might classify its iPhone as a star due to its high market share and strong growth rate in the smartphone industry. Meanwhile, iTunes could be considered a cash cow, as it holds a large share of a mature market with steady, reliable revenue but limited growth potential. Apple TV could be labeled a question mark, as it has potential but still struggles to achieve a dominant market position in the highly competitive streaming industry. The auditor can add the sales volume of each audited brand as an additional dimension to the traditional methodology. The new dimension should be represented by the size of bubbles in the BCG matrix. Furthermore, the company's archives can be used as extra data to complete the BCG matrix in order to better categorize the audited brands. The matrix acts a visualization of brand portfolio, showing its diversification and which brand is the most powerful one that drives the company's business.

The third step in the brand architecture redesign relates to the brand architecture strategy. The first stage consists of the analysis of the current brand architecture strategy using several data sources to obtain a deeper understanding of the organization and its brands as proposed by Aaker and Joachimsthaler (2000). For situations in which the company does not have a formal structure of its brand portfolio, participant observation is considered the most effective way to collect information.

Sometimes, a brand audit reveals internal disagreements and confusion among staff regarding the current brand architecture. Employees may fail to recognize certain brand logos or mistakenly include discontinued brands in the portfolio, reflecting a lack of clarity. This often stems from companies using inconsistent and different designations for different products and services, with limited connection to the overarching corporate brand. Additionally, many companies implement hybrid brand architecture strategies, applying different approaches to various brand types, which can create further confusion. As a result, the brand architecture becomes ambiguous, leaving staff uncertain about the brand's structure and strategic direction. This issue typically arises from the absence of a cohesive, strategic approach to the brand architecture, causing the company to miss out on its full potential and benefits, as shown during the audit to DouroAzul (Brandão et al., 2020).

To resolve this unclarity, brand auditors can analyze the company's archives such as brand brochures, press releases and organizational charts, among many other communication materials. More specifically, the auditor can use interviews to investigate staff perceptions of the ideal portfolio organization as well as brand interrelationships. From a methodological perspective, informants can be shown different logos of existing brands, future brands or projects, extinct brands, companies that were not related to brands and external brands. The auditor should actively mix the logos in order to assess whether the informants were able to easily identify the brands included in the brand portfolio. Furthermore, the auditor should ask the participants to design the ideal portfolio structure using the given logos and to show the brand interrelationships. To conclude this stage, the auditor should revise the current brand architecture and propose the most suitable strategy for the brand portfolio.

The fourth and last step of the brand architecture redesign relates to the Portfolio Structure. As the name suggests, the portfolio structure is the visible outcome of all previous steps. Before designing the portfolio structure, it is advisable for the auditor to start by identifying the product-defining roles (Aaker, 2004a, 2004b; cited by Brandão et al., 2020). Afterward, the portfolio structure redesign can be done using brand networks or brand hierarchy trees so that all the brand interrelationships are correctly represented. For example, the auditor of DouroAzul proposed a revised brand architecture in which DouroAzul remains the corporate brand (internally and externally), since DouroAzul scored high in all three dimensions of the brand portfolio audit scorecard. Secondly, five segments were included in the portfolio structure, namely, Space, Cruises, Hotels, Sightseeing and Attractions. Yet, the brand DouroAzul – Agencia de Viagens was not added to the five segments, since the brand is transversal to them. Lastly, the auditor proposed a revised brand architecture as follows:

a. master band as driver strategy (DouroAzul – Agencia de Viagens);
b. House of brands – not connected (Caminho das Estrelas, Monumental Palace Hotel, Douro Marina Hotel and World of Discoveries) and
c. House of brands – Shadow endorser (Mystic Cruises, BlueTours, Helitours); endorsed brands – strong endorsement (Trafaria Praia and Mundo dos Sabores) and endorsed brands – token endorsement (Welcome Tourist and Business Center).

It should be stressed that the revised brand architecture strategy is context-dependent and can vary significantly across different companies and sectors. For some businesses, a branded house strategy, where the corporate brand dominates and drives the identity of all sub-brands, may be the most beneficial. For instance, Virgin exemplifies this approach, with Virgin Atlantic, Virgin Books and Virgin Hotels all aligned under the same core brand. However, in other cases, particularly in industries with diverse consumer segments or distinct product categories, a house of brands strategy may be more advantageous. Procter & Gamble (P&G) employs this brand architecture, where brands such as Ariel, Pampers and Gillette operate independently without overt ties to the corporate brand. This approach allows P&G to target specific market needs, ensuring that each brand maintains its unique identity, which is crucial in the highly competitive FMCG sector. For companies operating in industries that require both differentiation and credibility, an endorsed brand strategy might be more effective. Marriott Hotels, for example, uses this strategy with sub-brands like Courtyard by Marriott and Springhill Suites by Marriot, which are individually branded but benefit from the credibility and trust associated with the Marriott name. Similarly, Nestlé applies this approach with brands like Nescafé and Nestlé Crunch, where the parent brand adds credibility, but the sub-brands retain independent identities. This brand architecture works particularly well when there is a need to balance the equity of the parent brand with the distinct positioning of individual products or services.

In some cases, companies may find a hybrid brand strategy to be the most flexible and effective. Coca-Cola follows this approach by using a branded house for its flagship product Coca-Cola, while managing independent brands like Minute Maid and Powerade under a house of brands strategy. This hybrid brand architecture allows Coca-Cola to retain a unified global identity while also catering to diverse consumer preferences in different beverage categories.

For companies in the tech sector, a branded house model is often more beneficial, as a strong, unified brand can help reinforce brand equity. Apple effectively uses this strategy with its products such as iPhone, iPad and MacBook, all closely tied to the Apple brand, creating a cohesive and compelling consumer experience. On the other hand, in industries like motorcycles, a house of brands model might be more effective. Honda uses this strategy by maintaining separate identities for its automotive brand and its motorcycle brands (e.g., Yamaha and Kawasaki), allowing for specialization in different product categories.

In conclusion, the choice of brand architecture strategy is highly context-dependent, influenced by factors such as industry dynamics, market trends and the specific objectives of the business. Both the brand relationship spectrum and the product-defining roles framework offer valuable perspectives, but they focus on different dimensions of brand portfolio management. The brand relationship spectrum helps determine the structural organization of a brand portfolio, guiding whether a company should unify its brands under a single parent brand (branded house) or maintain distinct, independent identities (house of brands). In contrast, the product-defining roles framework provides insight into the strategic positioning of individual brands, categorizing brands according to their role in the portfolio.

Ultimately, the decision to use one framework or combine both depends on the company's strategic goals and the nature of its brand portfolio. The brand relationship spectrum is particularly valuable when deciding how tightly or loosely connected different brands should be within the company's brand portfolio. On the other hand, the product-defining roles framework focuses more on determining the specific role played by each brand in maximizing the overall brand portfolio performance. By understanding the strengths of each framework, companies can design a more cohesive, effective brand architecture that aligns with their broader business objectives, optimizes market positioning and meets consumer needs.

CONCLUSION

Auditing brand portfolios on a regular and detailed basis and redesigning the brand architecture is crucial for companies so as to remain relevant in a highly competitive market. The brand audit framework proposed by Brandão et al. (2020) allows marketeers to use a diagnosis tool to perform a comprehensive, systematic, periodic and independent examination of brands within a company. It also considers the growing need to combine both supply- and demand-side measures of brands, something not incorporated in previous frameworks. This dual assessment is necessary to aligning the portfolio strategy with the business objectives and consumer perceptions (Brandão et al., 2020; Nguyen et al., 2018; Uggla, 2015). In addition, the proposed brand audit score facilitates brand portfolio audits. Moreover, this framework combines for the first time, two dimensions (brand portfolio and brand architecture), allowing auditors to rely on a more dynamic and holistic assessment of the brand portfolio. Hence, it enables companies to make strategic decisions on their brand portfolio and to redesign their brand architecture more effectively (Brandão et al., 2020). Lastly, this framework has been applied and tested in real business settings, more precisely in three B2B and B2C Portuguese companies. The findings demonstrate that the framework is flexible and applicable to several types of companies from different sectors and sizes.

Suggestions for Future Research

Suggestions for future research could include exploring the impact of digital technologies on how brands systematically collect information related to their brand portfolio. For instance, integrating big data and machine learning algorithms could provide deeper insights into brand performance, enabling brand managers to make more informed and strategic decisions. According to the resource-based view theory, the adoption of innovative resources within companies is crucial in rapidly evolving business environments and can create competitive advantages (Han et al., 2025). Nevertheless, little is known on how brand managers can integrate big data and machine learning algorithms into brand portfolio audits. Hence, some potential research questions arise:

RQ1: What are the challenges and opportunities in adopting big data and machine learning algorithms in brand portfolio management?

RQ2: How do brand managers with different resource capabilities use big data analytics and machine learning algorithms in brand audits, and what is its impact on brand portfolio and brand architecture?

Another promising area of research is that of examining the role of artificial intelligence (AI) in optimizing brand architecture design. AI has the potential to revolutionize brand management by offering predictive analytics and automated brand management processes, leading to more agile and responsive changes in brand portfolios and brand architecture. Despite the perceived ease of use of AI, its adoption also raises important issues related to virtual moral agency (Coeckelbergh, 2009) in brand management. Hence, another potential research question could be:

RQ3: How can ethical concerns be mitigated when AI is used to audit brand portfolios and redesign brand architecture?

Additionally, future research could focus on incorporating cultural nuances into brand audits to account for how cultural differences impact brand perceptions. In the light of cultural identity theory, individuals with a particular culture acknowledge and connect with key elements that distinguish their culture from others (Clark, 1990). As such, pertinent research questions could investigate:

RQ5: In what ways can brand audits be adjusted to account for cultural nuances and what tools should be developed to assist brand auditors?

Lastly, examining the practical challenges and best practices in implementing the brand audit score across various industries and organizational contexts would be beneficial. This research could identify potential barriers to adoption and offer solutions to enhance the framework's applicability and effectiveness in different business environments. Investigating these practical challenges and identifying different metrics could lead to frameworks that successfully integrate brand audits into diverse organizational settings, thus making the brand audit score more applicable and effective across different contexts. Accordingly, additional research questions could further investigate:

RQ6: What are the key barriers to the adoption and implementation of the brand audit score across various types of companies?

REFERENCES

Aaker, D. A. (2004a). *Brand portfolio strategy: Creating relevance, differentiation, energy, leverage, and clarity*. Free Press.

Aaker, D. A. (2004b). Even brands need spring cleaning. *Brandweek*, *45*(10), 36–40.

Aaker, D. A., & Joachimsthaler, E. (2000). The brand relationship spectrum: The key to the brand architecture challenge. *California Management Review*, *42*(4), 8–23. https://doi.org/10.2307/41166051

Baumgarth, C., Kaluza, M., & Lohrisch, N. (2016). Brand audit for cultural institutions (BAC): A validated and holistic brand controlling tool. *International Journal of Arts Management*, *19*(1), 54–68.

Brandão, A., Sousa, J. C. C., & Rodrigues, C. (2020). A dynamic approach to brand portfolio audit and brand architecture strategy. *European Business Review*, *32*(2), 181–210. https://doi.org/10.1108/EBR-12-2018-0206

Chailan, C. (2009). Brand architecture and brands portfolio: A clarification. *EuroMed Journal of Business*, *4*(2), 173–184. https://doi.org/10.1108/14502190910976529

Clark, T. (1990). International marketing and national character: A review and proposal for an integrative theory. *Journal of Marketing*, *54*(4), 66–79. https://doi.org/10.1177/002224299005400406

Coeckelbergh, M. (2009). Virtual moral agency, virtual moral responsibility: On the moral significance of the appearance, perception, and performance of artificial agents. *AI and Society*, *24*(2), 181–189. https://doi.org/10.1007/s00146-009-0208-3

DelVecchio, D. (2000). Moving beyond fit: The role of brand portfolio characteristics in consumer evaluations of brand reliability. *The Journal of Product and Brand Management*, *9*(7), 457–471. https://doi.org/10.1108/10610420010351411

Devlin, J. F., McKechnie, S., de Chernatony, L., Christodoulides, G., Abimbola, T., & Roper, S. (2008). Consumer perceptions of brand architecture in financial services. *European Journal of Marketing*, *42*(5/6), 654–666. https://doi.org/10.1108/03090560810862561

Esbjerg, L., & Bech-Larsen, T. (2009). The brand architecture of grocery retailers: Setting material and symbolic boundaries for consumer choice. *Journal of Retailing and Consumer Services*, *16*(5), 414–423. https://doi.org/10.1016/j.jretconser.2009.06.002

Fang, X., & Wang, X. (2018). Examining consumer responses to cross-border brand acquisitions. *European Journal of Marketing*, *52*(7/8), 1727–1749. https://doi.org/10.1108/EJM-04-2016-0200

Freire, J. R. (2016). Managing destination brand architecture—The case of Cascais municipality. *Place Branding and Public Diplomacy*, *12*(1), 78–90. https://doi.org/10.1057/pb.2015.23

Han, W., Weijie, Z., Zhaoli, S., & Ruoyu, L. (2025). Innovative resources driven artificial intelligence orientation: The moderating role of environmental and executives' characteristics. *Technology in Society*, *81*, 102837. https://doi.org/10.1016/j.techsoc.2025.102837

Hill, S., Ettenson, R., & Tyson, D. (2005). Achieving the ideal brand portfolio. *Sloan Management Review*, *46*(2), 85–90.

Hsu, L., Fournier, S., & Srinivasan, S. (2016). Brand architecture strategy and rm value: How leveraging, separating, and distancing the corporate brand affects risk and returns. *Journal of the Academy of Marketing Science*, *44*(2), 261–280. https://doi.org/10.1007/s11747-014-0422-5

Johnson, G., Scholes, K., & Whittington, R. (2008). *Exploring corporate strategy* (8th ed.). Financial Times Prentice Hall.Kapferer, J. N. (1992). *Strategic brand management: New approaches to creating and evaluating brand equity*. Kogan Page.

Kapferer, J. N. (2008). *The new strategic brand management*. Kogan Page.

Katsanis, L. P., Williams, A., & Srirangan, K. (2023). Is your company competent, interpersonal or community focused? The effect of values and brand portfolio on company reputation. *International Journal of Pharmaceutical and Healthcare Marketing*, *17*(4), 585–608. https://doi.org/10.1108/IJPHM-11-2021-0106

Keller, K. L. (2013). *Strategic brand management: Building, measuring, and managing brand equity* (4th ed.). Pearson Education.

Keller, K. L. (2015). Designing and implementing brand architecture strategies. *Journal of Brand Management*, *21*(9), 1–14. https://doi.org/10.1057/bm.2014.38

Kumar, N. (2003). Kill a brand, keep a customer. *Harvard Business Review*, *81*(12), 86–95.

Laforet, S. (2017). Effects of organisational culture on brand portfolio performance. *Journal of Marketing Communications*, *23*(1), 92–110. https://doi.org/10.1080/13527266.2014.956230

Laforet, S., & Saunders, J. (1994). Managing brand portfolios: How the leaders do it. *Journal of Advertising Research*, *34*(5), 64–77. https://doi.org/10.1080/00218499.1994.12466972

Laforet, S., & Saunders, J. (2005). Managing brand portfolios: How strategies have changed. *Journal of Advertising Research*, *45*(3), 314–327. https://doi.org/10.1017/S0021849905050397

Lederer, C., & Hill, S. (2001). See your brands through your customers' eyes. *Harvard Business Review*, *79*(6), 125.

Leijerholt, U., Chapleo, C., & O'Sullivan, H. (2019). A brand within a brand: An integrated understanding of internal brand management and brand architecture in the public sector. *The Journal of Brand Management*, *26*(3), 277–290. https://doi.org/10.1057/s41262-018-0128-y

Louro, M. J., & Cunha, P. V. (2001). Brand management paradigms. *Journal of Marketing Management*, *17*(7/8), 849–875. https://doi.org/10.1362/026725701323366845

Muzellec, L., & Lambkin, M. C. (2009). Corporate branding and brand architecture: A conceptual framework. *Marketing Theory*, *9*(1), 39–54. https://doi.org/10.1177/1470593108100060

Nguyen, H. T., Zhang, Y., & Calantone, R. J. (2018). Brand portfolio coherence: Scale development and empirical demonstration. *International Journal of Research in Marketing*, *35*(1), 60–80. https://doi.org/10.1016/j.ijresmar.2017.11.003

Olins, W. (1989), *Corporate identity: Making business strategy visible through design*. Thames and Hudson.

Petromilli, M., Morrison, D., & Million, M. (2002). Brand architecture: Building brand portfolio value. *Strategy and Leadership*, *30*(5), 22–28. https://doi.org/10.1108/10878570210442524

Rajagopal. (2008). Measuring brand performance through metrics application. *Measuring Business Excellence*, *12*(1), 29–38. https://doi.org/10.1108/13683040810864369

Rashbass, H. (2024, October 18). *'We needed to simplify the story': How one B2B business rebranded after multiple acquisitions.* Marketingweek. Retrieved October 30, 2024, from www.marketingweek.com/portfolio-fit-for-purpose/

Rashid, A., Spry, L., & Pich, C. (2024). A proposed brand architecture model for UK fashion brands.

The Journal of Brand Management, *31*(5), 516–528. https://doi.org/10.1057/s41262-024-00358-9

Rogers, C. (2019, June 26). *Is your brand portfolio fit for purpose? Marketing week*. Retrieved September 30, 2024, from www.marketingweek.com/portfolio-fit-for-purpose/

Sarabia-Sanchez, F. J., & Cerda-Bertomeu, M. J. (2017). Place brand developers' perceptions of brand identity, brand architecture and neutrality in place brand development. *Place Branding and Public Diplomacy*, *13*(1), 51–64. https://doi.org/10.1057/s41254-016-0017-7

Serota, K., & Bhargava, M. (2010). Brand-usage networks: A demand side approach to brand architecture. *Journal of Strategic Marketing*, *18*(6), 451–471. https://doi.org/10.1080/0965254X.2010.525248

Shah, P. (2015). Kill it or keep it? The weak brand retain-or-discard decision in brand portfolio management. *Journal of Brand Management*, *22*(2), 154–172. https://doi.org/10.1057/bm.2015.11

Spry, L., Foster, C., Pich, C., & Peart, S. (2020). Managing higher education brands with an emerging brand architecture: The role of shared values and competing brand identities. *Journal of Strategic Marketing*, *28*(4), 336–349. https://doi.org/10.1080/0965254X.2018.1501412

Strebinger, A. (2004). Strategic brand concept and brand architecture strategy—A proposed model. *Advances in Consumer Research*, *31*(1), 656–661.

Uggla, H. (2015). Aligning brand portfolio strategy with business strategy. *IUP Journal of Brand Management*, *12*(3), 8–17.

Uggla, H., & Filipsson, D. (2009). Business and brand strategy: A framework for integration. *ICFAI Journal of Business Strategy*, *6*(2), 27–42.

Varadarajan, R. (2006). Brand portfolio, corporate image, and reputation: Managing brand deletions. *Journal of the Academy of Marketing Science*, *34*(2), 195–205. https://doi.org/10.1177/0092070305284988

Zelenskaya, E., & Elkanova, E. (2021). Designing place brand architecture: The potential of a sub-brands strategy. *The Journal of Product and Brand Management*, *30*(1), 167–179. https://doi.org/10.1108/JPBM-08-2019-2551

Zinkan, R. (2018). Brand architecture in higher education. *Journal of Brand Strategy*, *7*(1), 84–91. https://doi.org/10.69554/EDGU1772

14

'What's in a Name?' A Discourse on Brand Naming

Sunny Vijay Arora, Arti D. Kalro, and Dinesh Sharma

The American Marketing Association defines a brand as 'any distinctive feature like a name, term, design, or symbol, that identifies goods or services'.[1] A brand name, as a key element of branding, can convey valuable information about a brand (Klink, 2003; Klink & Wu, 2014). It can also effectively signal unobservable qualities (Rao et al., 1999) and help boost consumer awareness and favorable impressions of a product (Aaker & Keller, 1990). According to Aaker (2009), greater brand awareness contributes to stronger brand equity, meaning that a well-chosen brand name can enhance both awareness and equity. Gardner and Levy (1955) argued that a brand name goes beyond merely being a label – it reflects the ideas and attributes associated with an organization's products, aiding consumers in making choices (Davcik et al., 2015; Gardner & Levy, 1955).

The need for new product names is just as vital for brand managers as it is for advancing the literature on brand naming. Over the past decade, the rise of direct-to-consumer (D2C) brands has been remarkable. E-commerce sales by direct-to-consumer brands increased from USD 76.57 billion in 2019 to an estimated USD 212.9 billion in the USA alone.[2] These brands often introduce numerous product lines, all requiring fresh names. Hence, industry professionals today recognize the importance of a structured approach to naming products, as this task has become increasingly difficult. Due to information overload and shorter consumer attention spans, creating new product names has become more challenging (Arora et al., 2015). Not all brands have a long-standing heritage (Wiedmann et al., 2011), meaning a random name may not necessarily be effective.

As the penetration of the Internet grows, challenges like trademark disputes arise, and there is an increased need for new web names. These web addresses, or top-level domain names, include suffixes such as .com, .org and .net, with new ones such as .hitachi and .paris likely to emerge in the future (Crovitz, 2012).

To capture consumer attention, managers often employ creative strategies for brand naming. For example, PUMA recently launched a campaign in India, temporarily rebranding itself as PVMA,

[1] American Marketing Association. Branding. Retrieved March 19, 2025, from www.ama.org/topics/brand-and-branding/

[2] eMarketer (@eMarketer). (August 10, 2022). Direct-to-consumer (D2C) e-commerce sales in the United States from 2019 to 2024 (in billion U.S. dollars) [Graph]. In *Statista*. Retrieved December 05, 2024, from www-statista-com-spjimrlibrary.knimbus.com/statistics/1109833/usa-d2c-ecommerce-sales/

honoring the badminton superstar and two-time Olympic medalist, PV Sindhu (TOI Lifestyle Desk, 2025). However, creating new brand names could also lead to complications. For instance, Ben & Jerry's faced backlash for naming one of its ice cream flavors as 'Hazed & Confused', which was interpreted by some people as a reference to a negative 'hazing' tradition at an American university (Stanford, 2014). Additionally, some brands fail because of their name choices, such as Ford's infamous, Edsel (Haig, 2005). Brand naming is both an art and a science; brand managers need not only creativity but also a structured approach to naming or renaming their brands.

This chapter aims to synthesize early discussions and narratives on brand naming in the literature and integrate them with the most contemporary research in the field. Additionally, it explores the impact of brand-naming strategies on consumer attitudes and behavior. We aim to (1) summarize the literature on brand naming, (2) describe the role and applications of sound symbolism in brand naming studied in extant research, (3) present a comprehensive framework for brand naming and present a set of future research directions.

HISTORICAL DEVELOPMENT OF BRAND-NAMING LITERATURE

Naming literature has evolved slower than how brand-naming practices have progressed in the industry, but research is rapidly striving to bridge the gap. Prominent academic research on brand names dates back to the early 1960s. Until 2000, rules of thumb for brand name creation, such as the length of the name, its memory and pronunciation, were considered important. Early research studies suggested that the more fitting (resemblance with the product class) and meaningful (word or a non-word) a brand name is, the better its recall would be (Kanungo, 1968). The association of 'remindfulness' of coined brand names and product categories was explored (Peterson & Ross, 1972). The variables of interest were the number of syllables in brand names and whether the brand name was singular or plural. Brand names with a single syllable were more 'remindful' than those with three syllables. Plural names were 'remindful' of some categories, such as cereals, and singular names were perceived as more 'remindful' of categories, such as laundry detergents. The heuristics for naming a new brand was a simple prescription that the name should be short, easily pronounceable and easy to remember, and it should suggest the product's positioning (Feakins, 1980). In this evolution of the brand-naming literature, researchers have focused on the letters, numbers and words forming the brand name.

Letters in Brand Names

The letters used to create brand names, especially the initial letters in a name, hold a special significance. Some letters continue to be used in high frequency, and others gain prominence in certain contexts. Schloss (1981) and Vanden Bergh (1982/83) analyzed the list of brand names from Marketing and Media Decisions and highlighted that brand names with plosive sounds like *k* and *p* were used more frequently. Plosives are consonants pronounced when air is expelled from our lungs and held in the mouth until the sound is completed. Then, the sound leaves the mouth with a popping noise. This more frequent use of *k* and *p* changed over the years. In an analysis of the top 100 brand names from the list of brands released by Interbrand, an overrepresentation of sounds like *m* (in the name, Marriott) and *s* (in Sprite) and an underrepresentation of sounds like *u* (in Budweiser) were found (Pogacar et al., 2015). Another study found an overrepresentation of *A* and *J* as the initial letters in top company names, which is in contrast to *S* being underrepresented (Van Doorn et al., 2016). The most underrepresented vowel sounds recently have been the sounds (in bold) in names such as S**ou**thwest Airlines, J**er**gens, T**oy**s 'R' Us and CBS C**or**poration. Similarly, the overrepresented vowel sounds are in V**i**sa and Cisc**o**, and consonant sounds are in **Y**amaha, **Z**ara, **F**ord, **J**eep, **P**ayPal and **T**ide. The underrepresented consonant sounds are the ones in brand names such as **R**evlon, mea**s**ure, **L**'Oréal and ma**th** (Pathak et al., 2020b).

Numbers in Brand Names: The Alphanumeric Brand Names

Alphanumeric brand names (ABNs) were initially defined as the mixing of proper nouns with numbers. Such names gained marketers' attention because of the proliferation of technology, lack of availability of English words for brand names, market segmentation fit, shorter product life cycles and multinational product marketing (Boyd, 1985). About a decade later, ABNs were redefined as 'names that contain one or more numbers either in digit form or in written form' (Pavia & Costa, 1993). It has been recognized that using ABNs suits technological products but ABNs are not suited for categories such as lingerie or home furniture. The use of ABNs has been seen to be more appropriate for brands with multigenerational technological product improvements and product differentiation (Auh & Shih, 2009). Research has also shown that customers with a low need for cognition follow the 'the higher, the better' heuristic to choose brands with higher numbers (Gunasti & Ross, 2010). Numbers in the ABNs can become implicit anchors that may bias consumers' product's price assessment and other numerical attributes when the numerical component is relevant and product attributes are evaluated superficially. For example, the Airbus A330 may be perceived to have 330 seats (Yan & Duclos, 2013).

Influence of Words Forming a Brand Name

Researchers have analyzed the role of linguistics in brand naming. For instance, Vanden Bergh et al. (1987) studied the linguistic characteristics of brand names listed in the Marketing and Media Decisions' lists of the top 200 brands from 1971 to 1985. The words forming the brand names were classified as phonetic, orthographic, morphological and semantic devices. They were further sub-classified as alliteration (consonant repetition, e.g., Coca-Cola), unusual spellings (e.g., Kool-Aid) and affixation (e.g., Jell-O), among others. These classifications and sub-classifications not only provided strategic naming implications for brand managers but also provided interesting research gaps for academics in the area of branding. These implications gave rise to many journal articles using empirical studies to test the effect of these word-based classifications on consumer responses.

Research has highlighted that the repetition of sounds in brand names (e.g., Lululemon) generates a positive affect and favorably influences the reactions to cross-selling, brand evaluations and product choices of consumers (Argo et al., 2010). Also, it is seen that brand names are evaluated more favorably when they are typical (reminds of the product category; Zinkhan & Martin, 1987), meaningful (Kohli et al., 2005) and descriptive (Kohli & Suri, 2000). Furthermore, early studies in brand naming have shown that brand names formed with high-frequency words help consumers remember the information relevant to the brand better when small sets of associations are tied to the brand names compared to when the associations are large. In contrast, for names formed with low-frequency words, memory for brand-related material, such as brands' product categories and the brands' message phrases, is not much influenced by the association set size (Meyers-Levy, 1989). Research has also shown that brand recognition for non-word names (e.g., Monit, a camera's name) is higher than for word names (e.g., Ultimate), but the recall of word names is higher (Lerman & Garbarino, 2002). Both brand recall and recognition for irrelevant word names (e.g., Parade) are higher than for relevant word names (e.g., Simplicity). Furthermore, suggestive and nonsuggestive brand names influence memory differently. A brand name that explicitly highlights a product benefit (a suggestive brand name) enhances the recall of advertised benefit claims aligned with its meaning more effectively than a nonsuggestive brand name. However, a suggestive brand name results in a lower brand recall of subsequently advertised claims unrelated to the product's meaning compared to a nonsuggestive brand name (Keller et al., 1998).

SOUND SYMBOLISM IN BRAND NAMES

Research on brand naming has advanced significantly with the introduction of sound symbolism, a concept borrowed from linguistics. Sound symbolism refers to the linguistic phenomenon where the sounds of a word provide cues about its meaning (Yorkston & Menon, 2004). The use of sound symbolism in brand names influences product perception, brand perception, brand name perception, product evaluation, product preference, brand name preference, brand personality, brand liking, purchase intention, brand meaning perception, brand equity, likelihood to recommend the brand, product choice and product positioning. Multiple studies have empirically tested this phenomenon in brand names of products with specific attributes. A review of the literature on sound symbolism in brand names highlights that the tested names vary by syllabic length and sound type (see Table 14.1).

A foundational study by Sapir (1929) demonstrated the effect of sound symbolism. Participants were told to associate two fictitious words, 'mil' and 'mal', with a large table and a small table. Approximately 80% of respondents associated 'mal' with the large table and 'mil' with the small table, highlighting the intuitive connections between sounds and perceived meanings. The author found an association between the *a* and the *i* sounds with large and small sizes, respectively, termed size-sound symbolism. Over the years, many such associations of sounds with objects have been tested, namely, power, dark-light contrast, soft-hard contrast, mildness, thick-thin contrast, weak-strong contrast, light-heavy contrast, fast-slow contrast, cold-warm contrast, prettiness, bitter-sweet contrast, friendliness and sharp-blunt contrast (Klink, 2000). Klink (2000) applied the concept of sound symbolism to study how specific

Table 14.1 Review of literature on sound symbolism in brand names

Author(s) (Year of Publishing)	*Sample Products (Attributes)*	*Sound Type (Vowels/ Consonants)*	*Brand Name Length (No. of Syllables)*
Klink (2000)	Car (small), deodorant (masculine)	Vowels, consonants	One, two
Klink (2001)	Shampoo (soft)	Combinations[a]	Two
Klink (2003)	Beer (dark)	Vowels, consonants	One, two
Yorkston and Menon (2004)	Ice cream (rich, creamy and smooth)	Vowels	One
Lowrey and Shrum (2007)	SUV (large), knife (sharp)	Vowels	Two
Klink and Athaide (2012)	Body fragrance (sincerity, sophistication and ruggedness)	Vowels	Two
Shrum et al. (2012)	4 × 4 vehicle (large), two-seater convertible (small)	Vowels	One, two
Kuehnl and Mantau (2013)	SUV/convertible (small, fast and light)	Vowels, consonants	Two
Wu et al. (2013)	Spring water/deodorant (masculine/feminine brand personality)	Vowels	One
Baxter and Lowrey (2014)	Car (small)	Vowels	Two
Klink and Wu (2014)	Car (small, fast)	Vowels, consonants, combinations[a]	Two
Guèvremont and Grohmann (2015)	Toothpaste/jeans (masculine/feminine brand personality)	Consonants	Two
Lieven et al. (2015)	Fragrance/apparel (masculine/feminine brand personality)	Vowels	One, three
Klink and Wu (2017)	Bottled water (ethical)	Combinations[a]	Two
Joshi and Kronrod (2020)	Pen/sunscreen (eco-friendly)	Consonants	One, two, three
Pathak and Calvert (2020)	Chocolate (sweet/bitter)	Consonants	Three
Pathak, Calvert, and Lim (2020)	Toilet cleaner/beer (harsh/soft)	Consonants	Three
Pathak et al. (2022)	Bottled water (carbonated/still)	Consonants	Two
Arora et al. (2023)	Car (small), deodorant (masculine), mobile app (friendly) and chocolate ice cream (rich)	Vowels, consonants, combinations[a]	Two, three
Motoki and Pathak (2023)	Sandwich (healthy)	Combinations[a]	Two, five

Source: Adapted from Arora et al. (2023) and modified.

[a]Combinations of vowel and consonant sounds.

sounds in brand names are associated with product attributes. Products with fictitious brand names with front vowel sounds (*ee* sound in flea and *i* sound in fly), compared to those with back vowel sounds (*ow* sound in bout and *oo* sound in boot), are perceived as more feminine, friendlier, smaller, thinner, softer, lighter, milder, faster, colder, more bitter, weaker and prettier. For producing front vowel sounds, the tongue's highest position occurs more toward the front of the mouth as opposed to its back that helps produce back vowels. According to the laws of physics, an inverse relationship exists between the mass and frequency of the vibrating tissue (Morton, 1994). Sounds that are of higher frequency convey a smaller size. On the other hand, the lower-frequency sounds convey a bigger size. Similar associations were found for consonant sounds: products with brand names having fricatives (e.g., *f* or *s*) are seen as lighter, sharper, smaller, faster, softer and more feminine compared to those with stops (e.g., *b* or *d*). Furthermore, brand names with voiceless stops and fricatives, as opposed to their voiced counterparts, are associated with lighter, sharper, softer, smaller, faster and more feminine perceptions. Front vowels and fricative consonants are of a higher frequency than stop consonants and back vowels. Researchers have found other associations with sounds in brand names with varying frequencies: front vowels with personality dimensions of sophistication and sincerity and back vowels with ruggedness (Klink & Athaide, 2012); brand names with higher-frequency sounds are considered more ethical (Klink & Wu, 2017) and increase the perception of luxury of hospitality brands (Motoki et al., 2023), and brands with voiced consonants (*g*, *z*, *v*, *b* and *d*) are seen as harsh (Pathak et al., 2020a), whereas brands with voiceless consonant sounds (*p*, *t* and *k*) are perceived as more environmentally friendly (Joshi & Kronrod, 2020). Brand names with voiceless consonants are associated with carbonated beverages and spikiness, while those with voiced consonants are associated with still water and roundness (Pathak et al., 2022). The preference for certain vowel sounds, such as back vowels, influences the brand perceptions of the same product depending on the product's attributes. For instance, a beer brand might benefit from back vowels, if described as smooth, mellow and rich instead of descriptions such as cold, clean and crisp (Lowrey & Shrum, 2007). The famous *Frish/Frosh* study by Yorkston and Menon (2004) showed that sound symbolism operates automatically, meaning it is an effortless, unintentional and uncontrollable process used outside of the consumer's awareness.

In many studies on sound symbolism in brand names, the first syllable typically holds the symbolic imbed. However, Klink and Wu (2014) validated that placing these imbeds later in the brand name still conveys the brand meaning effectively. Additionally, vowels generally convey brand meaning better than consonants. When both vowel and consonant imbeds with the same sound frequency (either high or low, termed consistent imbeds) are used, the additive effect strengthens the communication of brand meaning. Brand names that incorporate both sound-symbolic and semantic imbeds tend to communicate product benefits more effectively than those with only sound-symbolic imbeds (Klink, 2001). It is seen that the products, these brand names represent, are liked more favorably by the consumers.

While previous research studied sound symbolism in simple English brand names, research later documented the sound-symbolic perceptions of products with blended brand names (BBNs) (Arora et al., 2023). BBNs are formed with at least one semantic component (the meaningful imbed) and one nonsemantic component (the sound-symbolic imbed) in a name. Such names meet the needs of brand managers, who want to avoid trademark-related concerns but wish to have a product-related association in their brand names. The vowel sounds in the BBNs connote product attribute properties better than a combination of vowel and consonant sounds, which in turn does better than consonant sounds alone. Arora et al. (2023) extended the extant knowledge of associations of sounds in brand names with product attributes to incorporate the influence of product-level categorization in influencing consumers' product perceptions. For instance, for an SUV to be positioned as friendly, the name *limauto* should have been considered more suitable than *lomauto* as the *i* sound in the name can be associated with friendliness, as suggested by the extant literature (Klink, 2000). However, according to Arora et al. (2023), for maximum effectiveness in influencing consumer perceptions and conveying the intended positioning through blended brand names, an SUV – being a subordinate category of a car – should be associated with a concrete attribute like 'bigness' rather than an abstract attribute like 'friendliness' and is better off being named *lomauto*, instead.

Researchers have expanded the study of sound symbolism in brand names to include brand marks and other brand elements. For instance, fictitious brand names containing front vowels are more closely associated with brand marks that feature lighter colors, lighter shades of the same color, angular shapes and smaller sizes (Klink, 2003). These front-vowel brand names also tend to align with brand personalities characterized by sophistication and sincerity, while back vowels are linked to brand personalities of ruggedness (Klink & Athaide, 2012). Additionally, brand names with front vowels are often associated with a feminine brand personality, while those with back vowels are linked to a masculine brand personality. Brands with sounds in the name as congruent with the targeted genders are liked more and gain higher purchase intention (Wu et al., 2013). Brand names containing stops (such as *b* or *d*) tend to increase perceptions of masculinity, while those with fricatives (such as *s* or *f*) are associated with femininity. This influence extends to the likelihood of recommending the brand, particularly when brand masculinity or femininity is made salient (Guèvremont & Grohmann, 2015). Additionally, brand masculinity or femininity is accentuated by logo shapes and type fonts that align with these traits, with angular and bold logos enhancing masculinity and round and slender logos conveying femininity. When there is greater congruence between the brand's masculinity/femininity and the product category's masculinity/femininity, brand preferences are stronger (Lieven et al., 2015).

Brand names with a voiced obstruent are associated with bitter-tasting products, whereas those with a voiceless obstruent are with sweet-tasting products (Pathak & Calvert, 2020). An obstruent is a speech sound produced when airflow is obstructed in the oral cavity. Examples of voiced obstruents include *b*, *d*, *g*, *z* and v, and voiceless obstruents are *p*, *t*, *k*, *s* and *f*. Also, it is highlighted in research that brand names with voiced obstruents are perceived as harsh. In contrast, brand names with voiceless obstruents are perceived as soft or mild (Pathak et al., 2020a). Most literature on sound-symbolic imbeds in brand names tested shorter names, usually monosyllabic (names with one syllable) or names with two syllables. Evidence for the effect of sound symbolism on product perceptions in longer names containing three syllables was provided more recently (Arora et al., 2023). Longer names are less frequently used than shorter names in everyday conversation as they are perceived as complex, distant and abstract. This property of longer names helps connote luxuriousness in brands. In contrast, shorter names are more appropriate for basic brands (Pathak et al., 2019). Brands with shorter names of foods are preferred as they are perceived as healthier because of perceptions of less potency (Motoki & Pathak, 2023).

Concerns regarding the true effects of sound symbolism have also been raised. When the customer visually evaluates a brand name, the typeface can influence the consumer response in similar ways as do sound-symbolic imbeds. The typeface, thus, provides a plausible alternative explanation of the sound-symbolic effects (Doyle & Bottomley, 2011).

BRAND NAME CLASSIFICATION FRAMEWORKS

Extant literature on brand naming did suggest useful strategies for managers to name their brands. However, the suggestions were piecemeal and not necessarily compatible with each other. It thus warranted a comprehensive guidebook on brand naming, given the practical significance of the topic. Over the years, researchers have created multiple brand-naming classifications that suit different contexts (see Table 14.2).

An early classification of brand names was proposed in 1967: invented names with no particular expressive value (e.g., Omo); invented names with a phonetically symbolic value (e.g., Soflan, suggesting gentleness in a woolen material); names with a known semantic significance (e.g., Mars) and names with both semantic and expressive value (e.g., Crunchie) (Dogana, 1967). Concerns with trademark-related issues in naming products bothered researchers (Melton, 1979). Names were suggested to be generic (e.g., shampoo), descriptive (e.g., LaserJet), suggestive (e.g., Dove), arbitrary (e.g., Apple) and coined (e.g., Exxon), suggesting a higher trademark protection for the latter. Brand names could also be classified following the Juliet and Joyce principles, referring to Shakespeare's work, Romeo and Juliet and James Joyce's Finnegan's Wake, respectively (Collins, 1977). The Juliet principle suggests that the verbal form of a name is irrelevant; instead, the associations we attach to that verbal form define the name's meaning ('A rose by any other name would smell as sweet'). In his book, James Joyce used sound symbolism instead of actual words to communicate.

Service brand names can be classified into various dimensions based on their characteristics. Descriptive names emphasize a key benefit or feature of the service, such as Nutrisystem and Sprint. Person-based names are derived from the names of owners, partners or prominent individuals, like Ford. Associative names use fabricated or unconventional words that acquire meaning through branding and promotion, as seen with Discover. Geographic names draw on local folklore, regional identity or terms like 'American' or 'US' to evoke patriotism or create an exotic appeal, exemplified by American Airlines. Finally, alphanumeric names combine letters and numbers, either in numerical form or written out, to represent the brand, such

Table 14.2 Brand-naming classifications

Author(s)	*Classification*	*Dimensions*
Dogana (1967)	Invented names	Invented names with and without phonetically symbolic value, semantic, semantic + expressive
Collins (1977)	Juliet-Joyce dichotomy	Semantic names, sound-symbolic names
Melton (1979)	Hierarchy of brand naming	Generic, descriptive, suggestive, arbitrary and coined
Turley and Moore (1995)	Naming for services	Descriptive, person-based, associative, geographic and alphanumeric names
Klink (2000)	Sound-symbolic names	Corporeal, imitative, conventional, synesthetic
Lencastre and Beirao (2004)	Word-based and initial-letter-based names	Acronyms, adjectives, verbs and nouns
Zaichkowsky (2010)	Degree of distinctiveness	Invented, irrelevant, descriptive and suggestive names
Arora et al. (2015)	Comprehensive categorization of names	Word-based semantic names, word-based invented names and non-word names

Source: Adapted from Arora et al. (2015) and modified.

as VH1 (Turley & Moore, 1995). The discussion on sound symbolism in brand names was extended by Klink (2000). Sound symbolism-based names can be categorized by the degree of connection between sound and meaning. Corporeal names use sounds to convey the speaker's emotional or physical states, such as 'Aaugh' or 'Achoo'. Imitative names rely on onomatopoeia, where the word phonetically mimics the source of the sound, like 'bang'. Conventional names form analogical associations between particular phonemes or clusters and specific meanings, as seen in the 'gl' of words such as glitter, glisten, glow and glimmer. Synesthetic names use vowels and consonants to represent visual, tactile or proprioceptive properties of objects, such as size or shape.

Furthermore, names could be classified based on acronyms, adjectives, verbs and nouns (Lencastre & Beirao, 2004). Naming types can be classified into four categories based on their distinctiveness and connection to the goods or services they represent. Invented names are highly distinctive and consist of coined letter combinations with no inherent meaning, such as Accenture. Irrelevant names are moderately distinctive and involve meaningful words in English that bear no direct reference to the goods or services, like Crest. Suggestive names are relatively weaker in distinctiveness, suggestive of the character or quality of the goods or services without being directly descriptive, as in Sunkist. Descriptive names are the weakest in distinctiveness, describing – though not explicitly – the character or quality of the goods or services, such as Gardenfresh (Zaichkowsky, 2010).

With as many brand-naming classifications available, most appeared fragmented and focused on a few dimensions of brand naming, and it may have been difficult to choose from and apply. A brand manager or entrepreneur often seeks a comprehensive framework to generate and evaluate potential names for their brand or company efficiently. A comprehensive brand-naming framework that not only subsumes inputs from the existing frameworks but also identifies newer dimensions for the framework's comprehensiveness was proposed by Arora et al. (2015), and the updated and modified version is presented here (as shown in Figure 14.1).

According to this framework, brand names were classified as word-based and non-word names. The word-based names were further divided into semantic and invented names. Semantic names are those that carry a verbal assigned meaning. These names could be product-related (e.g., the car named 'Swift' by Maruti Suzuki) or unrelated to the product. The unrelated names could either be metaphorically described (e.g., the car named 'Spark' by Chevrolet) or be non-metaphorically (e.g., the car named 'Polo' by Volkswagen). Invented names have been divided into semantic invented names and names primarily based on sound symbolism (termed in the framework as expressive and synesthetic). Semantic invented names contain a semantic association but are lexically meaningless overall. These can be created using various linguistic techniques. Blending involves combining parts of two or more words, such as Intel or Vodafone. Affixation forms names by adding prefixes, suffixes or infixes to existing words, like Jell-O or Motorola. Compounding creates names by joining two or more complete words, as seen with Airbus, Bank of America or Coca-Cola. Clipping reduces a word to one of its parts, resulting in names like Cisco or Fanta. Finally, unusual spellings use modified versions of expected spellings to create distinctive names, such as Publix. Recent research unpacked two of its subdimensions, viz., *pseudohomophone* brand names and vowel-less brand names. *Pseudohomophone* brand names are non-words that sound like real words; for example, *Whyte* suggests *White*. In processing these names, the associative meaning gets primed by retrieving the phonology (sound) of the word, but only when the consumers lack knowledge of the brand (Baxter et al., 2017). Brands with vowel-less names, such as Lyft, Tumblr and Qzzr are perceived as more rugged compared to brands with voweled names, which in turn are perceived as more competent, sincere and sophisticated. Food brands with vowel-less brand names are rated lower in taste expectation, expensiveness, willingness to pay, quality and healthfulness (Pathak & Motoki, 2022). Arora et al. (2015) concluded that compounding and blending were the most used brand-naming strategies among the semantic invented names. Non-word names were classified as either number-based or shortened forms of words. The authors defined number-based names as 'names containing a number, irrespective of whether they contain another word'. Therefore, this category includes the ABNs (e.g., the car named 'XUV500' by Mahindra & Mahindra). An abbreviation is a name that expresses words or a phrase, formed by the initial letters of the words, but is not a word itself (e.g., BMW, which stands for Bayerische Motoren Werke). An acronym is a name that expresses words or a phrase, formed by the initial letters of the words, and that sounds like a word itself. Acronyms were further subclassified as semantically related to the product (e.g., Seat, which stands for Sociedad Española de Automóviles de Turismo, a Spanish car manufacturer) or semantically unrelated (e.g., Fiat, which stands for Fabbrica Italiana Automobili Torino, an Italian automobile manufacturer). The acronyms may also be nonsemantic or meaningless

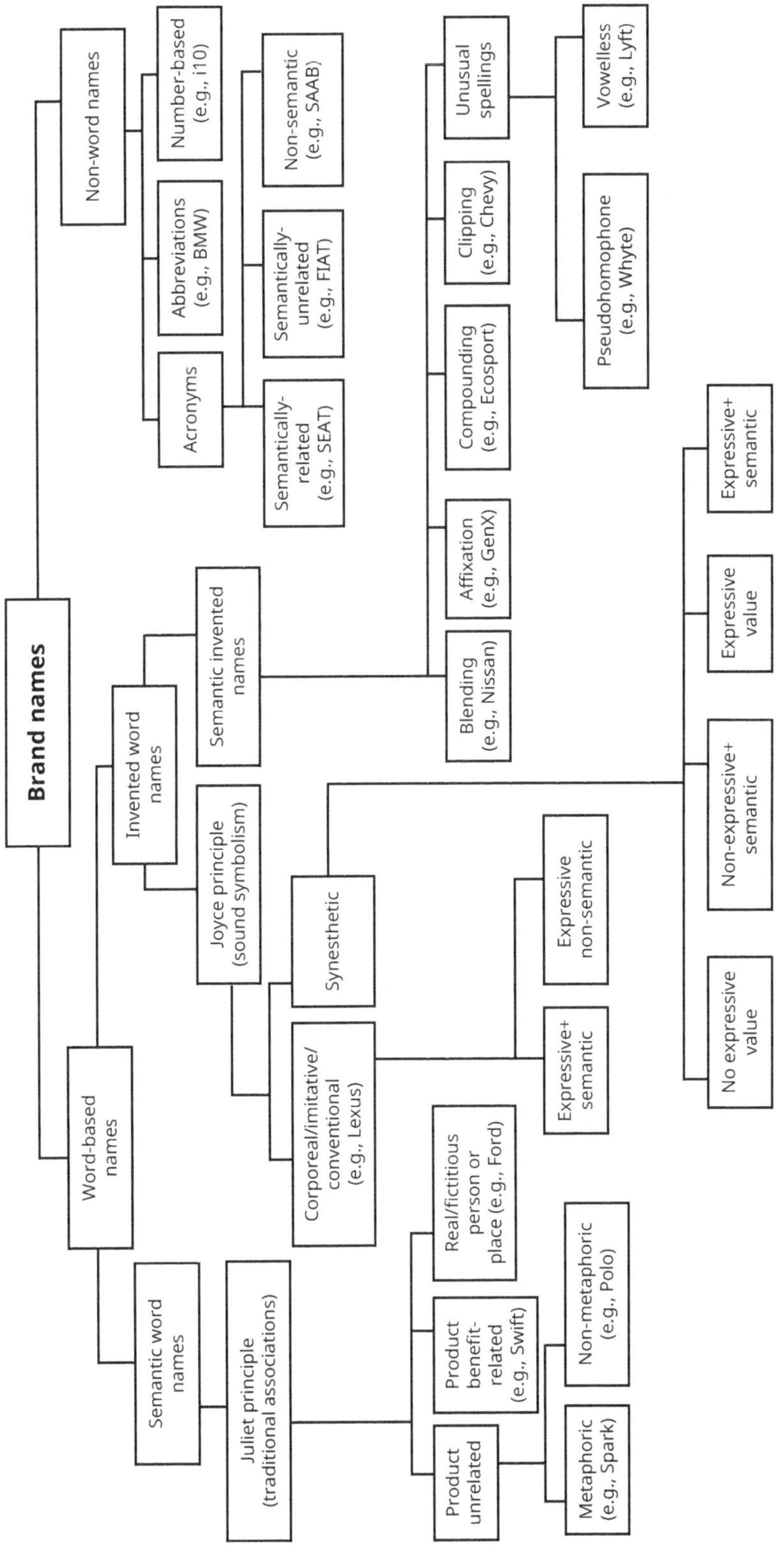

Figure 14.1 Modified Arora–Kalro–Sharma framework for brand name classification

Source: Adapted from Arora et al. (2015) and modified.

(e.g., Saab, which stands for Svenska Aeroplan Aktiebolaget, a Swedish aerospace and defense company).

MORE ON BRAND NAMING: BEYOND BRAND NAME ATTRIBUTES

Brand names have been researched in many contexts other than those discussed above. Some of the topics gathered significant research attention. These include foreign branding and country-of-origin (COO) effects, language translation and transliteration, and line and brand extensions.

Foreign Branding and COO Effects

Foreign names of brands or foreign branding can influence product perceptions and attitudes; for example, French brand names enhance attitudes toward hedonic products (Leclerc et al., 1994). COO described by the 'Made in (country name)' can evoke certain product qualities and influence product evaluations (Ettenson et al., 1988). Emerging market firms prefer a developed-country brand name as it positively influences consumers' purchase intentions compared to an emerging-country brand name (Witek-Hajduk & Grudecka, 2022). A product with a foreign brand name may not necessarily be manufactured in the implied country. When the implied COO is perceived as incongruent with the actual COO, consumers' purchase likelihood decreases for hedonic products, especially in emerging countries (Melnyk et al., 2012). When the COO of local brands using foreign brand names is revealed to consumers, their purchase intention reduces (Chen, 2021). Where consumers speak a different language and have a distinct cultural background, featuring a foreign celebrity and using an English brand name may pose a disadvantage due to ethnocentrism (Chao et al., 2005). Bicultural Japanese-American consumers perceive products as being of higher quality when the brand name is written in Japanese rather than in English because these products are closely related to their ethnicity (Moriuchi & Jackson, 2017). English versions of Chinese brand names, when shorter in length and with semantic relevance to English (e.g., Chery vs. Changfeng), are perceived as more memorable (Fetscherin et al., 2015). A bilingual brand name (in both English and Chinese) creates a less luxurious perception of the brand than a foreign brand name, particularly when the endorser is a Western celebrity instead of a Chinese celebrity (Kim et al., 2020). When a brand name contains letters and sounds in a foreign language, consumers choose a shape that matches the sound characteristics of the names (the sound symbolism effect). Contrarily, if a brand name is in a familiar language, consumers could match the curvatures of the letters in the names with associated shapes (Jang et al., 2024).

For young Korean bilingual consumers, advertisements presenting a brand name in a foreign language (English Roman alphabet) and using the local language (Hangul) for the body copy message, both as phonetic languages, helped enhance the brand name (as it is more distinctive in foreign language) and the message (because of language familiarity) recall and recognition (Ahn & Ferle, 2008). The sound symbolism effect in brand names with sounds matching product attributes persisted for consumers speaking French, Spanish and Chinese and bilingual in English irrespective of whether it was tested in their first or second language, suggesting the universality of the effect (Shrum et al., 2012). In a related study, Kuehnl and Mantau (2013) argued that native speakers of English, French, German and Spanish preferred plosives (*k* in key) in international brand names for sports utility vehicles. However, native English consumers preferred front vowels (*e* in bed) regardless of car type.

Language Translation and Transliteration

Researchers have tried to understand how brand names adapt to different cultures and languages. Significant work has been done studying the Chinese and English languages. Managers have three options: translation of the brand name [semantic equivalence with the original brand name; e.g., Apple to Píngguǒ (苹果)], transliteration [maintaining phonetic equivalence of the brand name; e.g., Disney to 迪士尼 (pronounced Di Shi Ni)] or a new name (Francis et al., 2002). English is a phonetic language (representing words as sounds), and Chinese is logographic (representing words and concepts in the form of certain sign symbols). Translations can happen in three ways: phonetic (by sound), semantic (by meaning) and *phonosemantic* (by sound and meaning) (also in Hanyu Pinyin, which is by romanizing Chinese phonetic rules; Kum et al., 2011). It is suggested that phonetic translations be preferred when the emphasis is on the English component in the brand name instead of on the Chinese component. The reverse is true for semantic translation, and a *phonosemantic* translation is evaluated equally under both conditions (Zhang & Schmitt, 2001). A phonetic translation may be necessary for an unknown brand (Hong et al., 2002). Retaining the original name may be a good idea for an existing strong brand name. While processing dual brand names (an English brand name and its localized Chinese version), highly language-proficient individuals prefer sound translation when the English name is emphasized. The same individuals prefer meaning translation when the Chinese name is emphasized. However, less proficient bilinguals prefer meaning translation of the dual names (Zhang & Schmitt, 2004).

Similarity and informativeness of brand names of Hollywood movies have been shown to impact box office revenues in China. The Chinese box office revenue increased when the translated movie name was both informative and similar to the original name. However, the effect of informativeness was stronger for Hollywood movies, which have a greater cultural gap in the Chinese market. Here, the cultural gap means that foreign audiences who lack the cultural background and knowledge required for full appreciation of the product, value the product lesser (Gao et al., 2020).

Line and Brand Extensions

Names could be chosen at a general level (e.g., Maxima) to connote overall product favorability or at a specific level (e.g., Lean Cuisine) that are suggestive of category- or brand-specific attribute or benefit 'positioning' information to support subsequent brand extensions. Specific brand names lead to better recall of factual details after choice tasks, while general names facilitate access to abstract evaluations after judgment tasks (Sen, 1999). Adults and children process brand information differently cognitively to evaluate a brand. Children rely more on surface cues (e.g., brand names) than deep cues (e.g., category similarity). Adults favor near extensions over far extensions based on category similarity (e.g., iced tea vs. coffee for Coca-Cola). Children respond positively to extensions with rhyming names (e.g., Coca-Cola Gola iced tea vs. Coca-Cola Higley iced tea), while adults do not show significant preference (Zhang & Sood, 2002). Products with moderately incongruent brand names (e.g., a book on Steak by the Dairy Association) are preferred to those with either congruent (e.g., a book on Vitamin D by the Dairy Association) or extremely incongruent brand names (e.g., a book on Steak by Coppertone) because of the greater elaboration of the incongruent names to resolve the incongruity (Meyers-Levy et al., 1994). Familiar prototypical brands (e.g., Toyota for SUVs; the degree to which a category member has attributes in common with other category members) increase consumer acceptance of novel extensions, for both close (e.g., independent four-wheel-drive) and distant product categories (e.g., foldable city scooter) because prototypical brands reduce consumer risk more than their disadvantage of being rigidly anchored in their representative product category (Goedertier et al., 2015). A Janus fit brand extension, which is an extension with both fitting and unfitting associations (e.g., Apple Gym, a video-streaming service focused on physical and sports training material as an extension of the parent brand Apple), is perceived as more innovative than both a traditional high-fit extension (e.g., Apple Navigator) and a low-fit extension (e.g., Apple Drill-screwdriver). This is because of its moderately high Eureka surprise experience, which is an initial feeling of surprise, followed by the sudden realization of it making sense for the parent brand (Falana et al., 2024). Similar brand extensions (e.g., CNN weekly magazine) are evaluated more favorably compared to less similar brand extensions (e.g., CNN movie channel), when consumers are chronically or momentarily prevention-focused (concerned with the absence or presence of negative outcomes) as they assign a higher weight to risk perceptions than to hedonic value (new product enjoyment) of the extension. In contrast, chronically or momentarily promotion-focused consumers (concerned with the presence or absence of positive outcomes) evaluate similar brand extensions no more favorably because they consider the hedonic value primarily for evaluation (Yeo & Park, 2006). Brand extensions that have a benefit overlap with the parent brand are evaluated more favorably by promotion-focused consumers. Prevention-focused consumers favor product category similarity extensions more (Chang et al., 2011). ABNs with ascending order of letters are evaluated more favorably for a line extension for reasons of ordinal superiority. Line extensions are perceived as a larger improvement of an existing product, when in ABNs the number component increases as compared to the increase in the order of the letter component. For example, from A70 to A80 instead of A70 to B70 (Kara et al., 2015). Multi-context numbers (e.g., 20; a multiple of 2, 2.5, 5 and 10), defined as 'numbers that can be favored in numerous contexts and transfer their favorability to different product categories', could be added to brand names forming ABNs. Such ABNs generate higher preferences for product extensions and more favorable consumer attitudes (Ozcan & Gunasti, 2019). For cross-gender brand extensions, extending female patronymic brands to men by adding the descriptor 'Men' is not an effective extension strategy. Female patronymic brands are those that are named after a woman founder. Using the surname Lauder (from Estée Lauder) before 'Men' instead increases brand extension attitude and purchase intention as the new brand name maintains a moderate degree of similarity with the existing one (Ulrich et al., 2020).

CREATIVE BRAND-NAMING STRATEGIES AND FUTURE DIRECTIONS

Researchers have attempted to explore the dimensions of brand naming discussed in the brand-naming framework earlier. However, the depth of knowledge of the naming dimensions either is insufficient or remains largely unexplored. For example, the use of unusual or unconventional spellings of brand names was recently explored by Costello et al. (2023). Choosing the name 'Lyft' over 'Lift' for a brand could have negative effects, as it may come across as less sincere. However, this approach might be desirable when consumers seek memorable experiences, like staying at an ice hotel. A brand name with minor misspellings (Tyme) can be as effective as a brand name with correct spellings by enhancing its conceptual fluency. If perceived as relevant, a brand with major misspellings (Komyuniti) can also be effective (Smith & Abell, 2025).

Other dimensions from the framework, such as affixation, compounding, clipping and even blending, have very limited theoretical understanding and must be explored. Heuristics and some empirical evidence suggest that brand names could be suggestive of the product category (Bali et al., 2024). However, less is understood regarding consumers' reactions when the product suggestiveness is only metaphorically related (e.g., the car named 'Spark') and not directly related (e.g., the car named 'Swift'). Shortening of brand names is another popular naming strategy (e.g., Reebok changed to Rbk). Again, little is known about the use of abbreviations as brand names. Furthermore, should the consumers react favorably when acronyms as brand names are related semantically (e.g., Seat, a Spanish car manufacturer) to the product versus when they are not (e.g., Fiat, an Italian automobile manufacturer)?

Over the years, brands have been named after a person's name (e.g., Ford). Brand names could be related to the first name. Consumers will prefer a brand with letters in the brand name starting with letters from their name, termed name letter branding (Brendl et al., 2005). The behavior can be explained by implicit egotism, that is, the need to self-enhance, which increases the positive valence of name letters. Brand names could also be related to one's surname (Howard & Kerin, 2013). Termed as the 'surname brand preference' effect, consumers prefer brands with names matching their surnames. Extending the research on self-concept in brand names, Kachersky & Carnevale (2015) provided guidance regarding the use of pronouns in brand names. They suggested that the use of 'you' in a brand name (e.g., YouTube) elicits a more favorable brand attitude when the brand prefers a positioning on social benefits. In contrast, 'I' will receive a more favorable consumer response, when the brand prefers a positioning on personal benefits (e.g., iMac).

There are other creative ways to name brands, such as geography-based, sensorial and using supernatural agents. Products by companies with small-sized geographic brand names are perceived as more authentic. Small geographic brand name size is based on the small administrative level of geography. For example, Cognac is smaller than France (Chen et al., 2024). Specificity in a scent brand name (Lavender Bouquet vs. Floral Bouquet) tends to reduce purchase intention, as it generates vivid olfactory imagery that induces a disconfirmation between imagined and experienced scents (Meng et al., 2021). Angelic brand names (Godly Gains, a brand name that focuses on building an image of a benevolent character or nature that is kind and loving) result in healthfulness perceptions of products because of the activation of brand virtuousness perceptions (Ilicic & Brennan, 2023).

Literature on brand naming has also been explored across multiple dimensions from linguistics. As presented above, phonetics and sound symbolism have garnered much attention as trademark-related concerns have risen of late. The Internet industry faces challenges related to cybersquatting. This practice involves registering web addresses, particularly those associated with well-known companies, as domain names with the aim of selling them later for a profit (Arora et al., 2015). This has necessitated innovation in brand naming. Words used as brand names can be articulated as inward (e.g., Bako) or outward (e.g., Kabo). When the articulation spots of consonants in a name move in the mouth from the front to the back, it is called inward articulation, and the reverse is called outward articulation (Topolinski et al., 2014). Products with brand names pronounced as inward are liked more, have higher purchase intentions and have a higher willingness to pay for. Food tastes more palatable and is consumed more when named as inward (Topolinski, 2017). Inward names are preferred when embedded in labels, logos and product packages (Godinho & Garrido, 2017). On another note, sound symbolism effects were found to be stronger than the in/out effect in sound–taste and sound–shape associations. Brand names did not follow the in/out results when sound-symbolic imbeds were included in the study (Pathak et al., 2021).

Recently, Lowe and Haws (2017) studied another linguistic property in brand names, namely, the acoustic pitch, to conclude that a lower pitch in voice or music helps draw an inference of a larger product size. Baxter and Lowrey (2014) tested sound symbolism perceptions of brand names in children from South America and Australia with differing English accents. Due to the back position of the tongue, natural speakers of Australian English perceive a magnified sound-symbolic effect compared to natural speakers of Southern American English. The morphology of brand names has also been explored of late. Reduplicated sounds (part or all of a word is repeated, e.g., *kuku* in which the syllable *ku* is doubled) in brand names enhance the brand's appeal by triggering associations with baby-schema cuteness (Motoki et al., 2025). Plural brand names (e.g., Dunkin' Donuts) compared to singular names (e.g., Dunkin' Donut) elicit a more favorable brand attitude. This is due to the perceptions of brand entitativity (Gupta et al., 2024). Entitativity is the perception of a collection of individuals as a cohesive group that shares common goals, similarities and organization. Companies may create complex brand names (Suunto, complex for Chinese consumers) because as compared to simple brand names (Suntuo, simple for Chinese consumers), they can make the brand appear more unique and increase its patronage intention. However, a complex name can also create a psychological distance, reducing the patronage intention. The psychological distance can be reduced if the company practices brand self-introduction. Brand self-introduction is a proactive behavior to pronounce the brand name to greet consumers during consumer–brand interactions, for example, 'Welcome to Uniqlo!' (Chen et al., 2025). A list of linguistic devices that could be thought starters for researchers to create new brand names was published by Vanden Bergh et al. (1987). New ideas can be generated through the use of sound play: onomatopoeia, clipping and blending; the use of word play: paronomasia and oxymorons; metaphors and metonymy; and abbreviations and acronyms. As we have discussed in this chapter, the sound frequency in brand names is well-researched. Similarly, other properties of sound, such as amplitude, timbre and pitch, can be considered for further research in brand naming.

CONCLUSION

Branding is key to marketing, and a brand's name is a very critical brand element. Trademark-related concerns have helped facilitate innovation in the domain of brand naming. Researchers and managers alike are finding newer and more creative ways to create new names. Arora et al. (2015) consolidated existing brand-naming frameworks and proposed a comprehensive framework to serve as a 'one-stop-shop' solution for brand managers to consult to name their brands and to help researchers probe unexplored properties of names that can influence consumer behavior. The manipulation of sound frequency in brand names has gathered immense interest from researchers. Sound symbolism influences consumer behavior automatically and outside of awareness (Yorkston & Menon, 2004). Hence, the overt use of this method to create names is not discussed much in practice. Other discussed linguistic devices have been explored in this chapter. Innovations in brand names will continue to garner more attention from marketers and academics, and this chapter aims to help generate newer avenues for research and practice.

REFERENCES

Aaker, D. A. (2009). *Managing brand equity*. Simon and Schuster.

Aaker, D. A., & Keller, K. L. (1990). Consumer evaluations and brand extensions. *Journal of Marketing, 54*(1), 27–41. https://doi.org/10.1177/002224299005400102

Ahn, J., & Ferle, C. L. (2008). Enhancing recall and recognition for brand names and body copy: A mixed-language approach. *Journal of Advertising, 37*(3), 107–117. https://doi.org/10.2753/JOA0091-3367370308

Argo, J. J., Popa, M., & Smith, M. C. (2010). The sound of brands. *Journal of Marketing, 74*(4), 97–109. https://doi.org/10.1509/jmkg.74.4.097

Arora, S., Kalro, A. D., & Sharma, D. (2015). A comprehensive framework of brand name classification. *Journal of Brand Management, 22*(2), 79–116. https://doi.org/10.1057/bm.2015.8

Arora, S. V., Kalro, A. D., & Sharma, D. (2023). Positioning products through names: Effect of sound symbolism on perception of products with blended brand names. *Journal of Product & Brand Management, 32*(3), 361–378. https://doi.org/10.1108/JPBM-12-2021-3794

Auh, S., & Shih, E. (2009). Brand name and consumer inference making in multigenerational product introduction context. *Journal of Brand Management, 16*(7), 439–454. https://doi.org/10.1057/palgrave.bm.2550104

Bali, L. M., Anesbury, Z. W., Phua, P., & Sharp, B. (2024). How prevalent are suggestive brand names and Distinctive Assets? An AI-human approach. *International Journal of Market Research, 66*(5), 631–649. https://doi.org/10.1177/14707853241251954

Baxter, S., Ilicic, J., & Kulczynski, A. (2017). You see Froot, you think fruit: Examining the effectiveness of pseudohomophone priming. *European Journal of Marketing*, *51*(5/6), 885–902. https://doi.org/10.1108/EJM-01-2016-0038

Baxter, S., & Lowrey, T. (2014). Examining children's preference for phonetically manipulated brand names across two English accent groups. *International Journal of Research in Marketing*, *31*(1), 122–124. https://doi.org/10.1016/j.ijresmar.2013.10.005

Boyd, C. W. (1985). Alpha-numeric brand names. *Journal of Advertising Research*, *25*(5), 48–52. https://doi.org/10.1080/00218499.1985.12467895

Brendl, C. M., Chattopadhyay, A., Pelham, B. W., & Carvallo, M. (2005). Name letter branding: Valence transfers when product specific needs are active. *Journal of Consumer Research*, *32*(3), 405–415. https://doi.org/10.1086/497552

Chang, C. C., Lin, B. C., & Chang, S. S. (2011). The relative advantages of benefit overlap versus category similarity in brand extension evaluation: The moderating role of self-regulatory focus. *Marketing Letters*, *22*(4), 391–404. https://doi.org/10.1007/s11002-010-9131-0

Chao, P., Wührer, G., & Werani, T. (2005). Celebrity and foreign brand name as moderators of country-of-origin effects. *International Journal of Advertising*, *24*(2), 173–192. https://doi.org/10.1080/02650487.2005.11072913

Chen, B. (2021). When foreign brands appear local, and local brands appear foreign: The asymmetric effects of foreign branding in developing countries. *Asia Pacific Journal of Marketing and Logistics*, *33*(1), 145–161. https://doi.org/10.1108/APJML-06-2019-0396

Chen, C., Luo, J., & Hu, J. (2025). Balancing uniqueness and patronage: The dual impact of brand name complexity on consumer behavior. *Asia Pacific Journal of Marketing and Logistics*. https://doi.org/10.1108/APJML-08-2024-1153

Chen, J., Wang, L., Pang, S., Zhang, Y., & Jiang, Y. (2024). Small = authentic: The effect of geographic brand name size on perceived product authenticity. *Journal of Marketing Theory and Practice*, 1–15. https://doi.org/10.1080/10696679.2024.2397768

Collins, L. (1977). A name to compare with a discussion of the naming of new brands. *European Journal of Marketing*, *11*(5), 337–363. https://doi.org/10.1108/EUM0000000005020

Costello, J. P., Walker, J., & Reczek, R. W. (2023). 'Choozing' the best spelling: Consumer response to unconventionally spelled brand names. *Journal of Marketing*, *87*(6), 889–905. https://doi.org/10.1177/00222429231162367

Crovitz, L. G. (2012, January 9). A new challenge for web freedom; A vast increase of top-level domain names will put the internet's self-regulating body to a test. *Wall Street Journal (Online)*. www.wsj.com/articles/SB10001424052970203471004577145132261409846

Davcik, N. S., Vinhas da Silva, R. & Hair, J. F. (2015). Towards a unified theory of brand equity: Conceptualizations, taxonomy and avenues for future research. *Journal of Product & Brand Management*, *24*(1), 3–17. https://doi.org/10.1108/JPBM-06-2014-0639

Dogana, F. (1967). Psycholinguistic contributions to the problem of brand names. *European Marketing Research Review*, *2*(1), 50–58.

Doyle, J. R., & Bottomley, P. A. (2011). Mixed messages in brand names: Separating the impacts of letter shape from sound symbolism. *Psychology & Marketing*, *28*(7), 749–762. https://doi.org/10.1002/mar.20410

Ettenson, R., Wagner, J., & Gaeth, G. (1988). Evaluating the effect of country of origin and the 'Made in the USA' campaign: A conjoint approach. *Journal of Retailing*, *64*(1), 85–100.

Falana, W. O., Aspara, J., & Frösén, J. (2024). The impact of Janus fit brand extensions on perceived brand innovativeness. *Journal of Business Research*, *179*, 114674. https://doi.org/10.1016/j.jbusres.2024.114674

Feakins, K. (1980). What's in a name? Ogilvy and Mather Research: The Research File no. 17.

Fetscherin, M., Diamantopoulos, A., Chan, A., & Abbott, R. (2015). How are brand names of Chinese companies perceived by Americans? *Journal of Product & Brand Management*, *24*(2), 110–123. https://doi.org/10.1108/JPBM-02-2014-0501

Francis, J. N., Lam, J. P., & Walls, J. (2002). Executive insights: The impact of linguistic differences on international brand name standardization: A comparison of English and Chinese brand names of Fortune 500 companies. *Journal of International Marketing*, *10*(1), 98–116. https://doi.org/10.1509/jimk.10.1.98.19528

Gao, W., Ji, L., Liu, Y., & Sun, Q. (2020). Branding cultural products in international markets: A study of Hollywood movies in China. *Journal of Marketing*, *84*(3), 86–105. https://doi.org/10.1177/0022242920912704

Gardner, B., & Levy, S. (1955). The product and the brand. *Harvard Business Review*, *33*(2), 33–39.

Godinho, S., & Garrido, M. V. (2017). Branding with the in-out effect: The impact of consonantal articulation on brand evaluation. *Psychology & Marketing*, *34*(9), 904–911. https://doi.org/10.1002/mar.21031

Goedertier, F., Dawar, N., Geuens, M., & Weijters, B. (2015). Brand typicality and distant novel extension acceptance: How risk-reduction counters low category fit. *Journal of Business Research*, *68*(1), 157–165. https://doi.org/10.1016/j.jbusres.2014.04.005

Guèvremont, A., & Grohmann, B. (2015). Consonants in brand names influence brand gender perceptions. *European Journal of Marketing*, *49*(1/2), 101–122. https://doi.org/10.1108/EJM-02-2013-0106

Gunasti, K., & Ross, W. T., Jr. (2010). How and when alphanumeric brand names affect consumer preferences. *Journal of Marketing Research*, *47*(6), 1177–1192. https://doi.org/10.1509/jmkr.47.6.1177

Gupta, T., Chen, S., & Mohanty, S. (2024). More the merrier: Effects of plural brand names on perceived entitativity and brand attitude. *Journal of Consumer Psychology*, *35*, 150–157. https://doi.org/10.1002/jcpy.1409

Haig, M. (2005). *Brand failures: The truth about the 100 biggest branding mistakes of all time*. Kogan Page.

Hong, F. C., Pecotich, A., & Shultz, C. J. (2002). Brand name translation: Language constraints, product attributes, and consumer perceptions in East and Southeast Asia. *Journal of International Marketing*, *10*(2), 29–45. https://doi.org/10.1509/jimk.10.2.29.19534

Howard, D., & Kerin, R. (2013). A surname brand effect explanation for consumer brand preference and advocacy. *Journal of Product & Brand Management*, *22*(5/6), 362–370. https://doi.org/10.1108/JPBM-01-2013-0238

Ilicic, J., & Brennan, S. M. (2023). Angelic brand name priming: Saintly branded food influences brand healthfulness perceptions. *European Journal of Marketing*, *57*(4), 1099–1129. https://doi.org/10.1108/EJM-09-2021-0719

Jang, H., Jang, J. Y., & Kim, D. Y. (2024). How brand names affect consumer perceptions: An experimental study on the sound symbolism of foreign brand names. *Journal of Global Marketing*, *37*(2), 119–137. https://doi.org/10.1080/08911762.2023.2299011

Joshi, P., & Kronrod, A. (2020). Sounds of green: How brand name sounds metaphorically convey environmental friendliness. *Journal of Advertising*, *49*(1), 61–77. https://doi.org/10.1080/00913367.2019.1696720

Kachersky, L., & Carnevale, M. (2015). Effects of pronoun brand name perspective and positioning on brand attitude. *Journal of Product & Brand Management*, *24*(2), 157–164. https://doi.org/10.1108/JPBM-02-2014-0495

Kanungo, R. N. (1968). Brand awareness: Effects of fittingness, meaningfulness, and product utility. *Journal of Applied Psychology*, *52*(4), 290–295. https://doi.org/10.1037/h0026039

Kara, S., Gunasti, K., & Ross, W. T. (2015). Is it the 'alpha' or the 'numeric'?: Consumers' evaluation of letter versus number changes in alphanumeric brand names. *Journal of Brand Management*, *22*(6), 515–533. https://doi.org/10.1057/bm.2015.28

Keller, K. L., Heckler, S. E., & Houston, M. J. (1998). The effects of brand name suggestiveness on advertising recall. *Journal of Marketing*, *62*(1), 48–57. https://doi.org/10.1177/002224299806200105

Kim, S., Yi Luk, K., Xia, B., Xu, N., & Yin, X. (2020). Brand name and ethnicity of endorser in luxury goods: Does a glocalization strategy work in China? *International Journal of Advertising*, *39*(6), 824–842. https://doi.org/10.1080/02650487.2018.1548197

Kohli, C., & Suri, R. (2000). Brand names that work: A study of the effectiveness of different types of brand names. *Marketing Management Journal*, *10*(2), 112–120.

Kohli, C. S., Harich, K. R., & Leuthesser, L. (2005). Creating brand identity: a study of evaluation of new brand names. *Journal of Business Research*, *58*(11), 1506–1515. https://doi.org/10.1016/j.jbusres.2004.07.007

Klink, R. R. (2000). Creating brand names with meaning: The use of sound symbolism. *Marketing Letters*, *11*(1), 5–20. https://doi.org/10.1023/A:1008184423824

Klink, R. R. (2001). Creating meaningful new brand names: A study of semantics and sound symbolism. *Journal of Marketing Theory and Practice*, *9*(2), 27–34. https://doi.org/10.1080/10696679.2001.11501889

Klink, R. R. (2003). Creating meaningful brands: The relationship between brand name and brand mark. *Marketing Letters*, *14*(3), 143–157. https://doi.org/10.1023/A:1027476132607

Klink, R. R., & Athaide, G. A. (2012). Creating brand personality with brand names. *Marketing Letters*, *23*(1), 109–117. https://doi.org/10.1007/s11002-011-9140-7

Klink, R. R., & Wu, L. (2014). The role of position, type, and combination of sound symbolism imbeds in brand names. *Marketing Letters*, *25*(1), 13–24. https://doi.org/10.1007/s11002-013-9236-3

Klink, R. R., & Wu, L. (2017). Creating ethical brands: The role of brand name on consumer perceived ethicality. *Marketing Letters*, *28*(3), 411–422. https://doi.org/10.1007/s11002-017-9424-7

Kuehnl, C., & Mantau, A. (2013). Same sound, same preference? Investigating sound symbolism effects in international brand names. *International Journal of Research in Marketing*, *30*(4), 417–420. https://doi.org/10.1016/j.ijresmar.2013.05.002

Kum, D., Lee, Y. H., & Qiu, C. (2011). Testing to prevent bad translation: Brand name conversions in Chinese–English contexts. *Journal of Business Research*, *64*(6), 594–600. https://doi.org/10.1016/j.jbusres.2010.06.015

Leclerc, F., Schmitt, B. H., & Dubé, L. (1994). Foreign branding and its effects on product perceptions and attitudes. *Journal of Marketing Research*,

31(2), 263–270. https://doi.org/10.1177/002224379403100209

Lencastre, P. D., & Beirao, A. F. (2004). The figurativeness of brand signs: An empirical research on names and logos memorization. In Conference Proceedings, 3rd International Conference on Research in Advertising (pp. 36–44).

Lerman, D., & Garbarino, E. (2002). Recall and recognition of brand names: A comparison of word and nonword name types. *Psychology & Marketing*, *19*(7–8), 621–639. https://doi.org/10.1002/mar.10028

Lieven, T., Grohmann, B., Herrmann, A., Landwehr, J. R., & Van Tilburg, M. (2015). The effect of brand design on brand gender perceptions and brand preference. *European Journal of Marketing*, *49*(1/2), 146–169. https://doi.org/10.1108/EJM-08-2012-0456

Lowe, M. L., & Haws, K. L. (2017). Sounds big: The effects of acoustic pitch on product perceptions. *Journal of Marketing Research*, *54*(2), 331–346. https://doi.org/10.1509/jmr.14.0300

Lowrey, T. M., & Shrum, L. J. (2007). Phonetic symbolism and brand name preference. *Journal of Consumer Research*, *34*(3), 406–414. https://doi.org/10.1086/518530

Melnyk, V., Klein, K., & Völckner, F. (2012). The double-edged sword of foreign brand names for companies from emerging countries. *Journal of Marketing*, *76*(6), 21–37. https://doi.org/10.1509/jm.11.0349

Melton, C. A. (1979). Generic term or trademark: Confusing legal standards and inadequate protection. *American University Law Review*, *29*, 109.

Meng, H., Zamudio, C., & Jewell, R. D. (2021). What's in a name? Scent brand names, olfactory imagery, and purchase intention. *Journal of Product & Brand Management*, *30*(2), 281–292. https://doi.org/10.1108/JPBM-06-2019-2418

Meyers-Levy, J. (1989). The influence of a brand name's association set size and word frequency on brand memory. *Journal of Consumer Research*, *16*(2), 197–207. https://doi.org/10.1086/209208

Meyers-Levy, J., Louie, T. A., & Curren, M. T. (1994). How does the congruity of brand names affect evaluations of brand name extensions? *Journal of Applied Psychology*, *79*(1), 46–53. https://doi.org/10.1037/0021-9010.79.1.46

Moriuchi, E., & Jackson, P. R. (2017). Role of brand names and product types on bicultural consumers' purchase intentions. *Journal of Consumer Marketing*, *34*(1), 53–65. https://doi.org/10.1108/JCM-10-2014-1190

Morton, E. S. (1994). Sound symbolism and its role in non-human vertebrate communication. In L. Hinton, J. Nichols, & J. J. Ohala (Eds.), *Sound symbolism* (pp. 348–365). Cambridge University Press.

Motoki, K., Iseki, S., & Pathak, A. (2025). Sounds cute: Exploring the role of sound reduplication in brand names. *International Journal of Research in Marketing*. https://doi.org/10.1016/j.ijresmar.2025.02.002

Motoki, K., Park, J., Pathak, A., & Spence, C. (2023). Creating luxury brand names in the hospitality and tourism sector: The role of sound symbolism in destination branding. *Journal of Destination Marketing & Management*, *30*, 100815. https://doi.org/10.1016/j.jdmm.2023.100815

Motoki, K., & Pathak, A. (2023). The length of brand names influences the expectation of healthiness in foods and preference for healthy foods. *Psychology & Marketing*, *40*(9), 1850–1862. https://doi.org/10.1002/mar.21859

Ozcan, T., & Gunasti, K. (2019). How associations between products and numbers in brand names affect consumer attitudes: Introducing multi-context numbers. *Journal of Brand Management*, *26*(2), 176–194. https://doi.org/10.1057/s41262-018-0125-1

Pathak, A., & Calvert, G. A. (2020). Sounds sweet, sounds bitter: How the presence of certain sounds in a brand name can alter expectations about the product's taste. *Food Quality and Preference*, *83*, 103918. https://doi.org/10.1016/j.foodqual.2020.103918

Pathak, A., Calvert, G. A., & Lim, L. K. (2020a). Harsh voices, sound branding: How voiced consonants in a brand's name can alter its perceived attributes. *Psychology & Marketing*, *37*(6), 837–847. https://doi.org/10.1002/mar.21346

Pathak, A., Calvert, G. A., & Motoki, K. (2021). Sound symbolism overrides articulation dynamics in the taste continuum. *Food Quality and Preference*, *91*, 104186. https://doi.org/10.1016/j.foodqual.2021.104186

Pathak, A., & Motoki, K. (2022). Evaluating brand names without vowels. *Food Quality and Preference*, *97*, 104450. https://doi.org/10.1016/j.foodqual.2021.104450

Pathak, A., Motoki, K., Techawachirakul, M., & Calvert, G. A. (2022). Spiky sounds sparkling: How voiceless consonants present in the brand name of a beverage are more appropriate in conveying its carbonation strength. *Food Quality and Preference*, *96*, 104404. https://doi.org/10.1016/j.foodqual.2021.104404

Pathak, A., Velasco, C., Petit, O., & Calvert, G. A. (2019). Going to great lengths in the pursuit of luxury: How longer brand names can enhance the luxury perception of a brand. *Psychology & Marketing*, *36*(10), 951–963. https://doi.org/10.1002/mar.21247

Pathak, A., Velasco, C., & Spence, C. (2020b). The sound of branding: An analysis of the initial phonemes of popular brand names. *Journal of Brand*

Management, *27*(3), 339–354. https://doi.org/10.1057/s41262-019-00183-5

Pavia, T. M., & Costa, J. A. (1993). The winning number: Consumer perceptions of alpha-numeric brand names. *Journal of Marketing*, *57*(3), 85–98. https://doi.org/10.1177/002224299305700306

Peterson, R. A., & Ross, I. (1972). How to name new brands. *Journal of Advertising Research*, *12*(6), 29–34.

Pogacar, R., Plant, E., Rosulek, L. F., & Kouril, M. (2015). Sounds good: Phonetic sound patterns in top brand names. *Marketing Letters*, *26*(4), 549–563.

Rao, A. R., Qu, L., & Ruekert, R. W. (1999). Signaling unobservable product quality through a brand ally. *Journal of Marketing Research*, *36*(2), 258–268. https://doi.org/10.1177/002224379903600209

Sapir, E. (1929). A study in phonetic symbolism. *Journal of Experimental Psychology*, *12*(3), 225–239. https://doi.org/10.1037/h0070931

Schloss, I. (1981). Chickens and pickles. *Journal of Advertising Research*, *21*, 47–49. https://doi.org/10.1080/00218499.1981.12468144

Sen, S. (1999). The effects of brand name suggestiveness and decision goal on the development of brand knowledge. *Journal of Consumer Psychology*, *8*(4), 431–455. https://doi.org/10.1207/s15327663jcp0804_04

Shrum, L. J., Lowrey, T. M., Luna, D., Lerman, D. B., & Liu, M. (2012). Sound symbolism effects across languages: Implications for global brand names. *International Journal of Research in Marketing*, *29*(3), 275–279. https://doi.org/10.1016/j.ijresmar.2012.03.002

Smith, L. W., & Abell, A. (2025). The art of misspelling: Unraveling the diverging effects of misspelled brand names on consumer responses. *Journal of Consumer Research*. https://doi.org/10.1093/jcr/ucaf020

Stanford, D. D. (2014, October 18). Ben & Jerry's refuses to change 'Hazed & Confused' name. *BloombergBusiness*. Retrieved February 10, 2025, from www.bloomberg.com/news/articles/2014-10-17/ben-jerry-s-won-t-rename-hazed-confused-after-complaints

TOI Lifestyle Desk. (2025). Why did PUMA rebrand itself as PVMA? Retrieved February 10, 2025, from https://timesofindia.indiatimes.com/life-style/fashion/luxury/fashion/why-did-puma-rebrand-itself-as-pvma-/articleshow/117244110.cms

Topolinski, S. (2017). Articulation patterns in names: A hidden route to consumer preference. *Journal of the Association for Consumer Research*, *2*(4), 382–391. https://doi.org/10.1086/692820

Topolinski, S., Maschmann, I. T., Pecher, D., & Winkielman, P. (2014). Oral approach–avoidance: Affective consequences of muscular articulation dynamics. *Journal of Personality and Social Psychology*, *106*(6), 885–896. https://doi.org/10.1037/a0036477

Turley, L. W., & Moore, P. A. (1995). Brand name strategies in the service sector. *Journal of Consumer Marketing*, *12*(4), 42–50. https://doi.org/10.1108/07363769510095298

Ulrich, I., Azar, S. L., & Aimé, I. (2020). Stay close but not too close: The role of similarity in the cross-gender extension of patronymic brands. *Journal of Business Research*, *120*, 157–174. https://doi.org/10.1016/j.jbusres.2020.07.027

Van Doorn, G., Paton, B., & Spence, C. (2016). Is J the new K? A failure to replicate Schloss (1981). *Journal of Brand Management*, *23*(6), 666–678. https://doi.org/10.1057/s41262-016-0007-3

Vanden Bergh, B. (1982/83). Feedback: More chickens and pickles. *Journal of Advertising Research*, *22*(6), 44. https://doi.org/10.1080/00218499.1982.12468070

Vanden Bergh, B., Adler, K., & Oliver, L. (1987). Linguistic distinction among top brand names. *Journal of Advertising Research*, *27*(4), 39–44.

Wiedmann, K. P., Hennigs, N., Schmidt, S., & Wuestefeld, T. (2011). The importance of brand heritage as a key performance driver in marketing management. *Journal of Brand Management*, *19*(3), 182–194. https://doi.org/10.1057/bm.2011.36

Witek-Hajduk, M. K., & Grudecka, A. (2022). Does the developed-country brand name still matter? Consumers' purchase intentions and ethnocentrism and materialism as moderators. *Journal of Product & Brand Management*, *31*(6), 854–869.

Wu, L., Klink, R. R., & Guo, J. (2013). Creating gender brand personality with brand names: The effects of phonetic symbolism. *Journal of Marketing Theory and Practice*, *21*(3), 319–330. https://doi.org/10.2753/MTP1069-6679210306

Yan, D., & Duclos, R. (2013). Making sense of numbers: Effects of alphanumeric brands on consumer inference. *International Journal of Research in Marketing*, *30*(2), 179–184. https://doi.org/10.1016/j.ijresmar.2012.09.007

Yeo, J., & Park, J. (2006). Effects of parent-extension similarity and self regulatory focus on evaluations of brand extensions. *Journal of Consumer Psychology*, *16*(3), 272–282. https://doi.org/10.1207/s15327663jcp1603_9

Yorkston, E., & Menon, G. (2004). A sound idea: Phonetic effects of brand names on consumer judgments. *Journal of Consumer Research*, *31*(1), 43–51. https://doi.org/10.1086/383422

Zaichkowsky, J. L. (2010). Strategies for distinctive brands. *Journal of Brand Management*, *17*(8), 548–560. https://doi.org/10.1057/bm.2010.12

Zhang, S., & Sood, S. (2002). 'Deep' and 'surface' cues: Brand extension evaluations by children and adults. *Journal of Consumer Research*, *29*(1), 129–141. https://doi.org/10.1086/338207

Zhang, S., & Schmitt, B. H. (2001). Creating local brands in multilingual international markets. *Journal of Marketing Research*, *38*(3), 313–325. https://doi.org/10.1509/jmkr.38.3.313.18869

Zhang, S., & Schmitt, B. H. (2004). Activating sound and meaning: The role of language proficiency in bilingual consumer environments. *Journal of Consumer Research*, *31*(1), 220–228. https://doi.org/10.1086/383437

Zinkhan, G. M., & Martin, C. R., Jr. (1987). New brand names and inferential beliefs: Some insights on naming new products. *Journal of Business Research*, *15*(2), 157–172. https://doi.org/10.1016/0148-2963(84)90046-8

15

Co-Branding Strategy: Theoretical Perspectives, Contemporary Practices and Research Directions

Ceyda Paydas Turan

INTRODUCTION

Imagine yourself jogging rhythmically with your Apple Watch Nike on your wrist and The North Face × Gucci hoodie on your back, burning off the calories from the last Doritos Locos Tacos you ate at Taco Bell followed by an Oreo McFlurry. An increasing number of brands today engage in collaborations like these, seamlessly integrating into consumers' daily lives.

Co-branding, a brand management strategy, whereby two or more brands are intentionally brought together and presented to the consumers in a manner that leverages each brand through the transfer of associations from one brand to the other, has received considerable interest from academics and practitioners alike (Paydas Turan, 2022). In today's highly competitive business environment where there are finite resources to meet consumer demands, managers are increasingly recognizing the value of collaborating with other brands to maximise brand potential. According to Forbes, some brands generate over 28% of their total revenue through brand partnerships, with year-on-year revenue growth exceeding 50% due to amplified revenue streams and an expanded customer base (Garcia, 2024). Although a properly executed co-branding strategy can be a strategic brand and business development tool, the process is challenging, and failures are prevalent in practice.

A comprehensive understanding of co-branding strategy is essential to effectively leverage its opportunities while mitigating associated risks. This chapter aims to deepen the understanding of co-branding strategy by examining the following key aspects: 1) its differentiation from other brand alliance strategies; 2) contemporary co-branding practices; 3) motivations for adopting co-branding strategy; 4) theoretical underpinnings of co-branding strategy; 5) key success factors and 6) managerial implications and future research directions. Thus, this chapter aims to provide readers with a state-of-the-art review of the co-branding literature, offer insights to guide managerial decision-making and outline key directions for future research.

Co-branding strategy, when properly executed, creates competitive advantages for brands. It enhances the value and drives financial outcomes as well as brand mindset metrics (Swaminathan et al., 2022). However, despite these successful practices demonstrating the benefits of brand alliance, co-branding arrangements entail some risks (Paydas Turan, 2022; Shan et al., 2022). By delving into the co-branding literature with the objectives of highlighting various conceptualizations, exploring its theoretical foundations, identifying the opportunities it presents and analysing key success factors, this chapter aims to offer both theoretical insights and practical managerial implications for co-branding strategy.

CO-BRANDING VERSUS OTHER BRAND ALLIANCE STRATEGIES

Despite the strong interest in co-branding strategy, ambiguity remains regarding the precise boundaries of the term 'co-branding'. Some researchers adopt a broader definition of co-branding, whereas others use a narrow definition (Han et al., 2023). When defined broadly, the term 'co-branding' has often been used interchangeably with 'brand alliance', referring to a marketing partnership strategy between two brands across various marketing contexts, including advertising, distribution channels and sales promotions (Besharat & Langan, 2014; Paydas Turan, 2022). The narrow definition of co-branding, on the other hand, construes it as a specific type of branding alliance. The formation of one single product or service through an alliance of two brands is the criterion most generally acknowledged to distinguish co-branding from other types of brand alliances (Besharat, 2010).

Co-branding in this chapter is defined as a long-term brand alliance strategy in which one product or service is branded simultaneously by two brands. For a brand alliance to be identified as a co-branding, the following criteria are essential and required: 1) a co-branded product or service should consist of two independent brands that are visible to the potential customers on an independent new product/service (Helmig et al., 2008; Rao et al., 1999); 2) these partner brands continue their independent existence in the market after co-branding launch (Chiambaretto & Gurău, 2017; Miller et al., 2014) and 3) the two independent partner brands coming together on a new product or service is executed strategically on purpose by these brands to create an additional value (Blackett & Russell, 2000). Table 15.1 presents a list of examples showcasing co-branding practices across various industries.

CONTEMPORARY CO-BRANDING PRACTICES

As the list of co-branding practices in Table 15.1 demonstrates, these partners exist as individual brands, partner up with each other on purpose and are exposed to potential customers simultaneously on relevant co-branded product or service. For example, Malibu, white rum-based coconut spirit brand, and Oatly, oat drink brand, successfully launched Piña Oatlada, a dairy-free piña colada-flavoured soft-serve ice cream, with a

Table 15.1 Contemporary co-branding examples

Co-branding	*Partner Brand X*	*Partner Brand Y*
Malibu × Oatly	Malibu (rum-based coconut spirit)	Oatly (oat milk)
Bianchi and Ducati	Bianchi (high-performance sports equipment, bicycle)	Ducati (high-performance motorcycles)
Bianchi and Emporio Armani	Bianchi (high-performance sports equipment, bicycle)	Emporio Armani (luxury fashion)
The North Face × Gucci	The North Face (outdoor performance gear and clothing)	Gucci (luxury fashion)
Coke Light with NutraSweet	Coca Cola Light (low-calorie carbonated drink)	NutraSweet (artificial sweetener)
Jacobs Instant Coffee with Daim Flavour	Daim (confectionery)	Jacobs (coffee)
Barbour × GANNI	Barbour (fashion)	GANNI (fashion)
Tefal and Teflon	Tefal (frying pan)	Teflon (non-stick chemical coating)
Oreo McFlurry	Oreo (cocoa biscuit cookie)	McDonalds (fast food)
Tefal × Le Cordon Bleu	Tefal (high-quality cookware)	Le Cordon Bleu (French culinary academy)
Versace for H&M	Versace (luxury fashion house)	H&M (fast-fashion retailer)
Mentos Fanta	Mentos (confectionary)	Coca Cola (carbonated soft drink)

Source: The author.

touch of alcohol. While Malibu manages to bring out the spirit of summer and enable great experiences, Oatly guides its customers in exploring unexpected ways to experience the glory of oats. The tag line for this innovative co-branding collaboration between Malibu and Oatly is creatively crafted: 'Lick Responsibly'. This co-branding succeeds as both brands, known for their great taste, have successfully merged to deliver a distinctive seasonal flavour. Another quintessential example of co-branding is Tefal × Le Cordon Bleu, where two highly respected French brands, Tefal, known for its high-quality cookware, and Le Cordon Bleu, a prestigious culinary academy, join forces to develop and launch a premium product line tailored for both professional chefs and home cooks. This co-branding partnership reflects their shared expertise and commitment to excellence in the culinary world. As demonstrated by the successful co-branding examples in Table 15.1, co-branding can be established between partner brands from the same (i.e., The North Face × Gucci, Barbour × Ganni) or different industries (i.e., Mentos Fanta, Malibu × Oatly, Bianchi & Emporio Armani, Jacobs Instant Coffee with Daim Flavour, Tefal & Teflon, and Oreo McFlurry), as well as through collaborations between a product and a service brand (i.e., Tefal × Le Cordon Bleu) or between a luxury and a mass-market brand (i.e., Versace for H&M).

Although branding strategies share similarities, such as the simultaneous presence of two distinct brands, other strategies and tactics depicted in Table 15.2 such as product bundling (i.e., McDonald's Happy Meal with a Disney Toy), advertising partnerships, including celebrity endorsements (i.e., Brad Pitt and DeLonghi), co-location projects (i.e., Shell and Waitrose Express)

Table 15.2 Co-branding among other brand alliance strategies

Brand Alliance Strategies

	Definition	*Characteristic*	*Perceived Integration*	*Example*
Value creation at the product/service level				
Co-branding				
Ingredient branding	One brand is incorporated into another as a component (Giakoumaki et al., 2016).	Physically inseparable	High	Oreo McFlurry; Mentos Fanta; Häagen-Dazs and Baileys
Co-developed branding	Two brands merge brand resources to develop a new product (Newmeyer et al., 2018)	Physically inseparable	High	The North Face × Gucci; Barbour × GANNI; Nike Air Jordan; Malibu × Oatly
Value delivery and communication at the distribution and advertising level				
Celebrity endorsement	An individual with high public recognition appears in an advertisement of a brand to leverage their reputation to support the brand (Knoll & Matthes, 2017)	Physically independent	Low/ Medium	Brad Pitt and DeLonghi Coffee
Co-promotion	Two independent brands come together to communicate value through co-coordinated marketing activity	Physically independent	Low	Mc Donald's Happy Meals with Disney toys
Joint sales promotion/ product bundling	Pooling brands' resources to capitalise on joint sales opportunities (Singh et al., 2016)	Physically independent	Low	Doritos with Pepsi Cola; McDonald's Happy Meal with a Disney Toy
Co-location	Pooling brands' resources to reduce search and increase variety (Newmeyer et al., 2018)	Physically independent	Medium	Little Waitrose and Partners at Shell

Source: The author.

and joint sales promotions (i.e., Starbucks and Spotify offering Spotify Premium subscribers exclusive benefits such as free beverages at Starbucks stores) are not considered co-branding. This distinction arises because these partnerships do not present potential customers with an inseparable product or service that is simultaneously branded by two brands (Helmig et al., 2008; Newmeyer et al., 2014, 2018). Co-branding can introduce a new product or service within an industry where one or both brands previously operated independently or expand into an entirely new industry where neither brand has existed before. When a co-branded product is launched in a new category that the brand(s) did not exist before, it is identified as a brand extension to a new category, leveraging the established brand equity of the partners (Malhotra & Bhattacharyya, 2022). Since the end product is co-branded, this branding strategy is specifically defined as a co-branding strategy. However, not every brand extension qualifies as co-branding, as brands can also choose to extend their single brand into a new product category without partnering with another brand. Every co-branded product serves as an alternative brand extension for the respective partner brands, whether in the form of a vertical or horizontal line extension or a category extension (Besharat & Langan, 2014).

Co-branding can be categorised into two types based on the level of integration between the partner brands: Ingredient branding and co-developed branding (Helmig et al., 2008). Ingredient branding, which is also known as vertical co-branding, entails the integration of a product part (i.e., ingredient) within another product (Desai and Keller, 2002; Paydas Turan, 2021b). The McFlurry ice cream with pieces of Oreo cookie is an example of vertical co-branding, where a well-known ingredient brand (Oreo) is integrated into the end product (McFlurry) to enhance its value and appeal. McFlurry, McDonald's frozen soft-serve dessert brand, incorporates Oreo, a cookie brand owned by Mondelez International, to create an ingredient branded product, Oreo McFlurrry, within its portfolio.

In horizontal co-branding, a co-developed product or service offering is formed by more than one producer at the same step in the value chain with similar or complementary resources, for example, The North Face × Gucci (composite product of The North Face and Gucci brands) (Helmig et al., 2008; Naidoo & Hollebeek, 2016). The North Face and Gucci brands collaborate to create this co-branding, drawing on the values of self-discovery and self-expression that define both brands.

A different typology used to define co-branding is physical (functional) versus symbolic co-branding (Lanseng & Olsen, 2012). Physical (functional) co-branding refers to an alliance where one brand incorporates another brand as a component or an ingredient. Häagen-Dazs Baileys is an example for functional co-branding since Baileys brand is an ingredient in Häagen-Dazs ice cream. In physical (functional) co-branding, the ingredient brand acts as a cue that signals the unique attributes of the host brand such as the quality (Desai et al., 2014). Symbolic co-branding, on the other hand, refers to a co-branding formed by two brands that are not functionally linked but rather share the symbolic meanings such as the image, status and values (Lanseng & Olsen, 2012). An example of this is the Louis Vuitton × Supreme collaboration, where Louis Vuitton, a French luxury fashion brand, and Supreme, a streetwear brand, combine forces to create a fusion of their distinct brand identities. Louis Vuitton brings its high-end luxury and heritage, while Supreme brings its youthful and edgy street culture, resulting in a co-branded offering that blends the two worlds.

MOTIVATIONS FOR ADOPTING CO-BRANDING STRATEGY

In today's highly competitive business landscape, managers are increasingly leveraging co-branding strategies as a powerful approach to enhance the brand potential. It all begins with the fundamental questions: 'What makes a brand strong?' and 'How do managers build strong brands?'. Customer-based brand equity highlights that the power of a brand lies in the minds and hearts of the customers (Keller, 1993). The challenge for brand managers is to create the right products and services and meaningful experiences through strategic marketing efforts to cultivate strong brand associations and positive customer perceptions. A brand that successfully builds a positive customer-based brand equity becomes well known among consumers, evokes favourable associations and generates positive judgements and emotions. When a brand resonates with its potential customers, it increases the likelihood of both initial purchases and long-term loyalty through repeat purchases (Keller, 1993). Every marketing effort made for a brand has the potential to either enhance or diminish its brand equity. Since every brand aims to strengthen its presence in the minds and hearts of existing and potential customers, they may seek additional support from other entities to enhance brand equity (Paydas Turan, 2021a). Although a properly executed co-branding can offer a strategic business success opportunity, the process is challenging, and failures are common in practice. When executed successfully, a co-branding strategy can enable focal brands to establish and/or enhance their brand identity by transferring relevant and positive associations from their co-branding partner (Aaker & Keller, 1990); create appropriate brand meanings and positioning; elicit desired brand responses; build the right brand relationships with the customers (Blackett & Boad, 1999); gain access to a new market and tap into new customers (Kalafatis et al., 2012; Pinello et al., 2022; Washburn et al., 2000). Co-branding helps firms develop brand resources and strengthen their brand equities (Han et al., 2023). Challenges that lead to failures are also evident in practice, demonstrating the impact of negative spill over effects that harm partner brands (Ahn et al., 2009; Lanseng & Olsen, 2012; Paydas Turan, 2021a; Singh et al., 2020). In order to build successful co-branding, it is crucial to understand the theoretical underpinnings of co-branding strategy and its key success factors. In the co-branding literature, 'success' generally refers to the consumers' positive and favourable attitudes, quality perceptions and purchasing intentions towards the co-branded product or service (Aaker & Keller, 1990; Besharat, 2010; Paydas Turan, 2021a; Singh et al., 2016).

The popularity of co-branding strategy in practice stems from its various promises: It can enable brands to enhance their brand equities (Kalafatis et al., 2012; Washburn et al., 2004), differentiate their brands in competitive environments (Helmig et al., 2008); reduce costs and speed up the product development process (Chiambaretto et al., 2016), help access new markets and address new target audience (Dahlstrom & Nygaard, 2016; Leuthesser et al., 2003; Uggla & Åsberg, 2010), leverage shared resources and competencies (Bengtsson & Servais, 2005), create synergies, boost awareness, enhance the value of the partner brands (Aaker, 1991; Simonin & Ruth, 1998) and boost sales revenue (Besharat, 2010; Swaminathan et al., 2022).

When two experts in their field join forces to develop a co-branding, this agreement can lower product development and production costs (Blackett & Boad, 1999; Chiambaretto et al., 2016). Another advantage of co-branding strategy is that brands can gain access to the target audience of their partners and hence extend their potential customer base (Uggla & Åsberg, 2010). This strategy is also viable when a brand seeks opportunities of access to a foreign market (Abratt & Motlana, 2002). When entering a foreign market, a brand can engage in co-branding with a well-established local brand to leverage its reputation within the region (Bluemelhuber et al., 2007; Rodrigue & Biswas, 2004). Co-branding strategy can be beneficial not only when entering a foreign market but also when expanding into a different industry. A cross-industry co-branding is perceived as a strategic shift in market boundaries, where two brands from different industries collaborate to create unique attributes that differentiate their co-branded offering (Chiambaretto et al., 2016; Smarandescu et al., 2013).

In the life span of any co-branding, partner brands come together to be successful, and the strategy is executed on the premise that the positive transfer of associations will create added value for the partner brands (Rao & Ruekert, 1994; Senechal et al., 2014; Singh et al., 2016). Co-branding establishes multiple pathways for the transfer of associations including those between the partner brands, from the partner brands to the co-branded offering and from the co-branded offering back to the partner brands (Baumgarth, 2004; Lafferty et al., 2004; Rao & Ruekert, 1994; Simonin & Ruth, 1998). When two brands come together to form the co-branding offer, they are also tied up in the minds of their consumers. Co-branding signals an implicit message that both brands share a common universe of values (Simonin & Ruth, 1998). Although some researchers argue that the brands with low equity are the ones benefiting the most from the transfer of association from their more reputable partner brands (Park et al., 1996), others find support for also high-equity brands having incentives to form alliance with lower-equity brands since co-branding arrangement helps them to increase brand awareness and has a positive effect on purchase intention (Vaidyanathan & Aggarwal, 2000; Washburn et al., 2004). Similarly, the co-branded product or service will also be affected by the transfer of associations coming from the partner brands. Research findings indicate that individual brand characteristics of partner brands such as the relevant associations, attitudes and beliefs about the brands are positively related to the evaluation of co-branding (Paydas Turan, 2021a; Rodrigue & Biswas, 2004). Conversely, a co-branded product or service can also trigger positive or negative transfer of associations from the co-branding initiative back to the partner brands, influencing their brand perception (Simonin & Ruth, 1998). While the transfer effect is stronger for low-equity brands when compared to high-equity brands (Washburn et al., 2004), both partners need to be cautious since these transfer effects are not always positive. If a co-branded product or service fails to meet the consumer's expectations, the resulting negativity may be attributed to the respective partner brands, leading to negative spillover effects where unfavourable perceptions from the co-branding transfer to the individual brands involved (Paydas Turan, 2022). Even a strong host brand is not protected against negative spillover effects when a negativity occurs at the co-branded offering (Radighieri et al., 2014). Therefore, overarching aim of this chapter is to review the co-branding literature and deepen the understanding of what co-branding is, and how it can maximise brand potential, with a focus on the theoretical underpinnings of the strategy.

THEORETICAL UNDERPINNINGS OF CO-BRANDING STRATEGY

The extensive co-branding literature explores various theories that explain the transfer of associations between partner brands and the co-branded offering. The most dominant theories used to understand how co-branding works and its impact on partner brands include signalling theory (Spence, 1973), information integration theory (Anderson, 1981), balance theory (Heider, 1946), associative network theory (Anderson, 1983), attitude accessibility theory (Fazio et al., 1982), attribution theory (Kelley, 1967), categorisation theory (Rosch, 1973, 1975) and schema congruity theory (Mandler, 1982). Some studies apply two or more of these theories, summarised in Table 15.3, to explain the co-branding phenomenon, highlighting the interdisciplinarity nature of co-branding research.

Signalling theory plays a central role in the co-branding literature (Pinello et al., 2022). It explains how people rely on perceivable cues to infer attributes that are not directly observable (Spence, 1973). Signalling theory (Spence, 1973) has been used as a prominent theory explaining the role that brands play in transmitting credible signals of product quality in marketing field (i.e., Bleijerveld et al., 2015; Helm & Ozergin, 2015; Ma et al., 2018; McCarthy & Norris, 1999; Naidoo & Hollebeek, 2016; Park et al., 1996; Rao et al., 1999; Singh et al., 2014; Xiang & Mishra, 2002). In the co-branding context, the presence of two reputable brands provides consumers even more powerful signals regarding the product's quality than in the case of a single brand, especially when the direct assessment of quality is challenging due to the lack of available information (Rao & Ruekert, 1994). The brand positionings of two partner brands are perceived as signals by the consumers when they are forming their attitudes towards the co-branded product, and hence, the positioning strategies of each partner brand are positively related with the co-branded product's positioning (Singh et al., 2014). Signalling theory is applied to show the positive effect of the presence of an ingredient branding on consumers' perception of the end product's quality, whether the host brand is perceived as of higher or lower quality (Helm & Ozergin, 2015). The presence of a well-known ingredient brand serves as a credible signal of quality, enhancing consumer confidence in the overall product.

Information integration theory (Anderson, 1981) that is widely used in consumer behaviour research explains how people receive information from different sources and by adding and weighing such information they form an attitude and decide how to behave. In the co-branding context, information integration theory shows how people integrate attitudes and beliefs about partner brands to form an evaluation of the final co-branded offering (Paydas Turan, 2021a; Simonin & Ruth, 1998). Prior brand attitudes are positively related to the attitude towards the co-branding (Rodrigue & Biswas, 2004). Research shows that individual brand characteristics of partner brands, which cover all the associations, attitudes and beliefs about the brands, are to some extent related to the evaluation of co-branding (Paydas Turan, 2021a). Information integration theory is employed among others in studies by Bouten et al. (2011); Naidoo and Hollebeek (2016); Mazodier and Merunka (2014); Rodrigue and Biswas (2004); Simonin and Ruth (1998) and Washburn et al. (2000).

Balance theory (Heider, 1946) is another theory employed in co-branding literature to explain how consumers' pre-existing attitudes towards partner brands affect their evaluation of the co-branded offering. It draws on the theory that explains how people seek consistency in their attitudes and relationships. Ahn et al. (2020), Bouten et al. (2011), Lanseng and Olsen (2012) and Senechal et al. (2014) are among the researchers that employ 'balance theory' in their co-branding studies. It is argued that that consumers' attitudes towards co-branding grow more positive when the product categories of partner brands fit well together (Bouten et al., 2011; Lanseng & Olsen, 2012), and there is perceived relevancy and perceived expectancy (Senechal et al., 2014). This is explained by balance theory (Heider, 1946) as consumers prefer situations that help retain their inner balance and maintain consistency.

Associative network theory (Anderson, 1983) is a cognitive theory that explains how human memory stores and retrieves information, which are represented as a network of interconnected nodes. Each node represents a concept, and the links between nodes form the associations in the human mind. In the co-branding context, the associative network theory explains how consumers form perceptions of co-branded products by drawing on the stored and retrieved associations of the partner brands from their memories or experiences.

Table 15.3 Theories applied in co-branding research

Theory	*Key Insight*	*Application in Co-branding*
Signalling theory (Spence, 1973)	In the case of asymmetric information between the two parties, individuals lacking the information rely on signals as perceived cues of information that is unavailable or unobservable to them.	How does the presence of a familiar and strong brand in a co-branding send signals of quality and credibility for the less familiar partner brand and/or the co-branded offering?
Information integration theory (Anderson, 1981)	Individuals form and modify their attitudes or beliefs as they receive and interpret new information, integrating it with their existing attitudes and beliefs.	How do customers integrate and weigh attitudes towards individual partner brands when forming perceptions of a co-branded offering?
Balance theory (Heider, 1946)	Individuals aim to maintain a consistency in their sentiments and behaviours when interacting with other people or objects.	How do consumers develop attitudes towards the co-branding partner of a favoured brand to maintain cognitive balance?
Associative network theory (Anderson, 1983)	Memory consists of interconnected nodes (individual pieces of information and concepts) that get recalled when stimulated.	How do consumers associate the stimulus about one of the partner brands to the other partner when the co-branding is reinforced through a co-branding ad?
Attitude accessibility theory (Fazio et al., 1982)	When individuals encounter with an object, associated evaluations can be triggered, and the likelihood of this activation is determined by the strength of the attitude. The stronger the attitude, the easier it is retrieved from memory in the presence of a relevant stimulus.	How does the attitude towards one of the partner brands get retrieved automatically with a relevant strong stimulus (i.e., immediate exposure to the brand's ad) and transferred to the partner brand or the co-branded offering?
Attribution theory (Kelley, 1967)	It explains how individuals assign causal inferences and their effect on attitudes and behaviours. Causal inferences have three dimensions: Locus, control, and stability.	How do consumers form judgements about partner brands in response to the success or failure of a co-branding partnership?
Categorisation theory (Rosch, 1973)	Individuals organise information by grouping objects, people, situations, etc., into categories based on shared features to ease the information processing.	How do consumers' pre-existing mental categories partner brands influence their evaluation of a co-branded offering?
Schema congruity theory (Mandler, 1982)	When individuals process new information by comparing it to existing mental schemas, responding to moderate incongruity (mismatch between features of a product and an activated category schema) leads to more favourable evaluation than does the process of responding to either congruity or extreme incongruity.	How does the level of perceived fit between partner brands across image, attributes and industry alignment impact consumer evaluation of a co-branded offering?

Source: The author.

These associations influence how consumers evaluate the co-branded offering and the extent to which they transfer existing brand perceptions to the new collaboration. This theory (1983) helps to highlight the process through which beliefs about brand alliances are formed in a person's mind (Naidoo & Hollebeek, 2016). An essential condition for associative network theory is that stimulus and response occur together. In the co-branding context, consumers can associate the stimulus about one partner brand to the other if the presence of co-branding is reinforced through advertising or any other marketing communication tools. Balachander and Ghose (2003), James (2005), Kalafatis et al. (2016) and Samu et al. (1999) are some of the academics employing associative network theory in their co-branding research.

Attitude accessibility theory (Fazio et al., 1982, 1989) explains how the accessibility of the attitudes stored in memory influences our judgements and behaviours. The accessibility of an attitude is the level of retrievability from memory in the presence of a relevant stimulus. This theory has been applied in co-branding research by Lafferty et al. (2004), Helmig et al. (2008) and Vaidyanathan and Aggarwal (2000) to explain how consumers' pre-existing attitudes towards partner brands shape their evaluations of the co-branded offering. Consumers are more likely to access attitudes related to a brand that are more salient or accessible. For example, the association of a branded ingredient with a private-brand product that is relatively less salient can have a positive impact on consumer evaluation of that unfamiliar private-brand product by leveraging the credibility of the more salient ingredient brand (Vaidyanathan & Aggarwal, 2000). Although stronger or more familiar brands are more accessible to consumers, research suggests that both partner brands can still gain advantages from co-branding. A well-known brand may still find value in partnering with a less salient brand if the attitudes towards the partners and the perception of brand fit are not negative (Simonin & Ruth, 1998).

Attribution theory developed by Kelley (1967), later expanded by Weiner (1985), explains how individuals infer the causes of events or behaviours, linking them either to internal factors (e.g., abilities or intentions) or external factors (e.g., situational circumstances). In the co-branding context, the attribution theory explains how consumers assign credit or blame to partner brands based on their pre-existing knowledge and perceptions of those brands. It is argued that in the event of an unfavourable evaluation of the co-branded product, more blame is likely to be attributed on the private brand that is less salient and less familiar rather than the national brand, which is more salient and familiar to the consumers (Vaidyanathan & Aggarwal, 2000). Research states that consumers can also discount the effect of a possible cause when alternative causes are feasible (Alcañiz et al., 2010). In the context of co-branding, dealing with a negative event occurring at one of the partner brands can be highly complex since the blame could be attributed to either brand to varying degrees, depending on the level of integration between them (Paydas Turan, 2022). Drawing on the attribution theory (Kelley, 1967), it is explained that consumers attribute blame to not only the partner brand that is the locus of the failure but also, to some extent, to the partner brand associated with the locus of failure through the co-branding agreement (Paydas Turan, 2022).

Categorisation theory (Rosch, 1973) is one of the other theories used in co-branding literature to explain how consumers evaluate co-branded products based on the attributes they assign for the partner brands. A brand can be perceived as a 'category' in consumers' minds (Aaker & Keller, 1990; Ahn & Sung, 2012; Bhat & Reddy, 2001). The pre-existing mental categories that consumers have for the partner brands have impact on how they evaluate the co-branded offering. When consumers' responses to an ingredient branding strategy for a luxury brand with a non-luxury ingredient brand are examined, if the parent brand has strong and favourable associations in memory, then consumers evaluate a co-branded offering that has high fit with the parent brand more favourably when compared to a brand that has poor fit with the parent brand (Moon & Sprott, 2016). Research shows that both the brand image and product category fit positively influence purchase intentions of the co-branded product, highlighting the prominence of categorisation theory in co-branding context (Moon & Sprott, 2016). The fit between partner brands, which plays a crucial role in shaping co-branding evaluations, can be a function of both functional and symbolic dimensions (Ahn & Sung, 2012).

Similarly, schema congruity theory (Mandler, 1982) describes the processing of new information by comparing it to existing mental schemas (i.e., cognitive structures or frameworks based on past experiences). Cognitive alignment or cognitive fluency is an important factor in the evaluation of any stimulus, and in a co-branding context, this refers to the relatedness, complementarity, similarity and match between the partner brands (Han et al., 2023). It is theorised that responding to moderate incongruity, which is a mismatch between features of a product and an activated category schema, leads to more favourable evaluation compared to either congruity or extreme incongruity. This occurs because of increased elaboration required to resolve moderate incongruity. Successful resolution of moderate incongruity is satisfying and rewarding and, thus, leads to favourable evaluation of the stimulus. In the context of co-branding, the level of congruity between partner brands matters, and the evaluation of the co-branded offering is sensitive to 'processing' condition (Walchli, 2007). The likelihood of positive evaluation for the co-branded offering is highest when partner brands have moderate incongruity, which requires further processing to resolve. Though, if the consumers have low involvement with the product category when processing the 'moderate incongruity', it is recommended that the relationship between partner brands be clearly explained and reinforced in the marketing communication for this co-branded offering to enhance consumer understanding (Walchli, 2007).

KEY SUCCESS FACTORS FOR CO-BRANDING[1]

Although a properly executed co-branding can create a success story for partner brands, the process is challenging, and failures are common in practice (Paydas Turan, 2021a). Consumer evaluation of co-branding is shaped by several factors, including attitudes toward the partner brands, perceived brand quality, brand equity, brand familiarity and perceived fit between brands. Additionally, individual characteristics such as variety-seeking behaviour, need for uniqueness and brand consciousness influence how co-branded products are evaluated (Paydas Turan, 2021a). The concept of brand fit has garnered significant attention from co-branding researchers, as it plays a crucial role in the overall success of co-branding partnerships. While some state that brand image fit has the highest impact on attitude and purchase intention (i.e., Ahn et al., 2009; Simonin & Ruth, 1998), others find that product category fit is more influential on consumer evaluation (Helmig et al., 2007). A more integrated perspective suggests that both brand fit and product fit contribute to positive evaluations, while pre-existing attitudes toward the individual brands play a less influential role (Senechal et al., 2014). Despite these insights, not all research aligns on the roles of product and brand fit. Some findings indicate that neither product nor brand fit significantly influences consumer evaluations of co-branded products (Singh et al., 2014). Similarly, the findings that pre-existing attitudes towards brands shape co-branding perceptions have been challenged (Rodrigue & Biswas, 2004). Other studies have confirmed the positive impact of brand attitude and brand fit on co-branding evaluation but found little evidence supporting the role of product category fit (Baumgarth, 2004; Lafferty et al., 2004). On the other hand, some research has shown that product fit, brand fit, and pre-existing brand attitudes towards partners collectively enhance consumer evaluations of co-branding, whereas brand familiarity towards the partner brands does not play a major role (Bouten et al., 2011).

While previous research has emphasised the importance of product category fit and brand concept consistency, assigning varying degrees of significance to these factors, recent studies on masstige co-branding have drawn attention to partnerships that involve conflicting brand concepts such as mass and prestige, accessibility and exclusivity or affordability and luxury (Shan et al., 2022; Suzuki & Kanno, 2022). These studies have demonstrated the effectiveness of co-branding strategy when executed correctly. The brand coolness of a masstige co-branding partnership, formed by a mass (or affordable) brand and a prestige (or luxury) brand, is shown to be a key attribute in fostering perceived congruence between luxury and mass brands, which positively influences consumer attitudes and purchase intentions towards the co-branded offering (Suzuki & Kanno, 2022). Further research attracts attention to the interaction effect of brand personality fit and product category fit on perceived masstige, being mediated by perceived novelty and processing fluency (Shan et al., 2022). Recent research on heritage brands (i.e., Chinese liquor heritage brand Luzhou Laojiao) highlights the potential of brand extension and co-branding strategies as effective approaches to product innovation and market entry. However, it also emphasises that heritage brands must exercise caution when pursuing co-branding initiatives (Zhang et al., 2025; Zhang & Guo, 2023). Heritage brands might aim to grab young consumers' attention and enhance brand awareness with co-branding practices. However, in a co-branding context, consumers tend to attribute less responsibility to the heritage brand compared to a brand extension, leading to a weaker perception of new product authenticity (Zhang et al., 2025). To strengthen perceived authenticity and increase purchase intention, advertising strategies can activate consumers' growth mindset by explicitly communicating the heritage brand's role in the co-branded offering (Zhang et al., 2025). These challenges highlight the need for further research on the various dimensions of the 'fit' concept and how potential consumers of co-branded offerings perceive it.

Although individual brand characteristics and the relationship between partner brands have been widely studied in co-branding literature, empirical research on the impact of consumer-related variables such as brand consciousness (Helmig et al., 2007; Mazodier & Merunka, 2014), brand involvement (Helmig et al., 2007; Mazodier & Merunka, 2014), need for uniqueness (Mazodier & Merunka, 2014), self-congruity (Mazodier & Merunka, 2014; Wang et al., 2020), variety seeking (Helmig et al., 2007; Mazodier & Merunka, 2014) and perceived

[1] This section builds upon the author's previous work, 'Success Drivers of Co-Branding: A Meta-Analysis' (Paydas Turan, 2021a), published in the *International Journal of Consumer Studies*. While drawing on its key findings, this chapter expands the discussion by covering recent studies and exploring co-branding within a broader framework, including its distinctions from other brand alliances, contemporary practices, underlying motivations, theoretical foundations, managerial implications, and directions for future research.

economic mobility (Nie et al., 2024) remains limited. However, consumer-related characteristics such as variety seeking, brand consciousness and product category involvement can be substantial predictors of symbolic co-branded purchase intention (Helmig et al., 2007; Mazodier & Merunka, 2014). Research shows that self-congruity with the secondary brand and need for uniqueness have positive impacts on symbolic co-branding purchase (Mazodier & Merunka, 2014). Moreover, consumers' involvement with the product category enhances the impact of self-congruity on purchase intention (Mazodier & Merunka, 2014). Not all co-branding partnerships are formed between brands with a high degree of fit. When analysing co-branding offerings formed by two brands with low fit (distant co-branding), consumers with high perceived economic mobility adopt a more holistic processing approach, leading to a more favourable evaluation of low-fit (distant) co-branding compared to those with low perceived economic mobility (Nie et al., 2024). These consumer-related characteristics are, therefore, important explanatory variables that can explain the inconclusive findings of former research and provide managers further insights for enhancing co-branding effectiveness.

The fragmented and ambiguous empirical evidence on success factors is largely due to the emphasis on different factors across various contexts (Dalman & Puranam, 2017; Newmeyer et al., 2014). A meta-analysis synthesising these contradictory findings in the literature reveals that while both individual brand characteristics and the relationship between brands are positively correlated with attitude towards co-branding, the correlation for the relationship between brands is significantly stronger when compared pairwise to that of individual brand characteristics (Paydas Turan, 2021a).

Whether co-branding occurs in a service or non-service business can serve as a contextual moderator that influences the success of co-branding. Findings indicate that the effect of relationship between brands on attitude towards co-branding is significantly stronger for the non-service sector when compared to the service sector (Paydas Turan, 2021a). Though, the business setting, another contextual moderator studied in the meta-analysis (2021) shows no significant difference in the correlation of success drivers and the attitude towards co-branding. In both business settings, B2C and B2B, relationship between brands has a higher correlation than individual brand characteristics of partners (Paydas Turan, 2021a).

The dyadic relationship between brands plays a key role in the evaluation of co-branding. As co-branding continues to gain popularity in today's competitive marketplace, selecting the right partner emerges as a critical determinant of success (Ahn et al., 2009; Phelps, 2016; Singh et al., 2014). Therefore, brands must focus their attention on finding the right partners for them, the 'right' partner is proved to be the one with whom they have a high degree of brand image fit (Paydas Turan, 2021a).

A meta-analysis synthesising studies conducted across different contexts finds that the congruence of consumer perceptions and associations regarding partner brands' images is more influential than the similarity and compatibility of their product categories (Paydas Turan, 2021a). The findings are generalisable to both co-branding strategies, vertical and horizontal, despite the varying levels of integration between partner brands. While the finding that 'the relationship between brands is key to the success of co-branding' is generalisable across all business types, the meta-analysis highlights the significance of consumer-related variables (e.g., customer involvement with the brands and variety-seeking behaviour) in the B2B context. It further reveals that the correlation between consumer-related variables and behavioural intention towards co-branding is significantly stronger in the B2B context than in the B2C context. This is presumably because the decision-making process in B2B contexts is more complex than it is in B2C and requires more customer involvement; this naturally increases the importance of consumer-related success factors (Paydas Turan, 2021a). Customer-specific explanations or tailor-made qualities might be more important in co-branding offerings in B2B markets. Further research on consumer-related variables (i.e., consumer characteristics) is therefore recommended in co-branding field.

Although marketers have leveraged the synergies of co-branding strategy for decades, empirical research using modern digital approaches to identify potential co-branding alliances and obtain broader insights across diverse categories remains scarce (Malhotra & Bhattacharyya, 2022). Recent studies employ automated implicit brand network analysis to identify cross-category co-branding opportunities by measuring the brand overlap among followers on X (formerly Twitter) and analysing brand users' co-interests and taste similarities (i.e., Malhotra & Bhattacharyya, 2022). This approach enables managers to explore viable co-branding opportunities across a broad band ecosystem.

MANAGERIAL IMPLICATIONS AND FUTURE RESEARCH AGENDA

In addition to contributing to a better understanding of co-branding strategy and outlining academic and managerial implications, this chapter offers guidance for future research in co-branding.

In practice, co-branding initiatives lead to both notable successes and failures. To achieve the desired positive outcome, it is essential for managerial decision-makers to identify the key success factors for co-branding. Academic research in co-branding informs managers about the importance of fit between partner brands. Managers must effectively prioritise their search criteria for the right partners. The findings indicate that the correlation between the relationship between partner brands and co-branding evaluation is significantly stronger than that of individual brand characteristics. Co-branding, by its nature, requires some interdependence between partner brands (Blackett & Boad, 1999; Newmeyer et al., 2014). Managers need to pay careful attention to the relationship between the partner brands and its effects on the evaluation of co-branding. Therefore, managers must ensure that the brands fit well with each other. When comparing the relative importance of brand image fit and product category fit, brand image fit should be assigned greater weight in the partner selection and decision-making process (Paydas Turan, 2021a). If the partner brands successfully establish a seamless connection within their combined offer, consumers are more likely to evaluate the co-branding positively. Further exploratory research on fit is recommended, as understanding how consumers perceive 'fit', particularly in terms of commonality or complementarity in values beyond image, equity or functionality, remains invaluable.

Managers are recommended to consider the impact of the type of industry and business in which they operate. While the relationship between brands is highly relevant to non-service industries, individual brand characteristics are more important to businesses in the service sector. Due to the intangible characteristics of services, consumers need to be offered cues that reduce the uncertainty that comes with the intangibility of the offer (Zeithaml et al., 1985). Therefore, in the context of service industries, consumers benefit significantly more from brand characteristics that act as quality signalling cues in forming their behavioural intention towards co-branding, when compared to non-service context (Paydas Turan, 2021a; Rao & Ruekert, 1994). When adopting co-branding strategy, managers in the service sector should ensure that they associate their brand with a partner from which they can derive incremental benefit in terms of signalling unobserved attributes. In non-B2C businesses, consumer-related characteristics play a significant role in customers' evaluation of co-branding (Paydas Turan, 2021a). This is an area that deserves further attention. It has been shown that consumer-related characteristics might be important explanatory variables in branding studies (Barone et al., 2000; Czellar, 2003). Consumer innovativeness and risk acceptance level are two of the consumer-related characteristics that, although neglected in the co-branding literature, have been examined in other branding studies (Klink & Daniel, 2001). Incorporating these consumer-related variables (i.e., consumer innovativeness, variety seeking and risk acceptance level) among others into co-branding studies would be valuable, as these factors influence how consumers perceive and respond to co-branding designed to create added value (Blackett & Boad, 1999).

Given the significant impact of marketing context on the success of brand extensions (Völckner & Sattler, 2006), further research on contextual antecedents (i.e., marketing support and retailer acceptance) would be valuable in advancing the understanding of co-branding success factors (Paydas Turan, 2021a). Moreover, the concept of fit needs further exploratory research because consumers may perceive fit beyond the image or category-related dimensions often examined in the literature. Fit between brands might also entail price fit, usage fit, complementarity, positioning and quality fit, all of which warrant further empirical research (Paydas Turan, 2021a; Zickermann, 2014). Expanding the understanding of fit perceptions could provide deeper insights into how consumers evaluate co-branding.

Another research context that has received limited attention is that of the online alliance. Given the increasing prevalence of digital partnerships (e.g., Spotify and Starbucks), the online co-branding landscape warrants further academic exploration (Jayawardhena et al., 2007; Singh et al., 2016). Further academic research in this area could provide valuable insights into navigating digital co-branding strategies for managers.

Co-branding have often analysed the consumers' brand evaluation at a single point in time, whereas it would be interesting to collect more evidence with longitudinal measurements (such as scanner data) providing actual field data. Identifying the potential longitudinal effects of the co-branding success factors would have considerable implications for management (Hogreve et al., 2017; Murtas et al., 2025). The reliance on cross-sectional data fails to capture consumer attitude changes towards co-branding across different stages of its life cycle. Additionally, incorporating actual sales data could provide new insights that complement the attitude and intention-based studies, which currently dominate the co-branding literature. It is accepted that an individual's behaviour intentions do not always translate into real behaviours; therefore, collecting actual field data would contribute to the literature and offer practical implications (Dalman

Table 15.4 Future research agenda

Research Directions
Factors that influence co-branding
Beyond brand image and product category, what additional dimensions of 'fit' should be considered when selecting co-branding partners?
What is the influence of marketing context (i.e., online vs. offline, retailer acceptance, intensity of competition and marketing investment) on consumer evaluation of co-branding?
How do consumer-related variables (e.g., need for closure, risk averseness) influence the acceptance of co-branding offerings?
Outcomes of co-branding
What are the alternative success metrics for co-branding beyond traditional performance indicators (i.e., resonance level, value perceptions, growth, market share, search effectiveness and followership)
How do consumer attitudes and behavioural intentions towards co-branding translate into firms' actual sales and profitability?
How does a brand alliance strategy impact a firm's short-term financial performance and long-term objectives, such as brand value and brand equity?
Contextual Factors
How do the distinct characteristics of B2C and B2B markets impact consumer evaluation of co-branding?
How can online and offline brands collaborate through co-branding to enhance customer experience?
How can service businesses leverage co-branding strategy to enhance their competitive advantage and customer value?
How does a firm's brand positioning influence consumer acceptance of ingredient branding?
Alternative Research Methods
What is the long-term impact of co-branding strategy on consumer evaluation, and how does it evolve over time? (longitudinal analysis recommended)
How can in-depth consumer insights be gathered on the negative spillover effects of co-branding failures? (qualitative research recommended for further exploration)
How do consumers perceive the fit between partner brands across various dimensions (i.e., brand recall, brand image fit, product category fit, marketing budget fit, positioning fit and conceptual fit)? (qualitative research recommended for exploring the meaning of fit)
How can network-based methods (i.e., implicit brand networks in social media) be utilised to identify and analyse co-branding opportunities across different product categories?

Source: The author.

& Puranam, 2017). Qualitative research could help uncover the underlying psychological processes involved in evaluating brand fit in co-branding and explore the potential transfer of association between partner brands. Moreover, network-based methods (i.e., using implicit brand networks on social media) can also provide novel and scalable opportunities for future co-branding research (Malhotra & Bhattacharyya, 2022).

In summary, as depicted in Table 15.4, future academic research on co-branding should focus on understudied variables that might shape consumer decision-making, the outcomes of co-branding, contextual factors influencing co-branding effectiveness and alternative research methods beyond those commonly used. Addressing these areas would contribute to a more comprehensive understanding of this promising strategy, helping to maximise its benefits while mitigating potential risks.

Co-branding is a powerful brand alliance strategy for unlocking brand potential and driving growth. Whether the strategic objectives involve attracting attention and differentiating from competitors, transferring positive associations between partner brands, expanding the customer base, entering new markets or increasing sales, co-branding offers significant opportunities for value creation.

REFERENCES

Aaker, D. A. (1991). *Managing brand equity: Capitalizing on the value of a brand name*. Free press.

Aaker, D. A., & Keller, K. L. (1990). Consumer evaluations of brand extensions. *Journal of Marketing, 54*(1), 27–41. https://doi.org/10.1177/002224299005400102

Abratt, R., & Motlana, P. (2002). Managing co-branding strategies: Global brands into local markets. *Business Horizons*, *45*(5), 43–50. https://doi.org/10.1016/S0007-6813(02)00242-2

Ahn, H., & Sung, Y. (2012). A two-dimensional approach to between-partner fit in co-branding evaluations. *Journal of Brand Management*, *19*(5), 414–424. https://doi.org/10.1057/bm.2011.49

Ahn, J., Kim, A., & Sung, Y. (2020). The effects of sensory fit on consumer evaluations of co-branding. *International Journal of Advertising*, *39*(4), 486–503. https://doi.org/10.1080/02650487.2019.1652518

Ahn, S., Kim, H., & Forney, J. (2009). Co-marketing alliances between heterogeneous industries: Examining perceived match-up effects in product, brand and alliance levels. *Journal of Retailing and Consumer Services*, *16*(6), 477–485. https://doi.org/10.1016/j.jretconser.2009.08.003

Alcañiz, E. B., Cáceres, R. C., & Pérez, R. C. (2010). Alliances between brands and social causes: The influence of company credibility on social responsibility image. *Journal of Business Ethics*, *96*(2), 169–186. https://doi.org/10.1007/s10551-010-0461-x

Anderson, N. H. (1981). *Foundations of information integration theory*. Academic Press.

Anderson, J. R. (1983). A spreading activation theory of memory. *Journal of Verbal Learning and Verbal Behaviour*, *22*(3), 261–295. https://doi.org/10.1016/S0022-5371(83)90201-3

Balachander, S., & Ghose, S. (2003). Reciprocal spill over effects: A strategic benefit of brand extensions. *Journal of Marketing*, *67*(1), 4–13. https://doi.org/10.1509/jmkg.67.1.4.18594

Barone, M. J., Miyazaki, A. D., & Taylor, K. A. (2000). The influence of cause-related marketing on consumer choice: Does one good turn deserve another? *Journal of the Academy of Marketing Science*, *28*(2), 248–262. https://doi.org/10.1177/0092070300282006

Baumgarth, C. (2004). Evaluations of co-brands and spill over effects: Further empirical results. *Journal of Marketing Communications*, *10*(2), 115–131. https://doi.org/10.1080/13527260410001693802

Bengtsson, A., & Servais, P. (2005). Co-branding on industrial markets. *Industrial Marketing Management*, 34(7), 706–713. https://doi.org/10.1016/j.indmarman.2005.06.004

Besharat, A. (2010). How co-branding versus brand extensions drive consumers' evaluations of new products: A brand equity approach. *Industrial Marketing Management*, *39*(8), 1240–9. https://doi.org/10.1016/j.indmarman.2010.02.021

Besharat, A., & Langan, R. (2014). Towards the formation of consensus in the domain of co-branding: Current findings and future priorities. *Journal of Brand Management*, *21*(2), 112–32. https://doi.org/10.1057/bm.2013.25

Bhat, S., & Reddy, S. K. (2001). The impact of parent brand attribute associations and affect on brand extension evaluation. *Journal of Business Research*, *53*(3), 111–22. https://doi.org/10.1016/S0148-2963(99)00115-0

Blackett, T., & Boad, B. (1999). *Co-branding: The science of alliance*. MacMillan Press.

Blackett, T., & Russell, N. (2000). Co-branding: The science of alliance. *Journal of Brand Management*, *7*(3), 161–70. https://doi.org/10.1057/bm.2000.3

Bleijerveld, J. F., Gremler, D. D., & Lemmink, M. (2015). Service alliances between unequals: The apple does not fall far from the better tree. *Journal of Service Management*, *26*(5), 807–22. https://doi.org/10.1108/JOSM-06-2015-0183

Bluemelhuber, C., Carter, L. L., & Lambe, C. J. (2007). Extending the view of brand alliance effects: An integrative examination of the role of country of origin. *International Marketing Review*, *24*(4), 427–43. https://doi.org/10.1108/02651330710761008

Bouten, L. M., Snelders, D., & Hultink, E. J. (2011). The impact of fit measures on the consumer evaluation of new co-branded products. *Journal of Product Innovation Management*, *28*(4), 455–69. https://doi.org/10.1111/j.1540-5885.2011.00819.x

Chiambaretto, P., & Gurău, C. (2017). David by goliath: What is co-branding and what is in it for SMEs. *International Journal of Entrepreneurship and Small Business*, *31*(1), 103–22. https://doi.org/10.1504/IJESB.2017.083805

Chiambaretto, P., Gurău, C., & Le Roy, F. (2016). Coopetitive branding: Definition, typology, benefits, and risks. *Industrial Marketing Management*, *57*, 86–96. https://doi.org/10.1016/j.indmarman.2016.05.009

Czellar, S. (2003). Consumer attitude towards brand extensions: An integrative model and research propositions. *International Journal of Research in Marketing*, *20*(1), 97–115. https://doi.org/10.1016/S0167-8116(02)00124-6

Dahlstrom, R., & Nygaard, A. (2016). The psychology of co-branding alliances: The business-to-business relationship outcomes of role stress. *Psychology and Marketing*, *33*(4), 267–82. https://doi.org/10.1002/mar.20874

Dalman, M. D., & Puranam, K. (2017). Consumer evaluation of ingredient branding strategy. *Management Research Review*, *40*(7), 768–82. https://doi.org/10.1108/MRR-04-2016-0092

Desai, K., Gauri, D., & Ma, Y. (2014). An empirical investigation of composite product choice. *Journal of Retailing*, *90*(4), 493–510. https://doi.org/10.1016/j.jretai.2014.09.002

Desai, K. K., & Keller, K. L. (2002). The effects of ingredient branding strategies on host brand extendibility. *Journal of Marketing*, *66*(1), 73–93. https://doi.org/10.1509/jmkg.66.1.73.18450

Fazio, R. H., Chen, J. M., McDonel, E. C., & Sherman, S. J. (1982). Attitude accessibility, attitude-behaviour consistency, and the strength of the object-evaluation association. *Journal of Experimental Social Psychology*, *18*(4), 339–57. https://doi.org/10.1016/0022-1031(82)90058-0

Fazio, R. H., Powell, M. C., & Williams, C. J. (1989). The role of attitude accessibility in the attitude-to-behaviour process. *Journal of Consumer Research*, *16*(3), 280–8. https://doi.org/10.1086/209214

Garcia, C. (2024). Council post: Unlocking the potential of brand-creator collaborations: A path to elevating sales and amplifying brand visibility. *Forbes*. Retrieved February 4, 2025, from www.forbes.com/councils/forbescommunicationscouncil/2023/11/30/unlocking-the-potential-of-brand-creator-collaborations-a-path-to-elevating-sales-and-amplifying-brand-visibility/?utm_source=chatgpt.com

Giakoumaki, C., Avlonitis, G. J., & Baltas, G. (2016). Does ingredient advertising work? Some evidence for its impact. *Journal of Business and Industrial Marketing*, *31*(7), 901–13. https://doi.org/10.1108/JBIM-02-2015-0027

Han, J., Wang, D., & Yang, Z. (2023). Acting like an interpersonal relationship: Cobrand anthropomorphism increases product evaluation and purchase intention. *Journal of Business Research*, *167*, 114194. https://doi.org/10.1016/j.jbusres.2023.114194

Heider, F. (1946). Attitudes and cognitive organization. *Journal of Psychology*, *21*(1), 107–12. https://doi.org/10.1080/00223980.1946.9917275

Helm, S. V., & Ozergin, B. (2015). Service inside: The impact of ingredient service branding on quality perceptions and behavioural intentions. *Industrial Marketing Management*, *50*, 142–9. https://doi.org/10.1016/j.indmarman.2015.04.003

Helmig, B., Huber, J. A., & Leeflang, P. (2007). Explaining behavioural intentions towards co-branded products. *Journal of Marketing Management*, *23*(3), 285–304. https://doi.org/10.1362/026725707X196387

Helmig, B., Huber, J., & Leeflang, P. (2008). Co-branding the state of the art. *Schmalenbach Business Review*, *60*(4), 359–77. https://doi.org/10.1007/BF03396775

Hogreve, J., Iseke, A., Derfuss, K., & Eller, T. (2017). The service–profit chain: A meta-analytic test of a comprehensive theoretical framework. *Journal of Marketing*, *81*(3), 41–61. https://doi.org/10.1509/jm.15.0395

James, D. (2005). Guilty through association: Brand association transfer to brand alliances. *Journal of Consumer Marketing*, *22*(1), 14–24. https://doi.org/10.1108/07363760510576518

Jayawardhena, C., Wright, L. T., & Dennis, C. (2007). Consumers online: Intentions, orientations, and segmentation. *International Journal of Retail and Distribution Management*, *35*(6), 515–26. https://doi.org/10.1108/09590550710750377

Kalafatis, S. P., Remizova, N., Riley, D., & Singh, J. (2012). The differential impact of brand equity on B2B co-branding. *Journal of Business and Industrial Marketing*, *27*(8), 623–34. https://doi.org/10.1108/08858621211273574

Kalafatis, S. P., Ledden, L., Riley, D., & Singh, J. (2016). The added value of brand alliances in higher education. *Journal of Business Research*, *69*(8), 3122–32. https://doi.org/10.1016/j.jbusres.2016.01.028

Keller, K. L. (1993). Conceptualizing, measuring, and managing customer-based brand equity. *Journal of Marketing*, *57*(1), 1–22. https://doi.org/10.1177/002224299305700101

Kelley, H. (1967). Attribution theory in social psychology. In D. Levine (Ed.), *Nebraska symposium of motivation* (pp. 192–238). University of Nebraska Press.

Klink, R., & Daniel, C. S. (2001). Threats to the external validity of brand extension research. *Journal of Marketing Research*, *38*(8), 326–35. https://doi.org/10.1509/jmkr.38.3.326.18864

Knoll, J., & Matthes, J. (2017). The effectiveness of celebrity endorsements: A meta-analysis. *Journal of the Academy of Marketing Science*, *45*(1), 55–75. https://doi.org/10.1007/s11747-016-0503-8

Lafferty, B., Goldsmith, R. E., & Hult, G. (2004). The impact of the alliance on the partners: A look at cause-brand alliances. *Psychology and Marketing*, *21*(7), 509–31. https://doi.org/10.1002/mar.20017

Lanseng, E. J., & Olsen, L. E. (2012). Brand alliances: The role of brand concept consistency. *European Journal of Marketing*, *46*(9), 1108–26. https://doi.org/10.1108/03090561211247874

Leuthesser, L., Kohli, C., & Suri, R. (2003). 2 + 2 = 5? A framework for using co-branding to leverage a brand. *Journal of Brand Management*, *11*(1), 35–47. https://doi.org/10.1057/palgrave.bm.2540146

Ma, B., Cheng, F., Bu, J., & Jiang, J. (2018). Effects of brand alliance on brand equity. *Journal of Contemporary Marketing Science*, *1*(1), 22–33. https://doi.org/10.1108/JCMARS-08-2018-0007

Malhotra, P., & Bhattacharyya, S. (2022). Leveraging co-followership patterns on social media to identify brand alliance opportunities. *Journal of Marketing*, *86*(4), 17–36. https://doi.org/10.1177/00222429221083668

Mandler, G. (1982). The structure of value: Accounting for taste. In M. S. Clark, & S. T. Fiske (Eds.), *Affect and cognition: The 17th annual Carnegie symposium* (pp. 3–36). Lawrence Erlbaum Associates.

Mazodier, M., & Merunka, D. (2014). Beyond brand attitude: Individual drivers of purchase for symbolic cobranded products. *Journal of Business Research*, *67*(7), 1552–8. https://doi.org/10.1016/j.jbusres.2014.01.015

McCarthy, M., & Norris, D. (1999). Improving competitive position using branded ingredients. *Journal of Product and Brand Management*, *8*(4), 267–85. https://doi.org/10.1108/10610429910284210

Miller, D., Merrilees, B., & Yakimova, R. (2014). Corporate rebranding: an integrative review of major enablers and barriers to the rebranding process. *International Journal of Management Reviews*, *16*(3), 265–89. https://doi.org/10.1111/ijmr.12020

Moon, H., & Sprott, D. E. (2016). Ingredient branding for a luxury brand: The role of brand and product fit. *Journal of Business Research*, *69*(12), 5768–74. https://doi.org/10.1016/j.jbusres.2016.04.173

Murtas, G., Pedeliento, G., Mangiò, F., & Andreini, D. (2025). Co-branding strategies in luxury fashion: The off-white case. *Journal of Strategic Marketing*, *33*(4), 484–503. https://doi.org/10.1080/0965254X.2022.2160484

Naidoo, V., & Hollebeek, L. D. (2016). Higher education brand alliances: Investigating consumers' dual-degree purchase intentions. *Journal of Business Research*, *69*(8), 3113–21. https://doi.org/10.1016/j.jbusres.2016.01.027

Newmeyer, C., Venkatesh, R., & Chatterjee, R. (2014). Cobranding arrangements and partner selection: a conceptual framework and managerial guidelines. *Journal of the Academy of Marketing Science*, *42*(2), 103–18. https://doi.org/10.1007/s11747-013-0343-8

Newmeyer, C., Venkatesh, R., Ruth, J., & Chatterjee, R. (2018). A typology of brand alliances and consumer awareness of brand alliance integration. *Marketing Letters*, *29*(3), 275–89. https://doi.org/10.1007/s11002-018-9467-4

Nie, X., Wang, L., & Chan, E. Y. (2024). Perceived economic mobility predicts evaluation of low-fit co-brands. *Psychology & Marketing*, *41*(7), 1562–73. https://doi.org/10.1002/mar.21997

Park, C. W., Jun, S. Y., & Shocker, A. D. (1996). Composite branding alliances: An investigation of extension and feedback effects. *Journal of Marketing Research*, *33*(4), 453–66. https://doi.org/10.1177/002224379603300407

Paydas Turan, C. (2021a). Success drivers of co-branding: A meta-analysis. *International Journal of Consumer Studies*, *45*(4), 911–36. https://doi.org/10.1111/ijcs.12682

Paydas Turan, C. (2021b). What's inside matters: The impact of ingredient branding on consumers' purchasing behaviours in services. *Journal of Retailing and Consumer Services*, *63*, 102690. https://doi.org/10.1016/j.jretconser.2021.102690

Paydas Turan, C. (2022). Deal or deny: The effectiveness of crisis response strategies on brand equity of the focal brand in co-branding. *Journal of Business Research*, *149*, 615–29. https://doi.org/10.1016/j.jbusres.2022.05.053

Phelps, M. (2016). *Build, buy or collaborate: 5 secrets for success*. Retrieved, December 5, 2018, from www.forbes.com/sites/marshallphelps/2016/01/25/5-secrets-to-innovation-success/#778ceac753ba

Pinello, C., Picone, P. M., & Destri, A. M. L. (2022). Co-branding research: Where we are and where we could go from here. *European Journal of Marketing*, *56*(2), 584–621. https://doi.org/10.1108/EJM-02-2021-0073

Radighieri, J., Mariadoss, B., Gregoire, Y., & Johnson, J. (2014). Ingredient branding and feedback effects: The impact of product outcomes, initial parent brand strength asymmetry, and parent brand role. *Marketing Letters*, *25*(2), 123–38. https://doi.org/10.1007/s11002-013-9231-8

Rao, A., & Ruekert, R. (1994). Brand alliances as signals of product quality. *Sloan Management Review*, *36*(1), 87–97.

Rao, A., Qu, L., & Ruekert, R. (1999). Signalling unobservable product quality through a brand ally. *Journal of Marketing Research*, *36*(2), 258. https://doi.org/10.1177/002224379903600209

Rodrigue, C. S., & Biswas, A. (2004). Brand alliance dependency and exclusivity: An empirical investigation. *Journal of Product and Brand Management*, *13*(7), 477–87. https://doi.org/10.1108/10610420410568417

Rosch, E. (1973). *On the internal structure of perceptual and semantic categories. Cognitive development and the acquisition of language*. Academic Press.

Rosch, E. (1975). Cognitive representations of semantic categories. *Journal of Experimental Psychology: General*, *104*(3), 192. https://doi.org/10.1037/0096-3445.104.3.192

Samu, S., Krishnan, H. S., & Smith, R. E. (1999). Using advertising alliances for new product introduction: interaction between product complementarity and promotional strategy. *Journal of Marketing*, *63*(1), 57–74. https://doi.org/10.1177/002224299906300105

Senechal, S., Georges, L., & Pernin, J. (2014). Alliances between corporate and fair-trade brands: Examining the antecedents of overall evaluation of the co-branded product. *Journal of Business Ethics*, *124*(3), 365–81. https://doi.org/10.1007/s10551-013- 1875

Shan, J., Lu, H., & Cui, A. P. (2022). 1 + 1 > 2? Is co-branding an effective way to improve brand masstige? *Journal of Business Research*, *144*, 556–71. https://doi.org/10.1016/j.jbusres.2022.01.058

Simonin, B. L., & Ruth, J. A. (1998). Is a company known by the company it keeps? Assessing the spill over effects of brand alliances on consumer brand attitudes. *Journal of Marketing Research*, *35*(1), 30–42. https://doi.org/10.1177/002224379803500105

Singh, J., Crisafulli, B., & Quamina, L. (2020). Corporate image at stake: The impact of crises and response strategies on consumer perceptions of corporate brand alliances. *Journal of Business Research*, *117*, 839–49. https://doi.org/10.1016/j.jbusres.2019.01.014

Singh, J., Kalafatis, S. P., & Ledden, L. (2014). Consumer perceptions of cobrands: The role of brand positioning strategies. *Marketing Intelligence and Planning*, *32*(2), 145–59. https://doi.org/10.1108/MIP-03-2013-0055

Singh, J., Quamina, L., & Kalafatis, S. (2016). Strategic brand alliances. Research advances and practical applications. In F. Riley, J. Singh, & C. Blankson (Eds.), *The Routledge companion to contemporary brand management* (pp. 20–135). Routledge.

Smarandescu, L., Rose, R., & Wedell, D. H. (2013). Priming a cross-category brand alliance: The moderating role of attribute knowledge and need for cognition'. *Psychology and Marketing*, *30*(2), 133–47. https://doi.org/10.1002/mar.20593

Spence, M. (1973). Job market signalling. *Quarterly Journal of Economics*, *87*(3), 355–74. https://doi.org/10.2307/1882010

Suzuki, S., & Kanno, S. (2022). The role of brand coolness in the masstige co-branding of luxury and mass brands. *Journal of Business Research*, *149*, 240–9. https://doi.org/10.1016/j.jbusres.2022.04.061

Swaminathan, V., Gupta, S., Keller, K. L., & Lehmann, D. (2022). Brand actions and financial consequences: A review of key findings and directions for future research. *Journal of the Academy of Marketing Science*, *50*(4), 639–64. https://doi.org/10.1007/s11747-022-00866-7

Xiang, F., & Mishra, S. (2002). The effect of brand alliance portfolio on perceived quality of an unknown brand. *Advances in Consumer Research*, *29*, 519–20.

Uggla, H., & Åsberg, P. (2010). The benefits and risks of strategic brand collaboration. *IUP Journal of Brand Management*, *7*(3), 35–48.

Vaidyanathan, R., & Aggarwal, P. (2000). Strategic brand alliances: Implications of ingredient branding for national and private label brands. *Journal of Product and Brand Management*, *9*(4), 214–28. https://doi.org/10.1108/10610420010344013

Völckner, F., & Sattler, H. (2006). Drivers of brand extension success. *Journal of Marketing*, *70*(2), 18–34. https://doi.org/10.1509/jmkg.70.2.018

Walchli, S. B. (2007). The effects of between-partner congruity on consumer evaluation of co-branded products. *Psychology & Marketing*, *24*(11), 947–73. https://doi.org/10.1002/mar.20191

Wang, W., Chen, C. H. S., Nguyen, B., & Shukla, P. (2020). Collaboration between East and West: Influence of consumer dialectical self on attitude towards co-brand personality traits. *International Marketing Review*, *37*(6), 1155–80. https://doi.org/10.1108/IMR-01-2019-0012

Washburn, J. H., Till, B. D., & Priluck, R. (2000). Co-branding: Brand equity and trial effects. *Journal of Consumer Marketing*, *17*(7), 591–602. https://doi.org/10.1108/07363760010357796

Washburn, J., Till, B., & Priluck, R. (2004). Brand alliance and customer-based brand-equity effects. *Psychology and Marketing*, *21*(7), 487–508. https://doi.org/10.1002/mar.20016

Weiner, B. (1985). An attributional theory of achievement motivation and emotion. *Psychological Review*, *92*(4), 548. https://doi.org/10.1037/0033-295X.92.4.548

Zeithaml, V. A., Parasuraman, A., & Berry, L. L. (1985). Problems and strategies in services marketing. *Journal of Marketing*, *49*(2), 33–46. https://doi.org/10.1177/002224298504900203

Zhang, Y., & Guo, X. (2023). New and old: Consumer evaluations of co-branding between new brands and Chinese time-honoured brands. *Journal of Retailing and Consumer Services*, *73*, 103293. https://doi.org/10.1016/j.jretconser.2023.103293

Zhang, Y., Guo, X., & Qu, Y. (2025). Brand extension or co-branding: The consumer's attribution of responsibility to the crossover strategies of heritage brands. *Journal of Retailing and Consumer Services*, *82*, 104133. https://doi.org/10.1016/j.jretconser.2024.104133

Zickermann, P. (2014). *Co-branding: Fit factors between partner brands*. Anchor Academic Publishing.

16

Brand Relationships

Cleopatra Veloutsou, Asli Tolunay,
Sergio Andrés Osuna-Ramírez, and Hui Chen

INTRODUCTION

Brands are '*evolving mental collections of actual (offer related) and emotional (human-like) characteristics and associations which convey benefits of an offer identified through a symbol, or a collection of symbols, and differentiates this offer from the rest of the marketplace*' (Veloutsou & Delgado-Ballester, 2018, p. 257). Starting from an early age, and for all their lifetime (Rodhain & Aurier, 2016), consumers build relational bonds with brands' cluster of functional and emotional attributes (Fetscherin & Heinrich, 2014), attaching symbolic meanings and values to brands beyond their utilitarian benefits (Bagozzi et al., 2021; Veloutsou, 2023).

The relevance of customer–brand bonds should be acknowledged. As a principle, consumer–brand relationships are individual brand-centric bonds/connections that occur when consumers act as independent entities and relate to brands and develop links primarily of emotional or even functional natures with brands (Veloutsou & Ruiz Mafe, 2020), and the concept is not different for other than consumer audiences. Strong brand relationships indicate brand strength, and they are essential for brands looking to differentiate from competitive offers and create lasting connections with various customer groups. Strong brands are not indifferent (Veloutsou et al., 2020) and occupy a high share of mind and heart for the consumers, providing value (Schultz, 2016). Given the associated value, individuals develop relationships with brands that allow them to express who they are and become a source of interaction and development of experiences, making brands a relational market-based asset (Iglesias et al., 2019).

The significance of brand relationships extends beyond consumer–brand dynamics as they are also key for business-to-business (B2B) brands (Koponen & Julkunen, 2022). In the B2B context, brand relationships are primarily functional-based bonds supporting the business scope. They go beyond simply purchasing and using (or not) a brand, encompassing a deep brand involvement. They vary in type depending on the intensity/passion (low vs. high) and valence (positive vs. negative) (Alvarez et al., 2023) and can range from deep affection to intense aversion (Alvarez & Fournier, 2016). The bond between the two parties can be affective or rational and based on financial, physical or emotional benefits. These relationships are not static but evolve over time (Tolunay & Veloutsou, 2025).

Against this background, some researchers use the term 'brand relationship' less precisely. These researchers often use many terms to describe the core of brand relationships (Albert & Thomson, 2018, 2024) or capture the concept through relationship quality, incorporating indicators not always clearly linked with the core emotional aspect of the relationship itself but with behavioural indicators such as loyalty or satisfaction (Albert & Thomson, 2018). This makes understanding brand relationships even more essential when aiming to build strong, lasting connections with the target audience in both consumer (Bagozzi et al., 2021) and B2B markets (Koponen & Julkunen, 2022). For all customers (consumers and organisations) and for other audiences, weak or strong and positive or negative relationships are not only crucial for understanding the existence or absence and the levels of brand loyalty and advocacy but also to influence purchasing behaviour, brand perception, and long-term brand success (Veloutsou, 2023).

Since the publication of the early work by Blackston's (1993), Fajer and Schouten's (1995) and Fournier's (1998) seminal paper, the study of brand relationships has become a prominent topic in both marketing literature and practice (Alvarez et al., 2023). Recent bibliometric analysis suggests that the literature in this stream of research is in its maturity (Fetscherin & Veloutsou, 2024); this is the time to try to summarize and present the key brand relationship aspects.

This chapter defines brand relationships, provides insights into their nature, including the metaphors this work is based on, and explains their forms and the role of passion in their development and growth. It also presents the dynamic brand relationships nature, the lack of clarity on brand relationships in the situation of ambivalence and relationships that consumer groups form with the same brand with different valance (brand polarization), as well as the evolution of these relationships over time.

BRAND RELATIONSHIPS' COMPREHENSIVE INSIGHTS

As brand relationships' literature has evolved in the last 30 years (Fetscherin & Veloutsou, 2024), and evidence that relationships can flourish in different contexts, such as online and offline (Veloutsou & Ruiz Mafe, 2020), has emerged, a variety of views on what the key brand relationship components and assumptions have been proposed. The ongoing stance is that customers connect and interact with brands, creating value, and brands can be active and contributing partners in this process (Bagozzi et al., 2021).

A key point of discussion in this field is the diversity of forms brand relationships can take, ranging from arranged and convenience marriages to friendships (Alvarez et al., 2023; Fournier, 1998). These relationships can vary along multiple dimensions, as they can be '*voluntary versus imposed, long term versus short term, public versus private, formal versus informal, distant versus close and symmetric versus asymmetric*' (Veloutsou & Moutinho, 2009, p. 316). The diversity of brand relationships underscores their complex nature.

To better appreciate brand relationships, the key metaphors used to approach these relationships and some of the most essential brand relationship characteristics helpful for a deeper understanding of the concept are presented.

Brand Relationship Metaphors

Research on brand relationships often relies on metaphors, either explicitly stated or implicitly suggested. Common metaphorical frameworks to examine relationships with customers, including consumers and organizations buyers, or other audiences include interpersonal, parasocial and business relationships.

Starting from the last, the business relationship metaphor assumes that brand relationships are deep, long-lasting, highly interactive and often described as a marriage (Johnston & Hausman, 2006; Ojansivu et al., 2020). Specific relational norms govern these relationships as a key element in understanding their nature (Heide & John, 1992). Relational norms work as a governance mechanism of opportunism, which disciplines and excludes certain behaviours in exchange relationships (Morgan & Hunt, 1994). The two relational partners share values and know-how, a process that paves the way towards developing collaborative partnerships (Joshi & Arnold, 1998). This metaphor is better suited to B2B contexts and for consumer segments that are developing relationships primarily based on rationality.

The parasocial relationship metaphor draws from the parasocial interaction theory, assuming one-sided and autonomous bonds between the relationship partners (Horton & Richard Wohl, 1956), that is, the customer and the brand in the context of brand relationships. This approach is the dominant one for human brands and brands with media presence, including television, radio and social media (Labrecque, 2014; Lacap et al., 2024; Wang & Liu, 2023), primarily because of its origins. An interesting observation is that, despite brand management research reports lacking engagement from brands in brand relationships – indicating that the most appropriate paradigm is the parasocial relationship metaphor – the interpersonal relationship metaphor remains the predominantly adopted approach in this literature.

The interpersonal relationship metaphor is, therefore, by far the most widely used one. It assumes that customers have feelings for their brands and that brands are active actors that may return things of behavioural or even emotional nature to them (Fournier, 1998; Veloutsou, 2007). Interaction between the two relationship actors, customers and brands, is the core assumption that this metaphor is built on since a relationship cannot be achieved without interaction (Veloutsou, 2007). Based on this metaphor, research indicates that customers and brands can experience a large variety of relationship forms (Fournier, 1998; Zarantonello et al., 2018) ranging from positive to negative and from strong to weak, with passion as the common factor (Fetscherin et al., 2019). Researchers refer to the '*emotional connection consumers develop over time with their favourite brands*' (Pourazad et al., 2019, p. 2), indicating that the approach suggesting an ongoing process that evolves is appreciated in numerous consumer–brand relationships.

Brand Relationships Sentiment/ Valance: Positive Versus Negative

From the customers' side, brand relationships are meaningful connections between themselves and brands. These connections can be based on a positive or a negative sentiment, forming a positive or negative brand relationship (Fetscherin et al., 2019, 2021). A positive brand relationship is based on a favourable brand attitude and/or recognized functional brand value, where individuals appreciate and support the brand and often see benefits because of the existence of their relationship with it. Brands benefit from positive relationships by getting positive cognitive, affective and behavioural responses in exchange (Fetscherin et al., 2019). In contrast, a negative brand relationship is an inverse customer–brand connection expressed through negative affective brand attitude or/and dis-appreciation of brand's functional value. A negative brand relationship is different from a lack of brand relationship since the latter does not involve an emotional or functional connection with the brand. Negative brand relationships are more detrimental for brands, causing several unfavourable consequences (Fetscherin et al., 2021) such as vengeance (Bechwati & Morrin, 2003), anti-consumption and brand avoidance (Hegner et al., 2017; Lee et al., 2009), as well as negative word of mouth (NWoM) and retaliation (Hegner et al., 2017).

Brand Relationships Passion Intensity: Close/Strong/Deep Versus Distant/ Weak/Shallow

Brand relationships can vary in closeness, ranging from close to distant, and in strength, being strong or weak. The closeness/strength of the relationship, apart from the valence, is primarily determined by the space this relationship occupies within the consumer. This engagement is expressed through the intensity of passion, giving rise to different forms of relationships ranging from strong negative (hate) to strong positive (love) (Fetscherin et al., 2019).

Some research in brand management and marketing suggests that passion is only present in positive relationships (Gilal et al., 2023). This work sees brand passion as a strong desire for a brand (Batra et al., 2012), an extraordinarily positive and primarily affective attitude towards a brand that drives emotional attachment (Herrando et al., 2017), defined as '*a psychological construct comprised of excitation, infatuation, and obsession for a brand*' (Albert et al., 2013, p. 905). Based on this approach, there is some discussion on consumer devotion, a state of passionate dedication to a brand that partially supports consumers' identity expression (Ortiz et al., 2013), and brand addiction, the '*consumer's psychological state that involves a mental and behavioural preoccupation with a particular brand, driven by uncontrollable urges to possess the brand's products, and involving positive affectivity and gratification*' (Cui et al., 2018, p. 124). The same stream of research appreciates that this positive brand passion may be harmonic but also may be brand obsession, causing stress (Gilal et al., 2023).

Another more general approach appreciates that brand passion has the potential to exist in relationships of any valence, including negative relationships (Zarantonello et al., 2016). Dictionary definitions of passion explicitly acknowledge its existence in both positive and negative relationships, presenting it as 'a very strong feeling of love, hate, anger, enthusiasm, etc.' (Oxford Dictionary) or 'a very powerful feeling, such as sexual attraction, love, hate, anger, or other emotions' (Cambridge Dictionary). In line with this approach, in the brand management literature, brand passion is also considered a strong emotional connection to a particular brand (Das et al., 2018), an extreme and emotional form of a relationship (Füller et al., 2008), defined as '*a psychological phenomenon constituted of excitation, infatuation, and obsession for a brand*' (Osuna Ramírez et al., 2024, p. 5). To cultivate passion, brands must be positioned as embodying active beliefs and confidence and stay vibrant in an ever-evolving world.

Brand Relationships Basis: Symbolic Versus Functional

Strong brand relationships stem from important for the individuals who develop feelings of brand-related real or imagery features. The basis of the customer–brand bond can be symbolic, functional or a combination of the two. This is because the link can be established through any of the knowledge components comprising the brand, namely, what the brand is (symbol, product and person) and what the brands does (user imagery and experience imagery) (Veloutsou & Ballester, 2025).

In consumer–brand relationships, most existing work implies that the bond is based primarily on symbolism, intangible advantages or value beyond the brand's practical utility. Researchers highlight that '*consumers are more strongly attached to brands that offer hedonic value than to more functional value-oriented brands*' (Karjaluoto et al., 2016, p. 530). For example, strong positive relationships (brand love) may be developed due to the contribution of the brand to the perceived well-being (Junaid et al., 2020), perceived brand value (Dias & Cavalheiro, 2022; Touni et al., 2022), value congruence (Kaufmann et al., 2016), self-brand identification or the degree that allows the consumers to self-express (Carroll & Ahuvia, 2006; Huber et al., 2015; Karjaluoto et al., 2016) and improve their standing within their social surroundings (Huber et al., 2015; Wallace et al., 2014). Symbolic brand attributes generate pleasurable benefits, such as social desirability and self-expressive value, fulfilling higher-level consumer needs (Bian & Yan, 2022; Fernandes & Moreira, 2019; Hwang & Kandampully, 2012). Similarly, a strong negative brand relationship (brand hate) is often generated from symbolic elements such as incongruity between brand's symbolic meaning and consumer's sense of self (Bryson et al., 2013; Hegner et al., 2017; Zarantonello et al., 2016), brand embarrassment (Sarkar et al., 2020), negative brand personality (Roy et al., 2022), moral incongruity (Demirbag-Kaplan et al., 2015) or symbolic incongruity (Hegner et al., 2017; Pinto & Brandão, 2021).

Limited attention is paid to the functional brand relationships (Leung et al., 2014). In terms of functional benefits, customers primarily value the brand for its practical advantages, utilitarian and objective characteristics, like efficiency or reliability, and inherent characteristics of brand attributes (e.g., quality, price or reliability) (Fernandes & Moreira, 2019; Fetscherin & Heinrich, 2014). These characteristics predominantly come from the brand as a product brand component (Veloutsou, 2023; Veloutsou & Ballester, 2025). Strong positive relationships can be based on elements such as brand performance satisfaction (Loureiro & Kaufmann, 2012) and brand uniqueness (Rahman et al., 2021), while strong negative brand relationships may occur on the basis of high levels of dissatisfaction with the brand's performance and negative past experience (Bryson et al., 2013; Hegner et al., 2017; Yang & Mundel, 2022), leading to a violation of trust, necessitating a more apologetic brand response (Hudders et al., 2022), all related to functional brand characteristics.

With many brands not being separable from their tangible attributes, some argue that the functional value alone is not enough for the formation of a strong relationship since satisfied consumers with the functional brand attributes but without emotional connections might switch to another brand in the case of a negative value proposition (price versus functionality) (Fetscherin & Heinrich, 2014). Following this understanding, research suggests that the customers engaging with brands based on both utilitarian and symbolic significance foster functional and emotional brand connections simultaneously (Albert & Merunka, 2013; Bairrada et al., 2018; Fernandes & Moreira, 2019).

TYPES OF BRAND RELATIONSHIPS BASED ON THE LEVEL OF PASSION AND SENTIMENT

Consumer–brand relationships might be organized according to the sentiment range (positive-negative) and the passion intensity (strong–weak) (Fetscherin et al., 2019). This organization leads to four distinct types of relationships, being the absence of sentiment and passion intensity a fifth relevant state (Figure 16.1). These five states are further discussed in this section.

High Passion: Brand Love and Brand Hate

Brand relationships with high levels of passion take the form of brand love or brand hate, depending on the sentiment polarity.

Brand love is a strong and passionate positive brand relationship, a deeper and longer-lasting feeling than simple preference (Ahuvia, 1993) and extensively researched in the literature (Albert et al., 2008; Alvarez et al., 2023; Batra et al., 2012; Bauer, 2023; Fetscherin et al., 2019). It is defined as '*the degree of passionate emotional attachment a satisfied consumer has for a particular trade name*' (Carroll & Ahuvia, 2006, p. 81) or '*an intimate, passionate and*

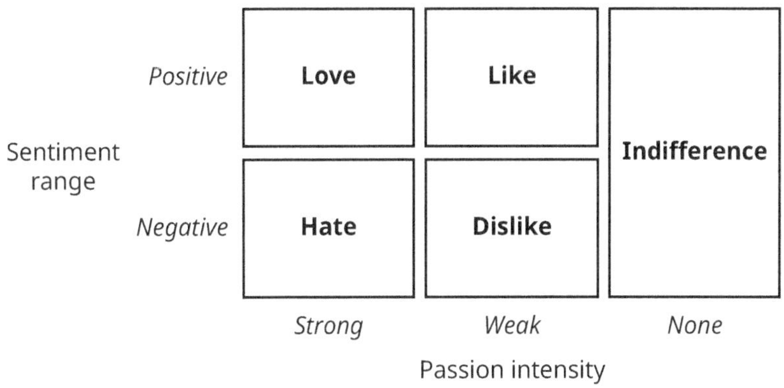

Figure 16.1 Consumer–brand relationship on the individual level based on the passion intensity and sentiment range

Source: Fetscherin et al. (2019).

engaged relationship between a consumer and a particular brand' (Keh et al., 2007, p. 84). Several researchers approach brand love as having different components or dimensions (Alvarez et al., 2023). For example, Batra et al. (2012) recognized seven dimensions of brand love: Self-brand integration, passion-driven behaviours, positive emotional connection, long-term relationship, anticipated separation distress, attitude valence and attitude strength. In any case, a loved brand is used as a self-expressiveness tool, through which consumers project their selves to others (Carroll & Ahuvia, 2006; Huber et al., 2015).

An equally strong bond in terms of passion but with a negative sentiment is brand hate (Fetscherin et al., 2019; Hegner et al., 2017; Zarantonello et al., 2016), defined as '*a psychological state in which a consumer forms an intense negative emotion and hatred toward a brand*' (Kucuk, 2018, p. 566), '*an extreme form of dislike of the brand*' (Zarantonello et al., 2016, p. 13) or '*an intense negative emotional affect towards the brand*' (Bryson et al., 2013, p. 395). A stream of research approaches brand hate as a combination of various negative feelings, suggesting that it can be active or passive (Zarantonello et al., 2016), each represented by sets of negative emotions. Given the different approaches to brand hate, it is not surprising that the literature distinguishes brand hate as an emotion and as a relationship (Aziz & Rahman, 2022).

Clearly, brand love brings many positive brand outcomes, including brand loyalty (Carroll & Ahuvia, 2006; Shetty & Fitzsimmons, 2022; Torres et al., 2022), positive word-of-mouth (Papista & Dimitriadis, 2019), willingness to pay a price premium (Hemonnet-Goujot & Valette-Florence, 2022), active engagement (Choi et al., 2022; Dias & Cavalheiro, 2022) and forgiveness behaviour (Rahman et al., 2021). Amidst the outcomes of brand hate are brand rejection, either by purchasing a competitor's brand or by stopping its consumption (Hegner et al., 2017; Zarantonello et al., 2016), or negative voicing via brand complaining (Zarantonello et al., 2016; Zhang & Laroche, 2020) and negative WoM (Hegner et al., 2017).

Low Passion: Brand Like and Brand Dislike

When the passion is lower, and the sentiment is positive or negative, the relationships with brands still exist and take the forms of brand like or brand dislike. Although some do not appreciate the differences between love/like and hate/dislike, recent work indicates that they are conceptually distinct from their higher in terms of passion counterparts, brand love and brand hate (Fetscherin, 2019).

In terms of meaning, brand like relates to favourable memory-stored band associations (Aaker & Moorman, 2017) but with moderate importance or/and strength. Brand liking derives positive brand attitudes and the perception that the liked brand cares (Haefner et al., 2011). On the other hand, brand dislike is a weaker than brand hate type of aversion, representing consumers' illusion of a brand as an inadequate relationship partner (Dalli et al., 2006). Because of its moderate negative strength or less significant brand associations, violations of trust require more apologetic management responses (Hudders et al., 2022), introducing a negative bias.

While brand love and hate are extensively studied both as concepts and as consumer behaviour triggers, brand like and dislike are relatively under-researched. However, in accordance with Fetscherin et al. (2019), they still have important roles in shaping consumer perceptions and behaviours. Brand like denotes a competitive advantage for the brand through an affective response associated with brand preference, leading to loyalty (Hayran & Ceylan, 2023) and to solid behavioural responses such as positive word-of-mouth (Wallace et al., 2014), conviction and purchase (Duffett et al., 2019). Conversely, brand dislike results in negative word-of-mouth (Romani et al., 2012), brand avoidance and switching (Romani et al., 2012).

Lack of Passion: Brand Indifference

Recent knowledge on different forms of consumer–brand relationships denotes that depending on the level of passion and its valence, relationships may take different forms, and passion may be absent (Fetscherin et al., 2019). Clearly, not all brands will enjoy passionate forms of relationships, and some brands will not even evoke any feelings, thus being indifferent for some consumers.

A lack of emotional engagement exemplifies indifferent brands. Such brands do not evoke powerful emotions and passion (Fetscherin & KC, 2021) but are characterized by a sense of neutrality among consumers. The zone of indifference is marked by the lack of any brand thoughts (Cluley, 2020), positive or negative, or any motivating factors that would make consumers support or oppose the brand (Park et al., 2013a).

The brands in the 'grey zone' of indifference are ignored by consumers, making them weak in the marketplace. Indifferent brands seem to have lost their scope of existence, as they fail to attract meaningful consumer interest, connection or interaction (Fetscherin et al., 2019). Next to negative brand relationships, this position is the most unpleasant a brand may occupy (Veloutsou & Delgado-Ballester, 2018). As such, managers should try their best to avoid being in this position within the minds of consumer segments of interest for their brands (Osuna Ramírez et al., 2019). However, interestingly, the existing literature donates limited comparative attention to brand indifference.

BRAND RELATIONSHIPS OUT OF THE COMMONLY EXPECTED FORMS

Although these general categories of brand relationships exist, as organized by the sentiment and level of passion, customers do not always feel the same for a brand both over time and compared to other customers. In particular, they may change their relationship, they may have mixed feelings towards the brand or they may be in a group of customers with a similar relationship, coexisting with another group of customers with precisely the opposite relationship with the same brand. These out of the commonly expected brand relationship forms are presented next.

Moving From One Relationship Type to Another

Similar to any relationship, brand relationships also evolve over time. They may change in strength and polarity, giving rise to different paths experienced throughout the relationship lifespan (Zarantonello et al., 2018). Although recent research, to some extent, is still concentrating on the extremes (i.e., love and hate) (Alvarez et al., 2023; Fetscherin & Veloutsou, 2024) and reflecting a static perspective (Attiq et al., 2023), some work started to recognize the potential for the emotional shifts within a single relationship (Aggarwal & Shi, 2018; Aziz & Rahman, 2022; Brandão et al., 2023; Robertson et al., 2022; Veloutsou et al., 2020; Yadav & Chakrabarti, 2022; Zarantonello et al., 2018).

Studies appreciating brand relationship evolution over time show that several factors are seen as relationship violations. Relationship violations may take the form of symbolic inconsistencies (Roy et al., 2022; Tolunay & Veloutsou, 2025), unsatisfied or changed expectations (Tolunay & Veloutsou, 2025; Zhang et al., 2020), or moral mismatch between the brand and the consumer (Akrout & Mrad, 2023; Tolunay & Veloutsou, 2025), and consumers may start to hate brands that they once loved. Contrary to previous findings supporting a buffering effect of previously positive feelings on company wrongdoings (Kennedy & Guzmán, 2021; Lee et al., 2021), there is also recent evidence suggesting that positively connected consumers may respond even more strongly when they experience a relationship violation (Brandão et al., 2023: Costa & Azevedo, 2023; Tolunay & Veloutsou, 2025).

Though not studied as frequently as the 'love-becomes-hate' phenomenon, consumers' hate can turn to love (Lopez, 2021) as well. These findings imply that while most research suggests that individuals relate either positively or negatively with a specific brand, brand relationships are dynamic and may move from one to another (Zarantonello et al., 2018).

Having Mixed Feelings Towards the Brand: Brand Ambivalence

At times, customers do not have exclusively positive or negative feelings towards a brand, a phenomenon called brand ambivalence (Mikulincer et al., 2010; Priester & Petty, 2001). Ambivalence is described in marketing as 'a psychological state of conflict associated with an attitude object' (Priester & Petty, 1996, p. 432) and as a 'simultaneous or sequential experience of multiple emotional states, as a result of the interaction between internal factors and external objects, people, institutions, and/or cultural phenomena in market-oriented contexts, that can have direct and/or indirect ramifications on prepurchase, purchase or postpurchase attitudes and behaviour' (Otnes et al., 1997, p. 83). Ambivalence contains an evaluative inconsistency causing mixed cognitive, affective (Eagly & Chaiken, 1998; Thompson et al., 1995) and behavioural responses (Hamby & Russell, 2022), influencing the attitude–behaviour relationship (Conner et al., 2021).

While extensive research has examined the impact of emotions on individuals, the influence of mixed emotions has been less explored within consumer behaviour (Lunardo & Saintives, 2018; Otnes et al., 1997; Williams & Aaker, 2002). Research shows that ambivalence causes emotional solid responses (De Liver et al., 2007) and discomfort (Williams & Aaker, 2002), influences consumers' decision-making during pre- and post-purchase (Jewell et al., 2002; Otnes et al., 1997; Roster & Richins, 2009) as well as satisfaction and loyalty (Olsen et al., 2005) and thus triggers subsequent consumer reactions (Lunardo & Saintives, 2018; Otnes et al., 1997; Watson & Spence, 2007). The limited literature on ambivalence within brand relationships indicates the co-existence of mixed emotions during these relationships (Evanschitzky et al., 2020; Zarantonello et al., 2018) such that individuals may love the brand in general but hate any entity related to this brand (Park et al., 2013b), including the offering, its users or retail environment (Penz & Hogg, 2011) or the parent company (Tugrul & Taqi, 2018), while the opposite may also happen. When consumers evaluate different symbolic or functional brand benefits, they may also love some but hate others, experiencing a conflict between cognitive and affective evaluations (Conner et al., 2021) and, thus, ambivalence (Sipilä et al., 2017). Image incongruence (Zarantonello et al., 2018), cultural, individual differences and situational factors might further initiate conflicting emotions (Aaker et al., 2008) in ongoing strong relationships when a mismatch between the brand offering and the consumer interest causes the relationship to fade (Evanschitzky et al., 2020).

Brand ambivalence may lead consumers to opt for different alternatives (Zarantonello et al., 2018), generate brand hate (Zarantonello et al., 2018), make consumers oversee the negatives following a cost–benefit analysis (Evanschitzky et al., 2020) or cause constructive criticism in hopes that changes in brands' actions will return the relationship to its origins (Zarantonello et al., 2018).

Simultaneous Opposing Passionate Feelings to Different Consumer Groups: Brand Polarization

Brand polarization arises when passionate love and frantic hate for a brand co-exist, and it is defined as 'an affective and cognitive phenomenon where beliefs and emotions of a significant number of individual consumers induce a simultaneous split into the extremes involving positive and negative passionate feelings and convictions towards the brand, like-minded consumers, and opposite-minded consumers' (Osuna Ramírez et al., 2024, p. 4). Brand polarization is encountered when brands take bold positions, embrace controversial advertising or offer niche products that appeal deeply to specific consumer groups but alienate others (Milfeld & Flint, 2021). The polarized reactions stem from the brand's identity, values or the experience it offers, leading to an emotional connection or rejection from different customer groups (Monahan et al., 2023).

This emerging topic in the branding literature may be captured by four dimensions: Brand passion, self-brand benchmarking, intra-group identification and inter-group dissociation (Osuna Ramírez et al., 2024). Brand passion embodies intensified feelings targeted towards the brand, covering both extremes of the emotional spectrum (love and hate). Self-brand benchmarking signals robust adjustment or misalignment between the consumer's and the brand's personality. Intra-group identification indicates the individual's affinity with consumers who share the same feelings towards the brand. Finally, inter-group dissociation represents the level of separateness exhibited by the consumer from others who have opposite feelings about the brand.

A polarizing brand might offer distinct advantages for various parties (Osuna Ramírez et al., 2019). Polarization can bring benefits for the brand, as its positioning strategy is supported, and the brand's strength perception is enhanced. The brand management team can rely on the phenomenon, as it serves as a guide to constantly improve, stay focused and gain respect. Brand polarization is also advantageous for consumers, as it allows enjoyment, self-expression and belonging to a group. The phenomenon can be a powerful strategic tool for differentiation, loyalty-building and visibility, but it also requires careful management (Luo et al., 2013a). Companies must align their polarizing stances with their core values, manage risks effectively and maintain a long-term strategic vision (Luo et al., 2013b).

LOOKING INTO THE FUTURE – RESEARCH DIRECTIONS

By acknowledging the dynamic nature of the consumer–brand relationships field (Fetscherin & Veloutsou, 2024), several gaps and shortcomings are yet to be filled. Looking at these uncharted areas in this field is crucial and holds significant managerial relevance since developing and fostering connections between customers and brands are a key concern of practicing managers as they try to cultivate desired consumer behavioural responses (Bagozzi et al., 2021; Veloutsou, 2023).

First and foremost, there are conceptual differences in the way that brand relationships are approached by scholars that need to be clarified. While extreme and more common forms of consumer–brand relationships have been studied extensively (Fetscherin & Veloutsou, 2024), there are still disagreements on the actual conceptualization and operationalisation of the concept itself (Alvarez et al., 2023). This is also evident in the various brand relationship forms. For instance, although ambivalence is consistently approached as mixed solid emotions, some view it as a state of mixed emotions felt at the same time (Priester & Petty, 1996), while others suggest that it can also happen sequentially within the relationship (Evanschitzky et al., 2020; Otnes et al., 1997; Rempel & Burris, 2005). Similar issues exist in the conceptualisation of other more mainstream terms, such as brand love or brand hate, let alone the operationalisation of all brand relationships' relevant terms. Different brand relationship types lead to different outcomes, but the conceptual inconsistency does not allow these connections to be clearly mapped.

The existing research does not address all the brand relationship bases equally. Brand relationship studies, particularly in the realms of emotional and functional connections, often fall short of fully capturing the inherent complexity and dynamism of these relationships (Fernandes & Moreira, 2019). Particularly, business brand relationships, which have predominantly been examined on a functional level, tend to overlook or underemphasize crucial for consumer–brand relationship elements, including emotional connection aspects such as identification (Mingione & Leoni, 2020).

The imbalance between research on positive and negative brand relationships is notorious. Work on positive brand relationships significantly outnumbers those on negative brand relationships (Fetscherin & Veloutsou, 2024). While there has been a growing interest in the extremely negative relationships, brand hate, in particular, more efforts are needed to explore the negative aspects of the consumer–brand relationship spectrum.

Likewise, current research on brand passion tends to view the construct solely as a positively valenced set of strong emotions. This approach totally overlooks brand passion's irrelevantness to the emotion valence strength of emotion attribute. There is clear evidence that brand passion also exists in brand relationships with a strong negative valence (Osuna Ramírez et al., 2024). Future research incorporating brand passion should embrace a more balanced and flexible approach and facilitate the exploration of intense negative feelings.

Brand relationship research tends to overlook the nuanced, context-dependent and evolving relationship nature of brand relationships outside the commonly expected forms. For example, a consumer's emotional bond with a brand can fluctuate considerably due to various external factors, including cultural shifts (Pontinha & Coelho do Vale, 2020). Moreover, while recent studies have predominantly explored how consumers develop positive relationships with brands, there is limited investigation into how consumers fall out of love and the mechanisms for repairing such conditions (Fetscherin, 2019; Kashif et al., 2021; Zhang et al., 2020). Although there is evidence that relationships evolve and their polarity and strength may change (Tolunay & Veloutsou, 2025), existing research often treats emotional responses as static or linear, thereby failing to account for the dynamic processes that truly characterize brand relationships. Consumers with a strong brand connection and closeness (Park et al., 2013b) may also experience a mix of emotions (Aaker et al., 2008), leading to conflicted brand relationships (Zarantonello et al., 2018). This ambivalence has the potential to transform the brand relationship nature and thus requires careful attention (Fournier & Alvarez, 2013). Lastly, there is scarcity of research on situations where extreme positive and negative feelings towards a brand are simultaneously experienced by different consumer groups or brand polarization (Osuna Ramírez et al., 2024). More research is needed to grasp a better understanding of this construct.

While brand relationship research has reached a mature stage (Fetscherin & Veloutsou, 2024), substantial gaps remain that require further exploration. Engaging with research in this area can not only clarify inconsistencies and uncertainties but also uncover new and uncharted dimensions within the broader field of brand relationships. Addressing these complexities will enhance our understanding and contribute to the ongoing development of the discipline.

REFERENCES

Aaker, D. A., & Moorman, C. (2017). *Strategic market management*. John Wiley & Sons.

Aaker, J., Drolet, A., & Griffin, D. (2008). Recalling mixed emotions. *Journal of Consumer Research*, *35*(2), 268–78. https://doi.org/10.1086/588570

Aggarwal, P., & Shi, M. (2018). Monogamous versus polygamous brand relationships. *Journal of the Association for Consumer Research*, *3*(2), 188–201. https://doi.org/10.1086/697078

Ahuvia, A. C. (1993). *I love it! Towards a unifying theory of love across diverse love objects* [Unpublished PhD dissertation]. Northwestern University.

Akrout, H., & Mrad, M. (2023). Measuring brand hate in a cross-cultural context: Emic and Etic scale development and validation. *Journal of Business Research*, *154*, 113289. https://doi.org/10.1016/j.jbusres.2022.08.053

Albert, N., & Merunka, D. (2013). The role of brand love in consumer-brand relationships. *Journal of Consumer Marketing*, *30*(3), 258–266. https://doi-org.ezproxy2.lib.gla.ac.uk/10.1108/07363761311328928

Albert, N., Merunka, D., & Valette-Florence, P. (2008). When consumers love their brands: Exploring the concept and its dimensions. *Journal of Business Research*, *61*(10), 1062–75. https://doi.org/10.1016/j.jbusres.2007.09.014

Albert, N., Merunka, D., & Valette-Florence, P. (2013). Brand passion: Antecedents and consequences. *Journal of Business Research*, 66(7), 904–9. https://doi.org/10.1016/j.jbusres.2011.12.009

Albert, N., & Thomson, M. (2018). A synthesis of the consumer-brand relationship domain: Using text mining to track research streams, describe their emotional associations, and identify future research priorities. *Journal of the Association for Consumer Research*, *3*(2), 130–46. https://doi.org/10.1086/696825

Albert, N., & Thomson, M. (2024). Epistemological jangle and jingle fallacies in the consumer–brand relationship subfield: A call to action. *Journal of Consumer Research*, *51*(2), 383–407. https://doi.org/10.1093/jcr/ucad064

Alvarez, C., David, M. E., & George, M. (2023). Types of consumer–brand relationships: A systematic review and future research agenda. *Journal of Business Research*, 160, Article 113753. https://doi.org/10.1016/j.jbusres.2023.113753

Alvarez, C., & Fournier, S. (2016). Consumers' relationships with brands. *Current Opinion in Psychology*, *10*, 129–35. https://doi.org/10.1016/j.copsyc.2015.12.017

Attiq, S., Hasni, M. J. S., & Zhang, C. (2023). Antecedents and consequences of brand hate: A study of Pakistan's telecommunication industry. *Journal of Consumer Marketing*, *40*(1), 1–14. https://doi.org/10.1108/JCM-04-2021-4615

Aziz, R., & Rahman, Z. (2022). Brand hate: A literature review and future research agenda. *European Journal of Marketing*, *56*(7), 2014–51. https://doi.org/10.1108/EJM-03-2021-0189

Bagozzi, R. P., Romani, S., Grappi, S., & Zarantonello, L. (2021). Psychological underpinnings of brands. *Annual Review of Psychology*, *72*(1), 585–607. https://doi.org/10.1146/annurev-psych-010419-051008

Bairrada, C. M., Coelho, F., & Coelho, A. (2018). Antecedents and outcomes of brand love: Utilitarian and symbolic brand qualities. *European Journal of Marketing*, *52*(3/4), 656–82. https://doi.org/10.1108/EJM-02-2016-0081

Batra, R., Ahuvia, A., & Bagozzi, R. P. (2012). Brand love. *Journal of Marketing*, *76*(2), 1–16. https://doi.org/10.1509/jm.09.0339

Bauer, B. C. (2023). Strong versus weak consumer-brand relationships: Matching psychological sense of brand community and type of advertising appeal. *Psychology & Marketing*, *40*(4), 791–810. https://doi.org/10.1002/mar.21784

Bechwati, N. N., & Morrin, M. (2003). Outraged consumers: Getting even at the expense of getting a good deal. *Journal of Consumer Psychology*, *13*(4), 440–53. https://doi.org/10.1207/S15327663JCP1304_11

Bian, W., & Yan, G. (2022). Analyzing intention to purchase brand extension via brand attribute associations: The mediating and moderating role of emotional consumer-brand relationship and brand commitment. *Frontiers in Psychology*, *13*, 884673. https://doi.org/10.3389/fpsyg.2022.884673

Blackston, M. (1993). Beyond brand personality: Building brand relationships. In Aaker, D. A., & Biel, A. L. (Eds.), *Brand Equity and Advertising: Advertising's Role in Building Strong Brands* (pp. 113–124). Lawrence Erlbaum Associates.

Brandão, A., Ribeiro, B., & Gadekar, M. (2023). You ruined our love story, but I just cannot hate you – A moderation–mediation analysis of past experienced brand love and brand hate. *International Journal of Consumer Studies*, *47*(3), 1126–38. https://doi.org/10.1111/ijcs.12892

Bryson, D., Atwal, G., & Hultén, P. (2013). Towards the conceptualisation of the antecedents of extreme negative affect towards luxury brands. *Qualitative Market Research: An International Journal*, *16*(4), 393–405. https://doi.org/10.1108/QMR-06-2013-0043

Cambridge Dictionary. (n.d.). Passion. In *Cambridge Dictionary*. Retrieved August 27, 2024, from https://dictionary.cambridge.org/us/dictionary/english/passion

Carroll, B. A., & Ahuvia, A. C. (2006). Some antecedents and outcomes of brand love. *Marketing Letters*, *17*(2), 79–89. https://doi.org/10.1007/s11002-006-4219-2

Choi, L., Kim, M. R., & Kwon, H. B. (2022). Impact of customer-based corporate reputation on customer engagement behaviors: Customer identification and brand love as mediators and industry type as a moderator. *Journal of Brand Management*, *29*(3), 213–229. https://doi.org/10.1057/s41262-021-00269-4

Cluley, R. (2020). Complaining about rivals: Indifference, cooperation, and competition in the governance of advertising. *Regulation & Governance*, *14*(2), 316–27. https://doi.org/10.1111/rego.12211

Conner, M., Wilding, S., van Harreveld, F., & Dalege, J. (2021). Cognitive-affective inconsistency and ambivalence: Impact on the overall attitude–behavior relationship. *Personality and Social Psychology Bulletin*, *47*(4), 673–87. https://doi.org/10.1177/0146167220945900

Costa, J., & Azevedo, A. (2023). Beyond brand hate: Are you willing to forgive a negative experience with your smartphone mobile communications' brand? *Corporate Reputation Review*, *26*(2), 83–96. https://doi.org/10.1057/s41299-022-00139-7

Cui, C., Mrad, M., & Hogg, M. (2018). Brand addiction: Exploring the concept and its definition through an experiential lens. *Journal of Business Research*, *87*, 118–27. https://doi.org/10.1016/j.jbusres.2018.02.028

Dalli, D., Romani, S., & Gistri, G. (2006). Brand dislike: Representing the negative side of consumer preferences. *Advances in Consumer Research*, *33*, 87–95.

Das, G., Agarwal, J., Malhotra, N. K., & Varshneya, G. (2018). Does brand experience translate into brand commitment?: A mediated- moderation model of brand passion and perceived brand ethicality. *Journal of Business Research*, *95*, 479–90. https://doi.org/10.1016/j.jbusres.2018.05.026

De Liver, Y., Van Der Pligt, J., & Wigboldus, D. (2007). Positive and negative associations underlying ambivalent attitudes. *Journal of Experimental Social Psychology*, *43*(2), 319–26. https://doi.org/10.1016/j.jesp.2006.02.012

Demirbag-Kaplan, M., Yildirim, C., Gulden, S., & Aktan, D. (2015). I love to hate you: Loyalty for disliked brands and the role of nostalgia. *Journal of Brand Management*, *22*(2), 136–53. https://doi.org/10.1057/bm.2015.10

Dias, P., & Cavalheiro, R. (2022). The role of storytelling in the creation of brand love: The PANDORA case. *Journal of Brand Management*, *29*(1), 58. https://doi.org/10.1057/s41262-021-00254-6

Duffett, R., Petroşanu, D. M., Negricea, I. C., & Edu, T. (2019). Effect of YouTube marketing communication on converting brand liking into preference among millennials regarding brands in general and sustainable offers in particular. Evidence from South Africa and Romania. *Sustainability (Switzerland)*, *11*(3), 1–24. https://doi.org/10.3390/su11030604

Eagly, A. H., & Chaiken, S. (1998). Attitude structure and function. In D. T. Gilbert, S. T. Fiske, & G. Lindzey (Eds.), *Handbook of Social Psychology* (4th ed., Vol. 1, pp. 269–322). McGraw-Hill.

Evanschitzky, H., Ramaseshan, B., Brady, M. K., Rabbanee, F. K., Brock, C., & Pokorska-Zare, J. (2020). Consumer relationship fading. *Psychology & Marketing*, *37*(6), 815–36. https://doi.org/10.1002/mar.21343

Fajer, M. T., & Schouten, J. W. (1995). Breakdown and dissolution of person–brand relationships. *Advances in Consumer Research*, *22*, 663–667.

Fernandes, T., & Moreira, M. (2019). Consumer brand engagement, satisfaction and brand loyalty: A comparative study between functional and emotional brand relationships. *Journal of Product & Brand Management*, *28*(2), 274–86. https://doi.org/10.1108/JPBM-08-2017-1545

Fetscherin, M. (2019). The five types of brand hate: How they affect consumer behavior. *Journal of Business Research*, *101*, 116–27. https://doi.org/10.1016/j.jbusres.2019.04.017

Fetscherin, M., Guzman, F., Veloutsou, C., & Cayolla, R. R. (2019). Latest research on brand relationships: Introduction to the special issue. *Journal of Product and Brand Management*, *28*(2), 133–9. https://doi.org/10.1108/JPBM-12-2018-2167

Fetscherin, M., & Heinrich, D. (2014). Consumer brand relationships: A research landscape. *Journal of Brand Management*, *21*(5), 366–71. https://doi.org/10.1057/bm.2014.22

Fetscherin, M., & KC, R. P. (2021). Anti-consumption in the context of brand relationships. *Strategic Change*, *30*(1), 53–8. https://doi.org/10.1002/jsc.2386

Fetscherin, M., & Veloutsou, C. (2024). Guest editorial: 30 years of brand relationship research. *Journal of Product and Brand Management*, *33*(4), 413–8. https://doi.org/10.1108/JPBM-05-2024-024

Fetscherin, M., Veloutsou, C., & Guzmán, F. (2021). Models for brand relationships: Guest editorial. *Journal of Product & Brand Management*, *30*(3), 353–9. https://doi.org/10.1108/JPBM-04-2021-012

Fournier, S. (1998). Consumers and their brands: Developing relationship theory in consumer research. *Journal of Consumer Research*, *24*(4), 343–73. https://doi.org/10.1086/209515

Fournier, S., & Alvarez, C. (2013). Relating badly to brands. *Journal of Consumer Psychology*, *23*(2), 253–64. https://doi.org/10.1016/j.jcps.2013.01.004

Füller, J., Matzler, K., & Hoppe, M. (2008). Brand community members as a source of innovation. *Journal of Product Innovation Management*, *25*(6), 608–19. https://doi.org/10.1111/j.1540-5885.2008.00325.x

Gilal, F. G., Paul, J., Thomas, A., Zarantonello, L., & Gilal, R. G. (2023). Brand passion: A systematic review and future research agenda. *Journal of Brand Management*, *30*(6), 490–515. https://doi.org/10.1057/s41262-023-00324-x

Haefner, J. E., Deli-Gray, Z., & Rosenbloom, A. (2011). In consumer decision making: Insights from Bulgarian and Hungarian Consumers during the global economic crisis. *Managing Global Transitions*, *9*(3), 249–73.

Hamby, A., & Russell, C. (2022). How does ambivalence affect young consumers' response to risky products? *Journal of the Academy of Marketing Science*, *50*(4), 841–63. https://doi.org/10.1007/s11747-021-00834-7

Hayran, C., & Ceylan, M. (2023). Impact of social media brand blunders on brand trust and brand liking. *International Journal of Market Research*, *65*(4), 466–83. https://doi.org/10.1177/14707853221132216

Hegner, S. M., Fetscherin, M., & van Delzen, M. (2017). Determinants and outcomes of brand hate. *Journal of Product and Brand Management*, *26*(1), 13–25. https://doi.org/10.1108/JPBM-01-2016-1070]

Heide, J. B., & John, G. (1992). Do norms matter in marketing relationships? *Journal of Marketing*, *56*(2), 32–44. https://doi.org/10.1177/002224299205600020

Hemonnet-Goujot, A., & Valette-Florence, P. (2022). 'All you need is love' from product design value perception to luxury brand love: An integrated framework. *Journal of Business Research*, *139*, 1463–75. https://doi.org/10.1016/j.jbusres.2021.10.066

Herrando, C., Jiménez-Martínez, J., & Martín-De Hoyos, M. J. (2017). Passion at first sight: How to engage users in social commerce contexts. *Electronic Commerce Research*, *17*(4), 701–20. https://doi.org/10.1007/s10660-016-9251-6

Horton, D., & Richard Wohl, R. (1956). Mass communication and parasocial interaction: Observations on intimacy at a distance. *Psychiatry*, *19*(3), 215–29. https://doi.org/10.1080/00332747.1956.11023049

Huber, F., Meyer, F., & Schmid, D. A. (2015). Brand love in progress – The interdependence of brand love antecedents in consideration of relationship duration. *Journal of Product & Brand Management*, *24*(6), 567–79. https://doi.org/10.1108/JPBM-08-2014-0682

Hudders, L., Lou, C., & de Brabandere, M. (2022). Understanding the impact of influencers' responses to negative follower comments on the persuasiveness of sponsored Instagram posts. *International Journal of Advertising*, *41*(1), 178–204. https://doi.org/10.1080/02650487.2021.1963554

Hwang, J., & Kandampully, J. (2012). The role of emotional aspects in younger consumer-brand relationships. *Journal of Product & Brand Management*, *21*(2), 98–108. https://doi.org/10.1108/10610421211215517

Iglesias, O., Markovic, S., & Rialp, J. (2019). How does sensory brand experience influence brand equity? Considering the roles of customer satisfaction, customer affective commitment, and employee empathy. *Journal of Business Research*, *96*, 343–54. https://doi.org/10.1016/j.jbusres.2018.05.043

Jewell, R. D., Coupey, E., & Jones, M. T. (2002). Catch a tiger by his toe: Ambivalence in decision making in the 2000 presidential election. In S. M. Broniarczyk, & K. Nakamoto (Eds.), *Advances in Consumer Research*, (Vol. 29, pp. 333–38). https://doi.org/10.1080/10447318.2022.2097785

Johnston, W. J., & Hausman, A. (2006). Expanding the marriage metaphor in understanding long-term business relationships. *Journal of Business & Industrial Marketing*, *21*(7), 446–52. https://doi.org/10.1108/08858620610708939

Joshi, A. W., & Arnold, S. J. (1998). How relational norms affect compliance in industrial buying. *Journal of Business Research*, *41*(2), 105–14. https://doi.org/10.1016/S0148-2963(97)00017-9

Junaid, M., Hussain, K., Basit, A., & Hou, F. (2020). Nature of brand love: Examining its variable effect on engagement and well-being. *Journal of Brand Management*, *27*(3), 284–99. https://doi.org/10.1057/s41262-019-00179-1

Karjaluoto, H., Munnukka, J., & Kiuru, K. (2016). Brand love and positive word of mouth: The moderating effects of experience and price. *Journal of Product & Brand Management*, *25*(6), 527–37. https://doi.org/10.1108/JPBM-03-2015-0834

Kashif, M., Korkmaz Devrani, T., Rehman, A., & Samad, S. (2021). Love is not blind: Investigating a love-hate transition among luxury fashion brand consumers. *Journal of Fashion Marketing and Management: An International Journal*, *25*(4), 625–43. https://doi.org/10.1108/JFMM-04-2020-0058

Kaufmann, H. R., Loureiro, S. M. C., & Manarioti, A. (2016). Exploring behavioural branding, brand love and brand co-creation. *Journal of Product & Brand Management*, *25*(6), 516–26. https://doi.org/10.1108/JPBM-06-2015-0919

Keh, H.-T., Pang, J., & Peng, S. (2007). Understanding and measuring brand love. In J. R. Priester, D. J. MacInnis, & C. W. Park (Eds.), *Conference proceedings of the Advertising and Consumer Psychology Conference: New Frontiers in Branding: Attitudes, Attachments, and Relationships* (pp. 84–88). June 2007, Society for Consumer Psychology/National Bureau of Economic Research. https://doi.org/10.2501/S0021849907070468

Kennedy, E., & Guzmán, F. (2021). No matter what you do, I still love you: An examination of consumer reaction to brand transgressions. *Journal of Product & Brand Management*, *30*(4), 594–608. https://doi.org/10.1108/JPBM-07-2019-2450

Koponen, J. P., & Julkunen, S. M. (2022). Development of long-term B2B customer relationships: The role of self-disclosure and relational cost/benefit evaluation. *European Journal of Marketing*, *56*(13), 194–235. https://doi.org/10.1108/EJM-07-2020-0492

Kucuk, S. U. (2018). Macro-level antecedents of consumer brand hate. *Journal of Consumer Marketing*, *35*(5), 555–64. https://doi.org/10.1108/JCM-10-2017-2389

Labrecque, L. I. (2014). Fostering consumer–brand relationships in social media environments: The role of parasocial interaction. *Journal of Interactive Marketing*, *28*(2), 134–48. https://doi.org/10.1016/j.intmar.2013.12.003

Lacap, J. P. G., Cruz, M. R. M., Bayson, A. J., Molano, R., & Garcia, J. G. (2024). Parasocial relationships and social media interactions: Building brand credibility and loyalty. *Spanish Journal of Marketing – ESIC*, *28*(1), 77–97. https://doi.org/10.1108/SJME-09-2022-0190

Lee, J.-S., Kim, J., Hwang, J., & Cui, Y. (2021). Does love become hate or forgiveness after a double deviation? The case of hotel loyalty program members. *Tourism Management*, *84*, 104279. https://doi.org/10.1016/j.tourman.2020.104279

Lee, M. S., Motion, J., & Conroy, D. (2009). Anti-consumption and brand avoidance. *Journal of Business Research*, *62*(2), 169–80. https://doi.org/10.1016/j.jbusres.2008.01.024

Leung, L.C., Bougoure, U.S., & Miller, K.W. (2014). The effects of affective and utilitarian brand relationships on brand consideration. *Journal of Brand Management*, *21*(6), 469–484. https://doi.org/10.1057/bm.2014.15

Lopez, A. (2021). Can we get back together? Measuring brand relationship breakup. *Journal of Consumer Behaviour*, *20*(3), 681–94. https://doi.org/10.1002/cb.1895

Loureiro, S. C., & Kaufmann, H. (2012). Explaining love of wine brands. *Journal of Promotion Management*, *18*(3), 329–43. https://doi.org/10.1080/10496491.2012.696460

Lunardo, R., & Saintives, C. (2018). Coping with the ambivalent emotions of guilt and pride in the service context. *Journal of Services Marketing*, *32*(3), 360–70. https://doi.org/10.1108/JSM-01-2017-0003

Luo, X., Wiles, M. A., & Raithel, S. (2013a). Make the most of a polarizing brand. *Harvard Business Review*, *91*(11), 29–31.

Luo, X., Wiles, M. A., & Raithel, S. (2013b). The impact of brand rating dispersion on firm value. *Journal of Marketing Research*, *50*(3), 399–415. https://doi.org/10.1509/jmr.12.0188

Mikulincer, M., Shaver, P. R., Bar-On, N., & Ein-Dor, T. (2010). The pushes and pulls of close relationships: Attachment insecurities and relational ambivalence. *Journal of Personality and Social Psychology*, *98*(3), 450–68. https://doi.org/10.1037/a0017366

Milfeld, T., & Flint, D. J. (2021). When brands take a stand: The nature of consumers' polarized reactions to social narrative videos. *Journal of Product & Brand Management*, *30*(4), 532–48. https://doi.org/10.1108/JPBM-10-2019-2606

Mingione, M., & Leoni, L. (2020). Blurring B2C and B2B boundaries: Corporate brand value co-creation in B2B2C markets. *Journal of Marketing Management*, *36*(1–2), 72–99. https://doi.org/10.1080/0267257X.2019.1694566

Monahan, L., Espinosa, J. A., Langenderfer, J., & Ortinau, D. J. (2023). Did you hear our brand is hated? The unexpected upside of hate-acknowledging advertising for polarizing brands. *Journal of Business Research, 154*, Article 113283. https://doi.org/10.1016/j.jbusres.2022.08.047

Morgan, R. M., & Hunt, S. D. (1994). The commitment-trust theory of relationship marketing. *Journal of Marketing*, *58*(3), 20–38. https://doi.org/10.1177/002224299405800302

Ojansivu, I., Hermes, J., & Laari-Salmela, S. (2020). Business relationships in the industrial network literature: Three approaches and their underlying assumptions. *Industrial Marketing Management*, *87*, 181–95. https://doi.org/10.1016/j.indmarman.2019.11.016

Olsen, S. O., Wilcox, J., & Olsson, U. (2005). Consequences of ambivalence on satisfaction and loyalty. *Psychology & Marketing*, *22*(3), 247–69. https://doi.org/10.1002/mar.20057

Ortiz, M. H., Reynolds, K. E., & Franke, G. R. (2013). Measuring consumer devotion: Antecedents and consequences of passionate consumer behavior. *The Journal of Marketing Theory and Practice*,

21(1), 7–29. https://doi.org/10.2753/MTP1069-6679210101

Osuna Ramírez, S. A., Veloutsou, C., & Morgan-Thomas, A. (2019). I hate what you love: Brand polarization and negativity towards brands as an opportunity for brand management. *Journal of Product and Brand Management*, *28*(5), 614–32. https://doi.org/10.1108/JPBM-03-2018-1811

Osuna Ramírez, S. A., Veloutsou, C., & Morgan-Thomas, A. (2024). On the antipodes of love and hate: The conception and measurement of brand polarization. *Journal of Business Research, 179*, Article 114687. https://doi.org/10.1016/j.jbusres.2024.114687

Otnes, C., Lowrey, T. M., & Shrum, L. J. (1997). Toward an understanding of consumer ambivalence. *Journal of Consumer Research*, *24*(1), 80–93. https://doi.org/10.1086/209495

Oxford Dictionary. (n.d). *Passion. In Oxford Dictionary*. Retrieved August 27, 2024, from www.oxfordlearnersdictionaries.com/us/definition/english/passion?q=passion

Papista, E., & Dimitriadis, S. (2019). Consumer–green brand relationships: Revisiting benefits, relationship quality and outcomes. *Journal of Product & Brand Management*, *28*(2), 166–87. https://doi.org/10.1108/JPBM-09-2016-1316

Park, C. W., Eisingerich, A. B., & Park, J. W. (2013a). Attachment-aversion (AA) model of customer-brand relationships. *Journal of Consumer Psychology*, *23*(2), 229–48. https://doi.org/10.1016/j.jcps.2013.01.002

Park, C. W., Eisingerich, A. B., & Park, J. W. (2013b). From brand aversion or indifference to brand attachment: Authors' response to commentaries to Park, Eisingerich, and Park's brand attachment–aversion model. *Journal of Consumer Psychology*, *23*(2), 269–74. https://doi.org/10.1016/j.jcps.2013.01.006

Penz, E., & Hogg, M. K. (2011). The role of mixed emotions in consumer behaviour: Investigating ambivalence in consumers' experiences of approach-avoidance conflicts in online and offline settings. *European Journal of Marketing*, *45*(1/2), 104–32. https://doi.org/10.1108/03090561111095612

Pinto, O., & Brandão, A. (2021). Antecedents and consequences of brand hate: Empirical evidence from the telecommunication industry. *European Journal of Management and Business Economics*, *30*(1), 18–35. https://doi.org/10.1108/EJMBE-04-2020-0084

Pontinha, V. M., & Coelho do Vale, R. (2020). Brand love measurement scale development: An intercultural analysis. *Journal of Product & Brand Management*, *29*(4), 471–89. https://doi.org/10.1108/JPBM-10-2018-2094

Pourazad, N., Stocchi, L., & Pare, V. (2019). Brand attribute associations, emotional consumer-brand relationship and evaluation of brand extensions. *Australasian Marketing Journal*, *27*(4), 249–60. https://doi.org/10.1016/j.ausmj.2019.07.004

Priester, J. R., & Petty, R. E. (1996). The gradual threshold model of ambivalence: Relating the positive and negative bases of attitudes to subjective ambivalence. *Journal of Personality and Social Psychology*, *71*(3), 431–49. https://doi.org/10.1037/0022-3514.71.3.431

Priester, J. R., & Petty, R. E. (2001). Extending the bases of subjective attitudinal ambivalence: Interpersonal and intrapersonal antecedents of evaluative tension. *Journal of Personality and Social Psychology*, *80*(1), 19–34. https://doi.org/10.1037/0022-3514.80.1.19

Rahman, R., Langner, T., & Temme, D. (2021). Brand love: Conceptual and empirical investigation of a holistic causal model. *Journal of Brand Management*, *28*(6), 609–42. https://doi.org/10.1057/s41262-021-00237-7

Rempel, J. K., & Burris, C. T. (2005). Let me count the ways: An integrative theory of love and hate. *Personal Relationships*, *12*(2), 297–313. https://doi.org/10.1111/j.1350-4126.2005.00116.x

Robertson, J., Botha, E., Ferreira, C., & Pitt, L. (2022). How deep is your love? The brand love-loyalty matrix in consumer-brand relationships. *Journal of Business Research*, *149*, 651–62. https://doi.org/10.1016/j.jbusres.2022.05.058

Rodhain, A., & Aurier, P. (2016). The child–brand relationship: Social interactions matter. *Journal of Product & Brand Management*, *25*(1), 84–97. https://doi.org/10.1108/JPBM-03-2015-0835

Romani, S., Grappi, S., & Dalli, D. (2012). Emotions that drive consumers away from brands: Measuring negative emotions toward brands and their behavioral effects. *International Journal of Research in Marketing*, *29*(1), 55–67. https://doi.org/10.1016/j.ijresmar.2011.07.001

Roster, C. A., & Richins, M. L. (2009). Ambivalence and attitudes in consumer replacement decisions. *Journal of Consumer Psychology*, *19*(1), 48–61. https://doi.org/10.1016/j.jcps.2008.12.008

Roy, S. K., Sharma, A., Bose, S., & Singh, G. (2022). Consumer-brand relationship: A brand hate perspective. *Journal of Business Research*, *144*, 1293–304. https://doi.org/10.1016/j.jbusres.2022.02.065

Sarkar, A., Sarkar, J. G., Sreejesh, S., Anusree, M. R., & Rishi, B. (2020). You are so embarrassing, still, I hate you less! Investigating consumers' brand embarrassment and brand hate. *Journal of Brand Management*, *27*(1), 1–15. https://doi.org/10.1057/s41262-019-00164-8

Schultz, D. (2016). Market brand equity: Lost in terminology and techniques? *Journal of Product & Brand Management*, *25*(6), 507–15. https://doi.org/10.1108/JPBM-07-2016-1260

Shetty, K., & Fitzsimmons, J. R. (2022). The effect of brand personality congruence, brand attachment and brand love on loyalty among HENRY's in the luxury branding sector. *Journal of Fashion Marketing and Management: An International Journal*, *26*(1), 21–35. https://doi.org/10.1108/JFMM-09-2020-0208

Sipilä, J., Sundqvist, S., & Tarkiainen, A. (2017). Winding paths: Ambivalence in consumers' buying processes. *Journal of Consumer Behaviour*, *16*(6), e93–112. https://doi.org/10.1002/cb.1662

Thompson, M. M., Zanna, M. P., & Griffin, D. W. (1995). Let's not be indifferent about (attitudinal) ambivalence. In R. E. Petty, & J. A. Krosnick (Eds.), *Attitude Strength: Antecedents and Consequences* (pp. 361–386). Erlbaum.

Tolunay, A., & Veloutsou, C. (2025). Don't make me hate you, my love! Perceived brand betrayal and the love-becomes-hate phenomenon. *Journal of Business Research*, *187*, 115060. https://doi.org/10.1016/j.jbusres.2024.115060

Torres, P., Augusto, M., & Neves, C. (2022). Value dimensions of gamification and their influence on brand loyalty and word-of-mouth: Relationships and combinations with satisfaction and brand love. *Psychology & Marketing*, *39*(1), 59–75. https://doi.org/10.1002/mar.21573

Touni, R., Kim, W. G., Haldorai, K., & Rady, A. (2022). Customer engagement and hotel booking intention: The mediating and moderating roles of customer-perceived value and brand reputation. *International Journal of Hospitality Management*, *104*, 103246. https://doi.org/10.1016/j.ijhm.2022.103246

Tugrul, T. O., & Taqi, M. (2018). *Construal level theory approach to mixed emotions of brand hate and brand love. In Proceedings of the 32nd International Business Information Management Association Conference,* November 2018, (pp. 515–523). International Business Information Management Association (IBIMA).

Veloutsou, C. (2007). Identifying the dimensions of the product-brand and consumer relationship. *Journal of Marketing Management*, *23*(1/2), 7–26. https://doi.org/10.1362/026725707X177892

Veloutsou, C. (2023). Enlightening the brand building–audience response link. *Journal of Brand Management*, *30*(6), 550–66. https://doi.org/10.1057/s41262-023-00331-y

Veloutsou, C., & Ballester, E. (2025). A typology of brand knowledge associations projected in brand-generated signals. *Journal of Product & Brand Management*, *34*(3), 376–97. https://doi-org.ezproxy2.lib.gla.ac.uk/10.1108/JPBM-03-2024-5022

Veloutsou, C., Chatzipanagiotou, K., & Christodoulides, G. (2020). The consumer-based brand equity deconstruction and restoration process: Lessons from unliked brands. *Journal of Business Research*, *111*, 41–51. https://doi.org/10.1016/j.jbusres.2019.12.029

Veloutsou, C., & Delgado-Ballester, E. (2018). New challenges in brand management. *Spanish Journal of Marketing – ESIC*, *22*(3), 254–71. https://doi.org/10.1108/SJME-12-2018-036

Veloutsou, C., & Mafe, C. R. (2020). Brands as relationship builders in the virtual world: A bibliometric analysis. *Electronic Commerce Research and Applications*, *39*, 100901. https://doi.org/10.1016/j.elerap.2019.100901

Veloutsou, C., & Moutinho, L. (2009). Brand relationships through brand reputation and brand tribalism. *Journal of Business Research*, *62*(3), 314–22. https://doi.org/10.1016/j.jbusres.2008.05.010

Wallace, E., Buil, I., & De Chernatony, L. (2014). Consumer engagement with self-expressive brands: Brand love and WOM outcomes. *Journal of Product & Brand Management*, *23*(1), 33–42. https://doi.org/10.1108/JPBM-06-2013-0326

Wang, S., & Liu, M. T. (2023). Celebrity endorsement in marketing from1960 to 2021: A bibliometric review and future agenda. *Asia Pacific Journal of Marketing and Logistics*, *35*(4), 849–73. https://doi.org/10.1108/APJML-12-2021-0918

Watson, L., & Spence, M. T. (2007). Causes and consequences of emotions on consumer behaviour: A review and integrative cognitive appraisal theory. *European Journal of Marketing*, *41*(5/6), 487–511. https://doi.org/10.1108/03090560710737570

Williams, P., & Aaker, J. L. (2002). Can mixed emotions peacefully coexist? *Journal of Consumer Research*, *28*(4), 636–49. https://doi.org/10.1086/338206

Yadav, A., & Chakrabarti, S. (2022). Brand hate: A systematic literature review and future research agenda. *International Journal of Consumer Studies*, *46*(5), 1992–2019. https://doi.org/10.1111/ijcs.12772

Yang, J., & Mundel, J. (2022). Effects of brand feedback to negative eWOM on brand love/hate: An expectancy violation approach. *Journal of Product & Brand Management*, *31*(2), 279–92. https://doi.org/10.1108/JPBM-05-2020-2900

Zarantonello, L., Romani, S., Grappi, S., & Bagozzi, R. P. (2016). Brand hate. *Journal of Product & Brand Management*, *25*(1), 11–25. https://doi.org/10.1108/JPBM-01-2015-0799

Zarantonello, L., Romani, S., Grappi, S., & Fetscherin, M. (2018). Trajectories of brand hate. *Journal of Brand Management*, *25*(6), 549–60. https://doi.org/10.1057/s41262-018-0105-5

Zhang, C., & Laroche, M. (2020). Brand hate: A multidimensional construct. *Journal of Product & Brand Management*, *30*(3), 392–414. https://doi.org/10.1108/JPBM-11-2018-2103

Zhang, Y., Zhang, J., & Sakulsinlapakorn, K. (2020). Love becomes hate? Or love is blind? Moderating effects of brand love upon consumers' retaliation towards brand failure. *Journal of Product & Brand Management*, *30*(3), 415–32. https://doi.org/10.1108/JPBM-07-2019-2470

17

Brand Management in Times of Crisis

Robert Karaszewski

INTRODUCTION

Modern organizations face an unprecedented range of crises – from negative product publicity and industrial disasters to public health emergencies and ethical lapses. These crises can swiftly erode decades of brand building, dissolve stakeholder confidence and even threaten an organization's survival. In the present information age, the speed and spread of information (and misinformation) amplify threats to brand reputation more than ever before.

Crisis communication has thus become a critical competency for brand management, demanding not only quick reactions but also strategic foresight and ethical clarity.

The objective of this chapter is to examine how foundational crisis communication theories, particularly situational crisis communication theory (SCCT) and discourse of renewal theory (DRT), can be applied and evolved to manage brand crises effectively in a dynamic landscape. The author focused on integrating traditional principles with modern considerations such as social media dynamics and artificial intelligence (AI) tools. By analyzing SCCT and DRT, we highlight their guidance for crisis response and the gaps that emerge under contemporary conditions. We also explore how **AI** can augment crisis management – from early threat detection to stakeholder engagement – while underscoring the ethical imperatives that accompany these technologies. Ultimately, this chapter aims to provide young researchers and practitioners with a comprehensive understanding of brand crisis management principles and a forward-looking perspective on emerging challenges and research directions.

Organizations today must prepare in advance with effective leadership and brand management strategies for crises. This includes understanding different **typologies of brand crises** and tailoring responses accordingly. Crises can be categorized as *performance related* (e.g., product failures or safety issues), *value related* (ethical breaches or corporate social responsibility [CSR] failures), *victim related* (when the organization is an unintended victim of external events) or *perception related* (gaps between brand promises and public perceptions). While such classifications help in identifying the nature of a crisis, managers must also apply robust communication theories and adapt to the situational nuances of each crisis. This involves the merging of crisis management in the field of communication, consumer behavior, ethics and AI. It aims to create a workable framework for crisis management with a focus on core values, ethical approach, understanding of all stakeholders and effective brand management during and after the storm. In the current world which is dynamic and integrated, organizations must be realistic and prepare well in advance regarding effective leadership and management of the brand during crises (Drewniak & Karaszewski, 2016; James et al., 2011; Kim et al., 2021; O'Reilly et al., 2015).

CRISIS COMMUNICATION THEORIES IN PRINCIPLE AND PRACTICE

Situational Crisis Communication Theory

The **SCCT**, developed by W. Timothy Coombs and colleagues, provides a systematic framework linking crisis types to specific response strategies. SCCT classifies crises into three main categories based on attributed responsibility: **victim crises** (minimal organizational responsibility), **accidental crises** (low responsibility) and **preventable crises** (high responsibility). For each category, SCCT prescribes aligned communication strategies ranging along a defensive-accommodative continuum. For example, in a *victim-type* crisis (e.g., rumors or natural disasters affecting the firm), organizations are advised to use defensive strategies like denial or scapegoating to assert innocence. In an *accidental* crisis (unintentional but internal failures), diminishment strategies such as excuses or justifications may be appropriate. In *preventable* crises (caused by misdeeds or negligence), SCCT recommends accommodative strategies like apologies or full remediation to rebuild trust. This tiered approach helps crisis managers answer *when* to use certain response tactics based on how much stakeholders blame the organization (Bublitz-Berg et al., 2024; Coombs, 2007; Garcia-Collart, 2024; Wagner et al., 2009).

While SCCT offers clear guidance and has been a dominant approach in crisis communication for decades, its **simplicity is increasingly challenged by the complexity of modern crises**. Real-world crises often don't fit neatly into one category or may evolve from one type to another. Moreover, the theory was developed in a presocial media context and focused largely on the organization's perspective. **Contemporary crisis scenarios unfold rapidly and publicly on social media, involving multiple voices and high uncertainty**, which can undermine SCCT's one-size-fits-all categorizations. Researchers have noted that SCCT did not fully account for the influence of new media; it uses a general notion of 'stakeholders' without distinguishing how different stakeholder groups engage via social platforms. Stakeholders online today do not just passively receive crisis messages; they actively shape the narrative, demand transparency and even organize responses (e.g., boycotts or viral campaigns). Coombs' model provides a starting template, but **organizations must complement SCCT with real-time monitoring and a stakeholder-centric approach** to remain effective. For example, SCCT might suggest a *deny* response in a baseless rumor crisis, but if misinformation is exploding on Twitter and being believed, a simple denial may not suffice without proactive clarification and engagement. Additionally, **social media crises blur the lines between crisis types** – a minor issue can quickly escalate due to public perception, or a victim-type crisis can prompt scrutiny of the past issues, making the situation 'preventable' in the public eye. Thus, **modern crisis communication demands flexibility beyond SCCT's initial prescriptions**, integrating **real-time insights** and **ethical transparency** when choosing responses. Scholars argue that purely defensive postures often falter in a climate where authenticity and accountability are prized by stakeholders. In summary, SCCT remains a useful framework for classifying crises and considering response strategies, but practitioners should adapt its guidelines to the **hyper-connected, fast-evolving media landscape** and use SCCT as part of a broader, more responsive crisis strategy (Coombs, 2007; Yolbulan Okan, 2014).

Discourse of Renewal Theory

The **DRT** offers a contrasting and in many ways complementary approach to crisis communication. Developed by scholars like Ulmer, Seeger and Sellnow, DRT views a crisis not just as a threat to be deflected, but as an opportunity for **organizational learning, ethical growth and renewal**. Instead of focusing on whom to blame or how to defend the organization's image, DRT emphasizes responding to crises through **optimism, ethical communication and forward-looking change**. Key principles of DRT include **organizational introspection** (acknowledging and addressing the underlying issues that led to the crisis), **commitment to stakeholders** (communicating with transparency and compassion) and a vision for a **better future post-crisis**. In practice, this means that during a crisis, leaders should highlight their plans for corrective action and improvement, thereby framing the event as a catalyst for positive change rather than a purely negative incident (Seeger et al., 2005).

DRT's relevance has grown in an era where stakeholders and the general public have **elevated expectations for corporate accountability and**

values-driven action. Today's stakeholders are not satisfied with perfunctory apologies or symbolic gestures; they expect real change and evidence of learning. In fact, many crises give rise to calls for boycotts or regulatory scrutiny precisely because stakeholders feel an organization's initial response is insufficient or insincere. DRT addresses this by advocating for genuine transformation and **building a narrative of renewal**. This approach aligns with modern principles of CSR and sustainability, where companies are encouraged to continually improve and align their operations with societal values. A crisis can thus be a defining moment that, if handled with integrity, **strengthens stakeholder trust in the long run**. For instance, companies that have successfully navigated product failures or scandals often do so by openly fixing the problem and inviting stakeholder input, thereby showing that they value their consumers' well-being above short-term image protection (Kurucz et al., 2008; Liu & Xin, 2015; Standop & Grunwald, 2009).

However, embracing DRT is not without challenges. Genuine renewal requires deep reflection and sometimes difficult changes within an organization's culture and leadership. It may involve '*giving up control and power differentials*' to allow more stakeholder involvement and oversight.

In practice, this could mean empowering independent ethics boards, engaging with external critics or increasing transparency to a level that leaders might be initially uncomfortable with. Moreover, not every crisis neatly presents an opportunity for positive change – some crises are exogenous (like natural disasters) where the focus might be more on resilience than internal reform. Even so, DRT suggests that how an organization communicates about any crisis can still emphasize hope and commitment to a better future (e.g., a city rebuilding after a flood can renew public trust by vowing improved infrastructure and preparedness). **In the digital age, DRT's focus on ethical communication and stakeholder engagement is especially pertinent**: social media amplifies public scrutiny, but it also provides channels for dialogue where organizations can demonstrate accountability and responsiveness. By actively engaging stakeholders online with honest updates and listening to their concerns, organizations can begin to repair relationships during the crisis itself – a strategy very much in line with renewal discourse (Gillespie et al., 2014; Holland et al., 2021).

In summary, **DRT expands the scope of crisis communication from damage control to transformative potential**. It complements SCCT by addressing aspects that SCCT underplays: the **moral dimension** of crises and the expectation that organizations should *learn and improve*, not just restore the status quo. Modern organizations can benefit from integrating DRT with SCCT – for example, using SCCT to stabilize an immediate situation (through appropriate initial responses) while employing DRT to guide long-term recovery and reforms. By doing so, companies not only survive a crisis but also can **enhance their brand resilience and reputation** by demonstrating values of accountability, transparency and improvement (Moberg, 2006; Seeger et al., 2005; Ulmer et al., 2007; Wagner et al., 2009; Xu, 2018).

EVOLVING CHALLENGES: SOCIAL MEDIA, STAKEHOLDERS AND SPEED

Both SCCT and DRT emerged from a time before social media's dominance and before AI-driven information dynamics. Today's crisis communication landscape is defined by **rapid information spread, heightened stakeholder activism and new technological risks and opportunities**. It is crucial to analyze how these factors demand an evolution in crisis communication strategies:

- **Social Media and Information Velocity:** Social media platforms have become both a source of crises and a critical channel for managing them. News (and rumors) can go viral within hours or minutes, meaning that the **golden hour** for response is dramatically shortened. SCCT's recommendations assume the organization can control the narrative to an extent by issuing carefully crafted statements. In reality, during a Twitter- or Instagram-fueled crisis, organizations must respond *faster and more continuously*, often engaging in two-way communication. Research in social-mediated crisis communication (SMCC) shows that traditional strategies must be adjusted for interactivity and dialogue. Additionally, the choice of platform matters – a video apology on YouTube or a live Q&A session on Twitter might be more effective for reaching certain audiences than a text statement on a website. The social media environment also means crisis communicators have to monitor *sentiment in real time*; public perception can shift quickly, and strategies may need to pivot accordingly (something SCCT's static categorizations don't account for). On the positive side, social media allows direct engagement with stakeholders, which aligns with DRT's emphasis on open dialogue and transparency. However, it also means that any misstep by the company is immediately visible and can exacerbate the situation. **Misinformation** is another major challenge – false narratives can spread as fast as true information, if not faster. Crisis managers now must include rumor management and fact-checking as part of their strategy, often collaborating with media or using the company's channels to debunk myths. This complexity underscores why crisis communication in practice requires blending the clarity of SCCT with the adaptive, value-centric approach of DRT.

- **Shifting Stakeholder Expectations:** Stakeholders today – whether customers, employees or the general public – **expect more from organizations in crisis**. Transparency, empathy and accountability are the watchwords. Simply put, people demand that organizations 'do the right thing' and do it visibly. This is partly a cultural shift (with concepts like CSR and accountability trending in public discourse) and partly fueled by social media (which gives individuals a platform to voice expectations and rally others). The implication for crisis communication is that **defensive postures or half-hearted apologies can backfire severely**. An audience who perceives an organization as prioritizing its image over genuine concern will likely respond with anger or cynicism, potentially turning a short-term incident into a protracted reputational crisis. For example, if a company is slow to recall a defective product or appears to downplay safety issues, consumers may organize boycotts and regulators might step in, prolonging the crisis impact. SCCT does advise more accommodative strategies when responsibility is high, but even in *accidental* cases, the tolerance for excuses is shrinking. Many stakeholders apply a **zero-tolerance mindset** to issues like discrimination, data privacy or environmental harm – even if the crisis was unintended, they expect a robust response and corrective action. This trend pushes companies toward integrating DRT principles: showing empathy (acknowledging harm caused to victims), taking responsibility where appropriate and outlining improvements. **Employee perspectives** are also crucial; internal stakeholders expect their organization to protect them and to live its espoused values. Crises often cause internal strain (as noted in many cases of CEO misbehavior or scandals), and transparent internal communication is as important as external communication. In sum, meeting stakeholder expectations today often means *overcommunicating* rather than undercommunicating, and focusing on **ethical commitments** in every message.
- **Complex, Intersectional Crises:** Modern crises often cut across multiple domains – consider a scenario that is simultaneously a public health issue, a supply chain problem and a social media misinformation battle (e.g., the COVID-19 pandemic for many companies). Such crises don't fit into neat categories and may trigger multiple stakeholder concerns at once. An overemphasis on any single aspect can leave other concerns unaddressed. Thus, crisis communication strategies must be multifaceted and coordinated across disciplines (legal, technical, communications, etc.). This complexity reinforces the need for an **integrated approach**: organizations should develop a crisis team that brings together different expertise, and communication should be consistent across channels to avoid confusion. Importantly, **ethical considerations** (like equity, fairness and human impact) should be embedded at each step because stakeholders will scrutinize decisions (e.g., who gets help first, what information is prioritized). DRT's call for 'responsible leadership' becomes very concrete in intersectional crises – leaders must demonstrate competence *and* moral integrity.

In light of these evolving challenges, scholars and practitioners are extending traditional theories. There are calls to refine SCCT by incorporating variables like **social media channel selection, message tone and stakeholder interaction**. Similarly, the principles of DRT are being applied to new contexts, encouraging organizations to engage in **dialogic communication** (two-way conversations) and to view stakeholders as partners in recovery rather than passive recipients of messages. The convergence of these ideas is leading toward more **holistic crisis communication models** that emphasize agility, stakeholder engagement and ethical clarity (Bradbury, 1994; Goodijk, 2002).

INTEGRATED CRISIS MANAGEMENT STRATEGIES

Beyond theory, effective brand management in crises involves practical strategies that span **precrisis preparedness, real-time response and post-crisis recovery**. Research and practice have identified several key principles and tactics that can help organizations navigate crises while protecting (or even strengthening) their brand:

- **Integrated Communication and Stakeholder Alignment: Communication sits at the heart of effective crisis management**, directly influencing how stakeholders perceive the brand. A solid, integrated crisis communication strategy typically unfolds in three key stages (often aligned with principles of integrated marketing communications [IMCs]): **sensing, informing and responding**. In the **sensing stage**, brands actively monitor their environment for potential threats or negative signals. This includes social media listening, customer feedback tracking and horizon scanning for issues in the industry. Next, the **informing stage** focuses on delivering clear, honest and timely information about the crisis. Both internal stakeholders (employees, partners) and external audiences (customers, regulators, public) need to know what is happening and what it means. Transparency here is crucial – acknowledging uncertainty or admitting a lapse can be better than issuing overly vague statements. Finally, the **responding stage** involves concrete actions to address and resolve the crisis, accompanied by communication about those actions. Throughout these stages, consistency is a key: everyone in the organization should relay aligned messages to prevent confusion. When done right, this coordinated approach maintains trust and manages stakeholder expectations effectively, thereby reducing potential damage. It's worth noting that **empathy and reassurance** should permeate communications – stakeholders need to feel that the organization cares and is in control. Simple practices like expressing concern for those affected and providing regular updates go a long way in preserving a brand's image during turmoil (Grossman, 2020; Johar et al., 2010).
- **Leveraging Brand Equity and Partnerships:** An organization's **brand equity** (the goodwill and trust it has accumulated) can act as a buffer during crises. High brand equity often means customers are more forgiving of accidental missteps, as they give the company the benefit of the doubt based on positive experiences. Interestingly, research suggests that during *accidental crises*, a strong prior reputation can indeed soften the blow, whereas in *preventable crises* (where the company is clearly at fault), brands with previously stellar reputations might face harsher criticism due to higher expectations. Therefore, companies should not be complacent even if they are industry leaders; they must respond earnestly regardless of past goodwill. **Corporate brand partnerships** (alliances, co-branding, sponsorships) can complicate crisis management, because a crisis affecting one can spill over to others (Johar et al., 2010; Riggio & Newstead, 2022).
- **Audience-Centric Messaging:** Different stakeholder groups may need different messaging during a crisis, even if the core information remains the same. **Cultural and regional sensitivity** can be crucial, as what reassures one demographic might not resonate with another. For example, an apology framed in a very direct manner may be appreciated in one culture but seen as insufficiently humble in another. Brands operating globally (as in the case of Swedish companies facing backlash in Muslim markets) have learned to tailor their crisis communication to respect cultural norms and values. This might involve translating messages not just linguistically but also conceptually – emphasizing respect, citing values or authorities that local stakeholders trust, and engaging community or religious leaders where appropriate.
- *Stakeholder mapping* is a useful exercise: identify key groups (customers, employees, local communities, investors, regulators, etc.) and ensure each is addressed. While messaging should be aligned, the tone and channel might differ (Boaz et al., 2018; Karlsen, 2002).
- **Learning and Evolving:** Every crisis provides lessons. Organizations that treat a crisis as a learning opportunity will refine their processes and hopefully prevent similar issues in the future. This ties back to DRT's ethos of renewal. After the dust settles, a **post-crisis analysis** should be conducted. What went wrong? What was handled well and what wasn't? How did the public react, and why? These questions can inform updates to crisis plans and even business practices. Many forward-thinking companies also publish their learnings or share them at conferences, contributing to industry-wide improvements (and demonstrating transparency). **CSR** initiatives often get a boost post-crisis, as firms invest in rebuilding trust – for example, a company implicated in an environmental spill might launch new environmental programs to show commitment to the cause. Importantly, com-

municating these changes closes the loop with stakeholders: it shows that feedback was heard and acted upon. Over time, a history of responsible crisis handling and continuous improvement becomes part of a brand's identity, reinforcing resilience (Ardiansyah & Alnoor, 2024; Johar et al., 2010).

These integrated strategies underline that **effective crisis management is not solely the domain of the public relations (PR) team**; it requires a holistic organizational effort. Marketing, operations, legal, HR and leadership all have roles to play in alignment. The ultimate goal is to ensure that when crisis strikes, the organization responds in a way that is **swift, smart and principled**, thereby safeguarding the brand's reputation. In the next section, we delve deeper into one of the most significant new facets of crisis management: the use of **AI** to predict, manage and communicate during crises, along with the ethical considerations it entails.

PRACTICAL INTEGRATION OF AI IN CRISIS MANAGEMENT

AI's current contributions to crisis management are already significant, and future applications promise to take it further. Today, organizations widely use **AI-driven social media monitoring** and **sentiment analysis** to keep a finger on the pulse during a crisis. These tools can instantly aggregate what thousands of stakeholders are saying and feeling, giving companies real-time feedback on their crisis response. AI chatbots are also employed on websites or customer service lines to handle the surge of inquiries that often accompany a crisis (such as flight cancellations or product recall information). When designed well, these bots can provide timely, accurate information and free up human reps to handle more complex or sensitive interactions. The key is ensuring that the chatbot knows its limits and routes people to a human when needed, to avoid frustration.

Looking to the future, one can envision **advanced AI applications** that further enhance crisis preparedness and response:

- **Predictive Crisis Analytics:** Building on current predictive tools, future AI may leverage **Big Data** in unprecedented ways to foresee crises. This could include analyzing global news, climate data political developments, and even employee chatter to anticipate crises stemming from external events (like geopolitical conflicts affecting supply chains) or internal issues (like workforce unrest). Some companies are already exploring AI 'digital twins' – virtual models of their operations – which could be stress-tested under simulated crisis scenarios to see how the organization would hold up and where weaknesses lie (Fuller et al., 2020).
- **AI-Enhanced Decision Support Systems:** During a crisis, leaders face high-pressure decisions with incomplete information. AI can serve as a decision support assistant by rapidly crunching numbers and predicting outcomes of various choices. For example, if facing a product contamination issue, an AI might instantly run models on the outcomes of a full recall versus a targeted recall versus shutting down production, including financial cost, impact on public perception and legal implications. While the final decision rests with leaders (who will consider factors beyond what data can capture), having those projections in seconds can make the decision both faster and more informed. This is analogous to how AI helps in medical decisions by suggesting diagnoses – the doctor (or in this case, the crisis manager) remains the ultimate arbiter (Debnath et al., 2020; Kumar et al., 2024).
- **Generative AI for Communication:** As natural language generation AI (like GPT models) becomes more sophisticated, it could assist in drafting crisis communication materials under human guidance. We are not far from a scenario where an AI can produce a decent first draft of a press release or a Q&A document based on inputs about the situation. This could save valuable time in the early moments of a crisis. However, as noted, organizations will need to use this carefully, ensuring a human reviews and infuses authenticity. Another application is personalized communication at scale – AI might help tailor messages to different stakeholder segments automatically (for instance, generating slightly different versions of an update for customers vs. suppliers, each addressing their specific concerns) (Fourie, 2024; Kirkpatrick, 2017).
- **AI in Misinformation Management:** One of the hardest aspects of modern crises is battling rumors and fake news. AI and machine learning can be trained to detect likely misinformation by cross-referencing claims with reliable data sources or identifying coordinated disinformation campaigns (e.g., spotting when many new social

accounts repeat the same false claim, indicating bot activity). Early detection of false narratives allows the organization to respond with corrections before those narratives harden into public belief. In the future, we might see AI systems that can engage directly with misinformation spreaders – for instance, automatically replying to a tweet that contains a common false rumor with a courteous correction and a link to factual information. This takes the burden off the communications team to manually counter every piece of fake news (Anderson, 2018; Vo & Lee, 2020).

- **Virtual Crisis Training and Simulation:** AI can power immersive training programs for crisis management teams. Imagine a simulation where an AI generates a realistic unfolding crisis (complete with fake news reports, social media posts and stakeholder reactions) to which a team must respond. The AI can adapt the scenario based on the team's actions – for example, if the team's statement is slow, the AI simulation increases the pressure with mounting public criticism. Such training, possibly using virtual or augmented reality, could greatly improve readiness by providing lifelike practice that goes beyond static drills. It also allows for testing how different strategies (maybe one informed by SCCT vs. another by DRT principles) play out in a controlled environment (Hoang et al., 2020; Hsu et al., 2013).

With these opportunities come **ethical implications** that must be front and center. **Privacy** is a big concern: predictive analytics might involve monitoring what employees say or scraping user content online, which should be done with caution and respect rights. **Transparency** to stakeholders about AI use is another issue – for example, should a company disclose that an online chat assistant is an AI during a crisis? (Most likely yes, to avoid deception.) And as AI takes on more sophisticated tasks, questions of **accountability** loom larger: If an AI-recommended action leads to harm, who is accountable? Legally and ethically, the organization deploying the AI is responsible, so there must be governance frameworks in place. Some experts advocate for an 'AI ethics officer' role in organizations, which could be pertinent during crises to evaluate AI-driven actions.

Incorporating AI into crisis management is thus a double-edged sword: it provides powerful tools that can help manage crises better and faster, but it introduces a new layer of complexity in decision-making and ethics. For young scholars, this convergence of AI and crisis communication presents fertile ground for research – exploring how AI can be leveraged without losing the human touch that effective crisis communication requires.

Managing a brand during a crisis is never straightforward – it requires quick thinking, early identification of the problem and flexible strategic adjustments. Spotting potential crises early gives companies a critical advantage, allowing them to react swiftly and minimize long-term damage. For instance, practical experiences from Turkish brands clearly demonstrate why it's vital to have a solid crisis management plan ready. Situations like product recalls or boycotts can severely damage the brand's reputation if handled poorly, emphasizing the need for detailed preparation. Being proactive means developing thorough, scenario-based strategies that protect your brand's carefully crafted image and overall trustworthiness (Johar et al., 2010).

Additionally, AI-driven risk prediction tools have revolutionized how brands prepare for crises by enabling proactive rather than reactive strategies. These tools analyze historical data, current trends and external events to predict potential risks, allowing organizations to develop comprehensive contingency plans. Proactive preparedness empowered by AI means that crisis responses can be strategically aligned with stakeholder needs, ensuring interventions are both relevant and impactful.

Furthermore, generative AI technologies offer significant advantages in streamlining crisis communication through automated content creation. These technologies can quickly produce consistent and carefully tailored messages that resonate emotionally with stakeholders and align clearly with organizational values. This consistency is crucial during crises when clarity and uniformity of communication can determine stakeholder trust and organizational credibility.

However, reliance on AI in crisis management demands careful ethical oversight and algorithmic transparency. AI tools, if not monitored closely, could inadvertently amplify biases or misinformation, complicating rather than clarifying crisis responses. Ensuring transparency in how AI algorithms function and making their decision-making processes understandable to stakeholders is essential for maintaining trust and accountability. Therefore, integrating AI into crisis management requires a balanced approach that leverages technological strengths while consciously mitigating ethical risks (Guan et al., 2022; Uddin, 2023).

When it comes to corporate brand partnerships, managing a crisis gets even trickier because multiple reputations are at stake. Interestingly, having high brand equity can act like a shield during accidental crises, softening the negative impact due to existing consumer goodwill. But in cases of preventable crises, brands with lower equity might actually fare better, as customers typically have fewer expectations. Therefore, companies must carefully assess the specific crisis context and the brand equity of each partner involved when crafting their crisis response strategy (Lucero et al., 2009; Pangarkar, 2016).

A solid integrated crisis communication strategy typically unfolds in three key stages: sensing, informing and responding. In the sensing phase, brands monitor signals and environments closely for potential threats. The informing stage focuses on clear, honest and timely communication, both internally and externally, about what is happening and what the implications are. Finally, responding involves taking concrete actions to actively address and resolve the crisis. Ensuring that everyone in the organization is aligned and communicating at each of these stages is crucial for maintaining trust among stakeholders and effectively managing their expectations. Done right, this coordinated approach can significantly reduce the potential damage of crises, reflecting the core principles of IMCs (Gramegna & Giudici, 2021; Lasker, 2024).

AI AS CRISIS ORACLE: POTENTIALS AND PITFALLS

The discourse of renewal perspective is useful for crisis leadership; however, contemporary practice should not only deal with crisis and atonement. Certainly, the peak innovations in crisis preparedness and brand protection must include vision – the ability to foresee catastrophes, discover hidden dangers and resolve tensions before they erupt into escalation. It is this vanguard aspiration where AI reveals its potential as both a radically utilitarian technology and an ethical decision augmentation and augmentation apparatus (Myne et al., 2022; Swasdee et al., 2020; Vinuesa et al., 2020).

Companies have proven that they can rely on AI's predictions of a crisis as a competitive advantage, to avoid the worst scenarios. As AI systems consider all the data across different channels, including customer sentiment, they are improvement tools that detect change based on inquiry sooner rather than later giving management a chance to act on it. This helps the brands readjust their communications and strategies in consideration of the trust and loyalty of their consumers during adverse times.

Nonetheless, the use of AI in the management of crises has its good side as well as bad side. One of the middle worries is data bias concerns that are particular components in fact analysis leading to the opposite of mitigation. Further, heavy dependency on AI takes away some elements, which tend to be very crucial in combating crises, human emotions that inform understanding of the situation.

Moreover, 'black box' algorithms are opaque in that their logic is hidden, and this creates a big problem with both accountability and transparency and both are necessary for brand trust. Stakeholders would resist the idea of AI making decisions and rationalizing those decisions in an opaque manner without accountability. This would decrease trust and loyalty that are critical in times of crisis.

Quite obviously, the strength of AI technologies lies in their ability to quickly analyze big, diversified information sets such as internal documentation, multimedia coverage, voice and social media conversations and others on corporate matters. Thanks to the growth of self-supervised learning and novel GE transformer mechanisms, there are prospects that AI can always be available to the organization as a crisis expert and forecast future risks facing the organization. Various arbitral incidents or some deviations from acceptable parameters could automatically activate escalation management plans enabling organizations to prevent crises from escalating into serious threats to their reputations growing from mere organ fascicles to cancerous growths (Banja, 2009; Grissinger, 2017; Redfern et al., 2019).

What is further, some understanding of the AI capabilities and their object-related rapid data synthesis and structural patterns recognition can potentially address the largely complex networks of interdependent decisions, interrelationships and situational occurrences that result in such events as crises. In the same context, this capacity for mapping out the causes facilitates an advanced level of the root cause analysis while overlaying the grappled issues of governance and ethics and poorly defined processes that require a radical overhaul under the discourse of renewal approach (Dillon et al., 2021; Gelman et al., 2023; Jose et al., n.d.).

In the domain of the crisis management, AI has also found one of the most productive use cases, which is the preparation of very specific crisis communications within the framework of the brand's voice, image and values. The advances made in recent years in the development of, for instance, large language models and multimodal generative AI help indeed in producing relevant stories that are emotionally appealing, through simple traditional media to elaborate digital stories, targeting and addressing the emotions of specific investors, employees and consumers (Chamola et al., 2023; Epstein et al., 2023; Ibarrola et al., 2023).

Nevertheless, although we have a profound optimism about the role of AI in managing some crisis situations, this must be balanced with an unflattering view of the risks and ethical practices that AI poses when it is allowed to run, sometimes, without sensible management controls. With the ever-increasing scope and power of these technological behemoths and the use of all encroaching data, so do the dangers associated with them – promotion of established social discrimination, invasion of privacy or achievement of a level of complexity whereby the system loses coherence and actionable information from human understanding – become issues that are very hard to ignore.

THE ETHICAL AI PARADIGM: A PATHWAY TO TRUSTED CRISIS LEADERSHIP

As moral stewardship is upheld, a refined approach to crisis leadership must be developed, charting a principled path that harmonizes the transformative capabilities of AI with established ethical reasoning, empathy for stakeholders and reverence for human rights. The vision entails 'ethical AI' emerging not as a replacement for human decision-making but as an enlightened system augmenting decisions based on immutable ethical precepts. This approach advocates for the integration of AI to support and amplify human capacities, ensuring that technological advancements serve humanity ethically and responsibly, with a steadfast commitment to uphold and promote universal moral values in every action and decision (Floridi et al., 2020; Karaszewski, 2011; Shahriari & Shahriari, 2017; Tamburrini, 2022; Vinuesa et al., 2020).

The imperative necessitates the purposeful training of AI models on curated corpora that span the breadth of moral philosophy, from Aristotelian virtue ethics and Kantian deontological frameworks to Abrahamic theories and the compassion-centric tenets of Buddhist thought. By doing so, these AI architectures are endowed with a foundational capacity for nuanced moral reasoning, termed 'moralituition' – the ability to impartially adjudicate ethical quandaries, surface potential pitfalls and guide decision-making toward outcomes aligned with inviolable human rights and stakeholder interests (Hagendorff, 2020; Papouli, 2018; Stahl, 2021; Thiebes et al., 2021; Zhou et al., 2020).

Moreover, addressing the 'black box' opacity that has long undermined trust in AI systems is crucial. Techniques like Local Interpretable Model-agnostic Explanations (LIME), SHapley Additive exPlanations (SHAP) and other emerging methods for interpretable and explainable AI can reveal the logical underpinnings, precedential justifications and data-driven insights shaping AI's outputs during crisis situations. This commitment to 'explicable AI' crystallizes transparency as a core operating principle, fostering accountability while allowing for continuous refinement of AI's ethical training corpora as societal values evolve. Integrating these elements – morality intuition, transparency and explainability – into the development and deployment of AI systems can pave the way for a new paradigm of ethical AI that inspires trust, safeguards human rights and enables inclusive and equitable crisis leadership (Gilbert et al., 2023a, 2023b; Gramegna & Giudici, 2021; Pizzi et al., 2020).

The democratization of AI's reasoning processes also unlocks elevated human–AI collaborative intelligence. Rather than fully automated decisions, a symbiotic synergy emerges where ethical AI furnishes guidance rooted in moral philosophy while human experts lend experiential wisdom, empathic intelligence and situational contextualization. This harmonious concordance between machine elucidation and human discernment is the illuminated path.

Ultimately, the praxeological vision is one where 'ethical AI' serves not as a supplantive crisis deus ex machina, but as a decision augmentation apparatus upholding transparency, stakeholder accountability and moral rectitude as irreproachable virtues of brand resilience and crisis leadership. It is a future where human values reign supreme, amplified by AI's radical capabilities in service of a common good while also navigating complex ethical considerations with deliberation and wisdom (Ferrario et al., 2019; Sewpersadh, 2023).

RESEARCH IMPLICATIONS AND FUTURE TRAJECTORIES

This multidisciplinary research has myriad implications. From a theoretical perspective, it heterointegrates foundational crisis communication frameworks like the discourse of renewal with cutting-edge AI and machine learning capabilities, forging a new holistic praxis. The injunction to develop 'ethical AI' architectures also represents an evolution of the field of machine ethics and its moral philosophy underpinnings (Floridi et al., 2018; Savage, 2023; Turini, 2024; Winfield et al., 2019).

For the practitioners involved in crisis management, this work offers a practical guiding architecture compromising the efficiency-oriented ethical safe AI framework that has the potential to augment risk identification, cause analysis and address effective crisis management within normative principles of equity, privacy and transparency. It emphasizes the importance of developing sound governance structures in relation to AI usage so that such use is consistent with the ethical standards of the organization.

It is noteworthy how converging various disciplines and approaches leads to a remarkable and socially responsible advancement of brand crisis management and recovery. This is a path paved by human wisdom and conscience but reinforced by AI willing to make the impossible possible – becoming a new type of able to see the invisible and bring untapped risks, invisible patterns and domain geometry of institutional narratives in a real-world driven by real behavioral ethics. Such a path will encounter obstacles – gaining support from stakeholders for 'ethical AI' governance or overcoming social, economic and regulatory issues. For institutions timbering frontiers of this vanguard, however, there is no more privilege than this sense of purpose: to be at the forefront of this onslaught toward principles-driven change (Campbell et al., 2020; Chen et al., 2021; Gilbert et al., 2023a, 2023b; Hickok, 2020; Imran et al., 2020; Kruspe et al., 2021; Stahl, 2021; Tahaei et al., 2023).

CONCLUDING RECOMMENDATIONS FOR FUTURE RESEARCH

In this study, an effort was made to formulate a comprehensive paradigm of crisis leadership and brand resilience by integrating human intelligence, a moral framework and changing ethical AI. The highlight of the study was a critique of the SCCT's character as well as its weaknesses relative to the more contemporary discourse of renewal, whose thrust is responsiveness, ethical authority and significant change in organizations. In fact, it functions as a 'god' bestowing all knowledge including danger and outlining its dynamics and brings forth effective crisis strategies to a brand. However, necessary technology focus enthusiastic support was warned against by showing the dangers of AI such as bias, privacy abuse and opaque analytic box.

The novel application that was suggested entailed developing virtue ethics based on the AI of computer-owned agents, who perform learning via the application of various ethical frameworks. Such 'ethical AI' would help address these issues by permitting the objective assessment of various problems with regard to human rights and the anticipated human rights violations. Also, it was argued that there should be the use of explainable AI approaches to improve how stakeholders understand and trust the organization.

The intersection of brand management, crisis communication and emerging technologies presents numerous opportunities for scholarly exploration. Key future research directions may include:

- **Comparative Effectiveness of Integrated Crisis Models:** Investigate how traditional theories like SCCT and DRT can be integrated or applied in tandem during modern crises. For example, researchers could analyze real-world cases to see if responses that combined situational strategies (per SCCT) with renewal-focused messaging (per DRT) achieved better stakeholder outcomes than those relying on a single approach. Such studies would shed light on the *complementarity* of these theories and possibly lead to an evolved crisis communication model that accounts for both immediate response and long-term renewal.
- **Crisis Communication in the Social Media Era:** Examine the impact of social media on crisis communication strategies and outcomes. This could involve studying how the speed of information flow and the proliferation of user-generated content are changing the efficacy of response strategies. Researchers might develop or test frameworks for **SMCC** that update SCCT's assumptions, exploring questions like: What are the best practices for choosing platforms and crafting messages for different types of crises? How do factors such as message tone, timing and engagement (e.g., responding to comments) influence public trust and the resolution of a crisis?
- **Mitigating Digital Misinformation during Crises:** Develop strategies and tools to combat the spread of misinformation and disinformation in crises. Future research can focus on identifying the most effective techniques for timely correction of false rumors (e.g., is it through official press releases, social media engagement, third-party fact-checkers or influencers?). Additionally, studying audience psychology in crises – why people believe or share certain false information – can inform more nuanced communication strategies that preempt misinformation. Given the rise of deepfakes and AI-generated fake content, this research area is both critical and urgent.

- **Enhancing AI Transparency and Ethics in Crisis Management:** Explore ways to improve the transparency of AI algorithms used for crisis prediction and response, and address the ethical challenges they pose. For instance, scholars could work on developing **explainable AI models specifically tailored to crisis contexts**, ensuring that crisis managers can interpret and justify AI recommendations to stakeholders. Research might also investigate stakeholder perceptions: under what conditions would the public trust an AI-informed decision in a crisis? Understanding this could guide how organizations communicate about their use of AI (e.g., being open about AI's role, or conversely, keeping it behind the scenes).
- **Cross-Cultural and Cross-Industry Crisis Response Analysis:** Conduct comparative studies on how brand crises and effective responses may differ across cultures and industries. Cultural values can influence what stakeholders expect (e.g., the concept of 'saving face' in some Asian cultures might affect how apologies are received). Industries also have specifics – a crisis in the tech sector might play out differently from one in the food industry. By analyzing diverse scenarios, researchers can determine which crisis communication principles are universal and which need adaptation. This line of inquiry will help global brands customize their crisis strategies for different markets and help refine theories like SCCT/DRT to account for cultural variables.
- **Longitudinal Studies of Brand Resilience Post-crisis:** There is a need for longitudinal research that follows brands *after* a crisis to understand the long-term impacts and recovery patterns. Questions to explore include: How long does it take for consumer trust and brand equity to rebound, if at all? What factors influence recovery – is it the initial response, consistent follow-up actions, external environmental changes or the presence of loyal customer segments? Long-term case studies (spanning years) of companies that faced major crises would be invaluable. These could also test the tenets of DRT – did the companies that professed renewal actually implement changes that prevented future crises or improved performance? By tracking outcomes over time, scholars can better correlate certain crisis response strategies with sustained brand health.
- **Multi-Stakeholder Engagement Frameworks:** Develop frameworks for engaging multiple stakeholder groups simultaneously during crises. Future research can delve into stakeholder mapping models and communication strategies that ensure *no key stakeholder is left behind* in the crisis response. This includes not just customers and media, but employees (often understudied in crisis scenarios), supply chain partners, regulators and community groups. How can organizations coordinate messages and actions that address the concerns of all these parties effectively? There may be trade-offs – a message that appeases customers might worry investors, for instance – and exploring how companies navigate these trade-offs is a rich area for the study. The goal would be to propose guidelines or models for holistic stakeholder communication during crises, possibly supported by case evidence or simulation experiments.
- **AI-Driven Crisis Communication Strategies:** Building on the earlier discussion, the research studies could specifically focus on the role of AI in crafting and delivering crisis communications. For example, experiments could test audience reactions to AI-generated crisis statements versus human-written ones to quantify any differences in credibility or acceptance. Another angle is the use of AI chatbots in high-stress scenarios – what design features make them more helpful than frustrating? And how does one measure their effectiveness?

REFERENCES

Anderson, K. E. (2018). Getting acquainted with social networks and apps: Combating fake news on social media. In *Library Hi Tech News* (Vol. 35, No. 3, p. 1–6). Rutgers University. https://doi.org/10.7282/T32J6GGK

Ardiansyah, M., & Alnoor, A. (2024). Integrating corporate social responsibility into business strategy: Creating sustainable value. *Involvement International Journal of Business*, *1*(1), 29. https://doi.org/10.62569/iijb.v1i1.5

Banja, J. D. (2009). The normalization of deviance in healthcare delivery. *Business Horizons*, *53*(2), 139. https://doi.org/10.1016/j.bushor.2009.10.006

Boaz, A., Hanney, S., Borst, R., O'Shea, A., & Kok, M. (2018). How to engage stakeholders in research: Design principles to support improvement. *Health Research Policy and Systems*, *16*, 60. https://doi.org/10.1186/s12961-018-0337-6

Bradbury, J. (1994). Risk communication in environmental restoration programs. *Risk Analysis*, *14*(3),

357. https://doi.org/10.1111/j.1539-6924.1994.tb00252.x

Bublitz-Berg, E., Platt, C. A., & Hill, B. (2024). Employee perceptions of responses to toxic leadership in the modern workplace: A Q methodological study. *In Leadership & Organization Development Journal*, *45*(7), 1205–1219. https://doi.org/10.1108/LODJ-09-2023-0512.

Campbell, C., Sands, S., Ferraro, C., Tsao, H., & Mavrommatis, A. (2020). From data to action: How marketers can leverage AI. *Business Horizons*, *63*(2), 227. https://doi.org/10.1016/j.bushor.2019.12.002

Chamola, V., Bansal, G., Das, T., Hassija, V., Reddy, N., Wang, J., Zeadally, S., Hussain, A., Yu, F., Guizani, M., & Niyato, D. (2023). *Beyond reality: The pivotal role of generative AI in the metaverse*. Cornell University. arXiv (Cornell University).

Chen, Q., Leaman, R., Allot, A., Luo, L., Wei, C.-H., Yan, S., & Lu, Z. (2021). Artificial intelligence in action: Addressing the COVID-19 pandemic with natural language processing. *Annual Review of Biomedical Data Science*, *4*, 313–339. https://doi.org/10.1146/annurev-biodatasci-021821

Coombs, W. T. (2007). Protecting organization reputations during a crisis: The development and application of situational crisis communication theory. *Corporate Reputation Review*, *10*(3), 163. https://doi.org/10.1057/palgrave.crr.1550049

Debnath, S., Barnaby, D. P., Coppa, K., Makhnevich, A., Kim, E. J., Chatterjee, S., Tóth, V., Levy, T., Paradis, M. D., Cohen, S. L., Hirsch, J. S., Zanos, T. P., Becker, L. B., Cookingham, J., Davidson, K. W., Dominello, A. J., Falzon, L., McGinn, T., Mogavero, J. N., & Osorio, G. A. (2020). Machine learning to assist clinical decision-making during the COVID-19 pandemic. *Bioelectronic Medicine*, *6*(1), Article 14. https://doi.org/10.1186/s42234-020-00050-8

Dillon, R., Klein, G., & Rogers, E. (2021). *A monitoring and warning framework for risks*. https://ieeexplore.ieee.org/document/9438256/

Drewniak, R., & Karaszewski, R. (2016). Brand management in a situation of an economic crisis. *Asia Pacific Journal of Marketing and Logistics*, *28*(4), 743. https://doi.org/10.1108/APJML-07-2015-0117

Epstein, Z., Hertzmann, A., Herman, L., Mahari, R., Frank, M., Groh, M., Schroeder, H., Smith, A., Akten, M., Fjeld, J., Farid, H., Leach, N., Pentland, A., & Russakovsky, O. (2023). *Art and the science of generative AI: A deeper dive*. Cornell University. arXiv (Cornell University).

Ferrario, A., Loi, M., & Viganò, E. (2019). In AI we trust incrementally: A multi-layer model of trust to analyze human-artificial intelligence interactions. *Philosophy & Technology*, *33*(3), 523. https://doi.org/10.1007/s13347-019-00378-3

Floridi, L., Cowls, J., Beltrametti, M., Chatila, R., Chazerand, P., Dignum, V., Luetge, C., Madelin, R., Pagallo, U., Rossi, F., Schafer, B., Valcke, P., & Vayena, E. (2018). AI4People – An ethical framework for a good AI society: Opportunities, risks, principles, and recommendations. *Minds and Machines*, *28*(4), 689–707. https://doi.org/10.1007/s11023-018-9482-5

Floridi, L., Cowls, J., King, T., & Taddeo, M. (2020). How to design AI for social good: Seven essential factors. *Science and Engineering Ethics*, *26*(3), 1771. https://doi.org/10.1007/s11948-020-00213-5

Fourie, A. (2024). *Crisis management & AI: Revolutionise your response*. www.crises-control.com/blogs/crisis-management-ai/

Fuller, A., Fan, Z., Day, C., & Barlow, C. (2020). Digital twin: Enabling technologies, challenges and open research. *IEEE Access*, *8*, 108952. https://doi.org/10.1109/ACCESS.2020.2998358

Garcia-Collart, T. (2024). Speak up! Brands' responsiveness matters: consumer reactions to brand communications in the early stages of a crisis. *Journal of Product & Brand Management*, *33*(4), 449–459. https://doi.org/10.1108/JPBM-01-2023-4311

Gelman, B., Salma, T., Vörös, T., & Berlin, K. (2023). That escalated quickly: An ML framework for alert prioritization. *arXiv preprint arXiv*:2302.06648. https://doi.org/10.48550/arXiv.2302.06648

Gilbert, T. K., Brozek, M. W., & Brozek, A. (2023a). *Beyond bias and compliance: Towards individual agency and plurality of ethics in AI. arXiv preprint arXiv:2302*.12149. https://doi.org/10.48550/arXiv.2302.12149

Gilbert, T. K., Brozek, M. W., & Brozek, A. (2023b). *Beyond bias and compliance: Towards individual agency and plurality of ethics in AI*. Cornell University. arXiv (Cornell University).

Gillespie, N., Dietz, G., & Lockey, S. (2014). Organizational reintegration and trust repair after an integrity violation: A case study. *Business Ethics Quarterly*, *24*(3), 371. https://doi.org/10.5840/beq2014437

Goodijk, R. (2002). Partnership at corporate level: The meaning of the stakeholder model. *Journal of Change Management*, *3*(3), 225. https://doi.org/10.1080/714042537

Gramegna, A., & Giudici, P. (2021). SHAP and LIME: An evaluation of discriminative power in credit risk. *Frontiers in Artificial Intelligence*, *4*, 752558. https://doi.org/10.3389/frai.2021.752558

Grissinger, M. (2017). Disrespectful behavior in health care: Its impact, why it arises and persists, and how to address it – Part 2. *Pharmacy and Therapeutics*, *42*(2), 74. https://pubmed.ncbi.nlm.nih.gov/28163550

Grossman, V. A. (2020). Leadership essentials during a disaster. *Journal of Radiology Nursing*, *39*(3),

156. https://doi.org/10.1016/j.jradnu.2020.04.006
Guan, H., Dong, L., & Zhao, A. (2022). Ethical risk factors and mechanisms in artificial intelligence decision making. *Behavioral Sciences*, *12*(9), 343. https://doi.org/10.3390/bs12090343
Hagendorff, T. (2020). The ethics of AI ethics: An evaluation of guidelines. *Minds and Machines*, *30*(1), 99. https://doi.org/10.1007/s11023-020-09517-8
Hickok, M. (2020). Lessons learned from AI ethics principles for future actions. *AI and Ethics*, *1*(1), 41. https://doi.org/10.1007/s43681-020-00008-1
Hoang, T. N., LaPorta, A. J., Malone, J. D., Champagne, R. A., Lavell, K., Rosa, G. M. D. L., Gaul, L., & Dukovich, M. (2020). Hyper-realistic and immersive surgical simulation training environment will improve team performance. *Trauma Surgery & Acute Care Open*, *5*(1), e000393. https://doi.org/10.1136/tsaco-2019-000393
Holland, D., Seltzer, T., & Kochigina, A. (2021). Practicing transparency in a crisis: Examining the combined effects of crisis type, response, and message transparency on organizational perceptions. *Public Relations Review*, *47*(2), 102017. https://doi.org/10.1016/j.pubrev.2021.102017
Hsu, E. B., Li, Y., Bayram, J. D., Levinson, D., Yang, S., & Monahan, C. (2013). State of virtual reality based disaster preparedness and response training. *PLoS Currents*, *5*, Article ecurrents.dis.1ea2b2e71237d5337fa53982a38b2aff. https://doi.org/10.1371/currents.dis.1ea2b2e71237d5337fa53982a38b2aff.
Ibarrola, F., Lulham, R., & Grace, K. (2023). *Affect-conditioned image generation*. Cornell University. arXiv (Cornell University).
Imran, M., Ofli, F., Caragea, D., & Torralba, A. (2020). Using AI and social media multimodal content for disaster response and management: Opportunities, challenges, and future directions. *Information Processing & Management*, *57*(5), 102261. https://doi.org/10.1016/j.ipm.2020.102261
James, E., Wooten, L., & Dushek, K. (2011). Crisis management: Informing a new leadership research agenda. *The Academy of Management Annals*, *5*(1), 455. https://doi.org/10.5465/19416520.2011.589594
Johar, G. V., Birk, M. M., & Einwiller, S. A. (2010). How to save your brand in the face of crisis. *MIT Sloan Management Review*, *51*(4), 57–64.
Jose, S., Arango, G., Flichy, P., Featherly, J., & Hughes, B. (n.d.). *Trusted operations–integrating operational performance, safety and security assurance*. Retrieved April 20, 2024, from https://onepetro.org/SPEIE/proceedings/14IE/All-14IE/Utrecht,%20The%20Netherlands/212213
Karaszewski, R. (2011). Przywództwo – aspekty etyczne. *Prakseologia*, *151*, 85.
Karlsen, J. T. (2002). Project stakeholder management. *Engineering Management Journal*, *14*(4), 19. https://doi.org/10.1080/10429247.2002.11415180
Kim, J., Oh, H., & Ham, C. (2021). The impact of the CSR-embedded crisis response: The role of values congruence between leadership styles and CSR motives. *Management Communication Quarterly*, *36*(1), 92. https://doi.org/10.1177/08933189211025322
Kirkpatrick, K. (2017). AI in contact centers. *Communications of the ACM*, *60*(8), 18. https://doi.org/10.1145/3105442
Kruspe, A., Kersten, J., & Klan, F. (2021). Review article: Detection of actionable tweets in crisis events. *Natural Hazards and Earth System Sciences*, *21*(6), 1825. https://doi.org/10.5194/nhess-21-1825-2021
Kumar, J. R. R., Kalnawat, A., Pawar, A. M., Jadhav, V. D., Srilatha, P., & Khetani, V. (2024). Transparency in algorithmic decision-making: Interpretable models for ethical accountability. *E3S web of conferences* (2024) (Vol. 491, p. 2041). EDP Sciences 2024.
Kurucz, E. C., Colbert, B. A., & Wheeler, D. (2008). The business case for corporate social responsibility. In A. Crane, A. McWilliams, D. Matten, J. Moon, & D. Siegel (Eds.), *The Oxford handbook of corporate social responsibility* (pp. 83–112). Oxford University Press.
Lasker, A. (2024). Exploring ethical considerations in generative AI. *International Journal of Advanced Research*, *12*(4), 531. https://doi.org/10.21474/IJAR01/18578
Liu, Q.-H., & Xin, Z. (2015). Corporate product recall and its influence on corporate performance. In *Advances in computer science research: Proceedings of the 2015 3rd international conference on advanced information and communication technology for education* (pp. 241–246). Atlantis Press. https://doi.org/10.2991/icaicte-15.2015.59
Lucero, M., Kwang, A. T. T., & Pang, A. (2009). Crisis leadership: When should the CEO step up? *Corporate Communications an International Journal*, *14*(3), 234. https://doi.org/10.1108/13563280910980032
Moberg, D. (2006). Ethics blind spots in organizations: How systematic errors in person perception undermine moral agency. *Organization Studies*, *27*(3), 413. https://doi.org/10.1177/0170840606062429
Myne, A., Leahy, K., & Soklaski, R. (2022). *Knowledge-integrated informed AI for national security*. Cornell University. arXiv (Cornell University).
O'Reilly, D., Leitch, C. M., Harrison, R. T., & Lamprou, E. (2015). Introduction: Leadership in a crises-constructing world. *Leadership*, *11*(4), 387–395. https://doi.org/10.1177/1742715015596633

Pangarkar, N. (2016). A framework for effective crisis response. *Journal of Organizational Change Management*, *29*(4), 464. https://doi.org/10.1108/JOCM-04-2015-0063

Papouli, E. (2018). Aristotle's virtue ethics as a conceptual framework for the study and practice of social work in modern times. *European Journal of Social Work*, *22*(6), 921. https://doi.org/10.1080/13691457.2018.1461072

Pizzi, M., Romanoff, M., & Engelhardt, T. (2020). AI for humanitarian action: Human rights and ethics. *International Review of the Red Cross*, *102*(913), 145. https://doi.org/10.1017/S1816383121000011

Redfern, O., Griffiths, P., Maruotti, A., Recio-Saucedo, A., & Smith, G. B. (2019). The association between nurse staffing levels and the timeliness of vital signs monitoring: A retrospective observational study in the UK. *BMJ Open*, *9*(9), e032157. https://doi.org/10.1136/bmjopen-2019-032157

Riggio, R. E., & Newstead, T. (2022). Crisis leadership. *Annual Review of Organizational Psychology and Organizational Behavior*, *10*(1), 201. https://doi.org/10.1146/annurev-orgpsych-120920-044838

Savage, N. (2023). *How robots can learn to follow a moral code*. www.nature.com/articles/d41586-023-03258-1

Seeger, M., Ulmer, R., Novak, J., & Sellnow, T. (2005a). Post-crisis discourse and organizational change, failure and renewal. *Journal of Organizational Change Management*, *18*(1), 78. https://doi.org/10.1108/09534810510579869

Sewpersadh, N. S. (2023). Disruptive business value models in the digital era [Review of disruptive business value models in the digital era]. *Journal of Innovation and Entrepreneurship*, *12*(1), Article 2, 1–27. https://doi.org/10.1186/s13731-022-00252-1

Shahriari, K., & Shahriari, M. (2017). *IEEE standard review – Ethically aligned design: A vision for prioritizing human well-being with artificial intelligence and autonomous systems*. In *Proceedings of the 2017 IEEE Canada international humanitarian technology conference (IHTC)* (pp. 197–201). IEEE. https://doi.org/10.1109/IHTC.2017.8058187

Stahl, B. (2021). Ethical issues of AI. In *Artificial intelligence for a better future: An ecosystem perspective on the ethics of AI and emerging digital technologies* (pp. 35–53). Springer. https://doi.org/10.1007/978-3-030-69978-9_4

Standop, D., & Grunwald, G. (2009). How to solve product-harm crises in retailing? *International Journal of Retail & Distribution Management*, *37*(11), 915. https://doi.org/10.1108/09590550910999352

Swasdee, A., Anshari, M., & Hamdan, M. (2020). *Artificial intelligence as decision aid in humanitarian response. 2020 International Conference on Decision Aid Sciences and Application (DASA)*2020.

Tahaei, M., Constantinides, M., Quercia, D., Kennedy, S., Muller, M., Stumpf, S., Liao, Q.V., Baeza-Yates, R., Aroyo, L., Holbrook, J., Luger, E., Madaio, M., Blumenfeld, I.G., De-Arteaga, M., Vitak, J., & Olteanu, A. (2023). Human-centered responsible artificial intelligence: Current & future trends. In A. Schmidt, K. Väänänen, T. Goyal, P.O. Kristensson, & A. Peters (Eds.), *Extended abstracts of the 2023 CHI conference on human factors in computing systems* (pp. 1–4). Association for Computing Machinery. https://doi.org/10.1145/3544549.3583178

Tamburrini, G. (2022). Digital humanism and global issues in artificial intelligence ethics. In H. Werthner, E. Prem, E. A. Lee, & C. Ghezzi (Eds.), *Perspectives on digital humanism*. Springer, Cham. https://doi.org/10.1007/978-3-030-86144-5

Thiebes, S., Lins, S., & Sunyaev, A. (2021). Trustworthy artificial intelligence. *Electronic Markets*, *31*(2), 447–464. https://doi.org/10.1007/s12525-020-00441-4

Turini, S. (2024). The algorithmic decalogue: A comprehensive examination of the A.I. ten commandments. https://doi.org/10.32388/1PMJ81

Uddin, A. S. M. A. (2023). The era of AI: Upholding ethical leadership. *Open Journal of Leadership*, *12*(4), 400. https://doi.org/10.4236/ojl.2023.124019

Ulmer, R. R., Seeger, M. W., & Sellnow, T. L. (2007). Post-crisis communication and renewal: Expanding the parameters of post-crisis discourse. *Public Relations Review*, *33*(2), 130–134. https://doi.org/10.1016/j.pubrev.2006.11.015

Vinuesa, R., Azizpour, H., Leite, I., Balaam, M., Dignum, V., Domisch, S., Felländer, A., Langhans, S. D., Tegmark, M., & Nerini, F. F. (2020). The role of artificial intelligence in achieving the sustainable development goals. *Nature Communications*, *11*(1), Article 233. https://doi.org/10.1038/s41467-019-14108-y

Vo, N., & Lee, K. (2020). Where are the facts? Searching for fact-checked information to alleviate the spread of fake news. *In Proceedings of the 2020 conference on empirical methods in natural language processing (EMNLP)* (pp. 7717–7731). *Association for Computational Linguistics*. https://doi.org/10.18653/v1/2020.emnlp-main.621

Wagner, T., Lutz, R. J., & Weitz, B. A. (2009). Corporate hypocrisy: Overcoming the threat of inconsistent corporate social responsibility perceptions. *Journal of Marketing*, *73*(6), 77. https://doi.org/10.1509/jmkg.73.6.77

Winfield, A. F., Michael, K., Pitt, J., & Evers, V. (2019). Machine ethics: The design and governance of ethical AI and autonomous systems [scanning the issue]. *In Proceedings of the IEEE*, *107*(3), 509–517. https://doi.org/10.1109/JPROC.2019.2900622

Xu, S. (2018). *Discourse of renewal: Developing multiple-item measurement and analyzing effects on relationships*. www.sciencedirect.com/science/article/pii/S0363811116304891

Yolbulan Okan, E. (2014). Managing brands at risk. *In Advances in marketing, customer relationship management, and e-services book series* (Vol. *177*). IGI Global.

Zhou, J., Chen, F., Berry, A., Reed, M., Zhang, S., & Savage, S. (2020). *A survey on ethical principles of AI and implementations. 2020 IEEE Symposium Series on Computational Intelligence (SSCI)*. IEEE 2020.

18

Managing Luxury Brands: Strategies in Brand Management

Gabriele Murtas and George Christodoulides

DEFINING THE MEANING(S) OF LUXURY

The definition of what constitutes luxury remains among the most debated topics in both academic research and industry discourse (Berthon et al., 2009; Cristini et al., 2017; Kapferer, 2012; Kestenbaum, 2021; Ko et al., 2019). To date, there is no universally agreed-upon meaning of the term. Luxury is a concept with fuzzy boundaries, making it difficult to define strictly. It is arguably a complex phenomenon with multiple facets, such as hedonistic experience, ties to heritage, know-how (*savoir-faire*) and culture, and its role as a social marker (Kapferer & Bastien, 2012). Additionally, luxury is *subjective* – what is considered luxury for one person may not hold the same meaning for another. It is also *context specific* – what is deemed luxury in one society or group may not be regarded as such in another. Furthermore, luxury is a *dynamic* concept, as what is considered luxurious evolves over time (Cristini et al., 2017). For instance, caviar is seen as a luxury today, but in the 1800s, it was served as a complimentary snack in bars. Similarly, car phones were viewed as status symbols in the 1990s, while their successor – mobile phones – is now widely diffused in society. Historically, luxury was considered a symbol of wealth, power and social status, accessible only to those deemed deserving by virtue of their lineage and societal position, serving as the visible outcome of an inherited social stratification system. Veblen's concept of *conspicuous consumption* (Veblen, 1899) suggests how the elite leveraged luxury goods to display their affluence and reinforce their superiority within established and often rigid social hierarchies. Indeed, in ancient Rome, rare items such as silk, exotic spices and intricate jewelry were reserved for the ruling classes (i.e., *Patricians*), symbolizing the right of noble families to indulge in opulence and reinforce their prestige within the society. As such, goods that were regarded as luxurious often conveyed a sense of exclusivity and inaccessibility from the masses, that is, *plebeians* (Cristini et al., 2017; Kapferer & Bastien, 2009).

In today's world, however, the definition of the term has undergone a profound transformation, mainly driven by a confluence of cultural, economic and technological forces (Kapferer & Bastien, 2009; Liu et al., 2021; Pantano et al., 2022). As a result, luxury is now predominantly associated with powerful brands that meticulously manage their brand identities (Ko et al., 2019), leveraging their heritage, craftsmanship and exclusivity to cultivate a sense of aspiration and desire among consumers (Kapferer & Bastien, 2012). Unlike in the past, when the meanings of luxury were primarily tied to the rarity of materials and the owner's social status, modern luxury is often defined by the prestigious image of a brand rooted in the emotional connection it fosters with consumers (Cristini et al., 2017). In addition, as societies have progressed and modern democracies have emerged, luxury has witnessed a similar process of 'democratization' (Christodoulides et al., 2021; Rosendo-Rios & Shukla, 2023) that has made it accessible to broader cohorts of consumers. Nowadays, luxury is everywhere (Kapferer & Bastien, 2009), with an ever-increasing number of brands positioning their standardized, mass-produced offerings as 'luxurious'. To differentiate such emerging strategies from traditional notions of luxury, academic researchers have introduced new terminologies that better encapsulate these modern concepts, such as 'premium' (Kapferer, 2014), 'masstige' (i.e., a combination of '*mass*-market' goods with a 'pres*tige*' appeal; see Boisvert et al., 2023) or affordable luxury (Chen et al., 2022). Nevertheless, the attempts to distinguish these overlapping interpretations have further fueled the ongoing debates over the definition of the term.

Adding to the complexity of defining luxury is its multifaceted nature, which encompasses three distinct elements (Berthon et al., 2009; Kapferer & Bastien, 2012). On the one hand, luxury has an objective dimension closely tied to the product's material qualities, including exceptional craftsmanship, the use of high-quality materials and an unparalleled design (Berthon et al., 2009; Ko et al., 2019). Beyond the material aspects, luxury also has a subjective dimension (i.e., *luxury for oneself*), as it is often experienced as a personal indulgence (Kapferer & Bastien, 2009). From this perspective, luxury can be viewed as a source of hedonic pleasure, offering deep emotional gratification (Hirschman & Holbrook, 1982). This feeling of fulfillment often stems from exclusivity, as well as the sense of personal accomplishment and self-reward that comes from owning such expensive and rare items (Ki et al., 2017). Finally, luxury embodies a social dimension (i.e., *luxury for others*), which emphasizes the status and recognition that luxury products confer on their owners (Kapferer & Bastien, 2009). Indeed, luxury goods continue to act as powerful symbols of social distinction, a function rooted in the prestigious image that they convey to others (Han et al., 2010). In an era where democratic ideals blur social hierarchies, the luxury's signaling effect becomes ever more important to distinguish oneself from others, thus fulfilling the long-lasting human dream of belonging to a higher social class (Kapferer & Bastien, 2009; Kapferer, 2012). Bourdieu's arguments further emphasize this subconscious desire, suggesting that luxury consumption provides a means for individuals to assert both their economic and cultural superiority within increasingly egalitarian societies (Bourdieu, 1984).

Aligning with the modern interpretation of luxury as embodied by luxury brands, recent studies have attempted to develop a generally applicable definition by synthesizing the findings from existing literature (Cristini et al., 2017; Ko et al., 2019), which are summarized in Table 18.1. Ko et al. (2019) identified five key elements that characterize a brand whose offerings are perceived as luxurious. First, a luxury brand must be perceived as delivering products or services of exceptionally high quality, setting it apart from competitors. Second, it should offer authentic value through functional (e.g., rare materials) and emotional (e.g., hedonic pleasure) benefits. Third, the brand must possess a prestigious image rooted in exceptional craftsmanship or artisanship that should reinforce its exclusivity and heritage. Fourth, the brand should be worthy of commanding a high

Table 18.1 Core elements of luxury brands

Key Elements	*Brief Description*
High product quality	Products must meet exceptionally high standards, from materials to craftsmanship.
Authentic value	Luxury items must offer functional as well as emotional benefits.
Prestigious image	Luxury maisons must have a brand image rooted in craftsmanship or artisanship, reinforcing their exclusivity and heritage.
High price	Luxury brands must command a premium price compared to existing similar offerings in the market.
Emotional bond	Luxury brands must build deep emotional connections with consumers, beyond the product itself.
Exclusivity	Exclusivity enhances desirability, creating rarity that drives the brand's allure.
Distinctive brand signals and creativity	Distinctive designs and creativity distinguish luxury brand from more conventional offerings.

Source: The authors.

price compared to similar offerings in the market. Lastly, a luxury brand should foster a strong emotional bond with consumers, thus creating a sense of attachment beyond the product itself. Similarly, Cristini et al. (2017) identified product quality as a fundamental factor determining whether a brand qualifies as 'luxury'. In addition, the authors emphasize the importance of exclusivity in creating desirability while also highlighting creativity and distinctive brand signals (e.g., highly recognizable designs) as crucial for offering unique goods that instantly convey the brand's luxury status.

Building a brand image that conveys these core elements (see Table 18.1) requires the adoption of a unique and peculiar branding strategy, which carefully balances exclusivity, desirability and product quality to create a lasting connection with loyal customers and attract new aspirational consumers. The following section explores the distinctive strategy luxury brands employ to achieve these objectives and sustain their unique market position.

EXPLORING THE LUXURY BRANDING STRATEGY

In the previous section, we explored the core elements that define a luxury brand, emphasizing how luxury can be interpreted in terms of its objective (i.e., material), subjective (i.e., luxury for oneself) and social (i.e., luxury for others) dimensions (Berthon et al., 2009; Kapferer & Bastien, 2009; Ko et al., 2019). Building on these pivotal aspects, the branding strategy of luxury brands revolves around carefully considering and balancing three key components (see Figure 18.1): 1) *functional value* (i.e., objective dimension), rooted in the superior quality, handmade processes and craftsmanship of luxury goods; 2) *experiential value* (i.e., subjective dimension), which focuses on the personal and emotional gratification of owning/using a luxury product; 3) *symbolic value* (i.e., social dimension), which emphasizes the social status and recognition that possessing a luxury item confers to the individual (Berthon et al., 2009; Kapferer & Bastien, 2012). This strategic approach, often referred to as the 'anti-laws' of luxury (Kapferer, 2012), defies traditional marketing principles by promoting exclusivity and scarcity over accessibility and availability, thereby cultivating emotional allure and a craving desire.

To reinforce the *functional value* of their products, luxury brands implement several strategic practices aimed at ensuring their offerings consistently meet the highest standards of excellence (Ko et al., 2019). One of the most fundamental practices is avoiding the delocalization of products to low-cost countries, as keeping the production local allows the brands to draw upon a rich tradition of skilled artisanship while capitalizing on the prestige and heritage associated with a specific nation (Kapferer, 2012; Kapferer & Bastien, 2012). As a result, many luxury brands deliberately maintain the manufacturing process in their home country or delocalize in regions famed for their craftsmanship to preserve both the quality and authenticity of their products. Consider Gucci shoes, globally renowned for their premium

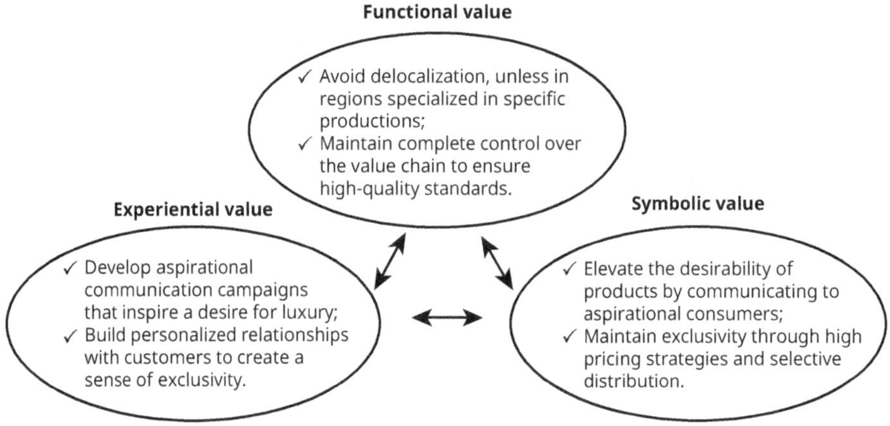

Figure 18.1 Key aspects of the luxury branding strategy

Source: The authors.

leather, with much of their prestige linked to the iconic 'Made in Italy' label, reflecting their production in the Tuscany region. This Italian area evokes a century-old tradition of artisanal expertise and a high-quality leatherwork that cannot be replicated elsewhere. Existing research supports the notion that consumers associate locally produced goods with higher standards and uniqueness – key elements in sustaining the functional value of luxury products (Wilcox et al., 2024). Connected to this point is the fact that luxury brands maintain complete control of their value chain to ensure that every step – from sourcing raw materials to final production – aligns with their strict standards. Indeed, luxury brand managers should be aware that issuing licenses and subcontracting could potentially dilute the very attributes that make luxury goods unique (Kapferer & Bastien, 2012). The importance of maintaining this stringent control on the supply chain was recently tested by brands like Dior and Armani, who faced significant challenges when investigations uncovered labor exploitation in subcontracted factories (Kostov, 2024). In outsourcing parts of their production, these brands compromised both the quality of their products and jeopardized the ethical integrity of their operations. With luxury consumers increasingly emphasizing ethical responsibility, such failures can irreparably undermine the reputation these companies have carefully built over time.

Regarding the *experiential value*, which focuses on the personal gratification that luxury provides to the individual, luxury brands implement several strategies aimed at deepening the consumer's emotional connection with the product being sold (Berthon et al., 2009; Kapferer & Bastien, 2012). The first key branding principle related to this aspect is to avoid advertising with the sole purpose of selling; instead, luxury brands should focus on creating a dream that consumers aspire to be part of (Ma et al., 2023). The goal – unlike traditional advertising, which aims to drive immediate sales – is to craft a narrative around the brand that resonates with consumers on an emotional level, making them crave to be part of the luxury realm. To illustrate this concept, the advertising campaign of Louis Vuitton's Art of Living collection offers a practical example (Louis Vuitton, 2023). Rather than highlighting specific product features, the ad integrates LV's products into a vision of a luxurious lifestyle, tapping into the consumer's emotional desire for an elevated way of living. Another proven strategy for fostering a deeper bond with the brand is to cultivate direct one-to-one relationships with clients (Kapferer & Bastien, 2012). Luxury brands excel in crafting personalized experiences that make each customer feel uniquely valued, elevating the act of purchase from a mere transaction to an expression of indulgence.

To conclude, the *symbolic value* of luxury branding focuses on the external perception of owning luxury products (Berthon et al., 2009; Kapferer & Bastien, 2012). Indeed, the strategies luxury maisons employ are specifically designed not only to deliver personal satisfaction but also to ensure that their products serve as symbols of status, thus elevating the owners' social standing. In order to achieve such an objective, luxury brands usually communicate to non-targets (Kapferer, 2012; Kapferer & Valette-Florence, 2018) so that even those who cannot afford the brand are aware of its prestige and image. For instance, Cartier leverages its partnership with the Venice International Film Festival (Cartier, 2021) to ensure that its products are seen in a high-profile setting by a global audience, including consumers not explicitly targeted for sales. This widespread visibility allows the brand to subtly communicate its distinctive brand signals, further amplifying its awareness and desirability. Despite aiming to increase brand recognition, luxury brands must continue to be perceived as rare and exclusive, avoiding that the increased exposure results in a brand dilution effect (Kapferer & Valette-Florence, 2018). To maintain this delicate balance, luxury brands frequently increase their average prices to keep their products aspirational and beyond the reach of the middle class (Han et al., 2010). This counterintuitive pricing strategy reinforces the exclusivity of the brand while also enabling the company to earn higher profit margins, as consumers are willing to pay a premium for the perceived rarity of an item. An additional strategy used by luxury brands to make sure that their items retain the sought-after aspirational appeal is maintaining strict control over the distribution (Kapferer, 2012; Kapferer & Bastien, 2012). By fully controlling how and when products are available, brand managers can easily create the perception of scarcity even for items that are widely available (Shi et al., 2020).

Influenced by the growing 'democratization' of the industry (Christodoulides et al., 2021), the distinct strategies of luxury, fashion and premium brands have gradually converged, giving rise to hybrid models or 'new forms of luxury' (Kapferer & Laurent, 2016; Thomsen et al., 2020). These emerging approaches selectively combine elements from each branding strategy, allowing brands to stand out in an increasingly crowded and competitive market. In the following section, we present the distinctions between luxury, fashion and premium strategies and provide an overview of the factors that have led to this hybridization process.

THE BLURRING BOUNDARIES BETWEEN LUXURY, FASHION AND PREMIUM STRATEGIES

As outlined in the first section of this chapter, luxury brands are characterized by their emphasis on superior craftsmanship, exclusivity and inaccessibility, largely driven by their elevated price points (see Table 18.1). In contrast to these unique elements, fashion brands prioritize trends and seasonality, rapid product turnover and mass-market appeal, often at the expense of the overall quality of their products and the image of a brand rooted in heritage and tradition (Kapferer & Bastien, 2012). What is in fashion quickly goes out of fashion, which stands in contrast to the timelessness of luxury. Consequently, fashion brands' marketing strategies heavily rely on product-focused advertisements specifically designed to drive repeat purchases (Taylor & Costello, 2017). This strategy fosters a culture of 'fast' fashion, encouraging the consumers to frequently update their wardrobes to stay trendy and chase the latest styles. The significant distinction between luxury and fashion branding can be partly understood through the economic concepts of the bandwagon and the snob effects (Leibenstein, 1950). On the one hand, fashion brands capitalize on the bandwagon effect, where popularity grows as more consumers purchase and adopt the brand's goods. In fact, the widespread diffusion of a bandwagon item increases its appeal, as consumers are influenced by the purchasing behaviors of others and the desire to conform to current trends (see 'mimetic desire' – Girard, 1961). On the contrary, luxury brands typically thrive on the snob effect, as desirability increases when ownership is restricted, reinforcing the value of exclusivity and scarcity within their branding strategy (Leibenstein, 1950). Positioned as an alternative strategy between luxury and fashion, the premium strategy occupies a distinct space that is arguably more rational than luxury, which primarily appeals to consumers' emotions (see Figure 18.2). This realist approach is adopted by companies that aim to offer the best value-for-money products, justifying their costs based on superior or additional features (Kapferer & Bastien, 2012; Kapferer, 2014). In this rational space, there is often a significant amount of justification, argument and persuasion. Luxury, on the other hand, sells dreams and is non-comparable. Each luxury brand presents a unique dream of exception, differentiated from others by intangible qualities. Ultimately, the price of luxury far exceeds what functional utility might suggest, unlike premium products. Swarovski and Coach are examples of brands that effectively leverage this strategy, offering premium-quality products at prices that feel justified by the value and features they provide. While premium products are typically more affordable than luxury items, there are instances where the most expensive Seiko (a *premium* brand) may be more expensive than an entry-level Rolex watch.

Today more than ever, these once clear boundaries between luxury, fashion and premium branding strategies have blurred in response to shifting consumer preferences, increasing demand for accessibility and the growing influence of digital technologies (Christodoulides et al., 2021; Kim, 2019; Liu et al., 2021; Pantano et al., 2022). As a result, some luxury brands have started adopting fashion-based tactics like rapid trend responsiveness (Bao et al., 2024; Murtas et al., 2024; Sung et al., 2023) and collaborative collections (Mrad et al., 2019; Murtas et al., 2022; Pantin-Sohier et al., 2023) to engage a younger consumer demographic while still preserving the

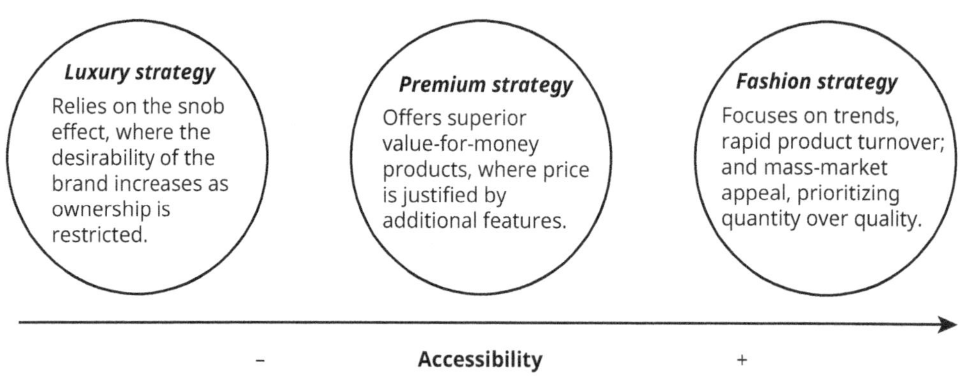

Figure 18.2 Comparison of luxury, premium and fashion branding strategies

Source: The authors.

symbolic and experiential value conveyed by the luxury branding strategy. Brands like Balenciaga, Louis Vuitton and even Audemars Piguet have approached popular streetwear-inspired designs in order to attract younger, trend-conscious consumers who are becoming the primary target of luxury brands (Bain & Co., 2024a). At the same time, social media has fueled the rapid success of modern luxury brands such as Off-White and Chrome Hearts, which blend the core elements of luxury and conspicuous brand signals with the street culture, making their products easily recognizable and appealing to new cohorts of consumers seeking status through visible brand symbols (Pedeliento et al., 2021). The rise of e-commerce has also further increased the accessibility of luxury goods, pushing luxury brands to adopt innovative marketing strategies traditionally associated with fashion brands (Kim, 2019). As a matter of fact, luxury maisons now offer (or '*drop*', see Suen, 2019) limited-edition online exclusive releases through their websites, staging the exclusivity of luxury and merging it with the urgency and immediacy typically associated with fashion brands. Reflecting the trend toward greater accessibility, some luxury brands have also increasingly embraced a premium-like strategy by introducing a broad range of entry-level items to attract a wider audience. For instance, Burberry has recently introduced more accessible products, while Chloé launched its diffusion line – 'See by Chloé' – offering more affordable options to attract aspirational consumers. In contrast, some luxury maisons have opted to maintain a more traditional distribution strategy and inconspicuous aesthetic, staying true to their heritage and timeless designs.

Given the multitude of strategies luxury brands employ today, it becomes imperative to organize these different approaches systematically to provide a clearer understanding of their differences and similarities. To address this aim, the following section offers a structured framework aimed at categorizing and elucidating these novel hybrid luxury branding strategies, offering valuable insights for academic researchers contributing to this domain and industry practitioners operating in the ever-evolving luxury sector.

INTRODUCING THE FRAMEWORK FOR EVOLVING LUXURY BRANDING STRATEGIES

Building on the insights from the previous section, it is clear that – nowadays – luxury brands can no longer be defined solely by the elements traditionally associated with their branding strategy (Berthon et al., 2009; Kapferer, 2014; Kapferer & Bastien, 2012). Indeed, the luxury market is increasingly characterized by a wide array of hybrid approaches that have emerged in response to evolving consumer preferences and the dynamic nature of the luxury concept and, hence, the luxury industry (Christodoulides et al., 2021; Pantano et al., 2022; Rosendo-Rios & Shukla, 2023). As these strategies blur the boundaries between traditional luxury, fashion and premium branding in distinct and varied ways, it becomes essential to categorize them systematically to identify the unique positioning and competitive advantages of each approach. Doing so provides a deeper understanding of how contemporary luxury brands take different approaches to balancing the inherently contradictory elements of exclusivity (*luxury strategy*) versus accessibility (*fashion* and *premium strategies*), timelessness (*luxury strategy*) versus mass appeal and trendiness (*fashion strategy*) and emotional (*luxury strategy*) versus rational value (*premium strategy*).

In this section, we propose a strategic framework that categorizes innovative luxury branding strategies along two key dimensions: 1) traditionalism–modernism and 2) conspicuous–inconspicuous brand signals (see Figure 18.3). On the one hand, *traditionalism* versus *modernism* reflects how brands balance their heritage with the adoption of modern designs and cultural trends (Kapferer & Bastien, 2012). On the other hand, *conspicuousness* versus *inconspicuousness* captures the degree to which brands leverage visible brand signals and overt status symbols in their products (Eckhardt et al., 2015; Veblen, 1899). This influences consumer perceptions of luxury as either a means of social signaling or personal gratification, affecting how brands communicate their value and connect with their target audience. Both dimensions were chosen due to their growing relevance in recent literature on luxury branding. The tension between preserving heritage and embracing modern aesthetics and innovations that appeal to a broad spectrum of consumers (Carpenter & Barlier, 2021; Mrad et al., 2019; Murtas et al., 2022) alongside the emphasis on inconspicuous consumption (Bardhi & Eckhardt, 2017; Eastman et al., 2022; Eckhardt et al., 2015) has become central in scholarly discourses, pushing brands to re-evaluate and adapt the traditional elements of their branding strategy (Kapferer & Bastien, 2012). Next, we present a detailed analysis of the four quadrants in the framework, offering practical examples of brands that exemplify each strategy.

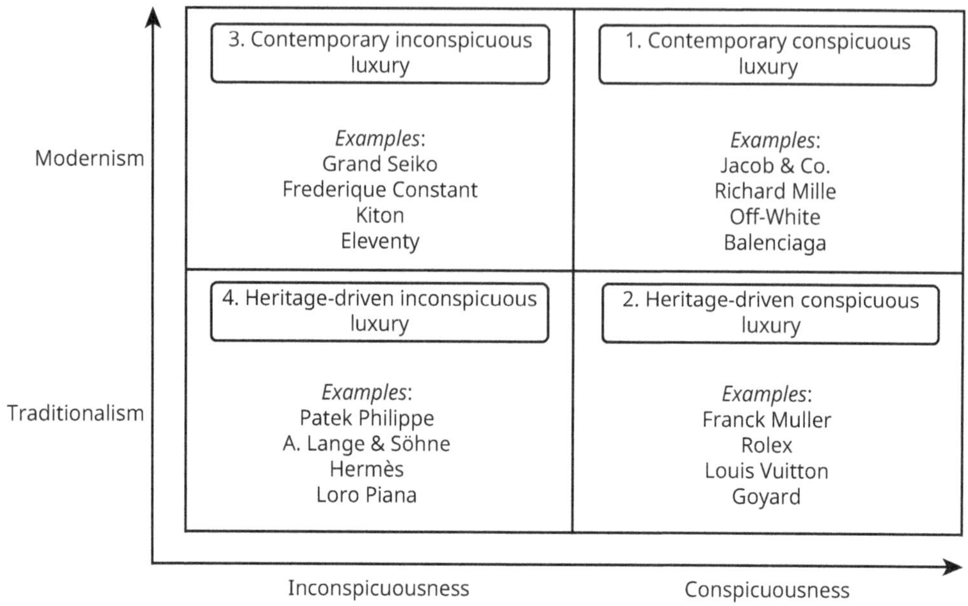

Figure 18.3 The framework for evolving luxury branding strategies

Source: The authors.

Quadrant I: Contemporary Conspicuous Luxury

Luxury brands positioned in this quadrant leverage conspicuous brand signals while embracing contemporary cultural movements. By incorporating bold logos and innovative aesthetics, these brands appeal to younger consumers who seek instantly recognizable luxury products that serve as powerful status symbols (Han et al., 2010) and are drawn to modern designs that resonate with their lifestyles. Heavily influenced by the fashion strategy, modern and conspicuous luxury brands constantly follow the latest trends, prioritizing innovative designs over timelessness. To sustain this market positioning, these luxury brands frequently engage in limited-edition collaborations (Mrad et al., 2019), capitalizing on the 'fear of missing out' (FOMO, see Good & Hyman, 2020) by creating exclusive product releases that drive demand through artificially-induced scarcity (see '*abundant rarity*', Kapferer, 2012). Social media plays a key role in amplifying this sense of urgency, creating buzz around co-branding initiatives (Murtas et al., 2022). The digital-first approach enhances brand awareness and appeal, particularly among younger audiences deeply connected to social media culture (Bazi et al., 2020). While this strategy successfully keeps the brand popular, it also presents significant drawbacks. The emphasis on trendiness and rapid product cycles may compromise the timelessness and superior quality traditionally associated with the luxury branding strategy. As a matter of fact, by focusing on short-term appeal, these brands often downplay the importance of material excellence and craftsmanship. Instead, they purposefully exploit the 'Made in' effect, where the prestige associated with the product's origin reinforces their luxury status without necessarily relying on high-quality materials and/or production processes (Arora et al., 2015). The reliance on contemporary designs also increases the risk of the brand falling 'out of fashion'. Thus, this approach challenges the brand's ability to maintain consistency, potentially diluting the brand's core identity.

Two notable examples of this modern, conspicuous luxury approach are Off-White and Balenciaga. Off-White, founded by Virgil Abloh in 2013 in Milan, exemplifies the modern and conspicuous luxury brand (Pedeliento et al., 2021). Off-White merges streetwear aesthetics with the main elements of the luxury branding strategy, offering products that are both synonyms with contemporary culture and exclusive due to their high price points. The brand's distinctive use of bold design elements (i.e., quotation marks, diagonal stripes, and the four-arrow logo) ensures that Off-White products are instantly recognizable, while the 'Made in Italy' effect reinforces the brand's prestige, even if high-quality materials are not always their primary focus. Despite its rich tradition in couture, even Balenciaga – particularly under the creative direction of Demna Gvasalia – can be considered as being part of this category. Balenciaga has recently pushed the boundaries of traditional luxury by introducing avant-garde designs and embracing urban influences. Products such as the Triple S sneakers feature exaggerated silhouettes and prominent brand signals, appealing to status-seeking consumers who wish to align themselves with the latest fashion trends.

Quadrant II: Heritage-Driven Conspicuous Luxury

Luxury brands falling in this quadrant employ conspicuous brand signals while maintaining traditional luxury values rooted in heritage and timelessness. These luxury brands incorporate iconic and well-known bold logos, monograms and signatures into their designs, appealing to consumers who not only desire luxury products that easily convey prestige and status (Han et al., 2010) but also carry a rich historical legacy (Cristini et al., 2017). Unlike modern luxury brands that frequently adapt to trends, the traditional and conspicuous brands maintain consistency in their core designs and brand imagery. Indeed, the strategy of these brands often aims to celebrate their heritage through timeless aesthetics, reinforcing the authenticity of their brand image (Pecot et al., 2019). They capitalize on the enduring appeal of their classic products, which are seen as investments and symbols of everlasting elegance. To sustain this strategic approach, these luxury brands carefully curate exhibitions, establish foundations and host exclusive events that celebrate their rich history and iconic symbols (Chailan, 2018). As the conspicuous signals are central to their branding strategy, these brands might prioritize bold elements at the expense of rare materials, thus focusing on their strong visual identity as a primary driver of their luxury status. While this strategy effectively reinforces the brand's timeless appeal, the heavy use of bold brand signals carries certain risks. Existing literature suggests how conspicuous branding elements can result in problems of overexposure and increase the likelihood of counterfeiting, which may both dilute the brand's exclusivity and desirability (Wilcox et al., 2009). To mitigate these risks, traditional and conspicuous luxury brands must strike a careful balance between visibility and exclusivity, ensuring their branding approach does not erode the brand's perceived value.

Louis Vuitton and Goyard can be considered two examples of this traditional, conspicuous luxury approach. Louis Vuitton, founded in 1854, is renowned for its iconic monogram canvas featuring the 'LV' initials and floral motifs, which have become synonymous with luxury and elegance. Louis Vuitton leverages its rich heritage and history to create products that are both timeless and instantly recognizable. The conspicuous display of the monogram serves as a powerful status symbol, appealing to consumers who wish to showcase their sophisticated taste. Similarly, Goyard, established in 1853, embodies the traditional and easily recognizable luxury brand with a focus on heritage and conspicuousness. Goyard is known for its signature 'Goyardine' canvas adorned with a distinctive chevron pattern and the subtle incorporation of the brand name into the design. To counterbalance the risks of overexposure, Goyard maintains a sense of exclusivity by limiting its retail presence to select boutiques worldwide and refraining from e-commerce and advertising. This strategy relies on word-of-mouth and the allure of rarity to attract discerning customers.

Quadrant III: Heritage-Driven Inconspicuous Luxury

Luxury brands in this quadrant adopt a more traditional luxury branding strategy, as they often emphasize their superior craftsmanship, the use of exquisite and rare materials and heritage (Kapferer & Bastien, 2012; Ko et al., 2019). These luxury brands maintain a low-profile approach by avoiding conspicuous logos, appealing to consumers who value subtlety and the intrinsic quality of the products rather than external social recognition (Seo & Buchanan-Oliver, 2019). As a result, these brands create understated yet exceptional items, with a strong focus on the functional and experiential values to convey their luxury status (see Figure 18.1). Their branding strategy aims to highlight their timeless artisanal production methods, meticulous attention to details and commitment to excellence (Kapferer & Bastien, 2012). While this strategy effectively preserves the brand's core identity and appeal to discerning consumers (Han et al., 2010), it also presents certain challenges. Avoiding conspicuous branding elements may result in lower brand awareness among the general public, though these brands are often regarded by the elites. Additionally, the resistance to adopting contemporary trends might make it difficult to attract younger luxury consumers seeking innovation and modern aesthetics. To address these challenges, traditional and inconspicuous luxury brands must find ways to subtly innovate their products, ensuring they remain relevant without compromising their core values rooted in craftsmanship and quality.

Two luxury brands adopting this traditional and inconspicuous approach are Hermès and Loro Piana. Founded in 1837, Hermès is renowned for its emphasis on exceptional craftsmanship and the use of the finest materials. The brand's products, such as the iconic Birkin and Kelly bags, are handcrafted by skilled artisans, with each piece requiring numerous hours to complete. Hermès avoids conspicuous logos on many of its products, opting instead for subtle design elements that signify the brand to those in the know (Han et al., 2010). The brand also maintains strict control over its production and distribution, limiting the availability of its most coveted items to preserve exclusivity. Loro Piana specializes in luxury textiles and apparel made from rare and high-quality materials such as vicuña, cashmere and baby cashmere. The brand strongly emphasizes sourcing the finest raw materials directly from their origins, ensuring unparalleled softness and quality in their products. Their designs are simple, elegant and timeless, without prominent logos or branding.

Quadrant IV: Contemporary Inconspicuous Luxury

To conclude, the last quadrant includes the modern luxury brands that adopt an inconspicuous approach, prioritizing subtle design and understated branding elements. Without the advantage of a long-standing heritage, these brands often emphasize the superior quality of their materials and advanced artisanal techniques to compete directly with more traditional luxury brands, thus involuntarily focusing on comparability – a strategy avoided by luxury brands to maintain a sense of uniqueness and incommensurability (Kapferer & Bastien, 2012). Consequently, the modern and inconspicuous luxury brands adopt a branding strategy similar to the premium brands, as they offer consumers a rational justification for their premium pricing based on tangible product attributes (Kapferer, 2014). Indeed, they usually engage in more rational marketing communications, highlighting the quality of materials, production techniques and the expertise of their artisans. These brands appeal to consumers who value understated elegance and the intrinsic qualities of luxury products over external status symbols (Han et al., 2010; Seo & Buchanan-Oliver, 2019). As per previous strategies, even luxury brands falling in this quadrant face important drawbacks. The lack of a history or iconic legacy may result in the brand being perceived as less authentic, making it harder to attract consumers (Pecot et al., 2019). In addition, by focusing on the comparable aspects of their goods, these brands risk being perceived as less unique compared to their more traditional counterparts.

Two brands leveraging this strategy are Kiton and Eleventy. Kiton, founded in 1968, exemplifies the modern and inconspicuous luxury brand. Despite being relatively young compared to centuries-old luxury houses, Kiton has established a reputation for exceptional quality and craftsmanship in men's tailoring. The brand specializes in creating bespoke suits and apparel using the finest fabrics and traditional Neapolitan tailoring techniques. Kiton avoids conspicuous logos, allowing the excellence of its craftsmanship and the quality of its materials to communicate its luxury status. Similarly, Eleventy, established in 2007 in Milan, represents the modern and inconspicuous luxury brand that combines contemporary design with high-quality materials. Since the brand cannot rely on its own history, it leverages the 'Made in Italy' reputation to draw on the heritage of Italian craftsmanship. This allows the brand to emphasize both the functional and symbolic values of its products, combining premium fabrics with timeless designs rooted in Italian tradition to create a sense of luxury.

Key Insights From the Framework

The framework for evolving luxury branding strategies offers a comprehensive matrix for analyzing and understanding the diverse hybrid strategies employed by luxury brands in today's market. By categorizing brands along the dimensions of *traditionalism* versus *modernism* and *conspicuousness* versus *inconspicuousness*, this framework helps identify how contemporary luxury brands position themselves, acknowledging that while they may share common foundations rooted in the luxury branding approach, their strategies can differ significantly based on how they embrace tradition versus modernity and their approach to visible brand signals. Figure 18.4 summarizes the main concepts presented in the previous sections, illustrating the key points that define each quadrant.

However, as outlined in the first section of this chapter, it is important to acknowledge that the meanings of luxury – along with the industry itself – are in a state of constant evolution (Berthon et al., 2009; Cristini et al., 2017; Kapferer & Bastien, 2012). The advent of modern technologies is currently transforming not only how luxury brands operate (Pantano et al., 2022) but also how consumers engage with these brands (Liu et al., 2021). At the same time, the growing consumer demand for circular consumption models is pushing luxury brands to reassess their practices and

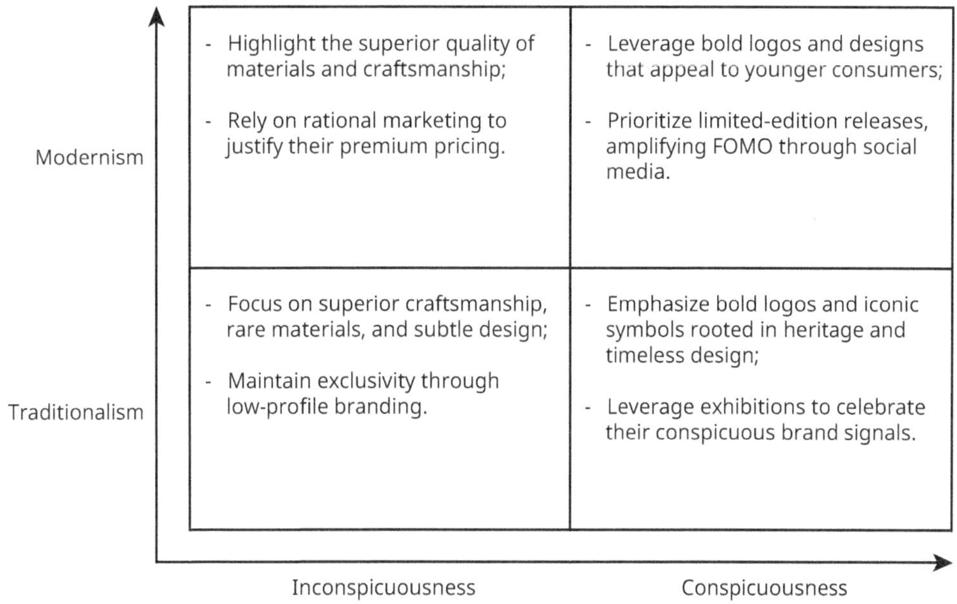

Figure 18.4 Summary of key concepts in current luxury branding strategies

Source: The authors.

value propositions (Kessous & Valette-Florence, 2019; Mrad et al., 2025; Turunen et al., 2020). Once again, emerging contemporary challenges require luxury brands to adapt strategically to maintain their relevance and competitive advantage. In the last part of the chapter, we provide an overview of these topics and offer valuable insights for scholars researching these areas, as well as for luxury brand managers.

EMERGING CHALLENGES IN LUXURY BRANDING

The Rise of New Technologies

The emergence of the latest digital technologies – such as artificial intelligence (AI), augmented and virtual reality (AR & VR) and the blockchain – has recently opened new avenues for luxury brands to enhance the customer experience, personalize offerings, strengthen brand loyalty and attract new cohorts of consumers (Javornik et al., 2021; Murtas et al., 2024; Nawres et al., 2024; Pantano et al., 2022). One of the most impactful technological developments is the integration of AR into the purchasing journey (Nawres et al., 2024). For instance, Cartier has recently partnered with Snapchat to offer a virtual try-on experience for its iconic Trinity ring, allowing customers to explore the product in an interactive and interactive way (Lee, 2024). Similarly, VR technologies have been used to create virtual showrooms and fashion shows, providing exclusive access to luxury brand events from anywhere in the world (Murtas et al., 2024). AI is another technology revolutionizing luxury branding. AI-powered chatbots and virtual assistants enable brands to offer 24/7 customer service, providing instant responses and personalized recommendations based on consumer data (Bain & Co., 2024b; Sahota, 2024). Conglomerates such as LVMH have started leveraging AI to analyze customer preferences and tailor marketing campaigns accordingly, enhancing the effectiveness of their communication strategies (McDowell, 2024). The implementation of blockchain technology has also introduced new possibilities for enhancing transparency and authenticity in the luxury market (de Boissieu et al., 2021), thereby instilling confidence in growing secondary markets. In addition, blockchain enables the creation of non-fungible tokens (NFTs), allowing luxury brands to offer digital collectibles and exclusive virtual assets, opening new revenue streams as well as opportunities to engage with tech-savvy consumers (Bao et al., 2024; Murtas et al., 2024; Sung et al., 2023). To conclude, social media platforms remain pivotal in shaping the way luxury brands interact with their audiences (Creevey et al., 2022; Liu et al., 2021). Luxury brands leverage platforms like Instagram, Facebook and TikTok to reach younger consumers, employing influencers to create authentic connections and drive brand narratives (Fronzetti Colladon et al., 2024). However, while these innovative technologies offer numerous opportunities, luxury brands must always ensure that digital initiatives align with their brand values and do not compromise the exclusivity and personalized experiences that define their specific brand positioning (Murtas et al., 2024) nor do they push these brands into ephemeral trends associated with the fashion business model.

The Rise of Sustainability and Circularity

The growing consumer demand for sustainability and circular practices is another contemporary challenge reshaping the luxury industry, pushing luxury brands to reassess their linear business models (Kessous & Valette-Florence, 2019). Consumers are seeking brands that not only offer high-quality products but also demonstrate a commitment to sustainability and responsible production, including the use of environmentally friendly materials, ethical sourcing, reduction of carbon footprints and transparent supply chains (Kapferer & Michaut-Denizeau, 2019). For instance, the LVMH group, through its LIFE 360 program, has been a pioneer in adopting sustainable practices, emphasizing the use of organic and recycled materials, as well as eco-friendly production processes (LVMH, 2021). Similarly, Kering has demonstrated leadership in sustainability by launching its 'Environmental Profit and Loss' accounting framework, which measures the environmental impact of its operations and supply chain (Kering, 2024). Besides advancements in sustainable practices, the adoption of circular consumption models is another significant challenge faced by the luxury sector. These models focus on extending the lifecycle of products through reuse, recycling and upcycling, reducing waste and promoting a more sustainable approach to consumption (European Parliament, 2023). Luxury brands are exploring ways to incorporate circularity into their business models, such as offering second-hand goods (Kessous & Valette-Florence, 2019; Turunen et al., 2020) or repairs (Mrad et al., 2025). Rimowa, for example, has embraced this approach by selling second-hand luggage directly on its website, thereby extending its product lifecycles (Rimowa, 2024). Third-party second-hand luxury platforms and luxury rental services are also gaining popularity. Marketplaces like The RealReal and Vestiaire Collective facilitate the resale of pre-owned luxury goods, appealing to consumers interested in sustainable consumption and access to luxury at lower price points (Benissan, 2022; The RealReal, 2022). Many luxury brands have started recognizing the influence of these emerging platforms, with some even establishing direct collaborations with them (Davis, 2023). However, even integrating sustainability and circular models presents challenges for luxury brands. Indeed, while the superior quality of luxury products is often perceived as a marker of longevity and sustainability (Sun et al., 2021), the principles of circularity may contrast with the traditional elements of inaccessibility and exclusivity (Kapferer & Michaut-Denizeau, 2019).

CONCLUDING REMARKS

In conclusion, it is important to note that when facing the challenges that lie ahead, luxury brands must constantly take into account the unique elements of their branding strategy to ensure they remain true to their core values. Indeed, although the sector demonstrated remarkable resilience after the COVID-19 pandemic (Bain & Co., 2023), more recent economic crises have revealed that not all luxury brands are equally prepared to deal with turbulent times. For example, amid the decline in sales experienced by major luxury conglomerates (Guilbault, 2024; Partridge, 2024), Brunello Cucinelli has continued to thrive by prioritizing high-quality materials and artisanal craftsmanship, two principles that deeply resonate with its clientele (Smolak, 2024). This commitment to the core principles of the luxury branding strategy has helped fortify the brand against market volatility. On the other hand, those luxury brands that have increasingly adopted fashion-oriented strategies – prioritizing trends and mass appeal – are now facing a significant slowdown, reflecting the contradiction of sustaining long-term relevance (i.e., timelessness) with a trend-driven approach (Spencer, 2024). The juxtaposition of brands thriving through traditional luxury strategies against those struggling after adopting fashion-centric approaches underscores the potential risks of diluting core luxury values. While embracing innovation, new technologies and sustainability initiatives is crucial in today's market, these efforts should always enhance rather than compromise the unique principles of luxury branding. As the luxury industry continues to evolve, achieving a balance between the heritage and innovation will be a key factor distinguishing winners from losers. Luxury brands that successfully achieve this balance are likely to strengthen their market presence and emerge as industry leaders in the years ahead.

REFERENCES

Arora, A. S., McIntyre, J. R., Wu, J., & Arora, A. (2015). Consumer response to diffusion brands and luxury brands: The role of country of origin and country of manufacture. *Journal of International Consumer Marketing*, *27*(1), 3–26. https://doi.org/10.1080/08961530.2014.974117

Bain & Co. (2023). *Renaissance in uncertainty: Luxury builds on its rebound*. www.bain.com/insights/renaissance-in-uncertainty-luxury-builds-on-its-rebound/

Bain & Co. (2024a). *Long live luxury: Converge to expand through turbulence*. www.bain.com/insights/long-live-luxury-converge-to-expand-through-turbulence/

Bain & Co. (2024b). *Luxury and technology*. www.bain.com/globalassets/noindex/2024/bain_report_luxury_and_technology_artificial_intelligence_the_quiet_revolution.pdf.pdf

Bao, W., Hudders, L., Yu, S., & Beuckels, E. (2024). Virtual luxury in the metaverse: NFT-enabled value recreation in luxury brands. *International Journal of Research in Marketing. In press*. https://doi.org/10.1016/j.ijresmar.2024.01.002

Bardhi, F., & Eckhardt, G. M. (2017). Liquid consumption. *Journal of Consumer Research*, *44*(3), 582–97. https://doi.org/10.1093/jcr/ucx050

Bazi, S., Filieri, R., & Gorton, M. (2020). Customers' motivation to engage with luxury brands on social media. *Journal of Business Research*, *112*, 223–35. https://doi.org/10.1016/j.jbusres.2020.02.032

Benissan, E. (2022). Vestiaire collective 'supercharges' US push by shutting down Tradesy. *Vogue*. www.voguebusiness.com/companies/vestiaire-collective-supercharges-us-push-by-shutting-down-tradesy

Berthon, P., Pitt, L., Parent, M., & Berthon, J. P. (2009). Aesthetics and ephemerality: Observing and preserving the luxury brand. *California Management Review*, *52*(1), 45–66. https://doi.org/10.1525/cmr.2009.52.1.45

Boisvert, J., Christodoulides, G., & Khan, M. S. (2023). Toward a better understanding of key determinants and consequences of masstige consumption. *Journal of Business Research*, *161*, 113871. https://doi.org/10.1016/j.jbusres.2023.113871

Bourdieu, P. (1984). *A social critique of the judgement of taste*. Harvard University Press.

Carpenter, G. S., & Barlier, X. (2021). Legendary luxury brands: Inventing the future by reaching to the past. *AMS Review*, *11*(3), 464–70. https://doi.org/10.1007/s13162-021-00207-x

Cartier. (2021). *Venice international film festival*. www.cartier.com/en-gb/maison/cartiers-commitments/art-culture/venice-film-festival

Chailan, C. (2018). Art as a means to recreate luxury brands' rarity and value. *Journal of Business Research*, *85*, 414–23. https://doi.org/10.1016/j.jbusres.2017.10.019

Chen, N., Petersen, F. E., & Lowrey, T. M. (2022). The effect of altruistic gift giving on self-indulgence in affordable luxury. *Journal of Business Research*, *146*, 84–94. https://doi.org/10.1016/j.jbusres.2022.03.050

Christodoulides, G., Athwal, N., Boukis, A., & Semaan, R. W. (2021). New forms of luxury consumption in the sharing economy. *Journal of Business Research*, *137*, 89–99. https://doi.org/10.1016/j.jbusres.2021.08.022

Creevey, D., Coughlan, J., & O'Connor, C. (2022). Social media and luxury: A systematic literature review. *International Journal of Management Reviews*, *24*(1), 99–129. https://doi.org/10.1111/ijmr.12271

Cristini, H., Kauppinen-Räisänen, H., Barthod-Prothade, M., & Woodside, A. (2017). Toward a general theory of luxury: Advancing from workbench definitions and theoretical transformations. *Journal of Business Research*, *70*, 101–7. https://doi.org/10.1016/j.jbusres.2016.07.001

Davis, J. (2023). Burberry partners with Vestiaire collective on circular fashion project. *Harper's Bazaar*. www.harpersbazaar.com/uk/fashion/fashion-news/a45650141/burberry-vestiaire-collective-resale/

de Boissieu, E., Kondrateva, G., Baudier, P., & Ammi, C. (2021). The use of blockchain in the luxury industry: Supply chains and the traceability of goods. *Journal of Enterprise Information Management*, *34*(5), 1318–38. https://doi.org/10.1108/JEIM-11-2020-0471

Eastman, J. K., Iyer, R., & Babin, B. (2022). Luxury not for the masses: Measuring inconspicuous luxury motivations. *Journal of Business Research*, *145*, 509–23. https://doi.org/10.1016/j.jbusres.2022.03.022

Eckhardt, G. M., Belk, R. W., & Wilson, J. A. (2015). The rise of inconspicuous consumption. *Journal of Marketing Management*, *31*(7-8), 807–26. https://doi.org/10.1080/0267257X.2014.989890

European Parliament. (2023). *Circular economy: Definition, importance and benefits*. www.europarl.europa.eu/topics/en/article/20151201STO05603/circular-economy-definition-importance-and-benefits

Fronzetti Colladon, A., Matarazzo, M., Petruzzellis, L., & Visentin, M. (2024). Exploring user reactions to luxury brand videos on YouTube: A comparative study of influencers and brand-official channels.

International Journal of Advertising, *43*(7), 1172–1194. https://doi.org/10.1080/02650487.2024.2367316

Girard, R. (1961). *Mensonge romantique et vérité romanesque*. Grasset.

Good, M. C., & Hyman, M. R. (2020). 'Fear of missing out': Antecedents and influence on purchase likelihood. *Journal of Marketing Theory and Practice*, *28*(3), 330–41. https://doi.org/10.1080/10696679.2020.1766359

Guilbault, L. (2024). Kering warns on profits after sales fall 16% in Q3. *Vogue*. www.voguebusiness.com/story/companies/kering-warns-on-profits-after-sales-fall-16-in-q3

Han, Y. J., Nunes, J. C., & Drèze, X. (2010). Signaling status with luxury goods: The role of brand prominence. *Journal of Marketing*, *74*(4), 15–30. https://doi.org/10.1509/jmkg.74.4.015

Hirschman, E. C., & Holbrook, M. B. (1982). Hedonic consumption: Emerging concepts, methods and propositions. *Journal of Marketing*, *46*(3), 92–101. https://doi.org/10.1177/002224298204600314

Javornik, A., Duffy, K., Rokka, J., Scholz, J., Nobbs, K., Motala, A., & Goldenberg, A. (2021). Strategic approaches to augmented reality deployment by luxury brands. *Journal of Business Research*, *136*, 284–92. https://doi.org/10.1016/j.jbusres.2021.07.040

Kapferer, J. N. (2012). Abundant rarity: The key to luxury growth. *Business Horizons*, *55*(5), 453–62. https://doi.org/10.1016/j.bushor.2012.04.002

Kapferer, J. N. (2014). The future of luxury: Challenges and opportunities. *Journal of Brand Management*, *21*(9), 716–26. https://doi.org/10.1057/bm.2014.32

Kapferer, J. N., & Bastien, V. (2009). The specificity of luxury management: Turning marketing upside down. *Journal of Brand Management*, *16*(5–6), 311–22. https://doi.org/10.1057/bm.2008.51

Kapferer, J. N., & Bastien, V. (2012). *The luxury strategy: Break the rules of marketing to build luxury brands*. Kogan Page Publishers.

Kapferer, J. N., & Laurent, G. (2016). Where do consumers think luxury begins? A study of perceived minimum price for 21 luxury goods in 7 countries. *Journal of Business Research*, *69*(1), 332–40. https://doi.org/10.1016/j.jbusres.2015.08.005

Kapferer, J. N., & Michaut-Denizeau, A. (2019). Are millennials really more sensitive to sustainable luxury? A cross-generational international comparison of sustainability consciousness when buying luxury. *Journal of Brand Management*, *27*, 35–47. https://doi.org/10.1057/s41262-019-00165-7

Kapferer, J. N., & Valette-Florence, P. (2018). The impact of brand penetration and awareness on luxury brand desirability: A cross country analysis of the relevance of the rarity principle. *Journal of Business Research*, *83*, 38–50. https://doi.org/10.1016/j.jbusres.2017.09.025

Kering. (2024). *Sustainability – Our EP&L*. www.kering.com/en/sustainability/measuring-our-impact/our-ep-l/

Kessous, A., & Valette-Florence, P. (2019). 'From Prada to Nada': Consumers and their luxury products: A contrast between second-hand and first-hand luxury products. *Journal of Business Research*, *102*, 313–27. https://doi.org/10.1016/j.jbusres.2019.02.033

Kestenbaum, R. (2021). The definition of luxury is expanding and changing. *Forbes*. www.forbes.com/sites/richardkestenbaum/2021/12/16/the-definition-of-luxury-is-expanding-and-changing/

Ki, C., Lee, K., & Kim, Y. K. (2017). Pleasure and guilt: How do they interplay in luxury consumption? *European Journal of Marketing*, *51*(4), 722–47. https://doi.org/10.1108/EJM-07-2015-0419

Kim, J. H. (2019). Imperative challenge for luxury brands: Generation Y consumers' perceptions of luxury fashion brands' e-commerce sites. *International Journal of Retail & Distribution Management*, *47*(2), 220–44. https://doi.org/10.1108/IJRDM-06-2017-0128

Ko, E., Costello, J. P., & Taylor, C. R. (2019). What is a luxury brand? A new definition and review of the literature. *Journal of Business Research*, *99*, 405–13. https://doi.org/10.1016/j.jbusres.2017.08.023

Kostov, N. (2024). Raids find luxury handbags being made by exploited workers in Italy. *The Wall Street Journal*. www.wsj.com/business/retail/dior-armani-italy-supply-chain-labor-36b14a85

Lee, A. (2024). Cartier's trinity ring arrives in virtual form at snapchat. *Women's Wear Daily*. wwd.com/business-news/technology/cartier-trinity-ring-ar-virtual-try-on-snapchat-1236307330/

Leibenstein, H. (1950). Bandwagon, snob ve veblen effects in the theory of consumers' demand. *Quarterly Journal of Economics*, *64*(2), 183–207. https://doi.org/10.2307/1882692

Liu, X., Shin, H., & Burns, A. C. (2021). Examining the impact of luxury brand's social media marketing on customer engagement: Using big data analytics and natural language processing. *Journal of Business Research*, *125*, 815–26. https://doi.org/10.1016/j.jbusres.2019.04.042

Louis Vuitton. (2023). *Art of living collections*. https://eu.louisvuitton.com/eng-e1/stories/art-of-living-campaign

LVMH. (2021). *Life 360*. www.lvmh.com/en/commitment-in-action/for-the-environment/life-360-lvmh

Ma, J., Zhao, Y., & Mo, Z. (2023). Dynamic luxury advertising: Using lifestyle versus functional advertisements in different purchase stages. *Journal of Advertising*, *52*(1), 39–56. https://doi.org/10.1080/00913367.2021.1951402

McDowell, M. (2024). Inside LVMH's AI factory. *Vogue*. www.voguebusiness.com/story/technology/inside-lvmhs-ai-factory?utm_source=chatgpt.com

Mrad, M., Farah, M. F., & Haddad, S. (2019). From Karl Lagerfeld to Erdem: A series of collaborations between designer luxury brands and fast-fashion brands. *Journal of Brand Management*, *26*(5), 567–82. https://doi.org/10.1057/s41262-018-00146-2

Mrad, M., Semaan, R. W., Christodoulides, G., & Prandelli, E. (2025). Give me a second life! Extending the life-span of luxury products through repair. *Journal of Retailing and Consumer Services*, *82*, 104055. https://doi.org/10.1016/j.jretconser.2024.104055

Murtas, G., Pedeliento, G., & Mangiò, F. (2024). Luxury fashion brands at the gates of the Web 3.0: An analysis of early experimentations with NFTs and the metaverse. *Journal of Global Fashion Marketing*, *15*(1), 90–114. https://doi.org/10.1080/20932685.2023.2249476

Murtas, G., Pedeliento, G., Mangiò, F., & Andreini, D. (2022). Co-branding strategies in luxury fashion: The Off-White case. *Journal of Strategic Marketing*, *33*(4), 484–503. https://doi.org/10.1080/0965254X.2022.2160484

Nawres, D., Nedra, B. A., Yousaf, A., & Mishra, A. (2024). The role of augmented reality in shaping purchase intentions and WOM for luxury products. *Journal of Business Research*, *171*, 114368. https://doi.org/10.1016/j.jbusres.2023.114368

Pantano, E., Pedeliento, G., & Christodoulides, G. (2022). A strategic framework for technological innovations in support of the customer experience: A focus on luxury retailers. *Journal of Retailing and Consumer Services*, *66*, 102959. https://doi.org/10.1016/j.jretconser.2022.102959

Pantin-Sohier, G., Sohier, R., Sohier, A., Hofmann, J., & Billot, S. (2023). The impact of moderately incongruent rap music endorsers on luxury brand personality and brand coolness. *Journal of Strategic Marketing*, *33*(4), 542–558. https://doi.org/10.1080/0965254X.2023.2232805

Partridge, J. (2024). Louis Vuitton owner LVMH reports surprise sales drop amid China slowdown. *The Guardian*. www.theguardian.com/business/2024/oct/16/louis-vuitton-owner-lvmh-surprise-sales-drop-china-slowdown

Pecot, F., Valette-Florence, P., & De Barnier, V. (2019). Brand heritage as a temporal perception: Cconceptualisation, measure and consequences. *Journal of Marketing Management*, *35*(17-18), 1624–43. https://doi.org/10.1080/0267257X.2019.1667414

Pedeliento, G., Mangiò, F., Littlewood, A. V., Murtas, G., & Manfrini, G. N. (2021). *A new paradigm in the luxury fashion industry: Off-White and the rise of luxury streetwear*. Sage Publications.

The RealReal. (2022). *Annual report 2021*. https://investor.therealreal.com/static-files/7a65e66b-b112-4235-b302-6fe02de414df

Rimowa. (2024). *Pre-loved luggage*. www.rimowa.com/it/en/pre-owned-luggage

Rosendo-Rios, V., & Shukla, P. (2023). When luxury democratizes: Exploring the effects of luxury democratization, hedonic value and instrumental self-presentation on traditional luxury consumers' behavioral intentions. *Journal of Business Research*, *155*, 113448. https://doi.org/10.1016/j.jbusres.2022.113448

Sahota, N. (2024). Weaving elegance with intelligence: How luxury brands are embracing AI. *Forbes*. www.forbes.com/sites/neilsahota/2024/03/15/weaving-elegance-with-intelligence-how-luxury-brands-are-embracing-ai/

Seo, Y., & Buchanan-Oliver, M. (2019). Constructing a typology of luxury brand consumption practices. *Journal of Business Research*, *99*, 414–21. https://doi.org/10.1016/j.jbusres.2017.09.019

Shi, X., Li, F., & Chumnumpan, P. (2020). The use of product scarcity in marketing. *European Journal of Marketing*, *54*(2), 380–418. https://doi.org/10.1108/EJM-04-2018-0285

Smolak, H. (2024). Brunello cucinelli backs growth targets as sales defy luxury slowdown. *The Wall Street Journal*. www.wsj.com/business/earnings/brunello-cucinelli-revenue-growth-beats-market-views-despite-luxury-sector-slowdown-32c4774e

Spencer, M. (2024). *France's Kering warns on 2024 operating profit as Gucci sales fall*. Reuters. www.reuters.com/business/retail-consumer/gucci-owner-kering-posts-16-fall-q3-sales-weak-china-demand-2024-10-23/

Suen, Z. (2019). *How to use drops in the Instagram age*. Business of Fashion. www.businessoffashion.com/articles/luxury/how-to-use-drops-in-the-instagram-age/

Sun, J. J., Bellezza, S., & Paharia, N. (2021). Buy less, buy luxury: Understanding and overcoming product durability neglect for sustainable consumption. *Journal of Marketing*, *85*(3), 28–43. https://doi.org/10.1177/0022242921993172

Sung, E., Kwon, O., & Sohn, K. (2023). NFT luxury brand marketing in the metaverse: Leveraging blockchain-certified NFTs to drive consumer behavior. *Psychology & Marketing*, *40*(11), 2306–25. https://doi.org/10.1002/mar.21854

Taylor, C. R., & Costello, J. P. (2017). What do we know about fashion advertising? A review of the literature and suggested research directions. *Journal of Global Fashion Marketing*, *8*(1), 1–20. https://doi.org/10.1080/20932685.2016.1255855

Thomsen, T. U., Holmqvist, J., von Wallpach, S., Hemetsberger, A., & Belk, R. W. (2020). Conceptualizing unconventional luxury. *Journal of Business*

Research, *116*, 441–5. https://doi.org/10.1016/j.jbusres.2020.01.058

Turunen, L. L. M., Cervellon, M. C., & Carey, L. D. (2020). Selling second-hand luxury: Empowerment and enactment of social roles. *Journal of Business Research*, *116*, 474–81. https://doi.org/10.1016/j.jbusres.2019.11.059

Veblen, T. (1899). *The theory of the leisure class*. Routledge.

Wilcox, K., Kim, H. M., & Sen, S. (2009). Why do consumers buy counterfeit luxury brands? *Journal of Marketing Research*, *46*(2), 247–59. https://doi.org/10.1509/jmkr.46.2.247

Wilcox, K., Laporte, S., & Ward, G. (2024). How traditional production shapes perceptions of product quality. *Journal of Consumer Research*, *51*(2), 256–75. https://doi.org/10.1093/jcr/ucad073

19

Business-to-Business Brand Management: Insights for Entrepreneurship

Susan M. Mudambi and Jessica Keech

INTRODUCTION AND MOTIVATION

Business-to-business (B2B) markets have generally been thought of as a battleground for large corporations, yet brand management can also make a difference for smaller firms and entrepreneurial ventures (Inskip, 2004). Entrepreneurship plays a significant and ongoing role in economic growth (Urbano et al., 2019; Wennekers & Thurik, 1999). Entrepreneurial ventures bring innovation, agility and disruption into marketplaces. However, entrepreneurs confront many unique challenges when it comes to managing B2B brands effectively.

Entrepreneurs often rely on their personal brand to secure initial success, with their effectiveness often associated with the concepts of the entrepreneurial mindset and entrepreneurial orientation. In contrast, brand management and brand orientation within the B2B space typically take a more structured, strategic approach to business growth. B2B brand management emphasizes not only personal reputation but also the development of corporate, product and service brands that resonate with diverse stakeholders over time (Kotler & Pfoertsch, 2006).

An integration of the two approaches of brand orientation and entrepreneurial orientation has the potential to be beneficial in providing insights regarding how to build brands in an entrepreneurial economy. Many B2B entrepreneurs struggle to scale their ventures beyond the initial stages of growth. They are unable to build the necessary brand equity that leads to long-term success. There is little academic research on how to integrate brand orientation and entrepreneurial orientation as part of a strategy for effectively navigating entrepreneurial business challenges. This chapter aims to fill this gap.

The chapter is structured as follows: First, we summarize key concepts and principles from the academic literature on B2B brand management and from the academic literature on entrepreneurship. Second, we compare and contrast these concepts and principles to enable the identification of areas of potential synergy and conflict. Third, we describe several ongoing and emerging challenges facing B2B entrepreneurs, including building awareness and reputation; managing long sales cycles; customer acquisition and retention; employee recruitment and retention and scalability and managing growth. Fourth, we explore how B2B brand orientation and entrepreneurial orientation principles can be applied to each of these challenges. Finally, we identify brand management questions that arise from viewing these business challenges from both the brand management and entrepreneurship perspectives. From this, we propose an agenda for future academic research on B2B brand management in an entrepreneurial economy. This agenda includes research ideas for developing insights into effective branding practices for B2B entrepreneurs.

LITERATURE REVIEW

To develop a thoughtful new research agenda, it is important to acknowledge established academic foundations and to reassess them within the current context. In this section, we summarize key concepts and principles from the academic literature of B2B brand management and of entrepreneurship. This lays the groundwork for drawing out new insights and for developing a future research agenda.

B2B Brand Management and Brand Orientation

Brand management in B2B markets has traditionally focused on corporate brands and the value they provide (Aspara & Tikkanen, 2008). A corporate brand is comprised of a corporate identity, the internal aspect or dimension of a brand and a reputation (Koporcic, 2017). A company's reputation can play an important role in B2B decision-making. The perception of how a company is perceived by other companies, how well it meets its commitments as well as how it is perceived by all company stakeholders form the reputation of a firm (Cretu & Brodie, 2007). Corporate identity is how the company wants to be presented to its customers and how it is perceived externally (Kotler & Pfoertsch, 2006). A strong brand can result in a market position that distinguishes it from competition. In B2B contexts, products and services may not vary greatly from each other, and so a strong brand can help the firm differentiate itself from competition (Hague, 2024). Product brands also rise in importance, especially in some markets. Because B2B buyers typically purchase a very wide range of products, they must approach procurement in a systematic way.

Traditionally, in B2B contexts, tangible aspects such as price and product quality were considered as more important criteria. Reducing risks and minimizing costs are often the paramount considerations (Bygballe, 2017; Mitchell & Moutinho, 2003), even as risk reduction and cost reduction exist somewhat in opposition to each other. Unlike business-to-consumer (B2C) branding, where emotional appeal often plays a central role, the decision-making process in B2B contexts is generally seen as more rational. However, emotions and intangible values can be important in B2B purchase decisions (Mudambi et al., 1997), especially to certain types of buyers (Mudambi, 2002).

The B2B brand management literature is extensive and examines a wide range of concepts and principles. One important concept is brand orientation. Various definitions of brand orientation have been offered in the literature (e.g., Chang et al., 2018; Urde, 1999; Urde et al., 2013). With brand orientation, the brand is a central and strategic asset of the firm. The strategic emphasis is on developing and maintaining a consistent, strong and distinctive brand identity across customer touchpoints and communication channels. Indeed, Chang et al. (2018) find that brand orientation positively impacts brand success and brand performance both directly and indirectly by influencing customer value co-creation.

The following section highlights six concepts that have been important in the past and that are likely to continue to be important to B2B brand management and B2B entrepreneurship in the future. See Table 19.1 for a summary.

- **Corporate branding and product branding.** B2B firms typically manage both corporate and product brands simultaneously. Corporate brands convey a company's overall reputation and credibility and appeal to multiple stakeholders. Product brands focus on the specific attributes and benefits of individual offerings from the buyer perspective. Brand differentiation at the product level is challenging due to the high quantity and range of product offerings and the specialized and often technical nature of the products (Kotler & Pfoertsch, 2006). While it is assumed that most decisions in B2B environments are made rationally, a growing body of literature focuses on the emotions involved within this context. Even in B2B contexts, emotions lead to action (Kotler & Pfoertsch, 2006), and both rational and emotional brand values influence organizations (Lynch & De Chernatony, 2004). Overall, it is essential for brands to find ways to incorporate rational and emotional reasons into strategies for building and maintaining B2B brands.
- **Brand equity and brand value.** Brand equity is one of the most heavily researched aspects of brand management, yet it remains elusive and dynamic. Brand equity has been defined as the additional value a product receives from its

Table 19.1 B2B brand management principles and key literature

Concepts and Principles	*Authors (Year)*
Corporate branding and product branding	Kotler and Pfoertsch (2006); Lynch and De Chernatony (2004)
Brand equity and brand value	Aaker (1991, 1992, 1996); Erdem and Swait (1998); Farquhar (1989); Keller (1993); Leek and Christodoulides (2011); Lindgreen and Wynstra (2005); Mudambi et al. (1997); Netemeyer et al. (2004); Yoo and Donthu (2001)
Brand consistency	Broniarczyk and Alba (1994); Erdem and Swait (1998); Kapferer (2004); Keller (2013); Liu et al. (2017); Park et al. (1991); Randall et al. (1998)
Differentiation	Kapferer (2004); Keller (2013)
Trust and relationship building	Bendixen et al. (2004); Bone et al. (2015); Hohenschwert and Geiger (2015); Lindgreen and Wynstra (2005); Mudambi (2002); Payne et al. (2008); Sharma and Patterson (1999)
Internal branding	Foster et al. (2010); Keller and Kotler (2016); King and Grace (2008)

Source: The authors.

brand name (Farquhar, 1989). Brand equity has also been defined as the 'set of brand assets and liabilities linked to a brand, its name and symbol, that add to or subtract from the value provided by the product or service to a firm and/or to that firm's customers' (Aaker, 1991, p. 15). In essence, brand equity is the incremental value associated with a product due to its brand image. Brand equity has been conceptualized as a multifaceted concept driven by consumer perceptions of quality, value and uniqueness (Netemeyer et al., 2004), as well as in terms of the consequences of such perceptions on marketplace consumer behaviors such as a greater willingness to pay a price premium, increased choice likelihood, repeat purchase behavior, etc. (Aaker, 1991, 1996; Keller, 1993; Yoo & Donthu, 2001).

Brand equity is conceived of as being beneficial to both consumers and firms (Aaker, 1991). From the consumer's perspective, relying on brand information can ease the decision-making process by providing shoppers with an easy-to-rely-upon, heuristic measure of quality (Aaker, 1992; Erdem & Swait, 1998). From the firm's perspective, brand equity reflects points of product differentiation that provide the firm with sustainable competitive advantages (Aaker, 1991). Similarly, there has been extensive research on the sources of B2B brand value and on the identification and communication of sources of brand value to customers. Brand values can stem from both tangible and intangible sources. The foundation of brand value is fundamentally awareness, perceived quality and brand associations (Keller, 1993). In the B2B context, the key sources of value have been described as product performance, distribution (ordering and delivery) performance, support services performance and company performance (Mudambi et al., 1997). B2B brand value has also been identified as involving reliability, performance, reputation (Webster & Keller, 2004), trust, loyalty and differentiation (Leek & Christodoulides, 2011). For a comprehensive review of brand value in business markets, see Lindgreen and Wynstra (2005).

- **Brand consistency.** One dominant theme in the literature is the need for a consistent brand image over time. This includes consistency with brand extensions, product design and messages across time and communication channels. The advantages of maintaining a consistent brand image include high brand awareness, marketing communication efficiencies of scale and overall increases in brand equity (Kapferer, 2004; Keller, 2013). To that end, the brand extension literature has focused particularly on brand concept consistency as it relates to similarity across brand extensions (Broniarczyk & Alba, 1994; Randall et al., 1998). Brand extensions with higher brand consistency and product feature similarity are more favorable (Park et al., 1991). Consistent communication is favored because it is thought to increase credibility and clarity in consumers' minds (Erdem & Swait, 1998). Research also indicates that consumers prefer the aesthetic design of a product to be more consistent with its brand image especially for luxury (vs. economy) products (Liu et al., 2017). Overall, since inconsistency can create unwanted tension (Pepitone, 1966), brand managers must maintain a consistent identity and image in their brand strategies.

- **Differentiation.** Another consistent theme at the core of brand management is the strategic focus on differentiation of the brand from competitor offers. Indeed, one of the sole purposes of branding is to create a competitive advantage by differentiating a brand from its competitors. Points of difference, the attributes that consumers strongly associate with a brand, are the key to establishing differentiation (Keller, 2013), and differentiation must be meaningful to the target audience and resonate with their needs. Creating unique values can distinguish a brand from competitors (Kapferer, 2004). The true essence of differentiation is about creating meaningful value to consumers that cannot be easily replicated by competitors.
- **Trust and relationship building.** B2B transactions often involve long-term relationships with multiple stakeholders, each of which has distinct objectives and concerns. The relationship perspective depends on trust. Relationship quality, trust and satisfaction are fundamental (Bendixen et al., 2004). B2B relationships develop between sales teams and procurement teams and between service teams and product users. Buyer–supplier relationships have considerable values (Lindgreen & Wynstra, 2005) and often focus on problem solving, at both the pre-purchase and after-purchase stages (Sharma & Patterson, 1999; Bone et al., 2015). Relationships can involve collaborative product development, customized solutions and ongoing support. Salespeople use interpersonal influence during complex B2B sales. As informed advisors, salespeople assist buyers in the decision-making process and positively affect the perceived relationship value (Hohenschwert & Geiger, 2015). B2B brand value is built not only on the characteristics of the company and the product but also on the co-creation of value with customers (Payne et al., 2008). This idea builds on the concept of service-dominant logic in marketing (Vargo & Lusch, 2004) that places service as the common dominator in exchange. The emphasis is that value is created not when the product or service is manufactured, but rather when it is consumed or used.
- **Internal branding.** Employees are critical assets for building a consistent brand identity and image. Internal branding is also increasingly important in markets characterized by shortages of unskilled and skilled labor and worker turnover. B2B internal branding focuses mostly at the corporate level, as most B2B brands often do not have deep associations with specific values (Keller & Kotler, 2016). Especially important are the mechanisms and outcomes of internal branding. Internal branding is linked to employee brand commitment and brand citizenship behaviors, behaviors that go beyond formal job requirements (King & Grace, 2008). Investment in internal branding results in employees who act like brand ambassadors, leading to improved customer satisfaction and brand loyalty (King & Grace, 2008). Also important is the alignment of employee behavior with the brand promise (Foster et al., 2010). Effective internal branding can lead to improved brand consistency and organizational performance via enhanced employee role clarity, brand identification and engagement (Foster et al., 2010). Looking internally to build the B2B brand can have external benefits.

Entrepreneurship and Entrepreneurial Orientation

Entrepreneurs think and act differently than typical B2B business leaders, and that unique energy is a spark for the economy. The entrepreneurial mindset is the 'true source of innovation and entrepreneurship' and is 'an ability and perspective that resides within each one of us' (Kuratko et al., 2021, p. 1681). The entrepreneurial mindset is often characterized by personal drive, innovation and a willingness to take risks. From the organizational perspective, entrepreneurial orientation is the strategic approach of entrepreneurs, or 'the strategy-making processes that provide organizations with a basis for entrepreneurial decisions and actions' (Rauch et al., 2009, p. 761). Entrepreneurial orientation is generally discussed as a firm-level concept (Vecchio, 2003) but is also presented as a propensity of an individual.

Entrepreneurship orientation research has emphasized three main dimensions: Proactiveness, innovativeness and risk-taking (Miller, 1983). Entrepreneurs and entrepreneurial firms proactively seek new opportunities, embrace innovation and take calculated risks to exploit market dynamics. They prioritize ventures into new markets and developing innovative new goods and services. The entrepreneurial focus is on creating value through novel solutions, with a tendency to prioritize rapid execution and growth over long-term strategic planning.

Table 19.2 Entrepreneurship principles and key literature

Concepts and Principles	*Authors (Year)*
Personal branding	Littunen (2000); Resnick et al. (2016)
Opportunity recognition	Baron (2006); McMullen et al. (2007)
Risk-taking	Brown et al. (2011a); Miller (1983)
Competitive aggressiveness	Covin and Covin (1990); Miller (2015)
Innovativeness	Marcati et al. (2008); Miller (1983)
Thought leadership	McCrimmon (2005); Neuhaus et al. (2022); Taylor et al. (2022)

Source: The authors.

The entrepreneurship literature is extensive and examines a wide range of ideas. The following section highlights six concepts that have been important in the past and are likely to continue to be important in the future, especially in the context of B2B brand management. See Table 19.2 for a summary.

- **Personal branding.** Entrepreneurs often rely on their personality characteristics (Littunen, 2000) and reputation to drive initial sales. This can be effective for building acceptance with the initial early adopters and initial investors. However, reliance on the founder's personality and brand limits business growth. When founders perceive themselves as the brand, it is difficult for them to delegate, and this hinders the business from becoming more established (Resnick et al., 2016).
- **Opportunity recognition**. Entrepreneurs are skilled at recognizing opportunities (Baron, 2006). They identify market gaps and capitalize on emerging opportunities. This ability is crucial for the early success of B2B ventures. Entrepreneurs value agility and often make quick decisions to pivot to new approaches in response to market feedback and changing conditions. Opportunity involves both discovery and exploitation (McMullen et al., 2007).
- **Risk-taking.** Entrepreneurs generally are characterized as being risk takers (Miller, 1983). The old expression of 'no risk, no reward' is motivating to many entrepreneurs. However, the aftermath of risk-taking merits further attention, as negative consequences of the risks often fall to a different set of individuals than do the positive rewards or consequences. For example, investors may fare differently from risk-taking than employees or suppliers. Brand identity can be hurt by risky communications or risky brand extensions (Brown et al., 2011a).
- **Competitive aggressiveness.** Successful entrepreneurs maintain a keen awareness of customer needs and of competitor activity. Beyond competitor intelligence gathering, entrepreneurial firms can implement aggressive pricing, negotiation and communication actions. Competitive aggressiveness is often associated with the financial performance of small and medium size enterprises (SMEs) (Covin & Covin, 1990). Yet aggressive responses can have a downside (Miller, 2015). Aggressive tactics can reduce trust and can take resources away from brand development and brand differentiation.
- **Innovativeness.** B2B entrepreneurs often build their reputations on their innovativeness (Miller, 1983) and their ability to bring new ideas to market. Innovativeness has both general and specific dimensions (Marcati et al., 2008) and is best placed within a broad context of risk management. In some markets, innovativeness takes the form of new product development championed by employees from an engineering or R&D background, who enjoy applying the latest technologies. However, B2B customers may be skeptical about change, especially when agreement from the end users of the product is needed. An appreciation of entrepreneurial innovativeness requires trust, strong buyer–seller relationships and a commitment to value co-creation.
- **Thought leadership.** B2B entrepreneurs are often externally focused, and many aim to be recognized as thought leaders in their fields. They may seek recognition and attention for their ideas, rather than for their products (Neuhaus et al., 2022). Although that can be personally fulfilling and beneficial (McCrimmon, 2005), there may be little connection to that recognition and firm financial performance in the short term. CEOs who leverage social media to develop

Table 19.3 Brand orientation versus entrepreneurial orientation

Brand Orientation	*Entrepreneurial Orientation*
Corporate branding and product branding	Personal branding
Brand equity and brand value	Opportunity recognition
Brand consistency	Risk-taking
Differentiation	Competitive aggressiveness
Trust and relationship building	Innovativeness
Internal branding	Thought leadership

Source: The authors.

thought leadership find it to be worth the trade-offs involved (Taylor et al., 2022), yet the thought leadership does not necessarily enhance teamwork and the broader brand building activities of the firm.

This brief overview of two large bodies of literature is not complete and comprehensive, but it serves to highlight several important aspects. Identifying common themes and theoretical principles in the B2B brand management and entrepreneurship literatures can open the door to insights and literature integration. Of particular interest is the potential for conflict – and for synergy – between brand orientation and entrepreneurial orientation for B2B firms. For example, an entrepreneur's emphasis on risk-taking and innovativeness can hurt brand consistency due to a fragmented or inconsistent brand image. Entrepreneurial capabilities must be balanced with the need for long-term investment in brand development.

An initial effort to compare and contrast brand and entrepreneurial orientation is summarized in Table 19.3. This acknowledges the potential for synergy and conflict in strategic development.

As summarized in Table 19.3, brand orientation emphasizes corporate and product branding, while entrepreneurial orientation emphasizes personal branding. Other contrasts include brand equity and brand value building versus opportunity recognition and agility; brand consistency versus risk-taking; trust and relationship building versus innovativeness and internal branding versus thought leadership. Taking this fresh look at brand orientation and entrepreneurial orientation can help to highlight connections and conflicts between the underlying theoretical principles. This understanding can build a realistic approach for facing current managerial challenges.

The entrepreneurial emphasis on new ideas and fast growth can sometimes lead to a neglect of brand management, an important aspect of firm strategy. Yet brand management can be too static, with an overemphasis on being true to past brand values and images and an underemphasis on innovation and adaptation. Brand management can be lacking in the agility to embrace new technologies and communication methods that are difficult to coordinate. Entrepreneurial, proactive approaches can be beneficial for addressing the brand management challenges facing B2B entrepreneurs.

BRAND MANAGEMENT CHALLENGES FACING B2B ENTREPRENEURS

In this section, we examine a few of the major brand management challenges facing B2B entrepreneurs. They include the following:

- building brand awareness and reputation;
- long sales cycles;
- customer acquisition and retention;
- employee recruitment and retention and
- scalability and managing growth.

Although some of these challenges are not unique to the B2B marketplace, they are dominant B2B concerns. They often present complexities that require both theoretical rethinking and practical solutions. In the following section, we discuss how these challenges affect brand management and business growth. We draw on academic research to explore how the key concepts and principles of B2B brand management and entrepreneurship apply. Additionally, we highlight questions raised by these challenges and offer avenues for future research.

Building Brand Awareness and Reputation

Building B2B brand awareness is a substantial challenge, as documented in both the academic literature and in the practitioner literature. A practical definition of brand awareness is 'the buyer's ability to identify the brand in sufficient detail to make a purchase' (Rossiter, 2014, p. 534). Brand awareness is the level of familiarity a potential buyer has with a brand and its attributes and is usually assessed by the extent of recognition or recall of the brand. If a buyer is not sufficiently aware of a brand, purchase consideration is certainly unlikely. Yet, brand awareness alone is insufficient. Building awareness must take place alongside the development of positive brand attitudes and brand reputation.

B2B entrepreneurs often find it difficult to build brand awareness for the firm, especially when they operate in niche markets or compete with larger, established firms. For SMEs, the initial brand awareness and brand reputation are synonymous or closely tied to the entrepreneur. The entrepreneur's professional network provides the foundation. The reputation of the entrepreneur enables a venture to find startup capital and get off the ground. An entrepreneur's reputation can be multifaceted yet is contingent on personal and professional networks. To grow, the focus must shift toward developing a corporate brand reputation that goes beyond the entrepreneur's personal network and that is distinct from the entrepreneur's identity and image.

In B2B markets, brand reputation serves as a critical factor in buyer decision-making. Trust plays a crucial role, especially due to high perceived risk and the long-term nature of B2B relationships (Blois, 1999; Ganesan, 1994). A branding strategy includes building consistent messaging, positioning the brand within a competitive landscape and ensuring visibility through advertising (Swani et al., 2020), social media (Swani et al., 2014) and industry events (Brown et al., 2017).

Insights From the B2B Brand Management Literature

- Trust and expertise. Trust is a key driver of brand success in B2B product markets (Mudambi, 2002) and in B2B services (Doney et al., 2007). Building a reputation for expertise and reliability (Leek & Christodoulides, 2012) is essential for entrepreneurs looking to establish themselves in the marketplace. Academic research also emphasizes the importance of social media as a tool for building trust and for developing thought leadership.
- Corporate versus personal branding. A strong corporate brand can build brand equity and enhance the perceived value of a firm's offerings (Bendixen et al., 2004). However, in entrepreneurial ventures, the founder's personal brand often takes precedence, especially in the early stages. Even well-established B2B firms struggle with how visible and vocal the CEO should be. Firms seek the right balance between leveraging the CEO's personal reputation online (Mudambi et al., 2019) and investing in the development of a broader corporate branding strategy. This raises the question of when entrepreneurs should transition from a personal branding focus to a corporate branding strategy. Exploring the strategic timing could provide insights into how entrepreneurs can effectively scale their reputations as their ventures grow.

Insights From the Entrepreneurship Literature

- Leveraging personal networks. Entrepreneurs often rely heavily on personal networks to build initial awareness. Academic studies highlight the use of the entrepreneur's social capital (Adler & Kwon, 2002). Networks are important, both offline and online (Smith et al., 2017), to drive brand growth. However, over-reliance on personal branding can limit scalability, particularly when the entrepreneur becomes synonymous with the brand.
- Adaptability. The entrepreneurial mindset embraces adaptability and new ideas. The integration of thoughts, actions and feelings constitutes the entrepreneurial mindset (Kuratko et al., 2021). Entrepreneurs can creatively experiment to see what resonates best with their target audiences and adjust based on resource availability and market realities. However, too much adjustment can conflict with brand management priorities and strategies for a consistent brand image. Keller and Lehmann (2009) note the 'delicate balancing act between consistency and change' (p. 11) and the difficulties of maintaining brand differentiation.

Questions for Future Research

- How do entrepreneurs effectively balance personal and corporate branding to maximize brand equity in B2B markets? When should entrepreneurs transition from a personal branding focus to a corporate branding strategy?
- What role do personal networks play in the early stages of B2B branding, and how can entrepreneurs leverage personal and professional networks for long-term brand building?

- How can B2B entrepreneurs embrace adaptability and flexibility while maintaining a consistent brand identity?

Long Sales Cycles

Access to capital is a significant barrier to entrepreneurs. B2B sales cycles are typically longer than B2C sales cycles due to the involvement of multiple decision-makers, higher levels of perceived risk, long negotiations and the expectation of customized products and services (Hancock et al., 2005). For B2B entrepreneurs, product complexity makes it harder to tell the investment story. Once initial funding is obtained, some B2B entrepreneurs struggle with the next steps. Entrepreneurs need to continue to build the brand and attract new funding to weather the lag before revenue is received.

Entrepreneurs can become frustrated by the slow pace of revenue generation, especially in the early stages of the venture. Converting leads to sales is a long process in a sales environment based on relationship building, rather than by taking a simpler transactional perspective (Monat, 2011). In the initial stages, building a brand while managing cash flow involves trade-offs. To expand, B2B entrepreneurs must be prepared to invest in relationship-building activities but must also keep expenses low. Long sales cycles make it difficult for entrepreneurs to manage cash flow while building the brand, especially during periods of economic uncertainty. Both brand management and financial management skills are critical. Additional research is needed on how brand management can help mitigate the challenges associated with long sales cycles.

Insights From the B2B Brand Management Literature

- Reducing perceived risk. Strong B2B brands reduce perceived risk by signaling quality and reliability to buyers (Kotler & Pfoertsch, 2006). This is especially important in long sales cycles, where buyers need frequent reassurance that the brand can meet their needs. Brand sensitivity often has a U-shaped relationship with risk, as brand sensitivity is highest when the purchasing situations are either relatively of low risk or of very high risk (Brown et al., 2011b).
- Content marketing. Content marketing is an inbound marketing practice that takes a publishing approach to building trust in the brand through creating content on websites and social media (Holliman & Rowley, 2014). Content marketing can increase trust and potentially shorten the sales cycle (Järvinen & Taiminen, 2016). By becoming content experts, B2B entrepreneurs can enable trust building with prospective buyers before they even enter the sales funnel. This can accelerate the decision process, the lead conversion time and the path to revenue. The effectiveness of the traditional interruptive marketing can decline over long sales cycles, and content marketing has a role to play in sustaining trust (Holliman & Rowley, 2014).

Insights From the Entrepreneurship Literature

- Relationship building. The entrepreneurial mindset is often relationship driven (Adler & Kwon, 2002), which aligns with the long sales cycles of B2B. Entrepreneurs excel at building personal relationships with potential clients, a critical factor in managing long sales. B2B relationships contribute to long-term brand loyalty. The challenge for entrepreneurs is to transfer the loyalty that comes from personal relationships to the brand.
- Resilience. The ability to persist through long sales cycles is a hallmark of entrepreneurship (Bullough & Renko, 2013). Entrepreneurs need to integrate persistence and patience into their strategies. Resilience involves being professionally patient, and entrepreneurial resilience is about bouncing back from setbacks and uncertainty. By developing resilience, firms can sustain operations while waiting for sales leads to convert and after unexpected shocks or downturns. What remains unclear is under what conditions buyers perceive resilience as a valuable B2B brand characteristic.

Questions for Future Research

- How can B2B entrepreneurs use brand-building activities to reduce perceived risk and shorten the sales cycle? How can entrepreneurs transform loyalty from personal relationships into brand loyalty?
- What role does content marketing play in building and sustaining long-term relationships with potential clients during long sales cycles?
- How can B2B entrepreneurs develop brand management strategies in parallel with broader resil-

ience strategies during long sales cycles? Under what conditions do buyers perceive resilience as a valuable B2B brand association?

Customer Acquisition and Retention

Acquiring and retaining new customers is essential for the survival and growth of businesses and is especially challenging for B2B entrepreneurial ventures. The organizational buying process is complex, formalized and highly competitive (Sheth, 1996). Acquisition is more complex in B2B markets, where purchasing decisions are multifaceted and involve long-term commitments. Retention is equally challenging, as customers expect ongoing value from their partnerships.

The strategies for acquisition and retention can be in conflict, similar to the differences of hunting versus farming (Nijssen et al., 2017). There can also be trade-offs regarding product innovation, with an acquisition focus more aligned with radical innovation and a retention focus more aligned with incremental innovation (Arnold et al., 2011). Entrepreneurs can come across as hunters and can be seen as offering radical innovation. That makes it a challenge to build a brand with a strategic balance between acquisition and retention. Retention requires brand loyalty, and B2B entrepreneurs need to demonstrate values over time. Superior customer support, ongoing education about the product or service and consistently delivering on brand promises are the foundation.

The rise of digital technologies and artificial intelligence (AI) presents opportunities and threats. Digital tools can streamline operations and improve customer experiences, and the failure to adopt these technologies can leave entrepreneurs at a competitive disadvantage. However, businesses based on relationships and a customer-centric strategy need to manage tech/touch trade-offs, as they can weaken that personal 'touch' foundation by leaning too much into 'tech' interfaces (Makarem et al., 2009). Increasing reliance on digital tools is a mixed blessing, as it can be difficult for firms to develop brand-building relationships that are essential for customer retention.

Insights From the B2B Brand Management Literature

- Loyalty and long-term value creation. Branding in B2B markets is heavily focused on creating long-term value and fostering customer loyalty (Beverland et al., 2007). B2B firms need to consistently deliver on their promises. To avoid competing solely on price, new entrants need to identify areas where competitors have not always kept their promises and build that into their brand identity. Yet, customers must first be attracted and acquired before loyalty strategies can begin. Entrepreneurs need a brand image that attracts the initial attention that gets them on the buyer's consideration list.
- Customer-centric branding. B2B customers expect solutions tailored to their unique needs. Working together can create value for the customers and the firms. Co-creating value with customers can strengthen brand loyalty (Cova & Salle, 2008). When entrepreneurs involve customers in the development of new products or services, this can foster a sense of co-ownership and long-term commitment. The co-creation of brand value is important for both acquisition and retention strategies. This involves developing a brand within a dynamic service ecosystem (Vargo & Lusch, 2011).

Insights From the Entrepreneurship Literature

- Retention through relationship management. Entrepreneurs excel at building personal relationships with clients, and these relationships can serve as a strong foundation for customer retention. However, as the business scales up, these relationships need to be institutionalized to ensure long-term loyalty. Loyalty requires both attitudinal and behavioral loyalty (Rauyruen & Miller, 2007).
- Agility in customer acquisition. Entrepreneurs are known as good hunters (Nijssen et al., 2017) for their agility in identifying and pursuing new customers. Rapid feedback can help them to refine their offerings based on customer needs. Entrepreneurs are often able to experiment with customer acquisition strategies to find the most effective approach.

Questions for Future Research

- How can B2B entrepreneurs balance brand consistency with the need for customization in customer acquisition and retention strategies?
- What are best practices for using digital technology and AI in customer retention strategies? When does usage of digital tools and AI make it more difficult for firms to develop the brand relationships that are essential for customer retention?

- What role does the entrepreneurial mindset play in developing agile customer acquisition strategies in B2B markets? Which customer acquisition strategies are the most effective for B2B entrepreneurs?

Employee Recruitment and Retention

Recruiting and retaining talented employees is difficult for firms of all sizes, and ideas regarding best practice frequently change. Chief Talent Officer is a title that started to become widespread around the time of the publication of the book, *The War for Talent* (Michaels et al., 2001). Twenty years later, the title of Chief People Officer started to gain popularity (Harrington, 2024). Whatever executive title is used, companies are signaling that they prioritize employee recruitment and retention.

Smaller B2B firms often struggle to compete with larger corporations in attracting and keeping employees due to fewer resources and low brand recognition. It is difficult for them to compete on salary and benefits and on established career paths. For newer B2B ventures, recruitment and retention are critical for scaling up from their initial start. The mission and values of the firm can be an important signal, especially to employees early in their careers. Since entrepreneurial B2B firms have the liability of newness (Yang & Aldrich, 2017), building a strong employer brand is essential, especially one that emphasizes company culture, opportunities for growth and the ability to make a significant impact.

Internal branding helps to ensure that employees are aligned with the company's mission and values. This can be difficult to develop if a firm has a strong founder-focused company culture. Collaboration, team building and empowerment are enabled through internal brand ambassadors and consensus building regarding the brand value of the firm (Schmidt & Baumgarth, 2018).

Insights From the B2B Brand Management Literature

- Employer branding. Employer branding is important in B2B contexts. Companies with reputations as good employers are more likely to attract and retain top talent (e.g., Backhaus & Tikoo, 2004). For entrepreneurs, building a brand that emphasizes culture, innovation and impact can be a powerful tool for recruiting employees. Yet, research has found mixed results regarding the relationship between corporate reputation more generally and employee retention (Schulze & Dada, 2025).
- Internal branding. The brand commitment of employees is essential for building a strong B2B brand (Schmidt & Baumgarth, 2018). Employee retention is often connected to strong internal branding initiatives. Internal branding strategies (Burmann & Zeplin, 2005) can help ensure that employees are aligned with the company's brand values, which, in turn, enhances employee satisfaction and retention. Internal branding can also lead to enhanced financial performance (Iyer et al., 2018).

Insights From the Entrepreneurship Literature

- Vision and leadership. A strategy of standing out through continuous streams of innovative ideas and products can help entrepreneurial ventures to attract and recruit employees (Schulze & Dada, 2025). Entrepreneurs often inspire loyalty in their employees by communicating a compelling vision for the company.
- Employee perspective. Vision-driven leadership can foster a sense of commitment and purpose among employees (Baum et al., 1998), even in the absence of high salaries or traditional benefits. The entrepreneurial mindset often values flexibility and empowerment, which can be attractive to employees looking for more autonomy in their work. Internal branding can also be very empowering, and once started, it can be unstoppable (Causon, 2004).

Questions for Future Research

- How can B2B entrepreneurs use employer branding to attract and retain top talent in a competitive job market?
- What are the best practices for internal branding in B2B firms?
- What explains the inconsistent relationship between corporate reputation and employee retention in B2B firms?

Scalability and Managing Growth

Scaling up and growing a B2B business presents unique challenges, starting with access to capital. There can be difficult trade-offs involving growth, operational efficiency and maintaining high service quality. Managing cash flow, operational bottlenecks and delegation of decision-making can all be problematic. Growth is not inevitable. Research has not satisfactorily answered the questions of how firms grow and why they grow (Wright & Stigliani, 2013).

The role of brand strategies in encouraging and managing growth is also not well established. The relationship between brand orientation and growth may be more positive in developed markets than in emerging markets (Reijonen et al., 2015). Brand consistency becomes more difficult to maintain as the business grows. Entrepreneurs need to develop scalable systems for ensuring that the brand message is communicated clearly across all customer touchpoints. As more employees are added, internal brand communications also become increasingly important.

Insights From the B2B Brand Management Literature

- Brand equity and investor appeal. Investors are attracted by firms with strong brand equity (Aaker, 1991). For B2B entrepreneurs, building strong brand equity can increase their chances of securing investment, as investors are more likely to back companies with a well-defined brand and clear value proposition. Being unconventional in brand building activities, especially when supported with a public relations strategy, can also create positive attention from investors and customers (Bresciani & Eppler, 2010). More generally, for B2B entrepreneurs, positioning the brand as financially stable and growth oriented can enhance its appeal to customers and potential investors.
- Consistency across touchpoints. As businesses scale, maintaining brand consistency across all customer touchpoints becomes more difficult but no less important. A cohesive brand identity helps to ensure consistency as the business grows (Keller, 2013). The form of corporate brand building changes at different stages of small business growth (Juntunen et al., 2010). Entrepreneurs are often skilled at scaling their businesses rapidly, but this can come at the expense of brand consistency across customer touchpoints.
- Scaling customer relationships. One of the key challenges in scaling a B2B venture is maintaining the personal relationships that were critical in the early stages of the business. Customer relationship management (CRM) systems can help entrepreneurs maintain strong relationships with clients as the business grows (Ocker & Mudambi, 2003; Payne & Frow, 2005).

Insights From the Entrepreneurship Literature

- Bootstrapping. Entrepreneurs are often skilled at bootstrapping, the practice of using limited resources to achieve growth. This depends on their ability to garner and utilize their human and social capital (Grichnik et al., 2014), rather than seeking external resources.
- Resourcefulness. Entrepreneurial resourcefulness is about leveraging available resources rather than seeking additional funding for growth. Their resourcefulness can take two main forms, self-reliant behaviors and joint resourcefulness behaviors, and that can have performance implications (Michaelis et al., 2022).

Questions for Future Research

- How can B2B entrepreneurs use brand equity to attract investors and secure capital?
- How can B2B entrepreneurs maintain brand consistency and customer relationships while scaling and growing their businesses?
- What are the best practices regarding bootstrapping and resourcefulness for growing a B2B brand?
- How do entrepreneurs assess the trade-offs between building a brand using bootstrapping and resourcefulness versus using external networks?

Overall, by examining numerous strategic challenges facing B2B entrepreneurs from the perspectives of brand management and entrepreneurship, insights and many new research questions have emerged. There is considerable potential for new B2B branding research in each of the areas of building brand awareness and reputation, long sales cycles, customer acquisition and retention, employee recruitment and retention and scalability and managing growth.

CONCLUSIONS FOR A RESEARCH AGENDA

B2B entrepreneurs face a unique set of challenges regarding brand management. By integrating insights from the academic literature on B2B brand management and the academic literature on entrepreneurship, this chapter has highlighted insights and practical strategies for overcoming challenges and building strong, resilient brands. Future research could pursue the questions emerging from this analysis of the intersection of these two topic areas. As presented in Table 19.4, the research questions that emerged from the gaps in the literature can draw on a range of theories and concepts and be addressed in multiple ways.

Both qualitative and quantitative research methodologies have potential to add to understanding. Qualitative and inductive approaches could include detailed case studies of B2B entrepreneurial ventures that explore how their brand management practices evolved over time and in response to changing market conditions. The case studies could involve in-depth interviews with B2B entrepreneurs regarding how they navigate the challenges of brand management, customer acquisition, employee recruitment and retention and growth. These interviews could also provide a deeper understanding of how the entrepreneurial mindset and entrepreneurial orientation influence brand management decisions.

Future research can also employ quantitative and deductive approaches to examining the many gaps in the B2B research regarding brand equity and business performance. Secondary data could be tapped to track the effectiveness of B2B brand management over time and under specific conditions. Surveys of buyer and seller dyads could examine perceived importance of attributes such as content area expertise and supplier resilience. To better understand employee perspectives, recruiters and job seekers could be asked about their perceived value of employer brand attributes and internal branding practices.

Controlled experiments could test different branding strategies to determine which are the most effective at various stages of business growth and to examine trade-offs. For instance, experiments could examine the roles of personal branding, corporate branding and product branding on customer trust and loyalty. Experiments could also be used to analyze the potential upsides and downsides of incorporating AI into B2B business processes. Choice-based conjoint analysis can be used

Table 19.4 Research agenda for B2B branding and entrepreneurship

Research Topics	*Theory and Literature Foundation*
Brand awareness and reputation	
Balancing personal and corporate branding for entrepreneurs	Personal and corporate branding
Role of personal and professional networks in brand building	Networking theory
Trade-offs between adaptability and brand consistency	Brand consistency
Long sales cycles	
How branding reduces perceived risk and shortens the sales cycle	Brand risk reduction
Role of content marketing in during long sales cycles	Content marketing
Perceived value of resilience as a brand association	Resilience
Customer acquisition and retention	
Best practices for using digital technology and AI in customer acquisition strategies; conditions under which using digital tools and AI hurt brand relationships and customer retention	Business relationships Artificial intelligence (AI)
Role of the entrepreneurial mindset in customer acquisition strategies	Entrepreneurial mindset
Employee recruitment and retention	
How B2B entrepreneurs use employer branding to attract and retain top talent in a competitive job market	Employer branding
Best practices for internal branding in B2B firms	Internal branding
Scalability and managing growth	
How B2B entrepreneurs use brand equity to attract investors and secure capital	Brand equity Investment attraction
How B2B entrepreneurs maintain brand consistency and customer relationships while scaling and growing their businesses	Branding growth strategies
Bootstrapping practices for growing a B2B brand	Bootstrapping
How entrepreneurs perceive trade-offs between bootstrapping versus external networks	Internal versus external brand building

Source: The authors.

to examine the trade-offs customers make across brand attributes (Chitturi & Mudambi, 2018), such as the trade-offs between brand adaptability and brand consistency.

There remains substantial potential for research on how entrepreneurs can effectively scale their businesses, maintain brand consistency and brand differentiation in an increasingly competitive marketplace. Insights are needed on the trade-offs between internally focused brand building strategies and externally focused brand strategies. Insights are also needed on how to navigate digital transformation and AI challenges in the decades ahead. Entrepreneurial strategies and branding strategies often involve weighing contradictory evidence and advice. By embodying principles of brand orientation and entrepreneurial orientation, managers can help B2B brands to remain relevant and valuable to firms, employees and customers.

REFERENCES

Aaker, D. A. (1991). *Managing brand equity*. The Free Press.

Aaker, D. A. (1992). The value of brand equity. *Journal of Business Strategy, 13*(4), 27–32. https://doi.org/10.1108/eb039503

Aaker, D. A. (1996). Measuring brand equity across products and markets. *California Management Review, 38*(3), 102–20. https://doi.org/10.2307/41165845

Adler, P. S., & Kwon, S.-W. (2002). Social capital: Prospects for a new concept. *Academy of Management Review, 27*(1), 17–40. https://doi.org/10.2307/4134367

Arnold, T. J., Fang, E. (Er), & Palmatier, R. W. (2011). The effects of customer acquisition and retention orientations on a firm's radical and incremental innovation performance. *Journal of the Academy of Marketing Science, 39*(2), 234–51. https://doi.org/10.1007/s11747-010-0203-8

Aspara, J., & Tikkanen, H. (2008). Significance of corporate brands for business-to-business companies. *The Marketing Review, 8*(1), 43–60. https://doi.org/10.1362/146934708X290241

Backhaus, K., & Tikoo, S. (2004). Conceptualizing and researching employer branding. *Career Development International, 9*(5), 501–17. https://doi.org/10.1108/13620430410550754

Baron, R. A. (2006). Opportunity recognition as pattern recognition: How entrepreneurs "connect the dots" to identify new business opportunities. *Academy of Management Perspectives, 20*(1), 104–19. https://doi.org/10.5465/amp.2006.19873412

Baum, J. R., Locke, E. A., & Kirkpatrick, S. A. (1998). A longitudinal sudy of the relation of vision and vision communication to venture growth in entrepreneurial firms. *Journal of Applied Psychology, 83*(1), 43. https://doi.org/10.1037/0021-9010.83.1.43

Bendixen, M., Bukasa, K. A., & Abratt, R. (2004). Brand equity in the business-to-business market. *Industrial Marketing Management, 33*(5), 371–80. https://doi.org/10.1016/j.indmarman.2003.10.001

Beverland, M., Napoli, J., & Lindgreen, A. (2007). Industrial global brand leadership: A capabilities view. *Industrial Marketing Management, 36*(8), 1082–93. https://doi.org/10.1016/j.indmarman.2006.08.007

Blois, K. J. (1999). Trust in business to business relationships: An evaluation of its status. *Journal of Management Studies, 36*(2), 197–215. https://doi.org/10.1111/1467-6486.00133

Bone, S. A., Fombelle, P. W., Ray, K. R., & Lemon, K. N. (2015). How customer participation in B2B peer-to-peer problem-solving communities influences the need for traditional customer service. *Journal of Service Research, 18*(1), 23–38. https://doi.org/10.1177/1094670514537710

Bresciani, S., & Eppler, M. J. (2010). Brand new ventures? Insights on start-ups' branding practices. *Journal of Product & Brand Management, 19*(5), 356–66. https://doi.org/10.1108/10610421011068595

Broniarczyk, S. M., & Alba, J. W. (1994). The importance of the brand in brand extension. *Journal of Marketing Research, 31*(2), 214–28. https://doi.org/10.1177/002224379403100206

Brown, B. P., Mohan, M., & Eric Boyd, D. (2017, December). Top management attention to trade shows and firm performance: A relationship marketing perspective. *Journal of Business Research, 81*, 40–50. https://doi.org/10.1016/j.jbusres.2017.07.020

Brown, B. P., Sichtmann, C., & Musante, M. (2011a). A model of product-to-service brand extension success factors in B2B buying contexts. *Journal of Business & Industrial Marketing, 26*(3), 202–10. https://doi.org/10.1108/08858621111115921

Brown, B. P., Zablah, A. R., Bellenger, D. N., & Johnston, W. J. (2011b). When do B2B brands influence the decision making of organizational buyers? An examination of the relationship between purchase risk and brand sensitivity. *International Journal of Research in Marketing, 28*(3), 194–204. https://doi.org/10.1016/j.ijresmar.2011.03.004

Bullough, A., & Renko, M. (2013). Entrepreneurial resilience during challenging times. *Business Horizons, 56*(3), 343–50. https://doi.org/10.1016/j.bushor.2013.01.001

Burmann, C., & Zeplin, S. (2005). Building brand commitment: A behavioural approach to internal brand management. *Journal of Brand Management, 12*(4), 279–300. https://doi.org/10.1057/palgrave.bm.2540223

Bygballe, L. E. (2017). Toward a conceptualization of supplier-switching processes in business relationships. *Journal of Purchasing and Supply Management, 23*(1), 40–53. https://doi.org/10.1016/j.pursup.2016.04.007

Causon, J. (2004). The internal brand: Successful cultural change and employee empowerment. *Journal of Change Management, 4*(4), 297–307. https://doi.org/10.1080/1469701042000259631

Chang, Y., Wang, X., & Arnett, D. B. (2018). Enhancing firm performance: The role of brand orientation in business-to-business marketing. *Industrial Marketing Management, 72*, 17–25. https://doi.org/10.1016/j.indmarman.2018.01.031

Chitturi, P., & Mudambi, S. M. (2018). Building brand value in business markets. In C. Baumgarth (Ed.), *B-to-B Marketnfuhrung: Grundlagen, Konzepte und Best Practices [B-to-B brand management: Fundamentals, concepts, and best practices]* (2nd ed.) (pp. 181–98). Springer. ISBN 978-3-658-05096-2.

Cova, B., & Salle, R. (2008). Marketing solutions in accordance with the SD logic: Co-creating value with customer network actors. *Industrial Marketing Management, 37*(3), 270–7. https://doi.org/10.1016/j.indmarman.2007.07.005

Covin, J. G., & Covin, T. J. (1990). Competitive aggressiveness, environmental context, and small firm performance. *Entrepreneurship Theory and Practice, 14*(4), 35–50. https://doi.org/10.1177/104225879001400406

Cretu, A. E., & Brodie, R. J. (2007). The influence of brand image and company reputation where manufacturers market to small firms: A customer value perspective. *Journal of Industrial Marketing Management, 36*(2), 230–40. https://doi.org/10.1016/j.indmarman.2005.08.013

Doney, P. M., Barry, J. M., & Abratt, R. (2007). Trust determinants and outcomes in global B2B services. *European Journal of Marketing, 41*(9/10), 1096–116. https://doi.org/10.1108/03090560710773363

Erdem, T., & Swait, J. (1998, April). Brand equity as a signaling phenomenon. *Journal of Consumer Psychology, 7*(2), 31–57. https://doi.org/10.1207/s15327663jcp0702_02

Farquhar, P. H. (1989). Managing brand equity. *Marketing Research, 1*(3), 23–33.

Foster, C., Punjaisri, K., & Cheng, R. (2010). Exploring the relationship between corporate, internal and employer branding. *Journal of Product & Brand Management, 19*(6), 401–9. https://doi.org/10.1108/10610421011085712

Ganesan, S. (1994, April). Determinants of long-term orientation in buyer-seller relationships. *Journal of Marketing, 58*, 1–19. https://doi.org/10.1177/002224299405800201

Grichnik, D., Brinckmann, J., Singh, L., & Manigart, S. (2014). Beyond environmental scarcity: Human and social capital as driving forces of bootstrapping activities. *Journal of Business Venturing, 29*(2), 310–26. https://doi.org/10.1016/j.jbusvent.2013.02.006

Hague, P. (2024). *B2B branding: How to build a B2B brand strategy*. Retrieved December 30, 2024, from www.b2binternational.com/publications/b2b-branding/

Hancock, M. Q., John, R. H., & Wojcik, P. J. (2005). Better B2B selling. *McKinsey Quarterly, 38*(3), 15.

Harrington, S. (2024). *Chief people officer: The new power player in the C-suite,* The People Space. Retrieved December 1, 2025, from www.thepeoplespace.com/ideas/articles/chief-people-officer-new-power-player-c-suite

Hohenschwert, L., & Geiger, S. (2015). Interpersonal influence strategies in complex B2B sales and the socio-cognitive construction of relationship value. *Industrial Marketing Management, 49*, 139–50. https://doi.org/10.1016/j.indmarman.2015.05.027

Holliman, G., & Rowley, J. (2014). Business to business digital content marketing: Marketers' perceptions of best practice. *Journal of Research in Interactive Marketing, 8*(4), 269–93. https://doi.org/10.1108/JRIM-02-2014-0013

Inskip, I. (2004). Corporate branding for small to medium-sized businesses: A missed opportunity or an indulgence? *Journal of Brand Management, 11*(5), 358–65. https://doi.org/10.1057/palgrave.bm.2540181

Iyer, P., Davari, A., & Paswan, A. (2018). Determinants of brand performance: The role of internal branding. *Journal of Brand Management, 25*(3), 202–16. https://doi.org/10.1057/s41262-018-0097-1

Järvinen, J., & Taiminen, H. (2016). Harnessing marketing automation for B2B content marketing. *Industrial Marketing Management, 54*, 164–75. https://doi.org/10.1016/j.indmarman.2015.07.002

Juntunen, M., Saraniemi, S., Halttu, M., & Tähtinen, J. (2010). Corporate brand building in different stages of small business growth. *Journal of Brand Management, 18*(2), 115–33. https://doi.org/10.1057/bm.2010.34

Kapferer, J.-N. (2004). *The new strategic brand management: Creating and sustaining brand equity long term* (3rd ed.). Kogan Page.

Keller, K. L. (1993). Conceptualizing, measuring, and managing customer-based brand equity. *Journal of Marketing, 57*(1), 1–22. https://doi.org/10.1177/002224299305700101

Keller, K. L. (2013). *Strategic brand management: Building, measuring, and managing brand equity* (4th ed.). Pearson Education.

Keller, K. L., & Kotler, P. (2016). *Marketing management* (15th ed.). Pearson Education.

Keller, K. L., & Lehmann, D. R. (2009). Assessing long term brand potential. *Journal of Brand Management*, *17*(1), 6–17. https://doi.org/10.1057/bm.2009.11

King, C., & Grace, D. (2008). Internal branding: Exploring the employee's perspective. *Journal of Brand Management*, *15*(5), 358–72. https://doi.org/10.1057/palgrave.bm.2550136

Koporcic, N. (2017). *Developing interactive network branding in business markets: Case studies of SMEs from developed and emerging business Barkets* [Doctoral dissertation]. Abo Akademi University.

Kotler, P., & Pfoertsch, W. (2006). *B2B brand management*. Springer.

Kuratko, D. F., Fisher, G., & Audretsch, D. B. (2021). Unraveling the entrepreneurial mindset. *Small Business Economics*, *57*(4), 1681–91. https://doi.org/10.1007/s11187-020-00372-6

Leek, S., & Christodoulides, G. (2011). A literature review and future agenda for B2B branding: Challenges of branding in a B2B context. *Industrial Marketing Management*, *40*(6), 830–7. https://doi.org/10.1016/j.indmarman.2011.06.006

Leek, S., & Christodoulides, G. (2012). A framework of brand value in B2B markets: The contributing role of functional and emotional components. *Industrial Marketing Management*, *41*(1), 106–14. https://doi.org/10.1016/j.indmarman.2011.11.009

Lindgreen, A., & Wynstra, F. (2005). Value in business markets: What do we know? Where are we going?. *Industrial Marketing Management*, *34*(7), 732–48. https://doi.org/10.1016/j.indmarman.2005.01.001

Littunen, H. (2000). Entrepreneurship and the characteristics of the entrepreneurial personality. *International Journal of Entrepreneurial Behavior and Research*, *6*(6), 295–310. https://doi.org/10.1108/13552550010362741

Liu, Y., Li, K. J., Chen, H. (Allen), & Balachander, S. (2017). The effects of products' aesthetic design on demand and marketing mix effectiveness: The role of segment prototypicality and brand consistency. *Journal of Marketing*, *81*(1), 83–102. https://doi.org/10.1509/jm.15.0315

Lynch, J., & De Chernatony, L. (2004). The power of emotion: Brand communication in business-to-business markets. *Journal of Brand Management*, *11*(5), 403–19. https://doi.org/10.1057/palgrave.bm.2540185

Makarem, S. C., Mudambi, S. M., & Podoshen, J. S. (2009). Satisfaction in technology-enabled service encounters. *Journal of Services Marketing*, *23*(3), 134–144. https://doi.org/10.1108/08876040910955143

Marcati, A., Guido, G., & Peluso, A. M. (2008). The role of SME entrepreneurs' innovativeness and personality in the adoption of innovations. *Research Policy*, *37*(9), 1579–90. https://doi.org/10.1016/j.respol.2008.06.004

McCrimmon, M. (2005). Thought leadership: A radical departure from traditional, positional leadership. *Management Decision*, *43*(7/8), 1064–70. https://doi.org/10.1108/00251740510610062

McMullen, J. S., Plummer, L. A., & Acs, Z. J. (2007). What is an entrepreneurial opportunity? *Small Business Economics*, *28*(4), 273–83. https://doi.org/10.1007/s11187-006-9040-z

Michaelis, T. L., Scheaf, D. J., Carr, J. C., & Pollack, J. M. (2022). An agentic perspective of resourcefulness: Self-reliant and joint resourcefulness behaviors within the entrepreneurship process. *Journal of Business Venturing*, *37*(1), 106083. https://doi.org/10.1016/j.jbusvent.2020.106083

Michaels, E., Handfield-Jones, H., & Axelrod, B. (2001). *The war for talent*. Harvard Business School Press.

Miller, D. (1983). The correlates of entrepreneurship in three types of firms. *Management Science*, *29*(7), 770–91. https://doi.org/10.1287/mnsc.29.7.770

Miller, D. (2015). A downside to the entrepreneurial personality? *Entrepreneurship Theory and Practice*, *39*(1), 1–8. https://doi.org/10.1111/etap.12130

Mitchell, V.-W., & Moutinho, L. (2003). Risk reduction in purchasing organisational professional services. *The Services Industries Journal*, *23*(5), 1–19. https://doi.org/10.1080/02642060308565621

Monat, J. P. (2011). Industrial sales lead conversion modeling. *Marketing Intelligence & Planning*, *29*(2), 178–94. https://doi.org/10.1108/02634501111117610

Mudambi, S. (2002). Branding importance in business-to-business markets: Three buyer clusters. *Industrial Marketing Management*, *31*(6), 525–33. https://doi.org/10.1016/S0019-8501(02)00184-0

Mudambi, S. M., Doyle, P., & Wong, V. (1997). An exploration of branding in industrial markets. *Industrial Marketing Management*, *26*(5), 433–46. https://doi.org/10.1016/S0019-8501(96)00151-4

Mudambi, S. M., Sinha, J. I., & Taylor, D. S. (2019). Why B-to-B CEOs should be more social on social media. *Journal of Business-to-Business Marketing*, *26*(1), 103–5. https://doi.org/10.1080/1051712X.2019.1565144

Netemeyer, R. G., Krishnan, B., Pullig, C., Wang, G., Yagci, M., Dean, D., Ricks, J., & Wirth, F. (2004). Developing and validating measures of facets of customer-based brand equity. *Journal of Business Research*, *57*(2), 209–24. https://doi.org/10.1016/S0148-2963(01)00303-4

Neuhaus, T., Millemann, J. A., & Nijssen, E. (2022). Bridging the gap between B2B and B2C: Thought leadership in industrial marketing: A systematic literature review and propositions. *Industrial Marketing Management*, *106*, 99–111. https://doi.org/10.1016/j.indmarman.2022.08.006

Nijssen, E. J., Guenzi, P., & Van der Borgh, M. (2017). Beyond the retention – acquisition trade-off: Capabilities of ambidextrous sales organizations. *Industrial Marketing Management*, *64*, 1–13. https://doi.org/10.1016/j.indmarman.2017.03.008

Ocker, R., & Mudambi, S. M. (2003, January, 6–9). Assessing the readiness of firms for CRM: A literature review and research model. In *Proceedings of the 2003 Hawaii international conference on systems sciences (HICSS)*.

Park, C. W., Milberg, S., & Lawson, R. (1991). Evaluation of brand extensions: The role of product feature similarity and brand concept consistency. *Journal of Consumer Research*, *18*(2), 185–93. https://doi.org/10.1086/209251

Payne, A. F., & Frow, P. (2005). A strategic framework for customer relationship management. *Journal of Marketing*, *69*(4), 167–76. https://doi.org/10.1509/jmkg.2005.69.4.167

Payne, A. F., Storbacka, K., & Frow, P. (2008). Managing the co-creation of value. *Journal of the Academy of Marketing Science*, *36*(1), 83–96. https://doi.org/10.1007/s11747-007-0070-0

Pepitone, A. (1966). Some conceptual and empirical problems of consistency models. In S. Feldman (Ed.), *Cognitive consistency: Motivational antecedents and behavior consequents* (pp. 257–97). Academic Press.

Randall, T., Ulrich, K., & Reibstein, D. (1998). Brand equity and vertical product line extent. *Marketing Science*, *17*(4), 356–79. https://doi.org/10.1287/mksc.17.4.356

Rauch, A., Wiklund, J., Lumpkin, G. T., & Frese, M. (2009). Entrepreneurial orientation and business performance: An assessment of past research and suggestions for the future. *Entrepreneurship Theory and Practice*, *33*(3), 761–87. https://doi.org/10.1111/j.1540-6520.2009.00308.x

Rauyruen, P., & Miller, K. E. (2007). Relationship quality as a predictor of B2B customer loyalty. *Journal of Business Research*, *60*(1), 21–31. https://doi.org/10.1016/j.jbusres.2005.11.006

Reijonen, H., Hirvonen, S., Nagy, G., Laukkanen, T., & Gabrielsson, M. (2015). The impact of entrepreneurial orientation on B2B branding and business growth in emerging markets. *Industrial Marketing Management*, *51*, 35–46. https://doi.org/10.1016/j.indmarman.2015.04.016

Resnick, S. M., Cheng, R., Simpson, M., & Lourenço, F. (2016). Marketing in SMEs: A '4Ps self-branding model. *International Journal of Entrepreneurial Behavior and Research*, *22*(1), 155–74. https://doi.org/10.1108/IJEBR-07-2014-0139

Rossiter, J. (2014). 'Branding' explained: Defining and measuring brand awareness and brand attitude. *Journal of Brand Management*, *21*(7/8), 533–40. https://doi.org/10.1057/bm.2014.33

Schmidt, H. J., & Baumgarth, C. (2018). Strengthening internal brand equity with brand ambassador programs: Development and testing of a success factor model. *Journal of Brand Management*, *25*(3), 250–65. https://doi.org/10.1057/s41262-018-0101-9

Schulze, A., & Dada, O. (2025). Building strategic human capital resources: The effects of strategic entrepreneurship on employee recruitment and retention. *Journal of Small Business Management*, *63*(1), 388–421. https://doi.org/10.1080/00472778.2024.2322985

Sharma, N., & Patterson, P. G. (1999). The impact of communication effectiveness and service quality on relationship commitment in consumer, professional services. *Journal of Services Marketing*, *13*(2), 151–70. https://doi.org/10.1108/08876049910266059

Sheth, J. N. (1996). Organizational buying behavior: Past performance and future expectations. *Journal of Business & Industrial Marketing*, *11*(3/4), 7–24. https://doi.org/10.1108/08858629610125441

Smith, C., Brock Smith, J., & Shaw, E. (2017). Embracing digital networks: Entrepreneurs' social capital online. *Journal of Business Venturing*, *32*(1), 18–34. https://doi.org/10.1016/j.jbusvent.2016.10.003

Swani, K., Brown, B. P., & Milne, G. R. (2014). Should tweets differ for B2B and B2C? An analysis of fortune 500 companies' twitter communications. *Industrial Marketing Management*, *43*(5), 873–81. https://doi.org/10.1016/j.indmarman.2014.04.012

Swani, K., Brown, B. P., & Mudambi, S. M. (2020, August). The untapped potential of B2B advertising: A literature review and future agenda. *Industrial Marketing Management*, *89*, 581–93. https://doi.org/10.1016/j.indmarman.2019.05.010

Taylor, J., Chitturi, P., & Mudambi, S. (2022). #THOUGHTLEADER: Tradeoffs in social media strategies for B2B CEOs. *Fox Business Review*, *1*(2), 3–7. https://fliphtml5.com/actmp/hhun/basic

Urbano, D., Aparicio, S., & Audretsch, D. (2019). Twenty-five years of research on institutions, entrepreneurship, and economic growth: What has been learned? *Small Business Economics*, *53*(1), 21–49. https://doi.org/10.1007/s11187-018-0038-0

Urde, M. (1999). Brand orientation: A mindset for building brands into strategic resources. *Journal of Marketing Management*, *15*(1-3), 117–33. https://doi.org/10.1362/026725799784870504

Urde, M., Baumgarth, C., & Merrilees, B. (2013). Brand orientation and market orientation – From alternatives to synergy. *Journal of Business Research*, *66*(1), 13–20. https://doi.org/10.1016/j.jbusres.2011.07.018

Vargo, S. L., & Lusch, R. F. (2004). Evolving to a new dominant logic for marketing. *Journal of Marketing*, *68*(1), 1–17. https://doi.org/10.1509/jmkg.68.1.1.24036

Vargo, S. L., & Lusch, R. F. (2011). It's all B2B… and beyond: Toward a systems perspective of the market. *Industrial Marketing Management*, *40*(2), 181–7. https://doi.org/10.1016/j.indmarman.2010.06.026

Vecchio, R. P. (2003). Entrepreneurship and leadership: Common trends and common threads. *Human Resource Management Review*, *13*(2), 303–27. https://doi.org/10.1016/S1053-4822(03)00019-6

Webster, F. E., Jr., & Keller, K. L. (2004). A roadmap for branding in industrial markets. *Journal of Brand Management*, *11*(5), 388–402. https://doi.org/10.1057/palgrave.bm.2540184

Wennekers, S., & Thurik, R. (1999). Linking entrepreneurship and economic growth. *Small Business Economics*, *13*(1), 27–56. https://doi.org/10.1023/A:1008063200484

Wright, M., & Stigliani, I. (2013). Entrepreneurship and growth. *International Small Business Journal*, *31*(1), 3–22. https://doi.org/10.1177/0266242612467359

Yang, T., & Aldrich, H. E. (2017). 'The liability of newness' revisited: Theoretical restatement and empirical testing in emergent organizations. *Social Science Research*, *63*, 36–53. https://doi.org/10.1016/j.ssresearch.2016.09.006

Yoo, B., & Donthu, N. (2001). Developing and validating a multidimensional consumer-based brand equity scale. *Journal of Business Research*, *52*(1), 1–14. https://doi.org/10.1016/S0148-2963(99)00098-3

PART 4

Brand Management Performance

20

Positive Brand-Related Constructs: Antecedents, Outcomes and Moderators

Faheem Gul Gilal, Jian Zhang, Zhiyong Yang, and Shadma Shahid

INTRODUCTION TO POSITIVE BRAND-RELATED CONSTRUCTS

Positive brand-related constructs play a crucial role in shaping consumer perceptions, fostering emotional connections and driving long-term brand success (Amoroso et al., 2021; Kwun & Kang, 2024). This chapter focuses on key constructs such as brand love, brand passion, brand attachment, brand loyalty, brand heroes, brand resurrection movements and brand storytelling. These constructs are unified by their ability to generate emotional, cognitive and behavioral engagement, underscoring their strategic importance in contemporary marketing (Alnawas & Hemsley-Brown, 2018; Ma et al., 2022).

While traditionally labeled as 'positive brand-related constructs,' many of these constructs transcend pure emotional engagement and encompass cognitive and behavioral dimensions. The constructs can be categorized into three primary domains: emotional constructs, cognitive constructs and behavioral constructs (Ahn & Back, 2020; Cheung et al., 2021; Hung & Lu, 2018). Each domain reflects distinct but interrelated aspects of consumer–brand relationships (Chatzi et al., 2024; Kumar, 2020).

Emotional Constructs

Brand love

Brand love embodies a profound emotional attachment between consumers and brands, similar to interpersonal love (Junaid et al., 2019). Carroll and Ahuvia (2006) defined it as the emotional connections formed by happy customers, characterized by intense emotional involvement. Batra et al. (2012) further conceptualized it as a multidimensional construct encompassing cognitions, emotions and behaviors. Studies across contexts – ranging from mobile apps (Hsu, 2023) to luxury products (Hemonnet-Goujot & Valette-Florence, 2022) – highlight its role in driving customer advocacy and loyalty.

The brand love scale, initially developed by Batra et al. (2012), comprises six items. All items are measured using a seven-point scale, and the detailed items are provided in Table 20.1.

Brand passion

Brand passion signifies an intense and enduring emotional bond, transcending mere satisfaction (Albert et al., 2013). Rooted in Vallerand et al. (2003) dual model, it can manifest as harmonious passion (intrinsically motivated) or obsessive

Table 20.1 Scale items of brand love

Scale Dimensions	*Scale Items*
Current self-identity	To what extent do you feel that... • Wearing of [American Eagle Outfitters] says something 'true' and 'deep' about whom you are as a person?
Passionate desire to use	To what extent do you feel yourself... • Desiring to wear [American Eagle] clothing?
Emotional attachment	Please express the extent to which you... • You feel emotionally connected to [American Eagle Outfitters]?
Long-term relationship	Please express the extent to which you... • Believe that you will be wearing [American Eagle Outfitters] for a long time.
Anticipated separation distress	Suppose [American Eagle Outfitters] were to go out of existence, to what extent would you feel... • Anxiety • Apprehension
Attitude valence	Please express your overall feelings and evaluations toward [American Eagle Outfitters]. • 7-point negative-positive • 7-point unfavorable-favorable

passion (externally driven). Passionate consumers advocate for brands, engage in word-of-mouth (WOM) and exhibit strong identity alignment (Gilal et al., 2023; Swimberghe et al., 2014).

The brand passion scale contains 14 items, with two dimensions: harmonious passion and obsessive passion, each comprising seven items (Swimberghe et al., 2014; Vallerand et al., 2003). All items are measured using a five-point scale, and the detailed items are provided in Table 20.2.

Cognitive Constructs

Brand attachment

Grounded in attachment theory (Bowlby, 1969), brand attachment refers to the bond connecting consumers and brands (Park et al., 2010). The construct encompasses affection, passion and connection, all of which contribute to self-brand congruence and prominence in consumers' self-identity (Ahmad & Akbar, 2023).

Table 20.2 Scale items of brand passion

Scale Dimensions	*Scale Items*
Harmonious brand passion	• I cannot imagine my life without being connected to [XYZ Brand]. • Engaging with [XYZ Brand] provides me with a variety of enjoyable and enriching experiences. • Interacting with [XYZ Brand] helps me discover new aspects of its products, which deepens my appreciation for them. • Activities related to [XYZ Brand] allow me to create memorable and fulfilling experiences. • Engaging with [XYZ Brand] reflects qualities I value about myself. • My engagement with [XYZ Brand] fits well with the other aspects of my life, enhancing my overall well-being. • The passion I have for [XYZ Brand] remains a positive part of my life, one that I can manage and control.
Obsessive brand passion	• The desire to engage with [XYZ Brand] is so intense that I feel compelled to follow it constantly • I find it difficult to imagine my life without being deeply involved with [XYZ Brand]. • I feel emotionally dependent on following and engaging with [XYZ Brand]. • I struggle to control my urge to constantly engage with [XYZ Brand]. • My feelings toward [XYZ Brand] sometimes border on obsession, and I can't stop thinking about it. • My emotional state often depends on how much I can interact with [XYZ Brand]. • The urge to follow and engage with [XYZ Brand] is so overwhelming that I find it hard to resist.

The Brand Attachment Scale has evolved over time through contributions from various scholars, enhancing our understanding of the emotional connections that consumers form with brands. Originally developed by Thomson et al. (2005), the scale identified three dimensions of brand attachment, capturing the affection, loyalty and personal connection consumers feel toward brands. This model was later refined by Park et al. (2010), who introduced a more personalized focus on how brands become part of consumers' identities, reducing the scale to two dimensions and four items. Jiménez and Voss (2014) simplified the scale further, emphasizing the emotional intensity of brand attachment through four items, exploring the strength of consumers' emotional ties. Shimul et al. (2019) advanced the scale by incorporating seven items, highlighting the role of brands in helping consumers achieve personal fulfillment and self-expression. The detailed items are provided in Table 20.3.

Brand storytelling

Brand storytelling facilitates cognitive engagement by crafting narratives that convey brand values and identity. These stories emotionally engage consumers, enhance trust and foster shared values (Dias & Cavalheiro, 2022). Mancuso and Stuth (2014) emphasized storytelling's ability to connect and inspire individuals.

To the best of our knowledge, no specific scale currently exists to measure brand storytelling. Therefore, future research could benefit from developing and validating a dedicated brand storytelling scale. Additionally, brand storytelling can be assessed using experimental conditions to further explore its impact.

Behavioral Constructs

Brand loyalty

Brand loyalty represents consumers' consistent preference for and commitment to a brand over time

Table 20.3 Brand attachment scale items

Scale	*Item*
Shimul et al. (2019)	• I am deeply passionate about this luxury brand.
	• I am deeply in love with this luxury brand.
	• When I think of this luxury brand, I feel a sense of joy.
	• I have a deep emotional connection to this luxury brand.
	• I would feel a sense of loss if this luxury brand is no longer available.
	• I feel this luxury brand helps me achieve what I want.
	• I feel a sense of exquisiteness from this luxury brand.
Jiménez and Voss (2014)	• No emotional bond/Strong emotional bond.
	• Not emotionally connected/Emotionally connected.
	• Not linked by feelings/Linked by feelings.
	• No feelings of attachment/Strong feelings of attachment.
Park et al. (2010)	• To what extent is [brand name] part of you and who you are?
	• To what extent do you feel personally connected to [brand name]?
	• To what extent are your thoughts and feelings toward [brand name] automatic and spontaneous?
	• To what extent do your thoughts and feelings toward [brand name] come to your mind naturally and instantly?
Thomson et al. (2005)	• Affectionate
Affection	• Friendly
	• Loved
	• Peaceful
Passion	• Passionate
	• Delighted
	• Captivated
Connection	• Connected
	• Bonded
	• Attached

(Møller Jensen & Hansen, 2006). Oliver (1999) described it as a deeply held commitment involving cognitive, affective and conative stages, ultimately fostering advocacy and repurchase intentions.

The brand loyalty scale, originally developed by Yoo and Donthu (2001), consists of three items. These items are measured using a five-point scale, with responses ranging from *strongly disagree* (1) to *strongly agree* (5). The detailed items are provided in Table 20.4 below.

Brand engagement

Brand engagement encompasses active consumer participation in brand-related activities. Gamification, augmented reality (AR) and social media interactions are critical drivers of engagement, fostering emotional and behavioral loyalty (Lin et al., 2022; McLean & Wilson, 2019).

The brand engagement scale, originally developed by Hollebeek et al. (2014), consists of 10 items. These items are measured using a five-point scale, with responses ranging from *strongly disagree* (1) to *strongly agree* (5). The detailed items are provided in Table 20.5 below.

Brand heroes

Brand heroes are influential advocates who passionately promote brands, often through persuasive WOM (Lin et al., 2023). These individuals create symbolic value and inspire brand communities.

The brand heroes scale, originally developed by Lin et al. (2023), consists of six items. These items are measured using a five-point scale, with responses ranging from *strongly disagree* (1) to *strongly agree* (5). The detailed items are provided in Table 20.6 below.

Brand resurrection movements

These movements involve consumer-driven efforts to revive discontinued brands. Nostalgic attachment and psychological reactance drive such initiatives, often facilitated by social media (Davari et al., 2017; Gilal et al., 2020).

Table 20.4 Brand loyalty scale items

Scale Dimension	*Scale Items of Brand Loyalty*
Brand Loyalty	• I consider myself to be loyal to [XYZ Brand]. • [XYZ Brand] would always be my first choice. • I will not buy other brands if [XYZ Brand] is available at the store.

Table 20.5 Brand engagement scale items

Scale Dimension	*Scale Items*
Brand Engagement	• Using [XYZ Brand/Tourism Site] makes me think about it more. • I frequently think about [XYZ Brand/Tourism Site] when I'm using it. • Using [XYZ Brand/Tourism Site] sparks my interest in learning more about it. • I feel very positive when I use [XYZ Brand/Tourism Site]. • Using [XYZ Brand/Tourism Site] makes me happy. • I feel good whenever I use [XYZ Brand/Tourism Site]. • I feel proud to use [XYZ Brand/Tourism Site]. • I spend more time using [XYZ Brand/Tourism Site] compared to other tourism sites. • Whenever I use tourism sites, I often choose [XYZ Brand/Tourism Site]. • [XYZ Brand/Tourism Site] is one of the most frequently used tourism sites for me.

Table 20.6 Brand heroes scale items

Scale Dimension	*Scale Items*
Brand Heroes	• I am quite persuasive at convincing others how great [XYZ Brand] is. • I want to change how other people think about or understand [XYZ Brand]. • I talk about [XYZ Brand] whenever I find an opportunity to do so. • I tell others about [XYZ Brand] because I am passionate about it. • I deeply appreciate the emotional experiences I've had from using [XYZ Brand]. • When I talk to others about [XYZ Brand], I tend to be excited and emotional.

Table 20.7 Brand resurrection movement scale items

Scale Dimension	*Scale Items*
Brand Resurrection Movement	• I would push retailers to bring [XYZ Brand]back. • I would actively participate in a consumer movement to relaunch [XYZ Brand]. • I would encourage others to join the consumer movement for relaunching [XYZ Brand]. • I would consider donating to the consumer movement aimed at relaunching [XYZ Brand]. • I would consider starting a movement to bring [XYZ Brand] back if no consumer movement exists.

The brand resurrection movement scale, originally developed by Davari et al. (2017), consists of five items. These items are measured using a five-point scale, with responses ranging from *strongly disagree* (1) to *strongly agree* (5). The detailed items are provided in Table 20.7 above.

ANTECEDENTS OF POSITIVE BRAND-RELATED CONSTRUCTS

Positive brand-related constructs, such as brand love, brand passion and brand loyalty, are often driven by various antecedents that span psychological, brand-related and social domains. These antecedents form the foundation for fostering emotional and behavioral engagement with brands. Below, the discussion focuses on key psychological drivers, brand-related factors and social influences, with propositions elaborating on why they hold and are supported by relevant citations (see Figure 20.1 for the conceptual framework).

Psychological Drivers

Self-congruence

We propose that self-congruence positively influences emotional brand constructs such as brand love and brand passion. Self-congruence, the alignment between a consumer's self-concept and a brand's identity (Ahn, 2019; Astakhova et al., 2017), is a foundational antecedent of positive brand-related constructs. This alignment fosters emotional constructs such as brand love and passion by enhancing self-connection. When consumers perceive a brand as reflecting their values, personality or aspirations, they are more likely to form a deeper emotional attachment to the brand. For instance, Malär et al. (2011) found that self-congruence strengthens brand attachment by creating a sense of identity reinforcement and emotional resonance. For example, consumers who view a luxury brand as aligned with their self-image are more likely to experience brand passion and demonstrate long-term loyalty. Similarly, Shimul and Phau (2023) argued that self-congruence acts as a psychological driver for brand loyalty and advocacy by making the consumer–brand relationship feel more personal and meaningful. Therefore, we propose:

Proposition 1: Self-congruence positively influences emotional brand constructs such as brand love and brand passion.

Needs satisfaction

We also propose that needs satisfaction positively impacts consumer engagement with brands. The satisfaction of intrinsic psychological needs – autonomy, competence and relatedness – plays a pivotal role in driving positive brand-related constructs. According to self-determination theory (Ryan & Deci, 2000), fulfilling these intrinsic needs fosters motivation, emotional well-being and deeper engagement. Brands that empower consumers to feel autonomous, competent and socially connected strengthen emotional and behavioral engagement. Escalas and Bettman (2017) highlighted that brands integrated into consumers' narratives often fulfill these intrinsic needs, leading to greater attachment and loyalty. Gilal et al. (2025) further showed that satisfying these needs drives brand passion, as consumers perceive these brands as sources of personal fulfillment. When brands provide consumers with opportunities to express independence (autonomy), achieve mastery (competence) or feel socially connected (relatedness), they foster emotional constructs such as brand passion and behavioral constructs like loyalty. For instance, fitness brands that empower users through customizable training programs and community support meet these intrinsic needs, deepening engagement (Chamorro et al., 2021). Thus, we propose:

Proposition 2: The satisfaction of intrinsic psychological needs (autonomy, competence and relatedness) positively impacts consumer engagement with brands.

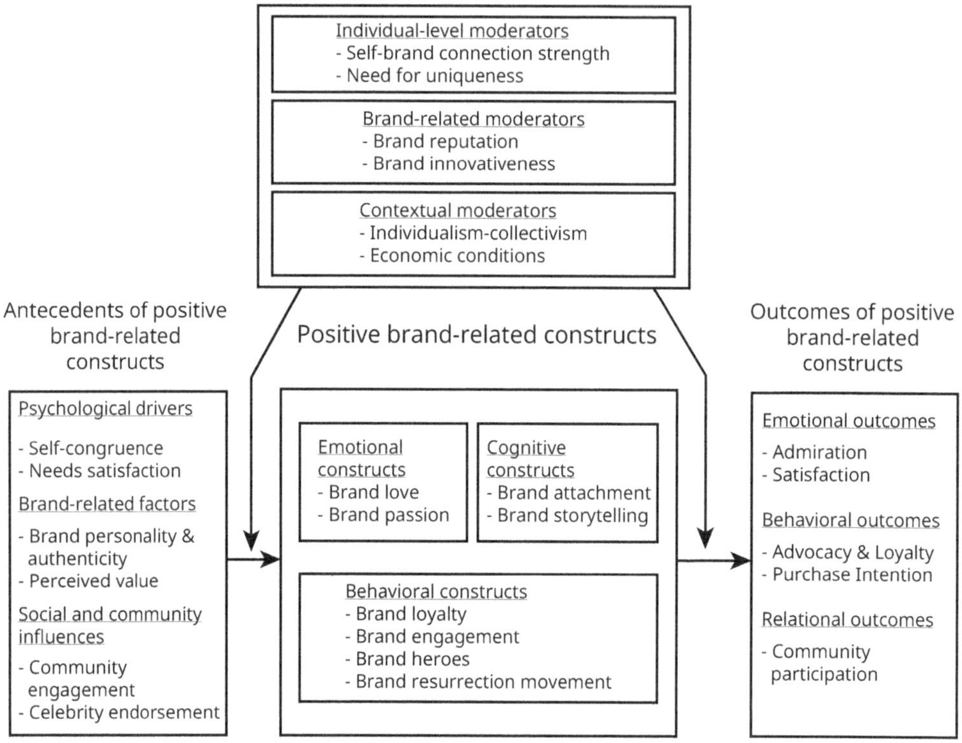

Figure 20.1 Theoretical framework

Source: The authors.

Brand-Related Factors

Brand personality and authenticity

We further propose that brand authenticity and credibility positively affect brand attachment and brand storytelling. Brands perceived as authentic and credible are better positioned to foster emotional bonds and encourage storytelling. Authenticity signals consistency, reliability and alignment with core values, which fosters trust and emotional attachment. According to Morhart et al. (2015), authenticity strengthens brand attachment by creating an emotional connection that feels genuine and meaningful. Heinberg et al. (2021) further emphasized that credibility enhances trust, which serves as the foundation for long-term emotional engagement and loyalty. Consumers are more likely to share meaningful stories about brands they perceive as authentic (Key et al., 2023). For instance, outdoor brands like Patagonia, known for their environmental activism and consistent messaging, inspire consumers to engage in storytelling by sharing their own experiences with the brand's products (Bulmer et al., 2024). Formally, we have:

Proposition 3: Brand authenticity and credibility positively influence brand attachment and brand storytelling.

Perceived value

The perceived value of a brand, encompassing hedonic, utilitarian and symbolic dimensions, is anticipated to significantly drive emotional and behavioral constructs. Hedonic value offers pleasure and enjoyment, utilitarian value ensures practicality and functionality and symbolic value enables self-expression and identity reinforcement (Aleem et al., 2024; Hasan, 2022). Bairrada et al. (2018) found that these dimensions of value collectively enhance the consumer–brand relationship by making interactions more meaningful. For example, a brand that offers both functional utility and symbolic resonance is more likely to foster brand love and loyalty (Esmaeilpour, 2015; Khan et al., 2021). A luxury fashion brand that provides aesthetic pleasure (hedonic value), durable quality (utilitarian value) and status signaling (symbolic value) creates a multidimensional bond with consumers (Loureiro et al., 2020; Ugalde et al., 2023; Yang & Mattila, 2016).

Proposition 4: Perceived value (hedonic, utilitarian and symbolic) positively influences emotional and behavioral constructs such as brand love and loyalty.

Social and Community Influences

Community engagement

Community engagement, both online and offline, is anticipated to foster a sense of belonging that amplifies brand loyalty and advocacy. Brand communities create platforms for shared experiences, allowing consumers to interact and collaborate, which strengthens emotional bonds with the brand (Chang et al., 2020; Coelho et al., 2019). Trivedi and Sama (2021) argued that participation in brand communities fosters a collective identity that deepens loyalty and encourages WOM advocacy. For example, Harley-Davidson's brand community cultivates strong emotional connections by organizing events and fostering social interactions among riders. Consumers who feel a sense of belonging within brand communities are more likely to advocate for the brand (Fazli-Salehi et al., 2024; Huang et al., 2022). For instance, active participation in online forums or in-person events strengthens consumer–brand relationships by fostering a shared identity (Burnasheva et al., 2019; Lee & Hsieh 2022). Taken together, we have:

Proposition 5: Community engagement (online and offline) positively influences brand advocacy and loyalty.

Celebrity endorsements

We anticipate that celebrity endorsements positively affect emotional brand constructs such as brand love and brand passion. Celebrity endorsements link brands with aspirational figures, enhancing their symbolic value and emotional appeal. When consumers admire a celebrity, they transfer these positive emotions to the endorsed brand. For example, Zhou et al. (2020) found that celebrity endorsements foster brand passion by associating the brand with qualities such as prestige, desirability and aspirational goals. In essence, consumers' admiration for a celebrity translates into a deeper emotional connection with the brand. For example, Nike's association with athletes like Serena Williams and Michael Jordan has enhanced the brand's emotional appeal and passion among consumers (Smith et al., 2017; Williams et al., 2022).

Proposition 6: Celebrity endorsements positively influence emotional brand constructs such as brand love and brand passion.

OUTCOMES OF POSITIVE BRAND-RELATED CONSTRUCTS

Positive brand-related constructs, such as brand love, passion and attachment, have significant implications for emotional, behavioral and relational outcomes. These outcomes highlight the value of fostering strong emotional bonds between consumers and brands. Below, the discussion elaborates on key emotional, behavioral and relational outcomes of positive brand-related constructs, with propositions supported by relevant literature.

Emotional Outcomes

A major emotional outcome is brand admiration and satisfaction, which are driven by positive brand-related constructs. Positive emotions associated with brand love, passion and attachment enhance the overall brand experience, creating a sense of fulfillment and joy in interacting with the brand. Wang and Tsai (2017) found that emotional attachment fosters admiration for brands by reinforcing the positive associations that consumers form. Similarly, Schnebelen and Bruhn (2018) argued that these emotions contribute to higher levels of satisfaction, as consumers feel validated in their decision to engage with the brand. In essence, brands that evoke strong positive emotions create lasting impressions and elevate the perceived quality of the interaction. For example, consumers who feel a deep emotional connection to a luxury brand like Chanel report higher satisfaction and admiration due to the brand's ability to align with their self-image and emotional needs.

Proposition 7: Positive brand-related constructs enhance brand admiration and satisfaction by fostering emotional fulfillment and a superior brand experience.

Behavioral Outcomes

Advocacy and loyalty

Brand love, passion and attachment drive advocacy (e.g., positive WOM) and loyalty behaviors, encouraging consumers to repeatedly choose the brand and recommend it to others. Carroll and Ahuvia (2006) demonstrated that brand love is a strong predictor of advocacy, as it motivates consumers to share their positive experiences. Rodrigues and Rodrigues (2019) further highlighted the role of passion in fostering loyalty, as emotionally invested consumers are more likely to stay committed to the brand despite competitive pressures. Indeed, strong emotional bonds with brands lead consumers to actively endorse them to others. For instance, Apple enthusiasts often advocate for the brand, sharing their experiences and persuading others to adopt its products, driven by their emotional connection and loyalty.

Proposition 8: Positive brand-related constructs foster advocacy and loyalty, encouraging repeat purchases and positive WOM.

Purchase intentions

Positive brand-related constructs significantly influence consumers' purchase intentions, including their willingness to pay a premium and prioritize the brand over competitors. Verma (2021) found that emotional attachment and passion for a brand increase consumers' perceived value of its products, leading to stronger purchase intentions. When consumers feel emotionally connected to a brand, they are more likely to pay higher prices, as the emotional benefits outweigh financial considerations. Consistent with our argument, consumers who feel emotionally invested in a brand perceive its products as more desirable and valuable (Malär et al., 2011; Thomson et al., 2005). For example, fans of Tesla are willing to pay a premium for the brand's electric vehicles, driven by their admiration for its innovative and sustainable image.

Proposition 9: Positive brand-related constructs enhance purchase intentions by increasing consumers' willingness to pay a premium and prioritize the brand.

Relational Outcomes

Community participation

Positive brand-related constructs foster active participation in brand communities, where consumers co-create value and strengthen their connection to the brand. These emotional bonds motivate consumers to engage with others who share similar brand affinities, enhancing their sense of belonging and involvement. Takamatsu (2021) highlighted that brand passion and attachment encourage community participation by creating shared experiences and collective identity among consumers. Consumers with strong emotional connections to a brand derive social and emotional value from participating in brand communities (Paruthi et al., 2023; Santos et al., 2022). For example, members of the LEGO Ideas community actively contribute new product designs and engage with other fans, reinforcing their connection to the brand and its values.

Proposition 10: Positive brand-related constructs encourage active community participation, leading to value co-creation and deeper brand relationships.

MODERATORS OF POSITIVE BRAND-RELATED CONSTRUCTS

The impact of antecedents on positive brand-related constructs and their subsequent outcomes is often moderated by various factors. These moderators influence the strength and direction of the relationships within the framework, adding complexity to consumer–brand dynamics. Below, the discussion elaborates on key individual, brand-related and contextual moderators, with propositions and supporting justifications.

Individual-Level Moderators

Self-brand connection strength

The strength of a consumer's self-brand connection moderates the relationship between self-congruence and positive brand-related constructs. Consumers with a stronger self-brand connection are more likely to develop intense emotional bonds such as brand love and passion when their self-concept aligns with the brand's identity. For instance, a consumer with a strong connection to a fitness brand like Nike is more likely to develop brand love when the brand's values align with their self-concept, compared to a consumer with a weaker connection. In the same vein, Malär et al. (2011) found that consumers with high self-brand connection experience amplified emotional responses, as they integrate the brand into their self-concept more deeply. Therefore, we have:

Proposition 11: The strength of self-brand connection moderates the relationship between self-congruence and emotional brand constructs, such that the relationship is stronger for consumers with a higher self-brand connection.

Need for uniqueness

The need for uniqueness moderates the relationship between perceived brand authenticity and emotional constructs like brand attachment. Consumers with a higher need for uniqueness are more likely to form stronger attachments to authentic brands because these brands help them express their individuality. Tian et al. (2001) demonstrated that consumers who value uniqueness are more sensitive to brands that emphasize authenticity and distinctiveness. Unique and authentic brands allow consumers to differentiate themselves, thereby strengthening their attachment. For example, consumers who prioritize individuality are more likely to feel emotionally connected to niche, artisanal brands like Allbirds due to their perceived authenticity. Thus, we propose:

Proposition 12: The need for uniqueness moderates the relationship between perceived brand authenticity and brand attachment, such that the relationship is stronger for consumers with a higher need for uniqueness.

Brand-Related Moderators

Brand reputation

Brand reputation moderates the relationship between community engagement and brand advocacy. Brands with a strong reputation provide a more credible platform for community engagement, amplifying advocacy behaviors. Helm (2011) argued that a positive brand reputation strengthens trust, which enhances consumers' willingness to advocate for the brand. A reputable brand creates a sense of pride and credibility among community members, motivating them to advocate for it (Gordon et al., 2021; Nandy & Sondhi, 2022; Zhou et al., 2023). For example, consumers in Apple's community are more likely to engage in advocacy because of the brand's globally recognized reputation for innovation and quality.

Proposition 13: Brand reputation moderates the relationship between community engagement and brand advocacy, such that the relationship is stronger for brands with a higher reputation.

Brand innovativeness

The strength of the relationship between perceived value and purchase intentions depends on the level of brand innovativeness. When a brand is perceived as highly innovative, consumers are more likely to use its innovativeness as a heuristic cue, reinforcing the weight of perceived value in their purchase decisions (Cheng et al., 2014). In contrast, when a brand is perceived as less innovative, perceived value alone may be less persuasive in driving purchase intentions, as consumers may be more skeptical about the brand's long-term relevance or ability to deliver sustained benefits. For example, Tesla's innovation amplifies the extent to which perceived value translates into actual purchase behavior. Empirical research supports this moderating role, demonstrating that perceived value has a stronger impact on purchase decisions when the brand signals high innovation (Sethi et al., 2001).

Proposition 14: Brand innovativeness moderates the relationship between perceived value and purchase intentions, such that the relationship is stronger for brands perceived as more innovative.

Contextual Moderators

Individualism–collectivism

Individualism–collectivism cultural orientation is anticipated to moderate the relationship between intrinsic need satisfaction (e.g., autonomy, competence and relatedness) and emotional brand constructs. Collectivist cultures emphasize relatedness and community, whereas individualist cultures prioritize autonomy and self-expression. Hofstede (2001) found that cultural differences significantly influence consumer motivations and emotional responses to brands. Cultural values shape the relative importance of intrinsic needs. For example, consumers in collectivist cultures like Japan may form stronger emotional bonds with brands that foster social connection, whereas those in individualist cultures like the USA value brands that support independence. Thus, we predict:

Proposition 15: Cultural orientation moderates the relationship between intrinsic need satisfaction and emotional brand constructs, such that relatedness is more impactful in collectivist cultures, while autonomy is more impactful in individualist cultures.

Economic conditions

Economic conditions moderate the relationship between perceived value and purchase intentions. During economic downturns, consumers place greater emphasis on utilitarian value, prioritizing functional benefits and cost-effectiveness, whereas in stable economic periods, hedonic and symbolic values exert a stronger influence on purchase decisions (Choi & Mela, 2019; Zhou & Hui, 2003). For example, while Costco's affordability and practicality may always offer perceived value, this value becomes a stronger predictor of purchase intentions during recessions. Conversely, in stable economic conditions, the prestige and emotional appeal of premium brands like LVMH play a more dominant role in shaping purchase intentions. Consequently, we have:

Proposition 16: Economic conditions moderate the relationship between perceived value and purchase intentions, such that utilitarian value is a stronger predictor during economic downturns, whereas hedonic and symbolic values are stronger predictors during stable conditions.

FUTURE RESEARCH DIRECTIONS

Future research should focus on empirically validating the proposed framework across diverse contexts to uncover its robustness and generalizability. This includes examining how the framework applies to different types of brands, consumer groups and consumption scenarios, as well as investigating the dynamic interactions among the antecedents, moderators and outcomes. Below are several promising areas for future exploration:

Validation Across Brand Types

One important avenue for future research is to assess how the relationships within the framework vary between luxury and utilitarian brands. Luxury brands, which emphasize hedonic and symbolic value, may generate stronger emotional outcomes such as brand love and passion, whereas utilitarian brands, which focus on functional value, may evoke more behavioral outcomes like loyalty and purchase intentions. For example, research could examine whether self-congruence has a greater impact on emotional attachment for luxury brands compared to utilitarian brands or if perceived value plays a more significant role for functional products like household appliances. Empirical studies could also explore whether the moderating effects of factors such as brand innovativeness or reputation differ based on brand type.

Cultural Differences

The framework's applicability across cultural contexts warrants further investigation. As cultural orientation significantly influences consumer behavior, future research should explore how collectivist versus individualist cultures shape the relationships among the antecedents, moderators and outcomes. For example, intrinsic need satisfaction may operate differently across cultures, with relatedness having a stronger effect in collectivist cultures and autonomy being more impactful in individualist cultures. Studies could also examine how cultural norms influence emotional outcomes, such as the expression of brand love, and behavioral outcomes, like advocacy. Cross-cultural comparisons would enhance the framework's global relevance and provide valuable insights for international marketing strategies.

Digital Versus Physical Brand Presence

With the increasing integration of digital and physical brand interactions, future research should examine how the framework operates in these distinct environments. Brands that primarily exist in digital spaces (e.g., e-commerce platforms or social media-native brands) may elicit different antecedents and outcomes compared to those with a strong physical presence (e.g., retail stores or tangible products). For instance, brand communities in digital environments may rely more heavily on online engagement to foster advocacy, whereas physical brand communities might emphasize in-person interactions. Research could also investigate how brand authenticity and perceived value are evaluated differently in digital versus physical contexts, as well as how these evaluations influence emotional and behavioral constructs.

Longitudinal Studies on Dynamic Interactions

Another critical direction is to explore the temporal dynamics of the framework. The relationships among antecedents, moderators and outcomes are likely to evolve over time as consumers interact with brands. For example, the role of community engagement in fostering brand advocacy may strengthen or weaken depending on the duration and intensity of participation. Longitudinal studies could also examine how positive brand-related constructs such as brand love and attachment develop and change across the customer journey, from initial exposure to long-term loyalty. Additionally, tracking the dynamic influence of moderators, such as economic conditions or brand innovativeness, could provide insights into how external factors shape consumer–brand relationships over time.

Interaction Between Constructs

Future research should investigate interactions among antecedents, moderators and outcomes to uncover synergistic or conflicting effects. For example, how does the interplay between self-congruence and intrinsic need satisfaction affect emotional outcomes like brand admiration? Similarly, how do individual-level moderators, such as self-brand connection, interact with brand-related moderators, like brand reputation, to influence purchase intentions? Studies focusing on these complex interactions would deepen our understanding of the multifaceted nature of consumer–brand relationships.

The Role of Emerging Technologies

Emerging technologies such as artificial intelligence, AR and virtual reality provide new contexts for testing the framework. These technologies create immersive brand experiences that may amplify emotional and behavioral outcomes. For instance, how do self-congruence and perceived value influence consumer attachment to virtual brands or metaverse-based brand interactions? Research could also examine whether digital innovations enhance or diminish the perceived authenticity of a brand and its subsequent outcomes.

Incorporating Negative Constructs

While the current framework focuses on positive brand-related constructs, future research could explore how negative constructs, such as brand avoidance or dissatisfaction, interact with positive ones. For example, under what conditions does dissatisfaction negate the effects of brand love or attachment? Investigating these dualities could provide a more comprehensive view of consumer–brand relationships and help brands mitigate risks while enhancing positive outcomes.

REFERENCES

Ahmad, B., & Akbar, M. I. U. D. (2023). Validating a multidimensional perspective of relationship marketing on brand attachment, customer loyalty and purchase intentions: A serial mediation model. *Journal of Strategic Marketing*, *31*(3), 669–692. https://doi.org/10.1080/0965254X.2021.1969422

Ahn, J. (2019). Cognitive antecedents and affective consequences of customers' self-concept in brand management: A conceptual model. *International Journal of Contemporary Hospitality Management*, *31*(5), 2114–2128. https://doi.org/10.1108/IJCHM-09-2018-0712

Ahn, J., & Back, K. J. (2020). The structural effects of affective and cognitive elaboration in formation of customer–brand relationship. *The Service Industries Journal*, *40*(3–4), 226–242. https://doi.org/10.1080/02642069.2018.1460358

Albert, N., Merunka, D., & Valette-Florence, P. (2013). Brand passion: Antecedents and consequences. *Journal of Business Research*, *66*(7), 904–909. https://doi.org/10.1016/j.jbusres.2011.12.009

Aleem, A., Loureiro, S. M. C., Schivinski, B., & Aguiar, M. (2024). What if utilitarian products are regarded as high-status? The moderate role of iconic and popular as two dimensions of brand coolness. *Journal of Marketing Communications*, *30*(4), 508–528. https://doi.org/10.1080/13527266.2022.2152077

Alnawas, I., & Hemsley-Brown, J. (2018). The differential effect of cognitive and emotional elements of experience quality on the customer-service provider's relationship. *International Journal of Retail & Distribution Management*, *46*(2), 125–147. https://doi.org/10.1108/IJRDM-03-2017-0058

Amoroso, S., Pattuglia, S., & Khan, I. (2021). Do Millennials share similar perceptions of brand experience? A clusterization based on brand experience and other brand-related constructs: The case of Netflix. *Journal of Marketing Analytics*, *9*(1), 33–43. https://doi.org/10.1057/s41270-021-00103-0

Astakhova, M., Swimberghe, K. R., & Wooldridge, B. R. (2017). Actual and ideal-self congruence and dual brand passion. *Journal of Consumer Marketing*, *34*(7), 664–672. https://doi.org/10.1108/JCM-10-2016-1985

Bairrada, C. M., Coelho, F., & Coelho, A. (2018). Antecedents and outcomes of brand love: Utilitarian and symbolic brand qualities. *European Journal of Marketing*, *52*(3/4), 656–682. https://doi.org/10.1108/EJM-02-2016-0081

Batra, R., Ahuvia, A., & Bagozzi, R. P. (2012). Brand love. *Journal of Marketing*, *76*(2), 1–16. https://doi.org/10.1509/jm.09.0339

Bowlby, J. (1969). *Attachment and loss: Attachment* (Vol. *1*). Basic Books.

Bulmer, S., Palakshappa, N., Dodds, S., & Harper, S. (2024). Sustainability, brand authenticity and Instagram messaging. *Journal of Business Research*, *175*(1), 1–13. https://doi.org/10.1016/j.jbusres.2024

Burnasheva, R., Suh, Y. G., & Villalobos-Moron, K. (2019). Sense of community and social identity effect on brand love: Based on the online communities of a luxury fashion brands. *Journal of Global Fashion Marketing*, *10*(1), 50–65. https://doi.org/10.1080/20932685.2018.1558087

Carroll, B. A., & Ahuvia, A. C. (2006). Some antecedents and outcomes of brand love. *Marketing Letters*, *17*(2), 79–89. https://doi.org/10.1007/s11002-006-4219-2

Chamorro, J., Alcaraz, S., Sánchez-Oliva, D., García-Calvo, T., & Torregrossa, M. (2021). Fuelling the passion: Psychological needs and behavioral regulations as antecedents of passion for football. *Journal of Sports Sciences*, *39*(6), 653–662. https://doi.org/10.1080/02640414.2020.1840056

Chang, C. W., Ko, C. H., Huang, H. C., & Wang, S. J. (2020). Brand community identification matters: A dual value-creation routes framework. *Journal of Product & Brand Management*, *29*(3), 289–306. https://doi.org/10.1108/JPBM-02-2018-1747

Chatzi, S., Peitzika, E., & Konsolaki, G. (2024). Enhancing brand loyalty: A relationship marketing perspective within the context of contractual services. *Journal of Relationship Marketing*, *23*(4), 272–304. https://doi.org/10.1080/15332667.2024.2306019

Cheng, C. C., Yang, C. L., & Sheu, C. (2014). The link between eco-innovation and business performance: A Taiwanese industry context. *Journal of Cleaner Production*, *64*, 81–90. https://doi.org/10.1016/j.jclepro.2013.09.050

Cheung, M. L., Pires, G. D., Rosenberger, P. J., Leung, W. K., & Sharipudin, M. N. S. (2021). The role of consumer-consumer interaction and consumer-brand interaction in driving consumer-brand engagement and behavioral intentions. *Journal of Retailing and Consumer Services*, *61*, 1–20. https://doi.org/10.1016/j.jretconser.2021.102574

Choi, H., & Mela, C. F. (2019). Monetizing online marketplaces. *Marketing Science*, *38*(6), 948–972. https://doi.org/10.1287/mksc.2019.1197

Coelho, A., Bairrada, C., & Peres, F. (2019). Brand communities' relational outcomes, through brand love. *Journal of Product & Brand Management*, *28*(2), 154–165. https://doi.org/10.1108/JPBM-09-2017-1593

Davari, A., Iyer, P., & Guzmán, F. (2017). Determinants of brand resurrection movements: Why consumers want dead brands back? *European Journal of Marketing*, *51*(11/12), 1896–1917. https://doi.org/10.1108/EJM-02-2016-0096

Dias, P., & Cavalheiro, R. (2022). The role of storytelling in the creation of brand love: The PANDORA case. *Journal of Brand Management*, *29*(1), 58–71. https://doi.org/10.1057/s41262-021-00254-6

Escalas, J. E., & Bettman, J. R. (2017). Connecting with celebrities: How consumers appropriate celebrity meanings for a sense of belonging. *Journal of Advertising*, *46*(2), 297–308. https://doi.org/10.1080/00913367.2016.1274925

Esmaeilpour, F. (2015). The role of functional and symbolic brand associations on brand loyalty: A study on luxury brands. *Journal of Fashion Marketing and Management*, *19*(4), 467–484. https://doi.org/10.1108/JFMM-02-2015-0011

Fazli-Salehi, R., Torres, I. M., Madadi, R., & Zúñiga, MÁ. (2024). Multicultural advertising: Impact of consumers' need to belong and brand use on self-brand connection and communal-brand connection. *Journal of Marketing Communications*, *30*(1), 74–101. https://doi.org/10.1080/13527266.2022.2099953

Gilal, F. G., Paul, J., Thomas, A., Zarantonello, L., & Gilal, R. G. (2023). Brand passion: A systematic review and future research agenda. *Journal of Brand Management*, *30*(6), 490–515. https://doi.org/10.1057/s41262-023-00324-x

Gilal, F. G., Zhang, J., Arijo, S. H., Gilal, R. G., & Chen, C. (2025). Psychological needs, brand attachment, and passion for themed-restaurant brands: A generational perspective. *Journal of Retailing and Consumer Services*, *83*(1), 41–55. https://doi.org/10.1016/j.jretconser.2024

Gilal, N. G., Gilal, F. G., Zhang, J., Gilal, R. G., Gong, Z., & Gilal, W. G. (2020). The role of endorsers in bringing defunct brands back to life: Theory and evidence. *Journal of Product & Brand Management*, *30*(5), 671–690. https://doi.org/10.1108/JPBM-03-2019-2315

Gordon, B. S., Yoshida, M., Nakazawa, M., & Bass, J. (2021). The role of pride feelings in the team and fan community identification processes: An empirical examination in professional sport. *Corporate Reputation Review*, *24*(2), 76–94. https://doi.org/10.1057/s41299-019-00092-y

Hasan, A. A. T. (2022). Technology attachment, e-Attitude, perceived value, and behavioral intentions towards Uber-ridesharing services: The role of hedonic, utilitarian, epistemic, and symbolic value. *Journal of Contemporary Marketing Science*, *5*(3), 239–265. https://doi.org/10.1108/JCMARS-01-2022-0002

Heinberg, M., Liu, Y., Huang, X., & Eisingerich, A. B. (2021). A bad job of doing good: Does corporate transparency on a country and company level moderate corporate social responsibility effectiveness? *Journal of International Marketing*, *29*(2), 45–61. https://doi.org/10.1177/1069031X20981870

Helm, S. (2011). Employees' awareness of their impact on corporate reputation. *Journal of Business Research*, *64*(7), 657–663. https://doi.org/10.1016/j.jbusres.2010.09.001

Hemonnet-Goujot, A., & Valette-Florence, P. (2022). "All you need is love" from product design value perception to luxury brand love: An integrated framework. *Journal of Business Research*, *139*(1), 1463–1475. https://doi.org/10.1016/j.jbusres.2021.10.066

Hofstede, G. (2001). Culture's consequences: Comparing values, behaviors, institutions, and organizations across nations. In *International educational and professional*. Sage Publications.

Hollebeek, L. D., Glynn, M. S., & Brodie, R. J. (2014). Consumer brand engagement in social media: Conceptualization, scale development and validation. *Journal of Interactive Marketing*, *28*(2), 149–165. https://doi.org/10.1016/j.intmar.2013.12.002

Hsu, C. L. (2023). Enhancing brand love, customer engagement, brand experience, and repurchase intention: Focusing on the role of gamification in mobile apps. *Decision Support Systems*, *174*(1), 1–12. https://doi.org/10.1016/j.dss.2023

Huang, T. K., Wang, Y. T., & Lin, K. Y. (2022). Enhancing brand loyalty through online brand communities: The role of community benefits. *Journal of Product & Brand Management*, *31*(5), 823–838. https://doi.org/10.1108/JPBM-08-2020-3027

Hung, H. Y., & Lu, H. T. (2018). The rosy side and the blue side of emotional brand attachment. *Journal of Consumer Behaviour*, *17*(3), 302–312. https://doi.org/doi:10.1002/cb.1712

Jiménez, F. R., & Voss, K. E. (2014). An alternative approach to the measurement of emotional attachment. *Psychology & Marketing*, *31*(5), 360–370. https://doi.org/10.1002/mar.20700

Junaid, M., Hussain, K., & Hou, F. (2019). Addressing the dichotomy of brand love. *International Journal of Market Research*, *61*(6), 577–580. https://doi.org/10.1177/1470785319853468

Key, T. M., Keel, A. L., Czaplewski, A. J., & Olson, E. M. (2023). Brand activism change agents: Strategic storytelling for impact and authenticity. *Journal of Strategic Marketing*, *31*(7), 1339–1355. https://doi.org/10.1080/0965254X.2021.1904435

Khan, M. A., Zulqarnain, M., Bhatti, Z. A., & Raza, A. (2021). Higher-order utilitarian and symbolic antecedents of brand love and consumers' behavioral consequences for smartphones. *Journal of Relationship Marketing*, *20*(3), 177–203. https://doi.org/10.1080/15332667.2020.1756026

Kumar, V. (2020). Building customer-brand relationships through customer brand engagement. *Journal of Promotion Management*, *26*(7), 986–1012. https://doi.org/10.1080/10496491.2020.1746466

Kwun, D., & Kang, J. (2024). Consequences of consumer-brand relationships: Review of ten major constructs. *Consumer Brand Relationships in Tourism: An International Perspective*, *72*, 37–61. https://doi.org/10.1007/978-3-031-59535-6_3

Lee, C. T., & Hsieh, S. H. (2022). Can social media-based brand communities build brand relationships? Examining the effect of community engagement on brand love. *Behaviour & Information Technology*, *41*(6), 1270–1285. https://doi.org/10.1080/0144929X.2021.1872704

Lin, C. W., Chien, C. Y., Ou Yang, C. P., & Mao, T. Y. (2022). Encouraging sustainable consumption through gamification in a branded app: A study on consumers' behavioral perspective. *Sustainability*, *15*(1), 589–603. https://doi.org/10.3390/su15010589

Lin, Y. T., Foscht, T., & Eisingerich, A. B. (2023). A time for heroes? Conceptualization, development and validation of the brand hero scale. *European Journal of Marketing*, *57*(13), 1–26. https://doi.org/10.1108/EJM-09-2021-0700

Loureiro, S. M. C., Jiménez-Barreto, J., & Romero, J. (2020). Enhancing brand coolness through perceived luxury values: Insight from luxury fashion brands. *Journal of Retailing and Consumer Services*, *57*, 10–22. https://doi.org/10.1016/j.jretconser.2020.102211

Ma, L., Ou, W., & Lee, C. S. (2022). Investigating consumers' cognitive, emotional, and behavioral engagement in social media brand pages: A natural language processing approach. *Electronic Commerce Research and Applications*, *54*, 1–11. https://doi.org/10.1016/j.elerap.2022.101179

Malär, L., Krohmer, H., Hoyer, W. D., & Nyffenegger, B. (2011). Emotional brand attachment and brand personality: The relative importance of the actual and the ideal self. *Journal of Marketing*, *75*(4), 35–52. https://doi.org/10.1509/jmkg.75.4.35

Mancuso, J., & Stuth, K. (2014). Storytelling and marketing: The perfect pairing? *Marketing Insights*, *26*(3), 3–8.

McLean, G., & Wilson, A. (2019). Shopping in the digital world: Examining customer engagement through augmented reality mobile applications. *Computers in Human Behavior*, *101*, 210–224. https://doi.org/10.1016/j.chb.2019.07.002

Møller Jensen, J., & Hansen, T. (2006). An empirical examination of brand loyalty. *Journal of Product & Brand Management*, *15*(7), 442–449. https://doi.org/10.1108/10610420610712829

Morhart, F., Malär, L., Guèvremont, A., Girardin, F., & Grohmann, B. (2015). Brand authenticity: An integrative framework and measurement scale. *Journal of Consumer Psychology*, *25*(2), 200–218. https://doi.org/10.1016/j.jcps.2014.11.006

Nandy, S., & Sondhi, N. (2022). Brand pride in consumer–brand relationships: Towards a conceptual framework. *Global Business Review*, *23*(5), 1098–1117. https://doi.org/10.1177/0972150919878072

Oliver, R. L. (1999). Whence consumer loyalty? *Journal of Marketing*, *63*(I1), 33–44. https://doi.org/10.1177/00222429990634s105

Park, C. W., MacInnis, D. J., Priester, J., Eisingerich, A. B., & Iacobucci, D. (2010). Brand attachment and brand attitude strength: Conceptual and empirical differentiation of two critical brand equity drivers. *Journal of Marketing*, *74*(6), 1–17. https://doi.org/10.1509/jmkg.74.6.1

Paruthi, M., Kaur, H., Islam, J. U., Rasool, A., & Thomas, G. (2023). Engaging consumers via online brand communities to achieve brand love and positive recommendations. *Spanish Journal of Marketing-ESIC*, *27*(2), 138–157. https://doi.org/10.1108/SJME-07-2022-0160

Rodrigues, C., & Rodrigues, P. (2019). Brand love matters to millennials: The relevance of mystery, sensuality and intimacy to neo-luxury brands. *Journal of Product & Brand Management*, *28*(7), 830–848. https://doi.org/10.1108/JPBM-04-2018-1842

Ryan, R. M., & Deci, E. L. (2000). Intrinsic and extrinsic motivations: Classic definitions and new directions. *Contemporary Educational Psychology*, *25*(1), 54–67. https://doi.org/10.1006/ceps.1999.1020

Santos, Z. R., Coelho, P. S., & Rita, P. (2022). Fostering consumer–brand relationships through social media brand communities. *Journal of Marketing Communications*, *28*(7), 768–798. https://doi.org/10.1080/13527266.2021.1950199

Schnebelen, S., & Bruhn, M. (2018). An appraisal framework of the determinants and consequences of brand happiness. *Psychology & Marketing*, *35*(2), 101–119. https://doi.org/10.1002/mar.21073

Sethi, R., Smith, D. C., & Park, C. W. (2001). Cross-functional product development teams, creativity, and the innovativeness of new consumer products. *Journal of Marketing Research*, *38*(1), 73–85. https://doi.org/10.1509/jmkr.38.1.73.18833

Shimul, A. S., & Phau, I. (2023). The role of brand self-congruence, brand love and brand attachment on brand advocacy: A serial mediation model. *Marketing Intelligence & Planning*, *41*(5), 649–666. https://doi.org/10.1108/MIP-10-2022-0443

Shimul, A. S., Phau, I., & Lwin, M. (2019). Conceptualising luxury brand attachment: Scale development and validation. *Journal of Brand Management*, *26*(6), 675–690. https://doi.org/10.1057/s41262-019-00158-6

Smith, A. C., Stavros, C., & Westberg, K. (2017). *Brand fans: Lessons from the world's greatest sporting brands*. Springer.

Swimberghe, K. R., Astakhova, M., & Wooldridge, B. R. (2014). A new dualistic approach to brand passion: Harmonious and obsessive. *Journal of Business Research*, *67*(12), 2657–2665. https://doi.org/10.1016/j.jbusres.2014.04.003

Takamatsu, S. (2021). The effect of sport team reputation on team attachment and community attachment: A comparison of fans, local residents, and sponsors. *Sport Management Review*, *24*(4), 620–641. https://doi.org/10.1080/14413523.2021.1879557

Thomson, M., MacInnis, D. J., & Whan Park, C. (2005). The ties that bind: Measuring the strength of consumers' emotional attachments to brands. *Journal of Consumer Psychology*, *15*(1), 77–91. https://doi.org/10.1207/s15327663jcp1501_10

Tian, K. T., Bearden, W. O., & Hunter, G. L. (2001). Consumers' need for uniqueness: Scale development and validation. *Journal of Consumer Research*, *28*(1), 50–66. https://doi.org/10.1086/321947

Trivedi, J., & Sama, R. (2021). Determinants of consumer loyalty towards celebrity-owned restaurants: The mediating role of brand love. *Journal of Consumer Behaviour*, *20*(3), 748–761. https://doi.org/10.1002/cb.1903

Ugalde, C., Vila-Lopez, N., & Kuster-Boluda, I. (2023). Brand attachment toward functional, symbolic and hedonic brands. *Journal of Fashion Marketing and Management: An International Journal*, *27*(3), 470–488. https://doi.org/10.1108/JFMM-09-2021-0228

Vallerand, R. J., Blanchard, C., Mageau, G. A., Koestner, R., Ratelle, C., Léonard, M., Gagné, M., & Marsolais, J. (2003). Les passions de l'ame: On obsessive and harmonious passion. *Journal of Personality and Social Psychology*, *85*(4), 756–767. https://doi.org/10.1037/0022-3514.85.4.756

Verma, P. (2021). The effect of brand engagement and brand love upon overall brand equity and purchase intention: A moderated–mediated model. *Journal of Promotion Management*, *27*(1), 103–132. https://doi.org/10.1080/10496491.2020.1809591

Wang, Y. C., & Tsai, C. T. S. (2017). Feeling better when buying more? Harmonious passion and obsessive passion in online food group buying. *British Food Journal*, *119*(6), 1263–1275. https://doi.org/10.1108/BFJ-07-2016-0309

Williams, A. S., Pedersen, Z. P., & Brummett, K. J. (2022). Legacy branding: The posthumous utilization and management of athlete brands. *International Journal of Sport Communication*, *15*(2), 85–92. https://doi.org/10.1123/ijsc.2021-0114

Yang, W., & Mattila, A. S. (2016). Why do we buy luxury experiences? Measuring value perceptions of luxury hospitality services. *International Journal of Contemporary Hospitality Management*, *28*(9), 1848–1867. https://doi.org/10.1108/IJCHM-11-2014-0579

Yoo, B., & Donthu, N. (2001). Developing and validating a multidimensional consumer-based brand equity scale. *Journal of Business Research*, *52*(1), 1–14. https://doi.org/10.1016/S0148-2963(99)00098-3

Zhou, F., Mou, J., Su, Q., & Wu, Y. C. J. (2020). How does consumers' perception of sports stars' personal brand promote consumers' brand love? A mediation model of global brand equity. *Journal of Retailing and Consumer Services*, *54*, 1–10. https://doi.org/10.1016/j.jretconser.2019

Zhou, L., & Hui, M. K. (2003). Symbolic value of foreign products in the People's Republic of China. *Journal of International Marketing*, *11*(2), 36–58. https://doi.org/10.1509/jimk.11.2.36.20163

Zhou, Z., Wang, Y., Zheng, Y., & Liu, S. (2023). Effects of brand community social responsibility: Roles of collective self-esteem and altruism. *Journal of Brand Management*, *30*(4), 347–366. https://doi.org/10.1057/s41262-022-00306-5

21

Negative Emotions Towards Brands: Theoretical Perspectives, Measurement and Future Research

Daniela Andreini and Lia Zarantonello

INTRODUCTION

Consumers' negative emotions towards brands have traditionally received less attention in the literature compared to positive emotions (Grappi et al., 2019). Historically, research has concentrated on understanding and leveraging the positive emotions that consumers develop for brands. However, in the past two decades, there has been a growing interest in exploring negative emotions (Khatoon & Rehman, 2021). Researchers have recognised the significant impact that not only positive emotions, but also negative emotions, can have on consumer behaviour. This is particularly relevant in today's hyper-connected, social-media-driven world, where consumers can share their negative experiences with brands instantly, amplifying the impact of these emotions and potentially causing severe consequences for the brands involved. Recent examples include Italian fashion influencer Chiara Ferragni, who faced public backlash and triggered anger from her followers due to allegations of fraud and her highly publicised divorce, which resulted in a loss of brand partnerships and followers (Il Messaggero, 2024). Similarly, H&M faced disappointment and betrayal from consumers after being accused of misleading sustainability claims, leading to a shift in consumer preference towards more ethically transparent brands (Ferris et al., 2023).

The present chapter aims to examine negative emotions in the brand management literature by highlighting how they have been defined and measured, the theoretical perspectives used in their investigation and the frameworks associated with them. The objective is to review key contributions in the field and offer a research agenda that may inspire future studies.

TYPES OF NEGATIVE EMOTIONS TOWARDS BRANDS

Different types of negative emotions have been examined in relation to brands. These include both primary (e.g., fear) and complex (e.g., brand hate) emotions; emotions that are felt individually by consumers (e.g., disgust) and others that assume the real or imaginary presence of other consumers and are influenced by social dynamics (e.g., brand embarrassment); emotions that arise within the context of a consumer–brand relationship (e.g., brand jealousy) and those that do not require such a relationship (e.g., brand dislike). These emotions are reviewed in the following and summarised in Table 21.1.

Table 21.1 Summary of key negative emotions towards brands

	Type of Emotion	*Assumes the Presence of Other Consumers*	*Assumes a Consumer–Brand Relationship*	*Psychometric Scale/Examples of Measurement Items it if Scale Not Available*
Anticipated separation distress	Complex emotion which includes feelings of anxiety, worry, fear and apprehension (Bagozzi et al., 2017; Batra et al., 2012)	No	Yes	• Two-item dimension from brand love prototype scale (Bagozzi et al., 2017) scale • Four-item dimension from short brand love prototype scale (Batra et al., 2012)
Brand dislike	Primary emotion (Dalli et al., 2007)	No	No	• Three-item dimension from NEB scale (Romani et al., 2012)
Brand embarrassment	Complex emotion which includes social anxiety, shame, guilt and regret (Grant & Walsh, 2009)	Yes	Yes	• Nine-item unidimensional scale (Walsh et al., 2016)
Brand hate	Complex emotion; defined as anger, contempt, disgust, fear, disappointment, shame and dehumanisation (Zarantonello et al., 2016); disgust, anger/fear and contempt (Romani et al., 2015); anger, sadness and fear (Zhang & Laroche, 2020); feelings of aversion and resentment (Akrout & Mrad, 2023); disgust, contempt and anger (Fetscherin, 2019)	No	No	• 18-item multidimensional scale and 4-item 'overall brand hate' scale (Zarantonello et al., 2016) • Nine-item multidimensional scale (Zhang & Laroche, 2020) • Seven-item cross-cultural, multidimensional scale (Akrout & Mrad, 2023)
Brand jealousy	Complex emotion (Sarkar & Sreejesh, 2014; Bıçakcıoğlu et al., 2017).	Yes	Yes	• Three-item unidimensional scale (Sarkar & Sreejesh, 2014)
Brand-related schadenfreude	Complex emotion (Sundie et al., 2009)	Yes	No	• Scale not available; varying type and number of items, e.g., 4 items from Sundie et al. (2009)
Negative brand nostalgic emotions	Complex emotion (Ford et al., 2018)	No	Yes	• Six-item dimension from cross-cultural brand nostalgia scale (Ford et al., 2018)
Other negative emotions: discontent, distress, feelings of rejection, frustration, rage	• Rage: primary emotion • Discontent, distress, feelings of rejection, frustration: complex emotions; Khatoon & Rehman, 2021; Romani et al., 2012)	No	No	• Discontent: Three-item dimension from NEB scale (Romani et al., 2012) • Frustration and rage: six 9-point semantic differential scales • Distress and feelings of rejection: scale not available (varying number/type of items; see Khatoon & Rehman, 2021)

Source: The authors.

Anticipated Separation Distress

Consumers who are in a positive relationship with a brand may still experience negative emotions. According to the brand love prototype framework, consumers may experience anticipated separation distress, a complex emotion encompassing feelings of anxiety, worry, fear and apprehension (Bagozzi et al., 2017; Batra et al., 2012).

Anticipated separation distress may arise when consumers foresee or experience distancing from a beloved brand and the potential loss of access to it. This might originate from concerns regarding the brand's future viability (e.g., distress over the possibility that a brand may go out of business or become financially unstable), the potential discontinuation of the brand (e.g., distress over the discontinuation of a favourite product line), or the brand's efficacy in fulfilling the consumer's needs and expectations (e.g., distress over the brand's products or services no longer meeting their evolving needs and desires) (Batra et al., 2012).

The psychometric scale to measure anticipated separation distress is part of the brand love prototype construct and includes two items ('practical', short scale; see Bagozzi et al., 2017) or four items (full scale: Batra et al., 2012).

Brand Dislike

Brand dislike is conceptualised as a temporary, negative emotional reaction to a brand (Dalli et al., 2007; Romani et al., 2012). This definition of emotional brand dislike differs from dispositional brand dislike, which refers to the negative attitudes consumers develop towards brands over time. Dispositional brand dislike can influence emotional brand dislike, making consumers more likely to momentarily dislike a brand if they already dislike its broader category.

Brand dislike can occur at different levels: at the product brand level, when consumers are dissatisfied with product characteristics; at the user brand level, when they associate the brand with an unfavourable stereotype; and at the corporate brand level, when they perceive the company as immoral or unfair (Dalli et al., 2006). Brand dislike is linked to negative outcomes such as complaints, negative word-of-mouth and brand switching (Romani et al., 2012). However, it does not always lead to abandonment or reduced consumption, as consumers may continue their relationship with the brand due to factors such as a lack of better alternatives, lower costs or inertia (Demirbag-Kaplan et al., 2015).

Brand dislike is measured through three items that form a dimension of the negative emotions towards the brand construct (Romani et al., 2012).

Brand Embarrassment

Brand embarrassment is a form of social anxiety that arises when a consumer's public identity is threatened (Grant & Walsh, 2009; Sarkar & Sarkar, 2017). It involves not only anxiety but also other negative emotions, including shame, guilt and regret (Krishna et al., 2019). It can arise when consumers feel awkward or uncomfortable when using a brand, whether in social situations with real observers or in private settings where judgment is imagined; this embarrassment can be experienced in anticipation, during or after the brand encounter (Grant & Walsh, 2009).

Brand embarrassment is influenced by personal self-factors and brand relationships (Grant & Walsh, 2009). Personal factors include perceived threats related to social class, status, self-perception, identity and traits such as self-confidence and personality. For example, a consumer may feel embarrassed if a brand has a poor country of origin, negative publicity, counterfeit associations, low prestige or an intergenerational gap in brand perception (Sarkar & Sarkar, 2017). A consumer's relationship with a brand also shapes brand embarrassment, affecting how consumers perceive and engage with it and determining whether they embrace, maintain or distance themselves from it (Grant & Walsh, 2009).

Brand embarrassment can lead to various outcomes, including a tendency to conform, brand consciousness, frugality, material values, reduced buying intention and reduced consumer–brand identification (Walsh et al., 2016). It can also result in social isolation, decreased intention to consume the brand publicly (Sarkar & Sarkar, 2017), and changes in brand conspicuousness (Song et al., 2017). Brand embarrassment can act as a mediator for brand hate (Sarkar et al., 2020).

Brand embarrassment is measured using a nine-item brand embarrassment scale, which can assess both the tendency of consumers to feel embarrassed by brands in general and the degree to which a consumer feels embarrassed by a specific brand (Walsh et al., 2016).

Brand Hate

Brand hate is viewed as a multidimensional concept in the literature, although conceptualisations of unidimensional brand hate are also present (Yadav & Chakrabarti, 2022). While the majority of scholars agree that brand hate can be seen as a 'constellation of negative emotions' (Zarantonello et al., 2016), there is no agreement on the specific emotions included. This constellation may include anger, contempt, disgust, fear, disappointment, shame and dehumanisation (Zarantonello et al., 2016); disgust, anger/fear and contempt (Romani et al., 2015); anger, sadness and fear (Zhang & Laroche, 2020); feelings of aversion and resentment (Akrout & Mrad, 2023); disgust, contempt and anger (Fetscherin, 2019). These multiple conceptualisations of brand hate are reflected in the various psychometric scales developed to measure this negative emotion, which contain a varied number of dimensions and items, covering the different negative emotions identified in the literature

(Akrout & Mrad, 2023; Zarantonello et al., 2016; Zhang & Laroche, 2020).

Brand hate can arise from negative past experiences with the brand, symbolic incongruity and ideological incompatibility (Hegner et al., 2017). It does not necessarily require the presence of an existing consumer–brand relationship: consumers may develop hate towards brands they dislike or those that promote a value system different from their own, without ever purchasing or using them (Zarantonello et al., 2018). Brand hate can thus develop within the context of a consumer–brand relationship, as part of an evolution of consumer feelings towards a brand over time, as well as outside of any consumer–brand relationship, in cases where consumers have never purchased from the brand and do not intend to buy from it in the future.

Brand hate is associated with various consumer outcomes, including behavioural outcomes on both the individual level (e.g., patronage reduction) and the group level (e.g., anti-brand communities), as well as cognitive (non-repurchase intention) and physiological responses (e.g., gut-wrenching) (Aziz & Rahman, 2022). Some of these outcomes are passive responses (e.g., avoiding the brand), whereas others are active, involving direct active anti-brand behaviours consumers engage in (e.g., brand revenge) (Aziz & Rahman, 2022; Zarantonello et al., 2016).

Brand Jealousy

Brand jealousy, or 'romantic brand jealousy', refers to the emotional reaction consumers experience when they feel excluded or unable to access a brand or its offerings, often because they perceive that others have a closer or more privileged relationship with the brand (Sarkar & Sreejesh, 2014). This emotion typically arises in relation to brands with which consumers have a strong, positive attachment, particularly when they are unable to access a product or experience that others can. This can happen with limited-edition products, exclusive releases or regional availability (Sarkar & Sreejesh, 2014).

Brand jealousy can act as mediator in brand love and hate relationships (Saini et al., 2023; Siddique & Rajput, 2022) and can lead to a variety of outcomes. These include positive outcomes such as increased brand attachment (Rana et al., 2021), active engagement (Sarkar & Sreejesh, 2014), purchase intention (Sarkar & Sreejesh, 2014 and willingness to pay a premium price (Bıçakcıoğlu et al., 2017; Rana et al., 2021). Negative outcomes of brand jealousy include brand switching or rejection (Saini et al., 2023), negative word of mouth (WOM) (Sarkar & Sreejesh, 2014) and brand addiction (Ghorbanzadeh, 2024).

Brand jealousy is measured through a three-item scale (Sarkar & Sreejesh, 2014).

Brand-Related Schadenfreude

Schadenfreude is a German word that refers to the pleasure derived from the suffering of others (van de Ven et al., 2011). In the context of branding, schadenfreude can refer to a consumer's enjoyment or satisfaction in observing the misfortune of: (1) another consumer in their relationship with a brand (e.g., a consumer might feel gratified if a luxury car they spot on the road suddenly breaks down in a cloud of smoke) (Sundie et al., 2009); (2) a consumer associated with a rival brand (e.g., Apple fans might feel schadenfreude when a competitor's phone gets negative reviews or major flaws) (Jansen & Schröder, 2021; Phillips-Melancon & Dalakas, 2014) or (3) a brand itself, its representatives or the company behind it (e.g., consumers might feel schadenfreude when a brand faces backlash over a controversial ad, influencer or CEO associated with the brand) (Dijk et al., 2006). Although schadenfreude is a form of joy, it is typically considered a negative emotion because it results from hostility and envy towards other consumers and their brands, reflecting a lack of empathy and a desire for social comparison or superiority (Sundie et al., 2009).

Brand schadenfreude is influenced by personal factors such as consumers' need for uniqueness (Shimul et al., 2021), narcissism and jealousy (Manna, 2024). It can lead to positive outcomes for one's preferred brand, including increased brand commitment, affect and purchase intention (Hayes & Carr, 2020), as well as negative outcomes for the brand that is the target of schadenfreude (Marticotte & Arcand, 2017).

No psychometric scale has been developed to measure brand *schadenfreude* yet, although there are items that have been validated in the measurement of this feeling (e.g., Sundie et al., 2009).

Negative Brand Nostalgic Emotions

Brand nostalgia can be viewed as an ambivalent emotion (Kessous et al., 2015). Although it evokes positive emotions that consumers associate with a brand they once used, brand nostalgia can also trigger negative emotions linked to past experiences with the brand (Ford et al., 2018). These may include unpleasant times from one's past, difficult moments in life, painful childhood memories, challenging times with family or feelings of sadness associated with the past (Ford et al., 2018).

Similar to how positive nostalgic emotions towards a brand can offer advantages to both consumers and the brand (Weingarten & Wei, 2023), negative nostalgic emotions can adversely impact the consumer–brand relationship, leading to negative outcomes such as decreased brand attachment, lower brand trust, a weakened self-brand connection, reduced self-congruence and diminished intentions to recommend or purchase the brand (Ford et al., 2018).

Negative nostalgic emotions towards brands are assessed as a dimension within the cross-cultural brand nostalgia scale (Ford et al., 2018).

Other Negative Brand Emotions

In addition to the key emotions mentioned above, which are central to the literature, brand management scholars also examine other negative emotions that consumers experience in relation to brands. These include discontent (Romani et al., 2012), frustration and rage, as well as distress and feelings of rejection (Khatoon & Rehman, 2021). Although some of these emotions are underexplored (Khatoon & Rehman, 2021), the impact of others on consumer behaviours has been examined: discontent results in brand switching (Romani et al., 2012); frustration and rage lead to negative word-of-mouth, brand switching, online and offline complaining, brand avoidance and revenge.

The measurement of these emotions varies. Discontent is included in the negative emotions towards brands scale (Romani et al., 2012). Frustration and rage are assessed using six items each, measuring intensity, duration, control, activity, physical effort and mental effort as part of an evaluation of negative consumer emotions towards brands. Finally, distress and feelings of rejection are measured using various sets of items that have been validated in the literature (Khatoon & Rehman, 2021).

THEORETICAL PERSPECTIVES ON NEGATIVE EMOTIONS TOWARDS BRANDS

Theoretical perspectives on negative emotions towards brands are essential for understanding adverse consumer behaviours such as brand switching, negative WOM and organised consumer boycotts. Since the 50s, it has been noted that consumers' behaviour is influenced not only by functional product features, but also by the feelings, emotions and meanings that consumers associate with selected products (Levy, 1959). This also applies to brands, which are considered symbols socially constructed by all stakeholders (Hatch & Schultz, 2010; Iglesias et al., 2013). Stakeholders may experience cognitive, self-expressive and emotional benefits when connecting with a brand (Aaker, 1996; de Chernatony et al., 2006). Consequently, brand value is built through rational arguments, tangible manifestations and its impact at the emotional level of feelings (Iglesias & Bonet, 2012).

Cognitive-affective theories suggest that consumers' emotional responses are dependent on their cognitive appraisals of brand-related stimuli. Consumer animosity, including emotions like anger and fear, is shaped by cognitive assessments of international disputes, leading to behaviours such as product avoidance and negative WOM. This highlights the importance of understanding cognitive processes that precede emotional reactions towards brands.

Even without direct interactions with brands, consumers can develop negative feelings towards them due to various factors. Individual taste preferences may result in dislike or aversion towards certain brands (Bryson et al., 2013). These negative emotions do not necessarily require consumption or purchase and can arise from ideological differences or perceived societal impacts (Romani et al., 2012; Zarantonello et al., 2018).

From an attachment theory perspective, the emotional investment consumers place in these relationships mirrors the dynamics of interpersonal bonds. Consequently, when brands fail to meet expectations, deviate from perceived 'personalities', or violate implicit relational contracts, consumers experience a spectrum of negative emotions, ranging from mild disappointment to profound betrayal (Fournier & Alvarez, 2013).

Finally, negative brand emotions often arise in social contexts when consumers perceive social evaluation while expressing their social identity (Miller, 1996) or when brand images conflict with the self-image in the eyes of others (Sarkar et al., 2020). Combining the social contexts and the related social theoretical approaches allows to enrich the theoretical frameworks able to capture the dynamics of the negative brand emotions.

The previous section outlines how consumers' negative emotions towards brands have been conceptualised in four different theoretical contexts, summarised in Table 21.2. This is based on whether consumers' negative emotions towards brands assume the presence of a relationship with the brand and/or the presence of other consumers. Accordingly, we have categorised the studies of

Table 21.2 Theoretical grid on negative emotions towards brands

		Assumes Consumer–Brand Relationship	
		No	*Yes*
Assumes the presence of other consumers	No	Appraisal theories	Consumer–brand attachment
	Yes	Social influence theory	Social identity theory

Source: The authors.

negative emotions towards brands into four quadrants: the first quadrant includes studies that used appraisal theory; the second quadrant includes studies based on consumer–brand attachment theories; the third quadrant gathers studies related to social influence theory; and the fourth quadrant includes studies grounded on social identity theory.

The First Quadrant

The first quadrant includes negative emotions that consumers experience in the absence of a relationship with the brand and/or with other consumers. These negative or hateful emotions towards brands can arise in cases involving differences in taste preferences, associations formed with the brand and its users or corporate behaviours and practices that are not accepted by consumers, which do not necessarily require the consumption or purchase of the brand (Bryson et al., 2013; Zarantonello et al., 2018). People interpret or appraise situations along a variety of different dimensions, and according to cognitive appraisal theories of emotion, the specific manner in which people appraise their situations characterises the specific emotions they feel. Cognitive appraisal theories propose that emotional responses are determined by an individual's evaluation of a situation, which involves assessing its significance for their personal well-being.

Appraisal theories suggest that emotions are not just reactions to events but are influenced by how individuals interpret those events. For example, the same event can be perceived differently by different people, leading to different emotional outcomes. This process of interpretation is known as appraisal. Various components of appraisal include the relevance of the event to personal goals, the congruence with one's values and beliefs, and the ability to cope with the consequences of the event (Smith & Ellsworth, 1985).

Consumers can reassess their initial evaluation of a situation, leading to a change in how they perceive and regulate their emotions. Therefore, it is not the specific situation itself that generates particular emotions, but rather the individual's subjective appraisal of the situation that results in emotional responses (Yeo & Ong, 2024).

Brand avoidance can be viewed through the lens of appraisal theories. When consumers encounter a brand, they appraise it based on their personal values, past experiences and social identity (Bryson et al., 2013; Zarantonello et al., 2018). The negative appraisals can arise from unmet expectations, symbolic incongruence with one's identity or ideological conflicts with the brand's values, resulting in experiential, identity and moral brand avoidance, respectively (Lee et al., 2009a).

The Second Quadrant

The second quadrant of research on consumer negative emotions builds upon the foundational understanding that consumers form emotional bonds with brands, akin to interpersonal attachments. While Susan Fournier's (1998) work initially framed these bonds as 'relationships', a more nuanced perspective can be gained by applying the principles of attachment theory. This approach emphasises the emotional security and dependency consumers develop towards brands, viewing brands as attachment figures that provide comfort, stability and a sense of belonging.

From an attachment perspective, the strength and quality of consumer–brand bonds are determined by the perceived availability and responsiveness of the brand, mirroring the dynamics of caregiver–infant attachments. Research has explored various attachment-related constructs within the consumer-–brand context, including attachment itself (Park et al., 2010), which examines the emotional connection and dependence consumers feel towards brands. Other relevant constructs such as trust (Delgado-Ballester & Munuera-Alemán, 2001) and identification (Bhattacharya & Sen, 2003) can be interpreted as indicators of a secure attachment, where consumers feel safe and aligned with the brand's values.

However, attachment theory also highlights the vulnerability inherent in these emotional bonds. When brands fail to meet consumers' attachment needs or exhibit behaviours that undermine perceived security, negative emotions arise. The comprehensive taxonomies of negative emotions provided in the literature (Khatoon & Rehman, 2021) are particularly relevant in this context, as they illustrate how specific negative emotions such as anger, sadness and disgust can arise from attachment-related anxieties, including perceived abandonment, unresponsiveness or betrayal (Khatoon & Rehman, 2021).

The attachment framework also acknowledges the potential for anxiety, worry, fear and apprehension within consumer–brand attachments, particularly in cases of brand love (Batra et al., 2012). These emotions reflect the consumer's concern about losing the brand or experiencing disruptions in the attachment bond. The consumer's ability to recover from attachment ruptures depends on factors related to the brand's responsiveness and the consumer's attachment style (Fournier, 1998; Grégoire et al., 2009; Thomson et al., 2012). Furthermore, past attachment experiences with a brand can evoke nostalgia (Ford et al., 2018), which, while often positive, can also include negative emotions tied to loss or change.

By applying attachment theory, we gain a more profound understanding of the emotional dynamics that drive consumer–brand interactions. This perspective highlights the importance of brands fostering secure attachments by providing consistent, reliable and responsive experiences, thereby minimising the risk of negative emotions and cultivating enduring consumer loyalty.

The Third Quadrant

The third quadrant encompasses consumers' negative emotions towards brands developed by individuals but generated and influenced by social groups (e.g., communities, cultural contexts, territories) even in the absence of consumers' direct relationship with brands. Negative brand emotions are frequently embedded within sociocultural contexts, wherein social evaluation and perceived conflicts between brand image and self-image play significant roles.

Utilising social influence refers to human responses guided by the dominant group's social behaviour. Research in the domain of social appraisal has found humans typically conform to the dominant view in a social setting (Cialdini & Goldstein, 2004) and identify with certain social groups or act to be identified as a part of a majority. The fear of possibly being branded as an outlier is the main motivation for people to adapt their views to conform to social norms. The influence of social identity and self-presentation shapes emotional responses (Miller, 1996; Sarkar et al., 2020). Thus, the negative emotions towards brands that can develop within a group and can be related to brand embarrassment and brand jealousy integrate psychological phenomena, such as existential phenomenology, with social identity theories (Haidt, 2003; Miller, 1996).

The Fourth Quadrant

The fourth quadrant represents the consumers' negative emotions towards brands that assume both the presence of a relationship with the brand and the social dimension with other consumers. Social identity theory posits that people define themselves in terms of the groups they belong to (Abrams & Hogg, 1988). In the brand hate literature, social identity theory has been used to explain how consumers legitimise their actions through community participation against brands perceived as misbehaving (Dessart et al., 2020). From the perspective of social identity theory, brand communities may express their dissatisfaction with a brand by rejecting it or disidentifying from it (Khalifa & Shukla, 2017) within a group, sharing negative WOM (Hegner et al., 2017; Romani et al., 2012; Ullrich & Brunner, 2015), participate in brand boycotts (Klein et al., 2004), or align with other consumers who hold unfavourable views of a brand.

Moreover, social influence theory plays a significant role. Humans tend to conform to the dominant views prevailing in a social setting, primarily to avoid being branded as outliers (Cialdini & Goldstein, 2004). This conformity can result in negative emotions towards brands, especially when the brand contradicts the group's values. Research has demonstrated that social groups can foster brand embarrassment and brand jealousy, integrating psychological phenomena like existential phenomenology with social identity theories (Haidt, 2003; Miller, 1996). Social influence can amplify these emotions, leading to collective actions against the brand, such as organised protests or online campaigns (Haidt, 2003; Sarkar et al., 2020). Understanding these dynamics is crucial for brands to navigate and manage consumer perceptions effectively.

THEORETICAL FRAMEWORKS AND RESEARCH AGENDA

Negative emotions often arise from various antecedents and lead to diverse outcomes, affecting both consumers and brands. Theoretical frameworks explaining negative emotions towards brands discussed in the previous section are here detailed and used to address future research.

Appraisal Theories and Cognitive Perspectives

Understanding appraisal theories provides insight into why consumers may develop negative emotions towards brands, emphasising the role of personal interpretation and the dynamic nature of emotional responses. Negative appraisals can lead to negative emotions and subsequent brand avoidance behaviours.

These theories state that individuals appraise stimuli which lead to the development of emotions. These appraisals define the emotions that are developed. The process of negative emotions and subsequent behaviours begins when consumers encounter brand-related stimuli that conflict with the consumers' value system. These stimuli can be both consumer-related (product/service failure) and brand-related (company's actions) (Kähr et al., 2016).

Brand-related stimuli pertain to the company's perceived values that lead to appraisal in the form of emotions such as hate, frustration and outrage, which further lead to anti-brand activities. Also, appraisal defines brand-directed emotions that occur both at the situational and brand levels and take into account brand-related aspects (Bruhn & Schnebelen, 2017).

Congruence between consumers' values/goals and the stimulus defines the valence of emotions (Bruhn & Schnebelen, 2017) and any incongruity results in the development of negative emotions. This is consistent with existing brand hate literature, which considers incongruity, be it symbolic (e.g., Rodrigues et al., 2021), functional or image (e.g., Zarantonello et al., 2018) incongruity, as leading to brand hate. Therefore, any incongruence between perceived brand personality and consumers' values and personal goals should lead to hate, and the appraisal theory-based model can help delineate how such incongruence-based negative cognitions and appraisals of brand-related stimuli lead to anti-brand behaviour. Brand hate literature, for instance, has extensively highlighted how corporates' immoral (e.g., Kähr et al., 2016) and inability to perform their CSR.

Disidentification theory explains how consumers protect their self-concept by distancing themselves from brands that conflict with their image and values (Lee et al., 2009b). This theory shows that identity avoidance leads to brand hate when consumers feel that a brand's ideology does not align with their beliefs (Rodrigues et al., 2021), resulting in a loss of identity and subsequent brand disidentification (Odoom et al., 2019).

The Big Five personality traits can moderate the relationship between brand personality and negative emotions like brand hate (Yadav, 2024). Traits such as extraversion, conscientiousness and neuroticism significantly influence behavioural outcomes like negative WOM intensity, boycott and sabotage.

The disidentification theory and the Big Five personality traits could lead future research to explore how generative artificial intelligence can detect, anticipate and moderate consumers' disidentification signals from brands and how chatbots can influence consumers' emotions through highly personalised brand experience. personality traits. Technologies like AI, VR and AR are applied to allow consumer access to new imaginative realities (e.g., Scholz & Smith, 2016). These immersive technologies, and the contexts they create, enable consumers to fantasise more and increase their feeling of engagement, and to develop new and untapped personalised scenarios reducing the dissonances between single consumers and their brands (Mangiò et al., 2022). How the agentic role of AI can be perceived by consumers over time? How congruent can AI be perceived by consumers?

Consumer–Brand Attachment

Research, increasingly informed by attachment theory, posits that consumer–brand bonds are fundamental in shaping meaning and self-identity (Park et al., 2010). Attachment theory's focus on emotional security and dependence offers a more nuanced perspective of the emotional connection consumers form with brands, viewing them as attachment figures that provide stability and comfort, and thus loyalty (Thomson et al., 2005).

This approach supports two key branches of studies. The first examines the classification of negative emotions arising from disruptions in these attachment bonds and their subsequent effects (Alvarez et al., 2023; Khatoon & Rehman, 2021). The second investigates the Attachment-Aversion continuum, specifically exploring how secure attachments can evolve into negative aversions when attachment needs are unmet (Fournier & Alvarez, 2013; Park et al., 2013). This continuum reflects the dynamic nature of consumer–brand attachments, influenced by perceived security and responsiveness.

Consistent with these studies, research has focused on how attachments can transform into negative emotions when consumers feel betrayed or cheated by brands (Jain & Sharma, 2019), experience company failures (Grégoire & Fisher, 2008) or undergo a 'divorce' from a brand (Batista Ferraz & Dallabrida, 2024). Brand transgression, defined as an 'act of violation of the implicit or explicit rules guiding consumer–brand relationship performance and evaluation' (Aaker et al., 2004, p. 2), is a primary antecedent of negative emotions rooted in this attachment-based understanding of consumer–brand interactions.

Corporate wrongdoing, including financial scandals and unethical practices, serves as a well-studied trigger for negative consumer emotions, such as anger, distrust and disappointment, significantly damaging brand reputation and loyalty

(Rodrigues & Borges, 2020). However, brand hate often stems not solely from the transgression itself, but from the brand's inability to manage consumer anxieties related to attachment insecurity, such as perceived abandonment or lack of responsiveness (Kucuk, 2010). A lack of meaningful engagement or deficient communication can exacerbate these negative emotions, as consumers feel undervalued or ignored, escalating to brand hate (Hashim & Kasana, 2019).

Future research should investigate how brands can incorporate consumers' individual attachment styles, such as anxiety and avoidance, to better predict anti-brand reactions beyond the main effects of other negative emotions (Japutra et al., 2018). This includes understanding how these styles influence consumer responses to corporate wrongdoing and how brands can mitigate feelings of threats to consumers' self-image and loss of attachment benefits.

Finally, understanding self-relevance, or how personally meaningful a brand is in fulfilling psychological, utilitarian, hedonic, social, symbolic or spiritual objectives, is crucial for comprehending the development of negative emotions. Brands with high self-relevance align with consumers' current needs and life projects, making attachment ruptures particularly distressing. In these cases, retaliatory behaviours can occur even without overt incidents. Future research should examine how specific emotions, particularly those related to self-esteem (e.g., pride, inspiration), influence the stability of attachment bonds over time (Park & MacInnis, 2018). Specifically, how do emotions affect the duration of brand attachments with high versus low self-relevance? Moreover, how do negative emotions evolve over time, and what strategies can brands employ to repair attachment ruptures?

Social Influence Theory

Socially constructed meanings and identities between brands and consumers revolve around a shared sense of identity and meaning within groups. The symbolic nature of consumption means that brands help establish consumers' sense of identity, status and self-esteem, also in communitarian contexts (Strizhakova et al., 2008).

Reference or peer groups play crucial roles in the socialised adoption and consumption of brands (Sirgy, 1982). Consumers construct self-concepts partially by imagining and experiencing how peers react to their consumption choices (Markus & Kunda, 1986). A shared emotional connection arises from the attitudes and actions of others, and the need for overt or tacit approval often leads consumers to consider the risks associated with purchasing or consuming particular branded products or services (Chaudhuri, 1997).

The importance of a brand to a group's identity directly correlates with the strength of normative peer influence on individual group members (Bagozzi & Dholakia, 2006; Strizhakova et al., 2008). Social appraisal and evaluations of likely consequences, therefore, play pivotal roles in defining brand acceptance or rejection. This framework underscores the significance of cognitive and social theories in studying consumers' negative emotions towards brands (Khatoon & Rehman, 2021).

When consumers perceive a threat to their social identity, especially if they have low collective self-esteem, they are likely to exhibit negative emotions towards brands associated with the threatened identity aspect. Accordingly, brand embarrassment is understood through approaches combining self-conscious emotions (Haidt, 2003) and desired social identity (Miller, 1996). Consumers' jealousy towards a brand can be explained by self-presentation and social exclusion theories (Sarkar & Sreejesh, 2014). These negative emotions highlight the intricate relationship between self-concept, social identity and brand perception.

As it concerns the outcomes, the intensity of electronic WOM (eWOM) is an immediate coping response to brand hate. Rather than the aggregate view of negative reviews, it has been found that it is the intensity of negatively valanced influencing behaviour that affects others' attitudes and behaviours, causing serious concern for marketers (Azer & Alexander, 2020; Bulut & Karabulut, 2018).

Considering that the expectation theory assumes that customers gather cognitive data regarding what to expect from a product or a brand through advertisements, various promotion channels, and, in our case, through other consumers' experiences (Oliver, 1977), future research could mix theories of expectation with social influence theories to understand how consumers' review-writing behaviours in the eWOM domain affect other consumers feelings, even without a direct experience with the brands (Ahmad & Guzmán, 2021).

In particular, it could be interesting to investigate which social groups have the most influence on consumers in developing negative emotions towards brands, and how dissociation from negative reference groups influences other consumers' brand avoidance (Charmley et al., 2013). Social comparison theory, which states that individuals evaluate themselves in comparison to others (Festinger, 1954), suggests that individuals not only compare themselves to alternative options, but also to the individuals who chose those alternatives.

Social Identity Theory

From these theoretical standpoints, consumers act not independently but as part of collectives (Hollenbeck & Zinkhan, 2006). Anti-brand communities comprise individuals who possess negative sentiments towards a brand and voluntarily form alliances to voice their discontent. Participation in brand communities is motivated by consumers' desire to connect with others sharing similar brand interests, engage in interactions and gain social validation as members of the group (Algesheimer et al., 2005; Veloutsou & Moutinho, 2009). Similarly, membership in groups expressing strong aversion to a brand enables consumers to cultivate a sense of belonging (Osuna-Ramirez et al., 2019). It can manifest as brand avoidance through boycotting and protests as a form to communicate consumer opposition to globalisation or capitalism. It can also occur as a means for consumers to communicate their misidentification or disidentification with a brand's meanings.

Brand retaliation is operationalised in the literature into three components: complaining to third parties, obsessing with negative internal ruminations about the brand, and engaging in payback behaviours designed to harm the brand intentionally (Thomson et al., 2012). Results suggest that self-relevance may motivate retaliation, even in the absence of a critical incident, illuminating previously unexplored mechanisms, including self-conscious emotional reactions, that motivate consumer hostility and retaliation (Johnson et al., 2011).

The rise of online firestorms (Delgado-Ballester et al., 2021) exemplifies the amplification of negative emotions through digital social networks. However, the use of harmful chatbots, the rise of fake news and misinformation can ignite consumers' negative emotions can lead to consumer activism, where individuals actively work to damage a brand image. This can include participation in anti-brand communities, where consumers collectively express their negative sentiments and organise campaigns against the brand (Brandão & Popoli, 2022) and the willingness to punish (Romani et al., 2012; Sweetin et al., 2013).

Anti-brand communities exist based on the social relationships among individuals who dislike a brand. Future researchers can utilise interdependence theory to explain how individuals join anti-brand communities to express their dissatisfaction with a brand. Interdependence theory suggests that individuals' behaviours are influenced by their interactions with others (Johnson & Johnson, 2005). Researchers can apply this theory to understand the dynamics within anti-brand communities.

Consumers participate in community activities for various reasons, including seeking social approval and support from others (Dessart et al., 2020; Marticotte et al., 2016; Sarkar et al., 2020). In addition to feelings, emotions, and social influence, shared rituals and traditions can impact consumer involvement in a brand community. Members may share brand-related information through these rituals and traditions. The shared practices within anti-brand communities can be examined using practice theory, as they affect members' engagement levels (Brandão & Popoli, 2022). Actions that provide shared meaning among users, create consumption opportunities or co-create value are considered practices according to practice theory (Holt, 1995). This theory can thus be applied to investigate brand hate.

Researchers can also employ regret theory. Consumers experience regret when their post-purchase evaluation is unsatisfactory (Herrmann et al., 1999). Literature indicates that consumers aim to avoid regretful decisions and may dislike or avoid brands that have caused them dissatisfaction and regret (Coricelli et al., 2005). Regret theory can thus be utilised to explain consumers' brand hate and its consequences.

CONCLUSION

The exploration of negative emotions towards brands and their implications for consumer behaviour has revealed significant insights into the complex dynamics of consumer–brand relationships. This chapter has explored various types of negative emotions, theoretical perspectives and the frameworks associated with them, offering a comprehensive understanding of how these emotions manifest and impact both consumers and brands.

Negative emotions towards brands are multifaceted, ranging from primary emotions like fear and disgust to complex emotions such as brand hate and jealousy. These emotions can arise from individual experiences, social interactions and cognitive appraisals, highlighting the diverse factors that contribute to negative brand perceptions. Understanding these emotions is crucial for brands to navigate the challenges posed by negative consumer sentiments and to develop strategies to mitigate their impact.

The chapter also highlighted the importance of understanding the theoretical perspectives and frameworks associated with negative emotions towards brands. Cognitive-affective theories, social identity theory, attachment theory and social influence theory provide valuable insights into the antecedents and outcomes of negative emotions. These frameworks help brands anticipate consumer behaviour and develop strategies to mitigate adverse reactions, investigating the impact of emerging technologies, social dynamics and cognitive processes on negative emotions towards brands. By deepening our understanding of these complex dynamics, managers can develop strategies to navigate the challenges posed by negative consumer emotions and cultivate positive ones. The insights gained from this chapter provide a foundation for future studies, offering valuable perspectives for brands to effectively manage consumer emotions and build resilient relationships in an increasingly dynamic and interconnected world.

REFERENCES

Aaker, D. A. (1996). Measuring brand equity across products and markets. *California Management Review, 38*(3), 102–120. https://doi.org/10.2307/41165845

Aaker, J., Fournier, S., & Brasel, S. A. (2004). When good brands do bad. *Journal of Consumer Research, 31*(1), 1–16. https://doi.org/10.1086/383419

Abrams, D., & Hogg, M. A. (1988). Comments on the motivational status of self-esteem in social identity and intergroup discrimination. *European journal of social psychology, 18*(4), 317–334.

Ahmad, F., & Guzmán, F. (2021). Negative online reviews, brand equity and emotional contagion. *European Journal of Marketing, 55*(11), 2825–2870. https://doi.org/10.1108/EJM-10-2019-0820

Akrout, H., & Mrad, M. (2023). Measuring brand hate in a cross-cultural context: Emic and etic scale development and validation. *Journal of Business Research, 154*, 113364. https://doi.org/10.1016/j.jbusres.2022.08.053

Algesheimer, R., Dholakia, U. M., & Herrmann, A. (2005). The social influence of brand community: Evidence from European car clubs. *Journal of Marketing, 69*(3), 19–34. https://doi.org/10.1509/jmkg.69.3.19.66363

Alvarez, C., David, M. E., & George, M. (2023). Types of consumer-brand relationships: A systematic review and future research agenda. *Journal of Business Research, 160*, 113753. https://doi.org/10.1016/j.jbusres.2023.113753

Azer, J., & Alexander, M. (2020). Negative customer engagement behaviour: The interplay of intensity and valence in online networks. *Journal of Marketing Management, 36*(3–4), 361–383. https://doi.org/10.1080/0267257X.2020.1735488

Aziz, R., & Rahman, Z. (2022). Brand hate: A literature review and future research agenda. *European Journal of Marketing, 56*(7), 2014–2051. https://doi.org/10.1108/EJM-03-2021-0189

Bagozzi, R. P., & Dholakia, U. M. (2006). Antecedents and purchase consequences of customer participation in small group brand communities. *International Journal of Research in Marketing, 23*(1), 45–61. https://doi.org/10.1016/j.ijresmar.2006.01.005

Bagozzi, R. P., Batra, R., & Ahuvia, A. (2017). Brand love: Development and validation of a practical scale. *Marketing Letters, 28*(1), 1–14. https://doi.org/10.1007/s11002-016-9406-1

Batista Ferraz, S., & Dallabrida, Y. M. (2024). Parting ways in the marketplace: Trajectories of divorce in consumer-brand relationships. *Journal of Marketing Management, 40*(15–16), 1437–1473. https://doi.org/10.1080/0267257X.2024.2435479

Batra, R., Ahuvia, A., & Bagozzi, R. P. (2012). Brand love. *Journal of Marketing, 76*(2), 1–16. https://doi.org/10.1509/jm.09.0339

Bhattacharya, C. B., & Sen, S. (2003). Consumer–company identification: A framework for understanding consumers' relationships with companies. *Journal of marketing, 67*(2), 76–88.

Bıçakcıoğlu, N., Ögel, İ. Y., & İlter, B. (2017). Brand jealousy and willingness to pay premium: The mediating role of materialism. *Journal of Brand Management, 24*(1), 33–48. https://doi.org/10.1057/s41262-016-0016-2

Brandão, A., & Popoli, P. (2022). "I'm hatin'it"! Negative consumer–brand relationships in online anti-brand communities. *European Journal of Marketing, 56*(2), 622–650. https://doi.org/10.1108/EJM-03-2020-0214

Bruhn, M., & Schnebelen, S. (2017). Integrated marketing communication–from an instrumental to a customer-centric perspective. *European journal of marketing, 51*(3), 464–489.

Bryson, D., Atwal, G., & Hultén, P. (2013). Towards the conceptualisation of the antecedents of extreme negative affect towards luxury brands. *Qualitative Market Research: An International Journal, 16*(4), 393–405. https://doi.org/10.1108/QMR-06-2013-0043

Bulut, Z. A., & Karabulut, A. N. (2018). Examining the role of two aspects of eWOM in online repurchase intention: An integrated trust–loyalty perspective. *Journal of Consumer Behaviour, 17*(4), 407–417. https://doi.org/10.1002/cb.1721

Charmley, R., Garry, T., & Ballantine, P. W. (2013). The inauthentic other: Social comparison theory and brand avoidance within consumer sub-cultures. *Journal of Brand Management, 20*(6), 458–472. https://doi.org/10.1057/bm.2012.53

Chaudhuri, A. (1997). Consumption emotion and perceived risk: A macro-analytic approach. *Journal of Business Research, 39*(2), 81–92. https://doi.org/10.1016/S0148-2963(96)00144-0

Cialdini, R. B., & Goldstein, N. J. (2004). Social influence: Compliance and conformity. *Annual Review of Psychology*, *55*(1), *591*–621. https://doi.org/10.1146/annurev.psych.55.090902.142015

Coricelli, G., Dolan, R. J., & Sirigu, A. (2005). Brain, emotion and decision making: The paradigmatic example of regret. *Trends in Cognitive Sciences*, *9*(6), 261–267. https://doi.org/10.1016/j.tics.2005.04.004

Dalli, D., Grappi, S., Romani, S., & Gistri, G. (2007). The brand dislike construct: Scale development and application to actual brands. In G. Fitzsimmons & V. Morwitz (Eds.), *Proceedings of the 2006 annual ACR conference* (pp. 153–157). September 28–October 1, 2006.

Dalli, D., Romani, S., & Gistri, G. (2006). Brand dislike: Representing the negative side of consumer preferences. In C. Pechmann, & L. Price (Eds.), *Advances in consumer research* (Vol. *33*, pp. 87–95). Association for Consumer Research.

de Chernatony, L., Cottam, S. M., & Segal-Horn, S. (2006). Building on services' characteristics to shape successful services brands. *Journal of Brand Management*, *13*(6), 423–440.

Delgado-Ballester, E., & Munuera-Alemán, J. L. (2001). Brand trust in the context of consumer loyalty. *European Journal of marketing*, *35*(11/12), 1238–1258.

Delgado-Ballester, E., López-López, I., & Bernal-Palazón, A. (2021). Why do people initiate an online firestorm? The role of sadness, anger, and dislike. *International Journal of Electronic Commerce*, *25*(3), 313–337. https://doi.org/10.1080/10864415.2021.1943173

Demirbag-Kaplan, M., Yildirim, C., Gulden, S., & Aktan, D. (2015). I love to hate you: Loyalty for disliked brands and the role of nostalgia. *Journal of Brand Management*, *22*(2), 136–153. https://doi.org/10.1057/bm.2015.10

Dessart, L., Veloutsou, C., & Morgan-Thomas, A. (2020). Brand negativity: A relational perspective on anti-brand community participation. *European Journal of Marketing*, *54*(7), 1761–1785. https://doi.org/10.1108/EJM-06-2018-0423

Dijk, W. W., Ouwerkerk, J. W., Goslinga, S., & Gallucci, M. (2006). When people fall from grace: Reconsidering the role of envy in schadenfreude. *Journal of Personality and Social Psychology*, *91*(5), 967–980.

Ferris, T., Lawlor, J., & Ketterer, E. (2023, June 2). *Guidance for "sustainable" claims after dismissal of H&M "greenwashing" class action*. Reuters. www.reuters.com/legal/legalindustry/guidance-sustainable-claims-after-dismissal-hm-greenwashing-class-action-2023-06-02/

Festinger, L. (1954). A theory of social comparison processes. *Human Relations*, *7*(2), 117–140. https://doi.org/10.1177/001872675400700202

Fetscherin, M. (2019). The five types of brand hate: How they affect consumer behavior. *Journal of Business Research*, *101*, 116–127. https://doi.org/10.1016/j.jbusres.2019.04.017

Ford, J. B., Merchant, A., Bartier, A.-L., & Friedman, M. (2018). The cross-cultural scale development process: The case of brand-evoked nostalgia in Belgium and the United States. *Journal of Business Research*, *83*, 19–29. https://doi.org/10.1016/j.jbusres.2017.09.049

Fournier, S. (1998). Consumers and their brands: Developing relationship theory in consumer research. *Journal of Consumer Research*, *24*(4), 343–373. https://doi.org/10.1086/209515

Fournier, S., & Alvarez, C. (2013). Relating badly to brands. *Journal of Consumer Psychology*, *23*(2), 253–264. https://doi.org/10.1016/j.jcps.2013.01.004

Ghorbanzadeh, D. (2024). The role of brand love and brand jealousy in the formation of brand addiction. *Current Psychology*, *43*(3), 2832–2846. https://doi.org/10.1007/s12144-023-04508-1

Grant, I., & Walsh, G. (2009). Exploring the concept of brand embarrassment: The experiences of older adolescents. In A. L. McGill, & S. Shavitt (Eds.), *NA – Advances in consumer research* (Vol. *36*, pp. 218–224). Association for Consumer Research.

Grappi, S., Romani, S., & Zarantonello, L. (2019). Consumer negativity towards brands. *Journal of Product & Brand Management*, *28*(5), 573–574. https://doi.org/10.1108/JPBM-05-2019-2359

Grégoire, Y., & Fisher, R. J. (2008). Customer betrayal and retaliation: When your best customers become your worst enemies. *Journal of the Academy of Marketing Science*, *36*(2), 247–261. https://doi.org/10.1007/s11747-007-0054-0

Grégoire, Y., Tripp, T. M., & Legoux, R. (2009). When customer love turns into lasting hate: The effects of relationship strength and time on customer revenge and avoidance. *Journal of Marketing*, *73*(6), 18–32. https://doi.org/10.1509/jmkg.73.6.18

Haidt, J. (2003). The moral emotions. In R. Davidson, & H. Goldsmith (Eds.), *Handbook of effective sciences* (pp. 852–870). Oxford University Press.

Hashim, S., & Kasana, S. (2019). Antecedents of brand hate in the fast food industry. *Spanish Journal of Marketing-ESIC*, *23*(2), 227–248. https://doi.org/10.1108/SJME-10-2018-0047

Hatch, M. J., & Schultz, M. (2010). Towards a theory of brand co-creation. *Journal of Brand Management*, *17*(8), 590–607. https://doi.org/10.1057/bm.2010.14

Hayes, R. A., & Carr, C. T. (2020). *Snark happens: Effects of schadenfreude on brand attitudes. Journal of Current Issues & Research in Advertising*, *41*(2), 243–256.

Hegner, S. M., Fetscherin, M., & van Delzen, M. (2017). Determinants and outcomes of brand hate. *Journal of Product & Brand Management, 26*(1), 13–25. https://doi.org/10.1108/JPBM-01-2016-1070

Herrmann, A., Huber, F., & Braunstein, C. (1999). Market-driven product and service design: Bridging the gap between customer needs, quality management, and customer satisfaction. *International Journal of Production Economics, 60*, 1–12.

Hollenbeck, C. R., & Zinkhan, G. M. (2006). Consumer activism on the internet: The role of anti-brand communities. *Advances in Consumer Research, 33*, 479.

Holt, D. B. (1995). How consumers consume: A typology of consumption practices. *Journal of Consumer Research, 22*(1), 1–16. https://doi.org/10.1086/209431

Iglesias, O., & Bonet, E. (2012). Cognitive-affective responses toward brand messages: The moderating role of brand image. *Journal of Brand Management, 19*(7), 589–606.

Iglesias, O., Ind, N., & Alfaro, J. (2013). The organic view of the brand: A brand value co-creation model. *Journal of Brand Management, 20*(6), 484–502.

Il Messaggero. (2024, December 26). Chiara Ferragni, Italian influencer investigated for fraud: "2024 was a tough year". *Il Messaggero*. www.ilmessaggero.it/en/chiara_ferragni_fraud_scandal_what_happened-8559471.html

Jain, K., & Sharma, I. (2019). Negative outcomes of positive brand relationships. *Journal of Consumer Marketing, 36*(7), 986–1002. https://doi.org/10.1108/JCM-07-2018-2764

Jansen, B. J., & Schröder, S. (2021). The role of schadenfreude in consumer rivalries: How consumers react to competitor brand failures. *Journal of Consumer Research, 47*(2), 305–321.

Japutra, A., Ekinci, Y., & Simkin, L. (2018). *Positive and negative behaviours resulting from brand attachment: The moderating effects of attachment styles. European Journal of Marketing, 52*(5/6), 1185–1202. https://doi.org/10.1108/EJM-10-2016-0566

Johnson, D. W., & Johnson, R. T. (2005). New developments in social interdependence theory. *Genetic, Social, and General Psychology Monographs, 131*(4), 285–358. https://doi.org/10.3200/MONO.131.4.285-358

Johnson, A. R., Matear, M., & Thomson, M. (2011). A coal in the heart: Self-relevance as a post-exit predictor of consumer anti-brand actions. *Journal of Consumer Research, 38*(1), 108–125. https://doi.org/10.1086/657924

Kähr, A. K., Nyffenegger, B., Krohmer, H., & Hennig-Thurau, T. (2016). Social media brand communities: The impact of participation on customer brand loyalty. *International Journal of Market Research, 58*(2), 21–39.

Kessous, A., Roux, E., & Chandon, J. L. (2015). Consumer–brand relationships: A contrast of nostalgic and non-nostalgic brands. *Psychology & Marketing, 32*(2), 187–202.

Khalifa, M. A., & Shukla, P. (2017). Brand avoidance: Antecedents and consequences. *Journal of Business Research, 79*, 217–225.

Khatoon, S., & Rehman, V. (2021). Negative emotions in consumer-brand relationships: A review and future research agenda. *International Journal of Consumer Studies, 45*(4), 719–749. https://doi.org/10.1111/ijcs.12665

Klein, J. G., Smith, N. C., & John, A. (2004). Why we boycott: Consumer motivations for boycott participation. *Journal of Marketing, 68*(3), 92–109. https://doi.org/10.1509/jmkg.68.3.92.34770

Krishna, A., Herd, K. B., & Aydınoğlu, N. Z. (2019). A review of consumer embarrassment as a public and private emotion. *Journal of Consumer Psychology, 29*(3), 492–516. https://doi.org/10.1002/jcpy.1086

Kucuk, S. U. (2010). Consumer alienation and brand rejection: The case of organic products. *Journal of Business Ethics, 91*(4), 560–591.

Lee, M. S., Motion, J., & Conroy, D. (2009b). Anti-consumption and brand avoidance. *Journal of Business Research, 62*(2), 169–180. https://doi.org/10.1016/j.jbusres.2008.01.024

Lee, Y. K., Back, K. J., & Kim, J. Y. (2009a). Family restaurant brand personality and its impact on customer's emotion, satisfaction, and brand loyalty. *Journal of Hospitality & Tourism Research, 33*(3), 305–328. https://doi.org/10.1177/1096348009338511

Levy, S. J. (1959). Symbols for sale. *Harvard Business Review, 37*(4), 117–124.

Mangiò, F., Pedeliento, G., & Andreini, D. (2022). Brand experience co-creation at the time of artificial intelligence. In O. Iglesias, N. Ind, & M. Schultz (Eds.), *The Routledge companion to corporate branding* (pp. 195–210). Routledge.

Manna, Y. (2024). Understanding the impact of narcissism and schadenfreude on e-consumers' purchase of counterfeit pro-environmental goods. *International Journal of Advanced and Applied Sciences, 11*(12), 22–33. https://doi.org/10.21833/ijaas.2024.12.003

Markus, H., & Kunda, Z. (1986). Stability and malleability of the self-concept: From situation to global self. *Journal of Personality and Social Psychology, 51*(4), 858–866. https://doi.org/10.1037/0022-3514.51.4.858

Marticotte, F., Arcand, M., & Baudry, D. (2016). The impact of brand evangelism on oppositional referrals towards a rival brand. *Journal of Product &*

Brand Management, *25*(6), 538–549. https://doi.org/10.1108/JPBM-06-2015-0920

Marticotte, F., & Arcand, M. (2017). Schadenfreude, attitude, and the purchase intentions of a counterfeit luxury brand. *Journal of Business Research*, *77*, 175–183. https://doi.org/10.1016/j.jbusres.2016.12.010

Miller, R. S. (1996). Is embarrassment a blessing or a curse? In R. S. Miller (Ed.), *Embarrassment: Poise and peril in everyday life* (pp. 245–262). Guildford Press.

Odoom, R., Anning-Dorson, J., & Acheampong, G. (2019). Online brand community identification and brand loyalty: The mediating role of brand trust and the moderating role of need for affiliation. *Journal of Brand Management*, *26*(5), 554–569.

Oliver, R. L. (1977). Effect of expectation and disconfirmation on postexposure product evaluations: An alternative interpretation. *Journal of Applied Psychology*, *62*(4), 480–486. https://doi.org/10.1037/0021-9010.62.4.480

Osuna-Ramirez, S. A., Veloutsou, C., & Morgan-Thomas, A. (2019). I hate what you love: Brand polarization and negativity towards brands as an opportunity for brand management. *Journal of Product & Brand Management*, *28*(5), 614–632. https://doi.org/10.1108/JPBM-03-2018-1811

Park, C. W., Eisingerich, A. B., & Park, J. W. (2013). Attachment–aversion (AA) model of customer–brand relationships. *Journal of Consumer Psychology*, *23*(2), 229–248. https://doi.org/10.1016/j.jcps.2013.01.002

Park, C. W., MacInnis, D. J., Priester, J., Eisingerich, A. B., & Iacobucci, D. (2010). Brand attachment and brand attitude strength: Conceptual and empirical differentiation of two critical brand equity drivers. *Journal of Marketing*, *74*(6), 1–17. https://doi.org/10.1509/jmkg.74.6.1

Park, J. K., & MacInnis, D. J. (2018). The role of self-esteem on brand attachment and its consequences. *Journal of Consumer Psychology*, *28*(2), 234–247. https://doi.org/10.1002/jcpy.1025

Phillips-Melancon, J., & Dalakas, V. (2014). Brand rivalry and consumers' schadenfreude: The case of Apple. *Services Marketing Quarterly*, *35*(2), 173–186. https://doi.org/10.1080/15332969.2014.885370

Rana, M. W., Mustafa, F., Quddoos, M. U., & Lodhi, R. N. (2021). How brand jealousy is an antidote for premium to pay more in the presence of materialism and brand attachment? *IRASD Journal of Management*, *3*(1), 35–45. https://doi.org/10.52131/jom.2021.0301.0024

Rodrigues, C., Brandão, A., & Rodrigues, P. (2021). I can't stop hating you: An anti-brand-community perspective on apple brand hate. *Journal of Product & Brand Management*, *30*(8), 1115–1133. https://doi.org/10.1108/JPBM-10-2019-2621

Rodrigues, P., & Borges, A. (2020). Corporate brand reputation and consumer reactions to brand transgressions. *Journal of Brand Management*, *27*(1), 127–141.

Romani, S., Grạppi, S., & Dalli, D. (2012). Emotions that drive consumers away from brands: Measuring negative emotions toward brands and their behavioral effects. *International Journal of Research in Marketing*, *29*(1), 55–67. https://doi.org/10.1016/j.ijresmar.2011.07.001

Romani, S., Grappi, S., Zarantonello, L., & Bagozzi, R. P. (2015). The revenge of the consumer! How brand moral violations lead to consumer anti-brand activism. *Journal of Brand Management*, *22*(8), 658–672. https://doi.org/10.1057/bm.2015.38

Saini, A., Kashif, M., & Platania, S. (2023). Temporary love: A love-hate transition among luxury fashion consumers in a mediation of brand jealousy and moderation of value-expressiveness. *Journal of Global Scholars of Marketing Science*, *33*(4), 513–535. https://doi.org/10.1080/21639159.2023.2209104

Sarkar, A., Sarkar, J. G., Sreejesh, S., Anusree, A., & Rishi, B. (2020). You are so embarrassing, still, I hate you less! Investigating consumers' brand embarrassment and brand hate. *Journal of Brand Management*, *27*(1), 93–107. https://doi.org/10.1057/s41262-019-00164-8

Sarkar, A., & Sreejesh, S. (2014). Examination of the roles played by brand love and jealousy in shaping customer engagement. *Journal of Product & Brand Management*, *23*(1), 24–32. https://doi.org/10.1108/JPBM-05-2013-0315

Sarkar, J. G., & Sarkar, A. (2017). You are an embarrassment: A qualitative investigation of brand embarrassment among young adolescents. *Qualitative Market Research*, *20*(3), 289–305. https://doi.org/10.1108/QMR-03-2016-0032

Scholz, J., & Smith, A. N. (2016). Augmented reality: Designing immersive experiences that maximize consumer engagement. *Business Horizons*, *59*(2), 149–161. https://doi.org/10.1016/j.bushor.2015.10.003

Shimul, A. S., Sung, B., & Phau, I. (2021). Effects of luxury brand attachment and perceived envy on schadenfreude: Does need for uniqueness moderate? *Journal of Consumer Marketing*, *38*(6), 709–720. https://doi.org/10.1108/JCM-09-2020-4125

Siddique, S., & Rajput, A. (2022). Self-expressiveness and hedonic brand affect brand love through brand jealousy. *Futuristic Business Journal*, *8*(1), 23. https://doi.org/10.1186/s43093-022-00136-6

Sirgy, M. J. (1982). Self-concept in consumer behavior. *Journal of Consumer Research*, *9*(3), 287–291. https://doi.org/10.1086/208924

Smith, C. A., & Ellsworth, P. C. (1985). Patterns of cognitive appraisal in emotion. *Journal of Personality and Social Psychology*, *48*(4), 813–838. https://doi.org/10.1037/0022-3514.48.4.813

Song, X., Huang, F., & Li, X. (2017). The effect of embarrassment on preferences for brand conspicuousness: The roles of self-esteem and self-brand connection. *Journal of Consumer Psychology*, *27*(1), 69–83. https://doi.org/10.1016/j.jcps.2016.05.001

Strizhakova, Y., Coulter, R. A., & Price, L. L. (2008). Branded products as a passport to global citizenship: Perspectives from developed and developing countries. *Journal of International Marketing*, *16*(4), 57–85. https://doi.org/10.1509/jimk.16.4.57

Sundie, J. M., Ward, J. C., Beal, D. J., Chin, W. W., & Geiger-Oneto, S. (2009). Schadenfreude as a consumption-related emotion: Feeling happiness about the downfall of another's product. *Journal of Consumer Psychology*, *19*(3), 356–373.

Sweetin, V. H., Knowles, L. L., Summey, J. H., & McQueen, K. S. (2013). Willingness-to-punish the corporate brand for corporate social irresponsibility. *Journal of Business Research*, *66*(10), 1822–1830. https://doi.org/10.1016/j.jbusres.2013.02.003

Thomson, M., MacInnis, D. J., & Park, C. W. (2005). The ties that bind: Measuring the strength of consumers' emotional attachments to brands. *Journal of Consumer Psychology*, *15*(1), 77–91. https://doi.org/10.1207/s15327663jcp1501_10

Thomson, M., Whelan, J., & Johnson, A. R. (2012). Why brands should fear fearful consumers: How attachment style predicts retaliation. *Journal of Consumer Psychology*, *22*(2), 289–298. https://doi.org/10.1016/j.jcps.2011.04.006

Ullrich, J., & Brunner, T. A. (2015). Consumer reactions to corporate wrongdoing: The effects of company-related attributes, consumer-related attributes and the type of wrongdoing. *Journal of Marketing Theory and Practice*, *23*(4), 411–430.

van de Ven, N., Zeelenberg, M., & Pieters, R. (2011). Why envy outperforms admiration. *Personality and Social Psychology Bulletin*, *37*(6), 784–795. https://doi.org/10.1177/0146167211400421

Veloutsou, C., & Moutinho, L. (2009). Brand relationships through brand reputation and brand tribalism. *Journal of Business Research*, *62*(3), 314–322. https://doi.org/10.1016/j.jbusres.2008.05.010

Walsh, G., Albrecht, A. K., Hofacker, C. F., Grant, I., & Takahashi, I. (2016). Developing and validating a scale of consumer brand embarrassment tendencies. *Journal of Business Research*, *69*(3), 1138–1147. https://doi.org/10.1016/j.jbusres.2015.08.029

Weingarten, E., & Wei, Z. (2023). Nostalgia and consumer behavior. *Current Opinion in Psychology*, *49*, 101555. https://doi.org/10.1016/j.copsyc.2022.101555

Yadav, A., & Chakrabarti, S. (2022). Brand hate: A systematic literature review and future research agenda. *International Journal of Consumer Studies*, *46*(5), 1992–2019. https://doi.org/10.1111/ijcs.12772

Yadav, A. (2024). When personalities collide: Examining the impact of consumer and brand personalities' interplay on brand hate development. *Journal of Product & Brand Management*, *33*(4), 460–476.

Yeo, V. C. S., & Ong, B. S. (2024). How do consumers react to service failure recovery on social media? The roles of appraisal and parasocial interaction. *Journal of Retailing and Consumer Services*, *78*, 103743. https://doi.org/10.1016/j.jretconser.2024.103743

Zarantonello, L., Romani, S., Grappi, S., & Bagozzi, R. P. (2016). Brand hate. *Journal of Product & Brand Management*, *25*(1), 11–25. https://doi.org/10.1108/JPBM-01-2015-0799

Zarantonello, L., Romani, S., Grappi, S., & Fetscherin, M. (2018). Trajectories of brand hate. *Journal of Brand Management*, *25*(6), 549–560. https://doi.org/10.1057/s41262-018-0105-5

Zhang, C., & Laroche, M. (2020). Brand hate: A multidimensional construct. *Journal of Product & Brand Management*, *30*(3), 392–414. https://doi.org/10.1108/JPBM-11-2018-2103

22

Enhancing Brand Experience in the Digital Transformation Age: Insights from Qualitative and Quantitative Research Methodologies

Michela Addis and Giulia Miniero

BRAND EXPERIENCE AND THE IMPACT OF DIGITAL TRANSFORMATION

Brand experience has been a central focus in marketing, grounded in the experiential view of consumer behavior (Holbrook, 2024; Schmitt et al., 2015; Zarantonello & Andreini, 2023). Over time, it has evolved to integrate new theoretical insights, positioning consumption experiences as pivotal for brand differentiation and long-term competitive advantage (Arici et al., 2022; McCarthy & Fader, 2020). Encompassing all interactions from initial awareness to post-purchase, brand experience spans the entire customer journey (Brakus et al., 2009; Lemon & Verhoef, 2016).

The rapid advancement of digital technology has transformed brand experience, creating both challenges and opportunities. Digital transformation, defined as leveraging innovative technologies to radically improve operations and redefine value propositions (Gong & Ribiere, 2021), necessitates a shift toward human-centered engagement at every touchpoint.

Technology drives innovative, customer-centric experiences (Sundbo, 2009). Over the last four decades, the focus has increasingly been on placing individuals at the heart of strategies. Today, digital tools provide the data required to implement such approaches, emphasizing human elements in brand interactions (D'Cruz et al., 2022; Puntoni et al., 2021).

Digital transformation offers substantial benefits, such as 'ephemeralization', which increases efficiency to achieve 'more with less' (Fuller, 2019), leading to resource savings, flexibility and agility. It expands brand interactions by seamlessly integrating online and offline touchpoints, including social media, mobile apps and digital advertising. These channels make brand experiences more dynamic, interactive and personalized. Ultimately, this evolution enables brands to focus on engaging consumers across all touchpoints in meaningful ways. Digital transformation has reshaped brand experience in four key areas (Figure 22.1).

Customized Brand Experiences

Big data empower brands to understand individual preferences and behaviors, enabling highly personalized messages, products and services. For example, Netflix uses algorithms to recommend content based on user interests and viewing habits, fostering stronger emotional connections (Addis, 2020). This data-driven personalization enhances customer

Customer-centric data-driven strategies

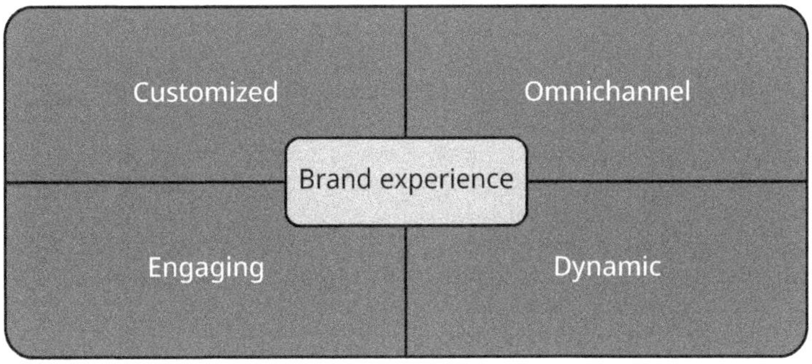

Figure 22.1 The impact of digital transformation on brand experience

Source: The authors.

experiences and supports value co-creation, where customers contribute their skills and knowledge to develop tailored products, enriching the brand experience (Vargo et al., 2008). Brand experience not only directly influences customer satisfaction but also mediates through variables such as hedonic and utilitarian benefits, brand love and brand personality (de Oliveira Santini et al., 2018). This extended model provides a deeper understanding of the relationships between brand experience, trust, loyalty and word-of-mouth, offering a valuable framework for developing branding strategies focused on creating meaningful experiences.

Omnichannel Experiences

Digital transformation has led to seamless omnichannel strategies, where brands integrate diverse platforms – physical and digital, internal and external – into unified customer journeys (Cui et al., 2022). By ensuring consistency across touchpoints, omnichannel experiences enhance convenience and foster brand loyalty (Edelman & Singer, 2015). Advanced technologies like machine learning and blockchain further improve integration, enabling richer customer data analysis and prediction capabilities (Barsoux et al., 2022; Govindarajan & Venkatraman, 2022).

Engaging Experiences

The digital era has transformed consumer–brand interactions, fostering engagement through interactive platforms like social media. Engagement, defined as a 'psychological state' (Brodie et al., 2013), thrives on dynamic exchanges on platforms such as Instagram and Facebook, which are now critical for building brand advocacy. Additionally, technologies like AR and VR offer immersive experiences, enhancing interactivity and co-creation across industries (Addis, 2020). Indeed, an innovative framework developed for immersive experiences through AR and VR highlights how these technologies can transform the way consumers engage with services and products (Zarantonello & Schmitt, 2023). These emerging technologies are particularly relevant for reducing service intangibility and expanding engagement opportunities throughout the customer journey.

Dynamic Experiences

Digital transformation enables real-time feedback, allowing brands to adapt swiftly to consumer needs. Insights from reviews, social media and service interactions help refine offerings and address issues promptly. By leveraging multiple touchpoints, brands gain a comprehensive view of customer journeys, shifting from market-oriented to customer-centric strategies. This approach captures emotional dimensions of experiences, enhancing satisfaction and engagement.

These features challenge researchers to adopt techniques that center on feelings, fantasy and fun. Comprehensive customer insights enable brands to craft holistic, pleasurable experiences, driving innovation and market success (Liedtka, 2015; Rosen et al., 1998). As digital transformation progresses, brands can better deliver customized, omnichannel and dynamic experiences, fostering customer loyalty and satisfaction (Addis, 2020).

DESIGNING BRAND EXPERIENCE THROUGH CUSTOMER JOURNEY MAP

Effective customer experiences are delivered through a careful planning and execution of every possible interaction through the steps of customer journey. Such exchanges between the customer and the product or service take place throughout the journey and shape the overall evaluation of the experience by the customer (Becker & Jaakkola, 2020).

Customer journeys, therefore, are considered an important framework to analyze and plan the customer experience, this notion being widely acknowledged in marketing literature (Rawson et al., 2013). By monitoring all the moments and touchpoints that contribute to shape the experience customers have with the product/brand, companies can gain insightful knowledge on how to improve and how to deliver the interaction in a way that meets and possibly exceeds the expectations of customers. For this reason, the steps of the customer journey represent the basis on which a great customer experience is built on with the latter being at the heart of a great brand equity (Lemon & Verhoef, 2016).

More in details, previous research has conceptualized the customer journey as consisting of four distinct stages, ranging from the pre-purchase stage (i.e., the phase in which customers develop an initial consideration for the good and search for it) to the actual purchase stage (i.e., the phase in which interactions with the product or service and its environment take place during the purchase process), the consumption stage (i.e., the stage in which customers interact with the product, forming impressions about its experiential value) and the post-purchase stage (i.e., the phase in which customers make concrete use of the product or service and therefore evaluate it and form opinions on future engagement and potential repurchase options) (Lemon & Verhoef, 2016; Voorhees et al., 2017). The customer journey comprises a series of touchpoints across the four stages before, during and after service provision or product delivery (Holz et al., 2024). Concentrating on the different phases of customer journey, rather than on the journey as a whole, enables the company to capture what customers do in their daily lives to achieve their goals, undertaking a perspective that is broader than the mere phases and thus accommodating the consumer interaction with multiple stakeholders beyond touchpoints with a single firm (Hamilton & Price, 2019; Heinonen et al., 2010).

Current marketing research suggests that a customer journey is considered effective if its touchpoints present a few features (Reitsamer et al., 2024): They share the same brand theme (i.e., journey cohesion), and they are perceived uniformly in their design (i.e., journey consistency) and fit the situational context of the customer (i.e., journey context sensitivity; Jaakkola & Terho, 2021; Kuehnl et al., 2019), making the cycle 'consistent and predictable' (Siebert et al., 2020). Consequently, assessing how customers evaluate their overall journey experience as driver of customers experience (Wirtz et al., 2003) comes with significant advantages for both customers and management.

RESEARCH METHODOLOGIES TO UNDERSTAND CUSTOMERS THROUGHOUT THEIR JOURNEY

Modern techniques for accessing the complex and subjective customer experience are vast and diverse, ranging from those rooted in anthropology to psychology, psychoanalysis, sociology, statistics and even neurology. There is no single market technique that is inherently superior, as each method is suited to specific conditions; moreover, engaging brands select the most appropriate technique for their objectives based on the particular circumstances of customer experiences. Identifying the right sources to capture the necessary customer insights for implementing a customer-centric approach is a challenging task (Ordenes et al., 2014). Additionally, recent technological and sociological changes not only encourage the continuous review of these methods but also their integration, as only the adoption of multiple research methodologies simultaneously can provide the insights needed to decipher the current complexity.

The presentation of the various available techniques is organized according to the phases of the customer journey map, as this framework is central to designing the brand experience. However, it is important to emphasize that assigning specific techniques to particular phases of the customer journey is ideal for maximizing their effectiveness based on the unique characteristics of each phase. In practice, brands can also extend the use of these techniques to other phases of the journey. Table 22.1 presents the techniques for each customer journey map step.

THE PRE-PURCHASE STEP

Focusing on the first step of the customer journey and collecting data on the interactions that take place between customers and the product at this stage are

Table 22.1 The research techniques by customer journey map steps

	Pre-Purchase Step	*Purchase Step*	*Consumption Step*	*Post-Consumption Step*
Techniques	Text Mining IoT and AR	Mystery Shopping Website analysis Metaverse	Individual and collective interviews Ethnographic and Netnography Analyses Photo-Elicitation Zaltman Metaphor-Elicitation Technique Multisensory Analysis	Personal Introspection Surveys Experimental design

Source: The authors.

very important for companies in order to get insights into potentially critical issues or pain points that might arise in the future. Traditionally, companies collect data on the overall customer experience at the end of the journey not acknowledging how the preliminary steps of the journey are crucial in shaping the entire outcome of the experience. This might bring researchers to overlook emerging pain points that might undermine the overall journey of the customer. Typically, survey data are collected at the end of the customer journey. This type of data does not offer real-time responses. Indeed, different types of data, collected with more recent techniques, based on big data and technological advancements, might be available to shed lights on consumers' evaluation. This suggests to organizations the opportunity to rely on other real-time customer data, such as big data analytics, that can empower firms in mastering their planned interactions with customers (Holmlund et al., 2020). Undeniably, it becomes complex for companies to collect data from the plethora of touchpoints that they employ for connecting with customers. In addition, analyzing and extracting insights from such a giant quantity of data pose some challenges to both companies and researchers that have to invest in organizing, processing and aggregating this amount of information in a meaningful way. New sources of data, such as text, sound, images and videos, web analytics, website cookies, Internet of Things that can be collected on social media platforms, websites and applications (Holmlund et al., 2020), offer a great potential to companies to research on the pre-purchase phase of the customer journey enabling the identification early on of critical pain points, unmasking underlying sources of friction on the various touchpoints and providing deeper insights into critical touchpoints. This allows organizations to strategize on how and where implementing changes to reduce friction more quickly.

Text Mining

The options and possibilities brought by technology in this realm are immense. Brands have now the chance to collect an explosion of data on different touchpoints.

In this domain, text mining techniques have become increasingly useful. Text mining – defined as the process of analyzing textual information to unveil implicit meanings – is based on a mix of data mining, machine learning, natural language processing and knowledge management (Yu et al., 2011). By leveraging on enormous amount of textual data collected on several digital platforms, text mining models convert unstructured textual data into structured data organized according to 'concepts' (Mikroyannidis & Theodoulidis, 2010). Relying on text mining techniques, firms can derive valuable insights into customer sentiment, reviews and feedback. In this area, it is crucial to acknowledge that the experiences customers have with products in the pre-purchase phase are highly dynamic and evolve over time. Consequently, the use of technologies based on big data, like text mining, presents a remarkable opportunity for researchers to capture these dynamics, focusing on the vocabulary and expressions consumers use when discussing the experiences they had with brands. In this context, sentiment analysis has gained significant traction as firms now have the capability to monitor conversations occurring on social media platforms that relate to product reviews, interactions customers have with brands and their subsequent feelings. More in details, text mining techniques are based on two fundamental steps:

- Crawling Social Media Data. The first essential step in sentiment analysis involves crawling data from social media sources to create a comprehensive database for subsequent analysis. This process requires the identification of key sources of information, which may include proprietary social media accounts managed by the brand and non-proprietary platforms where consumers freely share opinions, reviews and feedback about products. At this stage, the data collected are typically unstructured. This unstructured data often contain irrelevant or redundant information

(Zeng et al., 2010). The challenge for companies lies in extracting meaningful and relevant insights from this vast pool of raw data.

- Developing the Text Mining Model. A pivotal step in applying a text mining approach is the manual coding of the collected data. This preliminary coding enables researchers to gain a foundational understanding of the data and uncover initial insights. Subsequently, a robust text mining model can be developed, relying on linguistic patterns derived from existing text libraries (e.g., pre-built within text mining software) or custom-created for specific analytical needs. The depth and sophistication of the analysis required will dictate the specificity of the text library.

By systematically crawling, processing and analyzing social media data, sentiment analysis offers a powerful tool for brands to understand and adapt to customer perceptions dynamically. With advancements in text mining techniques and the ability to create context-specific libraries, companies and researchers can uncover nuanced insights that guide decision-making and enhance the customer experience throughout their journey.

IoT and AR

When analyzing the customer journey, bridging the online and offline touchpoints becomes paramount in order to picture the experience holistically. In this realm, the technological advancements now available will revolutionize the customer experience concept by profoundly modifying how individuals will experience the purchasing context (Hoyer et al., 2022). Specifically, the IoT, AR/VR/MR and virtual assistants/chatbots/robots will impact extensively the exchanges that companies can plan with customers on their touchpoints.

More in details, in the pre-transaction phase of the customer journey, IoT provides consumers with rich, detailed and relevant information that firms can leverage on to support the customer decision process.

IoT in the context of consumer experience entails the use of sensors or Bluetooth devices such as beacons in or outside of stores that locate customers' smartphones and send customers personalized messages with relevant product information or special discounts when they stand near specific product (Shankar et al., 2016). Moreover, IoT supports organizations in tracking the information that customers consult online, and at the same time, it can be employed to send customers relevant information on products when they are in a store of the same brand. This constitutes valuable data that can be collected and analyzed to assess how the pre-purchase stage of the customer journey is evolving.

By the same token, AR/VR/MR technologies are particularly important in the pre-transaction phase as these devices facilitate imagination, allowing consumers to experience and test products or services in 3D in real-world scenarios. This enhances the experience customers have with the product, even before actually purchasing it. Recording data on how customers interact with AR/VR/MR technologies offer valuable insights into both explicit and implicit reactions, enabling companies to fine-tune their offerings and improve customer satisfaction.

The data collected through AR/VR/MR can include a variety of touchpoints such as

- Interaction Data. This involves tracking how customers engage with virtual products, such as how long they interact with specific features, which elements they focus on (e.g., using gaze tracking), and the sequence of their interactions. These data points can reveal which features are most appealing or confusing, allowing companies to prioritize improvements. These data can be analyzed by creating heatmaps that can show which areas of a product or environment attract the most attention. This analysis helps companies understand the focal points of customer interest and areas that might need redesign.
- Behavioral Data. AR/VR/MR devices can monitor customer movements, such as gestures, head positioning or navigation patterns within a virtual environment. For instance, if customers consistently avoid a particular section of a virtual store, it might indicate design issues or disinterest in certain products. In this case, analyzing customer feedback such as verbal comments, survey responses or even sentiment inferred from tone of voice can provide a clearer picture of how customers feel about their virtual interactions.
- Emotional Data. Advanced AR/VR/MR setups equipped with emotion-tracking capabilities (e.g., facial expression analysis or biometric sensors) can capture customers' emotional responses to different features. Positive emotions like excitement or negative ones like frustration can provide insights into customer satisfaction or pain points. Analysis of these data might be conducted employing machine learning algorithms to identify patterns or clusters in customer behavior. For example, clustering techniques might group

customers by engagement levels, preferences or emotional responses.
- Preference Data. By analyzing the customization choices customers make – such as color, size or style options when visualizing products – companies can identify trends and preferences that inform product development or marketing strategies.

Through AR/VR/MR, companies can collect a rich array of data that goes beyond traditional metrics, offering a multidimensional understanding of preferences, emotions and behaviors in the pre-purchase phase of the journey. When analyzed effectively, these data provide actionable insights to refine product offerings, improve customer engagement and create more immersive and rewarding pre-purchase experiences.

THE PURCHASE STEP

Delivering an outstanding customer experience is crucial whenever potential interactions between customers and companies occur. This is particularly relevant for businesses managing retail stores across various industries, where the in-store experience significantly influences customer purchase decisions. The importance of customer experience extends to the banking and finance industry, where large retail prioritizes creating a positive atmosphere during client interactions at retail locations, as it plays a critical role in the presentation of financial products.

From a business perspective, measuring the effectiveness of the customer experience delivered is essential.

Mistery Shopping

One widely used research technique for assessing customer experience in the purchase stage of the journey is mystery shopping, where a researcher poses as a customer and interacts with an organization as naturally as possible to evaluate various aspects of the experience (Finn & Kayandé, 1999; Wilson, 1998). The primary goal of mystery shopping is to assess how a company stages its customer experience, providing a comprehensive, 360° evaluation. This technique is designed to collect data on the actual experience delivered by the brand, taking into account all the interferences and potential confounding factors that may arise in real-world settings. The co-presence of other clients, unpredictable elements and unplanned circumstances can challenge the implementation of the company's strategic directions, making such assessments invaluable. To ensure that the technique is applied effectively and yields actionable insights, several key steps are essential:

- Template Development. For mystery shopping to be effective, companies should develop structured templates that outline the critical components of the customer experience they plan to deliver. These templates guide the researcher in their observation and assessment and ensure consistency across visits. Brands can customize these templates to address the unique needs of the organization, retailer, or specific scenario being studied.
- Planning the Visits. Planning is a crucial phase that ensures the mystery shopping process captures a diverse range of scenarios. Researchers schedule visits across different times and days to observe how factors such as peak hours, crowd density or promotional events impact the customer experience.
- Conducting the Visits. This phase involves the actual data collection, where the researcher immerses themselves in the customer experience. Observations focus on both hard elements (e.g., store layout, lighting, furniture, product displays and availability of staff) and soft elements (e.g., overall ambiance, friendliness of staff, tone of voice, background music and scents). Acting as a potential customer, the researcher engages in various interactions with staff, tests customer service responses and, where appropriate, completes a purchase. This approach ensures that the data collected reflects a realistic representation of the purchasing phase of customer journey.
- Data Analysis. In the final step, researchers analyze the data collected during the visits. This process typically involves both qualitative and quantitative techniques. Thematic coding is often employed to organize and categorize data according to the themes or categories defined in the observation template. This allows researchers to extract meaningful insights from textual notes, visual impressions and audio recordings.

Website Analysis

When assessing the interactions customers have with the company in the purchase phase of their journey, the brand website is an important touchpoint to evaluate. It represents a key entry point into the buying phase and is a fundamental window to showcase the elements of the experience that the company is trying to convey. Therefore, using the website to collect information on how customers perceive the purchasing phase of the journey becomes very valuable for the company. To conduct a thorough website analysis for a company aiming to assess its customer experience, data on the following aspects of the website can be collected:

- Interactive and Communicative Functions. Measure if the website includes features that engage users actively, such as some fashion blogs do with 'featured outfit of the day' or similar interactive elements. Assess the interactivity of website components that encourage user interaction and enhance engagement with the brand's story and offerings.
- Depth of Shopping Information. Assess the level of detail provided in the website about products, including descriptions, specifications and other relevant data that support customers to make informed purchasing decisions. Test whether this information is easily accessible and comprehensive for customers by directly asking it on the website or with follow-up emails.
- Aesthetic Features. A very important dimension of the customer experience, online especially, is its aesthetic pleasantness. Companies, therefore, need to examine the visual appeal of the website by testing how customers perceive the product presentation, the usability and friendliness of the design interface together with the appeal of images, color schemes and the overall emotional impact of the website. More importantly, these elements should represent and be consistent with the overall identity of the brand so to reinforce a visually cohesive experience.
- Functional Features. In order to ensure that the online experience is effective, companies should include in their assessment also functional aspects like personalization options, ease of navigation, processing speed and security. Ensuring that the website is informative and consistent in layout and language to avoid any potential friction that might undermine the overall pleasantness of the experience in the purchasing phase. Additionally, evaluate any interactive shopping services (e.g., chatbots) and customer support features that can enhance user satisfaction.

Using these steps will help create a structured and holistic approach to website analysis, aimed at understanding and improving customer experience based on the quality of both interactive and aesthetic elements, as well as the website's technical functionality.

Metaverse

Among the more recent opportunities available to firms for collecting data during the purchasing stage of the customer journey, the metaverse presents a groundbreaking realm of possibilities. The metaverse, defined as 'a technology-mediated network of scalable and potentially interoperable extended reality environments merging the physical and virtual realities to provide experiences characterized by their level of immersiveness, environmental fidelity, and sociability' (Barrera & Shah, 2023, p. 6), offers firms and researchers multiple innovative options for assessing the customer experience.

One of the key advantages of the metaverse is its continuous and ongoing spatiotemporal accessibility, which allows users to interact with virtual environments at any time. This provides companies with the opportunity to collect real-time data on a large scale, enabling insights into behaviors, preferences and decision-making processes as they unfold. Unlike traditional methods of data collection, where information is gathered periodically or retrospectively, the metaverse facilitates a dynamic flow of data, capturing the nuances of customer interactions in virtual settings.

In the metaverse, detailed profiles of users are generated, which include information about media consumption habits, interests, preferences and behavioral patterns. These profiles are further enriched by the ability of companies to observe user interactions with virtual assets, such as avatars and digital products. For instance, when users create and customize their avatars or virtual items, companies gain access to highly individualized data about aesthetic preferences, functionality choices and purchasing behaviors. This level of granularity is particularly valuable for understanding customer preferences and predicting future behaviors (Dwivedi et al., 2022). Such insights can inform product development, marketing strategies and personalized customer experiences.

The devices used to access the metaverse – such as headsets, goggles, handheld controllers and haptic devices like wristbands and smart gloves – provide a wealth of data beyond traditional metrics. These devices can capture behavioral data, such as navigation patterns, object interaction frequencies and movement precision within the virtual environment. In addition, physiological data, including heart rate, eye tracking and even neural activity (where available), can be monitored to infer levels of engagement, excitement or stress. Emotional data, derived from facial expressions or biometric sensors, further enrich the understanding of how users feel during their virtual interactions.

By integrating behavioral, physiological and emotional data with user profiles and real-time interaction metrics, companies can create multidimensional insights into the purchasing phase of customer journey. For instance, analyzing how users engage with virtual storefronts or products can help brands identify friction points, optimize interface designs and enhance the overall customer experience. Furthermore, the immersive nature of the metaverse allows researchers to test different scenarios and track how users respond to changes in the environment, providing an experimental platform to refine offerings in a controlled yet realistic setting (Park & Kim, 2022).

THE CONSUMPTION STEP

The consumption phase of the customer journey is marked by intimacy, occurring in private spaces where brands have historically faced challenges accessing customer experiences. However, the importance of this phase in generating valuable insights has driven innovation in research methods. These methods aim to observe consumption in its natural context, capturing its sensory, cognitive and emotional dimensions. The success of these approaches depends on adopting the consumer's perspective and uncovering deeper, often subconscious, elements of the experience.

Research techniques for this phase are categorized into exploratory methods and measurement tools for descriptive and causal analysis. Exploratory techniques include individual and collective interviews, ethnographic analysis, photo-elicitation and Zaltman Metaphor-Elicitation Technique. The techniques to measure the consumption step of the customer experiences include multisensory analysis based on neurological-physiological reactions measured at both the peripheral and central levels, which have been significantly enhanced by the recent technological advancements.

Individual and Collective Interviews

This category of exploratory techniques involves conducting interviews with individuals or groups to access knowledge through deep linguistic exploration, emphasizing the cognitive dimension of consumption experiences. Exploratory interview techniques can be categorized based on the level of researcher control over interactions with participants:

- Guided Techniques: The researcher actively directs the interaction, using a structured or semi-structured approach. Examples include in-depth interviews and focus groups.
- Open-Ended Techniques: Participants control the flow of interaction, with the researcher adopting a passive, observational role. This approach is exemplified by phenomenological interviews.

Guided techniques involve a high level of researcher control, enabling a structured exploration of participants' experiences. These methods are particularly useful for ensuring consistency and focus, making them adaptable to various research contexts.

- In-Depth Interviews. In-depth interviews aim to delve into participants' personal and subjective experiences (Boyce & Neale, 2006; Gilgun & Sussman, 2014). Researchers guide the conversation using standardized protocols, which enhance the method's flexibility across industries and contexts. A distinctive feature of in-depth interviews is the use of the laddering technique, a method that uncovers underlying motivations and abstract consumer behavior processes by encouraging participants to articulate their values and decision-making drivers (Reynolds & Olson, 2001).
- Focus Groups. Focus groups are ideal for exploring the social dimensions of consumption, as they emphasize shared experiences and group dynamics. In these sessions, the researcher moderates discussions to ensure balanced participation and to maintain alignment with the study's objectives. Proper participant segmentation is critical for meaningful insights; poor group composition can undermine the quality and reliability of the findings. By fostering interaction among participants, focus groups reveal collective perspectives, which are particularly valuable when studying social influences on behavior.

Open-ended techniques, on the other hand, prioritize participant autonomy, allowing them to steer the conversation naturally. These methods provide deeper insights into lived experiences by capturing narratives that emerge organically.

- Phenomenological Interviews. Phenomenological interviews are designed to uncover the essence of participants' lived experiences by giving them control over the narrative. The process begins with an open-ended question, allowing the participant to guide subsequent interactions. Researchers avoid 'why' questions, as these may lead to abstract reasoning and detract from the authentic recounting of the phenomenon. This technique emphasizes the importance of context, ensuring that the participant's experiences are understood within their natural environment. The goal is to capture the 'phenomenon' as it emerges from the participant's perspective, free from researcher-imposed structures.

Data analysis across these techniques aims to preserve the richness of the collected narratives:

- Contextual Meanings: Focus on dimensions such as time, geographical space, interpersonal relationships and identity formation to understand the participant's lived experience.
- Textual Fidelity: Treat the respondent's language as an independent data source, avoiding external theories or interpretations not present in the participant's narrative.
- Collaborative Validation: Engage in group discussions among researchers to rigorously interpret data, ensuring a thorough understanding of elements not explicitly tied to the participant's narrative but relevant to the study.

Both guided and open-ended exploratory techniques are essential tools for understanding consumer behavior. Guided approaches, like in-depth interviews and focus groups, are particularly effective for structured investigations into specific topics or group dynamics. Open-ended techniques, such as phenomenological interviews, allow for authentic, nuanced narratives to emerge, providing a deeper understanding of participants' lived experiences. Regardless of the approach, rigorous data analysis ensures that the findings maintain their richness and validity, contributing valuable insights into consumer research.

Ethnographic and Netnography Analyses

Ethnographic analysis, rooted in anthropology, explores how culture shapes individuals' interpretive frameworks (Pettigrew, 2000). This naturalistic approach emphasizes understanding phenomena within their real-world contexts. Researchers immerse themselves in social groups as both observers and participants, building the intimacy required for effective insights.

The primary goal is to provide detailed accounts of phenomena through various data collection methods, including interviews, participant observation, photographs and recordings. Quantitative techniques may complement qualitative data, as seen in studies like American Thanksgiving consumption patterns (Wallendorf & Arnould, 1991). Regular updates to data interpretation are recommended throughout the research process.

The ethnographic method is particularly valuable in four contexts:

- Studying cultural consumption dimensions (e.g., rituals, myths and gift exchanges).
- Analyzing service interactions and everyday consumption behaviors.
- Uncovering hidden or irrational behaviors, such as extravagant purchases.
- Exploring unfamiliar cultures and subcultures.

A significant evolution of this method is netnography, which adapts ethnographic analysis to computer-mediated communication contexts (Kozinets, 2002).

Netnography adapts ethnography to online contexts, focusing on social and interactive dimensions of virtual experiences (Kozinets, 2002, 2015). Social media and online communities provide rich data on shared interests, interactions and knowledge exchange. This method has been applied in marketing to areas like music, gaming and salsa dancing experiences (García-Álvarez et al., 2009; Hamilton & Hewer, 2009; Kerrigan et al., 2014).

Emerging technologies suggest customizing netnography protocols to immersive contexts, promising significant future advancements (Heinonen & Medberg, 2018; Kozinets, 2022). However, its static nature limits its ability to capture experiential dynamics.

To address netnography's limitations, screencast videography focuses on dynamic, real-time experiences. This method uses video recordings of screen activities, capturing live interactions and patterns that reveal deeper insights into the experiential process (Kawaf, 2019). By repeatedly analyzing these videos, researchers can identify themes and better understand how online interactions evolve over time.

Photo-Elicitation

Initially applied in mental health studies during the 1950s, photo-elicitation has recently gained prominence in consumer research. This method employs photography to focus on the context of experiences, providing a versatile tool for documenting reality. Typically, photographs serve as stimuli, prompting participants to comment on the depicted scenes during interviews, making the images central to the data collection process.

The shift from disposable to digital cameras has significantly enhanced this method, enabling participants to take and review photographs instantly. This advancement has broadened the technique's applicability and efficiency. Depending on the approach, the researcher may capture moments in the participant's life (autodriving), or the participants themselves may take photos during their consumption experiences.

When participants create the photographic content, the emphasis is on elements they find personally significant, highlighting the subjective nature of their consumption experiences. This method underscores the consumer's perspective, allowing researchers to focus on aspects that might otherwise remain overlooked.

One specific approach within this method is the Collective Stereographic Photo Essay, introduced by Holbrook (1997). This technique leverages three-dimensional photographs to enhance realism, clarity and depth, helping to deepen the understanding of consumption experiences.

Whether researchers or participants generate the photos, the images are typically accompanied by brief explanatory texts or interviews. These visual and verbal elements are then analyzed together to identify common themes across experiences. This combined analysis offers rich, nuanced insights into consumer behavior that traditional research methods might miss.

Zaltman Metaphor-Elicitation Technique

Advances in psychology and neuroscience have shaped the Zaltman Metaphor-Elicitation Technique (ZMET), developed by Zaltman (1997, 2003) to study purchasing and consumption processes. Traditional research methods often assume that thought is largely conscious and can be analyzed procedurally using words. However, neuroscience, anthropology and psychology suggest that 95% of human thought, emotions and learning occur unconsciously (Zaltman, 2003).

Neuroscience indicates that unconscious thoughts are often structured as images and are only translated into words when individuals become aware of them. Based on this, metaphors – broadly defined to include similes, allegories and proverbs – play a crucial role in human cognition. Metaphors connect new stimuli to existing knowledge, allowing individuals to perceive the world more effectively. Metaphors embody the biological interplay of reason and emotion, with neither functioning effectively in isolation (Christensen & Olson, 2002).

ZMET unfolds through two main phases: Data collection and data analysis, offering a structured approach to uncovering deep, unconscious consumer insights.

- Data Collection. The Metaphor-Elicitation Phase. Eliciting metaphors is a nuanced process that taps into both superficial and deeply rooted unconscious thoughts. While some metaphors are easily identified, others are embedded in implicit cognitive structures, revealing valuable insights into purchasing and consumption behaviors. Metaphors are closely tied to individual memories, which can be explicit (conscious and easily recalled by the individual) and implicit (unconscious, not immediately accessible, yet influential in shaping behavior). Both types of memories interact dynamically with marketing strategies, shaping and being shaped by them.

  Before the interview, participants are tasked with selecting or creating images from various sources – such as magazines, books or personal drawings – that capture their feelings about the topic under discussion. These images are then arranged into a collage, offering a visual representation of the participant's perspective on the consumption experience.

  During the in-depth interview, participants narrate stories inspired by their collages. This process allows researchers to uncover key metaphors and identify connections between them, revealing deeper emotions, thoughts and associations tied to the participant's consumption experience.
- Data Analysis. Constructing the Consensus Map. The collected metaphors are synthesized into a consensus map, which visualizes the network of abstract concepts within participants' cognitive frameworks. This map highlights shared schemas and recurring constructs across multiple participants. The consensus mapping process is articulated into two activities: (1) The construct identification (constructs are recognized when they recur across multiple interviews, e.g., mentioned by at least five participants) and the (2) mapping relationships (relationships between constructs are visualized, with some acting as starting points and others serving as destinations

or connectors). The consensus map provides a comprehensive view of shared cognitive patterns, offering insights into how consumers perceive and experience specific topics.

ZMET combines the richness of metaphor analysis with rigorous qualitative research to uncover deep insights into unconscious consumer thought. By linking memory, emotion and cognition through visual and verbal storytelling, it offers a robust method for understanding complex purchasing and consumption behaviors (Zaltman, 1997, 2003).

Multisensory Analysis

Multisensory analysis measures physiological and neurological reactions to emotions, capturing insights that individuals may not consciously recognize or articulate (Zaltman, 2003). Later, the multisensory sculpting (MSS) method was developed to allow researchers to access embodied brand knowledge through the use of multisensory metaphors (Von Wallpach & Kreuzer, 2013). This innovative approach highlights the importance of integrating sensory and introspective data to uncover non-conscious brand associations, enriching traditional methodologies. MSS is particularly valuable for decoding the intricate dynamics of sensory stimuli during consumption, offering a comprehensive understanding of how consumers internalize and interact with brands.

This approach, which gained prominence with neuromarketing, focuses on how consumers respond to external and internal stimuli, offering valuable insights into emotions and memory processes that traditional methods often miss.

Peripheral measures assess unconscious responses to marketing stimuli, including facial expressions, pupil dilation and skin conductance. These reactions, often triggered by multisensory stimuli (e.g., visual, auditory or olfactory), provide real-time feedback that shapes the consumption experience (Petit et al., 2019; Yazdanparast & Spears, 2013). While foundational theories suggest universality in some physiological responses, such as facial expressions, cultural and contextual factors also influence emotional expression.

Modern technologies, such as biofeedback sensors, track immediate reactions like heart rate or sweat levels (Mullen & Johnson, 1990), while tools like eye tracking analyze attention patterns, helping refine user experiences.

Neurological techniques focus on brain activity to understand deeper cognitive and emotional responses. Two key categories include:

- Response Latency Techniques. Measure the time between stimulus and response to reveal subconscious associations. Methods like priming and the implicit association test (IAT) explore automatic connections between concepts, uncovering biases and preferences that participants may be unaware of (Zaltman, 2003).
- Neuroimaging Techniques. Visualize brain activity to study responses to stimuli. Examples include:
    - Functional Magnetic Resonance Imaging (fMRI). Tracks blood flow to reveal neural activity but requires significant investment and participant effort.
    - Functional Diffuse Optical Tomography (fDOT). Offers a less invasive alternative to fMRI, capturing activity near the brain's surface.
    - Positron Emission Tomography (PET). Provides detailed imaging but is invasive and costly.

Multisensory analysis, combining physiological and neurological methods, provides brands with a deeper understanding of consumer emotions and reactions. However, these techniques primarily focus on the emotional dimension and should be complemented with other approaches to capture the full complexity of the consumption experience.

POST-CONSUMPTION STEP

The post-consumption phase is the final and crucial stage of the customer journey, where the primary task of marketing research is to assess and analyze the value generated for the customer. Each brand will have a set of specific objectives, and it is in this phase that research determines whether, and to what extent, these goals have been achieved. To accomplish this, a variety of techniques are available, categorized into those that explore the brand experience and those that measure it. Among the exploratory techniques, personal introspection plays a significant role, manifesting as subjective personal introspection and diaries. In contrast, surveys, experimental design, web analysis and textual analysis are commonly used to measure the customer experience.

Personal Introspection

Personal introspection, while a relatively recent method in marketing, has a longstanding tradition in psychology.

In consumer experience research, introspection involves individuals analyzing their own experiences by exploring their stream of consciousness. The premise is that since the experience is personal and subjective, only the individual who lived it can fully interpret its meaning. This method encourages participants to deeply examine their sensations, emotions and perceptions. Typically, introspection revisits past consumption experiences through memory, though it can also address ongoing experiences, making it adaptable to various contexts.

Introspection offers two primary benefits in studying consumption experiences:

- Detailed Variable Identification. It reveals the variables contributing to the experience and their interactions.
- Capturing Dynamics. It traces how these variables and their effects evolve over time, offering insights into the fluid nature of consumption.

At the conclusion of an introspective study, reports should address three dimensions of the consumption experience (Hirschman & Holbrook, 1992):

- Cognitive Interpretation. The rational meaning attributed to the product.
- Emotional Reaction. The feelings and emotions elicited during consumption.
- Evaluation. The overall perception of the product, encompassing its individual and social value.

While introspection provides rich, detailed insights, it faces challenges in terms of external validity. To address this, researchers often involve larger samples, with participants conducting their own introspection to ensure broader applicability.

Technological advancements, particularly in machine learning for text analysis, have further enhanced introspective methods. The increased use of diaries has facilitated the transformation of qualitative data into quantitative insights, enabling a deeper understanding of customer experiences (Hirschman & Holbrook, 1992). These advancements make introspection a robust tool for exploring the nuanced dynamics of consumer behavior.

Surveys

Surveys are among the most widely used methods in marketing research, particularly for exploring causal relationships. They typically involve administering questionnaires to large, representative samples to measure and test variables related to customer experiences, such as the antecedents and outcomes of customer engagement.

Surveys provide a structured approach that follows an established protocol: Researchers select an interpretive model, define measurement scales, administer the questionnaire and analyze the data statistically. This process enables insights from large samples, yielding results that are both valid and comparable across groups and time periods.

Technological advancements, particularly in social media, have revitalized survey usage. Platforms like Facebook, Twitter and Instagram provide vast amounts of spontaneous consumer feedback and offer brands opportunities to gather self-reported attitudes and behaviors from specific target segments. These platforms are especially valuable for engaging younger demographics.

Despite their widespread use, surveys have notable limitations:

- Capturing Complexity. Traditional surveys often struggle to address the complex, non-linear relationships that shape consumption experiences. These methods fail to capture the intertwined nature of such experiences, where cause-and-effect relationships may not be straightforward (Hirschman & Holbrook, 1992).
- Emotional Depth. Surveys often assume that emotional experiences can be directly linked to specific stimuli, an assumption that may not always hold true. Experiences do not always require a direct external stimulus, meaning traditional surveys may miss key aspects of emotional consumption.
- Sampling Challenges. Defining the unit of analysis and sampling poses difficulties. Focusing on individual experiences, rather than individuals, complicates sampling and makes aggregating results into a cohesive framework more challenging.
- Scale Selection. The quality of survey results depends heavily on the selection of scales and underlying theoretical models, adding complexity to the research process.
- Reliance on Self-Reported Data. Surveys depend on participants' ability to articulate their emotions and experiences. However, self-reported data assume the absence of barriers like communicability, contextualization and awareness – barriers that are particularly challenging when studying emotions, as individuals may struggle to recognize or express them.

Despite these challenges, surveys remain a valuable tool in marketing research. They are relatively easy to administer, cost-effective and capable of collecting large-scale data from diverse populations. However, researchers must be mindful of their limitations, especially when investigating complex, emotionally driven consumption experiences. Adopting complementary methods and refining survey designs can help address these gaps, ensuring more comprehensive insights.

Experimental Design

Experimental studies, closely linked with quantitative data, are often considered the best method for identifying universal relationships. Although commonly used in physical sciences, this approach has also been applied to consumer behavior research (Applebaum & Spears, 1950; Perdue & Summers, 1986). The primary objective is to test relationships among variables by isolating specific variables while controlling others, ensuring strong internal validity (Singleton et al., 1993).

Conducting an experimental study requires hypothesizing the variables and their causal links in advance, typically grounded in a theoretical framework. The goal is to confirm or refute these causal links by manipulating independent variables and observing their effects on dependent variables under controlled conditions (Ryals & Wilson, 2005).

There are three primary experimental designs:

- After-Only Design. Measures are taken only after the treatment.
- Before–After Design. Measures are taken before and after the treatment, using the same group as both the control and experimental groups.
- Before–After Design With Control Group. This design uses two groups – a control group and an experimental group – to isolate the variable of interest while controlling for others. This method is particularly effective in studying consumer behavior (Ryals & Wilson, 2005).

'Quasi-experiments' are useful for studying natural settings, maintaining some control similar to laboratory experiments but facing challenges like the timing of treatments and subject selection. Despite smaller sample sizes, experiments can provide in-depth analyses of variable relationships (Holbrook, 1980).

Experiments, though more complex to design than surveys, allow researchers to control all research conditions. They often involve statistical analyses such as ANOVA, MANOVA, multidimensional scaling, regression, conjoint analysis and structural equation modeling.

A prominent application of experimental methods, especially in digital experiences, is A/B testing. This method compares two versions of a product or feature to determine which performs better in terms of user engagement or other metrics, optimizing design based on real user data.

Experimental research, while essential, can struggle with capturing the full complexity of consumption experiences. Despite relying on self-report data, other measures such as behavioral and psychophysiological responses can also be investigated, though these are often less clear-cut. Challenges include understanding the strength of associations, event sequences, potential intervening variables and measurement errors (Bagozzi, 1977).

It is fundamentally important to consider background variables for determining the external validity of experimental research as external validity depends on the interpretive models used to analyze phenomena (Lynch, 1982). Accurate identification of determinants allows for generalization of results. Thus, experimental techniques are most effective when based on prior exploratory research that identifies relevant variables, serving as a foundation for subsequent studies.

FUTURE DIRECTIONS

The digital transformation process offers profound benefits for organizations, reshaping how brands operate and deliver value. However, its success lies not merely in technology adoption but in leveraging these technologies to enhance brand experiences. By integrating digital technologies across all business areas, organizations can create customer-centric, data-driven strategies that enable customized, omnichannel and dynamic brand experiences.

A customer-based strategy begins with a comprehensive understanding of customer experiences, treating customers as a strategic knowledge source to foster competitive advantage. This process requires constant innovation and re-engineering, with organizations adopting a customer-centric approach that dissolves internal and external boundaries (Terho et al., 2022). Whether in front- or back-office roles, all employees contribute to creating engaging customer experiences and strengthening market relationships.

Customer centricity entails proactively involving customers in defining offerings, tracking their behaviors and profiling them down to personality traits and preferences. In this model, customers act as co-creators and equal stakeholders in shaping the brand experience. Every business process, not just marketing, must be aligned with customer needs and preferences (Gahler et al., 2023).

The digital transformation process increases efficiency, flexibility and agility, offering brands unprecedented opportunities to connect with consumers. It transforms the brand experience into one that is dynamic, interactive and personalized, fostering human-centered interactions at every touchpoint along the customer journey. By ensuring that every interaction contributes to a seamless, engaging brand experience, organizations can build deeper, lasting relationships with customers.

CHALLENGES OF DIGITAL TRANSFORMATION IN BRAND EXPERIENCE

While digital transformation offers numerous benefits, it also presents several challenges that brands must navigate to create a successful brand experience.

- Balancing Technology With Human Touch. As brands increasingly rely on digital technologies to enhance customer experience, there is a risk of losing the human touch that has traditionally been a cornerstone of brand relationships. Automated customer service, for example, can improve efficiency but may lack the empathy and understanding that human agents provide. Brands must find the right balance between leveraging technology and maintaining genuine human connections.
- Managing Data Privacy and Security. The use of consumer data to personalize experiences raises important concerns about privacy and security. Consumers are becoming more aware of how their data is being used and are demanding greater transparency from brands. Brands must ensure that they are not only compliant with data protection regulations but also that they build trust by being transparent about their data practices.
- Keeping Up With Rapid Technological Changes. The pace of technological change is another challenge for brands. New digital tools and platforms are constantly emerging, and brands must continuously adapt to stay relevant. This requires significant investment in technology as well as a willingness to experiment and innovate.

The digital transformation process equips organizations to connect with consumers in meaningful ways, creating personalized, human-centered experiences. However, the journey requires brands to balance technological advancements with the human touch, navigate data privacy concerns and remain agile in the face of rapid change. By addressing these challenges and prioritizing customer-centricity, organizations can unlock the full potential of digital transformation to enhance brand experiences and sustain long-term success.

FUNDING

This work was supported by Rome Technopole, PNRR grant M4-C2-Inv. 1.5 CUP F83B22000040006. In particular, the analysis of the research methodologies for the consumption and the post-consumption stage was funded by Rome Technopole.

REFERENCES

Addis, M. (2020). *Engaging brands: A customer-centric approach for superior experiences*. Routledge.

Applebaum, W., & Spears, R. F. (1950). Controlled experimentation in marketing research. *Journal of Marketing*, *14*(4), 505–17. https://doi.org/10.1177/002224295001400401

Arici, H. E., Köseoglu, M. A., & Sökmen, A. (2022). The intellectual structure of customer experience research in service scholarship: A bibliometric analysis. *The Service Industries Journal*, *42*(7–8), 514–50. https://doi.org/10.1080/02642069.2022.2043286

Bagozzi, R. P. (1977). Structural equation models in experimental research. *Journal of Marketing Research*, *14*(2), 209–26. https://doi.org/10.1177/002224377701400209

Barrera, K. G., & Shah, D. (2023). Marketing in the metaverse: Conceptual understanding, framework, and research agenda. *Journal of Business Research*, *155*, 113420. https://doi.org/10.1016/j.jbusres.2022.113420

Barsoux, J. L., Wade, M., & Bouquet, C. (2022). Identifying unmet needs in a digital age. *Harvard Business Review*, *100*(7–8), 150. Retrieved from https://hbsp.harvard.edu/product/R2204C-PDF-ENG

Becker, L., & Jaakkola, E. (2020). Customer experience: Fundamental premises and implications for research. *Journal of the Academy of Marketing Science*, *48*(4), 630–48. https://doi.org/10.1007/s11747-019-00718-x

Boyce, C., & Neale, P. (2006). *Conducting in-depth interviews: A guide for designing and conducting in-depth interviews for evaluation input* (Vol. *2*). Pathfinder International.

Brakus, J. J., Schmitt, B. H., & Zarantonello, L. (2009). Brand experience: What is it? How is it measured? Does it affect loyalty? *Journal of Marketing*, *73*(3), 52–62. https://doi.org/10.1509/jmkg.73.3.052

Brodie, R. J., Ilic, A., Juric, B., & Hollebeek, L. (2013). Consumer engagement in a virtual brand community: An exploratory analysis. *Journal of Business Research*, *66*(1), 105–14. https://doi.org/10.1016/j.jbusres.2011.07.029

Christensen, G. L., & Olson, J. C. (2002). Mapping consumers' mental models with ZMET. *Psychology & Marketing*, *19*(6), 477–501. https://doi.org/10.1002/mar.10021

Cui, X., Xie, Q., Zhu, J., Shareef, M. A., Goraya, M. A. S., & Akram, M. S. (2022). Understanding the omnichannel customer journey: The effect of online and offline channel interactivity on consumer value co-creation behavior. *Journal of Retailing and Consumer Services*, *65*, 102869. https://doi.org/10.1016/j.jretconser.2021.102869

D'Cruz, P., Du, S., Noronha, E., Parboteeah, K. P., Trittin-Ulbrich, H., & Whelan, G. (2022). Technology, megatrends and work: Thoughts on the future of business ethics. *Journal of Business Ethics*, *180*(3), 879–902. https://doi.org/10.1007/s10551-022-05240-9

de Oliveira Santini, F., Ladeira, W. J., Sampaio, C. H., & Pinto, D. C. (2018). The brand experience extended model: A meta-analysis. *Journal of Brand Management*, *25*(6), 519–35. https://doi.org/10.1057/s41262-018-0104-6

Dwivedi, Y. K., Hughes, L., Baabdullah, A. M., Ribeiro-Navarrete, S., Giannakis, M., Al-Debei, M. M., Dennehy, D., Metri, B., Buhalis, D., Cheung, C. M., & Conboy, K. (2022). Metaverse beyond the hype: Multidisciplinary perspectives on emerging challenges, opportunities, and agenda for research, practice and policy. *International Journal of Information Management*, *66*, 102542. https://doi.org/10.1016/j.ijinfomgt.2022.102542

Edelman, D. C., & Singer, M. (2015). Competing on customer journeys. *Harvard Business Review*, *93*(11), 88–100. Retrieved from: https://hbr.org/2015/11/competing-on-customer-journeys

Finn, A., & Kayandé, U. (1999). Unmasking a phantom: A psychometric assessment of mystery shopping. *Journal of Retailing*, *75*(2), 195–217. https://doi.org/10.1016/S0022-4359(99)00004-4

Fuller, R. B. (2019). *Nine chains to the moon: An adventure story of thought* (Vol. *165*). Birkhäuser.

Gahler, M., Klein, J. F., & Paul, M. (2023). Customer experience: Conceptualization, measurement, and application in omnichannel environments. *Journal of Service Research*, *26*(2), 191–211. https://doi.org/10.1177/10946705221126590

García-Álvarez, E., López-Sintas, J., & Zerva, K. (2009). A contextual theory of accessing music: Consumer behavior and ethical arguments. *Consumption, Markets and Culture*, *12*(3), 243–64. https://doi.org/10.1080/10253860903063253

Gilgun, J. F., & Sussman, M. B. (2014). *The methods and methodologies of qualitative family research*. Routledge.

Gong, C., & Ribiere, V. (2021). Developing a unified definition of digital transformation. *Technovation*, *102*, 102217. https://doi.org/10.1016/j.technovation.2020.102217

Govindarajan, V., & Venkatraman, N. V. (2022). The next great digital advantage. *Harvard Business Review*, *100*(3), 55–6. Retrieved from: https://hbr.org/2022/05/the-next-great-digital-advantage

Hamilton, K., & Hewer, P. (2009). Salsa magic: An exploratory netnographic analysis of the salsa experience. *Advances in Consumer Research*, *36*, 502–8. ISSN: 0098-9258

Hamilton, R., & Price, L. L. (2019). Consumer journeys: Developing consumer-based strategy. *Journal of the Academy of Marketing Science*, *47*(2), 187–91. https://doi.org/10.1007/s11747-019-00636-y

Heinonen, K., & Medberg, G. (2018). Netnography as a tool for understanding customers: Implications for service research and practice. *Journal of Services Marketing*, *32*(6), 657–79. https://doi.org/10.1108/JSM-08-2017-0294

Heinonen, K., Strandvik, T., Mickelsson, K. J., Edvardsson, B., Sundström, E., & Andersson, P. (2010). A customer-dominant logic of service. *Journal of Service Management*, *21*(4), 531–48. https://doi.org/10.1108/09564231011066088

Hirschman, E. C., & Holbrook, M. B. (1992). *Postmodern consumer research* (Vol. *1*). Sage.

Holbrook, M. B. (1980). Some preliminary notes on research in consumer esthetics. *Advances in Consumer Research*, *7*(1), 1. https://doi.org/10.1086/208787

Holbrook, M. B. (1997). Three-dimensional stereographic visual displays in marketing and consumer research. *Academy of Marketing Science Review*, *11*(1), 1–73.

Holbrook, M. B. (2024). *Consumer behavior: New essays on the study of consumption*. Taylor & Francis.

Holmlund, M., Van Vaerenbergh, Y., Ciuchita, R., Ravald, A., Sarantopoulos, P., Ordenes, F. V., & Zaki, M. (2020). Customer experience management in the age of big data analytics: A strategic framework. *Journal of Business Research*, *116*, 356–65. https://doi.org/10.1016/j.jbusres.2020.01.022

Holz, H. F., Becker, M., Blut, M., & Paluch, S. (2024). Eliminating customer experience pain points in complex customer journeys through smart service solutions. *Psychology & Marketing*, *41*(3), 592–609. https://doi.org/10.1002/mar.21938

Hoyer, W. D., Kroschke, M., Schmitt, B., Kraume, K., & Shankar, V. (2020). Transforming the customer experience through new technologies. *Journal of Interactive Marketing*, *51*(1), 57–71. https://doi.org/10.1016/j.intmar.2020.04.001

Jaakkola, E., & Terho, H. (2021). Service journey quality: Conceptualization, measurement and customer outcomes. *Journal of Service Management*, *32*(6), 1–27. https://doi.org/10.1108/JOSM-06-2020-0233

Kawaf, F. (2019). Capturing digital experience: The method of screencast videography. *International Journal of Research in Marketing*, *36*(2), 169–84. https://doi.org/10.1016/j.ijresmar.2018.11.002

Kerrigan, F., Larsen, G., Hanratty, S., & Korta, K. (2014). "Gimme shelter" experiencing pleasurable escape through the musicalisation of running. *Marketing Theory*, *14*(2), 147–66. https://doi.org/10.1177/1470593114521451

Kozinets, R. V. (2015). Management netnography: Axiological and methodological developments in online cultural business research. In *The Sage handbook of qualitative business and management research methods*. Sage.

Kozinets, R. V. (2002). The field behind the screen: Using netnography for marketing research in online communities. *Journal of Marketing Research*, *39*(1), 61–72. https://doi.org/10.1509/jmkr.39.1.61.18935

Kozinets, R. V. (2022). Immersive netnography: A novel method for service experience research in virtual reality, augmented reality and metaverse contexts. *Journal of Service Management*, *34*(1), 100–25. https://doi.org/10.1108/JOSM-12-2021-0481

Kuehnl, C., Jozic, D., & Homburg, C. (2019). Effective customer journey design: Consumers' conception, measurement, and consequences. *Journal of the Academy of Marketing Science*, *47*(3), 551–68. https://doi.org/10.1007/s11747-018-00625-7

Lemon, K. N., & Verhoef, P. C. (2016). Understanding customer experience throughout the customer journey. *Journal of Marketing*, *80*(6), 69–96. https://doi.org/10.1509/jm.15.0420

Liedtka, J. (2015). Perspective: Linking design thinking with innovation outcomes through cognitive bias reduction. *Journal of Product Innovation Management*, *32*(6), 925–38. https://doi.org/10.1111/jpim.12163

Lynch, Jr., J. G. (1982). On the external validity of experiments in consumer research. *Journal of Consumer Research*, *9*(3), 225–39. https://doi.org/10.1086/208919

McCarthy, D., & Fader, P. (2020). How to value a company by analyzing its customers. *Harvard Business Review*, *98*(1), 51–4.

Mikroyannidis, A., & Theodoulidis, B. (2010). Ontology management and evolution for business intelligence. *International Journal of Information Management*, *30*(6), 559–66. https://doi.org/10.1016/j.ijinfomgt.2009.10.002

Mullen, B., & Johnson, C. (1990). Distinctiveness-based illusory correlations and stereotyping: A meta-analytic integration. *British Journal of Social Psychology*, *29*(1), 11–28. https://doi.org/10.1111/j.2044-8309.1990.tb00883.x

Ordenes, F. V., Theodoulidis, B., Burton, J., Gruber, T., & Zaki, M. (2014). Analyzing customer experience feedback using text mining: A linguistics-based approach. *Journal of Service Research*, *17*(3), 278–95. https://doi.org/10.1177/1094670514524625

Park, S., & Kim, S. (2022). Identifying world types to deliver gameful experiences for sustainable learning in the metaverse. *Sustainability*, *14*(3), 1361. https://doi.org/10.3390/su14031361

Perdue, B. C., & Summers, J. O. (1986). Checking the success of manipulations in marketing experiments. *Journal of Marketing Research*, *23*(4), 317–26. https://doi.org/10.1177/002224378602300401

Petit, O., Velasco, C., & Spence, C. (2019). Digital sensory marketing: Integrating new technologies into multisensory online experience. *Journal of Interactive Marketing*, *45*(1), 42–61. https://doi.org/10.1016/j.intmar.2018.07.004

Pettigrew, S. F. (2000). Ethnography and grounded theory: A happy marriage? *Advances in Consumer Research*, *27*(1), 1. https://doi.org/10.1086/314305

Puntoni, S., Reczek, R. W., Giesler, M., & Botti, S. (2021). Consumers and artificial intelligence: An experiential perspective. *Journal of Marketing*, *85*(1), 131–51. https://doi.org/10.1177/0022242920953847

Rawson, A., Duncan, E., & Jones, C. (2013). The truth about customer experience. *Harvard Business Review*, *91*(9), 90–8. Retrieved from: https://hbr.org/2013/09/the-truth-about-customer-experience

Reitsamer, B. F., Stokburger-Sauer, N. E., & Kuhnle, J. S. (2024). How and when effective customer journeys drive brand loyalty: The role of consumer-brand identification. *Journal of Service Management*, *35*(6), 109–35. https://doi.org/10.1108/JOSM-08-2023-0374

Reynolds, T. J., & Olson, J. C. (2001). *Understanding consumer decision making: The means-end approach to marketing and advertising strategy*. Psychology Press.

Rosen, D. E., Schroeder, J. E., & Purinton, E. F. (1998). Marketing high tech products: Lessons in customer focus from the marketplace. *Academy of Marketing Science Review*, *6*, 1–17.

Ryals, L., & Wilson, H. (2005). Experimental methods in market research: From information to insight. *International Journal of Market Research*, *47*(4), 345–64. https://doi.org/10.1177/147078530504700402

Schmitt, B., Brakus, J. J., & Zarantonello, L. (2015). From experiential psychology to consumer experience. *Journal of Consumer Psychology*, *25*(1), 166–71. https://doi.org/10.1016/j.jcps.2014.09.001

Shankar, V., Kleijnen, M., Ramanathan, S., Rizley, R., Holland, S., & Morrissey, S. (2016). Mobile shopper marketing: Key issues, current insights, and future research avenues. *Journal of Interactive Marketing*, *34*(1), 37–48. https://doi.org/10.1016/j.intmar.2016.03.002

Siebert, A., Gopaldas, A., Lindridge, A., & Simões, C. (2020). Customer experience journeys: Loyalty loops versus involvement spirals. *Journal of Marketing*, *84*(4), 45–66. https://doi.org/10.1177/0022242920920262

Singleton, R. A., Straits, B. C., & Straits, M. M. (1993). *Approaches to social research* (2nd ed.). Oxford University Press.

Sundbo, J. (2009). Innovation in the experience economy: A taxonomy of innovation organisations. *The Service Industries Journal*, *29*(4), 431–55. https://doi.org/10.1080/02642060802283139

Terho, H., Mero, J., Siutla, L., & Jaakkola, E. (2022). Digital content marketing in business markets: Activities, consequences, and contingencies along the customer journey. *Industrial Marketing Management*, *105*, 294–310. https://doi.org/10.1016/j.indmarman.2022.06.006

Vargo, S. L., Maglio, P. P., & Akaka, M. A. (2008). On value and value co-creation: A service systems and service logic perspective. *European Management Journal*, *26*(3), 145–52. https://doi.org/10.1016/j.emj.2008.04.003

Von Wallpach, S., & Kreuzer, M. (2013). Multi-sensory sculpting (MSS): Eliciting embodied brand knowledge via multi-sensory metaphors. *Journal of Business Research*, *66*(9), 1325–31. https://doi.org/10.1016/j.jbusres.2012.02.032

Voorhees, C. M., Fombelle, P. W., Gregoire, Y., Bone, S., Gustafsson, A., Sousa, R., & Walkowiak, T. (2017). Service encounters, experiences and the customer journey: Defining the field and a call to expand our lens. *Journal of Business Research*, *79*, 269–80. https://doi.org/10.1016/j.jbusres.2017.04.014

Wallendorf, M., & Arnould, E. J. (1991). 'We gather together': Consumption rituals of Thanksgiving Day. *Journal of Consumer Research*, *18*(1), 13–31. https://doi.org/10.1086/209237

Wilson, A. M. (1998). The role of mystery shopping in the measurement of service performance. *Managing Service Quality: An International Journal*, *8*(6), 414–20.

Wirtz, J., Kimes, S. E., Theng, J. H. P., & Patterson, P. (2003). Revenue management: Resolving potential customer conflicts. *Journal of Revenue and Pricing Management*, *2*(3), 216–26. https://doi.org/10.1057/palgrave.rpm.5170068

Yazdanparast, A., & Spears, N. (2013). Can consumers forgo the need to touch products? An investigation of nonhaptic situational factors in an online context. *Psychology & Marketing*, *30*(1), 46–61. https://doi.org/10.1002/mar.20588

Yu, C. H., Jannasch-Pennell, A., & DiGangi, S. (2011). Compatibility between text mining and qualitative research in the perspectives of grounded theory, content analysis, and reliability. *Qualitative Report*, *16*(3), 730–44. Retrieved from: www.nova.edu/ssss/QR/QR16-3/yu.pdf

Zaltman, G. (1997). Rethinking market research: Putting people back in. *Journal of Marketing Research*, *34*(4), 424–37. https://doi.org/10.1177/002224379703400402

Zaltman, G. (2003). *How customers think: Essential insights into the mind of the market*. Harvard Business School Publishing.

Zarantonello, L., & Andreini, D. (2023). A roadmap of brand experience. In *A research agenda for brand management in a new era of consumerism* (pp. 123–141). Edward Elgar Publishing.

Zarantonello, L., & Schmitt, B. H. (2023). Experiential AR/VR: A consumer and service framework and research agenda. *Journal of Service Management*, *34*(1), 34–55. https://doi.org/10.1108/JOSM-12-2021-0479

Zeng, D., Chen, H., Lusch, R., & Li, S. H. (2010). Social media analytics and intelligence. *IEEE Intelligent Systems*, *25*(6), 13–6. https://doi.org/10.1109/MIS.2010.151

23

Brand Engagement Overview: Definitions, Measurements and Strategies

Valentina Mazzoli

INTRODUCTION

In the last 15 years, brand engagement has received considerable attention from both academics and practitioners, given the relevance of brand engagement for retaining customers and creating a successful competitive advantage for companies (Kumar & Pansari, 2016; Pansari & Kumar, 2017).

Given the renowned importance of brand engagement among brands, several consulting companies (Gligor et al., 2019) have developed reports and created their appropriate divisions to delve into the drivers and consequences of brand engagement, with the aim of exemplifying the most relevant brand strategies to nurture brand engagement.

Several practical and popular examples of these strategies include, for instance, Dove's 'Real Beauty' Campaign, whose main scope was the celebration of natural beauty and the promotion of body positivity. The campaign helped boost Dove's brand perception, solidifying its reputation for authenticity and social impact. This emotional connection with its audience translated to massive social media engagement and millions of views on social media channels (Feng et al., 2019).

Another example of brand engagement strategies was developed by the online eyewear company Warby Parker, offering augmented reality 'try-ons' for their customers to ease the purchasing process (Valdellon, 2021).

Similarly, the campaign 'Share a Coke' by Coca-Cola, by replacing the iconic Coca-Cola logo with popular names on its bottles, the brand made its product more personal. Consumers were encouraged to find and share bottles with their names or loved ones' names. This led to an increase in sales in many countries, such as Australia. Social media played a significant role, with user-generated content contributing to its global success across many countries (Vincent & Kolade, 2019).

Spotify's annual 'Wrapped' campaign turns its users into brand ambassadors by showcasing personalized listening habits from the year. The highly shareable nature of the campaign leads to significant social media buzz. Wrapped has become a cultural moment, contributing to increases in both daily active users and overall app downloads (Meidivia et al., 2023).

As shown by these few examples, brand engagement involves the consumer at different levels, such as at cognitive, affective and behavioral ones. Indeed, brand engagement has been conceptualized as a psychological state created through collaborative experiences involving cognitive, emotional and behavioral activities (Brodie et al., 2011; Hollebeek et al., 2014). However, from a conceptual level, the perceived overlap with other similar brand-related concepts has led to many conceptualizations of this construct with many definitions and dimensions. This chapter will review the main definitions of this concept, differentiating it from other brand-related concepts (i.e., brand attachment, brand involvement, brand love and brand experience).

Moreover, due to the multifaceted nature of measurements of brand engagement, this chapter will review the main tools to measure brand engagement.

As brand engagement plays a crucial role in building brand equity and sustaining a competitive advantage in today's marketplace, the aim of this chapter is also to review the brand engagement strategies at different levels of the consumer journey with the purpose of providing useful managerial guidelines to implement brand engagement strategies.

THEORETICAL FOUNDATIONS OF BRAND ENGAGEMENT

Definitions and Dimensions of Brand Engagement

The concept of brand engagement is part of the customer management literature (Pansari & Kumar, 2017), as it is seen as an evolutionary focus of marketing from transactions (up to the 1990s), to relationships (from the 1990s to the 2000s), and finally to engagement (from the first decade of the 2000s). Brand engagement is perceived as a construct that can take relationships to a higher level.

Thus, since the early 2000s, academics and practitioners have been dealing with engagement, trying to define it, identifying its antecedents and consequences, and metrics for its measurement. Engagement embeds a relationship with brands based on active participation, which in the past was conceptualized using a number of terms such as 'prosumer' or 'co-creator' (Toffler, 1980; Vargo & Lusch, 2004).

The great attention given to this topic depends on the now widespread belief that there is a positive relationship between levels of consumer engagement and business performance, demonstrated not only by academic research but also by accredited research institutions (Liadeli et al., 2023).

With the proliferation of social media, customer engagement has become even more central in the marketing literature, in which the study of interaction with focal objects, such as brands, has attracted the attention of many scholars and practitioners. Thus, as the concept of customer engagement has proliferated, other niche fields of research have gained constant attention such as customer brand engagement. Social media has emphasized the active participation of consumers in the value chain of brands, making the consumer the foremost supplier of operant resources in the business ecosystem (Cantone et al., 2022). The theoretical foundation of brand engagement refers to the Service-Dominant Logic (SDL), in which consumers are the active agents whose knowledge and capabilities are leveraged in the value co-creation process (Vargo & Lusch, 2004). Other theories have been applied to the study of brand engagement. To mention a few, the relationship marketing theory (e.g., Hollebeek, 2011); the stimulus-organism-response model (Islam & Rahman, 2017), the uses and gratifications theory (De Vries & Carlson, 2014); and the organization psychology theory (Dwivedi, 2015) have been used to extend the comprehension of brand engagement (Kumar & Nayak, 2019).

Traditionally, customer brand engagement is defined as 'the level of a customer's cognitive, emotional and behavioral investment in specific brand interactions' (Hollebeek, 2011, p. 656). Although many definitions of brand engagement have been developed (see Table 23.1), there is a strong consensus that brand engagement is a multidimensional construct that is composed of a cognitive dimension, an affective dimension and a behavioral dimension. All these dimensions characterize the relationship between the customer and the brand (Lourenço et al., 2022).

The cognitive dimension of brand engagement is related to the concept of human cognition, which considers the human processes of perception, elaboration and the storage of sensory inputs and stimuli (Neisser, 2014). Customer brand engagement literature has integrated specific components of cognition, such as the cognitive processing of the information retrieved by consumers during consumer–brand interactions (Hollebeek et al., 2014). Similarly, the level of consumer attention is as well a component of consumer cognition that leads to relational benefits with a brand (Hollebeek, 2011; Vivek et al., 2014). The highest level of attention is conceptualized as absorption, and it considers consumers as 'fully concentrated and happily engrossed in brand interaction' (Dwivedi, 2015, p. 100). The cognitive dimension of brand engagement has also been considered the perceived reduction of uncertainty due to the cognitive trust dimension that is based on shared values, experiences and information cues between the brand

Table 23.1 Definitions of engagement considered in the branding literature

Variable Label	*Definition*	*Source*
Customer engagement	'A psychological process that models the underlying mechanisms by which customer loyalty forms for new customers of a service brand as well as the mechanisms by which loyalty may be maintained for repeat purchase customers of a service brand' (p. 65)	Bowden (2009)
Customer brand engagement	'The level of an individual customer's motivational, brand-related and context-dependent state of mind characterized by specific levels of cognitive, emotional and behavioral activity in direct brand interactions' (p. 790)	Hollebeek (2011)
Consumer engagement	'A multi-dimensional concept comprising cognitive, emotional and/or behavioral dimensions, and plays a central role in the process of relational exchange where other relational concepts are engagement antecedents and/or consequences in iterative engagement processes within the brand community' (p. 3)	Brodie et al. (2013)
Consumer brand engagement	'A consumer's positively-valenced brand-related cognitive, emotional and behavioral activity during or related to focal consumer/brand interactions' (p. 154)	Hollebeek et al. (2014)
Brand engagement	'A customer's cognitive, emotional and behavioral investment in specific brand interactions' (p. 62)	Hollebeek and Chen (2014)
Consumer brand engagement	'A consumer's positive, fulfilling, brand-use-related state of mind that is characterized by vigor, dedication and absorption' (p. 101)	Dwivedi (2015)
Customer engagement	'A customer's motivationally driven, volitional investment of operant resources (including cognitive, emotional, behavioral, and social knowledge/skills) and operand resources (e.g., equipment) into brand interactions' (p. 166)	Hollebeek et al. (2019); Kumar et al. (2019)

Source: The author.

and consumers (Roy et al., 2018). The cognitive dimension in the social media environment depicts consumer interactions with brands (Schivinski et al., 2016). Although there are commonalities among different studies on brand engagement, they consider different elements of cognition (Gielens & Steenkamp, 2019). Moreover, they ignore all the unconscious cognitive processing elements that may enrich the conceptualization of brand engagement.

The affective dimension considers sentiments, emotions and, in general, affection-based reactions to brand situational perceptions. Although this dimension is widely used for the definition and measurement of brand engagement, a clear definition of it is still lacking. Affective engagement can be conceptualized as the overall level of emotions felt by a consumer, and it usually considers two subdimensions that are enthusiasm and enjoyment (Dessart et al., 2016). Despite the predominance of the behavioral perspective (Hollebeek et al., 2020, literature has confirmed that emotions strongly affect consumer–brand relationships (Richins, 2008). Emotional states are triggered by consumer–brand interactions, leading to specific behavior or intentions (Ivens et al., 2015). For instance, participation with enthusiasm refers to the passionate reactions when engaging with a brand (Vivek et al., 2014). Similarly, the valenced affective (both negative and positive) idea of brand perception is the passion dimension of engagement (Hollebeek & Chen, 2014). The affective responses are produced by consumers' cognitions. Thus, the processing feelings that emerge in the interplay of cognition and emotions toward a brand are responsible for the emotional dimension of engagement (Lourenço et al., 2022).

In the last few years, there has been a growing interest in the behavioral dimension of brand engagement (Hollebeek et al., 2019, 2024), whose measurement also reflects the main concern for practitioners (Roy et al., 2018; Schivinski et al., 2016). The behavioral dimension includes visible responses and explicit reactions as the result of consumer–brand interactions (Lourenço et al., 2022). The behavioral dimension or the 'activation' dimension refers to the 'consumer's level of energy, effort and time spent on a brand in a particular consumer/brand interaction' (Hollebeek et al., 2014, p. 154). In other words, the behavioral dimension of engagement refers to the manifestations toward the object of engagement (i.e., the brand), beyond purchase, resulting from motivational drivers (Dessart et al., 2016). This dimension of engagement is triggered by precedent cognitive and emotional dimensions.

Differentiating Brand Engagement from other Brand-Related Concepts

Despite the abundant conceptualizations of brand engagement, this construct has been criticized by several scholars, as it seems to overlap with other brand-related constructs in several ways (Cantone et al., 2022; Obilo et al., 2021). These include brand involvement (Zaichkowsky, 1985), brand experience (Brakus et al., 2009), brand attachment (Park et al., 2010) and brand love (Batra et al., 2012). The key element of all these constructs is the commitment consumers experience and show toward the brand.

Brand involvement

Significant research has been devoted to highlighting that, despite similarities, brand engagement and brand involvement are conceptually distinct constructs (Gligor et al., 2019; Haverila et al., 2022). Brand involvement can be conceptualized as the level of interest and personal relevance an individual has for a brand in terms of basic values, goals and self-concept (Mittal, 1995; Zaichkowsky, 1985). Brand engagement is a similar psychological state that an individual experiences for a brand, but it differentiates from brand involvement (Solem & Pedersen, 2016). Compared to brand engagement, brand involvement is more inert and, while considering the emotional and cognitive dimensions (Andersen, 2005), it overlooks the behavioral dimension. In this sense, brand engagement is a broader concept, which is thought to extend beyond mere involvement (Mollen & Wilson, 2010). Involvement concentrates the individual on the perceived importance of the brand, but it does not measure any activation toward it.

Brand experience

Brand experience, as well as brand engagement, is an important variable in the context of interactive service environments. When talking about brand experience, we refer to those 'sensations, feelings, cognitions and behavioral responses evoked by brand-related stimuli that are part of a brand's design and identity, packaging, communications and environments' (Brakus et al., 2009, p. 52). Thus, brand experience is mainly based on responses to brand-related stimuli. It does not assume a motivational psychological state, which is the core element of brand engagement (Brodie et al., 2011). Moreover, as brand experience can also be aroused by indirect communication activities, such as advertising, that are not included in the interactive experience with the brand, brand engagement embeds more customer proactivity in the interactive contexts (Hollebeek et al., 2014).

Brand attachment

Brand attachment refers to a strong emotional connection that a consumer experiences with a brand (Park et al., 2010; Shimul, 2022). Brand attachment and brand engagement both refer to the quality of the relationship, but brand attachment refers to the connection of the individual self-concept with the brand (Escalas, 2004), and it does not imply any interactivity with it, which is instead central for brand engagement. Moreover, brand attachment does not assume any motivational state, which features brand engagement. Brand attachment helps individuals in developing brand commitment (Dennis et al., 2016), spreading positive word-of-mouth (Magnoni et al., 2021) and pushing individuals to pay a higher price for the brand (Orth et al., 2012; Li et al., 2019).

Brand love

Brand love is conceptualized as the extreme positive connection that an individual has with a brand. Brand love usually includes seven elements: passion-driven behaviors that reflect the tough desire to interact with it by using it, and investing resources into it; self-brand integration that embeds the brand's ability to explicit consumers' identities and to join life's deeper meanings; positive emotional connection that includes a sense of positive attachment toward the brand; anticipated separation distress without the brand; long-term relationship, which refers to the commitment toward the brand in the long term; positive valence in terms of attitude and stable attitudes (Batra et al., 2012). These dimensions have many points in common with the three dimensions of brand engagement. However, brand love does not reflect the motivational state that characterizes brand engagement.

Brand Engagement and Individual Traits

The motivational power of brand engagement depends not only on the brand but also on the specific individual characteristics of the customer. Three latent segments of engaged consumers exist in online brand communities (Dessart et al., 2019). The first segment is composed of the 'emotional engagers'. For consumers of this segment, it is all about what they feel for the brand. In essence, the emotional connection that fuels a strong bond with a brand stems from consumers' sense of enjoyment during brand interactions and their excitement about the brand itself. These individuals do not actively engage in cognitive processing or take specific actions related to the brand. On the other hand, the second group, referred to as 'thinkers', is primarily driven by cognitive engagement, such as paying attention and becoming deeply absorbed when making repurchase decisions. For them, brand loyalty emerges solely through mental processing – focusing on the brand, maintaining attention and immersing themselves in brand-related experiences – rather than being influenced by emotions or behaviors. The third group is the 'active engagers'. They are the most loyal consumers. The motivational power toward the brand is manifested through active behaviors, such as sharing, learning from the brand and supporting it, which is the main reason for developing loyalty. These people need to feel close to the brand and actively participate in the community to develop repurchase behavior.

Moreover, individuals may experience a natural tendency, which can be higher or lower in developing relationships with brands. This natural tendency refers to the concept of *brand engagement in self-concept* (BESC; Sprott et al., 2009). BESC is defined as 'an individual difference representing consumers' propensity to include important brands as part of how they view themselves' (Sprott et al., 2009, p. 92). This concept is rooted in the cognitive schema theory, which considers the self as a group of schemas embodying a stable structure of knowledge (Markus, 1977). Individuals differ in specific self-schemas, driving perceptions and behaviors toward brands that fit with these schemas. Thus, BESC is concerned with how brands become important to consumers' self-schemas (Alden et al., 2016). Drivers of BESC can be related to self-determination theory embedding intrinsic aspirations and extrinsic aspirations (Razmus et al., 2017), while consequences of BESC motivate the relationship with specific brands in terms of brand loyalty and brand advocacy (Mazzoli et al., 2019). BESC drives stronger memory associations, leading to greater brand name recall. Consumers higher in BESC usually pay more attention to brands (e.g., selective attention) and display higher brand loyalty. Moreover, they tend to interact higher on brand websites (Alden et al., 2016) and are more likely to become ambassadors of brands (Samala & Singh, 2019). Thus, people with high BESC are more prone to establish strong relationships with brands and vice versa. Moreover, BESC also depends on culture or socioeconomic contexts (Razmus et al., 2020).

BESC differentiates from brand engagement as the former refers to the natural tendency of individuals to include brands as part of how they view themselves, while the latter indicates the motivational power an individual experiences toward a specific brand in terms of cognitive, affective and behavioral dimensions.

The BESC scale reflects this definition as it has eight items that measure the general tendency of the individual to establish a strong connection with brands (see Table 23.2).

Table 23.2 BESC scale

N	*Items*	*Source*
1	I have a special bond with the brands that I like	Sprott et al. (2009)
2	I consider my favorite brands to be a part of myself	
3	I often feel a personal connection between my brands and me	
4	Part of me is defined by important brands in my life	
5	I feel as if I have a close personal connection with the brands I most prefer	
6	I can identify with important brands in my life	
7	There are links between the brands that I prefer and how I view myself	
8	My favorite brands are an important indication of who I am	

Source: Sprott et al. (2009), p. 93.

KEY DRIVERS OF BRAND ENGAGEMENT

Literature on engagement has dedicated many studies to the investigation of the main antecedents of brand engagement. With the purpose of reviewing all the antecedents investigated by the literature, we organized them in fields of research or contexts (Gligor et al., 2023).

In the context of customer–brand relationships, brand involvement and participation (e.g., brand interactivity) have been proposed as the main antecedents of customer brand engagement (France et al., 2016; Leckie et al., 2016). Consumer involvement reflects the extent to which individuals recognize the significance of an object based on their personal needs, values and interests (Zaichkowsky, 1985), while consumer participation is one of the most important manifestations of customer voluntary performance revealed in customer-to-brand behavior. Participation refers to the degree to which the customer is involved in the production and delivery of services of the brand. In a service context, it entails the extent to which consumers provide helpful suggestions and constructive feedback on the service (Eisingerich et al., 2015). Stimulating customer participation is of crucial importance to the shift from a goods-centered logic to a Service-Dominant logic (Vargo & Lusch, 2004). Consumer participation in interactions that provide common interest to both the organization and consumers results in higher levels of enthusiasm, thereby leading to increased engagement with the brand (Leckie et al., 2016; Vivek et al., 2012). Qualitative studies showed that customers engage with brands perceived to listen to what customers are communicating and engage in two-way information exchange (Shao & Chen, 2021). Moreover, brands perceived as highly interactive are considered more willing to develop customized relationships (Sawhney et al., 2005). Consequently, customers feel encouraged to engage with the brand, further strengthening the relationship (Gligor et al., 2019). Similarly, brand self-congruity and customer brand identification reinforce brand engagement and the quality of the customer–brand relationship (France et al., 2016). Customer brand identification can be defined as 'a consumer's perception of the degree to which the specific brand reflects one's inner self' (Carroll & Ahuvia, 2006, p. 82). Customer–brand identification impacts affective and behavioral components of engagement (Leckie et al., 2016).

In highly interactive contexts such as restaurants and other services, brand trust, customer satisfaction (Nyadzayo et al., 2020), emotional brand attachment and the overall co-creation experience nurture brand engagement (Hussain et al., 2021).

In the retail shopping context, brand engagement is greater when individuals consume for status (Flynn et al., 2016). Status consumption is defined as 'the motivational process by which individuals strive to improve their social standing through the conspicuous consumption of consumer products that confer and symbolize status both for the individual and surrounding significant others' (Eastman et al., 1999, p. 41) and triggered by materialism, it is supposed to influence brand engagement (Flynn et al., 2016). Moreover, gamified shopping experiences affect brand engagement in the retail shopping context (Högberg et al., 2019). Gamification enhances engagement through hedonic value, which, together with reward satisfaction, drives continued engagement intention associated with brand engagement.

Given the relevance of brand engagement in social media contexts, many studies have focused on the investigation of the brand engagement antecedents in this context. The relevance of brand involvement and community involvement as main antecedents of brand engagement is also confirmed in the social media environment (Algharabat et al., 2018; Carvalho & Fernandes, 2018). Moreover, customer–brand identification is an important brand engagement driver, even in the social media context (Swani et al., 2021). Kumar and Nayak's study (2019) investigated the role of psychological ownership as a driver for brand engagement in online brand communities. Psychological ownership is 'that state in which individuals feel as though the target of ownership (material or immaterial in nature) or a piece of it is "theirs"' (Pierce et al., 2001, p. 299). Possessions tend to shape the identity of individuals as a relevant part of their extended self (Belk, 1988). In the customer–brand relationship, psychological ownership represents a relevant variable (Wiedmann, 2014). It was found that feelings of psychological ownership are stimulated not only from the possession of the product or the brand but also by merely touching the objects, naming the products and co-designing the innovations (Peck & Shu, 2009; Sembada, 2018). Based on that, individuals usually join brand communities for self-identity and/or self-enhancement and informational learning (Stokburger-Sauer, 2010), making the 'brand' an essential part of their identity. As a consequence, psychological ownership of the brand increases brand engagement (Sembada, 2018).

Overall, we can affirm that brand interactivity, brand involvement, brand trust, brand loyalty, satisfaction with the brand and brand commitment have been extensively investigated as potential drivers of brand engagement across several contexts. Different combinations of these factors may influence brand engagement differently (Gligor et al., 2019). However, brand interactivity results as the strongest predictor of brand engagement (France et al., 2016).

MAIN OUTCOMES OF BRAND ENGAGEMENT

Brand engagement drives relevant virtuous behaviors that nurture the customer–brand relationship over time (Kumar & Nayak, 2019).

Potential positive consequences coming from brand engagement refer to higher brand trust (Pongpaew et al., 2017), higher brand equity (Hepola et al., 2017) and insensitivity to premium prices (Dwivedi et al., 2018; Flynn et al., 2016). The value of brands is supposed to increase as the brand is able to trigger strong brand engagement among its customers (France et al., 2016; Xi & Hamari, 2021).

Brand experience and customer delight have been proposed as outcomes (e.g., Brodie et al., 2011; Nysveen & Pedersen, 2014).

In social media and online brand community contexts, brand engagement is often the driver of brand loyalty (Dessart et al., 2019). Particularly, each dimension of engagement affects brand loyalty in different ways. Affective engagement is the main predictor of brand loyalty, with behavioral engagement following closely behind. Notably, cognitive engagement is not a significant driver of brand loyalty (Dessart et al., 2019). This finding reinforces the idea that repeat purchases are primarily driven by emotional and relational factors (Kumar & Nayak, 2019). Similarly, brand engagement in online communities usually increases customer commitment, trust and cumulative satisfaction (Carvalho & Fernandes, 2018). This has led to potential inconsistencies in what has been considered an outcome or a driver. Thus, the relationships between brand engagement and several other relationship concepts remain unclear; for instance, attachment, commitment and trust may represent drivers or consequences, depending on the length of the customer relationship (e.g., Kumar & Nayak, 2019).

In the online and offline contexts, brand advocacy, word-of-mouth intentions and referrals are driven by brand engagement (Algharabat et al., 2018; Carvalho & Fernandes, 2018), which in certain situations is transformed into brand evangelism (Nyadzayo et al., 2020).

In general, brand engagement has been linked to several positive outcomes, such as improved brand image (Blasco-Arcas et al., 2016), brand value (France et al., 2016), self-brand connection and brand usage intent (Hollebeek et al., 2014). Further, customer engagement leads to greater performance, including profitability and sales growth (Pansari & Kumar, 2017). However, a drawback of brand engagement refers to the compulsive use of social media (Okazaki et al., 2021).

MEASURING BRAND ENGAGEMENT

Quantitative Scales

The majority of studies addressing brand engagement have relied on quantitative measures to capture brand engagement, its relationships with its drivers and its effects. To this aim, several scales have been developed for capturing in a quantitative way, the value of brand engagement for customers. Many scales have been developed considering the social media environment as the interactive nature of social media creates the opportunity for brands/firms to enhance brand engagement, especially considering the crucial role of brand interactivity in determining brand engagement (Gligor et al., 2019).

Some scales operationalize brand engagement as a multi-dimensional construct (e.g., Carlson et al., 2018; Hollebeek et al., 2014; Kumar & Pansari, 2016; Roy et al., 2018), while others as a unidimensional one (Blasco-Arcas et al., 2016; Campbell et al., 2015; France et al., 2016; Högberg et al., 2019).

The variety of items and dimensions included in the scales presented in Table 23.3 reflects the variety of definitions of brand engagement developed throughout the years.

One of the most used scales is the one developed by Hollebeek et al. (2014) and reflects the classic view of brand engagement as a multidimensional construct that embeds a cognitive (i.e., cognitive processing), an affective (i.e., affection) and a behavioral dimension (i.e., activation).

On the other hand, Roy et al. (2018), Kumar and Pansari (2016) and Carlson et al. (2018) essentially focus on customer behaviors toward the brands. Roy et al. (2018) investigate three dimensions, namely word of mouth, the customer helping customers and the customer helping company. This scale highlights the double relationship in which an engaged customer with a brand is embedded: the one with other customers and the one with the company. Similarly, Carlson et al. (2018) focus on the relationship between the customer and the brand, addressing the co-creation processes that might derive from customers' feedback toward the brand and customers' collaboration intentions with other users. Finally, Kumar and Pansari (2016) focus on four relevant dimensions that manifest engaged consumers, which are customer purchases, customer referrals, customer influence and customer knowledge. Although these dimensions mainly capture customers' behaviors that the brand may benefit from, the items included in these dimensions also capture the way how the customers experience the activity in an emotional way (e.g., 'owning the products/services of this brand makes me happy' or 'I love talking about my brand experience').

The scales developed by Blasco-Arcas et al. (2016), Campbell et al. (2015), Högberg et al. (2019) and France et al. (2016) mainly reflect the emotional dimension of engagement as suggested by items like these: 'I feel I have a special bond with this brand', 'I feel I have a close personal connection with this brand', 'I feel I have a special relationship with this brand' (Blasco-Arcas et al., 2016) or 'I am passionate about the brand', 'I have a sense of belonging to the brand', 'I am enthusiastic toward the brand' (France et al., 2016).

Table 23.3 Quantitative scales dimensions, items and sources for brand engagement

Source	*Dimensions*	*Items*
Hollebeek et al., 2014	Cognitive processing	• Using this brand gets me to think about the brand • I think about this brand a lot when I use it • Using this brand stimulates my interest to learn more about the brand
	Affection	• I feel very positive when I use this brand • Using this brand makes me happy • I feel good when I use this brand • I am proud to use this brand
	Activation	• I spend a lot of time using this brand, compared to other brands in the same category • Whenever I am using products/services belonging to the same brand category, I usually use this brand • This brand is one of the brands I usually use when I use products/services belonging to the same category
Roy et al., 2018	Word of mouth	• I say positive things about this brand to others • I recommend this brand to my peers • I encourage friends and relatives to purchase the products of this brand
	Customer helping customers	• I teach other customers how to use the products/services of this brand correctly • I help other customers when they don't know how to use the products/services of this brand • I explain to other customers how to use the products/services of this brand correctly
	Customer helping company	• I provide information when surveyed by this brand • I would provide helpful feedback to customer service • I would inform this brand about the service provided by their employees
Carlson et al., 2018	Feedback Intentions	• When I experience a problem with the brand I intend to notify the brand • When I have a useful idea on how to improve the brand, I intend to communicate it via its social media platform(s) • I intend to provide constructive suggestions to the brand via its social media platform(s) on how to improve it • I'm willing to complete a survey/provide feedback on its social media platform(s)
	Collaboration Intentions	• I intend to share my ideas about the brand with other social media users • I intend to help other social media users with brand issues • I intend to get help from other social media users
Blasco-Arcas et al., 2016		• My interaction with this brand makes me feel valuable • I feel I have a special bond with this brand • I feel I have a close personal connection with this brand • I feel I have a special relationship with this brand
Kumar and Pansari, 2016	Customer purchases	• I will continue buying the products/services of this brand in the near future • My purchase with this brand makes me content • I get my money's worth when I purchase this brand • Owning the products/services of this brand makes me happy
	Customer referrals	• Given that I use this brand, I refer my friends and relatives to this brand because of the monetary referral incentives • I promote the brand because of the monetary referral benefits provided by the brand • In addition to the value derived from the product, the monetary referral incentives also encourage me to refer this brand to my friends and relatives • I enjoy referring this brand to my friends and relatives because of monetary referral incentives

(*Continued*)

Table 23.3 (Continued)

Source	*Dimensions*	*Items*
	Customer influence	• I actively discuss this brand on any media • I love talking about my brand experience • I discuss the benefits that I get from this brand with others • I am part of this brand and mention it in my conversations
	Customer knowledge	• I provide feedback about my experience with the brand to the firm • I provide suggestions for improving the performance of the brand • I provide suggestions/feedback about the new products/services of the brand • I provide feedback/suggestions for developing new products/services for this brand
Högberg et al., 2019		• I feel very positive when I shop at this brand • Being with this brand makes me happy • I feel good when using products from this brand • I feel proud to use products from this brand
Campbell et al., 2015		• I like to talk about this brand that is advertised on social media networking sites • I am always interested in learning more about this brand that is present online • I would be interested in receiving communications from this brand via social networking sites • I am accepting of communication from this brand providing it seeks my permission • I am proud to have others know when I affiliate with this brand via social media networking sites • I like to browse through social networking related to this brand • Compared to other people, I closely follow news about this brand
France et al., 2016		• When I am dealing with the brand, I am deeply engrossed • I am passionate about the brand • I have a sense of belonging to the brand • I am enthusiastic toward the brand • When involved with the brand, my mind is focused on what is happening • When interacting with the brand, I concentrate entirely on the brand • I am a dedicated brand customer

Source: The author.

Other Methods to Capture Brand Engagement

When discussing brand engagement and its measurement, scholars have mainly focused on developing quantitative scales. In business practice, with the rapid growth of social media, practitioners use customer engagement metrics to assess the digital strategy efficacy. Over time, main social media platforms (e.g., Instagram, Facebook, LinkedIn and YouTube) developed metrics to measure engagement with brand-related content. Thus, the concept of brand engagement overlaps with the one of engagement with brand-related social media content. Accordingly, practitioners developed groups of indicators to monitor the engagement generated by social media marketing activities. As a result, marketers consider brand engagement captured through these metrics as the key metric to evaluate social media strategy success.

A recent study by Trunfio and Rossi (2021) mapped the main methods adopted by scholars and practitioners to measure brand engagement in the social media environment beyond self-reported measures (for a full review of metrics, see Trunfio & Rossi, 2021). They considered 41 articles published from 2013 to 2020. The majority of these articles considered quantitative metrics mainly based on the number of likes, number of comments, number of shares, number of mentions and number of platform followers (e.g., Gruner & Power, 2017; Medjani et al., 2019). Other studies have considered these absolute metrics, normalizing them with specific indexes, such as the sum of likes, comments and shares, divided by the total number of followers (e.g., Dolan et al., 2017; Mariani et al., 2018; Vlachvei & Kyparissis, 2017).

A smaller quantity of papers has considered qualitative metrics to 'measure' and interpret brand engagement and the success of social media strategies (e.g., Abuljadail & Ha, 2019; Michopoulou & Moisa, 2019). These metrics allow us to understand the quality of interactions and the quality of the relationship between the brand and the consumers. The term *metrics* for qualitative interpretation is not appropriate, as we refer to insights obtained through content or sentiment analyses. Sentiment analysis measures the tone of conversations about the brand, which can be positive, negative or neutral. It can be done using social listening platforms or by manual coding of comments, mentions and reviews. Content analysis can consider different elements such as the content relevance for the audience, measuring the congruence of the content with the audience's interests and values. To measure this, content can be classified considering if people share personal stories in their comments or monitor recurring themes in comments, mentions and reviews to assess the level of congruence with themes communicated. Moreover, comments, mentions and reviews can be analyzed in terms of tone and emotions conveyed, considering also the strength of the emotional valence.

STRATEGIES TO ENHANCE BRAND ENGAGEMENT

Brand engagement strategies are supported by the idea that consumers should interact and participate in brand initiatives. Given the multidimensional nature of brand engagement, brands should adopt a customer-centric approach where personalization and care of consumer pain points are prominent throughout the entire customer journey. Brands should design the brand experience considering the pivotal role of customer–brand interaction. Brand experience is no longer something that is related to brand communication; it is the essence of brand communication; thus, via brand experience, the brand can foster brand engagement and related virtuous behaviors.

As consumer participation is stimulated in an environment where they feel familiar and comfortable, the online brand community is a must for any marketing strategy focused on brand engagement. Brand communities stimulate brand interactions, which in turn drive consumer participation, which is the essence of brand engagement.

In the social media context, where brands are more than ever stories, brands should develop content marketing strategies, providing valuable and engaging content. The sense of community surrounding the brand can be emphasized by engaging stories on social media. Influencer marketing can be of crucial importance in content marketing strategies that drive engagement, reducing the perceived distance between the consumers and the brand.

In the following sections, we will delve into these strategies and explain how the company can achieve important brand engagement objectives.

The Importance of Adopting a Customer-Centric Approach to Design Brand Experiences for Brand Engagement

Adopting a customer-centric approach to brand engagement means designing brand experiences where consumer–brand interactions are protagonists. To embed this idea, it is relevant to design the brand experience considering the different stages of the customer journey. Customer journey is conceptualized as 'the process a customer goes through, across all stages and touchpoints, that makes up the customer experience' (Lemon & Verhoef, 2016, p. 71). Research assumes a crucial role in brand engagement in shaping the customer journey (Demmers et al., 2020; Mele & Russo-Spena, 2022).

Antecedents of brand engagement throughout the phases of customer journeys can be explored by using data from Facebook pages (Demmers et al., 2020). The effect of post characteristics, such as entertaining versus informational value, vividness and activation, depends on the stage of the journey. In the pre-consumption phase, higher levels of engagement are related to informative posts compared to entertaining posts, as they should fulfill the initial customer's need for information. Consistent with the need for more hedonic value in the consumption experience, it enriches the brand experience, which leads to higher brand engagement. In the post-consumption phase, no differences between informative and entertaining posts were found, as consumers in this phase seek information confirming that they have made the right choice in fulfilling their need for functional and hedonic information. Moreover, the level of vividness of posts is important in every stage of the customer journey. Finally, brand posts containing activating elements such as links, quizzes, polls and questions usually lead to a higher level of engagement in the pre-consumption and post-consumption phases, where the level of brand interaction might be lower compared to the consumption phase.

Similarly, smart technologies across the customer journey trigger brand engagement differently (Mele & Russo-Spena, 2022). Brands initiate conversations with customers to foster interactions in 'phygital' environments throughout stages and touchpoints, such as platforms, chatbots and apps. This allows companies to collect customers' real-time data that companies can use through systems of insights, which apply advanced analytics to get insights on what customers want and purchase and use to identify the best actions to take. Conversely, through systems of engagement, brands engage customers by delivering personalized offerings (e.g., clienteling) and context-appropriate responses using gamification, and next-generation devices, and infrastructures. By augmenting customers' senses, knowledge and capabilities, companies set the stage for an immersive engagement. The interplay between the system of insights and the system of engagement shapes the architecture of the phygital customer journey.

The Interplay Between Online Brand Communities and Brand Engagement

In the previous sections, we observed that brand interaction serves as a key factor in driving brand engagement by encouraging consumer participation, which lies at the core of engagement. Building on this understanding, the significance of brand communities becomes evident. Specifically, online brand communities foster greater interaction, which, in turn, enhances engagement. Therefore, marketers should prioritize the integration of an engaging brand community into the overall brand experience (Baldus et al., 2015).

However, merely creating a brand community is insufficient; it is crucial to design one that fosters engagement both with the brand and within the community itself (Kumar & Kumar, 2020). To achieve this, marketers should focus on strategies that enhance members' experiences and boost their self-esteem. This could involve inviting customers to take part in online activities such as brand-related quizzes, offering unique experiences, reinforcing self-beliefs, organizing offline events or planning trips through lottery systems. Incorporating a feedback mechanism can help assess the effectiveness of these activities in delivering experiences and improving self-esteem within the community.

Community administrators should actively recognize, support and reward individual contributions while creating an environment where members feel acknowledged and appreciated – a rare occurrence in many online brand communities due to their large size. Additionally, implementing measures to mitigate unwanted criticism and other negative behaviors can help maintain a positive atmosphere, reducing the risk of harming members' self-esteem (Verhoef et al., 2009).

Management should also make their investments in brand communities more transparent, demonstrating a commitment to nurturing customer relationships. Research suggests that brand communities should take the lead, with brands naturally aligning behind them (Fournier & Lee, 2009). Managers should strategically allocate resources – both financial and non-financial – to support community relationships and ensure the visibility of these investments. Many online brand communities are currently perceived as mere interaction platforms, with customers often viewing them as lacking genuine investment or effort from the brand, which can hinder engagement.

Finally, brand psychological ownership plays a significant role in enhancing brand engagement. Studies have shown that participation in brand community discussions increases this sense of ownership (Kumar & Nayak, 2019). To capitalize on this, managers should encourage and incentivize member participation, fostering a deeper connection with the brand.

The Power of Content Marketing and Influencer Marketing in Shaping Brand Engagement

Content marketing plays a pivotal role in driving brand engagement on social media. Recent studies have highlighted the importance of understanding key elements within digital content marketing. Informative, commercial, entertaining and emotional components are generally considered predictors of brand engagement (Odoom, 2023). However, their effectiveness is conditional and not universally positive – particularly when negative emotions are involved. While fear appeals might be effective in traditional advertising, they are often less suitable for digital content on social media. Consequently, brands must approach the use of emotional elements in their social media campaigns with care.

Interestingly, information-driven content, though sometimes perceived as 'dry', can still engage consumers effectively when tailored to the right context or presented innovatively, even for well-known brands. By strategically leveraging these key elements, marketing managers can create meaningful brand experiences and use digital content marketing as a powerful engagement tool.

Influencer marketing and content marketing can complement each other. Managers can amplify their digital content marketing efforts by collaborating with social media influencers and utilizing their branded content (Odoom, 2023). Influencers can enhance their parasocial relationships with followers by employing advanced digital tools to create content that fosters deeper psychological connections.

When selecting influencers to drive brand engagement, several factors must be considered. Hughes et al. (2019) offer valuable insights into managing influencer campaigns across different platforms. For awareness campaigns on blogging platforms, emphasizing the expertise and credibility of bloggers is crucial. In contrast, trial campaigns can achieve similar success with both expert and novice sources. On high-distraction platforms like Facebook, campaign strategies should align with the campaign's intent. For example, trial campaigns may benefit from hedonic, highly engaging content to capture attention.

When implementing strategies across multiple high-distraction platforms, it is advisable to collaborate with influencers who have a large follower base to maximize reach and engagement. Campaign success is also influenced by platform characteristics and intent. For blog platforms, managers should prioritize expertise and campaign incentives for awareness campaigns while leveraging hedonic content for trial campaigns. On platforms such as Facebook, Twitter or Instagram, it is recommended to avoid campaign incentives and focus instead on the hedonic appeal of the content to drive engagement in low-involvement environments.

Social media influencers significantly affect brand engagement, with the type of video content they create playing a key role at different stages of the customer journey (Delbaere et al., 2021). For example, in the beauty industry, videos showcasing product selections help consumers build an initial consideration set, while tutorials are more relevant during the post-purchase phase. Interestingly, the emotional responses to various video formats suggest that consumer preferences and affinities are more closely tied to their self-concept (actual or ideal self) than to the influencer's personality.

Among video types, 'hauls' and 'favorites' generate the highest brand mentions. These formats often feature influencers either enthusiastically introducing new brands (hauls) or discussing their most cherished products (favorites). This enthusiasm, combined with the parasocial bond between influencers and their followers, fosters a sense of friendship. Followers often strengthen this perceived connection by purchasing and using the brands the influencer promotes. Conversely, tutorials and first impressions yield fewer brand mentions. Tutorials tend to prioritize makeup techniques and achieving specific looks over brand promotion, leading followers to focus more on replicating the style rather than the products themselves. First impressions, on the other hand, may elicit skepticism from followers, as the brand featured has yet to establish itself as a favorite of the influencer.

Partnering with influencers for 'haul' or 'favorites' videos may be the most effective strategy for marketers aiming to promote cognitive engagement with their brands. However, tutorials and reviews offer a different dynamic if the goal is to elicit emotional responses. Tutorials, in particular, evoke strong positive and negative emotional reactions. While some followers may be inspired and eager to recreate a look (positive emotion), others may reject it entirely (negative emotion), making tutorials a high-risk, high-reward option. In contrast, hauls are a safer choice, generating fewer extreme emotional reactions.

Ultimately, marketers should align their choice of video format with their brand engagement objectives. For those prioritizing emotional connection, tutorials and reviews may deliver impactful results, while hauls offer a more reliable, steady form of engagement.

CONCLUSIONS AND FUTURE RESEARCH AGENDA

This chapter aims to clarify the concept of brand engagement in terms of definitions, measurements and strategies.

The significance of brand engagement stems from its ability to capture the depth and breadth of interactions between individuals and brands across various touchpoints and contexts. While the concept of brand engagement has gained prominence in recent years, its definition remains somewhat nebulous, reflecting its multifaceted nature. This uncertainty is also reflected in its measurement, where several quantitative scales have been developed throughout the years. While scholars have been involved in several conceptualizations of this phenomenon, at a business level, brand engagement clearly represents a relevant set of metrics to assess the efficacy of the social media strategy. These metrics can be enriched by more qualitative analysis to assess the quality of consumer brand interactions in terms of sentiment and content.

The abundant conceptualizations of brand engagement have blurred the systematization of its drivers and consequences. However, they might depend on the duration of the customer–brand relationship, where, for instance, the self-brand connection can be either a driver or a consequence. Similarly, brand attachment, brand trust and brand commitment can be either drivers or consequences depending on the duration of the relationship.

Future studies on brand engagement can focus on specific dimensions of engagement with the aim to identify specific antecedents and consequences of them. For instance, for the cognitive dimension of engagement, although studies consider different elements of cognition (Gielens & Steenkamp, 2019), they largely overlook the unconscious cognitive processing elements that may enrich the conceptualization of brand engagement.

Brand engagement strategies are manifold and extend across various industries and contexts. Overall, brand engagement is supported by a customer-centric approach to brand experience, according to which each initiative to foster brand engagement needs to be consistent throughout the customer journey and dedicated to brand interactions and consumer participation. Future studies can develop brand engagement strategies along the customer journey to provide actionable guidance for brands and retailers to trigger and nurture brand engagement. Such studies could also help develop metrics for measuring strategy efficacy, providing brands and retailers with a framework to monitor and optimize their engagement efforts.

As markets evolve, the challenges for brand engagement are expected to become more complex. Future challenges may include different aspects of managing brand engagement, such as adapting to emerging technologies. Brands integrating cutting-edge technologies, such as artificial intelligence, augmented reality and virtual reality, to create immersive experiences must be mindful of potential disconnects. Consumers may perceive these implementations as impersonal or intrusive if not executed thoughtfully. This aspect also includes the implementation of the metaverse in the brand engagement strategy. The implementation of virtual spaces to engage consumers requires creating authentic, innovative interactions while ensuring inclusivity and accessibility in these digital environments. Future studies can consider how the evolving technologies may challenge brand engagement both in terms of strategies and measurements. Relatively few studies have explored qualitative metrics for assessing and interpreting brand engagement and the success of digital strategies. Thus, future studies may consider how companies can implement qualitative measures to control the efficacy of brand engagement strategies in the digital environment.

Consumers increasingly demand personalized experiences, but growing privacy concerns and stricter regulations (e.g., General Data Protection Regulation (GDPR), and California Consumer Privacy Act (CCPA) require brands to find ways to offer tailored interactions without violating trust or legal boundaries. Future studies could explore how certain brand engagement strategies may inadvertently damage the consumer–brand relationship, particularly in the context of privacy concerns and regulatory constraints.

Future consumers, especially Gen Z and younger generations, prioritize brands aligned with their values. Failing to demonstrate genuine commitment to sustainability, social justice or other causes may alienate key audiences. As the consumer base becomes more diverse in age, brands will need to tailor their engagement strategies to resonate with younger and older generations without alienating either group. Future research could examine how different generations respond to brand engagement strategies, helping companies tailor their approaches to specific audience segments.

REFERENCES

Abuljadail, M., & Ha, L. (2019). Engagement and brand loyalty through social capital in social media. *International Journal of Internet Marketing and Advertising*, *13*(3), 197–217. https://doi.org/10.1504/IJIMA.2019.102557

Alden, D. L., Kelley, J. B., Youn, J. B., & Chen, Q. (2016). Understanding consumer motivations to interact on brand websites in the international marketplace: Evidence from the US, China, and South Korea. *Journal of Business Research*, *69*(12), 5909–5916. https://doi.org/10.1016/j.jbusres.2016.04.108

Algharabat, R., Rana, N. P., Dwivedi, Y. K., Alalwan, A. A., & Qasem, Z. (2018). The effect of telepresence, social presence and involvement on consumer brand engagement: An empirical study of non-profit organizations. *Journal of Retailing and Consumer Services*, *40*, 139–149. https://doi.org/10.1016/j.jretconser.2017.09.011

Andersen, P. H. (2005). Relationship marketing and brand involvement of professionals through web-enhanced brand communities: The case of Coloplast. *Industrial Marketing Management*, *34*(3), 285–297. https://doi.org/10.1016/j.indmarman.2004.07.007

Baldus, B. J., Voorhees, C., & Calantone, R. (2015). Online brand community engagement: Scale development and validation. *Journal of Business Research*, *68*(5), 978–985. https://doi.org/10.1016/j.jbusres.2014.09.035

Batra, R., Ahuvia, A., & Bagozzi, R. P. (2012). Brand love. *Journal of Marketing*, *76*(2), 1–16. https://doi.org/10.1509/jm.09.0339

Belk, R. W. (1988). Possessions and the extended self. *Journal of Consumer Research*, *15*(2), 139–168. https://doi.org/10.1086/209154

Blasco-Arcas, L., Hernandez-Ortega, B. I., & Jimenez-Martinez, J. (2016). Engagement platforms: The role of emotions in fostering customer engagement and brand image in interactive media. *Journal of Service Theory and Practice*, *26*(5), 559–589. https://doi.org/10.1108/JSTP-12-2014-0286

Bowden, J. L. H. (2009). The process of customer engagement: A conceptual framework. *Journal of Marketing Theory and Practice*, *17*(1), 63–74. https://doi.org/10.2753/MTP1069-6679170105

Brakus, J. J., Schmitt, B. H., & Zarantonello, L. (2009). Brand experience: What is it? How is it measured? Does it affect loyalty? *Journal of Marketing*, *73*(3), 52–68. https://doi.org/10.1509/jmkg.73.3.052

Brodie, R. J., Hollebeek, L. D., Jurić, B., & Ilić, A. (2011). Customer engagement: Conceptual domain, fundamental propositions, and implications for research. *Journal of Service Research*, *14*(3), 252–271. https://doi.org/10.1177/1094670511411703

Brodie, R. J., Ilic, A., Juric, B., & Hollebeek, L. (2013). Consumer engagement in a virtual brand community: An exploratory analysis. *Journal of Business Research*, *66*(1), 105–114. https://doi.org/10.1016/j.jbusres.2011.07.029

Campbell, C., Jewell, R. D., & Hessick, C. (2015). Developing a behavior-based measure of online brand-engagement. *Advances in Consumer Research*, *43*, 476–477.

Cantone, L., Testa, P., & Marrone, T. (2022). Issues in defining and placing consumer brand engagement. *Italian Journal of Marketing*, *2022*(2), 135–172. https://doi.org/10.1007/s43039-022-00054-z

Carlson, J., Rahman, M., Voola, R., & De Vries, N. (2018). Customer engagement behaviours in social media: Capturing innovation opportunities. *Journal of Services Marketing*, *32*(1), 83–94. https://doi.org/10.1108/JSM-02-2017-0059

Carroll, B. A., & Ahuvia, A. C. (2006). Some antecedents and outcomes of brand love. *Marketing Letters*, *17*(2), 79–89. https://doi.org/10.1007/s11002-006-4219-2

Carvalho, A., & Fernandes, T. (2018). Understanding customer brand engagement with virtual social communities: A comprehensive model of drivers, outcomes and moderators. *Journal of Marketing Theory and Practice*, *26*(1–2), 23–37. https://doi.org/10.1080/10696679.2017.1389241

Delbaere, M., Michael, B., & Phillips, B. J. (2021). Social media influencers: A route to brand engagement for their followers. *Psychology & Marketing*, *38*(1), 101–112. https://doi.org/10.1002/mar.21419

Demmers, J., Weltevreden, J. W., & van Dolen, W. M. (2020). Consumer engagement with brand posts on social media in consecutive stages of the customer journey. *International Journal of Electronic Commerce*, *24*(1), 53–77. https://doi.org/10.1080/10864415.2019.1683701

Dennis, C., Papagiannidis, S., Alamanos, E., & Bourlakis, M. (2016). The role of brand attachment strength in higher education. *Journal of Business Research*, *69*(8), 3049–3057. https://doi.org/10.1016/j.jbusres.2016.01.020

Dessart, L., Veloutsou, C., & Morgan-Thomas, A. (2016). Capturing consumer engagement: Duality, dimensionality and measurement. *Journal of Marketing Management*, *32*(5–6), 399–426. https://doi.org/10.1080/0267257X.2015.1130738

Dessart, L., Aldás-Manzano, J., & Veloutsou, C. (2019). Unveiling heterogeneous engagement-based loyalty in brand communities. *European Journal of Marketing*, *53*(9), 1854–1881.

De Vries, N. J., & Carlson, J. (2014). Examining the drivers and brand performance implications of customer engagement with brands in the social media environment. *Journal of Brand Management*, *21*(6), 495–515. https://doi.org/10.1057/bm.2014.18

Dolan, R., Conduit, J., Fahy, J., & Goodman, S. (2017). Social media: Communication strategies, engagement and future research directions. *International Journal of Wine Business Research*, *29*(1), 2–19. https://doi.org/10.1108/IJWBR-04-2016-0013

Dwivedi, A. (2015). A higher-order model of consumer brand engagement and its impact on loyalty intentions. *Journal of Retailing and Consumer Services*, *24*, 100–109. https://doi.org/10.1016/j.jretconser.2015.02.007

Eastman, J. K., Goldsmith, R. E., & Flynn, L. R. (1999). Status consumption in consumer behavior: Scale development and validation. *Journal of Marketing Theory and Practice*, *7*(3), 41–52. https://doi.org/10.1080/10696679.1999.11501839

Eisingerich, A. B., Chun, H. H., Liu, Y., Jia, H. M., & Bell, S. J. (2015). Why recommend a brand face-to-face but not on Facebook? How word-of-mouth on online social sites differs from traditional word-of-mouth. *Journal of Consumer Psychology*, *25*(1), 120–128. https://doi.org/10.1016/j.jcps.2014.05.004

Escalas, J. E. (2004). Narrative processing: Building consumer connections to brands. *Journal of Consumer Psychology*, *14*(1–2), 168–180. https://doi.org/10.1207/s15327663jcp1401&2_19

Feng, Y., Chen, H., & He, L. (2019). Consumer responses to femvertising: A data-mining case of dove's 'campaign for real beauty' on YouTube. *Journal of Advertising*, *48*(3), 292–301. https://doi.org/10.1080/00913367.2019.1602858

Flynn, L. R., Goldsmith, R. E., & Pollitte, W. (2016). Materialism, status consumption, and market involved consumers. *Psychology & Marketing*, *33*(9), 761–776. https://doi.org/10.1002/mar.20915

France, C., Merrilees, B., & Miller, D. (2016). An integrated model of customer-brand engagement: Drivers and consequences. *Journal of Brand Management*, *23*(2), 119–136. https://doi.org/10.1057/bm.2016.4

Fournier, S., & Lee, L. (2009). Getting brand communities right. Harvard Business Review, *87*(4), 105–111.

Gielens, K., & Steenkamp, J. B. E. (2019). Branding in the era of digital (dis) intermediation. *International Journal of Research in Marketing*, *36*(3), 367–384. https://doi.org/10.1016/j.ijresmar.2019.01.005

Gligor, D., Bozkurt, S., & Russo, I. (2019). Achieving customer engagement with social media: A qualitative comparative analysis approach. *Journal of Business Research*, *101*, 59–69. https://doi.org/10.1016/j.jbusres.2019.04.006

Gligor, D., Bozkurt, S., & Welch, E. (2023). Building theoretical sand castles: The case of customer brand engagement. *Journal of Marketing Analytics*, *11*(3), 297–316. https://doi.org/10.1057/s41270-023-00227-5

Gruner, R. L., & Power, D. (2017). What's in a crowd? Exploring crowdsourced versus traditional customer participation in the innovation process. *Journal of Marketing Management*, *33*(13–14), 1060–1092. https://doi.org/10.1080/0267257X.2017.1325389

Haverila, M., Haverila, K., McLaughlin, C., & Arora, M. (2022). Engagement, participation, and relationship quality in the context of co-creation in brand communities. *Journal of Marketing Analytics*, *10*, 232–249. https://doi.org/10.1057/s41270-021-00136-5

Hepola, J., Karjaluoto, H., & Hintikka, A. (2017). The effect of sensory brand experience and involvement on brand equity directly and indirectly through consumer brand engagement. *Journal of Product & Brand Management*, *26*(3), 282–293. https://doi.org/10.1108/JPBM-10-2016-1348

Högberg, J., Ramberg, M. O., Gustafsson, A., & Wästlund, E. (2019). Creating brand engagement through in-store gamified customer experiences. *Journal of Retailing and Consumer Services*, *50*, 122–130. https://doi.org/10.1016/j.jretconser.2019.05.006

Hollebeek, L. (2011). Exploring customer brand engagement: Definition and themes. *Journal of Strategic Marketing*, *19*(7), 555–573. https://doi.org/10.1080/0965254X.2011.599493

Hollebeek, L. D., & Chen, T. (2014). Exploring positively-versus negatively-valenced brand engagement: A conceptual model. *Journal of Product & Brand Management*, *23*(1), 62–74. https://doi.org/10.1108/JPBM-06-2013-0332

Hollebeek, L. D., Glynn, M. S., & Brodie, R. J. (2014). Consumer brand engagement in social media: Conceptualization, scale development and validation. *Journal of Interactive Marketing*, *28*(2), 149–165. https://doi.org/10.1016/j.intmar.2013.12.002

Hollebeek, L. D., Kumar, V., & Srivastava, R. K. (2020). From customer-, to actor-, to stakeholder engagement: Taking stock, conceptualization, and future directions. *Journal of Service Research*, *25*(2), 328–343. https://doi.org/10.1177/1094670520977680

Hollebeek, L. D., Menidjel, C., Sarstedt, M., Jansson, J., & Urbonavicius, S. (2024). Engaging consumers through artificially intelligent technologies: Systematic review, conceptual model, and further research. *Psychology & Marketing*, *41*(4), 880–898. https://doi.org/10.1002/mar.21957

Hollebeek, L. D., Srivastava, R. K., & Chen, T. (2019). SD logic–informed customer engagement: Integrative framework, revised fundamental propositions, and application to CRM. *Journal of the Academy of Marketing Science*, *47*(1), 161–185. https://doi.org/10.1007/s11747-016-0494-5

Hughes, C., Swaminathan, V., & Brooks, G. (2019). Driving brand engagement through online social influencers: An empirical investigation of sponsored blogging campaigns. *Journal of Marketing*, *83*(5), 78–96. https://doi.org/10.1177/0022242919854374

Hussain, K., Jing, F., Junaid, M., Zaman, Q. U., & Shi, H. (2021). The role of co-creation experience in engaging customers with service brands. *Journal of Product & Brand Management*, *30*(1), 12–27. https://doi.org/10.1108/JPBM-08-2019-2537

Islam, J. U., & Rahman, Z. (2017). The impact of online brand community characteristics on customer engagement: An application of stimulus-organism-response paradigm. *Telematics and Informatics*, *34*(4), 96–109. https://doi.org/10.1016/j.tele.2017.01.004

Ivens, B. S., Leischnig, A., Muller, B., & Valta, K. (2015). On the role of brand stereotypes in shaping consumer response toward brands: An empirical examination of direct and mediating effects of warmth and competence. *Psychology & Marketing*, *32*(8), 808–820. https://doi.org/10.1002/mar.20820

Khan, M. L. (2017). Social media engagement: What motivates user participation and consumption on YouTube? *Computers in Human Behavior*, *66*, 236–247. https://doi.org/10.1016/j.chb.2016.09.024

Kumar, J., & Kumar, V. (2020). Drivers of brand community engagement. *Journal of Retailing and Consumer Services*, *54*, 101949. https://doi.org/10.1016/j.jretconser.2019.101949

Kumar, J., & Nayak, J. K. (2019). Brand engagement without brand ownership: A case of non-brand owner community members. *Journal of Product &*

Brand Management, *28*(2), 216–230. https://doi.org/10.1108/JPBM-04-2018-1840

Kumar, V., & Pansari, A. (2016). Competitive advantage through engagement. *Journal of Marketing Research*, *53*(4), 497–514. https://doi.org/10.1509/jmr.15.0044

Kumar, V., Rajan, B., Gupta, S., & Pozza, I. D. (2019). Customer engagement in service. *Journal of the Academy of Marketing Science*, *47*(1), 138–160. https://doi.org/10.1007/s11747-017-0565-2

Leckie, C., Nyadzayo, M. W., & Johnson, L. W. (2016). Antecedents of consumer brand engagement and brand loyalty. *Journal of Marketing Management*, *32*(5–6), 558–578. https://doi.org/10.1080/0267257X.2015.1131735

Lemon, K. N., & Verhoef, P. C. (2016). Understanding customer experience throughout the customer journey. *Journal of Marketing*, *80*(6), 69–96. https://doi.org/10.1509/jm.15.0420

Li, Y., Lu, C., Bogicevic, V., & Bujisic, M. (2019). The effect of nostalgia on hotel brand attachment. *International Journal of Contemporary Hospitality Management*, *31*(2), 691–717. https://doi.org/10.1108/IJCHM-12-2017-0797

Liadeli, G., Sotgiu, F., & Verlegh, P. W. (2023). A meta-analysis of the effects of brands' owned social media on social media engagement and sales. *Journal of Marketing*, *87*(3), 406–427. https://doi.org/10.1177/00222429221123250

Lourenço, C. E., Hair, Jr., J. F., Zambaldi, F., & Ponchio, M. C. (2022). Consumer brand engagement concept and measurement: Toward a refined approach. *Journal of Retailing and Consumer Services*, *68*, 103053. https://doi.org/10.1016/j.jretconser.2022.103053

Magnoni, F., Valette-Florence, P., & De Barnier, V. (2021). Modeling the effects of place heritage and place experience on residents' behavioral intentions toward a city: A mediation analysis. *Journal of Business Research*, *134*, 428–442. https://doi.org/10.1016/j.jbusres.2021.04.069

Mariani, M., Baggio, R., Fuchs, M., & Höepken, W. (2018). Business intelligence and big data in hospitality and tourism: A systematic literature review. *International Journal of Contemporary Hospitality Management*, *30*(12), 3514–3554. https://doi.org/10.1108/IJCHM-07-2017-0461

Markus, H. (1977). Self-schemata and processing information about the self. *Journal of Personality and Social Psychology*, *35*(2), 63–78. https://doi.org/10.1037/0022-3514.35.2.63

Mazzoli, V., Acuti, D., Donvito, R., & Ko, E. (2019). Dressing your soul: The role of brand engagement in self-concept. *Mercati & Competitività* (2019/1).

Medjani, F., Rutter, R., & Nadeau, J. (2019). Social media management, objectification and measurement in an emerging market. *International Journal of Business and Emerging Markets*, *11*(3), 288–311. https://doi.org/10.1504/IJBEM.2019.102654

Meidivia, R. R., Novieningtyas, A., & Naumovska, L. (2023). The effectiveness of AI in marketing 'spotify wrapped': How it affects Indonesian customer's engagement. *International Journal of Business and Technology Management*, *5*(3), 260–269.

Mele, C., & Russo-Spena, T. (2022). The architecture of the phygital customer journey: A dynamic interplay between systems of insights and systems of engagement. *European Journal of Marketing*, *56*(1), 72–91. https://doi.org/10.1108/EJM-04-2019-0308

Michopoulou, E., & Moisa, D. G. (2019). Hotel social media metrics: The ROI dilemma. *International Journal of Hospitality Management*, *76*, 308–315. https://doi.org/10.1016/j.ijhm.2018.05.019

Mittal, B. (1995). A comparative analysis of four scales of consumer involvement. *Psychology & Marketing*, *12*(7), 663–682. https://doi.org/10.1002/mar.4220120708

Mollen, A., & Wilson, H. (2010). Engagement, telepresence and interactivity in online consumer experience: Reconciling scholastic and managerial perspectives. *Journal of Business Research*, *63*(9–10), 919–925. https://doi.org/10.1016/j.jbusres.2009.05.014

Neisser, U. (2014). Cognitive Psychology: Classic Edition. *Psychology press*.

Nyadzayo, M. W., Johnson, L. W., & Rossi, M. (2020). Drivers and outcomes of brand engagement in self-concept for luxury fashion brands. *Journal of Fashion Marketing and Management: An International Journal*, *24*(4), 589–609.

Nysveen, H., & Pedersen, P. E. (2014). Influences of cocreation on brand experience. *International Journal of Market Research*, *56*(6), 807–832. https://doi.org/10.2501/IJMR-2014-016

Obilo, O. O., Chefor, E., & Saleh, A. (2021). Revisiting the consumer brand engagement concept. *Journal of Business Research*, *126*, 634–643. https://doi.org/10.1016/j.jbusres.2019.12.023

Odoom, R. (2023). Digital content marketing and consumer brand engagement on social media-do influencers' brand content moderate the relationship? *Journal of Marketing Communications*, 1–24. https://doi.org/10.1080/13527266.2023.2249013

Okazaki, S., Schuberth, F., Tagashira, T., & Andrade, V. (2021). Sneaking the dark side of brand engagement into Instagram: The dual theory of passion. *Journal of Business Research*, *130* (C), 493–505. https://doi.org/10.1016/j.jbusres.2019.11.028

Pansari, A., & Kumar, V. (2017). Customer engagement: The construct, antecedents, and consequences. *Journal of the Academy of Marketing Science*, *45*(3), 294–311. https://doi.org/10.1007/s11747-016-0485-6

Park, C. W., MacInnis, D. J., Priester, J., Eisingerich, A. B., & Iacobucci, D. (2010). Brand attachment and brand attitude strength: Conceptual and empirical differentiation of two critical brand equity drivers. *Journal of Marketing*, *74*(6), 1–17. https://doi.org/10.1509/jmkg.74.6.1

Peck, J., & Shu, S. B. (2009). The effect of mere touch on perceived ownership. *Journal of Consumer Research*, *36*(3), 434–447. https://doi.org/10.1086/598614

Pierce, J. L., Kostova, T., & Dirks, K. T. (2001). Toward a theory of psychological ownership in organizations. *Academy of Management Review*, *26*(2), 298–310. https://doi.org/10.2307/259124

Pongpaew, W., Speece, M., & Tiangsoongnern, L. (2017). Social presence and customer brand engagement on Facebook brand pages. *Journal of Product & Brand Management*, *26*(3), 262–281. https://doi.org/10.1108/JPBM-08-2015-0956

Razmus, W., Jaroszyńska, M., & Palęga, M. (2017). Personal aspirations and brand engagement in self-concept. *Personality and Individual Differences*, *105*, 294–299. https://doi.org/10.1016/j.paid.2016.10.018

Razmus, W., Mazzoli, V., Acuti, D., & Grabner-Kräuter, S. (2020). Brand engagement in self-concept: A comparative study in Austria, Italy and Poland. *Journal of Consumer Marketing*, *37*(7), 785–794. https://doi.org/10.1108/JCM-09-2019-3412

Richins, M. L. (2008). Consumption emotions. In *Product experience* (pp. 399–422). Elsevier.

Roy, S. K., Shekhar, V., Lassar, W. M., & Chen, T. (2018). Customer engagement behaviors: The role of service convenience, fairness and quality. *Journal of Retailing and Consumer Services*, *44*, 293–304. https://doi.org/10.1016/j.jretconser.2018.07.018

Samala, N., & Singh, S. (2019). Millennial's engagement with fashion brands: A moderated-mediation model of brand engagement with self-concept, involvement and knowledge. *Journal of Fashion Marketing and Management*, *23*(1), 2–16. https://doi.org/10.1108/JFMM-04-2018-0045

Sawhney, M., Verona, G., & Prandelli, E. (2005). Collaborating to create: The Internet as a platform for customer engagement in product innovation. *Journal of Interactive Marketing*, *19*(4), 4–17. https://doi.org/10.1002/dir.20046

Schivinski, B., Christodoulides, G., & Dabrowski, D. (2016). Measuring consumers' engagement with brand-related social-media content: Development and validation of a scale that identifies levels of social-media engagement with brands. *Journal of Advertising Research*, *56*(1), 64–80. https://doi.org/10.2501/JAR-2016-004

Sembada, A. (2018). The two sides of empowering consumers to co-design innovations. *Journal of Services Marketing*, *32*(1), 8–18. https://doi.org/10.1108/JSM-02-2017-0062

Shao, Z., & Chen, K. (2021). Understanding individuals' engagement and continuance intention of MOOCs: The effect of interactivity and the role of gender. *Internet Research*, *31*(4), 1262–1289. https://doi.org/10.1108/INTR-10-2019-0416

Shimul, A. S. (2022). Brand attachment: A review and future research. *Journal of Brand Management*, *29*(4), 400–419. https://doi.org/10.1057/s41262-022-00279-5

Solem, B. A. A., & Pedersen, P. E. (2016). The role of customer brand engagement in social media: Conceptualisation, measurement, antecedents and outcomes. *International Journal of Internet Marketing and Advertising*, *10*(4), 223–254. https://doi.org/10.1504/IJIMA.2016.081344

Sprott, D., Czellar, S., & Spangenberg, E. (2009). The importance of a general measure of brand engagement on market behavior: Development and validation of a scale. *Journal of Marketing Research*, *46*(1), 92–104. https://doi.org/10.1509/jmkr.46.1.92

Stokburger-Sauer, N. (2010). Brand community: Drivers and outcomes. *Psychology & Marketing*, *27*(4), 347–368. https://doi.org/10.1002/mar.20335

Swani, K., Milne, G. R., & Miller, E. G. (2021). Social media services branding: The use of corporate brand names. *Journal of Business Research*, *125*, 785–797. https://doi.org/10.1016/j.jbusres.2019.04.033

Toffler, A. (1980). *The third wave/alvin toffler* (p. 544). Morrow.

Trunfio, M., & Rossi, S. (2021). Conceptualising and measuring social media engagement: A systematic literature review. *Italian Journal of Marketing*, *2021*(3), 267–292. https://doi.org/10.1007/s43039-021-00035-8

Valdellon, L. (2021). *8 clever customer engagement examples from top brands in 2021*. CleverTap. Retrieved April 20, 2023, from https://clevertap.com/blog/customer-engagement-examples/

Vargo, S. L., & Lusch, R. F. (2004). Evolving to a new dominant logic for marketing. *Journal of Marketing*, *68*(1), 1–17. https://doi.org/10.1509/jmkg.68.1.1.24036

Verhoef, P. C., Lemon, K. N., Parasuraman, A., Roggeveen, A., Tsiros, M., & Schlesinger, L. A. (2009). Customer experience creation: Determinants, dynamics and management strategies. *Journal of Retailing*, *85*(1), 31–41. https://doi.org/10.1016/j.jretai.2008.11.001

Vincent, E., & Kolade, A. (2019). Persuasive communication: Semiotic analysis of 'share-a-coke' advertising campaign. *World Journal of Innovative Research*, *7*(2), 1–6.

Vivek, S. D., Beatty, S. E., & Morgan, R. M. (2012). Customer engagement: Exploring customer relationships beyond purchase. *Journal of Marketing Theory and Practice*, *20*(2), 122–146. https://doi.org/10.2753/MTP1069-6679200201

Vivek, S. D., Beatty, S. E., Dalela, V., & Morgan, R. M. (2014). A generalized multidimensional scale for measuring customer engagement. *Journal of Marketing Theory and Practice*, *22*(4), 401–420. https://doi.org/10.2753/MTP1069-6679220404

Vlachvei, A., & Kyparissis, A. (2017). Museums on Facebook wall: A case study of Thessaloniki's museums. *Tourismos*, *12*(3), 75–96.

Wiedmann, K. P. (2014). The future of brand and brand management – Some provocative propositions from a more methodological perspective. *Journal of Brand Management*, *21*(9), 743–757. https://doi.org/10.1057/bm.2014.39

Xi, N., & Hamari, J. (2021). Shopping in virtual reality: A literature review and future agenda. *Journal of Business Research*, *134*, 37–58. https://doi.org/10.1016/j.jbusres.2021.04.075

Zaichkowsky, J. L. (1985). Measuring the involvement construct. *Journal of Consumer Research*, *12*(3), 341–352. https://doi.org/10.1086/208520

24

The Role of Consumption Communities in Brand Value Co-Creation and Co-Destruction

Daniele Dalli

INTRODUCTION

Consumption communities (CCs) are pervasive in contemporary consumer culture (Coffin et al., 2023) and significantly influence business development. According to McKinsey (2022), community-based business models grow faster and are more profitable than average. This growth is driven by the loyalty and advocacy of community customer bases, as well as the enhanced effectiveness of corporate processes rooted in communal co-creation (e.g., user-generated content (UGC) and innovation). Companies such as Lego (Antorini et al., 2012) and Threadless (Grant et al., 2023) exemplify communal value creation. However, community members can also be demanding and may react negatively when their expectations are unmet, as seen with loyalty programs (Wharton Baker Retailing Center, 2021). Consequently, CCs present both opportunities and challenges for marketing managers, for the role they play in market dynamics.

Theoretically, CCs are categorized into three main types (Canniford, 2011a): sub-cultures of consumption (Schouten & McAlexander, 1995), brand communities (Muñiz & O'Guinn, 2001) and consumer tribes (Cova, 1997). These forms share common traits, such as collective behavior patterns, dynamic interactions among members and engagement with products, brands or categories. However, they also exhibit differences: subcultures of consumption often feature deviant traits, brand communities are primarily brand-centric, and consumer tribes emphasize relationships between people and places.

CCs play a significant role in value co-creation (Galvagno & Dalli, 2014). Since the early 2000s, marketing and consumer researchers have demonstrated the critical role of CCs as intermediaries and active agents in the value-creation process across various contexts, including business-to-consumer, business-to-business and services (Schau et al., 2009). CCs contribute to product and service innovation, distribution, communication and even market creation (Martin & Schouten, 2014).

While significant attention has been paid to co-creation, the phenomenon of co-destruction has received less scrutiny despite its theoretical and practical importance (Echeverri & Skålén, 2021; Lumivalo et al., 2024). It is critical to recognize that consumers, individually or collectively, may not always support corporate or institutional initiatives. Although they frequently participate enthusiastically, ethical considerations, sustainability concerns, ideology or personal preferences can drive consumers away from brands and, in some cases, motivate them to act against them (Romani et al., 2012).

This chapter examines the ways in which CCs contribute to value creation (Schau et al., 2009) and highlights potential critical or destructive actions they may undertake. These actions include opposing corporate strategies by initiating social discourses through social networks and real-world activism (Nøjgaard, 2023), refusing to comply with corporate strategies, switching to alternative products and services, or developing their own entrepreneurial tribes (Cova & Guercini, 2024).

Finally, the chapter proposes a tentative framework for measuring CC outcomes from a corporate perspective, encompassing dimensions such as business performance (e.g., sales, market share) and social media metrics (e.g., engagement, electronic word-of-mouth).

CCs IN PRACTICE

CCs span a wide range of business categories, from fast-moving consumer goods and retail channels to services and entertainment. Large multinational companies, such as Nike, Adidas, Glossier and Sephora, design community programs to engage consumers in developing new products, services and related applications, fostering community-driven offerings, and providing reviews, peer-to-peer support and creative advertising.

In the durable goods sector, companies like Apple, Samsung and Microsoft cultivate communities that discuss product features, provide technical support and give feedback on updates or new releases. These communities play a critical role in refining product development and influencing purchase decisions.

In the automotive industry, brands such as Harley-Davidson, Ducati and BMW nurture passionate CCs that offer advice, organize events and discuss vehicle features, influencing potential buyers and fostering customer loyalty. However, these initiatives sometimes face crises when brand enthusiasts realize their idealized products or services are subject to corporate control and no longer align with their expectations.

In the entertainment and media sector, companies like Netflix, Disney and major video game developers rely heavily on CCs to build anticipation around new releases, products and experiences. Consumption practices in these categories have evolved from individual tasks to collective activities. Movie or TV series viewing, as well as internet-based gaming, has transformed into crowd-based events where consumers engage with content while interacting with others as co-consumers or spectators. This communal involvement adds layers of value derived from the community itself, rather than solely from the company.

In the fitness industry, brands like Peloton, CrossFit and Lululemon rely on their communities to foster a sense of belonging. These communities participate in challenges, share progress and promote lifestyle practices aligned with the brand's values. Similar dynamics are observed in gaming communities, where users discuss strategies, share game modifications (mods) and engage in e-sports tournaments. Major players such as Sony, Microsoft and Riot Games invest significantly in nurturing these communities.

Communities focused on dietary preferences (e.g., veganism, gluten-free), coffee aficionados and craft beer enthusiasts also play an essential role for food and beverage companies. Brands like Starbucks, Coca-Cola and niche players such as Blue Bottle Coffee utilize these communities to foster engagement and involve consumers in product development. Similarly, companies like Airbnb, Marriott and TripAdvisor rely on their communities to share experiences, provide travel tips and offer reviews. In these contexts, CCs significantly influence travel decisions, hotel and restaurant choices, and customer loyalty.

Even luxury brands, such as Rolex, Chanel and Lamborghini, cultivate tight-knit CCs where exclusivity, brand prestige and personal identity are central. These communities often influence product demand and sustain the mystique surrounding the brand.

To summarize, CCs create value for corporate marketing and business models in four major areas:

- Customer engagement: Communities foster engagement through discussions, content sharing and recommendations.
- Loyalty and retention: Communities build strong emotional connections with brands and among members, leading to higher customer retention and repeat purchases.
- Co-creation and feedback: Companies leverage CCs for product innovation, user feedback, customer service and customer-driven improvements.
- Amplified word-of-mouth: Communities act as organic marketing hubs, where advocates spread the word and influence others.

However, alongside these examples of value co-creation, CCs can also drive value co-destruction when their actions or dynamics harm brand equity, customer trust or overall market value.

Negative word-of-mouth arises when communities amplify grievances or negative experiences with a brand. This process is often accelerated through social media, where consumers express frustrations with products, services or communications. For example, in the 'United Breaks Guitars' case (2009), musician Dave Carroll's viral song highlighted United Airlines' poor customer service after his guitar was damaged. The song, widely shared by CCs on social media, caused significant brand damage, including a reported 10% drop in United Airlines' stock price and long-term reputational harm. Similarly, in 2017, Pepsi faced backlash for an advertisement featuring Kendall Jenner, which was criticized for trivializing social justice movements. The ad was pulled within 24 h, but the reputational damage and accusations of tone-deafness lingered.

Communities may also organize boycotts or protests in response to ethical concerns, dissatisfaction with products or political stances, leading to declines in sales and loyalty. A notable example is the longstanding boycott against Nestlé, which began in the 1970s and continues today, resulting in reputational harm and eroding consumer trust. More recently, companies that supported LGBTQ + initiatives faced boycotts in the USA, prompting some to retreat from these initiatives (Murray, Forbes, June 2024).

Boycotts also occur when products or services fail to meet expectations or when brands exploit their communities for profit without genuine engagement. In such cases, consumers perceive the brand as insincere, damaging trust and loyalty.

Failure to address community feedback can lead to public complaints, boycotts or migration to competitors. For instance, in 2018, Dolce & Gabbana faced backlash in China for a campaign criticized as stereotypical and misogynistic. The controversy quickly escalated, with e-retailers, social networks and even public agencies condemning the brand.

In sum, while CCs provide significant value, they must be carefully managed to avoid value destruction. Missteps – whether through poor communication, misaligned values or a lack of authentic engagement – can result in substantial brand damage in both the short and long term.

A BRIEF HISTORY OF CCs FROM A THEORETICAL PERSPECTIVE

Marketing and consumer researchers began addressing the collective dimension of consumption many years ago. Examples include the works of Arnould and Price (1993), Celsi et al. (1993), Reilly and Wallendorf (1987), Wallendorf and Arnould (1991), and Wallendorf and Reilly (1983). However, this body of literature did not explicitly identify CCs (or a similar term) as a distinct unit of analysis.

The studies widely recognized as precursors to this stream of research are Cova (1997), Muñiz and O'Guinn (2001), and Schouten and McAlexander (1995). These papers introduced the concepts of subcultures of consumption, consumer tribes and brand communities. While these concepts differ in their details, they are frequently grouped as prototypes or examples of CCs (Canniford, 2011a, 2011b; Chalmers Thomas et al., 2013).

These foundational works are grounded in sociological research traditions. For instance, Schouten and McAlexander (1995) draw on deviance studies, Muñiz and O'Guinn (2001) are informed by the sociology of consumption, and Cova (1997) reflects Maffesoli's neo-tribalism and postmodern thought (Firat & Venkatesh, 1995). These collectives are specific to consumption because they offer their members resources – such as practices, goods, brands and knowledge – that provide 'linking value' (Cova, 1997). This linking value does not derive from the intrinsic properties or utility of these resources but from the social bonds they enable. For example, a brand may carry linking value if it connects like-minded individuals within a shared context.

These early studies were theoretically and empirically based on the premise that CCs consist of individuals and the relationships among them, regardless of physical proximity. Many communities became global in scope, allowing members to feel a sense of belonging even without personal interaction.

During the 2000s, researchers used various terms to describe these phenomena, including marketplace cultures (Arnould & Thompson, 2005), new CCs (Bekin et al., 2005), consumer crowds (Kozinets et al., 2008), CCs (Chalmers Thomas et al., 2013), brand publics (Arvidsson & Caliandro, 2016) and consumer collectives (Arnould et al., 2021). Despite differences in terminology, most of these theorizations share two central characteristics: they are tied to consumption and to markets. Practically speaking, these communities are composed of individuals who buy goods or services in the marketplace and use them to satisfy their needs.

Consumer culture theory scholars have extensively demonstrated that the value derived from these activities is not solely embedded in products or services but is actively produced and reproduced at personal, collective and cultural levels. Brand communities, for example, engage in value-creating practices (Schau et al., 2009) within market contexts where companies interact with consumers as customers. Similar activities also occur in hybrid or non-corporate contexts, such as cooperative or peer-driven systems (Scaraboto, 2015). Hybrid economies, which exist between social and economic exchanges, illustrate how interactions within these communities can either enhance or undermine value circulation.

Such hybrid contexts extend beyond traditional buyer–seller relationships, emphasizing consumer-to-consumer dynamics, often mediated by digital platforms. In these collaborative or sharing economy settings, consumers orchestrate activities that create value through circulation (Figueiredo & Scaraboto, 2016; Scaraboto & Figueiredo, 2022) or sharing (Belk, 2010). These examples illustrate that communal value creation occurs both within and outside of markets, governed by distinct principles of social and economic exchange.

Empirical studies have documented CCs across diverse contexts, including bikers (Schouten & McAlexander, 1995), surfers (Canniford & Shankar, 2013), online skaters (Cova & Cova, 2001), off-road drivers (McAlexander et al., 2002), vintage car collectors (Leigh et al., 2006) and cosplayers (Seregina & Weijo, 2017). These studies, whether implicitly or explicitly, assume that CCs consist of groups of people interacting with one another. Even if these interactions are temporary or part-time, these collectives are defined as groups of individuals.

Arvidsson and Caliandro (2016), however, propose an alternative perspective, suggesting that CCs can exist as something between collectives and individuals. Brand publics, for example, are conceptualized as flows of affect – posts, likes and other digital traces – that are detached from the individuals who originated them. These publics occupy a space between individual and collective, reflecting broader shifts in social media dynamics.

In parallel, other scholars have introduced market-oriented perspectives of CCs. Mamali et al. (2018) describe consumer-constructed organizations as hybrid entities, while Guercini and Cova (2018) view them as unconventional forms of entrepreneurship. These organizations challenge traditional market boundaries by transitioning from demand-side consumers to supply-side competitors.

Actor-network and assemblage theories (Canniford & Bajde, 2015) have also pushed research on CCs into new territory. These perspectives highlight that such communities are inherently situational, defined by specific configurations of individuals, objects and interactions at a given time and place.

In this stream of research, thanks to Kozinets and Handelman (2004), we discover that communities become critical and destroy value, and/or they allow consumers to escape from the market (Bekin et al., 2005; Kozinets, 2002a) and participate in alternative chains of value creation and circulation. In essence, communities participate in corporate activities of value creation but also contrast them: they do it directly, for example, by promoting boycott campaigns which reduce a given company's turnover, and indirectly, by promoting alternative ways of obtaining goods and services (self-production, freecycle, sharing, etc.).

The digital era has further transformed CCs. Scholars studying online communities (Kozinets, 2002b) have observed how digital platforms diminish the importance of physical proximity while enabling broader, more dynamic interactions. These communities generate social capital (Mathwick et al., 2008), facilitate learning (Jayanti & Singh, 2010), amplify word of mouth (Kozinets et al., 2010) and provide benefits that enhance company profitability (Manchanda et al., 2015).

Recently, CCs have been reconceptualized as assemblages of individuals, objects and digital devices (Hoffman & Novak, 2018). For instance, IoT devices such as Alexa enable consumer-to-consumer interactions, transforming individual consumption into communal experiences. Material objects also play a central role in communal value co-creation, not only in an instrumental sense but in ethical or sustainability contexts. Communities criticism of unsustainable practices illustrate how material objects can be handled in such a way to shape alternative value pathways (Gollnhofer et al., 2019).

From an assemblage theory perspective, CCs are ephemeral and dynamic networks of individuals, objects, territories and other resources. In specific contexts, these networks create value for participants and, in some cases, for the environment (Diaz Ruiz et al., 2020; Morgan-Thomas et al., 2020). Rituals, gatherings and shared activities often generate collective atmospheres that produce value for participants and companies alike. However, these atmospheres are fragile and require consistent maintenance and engagement (Hill et al., 2022).

Recent scholarship suggests that, under certain conditions, CCs can evolve beyond their initial focus on consumption and transform into entrepreneurial entities (Cova & Guercini, 2024; Guercini & Cova, 2018) or structured organizations (Mamali et al., 2018). These transformations often leverage digital platforms and social networks to scale the community's influence and activities (Kozinets et al., 2021; Perren & Kozinets, 2018). CCs may transition into entrepreneurial ventures when members collectively mobilize resources, knowledge and social capital to pursue business objectives. This transformation is frequently driven by the community's ability to identify and exploit market opportunities.

Such entrepreneurial evolution is particularly evident in niche markets, where consumer passion and expertise contribute to product innovations or services tailored to the community's unique needs. For example, fan-based communities centered around specific products – such as craft beer enthusiasts or sustainable fashion advocates – often lay the foundation for entrepreneurial initiatives by identifying unmet needs within their consumption culture. Shared commitment to these needs fosters collaboration, which may lead to the creation of businesses serving both the community itself and external markets.

While entrepreneurial transformation is one potential trajectory, CCs can also evolve into more formalized organizational structures. Mamali et al. (2018) highlight that transitioning from an informal network to a structured entity often involves establishing governance mechanisms, role specialization and resource management practices. This process typically occurs when communities aim to scale their activities, formalize their goals or engage with external stakeholders. For example, hobbyist groups focused on open-source software development or urban gardening may adopt hierarchical structures to manage resources effectively, coordinate activities, or negotiate partnerships. Such organizational transitions allow communities to sustain their efforts over time while accommodating growth and diversification.

The digital age has further expanded the potential of CCs by enabling seamless integration with social networks and web platforms. Kozinets et al. (2021) and Perren and Kozinets (2018) explore how digital environments facilitate community interactions, amplify visibility and provide tools for monetization and collaboration. Platforms like Instagram, Facebook and TikTok enable CCs to maintain a constant online presence, engage with broader audiences and create content that strengthens their communal identity. This integration often catalyzes entrepreneurial and organizational transformations. For instance, content creators within a community might use social media platforms to promote community-driven programs, sell branded merchandise or establish subscription-based services. Similarly, digital platforms support communities transitioning into organizations by offering tools for coordination, fundraising and communication.

The conceptualization of communities has evolved significantly, reflecting shifts in theoretical frameworks, methodologies and sociotechnological contexts. While early studies emphasized shared identities, geographies or consumption practices as foundational to community formation, contemporary scholarship challenges and redefines these traditional perspectives. Scholars such as Hill et al. (2022) and Zwick and Bradshaw (2016) have contributed to this discourse by examining the emergent nature of communities and interrogating their ontological essence, respectively.

Hill et al. (2022) argue that contemporary community emergence diverges from earlier models, which often presumed static and homogeneous foundations. Instead, they propose that communities form through dynamic, fluid and contingent processes shaped by the interplay of cultural, technological and market forces. For instance, digital platforms enable highly transient and fragmented communities, where membership and engagement often arise from algorithmically mediated interactions rather than stable, pre-existing bonds. This contrasts sharply with the traditional view of communities as cohesive and enduring entities. Hill et al. emphasize that these emergent communities may coalesce around fleeting shared experiences – such as viral events or trending topics – rather than deep, sustained commonalities.

This rethinking of emergence aligns with broader shifts in social theory emphasizing complexity, hybridity and the performative nature of social formations. It highlights the roles of individuals and institutions as active co-creators of community structures, often responding to specific needs or contexts rather than following organic or predetermined pathways.

Parallel to this focus on emergence, Zwick and Bradshaw (2016) challenge the very ontological foundation of communities, questioning their existence as stable, coherent or even 'real' entities. Instead, they argue that communities are often discursively constructed or strategically mobilized, particularly in contexts such as marketing, political activism or digital environments.

From this perspective, the notion of 'community' functions as a rhetorical tool or ideological construct rather than a fixed sociological category. For example, brands frequently invoke the language of the community to cultivate emotional connections with consumers, fostering a sense of belonging that may not correspond to any actual social structure. Similarly, digital platforms often frame their user bases as communities despite lacking interpersonal bonds or shared purposes among users.

This ontological critique compels scholars to interrogate the motivations and power dynamics underlying the invocation of community. It also encourages a critical examination of how communities are commodified, managed and instrumentalized in contemporary society.

Table 24.1 A tentative chronology of consumption communities concepts

Concepts	*Description*	*References*
Collective consumption	Collective aspects of consumption: How social relations affect individual consumers and their activities	Arnould and Price (1993); Celsi et al. (1993); Reilly and Wallendorf (1987); Wallendorf and Arnould (1991); Wallendorf and Reilly (1983)
CCs precursors	Sub-cultures of consumption, consumer tribes and brand communities: consumers' collectives as units of analysis	Cova (1997); Muñiz and O'Guinn (2001); Schouten and McAlexander (1995)
Theoretical development	Marketplace cultures, new consumption communities, consumer crowds, consumption communities, brand publics, consumer collectives	Arnould et al. (2021); Arnould and Thompson (2005); Arvidsson and Caliandro (2016); Bekin et al. (2005); Chalmers Thomas et al. (2013); Kozinets et al. (2008)
Market and non-market-based communities	CCs create or destroy value at the crossroads of market economy and social exchange networks	Scaraboto (2015); Schau et al. (2009)
Brand publics	CCs detach from individual participants and acquire a new epistemological, meso-level, status	Arvidsson and Caliandro (2016)
Hybrid organizations	CCs as both consumer and corporate or institutional organizations	Guercini and Cova (2018); Mamali et al. (2018)
Critical CCs	CCs help consumers in escaping the market economy or fight against it	Bekin et al. (2005); Kozinets (2002a); Kozinets and Handelman (2004)
CCs turn digital	CCs become digital actors and expand their scope between direct interpersonal relationships	Kozinets (2002b)
Beyond human CCs	CCs incorporate digital resources and physical devices	Diaz Ruiz et al. (2020); Hill et al. (2022); Hoffman and Novak (2018); Morgan-Thomas et al. (2020); Perren and Kozinets (2018)
CCS as reifications	CCs can be seen as a projection of the theoretical discourse, beyond their members actual awareness	Zwick and Bradshaw (2016)

Source: The authors.

The divergence in conceptualizations of communities – whether through their emergent properties or their contested ontology – has profound implications for theoretical inquiry and practical application. Theoretically, these perspectives invite a more nuanced understanding of the fluidity, performativity and contextuality of social formations. Practically, they underscore the importance of critically evaluating the uses and misuses of 'community' as a concept in marketing, public policy and digital governance.

Organizations seeking to engage with communities must account for both their structural dynamics and the ethical implications of framing, representing or exploiting such groups. Policy-makers, likewise, can use these insights to design interventions that acknowledge the contingent and constructed nature of communities rather than assuming their stability or homogeneity.

These contributions enrich our understanding of social life, challenging conventional categories and encouraging us to embrace the evolving realities of collective existence. This discussion is synthesized in the following table, which outlines the implications of CC research across a tentative chronology (Table 24.1).

CO-CREATION AND CO-DESTRUCTION IN CCs

Several studies examine CCs as contexts for value co-creation and co-destruction. While most focus on one of these aspects, some discuss both (Buhalis et al., 2020; Hardcastle et al., 2025; Quach & Thaichon, 2017).

Co-creation within CCs has been explored across various empirical settings, including innovation and knowledge-sharing platforms (Akman et al., 2019; Alhashem et al., 2020; Chen et al.,

Table 24.2 Sources of value co-creation in consumption communities

	Description	*Example*	*References*
Shared purpose	A unifying goal or mission that drives community members to participate and create value collectively	Members of open-source communities contributing to software development to achieve a common goal	Akman et al. (2019); Jiang et al. (2024)
Knowledge sharing	The exchange of insights, expertise and experiences among community members to enhance collective understanding and individual troubleshooting	Users of online forums sharing troubleshooting tips for specific software issues	Chen et al. (2018); Zhu et al. (2022)
Collaborative innovation	Joint efforts by community members to develop new ideas, products, or services, often facilitated by brands	Participants in LEGO Ideas proposing and voting on new LEGO set designs	Chapman and Dilmperi (2022); Seraj (2012)
Community engagement	Active involvement of members in community activities, fostering interaction and collective engagement	Active discussions and event participation in a sports fan community	Healy and McDonagh (2013); Pongsakornrungsilp and Schroeder (2011)
Social connectedness	Emotional and social bonds among members that foster trust and a sense of belonging	Close friendships forming in online support groups, creating a safe environment for sharing experiences	Alhashem et al. (2020); Skålén et al. (2015)
Brand advocacy	Efforts by members to promote the brand through positive word-of-mouth and personal endorsements toward non-members and the public	Social media users enthusiastically sharing their love for a brand with their networks	Cova et al. (2015a); Gambetti and Graffigna (2015)

Source: The authors.

2018), brand communities and groups of sports or activity fans (Pongsakornrungsilp & Schroeder, 2011; Seraj, 2012).

The major areas where co-creation occurs in CCs are summarized in Table 24.2, along with examples and references. A shared purpose serves as the cornerstone of co-creation, uniting community members around a common goal. This collective mission fosters collaboration and meaningful engagement. For instance, members of open-source communities, such as contributors to Linux and similar projects, collaborate to develop and improve software. This dynamic has been extensively documented by Akman et al. (2019) and Jiang et al. (2024), who highlight the critical role of shared values in motivating sustained contributions.

Knowledge sharing involves the exchange of insights and expertise among community members to enhance both individual and collective problem-solving capacities. This process often takes place in digital environments, such as forums or social media groups, where users discuss troubleshooting tips and strategies. Studies by Chen et al. (2018) and Zhu et al. (2022) highlight the pivotal role of such exchanges in building community trust and fostering reciprocal learning.

Collaborative innovation refers to joint efforts to create new products, services or ideas, often involving direct collaboration with brands. A notable example is the LEGO Ideas platform, where users propose and vote on potential new designs. This participatory model not only drives innovation but also strengthens brand loyalty (Chapman

& Dilmperi, 2022). In the framework proposed by Seraj (2012), contributions to innovation by CCs can be classified as intellectual, integrating the social and cultural components of perceived value within online communities.

Community engagement takes shape through active participation in discussions, events and activities. Such engagement deepens collective interactions and strengthens bonds among members. For instance, sports fan communities often demonstrate this through dynamic debates, shared celebrations and organized events (Pongsakornrungsilp & Schroeder, 2011). Healy and McDonagh (2013) investigated a community of Liverpool football fans, identifying key roles that consumers play in supporting community cohesion and mutual value creation.

Social connectedness refers to the emotional and relational ties that bind community members. These bonds foster an environment of trust and belonging, as seen in online support groups where participants share personal experiences and offer mutual encouragement. Alhashem et al. (2020) demonstrate how collective value emerges through the interactions of passionate participants in Instructables, a do-it-yourself-focused community. Similarly, Skålén et al. (2015) emphasize the importance of specific rules and practices in structuring the relationship between the community and the company to effectively create value for both parties.

Brand advocacy arises when community members actively promote a brand through personal endorsements and positive word-of-mouth. Social media serves as a prominent platform for such advocacy, enabling users to share their enthusiasm for a brand with broader audiences (Cova et al., 2015a). Gambetti and Graffigna (2015) illustrate how advocacy and co-creation may be constrained by misalignments and internal tensions in meaning-making processes, which can result in ambiguous community identities and opportunistic member behaviors.

In Table 24.3, the theoretical conditions under which co-destruction arises are summarized. Resource misalignment occurs when resources are poorly aligned or inadequately integrated, leading to inefficiencies and diminished outcomes. For

Table 24.3 Sources of value co-destruction in consumption communities

	Description	*Example*	*References*
Resource misalignment	Occurs when resources are not effectively aligned or integrated, leading to inefficiencies and reduced value for one or more stakeholders.	A collaboration platform failing due to poor integration of skills and resources among team members.	Bidar et al. (2024); Li and Tuunanen (2022)
Miscommunication and expectation gaps	Happens when communication breakdowns or mismatched expectations create dissatisfaction and failed interactions.	Service providers overpromising and underdelivering on offerings, leading to customer dissatisfaction.	Buhalis et al. (2020); Echeverri and Skålén (2021)
Power dynamics and hierarchies	Arises when unequal power distribution or hierarchical decisions favor certain actors at the expense of others, causing conflict or resentment.	Corporate decisions prioritizing shareholder profits at the expense of worker well-being in collaborative environments.	Huang et al. (2025)
Technological overreach	Refers to technology overuse or misuse that causes alienation or value diminution for users.	Gaming platforms using predatory monetization models that frustrate players.	Lehtonen et al. (2022)
Negative social interactions	Includes toxic behaviors, conflicts or exclusionary practices within social or collaborative settings.	Trolling in online communities resulting in members disengaging from platforms.	Li and Tuunanen (2022); Quach and Thaichon (2017)
Intentional sabotage	Involves deliberate actions to undermine value creation, often motivated by competitive or personal reasons.	Competitors posting fake negative reviews to harm a business's reputation.	Hardcastle et al. (2025); Huang et al. (2025)

Source: The authors.

example, collaboration platforms may fail when team members lack complementary skills or resources, resulting in disorganized workflows and suboptimal results. Bidar et al. (2024) identify key sources of potential co-destruction in online collaborative networks, categorizing them into pre-existing conditions, process-related themes and post-process factors. Li and Tuunanen (2022) emphasize the critical role of information technology in service systems, particularly in promoting social interaction and facilitating resource integration to mitigate co-destruction risks.

Breakdowns in communication or mismatched expectations often lead to dissatisfaction and failed interactions. A common example is when service providers overpromise but underdeliver, eroding customer trust. Buhalis et al. (2020) examine the role of Airbnb in local communities, highlighting how its rapid development introduced critical issues that hinder co-creation and fuel co-destruction. Using a practice-theory perspective, Echeverri and Skålén (2021) explore how such gaps damage relationships and impede long-term collaboration.

Hierarchical decision-making and imbalanced power dynamics can create conflicts, resentment or perceptions of inequity within CCs. For example, corporate decisions prioritizing shareholder profits at the expense of employee well-being often demoralize teams and reduce productivity. Huang et al. (2025) emphasize that such imbalances undermine collective efforts and erode trust.

The overuse or misuse of technology can alienate users and diminish perceived value. For instance, gaming platforms employing predatory monetization models, such as excessive in-game purchases, frustrate players and reduce engagement. Lehtonen et al. (2022) investigate the negative effects of technological overreach on user satisfaction and loyalty.

Toxic behaviors, conflicts and exclusionary practices within communities often lead to disengagement and a loss of value for members. For example, trolling and harassment in online forums frequently drive users to abandon these platforms. Quach and Thaichon (2017) discuss how such negative interactions undermine community cohesion, discourage participation and promote value destruction.

Intentional sabotage involves deliberate actions to undermine value creation and can significantly impact community dynamics. For example, posting fake negative reviews to harm a business's reputation erodes consumer trust. Hardcastle et al. (2025) and Huang et al. (2025) examine the conditions under which community members deliberately hinder value co-creation, intentionally fostering value destruction.

The phenomena of communal value co-creation and co-destruction represent two intertwined aspects of collective interactions in contemporary academic discourse. Traditionally analyzed as distinct processes, recent studies highlight their frequent simultaneity within the same contexts. Scholars such as Buhalis et al. (2020), Hardcastle et al. (2025) and Li and Tuunanen (2022) advance our understanding of how communities simultaneously generate and diminish value, underscoring the complexity of these dynamics in communal and organizational environments.

Communities are dynamic ecosystems where interactions can produce both positive and negative outcomes. Peer-to-peer platforms like Airbnb and Uber foster co-creation as users share resources and build trust, enhancing mutual benefits. However, these interactions may also involve co-destruction, such as disputes over pricing, service quality or discriminatory practices. Similarly, in collaborative workspaces, sharing ideas may lead to innovation (co-creation), while unresolved conflicts or competition for recognition may simultaneously foster resentment (co-destruction).

The interplay between co-creation and co-destruction is particularly pronounced in contexts with high interdependence among community members, such as service ecosystems, digital platforms and social movements. In these settings, value creation may also trigger value destruction.

The dual nature of value co-creation and co-destruction has significant theoretical and practical implications. Theoretically, it challenges linear or binary models of communal interactions, advocating for a nuanced, systems-based understanding of value dynamics. Scholars must explore how these processes co-evolve and influence one another within specific contexts, emphasizing their temporal and relational dimensions.

Practically, organizations and community managers must recognize that fostering co-creation does not automatically eliminate co-destruction. Proactively managing tensions, aligning expectations and facilitating open communication are critical to minimizing co-destructive outcomes. For example, platform operators can implement moderation policies or design interventions to address sources of conflict without stifling positive engagement.

MEASUREMENT

Measuring the ability of CCs to create or destroy value requires a combination of quantitative metrics and qualitative insights to capture the impact of such activities on brand performance, customer behavior and brand perception. Some of these

Table 24.4 Value co-creation and value co-destruction measurement

Measure	*Purpose*	*Metrics*	*Insight*
Engagement	Gauge how actively the community is involved with the company/brand	Participation rate User-generated content Engagement levels	General measures of actual community members' involvement
Net promoter score	Measures customer loyalty and the likelihood of community members supporting the company/brand	NPS: Promoters – detractors	Relative measure of the support (or criticism) by customers and community members
Sentiment analysis	Evaluate the tone of discussions within the community toward the company/brand	Positive/negative sentiment ration: The balance of positive versus negative conversations Emotion analysis: positive and negative	Valence measures (relative and absolute) of the sentiment toward the company/brand
Customer lifetime value	Track the monetary impact of community participation on individual customer lifetime value	CLV measures the total worth of a customer to a business over the entirety of their relationship	General measure of the 'value' of the customers' community
Churn rate and retention	Track customer retention and the likelihood of community members remaining loyal to the company/brand	Churn Rate is the percentage of customers who disengage from the brand over a given period. Retention Rate is the percentage of community members who remain actively engaged with the brand over time.	Measures the ability of the company to retain customers and control disengagement
Brand equity	Assess the overall impact of consumption communities on brand strength, perception and market value	Brand awareness and favorability Brand Equity Market Share	Assesses the value and strength of the brand in terms of demand and market power
Sales and revenues	Directly measure the financial impact of consumption communities on revenue generation	Revenue growth from community members Customer acquisition cost Sales decline from negative campaigns	Evaluates the positive and negative impact of community value co-creation and co-destruction in financial terms

Source: The authors.

measures are general, and they are not necessarily related to the 'communal' side of the relationship between companies and their markets, while others are more specific (Table 24.4).

Engagement metrics aim to assess the level of participation and involvement of community members with a brand. Key indicators include:

1. Participation rate: This measures the percentage of active members contributing content, discussions or feedback. For example, a thriving online forum such as Reddit's r/fitness, where 70% of registered users actively post questions, share personal progress updates and respond to others' queries, reflects a high participation rate. Such forums foster robust interactions that amplify community engagement and co-create value by enabling peer-to-peer knowledge sharing. On the contrary, when the percentage is relatively lower or decreasing, it signals potential loss of engagement and eventual co-destruction.
2. UGC: The volume of posts, reviews and shared experiences created by the community can either enhance or detract from the brand's value. For instance, a travel community, such as TripAdvisor, posting detailed itineraries and positive reviews, helps co-create value for tourism brands by enhancing their credibility and providing potential customers with authentic insights and recommendations. Even in these cases, low or decreasing values of UGC denote loss of co-creation and potential co-destruction.
3. Engagement levels: Metrics such as likes, shares, comments and interactions on brand-related content across various platforms. For example, a viral

social media campaign with high engagement levels can significantly boost brand visibility and perception. Engagement usually brings value, but it is necessary to check for valence and sentiment analysis (see below).

Tools such as social media analytics platforms (e.g., Sprout Social, Hootsuite, Brandwatch) and community platforms (e.g., Discourse, Reddit metrics) provide insights into these dynamics. High participation rates and positive UGC indicate strong value co-creation, whereas spikes in negative engagement point to potential value co-destruction, such as when community members express collective dissatisfaction during a product recall. More in general, quantitative measures of engagement can be misleading if not paralleled with qualitative analysis oriented toward valence and sentiment analysis: in fact, higher levels of engagement could be due to strong criticism or dissatisfaction.

The Net Promoter Score is a widely used metric to measure customer loyalty and the likelihood of community members recommending the brand. Calculated by subtracting the percentage of detractors (those rating low in their likelihood to recommend the brand) from promoters (rating higher), the Net Promoter Score (NPS) reflects overall community commitment. High scores signify effective value co-creation, while low scores highlight dissatisfaction, potentially leading to value co-destruction. For instance, a community of fitness enthusiasts advocating for Zwift, known for its interactive exercise bikes and training and racing app, demonstrates value co-creation by generating enthusiastic testimonials and hosting group rides that promote the brand's offerings. Conversely, the backlash faced by Nike after a controversial ad campaign involving a polarizing athlete led to a dip in its NPS, illustrating value co-destruction through a division in public support. Monitoring shifts in NPS over time within CCs allows businesses to identify trends and areas requiring intervention.

Sentiment analysis focuses on evaluating the tone and emotional context of discussions within the community. Metrics include:

- Emotion analysis: Identifying emotional valences such as happiness, frustration or anger within community interactions. For instance, a gaming platform like Steam exemplifies this dynamic. Steam fosters co-creation by engaging its community through regular updates, such as introducing features like Steam Deck compatibility and seasonal sales that generate users' excitement. However, it has also faced co-destruction scenarios, such as user backlash over major technical glitches during the launch of updates or downtime during critical gaming events, highlighting the delicate balance of value dynamics in such communities.
- Positive/negative sentiment ratio: The balance of positive versus negative conversations around the brand. For example, a beauty brand such as Fenty Beauty, known for its inclusive product range and diverse marketing campaigns, exemplifies strong value co-creation through overwhelmingly positive reviews on social media. Community members frequently share testimonials, makeup tutorials and product reviews, creating a vibrant ecosystem of user-generated content that amplifies brand credibility and attitudes.

Artificial intelligence-driven sentiment analysis tools (e.g., Lexalytics, Brandwatch) and natural language processing platforms (e.g., IBM Watson, Google Cloud Natural Language API) assist in capturing and interpreting these dynamics. A higher ratio of positive sentiment and emotions such as excitement signals value co-creation, while negative sentiment spikes may suggest value co-destruction.

Customer lifetime value (CLV) measures their relationship with a brand, reflecting the financial impact of community participation. Higher CLV suggests that the community fosters loyalty and advocacy, leading to increased spending. For example, a tech community that actively supports and educates users about a software brand contributes to higher CLV by reducing churn and increasing upgrades. Conversely, declining CLV indicates disengagement and potential value destruction, such as when users leave due to unresolved service complaints.

Tools such as Salesforce and HubSpot offer comprehensive CLV tracking and reporting, helping businesses understand the financial contributions of their community.

Churn and retention metrics assess the likelihood of community members remaining loyal to the brand over time. Key indicators include:

- Churn rate: The percentage of customers who disengage or stop purchasing from the brand within a given period. For instance, a subscription service facing high churn rates may discover community members feeling neglected or dissatisfied. For example, Netflix experienced churn spikes in the past when certain popular shows were removed from its library, which led to

dissatisfaction among fans who felt their feedback on content preferences was ignored.
- Retention Rate: The percentage of community members who remain actively engaged with the brand over time. For example, a gaming community maintaining active participation through regular updates and events signals effective retention strategies.

Tools such as Recurly and Google Analytics track these metrics. A high retention rate reflects successful value co-creation while rising churn rates signal dissatisfaction and value co-destruction. For instance, a clothing brand losing customers after a poorly received product line might indicate significant co-destruction.

Brand equity evaluates the overall impact of CCs on brand strength, perception and market performance. Key metrics include:

- Brand awareness and favorability: Changes in how the brand is perceived by community members and the broader public. For example, a community-driven campaign promoting sustainability initiatives, such as Patagonia's 'Don't Buy This Jacket' campaign, can enhance brand favorability by aligning community values with corporate actions and fostering deeper engagement with ethically and sustainability-minded consumers.
- Market share impact: The extent to which communities drive loyalty and advocacy, maintaining or growing market share. For instance, an automobile brand gaining market share due to active support from a fan community demonstrates value co-creation.

Brand valuation firms like Interbrand and market research companies such as Ipsos are instrumental in tracking these dynamics. Increased brand equity and positive public perception signify value co-creation, while declines indicate community-driven value destruction. For instance, widespread negative press following a community boycott can erode brand equity.

Sales and revenues directly measure the financial impact of CCs on revenue generation. Key indicators include:

- Revenue growth from community members: Sales driven by engaged community participants. For example, Apple's iPhone experienced a surge in sales following a wave of community-driven product reviews and unboxings on YouTube, which showcased the phone's features and build quality, emphasizing user satisfaction.
- Customer acquisition cost (CAC): Communities that co-create value often reduce CAC by fostering organic acquisition through advocacy. For instance, a skincare brand like The Ordinary gaining new customers through word-of-mouth recommendations by community influencers on Instagram, where detailed product reviews and tutorials highlight its effectiveness and affordability, driving both awareness and trust.
- Sales decline from negative campaigns: Instances where community backlash leads to organized boycotts or reduced revenue. For example, Nestl√©, which faced declining sales following a viral campaign criticizing its palm oil sourcing practices, provides a compelling example of this dynamic. The campaign, led by environmental advocacy groups, highlighted deforestation and labor abuses, spurring a widespread consumer boycott that underscored the power of community-driven value co-destruction.

E-commerce platforms (e.g., Shopify, Magento) and financial analysis tools (e.g., QuickBooks, NetSuite) provide detailed insights into these financial metrics when integrated with customer relationship management tools. Increased sales and reduced CAC point to effective value co-creation, whereas declining revenues following negative campaigns reflect value co-destruction.

Case study analysis and qualitative research. To complement quantitative metrics, qualitative research methods such as case studies, focus groups and thematic analysis provide contextual insights. These approaches explore the motivations, perceptions, meanings and behaviors of community members, offering a nuanced understanding of value co-creation and co-destruction dynamics. For example, a focus group with active members of a given community might reveal why certain initiatives resonate better than others.

Tools such as NVivo and Dedoose assist in organizing and analyzing qualitative data, while social media listening platforms (e.g., Sprinklr, Talkwalker) track online discussions for thematic analysis. For instance, a thematic analysis of online complaints about a tech brand may uncover recurring issues causing value co-destruction.

Some of these measures focus on behaviors that are not directly related to co-creation or co-destruction. For example, growing engagement also depends on contextual factors, and it does not necessarily mean that consumers are bringing more value to the brand. In fact, higher engagement can also depend on negative campaigns. More in detail, some measures highlight collective behaviors and eventually more (or less) value without conscious and constructive (or destructive) practices. Consumers buy more or engage more, but they do not necessarily provide, for example, positive reviews, peer-to-peer support or new ideas for product development. On the other side, when consumers buy less or engage less, that does not mean they are criticizing or devaluing the brand. They simply stop buying. Therefore, it is necessary to use these measures in combination to cross-check insights from different metrics. For instance, engagement and sentiment analysis must be used together to check if more engagement is associated with positive sentiment and then value co-creation or the opposite. Secondly, it is always necessary to run qualitative analyses to verify if and how consumers are co-creating or co-destructing value, purposefully or not.

FUTURE RESEARCH

Research on CCs so far has been flourishing and has brought to light their emerging and changing properties. In some cases, the very nature of CCs has been questioned and how we define them is of major concern to fully exploit this research stream. From this perspective, it could be useful to deal with the following theoretical and epistemological issues:

- Which theory or theories could be used in CCs, research? This literature began with interpretive studies and soon gained attention from positivist scholars (Algesheimer et al., 2005, 2010; Bagozzi & Dholakia, 2006; Dholakia et al., 2004). Depending on the context, scale of analysis and research objectives, these approaches appear to be antagonistic. This is an argument that needs further discussion and consideration: is it really the case that these approaches cannot be integrated? Are there any further perspectives that could prove to be useful in representing CCs more holistically?
- Strictly related to the former argument, communities can be observed in their micro dimension (Leigh et al., 2006), such as when examining direct one-to-one relationships between members. At the same time, communities also exhibit a macro dimension (Arvidsson & Caliandro, 2016; Kozinets, 2002b), for example, when consumers worldwide identify with a brand, a rock star or a countercultural movement. Moreover, they are increasingly integrated into complex digital ecosystems in which they and their members interact with platforms, social networks and devices (Diaz Ruiz et al., 2020; Morgan-Thomas et al., 2020). These assemblages (Canniford & Bajde, 2015) present macro and micro, human and artificial, material and nonmaterial traits that need a thorough reconsideration of the literature to redefine the essence and the boundaries of CCs.
- Marketing and consumer research scholars have identified conditions in which societal arrangements can be designed or managed to 'facilitate' market(ing) processes (McAlexander et al., 2002; Schau et al., 2009). Others have highlighted the contrary perspective, involving antagonism, anti-market attitudes and market escape (Kozinets, 2002a; Kozinets & Handelman, 2004). In given conditions, CCs deviate from the traditional consumption domain and move toward the institutional and entrepreneurial realms, sometimes mimicking actual companies (Guercini & Cova, 2018; Mamali et al., 2018). More attention could be dedicated to deepening the relationship between social and economic exchanges and the role they play in promoting market and social development. Special attention should be dedicated to the interaction of the constructive (co-creation) and the critical (co-destructive) dimensions, which often occur together in the very same context and – not so paradoxically – contribute to institutional and social development.

SYNTHESIS AND TAKEAWAYS

CCs play a vital role in consumer culture, driving business growth through loyalty, advocacy and co-creation. They encompass subcultures, brand communities and consumer tribes, fostering innovation and value creation. However, CCs also present challenges, including co-destruction, activism and resistance. This chapter examines the dynamics and outcomes of CCs and proposes a framework for measuring their corporate impact.

CCs drive customer engagement, loyalty, co-creation and word-of-mouth across diverse industries, including technology, fitness, food and luxury. While they offer significant value, mismanagement or misaligned corporate actions can result in co-destruction, boycotts and reputational damage. To harness the potential of CCs while mitigating risks, companies must engage with them authentically and strategically.

Value co-creation and co-destruction are intertwined, dynamic processes that often occur simultaneously within CCs. These processes challenge traditional linear models, necessitating a systems-based approach that considers temporal and relational dimensions. The high interdependence inherent in CCs amplifies this duality, underscoring the importance of understanding the triggers for both value creation and destruction and their coexistence within shared contexts.

Companies and institutions engaging with CCs must adopt active management strategies to balance co-creation and minimize co-destruction. Key strategies include fostering open communication, aligning member and corporate expectations, addressing power imbalances and proactively managing conflicts. Effective moderation and thoughtful platform design are essential to sustaining engagement while minimizing the risks of value destruction, ensuring long-term positive outcomes for both communities and businesses.

Measuring value co-creation and co-destruction within CCs requires integrating quantitative and qualitative metrics. Engagement metrics, such as participation rates and sentiment analysis, should be paired with financial indicators like customer lifetime value and revenue growth to identify trends. Sentiment and valence analysis are critical for distinguishing positive engagement from criticism or dissatisfaction.

To ensure a nuanced understanding of member behaviors, managers should complement quantitative data with qualitative insights, such as thematic analysis and focus groups. Cross-referencing metrics with contextual factors helps avoid misinterpretations, enabling companies to develop proactive strategies that foster value co-creation while mitigating the risks of co-destruction, such as boycotts or disengagement driven by dissatisfaction.

REFERENCES

Akman, H., Plewa, C., & Conduit, J. (2019). Co-creating value in online innovation communities. *European Journal of Marketing*, *53*(6), 1205–1233. https://doi.org/10.1108/EJM-12-2016-0780

Algesheimer, R., Borle, S., Dholakia, U. M., & Singh, S. S. (2010). The impact of customer community participation on customer behaviors: An empirical investigation. *Marketing Science*, *29*(4), 756–769. https://doi.org/10.1287/mksc.1090.0555

Algesheimer, R., Dholakia, U. M., & Herrmann, A. (2005). The social influence of brand community: Evidence from European car clubs. *Journal of Marketing*, *69*(3), 19–34. https://doi.org/10.1509/jmkg.69.3.19.66363

Alhashem, M., Moraes, C., & Szmigin, I. T. (2020). Use and social value in peer-to-peer prosumption communities. *European Journal of Marketing*, *55*(1), 193–218. https://doi.org/10.1108/EJM-03-2019-0235

Antorini, Y. M., Muñiz, A. M. J., & Askildsen, T. (2012). Collaborating with customer communities: Lessons from the LEGO Group. *MIT Sloan Management Review*, *53*(3), 73.

Arnould, E. J., Arvidsson, A., & Eckhardt, G. M. (2021). Consumer collectives: A history and reflections on their future. *Journal of the Association for Consumer Research*, *6*(4), 415–428. https://doi.org/10.1086/716513

Arnould, E. J., & Price, L. L. (1993). River magic: Extraordinary experience and the extended service encounter. *Journal of Consumer Research*, *20*(1), 24–45. https://doi.org/10.1086/209331

Arnould, E. J., & Thompson, C. J. (2005). Consumer culture theory (CCT): Twenty years of research. *Journal of Consumer Research*, *31*(4), 868–882. https://doi.org/10.1086/426626

Arvidsson, A., & Caliandro, A. (2016). Brand public. *Journal of Consumer Research*, *42*(5), 727–748. https://doi.org/10.1093/jcr/ucv053

Bagozzi, R. P., & Dholakia, U. M. (2006). Antecedents and purchase consequences of customer participation in small group brand communities. *International Journal of Research in Marketing*, *23*(1), 45–61. https://doi.org/10.1016/j.ijresmar.2006.01.005

Bekin, C., Carrigan, M., & Szmigin, I. (2005). Defying marketing sovereignty: Voluntary simplicity at new consumption communities. *Qualitative Market Research: An International Journal*, *8*(4), 413–429. https://doi.org/10.1108/13522750510619779

Belk, R. W. (2010). Sharing. *Journal of Consumer Research*, *36*(5), 715–734. https://doi.org/10.1086/612649

Bidar, R., Jabbari, M., & Luck, E. (2024). Value co-destruction in online collaborative networks. *European Management Journal*, *42*(1), 98–107. https://doi.org/10.1016/j.emj.2022.08.001

Buhalis, D., Andreu, L., & Gnoth, J. (2020). The dark side of the sharing economy: Balancing value co-creation and value co-destruction. *Psychology & Marketing*, *37*(5), 689–704. https://doi.org/10.1002/mar.21344

Canniford, R. (2011a). A typology of consumption communities. In R. W. Belk, K. Grayson, A. M. Muñiz, & H. J. Schau (Eds.), *Research in consumer behavior* (pp. 57–75). Emerald.

Canniford, R. (2011b). How to manage consumer tribes. *Journal of Strategic Marketing*, *19*(7), 591–606. https://doi.org/10.1080/0965254X.2011.599496

Canniford, R., & Bajde, D. (2015). *Assembling consumption: Researching actors, networks and markets*. Routledge.

Canniford, R., & Shankar, A. (2013). Purifying practices: How consumers assemble romantic experiences of nature. *Journal of Consumer Research*, *39*(5), 1051–1069. https://doi.org/10.1086/667202

Celsi, R. L., Rose, R. L., & Leigh, T. W. (1993). An exploration of high-risk leisure consumption through skydiving. *Journal of Consumer Research*, *20*(1), 1–23. https://doi.org/10.1086/209330

Chalmers Thomas, T., Price, L. L., & Schau, H. J. (2013). When differences unite: Resource dependence in heterogeneous consumption communities. *Journal of Consumer Research*, *39*(5), 1010–1033. https://doi.org/10.1086/666616

Chapman, A., & Dilmperi, A. (2022). Luxury brand value co-creation with online brand communities in the service encounter. *Journal of Business Research*, *144*, 902–921. https://doi.org/10.1016/j.jbusres.2022.01.068

Chen, T., Drennan, J., Andrews, L., & Hollebeek, L. D. (2018). User experience sharing: Understanding customer initiation of value co-creation in online communities. *European Journal of Marketing*, *52*(5/6), 1154–1184. https://doi.org/10.1108/EJM-05-2016-0298

Coffin, J., Cova, B., & Shankar, A. (2023). Introduction to the special section: Tribal marketing after Covid. *Marketing Theory*, *23*(2), 267–273. https://doi.org/10.1177/14705931231153119

Cova, B. (1997). Community and consumption: Towards a definition of the 'linking value' of product or services. *European Journal of Marketing*, *31*(3/4), 297–316. https://doi.org/10.1108/03090569710162380

Cova, B., & Cova, V. (2001). Tribal aspects of postmodern consumption research: The case of French in-line roller skaters. *Journal of Consumer Behaviour*, *1*(1), 67–76. https://doi.org/10.1002/cb.54

Cova, B., & Guercini, S. (2024). Tribal entrepreneurs: Caught in the crossfire of the tribal and market logics? *Consumption Markets & Culture*, *27*(1), 1–16. https://doi.org/10.1080/10253866.2023.2252751

Cova, B., Pace, S., & Skålén, P. (2015a). Brand volunteering: Value co-creation with unpaid consumers. *Marketing Theory*, *15*(4), 465–485. https://doi.org/10.1177/1470593115568919

Dholakia, U. M., Bagozzi, R. P., & Pearo, L. K. (2004). A social influence model of consumer participation in network-and small-group-based virtual communities. *International Journal of Research in Marketing*, *21*(3), 241–263. https://doi.org/10.1016/j.ijresmar.2003.12.004

Diaz Ruiz, C. A., Peñaloza, L., & Holmqvist, J. (2020). Assembling tribes: An assemblage thinking approach to the dynamics of ephemerality within consumer tribes. *European Journal of Marketing*, *54*(5), 999–1024. https://doi.org/10.1108/EJM-08-2018-0565

Echeverri, P., & Skålén, P. (2021). Value co-destruction: Review and conceptualization of interactive value formation. *Marketing Theory*, *21*(2), 227–249. https://doi.org/10.1177/1470593120983390

Figueiredo, B., & Scaraboto, D. (2016). The systemic creation of value through circulation in collaborative consumer networks. *Journal of Consumer Research*, *43*(4), 509–533. https://doi.org/10.1093/jcr/ucw038

Firat, F. A., & Venkatesh, A. (1995). Liberatory postmodernism and the reenchantment of consumption. *Journal of Consumer Research*, *22*(3), 239–267. https://doi.org/10.1086/209448

Galvagno, M., & Dalli, D. (2014). Theory of value co-creation: A systematic literature review. *Managing Service Quality*, *24*(6), 643–683. https://doi.org/10.1108/MSQ-09-2013-0187

Gambetti, R. C., & Graffigna, G. (2015). Value co-creation between the 'inside' and the 'outside' of a company: Insights from a brand community failure. *Marketing Theory*, *15*(2), 155–178. https://doi.org/10.1177/1470593114545004

Gollnhofer, J. F., Weijo, H. A., & Schouten, J. W. (2019). Consumer movements and value regimes: Fighting food waste in Germany by building alternative object pathways. *Journal of Consumer Research*, *46*(3), 460–482. https://doi.org/10.1093/jcr/ucz004

Grant, A., Weijo, H., & Dacin, P. A. (2023). How institutional logics shape fairness in crowdsourcing: The case of Threadless. *International Journal of Research in Marketing*, *40*(2), 378–397. https://doi.org/10.1016/j.ijresmar.2022.10.002

Guercini, S., & Cova, B. (2018). Unconventional entrepreneurship. *Journal of Business Research*, *92*, 385–391. https://doi.org/10.1016/j.jbusres.2018.06.021

Hardcastle, K., Edirisingha, P., Cook, P., & Sutherland, M. (2025). The co-existence of brand value co-creation and co-destruction across the customer journey in a complex higher education brand. *Journal of Business Research*, *186*, 114979. https://doi.org/10.1016/j.jbusres.2024.114979

Healy, J. C., & McDonagh, P. (2013). Consumer roles in brand culture and value co-creation in virtual communities. *Journal of Business Research*, *66*(9), 1528–1540. https://doi.org/10.1016/j.jbusres.2012.09.014

Hill, T., Canniford, R., & Eckhardt, G. M. (2022). The roar of the crowd: How interaction ritual chains create social atmospheres. *Journal of Marketing*, *86*(3), 121–139. https://doi.org/10.1177/00222429211023355

Hoffman, D. L., & Novak, T. P. (2018). Consumer and object experience in the internet of things: An assemblage theory approach. *Journal of Consumer Research*, *44*(6), 1178–1204. https://doi.org/10.1093/jcr/ucx105

Huang, Y., Wu, W., & Qian, L. (2025). Explicit vs. Implicit? How different self-presentations of luxury tourism experience trigger others' value co-destruction intention in online travel communities. *Tourism Management*, *107*, 105058. https://doi.org/10.1016/j.tourman.2024.105058

Jayanti, R. K., & Singh, J. (2010). Pragmatic learning theory: An inquiry-action framework for distributed consumer learning in online communities. *Journal of Consumer Research*, *36*(6), 1058–1081. https://doi.org/10.1086/648689

Jiang, H., Meng, F., & Liu, B. (2024). Unlocking non-transactional value co-creation: Insights from online travel communities. *Journal of Travel Research*, *64*(5). https://doi.org/10.1177/00472875241237256

Kozinets, R. V. (2002a). Can consumers escape the market? Emancipatory illuminations from burning man. *Journal of Consumer Research*, *29*(1), 20–38. https://doi.org/10.1086/339919

Kozinets, R. V. (2002b). The field behind the screen: Using netnography for marketing research in online communities. *Journal of Marketing Research*, *39*(1), 61–72. https://doi.org/10.1509/jmkr.39.1.61.18935

Kozinets, R. V., De Valck, K., Wojnicki, A. C., & Wilner, S. J. S. (2010). Networked narratives: Understanding word-of-mouth marketing in online communities. *Journal of Marketing*, *74*(2), 71–89. https://doi.org/10.1509/jm.74.2.71

Kozinets, R. V., Ferreira, D. A., & Chimenti, P. (2021). How do platforms empower consumers? Insights from the affordances and constraints of reclame aqui. *Journal of Consumer Research*, *48*(3), 428–455. https://doi.org/10.1093/jcr/ucab014

Kozinets, R. V., & Handelman, J. M. (2004). Adversaries of consumption: Consumer movements, activism, and ideology. *Journal of Consumer Research*, *31*(3), 691–704. https://doi.org/10.1086/425104

Kozinets, R. V., Hemetsberger, A., & Schau, H. J. (2008). The wisdom of consumer crowds: Collective innovation in the age of networked marketing. *Journal of Macromarketing*, *28*(4), 339–354. https://doi.org/10.1177/0276146708325382

Lehtonen, M. J., Vesa, M., & Harviainen, J. T. (2022). Games-as-a-disservice: Emergent value co-destruction in platform business models. *Journal of Business Research*, *141*, 564–574. https://doi.org/10.1016/j.jbusres.2021.11.055

Leigh, T. W., Peters, C., & Shelton, J. (2006). The consumer quest for authenticity: The multiplicity of meanings within the MG subculture of consumption. *Journal of the Academy of Marketing Science*, *34*(4), 481–493. https://doi.org/10.1177/0092070306288403

Li, M., & Tuunanen, T. (2022). Information technology–supported value co-creation and co-destruction via social interaction and resource integration in service systems. *The Journal of Strategic Information Systems*, *31*(2), 101719. https://doi.org/10.1016/j.jsis.2022.101719

Lumivalo, J., Tuunanen, T., & Salo, M. (2024). Value co-destruction: A conceptual review and future research agenda. *Journal of Service Research*, *27*(2), 159–176. https://doi.org/10.1177/10946705231177504

Mamali, E., Nuttall, P., & Shankar, A. (2018). Formalizing consumer tribes: Towards a theorization of consumer-constructed organizations. *Marketing Theory*, *18*(4), 521–542. https://doi.org/10.1177/1470593118767723

Manchanda, P., Packard, G., & Pattabhiramaiah, A. (2015). Social dollars: The economic impact of customer participation in a firm-sponsored online customer community. *Marketing Science*, *34*(3), 367–387. https://doi.org/10.1287/mksc.2014.0890

Martin, D. M., & Schouten, J. W. (2014). Consumption-driven market emergence. *Journal of Consumer Research*, *40*(5), 855–870. https://doi.org/10.1086/673196

Mathwick, C., Wiertz, C., & De Ruyter, K. (2008). Social capital production in a virtual P3 community. *Journal of Consumer Research*, *34*(6), 832–849. https://doi.org/10.1086/523291

McAlexander, J. H., Schouten, J. W., & Koenig, H. F. (2002). Building brand community. *Journal of Marketing*, *66*(1), 38–54. https://doi.org/10.1509/jmkg.66.1.38.18451

McKinsey. (2022). *A better way to build a brand: The community flywheel*. www.mckinsey.com/capabilities/growth-marketing-and-sales/our-insights/a-better-way-to-build-a-brand-the-community-flywheel

Morgan-Thomas, A., Dessart, L., & Veloutsou, C. (2020). Digital ecosystem and consumer engagement: A socio-technical perspective. *Journal of Business Research*, *121*, 713–723. https://doi.org/10.1016/j.jbusres.2020.03.042

Muñiz, A. M. J., & O'Guinn, T. C. (2001). Brand community. *Journal of Consumer Research*, *27*(4), 412–432. https://doi.org/10.1086/319618

Nøjgaard, M. (2023). The value-translation model of consumer activism: How consumer watchdog organizations change markets. *Journal of Consumer Research*, *49*(6), 967–986. https://doi.org/10.1093/jcr/ucac025

Perren, R., & Kozinets, R. V. (2018). Lateral exchange markets: How social platforms operate in a networked economy. *Journal of Marketing*, *82*(1), 20–36. https://doi.org/10.1509/jm.14.0250

Pongsakornrungsilp, S., & Schroeder, J. E. (2011). Understanding value co-creation in a co-consuming brand community. *Marketing Theory*, *11*(3), 303–324. https://doi.org/10.1177/1470593111408178

Quach, S., & Thaichon, P. (2017). From connoisseur luxury to mass luxury: Value co-creation and co-destruction in the online environment. *Journal of Business Research*, *81*, 163–172. https://doi.org/10.1016/j.jbusres.2017.06.015

Reilly, M. D., & Wallendorf, M. (1987). A comparison of group differences in food consumption using household refuse. *Journal of Consumer Research*, *14*(2), 289–294. https://doi.org/10.1086/209113

Romani, S., Grappi, S., & Dalli, D. (2012). Emotions that drive consumers away from brands: Measuring negative emotions toward brands and their behavioral effects. *International Journal of Research in Marketing*, *29*(1), 55–67. https://doi.org/10.1016/j.ijresmar.2011.07.001

Scaraboto, D. (2015). Selling, sharing, and everything in between: The hybrid economies of collaborative networks. *Journal of Consumer Research*, *42*(1), 152–176. https://doi.org/10.1093/jcr/ucv004

Scaraboto, D., & Figueiredo, B. (2022). How consumer orchestration work creates value in the sharing economy. *Journal of Marketing*, *86*(2), 29–47. https://doi.org/10.1177/00222429211027777

Schau, H. J., Muñiz, A. M. J., & Arnould, E. J. (2009). How brand community practices create value. *Journal of Marketing*, *73*(5), 30–51. https://doi.org/10.1509/jmkg.73.5.30

Schouten, J. W., & McAlexander, J. H. (1995). Subcultures of consumption: An ethnography of the new bikers. *Journal of Consumer Research*, *22*(1), 43–61. https://doi.org/10.1086/209434

Seraj, M. (2012). We create, we connect, we respect, therefore we are: Intellectual, social, and cultural value in online communities. *Journal of Interactive Marketing*, *26*(4), 209–222. https://doi.org/10.1016/j.intmar.2012.03.002

Seregina, A., & Weijo, H. A. (2017). Play at any cost: How cosplayers produce and sustain their ludic communal consumption experiences. *Journal of Consumer Research*, *44*(1), 139–159. https://doi.org/10.1093/jcr/ucw077

Skålén, P., Pace, S., & Cova, B. (2015). Firm-brand community value co-creation as alignment of practices. *European Journal of Marketing*, *49*(3/4), 596–620. https://doi.org/10.1108/EJM-08-2013-0409

Wallendorf, M., & Arnould, E. J. (1991). 'We gather together': Consumption rituals of thanksgiving day. *Journal of Consumer Research*, *18*(1), 13–31. https://doi.org/10.1086/209237

Wallendorf, M., & Reilly, M. D. (1983). Ethnic migration, assimilation, and consumption. *Journal of Consumer Research*, *10*(3), 292–302. https://doi.org/10.1086/208968

Wharton Baker Retailing Center. (2021). *Understanding the boomerang effect of loyalty programs.* https://bakerretail.wharton.upenn.edu/wp-content/uploads/2021/04/Understanding-the-Boomerang-Effect-of-Loyalty-Programs-FINAL-APR2021.pdf

Zhu, T., Zhang, L., Zeng, C., & Liu, X. (2022). Rethinking value co-creation and loyalty in virtual travel communities: How and when they develop. *Journal of Retailing and Consumer Services*, *69*, 103097. https://doi.org/10.1016/j.jretconser.2022.103097

Zwick, D., & Bradshaw, A. (2016). Biopolitical marketing and social media brand communities. *Theory, Culture & Society*, *33*(5), 91–115. https://doi.org/10.1177/0263276415625333

25

Internal Branding for Practice and Research: Guidance for Its Definition, Implementation and Outcomes Measurement

David Barros-Arrieta

INTRODUCTION

The significance of employees as internal customers began to emerge in marketing literature during the 1970s, largely due to the contributions of Berry, Hensen and Burke. They identified employee engagement as a key factor in enhancing the service quality provided to external customers (García et al., 2018). Since then, the internal marketing approach has evolved to focus on understanding employees' needs and implementing strategies that benefit them, thereby increasing their satisfaction and motivation to improve their performance for external customers. Ultimately, this aims to achieve marketing objectives (Qiu et al., 2022). The concept of internal branding has emerged as a specific aspect of internal marketing, concentrating on promoting the brand within the organization so that employees internalize its values and understand how to represent it to customers and other external audiences (Du Preez et al., 2017; Ragheb et al., 2018). Internal branding serves as a brand management strategy that supports external branding efforts by ensuring consistency between the expectations set by external brand messages and the actual brand experience delivered through employee performance (Dechawatanapaisal, 2018). Employees play a crucial role in turning the brand promise into reality, and the effectiveness of the brand strategy is strengthened when their behaviors align with the brand attributes (Kang, 2016; Khairy et al., 2023).

Recent advancements in internal branding research have helped identify common elements, leading to a consensus on its definition, dimensions and outcomes. Literature reviews by Saleem and Iglesias (2016) and Barros and García (2021) have significantly contributed to consolidating knowledge in this area. However, despite these advancements in understanding internal branding, there remain opportunities for further research to reinforce existing agreements and deepen our understanding of the topic. Internal branding process is influenced by various organizational and contextual factors affecting its implementation and outcomes (Prashar & Maity, 2024). This indicates that discussions surrounding internal branding are still ongoing. It is essential to organize the existing knowledge about internal branding to support future research while promoting its application in business contexts.

A gap persists between research and practice in the field of internal branding (Ind, 2017). While researchers have made substantial contributions to building a solid understanding of this topic, the implementation of internal branding often remains limited to specific actions rather than being part of formal, structured programs that involve collaboration between the marketing and human resources departments. A previous study by Barros et al. (2024) aims to aid in the implementation of internal branding by outlining its key dimensions and specific activities. However, this work does not provide guidance on how to measure the anticipated outcomes of internal branding implementation.

In line with these observations, this chapter aims to discuss advancements in internal branding concerning its definition, the identification of its dimensions to facilitate implementation, and the expected outcomes, alongside guidelines for measuring these outcomes. The primary goal of this chapter is to enhance business practices through the implementation of formal internal branding programs while also promoting further research in the field, using the consensus established in this document as a foundation. The ideas presented in this chapter were developed based on previous studies conducted by the author (Barros et al., 2024; Barros & García, 2021), along with discussions from other contributions found in the internal branding literature. The chapter is organized as follows: first, it reviews the current state of the definition of internal branding, synthesizing contributions from various authors and identifying commonalities in definitions based on literature findings. Next, it provides a guide for implementing internal branding by examining its main dimensions and identifying specific actions within each dimension. It then details the outcomes of internal branding and offers methods for measuring these outcomes based on prior studies. The chapter concludes with final reflections and conclusions.

CURRENT STATUS OF INTERNAL BRANDING DEFINITION

Internal branding has garnered significant interest from researchers and practitioners in the marketing field since it emerged in the 1990s (Ragheb et al., 2018). It is considered a subset of internal marketing (Iyer et al., 2018) and focuses on managing a brand within organizations to ensure that employees exhibit the expected brand behaviors toward customers and other external stakeholders (Barros & García, 2021). In addition to internal branding, the literature has identified other subsets of internal marketing, such as employer branding (Špoljarić & Ozretić, 2023) and internal customer experience (Panneerselvam & Balaraman, 2022). These perspectives emphasize that employees are increasingly viewed as a crucial focus of marketing strategy, not only as executors of assigned tasks but also as a target audience for marketing efforts.

Researchers have noted a previous lack of consensus regarding the conceptualization of internal branding (Saleem & Iglesias, 2016). However, advancements in research have led to a consolidation of definitions, highlighting common elements that contribute to a unified understanding of the concept. Several definitions have emerged over time. For example, some authors (Foster et al., 2010; King & Grace, 2012; Punjaisri et al., 2009a; Punjaisri & Wilson, 2011) conceptualize internal branding as a process that focuses on employee intervention to ensure that employees internalize the brand and fulfill the brand promise for external stakeholders. Later definitions added new elements to these earlier conceptualizations to define internal branding as an effort to develop, strengthen and maintain a corporate brand internally, ensuring that employees 'live the brand values' and provide a brand-consistent experience that translates into quality service for customers (Du Preez & Bendixen, 2015; Pinar et al., 2016). Other authors (Iyer et al., 2018) view internal branding as an extension of internal marketing, focusing on creating symbolic connections between employees and brands through human capital development via training, workshops and communication for brand management. The common thread among these recent definitions is their emphasis on detailing the processes and activities involved in implementing internal branding.

Recently, the marketing literature has increasingly provided structured definitions that reflect advancements in the internal branding concept and offer insights into its implementation. Some documents define internal branding including communication, training and rewards as the main processes of internal branding (Goud & Sheena, 2024; Gulati et al., 2023). In previous research work, we defined internal branding based on their dimensions: brand-centered human resource management, internal brand communications and brand leadership as dimensions of internal branding (Barros & García, 2021). Other documents define internal branding as an inter-functional process involving the marketing and human resources departments (Barros et al., 2024).

Previous literature reviews (Barros & García, 2021; Saleem & Iglesias, 2016) present definitions of internal branding. However, for the purpose of this chapter, it is essential to emphasize the common themes that represent agreements in the conceptualization of internal branding. Below are key statements about internal branding, drawn from the literature review and my experience as a researcher in the field. These statements are intended to be useful for both marketing researchers and practitioners:

1. Internal branding stems from internal marketing strategy, which emphasizes the importance of internal customers, namely employees. Similar to how external branding considers the needs and expectations of customers and other external stakeholders, internal branding strategy focuses on understanding employees' needs and expectations to garner their support for the overall brand strategy.
2. The responsibility for planning, executing and monitoring the internal branding strategy does not rest solely with the marketing department. While the marketing team typically possesses more expertise in brand strategy, the human resources department must also play a significant role, as many actions fall under its purview. Consequently, internal branding requires a collaborative effort between the marketing and human resources departments.
3. Internal branding strategy bolsters external branding efforts by ensuring that the brand promise made to external customers is met. Internal and external branding should be regarded as complementary rather than independent components. Literature defines internal branding as the brand-related actions directed toward employees, which ultimately influence their performance in front of customers and other external stakeholders, thereby guaranteeing the fulfillment of the brand promise.
4. Although there is no single framework outlining the main dimensions or processes of internal branding, research and practice indicate that internal brand communication and brand training are the most commonly utilized mechanisms. Additionally, advancements in research have highlighted other essential components, particularly relating to leadership and the role of the human resources department, which should not be overlooked.
5. The internal branding process is expected to affect employees in several ways, including their cognitive, psychological, attitudinal and behavioral dimensions in relation to the brand. This employee impact also extends to how external customers and other stakeholders perceive the brand. In summary, internal branding enhances perceived brand equity for both internal and external audiences of the organization.

The subsequent sections of this document will delve into the implementation process of internal branding, its outcomes and methods for measuring its impact on employees. These insights will further enrich the understanding of internal branding, focusing on its dimensions and outcomes.

GUIDE TO IMPLEMENTING INTERNAL BRANDING BASED ON ITS DIMENSIONS

An important step in transferring knowledge from research to practice in the field of internal branding is how researchers present the implementation process. Executing internal branding is associated with the main dimensions or processes identified in the marketing literature. Fortunately, extensive academic research has provided valuable empirical evidence highlighting essential dimensions for implementing internal branding. Instead of offering a definitive and unified contribution, this section presents a set of internal branding actions identified in the literature. These actions can serve as reference points for researchers and marketing professionals to adapt to their specific needs. While some processes are common in internal branding strategies, particular needs may arise depending on the type of organization. Thus, this internal branding implementation guide serves as a reference framework that can be adjusted for each unique case.

If a company is considering implementing an internal branding program, it should first ask itself the following questions: Are we an organization oriented toward our internal market, meaning our employees? Does our organization view corporate brand management as a crucial component of our marketing and corporate strategies? These two questions are essential as they help determine how prepared a company is to implement an internal branding strategy. In previous research (Barros et al., 2024; Barros & García, 2021) we have suggested that internal market orientation and corporate brand orientation are key factors in the successful implementation of internal branding. This does not imply that companies cannot implement internal branding without these conditions. However, the process will be easier for companies that already understand and address employee needs and consider the corporate brand a vital element of their corporate strategy. Internal market orientation facilitates internal branding by motivating managers to create value for employees through various strategies, including brand initiatives (Boukis et al., 2017). Organizations focused on their corporate brand will likely receive more managerial support when implementing brand actions internally, as managers recognize the benefits these efforts bring (Iyer et al., 2018).

Piehler (2022) identifies three key antecedents of internal branding: brand orientation, brand climate and strategic branding. These elements are linked to the corporate brand strategy orientation discussed earlier. However, brand climate is specifically defined as the environment in which employees perceive brand efforts aimed at them, influencing their performance related to the brand. This suggests a scenario where internal branding actions are already in place. Additionally, Piehler (2022) highlights that market orientation, especially its focus on placing the customer at the center, and relationship orientation also serves as antecedents to internal branding. It is important to note that while market orientation focuses primarily on external customers, the ultimate goal of internal branding is to enhance the external customer experience with the brand. Relationship orientation emphasizes maintaining positive interactions with employees. This concept can be related to the idea of internal market orientation discussed previously.

Secondly, the internal branding strategy should be developed collaboratively by the marketing and human resources departments. Several authors emphasize the importance of involving human resources in this strategy (Barros et al., 2024; Barros & García, 2021; Dechawatanapaisal, 2018; Iyer et al., 2018; Piehler, 2022). While the marketing department typically has a strong grasp of the company's brand strategy, there are aspects of internal branding that fall under the purview of human resources (Saleem & Iglesias, 2016). In practice, challenges still exist when it comes to integrating these two departments within the internal branding strategy. Nevertheless, the goal of this chapter is to remind both researchers and practitioners in the fields of marketing and human resources that cooperation between these departments is essential throughout the design, implementation and evaluation of the internal branding strategy.

Internal branding aims to influence employees through a clear brand strategy, fostering a connection between them and the brand's values. When employees' personal values align with the brand's values, it becomes easier to engage and motivate them. To facilitate this alignment, researchers suggest that internal branding strategy should start during the recruitment process (Murillo & King, 2019a; Piehler et al., 2016; Saleem & Iglesias, 2016). This ensures that new hires share values that resonate with the brand. Marketing should collaborate with human resources to create tools for measuring the alignment of candidates' personal values with the brand values during recruitment. Additionally, both departments should monitor the brand-citizenship behaviors of new employees throughout their probationary period, where applicable.

Branding training programs have been one of the most frequently mentioned dimensions in the internal branding literature (Chiang et al., 2018; Gulati et al., 2023; Hofer & Grohs, 2018; Murillo et al., 2024; Zhang et al., 2016) because they effectively educates employees about various aspects related to the brand. The induction session is the first formal training that new employees receive, making it an ideal opportunity to teach them about the brand attributes, values and expected behaviors that align with the brand (Piehler, 2022). Brand training can occur in person through workshops, corporate events and coaching sessions, or virtually via online courses and virtual training sessions.

Another area where the marketing and human resources departments collaborate is in the implementation of reward systems (Barros & García, 2021; Saleem & Iglesias, 2016). Within the internal branding context, several authors (Dechawatanapaisal, 2018; Du Preez et al., 2017; Ragheb et al., 2018; Raj, 2020; Suomi et al., 2021) recommend establishing rewards for employees who exhibit results that support the brand. These results may include strong service orientation, acting as brand ambassadors, promoting the brand in digital environments, receiving positive customer feedback, contributing to the improvement of brand strategy or using branded clothing or products. Rewards can be financial, such as bonuses or cash payments, or non-financial, including gift products, extra days off, public recognition, trips, work flexibility and promotions (Barros et al., 2024).

Performance evaluation, overseen by the human resources department, should include indicators that assess brand-supportive behaviors. This integration helps employees understand that their contribution to the brand is a crucial part of their performance metrics (Chiang et al., 2018). As a result, evaluations among employees and between employees and superiors can reflect contributions of each one in advancing the corporate brand strategy (Lee et al., 2020). This aspect is vital for the effective implementation of internal branding, as performance assessments often focus solely on job-specific metrics, neglecting the impact of employees on the brand strategy. To enhance this process, the development of performance evaluation indicators should be a collaborative effort with the marketing department, relying on previously established criteria that align with brand-based rewards (Barros et al., 2024). Research has shown that brand-based performance evaluation is key to fostering a workplace culture that reinforces the brand (Barros & García, 2021; Piehler, 2018; Quaratino & Mazzei, 2018; Ragheb et al., 2018).

The aforementioned processes (brand-based recruitment, training, reward systems and brand-based performance evaluation) are collectively referred to as 'brand-centered human resource management' by various authors (Barros et al., 2024; Barros & García, 2021; Chiang et al., 2018; Helm et al., 2016; Piehler, 2018; Piehler et al., 2016). It is important to note that this does not suggest the human resources department should prioritize the brand over its other responsibilities. Instead, it emphasizes the need for HR processes to incorporate elements that reinforce the brand objectives within the organization.

Internal brand communications are an important dimension of internal branding that is often highlighted in the literature. Effective internal communication is crucial for internal branding efforts, as it helps employees understand and embrace the brand values, leading them to identify with and commit to the brand (Leijerholt et al., 2022). Employees receive brand communications from various sources, both internal and external; however, internal communications play a primary role in the internalization of the brand (Bravo et al., 2017). Therefore, organizations must ensure that brand information flows both horizontally among employees and vertically between leaders and their teams (Anees-ur-Rehman et al., 2018; Piehler, 2018). In previous research (Barros et al., 2024), we suggest several internal communication tools that can effectively promote the brand among employees, including daily briefings, newsletters, notices, corporate websites, email messages, social media posts, meetings, brand manuals, bulletin boards, corporate videos, brand books, corporate magazines and hymns.

Recent studies indicate that the success of internal branding also relies on the presence of leaders who inspire others to embody the brand (Binu Raj, 2022; Coffie et al., 2024; Lee et al., 2020; Piehler, 2022). Brand leadership refers to the role that managers or directors play as brand promoters, but also the leadership role that any employee can assume to promote the brand among their colleagues (Barros & García, 2021). This means that leaders can communicate the brand both horizontally within the organizational structure and vertically as supervisors guide and motivate their employees. Marketing managers are expected to function as brand leaders, with the goal of developing future leaders within their teams (Barros et al., 2024). An interesting perspective on this matter is offered by Zhang and Xu (2021), who argue that employees should also practice self-leadership, fostering their own cognitive and behavioral motivation to commit to and support the brand. Overall, brand leadership serves as a fundamental foundation for cultivating brand ambassadors within the organization.

The dimensions discussed in the previous paragraphs are the most frequently mentioned and developed within the internal branding literature. However, there are additional actions worth considering that researchers and marketing professionals may evaluate for inclusion in their strategic vision. Some authors (Devasagayam et al., 2010; Saleem & Iglesias, 2016) recommend promoting the creation of internal brand communities to strengthen employees' connections with the brand. These brand communities can exist in both physical workplace environments and digital spaces where interactions related to the brand occur. Distributing branded promotional products creates bonds between the brand and employees (Bodkin et al., 2016). Examples of such products include mugs, T-shirts, notebooks, pens and accessories. Additionally, brand ambassador programs are linked to the concepts of brand leadership and brand communities mentioned earlier (Murillo et al., 2024; Schmidt & Baumgarth, 2018). Some authors, such as Bravo et al. (2017), Hofer and Grohs (2018), and Piehler (2022), identify external brand communications as a significant mechanism of internal branding. However, it is essential to note that these communications are part of external branding strategies that indirectly impact employees and should not be strictly classified as an internal dimension of brand management.

Figure 25.1 summarizes the key ideas related to the dimensions of internal branding, which will aid in the implementation process.

EXPECTED OUTCOMES OF INTERNAL BRANDING AND GUIDELINES FOR THEIR MEASUREMENT

Internal branding aims to enhance employees' relationships with the brand. The literature indicates various outcomes resulting from internal branding efforts, with several established agreements worth discussing. This chapter outlines the expected outcomes of implementing internal branding and provides guidelines for measuring these outcomes, considering future empirical studies and the practical needs of marketing professionals.

The literature review shows that research on internal branding has identified numerous positive effects on employees and the strengthening of the corporate brand. Empirical evidence suggests that internal branding positively influences several key areas: brand commitment (Piehler, 2018), brand citizenship behaviors (Chhibber et al., 2024), brand identification (Piehler et al., 2016), brand loyalty (Hasni et al., 2018) and brand understanding (Afshardoost et al., 2021). The following paragraphs will explain each of these outcomes and

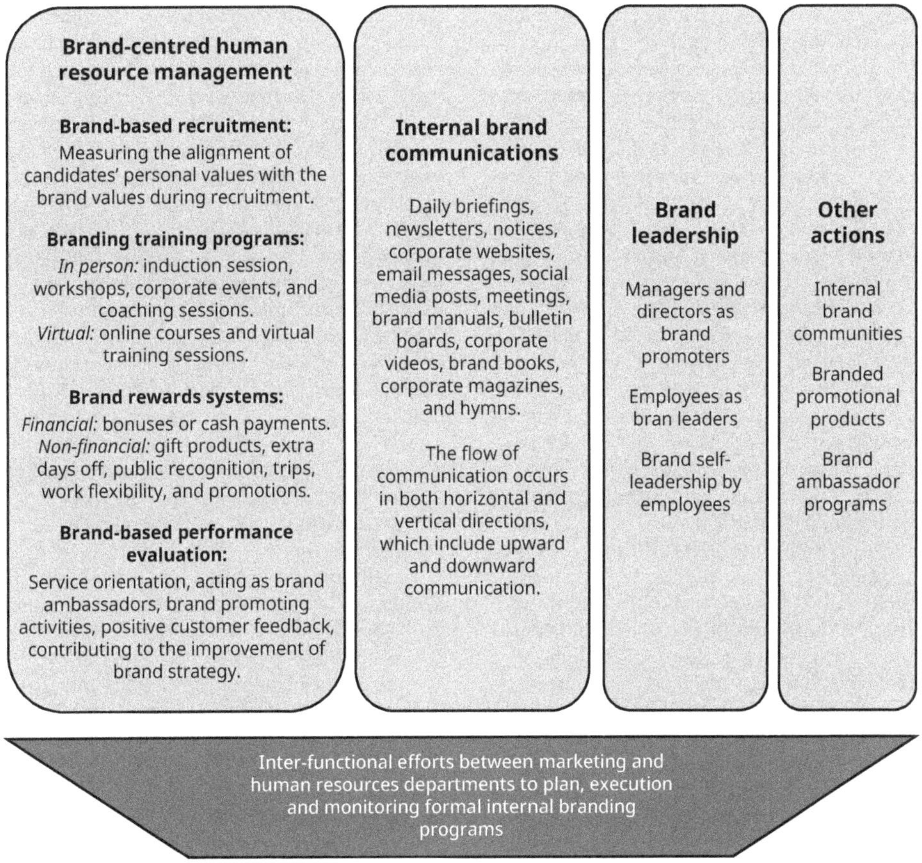

Figure 25.1 Dimensions of internal branding

Source: The author.

propose methods to measure them among employees. The sequence in which these internal branding outcomes are discussed follows a logical progression identified in a prior systematic review (Barros & García, 2021), reflecting the empirical evidence found in the literature.

The first significant impact of implementing internal branding strategies among employees is brand understanding. This is defined as employees acquiring knowledge and comprehension of all fundamental aspects related to the brand, such as its attributes, values and meanings, along with its relevance and the role they play in the brand strategy through their behavior (Murillo & King, 2019b). Brand understanding goes beyond simply knowing the brand; it involves a deep internalization that equips employees with the tools necessary to perform their roles effectively in support of the brand (Afshardoost et al., 2021). This step is particularly crucial for new or recently hired employees, as it helps them understand the brand and act in alignment with it. Piehler (2018) outlines how to measure brand understanding through four dimensions: (1) brand relevance: employees recognize that the brand is essential to the organization's success; (2) behavior relevance: employees comprehend that their behavior contributes to the brand success; (3) brand knowledge: employees are well-informed about the brand and understand what it represents; (4) brand confidence: employees can translate abstract brand identities and promises into specific behaviors that strengthen the brand in their daily work. Using these four components, measurement tools can be developed to assess how well employees understand the brand. Piehler et al. (2016, p. 1601) and Piehler (2018, pp. 232 and 233) provide specific items for measuring brand understanding, which can serve as a reference for scientific research or practical business assessments.

Once employees develop a deep understanding of the brand, they enter a phase of brand identification, where they cultivate a sense of belonging to the brand and connect with what it represents (Barros & García, 2021; Saleem & Iglesias, 2016). Brand identification enables employees to feel closer to the brand and exhibit improved behavior toward customers (Ngo et al., 2020). When employees identify with the brand, they perceive it as their own, experiencing the brand's successes and failures as if they were their own (Renjini, 2020). According to Piehler et al. (2016), brand identification comprises both cognitive and affective components. The cognitive component pertains to the perception of belonging to the brand, while the affective component relates to the positive emotions employees derive from being part of the brand. These authors outline specific items on page 1600 of their article to measure the extent of employees' brand identification.

A level beyond brand identification is brand commitment. Previous studies (Kimpakorn & Tocquer, 2010; Punjaisri et al., 2009b) have empirically shown that brand identification is a precursor to brand commitment, highlighting a direct connection between these two outcomes. Brand commitment is defined as the psychological attachment employees feel toward the brand, motivating them to exert additional effort in its support (Afshardoost et al., 2021). Earlier literature conceptualized brand commitment as a multidimensional construct. For instance, Burmann and Zeplin (2005) identified three key components of brand commitment: obedience, identification and internalization. Schulz et al. (2017) categorized brand commitment into affective, continuance and normative elements, while Kimpakorn and Tocquer (2010) measured it using three interrelated components – identification, affective commitment and loyalty. However, Piehler (2018) clarifies that brand commitment should be viewed as a unidimensional concept determined by the affective components in the employee–brand relationship. This chapter also considers identification and loyalty to the brand as independent outcomes rather than as components of brand commitment. Importantly, this chapter does not advocate for any specific measurement approach. Readers are encouraged to consult Piehler et al. (2016), which provides a measurement instrument focused on the affective dimension (p. 1600), and the study by Kimpakorn and Tocquer (2010), which shares a measurement instrument that includes affective commitment, identification and loyalty (p. 383).

The literature provides empirical evidence demonstrating the relationship between brand commitment and two additional outcomes of internal branding: brand loyalty (Punjaisri et al., 2009a) and brand citizenship behavior (Piehler, 2018; Piehler et al., 2016). Brand loyalty has traditionally been defined as the intention to stay working for an organization (Du Preez et al., 2017; Ragheb et al., 2018; Watson et al., 2018). However, brand loyalty not only involves the willingness to stay with the brand but also includes speaking positively about it, defending it and recommending it to other stakeholders (Ilyas et al., 2019). In this context, brand loyalty encompasses both attitudinal and behavioral elements. Studies that provide measurement instruments for brand loyalty primarily focus on the intention to stay with the brand. For example, Punjaisri and Wilson (2011, p. 1536), Hasni et al. (2018, p. 1064), and Soleimani et al. (2023, p. 151) utilize two questions to measure brand loyalty. This creates an opportunity to develop instruments that incorporate additional dimensions of brand loyalty, such as making positive remarks about the brand, defending it and recommending it to external stakeholders.

Brand citizenship behaviors are an important outcome of internal branding, with brand commitment serving as a key antecedent (Piehler, 2018). These behaviors are defined as the willingness of employees to engage in actions that benefit the brand, extending beyond formal responsibilities and expected performance (Burmann et al., 2009). Brand citizenship behaviors align with the brand identity and contribute to fulfilling the brand promise (Barros & García, 2021). In some research, the term 'brand citizenship behavior' has been used interchangeably with 'organizational citizenship behavior' (King & Grace, 2012). But, in the context of internal branding, brand citizenship behaviors specifically focus on aspects related to the brand rather than organizational-level behaviors (Afshardoost et al., 2021). Brand citizenship behaviors are seen as a multidimensional concept that includes various components. For example, Piehler (2018) identifies three components: brand compliance, brand endorsement and brand development. Alternatively, Hoppe (2018) defines components such as brand acceptance, brand promotion and brand participation. Literature about internal branding offers various instruments to measure brand citizenship behaviors. This chapter recommends reviewing the measurement tools proposed by Hoppe (2018, p. 467), Piehler (2018, p. 232) and Piehler et al. (2016, pp. 1599–1600), which approach the concept from a multidimensional perspective.

The outcomes of internal branding, as discussed earlier, positively influence brand equity at both internal and external levels (Barros et al., 2024). Some researchers (Anees-ur-Rehman et al., 2018; Barros & García, 2021; Poulis & Wisker, 2016) argue that the ultimate goal of internal branding is to create brand equity. Perceived brand equity refers to the perceptions individuals hold about a brand and how they generate value around it in their minds (Kimpakorn & Tocquer, 2010). It is essential to distinguish between internal brand equity and external brand equity, as internal branding directly affects brand equity for employees and indirectly influences brand equity for external stakeholders (Sousa & Ferreira, 2024). At the internal level, brand equity is known as employee-based brand equity (EBBE), which reflects the value employees perceive from the brand due to internal brand-building efforts. This perception fosters positive employee brand behavior (Baumgarth & Schmidt, 2010). Furthermore, the document published by Sousa and Ferreira (2024) defines EBBE as a process that creates value for employees through brand initiatives involving leadership, culture and context, which ultimately leads to positive employee attitudes and behaviors toward the brand. At the external level, customer-based brand equity (CBBE) represents the value perceived and developed by customers. This encompasses brand awareness, perceived quality, brand associations, emotional connections and brand loyalty (Çınar, 2020). Finally, it is important not to overlook the financial perspective of brand equity, known as financial-based brand equity. This perspective considers brand equity in terms of its monetary value, which can be crucial in situations such as mergers, acquisitions or divestitures (Kimpakorn & Tocquer, 2010).

EBBE has been identified by several authors as a multidimensional process. King et al. (2012) and Sousa and Ferreira (2024) outline three dimensions: (1) brand loyalty, which refers to employees' intentions to remain with the organization; (2) brand-consistent behavior, related to employees' voluntary actions that align with the brand and organizational values and (3) brand endorsement, which measures how willing employees are to share positive opinions about the brand with others. King and Grace (2010) describe EBBE through four key benefits: brand citizenship behavior, employee satisfaction, employee intention to stay and positive employee word of mouth. There are measurement instruments available for EBBE that can be consulted or adapted as needed. The first instrument, developed by King et al. (2013), can be found on pages 351–353 of their publication. Another instrument is provided by King and Grace (2010) and is accessible on pages 968 and 969. Each instrument presents a distinct perspective based on the previously discussed dimensions.

This chapter offers a more detailed explanation of EBBE due to its direct relevance to internal branding. However, readers are also encouraged to consider the impacts EBBE has on CBBE and financial-based brand equity. These two perspectives of brand equity are indirectly influenced by internal branding efforts, as their outcomes are mediated by other variables such as external branding initiatives and organizational performance. For those interested in exploring this topic further, it is recommended to review the study by Hasni et al. (2018), which examines the impact of internal branding on CBBE. The measurement instrument from this study can be found on page 1064 of their article. Additionally, the research conducted by Abrar et al. (2022) analyzes the literature findings to explain the relationship between EBBE and CBBE.

Table 25.1 summarizes the outcomes of internal branding, detailing their measurement components and identifying published instruments suitable for research on internal branding or for assessing the implementation impact by marketing and human resources professionals. The ways to measure internal branding outcomes vary. Each researcher or professional should evaluate the available proposals to choose the one that best suits their specific measurement needs.

Before starting an internal branding program, it is advisable to measure employees' current standings on several indicators, including brand understanding, brand identification, brand commitment, brand loyalty, brand citizenship behavior and EBBE. After implementing the program, these indicators should be re-evaluated to assess the actual impact of the internal branding program. Additionally, performing periodic measurements will allow for necessary strategy adjustments based on the findings. This monitoring process should involve collaboration between the marketing and human resources departments.

FINAL REFLECTIONS AND FUTURE RESEARCH AGENDA

It is often observed that research advances more rapidly than business practice. However, this gap presents an opportunity for marketing and human resources managers to leverage these publications to stay informed about developments in internal branding and translate this knowledge into actionable strategies. A persistent challenge is the integration of both departments in designing, executing and evaluating internal branding programs. Nonetheless, this gap is gradually closing as human resources managers become more involved in organizational processes where their role is crucial, including in branding strategies.

Table 25.1 How to measure outcomes of internal branding

Outcome	*Components*	*Description*	*Available Measuring Instruments*
Brand understanding	Brand relevance	Employees understand that the brand is important to the organization's success	Piehler (2016, p. 1601)
	Behavior relevance	Employees understand that they contribute, through their behavior to the brand's success)	
	Brand knowledge	Employees are informed about the brand, and they know what it represents	Piehler (2018, pp. 232 and 233)
	Brand confidence	Employees can translate abstract brand identities and brand promises into specific, brand strengthening behaviors in their daily work	
Brand identification	Cognitive	Refers to the perception of belonging to the brand	Piehler et al. (2016, p. 1601)
	Affective	Refers to the favorable feelings employees experience as part of the brand	
Brand commitment	Identification	Feeling part of the brand	Kimpakorn and Tocquer (2010, p. 383)
	Willingness to remain	Intention to stay with the brand	
	Affective	Emotional attachment to the brand	Kimpakorn and Tocquer (2010, p. 383) Piehler et al. (2016, p. 1600) Piehler (2018, p. 232)
Brand loyalty	Intention to stay	The intention to stay working for the brand	Punjaisri and Wilson (2011, p. 1536) Hasni et al. (2018, p. 1064) Soleimani et al. (2023, p. 151)
Brand citizenship behavior	Brand compliance	Following rules to ensure brand consistency	Piehler (2018, p. 232)
	Brand endorsement	It involves representing the brand positively and advocating for it to potential customers, colleagues and other stakeholders	
	Brand development	Behaviors that contribute to brand enhancement, such as developing expertise, participating in training programs, generating innovative ideas, taking on extra duties and responsibilities or suggesting ways to improve the customer brand experience	Piehler et al. (2016, pp. 1599–1600)
	Brand acceptance	Refers to how well employees align with the norms and codes of conduct associated with the brand	Hoppe (2018, p.467)
	Brand promotion	Active engagement with brand-related activities, such as the willingness to recommend the brand to others	
	Brand participation	Indicates the continuous development and involvement with the brand by seeking out and acquiring brand-related information	
Employee-based brand equity	Brand loyalty	Refers to employees' intentions to remain with the organization	King and Grace (2010, pp. 968 and 969)
	Brand-consistent behavior	Voluntary actions that align with the brand and organizational values	King et al. (2013, pp. 251–253)
	Brand endorsement	measures how willing employees are to share positive opinions about the brand with others.	
	Employee satisfaction	Sense of satisfaction from the job	King and Grace (2010, p. 968)

Source: The author.

Large companies have made quicker progress in implementing internal branding due to their robust organizational structures, well-defined corporate strategies and greater resource availability. In contrast, small businesses often face limitations regarding structure and resources, which hinder their ability to formalize internal branding efforts. Additionally, many small businesses lack a clear marketing strategy. This chapter encourages the exploration of proposed actions that can serve as a starting point for gradually implementing internal branding. Moreover, the chapter advocates for internal branding to be established as a formal program that includes phases of planning, execution and monitoring. Current business practices show that actions related to internal branding are often being implemented, but these efforts frequently consist of actions that do not form part of a formal program. Each company will need to design an internal branding program tailored to its unique needs, capacities and defined brand objectives.

Research on internal branding has primarily focused on the corporate brand perspective; however, there are instances where companies manage both corporate brands and product brands. Future research is needed to explore internal branding in the context of product brand management. While the relationships between the antecedents, dimensions and outcomes of internal branding have been empirically studied, most studies focus primarily on employees' perspectives. It is crucial to conduct more research that simultaneously examines internal brand outcomes alongside external brand outcomes by integrating both employee and customer perceptions within the same study. This would enhance our understanding of the effects of internal branding not only in the internal market but also on customers and other external stakeholders. The advancement of technology and communication has transformed many organizational processes, including internal branding. Future research should explore how new technologies have influenced internal branding programs. Specifically, it would be valuable to understand how artificial intelligence, virtual reality and augmented reality have been integrated into internal brand management. The use of artificial intelligence in marketing and human resources has rapidly increased, and internal branding is not exempt from this trend. Additionally, virtual reality and augmented reality create new scenarios for employees to engage with the brand. Conducting comparative studies on the implementation of internal branding in both large and small companies will help identify their similarities and differences, uncovering practical insights that benefit all types of organizations. Furthermore, analyzing cultural factors that may impact the implementation of internal branding is also an important area for investigation, as cultural aspects influence organizational behavior and, consequently, internal branding. In a previous literature review (Barros & García, 2021), we provide more research topics that could be explored in future studies about internal branding.

REFERENCES

Abrar, M., Khan, A. S., & Xiang, L. (2022). Impact of employee-based brand equity on customer-based brand equity. In M. W. Bari, M. Abrar, & E. Alaverdov (Eds.), *Antecedents and outcomes of employee-based brand equity* (pp. 16–30). IGI Global.

Afshardoost, M., Eshaghi, M. S., & Bowden, J. L. H. (2021). Internal brand management, brand understanding, employee brand commitment, and brand citizenship behavior: A meta-analysis. *Journal of Strategic Marketing*, *31*(5), 983–1011. https://doi.org/10.1080/0965254X.2021.2016896

Anees-ur-Rehman, M., Wong, H. Y., Sultan, P., & Merrilees, B. (2018). How brand-oriented strategy affects the financial performance of B2B SMEs. *Journal of Business & Industrial Marketing*, *33*(3), 303–315. https://doi.org/10.1108/JBIM-10-2016-0237

Barros, D., & García, E. (2021). Internal branding: Conceptualization from a literature review and opportunities for future research. *Journal of Brand Management*, *28*(2), 133–151. https://doi.org/10.1057/s41262-020-00219-1

Barros, D., Granados, A., Fuentes, L., Picalúa, V., & Ghisays, M. (2024). Internal branding workflow implementation based on inter-functional effort between marketing and human resources departments. *Procedia Computer Science*, *238*, 981–988. https://doi.org/10.1016/j.procs.2024.06.123

Baumgarth, C., & Schmidt, M. (2010). How strong is the business-to-business brand in the workforce? An empirically-tested model of 'internal brand equity' in a business-to-business setting. *Industrial Marketing Management*, *39*(8), 1250–1260. https://doi.org/10.1016/j.indmarman.2010.02.022

Binu Raj, A. (2022). Internal branding, employees' brand commitment and moderation role of transformational leadership: An empirical study in Indian telecommunication context. *Asia-Pacific Journal of Business Administration*, *14*(3), 285–308. https://doi.org/10.1108/APJBA-04-2021-0175

Bodkin, C. D., Peters, C., & Thomas, J. (2016). The impact of employee work perceptions on purchase intentions from a company store. *Journal of Product & Brand Management*, *25*(5), 479–489. https://doi.org/10.1108/JPBM-09-2015-0998

Boukis, A., Gounaris, S., & Lings, I. (2017). Internal market orientation determinants of employee brand enactment. *Journal of Services Marketing*, *31*(7), 690–703. https://doi.org/10.1108/JSM-07-2016-0272

Bravo, R., Buil, I., de Chernatony, L., & Martínez, E. (2017). Managing brand identity: Effects on the employees. *International Journal of Bank Marketing*, *35*(1), 2–23. https://doi.org/10.1108/IJBM-10-2015-0148

Burmann, C., & Zeplin, S. (2005). Building brand commitment: A behavioural approach to internal brand management. *Journal of Brand Management*, *12*(4), 279–300. https://doi.org/10.1057/palgrave.bm.2540223

Burmann, C., Zeplin, S., & Riley, N. (2009). Key determinants of internal brand management success: An exploratory empirical analysis. *Journal of Brand Management*, *16*(4), 264–284. https://doi.org/10.1057/bm.2008.6

Chhibber, P., Chahal, H., & Kaurav, R. P. S. (2024). Is brand commitment the missing link in the internal branding and brand citizenship behaviours relationship in services sector: A meta-analysis. *Management Review Quarterly*, *75*(2), 1259–1310. https://doi.org/10.1007/s11301-024-00408-1

Chiang, H. H., Han, T. S., & McConville, D. (2018). The attitudinal and behavioral impact of brand-centered human resource management: Employee and customer effects. *International Journal of Contemporary Hospitality Management*, *30*(2), 939–960. https://doi.org/10.1108/IJCHM-02-2016-0103

Çınar, K. (2020). Customer based brand equity models in hotel industry: A literature review. In A. Kavoura, E. Kefallonitis, & P. Theodoridis (Eds.), *Strategic innovative marketing and tourism: Springer proceedings in business and economics* (pp. 281–288). Springer.

Coffie, I. S., Müller, R.-A., Marfo, M., Ocloo, E. C., & de Klerk, N. (2024). Succession planning practices and succession success in family-owned businesses: The role of leadership style as internal branding mechanism. *Journal of Family Business Management*, *15*(3), 684–704. https://doi.org/10.1108/JFBM-09-2024-0207

Dechawatanapaisal, D. (2018). Employee retention: The effects of internal branding and brand attitudes in sales organizations. *Personnel Review*, *47*(3), 675–693. https://doi.org/10.1108/PR-06-2017-0193

Devasagayam, P. R., Buff, C. L., Aurand, T. W., & Judson, K. M. (2010). Building brand community membership within organizations: A viable internal branding alternative? *Journal of Product & Brand Management*, *19*(3), 210–217. https://doi.org/10.1108/10610421011046184

Du Preez, R., & Bendixen, M. T. (2015). The impact of internal brand management on employee job satisfaction, brand commitment and intention to stay. *International Journal of Bank Marketing*, *33*(1), 78–91. https://doi.org/10.1108/IJBM-02-2014-0031

Du Preez, R., Bendixen, M., & Abratt, R. (2017). The behavioral consequences of internal brand management among frontline employees. *Journal of Product & Brand Management*, *26*(3), 251–261. https://doi.org/10.1108/JPBM-09-2016-1325

Foster, C., Punjaisri, K., & Cheng, R. (2010). Exploring the relationship between corporate, internal and employer branding. *Journal of Product & Brand Management*, *19*(6), 401–409. https://doi.org/10.1108/10610421011085712

García, E., Barros, D., & Valle, A. (2018). Endomarketing desde el paradigma de la sostenibilidad organizacional: Una revisión de la literatura. *Desarrollo Gerencial*, *10*(2), 65–82. https://doi.org/10.17081/dege.10.2.3219

Goud, V., & Sheena, X. (2024). Exploring the Nexus between internal branding and front-line employees performance in Indian public sector banks: Serial mediation approach. *Vision*, *28*(5), 580–591. https://doi.org/10.1177/09722629211039348

Gulati, C., Mathur, G., & Upadhyay, Y. (2023). Internal branding: Connecting links to establish employees' brand behaviour in hospitality sector. *FIIB Business Review*, *0*(0), 1–15. https://doi.org/10.1177/23197145221143831

Hasni, M. J. S., Salo, J., Naeem, H., & Abbasi, K. S. (2018). Impact of internal branding on customer-based brand equity with mediating effect of organizational loyalty: An empirical evidence from retail sector. *International Journal of Retail & Distribution Management*, *46*(11/12), 1056–1076. https://doi.org/10.1108/IJRDM-07-2017-0148

Helm, S. V., Renk, U., & Mishra, A. (2016). Exploring the impact of employees' self-concept, brand identification and brand pride on brand citizenship behaviors. *European Journal of Marketing*, *50*(1/2), 58–77. https://doi.org/10.1108/EJM-03-2014-0162

Hofer, K. M., & Grohs, R. (2018). Sponsorship as an internal branding tool and its effects on employees' identification with the brand. *Journal of Brand Management*, *25*(3), 266–275. https://doi.org/10.1057/s41262-018-0098-0

Hoppe, D. (2018). Linking employer branding and internal branding: Establishing perceived employer brand image as an antecedent of favourable employee brand attitudes and behaviours. *Journal of Product & Brand Management*, *27*(4), 452–467. https://doi.org/10.1108/JPBM-12-2016-1374

Ilyas, M. A., Adeel, I., Alshuaibi, A. S. I., & Shaari, H. (2019). Conceptualizing the relationship between employer brand pride, employer brand reputation, employee engagement and employee brand loyalty. *International Journal of Innovation, Creativity and Change*, *7*(5), 346–361.

Ind, N. (2017). *Branding inside out: Internal branding in theory and practice*. Kogan Page Publishers.

Iyer, P., Davari, A., & Paswan, A. (2018). Determinants of brand performance: The role of internal branding. *Journal of Brand Management*, *25*(3), 202–216. https://doi.org/10.1057/s41262-018-0097-1

Kang, D. S. (2016). Turning inside out: Perceived internal branding in customer-firm relationship building. *Journal of Services Marketing*, *30*(4), 462–475. https://doi.org/10.1108/JSM-07-2015-0229

Khairy, H. A., Agina, M. F., Aliane, N., & Hashad, M. E. (2023). Internal branding in hotels: Interaction effects of employee engagement, workplace friendship, and organizational citizenship behavior. *Sustainability*, *15*(5), 4530. https://doi.org/10.3390/su15054530

Kimpakorn, N., & Tocquer, G. (2010). Service brand equity and employee brand commitment. *Journal of Services Marketing*, *24*(5), 378–388. https://doi.org/10.1108/08876041011060486

King, C., & Grace, D. (2010). Building and measuring employee-based brand equity. *European Journal of Marketing*, *44*(7/8), 938–971. https://doi.org/10.1108/03090561011047472

King, C., & Grace, D. (2012). Examining the antecedents of positive employee brand-related attitudes and behaviours. *European Journal of Marketing*, *46*(3/4), 469–488. https://doi.org/10.1108/03090561211202567

King, C., Grace, D., & Funk, D. C. (2012). Employee brand equity: Scale development and validation. *Journal of Brand Management*, *19*(4), 268–288. https://doi.org/10.1057/bm.2011.44

King, C., Grace, D., & Funk, D. C. (2013). Erratum: Employee brand equity: Scale development and validation. *Journal of Brand Management*, *20*(4), 350–354. https://doi.org/10.1057/bm.2012.60

Lee, Y. H., Hsiao, C., Chan, H. Y., & Lee, I. C. (2020). Explorations of employee-based brand equity in the banking industry from a perceived-leadership perspective. *International Journal of Bank Marketing*, *38*(2), 425–455. https://doi.org/10.1108/IJBM-05-2019-0166

Leijerholt, U., Biedenbach, G., & Hultén, P. (2022). Internal brand management in the public sector: The effects of internal communication, organizational practices, and PSM on employees' brand perceptions. *Public Management Review*, *24*(3), 442–465. https://doi.org/10.1080/14719037.2020.1834607

Murillo, E., & King, C. (2019a). Why do employees respond to hospitality talent management: An examination of a Latin American restaurant chain. *International Journal of Contemporary Hospitality Management*, *31*(10), 4021–4042. https://doi.org/10.1108/IJCHM-10-2018-0871

Murillo, E., & King, C. (2019b). Examining the drivers of employee brand understanding: A longitudinal study. *Journal of Product & Brand Management*, *28*(7), 893–907. https://doi.org/10.1108/JPBM-09-2018-2007

Murillo, E., Sádaba, T., Mir-Bernal, P., Terán-Bustamante, A., & López-Sánchez, O. (2024). Internal branding processes in a fashion organization: Turning employees into brand ambassadors. *Mercados Y Negocios*, *25*(52), 3–30. https://doi.org/10.32870/myn.vi52.7718

Ngo, L. V., Nguyen, N. P., Huynh, K. T., Gregory, G., & Cuong, P. H. (2020). Converting internal brand knowledge into employee performance. *Journal of Product & Brand Management*, *29*(3), 273–287. https://doi.org/10.1108/JPBM-10-2018-2068

Panneerselvam, S., & Balaraman, K. (2022). Employee experience: The new employee value proposition. *Strategic HR Review*, *21*(6), 201–207. https://doi.org/10.1108/SHR-08-2022-0047

Piehler, R. (2018). Employees' brand understanding, brand commitment, and brand citizenship behaviour: A closer look at the relationships among construct dimensions. *Journal of Brand Management*, *25*(3), 217–234. https://doi.org/10.1057/s41262-018-0099-z

Piehler, R. (2022). Branding inside-out: Development of the internal branding concept. In O. Iglesias, N. Ind, & M. Schultz (Eds.), *The Routledge companion to corporate branding* (pp. 419–441). Routledge.

Piehler, R., King, C., Burmann, C., & Xiong, L. (2016). The importance of employee brand understanding, brand identification, and brand commitment in realizing brand citizenship behaviour. *European Journal of Marketing*, *50*(9/10), 1575–1601. https://doi.org/10.1108/EJM-11-2014-0725

Pinar, M., Girard, T., Trapp, P., & Eser, Z. (2016). Services branding triangle: Examining the triadic service brand promises for creating a strong brand in banking industry. *International Journal of Bank Marketing*, *34*(4), 529–549. https://doi.org/10.1108/IJBM-04-2015-0043

Poulis, A., & Wisker, Z. (2016). Modeling employee-based brand equity (EBBE) and perceived environmental uncertainty (PEU) on a firm's performance. *Journal of Product & Brand Management*, *25*(5), 490–503. https://doi.org/10.1108/JPBM-04-2015-0852

Prashar, A., & Maity, M. (2024). Building employee commitment through internal branding – a meta-analytic study. *European Journal of Marketing*,

58(5), 1241–1274. https://doi.org/10.1108/EJM-12-2021-0983

Punjaisri, K., Evanschitzky, H., & Wilson, A. (2009a). Internal branding: An enabler of employees' brand-supporting behaviours. *Journal of Service Management*, *20*(2), 209–226. https://doi.org/10.1108/09564230910952780

Punjaisri, K., & Wilson, A. (2011). Internal branding process: Key mechanisms, outcomes and moderating factors. *European Journal of Marketing*, *45*(9/10), 1521–1537. https://doi.org/10.1108/03090561111151871

Punjaisri, K., Wilson, A., & Evanschitzky, H. (2009b). Internal branding to influence employees' brand promise delivery: A case study in Thailand. *Journal of Service Management*, *20*(5), 561–579. https://doi.org/10.1108/09564230910995143

Qiu, J., Boukis, A., & Storey, C. (2022). Internal marketing: A systematic review. *Journal of Marketing Theory and Practice*, *30*(1), 53–67. https://doi.org/10.1080/10696679.2021.1886588

Quaratino, L., & Mazzei, A. (2018). Managerial strategies to promote employee brand consistent behavior: The new frontier for brand building strategies. *EuroMed Journal of Business*, *13*(2), 185–200. https://doi.org/10.1108/EMJB-02-2017-0008

Ragheb, S., Ahmed, A., & Hussein, H. (2018). Internal corporate branding impact on employees' brand supporting behaviour. *Journal of Product & Brand Management*, *27*(1), 79–95. https://doi.org/10.1108/JPBM-03-2016-1112

Raj, A. B. (2020). Employee well-being through internal branding: An integrated approach for achieving employee-based brand outcomes. *Global Business Review*, *21*(4), 1065–1086. https://doi.org/10.1177/0972150918779161

Renjini, D. (2020). Impact of internal marketing on customer orientation of employees: Mediating role of employee brand identification. *International Journal of Management (IJM)*, *11*(12), 2300–2306. https://doi.org/10.34218/IJM.11.12.2020.217

Saleem, F. Z., & Iglesias, O. (2016). Mapping the domain of the fragmented field of internal branding. *Journal of Product & Brand Management*, *25*(1), 43–57. https://doi.org/10.1108/JPBM-11-2014-0751

Schmidt, H. J., & Baumgarth, C. (2018). Strengthening internal brand equity with brand ambassador programs: Development and testing of a success factor model. *Journal of Brand Management*, *25*(3), 250–265. https://doi.org/10.1057/s41262-018-0101-9

Schulz, S. A., Martin, T., & Meyer, H. M. (2017). Factors influencing organization commitment: Internal marketing orientation, external marketing orientation, and subjective well-being. *Journal of Management Development*, *36*(10), 1294–1303. https://doi.org/10.1108/JMD-12-2016-0334

Soleimani, M., Dana, L. P., Salamzadeh, A., Bouzari, P., & Ebrahimi, P. (2023). The effect of internal branding on organisational financial performance and brand loyalty: Mediating role of psychological empowerment. *Journal of Asian Business and Economic Studies*, *30*(2), 143–163. https://doi.org/10.1108/JABES-08-2021-0122

Sousa, B., & Ferreira, P. (2024). Employee based brand equity: A systematic review of literature, framework development, and implications for future research. *Journal of Management History*, *30*(3), 475–492. https://doi.org/10.1108/JMH-07-2023-0069

Špoljarić, A., & Ozretić, Đ. (2023). Employer brand and international employer brand: Literature review. *Corporate Communications: An International Journal*, *28*(4), 671–682. https://doi.org/10.1108/CCIJ-11-2022-0141

Suomi, K., Saraniemi, S., Vähätalo, M., Kallio, T., & Tevameri, T. (2021). Employee engagement and internal branding: Two sides of the same coin? *Corporate Reputation Review*, *24*(1), 48–63. https://doi.org/10.1057/s41299-019-00090-0

Watson, A. W., Taheri, B., Glasgow, S., & O'Gorman, K. D. (2018). Branded restaurants employees' personal motivation, flow and commitment: The role of age, gender and length of service. *International Journal of Contemporary Hospitality Management*, *30*(3), 1845–1862. https://doi.org/10.1108/IJCHM-02-2017-0075

Zhang, H., & Xu, H. (2021). Improving internal branding outcomes through employees' self-leadership. *Journal of Hospitality and Tourism Management*, *46*, 257–266. https://doi.org/10.1016/j.jhtm.2020.12.013

Zhang, J., Jiang, Y., Shabbir, R., & Zhu, M. (2016). How brand orientation impacts B2B service brand equity? An empirical study among Chinese firms. *Journal of Business & Industrial Marketing*, *31*(1), 83–98. https://doi.org/10.1108/JBIM-02-2014-0041

26

Unraveling the Complexity of Brand Performance: Holistic Framework and Practical Guidelines

M. Berk Ataman, Koen Pauwels, and Burcu Sezen

INTRODUCTION

Brands are recognized as one of the most valuable intangible assets for firms. Effective and efficient management of this asset necessitates a holistic approach and the establishment of a robust brand performance measurement system. Central to any attempt to create such a system should be the acknowledgment that brand value is generated through a series of interconnected events involving various stakeholders: the value a brand creates for customers through its marketing activities (producing consumer-market outcomes, resulting in customer-based brand equity) affects how well the brand performs in the marketplace (producing product-market outcomes, resulting in sales-based brand equity), which in turn influences the investment community (producing financial-market outcomes, resulting in financial brand equity). This understanding of the brand value chain, as delineated by Keller and Lehmann (2003) and further expanded by Katsikeas et al. (2016), serves as the foundational framework for our review.

Building upon this foundation, our chapter examines empirical studies published in leading marketing journals since 2000. Our primary goal is to offer a comprehensive perspective on brand performance measurement. To that end, we present a broad set of brand performance indicators (BPIs), organizing them across consumer-market, product-market and financial-market levels. This structure helps clarify how different indicators capture the multidimensional nature of brand performance and their relevance to various stakeholders. We also explore the methodologies used to measure, estimate or construct these indicators.

The rich and diverse set of consumer-market indicators, such as the numerous components of a brand's comparative advantage, brand awareness and loyalty, underscore the central role of consumer perceptions in defining brand value. At the same time, the field maintains a strong emphasis on product-market indicators such as brand sales and financial-market metrics such as firm value, reflecting an interest in quantifiable, outcome-oriented results. Beyond these perspectives, a distinct set of BPIs highlights the critical role of resources in creating value and sustaining brand performance. These emerging resource-market indicators provide a fresh perspective, extending the scope of performance measurement to reflect a brand's broader role in fostering stakeholder relationships and sustaining competitive advantage. We propose expanding the brand value chain to incorporate this dimension in recognition of its significance.

Emphasizing the importance of monitoring brand performance through a stakeholder-centric lens, we examine how this expanded brand value chain can be used to tailor performance indicator sets to the specific needs of brand managers, investors and other relevant parties. We then contrast academic approaches with those employed by commercial entities, highlighting the resemblance between the practical and theoretical approaches to brand performance measurement. We also explore how novel data sources and technologies (e.g., digital metrics, user-generated content and generative artificial intelligence, GenAI) are reshaping the practice of brand performance measurement. While novel data and technologies offer new opportunities for tracking brand performance with greater depth and efficiency, they bring challenges like noise, contextual limitations and demographic biases, requiring thoughtful implementation. Finally, we discuss the complexities of measuring brand performance in a global context, focusing on issues such as scale invariance, cultural influences and the aggregation of national measures into global metrics.

Collectively, our review underscores the importance of developing a comprehensive, stakeholder-driven, state-of-the-art measurement framework – integrating consumer-market, product-market, financial-market and resource-market indicators – that captures the multidimensional nature of brand performance, adapts to the complexities of the market environment and leverages the novel data sources, techniques and technologies.

UNPACKING THE LAYERS OF BRAND PERFORMANCE MEASUREMENT

Research in marketing uses a wide array of variables to measure brand performance, which can be grouped under predefined categories based on an established framework: the brand value chain (Keller & Lehmann, 2003).

Firms invest in their brands through marketing expenditures and actions, with the goal of creating value. The value of a brand, as Keller and Lehmann (2003) emphasize, ultimately resides with the customers and it is at this consumer level where brand value is initially created. This makes consumer-market level a natural starting point for measuring brand performance. These indicators capture what consumers know, feel and do in relation to the brand (e.g., brand awareness, customer satisfaction and brand loyalty). The collective mindset of consumers toward the brand determines its success in the marketplace. Consequently, the performance of a brand and the value it creates for the firm can be measured at the product-market level (e.g., market share and sales). Observing the outcomes at the product-market level and assessing the brand's prospects, investors assign financial value to the brand and the firm. These assessments are captured through financial-market level indicators (e.g., brand value, firm value and risk).

However, not all BPIs neatly align with the traditional categories of consumer-market, product-market or financial-market outcomes. These additional indicators share a common thread: they reflect the brand's ability to generate, manage and leverage critical resources and stakeholder relationships. Recognizing their importance in understanding a brand's broader performance impact, we propose a new category of BPIs: resource-market level indicators. This new category builds on the resource-based view outlined in Morgan (2012), which highlights marketing resources as one of the key drivers of sustainable competitive advantage. Resource-market level BPIs reflect how brands influence the firm's resource ecosystem, including relational, reputational, human and financial resources. These indicators extend our understanding of brand performance by demonstrating how a brand contributes to the firm's ability to maintain stakeholder relationships, attract financial capital and strengthen internal capabilities.

Incorporating resource-market indicators not only broadens our understanding of brand performance but also lays the groundwork for updating the classical brand value chain. This expanded perspective, discussed in subsequent sections, reflects the evolving role of brands as strategic assets in complex and interconnected business environments.

Consumer-Market Level BPIs

Consumer-market indicators of brand performance can be organized around eight constructs, which align with the components of established customer-based brand equity frameworks (e.g., Aaker, 1991; Keller, 1993) and the stages of consumer decision journey, reflecting how the relationship between a consumer and a brand evolves.

Brand awareness

The first of these constructs is brand awareness, defined as the degree to which consumers are familiar with a brand. This includes their ability to recognize and recall the brand, understand its messages and attributes, and associate it with specific experiences or characteristics. Brand awareness captures the accumulated direct and indirect experiences consumers have with the brand, shaping their perceptions and future behaviors.

Research assesses brand awareness through three primary approaches. Each captures a different aspect of consumers' familiarity with and memory of a brand. First, multi-item Likert scales are commonly used to measure consumers' self-reported familiarity with and understanding of a brand. Second, structured tasks, such as brand recall and recognition tasks, are used to evaluate consumers' ability to retrieve brand information from memory with or without prompting, reflecting the depth of brand knowledge stored in memory. Finally, behavioral indicators, though less frequently used, provide proxies for brand familiarity. Examples of such proxies include the number of days since a consumer's last purchase or digital actions such as bookmarking, following, searching for or favoriting the brand online (Qin et al., 2024; Zenetti & Pauwels, 2024). Table 26.1 displays the different ways in which extant research measures brand awareness as well as all other consumer-market indicators.

Brand associations

The second construct captures various aspects of brand associations, representing the set of attributes, perceptions and mental connections that consumers hold about a brand. These associations include functional and emotional attributes and benefits, symbolic meanings and human-like traits (e.g., brand personality).

The measurement of brand associations varies depending on one's goals. The strength, consistency and valence of associations across consumers can be assessed using single-item or multi-item Likert scales targeting specific functional or emotional attributes, brand personality traits or symbolic aspects of the intended brand image. Social network mining methods can also gauge whether and how strongly consumers associate brands with certain attributes, traits or symbols (Culotta & Cutler, 2016). Alternatively, one may seek to reveal the entire interconnected network of brand-related concepts in consumer memory (i.e., John et al., 2006), uncovering the core elements of the perceived brand image. These individual-level mental networks of brand associations can help assess the consistency of brand-related perceptions across consumer groups or guide strategic brand decisions. Advanced techniques, such as functional Magnetic Resonance Imaging (fMRI), can also capture the consistency of brand image across consumer groups or assess image alignment between different brand entities (Chan et al., 2018).

Brand advantage

The third construct captures consumers' evaluations and feelings toward a brand, covering both cognitive and emotional dimensions, influencing their purchase considerations, preferences and loyalty. Inspired by Lehmann et al. (2008), we refer to this rather broad category as brand advantage measures. Brand advantage is typically measured using multi-item Likert scales to reflect its multifaceted nature. However, single-item scales are occasionally employed for general evaluations of brand appeal.

Brand advantage measures include consumers' perceptions of the brand's quality and superiority compared to competitors (i.e., perceived brand quality) and their evaluation of the brand's worth relative to its price or the value derived from it (i.e., perceived brand value). Also included are measures of the degree to which a brand stands out from competitors (i.e., brand differentiation) and the personal importance of a brand to a consumer (i.e., brand relevance[1]). Emotional responses, such as liking and attraction (i.e., brand attitude) and respect and admiration for the brand's reliability and leadership (i.e., brand esteem), are also captured in this category. Furthermore, variables assessing consumers' satisfaction with the brand based on their experiences (i.e., brand satisfaction), their belief in the brand's reliability, dependability and integrity (i.e., brand trust), their perceptions of the brand's ability to adapt, innovate and meet future consumer needs (i.e., brand energy), their belief that the brand remains true to its core values, being genuine, credible and aligned with consumer expectations (i.e., brand authenticity and brand credibility) are also included in this category. See Table 26.1 for various measures of brand advantage.

Brand consideration

The fourth construct assesses brand consideration, which reflects the likelihood that consumers include a brand in their set of potential purchase options when making a purchase decision. It is often measured directly using single-item Likert scales or yes/no responses, as seen in tracking studies (e.g., Pauwels et al., 2013; Srinivasan et al., 2010).

Purchase intention

The fifth construct corresponds to purchase intention, representing the likelihood or willingness of consumers to buy a brand's products or services. Positioned between brand consideration and actual purchase in the consumer decision journey, purchase intention is typically measured through straightforward self-reported single-item Likert scales that capture consumers' intentions to buy (e.g., Desai & Ratneshwar, 2003; Henderson et al., 2025).

[1] BAV Group's BrandAsset Valuator pillars of knowledge, relevance, esteem, energy and differentiation and their measurement are discussed subsequently.

Table 26.1 Consumer-market level brand performance measures

Indicator (Measurement Approach)	*Scale Items/Question Wording*	*Source/Select References*
Brand Awareness (Scale)	'I know what [X] looks like' 'I can recognize [X] among other competing brands' 'I am aware of [X]' 'Some characteristics of [X] come to my mind quickly' 'I can quickly recall the symbol or logo of [X]' 'I have difficulty in imagining [X] in my mind'	Yoo et al. (2000)
	Scales constructed by a subset of the items above	Arnett et al. (2003); Baldauf et al. (2009)
	'I am familiar with [X]' 'I am aware of [X]' OR 'I can recognize [X] among other competing brands'	Becker-Olsen and Hill (2006); Heinberg et al. (2020)
Brand Awareness (Structured task)	'When you think of [CATEGORY CUE], what brands come to mind?' 'Which of the following brands of [CATEGORY CUE] have you heard of?' followed by a list of brands	Esch et al. (2012); Warlop et al. (2005)
Brand Advantage–Perceived Brand Quality (Scale)	'Rate the quality of [X] from low to high quality'	Dawar and Pillutla (2000); Hogreve et al. (2019)
	'[X] is of high quality' 'The likely quality of [X] is extremely high' 'The likelihood that [X] would be functional is very high' 'The likelihood that [X] is reliable is very high' '[X] must be of very good quality' '[X] appears to be of very poor quality'	Baldauf et al. (2009); Yoo et al. (2000)
	For service brands, versions of the scale: 'I felt the service [X] provided was excellent' 'I felt the service [X] provided was superior to my expectations' 'I felt the service [X] provided was at a high standard'	Hogreve et al. (2019); Petersen et al. (2018)
Brand Advantage–Perceived Brand Value (Scale)	'[X] is a very good value' 'The prices of [X] are acceptable' 'I would consider [X] to be a good buy'	Arnett et al. (2003)
	'The price-quality ratio of the product/service the firm is offering is good' 'I can buy this product/service at places that are convenient for me' 'I can make use of the product/service of this firm at any time and place I want'	Ou et al. (2014, 2017)
Brand Advantage–Brand Attitude (Scale)	'Rate your attitude toward [X] from "dislike a great deal" to "like a great deal"'	Mazodier et al. (2018); Srinivasan et al. (2010); Valenti et al. (2023)
	Semantic differential scales with a combination of bipolar adjective pairs: 'Positive/Negative' 'Good/Bad' 'Favorable/Unfavorable' 'Likable/Dislikeable' 'Low quality/High quality'	Dolbec and Chebat (2013); Lei et al. (2008); Mathur et al. (2023)

(Continued)

Table 26.1 (Continued)

Indicator (Measurement Approach)	*Scale Items/Question Wording*	*Source/Select References*
Brand Advantage–Brand Satisfaction (Scale)	'Rate your overall satisfaction with [X] from "very dissatisfied" to "very satisfied"'	Echambadi et al. (2013); Ramaswami and Arunachalam (2016)
	'I am happy about my decision to use [X]' 'I believe I did the right thing when I decided to use [X]' 'Overall, I am satisfied with my decision to use [X]'	Brady et al. (2008)
Brand Advantage–Brand Trust (Scale)	'I trust this brand' 'I rely on this brand' 'This is an honest brand' 'This brand is safe'	Chaudhuri and Holbrook (2001)
	Scales constructed by a subset of the items: '[X] is trustworthy' '[X] is dependable' '[X] is reliable'	Dawar and Pillutla (2000); Puzakova et al. (2013)
Brand Advantage–Brand Authenticity (Scale)	'The brand remains true to its espoused values' 'The brand refuses to compromise the values upon which it was founded' 'The brand has stuck to its principles'	Biraglia et al. (2023)
	'[X] remains true to its values' 'The brand always sticks to its principles' 'This brand is guided by sincere values'	Heinberg et al. (2020)
Brand Advantage–Brand Credibility (Scale)	'This brand delivers what it promises' 'This brand's product claims are believable' 'Over time, my experiences with this brand have led me to expect it to keep its promises, no more and no less' 'This brand is committed to delivering on its claims, no more and no less' 'This brand has a name you can trust' 'This brand has the ability to deliver what it promises'	Erdem et al. (2006) (see Erdem et al. (2002) for a shorter version)
	'[X] is trustworthy' '[X] is reputable' '[X] makes honest claims' '[X] has a long-lasting nature' 'In the past, today, and in the future, the values behind [X] will not change'	Rapp et al. (2013)
Brand Consideration (Structured task)	'Which of the following brands of [CATEGORY CUE] have you considered buying in the past [TIME WINDOW]?' followed by a list of brands	Pauwels et al. (2013); Srinivasan et al. (2010)
Purchase Intention (Scale)	'Rate your willingness to buy [X] from "definitely would not buy" to "definitely would buy"'	Desai and Ratneshwar (2003); Henderson et al. (2025)
	'The next time I buy a [CATEGORY CUE], I will take [X] into consideration' 'I can imagine buying [X]'	Puzakova et al. (2013)
	'How likely are you to purchase [X]?' 'How likely are you to frequent a store that sells [X]?' 'How often have you purchased products made by [X]?'	Martin and Stewart (2001)

(Continued)

Table 26.1 (Continued)

Indicator (Measurement Approach)	*Scale Items/Question Wording*	*Source/Select References*
	'I am likely to purchase [X]' 'If I were going to buy a [CATEGORY CUE], I would consider buying [X]' 'My willingness to buy [X] is high'	Mathur et al. (2023)
Brand Loyalty–Commitment to (repurchase) the brand (Scale)	'I consider myself to be loyal to [X]' '[X] would be my first choice' 'I will not buy other brands if [X] is available at the store'	Arnett et al. (2003); Baldauf et al. (2009); Barone and Jewell (2013); Yoo et al. (2000)
	'I consider [X] as my first choice for [CATEGORY CUE]' 'I will do more business with [X] in the next few years' 'If I had to do it over again, I would make the same choice'	Zhang and Bloemer (2008)
Brand Loyalty–Commitment to (repurchase) the brand (Scale)	'I am very loyal to [X]' 'I am very committed to [X]' 'I plan to conduct business with [X] in the future'	Petersen et al. (2018)
	'I will buy this brand the next time I buy [CATEGORY CUE]' 'I intend to keep purchasing this brand'	Chaudhuri and Holbrook (2001)
Brand Loyalty–Emotional Attachment (Scale)	'I feel emotionally connected to [X]' 'I feel a bond to [X]'	Heinberg et al. (2020)
	'I have the feeling that [X] knows exactly what I want' 'I feel at home with [X]' 'I feel committed to [X]'	Ou et al. (2014)
	'I feel emotionally attached to [X]' 'I feel like part of the family of [X]' 'I feel a strong sense of belonging with [X]' '[X] has a great personal meaning for me'	Zhang and Bloemer (2008)
	Multi-item commitment, intimacy, and passion scales	Nyffenegger et al. (2015)
	Multi-item affection, connection, and passion scales	Dolbec and Chebat (2013)
Brand Loyalty–Willingness to recommend or support (Scale)	Scales constructed by a subset of the items: 'If my friends were looking for [CATEGORY CUE], I would tell them to try [X]' 'I would speak favorably to others about [X]' 'I would recommend [X] to my friends'	Hogreve et al. (2019); Mathur et al. (2023); Nyffenegger et al. (2015); Zhang and Bloemer (2008)
Brand Equity (Scale)	'It makes sense to buy [X] instead of any other brand, even if they are the same' 'Even if another brand has the same features as [X], I would prefer to buy [X]' 'If there is another brand as good as [X], I prefer to buy [X]' 'If another brand is not different from [X] in any way, it seems smarter to purchase [X]'	Dolbec and Chebat (2013); Halbauer et al. (2022); Heinberg et al. (2020); Yoo et al. (2000)
	Other alternatives	Brady et al. (2008); Gao et al. (2020); Ou et al. (2014, 2017); Sirianni et al. (2013); Zhao et al. (2020)

Source: The authors.

Brand preference

The sixth construct pertains to brand preference, defined as the degree to which consumers favor a brand over competing alternatives during purchase decisions. This construct covers relative preference, the intensity of preference and actual brand choice behavior. Brand preference is frequently measured through experimental methods, such as discrete choice experiments, which record consumers' brand selection among competing options (e.g., Aribarg et al., 2014; Ferjani et al., 2009).

Brand loyalty

The penultimate construct is brand loyalty, which captures consumers' commitment and emotional attachment to a brand, manifested in consistent repeat purchases and a strong customer–brand relationship. Reflecting both behavioral and emotional aspects of loyalty, its measures span repeat purchase likelihood, the strength of the emotional bond and supportive behaviors such as recommending the brand to others or advocating for it.

Moreover, different measurement approaches enable capturing its attitudinal and behavioral dimensions. Use of multi-item scales assessing loyalty-related attitudes, such as commitment to (repurchase) the brand, emotional attachment to the brand and willingness to recommend or support the brand, is widespread in the literature (see Table 26.1 for various measures of brand loyalty). So is the use of direct questions measuring specific aspects of loyalty. Tracking actual (digital) consumer behavior facilitates assessing the behavioral aspect of brand loyalty through measures such as repeat purchase rates (e.g., Cleeren et al., 2008; Echambadi et al., 2013; Koll & Plank, 2022), customer lifetime value (e.g., Ramaswami & Arunachalam, 2016) and (online) brand-related engagement activities.

Brand equity

The final category represents customer-based brand equity, a higher-order, holistic construct that reflects the cumulative value a brand adds to a product or service as perceived by consumers. The measures aim to quantify the overall value that a brand contributes to a product or service, beyond its objective attributes or functional benefits. Because brand equity arises from consumers' knowledge of and associations with the brand and includes both cognitive judgments and emotional reactions, such as trust, credibility, quality perceptions and emotional attachments, measurement relies on multi-item scales reflecting the multidimensional nature of this intangible asset.

To conclude, the central role of consumer mindset in brand performance measurement remains widely recognized (Srinivasan et al., 2010). The unwavering focus on these indicators reinforces the notion that the value of a brand ultimately resides with the customer. While brand awareness, advantage and loyalty have long been foundational, shifts in consumer behavior and digital marketing practices suggest a rebalancing of emphasis (Court et al., 2009). Measures capturing consumer intent, such as brand consideration and purchase intention, may gain relevance to the detriment of brand preference as decision-making increasingly occurs in digital environments. Because, in these environments, brands may be added shortly before the purchase based on consumer reviews, retail media ads or price comparison sites (De Haan et al., 2016; Qin et al., 2024). Supporting this, Pauwels and van Ewijk (2013, 2020) report a lower sales elasticity for preference than for consideration or awareness, and attribute it to the low cost of online search.

Product-Market Level BPIs

Product-market level indicators of brand performance encountered in the literature can be classified under seven categories. The first two are direct measures of brand performance: *brand sales*, either volume (i.e., unit sales) or value sales (i.e., sales revenue) and *market share*. These indicators are readily available from company records or can be obtained from data aggregators. Though relevant for brand performance management purposes, they can be considered noisy measures of a brand's health; sales and market share exhibit substantial variability over time due to own and competing marketing actions (e.g., short-term oriented marketing actions, such as promotions, and long-term oriented marketing actions, such as new product/service introductions) as well as external factors (e.g., macroeconomic factors, such as business cycles; environmental factors, such as weather conditions; and geographical factors, such as local unemployment rates). Accordingly, a group of product-market level measures have been proposed to extract brand health indicators from these data. One encounters four such indicators in the literature.

In evaluating brand health at the product-market level, two interrelated indicators seek to capture the additional market success attributable to a brand's inherent value: the *market share premium* and the *quantity premium*. Both reflect the brand's ability to enhance sales performance beyond what can be explained by product attributes and marketing efforts. Specifically, *market share premium* is the incremental market share a brand achieves over competitors due to its brand name and reputation (e.g., Datta et al., 2017).[2] It captures the brand's ability to dominate the market by influencing consumer choices, leading to superior sales performance compared to private labels, generic alternatives or hypothetical unbranded equivalents. *Quantity premium* is the long-term, consistent sales volume a brand achieves due to its inherent value, independent of short-term marketing fluctuations (e.g., Ataman et al., 2008). It represents the baseline sales level attributed solely to the brand's strength and reputation.

While both indicators account for the residual value the brand adds to market performance after controlling for other factors, reflecting the intrinsic value of the brand, they differ primarily in terms of their focus. Whereas market share premium focuses on the brand's ability to capture a larger share of the market relative to competitors, highlighting competitive advantage and dominance, quantity premium concentrates on the consistent sales volume attributable to the brand's inherent value, emphasizing long-term sales stability. In terms of measurement or operationalization, they share more similarities than differences. Both rely on actual sales data, whether in units sold or market share percentages, to assess the brand's performance and both employ a residual approach, where the unexplained variance in sales or market share after accounting for known factors is attributed to the brand's influence. To isolate the brand's effect on performance, both use advanced econometric models (e.g., dynamic sales-response models, choice or market share attraction models) that control for product attributes, price, promotions, and other marketing mix variables (e.g., Rajavi et al., 2023; Sriram et al., 2007; Sriram & Kalwani, 2007). Alternatively, both can be measured using straightforward, non-model-based approaches that rely on comparing focal brand's performance to that of a generic alternative (e.g., Ailawadi et al., 2003).

Another one of these brand health indicators is *price premium*. It captures a brand's pricing power – a brand's ability to command higher prices than competitors and maintain sales volumes despite price increases. This power stems from the perceived value, reputation and consumer perceptions associated with the brand and reflects the strategic advantage a brand holds in its ability to leverage pricing for profitability without eroding its customer base. A brand with strong pricing power is characterized by its flexibility to charge a high enough price that signifies the substantial added value in the brand compared to alternatives, as perceived by the consumers, and to increase its prices while minimizing loss of sales.

Accordingly, the measurement of a brand's pricing power proceeds along two routes. First, the additional amount consumers are willing to pay for a product because of its brand name, over and above the price of generic or lower-priced alternatives, can be determined by calculating the price difference between branded products and private label or unbranded goods (e.g., Ailawadi et al., 2003). Another method involves measuring the ratio of the brand's price to that of its (leading) competitor, reflecting its relative price positioning in the market (e.g., Chaudhuri & Holbrook, 2001). Consumer surveys or experimental studies can also assess price premium by asking participants to indicate the maximum price they are willing to pay for the brand compared to alternatives, thereby gauging their willingness to pay extra due to brand perception (e.g., DelVecchio & Smith, 2005; Fernández-Barcala & González-Díaz, 2006). Additionally, hedonic pricing models can estimate the added value attributed to the brand name by analyzing how brand attributes contribute to product prices (e.g., Goldfarb et al., 2009). Second, unveiling the brand's capacity to adjust prices without significantly affecting consumer demand or sales volume involves deriving price elasticity parameters (i.e., regular, non-promotional price elasticity) from sales data using econometric models (e.g., Ataman et al., 2010; Datta et al., 2017). A lower price elasticity magnitude suggests stronger pricing power, as consumers are less responsive to price increases. Data from discrete choice experiments can also model how price adjustments impact consumer choice and demand, providing insights into the brand's capacity to adjust prices without significantly affecting sales.

The last of these brand health indicators is *revenue premium*, which is the additional revenue generated by a branded product over and above the revenue of a comparable unbranded or private label product (Ailawadi et al., 2003). This measure captures the incremental sales value that is directly attributable to the brand name, reflecting the brand's ability to command higher revenue through favorable consumer-market level outcomes. Revenue premium can be considered a financial measure of brand equity, though at the product-market level, as it quantifies the monetary advantage the brand name provides. While the methods for calculating revenue premium are varied, they fundamentally share a common approach centered on comparing the revenue generated by branded products to that of comparable unbranded or private label alternatives. The measure is obtained either through direct comparison of sales revenues, as in measuring the revenue premium by subtracting unbranded revenues

[2] While Datta et al. (2017) refer to this indicator as sales-based brand equity, we refer to it as market share premium because their brand health indicator is the time-varying brand-specific intercepts in a multinomial logit attraction model for market share, an aggregate analog of the individual brand choice model (Cooper & Nakanishi, 1988). Choice share premium can also be included in this category.

from branded revenues (Ailawadi et al., 2003), or isolating the incremental revenue attributable to the brand name by controlling for the influence of marketing activities and other potential drivers on sales revenues (e.g., Slotegraaf & Pauwels, 2008).

The final category of product-market level BPIs consists of measures designed to quantify overall *brand equity* (i.e., sales-based brand equity). These methods share a common foundation, defining brand equity as the incremental benefit – expressed in terms of revenue or profit – generated by a brand's unique attributes compared to unbranded equivalents. Despite this shared premise, these methods differ significantly in their scope, methodology and the level of detail they provide, reflecting varied priorities.

One can classify the product-market level brand equity measures into three groups based on their conceptual focus and methodological features. One group of measures focuses on outcome-oriented, static approaches that emphasize practical and accessible metrics of brand equity. These methods, such as Dubin's (1998), derive brand equity from straightforward comparisons with private-label or unbranded equivalents, highlighting outcomes like incremental profit. Their simplicity and reliance on readily available market data make them particularly appealing to managers. However, these methods are static in nature: they fail to account for the dynamic evolution of brand equity or incorporate strategic factors, such as competitive actions. As a result, they offer limited diagnostic capabilities for understanding how brand equity changes over time or interacts with broader market forces.

In contrast, dynamic and strategic models emphasize the evolving and strategic aspects of brand equity. These approaches highlight how brand equity interacts with market dynamics, such as entry deterrence, competition and advertising investments. For instance, Bar and Haviv (2023) explore how a strong brand can deter market entry, highlighting the strategic value of branding in influencing competitors' actions. Similarly, Borkovsky et al. (2017) examine the interplay between advertising, competition and the depreciation of brand equity, offering forward-looking insights into brand value. Goldfarb et al. (2009) integrate demand-side and supply-side dynamics within an equilibrium framework, capturing how brand equity influences firm and retailer decisions. While these models provide richer and more comprehensive insights, they require complex structural modeling and detailed data, making them less accessible to practitioners without technical expertise.

A third group of methods takes an individual-level, perceptual approach, linking consumer perceptions with financial outcomes. For example, Srinivasan et al. (2005) and Ferjani et al. (2009) derive dollar-metric values for brand equity using primary data, such as surveys or conjoint analysis. These approaches also capture the psychological and behavioral mechanisms underlying brand equity, providing valuable insights into consumer–brand relationships. However, their reliance on resource-intensive data collection methods may make them less practical for large-scale analyses.

In conclusion, discussions of product-market level brand performance have long centered on sales and market share, as these indicators provide direct insights into a brand's market success. The emphasis on brand sales indicates an unwavering focus on tangible outcomes in brand performance assessments (show us the money!), reflecting the industry's increasing demand for measurable results to justify branding efforts. Market share, on the other hand, remains an essential benchmark for understanding a brand's competitive standing, offering insights into penetration and positioning within a given market. The relevance of different product-market indicators is also shaped by broader industry and methodological trends. As competition becomes more complex, particularly in digital and omnichannel environments, the need for absolute performance measures that capture direct financial contributions, rather than comparative metrics, grows. This is consistent with shifts in modeling approaches that favor continuous variables over relative measures (Dekimpe & Hanssens, 1999; Reimer et al., 2014).

Beyond these foundational measures, product-market level brand health indicators offer additional perspectives on brand strength. While share premium highlights a brand's competitive advantage relative to others, quantity premium reflects its ability to drive volume and price premium speaks to its pricing power. The relative emphasis on these indicators has likely shifted over time as firms adapt to changing competitive landscapes and evolving measurement approaches. Notably, price premium remains a critical yet evolving construct, given branding's well-documented role in influencing consumer price sensitivity (Ataman et al., 2024).

Financial-Market Level BPIs

Financial-market level BPIs span six categories, overlapping significantly with the metrics for assessing investor response listed in Srinivasan and Hanssens (2009).

Cash flow, the first financial-market level BPI, captures the net amount of cash flowing into and out of a firm's operations and reflects the balance between revenues from sales and costs associated with producing and marketing the firm's offerings. It is typically measured using direct financial metrics from statements (i.e., Net Cash Flow from Operations, item 308 in Compustat) or proxies such as EBITDA. Importantly, it is the volatility of cash flows that is more informative for the financial community (e.g., Fischer et al., 2016). Therefore, this indicator is operationalized using dispersion metrics (e.g., coefficient of variation, variance or range) and used after standardizing across firms.

A second category comprises *return-based accounting performance* indicators. These are accounting-derived measures of profitability that quantify how efficiently a firm's assets (e.g., Mizik, 2014; Mizik & Jacobson, 2008; Nguyen & Feng, 2021) or shareholders' equity (e.g., Aaker & Jacobson, 2001; Nguyen & Feng, 2021) are converted into earnings. The most common measures are return-on-assets (ROA) and return-on-equity (ROE). By comparing operating or net income metrics to the firm's resource base, these indicators reflect both the immediate financial health of the organization and the strategic influence of intangible factors such as brand equity.[3]

The third category focuses on *stock returns*, premised on the idea that brands are key intangible drivers of firm value. Stock returns represent the way investors, through trading decisions and resulting price adjustments, incorporate brand-related information into the firm's market valuation. This indicator reflects how effectively a brand's intangible assets are converted into future cash flow expectations, long-term profitability and competitive advantage. In this sense, stock returns are a forward-looking, market-based measure that links brand strategies and consumer perceptions directly to financial outcomes.

Stock returns, calculated from price changes and dividends, are often adjusted for market effects to isolate firm-specific events or strategies. Specifically, abnormal stock returns are obtained by subtracting the expected return, derived from models like the market model (e.g., Dutordoir et al., 2015) or multifactor market models (e.g., Madden et al., 2006), from the actual stock return. Event studies are a common application of abnormal returns. They are used to assess stock price reactions to particular events, such as product launches or brand-related announcements. They rely on well-defined windows to capture short-term or long-term effects. Key metrics include Cumulative Abnormal Returns, which sum abnormal returns over an event window to measure total impact (e.g., Gielens et al., 2018) and Buy-and-Hold Abnormal Returns, which account for compounded returns over longer periods to evaluate sustained effects (e.g., Ertekin et al., 2018).

Stock returns not only reflect the financial market's valuation of a firm's performance but also capture the compensation investors demand for bearing both market-wide and firm-specific uncertainties. Accordingly, a fourth group of BPIs assess *risk*, which captures the uncertainty and variability in a firm's financial performance, expected cash flows and market valuation. Risk is often reflected in the volatility of the firm's share prices (e.g., Johansson et al., 2012; Rego et al., 2009). This indicator distinguishes between systematic (market-wide) and unsystematic (firm-specific) risk. Systematic risk, measured by market beta, highlights the firm's exposure to economy-wide shocks, industry cycles or market sentiment (e.g., Ha et al., 2021; Madden et al., 2006; Rego et al., 2009). Unsystematic (idiosyncratic) risk, in contrast, reflects vulnerabilities unique to the firm, such as the strength or weakness of its brand, the stability of its customer base, product quality issues, reputational setbacks or the success of its marketing and innovation efforts (e.g., Colicev et al., 2018; Luo et al., 2013). By considering both market-level and firm-level influences, risk serves as a forward-looking and strategic indicator, enabling investors, managers and other stakeholders to assess how well the firm can withstand external disturbances, maintain stable cash flows and protect shareholder value over time.

The fifth category measures *firm value*, which reflects the financial market's assessment of a firm's worth. This measure integrates tangible and intangible assets to capture a firm's potential for future cash flow generation. Metrics such as market capitalization (e.g., Nguyen & Feng, 2021) and Tobin's q (e.g., Angulo-Ruiz et al., 2014; Cao, 2022; McAlister et al., 2016) are commonly used.[4] By signaling how investors value intangible resources and growth opportunities, firm value serves as a forward-looking indicator of financial health and strategic market position.

The final category contains measures of *brand equity*, often quantified using off-the-shelf financial brand value estimates from sources like Interbrand or BrandZ. These commercial tools assess brand performance by integrating financial and brand-related factors and are discussed in the

[3] ROA is calculated as the firm's profitability (i.e., operating income or net income) divided by its total assets. It indicates how efficiently a firm uses its assets to generate earnings. ROE, on the other hand is calculated as the firm's profitability (i.e., net income) divided by shareholder's equity (i.e., the book value of equity). It indicates how effectively the firm generates earnings from invested capital.

[4] We caution readers about using Tobin's q as a measure of firm value. Bendle and Butt (2018) highlight the limitations of accounting-based approximations of Tobin's q and explain how these can result in a biased representation of firm value. For a concise discussion of these concerns and potential remedies, see Edeling et al. (2021).

section focusing on commercial products for measuring brand performance.

In sum, financial-market indicators have become increasingly central to brand performance assessment, reflecting the field's emphasis on capturing the financial impact of marketing investments and demonstrating the value brands create for financial stakeholders, particularly shareholders. While early assessments primarily focused on stock returns and return-based accounting measures, discussions have expanded to include brand value, firm value and risk, which offer broader perspectives on intangible assets and corporate worth. The growing attention to firm value, likely encouraged by the works of Srinivasan and coauthors (Edeling et al., 2021; Pauwels et al., 2004; Srinivasan & Hanssens, 2009), suggests that researchers and practitioners recognize their relevance in understanding long-term financial contributions, beyond immediate market fluctuations. Meanwhile, discussions around risk remain important in an increasingly complex business environment, where financial stability and strategic foresight are central concerns for firms (Malshe et al., 2023).

Emerging BPIs at the Resource-Market Level

The field has shown an interest in exploring alternative dimensions of brand performance through a set of novel measures that do not fit neatly in the former indicator categories yet share a common thread: the firm's resource ecosystem. These emerging BPIs, referred to as resource-market level indicators of brand performance, can be grouped under four categories.

Some of the indicators align with *relational resources*, which represent the strength and utility of the firm's partnerships and networks. For instance, one indicator captures the degree to which dealers advocate for a firm's products and services (Ramaswami & Arunachalam, 2016), while another one captures the trust and credibility the firm has built within its trading network (Davis & Mentzer, 2008). Similarly, a different indicator, the energy expended by channel intermediaries in promoting a brand, highlights the importance of cultivating strong relationships with external partners who play a key role in the brand's performance (Hughes & Ahearne, 2010).

Other indicators map onto *reputational resources*, such as innovation credit in Barone and Jewell (2013), which represents the intangible goodwill a brand earns through consumer perceptions of its innovativeness. This resource allows brands to deviate from category norms without penalty, underscoring the strategic importance of reputation in fostering flexibility and resilience in market performance.

The brand's influence on internal stakeholders is captured through *human resources* indicators. Employee-based brand equity exemplifies how brands affect employee attitudes, behaviors, satisfaction and retention (Baker et al., 2014; Tavassoli et al., 2014). A strong brand not only reduces costs, such as executive compensation, but also enhances organizational effectiveness by fostering a positive work environment and aligning employees with the firm's and brand's mission.

Lastly, several indicators pertain to *financial resources*, which represent the brand's role in securing and managing financial capital. Measures such as financial resources, credit spread, financial leverage and credit rating highlight the firm's financial health and its ability to attract and efficiently use internal and external capital (Fischer & Himme, 2017; Rego et al., 2009). These indicators reflect the brand's indirect impact on the firm's cost of capital, creditworthiness and ability to sustain long-term marketing investments.

In sum, resource-market level BPIs offer a more complete view of brand performance, highlighting the ripple effects of branding strategies on internal and external resource flows. They provide a structured framework for understanding how brands create value beyond consumer and product markets. These emerging indicators also lay the groundwork for an updated conceptualization of the brand value chain, which we discuss in the following section.

THE UPDATED BRAND VALUE CHAIN

The brand value chain, as articulated by Keller and Lehmann (2003), conceptualizes brand value as a series of interconnected outcomes that flow from marketing investments. Traditionally, these outcomes are organized into three core levels: consumer-market outcomes, product-market outcomes and financial-market outcomes. While this framework has served as the foundational guide for measuring brand performance, and for organizing the BPIs reviewed in this chapter, our review highlights the need for an update to fully capture brands' area of influence.

Specifically, we introduce resource-market outcomes as a fourth category within the brand value chain (see Figure 26.1). These outcomes reflect the brand's ability to influence relational, reputational, human and financial resources, which are essential for sustaining competitive advantage and driving performance across all levels. Resource-market outcomes may appear peripheral, yet they underpin the entire value creation process by providing the foundational assets and capabilities upon which branding success depends.

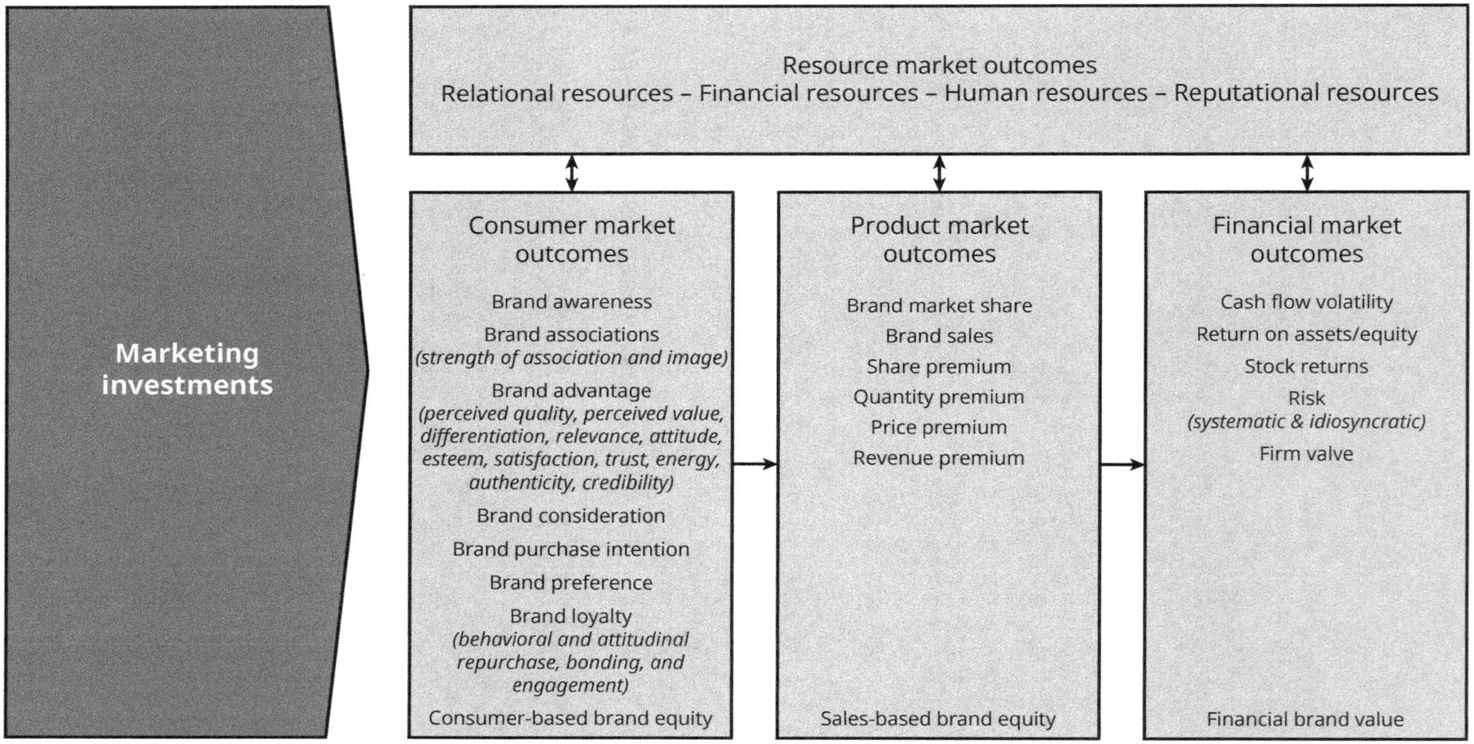

Figure 26.1 The revised brand value chain and brand performance indicators

Source: The authors.

The updated brand value chain recognizes the cascading effects among its four levels. Marketing investments initially manifest in consumer-market outcomes, shaping how consumers perceive, feel about and engage with the brand. These consumer-level responses drive product-market outcomes, including market share, sales volume and price premiums. Product-market success, in turn, informs financial-market outcomes, such as stock returns, firm value and risk assessments. At the base of this process, resource-market outcomes enable and sustain these effects by enhancing relational networks, financial resilience, employee engagement and brand reputation.

For example, strong relational resources may amplify product-market outcomes by improving distribution efficiency and brand availability. Similarly, robust financial resources may provide firms with the capital needed to maintain marketing investments that fuel consumer engagement and product-market success. Human resources may contribute to internal alignment and organizational effectiveness, while reputational resources may enhance the brand's adaptability and market resilience.

The inclusion of resource-market outcomes enhances the integrative nature of the brand value chain, providing a more holistic view of brand performance. This updated framework serves as the foundation for a robust brand performance measurement system as discussed subsequently.

DESIGNING A BRAND PERFORMANCE TRACKING SYSTEM BASED ON THE BRAND VALUE CHAIN

The updated brand value chain, with its expanded inclusion of resource-market outcomes, provides a comprehensive conceptual foundation for tracking brand performance. By systematically monitoring performance across the four levels – consumer-market, product-market, financial-market and resource-market outcomes – firms can gain actionable insights that inform strategic and tactical decision-making. However, for this effort to deliver practical value, it must be operationalized into a holistic brand performance tracking system that aligns with the specific needs of diverse stakeholders.

Accordingly, the first step is to identify which indicators to prioritize based on the firm's strategic objectives and the stakeholders it seeks to address. For example, consumer-market indicators such as brand awareness, brand associations and loyalty are critical for brand managers and marketing strategists tasked with shaping consumer perceptions and driving engagement. These measures serve as early warning signals for shifts in brand health and can inform decisions on messaging, positioning and resource allocation.

At the product-market level, indicators like market share, price premiums and revenue premiums provide direct feedback on a brand's market performance. This layer is particularly relevant for executive leadership, product development teams and retailers seeking to assess the competitive effectiveness of branding efforts in driving tangible market outcomes. For instance, tracking sales-based brand equity can help firms understand the link between consumer perceptions and market success.

Moving to the financial-market level, indicators such as stock returns, firm value and systematic risk provide critical insights for investors, financial analysts and executive leadership. These measures reflect the financial community's evaluation of branding efforts and their ability to deliver long-term value. By incorporating financial-market outcomes, firms can align brand strategies with shareholder interests and track their financial impact over time.

The addition of resource-market indicators fills a gap in traditional tracking systems. These indicators capture the brand's role in building and leveraging key resources such as relational, financial, human and reputational capital. Resource-market indicators are particularly relevant for internal stakeholders such as finance teams, human resource professionals and executive leadership, as well as external stakeholders like distributors and suppliers. For instance, tracking credit ratings or financial leverage allows firms to gauge their financial stability and capacity for sustained investments in brand-building activities.

Ultimately, the design of a brand performance tracking system can and should be tailored to the needs of the stakeholder being prioritized. Table 26.2 provides a stakeholder-centric perspective, highlighting which categories of indicators are most relevant for different groups. For example, while brand managers may require a balanced view of all four levels to guide brand strategy, investors are more likely to focus on financial-market outcomes and resource-market indicators that signal stability and growth potential. By prioritizing indicators based on stakeholder needs, firms can create a targeted tracking system that maximizes its relevance and utility. Such a tracking system is often visualized as an interactive dashboard, which is an important service to all stakeholders, from employees to external partners such as ad agencies (Pauwels et al., 2009).

In sum, the updated brand value chain, when operationalized into a performance tracking

Table 26.2 Stakeholder relevance matrix for brand performance indicator categories

Stakeholder	*Consumer-Market Indicators*	*Product-Market Indicators*	*Financial-Market Indicators*	*Resource-Market Indicators*
Brand Managers	Critical for understanding consumer behavior, essential for brand strategies	Critical for assessing market penetration and sales outcomes	Guide tracking financial outcomes but less central to daily brand decisions	Critical for leveraging relational and human resources
Marketing Strategists	Critical for designing campaigns and aligning brand messaging with consumer needs	Critical for evaluating product-market dynamics and competitive performance	Provides insights into financial viability and strategic alignment	Critical for integrating resource-based strategies
Executive Leadership	Provides insights into brand health and consumer sentiment	Critical for evaluating strategic market performance	Critical for assessing the firm's financial success and sustainability	Guides decisions about resource allocation and long-term investments
Finance Teams	Provides context for financial projections by linking consumer mindset to performance	Helps linking product-market performance with financial metrics	Critical for financial planning and assessing the impact of brand equity on profitability	Critical for supporting creditworthiness and resource management
Human Resource Teams				Critical for fostering employee-based brand equity
Product Development Teams	Helps aligning product features with consumer expectations	Critical for tracking product success and market acceptance		Helps to ensure resources support innovation and product quality
Sales Teams	Guides messaging and sales strategies for consumers	Critical for evaluating sales performance and setting targets		Critical for understanding distributor relationships and efforts
Retailers and Distributors	Critical for insights into consumer preferences and shopping behavior	Critical for determining product placement and pricing	Helps to assess financial stability and partnerships	Helps in fostering trust and collaboration in the supply chain
Suppliers	Provides an understanding of end-consumer demand trends	Helps in anticipating supply requirements and production planning	Helps to assess the financial stability of partner brands	Helps in supporting long-term supplier relationships and resource coordination
Investors/ Financial Analysts	Provides high-level insights into consumer engagement and brand equity	Useful for evaluating product-market success as part of investment analyses	Critical for understanding financial returns and risks associated with branding	For assessing a firm's creditworthiness and long-term resource sustainability
Advertising Agencies	Critical for crafting effective campaigns, ensuring alignment with branding strategies	Useful for aligning messaging with brand performance and competitive positioning		

Source: The authors.

system, offers a holistic and stakeholder-driven approach to measuring brand performance. By integrating indicators across consumer-market, product-market, financial-market and resource-market outcomes, firms can better understand, manage and leverage their brand assets to create sustainable value.

TOOLS OF THE TRADE: AN OVERVIEW OF BRAND PERFORMANCE MEASUREMENT PRODUCTS

Having established the conceptual foundations for measuring brand performance and provided a comprehensive list of BPIs encountered in the literature, we turn to the commercial methodologies most commonly employed. These methodologies, which we will refer to as 'brand valuation tools', provide structured approaches to assessing the value that brands contribute to businesses from the perspectives of different stakeholders.

In carrying out brand valuation, it is important to realize the purpose of the valuation. Within the industry, there are three primary purposes: (1) valuations for brand management purposes, (2) valuations for accounting purposes and (3) valuations for transactional purposes. Technical valuations (used for accounting and transactional purposes) and brand management valuations serve different objectives and, consequently, follow distinct methodologies.

Valuations for brand management purposes are critical for marketing strategy, marketing budget allocation, brand architecture and brand portfolio management decisions and for management scorecards. These valuations rely on dynamic business models that evaluate the role of the brand in influencing the model's key variables (Salinas, 2009). In contrast, valuations for *accounting or transactional purposes* are typically undertaken for balance sheet reporting, tax planning, litigation support, securitization, mergers and acquisitions and investor relations. These valuations emphasize determining a brand's value at a specific point in time.[5]

The following sections detail the brand valuation methods used by the five providers most frequently cited in the marketing literature. These particular brand valuation methods are used primarily for brand management purposes.

Young & Rubicam's Brand Asset Valuator

Young & Rubicam, an advertising agency, introduced the BrandAsset Valuator (BAV) model in the early 1990s to assess and measure brand equity. Originally, the model evaluated brands based on four key pillars – Knowledge, Differentiation, Relevance and Esteem – all of which represent consumer-market level indicators of brand performance. In 2005, a fifth pillar, Energy, was added to capture a brand's momentum and vitality (Fudge, 2005; Gerzema et al., 2005). The BAV model provides insights into a brand's health and trajectory through analysis of the relationships among these pillars. Of the four foundational pillars, Differentiation and Relevance combine to form Brand Strength, which reflects the brand's future growth potential. Esteem and Knowledge combine to form Brand Stature, which indicates the brand's current status and performance.

Research in marketing has leveraged BAV data to study links within consumer-market level BPIs (e.g., Luffarelli et al., 2023) and across consumer-market-level and product-market-level indicators, such as brand health indicators (e.g., Datta et al., 2017); consumer-market indicators and financial performance metrics, such as stock returns, systematic risk and firm valuation (e.g., Ha et al., 2021; Mizik, 2014; Mizik & Jacobson, 2008); and consumer-market indicators and resource-market outcomes (e.g., Tavassoli et al., 2014). Furthermore, BAV data are often paired with product or logo design properties to examine their combined effects on downstream-market outcomes (e.g., Affonso & Janiszewski, 2023; Heitmann et al., 2020; Luffarelli et al., 2019).

[5] Brand value can be calculated following one of three basic approaches. First, the cost approach determines brand value by taking into account the cost of devoting the brand (brand acquisition, creation or maintenance) during any and all phases of its development (testing, product concept R&D, product improvements, promotions). While calculating the brand value using the cost approach is straightforward, it does not capture the value added by the brand's competitive position or brand strength. Thus, it is used more commonly for valuing easily replaceable assets. Second, the market approach determines brand value by considering recent transactions such as sales, acquisitions, licenses that have involved similar brands for which data is available. The market approach is straightforward to calculate, provided the availability of data and it is more appropriate for valuing assets that are not unique. Third, the income approach necessitates the calculation of future income, profits or cash flow attributable to the brand over its expected remaining useful life and discounting them to present value. This method, though considered more subjective, is more suited for tracking brand value.

Harris Interactive's EquiTrend

Harris Interactive's EquiTrend is a comprehensive annual tracking study designed to measure and compare brand equity across a wide array of brands and categories. The Brand Equity Index is the cornerstone of the EquiTrend study, providing an understanding of a brand's overall strength. The index is a weighted composite score of three primary factors spanning several consumer-market level BPIs: Familiarity (i.e., whether consumers have prior exposure to the brand and if it is memorable), Perceived Quality (i.e., the brand's ability to meet or exceed consumer expectations) and Purchase Consideration (i.e., the likelihood that a consumer would purchase or recommend the brand in the future). While the specific weights assigned to each component are proprietary, they reflect the relative importance of each component in influencing consumer behavior and brand strength (Harris Interactive, n.d.). Harris Interactive supplements the Brand Equity Index with a broader set of metrics that provide deeper insights into consumer–brand relationships, such as Consumer Connection, which assesses the depth of emotional and aspirational resonance between consumers and the brand, and Brand Momentum, which tracks the brand's growth trajectory and its ability to adapt to changing consumer preferences and market trends.

EquiTrend data have been most frequently used to illustrate how strong brands mitigate financial and operational risks, serving as a bridge between marketing metrics and financial decision-making. Specifically, research has used EquiTrend data to explore the relationships across consumer-market-level and financial-market-level indicators, including stock performance, firm risk and financial leverage (e.g., Fischer & Himme, 2017; Johansson et al., 2012; Rego et al., 2009) and consumer-market indicators and operational performance metrics, such as warranty claims and costs (e.g., Cao, 2022).

YouGov's BrandIndex

An emerging commercial source is the YouGov BrandIndex: a versatile brand performance tracking tool used primarily for brand management purposes. YouGov tracks, daily, 16 key brand health metrics to provide a comprehensive view of a brand's overall performance. These metrics cover various stages of the consumer purchase funnel and are grouped into three main categories. Media and communication metrics examine public discourse about the brand, including measures such as advertising awareness, aided brand awareness, brand attention (i.e., the level of media focus on the brand), brand buzz (i.e., the volume and sentiment of brand-related conversations) and word-of-mouth exposure (i.e., the frequency of brand mentions in personal conversations). Purchase funnel metrics assess consumer engagement with the brand, including purchase intent, consideration, current customer and former customer metrics. Finally, brand perception metrics capture how consumers perceive and feel about the brand, incorporating measures such as general impression (i.e., consumer attitudes), customer satisfaction, quality, value, corporate reputation and recommendation. These metrics are also averaged to generate an overall brand health index, summarizing the brand's current status and perception in the market.

The literature primarily leverages YouGov's BrandIndex metrics to explore the relationship between consumer mindset indicators and firm-level financial outcomes, such as stock returns and idiosyncratic risk (e.g., Colicev et al., 2018; Luo et al., 2013). These metrics are also utilized to examine how brand equity serves as a moderator in strategic decision-making, influencing the effectiveness of managerial actions such as remedy choices in crisis scenarios (e.g., Mafael et al., 2022).

Interbrand

Interbrand's methodology focuses on the financial value a brand contributes to a business, positioning it primarily within the category of financial-market level indicators. However, the methodology also integrates a brand's consumer-market level success into its financial value calculations by accounting for the brand's role in consumer purchase decisions and overall strength. The process begins by determining the brand's direct financial contribution to the business, isolating the brand's financial impact from other operational aspects of the business. This financial contribution is then multiplied by the 'role of brand' index (RBI), which measures the portion of the purchase decision attributable to the brand, rather than other factors such as price or product features. The RBI quantifies the brand's influence on consumer choice as a percentage, capturing how important the brand is in driving consumer demand. Finally, Interbrand calculates the brand's financial value by discounting its potential future earnings to present value. This discounting accounts for a brand-specific risk rate, which is derived from the brand's strength score. The strength score evaluates the brand's ability to foster customer loyalty and sustain future demand, and it is assessed across ten internal and external dimensions (Interbrand, 2022).

Research leverages Interbrand's brand value estimates primarily to explore the relationship between brand equity and financial performance, emphasizing how strong brands contribute to shareholder value, reduce financial risk and enhance firm-level metrics such as stock returns and cost of capital (e.g., Dutordoir et al., 2015; Himme & Fischer, 2014; Johansson et al., 2012; Madden et al., 2006; Peterson & Jeong, 2010). Interbrand data are also utilized when studying the role of brand value in augmenting marketing effectiveness (e.g., Mazodier & Rezaee, 2013; Wiles & Danielova, 2009) and as an outcome variable when investigating the impact of broader strategic elements on brand equity (e.g., Pogacar et al., 2021; Torres et al., 2012).

Kantar BrandZ

Kantar's BrandZ brand valuation methodology consists of three steps similar to that of Interbrand's. The brand's financial value is multiplied with the brand contribution to result in the brand value. The process starts with the earnings associated with intangible assets of the company and the earnings linked exclusively to the brand. Next, akin to the way financial stock value is calculated, Kantar uses the 'brand multiple' to determine the future potential earnings of the brand, resulting in the branded business' financial value. This financial value is further multiplied with the 'brand contribution', which evaluates customer-based brand equity across three key dimensions: Meaningfulness, Difference and Salience. This final multiplication of the branded business' financial value with brand contribution brings about the brand value (Kantar, 2025). Kantar's BrandZ brand value estimates are only occasionally used in the literature (e.g., Affonso & Janiszewski, 2023).

BRAND PERFORMANCE MEASUREMENT WITH NEW DATA, METHODS AND TECHNOLOGIES

The proliferation of digital technologies and advanced analytical methods has introduced novel data sources for measuring brand performance, especially at the consumer-market level. These emerging sources leverage consumers' digital behavioral traces, structure of their social networks, textual and visual content they generate and even GenAI. Such data offer potential advantages, including richer insights, real-time accessibility and cost efficiencies. They either complement traditional consumer-market-level BPIs (i.e., by providing additional perspectives on consumer perceptions and behaviors), or in some cases, replace traditional methods (i.e., by achieving similar outcomes more efficiently). However, these innovations are not without limitations.

One type of new data is digital metrics: consumers' online traces. These include behavioral signals such as website visits, search engine activity and social media interactions. For example, search terms and page visits serve as proxies for consumer interest and purchase intent, providing firms with timely indicators of brand performance (e.g., Pauwels & van Ewijk, 2020). Compared to traditional surveys, these data excel at capturing short-term trends and behaviors, especially in high-involvement product categories. However, they remain susceptible to noise, particularly when consumer engagement is low, and they may not reflect deeper, enduring attitudes toward a brand.

Another source of new data is text-based user-generated content, such as online forum entries, user reviews and social tags. Analysis of these unstructured textual data primarily provides insights into brand perceptions and competitive positioning. For instance, Netzer et al. (2012) use text mining to map market structures by extracting associations between brands from online discussions. Social tags, as explored by Nam et al. (2017) and Nam and Kannan (2014), offer an alternative means to identify brand associations and track trends. Related, Culotta and Cutler (2016) propose quantifying brand associations by analyzing social network data. By bypassing user-generated posts and focusing instead on social connections, their approach also captures the perceptions of silent audiences who influence brand meaning but do not actively post content. The scalability and cost-effectiveness of these methods are their clear advantages. Yet, user-generated content introduces challenges such as selection biases, unstructured noise and ambiguities in interpreting meaning.

Visual and neuroimaging data represent another promising source. Analysis of consumer-generated images shared voluntarily on social media platforms (e.g., Liu et al., 2020) or brand collages solicited on visual elicitation platforms (e.g., Dzyabura & Peres, 2021) allow researchers to uncover unaided associations and emotional cues embedded in visual content. At a more granular level, neuroimaging techniques such as fMRI capture brain activity to quantify brand imagery (Chan et al., 2018). These approaches are particularly suited to uncovering implicit, nonverbal and multisensory brand perceptions. However, their reliance on sophisticated tools, significant costs and limited scalability may restrict their broader application in brand performance tracking.

GenAI introduces yet another layer of innovation. A burgeoning literature stream explores whether and to what extent large language models (LLMs) can simulate human behavior, raising the possibility of obtaining consumer-market-level BPIs without direct input from consumers. LLMs' ability to simulate consumer behavior and generate insights makes them particularly effective for exploratory and qualitative tasks, such as creating synthetic respondents and moderating discussions (Arora et al., 2025). LLMs also have been shown to replicate aggregate consumer preferences and construct perceptual maps that align with human data, making them cost-effective and scalable for tracking general trends (Brand et al., 2023; Li et al., 2024). However, this early evidence may not be sufficient to justify using data from synthetic respondents as a suitable substitute for human data when measuring brands' consumer-market level performance.

Despite their potential, LLMs' capabilities are bounded by significant challenges. Their dependence on the quality and scope of training data often leads to inaccurate or biased outputs, such as the over-representation of prominent brands and the failure to incorporate recent or domain-specific information, necessitating human validation (Arora et al., 2025; Li et al., 2024). Moreover, LLMs struggle to reflect demographic variability. They generate responses with reduced heterogeneity and fail to capture nuanced behaviors across consumer segments (Brand et al., 2023). These challenges are compounded by their inability to fully understand real-time cultural and contextual nuances, as they lack the psychological and emotional depth of real-world decision-making processes (Arora et al., 2025; Goli & Singh, 2024). Their inconsistent behavior across product categories, languages and model versions raises further concerns about their reliability in replicating human-like responses (Brand et al., 2023; Goli & Singh, 2024). All of these may limit their utility for producing dynamic metrics measuring consumer-market-level performance of brands.

Consumers' mindsets about brands rely on situational, emotional and experiential factors that off-the-shelf LLMs cannot contextualize due to their dependence on the training data. Moreover, these off-the-shelf LLMs do not reflect emerging patterns or contain up-to-date information. Metrics like purchase intention or brand consideration are shaped by real-time inputs, while constructs like brand loyalty require longitudinal tracking, which synthetic respondents are incapable of replicating. While fine-tuning and prompt engineering have been shown to improve the output of LLMs (Brand et al., 2023; Gui & Toubia, 2023; Li et al., 2024), these processes are resource-intensive, requiring substantial pre-existing data and careful validation. Whether these interventions can overcome the inherent limitations of LLMs for achieving consistent and accurate consumer mindset metrics remains an open question. Ongoing advancements in artificial intelligence (AI) training techniques and real-time data integration may address some of these gaps, opening avenues for more reliable applications in brand performance measurement.

MEASURING BRAND PERFORMANCE ACROSS BORDERS: ISSUES AND INSIGHTS

A substantial body of work almost exclusively focuses on single-country contexts, often overlooking the complexities associated with measuring the performance of globally operating brands. This gap highlights the need to rethink branding strategies and brand valuation approaches in international contexts (Roth, 1995). Despite its significance, research on brand performance measurement in a global context remains limited. In particular, key questions about how brand equity operates in international markets and how it can be effectively measured and managed across diverse cultural and economic environments remain largely unanswered (Broyles et al., 2010; Chatzipanagiotou et al., 2019; Pappu et al., 2006; Vukasović, 2016; Whitelock & Fastoso, 2007). Given the critical importance of this challenge, particularly for customer-based brand equity as a consumer-market-level indicator of brand success, our discussion focuses primarily on this dimension.

Global brand managers face significant gaps in actionable guidance on four critical issues concerning brand performance measurement in an international context. First, managers need to ensure that their measures of brand equity provide meaningful comparisons across markets. Without consistent measurement tools, evaluating brand equity across countries becomes difficult, posing significant challenges for decision-making. This challenge highlights the importance of achieving measurement invariance (i.e., ensuring that the widely recognized scales perform equivalently across diverse cultural and economic contexts).

Valid measures that work consistently across countries and product categories enable managers to position brands effectively, adapt communication strategies and make informed decisions about standardization versus adaptation by providing timely feedback on which strategies are working. Cross-nationally valid measures of brand equity are also essential for advancing academic knowledge in international branding, contributing to a better understanding of brand performance in global markets (Christodoulides et al., 2015). However, the literature presents mixed findings on the validity of brand equity models in a global context. While some studies demonstrate measurement invariance across countries (Broyles et al., 2010; Buil et al., 2008; Lehmann et al., 2008; Vukasović, 2016), others highlight challenges in cross-national applicability, including issues with scale discrimination and variance in brand equity dimensions (Christodoulides et al., 2015; Jung & Sung, 2008). These findings underscore the need for more research on ensuring consistent measurement across borders.

Second, as brands operate globally, managers face the challenge of aggregating national brand performance metrics to develop a cohesive understanding of global brand performance. Without robust models for consumer-market-level indicators, brand managers struggle to compare their brand's value against global competitors or track progress across diverse markets (Hsieh, 2004; Wang et al., 2008). This lack of integration hampers their ability to align global strategies with local performance outcomes.

Despite its importance, there is limited academic research addressing the aggregation of national measures of brand equity to the global level. An exception is Hsieh's (2004) National Brand Equity model, which offers a novel approach by decomposing customer-based brand equity into two distinct components: measured and unmeasured brand equity. The measured component focuses on the effectiveness of individual benefit associations across different countries, while the unmeasured component captures the value attached to the brand, not typically assessed through standard association metrics. This dual-component framework allows for a more nuanced understanding of how brand equity can be aggregated at a global level, taking into account the diverse consumer perceptions and market environments across nations (Hsieh, 2004).

Third, identifying the drivers of consumer-market-level outcomes across different markets presents a significant challenge. Factors influencing brand performance can vary widely across regions due to differences in consumer preferences, cultural norms and market conditions, underscoring the need to understand differential antecedents of brands' consumer-market level success across markets (Burgess & Steenkamp, 2006). This complexity highlights a critical gap in the literature, as building and managing the antecedents of brand equity in a global context remains under-researched (Buil et al., 2013; Davcik et al., 2015; Yoo et al., 2000).

While some studies, such as Broyles et al. (2010), suggest that antecedents of brand equity do not differ substantially across markets, a growing body of research indicates otherwise. For example, de Mooij and Hofstede (2010) argues that cultural, social and economic characteristics significantly influence the formation of high brand equity. Further, many scholars have identified international marketing dimensions that lead to differential brand equity formation (Cho & Hwang, 2020; Heinberg et al., 2020; Rajavi et al., 2019; Torelli & Stoner, 2015), while others find partial variance across markets (e.g., Yoo & Donthu, 2002).

Finally, translating customer-market outcomes into tangible product-market outcomes remains a critical challenge, as market-specific factors like competitive intensity, economic conditions and cultural differences significantly influence how brand equity contributes to sales and other outcomes (e.g., Pauwels et al., 2013). While the relationship between customer-based brand equity and behavioral outcomes is well-established (e.g., Cobb-Walgren et al., 1995; Keller, 2001), research on its boundaries, particularly in international contexts, remains limited. Studies highlight the moderating roles of culture (Krautz, 2017), brand globalness (Zarantonello et al., 2020), country of origin (Porto & Soyer, 2018; Septianto et al., 2022) and market maturity (Datta et al., 2017). For example, Pauwels et al. (2013) find that brand consideration drives sales differently in emerging and mature markets, emphasizing the need for generalizations based on national infrastructure and cultural factors. Similarly, Walsh et al. (2014) and Pergelova and Angulo-Ruiz (2017) identify national characteristics as significant moderators of advertising effectiveness. These findings underscore the importance of understanding market-specific factors to leverage brand equity effectively across diverse contexts.

CONCLUSIONS

This chapter painted a comprehensive picture of brand performance measurement by presenting a wide array of performance indicators organized under the interconnected blocks of the brand value chain framework. Within this framework, consumer-market metrics are abundant and remain popular, with brand awareness, advantage and loyalty taking center stage. Due to the low cost of online search, metrics such as brand preference become less important, while brand consideration and purchase intention gain prominence. Further down the value chain, product market measures, such as sales, market share, revenue premium and price premium, and financial market metrics, such as brand value and firm value, stand out. Metrics obtained from retail media, measures of risk, and resource-market outcomes are exciting new metrics, while social tags and generative AI offer new data sources and methods. In the end, we propose to add resource-market outcomes to complement the holistic brand value chain and encourage more research on these new metrics.

Moving beyond the brand value chain, we next discuss how a collection of BPIs can be tailored to the specific needs of brand managers, investors and other relevant parties. The contrast between academic and commercial approaches highlights this multi-stakeholder perspective. We detail five commercial measurements of brand performance, distinguishing valuations for brand management purposes (marketing internal stakeholders) from valuations for accounting or transactional purposes (for financial stakeholders). Finally, the global playing field of brands leads to a discussion of scale invariance, cultural influences and the aggregation of national measures into global metrics.

Overall, our review demonstrates that brand performance is rich and exciting in both academic and commercial work. While specific metrics and methods may come and go, new technology and globalization continue to add opportunities to better measure and manage the brand for the benefit of all stakeholders. In contrast to doomsday claims about the end of branding, brands are even more important in online and international environments. As a result, we foresee a second golden age of branding research.

REFERENCES

Aaker, D. A. (1991). *Managing brand equity*. Free Press.

Aaker, D. A., & Jacobson, R. (2001). The value relevance of brand attitude in high-technology markets. *Journal of Marketing Research*, *38*(4), 485–493. https://doi.org/10.1509/jmkr.38.4.485.18905

Affonso, F. M., & Janiszewski, C. (2023). Marketing by design: The influence of perceptual structure on brand performance. *Journal of Marketing*, *87*(5), 736–754. https://doi.org/10.1177/00222429221142281

Ailawadi, K. L., Lehmann, D. R., & Neslin, S. A. (2003). Revenue premium as an outcome measure of brand equity. *Journal of Marketing*, *67*(4), 1–17. https://doi.org/10.1509/jmkg.67.4.1.18688

Angulo-Ruiz, F., Donthu, N., Prior, D., & Rialp, J. (2014). The financial contribution of customer-oriented marketing capability. *Journal of the Academy of Marketing Science*, *42*(4), 380–399. https://doi.org/10.1007/s11747-013-0353-6

Aribarg, A., Arora, N., Henderson, T., & Kim, Y. (2014). Private label imitation of a national brand: Implications for consumer choice and law. *Journal of Marketing Research*, *51*(6), 657–675. https://doi.org/10.1509/jmr.13.0420

Arnett, D. B., Laverie, D. A., & Meiers, A. (2003). Developing parsimonious retailer equity indexes using partial least squares analysis: A method and applications. *Journal of Retailing*, *79*(3), 161–170. https://doi.org/10.1016/S0022-4359(03)00036-8

Arora, N., Chakraborty, I., & Nishimura, Y. (2025). AI – human hybrids for marketing research: Leveraging large language models (LLMs) as collaborators. *Journal of Marketing*, *89*(2), 43–70. https://doi.org/10.1177/00222429241276529

Ataman, M. B., Mela, C. F., & van Heerde, H. J. (2008). Building brands. *Marketing Science*, *27*(6), 1036–1054. https://doi.org/10.1287/mksc.1080.0358

Ataman, M. B., Pauwels, K., Srinivasan, S., & Vanhuele, M. (2024). *Advertising,s impact on brand price elasticity*. HEC Paris Research Paper.

Ataman, M. B., van Heerde, H. J., & Mela, C. F. (2010). The long-term effect of marketing strategy on brand sales. *Journal of Marketing Research*, *47*(5), 866–882. https://doi.org/10.1509/jmkr.47.5.866

Baker, T. L., Rapp, A., Meyer, T., & Mullins, R. (2014). The role of brand communications on front line service employee beliefs, behaviors, and performance. *Journal of the Academy of Marketing Science*, *42*(6), 642–657. https://doi.org/10.1007/s11747-014-0376-7

Baldauf, A., Cravens, K. S., Diamantopoulos, A., & Zeugner-Roth, K. P. (2009). The impact of product-country image and marketing efforts on retailer-perceived brand equity: An empirical analysis. *Journal of Retailing*, *85*(4), 437–452. https://doi.org/10.1016/j.jretai.2009.04.004

Bar, R. N., & Haviv, A. (2023). Brand building to deter entry and its impact on brand value. *Management Science*, *69*(9), 5418–5438. https://doi.org/10.1287/mnsc.2022.4608

Barone, M. J., & Jewell, R. D. (2013). The innovator's license: A latitude to deviate from category norms. *Journal of Marketing*, *77*(1), 120–134. https://doi.org/10.1509/jm.10.0145

Becker-Olsen, K. L., & Hill, R. P. (2006). The impact of sponsor fit on brand equity: The case of nonprofit service providers. *Journal of Service Research*, *9*(1), 73–83. https://doi.org/10.1177/1094670506289532

Bendle, N. T., & Butt, M. N. (2018). The misuse of accounting-based approximations of Tobin's q in a world of market-based assets. *Marketing Science*, *37*(3), 484–504. https://doi.org/10.1287/mksc.2018.1093

Biraglia, A., Fuchs, C., Maira, E., & Puntoni, S. (2023). When and why consumers react negatively to brand acquisitions: A values authenticity account. *Journal of Marketing*, *87*(4), 601–617. https://doi.org/10.1177/00222429221137817

Borkovsky, R. N., Goldfarb, A., Haviv, A. M., & Moorthy, S. (2017). Measuring and understanding brand value in a dynamic model of brand management. *Marketing Science*, *36*(4), 471–499. https://doi.org/10.1287/mksc.2016.1020

Brady, M. K., Cronin, Jr., J. J., Fox, G. L., & Roehm, M. L. (2008). Strategies to offset performance failures: The role of brand equity. *Journal of Retailing*, *84*(2), 151–164. https://doi.org/10.1016/j.jretai.2008.04.002

Brand, J., Israeli, A., & Ngwe, D. (2023). *Using LLMs for market research*. Harvard Business School Marketing Unit Working Paper, 23-062. www.hbs.edu/ris/Publication%20Files/23-062_ed720ebc-ec4d-4bc3-a6ba-bad8cfbd9d51.pdf

Broyles, S. A., Leingpibul, T., Ross, R. H., & Foster, B. M. (2010). Brand equity's antecedent/consequence relationships in cross-cultural settings. *Journal of Product & Brand Management*, *19*(3), 159–169. https://doi.org/10.1108/10610421011046148

Buil, I., De Chernatony, L., & Martinez, E. (2008). A cross-national validation of the consumer-based brand equity scale. *Journal of Product & Brand Management*, *17*(6), 384–392. https://doi.org/10.1108/10610420810904121

Buil, I., Martínez, E., & De Chernatony, L. (2013). The influence of brand equity on consumer responses. *Journal of Consumer Marketing*, *30*(1), 62–74. https://doi.org/10.1108/07363761311290849

Burgess, S. M., & Steenkamp, J. B. E. M. (2006). Marketing renaissance: How research in emerging markets advances marketing science and practice. *International Journal of Research in Marketing*, *23*(4), 337–356. https://doi.org/10.1016/j.ijresmar.2006.08.001

Cao, Z. (2022). Brand equity, warranty costs, and firm value. *International Journal of Research in Marketing*, *39*(4), 1166–1185. https://doi.org/10.1016/j.ijresmar.2022.02.002

Chan, H.-Y., Boksem, M., & Smidts, A. (2018). Neural profiling of brands: Mapping brand image in consumers' brains with visual templates. *Journal of Marketing Research*, *55*(4), 600–615. https://doi.org/10.1509/jmr.17.0019

Chatzipanagiotou, K., Christodoulides, G., & Veloutsou, C. (2019). Managing the consumer-based brand equity process: A cross-cultural perspective. *International Business Review*, *28*(2), 328–343. https://doi.org/10.1016/j.ibusrev.2018.10.005

Chaudhuri, A., & Holbrook, M. B. (2001). The chain of effects from brand trust and brand affect to brand performance: The role of brand loyalty. *Journal of Marketing*, *65*(2), 81–93. https://doi.org/10.1509/jmkg.65.2.81.18255

Cho, E., & Hwang, J. (2020). Drivers of consumer-based brand equity: A two-country analysis of perceived brand origin and identity expressiveness. *International Marketing Review*, *37*(2), 241–259. https://doi.org/10.1108/IMR-12-2018-0351

Christodoulides, G., Cadogan, J. W., & Veloutsou, C. (2015). Consumer-based brand equity measurement: Lessons learned from an international study. *International Marketing Review*, *32*(3/4), 307–328. https://doi.org/10.1108/IMR-10-2013-0242

Cleeren, K., Dekimpe, M. G., & Helsen, K. (2008). Weathering product-harm crises. *Journal of the Academy of Marketing Science*, *36*(2), 262–270. https://doi.org/10.1007/s11747-007-0022-8

Cobb-Walgren, C. J., Ruble, C. A., & Donthu, N. (1995). Brand equity, brand preference, and purchase intent. *Journal of Advertising*, *24*(3), 25–40. https://doi.org/10.1080/00913367.1995.10673481

Colicev, A., Malshe, A., Pauwels, K., & O'Connor, P. (2018). Improving consumer mindset metrics and shareholder value through social media: The different roles of owned and earned media. *Journal of Marketing*, *82*(1), 37–56. https://doi.org/10.1509/jm.16.0055

Cooper, L. G., & Nakanishi, M. (1988). *Market share analysis: Evaluating competitive marketing effectiveness*. Kluwer.

Court, D., Elzinga, D., Mulder, S., & Vetvik, O. J. (2009). The consumer decision journey. *McKinsey Quarterly*, *3*, 96–107. www.mckinsey.com/capabilities/growth-marketing-and-sales/our-insights/the-consumer-decision-journey

Culotta, A., & Cutler, J. (2016). Mining brand perceptions from twitter social networks. *Marketing Science*, *35*(3), 343–362. https://doi.org/10.1287/mksc.2015.0968

Datta, H., Ailawadi, K. L., & van Heerde, H. J. (2017). How well does consumer-based brand equity align with sales-based brand equity and marketing-mix response? *Journal of Marketing*, *81*(3), 1–20. https://doi.org/10.1509/jm.15.0340

Davcik, N. S., Vinhas da Silva, R., & Hair, J. F. (2015). Towards a unified theory of brand equity: Conceptualizations, taxonomy and avenues for future research. *Journal of Product & Brand Management*, *24*(1), 3–17. https://doi.org/10.1108/JPBM-06-2014-0639

Davis, D. F., & Mentzer, J. T. (2008). Relational resources in interorganizational exchange: The effects of trade equity and brand equity. *Journal of Retailing*, *84*(4), 435–448. https://doi.org/10.1016/j.jretai.2008.08.002

Dawar, N., & Pillutla, M. M. (2000). Impact of product-harm crises on brand equity: The moderating role of consumer expectations. *Journal of*

Marketing Research, *37*(2), 215–226. https://doi.org/10.1509/jmkr.37.2.215.18729

De Haan, E., Wiesel, T., & Pauwels, K. (2016). The effectiveness of different forms of online advertising for purchase conversion in a multiple-channel attribution framework. *International Journal of Research in Marketing*, *33*(3), 491–507. https://doi.org/10.1016/j.ijresmar.2015.12.001

Dekimpe, M. G., & Hanssens, D. M. (1999). Sustained spending and persistent response: A new look at long-term marketing profitability. *Journal of Marketing Research*, *36*(4), 397–412. https://doi.org/10.1177/002224379903600401

De Mooij, M., & Hofstede, G. (2010). The Hofstede model: Applications to global branding and advertising strategy and research. *International Journal of Advertising*, *29*(1), 85–110. https://doi.org/10.2501/S026504870920104X

DelVecchio, D., & Smith, D. C. (2005). Brand-extension price premiums: The effects of perceived fit and extension product category risk. *Journal of the Academy of Marketing Science*, *33*(2), 184–196. https://doi.org/10.1177/0092070304269753

Desai, K. K., & Ratneshwar, S. (2003). Consumer perceptions of product variants positioned on atypical attributes. *Journal of the Academy of Marketing Science*, *31*(1), 22–35. https://doi.org/10.1177/0092070302238600

Dolbec, P.-Y., & Chebat, J.-C. (2013). The impact of a flagship vs. a brand store on brand attitude, brand attachment and brand equity. *Journal of Retailing*, *89*(4), 460–466. https://doi.org/10.1016/j.jretai.2013.06.003

Dubin, J. A. (1998). The demand for branded and unbranded products – an econometric method for valuing intangible assets. In J. A. Dubin (Ed.), *Studies in consumer demand – econometric methods applied to market data* (pp. 77–127). Springer US. https://doi.org/10.1007/978-1-4615-5665-7_4.

Dutordoir, M., Verbeeten, F. H., & De Beijer, D. (2015). Stock price reactions to brand value announcements: Magnitude and moderators. *International Journal of Research in Marketing*, *32*(1), 34–47. https://doi.org/10.1016/j.ijresmar.2014.08.001

Dzyabura, D., & Peres, R. (2021). Visual elicitation of brand perception. *Journal of Marketing*, *85*(4), 44–66. https://doi.org/10.1177/0022242921996661

Echambadi, R., Jindal, R. P., & Blair, E. A. (2013). Evaluating and managing brand repurchase across multiple geographic retail markets. *Journal of Retailing*, *89*(4), 409–422. https://doi.org/10.1016/j.jretai.2013.05.005

Edeling, A., Srinivasan, S., & Hanssens, D. M. (2021). The marketing – finance interface: A new integrative review of metrics, methods, and findings and an agenda for future research. *International Journal of Research in Marketing*, *38*(4), 857–876. https://doi.org/10.1016/j.ijresmar.2020.09.005

Erdem, T., Swait, J., & Louviere, J. (2002). The impact of brand credibility on consumer price sensitivity. *International Journal of Research in Marketing*, *19*(1), 1–19. https://doi.org/10.1016/S0167-8116(01)00048-9

Erdem, T., Swait, J., & Valenzuela, A. (2006). Brands as signals: A cross-country validation study. *Journal of Marketing*, *70*(1), 34–49. https://doi.org/10.1509/jmkg.70.1.034.qxd

Ertekin, L., Sorescu, A., & Houston, M. B. (2018). Hands off my brand! The financial consequences of protecting brands through trademark infringement lawsuits. *Journal of Marketing*, *82*(5), 45–65. https://doi.org/10.1509/jm.17.0328

Esch, F.-R., Möll, T., Schmitt, B., Elger, C. E., Neuhaus, C., & Weber, B. (2012). Brands on the brain: Do consumers use declarative information or experienced emotions to evaluate brands? *Journal of Consumer Psychology*, *22*(1), 75–85. https://doi.org/10.1016/j.jcps.2010.08.004

Ferjani, M., Jedidi, K., & Jagpal, S. (2009). A conjoint approach for consumer- and firm-level brand valuation. *Journal of Marketing Research*, *46*(6), 846–862. https://doi.org/10.1509/jmkr.46.6.846

Fernández-Barcala, M., & González-Díaz, M. (2006). Brand equity in the European fruit and vegetable sector: A transaction cost approach. *International Journal of Research in Marketing*, *23*(1), 31–44. https://doi.org/10.1016/j.ijresmar.2006.01.004

Fischer, M., & Himme, A. (2017). The financial brand value chain: How brand investments contribute to the financial health of firms. *International Journal of Research in Marketing*, *34*(1), 137–153. https://doi.org/10.1016/j.ijresmar.2016.05.004

Fischer, M., Shin, H. S., & Hanssens, D. M. (2016). Brand performance volatility from marketing spending. *Management Science*, *62*(1), 197–215. https://doi.org/10.1287/mnsc.2014.2102

Fudge, A. (2005, November 3-4). Brand energy: A compass for navigating troubled waters. *Marketing science institute conference on connecting with customers in a complex world*, Chicago, IL.

Gao, L., Melero-Polo, I., & Sese, F. J. (2020). Customer equity drivers, customer experience quality, and customer profitability in banking services: The moderating role of social influence. *Journal of Service Research*, *23*(2), 174–193. https://doi.org/10.1177/1094670519856119

Gerzema, J., Lebar, E., & Sussman, M. (2005). *Brand energy: Quantifying the value of brand momentum*. Y&R White Paper.

Gielens, K., Geyskens, I., Deleersnyder, B., & Nohe, M. (2018). The new regulator in town: The effect of Walmart's sustainability mandate on supplier shareholder value. *Journal of Marketing*, *82*(2), 124–141. https://doi.org/10.1509/jm.16.0276

Goldfarb, A., Lu, Q., & Moorthy, S. (2009). Measuring brand value in an equilibrium framework.

Marketing Science, *28*(1), 69–86. https://doi.org/10.1287/mksc.1080.0376

Goli, A., & Singh, A. (2024). Frontiers: Can large language models capture human preferences? *Marketing Science*, *43*(4), 709–722. https://doi.org/10.1287/mksc.2023.0306

Gui, G., & Toubia, O. (2023). The challenge of using LLMs to simulate human behavior: A causal inference perspective. In *SSRN Electronic Journal*. arXiv preprint arXiv:2312.15524. https://doi.org/10.2139/ssrn.4650172

Ha, K. C., Song, R., & Erickson, G. (2021). Multidimensional brand equity and asymmetric risk. *International Journal of Research in Marketing*, *38*(3), 593–614. https://doi.org/10.1016/j.ijresmar.2020.10.002

Halbauer, I., Jacob, S., & Klarmann, M. (2022). Brand presentation order in voice shopping: Understanding the effects of sequential product presentation. *Journal of Retailing*, *98*(4), 759–778. https://doi.org/10.1016/j.jretai.2022.06.002

Harris Interactive. (n.d.). *The Harris Poll EquiTrend study*. https://theharrispoll.com/equitrend/

Heinberg, M., Katsikeas, C. S., Ozkaya, H. E., & Taube, M. (2020). How nostalgic brand positioning shapes brand equity: Differences between emerging and developed markets. *Journal of the Academy of Marketing Science*, *48*(5), 869–890. https://doi.org/10.1007/s11747-019-00637-x

Heitmann, M., Landwehr, J. R., Schreiner, T. F., & van Heerde, H. J. (2020). Leveraging brand equity for effective visual product design. *Journal of Marketing Research*, *57*(2), 257–277. https://doi.org/10.1177/0022243720904004

Henderson, C. M., Mazodier, M., & Khenfer, J. (2025). The positive effects of integrated advertising, featuring diverse ensembles, on societal identification and mainstream brand value. *Journal of the Academy of Marketing Science*, *53*(2), 617–642. https://doi.org/10.1007/s11747-023-00977-9

Himme, A., & Fischer, M. (2014). Drivers of the cost of capital: The joint role of non-financial metrics. *International Journal of Research in Marketing*, *31*(2), 224–238. https://doi.org/10.1016/j.ijresmar.2013.10.006

Hogreve, J., Bilstein, N., & Hoerner, K. (2019). Service recovery on stage: Effects of social media recovery on virtually present others. *Journal of Service Research*, *22*(4), 421–439. https://doi.org/10.1177/1094670519851871

Hsieh, M.-H. (2004). Measuring global brand equity using cross-national survey data. *Journal of International Marketing*, *12*(2), 28–57. https://doi.org/10.1509/jimk.12.2.28.32897

Hughes, D. E., & Ahearne, M. (2010). Energizing the reseller's sales force: The power of brand identification. *Journal of Marketing*, *74*(4), 81–96. https://doi.org/10.1509/jmkg.74.4.081

Interbrand. (2022). *Brand Valuation: A versatile strategic tool for business*. https://interbrand.com/wp-content/uploads/2023/09/IB-Brand-Valuation_220608b.pdf

Johansson, J. K., Dimofte, C. V., & Mazvancheryl, S. K. (2012). The performance of global brands in the 2008 financial crisis: A test of two brand value measures. *International Journal of Research in Marketing*, *29*(3), 235–245. https://doi.org/10.1016/j.ijresmar.2012.01.002

John, D. R., Loken, B., Kim, K., & Monga, A. B. (2006). Brand concept maps: A methodology for identifying brand association networks. *Journal of Marketing Research*, *43*(4), 549–563. https://doi.org/10.1509/jmkr.43.4.549

Jung, J., & Sung, E. (2008). Consumer-based brand equity: Comparisons among Americans and South Koreans in the USA and South Koreans in Korea. *Journal of Fashion Marketing and Management*, *12*(1), 24–35. https://doi.org/10.1108/13612020810857925

Kantar. (2025). *Kantar BrandZ: Most valuable global brands 2025*. www.kantar.com/campaigns/brandz-downloads/kantar-brandz-most-valuable-global-brands-2025

Katsikeas, C. S., Morgan, N. A., Leonidou, L. C., & Hult, G. T. M. (2016). Assessing performance outcomes in marketing. *Journal of Marketing*, *80*(2), 1–20. https://doi.org/10.1509/jm.15.0287

Keller, K. L. (1993). Conceptualizing, measuring, and managing customer-based brand equity. *Journal of Marketing*, *57*(1), 1–22. https://doi.org/10.1177/002224299305700101

Keller, K. L. (2001). *Building customer-based brand equity: A Blue print for creating strong brands*. MSI Report, 01-107.

Keller, K. L., & Lehmann, D. R. (2003). How do brands create value? *Marketing Management*, *12*(3), 26–26.

Koll, O., & Plank, A. (2022). Do shoppers choose the same brand on the next trip when facing the same context? An empirical investigation in FMCG retailing. *Journal of Retailing*, *98*(4), 576–592. https://doi.org/10.1016/j.jretai.2022.01.003

Krautz, C. (2017). A cross-cultural study of collective brand perceptions within the brand equity framework. *Journal of Marketing Theory and Practice*, *25*(3), 274–290. https://doi.org/10.1080/10696679.2017.1311218

Lehmann, D. R., Keller, K. L., & Farley, J. U. (2008). The structure of survey-based brand metrics. *Journal of International Marketing*, *16*(4), 29–56. https://doi.org/10.1509/jimk.16.4.29

Lei, J., Dawar, N., & Lemmink, J. (2008). Negative spillover in brand portfolios: Exploring the antecedents of asymmetric effects. *Journal of Marketing*, *72*(3), 111–123. https://doi.org/10.1509/JMKG.72.3.111

Li, P., Castelo, N., Katona, Z., & Sarvary, M. (2024). Frontiers: Determining the validity of large language models for automated perceptual analysis. *Marketing Science*, *43*(2), 254–266. https://doi.org/10.1287/mksc.2023.0454

Liu, L., Dzyabura, D., & Mizik, N. (2020). Visual listening In: Extracting brand image portrayed on social media. *Marketing Science*, *39*(4), 669–686. https://doi.org/10.1287/mksc.2020.1226

Luffarelli, J., Delre, S. A., & Landgraf, P. (2023). How has the effect of brand personality on customer-based brand equity changed over time? Longitudinal evidence from a panel data set spanning 18 years. *Journal of the Academy of Marketing Science*, *51*(3), 598–616. https://doi.org/10.1007/s11747-022-00895-2

Luffarelli, J., Stamatogiannakis, A., & Yang, H. (2019). The visual asymmetry effect: An interplay of logo design and brand personality on brand equity. *Journal of Marketing Research*, *56*(1), 89–103. https://doi.org/10.1177/0022243718820548

Luo, X., Raithel, S., & Wiles, M. A. (2013). The impact of brand rating dispersion on firm value. *Journal of Marketing Research*, *50*(3), 399–415. https://doi.org/10.1509/jmr.12.0188

Madden, T. J., Fehle, F., & Fournier, S. (2006). Brands matter: An empirical demonstration of the creation of shareholder value through branding. *Journal of the Academy of Marketing Science*, *34*(2), 224–235. https://doi.org/10.1177/0092070305283356

Mafael, A., Raithel, S., & Hock, S. J. (2022). Managing customer satisfaction after a product recall: The joint role of remedy, brand equity, and severity. *Journal of the Academy of Marketing Science*, *50*(1), 174–194. https://doi.org/10.1007/s11747-021-00802-1

Malshe, A. V., Yin, Y., Colicev, A., Bart, Y., & Pauwels, K. (2023). *How ESG reduces risk: The role of consumers and institutional investors*. Northeastern U. D'Amore-McKim School of Business Research Paper, 4410032. https://papers.ssrn.com/sol3/papers.cfm?abstract_id=4410032

Martin, I. M., & Stewart, D. W. (2001). The differential impact of goal congruency on attitudes, intentions, and the transfer of brand equity. *Journal of Marketing Research*, *38*(4), 471–484. https://doi.org/10.1509/jmkr.38.4.471.18912

Mathur, P., Malika, M., Agrawal, N., & Maheswaran, D. (2023). The context (In)dependence of low-fit brand extensions. *Journal of Marketing*, *87*(1), 114–132. https://doi.org/10.1177/00222429221076840

Mazodier, M., Henderson, C. M., & Beck, J. T. (2018). The long reach of sponsorship: How fan isolation and identification jointly shape sponsorship performance. *Journal of Marketing*, *82*(6), 28–48. https://doi.org/10.1177/0022242918807673

Mazodier, M., & Rezaee, A. (2013). Are sponsorship announcements good news for the shareholders? Evidence from international stock exchanges. *Journal of the Academy of Marketing Science*, *41*(5), 586–600. https://doi.org/10.1007/s11747-013-0325-x

McAlister, L., Srinivasan, R., Jindal, N., & Cannella, A. A. (2016). Advertising effectiveness: The moderating effect of firm strategy. *Journal of Marketing Research*, *53*(2), 207–224. https://doi.org/10.1509/jmr.13.0285

Mizik, N. (2014). Assessing the total financial performance impact of brand equity with limited time-series data. *Journal of Marketing Research*, *51*(6), 691–706. https://doi.org/10.1509/jmr.13.0431

Mizik, N., & Jacobson, R. (2008). The financial value impact of perceptual brand attributes. *Journal of Marketing Research*, *45*(1), 15–32. https://doi.org/10.1509/jmkr.45.1.15

Morgan, N. A. (2012). Marketing and business performance. *Journal of the Academy of Marketing Science*, *40*(1), 102–119. https://doi.org/10.1007/s11747-011-0279-9

Nam, H., Joshi, Y. V., & Kannan, P. K. (2017). Harvesting brand information from social tags. *Journal of Marketing*, *81*(4), 88–108. https://doi.org/10.1509/jm.16.0044

Nam, H., & Kannan, P. K. (2014). The informational value of social tagging networks. *Journal of Marketing*, *78*(4), 21–40. https://doi.org/10.1509/jm.12.0151

Netzer, O., Feldman, R., Goldenberg, J., & Fresko, M. (2012). Mine your Own business: Market-structure surveillance through text mining. *Marketing Science*, *31*(3), 521–543. https://doi.org/10.1287/mksc.1120.0713

Nguyen, H. T., & Feng, H. (2021). Antecedents and financial impacts of building brand love. *International Journal of Research in Marketing*, *38*(3), 572–592. https://doi.org/10.1016/j.ijresmar.2020.10.001

Nyffenegger, B., Krohmer, H., Hoyer, W. D., & Malär, L. (2015). Service brand relationship quality: Hot or cold? *Journal of Service Research*, *18*(1), 90–106. https://doi.org/10.1177/1094670514547580

Ou, Y.-C., De Vries, L., Wiesel, T., & Verhoef, P. C. (2014). The role of consumer confidence in creating customer loyalty. *Journal of Service Research*, *17*(3), 339–354. https://doi.org/10.1177/1094670513513925

Ou, Y.-C., Verhoef, P. C., & Wiesel, T. (2017). The effects of customer equity drivers on loyalty across services industries and firms. *Journal of the Academy of Marketing Science*, *45*(3), 336–356. https://doi.org/10.1007/s11747-016-0477-6

Pappu, R., Quester, P. G., & Cooksey, R. W. (2006). Consumer-based brand equity and country-of-origin relationships: Some empirical evidence. *European Journal of Marketing*, *40*(5/6), 696–717. https://doi.org/10.1108/03090560610657903

Pauwels, K., Ambler, T., Clark, B. H., LaPointe, P., Reibstein, D., Skiera, B., Wierenga, B., & Wiesel, T. (2009). Dashboards as a service: Why, what, how, and what research is needed? *Journal of Service Research*, *12*(2), 175–189. https://doi.org/10.1177/1094670509344213

Pauwels, K., Erguncu, S., & Yildirim, G. (2013). Winning hearts, minds and sales: How marketing communication enters the purchase process in emerging and mature markets. *International Journal of Research in Marketing*, *30*(1), 57–68. https://doi.org/10.1016/j.ijresmar.2012.09.006

Pauwels, K., Silva-Risso, J., Srinivasan, S., & Hanssens, D. M. (2004). New products, sales promotions, and firm value: The case of the automobile industry. *Journal of Marketing*, *68*(4), 142–156. https://doi.org/10.1509/jmkg.68.4.142.42724

Pauwels, K., & van Ewijk, B. (2013). Do online behavior tracking or attitude survey metrics drive brand sales? An integrative model of attitudes and actions on the consumer boulevard. *Marketing Science Institute Working Paper Series*, *13*(118), 1–49.

Pauwels, K., & van Ewijk, B. (2020). Enduring attitudes and contextual interest: When and why attitude surveys still matter in the online consumer decision journey. *Journal of Interactive Marketing*, *52*(1), 20–34. https://doi.org/10.1016/j.intmar.2020.03.004

Pergelova, A., & Angulo-Ruiz, F. (2017). Comparing advertising effectiveness in South-American and North-American contexts: Testing Hofstede's and Inglehart's cultural dimensions in the higher education sector. *International Journal of Advertising*, *36*(6), 870–892. https://doi.org/10.1080/02650487.2017.1364032

Petersen, J. A., Kumar, V., Polo, Y., & Sese, F. J. (2018). Unlocking the power of marketing: Understanding the links between customer mindset metrics, behavior, and profitability. *Journal of the Academy of Marketing Science*, *46*(5), 813–836. https://doi.org/10.1007/s11747-017-0554-5

Peterson, R. A., & Jeong, J. (2010). Exploring the impact of advertising and R&D expenditures on corporate brand value and firm-level financial performance. *Journal of the Academy of Marketing Science*, *38*(6), 677–690. https://doi.org/10.1007/s11747-010-0188-3

Pogacar, R., Angle, J., Lowrey, T. M., Shrum, L. J., & Kardes, F. R. (2021). Is Nestlé a lady? The feminine brand name advantage. *Journal of Marketing*, *85*(6), 101–117. https://doi.org/10.1177/0022242921993060

Porto, R. B., & Soyer, T. d. S. (2018). Is naming brands in english worth doing? Effects of foreignness and country of origin on brand equity. *Brazilian Business Review*, *15*(6), 606–623. https://doi.org/10.15728/bbr.2018.15.6.6

Puzakova, M., Kwak, H., & Rocereto, J. F. (2013). When humanizing brands goes wrong: The detrimental effect of brand anthropomorphization amid product wrongdoings. *Journal of Marketing*, *77*(3), 81–100. https://doi.org/10.1509/jm.11.0510

Qin, V., Pauwels, K., & Zhou, B. (2024). Data-driven budget allocation of retail media by ad product, funnel metric, and brand size. *Journal of Marketing Analytics*, *12*(2), 235–249. https://doi.org/10.1057/s41270-024-00294-2

Rajavi, K., Kushwaha, T., & Steenkamp, J.-B. E. (2019). In brands we trust? A multicategory, multicountry investigation of sensitivity of consumers' trust in brands to marketing-mix activities. *Journal of Consumer Research*, *46*(4), 651–670. https://doi.org/10.1093/jcr/ucz026

Rajavi, K., Kushwaha, T., & Steenkamp, J. B. E. (2023). Brand equity in good and bad times: What distinguishes winners from losers in CPG industries? *Journal of Marketing*, *87*(3), 472–489. https://doi.org/10.1177/00222429221122698

Ramaswami, S. N., & Arunachalam, S. (2016). Divided attitudinal loyalty and customer value: Role of dealers in an indirect channel. *Journal of the Academy of Marketing Science*, *44*(6), 770–790. https://doi.org/10.1007/s11747-015-0471-4

Rapp, A., Beitelspacher, L. S., Grewal, D., & Hughes, D. E. (2013). Understanding social media effects across seller, retailer, and consumer interactions. *Journal of the Academy of Marketing Science*, *41*(5), 547–566. https://doi.org/10.1007/s11747-013-0326-9

Rego, L. L., Billett, M. T., & Morgan, N. A. (2009). Consumer-based brand equity and firm risk. *Journal of Marketing*, *73*(6), 47–60. https://doi.org/10.1509/jmkg.73.6.47

Reimer, K., Rutz, O. J., & Pauwels, K. (2014). How online consumer segments differ in long-term marketing effectiveness. *Journal of Interactive Marketing*, *28*(4), 271–284. https://doi.org/10.1016/j.intmar.2014.05.002

Roth, M. S. (1995). Effects of global market conditions on brand image customization and brand performance. *Journal of Advertising*, *24*(4), 55–75. https://doi.org/10.1080/00913367.1995.10673489

Salinas, G. (2009). *The International Brand Valuation Manual: A complete overview and analysis of brand valuation techniques, methodologies and applications*. Wiley. https://doi/10.1002/9781119206408

Septianto, F., Japutra, A., Sung, B., & Seo, Y. (2022). The interaction effect of country-of-origin positioning and cultural distance on international advertising effectiveness: A construal level perspective. *International Marketing Review*, *39*(4), 931–954. https://doi.org/10.1108/IMR-10-2021-0291

Sirianni, N. J., Bitner, M. J., Brown, S. W., & Mandel, N. (2013). Branded service encounters: Strategically aligning employee behavior with the brand positioning. *Journal of Marketing*, *77*(6), 108–123. https://doi.org/10.1509/jm.11.0485

Slotegraaf, R. J., & Pauwels, K. (2008). The impact of brand equity and innovation on the long-term effectiveness of promotions. *Journal of Marketing Research*, *45*(3), 293–306. https://doi.org/10.1509/jmkr.45.3.293

Srinivasan, S., & Hanssens, D. M. (2009). Marketing and firm value: Metrics, methods, findings, and future directions. *Journal of Marketing Research*, *46*(3), 293–312. https://doi.org/10.1509/jmkr.46.3.293

Srinivasan, S., Vanhuele, M., & Pauwels, K. (2010). Mind-set metrics in market response models: An integrative approach. *Journal of Marketing Research*, *47*(4), 672–684. https://doi.org/10.1509/jmkr.47.4.672

Srinivasan, V., Park, C. S., & Chang, D. R. (2005). An approach to the measurement, analysis, and prediction of brand equity and its sources. *Management Science*, *51*(9), 1433–1448. https://doi.org/10.1287/mnsc.1050.0405

Sriram, S., Balachander, S., & Kalwani, M. U. (2007). Monitoring the dynamics of brand equity using store-level data. *Journal of Marketing*, *71*(2), 61–78. https://doi.org/10.1509/jmkg.71.2.061

Sriram, S., & Kalwani, M. U. (2007). Optimal advertising and promotion budgets in dynamic markets with brand equity as a mediating variable. *Management Science*, *53*(1), 46–60. https://doi.org/10.1287/mnsc.1060.0604

Tavassoli, N. T., Sorescu, A., & Chandy, R. (2014). Employee-based brand equity: Why firms with strong brands pay their executives less. *Journal of Marketing Research*, *51*(6), 676–690. https://doi.org/10.1509/jmr.13.0435

Torelli, C. J., & Stoner, J. L. (2015). Managing cultural equity: A theoretical framework for building iconic brands in globalized markets. In D. J. Macinnis & C. W. Park (Eds.), *Review of marketing research* (Vol. *12*, pp. 83–120). Emerald Group Publishing Limited. https://doi.org/10.1108/S1548-643520150000012004

Torres, A., Bijmolt, T. H., Tribó, J. A., & Verhoef, P. (2012). Generating global brand equity through corporate social responsibility to key stakeholders. *International Journal of Research in Marketing*, *29*(1), 13–24. https://doi.org/10.1016/j.ijresmar.2011.10.002

Valenti, A., Yildirim, G., Vanhuele, M., Srinivasan, S., & Pauwels, K. (2023). Advertising's sequence of effects on consumer mindset and sales: A comparison across brands and product categories. *International Journal of Research in Marketing*, *40*(2), 435–454. https://doi.org/10.1016/j.ijresmar.2022.12.002

Vukasović, T. (2016). An empirical investigation of brand equity: A cross-country validation analysis. *Journal of Global Marketing*, *29*(5), 251–265. https://doi.org/10.1080/08911762.2016.1194508

Walsh, G., Shiu, E., & Hassan, L. M. (2014). Cross-national advertising and behavioral intentions: A multilevel analysis. *Journal of International Marketing*, *22*(1), 77–98. https://doi.org/10.1509/jim.13.0091

Wang, H., Wei, Y., & Yu, C. (2008). Global brand equity model: Combining customer-based with product-market outcome approaches. *Journal of Product & Brand Management*, *17*(5), 305–316. https://doi.org/10.1108/10610420810896068

Warlop, L., Ratneshwar, S., & van Osselaer, S. M. (2005). Distinctive brand cues and memory for product consumption experiences. *International Journal of Research in Marketing*, *22*(1), 27–44. https://doi.org/10.1016/j.ijresmar.2004.02.001

Whitelock, J., & Fastoso, F. (2007). Understanding international branding: Defining the domain and reviewing the literature. *International Marketing Review*, *24*(3), 252–270. https://doi.org/10.1108/02651330710755285

Wiles, M. A., & Danielova, A. (2009). The worth of product placement in successful films: An event study analysis. *Journal of Marketing*, *73*(4), 44–63. https://doi.org/10.1509/jmkg.73.4.044

Yoo, B., & Donthu, N. (2002). Testing cross-cultural invariance of the brand equity creation process. *Journal of Product & Brand Management*, *11*(6), 380–398. https://doi.org/10.1108/10610420210445505

Yoo, B., Donthu, N., & Lee, S. (2000). An examination of selected marketing mix elements and brand equity. *Journal of the Academy of Marketing Science*, *28*(2), 195–211. https://doi.org/10.1177/0092070300282002

Zarantonello, L., Grappi, S., Formisano, M., & Brakus, J. (2020). How consumer-based brand equity relates to market share of global and local brands in developed and emerging countries. *International Marketing Review*, *37*(2), 345–375. https://doi.org/10.1108/IMR-05-2018-0176

Zenetti, G., & Pauwels, K. (2024). Amplifying off-site purchases with on-site retail media advertising. *Journal of Interactive Marketing*, *59*(4), 329–346. https://doi.org/10.1177/10949968241246257

Zhang, J., & Bloemer, J. M. M. (2008). The impact of value congruence on consumer-service brand relationships. *Journal of Service Research*, *11*(2), 161–178. https://doi.org/10.1177/1094670508322561

Zhao, Y., Zhang, Y., Wang, J., Schrock, W. A., & Calantone, R. J. (2020). Brand relevance and the effects of product proliferation across product categories. *Journal of the Academy of Marketing Science*, *48*(6), 1192–1210. https://doi.org/10.1007/s11747-020-00727-1

27

An Overview of Brand Metrics: Monitoring Brand's Competitive Standing

Jacek Kall

The prevailing approach to brand management is marked by an overreliance on visual and verbal elements, with numerical data being accorded comparatively less significance. Nevertheless, the management of entities that are inherently incapable of quantification remains challenging. Moreover, verbal descriptions of a brand's market standing are often characterised by vagueness and ambiguity, if absent of any quantifiable metrics.

Brand metrics are quantitative indicators that reflect either the behaviour of brand buyers or the mindsets of category buyers, which serve as a basis for evaluating the brand's market position, assessing its growth potential and identifying activities likely to enhance its performance. Such evaluations are achieved by comparing the metric in question to historical values, benchmark figures and/or the performance of competitors. The use of the plural is fully justified, as no single metric can reliably assess the brand's condition, in the same way that no single indicator can assess the strength of an economy or the health of an individual.

It is critical to underscore a significant distinction between metrics relating to corporate brands, which assess the health of the entire company, when the products offered are named after the company's name (*branded house*, see: Aaker, 2004), as opposed to entities operating a portfolio of brands (*house of brands*), where the health of individual brands is reflected in their individual metrics. Additionally, metrics can be analysed at the brand level, as well as at the level of individual models or versions of the product. Furthermore, it should be noted that some of the metrics examined in this chapter, for example, penetration or trial rate, find application in both the brand as well as the category (collective offering of all brands). This does not invalidate the usefulness of these metrics for analysing brand health, but rather underscores the necessity for meticulous delineation of the subject of analysis.

BRAND METRICS: A CONSUMER-BASED PERSPECTIVE

Brand metrics' analysis fits into two strains of management science, which are of rising importance: performance measurement and evidence-based marketing.

Performance measurement

As to the performance measurement, one of the pioneering concepts was Kaplan and Norton's (1996) *strategic scorecard*. To gain a more profound comprehension of a brand's performance within the market, a variety of metrics are employed by companies to assess its performance, with consumer surveys playing a prominent role (Lehmann et al., 2008). Brand metrics constitute a fundamental aspect of the *brand audit* (Lalaounis, 2021), a comprehensive evaluation aimed at diagnosing the brand's overall health, identifying its sources of equity and proposing strategic improvements. The brand audit encompasses two primary dimensions: the organisational perspective (*brand inventory*) and the consumer perspective (*brand exploratory*). A variety of qualitative and quantitative research is included in the latter category, with numerous brand metrics being derived from consumer surveys (*brand tracking studies*; Keller & Swaminathan, 2020). An effective brand measurement system helps businesses understand how the brand is performing against customer expectations, evaluate its performance relative to competitors, identify potential weaknesses before they become business problems, and pinpoint areas to focus on for brand-building efforts that drive business value. Three categories of brand metrics have been identified: perception (further subdivided into 'awareness' and 'familiarity and consideration'), performance (consisting of 'purchase decisions' and 'loyalty') and financial ones (Munoz & Kumar, 2004).

A number of prominent publications have addressed the subject of marketing metrics, including those pertaining to brands: Bendle et al. (2016), Binet and Field (2007), Davis (2000), Jeffery (2010) and Marr (2012). Brand metrics can be analysed within the framework of a customer-based approach to branding. Consumer-based brand performance measures can be broadly grouped into five principal categories: awareness, associations (i.e., image and beliefs), attitudes, attachment (i.e., loyalty) and activity (e.g., purchase, consumption, word of mouth), as suggested by Aaker (1996), Keller (2008) and Keller and Lehmann (2003). Keller and Lehmann (2006) further developed a conceptual model of the *brand value chain*, linking marketing programmes supporting building the brand, with the shareholder value. Marketing campaigns impact consumer mindset (awareness, attitude, propensity to purchase), which (under favourable marketplace conditions) turn into customer behaviour, influencing such performance outcomes like price premiums, market share, profitability and the like (see Figure 27.1). Those, in turn, are the foundation for shareholder value (Figure 27.1).

Evidence-Based Marketing

Evidence-based marketing operates within the broader concept of evidence-based practice, where business practice is supported by knowledge about market and business performance, emerging from the research (Rowley, 2012). Evidence-based marketing has been defined as marketing activities in which decisions are based on what currently constitutes the best, most reliable, and generalisable knowledge about how the world works, how consumers

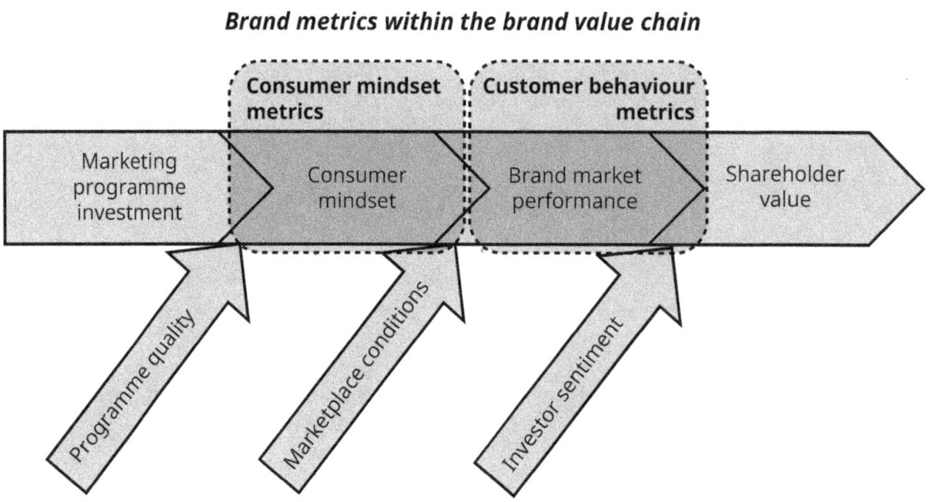

Figure 27.1 Brand metrics within the brand value chain

Source: Own based on Keller & Lehmann, 2006.

buy and how market interventions work, supported by the evidence and data relating to specific market situations (Sharp, 2019). Evidence-based marketing is primarily credited with the identification and propagation of several 'laws' related to the market and consumer behaviour, including double jeopardy, natural monopoly, buyer moderation and duplication of purchase, among others.

While researchers tend to focus on relationships between metrics and economic performance, practitioners suggest specific metrics for managers. Accordingly, numerous authors of publications have indicated that a variety of metrics are considered to be ideal for measuring brand health (Ambler, 2003; Davis, 2000; Marr, 2012). Typically, this includes brand awareness, penetration and loyalty, among others. The necessity for selecting metrics that correspond to specific business models is hereby underscored.

CONSUMER-MINDSET AND CUSTOMER-BEHAVIOUR METRICS

The proposed approach constitutes a simplification of Katsikeas et al. (2016) proposal. 'Customer mindset' effects influence customer behaviour (their acquisition and retention, but also non-purchase behaviour, such as brand recommendations), which in turn translates into 'product-market performance' (e.g., market share) and 'customer-level performance' (e.g., share-of-wallet (SOW) or lifetime value). Product-market performance impacts on 'accounting performance' (e.g., profit, margin), which in turn impacts 'financial-market performance' (e.g., investor returns). However elaborate the proposal is, it lacks key brand metrics such as e.g., penetration. As our focus is on brands, this proposal has been modified accordingly. With reference to the proposed model, brand metrics are divided into two categories:

1. Documenting behaviour (purchase), thus are called *'Customer-Behaviour Metrics' (CBMs)*, in which brand buyers' preferences are directly (through the purchase of a particular brand) revealed.
2. Exploring knowledge, perception and intentions regarding brands, which might be called the *'Consumer-Mindset Metrics*[1] (CMMs), in which their preferences are forthrightly revealed or can be deduced from.

It may be useful to organise brand metrics by assigning them to specific stages of the customer journey. Customer journey is a schematic representation of the process related to a brand that a consumer/customer goes through: from not being aware of it, to becoming its advocate. There are dozens of models of customer journey in the literature. Considering the possibility of measuring the mindset of consumers and customers' behaviour, six stages of the journey might be identified: Awareness – Consideration – Purchase – Satisfaction – Loyalty – Advocacy (see Figure 27.2).

In the context of brand management, CBMs have been shown to play a pivotal role in the reliable assessment of brand strength. While these metrics may lack the illustrative appeal of reports derived from brand image research and do not offer direct, actionable insights for addressing specific brand deficiencies (e.g., insufficient availability or low popularity among category buyers), they nonetheless provide clear guidance on prioritising strategic objectives. CBMs assess the outcomes of past customer acquisition and retention efforts, whereas CMMs are primarily employed to forecast the future health of a brand. Of all brand metrics, its market share is probably the most important in terms of analysing the brand's competitive standing, as only relating the brand's sales to the outcomes of all category suppliers gives a definite answer on how well the brand performs. Managers may sometimes overlook metrics that exhibit minimal short-term variability, despite their critical importance to a brand's profitability and long-term sustainability (Binet & Carter, 2018; Kantar, 2021). For instance, a mere 40% of companies surveyed by Deloitte (The CMO Survey, 2021) assert that they evaluate market share solely 'when needed' or never. However, it is the market share, and not brand sales, that constitutes the only reliable basis for strategic recommendations regarding future brand-building activities. Among other reasons why market share is more instructive than sales is that the latter tend to fluctuate constantly (month-on-month; quarter-on-quarter), while market share has a propensity to be fairly stable (at least, in the short term), which gives a better approximation of the brand's actual market standing.

CMMs are numerical indicators depicting category buyers' knowledge and attitudes towards the brand that may lead to a purchase and also declared evaluations of brand users. Srinivasan et al. (2010) found that CMM accounts for a third of the total explained variance in sales and may serve as valuable early warning signs of changes in market performance. And yet, an improvement in attitude

[1] The use of the term 'consumer' instead of 'customer' is deliberate, as these metrics refer to all category buyers, not just brand customers.

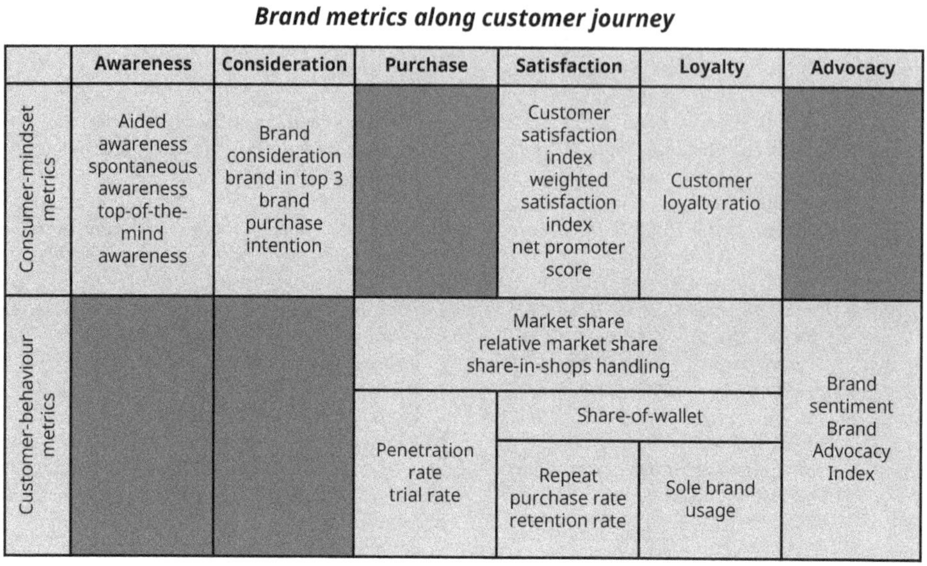

Figure 27.2 Brand metrics along customer journey

Source: The author.

does not necessarily translate into increased brand sales (Lalaounis, 2021), which once again underlines the importance of analysing CBM. While CBMs are based on actual sales, CMMs are based on respondents' declarations as revealed in surveys and are inherently subject to greater errors and noise.

BEFORE THE PURCHASE

Brand Awareness

Brand awareness is imperative for conscious brand selection, as sales can be driven by web search rankings, low price or pure convenience, with the buyer potentially being unaware of the brand. It is imperative for brands to achieve a level of consumer awareness that is sufficient to ensure their products or services are considered when making purchasing decisions. It is imperative that customers are cognizant of a brand's existence, its potential to address their needs, and its ability to deliver the promised benefits. Brand awareness is referred to as the buyer's ability to recognise a brand by seeing it on a shop shelf or website, or recall it from memory, sufficiently to make a purchase.

Aided (or prompted) awareness measures brand recognition and is the percentage of surveyed category buyers, who declare they have heard about the brand shown on a list. Many brands easily achieve scores of more than 80% or 90%. Should a negligible proportion of respondents indicate recognition of a particular brand, it is improbable that the brand exerts a substantial influence on purchase decisions.

Spontaneous (or unaided) awareness measures brand recall and is the percentage of surveyed category buyers who can retrieve the brand name from memory to the stimulus of the product category question. Only really strong brands achieve brand recall scores above 70%–80%, which is due to the low motivation to remember all brands within a category. Spontaneous awareness of a brand is usually 30–60 percentage points lower than assisted one. A strong correlation exists between brand awareness and brand trial, and in case of consumer-packaged goods, between spontaneous awareness and the brand's market share (Kall, 2021). The lower the involvement in a category purchase – due to the product being less important to the buyer and associated with relatively lower risk – the less motivated the buyer is to actively seek information beyond her/his memory (Stasiuk & Maison, 2014). In such a situation, if the brand is easily recalled, it has a greater chance of being selected, as the consumer is not stimulated to look around for alternatives.

A strong brand relationship is evidenced by the *top-of-the-mind awareness (TOMA)*, that is, the percentage of category buyers mentioning a particular brand as the first, when asked about brands recalled within a category. A brand is considered a favourite, the most frequently purchased, the most desired or the best in its category. Conversely, an obscure, minor or insignificant brand is unlikely to be mentioned as a top-of-mind choice. Brands with high market shares, and also high spontaneous awareness, differ significantly in terms of their TOMA indices (Romaniuk et al., 2004). Contrary to spontaneous awareness, it is not feasible for numerous brands to obtain figures in the order of a few tens of percentage points each for the TOMA. Consequently, while a high assisted awareness does not ensure a strong market position for a brand, a significant advantage in TOMA most likely signifies greater popularity (penetration) and/or a more favourable opinion.

Brand Consideration

In the context of substantial purchases and business-to-business (B2B) markets, brand consideration has the potential to supersede comprehensive brand image analyses. This signifies the brand's capacity to satisfy customers' needs and preferences. Brand consideration represents the proportion of category buyers aware of a particular brand, willing to contemplate purchasing that brand. It is typically gauged on a 5-point scale, known as the 'consideration scale': 'I would: definitely – rather – rather not – never consider buying this brand' (with the option 'Don't know/ Hard to say'). Alternatively, the '*brand in top 3*' metric reflects the percentage of category buyers aware of a particular brand, who state they would include a brand among the three brands most likely to be considered in the decision-making process. In the examination of hundreds of campaigns, it is the brand consideration that has emerged as the most influential factor in base sales, in two-thirds of cases. Typically, a one percentage point rise in brand consideration led to a 0.5–1.5 percentage increase in base sales (Ebiquity and Gain Theory, 2018). Many researchers have proved a strong correlation between brand awareness and brand consideration (Bergkvist & Taylor, 2022), while Mecredy et al. (2021) have demonstrated that brands with low awareness are 'doubly punished', with lower unaided brand recall, and lower purchase consideration.

Brand Purchase Intention

Brand purchase intention represents the percentage of category buyers aware of the brand, who state their intention to purchase a specific brand on their next purchase. It is calculated based on responses to the question, 'How likely is it that the next time you purchase... (what? for whom? at which store? in what context of use?), you will choose brand X?' Respondents use an 11-point scale proposed by Juster (East et al., 2008), ranging from 0 'no chance, almost no chance' to 10 'certain, practically certain'. Conclusions can be drawn about the brand's potential for high sales by comparing the metric with the competition. Brand purchase intention often serves as a more reliable predictor of future performance compared to the straightforward extrapolation of historical sales trends (Armstrong et al., 2000).

PURCHASE AND MARKET SHARE

Market share importance has been proved by the seminal paper by Buzzell et al. (1975). According to Boston Consulting Group, by doubling production output, companies used to achieve a 10%–15% decrease in costs. In the markets where economies of scale operate, higher market share reduces the unit costs and thus translates into higher profitability (Bendle & Bagga, 2016). Szymanski et al. (1993) meta-analysis also proved a positive correlation between a company's market share and its profits. According to Morgan and Rego (2009), the strong, positive relationship between relative market share and firms' Tobin's q as well as cash flow performance, suggests that, despite past debates, market share remains a valuable metric for evaluating marketing effectiveness. Furthermore, Edeling and Himme (2018) proved the impact of market share on profits, claiming that it is more pronounced in the case of manufactured goods, than in services, and is stronger for business-to-consumer (B2C) than for B2B industries. Apart from impact on profits, higher market share often leads to higher customer retention and satisfaction (O'Regan, 2002). On the other hand, Porter (1998) showed that also small (in terms of market share) brands, focusing on niches and providing customers with tailored-made offers can be highly profitable. Surprisingly, Boston Consulting Group claimed in subsequent publications that the probability of the market leader being also the most profitable brand in the category is close to zero (Reeves et al., 2014).

Market share (100 * brand sales in volume or value/total category sales, by volume or value) should be calculated based on actual sales to end users rather than intermediaries. For value market share calculations, it is essential to use transaction prices rather than list prices. Similarly, for volume market share, issues related to package comparability must be addressed by converting the number of items sold into their corresponding tonnage. It is imperative to establish precise definitions for the market, encompassing both the product dimension and the geographic dimension.

Half of the leading consumer packaged goods' (CPG) brands have volume market share between 10% and 30% (Europanel, 2020); with the average close to 29%, which is a little bit more than double the share of brand number 2, which in turn has a share twice that of the number 3 brand (Europanel, 2024a). In the case of some industrial goods, especially those in which the manufacturing process is extremely complex (e.g., photolithographic machines), the share of the leading supplier exceeds 60%, reaching in some cases even 90%. On the other hand, there are quite numerous examples of fragmented markets, where a few leading brands have similar market shares, in the range of 5%–10% each.

It follows that, to reliably assess a brand's position, it is necessary (as emphasised by Cooper & Nakanishi, 1988) to relate its market share to that of the leader (or, in the case of leaders, to the runner-up). *Relative market share* (sales in value or volume of a given brand/sales of the leading brand, or the brand being compared to, in value or volume), if close to 0, indicates plainly how weak the examined brand is. And the more relative market share exceeds 1, the larger the leader's advantage over its closest competitors. Analysis of a brand's relative market share over time allows a reliable assessment of whether the brand is weakening or strengthening. Bhattacharya et al. (2022) demonstrated that relative value market share is extremely useful in predicting profits, especially when referring to the three leading brands, not just the leader alone (particularly in the case of B2C service and B2B products brands).

The process of increasing a brand's market share is invariably a protracted one. According to Europanel (2023), over two-thirds of large and medium-sized CPG brands demonstrated stable market shares, exhibiting a change of no more than 0.2 percentage points between 2018 and 2021. If large brands lose their market share, it is usually due to their own mistakes, unforeseen major changes in the macro-environment (today, mainly technological), or the emergence of strong competitor/s with very attractive offer/s for customers, or a disruptive innovation.

Irrespective of the significance of achieving a high market share, it is not economically rational to pursue this objective through means such as protracted price reductions or unsustainable communication budgets (Reynolds & Phillips, 2005). Furthermore, there is no economic advantage in achieving a high market share in declining categories (Davis, 2018), where some companies, having obtained detailed market intelligence, withdraw from rivalry, leaving the market to be shared by the remaining competitors (whose market shares naturally increase).

Components of Market Share

From the perspective of buyers' behaviour, volume market share is the product of penetration rate, SOW and heavy usage index (Parfitt & Collins, 1968), and in the case of value market share, the above product must be multiplied by price index.

Heavy usage index

Heavy usage index (the number of product packages purchased by the average brand buyer/the number of product packages purchased by the average category buyer) typically hovers around a value of one. In practice, for brands with the largest market shares, their value tends to be slightly above one (around 1.1), whereas most brands have heavy usage indices slightly below one (approximately 0.9–0.95; Kall, 2021).

Price index

Brand's price index (100 * average retail price of a brand/average retail price of all brands in the category) provides an insight into how a brand's retail price compares to the average retail price across all brands within a category. A brand with a price index greater than 100 has its value market share higher than its volume market share (and vice versa). Consequently, both prestigious and economy brands can exhibit volume market shares significantly deviating from their value shares.

Penetration rate

Penetration rate (100 * number of brand buyers, even if only one-off/number of category buyers) is a measure of a brand's popularity among category buyers. The optimal source for computing brand penetration is panel research, but it can also be figured out from surveys, the results of which are subject to errors, due to the fleeting memory of respondents. Penetration does not increase in proportion to the extension of the period of analysis (e.g., from half a year to a year) because of the 'glass ceiling', which is becoming increasingly apparent. Every brand has a fraction of customers who have negative attitude towards it (disappointed buyers from the past, or category buyers who heard negative opinions about it), as well as category buyers who either have not heard of the brand, or cannot buy it (price barrier or availability problems), or consumers who are 100% loyal to other brands. Initially, an increase in brand penetration in subsequent periods is achieved through increasing its familiarity and accessibility; in the long term, penetration growth depends mainly on retaining as many trialists as possible. The category of non-buyers ends up comprising mainly lost customers and those fully loyal to other brands, and it is reasonable to expect this segment to amount to no less than a dozen to twenty-something per cent of all category buyers. That is why leading brands achieve yearly penetration rates exceeding 50%–60%, or even more. Small brands struggle to achieve a penetration of 5%–10%, and for the new brand to build a strong market position, it needs to reach at least 15% yearly penetration (Vishwanath et al., 2014). Penetration depends on two metrics: trial rate and repeat-purchase rate. Newly launched brands, to increase their penetration, in the first place need to increase their trial rate.

Trial rate

Trial rate is the percentage of category buyers who bought a particular brand for the first time, over a certain period. Reaching out to more and more category buyers is facilitated by their natural curiosity and openness to novelty. Trial depends in the first place on making the new brand widely available for buyers (Singh & Wright, 2016), as well as ensuring its recognition and initial interest in trying it out. Trial rate growth is hindered by the equally natural inertia of buyers (tendency to return to brands they already know well), by the marketing activities of competitors and, in the case of big-ticket items, by the high level of risk resulting from the high price. As a result, nowadays getting a trial rate of 10% in the first twelve months of market presence is very difficult. High trial rate is evidence of successful customer acquisition. As a result of trying out a new brand, a significant (if not dominant) proportion of trialists decide to return to it, and as the share of available first-time buyers starts to deplete over time, it is *the repeat-purchase rate* (see: 'After the purchase') that becomes crucial for future increase of penetration.

SOW (or share-of-requirements)

SOW (100 * brand purchases in volume or value/ category purchases made by brand buyers, in volume or value) is an explicit measure of customer satisfaction and brand loyalty/attachment, in the context of typical tendency of customers to use several brands within a category (Ehrenberg, 1998; Romaniuk & Sharp, 2022). If not estimated based on consumer panels, SOW can be roughly calculated if the results of buyers' survey managed to determine how many brands they buy on average within a given category, and which place in the ranking the brand occupies (Keiningham et al., 2011): [1 – rank of a brand in the repertoire/ (number of brands purchased + 1)] * (2/number of brands purchased). In 90% of cases, that estimate is pretty close to the actual value.

When a new brand enters the market, its SOW stabilises shortly after the launch. It is evident that brands which are poised to achieve market leadership, soon after launch, demonstrate a SOW which is similar to that of established market leaders. However, as the analysis period extends, a brand's SOW generally diminishes, due to the increased probability that consumers will opt for alternative brands within the category. Reasons for this switch can range from minor issues such as occasional availability problems, to choosing a different (than usual) store, perhaps due to factors like being on holidays.

A substantial increase in the brand's share of wallet must necessarily entail a concomitant decline in the SOW of competing brands. It is evident that elevating the SOW beyond the 50%–60% range would necessitate the elimination of an alternative brand from the repertoire, or a substantial alteration in customer preferences (induced by a notable price reduction, enhanced accessibility or a shift in brand perception), and/or satisfaction levels. The question remains as to how achievable this is, in a situation where competing brands are often perceived as offering similar utility.

SOW depends not only on category buyers' preferences and satisfaction provided by brands used, but also average number of brands purchased in the category by the typical buyer. Buyers may prefer purchasing a few brands over loyalty to the only one because of (East et al., 2008): convenience (easier shopping), seeking variety, an urge to be independent of price pressure (choosing from the repertoire the cheapest brand available), or the belief that different brands are perfect for different occasions.

The variation in SOW scores among brands in the same category is not as strong as differences in their penetration rates (Jones, 1998). The explanation for this phenomenon is relatively straightforward. SOW is influenced by three factors: the relative frequency of brand purchases (within a specified timeframe) and the relative number and size of packages purchased per shopping trip. It is evident that competing brands in the category typically offer packages of similar sizes. Furthermore, the mean number of packages purchased per shopping trip tends to be consistent across brands.

Consequently, disparities in SOW values primarily stem from variations in the frequency of brand purchases over an analysed period of time. Given that CPGs are typically purchased between one and twelve times per year (with an average of six purchases, according to Sharp, 2019), the SOW of the least frequently purchased brand within a repertoire is unlikely to fall below 10%, while that of the most frequently purchased brand rarely exceeds 50%. Average SOW for foodstuff brands is around 30% (East et al., 2008), while leading CPG brands reach SOW of 60% (Europanel, 2024b). In practice, the most significant disparities in brands' SOW scores within a category are ordinarily no greater than two-to-threefold. However, discrepancies in their penetration rates can reach levels 30–50 times higher, and in some cases, even greater.

Also in the context of infrequently purchased goods, brand penetration has been demonstrated to be a critical determinant of a brand's market share (Baldinger et al., 2002; Romaniuk et al., 2018). This is due to the fact that the SOW among competing brands within a given category is usually very similar and approaches 100%. To illustrate this point, consider the example of consumers who purchase a smartphone or automobile of a specific brand in any given year. The vast majority of these buyers purchase only a single unit of the product, resulting in an SOW of 100% for that brand. A small proportion of customers may purchase two items, probably from different brands, marginally reducing the SOW to just below 100%. Consequently, the sole metric that accounts for variations in market share across brands is their respective penetration rates.

It is important to recognise that *smaller brands typically face a double disadvantage: they tend to have lower penetration, and at the same time smaller than leaders SOW*. This is referred to as the *double jeopardy law* (Ehrenberg & Goodhardt, 2002). This occurs because those few buyers who purchase smaller brands often also include larger, more established brands in their repertoire. It naturally results in smaller brands having a lower SOW. However, the reverse is not true: consumers who primarily buy market leaders rarely feel compelled to purchase smaller brands. For the largest brands in a category, the opposite phenomenon occurs: both their penetration and their SOW are higher, compared to their rivals (Sharp, 2019).

The double-jeopardy law, as evidenced in CPG markets, serves as a foundational principle upon which evidence-based marketing strategies can be formulated. This principle provides a clear strategic recommendation for smaller brands, namely to prioritise increasing brand penetration. This focus stems from the natural consumer behaviour of purchasing a limited selection of brands within a category, with the position of each brand in the buyer's purchase hierarchy being primarily influenced by individual preferences. This tendency is evidenced by the observation that smaller brands typically exhibit lower SOW compared to market leaders. Consequently, for smaller brands, enhancing popularity among category buyers is of greater strategic importance than attempting to cultivate loyalty – a perspective that contrasts sharply with the emphasis on loyalty promotion commonly advocated in traditional marketing textbooks.

For a CPG brand, at least as important as CBMs are those relating to brand's availability. Especially that there is strong evidence of much greater impact on sales and market share, of increase in distribution, compared with an increase in communication or promotional budgets (Ataman et al., 2010; Wilbur & Farris, 2014). From the perspective of a brand's availability, its market share is the product of the brand's weighted distribution and its share in shops handling.

Weighted distribution

Weighted distribution (100 * category sales in volume or value, in stores carrying the brand/total category sales), also referred to as 'product category volume distribution', indicates the percentage of category sales attributed to points-of-sale carrying the brand. Therefore, weighted distribution measures a brand's availability in the most important outlets and indicates the maximum market share that a brand can achieve. Research (Jones & Slater, 2003) suggests that a new brand gaining customer acceptance usually achieves 70% weighted distribution within the first 8 months, demonstrating its availability in all major retail chains.

Share-in-shops handling

Share-in-shops handling (SISH) (100 * brand sales, in volume or value, in stores carrying the brand/category sales in stores carrying the brand, in volume or value), called also 'share in handlers', indicates the demand for a brand at points-of-sale where it is available. SISH can be considered as an indicator of shoppers' interest in a brand, as well as the effectiveness of the brand's merchandising, independent of the brand's availability. SISH is directly dependent on the number of brands within a category offered on shops' shelves, including private labels. In certain retail chains (predominantly discounters, though also supermarkets), private labels can account for up to 50% of category sales. Consequently, even the most successful of the remaining manufacturers' brands have SISH that rarely exceeds 20%–25%.

For newly introduced brands, SISH holds some predictive value: relatively high SISH, despite the brand's low availability, suggests that increasing weighted distribution could lead to a substantial increase in the market share. Conversely, a low SISH for a new brand may indicate either low customer appeal or the selection of an inappropriate distribution channel (store format). Initially, the market share of a newly launched brand typically rises due to an increase in numeric and weighted distribution. However, as a brand's availability improves, the importance of SISH is growing (Jones & Slater, 2003).

AFTER THE PURCHASE

Satisfaction

Satisfaction verifies whether brand promises have been delivered and is crucial for repeat purchases. Satisfaction is defined as an emotional reaction that occurs when customers compare their brand experience with their expectations. The experience is deemed satisfactory if it surpasses (or at the very least, matches) these expectations. It is important to note that satisfaction is a subjective experience and not based on the objective (as stated by experts) quality of a product or service. The concept of overall satisfaction is derived from the comprehensive brand experience, whereas partial satisfaction is associated with discrete stages of the purchase or specific attributes of the offer. The concept of current satisfaction pertains to the most recent purchase or consumption episode, whereas cumulative satisfaction encompasses long-term brand experiences. Ideally, satisfaction should be measured among typical (not 'heavy') users of a brand, as they often purchase multiple brands in the category and can provide a comparative perspective, rendering their opinions potentially the most 'objective' (Kall, 2021). Conversely, heavy users (i.e., the top 20% of consumers) account for half of brand consumption (Romaniuk & Sharp, 2022), yet, due to their exclusive engagement with a single brand, they are unable to provide a comparative perspective. It can be hypothesised that their satisfaction is high; otherwise, they would have switched brands.

The Customer Satisfaction Index

The Customer Satisfaction Index (CSI) represents the overall evaluation of a brand, based on attributes important to customers, without considering the varying importance of these attributes. A scale should be used (e.g., 1 to 5, –3 to +3, or 'very dissatisfied – rather dissatisfied – neither satisfied nor dissatisfied – rather satisfied – very satisfied'), ensuring an odd number of options, to include a neutral middle rating. In lieu of a focus on the 'top 2 boxes' as is customary in the practices of research companies (and suggested by Bendle et al., 2016, among others), the consideration of the mean should be incorporated into the analysis. Given the predominance of courteous customers, an average rating of 3.3–3.5 on a 5-point scale can be regarded as an 'average brand's' rating (Kall, 2021). More reliable is *The Weighted Satisfaction Index* (WSI), which is the overall evaluation of a brand based on attributes important to customers, accounting for the varying significance of these attributes to the customers (ratings are weighted by the importance of each attribute). While it is accepted that WSI is a good predictor of a brand's future economic health (Kall, 2021), it is important to remember that customer satisfaction surveys of different brands, with large and small market shares, do not reveal significant differences in their CSI nor WSI (Sharp et al., 2024). Rego et al. (2013) found: (1) typically negative relationship between market share and customer satisfaction (heterogeneity being the key explanation for that) and (2) that this negative relationship arises from the significant negative impact of a firm's current market share on its future ability to satisfy customers. Keiningham et al. (2015) demonstrated that relative ranked satisfaction is a superior indicator of brand's SOW, than absolute satisfaction.

Net Promoter Score

Net Promoter Score (NPS) is a straightforward measure of customer satisfaction, which is employed by approximately two-thirds of Fortune 1000 companies. It is determined by asking a question: 'How likely are you to recommend our brand/product/service to a friend or colleague?' Responses are given on an 11-point scale, from 'very unlikely' (0) to 'very likely' (10). NPS is calculated as the percentage of scores 9 and 10 (promoters) minus the percentage of scores 0–6 (detractors). Unfortunately, NPS fails to predict future economic health of the brand (Kall, 2021).

CBMs used for analysing satisfaction are: repeat purchase rate and retention rate.

Repeat Purchase Rate

Repeat purchase rate (a.k.a. repurchase rate) is calculated in three different ways, as the quotient of the number of brand buyers (in case of frequently purchased goods, over a period of a half a year or a year, and in case of infrequently purchased goods, in the purchase episode 'n'), divided by: (1) buyers of the brand in purchase episode 'n – 1' (for high ticket items, purchased every few years), (2) buyers who tried the brand for the first time in the period 'n – 1' or (3) brand buyers from any of the previous periods or purchase episodes. Over time, the repeat purchase rate tends to stabilise at a higher level than initially, because in the first phase of a new brand's presence on the market, consumer attitudes to and evaluation of the new brand, have not yet crystallised. Repeat purchase is a confirmation of the satisfaction provided by all customer touchpoints, but in particular by the product/service itself. Yet high repeat purchase rates may also result from the lack of alternatives (the only service provider in a small town), or barriers prohibiting brand change (in case of contract signed or subscription services), in which case, the proper metric of retaining customers is the retention rate.

Retention Rate

Retention rate (100 * number of customers who decided to prolong the subscription or membership/number of brand customers with the contract ending[2]) is the measure of efficacy of retention activities. Retention rates for service brands based on a subscription range from 80% to 96% (East et al., 2008). Defection of a small percentage of customers is quite natural, as some of them move to places where the brand is unavailable, or lose interest in the service as such, or simply pass away.

Loyalty

Loyalty is derived from customer satisfaction and engenders a deeper engagement between the consumer and the brand. Loyalty is widely recognised in the academic literature as a mixture of repeat purchases of a brand and a positive attitude towards it. It has been presented by numerous publications and consultants as the ultimate goal of marketing. The intricacies inherent in this construct, however, render it a formidable challenge to quantify. Simple way to measure it is to use the Customer Loyalty Ratio. *Customer Loyalty Ratio* measures the percentage of brand buyers who intend to purchase the brand again. It is based on survey responses using a scale from 'I will definitely buy this brand again' to 'I will certainly not buy it' (with 'it is difficult to say' included). The metrics are calculated as follows: Standard Loyalty Ratio is 100 multiplied by the number of 'I will definitely buy' plus 'I would rather buy' answers, divided by total brand buyers surveyed and Enhanced Loyalty Ratio equals 100 multiplied by 'I will definitely buy', divided by total brand buyers surveyed. Loyalty ratios tend to be higher for high-involvement services like banks and insurance, and lower for CPG.

An alternative way to measure loyalty is to use one CBM, namely 'sole brand usage'. *Sole brand users* (SBUs) are those of the brand buyers who purchase within a particular category only one brand (in their case, the brand's SOW equals 100). As Ehrenberg's *law of buying frequencies* demonstrates, the distribution of product purchase frequencies is left-skewed – each product has a majority of one-time (occasional) buyers and a very small percentage of heavy buyers (Romaniuk & Sharp, 2022). When analysing shorter periods (i.e., a month), a high percentage of SBU may be explained by a limited number of purchase occasions. Those consumers who make a single purchase are, by definition, 'SBUs', which does not accurately reflect the nature of their relationship with the brand. As the time period under analysis increases, the percentage of SBU tends to decrease, as consumers have more opportunities to explore other brands. In categories where purchases are frequent, the percentage of SBU is typically low – in CPG, SBUs usually constitute between a few and several percent of the brand buyers (Sharp, 2019). A relatively high number of SBU can stem from either strong satisfaction and loyalty, limited access to alternative options or a natural tendency of sticking to one brand within a category (e.g., gas, electricity) at a time. Also, market leaders often have a higher (sometimes even two times higher than smaller brands) proportion of SBU, though exceptions exist. For example, private labels, despite their smaller market shares, attract a disproportionately high number of exclusive users (as they stick to their favourite retailer).

Advocacy

Advocacy is characterised by a consumer's recommendation of a brand to others, based on their conviction of its superiority. The critical influence

[2] The calculation of the retention rate by dividing the number of a brand's customers at the end of the year by the number of customers at the beginning of the year, as proposed by Davis (2018), is an erroneous approach. This method conflates the retention of existing customers with the acquisition of new ones, thereby failing to isolate the metric's intended focus.

of other customers' opinions on the buyer's decision-making process is widely acknowledged, rendering the necessity of citing sources that argue otherwise seemingly redundant, given the apparent paucity of such research. Nevertheless, this acknowledgement does not imply that the relative significance of volume and valence of the opinions, whether conveyed through offline or online channels, has been definitively established. Meta-analyses by You et al. (2015) and by Floyd et al. (2014) demonstrated that online opinions' sentiment is supposed to be nearly twice as impactful as their volume. Another meta-analysis carried out by Babić et al. (2016) indicates that the volume has a stronger impact on sales than opinions' valence. What is more, in about two-thirds of cases, elasticities were below average, while You et al. (2015) proved that half of volume sales elasticities were below 0.1% (or even negative). In the case of sales elasticities related to the valence of online opinions, over one-third exhibited a negative relationship, indicating that more favourable sentiment was paradoxically associated with lower brand sales. In practice, companies tend to analyse the *volume* of brand opinions more often than their sentiment. Social media *sentiment* measures how customers discuss a brand online by calculating the difference between the percentage of positive and negative posts.

The Brand Advocacy Index

The Brand Advocacy Index (BAI), introduced by the Boston Consulting Group, measures the sentiment based on two assumptions: spontaneous opinions are twice as important as solicited ones, and critical opinions are twice as important as positive ones. BAI equals the percentage of spontaneous positive recommendations plus 0.5 * percentage of solicited positive recommendations minus (2 * percentage of spontaneous critical opinions plus percentage of solicited critical opinions). BAI thus ranges from −200 (all negative, spontaneous opinions) to +100 (all positive, spontaneous opinions). BCG's research shows a strong correlation (Pearson's value of 81%) between BAI and revenue growth (Esquivivas et al., 2013).

Finally, it is important to acknowledge that identifying a strong correlation between opinions and sales does not clarify the direction of causality. Specifically, it remains uncertain whether increased brand sales result from a growing number of opinions and/or a predominance of positive sentiment, or whether rising sales drive an increase in the volume of opinions, with positive sentiment prevailing due to general buyer satisfaction. Both directions of influence are equally plausible.

MANAGERIAL IMPLICATIONS

CMMs are employed to assess a brand's current market position (by comparing relevant metrics with the values obtained by competitors) and to predict future market performance (by analysing changes in relevant metrics over time). Furthermore, they can be utilised to evaluate the effectiveness of marketing campaigns, whether those campaigns are aimed at acquiring new customers (by impacting brand awareness, consideration and advocacy) or at improving the retention of existing customers (influencing satisfaction, loyalty, advocacy).

CBMs have the potential to inform the design of strategies for further brand development. For market leaders, the most significant metric is the brand's relative market share, which indicates the scale of its competitive advantage. A detailed analysis of the components of market share is essential for challengers to identify the pivotal tasks confronting their brand. These challenges may pertain to the necessity of enhancing the brand's popularity among category buyers, characterised by insufficient market penetration, or to fortifying brand loyalty among existing customers, characterised by a low SOW. Alternatively, the brand may need to address issues related to enhancing availability at crucial points of sale, characterised by a weighted distribution that is too low, or to stimulate heightened interest in the brand among shoppers, characterised by a share-in-shops-handling that is too low. For smaller brands, the analysis of market share yields limited practical insights; instead, their owners should prioritise metrics such as trial rate and penetration rate to assess potential market share growth. Additionally, brand managers should monitor weighted distribution to ensure sufficient brand availability, share-in-shop-handling to evaluate point-of-sale performance and SOW as a measure of customer loyalty.

In determining the most suitable brand metrics for utilisation, brand managers must consider the following factors: (1) relevance to marketing goals and business model, (2) actionability (providing insights that can lead to specific actions or strategies), (3) consistency over time (being stable enough to track progress over extended periods), (4) comparability (allowing for comparisons with competitors, industry benchmarks or past performance) and (5) cost-effectiveness (cost of gathering and analysing the data should be justified by the value of the insights gained). It is recommended that brand managers avoid an exclusive focus on CMMs, despite their relative ease of acquisition from research suppliers. It is recommended that managers examine the causal relationships between brand metrics and financial outcomes, with a view to mitigating the risk of brand decisions that are not aligned with long-term strategic objectives.

LIMITATIONS AND SUGGESTIONS FOR FUTURE RESEARCH

The issues concerning metrics pertain to consumer-mindset rather than customer-behaviour ones, a consequence of the limited depth of information obtainable from respondents in structured interviews applied to measure consumers' feelings, attitudes or emotions.

It should be noted that attitude measurement is subject to a number of limitations. Firstly, it is more important which brands spring to buyers' minds, when they consider buying a particular product, rather than what they think of individual brands (Romaniuk & Sharp, 2022). According to Sharp (2019), brand attitudes are probabilistic in nature, as evidenced by the finding that surveys conducted on the same sample demonstrate that only half of the respondents maintain a consistent attitude towards a particular brand. It has been observed that respondents frequently remain unaware of their sentiments towards a brand until they are prompted by a survey. In introspective methods, such as surveys, which are the standard in attitude measurement, consumers readily respond when asked about trivial matters, such as brand attitudes (Evans, 2017), and they 'make up' their opinions when asked to comment on brands with which they are not familiar (Dolnicar & Rossiter, 2008). Additionally, consumer mood can significantly influence brand evaluation (Stasiuk & Maison, 2014). Furthermore, researchers have noted a growing recognition among the academic community that consumers frequently lack awareness regarding the origins of their attitudes, which can be implicit yet influence their purchasing decisions. Consequently, there has been a discernible shift from introspective methods, such as surveys, towards indirect approaches that involve analysing reaction time (Stasiuk & Maison, 2014).

A multitude of issues have been identified as stemming from the utilisation of scales or ratings within survey instruments. The ambiguity of the scales is a factor in the level of noise observed. The interpretation of terms such as 'likely' or numerical ratings can vary significantly among respondents. Consequently, the utilisation of rankings as opposed to individual ratings is proposed as a superior alternative (Kahneman et al., 2022), given the reduced susceptibility of relative judgments to variability (noise) in comparison to absolute judgments. This is due to the human capacity for effective pairwise comparisons, whilst our aptitude for categorising objects on a fixed scale is more limited.

The analysis of brand health in academic publications frequently encompasses constructs that are intricate and ambiguous, such as 'loyalty'. Contrary to the pervasive recognition of brand loyalty as a pivotal factor in economic prosperity, Sharp (2019) challenges the very notion of loyalty in itself, attributing repeat brand purchases to a human tendency towards routine, rather than attributing it to the sophisticated efforts on the side of marketers. The reality of CPG markets is that the proportion of shoppers who purchase a single brand is very small, rarely exceeding 10%. Repeat purchases of a particular brand by a customer are indicative of convenience rather than a desire for a 'relationship' with the brand or exceptional loyalty (Sharp, 2019). Furthermore, the reliable investigation of loyalty extends beyond the simple question of customers' willingness to continue purchasing a particular brand.

In the domain of advocacy, it is imperative that metrics analysing the volume and sentiment of brand opinion encompass not only electronic word-of-mouth but also face-to-face conversations. Fay et al. (2019) conducted a longitudinal study tracking daily consumer discourse about products and brands alongside recorded purchases. The study found that only 9% of purchases were influenced solely by social media discussions, 10% by offline exchanges, and 80% by a combination of both, with online and offline interactions, varying between 60:40 and 40:60 impact on purchase decisions. Notably, face-to-face discussions impacted decisions more through conversation volume than sentiment, whereas on social media, sentiment was the primary factor. One major issue in sentiment analysis is that lexicographic method struggles with context-dependent adjectives (e.g., funny, lofty) that can be both positive and negative. Additionally, many customer opinions are neutral, and reviews often contain spelling errors, slang or sarcasm, complicating the analysis. A further challenge arises in the analysis of brand opinion volume, where issues of equivalence and comparability arise among the various forms of recommendations, such as verbal opinion versus product image (e.g., unboxing), detailed opinion versus simple 'I recommend' or 'I like it' statements and likes under posts versus self-written posts.

In addition to the indicated limitations in measuring brand health, four areas for further research are suggested as being the most fruitful:

1. Cross-disciplinary research which incorporates psychology, sociology and economics to refine brand metrics, for example, Rust et al. (2004) link brand equity to firm value and financial performance.
2. Longitudinal Brand Tracking examines brand metrics over time to identify trends and drivers of brand equity, crucial for understanding long-term impacts of strategic decisions.
3. Cross-Channel and Omnichannel Metrics assess brand performance across multiple touchpoints to ensure a seamless, integrated customer experience. Key research areas are: (a) Customer Journey Mapping – Lemon and Verhoef (2016) highlight the role of integrated metrics in omnichannel experiences, (b) Unified Measurement Frameworks – Neslin et al. (2006) propose methods for integrating cross-channel data, improving decision-making, (c) Attribution Modelling – enhancing accuracy in assigning brand impact across channels, especially in multi-touchpoint interactions.
4. AI in Brand Metrics revolutionises measurement through: (a) Real-Time Data Processing – AI-driven insights enhance predictive analytics (Huang & Rust, 2021; Timoshenko & Hauser, 2019), (b) Personalisation – AI enables individual-level brand metrics, refining segmentation and customer engagement (Davenport et al., 2020).

REFERENCES

Aaker, D. A. (1996). *Building strong brands*. The Free Press.

Aaker, D. A. (2004). *Brand portfolio strategy: Creating relevance, differentiation, energy, leverage, and clarity*. Free Press.

Ambler, T. (2003). *Marketing and the bottom line: The marketing metrics to pump up cash flow* (2nd ed.). Prentice Hall Financial Times.

Armstrong, J. S., Morwitz, V. G., & Kumar, V. (2000). Sales forecasts for existing consumer products and services: Do purchase intentions contribute to accuracy?. *International Journal of Forecasting*, *16*(3), 383–397. https://doi.org/10.1016/S0169-2070(00)00058-3

Ataman, M. B., Van Heerde, J. L., & Mela, C. F. (2010). The long-term effect of marketing strategy on brand sales. *Journal of Marketing Research*, *47*(5), 866–882. https://doi.org/10.1509/ jmkr.47.5.866

Babić R. A., Sotgiu, F., de Valck, K., & Bijmolt, T. H. A. (2016). The effect of electronic word of mouth on sales: A meta-analytic review of platform, product, and metric factors. *Journal of Marketing Research*, *53*(3), 297–318. https://doi.org/10.1509/ jmr.14.0380

Baldinger, A. L., Blair, E., & Echambadi, R. (2002). Why brands grow? *Journal of Marketing Research*, *42*(1), 7–14. https://doi.org/10.2501/JAR-42-1-6-14

Bendle, N. T., & Bagga, C. K. (2016). The metrics that marketers muddle. *MIT Sloan Management Review*, *57*(3), 73–82.

Bendle, N. T., Farris, P. W., Pfeifer, P. E., & Reibstein, D. J. (2016). *Marketing metrics: The manager's guide to measuring marketing performance* (3rd ed.). Pearson Education.

Bergkvist, L., & Taylor, C. R. (2022). Reviving and improving brand awareness as a construct in advertising research. *Journal of Advertising*, *51*(3), 294–307. https://doi.org/10.1080/0091 3367.2022.2039886

Bhattacharya, A., Morgan, N. A., & Rego, L. L. (2022). Examining why and when market share drives firm profit. *Journal of Marketing*, *86*(4), 73–94. https://doi.org/10.1177/00222429211. 031922.

Binet, L., & Carter, S. (2018). *How not to plan – 66 ways to screw it up*. APG Ltd. Matador.

Binet, L., & Field, P. (2007). *Marketing in the era of accountability: Identifying the marketing practices and metrics that truly increase profitability*. WARC.

Buzzell, R. D., Gale, B. T., & Sultan, G. M. (1975, January/February). Market share – a key to profitability. *Harvard Business Review*, *53*(1), 97–107.

The CMO Survey. (2021). *Managing and measuring marketing spending for growth and returns – highlights and insights report*. Duke University's Fuqua School of Business and American Marketing Association.

Cooper, L. G., & Nakanishi, N. (1988). *Market-share analysis: Evaluating competitive marketing effectiveness*. Kluwer Academic Publishers.

Davenport, T., Guha, A., Grewal, D., & Bressgott, T. (2020). How artificial intelligence will change the future of marketing. *Journal of the Academy of Marketing Science*, *48*(1), 24–42. https://doi.org/10.1007/s11747-019-00696-0

Davis, S. M. (2000). *Brand asset management: Driving profitable growth through your brands*. Jossey Bass Wiley.

Davis, J. A. (2018). *Measuring marketing – the 100+ essential metrics every marketer needs* (3rd ed.). Walter de Gruyter Inc.

Dolnicar, S., & Rossiter, J. (2008). The low stability of brand-attribute associations is partly due to measurement factors. *International Journal of Research in Marketing*, *25*(2), 104–108. https://doi.org/10.1016/j.ijresmar.2007.10.002

East, R., Wright, M., & Vanhuele, M. (2008). *Consumer behaviour: Applications in marketing*. SAGE.

Ebiquity and Gain Theory. (2018). *Profit ability: The business case for advertising*, special report.

Edeling, A., & Himme, A. (2018). When does market share matter? New empirical generalizations from a meta-analysis of the market share–performance relationship. *Journal of Marketing, 82*(3), 1–24. https://doi.org/10.1509/jm.16.0250

Ehrenberg, A. S. C. (1998). Repetitive advertising and the consumer. In J. P. Jones (Ed.), *How advertising works: The role of research* (pp. 63–81). SAGE.

Ehrenberg, A. S. C., & Goodhardt, G. (2002). Double jeopardy revisited, again. *Marketing Research, 14*(1), 40.

Esquivivas, P., Knox, S., Sanchez-Rodriguez, V., & Visser, J. (2013). *Fuelling growth through word of mouth: Introducing the brand advocacy index*. The Boston Consulting Group.

Europanel. (2020). *What the top dogs get.* Retrieved October 20, 2024, from visionplatform.europanel.com/what-the-top-dogs-get/

Europanel. (2023). *Comparing winning and losing brands for the period of 2018 to 2021*. Retrieved October 20, 2024, from visionplatform.europanel.com/pick-of-week-2023-29/

Europanel. (2024a). *How big are the biggest brands? (Part 1)*. Retrieved October 20, 2024, from visionplatform.europanel.com/pick-of-week-2024-12/

Europanel. (2024b). *They recently launched report State of the Grocery Retail Europe 2024*. Retrieved October 20, 2024, from visionplatform.europanel.com/pick-of-week-2024-17/

Evans, J. B. T. (2017). *Thinking and reasoning: A very short introduction*. Oxford University Press.

Fay, B., Keller, E., Larkin, R., & Pauwels, K. (2019). Deriving value from conversations about your brand. *MIT Sloan Management Review, 60*(2), 72–77.

Floyd, K., Freling, R., Alhoqail, S., Young Cho, H., & Freling, T. (2014). How online product reviews affect retail sales: A meta-analysis. *Journal of Retailing, 90*(2), 217–232. https://doi.org/10.1016/j.jretai.2014.04.004

Huang, M. H., & Rust, R. T. (2021). A strategic framework for artificial intelligence in marketing. *Journal of the Academy of Marketing Science, 49*(1), 30–50. https://doi.org/10.1007/s11747-020-00749-9

Jeffery, M. (2010). *Data-driven marketing: The 15 metrics everyone in marketing should know*. John Wiley & Sons.

Jones, J. P. (1998). Penetration, brand loyalty, and the penetration supercharge. In J. P. Jones (Ed.), *How advertising works: The role of research* (pp. 57–62). Sage.

Jones, J. P., & Slater, J. S. (2003). *What's in a name? Advertising and the concept of brands*. M.E. Sharpe.

Kahneman, D., Sibony, O., & Sunstein, C. R. (2022). *Noise: A flaw in human judgement*. HarperCollins.

Kall, J. (2021). *Brand metrics: Measuring brand efficacy along the customer journey*. Routledge.

Kantar. (2021). *A comprehensive guide to brand equity and growth*. Retrieved May 5, 2024, from www.kantar.com/campaigns/brand-equity-guide

Kaplan, R. S., & Norton, D. P. (1996). *The balanced scorecard: Translating strategy into action*. Harvard Business School Press.

Katsikeas, C. S., Morgan, N. A., Leoindou, L. C., & Hult, G. T. M. (2016). Assessing performance outcomes in marketing. *Journal of Marketing, 80*, 1–20. https://doi.org/10.1509/jm.15.0287

Keiningham, T. L., Aksoy, L., Buoye, A., & Cooil, B. (2011, October). Customer loyalty isn't enough. Grow your share of wallet. *Harvard Business Review, 89*, 29–31.

Keiningham, T. L., Cooil, B., Malthpuse, E. C., Buoye, A., Aksoy, L., De Keyser, A., & Lariviere, B. (2015). Perceptions are relative: An examinations of the relationship between relative satisfaction metrics and share of wallet. *Journal of Service Management, 26*(1), 2–43. https://doi.org/10.1108/JOSM-12-2013-0345

Keller, K. L. (2008). *Strategic brand management* (3rd ed.). Prentice Hall.

Keller, K. L., & Lehmann, D. R. (2003). How Do brands create value? *Marketing Management, 12*(3), 26–31.

Keller, K. L., & Lehmann, D. R. (2006). Brand and branding: Research findings and future priorities. *Marketing Science, 25*(6), 740–59. https://doi.org/10.1287/mksc.1050.0153

Keller, K. L., & Swaminathan, V. (2020). *Strategic brand management: Building, measuring, and managing brand equity (global edition)* (5th ed.). Pearson.

Lalaounis, S. T. (2021). *Strategic brand management and development: Creating and marketing successful brands*. Routledge.

Lehmann, D. R., Keller, K. L., & Farley, J. U. (2008). The structure of survey-based brand metrics. *Journal of International Marketing, 16*(4), 29–56. https://doi.org/10.1509/jimk.16.4.29

Lemon, K. N., & Verhoef, P. C. (2016). Understanding customer experience throughout the customer journey. *Journal of Marketing, 80*(6), 69–96. https://doi.org/10.1509/jm.15.0420

Marr, B. (2012). *Key performance indicators: The 75 measures every manager needs to know*. Pearson Financial Times Publishing.

Mecredy, P., Wright, M., Feetham, P., & Stern, P. (2021). Empirical generalisations in customer mindset metrics. *Journal of Consumer Behaviour, 21*(1), 102–120. https://doi.org/10.1002/cb.1961

Morgan, N. A., & Rego, L. L. (2009). Brand portfolio strategy and firm performance. *Journal of Marketing*, *73*(1), 59–74. https://doi.org/10.1509/jmkg.73.1.59

Munoz, T., & Kumar, S. (2004). Brand metrics: Gauging and linking brands with business performance. *Brand Management*, *11*(5), 381–387. https://doi.org/10.1057/palgrave.bm.2540183

Neslin, S. A., Grewal, D., Leghorn, R., Shankar, V., Teerling, M. L., Thomas, J. S., & Verhoef, P. C. (2006). Challenges and opportunities in multichannel customer management. *Journal of Service Research*, *9*(2), 95–112. https://doi.org/10.1177/1094670506293559

O'Regan, N. (2002). Market share: The conduit to future success? *European Business Review*, *14*(4), 287–293. https://doi.org/10.1108/09555340210434474

Parfitt, J. H., & Collins, B. J. K. (1968). Use of consumer panels for brand-share prediction. *Journal of Marketing Research*, *5*(2), 131–145. https://doi.org/10.1177/002224376800500201

Porter, M. E. (1998). *Competitive advantage: Creating and sustaining superior performance*. Free Press.

Reeves, M., Moose, S., & Venema, T. (2014). BCG Classics Revisited: The Growth Share Matrix. *BCG Perspectives*, *6*(14), 487.

Rego, L. L., Morgan, N. A., & Fornell, C. (2013). Reexamining the market share-customer satisfaction relationship. *Journal of Marketing*, *77*(5), 1–20. https://doi.org/10.1509/jm.09,0363

Reynolds, T. J., & Phillips, C. B. (2005). In search of true brand equity metrics: All market share ain't created equal. *Journal of Advertising Research*, *45*(02), 171–186. https://doi.org/10.1017/S0021849905050191

Romaniuk, J., Dawes, J., & Nenycz-Thiel, M. (2018). Modelling brand market share change in emerging markets. *International Marketing Review*, *35*(5), 785–805. https://doi.org/10.1108/IMR-01-2017-0006

Romaniuk, J., & Sharp, B. (2022). *How brands grow part 2* (revised ed.). Oxford University Press.

Romaniuk, J., Sharp, B., Paech, S., & Driesener, C. (2004). Brand and advertising awareness: A replication and extension of a known empirical generalisation. *Australasian Marketing Journal*, *12*(3), 70–80. https://doi.org/10.1016/S1441-3582(04)70107-X

Rowley, J. (2012). Evidence-based marketing. A perspective on the 'practice-theory divide'. *International Journal of Market Research*, *54*(4), 521. https://doi.org/10.2501/IJMR-54-4-521-541

Rust, R. T., Lemon, K. N., & Zeithaml, V. A. (2004). Return on marketing: Using customer equity to focus marketing strategy. *Journal of Marketing*, *68*(1), 109–127. https://doi.org/10.1509/jmkg.68.1.109.24030

Sharp, B. (2019). *Marketing: Theory, evidence, practice*. Oxford University Press.

Sharp, B., Dawes, J., & Victory, K. (2024). The market-based assets theory of brand competition. *Journal of Retailing and Consumer Services*, *76*, 1–13. https://doi.org/10.1016/j.jretconser.2023.103566

Singh, J., & Wright, M. (2016). New brands: Performance and measurement. In F. Dall'Olmo Riley, J. Singh, & C. Blankson (Ed.), *The Routledge companion to contemporary brand management* (pp. 186–189). Routledge.

Srinivasan, S., Vanhuele, M., & Pauwels, K. (2010). Mind-set metrics in market response models: An integrative approach. *Journal of Marketing Research*, *47*(4), 672–684. https://doi.org/10.1509/jmkr.47.4.672

Stasiuk, K., & Maison, D. (2014). *Psychologia konsumenta*. PWN.

Szymanski, D. M., Bharadwaj, S. G., & Varadarajan, P. R. (1993). An analysis of the market share-profitability relationship. *Journal of Marketing*, *57*(3), 1–18. https://doi.org/10.1177/ 002224299305700301

Timoshenko, A., & Hauser, J. R. (2019). Identifying customer needs from user-generated content. *Marketing Science*, *38*(1), 1–20. https://doi.org/10.1287/mksc.2018.1123

Vishwanath, V., Delaney, L., Meacham, M., & Tager, S. (2014, June 24). Winning with brands: What will it take to keep brands thriving. *Bain and Company Brief*. Retrieved March 25, 2024, from www.bain.com/insights/winning-with-brands/

Wilbur, K. C., & Farris, P. W. (2014). Distribution and market share. *Journal of Retailing*, *90*(2), 154–167. https://doi.org/10.1016/j.jretai.2013.08.003

You, Y., Vadakkepatt, & Joshi, A. M. (2015). A meta-analysis of electronic word-of-mouth elasticity. *Journal of Marketing*, *79*, 19–39. https://doi.org/10.1509/jm.14.0169

PART 5

Contemporary Issues in Brand Management

28

Brand Morality: A Critical Review and Contemporary Challenges

Yunyi Wei, Kokho (Jason) Sit, and Yuksel Ekinci

INTRODUCTION

This book chapter discusses the concept of brand morality and its growing significance in contemporary marketing. It explores the unique meanings and roles of brand morality, distinguishing it from brand ethics and emphasizes the importance of this differentiation in meeting evolving consumer expectations and shaping strategic brand directions. By discussing how brand morality influences consumer behavior and brand positioning, the chapter aims to provide academics and practitioners with a critical understanding of established and emerging perspectives. In addition, it identifies potential avenues for future research, offering valuable insights for advancing branding practices in an increasingly value-driven marketplace.

WHAT IS MORALITY?

Morality broadly refers to the principles and standards that govern individuals' behavior regarding right and wrong (Kesebir & Haidt, 2010). Historically, humans have used morality to guide and evaluate their and others' actions, typically along a 'right versus wrong' continuum (Rachels & Rachels, 2019). Recently, brands have integrated morality into their strategies to serve customers better and navigate ethical challenges (Mills & Wilner, 2023). A critical understanding of morality's meanings and applications can provide academics and practitioners with insights into their research and operational endeavors related to branding (Bravo & Chapa, 2024). Morality is a multifaceted concept with diverse interpretations depending on the theoretical lens, such as utilitarian, deontological, psychological and communitarian, as shown in Table 28.1.

The *utilitarian* perspective promotes welfare, justice and rights (Nucci & Turiel, 2009). The *deontological* perspective focuses on ethical principles and norms that guide behavior, emphasizing fairness, honesty, integrity and responsibility (Greenberg & Baron, 2008). The *psychological* perspective views morality as a mandatory psychological rule or standard (Beets, 2012). Finally, the *communitarian* perspective frames morality as rooted in community traditions and intuitions (Brandt & Rose, 2004).

The mentioned perspectives share three key commonalities. First, morality is evaluative, judging actions based on public motives that align with societal expectations (Cornwell & Higgins, 2019). Second, moral judgments are context-dependent and influenced by specific situations and cultural

Table 28.1 Theoretical perspectives of morality

Theoretical Perspective	*Focus*	*Description*	*References*
Utilitarian	Welfare, justice and rights	Promotes the greatest good for the most significant number, balancing harm and benefit	Nucci and Turiel (2009)
Deontological	Ethical principles and norms	Focuses on fairness, honesty, integrity, responsibility and other ethical standards	Greenberg and Baron (2008)
Psychological	Psychological rule or standard	Morality is viewed as a mandatory psychological rule or standard	Beets (2012)
Communitarian	Community traditions and intuitions	Morality is shaped by community norms, traditions and shared values	Brandt and Rose, (2004)

Source: The authors.

norms (McHugh et al., 2022). Third, brand morality involves normative dimensions, with ethical guidelines governing brand behavior to meet consumer expectations and societal values (Agu et al., 2024).

MORALITY VERSUS ETHICS

Table 28.2 illustrates a critical distinction between morality and ethics, though they are often conflated in branding literature.

Ethics emphasizes the objective attributes of transparency, fairness and honesty derived from corporate social responsibility (CSR) and sustainability frameworks (Carroll, 2021; Schwartz & Carroll, 2008). Morality tends to focus on the subjective attributes of care, emotional engagement, consumer well-being and societal concerns (Wei et al., 2024). While varied morality definitions exist, they share core attributes: morality as a psychological standard for right and wrong, its role in guiding behavior and its function in maintaining societal order (Graham et al., 2013).

However, unique attributes – such as the influence of community norms – highlight its complexity and contextual nature. Morality's malleability is evident in diverse cultural and economic contexts for brands. For example, the global fashion brand H&M faced contrasting reactions when it ceased sourcing cotton from Xinjiang due to alleged human rights abuses. Western consumers praised the decision, while Chinese consumers criticized it for misinterpreting national priorities and prioritizing political concerns over economic interests (Brenkert, 2016). This illustrates that morality often transcends binary notions of 'right' or 'wrong' and varies significantly across situations and cultures (Graham et al., 2013).

Significance of Brand Morality in Business and Society

The principle of 'avoiding evil and doing good' has historical, religious and philosophical roots but is now widely applied in commercial contexts, particularly in branding (Asamoah et al., 2025). Brands use this principle to develop ethical activities, such as ensuring fair wages (Zhou et al., 2025), maintaining product quality (Kopalle & Lehmann, 2015) and fostering inclusivity (Shaban, 2016). While ethical branding focuses on compliance with laws and regulations, moral branding extends to deeper commitments like authenticity, care and reciprocity (Nguyen & Dekhili, 2019; Thøgersen, 2021; Wei et al., 2024). From a *postmodern* perspective, moral branding fosters genuine stakeholder relationships beyond merely following ethical norms (Bhattacharjee et al., 2013). Consumer preferences have also evolved to

Table 28.2 Distinction between morality and ethics in branding

Concept	*Description*	*Defining Dimensions/Attributes*	*References*
Morality	A subjective standard for right and wrong, guided by societal and cultural norms	Care, emotional engagement, well-being, societal concerns	(Graham et al., 2013; Wei et al., 2024)
Ethics	Derived from CSR and sustainability frameworks, it emphasizes corporate responsibility	Transparency, fairness and honesty	(Carroll, 2021; Schwartz & Carroll, 2008)

Source: The authors.

favor brands that align with ethical values, such as social responsibility and fairness (Campbell & Winterich, 2018; Jeanes, 2013). Global challenges like climate change and social justice have further amplified the demand for brands to exhibit moral responsibility (Romani et al., 2015).

The growing emphasis on morality in branding stems from increasing social media scrutiny (Sansome et al., 2025), transparency demands (Hagelstein et al., 2021) and the need for authenticity (Park et al., 2023). Moral branding requires brands to move beyond compliance, fostering genuine care for stakeholders and collaborating with others to ensure societal well-being (Harrison et al., 2020). While ethical branding ensures regulatory adherence, moral branding builds deeper consumer trust through authentic care and responsibility (Freeman et al., 2020). Integrating morality into brand management is crucial for long-term sustainability, consumer loyalty and societal trust. As the business landscape evolves, moral branding will remain a fundamental strategy for success (Carroll et al., 2022).

Case studies are helpful to illustrate the impact of moral branding on consumer behavior, employee behavior and business performance. John Lewis Partnership showed that violating the moral principle of fairness can undermine the consumer trust built over the years (McCulloch, 2021; Nguyen & Dekhili, 2019). As one of the UK's largest employee-owned businesses, it brands its employees as 'partners' and shares profits with them, reflecting the reciprocity and loyalty principles under the moral cooperation (MaC) perspective and the care principle in moral foundation theory (Baumard et al., 2013; Haidt & Joseph, 2004). However, in 2021, the decision to pay bonuses only to senior managers amid financial difficulties attracted public criticism, as it was perceived to violate the principles mentioned earlier (McCulloch, 2021). This incident exemplifies how (perceived) violation of the moral tenets can undermine stakeholders' trust in a brand regardless of its heritage and status (Nguyen & Dekhili, 2019).

In contrast, Lush, a global skincare brand, provided a positive example of moral branding. In 2021, it voluntarily closed its Facebook, Instagram, Snapchat and TikTok accounts to protect users from harmful online content (Wood, 2021). Motivated by genuine concern rather than regulatory pressure, the decision earned the brand favorable publicity (Thøgersen, 2021). Lush's action exemplified the subtle distinction between simply fulfilling ethical guidelines and caring for vulnerable stakeholders morally (and proactively) (Campbell & Winterich, 2018).

BRAND MORALITY

Research on morality within branding, also known as brand morality, can be grouped into two broad domains: consumer-focused morality and business/brand-focused morality. These domains represent different perspectives on how morality influences consumer and brand relationships. *Consumer-focused morality* is more widely studied, and morality is examined through self-concepts, such as personal values, and their role in consumer decision-making and brand interactions. This area of research focuses on how individual consumers' ethical beliefs and value systems influence their purchasing decisions, brand loyalty and the overall consumer–brand relationship. It explores how moral considerations influence consumer preferences and behaviors, particularly in contexts such as ethical consumption, sustainable products and CSR. Furthermore, studies in this domain also investigate how consumers' perceptions of brand morality can shape brand image and affect market competitiveness.

On the other hand, brand-focused morality is less explored in existing branding literature. This gap in research highlights the need for a deeper understanding of how brands can embody and express moral values through their actions and messaging. There is a lack of theoretical models and frameworks to guide businesses in incorporating morality into their branding strategies or understanding consumer responses from a moral standpoint. This lack of theoretical clarity makes it challenging for companies to strategically align their brand identities with consumers' ethical expectations. As a result, businesses often struggle to understand how best to integrate moral values into their branding practices, whether through product offerings, advertising or corporate initiatives (Blackett & Russell, 2000). The following section discusses these two domains, elaborating on their characteristics and implications for brand management. The research aims to provide valuable insights for developing more ethically aligned branding strategies by addressing the theoretical and practical gaps in both consumer-focused and brand-focused morality.

Consumer-Focused Brand Morality

Consumer-focused morality conceptualizes morality as a personal construct that consumers use to express their identity rather than as a characteristic of brands. This moralistic communication occurs through the consumption of goods and services

Table 28.3 Consumer-focused morality

Concept	*Focus*	*Description*
Moral Judgment (Cognitive)	Ethical evaluation of brands by consumers.	Positive moral evaluations lead to favorable brand attitudes and purchasing decisions. Negative evaluations can lead to boycotts or brand rejection (Bhattacharjee et al., 2013).
Moral Emotions (Affective)	The emotional responses triggered by ethical or unethical brand actions.	Consumers experience positive emotions (e.g., pride) when brands act ethically, which fosters loyalty. Conversely, negative emotions (e.g., anger) arise when brands engage in unethical practices, prompting negative consumer actions (Grappi et al., 2013).
Moral Awareness (Mindset)	The recognition and evaluation of ethical issues in brand behavior.	Consumers with higher moral awareness critically assess corporate social responsibility (CSR) efforts, distinguishing between genuine ethical actions and those aimed solely at image management (Reynolds, 2006).
Moral Identity (Personal)	The role of personal morality in shaping consumer actions and preferences.	Individuals with a strong moral identity are more likely to choose brands that align with their ethical values and avoid those that conflict with their principles. This influences brand preferences and consumer engagement (Winterich et al., 2013).

Source: The authors.

(Ellemers et al., 2019). Four key perspectives define this domain, as shown in Table 28.3. These four perspectives collectively shape how morality influences consumer decision-making, brand perception and behavior.

The moral judgment perspective posits that consumers cognitively assess brands based on their moral traits, influencing their purchasing decisions and support (Bhattacharjee et al., 2013). Favorable moral judgments, such as viewing a brand as helpful, encourage patronage, while negative judgments, such as dishonesty, lead to consumer backlash. However, these judgments are subjective and vary across cultural and social contexts (e.g., collectivistic vs. individualistic values) (Xu, 2022). Unlike moral judgment, moral awareness determines whether consumers recognize a brand's moralistic actions without making a value judgment (Reynolds, 2006). Higher moral awareness increases consumer attention to CSR, affecting brand perception.

Moral emotions shape consumers' affective responses to brands. Positive emotions, such as pride, reinforce loyalty when brands engage in ethical behavior (Grappi et al., 2013). Conversely, negative emotions like anger can drive boycotts and negative word-of-mouth if a brand is perceived as immoral. Meanwhile, moral identity encompasses a holistic perspective, emphasizing morality as a core part of consumers' self-concept (Choi & Winterich, 2013). Those with strong moral identity is more likely to align their purchasing behavior with moral values and engage in ethical consumption (Winterich et al., 2013). Moral identity can also influence moral judgment, emotions and awareness.

Business-Focused Brand Morality

Business-focused morality has received less attention in the branding literature than consumer-focused morality. The three possible reasons are (1) morality is perceived as a human more than a branding concept and thus the popularity of the consumer-focused perspective, (2) morality is construed identical to ethics from a business perspective and (3) ethics is an easier-to-apply branding concept than morality.

Business-focused ethics is more favorable than business-focused morality, possibly because:

- **Clearer Guidelines**: Regulatory frameworks and industry standards associated with brand ethics provide concrete guidelines for ethical behavior, such as compliance with CSR expectations and sustainability reporting standards (Kotsantonis et al., 2016; Schwartz & Carroll, 2008).
- **Familiar Focus on Compliance**: Ethical frameworks emphasize adherence to legal and corporate governance policies, making ethical behavior more familiar to codify and integrate into business operations (Singh & Crisafulli, 2022).
- **Complex Morality**: Unlike ethics, brand morality involves deeper, subjective considerations of values, intent and care. It often requires intrinsic motivation and long-term value-driven commitments that align with societal expectations, which are more challenging to discern (Hunt & Vitell, 2006; Trevino & Nelson, 2021).

The challenges of operationalizing the concept also compound the negligence of business-focused morality. Unlike consumer-focused morality, to the author's best knowledge, no specific frameworks of business-focused morality can be identified in the extant branding literature. While some morality theories (e.g. moral as cooperation) (Curry et al., 2019) are detectable in the organizational behavior literature, the extent to which they are applicable to study business-focused morality in a branding context is unclear.

This chapter calls for more attention to business-focused morality in branding. It responds to consumers' increasing expectations for brands to display moralistic traits or behave moralistically, like caring for people and society beyond the scope of following regulations. Consumers seem to believe that commercial viability can coexist with moralistic behaviors when brands endeavor to achieve balance (He & Harris, 2020). This belief can be attributed to COVID-19. This pandemic unexpectedly created many deaths and changed the ways we work, live and interact with each other. Hence, consumers yearn to be cared for and can care for someone or something via personal consumption. Care, when appropriately practiced, can create a warm relationship between two parties and, in turn, foster customer advocacy (Kolbl et al., 2020) and their willingness to pay and recommend the brand to others (Xie et al., 2022).

Besides COVID-19, consumers' expectations of business-focused morality can also be driven by:

- Increased awareness of societal and environmental impacts (White et al., 2019);
- Media coverage of 'uncaring' business practices despite being ethical (e.g., the overuse of zero-hour contracts) (Toovey, 2023) and
- Widening the scope of CSR to include benevolent and ethical activities that benefit local communities (e.g., helping the sleeping roughs) (Gov.UK, 2023).

Multiple theoretical perspectives

Extant branding literature presents six theoretical perspectives on studying business-focused brand morality, each with unique pros and cons (see Table 28.4).

Deontological perspective

Compliance is the focal conduct of this perspective, emphasizing a brand's respect for and adherence

Table 28.4 Multiple theoretical perspectives of business-focused brand morality

Theoretical Perspective	*Core Focus*	*Key Dimensions*	*References*
Deontological Perspective	Emphasizes adherence to rules, duties or principles; outcomes are irrelevant.	Honesty, justice, fairness.	Kant (1785); Reidenbach and Robin (1990)
Virtue Ethics Perspective	It focuses on inherent moral traits and character, asking, 'What kind of brand is this?' rather than 'What does the brand do?'	Integrity, benevolence, authenticity, empathy.	Aristotle (350 BCE); Solomon (1992)
Consequentialist Perspective	Prioritizes outcomes of actions, with morality judged by the tangible social or environmental value created.	Social impact, beneficence, sustainability.	Mill (2016); Crane (2001)
Moral Foundations Perspective	Evaluates morality based on innate foundations; violations result in negative consequences like boycotts.	Care/harm, fairness/cheating, loyalty/betrayal, etc.	Haidt and Graham (2007); Graham et al. (2013)
Cooperation Perspective	Views morality as fostering cooperation and group well-being through collaborative relationships.	Reciprocity, group loyalty, conflict resolution, resource sharing.	Curry et al. (2019)
Integrated Multidimensional Perspective	Synthesizing the other perspectives, complementing one's weaknesses with other's strengths.	As many as needed, depending on the study context.	Developed for this book chapter

Source: The authors.

to the rules, duties or principles practiced by the operating markets or cultures (Kant, 1785). In this view, ethical actions are not liable for the outcomes they produce but for the intention and adherence to moral duties or principles, which are universally binding. Thus, this perspective values the defining dimensions of **honesty, justice and fairness.** A brand's commitment to these principles is essential for establishing trust with consumers, particularly in environments where ethical conduct is a key factor in decision-making. The outcomes of an action are immaterial in this perspective. This means that even if a brand's actions do not yield immediate benefits or profit, the mere adherence to moral guidelines ensures that the brand remains ethically grounded. For instance, a brand is perceived as moralistic when it champions transparency in marketing communications or offers fair wages to its employees. Such actions reflect a strong commitment to ethical principles and can differentiate a brand in a competitive market, where consumers are increasingly attentive to corporate integrity. Some scholars (Reidenbach & Robin, 1990) suggest this perspective particularly appeals to rule-following consumers who respect social norms and favor duty-bound behaviors.

Virtue ethics perspective

Virtue ethics are broadly about a person's character and virtues instead of achievements (Aristotle, 384-322 BCE, cited in Fisher & Dimmock, 2020). This framework shifts the focus from external actions or results to developing and expressing internal moral qualities. Like the deontological perspective, the outcomes of an action are less important in this perspective. The emphasis is placed on the intrinsic moral qualities that define a person or entity, rather than on the utilitarian consequences of their actions. When applied to brand morality, this perspective focuses on a brand's inherent moral traits or qualities in the eyes of consumers instead of its self-fulfilled commercial successes. Brands are assessed not just by their performance in the marketplace but by their moral character through their actions and the way they engage with consumers. It asks, '*What kind of brand is this?*' *and not* '*What does the brand do?*' This highlights a shift from a results-oriented view to one that prioritizes the ethical identity and values of a brand. Thus, it particularly emphasizes the dimensions of **integrity, benevolence, authenticity and empathy**. These qualities reflect how the brand connects with its consumers on a deeper, more human level, fostering trust and long-term loyalty. Under this perspective, consumers' perceived morality emerges when a brand displays the traits of compassion and genuineness towards them, other stakeholders (e.g., employees) and society at large (Solomon, 1992). Such traits are often seen as authentic indicators of a brand's ethical commitment, as they go beyond CSR and reflect a genuine concern for people and communities.

Consequentialist perspective

Unlike the two perspectives above, consequentialists particularly emphasize the outcomes of an action (Mill, 2016). This means that the morality of an action is assessed based on its tangible effects rather than the intent behind it. Accordingly, a brand is only deemed moralistic when it delivers its promises or tangible results, such as fulfilling commitments to customers, maintaining product quality or demonstrating transparency in business operations. Exhibiting moralistic inherent characters or qualities is less desirable in this perspective because intentions alone do not ensure real benefits to stakeholders. Hence, this perspective emphasizes **social impact, beneficence and sustainability**, which are evaluated based on observable and measurable contributions. To achieve moral credentials under this perspective, brands can undertake activities that benefit the local communities or markets in which they operate, like improving the social welfare of vulnerable individuals (e.g., rough sleepers) through housing initiatives, supporting altruistic activities such as charity partnerships or initiating sustainable commercial practices like reducing carbon footprints and minimizing waste in production (Crane, 2001).

Moral foundations perspective

Developed by Haidt and Graham (2007), this perspective suggests that a person's moral reasoning is based on innate, universal foundations, specifically around the dimensions of **care/harm**, **fairness/cheating**, **loyalty/betrayal**, **authority/subversion**, **sanctity/degradation** and **liberty/oppression** (Haidt, 2001; Hoppner & Vadakkepatt, 2019). According to this theory, these foundational values are hardwired into human cognition and form the basis of how people make moral judgments across different cultural and social contexts. When applied to brand morality, it argues that consumers evaluate a brand's credentials based on how well they align with the listed moral foundations. Brands that resonate with these core values are likely to foster stronger consumer relationships, as consumers perceive them as morally aligned with their own values. It also claims that the violations of any of the listed moral foundations by a brand are deemed immoral and will result in adverse consequences (e.g., brand boycott) (Graham et al., 2013). Such violations can significantly damage a brand's reputation, as they may lead to consumer outrage and a loss of trust, which can be challenging to rebuild. The moral foundation theory perspective broadly resonates with the deontological and virtue ethics perspectives, which consistently emphasize the fulfillment of moralistic benchmarks or traits instead of delivering moralistic outcomes. While all three perspectives emphasize adhering to moral principles, each has a unique lens through which it evaluates brand behavior. There is a subtle distinction between them, however. That is, they value different fundamental meanings of brand morality. For example, the deontological perspective focuses on righteousness and adherence to duty, while virtue ethics prioritizes authenticity and compassion. The moral foundation theory, in contrast, places greater emphasis on the brand's role in fostering social bonds and upholding communal values. The differences among these perspectives illustrate the complexity of brand morality, highlighting that brands can embody multiple moral dimensions depending on the context and the values they seek to promote.

Moral as cooperation perspective

As Curry et al. (2019) proposed, this perspective describes morality as a set of evolved cooperative behaviors essential to support individuals' and groups' well-being. Its defining dimensions include **reciprocity**, **group loyalty**, **conflict resolution** and **resource sharing**. These behaviors are fundamental to fostering trust, mutual support and long-term stability within a community or organization. When coupled with brand morality, this perspective suggests that a moralistic brand endeavors to support, form alliances and resolve conflicts with and amongst stakeholders, including competitors, in the operating markets. By promoting cooperation, brands can build stronger, more resilient relationships that benefit all parties involved. Its fundamental focus is establishing and maintaining cooperative relationships with stakeholders. In this regard, the moral as cooperation perspective overlaps with the moral foundations perspective. For instance, a brand can enhance its moral image by treating its employees as 'partners', developing reciprocal relationships and working together to create a successful and sustainable business. A practice that the UK's prominent department-store brand, John Lewis, has undertaken for about 160 years (JLP, 2024). Unlike the moral foundation's perspective, the MaC perspective explicitly emphasizes resource sharing in establishing cooperative relationships (Curry et al., 2019).

Integrated multidimensional perspective

This perspective integrates the earlier varied perspectives and does not deem them mutually exclusive. It champions a more 'inclusive' or rounded approach to understanding brand morality. It enables brands to target consumers who appreciate varied moralistic traits, recognizing that different individuals and cultures may prioritize different ethical dimensions (Schmidt & Ludlow, 2002). Some scholars (Firat & McPherson, 2010) assert that brands will unlikely adopt or rely on a single perspective when developing their moralistic credentials and activities, as doing so may limit their appeal and effectiveness in diverse markets. Instead, they will likely employ a combination of perspectives because of the constantly evolving business landscape, increasing consumer expectations and the multiple stakeholders they serve, including customers, employees, investors and regulators. For example, when trading in Malaysia, a brand can comply with the local laws and norms to uphold ethical business conduct (deontological ethics), emphasize its heritage in integrity and compassion to foster trust among consumers (virtue ethics) and support local charities to deliver tangible societal outcomes, such as working with World Vision Malaysia to overcome extreme poverty and injustice by funding education programs, healthcare services and sustainable development projects (consequentialist ethics).

Dimensions of Brand Morality

Like many brand concepts (e.g., brand personality), a single dimension, perspective or context cannot adequately define brand morality. Instead, multiplicity is necessary to capture the concept's rich meanings meaningfully. Scholars have approached brand morality differently, resulting in the existence of different contexts and defining dimensions, as shown in Table 28.5.

CSR is one of the most studied areas of brand morality because it inherently reflects moral principles such as responsibility, fairness and humanity, which align with consumers' moral expectations (e.g., Nadeau et al., 2020; Wang et al., 2020). This study area is central to understanding how businesses can align their operations with societal values and ethical norms, which are increasingly critical to brand perception in the marketplace. CSR provides consumers with clear and tangible evidence of whether a brand's actions can be deemed 'good' or 'bad' (Brunk, 2010). By engaging in CSR activities, brands enhance their public image and actively contribute to the social

Table 28.5 Dimensions of brand morality

Author/s & Year	*Focal Context*	*Description*	*Defining Dimensions*
van Prooijen and Bartels (2019)	CSR	Define brand morality as a series of morality traits (e.g., honesty, trustworthiness)	Honest, sincere and trustworthy
Choi and Winterich (2013)	Moral identity on in-group and out-group brand attitude	Morality is the degree to which a consumer perceives a brand as virtuous, a series of characteristics	Virtuous, principled and fair
Krishna and Kim (2021)	Brand misconduct	Brand morality is defined as people's judgment of brand behavior according to their moral principles	Principled, justice and responsible
Ilicic et al. (2021)	Advertising	The distinction between morality and immorality is defined as conformity and rebelliousness In theological form, morality is defined as compliance as a symbol of conformity and rebelliousness as immorality	Conformity and rebelliousness
Lopez and Rodriguez (2018)	Children	Branding morality is defined as 'good or bad' behavior	Good: Make you look better help the least fortunate Help you identify high-quality product self-products that help us in our lives Bad: Putting much advertising everywhere selling harmful products make us buy things we do not need
Cheng and Yu (2021)	Branding (general)	Brand morality is defined as a series of moral traits	Fairness, honesty, integrity and social responsibility
Kim and Ball (2021)	Advertising	Mentioned the brand morality as the perceived warmth	kindness, caring and friendliness
Schmeltz (2012)	CSR	Define morality in branding as a kind of morally oriented value	helpful, responsible and honest
Amos et al. (2021)	Food	For food brands, morality refers to people's moral intuition regarding the quality of food they eat. Moral/pure food is seen as benevolent and healthy-nurturing . In contrast to foods that are untouched and/or minimally altered, food that has been changed by modern agricultural practices is perceived as bad (immoral)	Nutritional, contaminant, benevolent
Kirmani et al. (2017)	Branding (general)	A series of moral traits	Being sincere, fair, principled, honest and trustworthy; socially conscious, organic or green)
Romani et al. (2015)	Manufacturing brand	When the brand's behavior conforms to the public's moral systems	Injustice, dishonesty, and unfair
Hoppner and Vadakkepatt (2019)	Moral authority	The moral value and what it stands for	Fairness, equality, care
Brown et al. (2003)	Branding(general)	A series of moral traits	Care, honesty, patriotism, sharing and authenticity
Nadeau et al. (2020)	CSR	A series of moral traits	Authentic, charitable, natural and positive
Wang et al. (2020)	CSR	A brand's social responsibility aims to fulfill moral obligations and conduct business with humane principles.	Humanity, fairness and justice

Source: The authors.

and environmental causes that resonate with their target audience. As consumer awareness of moral and ethical issues grows, socially responsible behavior has become a brand's baseline expectation. Consumers are becoming more discerning, often scrutinizing brands for evidence of genuine commitment to social responsibility rather than just marketing gimmicks. In a CSR context, brand morality's defining dimensions include honesty, sincerity, trustworthiness (van Prooijen & Bartels, 2019), humanity, fairness, justice (Wang et al., 2020), and authenticity, charity, and positivity (Nadeau et al., 2020). These dimensions are important to consumers and influence a brand's long-term success and reputation, as companies that align with these values tend to foster greater customer loyalty and trust.

Besides CSR, brand morality has been examined in other business contexts like food labeling and manufacturing. For instance, Amos et al. (2021) investigated moral attributes like purity and naturalness in food products, highlighting how consumers increasingly seek ethical food choices, where the moral qualities of the product are central to their purchasing decisions. Ilicic et al. (2021) reported conformity and rebelliousness as the moral dimensions of advertising. This suggests that consumers are also sensitive to how brands position themselves in relation to societal norms – whether they conform to or challenge established standards. Romani et al. (2015) studied moral violations in the manufacturing sector and identified the key characteristics such as injustice and dishonesty. Such violations underscore the ethical challenges brands face in maintaining transparency and fairness throughout their supply chains, which can significantly affect public perceptions and consumer trust.

The mentioned studies highlight that business-focused and consumer-focused brand morality overlap on many dimensions, such as kindness, fairness and integrity. These common values suggest that brand morality is not a siloed concept but a shared framework that bridges business operations and consumer expectations. This finding reinforces the widespread application of anthropomorphism in studying brand concepts (e.g., brand personality) (Austin et al., 2003), and business-focused brand morality is no exception. The use of anthropomorphic traits helps to humanize brands, making it easier for consumers to connect with them on an emotional level. There is a subtle distinction between the defining dimensions of brand morality in CSR and non-CSR contexts, where the former emphasizes more strategic dimensions like societal and charitable actions and the latter more on grounded dimensions like purity and dishonesty. This distinction is crucial for understanding how different business strategies align with varying consumer expectations across industries. The distinction illustrates the context-dependent nature of brand morality. In essence, brand morality is not a one-size-fits-all concept but must be tailored to the specific ethical landscape in which a brand operates.

Multiple research frameworks

Business-focused frameworks outnumber consumer-focused frameworks in the extant branding literature. Some are parsimonious, comprising only two dimensions, whereas some are complex, involving multiple dimensions. For example, Lopez and Rodriguez's framework (2018) succinctly describes brand morality as 'good' and 'bad' behaviors. Brown et al. (2003) offer a more intricate framework encompassing five dimensions: care, honesty, patriotism, sharing and authenticity. Kirmani et al. (2017) present a seven-dimensional framework comprising sincerity, fairness, principled, honesty, trustworthiness, social consciousness and organic and green.

The studies above highlight two key insights. Brand morality is highly context-dependent. The nature and number of defining dimensions vary significantly between contexts; thus, our knowledge of the concept remains dispersed. A study that critically reviews and synthesizes the wide range of defining dimensions and then provides a consolidated understanding of brand morality has yet to emerge. This chapter lays the groundwork for future studies pursuing this research direction.

Antecedents and consequences of brand morality

This chapter identifies three key antecedents and five essential consequences of brand morality, providing a focused framework for branding research and practice (see Table 28.6). While not exhaustive, these factors offer valuable insights into the study and application of brand morality.

Personal Values: Personal values, a consumer-oriented antecedent, represent the fundamental beliefs and principles that shape individuals' preferences, behaviors and decision-making. These values influence how consumers perceive and interact with brands and products. They are categorized into four broad orientations, each encompassing specific motives (Doran, 2009):

- Self-transcendence prioritizes collective well-being and moral responsibility, incorporating universalism, benevolence, self-direction and conformity/tradition.

Table 28.6 Potential antecedents and consequences of brand morality

Category	*Concept*	*Description*
Antecedents of Brand Morality	Personal values	The core beliefs and principles that direct one's actions and decision-making (Doran, 2009)
	Core Brand Values	Fundamental principles guiding a brand's vision and strategy. Internal values (honesty, transparency) and external values (sustainability, equity) shape perceptions based on alignment with societal norms (Agu et al., 2024)
	Corporate social responsibility orientation (CSRO)	Reflects a brand's commitment to ethical conduct and social responsibility. Strong CSRO promotes moral perceptions through support for social and environmental welfare (Ellemers & Chopova, 2021; Lin et al., 2021)
Consequences of Brand Morality	Brand Honesty	Brand honesty relates to fulfilling promises and establishing trust. It is a critical trait in the deontological perspective of brand morality (Hayes et al., 2006; Sloan et al., 2018)
	Brand Trust	Brand trust involves consumer belief in a brand's honesty, integrity, and reliability, closely connected to brand morality (Chaudhuri & Holbrook, 2001; Delgado-Ballester et al., 2003)
	Brand Satisfaction	Consumer evaluations of brands, influenced by traits like authenticity, fairness and integrity, contribute to brand satisfaction (Kotler & Armstrong, 2022; McDonald & Rundle-Thiele, 2008)
	Brand Reputation	Brand reputation is formed by traits like authenticity, fairness and integrity, which influence consumer loyalty and marketing strategies (Fombrun, 2005; Veloutsou & Moutinho, 2009)
	Self-Brand Connection	Consumers embrace brands as part of their identity, often for altruistic purposes like supporting sustainability and enhancing their image (Escalas & Bettman, 2003; Kaur & Manna, 2024)

Source: The authors.

- Self-enhancement focuses on personal success, power and individual satisfaction and is driven by achievement, power and hedonism.
- Conservation – Emphasizes stability, security and order linked to conformity/tradition and security motives.
- Openness to Change – Encourages personal growth, autonomy and novelty, associated with stimulation and self-direction motives.

Personal values are crucial in understanding consumer attitudes toward brand morality, aiding market segmentation and targeting (Hosseini & Shabani, 2015). Since these values shape consumer preferences, individuals with self-transcendence tendencies are more likely to support moral branding, as their universalism and benevolence motives align with morality's core principles of care and kindness (Joseph et al., 2022). Conversely, self-enhancement consumers, who prioritize success and status, may only engage with moral branding if convinced it aligns with their aspirations for recognition, power or enjoyment (Doran, 2009).

The influence of openness to change and conservation on brand morality is less clear. These values lack direct alignment with morality's defining attributes. However, brands can position their moral initiatives strategically. For instance, moral campaigns promoting self-respect and freedom of expression (e.g., #MeToo, #BlackLivesMatter) may appeal to openness to change consumers (Mirzaei et al., 2022). Similarly, moral campaigns focused on social protection and community belonging, such as supermarket partnerships with food banks, may resonate with conservation-oriented consumers (Smithers, 2020).

Core Brand Values: Core brand values are the fundamental principles that define a brand's identity and communicate its mission and ethos to the public (Agu et al., 2024). They shape a brand's character, influencing long-term and short-term strategies, and serve as a key connection point between brands and consumers (Keller, 2003; Nadeem et al., 2021).

These values fall into two categories:

- Internal Values – Focus on organizational culture and practices, such as honesty, transparency and employee welfare.
- External Values – Reflect a brand's engagement with broader societal issues, including environmental sustainability, social equity and community involvement (De Chernatony et al., 2006).

As a business-centric antecedent of brand morality, core brand values can have a positive or negative influence depending on their alignment with consumer expectations and societal norms. Brands championing workplace diversity and environmental responsibility are considered moral (Sen et al., 2006). However, their moral credibility diminishes when brands exploit social campaigns for self-interest, alienate societal groups or manipulate political figures. For instance, allegations that Meta removed Facebook and Instagram's fact-checking function to align with President Trump's views illustrate how brand values can be misused, harming moral perception (Zahn, 2025).

Corporate Social Responsibility Orientation: CSRO mirrors a corporation's moral standard, reflecting its commitment to ethical responsibility (Soliman & Ben-Amar, 2022). It drives positive managerial behaviors, such as transparent financial disclosures and a willingness to support colleagues beyond defined roles (Burton & Goldsby, 2009).

CSRO strengthens brand morality as a business-centric antecedent by encouraging engagement in moralistic activities, such as supporting vulnerable communities (Ellemers & Chopova, 2021) and advocating for social and environmental well-being (Lin et al., 2021). A strong CSRO signals a brand's dedication to ethical conduct, reinforcing consumer trust and long-term sustainability.

Brand Honesty: Brand honesty refers to a brand's perceived ability to fulfill promises, meet obligations and maintain a trustworthy image (Hayes et al., 2006). From a deontological perspective, brand morality is often equated with brand honesty, leading some scholars to measure them interchangeably (Sloan et al., 2018; Sung & Kim, 2010). Honesty is associated with attributes such as credible information (Esmaeilpour & Aram, 2016), consistent communication (Park & Kim, 2016) and altruistic motives (Doney & Cannon, 1997). A brand perceived as moral – exemplifying fairness and transparency – is more likely to be viewed as honest. Given its close relationship with morality, brand honesty can be considered both a consequence and a defining attribute of brand morality (Alwi et al., 2017). Further research is needed to explore the interplay between these concepts.

Brand Trust: Brand trust reflects consumers' belief in a brand's honesty, reliability and integrity (Deutsch, 1973). It comprises two key dimensions:

- Reliability – The brand's ability to meet expectations and fulfill promises (Delgado-Ballester et al., 2003).
- Intentionality – The brand's willingness to protect and prioritize consumer interests (Chaudhuri & Holbrook, 2001).

Brand trust emerges as a consequence of brand morality, as consumers tend to trust brands they perceive as moral in their ethos and actions. Moral traits such as empathy, cooperation and care are central to consumer trust, as discussed in the Moral Foundations Theory and MaC perspectives (Decety & Cacioppo, 2012; Willis & Todorov, 2006). The Lush case – where the brand voluntarily deactivated its social media accounts to protect users from harmful content – demonstrates how moral actions foster trust and public goodwill (Baker, 2021; Wood, 2021).

Brand Satisfaction: Brand satisfaction refers to consumers' overall evaluation of a brand, which can be favorable, unfavorable or neutral (Fornell, 1992). The criteria for this evaluation vary depending on individual preferences and situational factors (Oliver, 1999; Tse & Wilton, 1988). Because morality influences consumer judgments, brand morality plays a crucial role in shaping satisfaction. Research in non-branding domains links moral traits such as authenticity, fairness, honesty, integrity, empathy and care to positive consumer evaluations (Izogo & Ogba, 2015; Kim et al., 2004; Kotler & Armstrong, 2022; Lee & Heo, 2009; Luo & Bhattacharya, 2006; McDonald & Rundle-Thiele, 2008; Oh, 1999).

A relevant example is Patagonia, which transferred 98% of its stock to a non-profit organization dedicated to combating climate change. This moral initiative reinforced consumer satisfaction and brand loyalty (Rhodes, 2022).

Brand Reputation: Brand reputation is a multifaceted concept influenced by factors such as authenticity, fairness, integrity and innovation (Fombrun & Van Riel, 2004). A strong reputation enhances consumer loyalty (Veloutsou & Moutinho, 2009) and informs marketing strategies (Fombrun, 2005). This chapter considers brand reputation a key consequence of brand morality because consumers value morally upright brands (Rush, 2021). Unlike brand satisfaction, which situational factors can influence, brand reputation is more stable and reliable (Oliver, 1999). Consumers judge brands based on the morality of their actions. If a marketing campaign is perceived as moral or immoral, it directly impacts the brand's reputation. The John Lewis Partnership case, where the retailer awarded bonuses only to senior managers in 2021, sparked criticism for contradicting its cooperative values and damaging its reputation (McCulloch, 2021).

Self-Brand Connection: Self-brand connection refers to how consumers use brands to express their personal and social identities (Escalas & Bettman, 2003). Consumers select brands to:

- Convey self-image (Escalas, 2004; Escalas & Bettman, 2003; Schembri et al., 2010).

- Promote social status (Lin et al., 2021).
- Enhance self-esteem (Belk, 1988).

Brand morality significantly impacts self-brand connection, as consumers are more likely to identify with brands they perceive as ethical and socially responsible. The Lush example illustrates this, as its moral decision to deactivate social media accounts strengthened consumer attachment. Similarly, brands associated with sustainability, such as Vinted and CeX, appeal to consumers who value ethical consumption, reinforcing self-brand connections (Kaur & Manna, 2024).

IS IT NECESSARY TO DIFFERENTIATE BRAND MORALITY FROM ETHICS?

Considering the many shared dimensions (e.g., compliance) between brand morality and ethics, some scholars and practitioners naturally question the pedagogical value of differentiating the two concepts in this chapter. An indifferent approach by treating brand morality and ethics as identical offers several apparent benefits: reinforcing the popularity of brand ethics over morality, less effort in applying a single concept instead of two related concepts, and more straightforward defending brand ethics over morality. However, when we think more critically, the mentioned benefits are more methodological than theoretical, as they will restrict our understanding and the development of new knowledge about brand morality. Building on this logic, this chapter challenges the indifferent treatment of brand morality and ethics. It aims to provide a nuanced and fresh theoretical understanding of the two concepts.

Differentiating brand morality from ethics can be further justified on the following grounds:

- **Responding to consumer expectations.** Today's consumers become increasingly aware of global challenges – such as climate change, social inequality and unethical labor practices – and demand that brands embody moral principles aligned with their personal or cultural values (Carrington et al., 2014; Romani et al., 2015). The alignment goes beyond merely complying with the laws and regulations required by the operating markets. Brands that successfully integrate these moral values into their practices can forge deeper emotional connections with consumers, enhancing loyalty and trust (Nguyen et al., 2021). Younger generations are reported to favor brands that actively support or engage with social issues (e.g., gender equality). They are considered socially conscious consumers (Broccardo et al., 2023).
- **Enriching ethical positioning.** To prevent prosecutions from consumers and governing bodies (e.g., the UK Food Standards Agency), brands typically comply with the legal requirements of their operating markets (e.g., 'Halal' must be labeled on consumable products being sold to Muslim consumers). Compliance, however, does not equate to being caring, kind and generous, as the mentioned attributes are typically at the discretion of a brand. While non-compliance with laws and regulations can result in prosecutions and penalties by official bodies, being unkind, uncaring and ungenerous does not. However, because of COVID-19, consumers have yearned for more kindness, caring and generosity from society – and businesses are part of it to help them feel hopeful and energized with their lives. Brands that behave morally by being kind, caring and generous beyond simply adhering to laws and legislations are suggested to experience better reputations and deeper consumer connections (Cheng & Yu, 2021; Martin & Tao-Peng, 2017; van Prooijen & Bartels, 2019).

In brief, a more critical understanding of brand morality and ethics will better inform us how the two concepts relate and how we can leverage them as marketing strategies, individually and collectively. It will support personnel management efforts, as brands can enrich ethical compliance (e.g., providing mandatory training to perform a job) with moral generosity (e.g., sharing profits with employees). It will guide brands in addressing misinformation as the public expects them to care about and address this issue willingly and proactively without pressure from law enforcement (see Cision, 2024).

FUTURE RESEARCH AGENDA

We recognize that this chapter presents more questions than answers about business-focused brand morality. They serve as our work's 'unique selling propositions' and provide scholars and practitioners with many directions when pursuing brand morality knowledge. The directions can be grouped into five areas, as discussed below.

Which Theoretical Perspective to Apply?

We present six theoretical perspectives meaningful to studying brand morality: deontological, virtue ethics, consequentialist, moral foundation, moral as cooperation and integrated multidimensional perspectives. An immediate question scholars and practitioners may ask is, 'Which is the best perspective of brand morality?' A simple and perhaps idle response is, 'It depends', as each perspective has pros and cons. Despite that, we propose that more attention can be devoted to the integrated multidimensional perspective, precisely blending the moral foundations and moral as cooperation dimensions. Because of its shared nature with brand ethics, previous studies have frequently focused on honesty, integrity, fairness and justice. Because of the growing interest in CSRs, recent studies of brand morality have focused on social impact and sustainability (see Wei et al., 2025). The dimensions of care and benevolence appear to receive the least attention when studying brand morality. As stated earlier, the adverse consequences of COVID-19, to a large extent, have triggered consumers to yearn for more caring and kindness in society, including the brands they patronize.

Care and benevolence are intricately linked. Both are about brands being supportive and generous in managing customers and other stakeholders beyond complying with the laws and customs practiced by their operating markets (Kim & Ball, 2021). Both care and benevolence focus on the 'heart' (compassion) rather than the 'head' (conformity) (Hemberg & Wiklund Gustin, 2020). Scholars posit that care and benevolence when practiced genuinely, can help brands forge deeper relationships with their customers and secure their trust more (Singh & Crisafulli, 2022).

Which Key Dimensions of brand Morality Should be Prioritized?

While we encourage more attention to care and benevolence, it does not discount the importance of other defining dimensions of brand morality. Future research can be less concerned with determining the ideal composition of defining dimensions, but more interested in identifying whether the composition is consistent between consumers and settings of different characteristics. Stated differently, future research can seek to develop a set of brand morality's defining dimensions that are 'inclusive' for different consumer types (e.g., young versus older consumers), different national cultures (e.g., individualists versus collectivists, or different business sectors (e.g., supermarket versus fashion).

Which Antecedents and Consequences do You Apply?

This chapter has proposed three antecedents and five consequences as key factors in studying brand morality. While these provide a foundational framework, their theoretical and practical applications require further exploration and empirical validation.

Future research could offer new insights by:

1. Identifying and profiling consumers whose personal values influence their (dis)favorability toward brand morality.
2. Examining the role of CSRO and core brand values in shaping a brand's approach to moralistic initiatives.
3. Exploring the relationships between brand morality and key brand concepts, such as honesty, trust and satisfaction, to determine their interdependencies.

Given the vast scope of brand morality, our proposed antecedents and consequences represent only a partial perspective. We encourage further research to investigate factors contributing to a deeper understanding of this evolving concept.

What Challenges Will a Brand Morality Study Face?

As illustrated by the cases of John Lewis Partnership, Lush, Meta and Patagonia, consumer perceptions of brand morality are dynamic and can evolve alongside societal and cultural shifts. Whether an inclusive and adaptable framework of brand morality accounts for different societal and cultural shifts remains to be confirmed and, thus, a challenge. Another challenge is the extent to which technological advancement can dictate future research on brand morality. For instance, brands adopt chatbots as a customer service tool. Will consumers perceive the tool as less caring because of the lack of human-to-human interaction and thus less moralistic for usage? (see Press, 2023, on 'One negative chatbot experience drives away 30% of customers') When brands employ artificial intelligence to generate brand messages or mascots, will consumers perceive the strategy as lacking authenticity, integrity, or care and thus less moral? (see NZ Herald, 2024 on 'Coke's AI-generated commercials').

Does Brand Morality Apply in Crisis Contexts?

Brand morality has been largely overlooked in crisis contexts, with existing research focusing primarily on non-crisis scenarios (see Table 28.5). However, given the increasing prevalence of global crises – such as the wars in Gaza and Ukraine, wildfires in Los Angeles, flooding in England and Europe, and rising anti-social behavior – the need for moral branding has never been greater (Martin, 2024). People often experience despair, hopelessness, insecurity and anger in such times (Burkeman, 2019), highlighting the urgency for brands to inject kindness, care and generosity into society.

Brands can play a crucial role by adopting a moralistic mindset and engaging in altruistic initiatives. Examples include:

- Partnering with charities and food banks to support vulnerable communities (Smithers, 2020).
- Donating funds to humanitarian organizations (e.g., UNICEF) to provide essential services to disaster victims (Feitelberg, 2022).
- Collaborating to tackle anti-social behavior and raising awareness in local communities (PCC for Hampshire, 2024).

However, brands must approach crisis-driven morality strategically and authentically. Attempting to engage in every crisis or moralistic initiative may appear opportunistic and insincere. Instead, brands should carefully align their efforts with their core values and target consumers' personal values. A well-planned moral approach allows brands to be generous while fostering stronger community ties and environmental stewardship.

REFERENCES

Agu, E. E., Iyelolu, T. V., Idemudia, C., & Ijomah, T. I. (2024). Exploring the relationship between sustainable business practices and increased brand loyalty. *International Journal of Management & Entrepreneurship Research*, *6*(8), 2463–2475. https://doi.org/10.51594/ijmer.v6i8.1365

Alwi, S. F. S., Ali, S. M., & Nguyen, B. (2017). The importance of ethics in branding: Mediating effects of ethical branding on company reputation and brand loyalty. *Business Ethics Quarterly*, *27*(3), 393–422. https://doi.org/10.1017/beq.2017.20

Amos, C., King, J., & King, S. (2021). The health halo of morality- and purity-signifying brand names. *Journal of Product & Brand Management*, *30*(8), 1262–1276. https://doi.org/10.1108/JPBM-06-2020-2947

Asamoah, G., Kusi, L. Y., Coffie, I. S., Afum, E., & Bonsu-Owu, H. K. (2025). Corporate social responsibility, corporate brand image and employer attractiveness: perspectives of potential employees. *International Journal of Business and Emerging Markets*, *17*(1), 71–86. https://doi.org/10.1504/IJBEM.2025.142923

Austin, J. R., Siguaw, J. A., & Mattila, A. S. (2003). A re-examination of the generalizability of the Aaker brand personality measurement framework. *Journal of Strategic Marketing*, *11*(2), 77–92. https://doi.org/10.1080/0965254032000104469

Baker, H. (2021, November 23). *Is Lush mad to quit social media or will it be start of a trend?* Business Live. www.business-live.co.uk/retail-consumer/lush-mad-quit-social-media-22247322.

Baumard, N., André, J. B., & Sperber, D. (2013). A mutualistic approach to morality: The evolution of fairness by partner choice. *Behavioral and Brain Sciences*, *36*(1), 59–78. https://doi.org/10.1017/S0140525X11002202

Beets, P. A. (2012). Strengthening morality and ethics in educational assessment through ubuntu in South Africa. *Educational Philosophy and Theory*, 44(sup2), 68–83. https://doi.org/10.1111/j.1469-5812.2011.00796.x

Belk, R. W. (1988). Possessions and the extended self. *Journal of Consumer Research*, *15*(2), 139. https://doi.org/10.1086/209154

Bhattacharjee, A., Berman, J. Z., & Reed, A. (2013). Tip of the hat, wag of the finger: How moral decoupling enables consumers to admire and admonish. *Journal of Consumer Research*, *39*(6), 1167–1184. https://doi.org/10.1086/667786

Blackett, T., & Russell, N. (2000). Co-branding – the science of alliance. *Journal of Brand Management*, 7(3), 161–170. https://doi.org/10.1057/bm.2000.3

Brandt, D., & Rose, C. (2004). Global networking and universal ethics. *AI & Society*, *18*(4), 334–343. https://doi.org/10.1007/s00146-003-0289-3

Bravo, O. S. A. C., & Chapa, S. (2024). Testing the effects of moral intensity news frames on consumer boycott intention. *Journal of Consumer Marketing*, *41*(2), 226–238. https://doi.org/10.1108/JCM-06-2022-5413

Brenkert, G. G. (2016). Business ethics and human rights: An overview. *Business and Human Rights Journal*, *1*(2), 277–306. https://doi.org/10.1017/bhj.2016.1

Broccardo, L., Zicari, A., Jabeen, F., & Bhatti, Z. A. (2023). How digitalization supports a sustainable business model: A literature review. *Technological Forecasting and Social Change*, *187*, 122146. https://doi.org/10.1016/j.techfore.2022.122146

Brown, S., Kozinets, R. V., & Sherry J. F., Jr. (2003). Teaching old brands new tricks: Retro branding and the revival of brand meaning. *Journal of Marketing*, *67*(3), 19–33. https://doi.org/10.1509/jmkg.67.3.19.18657

Brunk, K. H. (2010). Exploring origins of ethical company/brand perceptions – A consumer perspective of corporate ethics. *Journal of Business Research*, *63*(3), 255–262. https://doi.org/10.1016/j.jbusres.2009.03.011

Burkeman, O. (2019, May 11). *The age of rage: are we really living in angrier times?* The Guardian: Lifestyle. www.theguardian.com/lifeandstyle/2019/may/11/all-fired-up-are-we-really-living-angrier-times

Burton, B. K., & Goldsby, M. (2009). Corporate social responsibility orientation, goals, and behavior: A study of small business owners. *Business & Society*, *48*(1), 88–104. https://doi.org/10.1177/0007650307305367

Campbell, M. C., & Winterich, K. P. (2018). A framework for the consumer psychology of morality in the marketplace. *Journal of Consumer Psychology*, *28*(2), 167–179. https://doi.org/10.1002/jcpy.1038

Carrington, M. J., Neville, B. A., & Whitwell, G. J. (2014). Lost in translation: Exploring the ethical consumer intention–behavior gap. *Journal of Business Research*, *67*(1), 2759–2767. https://doi.org/10.1016/j.jbusres.2012.09.022

Carroll, A. B. (2021). Corporate social responsibility: Perspectives on the CSR construct's development and future. *Business & Society*, *60*(6), 1258–1278. https://doi.org/10.1177/00076503211001765

Carroll, R., Cadet, F. T., & Kachersky, L. (2022). Authenticity attracts authenticity: The impact of brand authenticity and self-authenticity on brand loyalty. *Journal of Brand Strategy*, 10(4), 377–388. https://doi.org/10.69554/FOEC1670

Chaudhuri, A., & Holbrook, M. B. (2001). The chain of effects from brand trust and brand affect to brand performance: the role of brand loyalty. *Journal of Marketing*, *65*(2), 81–93. https://doi.org/10.1509/jmkg.65.2.81.18255

Cheng, G., & Yu, W. (2021). Brand attachment and oppositional loyalty: The moderating role of moral identity. *Social Behavior and Personality: An International Journal*, *49*(10), 1–18. https://doi.org/10.2224/sbp.10804

Choi, W. J., & Winterich, K. P. (2013). Can brands move in from the outside? How moral identity enhances out-group brand attitudes. *Journal of Marketing*, *77*(2), 96–111. https://doi.org/10.1509/jm.11.0544

Cision. (2024, November 30). *How brands can battle misinformation (and why they need to)*. Cision. www.cision.com/resources/articles/how-brands-can-battle-misinformation

Cornwell, J. F., & Higgins, E. T. (2019). Sense of personal control intensifies moral judgments of others' actions. *Frontiers in Psychology*, 10, 2261. https://doi.org/10.3389/fpsyg.2019.02261

Crane, A. (2001). Unpacking the ethical product. *Journal of Business Ethics*, *30*(4), 361–373. https://doi.org/10.1023/A:1010793013027

Curry, O. S., Chesters, M. J., & Van Lissa, C. J. (2019). Mapping morality with a compass: Testing the theory of 'morality-as-cooperation'with a new questionnaire. *Journal of Research in Personality*, 78, 106–124. https://doi.org/10.1016/j.jrp.2018.10.008

Decety, J., & Cacioppo, S. (2012). The speed of morality: A high-density electrical neuroimaging study. *Journal of Neurophysiology*, *108*(11), 3068–3072. https://doi.org/10.1152/jn.00473.2012

De Chernatony, L., Cottam, S., & Segal-Horn, S. (2006). Communicating services brands' values internally and externally. *The Service Industries Journal*, *26*(8), 819–836. https://doi.org/10.1080/02642060601011616

Delgado-Ballester, E., Munuera-Aleman, J. L., & Yague-Guillen, M. J. (2003). Development and validation of a brand trust scale. *International Journal of Market Research*, *45*(1), 1–18. https://doi.org/10.1177/147078530304500103

Deutsch, M. (1973). *The resolution of conflict: Constructive and destructive processes*. Yale University Press.

Doney, P. M., & Cannon, J. P. (1997). An examination of the nature of trust in buyer–seller relationships. *Journal of Marketing*, *61*(2), 35–51. https://doi.org/10.1177/002224299706100203

Doran, C. J. (2009). The role of personal values in fair trade consumption. *Journal of Business Ethics*, *84*(4), 549–563. https://doi.org/10.1007/s10551-008-9724-1

Ellemers, N., & Chopova, T. (2021). The social responsibility of organizations: Perceptions of organizational morality as a key mechanism explaining the relation between CSR activities and stakeholder support. *Research in Organizational Behavior*, *41*, 100156. https://doi.org/10.1016/j.riob.2022.100156

Ellemers, N., Van Der Toorn, J., Paunov, Y., & Van Leeuwen, T. (2019). The psychology of morality: A review and analysis of empirical studies published from 1940 through 2017. *Personality and Social Psychology Review*, *23*(4), 332–366. https://doi.org/10.1177/1088868318811759

Escalas, J. E. (2004). Narrative processing: Building consumer connections to brands. *Journal of*

Consumer Psychology, *14*(1–2), 168–180. https://doi.org/10.1207/s15327663jcp1401&2_19

Escalas, J. E., & Bettman, J. R. (2003). You are what they eat: The influence of reference groups on consumers' connections to brands. *Journal of Consumer Psychology*, *13*(3), 339–348. https://doi.org/10.1207/S15327663JCP1303_14

Esmaeilpour, M., & Aram, F. (2016). Investigating the impact of viral message appeal and message credibility on consumer attitude toward the brand. *Management & Marketing*, *11*(2), 470–483. https://doi.org/10.1515/mmcks-2016-0010

Feitelberg, R. (2022, February 28). *As Russian war continues, brands and retailers work to keep employees safe and offer relief.* Women's Wear Daily. wwd.com/fashion-news/fashion-scoops/as-russian-war-continues-brands-and-retailers-work-to-keep-employees-safe-and-offer-relief-1235108516/

Firat, R., & McPherson, C. M. (2010). Toward an Integrated Science of Morality. In S. Hitlin & S. Vaisey (Eds.), *Handbook of the sociology of morality. Handbooks of sociology and social research.* Springer.

Fisher, A., & Dimmock, M. (2020). *Philosophical thought: Aristotelian virtue ethics.* Retrieved from https://open.library.okstate.edu/introphilosophy/chapter/virtue-ethics/

Fombrun, C. J. (2005). Corporate reputations as economic assets. In M. A. Hitt, R. E. Freeman & J. S. Harrison (Eds.), *The blackwell handbook of strategic management* (pp. 285–308). Blackwell Publishers Ltd.

Fombrun, C. J., & Van Riel, C. B. (2004). *Fame & fortune: How successful companies build winning reputations.* Financial Times Press.

Fornell, C. (1992). A national customer satisfaction barometer: The Swedish experience. *Journal of Marketing*, *56*(1), 6–21. https://doi.org/10.1177/002224299205600103

Freeman, R. E., Phillips, R., & Sisodia, R. (2020). Tensions in stakeholder theory. *Business & Society*, *59*(2), 213–231. https://doi.org/10.1177/0007650318773750

Graham, J., Haidt, J., Koleva, S., Motyl, M., Iyer, R., Wojcik, S. P., & Ditto, P. H. (2013). Chapter Two - Moral foundations theory: The pragmatic validity of moral pluralism. In P. Devine, & A. Plant (Eds.), *Advances in experimental social psychology* (Vol. *47*, pp. 55–130). Academic Press. https://doi.org/10.1016/B978-0-12-407236-7.00002-4.

Grappi, S., Romani, S., & Bagozzi, R. P. (2013). Consumer response to corporate irresponsible behavior: Moral emotions and virtues. *Journal of Business Research*, *66*(10), 1814–1821. https://doi.org/10.1016/j.jbusres.2013.02.002

Greenberg, J., & Baron, R. A. (2008). *Behavior in Organizations* (10th ed.). Pearson.

Hagelstein, J., Einwiller, S., & Zerfass, A. (2021). The ethical dimension of public relations in Europe: Digital channels, moral challenges, resources, and training. *Public Relations Review*, *47*(4), 102063. https://doi.org/10.1016/j.pubrev.2021.102063

Haidt, J. (2001). The emotional dog and its rational tail: a social intuitionist approach to moral judgment. *Psychological Review*, *108*(4), 814. https://doi.org/10.1037/0033-295X.108.4.814

Haidt, J., & Graham, J. (2007). When Morality Opposes Justice: Conservatives Have Moral Intuitions that Liberals may not Recognize. *Social Justice Research*, *20*(1), 98–116. https://doi.org/10.1007/s11211-007-0034-z

Haidt, J., & Joseph, C. (2004). Intuitive ethics: How innately prepared intuitions generate culturally variable virtues. *Daedalus*, *133*(4), 55–66. https://doi.org/10.1162/0011526042365555

Harrison, D. E., Ferrell, O. C., Ferrell, L., & Hair J. F., Jr. (2020). Corporate social responsibility and business ethics: conceptualization, scale development and validation. *Journal of Product & Brand Management*, *29*(4), 431–439. https://doi.org/10.1108/JPBM-11-2018-2113

Hayes, S. C., Luoma, J. B., Bond, F. W., Masuda, A., & Lillis, J. (2006). Acceptance and commitment therapy: Model, processes and outcomes. *Behaviour Research and Therapy*, *44*(1), 1–25. https://doi.org/10.1016/j.brat.2005.06.006

He, H., & Harris, L. (2020). The impact of Covid-19 pandemic on corporate social responsibility and marketing philosophy. *Journal of Business Research*, *116*, 176–182. https://doi.org/10.1016/j.jbusres.2020.05.030

Hemberg, J., & Wiklund Gustin, L. (2020). Caring from the heart as belonging – The basis for mediating compassion. *Nursing Open*, *7*(2), 660–668. https://doi.org/10.1002/nop2.438

Hoppner, J. J., & Vadakkepatt, G. G. (2019). Examining moral authority in the marketplace: A conceptualization and framework. *Journal of Business Research*, *95*, 417–427. https://doi.org/10.1016/j.jbusres.2018.07.045

Hosseini, M., & Shabani, M. (2015). New approach to customer segmentation based on changes in customer value. *Journal of Marketing Analytics*, *3*(3), 110–121. https://doi.org/10.1057/jma.2015.10

Hunt, S. D., & Vitell, S. J. (2006). The general theory of marketing ethics: A revision and three questions. *Journal of Macromarketing*, *26*(2), 143–153. https://doi.org/10.1177/0276146706290923

Ilicic, J., Brennan, S. M., & Kulczynski, A. (2021). Sinfully decadent: priming effects of immoral advertising symbols on indulgence. *Marketing Letters*, *32*(1), 61–73. https://doi.org/10.1007/s11002-020-09544-6

Izogo, E. E., & Ogba, I. E. (2015). Service quality, customer satisfaction and loyalty in automobile repair

services sector. *International Journal of Quality & Reliability Management*, *32*(3), 250–269. https://doi.org/10.1108/IJQRM-05-2013-0075
Jeanes, E. L. (2013). The construction and controlling effect of a moral brand. *Scandinavian Journal of Management*, *29*(2), 163–172. https://doi.org/10.1016/j.scaman.2013.03.007
JLP. (2024, November 29). *Who we are*. John Lewis Partnership. https://apastyle.apa.org/learn/faqs/web-page-no-author
Joseph, K. G., Arinaitwe, E., & Muwaga, M. (2022). The relationship between mindfulness and sustainable consumer behaviour: The mediating effect of self-transcendence. *International Journal of Social Science and Humanities Research*, *10*(2), 94–101. https://doi.org/10.5281/zenodo.6500349
Kant, I. (1785). *Groundwork of the Metaphysics of Morals (1785)*. New Haven.
Kaur, M., & Manna, R. (2024). Sale of second-hand goods by consumers: mediating role of satisfaction between perceived value and behavioural intentions. *The International Review of Retail, Distribution and Consumer Research*, *35*(3), 291–312. https://doi.org/10.1080/09593969.2024.2393095
Keller, K. L. (2003). *Strategic brand management: Building, measuring, and managing brand equity*. Pearson Education.
Kesebir, S., & Haidt, J. (2010). Morality. In S. Fiske, D. Gilbert, & G. Lindzey (Eds.), *Handbook of social psychology* (pp. n.d.). SSRN. https://papers.ssrn.com/sol3/papers.cfm?abstract_id=1534423
Kim, M. K., Park, M. C., & Jeong, D. H. (2004). The effects of customer satisfaction and switching barrier on customer loyalty in Korean mobile telecommunication services. *Telecommunications Policy*, *28*(2), 145–159. https://doi.org/10.1016/j.telpol.2003.12.003
Kim, T., & Ball, J. G. (2021). Unintended consequences of warmth appeals: An extension of the compensation effect between warmth and competence to advertising. *Journal of Advertising*, *50*(5), 622–638. https://doi.org/10.1080/00913367.2021.1940393
Kirmani, A., Hamilton, R. W., Thompson, D. V., & Lantzy, S. (2017). Doing well versus doing good: The differential effect of underdog positioning on moral and competent service providers. *Journal of Marketing*, *81*(1), 103–117. https://doi.org/10.1509/jm.15.0369
Kolbl, Ž., Diamantopoulos, A., Arslanagic-Kalajdzic, M., & Zabkar, V. (2020). Do brand warmth and brand competence add value to consumers? A stereotyping perspective. *Journal of Business Research*, *118*, 346–362. https://doi.org/10.1016/j.jbusres.2020.06.048
Kopalle, P. K., & Lehmann, D. R. (2015). The truth hurts: How customers may lose from honest advertising. *International Journal of Research in Marketing*, *32*(3), 251–262. https://doi.org/10.1016/j.ijresmar.2014.12.003
Kotler, P., & Armstrong, G. (2022). *Principles of marketing* (18th ed.). Pearson.
Kotsantonis, S., Pinney, C., & Serafeim, G. (2016). ESG integration in investment management: Myths and realities. *Journal of Applied Corporate Finance*, *28*(2), 10–16. https://doi.org/10.1111/jacf.12169
Krishna, A., & Kim, S. (2021). Exploring the dynamics between brand investment, customer investment, brand identification, and brand identity fusion. *Journal of Business Research*, *137*, 267–277. https://doi.org/10.1016/j.jbusres.2021.08.039
Lee, S., & Heo, C. Y. (2009). Corporate social responsibility and customer satisfaction among US publicly traded hotels and restaurants. *International Journal of Hospitality Management*, *28*(4), 635–637. https://doi.org/10.1016/j.ijhm.2009.02.007
Lin, Y. H., Lin, F. J., & Wang, K. H. (2021). The effect of social mission on service quality and brand image. *Journal of Business Research*, *132*, 744–752. https://doi.org/10.1016/j.jbusres.2020.10.054
Lopez, A., & Rodriguez, R. (2018). Children and their brands: how young consumers relate to brands. *Journal of Consumer Marketing*, *35*(2), 130–142. https://doi.org/10.1108/JCM-06-2016-1842
Luo, X., & Bhattacharya, C. (2006). Corporate social responsibility, customer satisfaction, and market value. *Journal of Marketing*, *70*(4), 1–18. https://doi.org/10.1509/jmkg.70.4.001
Martin, F., & Tao-Peng, F. (2017). Morality matters? Consumer identification with celebrity endorsers in China. *Asian Business & Management*, *16*(4–5), 272–289. https://doi.org/10.1057/s41291-017-0022-6
Martin, N. (2024, September 9). *Anti-social behaviour concerns: Thousands of communities say their fears aren't being taken seriously by authorities*. Sky News. https://news.sky.com/story/anti-social-behaviour-concerns-thousands-of-communities-say-their-fears-arent-being-taken-seriously-by-authorities-13210576
McCulloch, A. (2021, September 23). *Employee anger at John Lewis over payments to managers*. Personnel Today. www.personneltoday.com/hr/employee-anger-at-john-lewis-over-payments-to-managers/
McDonald, L. M., & Rundle-Thiele, S. (2008). Corporate social responsibility and bank customer satisfaction. *International Journal of Bank Marketing*, *26*(3), 170–182. https://doi.org/10.1108/02652320810864643
McHugh, C., McGann, M., Igou, E. R., & Kinsella, E. L. (2022). Moral judgment as categorization (MJAC). *Perspectives on Psychological Science*,

17(1), 131–152. https://doi.org/10.1177/1745691621990636

Mill, J. S. (2016). Utilitarianism. In S. M. Cahn (Ed.), *Seven masterpieces of philosophy* (pp. 329–375). Routledge. https://doi.org/10.4324/9781315508818.

Mills, B., & Wilner, A. (2023). The science behind 'values': Applying moral foundations theory to strategic foresight. *Futures & Foresight Science*, *5*(1), e145. https://doi.org/10.1002/ffo2.145

Mirzaei, A., Wilkie, D. C., & Siuki, H. (2022). Woke brand activism: Authenticity or the lack of it. *Journal of Business Research*, 139, 1–12. https://doi.org/10.1016/j.jbusres.2021.09.044

Nadeau, J., Rutter, R., & Lettice, F. (2020). Social media responses and brand personality in product and moral harm crises: why waste a good crisis? *Journal of Marketing Management*, *36*(11–12), 1031–1054. https://doi.org/10.1080/0267257X.2020.1764080

Nadeem, W., Tan, T. M., Tajvidi, M., & Hajli, N. (2021). How do experiences enhance brand relationship performance and value co-creation in social commerce? The role of consumer engagement and self brand-connection. *Technological Forecasting and Social Change*, *171*, 120952. https://doi.org/10.1016/j.techfore.2021.120952

Nguyen, N. X., Tran, K., & Nguyen, T. A. (2021). Impact of service quality on in-patients' satisfaction, perceived value, and customer loyalty: A mixed-methods study from a developing country. *Patient Preference and Adherence*, *15*, 2523–2538. https://doi.org/10.2147/PPA.S333586

Nguyen, T. P., & Dekhili, S. (2019). Sustainable development in Vietnam: An examination of consumers' perceptions of green products. *Business Strategy & Development*, *2*(2), 127–136. https://doi.org/10.1002/bsd2.48

Nucci, L., & Turiel, E. (2009). Capturing the complexity of moral development and education. *Mind, Brain, and Education*, *3*(3), 151–159. https://doi.org/10.1111/j.1751-228X.2009.01065.x

NZ Herald. (2024, November 21). *Coca-Cola Christmas ad 2024: Coke's AI-generated commercials slammed by consumers*. New Zealand Herald. www.nzherald.co.nz/entertainment/coca-cola-christmas-ad-2024-cokes-ai-generated-commercials-slammed-by-consumers/YHGCFVAHY5HNPNLVJERVGUNA2E/

Oh, H. (1999). Service quality, customer satisfaction, and customer value: A holistic perspective. *International Journal of Hospitality Management*, *18*(1), 67. https://doi.org/10.1016/S0278-4319(98)00047-4

Oliver, R. L. (1999). Whence consumer loyalty? *Journal of Marketing*, *63*(4_suppl1), 33–44. https://doi.org/10.1177/00222429990634s105

Park, H., & Kim, Y. K. (2016). An empirical test of the triple bottom line of customer-centric sustainability: the case of fast fashion. *Fashion and Textiles*, *3*(1), 1–18. https://doi.org/10.1186/s40691-016-0077-6

Park, J., Hong, E., & Park, Y. N. (2023). Toward a new business model of retail industry: The role of brand experience and brand authenticity. *Journal of Retailing and Consumer Services*, *74*, 103426. https://doi.org/10.1016/j.jretconser.2023.103426

PCC for Hampshire. (2024, November 18). *Partnership approach tackling anti-social behaviour sees significant impact*. Police & Crime Commissioner (PCC) for Hampshire & Isle of Wight. www.hampshire-pcc.gov.uk/partnership-approach-tackling-anti-social-behaviour-sees-significant-impact

Press, G. (2023, February 1). *One negative chatbot experience drives away 30% of customers*. Forbes. www.forbes.com/sites/gilpress/2023/02/01/one-negative-chatbot-experience-drives-away-30-of-customers/

Rachels, J., & Rachels, S. (Eds.). (2019). *The right thing to do: Readings in moral philosophy*. Rowman & Littlefield.

Reidenbach, R. E., & Robin, D. P. (1990). Toward the development of a multidimensional scale for improving evaluations of business ethics. *Journal of Business Ethics*, *9*(8), 639–653. https://doi.org/10.1007/BF00383391

Reynolds, S. J. (2006). Moral awareness and ethical predispositions: investigating the role of individual differences in the recognition of moral issues. *Journal of Applied Psychology*, *91*(1), 233. https://doi.org/10.1037/0021-9010.91.1.233

Rhodes, C. (2022, September 20). *Patagonia's radical business move is great – but governments, not billionaires, should be saving the planet*. The Guardian: Opinion. www.theguardian.com/commentisfree/2022/sep/20/patagonia-billion-dollar-climate-initiative-philanthropy

Romani, S., Grappi, S., Zarantonello, L., & Bagozzi, R. P. (2015). The revenge of the consumer! How brand moral violations lead to consumer anti-brand activism. *Journal of Brand Management*, *22*(8), 658–672. https://doi.org/10.1057/bm.2015.38

Rush, L. (2021, June 15). *Want To Build Your Brand's Reputation? Try Enhancing The Customer Support Experience*. Forbes: Small Business. www.forbes.com/councils/forbesbusinesscouncil/2021/06/15/want-to-build-your-brands-reputation-try-enhancing-the-customer-support-experience/

Sansome, K., Conduit, J., & Wilkie, D. (2025). Consumers demand transparency… but do they actually engage? Exploring motives and interactions with brand transparency information. *Journal of Business Research*, *194*, 1–12. https://doi.org/10.1016/j.jbusres.2025.115386

Schembri, S., Merrilees, B., & Kristiansen, S. (2010). Brand consumption and narrative of the self. *Psychology & Marketing, 27*(6), 623–637. https://doi.org/10.1002/mar.20348

Schmeltz, L. (2012). Consumer-oriented CSR communication: focusing on ability or morality? *Corporate Communications: An International Journal, 17*(1), 29–49. https://doi.org/10.1108/13563281211196344

Schmidt, K., & Ludlow, C. (2002). *Inclusive branding: The why and how of a holistic approach to brands*. Palgrave Macmillan.

Schwartz, M. S., & Carroll, A. B. (2008). Integrating and unifying competing and complementary frameworks. *Business & Society, 47*(2), 148–186. https://doi.org/10.1177/0007650306297942

Sen, S., Bhattacharya, C. B., & Korschun, D. (2006). The role of corporate social responsibility in strengthening multiple stakeholder relationships: A field experiment. *Journal of the Academy of Marketing Science, 34*(2), 158–167. https://doi.org/10.1177/0092070305284978

Shaban, A. (2016). Managing and leading a diverse workforce: One of the main challenges in management. *Procedia-Social and Behavioral Sciences*, 230, 76–84. https://doi.org/10.1016/j.sbspro.2016.09.010

Singh, J., & Crisafulli, B. (2022). *Brands and consumers: A research overview*. Routledge.

Sloan, D. R., Aiken, D., & Mikkelson, A. C. (2018). Places in names: an investigation of regional geographic brand congruency. *Journal of Product & Brand Management, 27*(7), 781–792. https://doi.org/10.1108/JPBM-11-2017-1656

Smithers, R. (2020, March 30). *Morrisons gives food banks £10 m during coronavirus outbreak*. The Guardian. www.theguardian.com/world/2020/mar/30/morrisons-gives-food-banks-10m-during-coronavirus-outbreak

Soliman, M., & Ben-Amar, W. (2022). Corporate social responsibility orientation and textual features of financial disclosures. *International Review of Financial Analysis, 84*, 102400. https://doi.org/10.1016/j.irfa.2022.102400

Solomon, R. C. (1992). *Ethics and excellence: Cooperation and integrity in business*. Oxford University Press.

Sung, Y., & Kim, J. (2010). Effects of brand personality on brand trust and brand affect. *Psychology & Marketing, 27*(7), 639–661. https://doi.org/10.1002/mar.20349

Thøgersen, J. (2021). Consumer behavior and climate change: Consumers need considerable assistance. *Current Opinion in Behavioral Sciences*, 42, 9–14. https://doi.org/10.1016/j.cobeha.2021.02.008

Toovey, J. (2023, September 13). *Could a ban on zero-hours contracts backfire?* IPSE. Retrieved December 1, 2024, from www.ipse.co.uk/articles/could-a-ban-on-zero-hours-contracts-backfire

Trevino, L. K., & Nelson, K. A. (2021). *Managing business ethics: Straight talk about how to do it right* (8th ed.). Wiley.

Tse, D. K., & Wilton, P. C. (1988). Models of consumer satisfaction formation: An extension. *Journal of Marketing Research, 25*(2), 204–212. https://doi.org/10.1177/002224378802500209

UK Government. (2023, October 27). *Ministers ask businesses to help in drive to end rough sleeping*. GOV.UK. Retrieved December 1, 2024, from www.gov.uk/government/news/ministers-ask-businesses-to-help-in-drive-to-end-rough-sleeping

van Prooijen, A. M., & Bartels, J. (2019). Anthropomorphizing brands: The role of attributed brand traits in interactive CSR communication and consumer online endorsements. *Journal of Consumer Behaviour, 18*(6), 474–483. https://doi.org/10.1002/cb.1786

Veloutsou, C., & Moutinho, L. (2009). Brand relationships through brand reputation and brand tribalism. *Journal of Business Research, 62*(3), 314–322. https://doi.org/10.1016/j.jbusres.2008.05.010

Wang, Z., Li, W., & Bian, K. (2020). Corporate ethics and social responsibility. *Academic Journal of Humanities & Social Sciences, 3*(10), 9–15. https://doi.org/10.25236/AJHSS.2020.031002

Wei, Y., Ekinci, Y., & Sit, K. (2025). More than law-abiding: A multi-staged consumer study on brand morality. *Psychology & Marketing, 42*(2), 600–614. https://doi.org/10.1002/mar.22139

Wei, Y., Sit, K. J., & Ekinci, Y. (2024). Customer definitions of moral value for retail brands: a qualitative understanding. *Journal of Retailing and Consumer Services, 77*, 103697. https://doi.org/10.1016/j.jretconser.2023.103697

White, K., Habib, R., & Hardisty, D. J. (2019). How to SHIFT consumer behaviors to be more sustainable: A literature review and guiding framework. *Journal of Marketing, 83*(3), 22–49. https://doi.org/10.1177/0022242919825649

Willis, J., & Todorov, A. (2006). First impressions: Making up your mind after a 100-ms exposure to a face. *Psychological Science, 17*(7), 592–598. https://doi.org/10.1111/j.1467-9280.2006.01750.x

Winterich, K. P., Mittal, V., & Aquino, K. (2013). When does recognition increase charitable behavior? Toward a moral identity-based model. *Journal of Marketing, 77*(3), 121–134. https://doi.org/10.1509/jm.11.0477

Wood, Z. (2021, November 23). *Lush quits Facebook, Instagram, TikTok and Snapchat over safety concerns*. The Guardian-Business. www.theguardian.com/business/2021/nov/23/lush-quits-facebook-instagram-tiktok-snapchat-social-media

Xu, H. (2022). Confucian culture and filial piety. In D. Gu, & M. E. Durpe (Eds.), *Encyclopedia of gerontology and population aging* (pp. 1132–1135). Springer International Publishing.

Xie, G. X., Chang, H., & Rank-Christman, T. (2022). Contesting dishonesty: When and why perspective-taking decreases ethical tolerance of marketplace deception. *Journal of Business Ethics*, *175*(1), 117–133. https://doi.org/10.1007/s10551-020-04582-6

Zahn, M. (2025, January 7). *Here's why Meta ended fact-checking, according to experts*. ABC News. https://abcnews.go.com/US/why-did-meta-remove-fact-checkers-experts-explain/story?id=117417445

Zhou, Y., Lai, H., Chen, X., & Hu, C. (2025). Protecting labor rights: Contract design and coordination between brand firms and suppliers. *European Journal of Operational Research*, *320*(1), 69–84. https://doi.org/10.1016/j.ejor.2024.07.025

29

Brand Social Responsibility

Bianca Grohmann

Social responsibility (SR) reflects the notion that organizations and brands are responsible for their social and environmental impact (Cote, 2021). Amid consumers' growing support of global sustainability goals and participation in socially responsible consumption (Agrawal & Gupta, 2018), brands are increasingly called out for shortcomings related to SR. For example, fast fashion brands – renowned for cheaply and quickly moving fashion trends from design to retail stores – are criticized for negative environmental impacts resulting from chemical and water use, carbon emissions, waste production and microplastics (David Suzuki Foundation, n.d.). These brands are also accused of offering products manufactured in poor working conditions, not ensuring living wages, or using child labor (Rajvanshi, 2023). Brands operating in industries considered controversial due to their possible negative impact on the environment and human health – including brands operating in the biotechnology, pharmaceutical, energy, oil, mining, transport, food and resource industries (Conte et al., 2023) – face similar criticism.

Increasing consumer and regulatory focus on SR has also resulted in several methods of rating brands in terms of SR to inform consumer decision-making and facilitate more socially responsible consumption choices. Examples include the *Good on You Sustainable Fashion and Beauty Brand Ratings* (Good on You, n.d.) or the *Forbes Best Brands for Social Impact* (Schwarz, 2024). Similar approaches have been implemented to rank corporate brands and firms in terms of SR, such as in the *Company Environmental, Social and Governance (ESG) Risk Ratings* (Sustainalytics, n.d.).

Increasing transparency regarding SR practices, policies and investments has moved SR activities to the forefront not only of consumer decision-making, but also of investor and supply chain considerations. In recognition of the importance of SR, an increasing number of corporations publish corporate SR (CSR) reports summarizing objectives and achievements related to environmental, ethical, philanthropic and economic development activities (Cote, 2021). Although many countries do not mandate annual CSR reports, 96% of the 250 leading global companies publish sustainability or ESG reports (KPMG, 2022).

In line with these developments, research in brand management has investigated the impact of SR on consumer responses to product brands and corporate brands, as well as the implications of corporate brand SR for corporate brand equity and brand valuation. This chapter presents an overview of this literature and highlights areas in need of further inquiry.

SR: DEFINITION, SCOPE AND APPLICATION TO BRANDS

SR refers to discretionary activities aimed at enhancing societal, environmental and economic well-being (Sen et al., 2016). SR activities comprise socially responsible business practices, corporate philanthropy, cause-related marketing, sponsorships, environmental responsibility and sustainability, employee volunteerism and access to distribution channels (Lacey et al., 2015; Peloza & Shang, 2011). As a result, SR activities benefit various stakeholders, including consumers, employees, supply chain partners, the community and the environment (Lacey et al., 2015; Peloza & Shang, 2011). Furthermore, SR activities can be implemented at the firm, brand and product level (Grohmann & Bodur, 2015).

Corporate SR

Drawing on the literature on CSR in organizational research (e.g., Carroll, 1979; McWilliams & Siegel, 2001), the marketing literature initially focused on SR implemented at the firm level and its impact on firm financial performance (Luo & Bhattacharya, 2006), consumer perceptions of the firm (Becker-Olsen et al., 2006; Lichtenstein et al., 2004; Sen et al., 2006; Wagner et al., 2009) and consumer responses to the firm's products (Berens et al., 2005; Brown & Dacin, 1997; Gürhan-Canli & Batra, 2004; Mohr et al., 2001; Sen & Bhattacharya, 2001). This literature defined CSR as a firm's activities related to its perceived societal or stakeholder obligations (Brown & Dacin, 1997; Lichtenstein et al., 2004; Luo & Bhattacharya, 2006; Sen & Bhattacharya, 2001) or a firm's voluntary 'commitment to minimizing or eliminating any harmful effects and maximizing its long-run beneficial impact on society' (Mohr et al., 2001, p. 47). Other definitions consider CSR in terms of firm performance in terms of economic, ethical, legal or philanthropic dimensions (Golob et al., 2008; Maignan, 2001; Salmones et al., 2005). Consistent with this conceptualization, many CSR measures capture firms' resource allocation to or performance on a set of discrete CSR dimensions (Maignan & Ferrell, 2004; Salmones et al., 2005). More recently, the marketing literature has adopted the ESG framework to conceptualize dimensions of SR implemented by firms and to examine their effects (Ferrell, 2021; Lee et al., 2022; Paolone et al., 2022).

Brand SR

Unique to the marketing literature is a consideration of SR at the product brand level (Dincer & Dincer, 2012; Du et al., 2007; Grohmann & Bodur, 2015; Madrigal & Boush, 2008). Many consumer-centric SR activities (e.g., cause-related marketing, cause sponsorship, diversity and SR in advertising) are implemented at the brand rather than the firm level (Dincer & Dincer, 2012; Grohmann & Bodur, 2015). As a result of these activities, consumers develop brand SR perceptions (Grohmann & Bodur, 2015). The literature also examines brand SR as it relates to corporate brands. Corporate brands consist of gestalt-like associations that represent firms beyond their products and services (Balmer, 2012; Urde et al., 2007) and reflect 'the organization's personality, its distinctive ways of communicating, and the enduring values that underlie its promise to customers' (Greyser & Urde, 2019, p. 84). Corporate brands differ from product brands in terms of management responsibility (i.e., brand manager vs. chief marketing officer), functional and general responsibility (i.e., marketing employees vs. employees at large), communication channels (i.e., marketing vs. corporate communications mix), stakeholder focus (i.e., consumers/customers vs. internal and external stakeholder network) and values (brand-based vs. founder or corporate culture values) (Balmer, 2001, 2012).

Regardless of whether it involves a product or corporate brand, brand SR differs from CSR in several ways (Dincer & Dincer, 2012; Grohmann & Bodur, 2015; Vuong & Khanh Giao, 2020): First, CSR and brand SR relate to different entities (Grohmann & Bodur, 2015). Brand SR relates to a product or corporate brand, which represents an abstract mental network of brand associations (Balmer, 2012; Keller, 1993; Urde et al., 2007). CSR, on the other hand, relates to the firm as a concrete organizational entity.

A second difference relates to the stakeholder groups that SR activities are directed toward (Grohmann & Bodur, 2015; Vuong & Khanh Giao, 2020). Brand SR activities aim to enhance SR perceptions primarily among consumers or business-to-business customers, although some authors argue that corporate brand SR also considers additional internal and external stakeholders (Balmer, 2001). Firm CSR activities, on the other hand, always require the balancing of sometimes contradictory demands and expectations across multiple stakeholder groups (Shea, 2010). These stakeholder groups comprise organizational groups (i.e., customers, employees, shareholders, suppliers), the community (i.e., residents, special interest groups), regulatory entities (i.e., municipalities, states, lawmakers) and the media (Maignan & Ferrell, 2004). The fact that firm CSR initiatives are not primarily directed at consumers (Peloza & Shang, 2011) and, therefore, often remain unobserved, results in low consumer awareness (Kim, 2019; Sen et al., 2006) and frequently inaccurate consumer perceptions of firm CSR activities (Brunk, 2010).

Third, brand SR and CSR are associated with idiosyncratic outcomes. Given its consumer and customer focus, product brand SR influences consumer responses to the brand, including brand attitude and purchase intentions (Grohmann & Bodur, 2015; Madrigal & Boush, 2008) and brand sales (Nickerson et al., 2022). Corporate brand SR is generally examined in terms of its impact on corporate brand equity (e.g., Hur et al., 2014; Sharma & Jain, 2019) and corporate brand valuation (e.g., Bhattacharya et al., 2020; Bouvain et al., 2013; Melo & Galan, 2011). CSR-related outcomes investigated in the literature focus on the firm level and include consumers' perceptions of the firm (Becker-Olsen et al., 2006), firm reputation among stakeholders (Lin, 2024), firm financial performance (Beurden & Gössling, 2008; Luo & Bhattacharya, 2006) and investment and employment intent (Sen et al., 2006).

Finally, brand SR and CSR differ in terms of their conceptualization. Consistent with the literature on brand as knowledge structures in consumers' minds (Keller, 1993), brand SR is defined in terms of holistic (or gestalt-like) consumer perceptions of a brand's SR (Dincer & Dincer, 2012; Grohmann & Bodur, 2015; Madrigal & Boush, 2008). This conceptualization considers that consumers rely on mental summary representations in their evaluation of a target (Brunk & Blümelhuber, 2011). This holistic view of brand SR is consistently applied to product brands, whereas research on corporate brands employs both holistic (e.g., Grohmann & Bodur, 2015) and dimension-based conceptualizations of SR (e.g., Bhattacharya et al., 2020; Wang et al., 2021). CSR, on the other hand, is conceptualized in terms of organizational performance on a set of discrete CSR dimensions, such as the economic, ethical, legal or philanthropic dimensions (Golob et al., 2008; Maignan, 2001; Salmones et al., 2005). Performance on CSR dimensions is thereby viewed from the perspective of one or more stakeholder groups (Peloza & Shang, 2011; Sen et al., 2006) or defined by third-party rankings (e.g., the *MSCI KLD 400 Social Index*; *Sustainalytics's ESG Risk Ratings*). Overall, the literature reveals important conceptual and substantive differences between CSR and brand SR.

Product SR

The marketing literature also examines SR at the product level. Product SR is defined as SR pertaining to product attributes, including product ingredients (e.g., recycled, organic, vegan, sustainably harvested materials), product technology (e.g., hybrid or renewable energy technologies) or product functionality (e.g., safety features exceeding industry or legislative standards) (Grohmann & Bodur, 2015). Consumers' product SR perceptions arise from ethical product attributes that mitigate social (e.g., living wages, child labor) or environmental (i.e., waste, emissions, water consumption, pesticide use) concerns (Bodur et al., 2014; Luchs et al., 2010).

Counterintuitively, product SR is associated with both positive and negative effects: Initial research supported a positive relationship between consumers' product SR perceptions and product evaluations (Brown & Dacin, 1997). This relationship is moderated by consumers' resource synergy beliefs (Gupta & Sen, 2013), self-accountability (Peloza et al., 2013) and environmental concern (Lin & Chang, 2012). The effect of product SR is also contingent on congruity between ethical attribute benefits and product category benefits, as well as consumers' price-quality beliefs (Bodur et al., 2014).

The literature also documented negative effects of product SR, however. These arise in the form of a sustainability liability (Luchs et al., 2010), such that product evaluations and consumption amounts reflect an implicit trade-off between socially responsible product attributes and perceived product effectiveness (Lin & Chang, 2012; Luchs et al., 2010). More specifically, consumers prefer environmentally friendly products when gentleness is a valued product attribute (e.g., for baby shampoo), but not when product strength is a desired attribute (e.g., for car wash soap; Luchs et al., 2010). Similarly, when consumers value product strength (e.g., for hand sanitizers, mouthwash), they perceive environmentally friendly products as less effective and therefore consume greater amounts (Lin & Chang, 2012).

Product SR is conceptually distinct from CSR (Brown & Dacin, 1997) and evidence regarding a relationship between consumers' CSR and product SR perceptions is mixed (Brown & Dacin, 1997; Grohmann & Bodur, 2015). Product SR also differs from brand SR: Although brand SR comprises consumers' overall perception of product SR associated with the brand's products, brand SR also arises from the brand's (non-product) marketing and communication activities, such as pricing (e.g., embedded premium charity donations; Henderson & Arora, 2010), packaging (e.g., minimal, compostable, recycled or recyclable) and brand communication (e.g., cause-related marketing; Du et al., 2007; non-deceptive, non-predatory advertising practices; Brunk, 2010; suggestive brand names, such as tentree, Seventh Generation,

Table 29.1 Corporate, brand and product social responsibility

	Corporate Social Responsibility (CSR)	*Brand Social Responsibility*		*Product Social Responsibility*
Focal entity	*Firm*	*Corporate Brand*	*Product Brand*	*Product*
Primary stakeholders	Organizational groups Customers, employees, shareholders, supply chain partners Community groups Residents, special interest groups Regulatory entities Lawmakers, municipalities, states Media	Consumers Additional internal and external stakeholders and networks	Consumers	Consumers
Primary outcomes	Firm reputation Financial performance	Corporate brand equity Corporate brand valuation	Brand attitude Purchase intention Product brand equity	Product evaluation Consumption amount
Nature of the construct	Performance on CSR/ ESG dimensions	Corporate brand associations Performance on CSR/ ESG dimensions	Product brand associations	Product attribute-based

Source: The author.

or Beyond Meat). Research suggests that brands' integration of both product-related and marketing-related (compared to only marketing-related) SR activities enhances consumers' SR perceptions (Du et al., 2007).

Based on this review of the marketing and branding literature, Table 29.1 illustrates key differences between CSR, brand SR as it relates to corporate and product brands, and product SR.

PRODUCT BRAND SR

Definition, Conceptualization and Measurement

In the context of product brands, the marketing literature proposes three conceptualizations of brand SR. The first builds on the literature on brand personality – the set of human characteristics consumers associate with brands (Aaker, 1997, p. 347) and conceives SR as a brand personality characteristic that consumers infer from brand actions, such as environmentally friendly product offerings (Madrigal & Boush, 2008). SR as a brand personality trait mirrors the human personality trait of conscientiousness – one of the Big Five dimensions of human personality (Costa & McCrae, 1992; Digman, 1990) – and refers to a brand's sense of obligation to be accountable for its actions and their impact on society (Madrigal & Boush, 2008). Brand SR is, therefore, defined as 'an enduring, differentiating characteristic that describes a brand's actions with respect to its obligation to the society at large, and the individuals living in that society' (Madrigal & Boush, 2008, p. 540). A five-item descriptive adjective scale – the SR scale (Madrigal & Boush, 2008) – captures this conceptualization of brand SR. This scale shows discriminant validity against the five brand personality dimensions (i.e., sincerity, excitement, sophistication, ruggedness, excitement; Aaker, 1997). Application of the scale supports its nomological validity in that brand SR – as measured by the SR scale – positively relates to consumers' ad, brand and product attitudes, although this relationship is moderated by consumers' willingness to reward (Madrigal & Boush, 2008). The primary disadvantage associated with this measure of brand SR pertains to its relatively limited validation.

A second conceptualization of brand SR builds on the CSR literature. It defines brand SR as 'the extent to which consumers perceive that a brand and sustained voluntary activities associated with the brand improve the welfare of society' (Dincer & Dincer, 2012, p. 487). The measure associated with this conceptualization of brand SR consists of 25 items – a set of 18 descriptive adjectives that capture the brand's trustworthiness and awareness, and a set of 7 Likert-type statements that relate to a brand's philanthropic activities and community engagement (Dincer & Dincer, 2012). A study involving ten brands demonstrated discriminant validity between the two sub-scales (i.e., descriptive adjective scale and Likert-type statements) and between the two sub-scales and existing CSR measures (Dincer & Dincer, 2012). Results also indicated that the descriptive adjective (vs. statement) sub-scale performed better at correctly situating brands associated with higher (vs. lower) brand SR in consumers' perceptual space. In addition, the descriptive adjective (vs. statements) sub-scale was a better predictor of purchase likelihood of socially responsible brands; nonetheless, either sub-scale was a better predictor of purchase likelihood of socially responsible brands than CSR scales (Dincer & Dincer, 2012). Disadvantages associated with this measure of brand SR involve scale length, lack of evidence regarding the scale's dimensionality and the fact that validation was limited to one study. Furthermore, when comparing SR scores across two sets of two brands – owned by the same corporation but associated with low versus high brand SR – the descriptive adjective scale indicated a significant difference in brand SR for only one pair of brands. Given these somewhat mixed results, the authors called for more research into the relationship between SR of brands and corporations operating them (Dincer & Dincer, 2012).

The third conceptualization of brand SR builds on the brand anthropomorphism and brand personality literature and suggests that brand SR reflects consumers' perceptions of a brand's values related to fairness, humaneness, caring and compassion (Grohmann & Bodur, 2015). According to this perspective, brand SR is defined as 'consumers' perceptions of the extent to which a brand reflects the human values related to SR' (Grohmann & Bodur, 2015, p. 377). This conceptualization taps into consumers' holistic impressions of a brand's SR and considers brand SR as a unidimensional construct reflected in a four-item descriptive adjective scale (Grohmann & Bodur, 2015). This brand SR measure showed discriminant validity against CSR scales, as well as the five brand personality dimensions (Aaker, 1997). Convergent validity relative to the SR (Madrigal & Boush, 2008) measure of the construct was also established (Grohmann & Bodur, 2015). This brand SR measure was validated across seven studies and showed predictive validity above CSR measures associated with the brand's parent firm. Table 29.2 summarizes definitions and measures of brand SR.

Antecedents and Outcomes of Product Brand SR

In the context of product brands, the literature identified several antecedents and consumer-level outcomes of brand SR. Research on the antecedents of brand SR suggests that brand-related factors – including association of a brand with a charitable organization in advertisements (Saenger et al., 2020), perceived brand transparency (Montecchi et al., 2024), perceived brand globalness (Vuong & Khanh Giao, 2020) and brand authenticity (Guzmán et al., 2024) – influence consumers' brand SR perceptions. More specifically, research examining consumers' ethical self-perceptions following a self-threat and the opportunity to engage in word-of-mouth about a socially responsible (vs. control) brand successfully induced greater brand SR perceptions by presenting consumers with an advertisement that associated a product brand with a charity, compared to a brand-only control advertisement (Saenger et al., 2020). This indicates that cause-related advertising and marketing campaigns contribute to building brand SR.

Consumers' perceptions of brand transparency also influence perceived brand SR: Whereas brand transparency may relate to the disclosure of brand attributes such as origin, authenticity or pricing, it also relates strongly to the transparency of SR-related information to preclude stakeholder skepticism or impressions of greenwashing (Montecchi et al., 2024). Consistent with this argument, a study involving a sample of consumers who evaluated one of several brands indicated that higher levels of perceived brand transparency increased brand SR perceptions (Montecchi et al., 2024). Research also found that brand globalness – defined as the extent to which consumers perceive a brand as global (based on brand presence in other markets, media exposure, word-of-mouth or travel; Steenkamp et al., 2003) – positively related to brand SR perceptions among Vietnamese consumers of coffee shop brands (i.e., Highlands and Starbucks coffee) and fast-food restaurants (i.e., McDonald's and KFC) (Vuong & Khanh Giao, 2020). Brand SR – measured by three items of Dincer and Dincer's brand SR scale – in turn positively related to consumers' purchase intentions and partially mediated the relationship between perceived brand globalness and purchase intentions, in parallel with perceived brand prestige and perceived brand quality (Vuong & Khanh Giao, 2020).

Table 29.2 Brand social responsibility: Definitions and measures

Reference	*Construct Definition*	*Items*
Madrigal and Boush (2008)	An enduring, differentiating characteristic that describes a brand's actions with respect to its obligation to the society at large and the individuals living in that society.	☐ Social responsibility ☐ Corporate giving ☐ Environmentally friendly ☐ Cares about doing the right thing ☐ Accountable for its actions *not at all/extremely descriptive*
Dincer and Dincer (2012)	The extent to which consumers perceive that a brand and sustained voluntary activities associated with the brand improve the welfare of society.	☐ aware, caring, concerned, conscious, kind, fair, helpful, honest, honorable, human, loyal, pro-active, respectful, responsible, sincere, sustainable, thoughtful, trustworthy *not at all/very descriptive* ☐ This brand ensures that local people benefit from its contributions. ☐ This brand sponsors and finances voluntary service. ☐ This brand integrates charitable contributions into its business activities. ☐ This brand help solve the social problems. ☐ This brand regularly makes donations to charity. ☐ This brand is actively involved in the community. ☐ This brand is committed to ethics principles. *strongly disagree/strongly agree*
Grohmann and Bodur (2015)	Consumers' perceptions of the extent to which a brand reflects human values related to social responsibility.	☐ fair ☐ compassionate ☐ humane ☐ caring *not at all/very descriptive*

Source: The author.

A study involving a sample of U.S. participants working in a business-to-business context found positive relationships between perceptions of external stakeholders' expectations, internal stakeholder expectations and financial commitment to a cause and brand conscientiousness (operationalized and measured using Dincer and Dincer's brand SR scale), as well as a negative relationship between higher perceived risk and perceptions of brand conscientiousness (Guzmán et al., 2024). Furthermore, a positive and significant relationship between perceived brand authenticity and brand conscientiousness emerged (Guzmán et al., 2024). Brand authenticity partially mediated the relationship between strategic alignment and brand conscientiousness, between long-term commitment and brand conscientiousness, and between fulfilling brand promise and brand conscientiousness (Guzmán et al., 2024).

Research also examined the impact of brand SR on various consumer-related outcomes. SR initiatives at the product brand level influenced consumers' brand identification, loyalty and advocacy, such that brands that integrated SR into their core positioning (i.e., through product, packaging, cause support with a high brand-cause fit) elicited more positive consumer responses than brands focusing exclusively on cause-related activities (Du et al., 2007). Furthermore, in two studies involving a fictitious clothing brand and samples of North American consumers and students, brand SR positively and significantly influenced ad attitude, brand attitude and attitude toward the brand's product (Madrigal & Boush, 2008). This effect was moderated by consumers' willingness to reward, such that a higher (vs. lower) willingness to reward amplified the positive effect of brand SR (Madrigal & Boush, 2008). Similarly, in a study involving 10 brands from different industries and a sample of Turkish consumers, brand SR was significantly and positively correlated with consumers' purchase intentions of socially responsible brands, whereas the correlation between brand SR and purchase intentions was not significant for socially irresponsible brands (Dincer & Dincer, 2012). The significant relationship between brand SR and purchase intentions was subsequently replicated (Vuong & Khanh Giao, 2020).

In studies conducted in a North American context with pairs of product brands owned by the same corporation (i.e., Unilever: Dove, Lever 2000; Toyota: Prius, Tundra), brand SR emerged as a significant predictor of brand attitude, purchase intentions and consumer-based product brand equity (Grohmann & Bodur, 2015). Furthermore, brand SR uniquely predicted brand-related outcomes, such as consumers' brand attitude and purchase intention, whereas CSR uniquely predicted firm-related outcomes, such as investment intent and employment intent (Grohmann & Bodur, 2015). Moreover, the relationship between brand SR and brand attitude and purchase intentions was fully mediated by brand self-connection – the extent to which consumers integrate a brand into their self-concept and form a strong connection with it (Escalas & Bettman, 2003; Grohmann & Bodur, 2015). Customer-corporate identification (i.e., the degree of perceived congruence between consumers and a firm; Lichtenstein et al., 2004), on the other hand, mediated the relationship between CSR and firm-related outcomes (i.e., employment and investment intent), but did not mediate the relationship between brand SR and brand-related outcomes (Grohmann & Bodur, 2015).

Product Brand SR as Mediator and Moderator

The literature also suggests that product brand SR mediates several consumer responses to brands. Brand SR mediated the effect of CSR (except for the CSR economic dimension) and product-related SR (i.e., socially responsible product attributes including product ingredients, technology or functionality; Brown & Dacin, 1997) on product brand attitude, purchase intent and brand equity (Grohmann & Bodur, 2015). Furthermore, brand SR mediated the relationship between brand personality and brand attitude (Costa Pinto et al., 2019): In a study involving a sample of North American consumers evaluating an athletic shoe brand in an experiment manipulating brand personality and consumers' identity goals, a sincere (versus sophisticated or control) brand personality increased brand SR perceptions, but only when social identity goals were salient (Costa Pinto et al., 2019). When personal identity goals were salient, brand personality did not relate to brand SR (Costa Pinto et al., 2019). In addition, brand SR emerged as a significant mediator of the interactive effect of brand personality and consumers' identity goals on brand attitude (Costa Pinto et al., 2019).

In research involving a South Korean student sample, co-creation in the form of providing color and slogan ideas for a fictitious furniture brand resulted in greater happiness with the brand, compared to a control condition that did not allow for consumer co-creation (Nobi, 2024). The positive and significant relationship between co-creation and brand happiness was mediated by brand SR, such that co-creation enhanced brand SR perceptions and subsequent brand happiness (Nobi, 2024).

Research also supports product brand SR as a moderator of brand-related effects. In the context of a national brand affected by a consumer boycott, a study involving 275 Indonesian consumers demonstrated that brand SR moderated the relationship between brand hate and negative word-of-mouth (Rahimah et al., 2023). More specifically, brand SR perceptions mitigated the relationship of brand hate and negative word-of-mouth, whereas negative word-of-mouth positively related to protest behavior, brand avoidance and brand switching (Rahimah et al., 2023). This suggests that consumers' brand responsibility perceptions could play an important role in decreasing the impact of brand scandals on undesirable consumer responses.

CORPORATE BRAND SR

The preceding sections discussed the literature on consumer perceptions of product brand SR and empirical findings that emerged from consumer research. Brand SR also comprises consumer perceptions of corporate brands (Grohmann & Bodur, 2015), however. Corporate brands arise from branding activities aimed at creating corporate associations among consumers (Berens et al., 2005), although they may also include other internal or external stakeholders (Balmer, 2001). SR research in marketing examines corporate brands either in terms of the brand representing an organization (e.g., HSBC, Morgan Stanley) or the product brand carrying the parent firm's corporate name (e.g., Samsung, Tesla, BMW) – often without clarifying this distinction.

Consistent with the positive effects of brand SR observed in the product brand context, the literature generally supports a positive relationship between corporate brand SR and corporate brand equity or valuation. Two lines of research support this positive association: The first operationalizes SR in terms of the corporate brand's performance on discrete SR dimensions (i.e., community, product, diversity, environment, employees, human rights and governance, or ESG dimensions) – and examines its relationship with brand equity of the corporate brand. This literature generally employs panel data. The second line of research examines the relationship between consumer or business-to-business customer perceptions of corporate brand SR and corporate brand equity and is based on consumer surveys or experiments.

Corporate Brand SR and Corporate Brand Valuation

Findings regarding the impact of specific SR dimensions associated with the corporate brand on brand valuation are somewhat mixed, likely due to differences in the timeframe, industries and geographical markets examined across studies. Direct support for a positive relationship between corporate brand SR and brand equity arose in a study that operationalized corporate brand SR in terms of Dow Jones Sustainability Index ratings – which comprise corporate governance, corporate commitment, social engagement and environmental protection dimensions – and corporate brand equity as a function of prestige, loyalty and extensions, a risk-free interest (discount) rate, and the brand's price advantage (i.e., excess value) (Wang et al., 2021).

Research also suggests that corporate brand SR impacts specific dimensions of brand value – operationalized in terms of the Young & Rubicam Brand Asset Valuator (BAV) brand metric dimensions (i.e., differentiation, relevance, esteem and knowledge) (Bhattacharya et al., 2020): A panel study examining the impact of SR dimensions (i.e., an index aggregating the community, product, diversity, environment, employees, human rights and governance dimensions captured by the Kinder, Lydenberg and Domini (KLD) Research and Analytics database) on brand value (i.e., the overall Young & Rubicam BAV brand metric) of 137 corporate brands in 19 industries for the years 2007–2015 (including the recession years 2008 and 2009) found a positive, but not significant relationship between corporate brand SR and brand value (Bhattacharya et al., 2020). Corporate brand SR is nonetheless positively related to the BAV differentiation dimension in non-recession years (Bhattacharya et al., 2020). In recession years, a positive and significant relationship between corporate brand SR and overall brand value, and between corporate brand SR and perceived brand quality (i.e., the BAV esteem dimension) emerged (Bhattacharya et al., 2020). No association between corporate brand SR and the BAV brand relevance and knowledge dimensions was observed in this study (Bhattacharya et al., 2020).

The literature also explored the relative impact of SR dimensions on corporate brand equity. A panel regression study involving data from 48 U.S. corporate brands spanning the years 2001–2003 demonstrates a positive relationship between corporate brand SR (i.e., an index score of the KLD community, product, diversity, environment and employee dimensions, but excluding human rights and governance) and corporate brand value (Melo & Galan, 2011). An aggregate SR score comprising all KLD dimensions did not relate significantly to brand value, however (Melo & Galan, 2011). This suggests that some SR dimensions more strongly relate to corporate brand value.

Which SR dimensions influence brand value also depends on the geographical context considered (Bouvain et al., 2013): A comparison of the impact of corporate brand SR on corporate brand value in the East Asian and U.S. banking sector showed a positive relationship between SR and brand value driven by different SR dimensions (Bouvain et al., 2013). Employment-based SR most strongly influenced brand value in Japan and South Korea, community-based SR positively related to brand value in China, and environmental SR, corporate governance, and regulatory compliance were strongly associated with brand value in the United States (Bouvain et al., 2013).

A positive association between SR activities directed at various stakeholders (i.e., customers, shareholders, employees, suppliers and community) and brand equity also emerged in a panel regression study involving data from 57 global corporate brands based in the USA, Japan, South Korea, France, UK, Italy, Germany, Finland, Switzerland and the Netherlands for the years 2002–2008 (Torres et al., 2012). In this study, community-based SR reinforced positive effects of SR activities directed at other stakeholders, particularly those aimed at customers (Torres et al., 2012). Similarly, a study based on secondary KLD and Interbrand data, including 78 U.S. corporate brands for the years 2000–2014, demonstrated that diversity-related and governance-related SR were positively associated with corporate brand equity, whereas employee-related SR showed a negative relationship to brand equity (Yang & Basile, 2019). Product and employee-related SR moderated the relationship between other SR dimensions and corporate brand equity (Yang & Basile, 2019).

Furthermore, there is evidence of a differential effect of SR strengths and concerns on corporate brand value: A panel regression study considered the impact of SR strengths and concerns associated with seven KLD dimensions (i.e., community, diversity, employee relations, environment, product, corporate governance and human rights) on absolute and incremental brand value and rankings reported by Interbrand for 54 different brands owned by of 47 unique firms between 2003 and 2014 (Harjoto & Salas, 2017). This study found a positive association between SR strengths and absolute brand value, and a negative association between SR concerns and incremental brand value and brand rankings (Harjoto & Salas, 2017). Overall, this line of research points toward differential and possibly interactive effects of SR dimensions on corporate brand value and equity.

Corporate Brand SR and Customer-Based Brand Equity

A second research stream on corporate brand SR examines the relation between consumer perceptions of corporate brand SR and corporate brand equity in consumer-based survey and experimental studies. This research stream generally finds a positive relationship between corporate brand SR and corporate brand equity. For instance, consumer-based surveys support a positive relationship between consumer perceptions of SR and corporate brand equity in the Indian retail banking sector (Fatma et al., 2015) and the life insurance industry in Taiwan (Hsu, 2012). A positive relationship between brand SR and corporate brand equity also emerged in a large-scale consumer study involving four corporate product brands, and this relationship was mediated by corporate brand credibility and corporate reputation (Hur et al., 2014). In a business-to-business context, buyer perceptions of SR activities positively related to perceptions of corporate brand reputation, brand equity and brand performance (Lai et al., 2010). The positive relationship between SR and corporate brand equity was also replicated in the hospitality industry, such that consumers' SR perceptions positively related to the brand awareness, brand image, perceived quality and brand loyalty dimensions of customer-based brand equity (Martínez & Nishiyama, 2019). Moreover, an experiment involving Australian, USA and Spanish consumers found that a single exposure to SR communication enhanced consumer-based corporate brand equity (Muniz et al., 2019). The magnitude of this effect differed across countries, however (Muniz et al., 2019). A consumer-based study of the sportwear industry in India similarly demonstrated a positive and significant relationship between consumers' perceptions of SR initiatives and consumer-based brand equity (Sharma & Jain, 2019). Taken together, consumer-based and panel data studies generally support a significant and positive, but often moderated relationship between SR and corporate brand equity or corporate brand value. This suggests that SR has important implications for corporate brand performance.

Figure 29.1 summarizes empirical findings regarding the antecedents and outcomes of brand SR as it relates to product and corporate brands.

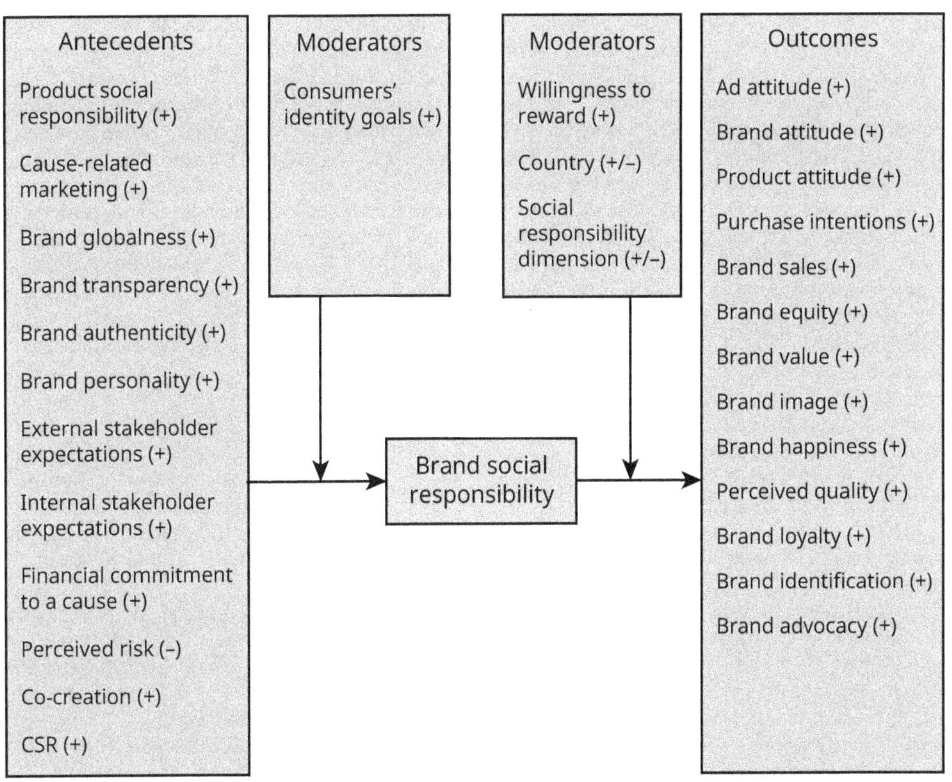

Figure 29.1 Brand social responsibility: A nomological network of empirical findings

RECIPROCAL EFFECTS OF CORPORATE AND PRODUCT BRAND SR

Building on the literature on product brand and corporate brand SR, research has begun to examine the relationship between consumers' corporate and product brand SR perceptions. Findings point to reciprocal spillover effects of SR associations across corporate and product brands (Grohmann & Bodur, 2015; Wang & Korschun, 2015). First, there is evidence that a product brand's SR activities impact consumer perceptions of the corporate brand and other product brands in a firm's brand portfolio (Wang & Korschun, 2015). More specifically, two experiments involving North American undergraduate students supported a spillover effect of one product brand's SR activities to the corporate brand (Wang & Korschun, 2015). Product brand SR also spilled over to another product brand in the corporation's brand portfolio, and this relationship was mediated by corporate brand SR (Wang & Korschun, 2015). In the context of utilitarian products (i.e., frozen yogurt, ice cream, soft drinks), this spillover was stronger when the corporate branding strategy was monolithic (vs. endorsed or stand-alone) and when the product category fit between the two brands was high (vs. low). In addition, the spillover enhanced consumer–company identification and positive word-of-mouth related to the corporate brand, but not product brand-related willingness to pay or purchase intentions (Wang & Korschun, 2015). For symbolic product categories (i.e., running shoes, T-shirts, watches), brand image similarity has a stronger impact on spillover across product brands than product category fit; furthermore, neither corporate brand nor product brand-level outcomes were influenced by the spillover of SR associations (Wang & Korschun, 2015). These findings indicate that brand architecture strategy, product-related (i.e., hedonic/utilitarian category, product category fit) and brand-related (i.e., brand image fit) factors interactively shape spillover effects.

Conversely, research also found that corporate brand SR positively relates to consumer responses to product brands. Examining the influence of corporate brand SR (operationalized in terms of consumers' ethicality perceptions of the corporate brand; Brunk, 2012) on European consumers' responses to FMCG product brands, a large-scale survey study supported a positive relationship between corporate brand SR and product brand trust, affect and loyalty (Singh et al., 2012). In research involving North American consumers evaluating an automotive corporate brand (Toyota) and its product brands (i.e., Prius, Tundra), corporate brand SR was positively related to product brand SR, which in turn was positively associated with product brand attitude and purchase intentions (Grohmann & Bodur, 2015). Although research on the joint and reciprocal effects of corporate and product brand SR is still scarce, these findings point to promising synergies that positively affect consumer responses to both the corporate and product brand.

CONCLUSIONS

The literature on brand SR shows growing and consistent evidence for a positive effect of product brand SR on consumers' responses to brands (e.g., brand attitudes, purchase intentions). Given the consistently positive effect of product brand SR on consumer responses, research has also identified several antecedents to product brand SR as well as consumer-based moderators (e.g., identity goals, willingness to reward) of the relationship between product brand SR and product brand outcomes. The literature on the relationship between corporate brand SR and corporate brand equity or valuation is more comprehensive, but shows mixed findings. As a result, research has begun to examine moderators of this relationship (e.g., country effects, interactive effects of SR domains).

For managerial practice, the empirical findings discussed in this chapter point toward a generally positive effect of product and corporate brand SR. Desirable outcomes include enhanced brand attitude, purchase intentions, brand equity and brand valuation. Critical antecedents to brand SR identified in the brand management literature can guide the development of brand SR in practice. These include product-related SR activities (e.g., ethical product attributes), non-product-related marketing activities (e.g., cause-related marketing, co-creation), and the development of positive brand associations (e.g., brand transparency, brand authenticity and brand personality). Considering the evidence supporting a reciprocal spillover across corporate to product brand SR associations, implementation of SR activities at both the product and corporate brand level likely generates important synergies.

Although research on brand SR has accelerated, many opportunities for future research remain. For example, this chapter highlighted the conceptual distinctions between corporate, brand and product SR. A review of the literature nonetheless strongly suggests that a more careful delineation of brand SR and CSR is called for. Especially secondary data-based research on corporate brand SR and consumer-based brand equity often fails to discuss the distinctions between the firm-based CSR literature – originating in management and focused on the organization – and the brand SR literature – rooted in marketing and focused on the product or corporate brand as the unit of analysis. A clear delineation between product SR, product and corporate brand SR, and firm-level CSR would encourage the use of adequate construct measures and would lend itself to a more nuanced investigation of unique antecedents, outcomes and interrelationships. For instance, product-related factors, such as materials, safety features or recalls, may have a significant impact on product SR and weaker – yet substantial – effects on product brand and corporate brand SR. Non-product-related factors, such as cause-related marketing, may impact product brand SR to a greater extent, despite being associated with the number of sales transactions at the product level. Philanthropy may relate more strongly to corporate brand SR perceptions. Firm-level CSR perceptions, on the other hand, may be more strongly influenced by CSR reporting, lobbying or reported penalties or fines. The relative impact of SR activities on product, product brand and corporate brand SR is currently not well understood but could offer important insights for theory development and managerial practice (e.g., resource allocation). Such insight would also have important implications for consumer adoption of socially responsible brands and significantly strengthen progress toward the achievement of the UN sustainable development goals.

Second, in research that employs dimension-based SR operationalizations, it is necessary to disentangle and clarify the relative effects of specific SR dimensions on corporate brand valuation or equity. Research on the relationship between corporate brand SR and corporate brand valuation often operationalizes SR as an index score capturing a corporate brand's performance across SR dimensions (e.g., Bhattacharya et al., 2020; Melo & Galan, 2011). To evaluate the relative and interactive effects of SR dimensions and provide empirically validated managerial guidance on what SR dimensions to prioritize, the use of individual dimension scores is strongly encouraged (Mattingly & Berman, 2006). Relatedly, the differential effects of strengths and concerns related to SR dimensions are not well understood. SR research relies on the use of difference scores (e.g., strengths minus concerns related to specific dimension; Rahman et al., 2019) or a summation of strength and concerns across all dimensions (Harjoto & Salas, 2017), although the use of individual strength and concern scores as they relate specific CSR dimensions would allow identification of asymmetric, null or compensatory effects. Higher levels of mandated SR reporting, the emergence of dimension-specific reporting standards and the increasing availability of more comprehensive SR databases will likely facilitate further investigations of the effects of SR dimensions, strengths and concerns.

Another area for future research is the reciprocal effect of brand SR within brand portfolios adopting alternative brand architecture strategies (e.g., house-of-brands, endorsed or mixed branding) as well as spillover effects between corporate and product brands. Based on the few articles that have examined such effects, the theoretical implications (in terms of consumers' association transfer) and managerial insights (in terms of synergistic returns on product brand and corporate brand investments) in this research domain are promising. Given the scarcity of studies on spillover effects, the literature would benefit from replication across a wider range of brands and product categories, and an investigation of alternative psychological mechanisms (e.g., product brand–corporate brand image fit, asymmetric strength of reciprocal mental associations between product and corporate brands). This chapter provided definitions, conceptualizations and a synthesis of findings to motivate future research on brand SR.

REFERENCES

Aaker, J. L. (1997). Dimensions of brand personality. *Journal of Marketing Research*, *34*, 347–356. https://doi.org/10.1177/002224379703400304

Agrawal, R., & Gupta, S. (2018). Consuming responsibly: Exploring environmentally responsible consumption behaviors. *Journal of Global Marketing*, *31*, 231–245. https://doi.org/10.1080/08911762.2017.1415402

Balmer, J. M. T. (2001). Corporate identity, corporate branding and corporate marketing – Seeing through the fog. *European Journal of Marketing*, *35*(3-4), 248–291. https://doi.org/10.1108/03090560110694763

Balmer, J. M. T. (2012). Strategic corporate brand alignment: Perspectives from identity-based views of corporate brands. *European Journal of Marketing*, *46*(7/8), 1064–1092. https://doi.org/10.1108/03090561211230205

Becker-Olsen, K. L., Cudmore, B. A., & Hill, R. P. (2006). The impact of perceived corporate social responsibility on consumer behavior. *Journal of Business Research*, *59*(1), 46–53. https://doi.org/10.1016/j.jbusres.2005.01.001

Berens, G., van Riel, C. B. M., & van Bruggen, G. H. (2005). Corporate associations and consumer product responses: The moderating role of corporate brand dominance. *Journal of Marketing*, *69*(3), 35–48. https://doi.org/10.1509/jmkg.69.3.35.66357

Beurden, P., & Gössling, T. (2008). The worth of values – A literature review on the relation between corporate social and financial performance. *Journal of Business Ethics*, *82*(2), 407–424. https://doi.org/10.1007/s10551-008-9894-x

Bhattacharya, A., Good, V., & Sardashti, H. (2020). Doing good when times are bad: The impact of CSR on brands during recessions. *European Journal of Marketing*, *54*(9), 2049–2077. https://doi.org/ 10.1108/EJM-01-2019-0088

Bodur, O., Gao, T., & Grohmann, B. (2014). The ethical attribute stigma: Understanding when ethical attributes improve consumer responses to product evaluations. *Journal of Business Ethics*, *122*, 167–177. https://soi.org/10.1007/s10551-013-1764-5

Bouvain, P., Baumann, C., & Lundmark, E. (2013). Corporate social responsibility in financial services: A comparison of Chinese and East Asian banks vis-à-vis American banks. *International Journal of Bank Marketing*, *31*(6), 420–439. https://doi.org/10.1108/IJBM-05-2012-0054

Brown, T. J., & Dacin, P. A. (1997). The company and the product: Corporate associations and consumer product responses. *Journal of Marketing*, *61*(January), 68–84. https://doi.org/10.1177/002224299706100106

Brunk, K. H. (2010). Exploring origins of ethical company/brand perceptions – A consumer perspective on corporate ethics. *Journal of Business Research*, *63*(3), 255–262. https://doi.org/10.1016/j.jbusres.2009.03.011

Brunk, K. H. (2012). Un/ethical company and brand perceptions: Conceptualising and operationalising consumer meanings. *Journal of Business Ethics*, *111*(4), 551–565. https://doi.org/10.1007/s10551-012-1339-x

Brunk, K. H., & Blümelhuber, C. (2011). One strike and you're out: Qualitative insights into the formation of consumers' ethical company or brand perceptions. *Journal of Business Research*, *64*, 134–141. https://doi.org/10.1016/j.jbusres.2010.02.009

Carroll, A. B. (1979). A three-dimensional conceptual model of corporate performance. *Academy of Management Review*, *4*(October), 497–505. https://doi.org/10.5465/amr.1979.4498296

Conte, F., Sardanelli, D., Vollero, A., & Siano, A. (2023). CSR signaling in controversial and noncontroversial industries: CSR policies, governance structures, and transparency tools. *European Management Journal*, *41*(2), 274–281. https://doi.org/10.1016/j.emj.2021.12.003

Costa, P. T., & McCrae, R. R. (1992). The five-factor model of personality and its relevance to personality disorders. *Journal of Personality Disorders*, *6*(4), 343–359. https://doi.org/10.1521/pedi.1992.6.4.343

Costa Pinto, D., Herter, M. M., Gonçalves, D., & Sayin, E. (2019). Can luxury brands be ethical? Reducing the sophistication liability of luxury brands. *Journal of Cleaner Production*, *233*, 1366–1376. https://doi.org/10.1016/j.jclepro.2019.06.094

Cote, C. (2021). *What is a CSR report & why is it important?* https://online.hbs.edu/blog/post/what-is-a-csr-report

David Suzuki Foundation. (n.d.). *The environmental cost of fast fashion*. Retrieved October 2, 2024 from https://davidsuzuki.org/living-green/the-environmental-cost-of-fast-fashion/

Digman, J. M. (1990). Personality structure: Emergence of the five-factor model. *Annual Review of Psychology*, *41*, 417–440. https://doi.org/10.1146/annurev.ps.41.020190.002221

Dincer, B., & Dincer, C. (2012). Measuring brand social responsibility: A new scale. *Social Responsibility Journal*, *8*(4), 484–494. https://doi.org/10.1108/17471111211272075

Du, S., Bhattacharya, C. B., & Sen, S. (2007). Reaping relational rewards from corporate social responsibility: The role of competitive positioning. *International Journal of Research in Marketing*, *24*(3), 224–241. https://doi.org/10.1016/j.ijresmar.2007.01.001

Escalas, J. E., & Bettman, J. R. (2003). You are what they eat: The influence of reference groups on consumers' connections to brands. *Journal of Consumer Psychology*, *13*(3), 339–348. https://doi.org/10.1207/S15327663JCP1303_14

Fatma, M., Rahman, Z., & Khan, I. (2015). Building company reputation and brand equity through CSR: The mediating role of trust. *International Journal of Bank Marketing*, *33*(6), 840–856. https://doi.org/10.1108/IJBM-11-2014-0166

Ferrell, O. C. (2021). Addressing socio-ecological issues in marketing: Environmental, social and governance (ESG). *AMS Review*, *11*, 140–44. https://doi.org/10.1007/s13162-021-00201-3

Golob, U., Lah, M., & Jančič, Z. (2008). Value orientations and consumer expectations of corporate social responsibility. *Journal of Marketing Communications*, *14*(2), 83–96. https://doi.org/10.1080/13527260701856525

Good on You. (n.d.). *Good on you – sustainable fashion and beauty brand ratings*. Retrieved November 18, 2024 from https://goodonyou.eco/

Gupta, R., & Sen, S. (2013). The effect of evolving resource synergy beliefs on the intentions–behavior discrepancy in ethical consumption. *Journal of Consumer Psychology*, *23*, 114–121. https://doi.org/10.1016/j.jcps.2012.07.004

Gürhan-Canli, Z., & Batra, R. (2004). When corporate image affects product evaluations: The moderating role of perceived risk. *Journal of Marketing Research, 41*(2), 197–205. https://doi.org/10.1509/jmkr.41.2.197.28667

Greyser, S. A., & Urde, M. (2019). What does your corporate brand stand for? *Harvard Business Review, 97*(1), 80–88. hbr.org/2019/01/what-does-your-corporate-brand-stand-for

Grohmann, B., & Bodur, H. O. (2015). Brand social responsibility: Conceptualization, measurement, and outcomes. *Journal of Business Ethics, 131*, 375–399. https://doi.org/10.1007/s10551-014-2279-4

Guzmán, F., Ahmad, F., & Johnson, R. W. (2024). What drives business-to-business brands to be conscientious? *Journal of Product & Brand Management, 33*(1), 138–161. https://doi.org/10.1108/JPBM-07-2023-4595

Harjoto, M. A., & Salas, J. (2017). Strategic and institutional sustainability: Corporate social responsibility, brand value, and Interbrand listing. *Journal of Product and Brand Management, 26*(6), 545–558. https://doi.org/10.1108/JPBM-07-2016-1277

Henderson, T., & Arora, N. (2010). Promoting brands across categories with a social cause: Implementing effective embedded premium programs. *Journal of Marketing, 74*(6), 41–60. https://doi.org/10.1509/jmkg.74.6.41

Hsu, K.-T. (2012). The advertising effect of corporate social responsibility on corporate reputation and brand equity: Evidence from the life insurance industry in Taiwan. *Journal of Business Ethics, 109*(2), 189–201. https://doi.org/10.1007/s10551-011-1118-0

Hur, W.-M., Kim, H., & Woo, J. (2014). How CSR leads to corporate brand equity: Mediating mechanism of corporate brand credibility and corporate reputation. *Journal of Business Ethics, 12*(1), 75–86. https://doi.org/10.1007/s10551-013-1910-0

Keller, K. L. (1993). Conceptualizing, measuring, and managing customer-based brand equity. *Journal of Marketing, 57*(1), 1–22. https://doi.org/10.1177/002224299305700101

Kim, S. (2019). The process model of corporate social responsibility (CSR) communication: CSR communication and its relationship with consumers' CSR knowledge, trust, and corporate reputation perception. *Journal of Business Ethics, 154*(4), 1143–1159. https://doi.org/10.1007/s10551-017-3433-6

KPMG. (2022). *Big shifts, small steps – survey of sustainability reporting 2022*. https://assets.kpmg.com/content/dam/kpmg/xx/pdf/2022/10/ssr-small-steps-big-shifts.pdf%20

Lacey, R., Kennett-Hensel, P., & Manolis, C. (2015). Is corporate social responsibility a motivator or hygiene factor? Insights into its bivalent nature. *Journal of the Academy of Marketing Science, 43*(3), 315–332. https://doi.org/10.1007/S11747-014-0390-9

Lai, C.-S., Chiu, C.-J., Yang, C.-F., & Pai, D.-C. (2010). The effects of corporate social responsibility on brand performance: The mediating effect of industrial brand equity and corporate reputation. *Journal of Business Ethics, 95*(3), 457–469. https://doi.org/10.1007/s10551-010-0433-1

Lee, M. T., Raschke, R. L., & Krishen, A. S. (2022). Signaling green! Firm ESG signals in an interconnected environment that promote brand valuation. *Journal of Business Research, 138*, 1–11. https://doi.org/10.1016/j.jbusres.2021.08.061

Lichtenstein, D. R., Drumwright, M. E., & Braig, B. M. (2004). The effect of corporate social responsibility on customer donations to corporate-supported nonprofits. *Journal of Marketing, 68*(October), 16–32. https://doi.org/10.1509/jmkg.68.4.16.42726

Lin, W. L. (2024). The role of corporate social responsibility and corporate social irresponsibility in shaping corporate reputation: An analysis of competitive action and innovation strategies. *Corporate Social Responsibility & Environmental Management, 31*(2), 1451–1468. https://doi.org/10.1002/csr.2640

Lin, Y. C., & Chang, C. A. (2012). Double standard: The role of environmental consciousness in green product usage. *Journal of Marketing, 76*(5), 125–134. https://doi.org/10.2307/41714513

Luchs, M. G., Naylor, R. W., Irwin, J. R., & Raghunathan, R. (2010). The sustainability liability: Potential negative effects of ethicality on product preference. *Journal of Marketing, 74*(5), 18–31. https://doi.org/10.1509/jmkg.74.5.018

Luo, X., & Bhattacharya, C. B. (2006). Corporate social responsibility, consumer satisfaction, and market value. *Journal of Marketing, 70*(4), 1–18. https://doi.org/10.1509/jmkg.70.4.001

Madrigal, R., & Boush, D. M. (2008). Social responsibility as a unique dimension of brand personality and consumers' willingness to reward. *Psychology & Marketing, 2*, 538–564. https://doi.org/10.1002/mar.20224

Maignan, I. (2001). Consumers' perceptions of corporate social responsibilities: A cross-cultural comparison. *Journal of Business Ethics, 30*(1), 57–72. https://doi.org/10.1023/A:1006433928640

Maignan, I., & Ferrell, O. C. (2004). Corporate social responsibility and marketing: An integrative framework. *Journal of the Academy of Marketing Science, 32*(1), 3–19. https://doi.org/10.1177/0092070303258971

Martínez, P., & Nishiyama, N. (2019). Enhancing customer-based brand equity through CSR in the hospitality sector. *International Journal of Hospitality & Tourism Administration, 20*(3), 329–353. https://doi.org/10.1080/15256480.2017.1397581

Mattingly, J. E., & Berman, S. L. (2006). Measurement of corporate social action: Discovering taxonomy in the Kinder Lydenberg Domini ratings data. *Business & Society*, *45*(1), 20–46. https://doi.org/10.1177/0007650305281939

McWilliams, A., & Siegel, D. (2001). Corporate social responsibility: A theory of the firm perspective. *Academy of Management Review*, *26*(January), 117–127. https://doi.org/10.2307/259398

Melo, T., & Galan, J. I. (2011). Effects of corporate social responsibility on brand value. *Journal of Brand Management*, *18*(6), 423–437. https://doi.org/10.1057/bm.2010.54

Mohr, L. A., Webb, D. J., & Harris, K. E. (2001). Do consumers expect companies to be socially responsible? The impact of corporate social responsibility on buying behavior. *Journal of Consumer Affairs*, *35*(1), 45–72. https://doi.org/10.1111/j.1745-6606.2001.tb00102.x

Montecchi, M., Plangger, K., West, D., & de Ruyter, K. (2024). Perceived brand transparency: A conceptualization and measurement scale. *Psychology & Marketing*, *41*(10), 2274–2297. https://doi.org/10.1002/mar.22048

Muniz, F., Guzmán, F., Paswan, A. K., & Crawford, H. J. (2019). The immediate effect of corporate social responsibility on consumer-based brand equity. *Journal of Product and Brand Management*, *28*(7), 864–879. https://doi.org/10.1108/JPBM-09-2018-2016

Nickerson, D., Lowe, M., Pattabhiramaiah, A., & Sorescu, A. (2022). The impact of corporate social responsibility on brand sales: An accountability perspective. *Journal of Marketing*, *86*(2), 5–28. https://doi.org/10.1177/00222429211044155

Nobi, B. (2024). Co-creation and brand happiness: Insights from a Korean perspective. *Journal of Consumer Marketing*, *41*(5), 540–548. https://doi.org/10.1108/JCM-08-2023-6185

Paolone, F., Cucari, N., Wu, J., & Tiscini, R. (2022). How do ESG pillars impact firms' marketing performance? A configurational analysis in the pharmaceutical sector. *Journal of Business & Industrial Marketing*, *37*(8), 1594–1606. https://doi.org/10.1108/JBIM-07-2020-0356

Peloza, J., & Shang, J. (2011). How can corporate social responsibility activities create value for stakeholders? A systematic review. *Journal of the Academy of Marketing Science*, *39*(2), 117–135. https://doi.org/10.1007/s11747-010-0213-6

Peloza, J., White, K., & Shang, J. (2013). Good and guilt-free: The role of self-accountability in influencing preferences for products with ethical attributes. *Journal of Marketing*, *77*(1), 104–119. https://doi.org/10.1509/jm.11.0454

Rahimah, A., Dang, H. P., Nguyen, T. T., Cheng, J. M., & Kusumawati, A. (2023). The subsequent effects of negative emotions: From brand hate to anti-brand consumption behavior under moderating mechanisms. *Journal of Product & Brand Management*, *32*(4), 618–631. https://doi.org/10.1108/JPBM-12-2021-3778

Rahman, M., Rodríguez-Serrano, A., & Lambkin, M. (2019). Brand equity and firm performance: The complementary role of corporate social responsibility. *Journal of Brand Management*, *26*, 691–704. https://doi.org/10.1057/s41262-019-00155-9

Rajvanshi, A. (2023). *Shein is the world's most popular fashion brand – at a huge cost to us all*. https://time.com/6247732/shein-climate-change-labor-fashion/

Saenger, C., Thomas, V. L., & Bock, D. E. (2020). Compensatory word of mouth as symbolic self-completion: When talking about a brand can restore consumers' self-perceptions after self-threat. *European Journal of Marketing*, *54*(4), 671–690. https://doi.org/10.1108/EJM-03-2018-0206

Salmones, M. M. G. d. l., Crespo, A. H., & Rodrígues del Bosque, I. (2005). Influence of corporate social responsibility on loyalty and valuation of services. *Journal of Business Ethics*, *61*(4), 369–385. https://doi.org/10.1007/s10551-005-5841-2

Schwarz, A. (2024). *Best brands for social impact*. www.forbes.com/lists/best-brands-social-impact/

Sen, S., & Bhattacharya, C. B. (2001). Does doing good always lead to doing better? Consumer reactions to corporate social responsibility. *Journal of Marketing Research*, *38*(May), 225–243. https://doi.org/10.1509/jmkr.38.2.225.18838

Sen, S., Bhattacharya, C. B., & Korschun, D. (2006). The role of corporate social responsibility in strengthening multiple stakeholder relationships: A field experiment. *Journal of the Academy of Marketing Science*, *34*(2), 158–166. https://doi.org/10.1177/0092070305284978

Sen, S., Du, S., & Bhattacharya, C. B. (2016). Corporate social responsibility: A consumer psychology perspective. *Current Opinion in Psychology*, *10*, 70–75. https://doi.org/10.1016/j.copsyc.2015.12.014

Sharma, R., & Jain, V. (2019). CSR, trust, brand loyalty and brand equity: Empirical evidences from sportswear industry in the NCR region of India. *Metamorphosis: A Journal of Management Research*, *18*(1), 57–67. https://doi.org/10.1177/0972622519853158

Shea, L. J. (2010). Using consumer perceived ethicality as a guideline for corporate social responsibility strategy: A commentary essay. *Journal of Business Research*, *63*, 263–264. https://doi.org/10.1016/j.jbusres.2009.04.021

Singh, J. J., Iglesias, O., & Batista-Foguet, J. M. (2012). Does having an ethical brand matter? The influence of consumer perceived ethicality on trust, affect and loyalty. *Journal of Business Ethics*, *111*, 541–549. https://doi.org/10.1007/s10551-012-1216-7

Steenkamp, J., Batra, R., & Alden, D. L. (2003). How perceived brand globalness creates brand value. *Journal of International Business Studies*, *34*(1), 53–65. https://doi.org/10.1057/palgrave.jibs.8400002

Sustainalytics. (n.d.). *Company ESG ratings*. Retrieved November 18, 2024 from www.sustainalytics.com/esg-ratings

Torres, A., Bijmolt, T. H. A., Tribó, J. A., & Verhoef, P. (2012). Generating global brand equity through corporate social responsibility to key stakeholders. *International Journal of Research in Marketing*, *29*(1), 13–24. https://doi.org/10.1016/j.ijresmar.2011.10.002

Urde, M., Greyser, S., & Balmer, J. (2007). Corporate brands with a heritage. *Journal of Brand Management*, *15*, 4–19. https://doi.org/10.1057/palgrave.bm.2550106

Vuong, B. N., & Khanh Giao, H. N. (2020). The impact of perceived brand globalness on consumers' purchase intention and the moderating role of consumer ethnocentrism: Evidence from Vietnam. *Journal of International Consumer Marketing*, *32*(1), 47–68. https://doi.org/10.1080/08961530.2019.1619115

Wagner, T., Lutz, R. J., & Weitz, B. A. (2009). Corporate hypocrisy: Overcoming the threat of inconsistent corporate responsibility perceptions. *Journal of Marketing*, *73*(November), 77–91. http://dx.doi.org/10.1509/jmkg.73.6.77

Wang, H.-M., Yu, T. H.-K., & Hsiao, C.-Y. (2021). The causal effect of corporate social responsibility and corporate reputation on brand equity: A fuzzy-set qualitative comparative analysis. *Journal of Promotion Management*, *27*(5), 630–641. https://doi.org/10.1080/10496491.2020.1851851

Wang, W., & Korschun, D. (2015). Spillover of social responsibility associations in a brand portfolio. *Journal of Product & Brand Management*, *24*(6), 596–609. https://doi.org/10.1108/JPBM-06-2014-0629

Yang, J., & Basile, K. (2019). The impact of corporate social responsibility on brand equity. *Marketing Intelligence & Planning*, *37*(1), 2–17. https://doi.org/10.1108/MIP-02-2018-0051

30

Diversity, Equity and Inclusion in Branding

Zoe Lee, Rossella C. Gambetti, and Sharifah Faridah Syed Alwi

BACKGROUND

The diversity, equity and inclusion (DEI) movement – which promotes diversity across various dimensions (e.g., race, ethnicity, gender, sexual orientation, age and disability, among others) (Arsel et al., 2022; Ferraro et al., 2023; Lee et al., 2024a) – has gained significant momentum in recent years and continues to shape the role of brand management in modern times. Despite the recent news suggesting DEI initiatives dying out (New York Times, 2024), this rise is driven by heightened awareness of systemic inequalities, changing demographics and a growing body of research demonstrating the business case for DEI for organisations, including enhanced innovativeness and profitability (Unstereotype Alliance, 2024), as well as the broader societal impact of brand activism (Gambetti & Biraghi, 2023; Lee et al., 2024b). A significant 39% of global consumers express dissatisfaction with brands, stating that 'not enough brands do a good job of representing people similar to me or my community' (Kantar Global Monitor, 2021). Events such as the global protest against racial injustice in 2020 (e.g., Black Lives Matter) and the United Nation's 2030 Agenda for Sustainable Development Goals have amplified the urgency of embedding DEI into all facets of life and society. Recognising these shifts, many organisations now view DEI as a strategic brand imperative and allocate resources to foster a more inclusive environment.

Inclusive brands refer to the intention to foster a sense of belonging and empowerment among individuals with often marginalised identities, such as race, gender, disabilities, age and others (Lee et al., 2024a; Licsandru & Cui, 2018; Park et al., 2023). Recent studies show that inclusive advertising can be reimagined for inclusive social impact outcomes (Rundle-Thiele et al., 2024; Zayer et al., 2023). Despite its promise, DEI initiatives are not without risks, and brands face challenges in navigating consumer expectations while maintaining authenticity. Recent high-profile controversies highlight these risks and news stories abound about companies withdrawing or pivoting their DEI strategies (e.g., Ford, Lowe's and Harley-Davidson) due to conservative activism (Gonzalez, 2024). For example, Bud Light experienced significant backlash in 2023 after a marketing campaign featuring a transgender influencer sparked polarised reactions. While some lauded the effort as a step towards inclusivity, others viewed it as a misalignment with the brand's perceived identity, leading to consumer boycotts and almost 25% drop in sales (Reuters, 2023). Similarly, Jaguar's recent rebranding strategy in the UK aimed to position the iconic brand as a modern, inclusive luxury automaker but received mixed responses. Critics argued that the rebrand overlooked the brand's heritage, alienating loyal customers and creating a perception of forced inclusivity. Some literature suggests that consumers view this inclusive brand strategy as a form of 'woke washing' (Sobande, 2019), where the symbolism of diversity and social justice is hijacked for commercial and short-term gains (Burgess et al., 2022). Others show that such transgression can be seen as violating social norms and, hence, result in negative consumer–brand relationships (Mazzoli et al., 2024). These examples underscore the delicate balance brands must strike between innovation and alignment with their core identity and positioning, as well as the potential for backlash if initiatives are perceived as inauthentic or poorly executed.

Hence, the integration of DEI into brand management has become a necessity, driven by societal changes and consumer demands for inclusivity and equity. However, achieving authentic DEI branding presents significant challenges, as brands must navigate a complex landscape where their actions are scrutinised for sincerity and alignment with values (Holt, 2002; Mirzaei et al., 2022). This chapter explores how brand managers can effectively integrate DEI into their frameworks by leveraging insights from intersectionality theory, signalling theory and consumer behaviours. To provide practical guidance, we present key strategies for promoting inclusivity, illustrated through three diverse case studies that highlight different perspectives and approaches. These examples not only demonstrate the transformative potential of DEI initiatives but also underscore the risks associated with misaligned or inauthentic efforts. By examining these strategies and their outcomes, this chapter sheds light on the mechanisms that make DEI successful in brand management, explores the conditions under which it may lead to negative consequences and identifies future research directions to advance knowledge in this domain.

THEORETICAL PERSPECTIVES

Conceptualising DEI in Branding Research

The concepts of DEI in branding are multifaceted and encompass a range of dimensions. Following Arsel et al. (2022) and Henderson et al. (2023), diversity is defined as recognising individuals' physical and sociocultural distinctions; equity refers to fairness and barrier-free experiences and inclusion focuses on integrating and valuing diverse groups to promote a sense of belonging and empowerment. In branding, diversity is most visible in advertising and product lines that strive to represent a broad spectrum of identities. For example, Fenty Beauty disrupted the beauty industry by launching a foundation line with 40 shades, addressing the long-standing neglect of darker skin tones by major beauty brands. This approach mirrors Khan and Kalra's (2022) perspective on surface-level differences, highlighting visible differences. However, brands must also address deep-level diversity, encompassing values, experiences and perspectives, to truly resonate with their audiences (Burgess et al., 2022). Beyond representation and to avoid tokenism, brands must demonstrate an authentic commitment to diversity to build trust and credibility (Lee et al., 2024a).

Equity, in contrast, moves beyond mere representation to focus on creating fair opportunities and outcomes for all individuals (Sterbenk et al., 2022). Unlike equality, which assumes identical treatment, equity acknowledges systemic barriers and seeks to address them through tailored strategies. Arsel et al. (2022) emphasise that equity requires a proactive approach to correcting imbalances in resource allocation and participation, particularly for marginalised communities. For instance, Nike's adaptive apparel line and its first hands-free shoes, designed for individuals with disabilities, exemplify equity in action (Fleming, 2021). By recognising and addressing the unique challenges faced by specific groups, such as those with mobility impairments, Nike illustrates how equity-centred branding can enhance accessibility and inclusivity.

Inclusion bridges diversity and equity by transforming them into meaningful brand experiences. It involves fostering an authentic connection with consumers, ensuring they feel valued, respected and empowered through the brand's messaging and actions (Lee et al., 2024a; Licsandru & Cui, 2018). Current DEI research has historically focused on gender, skin tone, body size (e.g., Kanwal et al., 2022; Michaelidou et al., 2022; Scaraboto & Fischer, 2013; Shoenberger et al., 2020) and race (Henderson et al., 2023). However, recently, we are beginning to see more research on less discussed facets of diversity such as disabilities (e.g., see D'Angelo et al., 2024; Grewal & van der Sluis, 2024; Kearney et al., 2019; van der Sluis et al., 2024) and sexual orientations (Eisend & Hermann, 2019).

Social Identity Theory (SIT) & Stigma Theory

SIT explains how individuals classify themselves and others into social groups, with group membership shaping self-concept and behaviour (Tajfel, 1974). Consumers will typically use their characteristics to determine their ingroup and outgroups. In brand management, SIT underscores the potential of DEI initiatives to resonate with consumers by aligning brand values with their social identities. It is especially important for companies' signalling as consumers choose brands with whom they can socially identify and it is perceived as more socially attractive (Jacobsen et al., 2025). Inclusive branding strategies, particularly those showcasing marginalised groups, can also strengthen consumer-brand connections, especially for underrepresented populations (Branca et al., 2024; Cheng et al., 2023; Chowdhury et al., 2023; Henderson et al., 2023). Despite these benefits, DEI in branding can create tensions when traditionally represented groups feel threatened by underrepresented groups in the brand's latest campaigns. This means that general consumers may react negatively or neutrally towards offerings developed for underrepresented consumers (Kipnis et al., 2013). For example, the recent backlash of Bud Light and transgender communities.

However, it is important to note that consumers do not always belong to one particular reference group. Recent studies show that consumers do belong to multiple groups and learn from other groups, depending on contexts and situations (Saint Clair & Forehand, 2020). This suggests that consumers who have traditionally been part of the majority group may be influenced by reference groups they do not belong to, particularly those that champion diversity and inclusion (D&I). As the recognition and celebration of D&I grow, consumers increasingly identify with and are inspired by underrepresented groups, even if those groups are not part of their original social ingroup. For example, a consumer who does not identify as nonbinary might appreciate a brand that offers gender-neutral clothing or uses inclusive pronouns in its messaging. This supports the idea of valuing inclusivity and recognising the importance of representation for others. In another example, a heterosexual consumer might identify with a brand's Pride Month campaign and purchase rainbow-themed merchandise, not because of personal identity but to support inclusivity and equality.

In contrast, **Stigma Theory** examines how attributes like disability, ethnicity or gender are devalued in social contexts (Crocker & Major, 1989; Harmeling et al., 2021). This devaluation leads to marginalisation and exclusion, which branding scholars seek to counter through innovative marketing and service strategies. For example, Mende et al. (2024) highlight the effectiveness of personalised communication in reducing stigma and promoting inclusion, leading to improved well-being. However, they caution against assuming that principles of interpersonal relationships, such as homophily, seamlessly transfer to human–technology interactions in artificial, digital, or robotic service contexts. In disability-focused advertising campaigns, such as the Paralympics' 'Yes I Can' ad, Matson-Barkat et al. (2022) demonstrate that the social sharing of emotions can empower marginalised groups and broader audiences, ultimately helping to destigmatise certain identities.

Integrating STI and Stigma Theory not only offers valuable insights into managing DEI in branding but also reveals tensions. SIT advocates for inclusive branding to enhance alignment with consumer identities, while Stigma Theory warns against reinforcing stereotypes or resorting to tokenism. Brands must navigate these complexities by emphasising authentic storytelling and building emotional connections that empower marginalised groups while engaging diverse audiences. By adopting this balanced approach, brands can mitigate stigma and foster greater societal inclusion (Branca et al., 2024; Matson-Barkat et al., 2022).

KEY STRATEGIES FOR INCLUSIVE BRANDING

Storytelling and Disability Inclusion

Storytelling plays a pivotal role in fostering inclusion. Lee et al. (2024a, p. 8) describe that 'developing powerful, warm and empathetic storytelling via narrative transportation can change consumers' beliefs and meanings, which will eventually lead to positive behaviours'. At its core, storytelling facilitates narrative transportation – the process by which individuals immerse themselves in a story, empathise with its characters and connect emotionally with its themes (Green & Brock, 2000; van Laer et al., 2019). These stories can manifest in heroic stories and empowerment stories that luxury consumers can relate to'. Hence, such stories can change negative attitudes towards stigmatised minorities and vulnerable groups (Hill & Sharma, 2020). These stories, when authentically crafted, can help brands foster deeper emotional connections while challenging stereotypes and reducing social exclusion (Campbell et al., 2025; Milfeld et al., 2021). Burgess et al. (2022) highlight the critical role of belief congruence in building audience connectedness, emphasising that campaigns resonate most when they align with consumer values and avoid perpetuating stereotypes. Through authentic inclusion, brands not only broaden their audience appeal but also contribute to a more equitable and inclusive marketplace.

Luxury fashion brands have increasingly adopted storytelling as a means to signal inclusivity. Gucci and Victoria's Secret, for example, have featured models such as Ellie Goldstein, the first model with Down Syndrome, and Winnie Harlow, who has vitiligo (Hogan, 2021; Yates, 2020). These narratives not only celebrate diversity but also position the brands as advocates for inclusivity, demonstrating their openness to societal change. Similarly, British Vogue's campaign showcasing disabled trailblazers has been praised for its ability to evoke admiration and empowerment, reinforcing the impact of inclusive storytelling on consumer perceptions (Mowbray, 2023).

An essential component of successful DEI storytelling is the creation of unique and credible narratives (Lee et al., 2024a). Effective storytelling goes beyond tokenistic representation, embedding disability narratives into a brand's identity in ways that resonate as authentic and meaningful (Janssen et al., 2017). Avoiding over-sanitised portrayals designed solely to evoke pity – commonly referred to as 'inspiration porn' (Grue, 2016) – is crucial. Instead, brands should focus on empowerment and authenticity, as seen in the creation of Kami, a virtual influencer with Down Syndrome. Developed in collaboration with women with Down Syndrome from around the world, Kami offers a nuanced representation of disability while normalising diversity in the digital space (Kozinets et al., 2023).

Furthermore, emotional engagement and consumer empowerment are other cornerstones of impactful storytelling. Narratives that highlight the challenges and achievements of disabled individuals can inspire admiration and encourage consumers to reconsider traditional notions of beauty and inclusivity. For example, luxury campaigns featuring disabled models in aspirational settings not only challenge societal stereotypes but also foster deeper emotional connections with the brand (Dessart & Pitardi, 2019). By focusing on shared human experiences and values, brands can drive stronger consumer identification with their messaging. Additionally, individuals feel more empowered when they believe that their voice is being heard and appreciated (Auh et al., 2019; Chauhan et al., 2025). Such positive imagery of disability inclusion imagery in brand communication could signal the brand's bravery in representing a diverse customer base and, hence, make consumers feel included and valued.

However, it is important to note that balancing inclusivity with aspirational branding requires careful consideration. It is not uncommon to find brands being accused of wokewashing (Middleton & Turnbull, 2021). While inclusivity inherently challenges the exclusivity associated with luxury branding, storytelling provides a pathway to reconcile these tensions. When brands embed disability narratives into their core messaging, they position themselves as cultural authorities advocating for inclusivity, without compromising the aspirational qualities that define luxury (Holt, 2002; Sarkar, 2018). This dual approach allows brands to align with shifting societal norms while maintaining their status as purveyors of aspiration and desirability.

In the context of luxury branding, storytelling helps mitigate perceived risks associated with disability inclusion. Some luxury shoppers may view inclusivity as incongruent with the exclusivity of luxury, potentially leading to scepticism or backlash. However, compelling and cohesive storytelling can have the potential to reframe inclusivity as a unique and valuable brand attribute, enhancing perceptions of authenticity and credibility (Foster & Pettinicchio, 2022; Michel et al., 2022). Narratives that celebrate the uniqueness of disabled individuals as part of a broader commitment to inclusivity can lead to greater consumer trust, loyalty and willingness to buy. Hence, storytelling serves as a bridge between inclusivity and traditional branding ideals, empowering brands to challenge societal norms while maintaining relevance in a competitive market. Inclusive narratives can enhance brand credibility, increase brand equity and align brands with evolving consumer expectations for social responsibility (Batat, 2022).

Disability Representation and Storytelling on Social Media

Most social media platforms in the past decade have shifted significantly in terms of the services provided to the users. The creators of social media platforms and apps have developed several features that are accessible to all users including minorities, making them a public space for the entire population. At the same time, social media has then become a primary place for critical discussion about cogent societal issues such as civil rights, social justice and social representation, freedom of self-expression and, of course, DEI discourse (Bitman, 2023; Sweet et al., 2020). In this regard, social media have been recently acknowledged as 'socio-cultural artefacts' (Vicari & Kirby, 2023), which means that as 'products located within pre-established circuits of discourse and meaning' (Lupton, 2014, p. 610), social media platforms are conceived of as participating in shaping sociocultural phenomena (Poell et al., 2021).

Along these lines, social media have recently accounted to play a significant cultural role in destigmatising disability by offering a plethora of options for disability representation on the web (Furr et al., 2016; Sweet et al., 2020). These options blend platforms, apps, affordances and algorithms, providing visibility, networking, legitimation and amplification opportunities to disabled individuals and their issues. Despite that the disability stigma perpetuated also in social media, the contemporary digital era and its collective neoliberal self-expression and self-entrepreneurship apparatus (Kozinets et al., 2023) have brought to the fore the representation of disability as one of the central concerns of contemporary DEI online discourse (Bitman, 2023). Central to the representation of disability is the imperative of creating a community around people who have disabilities and/or their caregivers and dear ones.

Social media represent a primary source for creating a community around disabled individuals and their issues. Scholars have recognised the critical importance of connecting individuals with disabilities to their communities (e.g., Cole et al., 2011), and social media offer social networking opportunities for individuals with mobility impairments or who use alternative forms of communication (e.g., Cole et al., 2011; Hynan et al., 2014). This ability to enable connectivity of social media also supports learning and the sharing of information (Sweet et al., 2020). Social media create and nurture community around disability and disabled individuals through displaying digital storytelling. Digital storytelling includes 'the whole range of personal stories now being told in potentially public form using digital media resources' (Couldry, 2008, p. 374). Social media provide an alternative mode of storytelling for marginalised groups, who can integrate, complicate or oppose the dominant media narrative (Liao, 2019; Moors, 2019). As Bitman (2023) notices, storytelling enables disabled activists to make their voices heard, in contrast to the traditionally non-disabled advocates speaking on their behalf, often as part of an offensive charitable narrative. While disabled storytellers aim to influence policy-makers and the media (Pearson & Trevisan, 2015; Trevisan, 2017), this focus on marginalised narratives demands increased control over activists' visibility enjoyed by users with stigmatised identities. Bitman (2023) points out that they can be selective about their public disclosures as they move between private and public spheres (Vivienne, 2016) and try to manage potential context collapse (Marwick & Boyd, 2011).

Digital storytelling relies on authenticity and personal engagement in the stories (Manning, 2020). However, a high level of personal engagement and visibility may oppress marginalised individuals (Banet-Weiser & Miltner, 2016), such as disabled activists, and expose them to societal pressure. Therefore, it is essential for disabled individuals to engage in digital storytelling that accurately balances the genuine representation of their marginalised voice with the slack, ephemeral and exploitative vein that characterises much of the social media discourse (Halupka, 2018; Smith et al., 2019). In the following section, we illustrate the case of a female disabled influencer, Lolo Spencer, who offers an effective example of how disability in social media can become a driver of personal empowerment and community building of marginalised individuals, of societal sensitisation and cultural destigmatisation of a diversity condition.

Case example: Lolo Spencer and the cultural destigmatisation of disability on social media

Lauren 'Lolo' Spencer is a disability lifestyle influencer, author, black model and actor who stars in HBO's comedy series 'The Sex Lives of College Girls' and who recently published the book 'Access Your Drive and Enjoy the Ride: A Guide on Achieving Your Dreams from a Person with a Disability'. Positivity is a choice that Lauren 'Lolo' Spencer had to consciously make at 14 years old when she stared down a daunting diagnosis of ALS – one that forced her into a wheelchair at the age of 19 and predicted that she had five years left to live (Rajani, 2023). This positive choice led her to venture into a lifestyle blog that later opened the way for a YouTube channel (Sitting Pretty) and an Instagram profile (itsololove) that currently counts 70,600 followers. Through her social media presence, Lauren decided to turn her illness into a public occasion for the education and empowerment of people with similar health issues and disabilities. Through her channels, she creates a community of disabled individuals and spreads public awareness about disability issues:

> *Since I started making lifestyle content on YouTube around nine years ago, I've always tried to advocate for being okay with having your disability. It's our body, so we can't escape it – and we might as well find ways to love it. [...] As I kept posting videos and content online, so many people sent messages, left comments, and shared their experiences and tips based on their particular disabilities. [...] I want people with disabilities to know that they can be independent, that they can be self-empowered, and if, for whatever reason, they don't have a life of full independence, they can still find joy in other ways.* (Wang, 2024)

In her social media accounts, Lauren engages in a personal, confessional-like storytelling that presents a cheerful and ironic tone of voice whereby she shares with the public every moment of her life, providing information, advice and support to the disabled community with her example. This light-hearted tone of voice is a unique marker of her digital storytelling ability to illuminate a dark situation and turn it into something positive and easy to talk about and share. In this regard, her Instagram account is populated with snapshots and posts about her travels, fashion shows, parties with friends and even disco nights.

But how does Lauren aggregate and give voice to a community around disability? Her major communication strategy is based on conducting a series of weekly interviews during her Instagram lives where she invites and engages in a conversation with other disabled influencers and creators to talk about their real lives and experiences of disability, interacting live with the audience. Among her guests are the Filipino influencer Lila Hart, affected by 'spina bifida', and Tamara Mena, a Latina actress and model who advocates for body positivity and disability, and she shared her difficulties in being accepted in the entertainment industry being plus size and disabled. Another communication strategy leverages Lauren's participation in challenges. One of the most important, for instance, was the challenge related to the hashtag #womensupportingwomen, where the intersection nature of her public persona found her most effective expression in supporting the actions of disabled women in the world (Figure 30.1 portrays an AI-prompted version of the post whereby Lolo Spencer accepted the #womensupporting-women challenge).

Figure 30.1 Lolo Spencer's empowering pride of being a disabled woman (AI-generated image prompted by the authors reproducing an Instagram post by Lolo Spencer)

Source: The authors.

This case shows how a disabled individual in the current digital age can leverage social media platforms and carefully curated digital storytelling that pays attention to blending public disclosure and disability issue sensitisation with light-heartedness, positivity and straightforwardness to craft a credible and effective representation of disability discourse that attempts to culturally destigmatise the issue.

DISNEY AND DIVERSITY

In recent years, there has been a notable increase in advertisers incorporating diversity into their campaigns. A report by McCormick (2025) indicates that 19% of global advertisements represent ethnic groups, 27% showcase diversity in skin tone, nearly 1% feature LGBTQIA + individuals and 4% include people aged 65 and older. While these figures reflect a growing commitment to inclusivity, many brands have encountered scepticism, with critics questioning the sincerity and depth of their efforts.

Disney exemplifies this tension. With a long history of incorporating diverse characters – dating back to films like Pocahontas (Phung, 2023) – the company has expanded its portfolio to include stories like Encanto, Raya and the Last Dragon, and Turning Red. However, despite these initiatives, Disney has faced criticism regarding the authenticity of its portrayals. For example, The Princess and the Frog, which introduced Princess Tiana as Disney's first Black princess. Yet, critics argue that her transformation into a frog for much of the film undermines her representation as a Black woman (Diep, 2023). Additionally, Tiana's working-class background starkly contrasts with the wealth and privilege of many other Disney princesses, reinforcing socioeconomic stereotypes about Black communities (Diep, 2023). These concerns highlight the complexities of corporate diversity efforts, where well-intended representation can sometimes perpetuate limiting narratives rather than dismantle them.

Recently, 'Encanto', which centres on a Colombian family, was criticised for generalising Latino culture rather than focusing specifically on Colombian traditions. Critics argue that the film presents a perspective of Colombia through

American eyes, leading to inauthentic storytelling and representations (Hermoza, 2024). Similarly, 'Turning Red', which highlights Chinese culture, has been accused of oversimplifying Chinese immigrant family experiences. The portrayal of the mother as a 'tiger mom' and the emphasis on academic excellence has been seen as reinforcing stereotypes about Asian families (Phung, 2023). Finally, 'Raya and the Last Dragon' aimed to introduce Southeast Asian representation but faced backlash for blending elements from various cultures into a single narrative. This amalgamation was viewed as homogenising distinct cultures (e.g., Malaysia, Thailand, Singapore and Indonesia), thereby erasing the unique experiences of multiple ethnic groups (Anwar, 2025; Phung, 2023).

These critiques highlight the challenges Disney faces in its efforts to promote D&I (Hart, 2022). While the company has made strides in featuring diverse characters and stories, questions about the authenticity and depth of these representations persist. Some argue that these efforts may be more about capitalising on diversity trends rather than genuine inclusivity, leading to accusations of 'woke-washing' (Anwar, 2025). In summary, although Disney has taken steps to incorporate diversity into its brand and storytelling, the legitimacy and sincerity of these efforts continue to be debated. The company must navigate the fine line between representation and appropriation to avoid perpetuating stereotypes and to ensure authentic portrayals of diverse cultures (Hart, 2022).

DISCUSSION AND FUTURE RESEARCH DIRECTIONS: INTEGRATING INCLUSIVITY INTO BRANDING RESEARCH

In this chapter, we set out to propose a move towards integrating DEI in branding research with the aim of providing a broad overview of the current state of the research that answers the calls for more inclusive marketing (Arsel et al., 2022). Our chapter indicates that it is important to distinguish between performative and authentic DEI efforts for long-term success. DEI is not being woke. Companies that retreat from DEI initiatives often have a history of performative, communications-led programmes, typically linked to virtue signalling (Berthon et al., 2023). Research has shown that such inauthentic inclusion can typically backfire (Ferraro et al., 2023). This occurs when brands project an illusion of inclusivity without meaningful investment in solving systemic issues or championing underrepresented groups. Hence, these efforts prioritise optics over substance, leaving consumers disillusioned and sceptical of the brand's integrity. In some cases, it may also lead to countermovements such as anti-DEI campaigns (Scott et al., 2025).

Authentic inclusion, by contrast, requires evidence of social impact and a commitment to addressing the barriers faced by underrepresented groups (Rundle-Thiele et al., 2024). Brands must go beyond surface-level declarations of inclusivity and engage in inclusive design practices that enhance accessibility and usability for diverse consumers (Patrick & Hollenbeck, 2021). By identifying and dismantling systemic barriers across the customer journey, brands can tailor their products and services to achieve greater market penetration and foster meaningful connections with a wider audience. Once actionable improvements are implemented, brands can communicate their efforts transparently, showcasing how these changes create tangible benefits for their customers. Merely claiming inclusivity or relying on third-party certifications is insufficient in today's market. As Aaker (2023) emphasised, creating signature social value programs that deliver measurable, lasting impact is essential. By consistently demonstrating the ways their offerings improve lives and contribute to societal well-being, brands can strengthen consumer loyalty and differentiate themselves as truly committed to equity and inclusion.

Finally, consistency is fundamental to achieving authentic inclusion and fostering trust and goodwill among both consumers and employees. An inclusive brand is not built overnight but through a sustained commitment to aligning external communications with internal practices. This alignment ensures that the brand's public image is not just a façade but a genuine reflection of its internal culture and values. Such coherence across all organisational facets – from marketing campaigns to workplace policies and customer interactions – creates a perception of dependability and authenticity. When consumers recognise this consistency, they are more likely to trust the brand, engage with it and develop long-term loyalty. Over time, this trust enhances brand equity, positioning the organisation as a leader in both social responsibility and market relevance.

In fact, the benefits of aligning employees with the brand extend well beyond consumer perceptions. Research by Moorman et al. (2024) demonstrates that when employees feel connected to and aligned with a brand's values and mission, they exhibit increased engagement, satisfaction and loyalty. This alignment fosters a sense of purpose and belonging, encouraging employees to become brand advocates both within and outside the organisation. Interestingly, such alignment can even lead to employees being more willing to accept lower

Table 30.1 Future research agenda

Themes (topics)	*Future Research Questions*
Conceptualisation of DEI in branding	• How can diversity, equity and inclusion be conceptually defined in the branding literature? • What are the core components of DEI in branding, and how do they differ across industries and cultural contexts? • How has the conceptualisation of DEI evolved over time in response to sociopolitical shifts and consumer expectations? • What is the role of intersectionality in defining DEI within branding and brand communications? (Uduehi et al., 2024)
Antecedents and consequences of DEI	• What organisational and market-driven factors motivate brands to engage with DEI? • How does brand activism influence consumer perceptions of a company's DEI efforts and overall brand experience? • What are the long-term consequences of DEI initiatives on brand equity, trust and loyalty? • To what extent does DEI influence financial and non-financial brand performance metrics? • How do DEI initiatives affect consumer well-being, particularly among marginalised communities? • What are the potential darksides of DEI in branding?
Internal aspects of DEI	a. *Employee and service-centric DEI* • How do employees perceive and respond to DEI branding initiatives within their organisation? • How does DEI impact employee engagement, job satisfaction and organisational commitment? • What challenges do frontline service employees face when delivering brand-led DEI initiatives? b. *Inclusive design in branding* • How can brands integrate inclusive design principles into their products, services and marketing strategies? • What role does accessibility play in inclusive branding, particularly for disabled consumers? c. *Corporate culture and barriers to DEI implementation* • What are the key cultural barriers that hinder the integration of DEI into corporate branding strategies? • How do organisations overcome resistance to DEI initiatives, both internally and externally? • How can companies ensure their DEI efforts are sustained and not performative? d. *Leadership and DEI* • What leadership styles are most effective in fostering DEI within branding strategies? • How do leadership attitudes towards DEI shape brand culture and corporate decision-making? • How do diverse leadership teams contribute to the authenticity of a brand's DEI efforts such as CEOs? • How do brands balance the tension between commercial objectives and genuine DEI commitments?
Theories, research methods, design	a. *Intersectionality in branding research* (Uduehi et al., 2024) • How has intersectionality been applied in branding and consumer behaviour research? • How can intersectional perspectives deepen our understanding of consumer responses to DEI initiatives, in relation to other psychology and sociology theories? b. *Innovative methodologies for studying DEI in branding* • How can text analysis be used to assess brand communications around DEI on social media? • What insights can netnography provide on how consumers engage with and respond to brands' DEI efforts on social media? • What role do AI and machine learning play in analysing large-scale DEI-related consumer data? c. *Longitudinal approaches to DEI in branding* • How do consumer attitudes towards DEI evolve over time? • What are the long-term impacts of DEI failures and crises on brand perception? • How does the effectiveness of DEI campaigns change across different generations of consumers?
Public policy and DEI	• How do government policies shape corporate approaches to DEI, especially the current rollback of DEI? • To what extent do brands engage in DEI initiatives to align with or resist political ideologies? • How do public discourses around DEI (e.g., anti-woke movements) affect brand strategies?

pay, highlighting the profound impact of authentic, values-driven brand identity on employee retention and morale. Ultimately, consistency in DEI efforts serves as the cornerstone of an inclusive brand, enabling organisations to attract, inspire and retain not only customers but also employees who share and uphold their vision of equity and inclusivity.

We summarise our research agenda in Table 30.1 by proposing a set of future research questions grouped around multiple themes:

CONCLUSION

The integration of DEI into brand management represents both a moral imperative and a strategic necessity in contemporary marketplaces. As brands navigate the evolving expectations of consumers and stakeholders, the challenge lies not only in increasing representation but in ensuring that inclusivity efforts are authentic, meaningful and impactful (Ferraro et al., 2023; Henderson et al., 2023; Lee et al., 2024a). The discussions in this chapter underscore that DEI is not a one-size-fits-all strategy; rather, it requires brands to adopt a nuanced, intersectional approach that extends beyond surface-level inclusivity (Arsel et al., 2022; Park et al., 2023). Theories such as STI (Tajfel, 1974) and stigma theory (Crocker & Major, 1989) provide useful frameworks for understanding consumer reactions to DEI initiatives, revealing both the opportunities and potential risks of misalignment. While brand activism and inclusive storytelling can foster stronger consumer connections (Branca et al., 2024; Lee et al., 2024a), brands must carefully balance their messaging to avoid perceptions of tokenism, 'woke-washing' (Sobande, 2019) or performative allyship (Mirzaei et al., 2022). Cases such as Disney, Bud Light and Jaguar illustrate the complex realities of embedding DEI into branding, highlighting the tensions between innovation, consumer perception and corporate identity (Gonzalez, 2024; Scott et al., 2025).

Looking ahead, future research should focus on the long-term implications of DEI strategies in branding, particularly in understanding how inclusivity shapes consumer trust, brand equity and corporate reputation over time (Burgess et al., 2022; Ferraro et al., 2023). More empirical studies are needed to assess the tangible impact of inclusive branding on financial performance, customer loyalty and employee engagement (Wilkie et al., 2023). Additionally, further exploration is required into underrepresented areas of DEI in branding, such as disability representation (Grewal & van der Sluis, 2024), neurodiversity and intersectional identities, to move beyond the dominant narratives of gender and race (Kearney et al., 2019; Matson-Barkat et al., 2022). Brands must also invest in sustained and measurable DEI initiatives that are deeply embedded in corporate structures rather than merely reflected in advertising campaigns. As societal expectations continue to evolve, the brands that succeed will be those that demonstrate an unwavering commitment to inclusivity, transparency and accountability. By embracing DEI as a foundational principle rather than a trend-driven marketing tool, brands can cultivate deeper, more meaningful relationships with consumers while contributing to a more equitable and representative marketplace.

REFERENCES

Aaker, D. (2023). *Four strategies define the future of purpose-driven branding.* www.ama.org/marketing-news/four-strategies-define-the-future-of-purpose-driven-branding/

Anwar, R. (2025). *Disney's diversity dilemma: Representation or false inclusivity?* https://stuyspec.com/article/disneys-diversity-dilemma-representation-or-false-inclusivity?

Arsel, Z., Crockett, D., & Scott, M. L. (2022). Diversity, equity, and inclusion (DEI) in the Journal of Consumer Research: A curation and research agenda. *Journal of Consumer Research, 48*(5), 920–933. https://doi.org/10.1093/jcr/ucab057

Auh, S., Menguc, B., Katsikeas, C. S., & Jung, Y. S. (2019). When does customer participation matter? An empirical investigation of the role of customer empowerment in the customer participation performance link. *Journal of Marketing Research, 56*(6), 1012–1033. https://doi.org/10.1177/0022243719866408

Banet-Weiser, S., & Miltner, K. M. (2016). # MasculinitySoFragile: Culture, structure, and networked misogyny. *Feminist Media Studies, 16*(1), 171–174. https://doi.org/10.1080/14680777.2016.1120490

Batat, W. (2022). Transformative luxury research (TLR): An agenda to advance luxury for well-being. *Journal of Macromarketing, 42*(4), 609–623. https://doi.org/10.1177/02761467221135547

Berthon, P. R., Ferguson, S. T. L., Pitt, L. F., & Wang, E. (2023). The virtuous brand: The perils and promises of brand virtue signaling. *Business Horizons, 66*(1), 27–36. https://doi.org/10.1016/j.bushor.2021.10.006

Bitman, N. (2023). 'Which part of my group do I represent?': Disability activism and social media users with concealable communicative disabilities.

Information, Communication & Society, *26*(3), 619–636. https://doi.org/10.1080/1369118X.2021.1963463

Branca, G., Grosso, M., & Castaldo, S. (2024). Value through diversity: A systematic literature review to understand diversity and inclusion in consumer research. *Psychology & Marketing*, *41*(11), 2854–2873. https://doi.org/10.1002/mar.22088

Burgess, A., Wilkie, D. C. H., & Dolan, R. (2022). Brand approaches to diversity: a typology and research agenda. *European Journal of Marketing*, *57*(1), 60–88. https://doi.org/10.1108/EJM-09-2021-0696

Campbell, C., Sands, S., McFerran, B., & Mavrommatis, A. (2025). Diversity representation in advertising. *Journal of the Academy of Marketing Science*, *53*, 588–616. https://doi.org/10.1007/s11747-023-00994-8

Chauhan, V., Gupta, M., & Das, G. (2025). Empowered by representation: How plus-size models create brand evangelists. *Psychology & Marketing*, *42*(1), 236–254. https://doi.org/10.1002/mar.22122

Cheng, Y., Zhou, X., & Yao, K. (2023). LGBT-inclusive representation in entertainment products and its market response: Evidence from field and lab. *Journal of Business Ethics*, *183*(4), 1189–1209. https://doi.org/10.1007/s10551-022-05075-4

Chowdhury, R. M. M. I., Arli, D., & Septianto, F. (2023). How religiosity affects attitudes toward brands that utilize LGBTQ-themed advertising. *Journal of Business Ethics*, *193*(1), 63–88. https://doi.org/10.1007/s10551-023-05578-8

Cole, J., Nolan, J., Seko, Y., Mancuso, K., & Ospina, A. (2011). GimpGirl grows up: Women with disabilities rethinking, redefining, and reclaiming community. *New Media & Society*, *13*(7), 1161–1179. https://doi.org/10.1177/1461444811398032

Couldry, N. (2008). Mediatization or mediation? Alternative understandings of the emergent space of digital storytelling. *New Media & Society*, *10*(3), 373–391. https://doi.org/10.1177/1461444808089414

Crocker, J., & Major, B. (1989). Social stigma and self-esteem: The self-protective properties of stigma. *Psychological Review*, *96*(4), 608. https://doi.org/10.1037/0033-295X.96.4.608

D'Angelo, J. K., Dunn, L., & Valsesia, F. (2024). Is this for me? Differential responses to skin tone inclusivity initiatives by underrepresented consumers and represented consumers. *Journal of Marketing*, *89*(2), 25–42. https://doi.org/10.1177/00222429241268634

Dessart, L., & Pitardi, V. (2019). How stories generate consumer engagement: An exploratory study. *Journal of Business Research*, *104*, 183–195. https://doi.org/10.1016/j.jbusres.2019.06.045

Diep, P. (2023). *Disney's problem with cultural representation*. https://medium.com/@paceyd/disneys-problem-with-cultural-representation-38a27c1cdd3d

Eisend, M., & Hermann, E. (2019). Consumer responses to homosexual imagery in advertising: A meta-analysis. *Journal of Advertising*, *48*(4), 380–400. https://doi.org/10.1080/00913367.2019.1628676

Ferraro, C., Hemsley, A., & Sands, S. (2023). Embracing diversity, equity, and inclusion (DEI): Considerations and opportunities for brand managers. *Business Horizons*, *66*(4), 463–479. https://doi.org/10.1016/j.bushor.2022.09.005

Fleming, S. (2021). *Nike's hands-free shoe is a step forward for inclusive clothing*. World Economic Forum. www.weforum.org/stories/2021/02/nike-hands-free-shoe-disability-inclusive-clothing/

Foster, J., & Pettinicchio, D. (2022). A model who looks like me: Communicating and consuming representations of disability. *Journal of Consumer Culture*, *22*(3), 579–597. https://doi.org/10.1177/14695405211022074

Furr, J. B., Carreiro, A., & McArthur, J. A. (2016). Strategic approaches to disability disclosure on social media. *Disability & Society*, *31*(10), 1353–1368. https://doi.org/10.1080/09687599.2016.1256272

Gambetti, R. C., & Biraghi, S. (2023). Branded activism: Navigating the tension between culture and market in social media. *Futures*, *145*, 103080. https://doi.org/10.1016/j.futures.2022.103080

Gonzalez, A. (2024). *The corporate retreat from DEI – a short-sighted strategy*. Forbes. www.forbes.com/sites/aliciagonzalez/2024/08/31/the-corporate-retreat-from-dei-a-short-sighted-strategy/

Green, M. C., & Brock, T. C. (2000). The role of transportation in the persuasiveness of public narratives. *Journal of Personality and Social Psychology*, *79*(5), 701–721. https://doi.org/10.1037/0022-3514.79.5.701

Grewal, L., & Van Der Sluis, H. (2024). Hidden barriers to marketplace disability accessibility: An empirical analysis of the role of perceived trade-offs. *Journal of Consumer Research*, *51*(1), 66–78. https://doi.org/10.1093/jcr/ucad051

Grue, J. (2016). The problem with inspiration porn: A tentative definition and a provisional critique. *Disability & Society*, *31*(6), 838–849. https://doi.org/10.1080/09687599.2016.1205473

Halupka, M. (2018). The legitimisation of clicktivism. *Australian Journal of Political Science*, *53*(1), 130–141. https://doi.org/10.1080/10361146.2017.1416586

Harmeling, C. M., Mende, M., Scott, M. L., & Palmatier, R. W. (2021). Marketing, through the eyes of the stigmatized. *Journal of Marketing Research*,

58(2), 223–245. https://doi.org/10.1177/0022243720975400

Hart, M. (2022). *Disney's lack of diversity and use of racial stereotypes... a tale as old as time*. https://shgreenwichkingstreetchronicle.org/115987/opinions/disneys-lack-of-diversity-and-use-of-racial-stereotypes-a-tale-as-old-as-time/

Henderson, C. M., Mazodier, M., & Khenfer, J. (2023). The positive effects of integrated advertising, featuring diverse ensembles, on societal identification and mainstream brand value. *Journal of the Academy of Marketing Science*, *53*, 617–642. https://doi.org/10.1007/s11747-023-00977-9

Hermoza, L. (2024). *How Disney's representation of culture and diversity has changed over the years*. https://insidethemagic.net/2024/12/how-disneys-representation-of-culture-and-diversity-has-changed-lh1/

Hill, R. P., & Sharma, E. (2020). Consumer vulnerability. *Journal of Consumer Psychology*, *30*(3), 551–570. https://doi.org/10.1002/jcpy.1161

Hogan, M. (2021). *Model Nina Marker driving autism awareness and inclusivity in fashion*. https://blog.portobelloinstitute.com/model-nina-marker-drives-autism-awareness-and-inclusivity-in-fashion

Holt, D. B. (2002). Why do brands cause trouble? A dialectical theory of consumer culture and branding. *Journal of Consumer Research*, *29*(1), 70–90. https://doi.org/10.1086/339922

Hynan, A., Murray, J., & Goldbart, J. (2014). 'Happy and excited': Perceptions of using digital technology and social media by young people who use augmentative and alternative communication. *Child Language Teaching and Therapy*, *30*(2), 175–186. https://doi.org/10.1177/0265659013519258

Jacobsen, L. F., Frank, D. A., Søndergaard, H. A., & Peschel, A. O. (2025). From diversity to distinction: Exploring the role of diversity and inclusion related to consumer perceptions of company innovativeness and attractiveness. *Journal of Business Research*, *189*, 115184. https://doi.org/10.1016/j.jbusres.2025.115184

Janssen, C., Vanhamme, J., & Leblanc, S. (2017). Should luxury brands say it out loud? Brand conspicuousness and consumer perceptions of responsible luxury. *Journal of Business Research*, *77*(1), 167–174. https://doi.org/10.1016/j.jbusres.2016.12.009

Kantar Global Monitor. (2021). *Inclusion and diversity: how to meet great expectations*. www.kantar.com/inspiration/brands/inclusion-and-diversity-how-to-meet-great-expectations

Kanwal, M., Burki, U., Ali, R., & Dahlstrom, R. (2022). Systematic review of gender differences and similarities in online consumers' shopping behaviour. *Journal of Consumer Marketing*, *39*(1), 29–43. https://doi.org/10.1108/JCM-01-2021-4356

Kearney, S., Brittain, I., & Kipnis, E. (2019). "Superdisabilities" vs "disabilities"? Theorizing the role of ableism in (mis) representational mythology of disability in the marketplace. *Consumption Markets & Culture*, *22*(5–6), 545–567. https://doi.org/10.1080/10253866.2018.1562701

Khan, U., & Kalra, A. (2022). It's good to be different: How diversity impacts judgments of moral behaviour. *Journal of Consumer Research*, *49*(2), 177–201. https://doi.org/10.1093/jcr/ucab061

Kipnis, E., Broderick, A. J., Demangeot, C., Adkins, N. R., Ferguson, N. S., Henderson, G. R., Johnson, G., Mandiberg, J. M., Mueller, R. D., Pullig, C., & Roy, A. (2013). Branding beyond prejudice: Navigating multicultural marketplaces for consumer well-being. *Journal of Business Research*, *66*(8), 1186–1194. https://doi.org/10.1016/j.jbusres.2012.08.011

Kozinets, R. V., Gretzel, U., & Gambetti, R. (2023). *Influencers and creators: Business, culture and practice*. Sage.

Lee, Z., Alwi, S. F. S., & Gambetti, R. (2024a). The thousand faces of beauty: How credible storytelling unlocks disability representation in inclusive luxury fashion branding. *Journal of Business Research*, *181*, 114744. https://doi.org/10.1016/j.jbusres.2024.114744

Lee, Z., Spry, A., Ekinci, Y., & Vredenburg, J. (2024b). From warmth to warrior: Impacts of non-profit brand activism on brand bravery, brand hypocrisy and brand equity. *Journal of Brand Management*, *31*(2), 193–211. https://doi.org/10.1057/s41262-023-00319-8

Liao, S. (2019). '# IAmGay# What about you?': Storytelling, discursive politics, and the affective dimension of social media activism against censorship in China. *International Journal of Communication*, *13*, 21.

Licsandru, T. C., & Cui, C. C. (2018). Subjective social inclusion: A conceptual critique for socially inclusive marketing. *Journal of Business Research*, *82*, 330–339. https://doi.org/10.1016/j.jbusres.2017.08.036

Lupton, D. (2014). *Digital sociology*. Routledge.

Manning, M. (2020). Crafting authenticity: Reality, storytelling, and female self-representation through instapoetry. *Storytelling, Self, Society*, *16*(2), 263–279. https://doi.org/10.13110/storselfsoci.16.2.0263

Marwick, A. E., & Boyd, D. (2011). I tweet honestly, I tweet passionately: Twitter users, context collapse, and the imagined audience. *New Media & Society*, *13*(1), 114–133. https://doi.org/10.1177/1461444810365313

Matson-Barkat, S., Puncheva-Michelotti, P., Koetz, C., & Hennekam, S. (2022). Destigmatisation through social sharing of emotions and empowerment: The case of disabled athletes and consumers of disability sports. *Journal of Business*

Research, *149*, 77–84. https://doi.org/10.1016/j.jbusres.2022.05.027

Mazzoli, V., Donvito, R., & Zarantonello, L. (2024). Brand transgressions in advertising related to diversity, equity and inclusion: implications for consumer–brand relationships. *Journal of Product & Brand Management*, *33*(5), 516–532. https://doi.org/10.1108/JPBM-02-2023-4352

McCormick, K. (2025). *Perspective-broadening stats about diversity & inclusion in marketing for 2025*. www.wordstream.com/blog/ws/2023/02/27/diversity-inclusion-marketing-statistics?

Mende, M., Scott, M. L., Ubal, V. O., Hassler, C. M. K., Harmeling, C. M., & Palmatier, R. W. (2024). Personalized communication as a platform for service inclusion? Initial insights into interpersonal and AI-based personalization for stigmatized consumers. *Journal of Service Research*, *27*(1), 28–48. https://doi.org/10.1177/10946705231188676

Michaelidou, N., Siamagka, N. T., Hatzithomas, L., & Chaput, L. (2022). Femvertising practices on social media: a comparison of luxury and non-luxury brands. *Journal of Product & Brand Management*, *31*(8), 1285–1300. https://doi.org/10.1108/JPBM-09-2020-3074

Michel, G., Stathopoulou, A., & Valette-Florence, P. (2022). Luxury is still alive and well: A spotlight on its multifaceted components. *Journal of Business Research*, *153*, 276–284. https://doi.org/10.1016/j.jbusres.2022.08.021

Middleton, K., & Turnbull, S. (2021). How advertising got "woke": The institutional role of advertising in the emergence of gender progressive market logics and practices. *Marketing Theory*, *21*(4), 561–578. https://doi.org/10.1177/14705931211035163

Milfeld, T., Haley, E., & Flint, D. J. (2021). A fresh start for stigmatized groups: The effect of cultural identity mindset framing in brand advertising. *Journal of Advertising*, *50*(5), 603–621. https://doi.org/10.1080/00913367.2021.1913264

Mirzaei, A., Wilkie, D. C., & Siuki, H. (2022). Woke brand activism authenticity or the lack of it. *Journal of Business Research*, *139*, 1–12. https://doi.org/10.1016/j.jbusres.2021.09.044

Moorman, C., Sorescu, A., & Tavassoli, N. T. (2024). Brands in the labor market: How vertical and horizontal brand differentiation impact pay and profits through employee–brand matching. *Journal of Marketing Research*, *61*(2), 204–224. https://doi.org/10.1177/00222437231184429

Moors, M. R. (2019). What is Flint? Place, storytelling, and social media narrative reclamation during the Flint water crisis. *Information, Communication & Society*, *22*(6), 808–822. https://doi.org/10.1080/1369118X.2019.1577477

Mowbray, N. (2023). *A necessary and overdue education: British Vogue dedicates five covers to disabled trailblazers*. https://edition.cnn.com/style/article/british-vogue-disabled-cover-stars-sinead-burke/index.html

New York Times. (2024). *D.E.I. goes quiet*. www.nytimes.com/2024/01/13/business/dealbook/dei-goes-quiet.html

Park, Y. W., Voss, G. B., & Voss, Z. G. (2023). Advancing customer diversity, equity, and inclusion: Measurement, stakeholder influence, and the role of marketing. *Journal of the Academy of Marketing Science*, *51*(1), 174–197. https://doi.org/10.1007/s11747-022-00883-6

Patrick, V. M., & Hollenbeck, C. R. (2021). Designing for all: Consumer response to inclusive design. *Journal of Consumer Psychology*, *31*(2), 360–381. https://doi.org/10.1002/jcpy.1225

Pearson, C., & Trevisan, F. (2015). Disability activism in the new media ecology: Campaigning strategies in the digital era. *Disability & Society*, *30*(6), 924–940. https://doi.org/10.1080/09687599.2015.1051516

Phung, A. (2023). *The reality of Disney's diversity*. https://pacificties.org/the-reality-of-disneys-diversity/

Poell, T., Nieborg, D. B., & Duffy, B. E. (2021). *Platforms and cultural production*. John Wiley & Sons.

Rajani, H. (2023, March 16). Lauren 'Lolo' spencer's book is a master class in finding joy as a young disabled person. *The Huffington Post*. Retrieved January 29, 2025, from www.huffpost.com/entry/lauren-lolo-spencer-interview_n_64135e76e4b0fef15242de7c#:~:text=In%20her%20new%20book%2C%20Lauren,sad%2Ddisabled%2Dperson%20trope.&text=Positivity%20is%20a%20choice%20that,five%20years%20left%20to%20live

Reuters. (2023). Bud Light loses top US beer spot after promotion with the transgender influencer. *Guardian*. www.theguardian.com/business/2023/jun/14/bud-light-loses-top-us-beer-spot-after-promotion-with-transgender-influencer

Rundle-Thiele, S., Mitchell, S. L., Lee, Z., & Hyde, F. (2024). Refocusing marketing effort to support net-positive social impact. *European Journal of Marketing*, *58*(7), 1806–1825. https://doi.org/10.1108/EJM-06-2023-0465

Saint Clair, J. K., & Forehand, M. R. (2020). The many-faced consumer: Consumption consequences of balancing multiple identities. *Journal of Consumer Research*, *46*(6), 1011–1030. https://doi.org/10.1093/jcr/ucz046

Sarkar, C. (2018, November 15). The case for brand activism – A discussion with Philip Kotler and Christian Sarkar. *The Marketing Journal*. www.marketingjournal.org/the-case-for-brand-activism-a-discussion-with-philipkotler-and-christian-sarkar/

Scaraboto, D., & Fischer, E. (2013). Frustrated fashionistas: An institutional theory perspective on consumer quests for greater choice in mainstream markets. *Journal of Consumer Research*, *39*(6), 1234–1257. https://doi.org/10.1086/668298

Scott, M. L., Mende, M., & Ramón, L. G. (2025). Inclusivity in the marketplace through the lens of social-movements and counter-movements theories. *Journal of Business Research*, *189*, 115058. https://doi.org/10.1016/j.jbusres.2024.115058

Shoenberger, H., Kim, E. A., & Johnson, E. K. (2020). # BeingReal about Instagram ad models: The effects of perceived authenticity: How image modification of female body size alters advertising attitude and buying intention. *Journal of Advertising Research*, *60*(2), 197–207. https://doi.org/10.2501/JAR-2019-035

Smith, B. G., Krishna, A., & Al-Sinan, R. (2019). Beyond slacktivism: Examining the entanglement between social media engagement, empowerment, and participation in activism. *International Journal of Strategic Communication*, *13*(3), 182–196. https://doi.org/10.1080/1553118X.2019.1621870

Sobande, F. (2019). Woke-washing: 'intersectional' femvertising and branding 'woke' bravery. *European Journal of Marketing*, *54*(11), 2723–2745. https://doi.org/10.1108/EJM-02-2019-0134

Sterbenk, Y., Champlin, S., Windels, K., & Shelton, S. (2022). Is femvertising the new greenwashing? Examining corporate commitment to gender equality. *Journal of Business Ethics*, *177*(3), 491–505. https://doi.org/10.1007/s10551-021-04755-x

Sweet, K. S., LeBlanc, J. K., Stough, L. M., & Sweany, N. W. (2020). Community building and knowledge sharing by individuals with disabilities using social media. *Journal of Computer Assisted Learning*, *36*(1), 1–11. https://doi.org/10.1111/jcal.12377

Tajfel, H. (1974). Social identity and intergroup behaviour. *Social Science Information*, *13*(2), 65–93. https://doi.org/10.1177/053901847401300204

Trevisan, F. (2017). *Disability rights advocacy online: Voice, empowerment and global connectivity*. Routledge.

Uduehi, E., Saint Clair, J. K., & Crabbe, R. (2024). Intersectionality in marketing: A paradigm for understanding understudied consumers. *Journal of Marketing*, *0*(0). https://doi.org/10.1177/00222429241258493

Unstereotype Alliance. (2024). *The business case for inclusive advertising*. www.unstereotypealliance.org/sites/default/files/2024-09/INCLUSIVE%20ADVERTISING%20%28Business%20case%29%20WEB.pdf

Van der Sluis, H., Samper, A., Kristofferson, K., & Hlava, T. (2024). How do physical disability cues influence assumptions about consumer tastes? Unpacking the disability preference stereotype. *Journal of Consumer Research*, ucae031.

Van Laer, T., Feiereisen, S., & Visconti, L. M. (2019). Storytelling in the digital era: A meta-analysis of relevant moderators of the narrative transportation effect. *Journal of Business Research*, *96*, 135–146. https://doi.org/10.1016/j.jbusres.2018.10.053

Vicari, S., & Kirby, D. (2023). Digital platforms as socio-cultural artifacts: developing digital methods for cultural research. *Information, Communication & Society*, *26*(9), 1733–1755. https://doi.org/10.1080/1369118X.2022.2027498

Vivienne, S. (2016). *Digital identity and everyday activism: Sharing private stories with networked publics*. Springer.

Wang, L. (2024, April 16). Lolo Spencer on building community and confidence as a disability advocate. *Women's Health Magazine*. Retrieved January 29, 2025, from www.womenshealthmag.com/life/a60400522/lolo-spencer/

Wilkie, D. C. H., Burgess, A. J., Mirzaei, A., & Dolan, R. M. (2023). Inclusivity in advertising: a typology framework for understanding consumer reactions. *Journal of Advertising*, *52*(5), 721–738. https://doi.org/10.1080/00913367.2023.2255252

Yates, J. L. (2020). *Ellie Goldstein, model with Down syndrome, stars in Gucci Beauty campaign*. www.goodmorningamerica.com/style/story/ellie-goldstein-model-syndrome-stars-gucci-beauty-campaign-71670206

Zayer, L. T., Coleman, C. A., & Gurrieri, L. (2023). Driving impact through inclusive advertising: An examination of award-winning gender-inclusive advertising. *Journal of Advertising*, *52*(5), 647–665. https://doi.org/10.1080/00913367.2023.2255233

31

Brands in the Firing Line: Unveiling the Cultural Controversies of Contemporary Brand Activism

Angela A. Beccanulli, Silvia Biraghi, and Rossella C. Gambetti

CULTURAL BRANDING AND BRAND ACTIVISM

The 2024 US presidential election unfolded with unexpected results for many, highlighting the deepening and widespread distrust Americans – and much of the world – harbor toward traditional institutions and media. Both supporters and critics of Donald Trump raised concerns about the legitimacy of the election process, voicing skepticism not only about the fairness of the election itself but also about the role of the media in shaping public perceptions and influencing decision-making (Raffio, 2024).[1]

This climate of skepticism is not new but rather the culmination of years of growing disillusionment. A Pew Research Center survey published in 2022 (Public Trust in Government 1958–2024) revealed in fact that only 20% of Americans trusted their government – the lowest level recorded in nearly 70 years. Similarly, fewer than 30% of individuals in major democracies believed that the media reported the news fairly, reflecting a global erosion of trust in the institutions designed to inform and govern. These troubling trends were confirmed in 2023 on a global scale by the Edelman Trust Barometer, which reported that only 43% of people worldwide trusted their governments to do what is right and only 37% of global citizens placed their faith in traditional media.

One of the most significant consequences of this erosion of trust over the years has been that individuals have increasingly turned to alternative sources of leadership and accountability, with brands emerging as pivotal players in this transformation (Gambetti & Biraghi, 2023; Moorman, 2020; Pimentel et al., 2024).

Consumers have progressively started viewing brands not merely as commercial entities but as influential institutions (Moorman, 2020), which are capable of shaping public opinion, influencing policy and so driving societal change due to their economic legitimacy (Kotler & Sarkar, 2020). This shift in expectations has prompted brands to redefine their rationale and relationship with society, ultimately taking on responsibilities once shouldered by traditional institutions (Gambetti & Biraghi, 2023).

Scholars such as Ahmad et al. (2024), Kotler and Sarkar (2017, 2020), and Matten and Crane (2005) have observed that, over the years, brands have increasingly stepped in to address societal needs and concerns often overlooked by traditional institutions. This trend has only intensified, with brands now actively engaging with cultural and societal themes that deeply resonate with their audiences.

---

1 https://today.usc.edu/trust-in-voting-how-misinformation-threatens-democracy/

In doing so, they have transformed into cultural resources, the dynamic entities both shaped by and shaping the socio-cultural contexts in which they operate (Schroeder, 2017). By intertwining their narratives with societal values and concerns, brands have positioned themselves as influential agents of cultural discourse and change. This approach is often referred to as 'cultural branding' (Askegaard, 2006; Cayla & Eckhardt, 2008; Holt, 2004), where brands function as cultural artifacts and as engaging and enticing bearers of cultural and ideological codes (Askegaard, 2006; Cayla & Eckhardt, 2008). Through cultural branding, brands help consumers construct their identities and life projects, finally offering support and actualizing values and desires once facilitated by traditional institutions (Gambetti & Biraghi, 2023).

Today, cultural branding has expanded to encompass *brand activism*, a brand's effort to 'promote, impede, or direct social, political, economic, and/or environmental reform or stasis with the desire to make improvements in society' (Sarkar, 2018, p. 554).

Brand activism involves brands publicly taking a stand on divisive social or political issues (Sarkar, 2018). This contentious nature of brand activism sets it apart from corporate social responsibility (Chernev & Blair, 2015; Luo & Bhattacharya, 2009; Verlegh, 2024), which typically concerns generally accepted, non-divisive, prosocial issues such as supporting healthcare, education or fighting natural disasters (Mukherjee & Althuizen, 2020). In brand activism, as the brand sides for divisive themes, it becomes not only a cultural resource – as in cultural branding and corporate social responsibility – but also a 'moral subject' (Sibai et al., 2021, p. 2) with the cultural authority to promote social, moral, legal, business, economic, political and environmental reform through its communication and practice (Gambetti, 2021; Moorman, 2020; Sarkar, 2018). Due to this, stakeholders increasingly perceive activist brands as 'purpose- and values-driven' (Vredenburg et al., 2020, p. 447), 'shouldering civic responsibilities as would a community pillar, acting as stalwart citizens of the community' (Holt, 2002, p. 88), which may challenge institutional powers and boost cultural and socio-political changes (Aßländer & Curbach, 2014; Matten & Crane, 2005; Moorman, 2020).

This evolving role of brands presents significant opportunities for them to enhance their image and reputation while aligning with consumers' values (Moorman, 2020). However, it also exposes brands to a delicate tension between market and culture. When championing social causes, consumers expect brands to exhibit a genuine and sustained commitment to societal betterment. To navigate this tension, brand activism must be deeply rooted in the brand's core identity and organizational culture (Biraghi et al., 2020). Such alignment ensures that activism becomes a deliberate and strategic component of the business, yielding dual benefits: contributing meaningfully to societal causes while enhancing the brand's image and reputation (Gambetti & Biraghi, 2023; Pimentel et al., 2024). Furthermore, effective brand activism necessitates authenticity, consistency, and concrete actions (Ahmad et al., 2024), demanding a clear, unequivocal and sustained commitment to the chosen cause over time.

Nevertheless, many brands often fall short of adhering to these conditions by aligning themselves with trending social or political themes solely for short-term marketing gains. This opportunistic approach typically involves a rushed attempt to capitalize on popular causes, leading to a misalignment with the brand's core identity or resulting in actions that appear ambiguous and superficial. When consumers detect this disconnect or lack of authenticity, their expectations get undermined, leading to frustration and a decline in brand loyalty. Typically, they accuse such brands of 'woke washing', a term that captures the perception of exploiting social causes for superficial gain. These accusations usually quickly escalate into widespread criticism against the brand, damaging its image and ultimately jeopardizing its reputation and revenues.

In the following paragraph, we will delve deeper into the concept of woke washing, exploring its origins and examining the broader implications of brands as they navigate the increasingly complex interplay between consumer expectations and business interests.

WOKE WASHING

Brand activism has offered significant benefits to consumers by allowing them to see their values and desires actualized in society, while also providing brands opportunities to enhance their image and reputation in the market. However, it has also intensified and provided brands with new subtle evidence of mismatch and inconsistencies between their identity, declared activism and conduct (Gambetti & Biraghi, 2023). These possible discrepancies form the foundations of what has been termed *woke washing* (Dowell & Jackson, 2020).

Woke washing refers to 'inauthentic brand activism in which activist marketing messaging about the focal socio-political issue is not aligned with the brand's purpose, values, and corporate practice' (Vredenburg et al., 2020, p. 445). This phenomenon has gained prominence in an era of public movements like #MeToo and #BlacklivesMatter that have brought critical social issues to the forefront, demanding attention and support. In response, many brands have responded by aligning themselves with these themes, bonding with consumers based on the relevance of the socio-political values they associate with. However, some of these brands have adopted an opportunistic approach, jumping on a trendy social issue not out of genuine commitment but as a calculated effort to obtain all the advantages of brand activism. Such brands typically employ a calculative approach to brand activism, treating it as a game of gains the brand seeks to win (Moorman, 2020). They champion societal themes that either lack alignment with their fundamental identity or, even when aligned, are treated superficially or ambiguously, as the primary goal is to capitalize on the immediate positive outcome of brand activism rather than engage effectively with the cause.

When consumers detect misalignments between a brand's proclaimed cause and its core identity or perceive ambiguity in its commitment, they are quick to accuse the brand of woke washing, so of free-riding on public interest to direct conversations toward their brands (Mirzaei et al., 2022). Nevertheless, woke washing is perceived as a marketing trick played out by brands that have 'unclear of indeterminate records of social cause practices' (Vredenburg et al., 2020), and when it gets noticed, it mobilizes criticism from consumers and stakeholders who start distrusting the brand, accusing it and damaging its image and reputation.

This criticism is highly potentiated in today's digital age as brand activism is mainly done on social media and these platforms provide fertile soil for rapid and widespread backlash. Sudden waves of criticism can escalate quickly on these platforms, leading to sanctions and collective retaliations that further harm the brand (Gomez-Mejia, 2020; Warren, 2022).

In the next paragraph, we will explore how social media platforms serve as dynamic arenas for brand activism while also acting as fertile ground for the polarization of opinions on specific social and political themes, either significantly enhancing the brand's reputation or subjecting it to criticism.

SOCIAL MEDIA AND POLARIZATIONS

In today's digital landscape, brand activism is predominantly carried out on social media platforms (Zhou et al., 2024). These platforms act as primary arenas for public discourse, where individuals articulate their social anxieties and aspirations (Holt, 2004), often inextricably linked to political and societal issues (Biraghi et al., 2020). These environments present brands with the unique opportunity to observe and, when appropriate, actively participate in real-time conversations surrounding the most pressing and widely debated topics among users (Allagui & Breslow, 2016). By leveraging these digital spaces, brands can stay attuned to the evolving pulse of public sentiment and engage in brand activism initiatives tied to the most pervasive and polarizing discussions as they unfold (Allagui & Breslow, 2016). Such timely and strategic engagement not only reinforces the brand's relevance but also fosters high levels of engagement and interaction (Angell et al., 2019).

However, social media use also exposes brand activism to intense social scrutiny. Social media aggregates and binds together communities of dispersed consumers, greatly increasing the pace and intensity of their interactions. Now that these communities are densely networked, their cultural influence also on brand actions has become direct and substantial (Holt, 2016). Consumers can seamlessly observe brand actions, evaluate them and support them with a comment, click or share when they perceive authenticity in the company's intent. This can generate widespread positive sentiment and enhance brand image in the short term and brand reputation in the long run. On the other hand, consumers can also readily detect any discrepancy between the brand action and the company's identity or any ambiguity and inconsistency in the activist action. When such dissonances are identified and consumers accuse the brand of 'woke washing', they spark collective mobilizations against the brand through 'dislikes' and sarcastic, polarizing and protesting comments that challenge the brand's power and authority (Gill, 2022).

Indeed, social media can facilitate both swift quick consensus and disapproval, with the latter often escalating into collective conversations, with extremized language, divisive ideas and polarization (Lee et al., 2014). This backlash can also lead to harsh anti-brand movements (Dessart et al., 2020; Ferrucci & Schauster, 2022; Rodrigues et al., 2021), where groups of consumers assume activist roles by voicing their opposition to corporate power and cultural authority (Brandão & Popoli, 2022; Popp et al., 2016).

The rapidity and intensity of these dichotomous behaviors are largely driven by the affordances and algorithmic mechanisms inherent to social media platforms. Affordances are defined as 'the mutuality of actor intentions and object capabilities that provide the potential for a particular action' (Majchrzak et al., 2013, p. 39). Examples include liking, commenting, sharing, tagging, hashtagging, using memes, GIFs and avatars. These features have significantly lowered the barriers for users to engage with content and between each other, enabling widespread consumer mobilization. Consumers through affordances can quickly form pro-brand or anti-brand movements, collectively scrutinizing, judging and reacting to a brand's conduct (Gill, 2022).

Algorithms, on the other hand, refer to formal processes or sets of step-by-step procedures, usually expressed mathematically, which categorize and sort people or concepts for further operations (Kozinets, 2022). They affect everything from search engine results to credit rating (Breidbach & Maglio, 2020) and play a specific influential role in determining the visibility of social media content (Kozinets, 2022), particularly favoring highly engaging or recent posts, thereby amplifying their reach.

When consumers use affordances like hashtags and tags to express their views on brand activism, the effects can significantly enhance polarizations and impact a brand's image and reputation.

For instance, if a brand's activism generates favorable responses, users may demonstrate their approval by tagging the brand in positive conversations or creating supportive hashtags. Over time, these actions embed the brand within a network of favorable associations, creating a long-lasting positive indexing effect in online content. This enhances the brand's intangible assets, strengthening its connection with consumers.

Conversely, criticism often leads to the proliferation of anti-brand hashtags and critical tagging. These negative associations typically become indexed to the brand, perpetuating ongoing criticism and creating reputational challenges in the long term. Once these negative perceptions take root, they are difficult to reverse, as criticism remains tightened to that brand in online discourses.

Moreover, when a brand activism campaign generates significant engagement–whether positive or negative–algorithms amplify its reach by repeatedly surfacing the content on users' feeds for weeks or even months. While this extended visibility increases awareness of the campaign, it also reinforces the dominant perception associated with it, whether supportive or critical.

In cases where the perception is negative and the brand faces accusations of woke washing, the consequences can be severe. Algorithmic mechanisms ensure that the negative narrative is continually exposed to a wider audience, keeping criticism at the forefront of public discourse. This ongoing reinforcement makes it exceedingly difficult for the brand to escape the 'woke washer' label, as most consumers encountering the content are likely to internalize or amplify the critical perception.

Despite the significant reputational risks, no research has considered so far how social media affordances and algorithms are enacted by consumers to spread and perpetuate woke-washing accusations and what is their impact in both the short and long term on the brand image and reputation. Understanding these dynamics is crucial for both scholars and practitioners navigating the complexities of digital image and reputation management. As platforms continue to introduce new affordances and update the algorithms, the mechanisms for expressing criticism and backlash become more complex, further complicating perceptions of brand activism and the solutions brands might take to recover from a 'woke-washing' label.

To illustrate these dynamics, the following section presents a case study conducted through a netnographic research lens (Kozinets, 2020) on a brand that, despite crafting brand activism campaigns aligned with its identity, conveyed ambiguous messages and engaged in inconsistent conduct. As a result, it became the target of woke-washing accusations, triggering widespread criticism on social media. This example underscores how rapidly online conversations can become polarized and how the interplay of tags, hashtags and algorithmic amplification exacerbates the challenges brands face when accusations of inauthentic activism arise. Ultimately, it highlights the pressing need for brands to critically assess not just the content of their activism but also the structural mechanisms that shape its reception and potential fallout in the digital sphere.

KELLOGG's 'CEREAL FOR DINNER' CASE STUDY

Kellogg's, founded in 1906, is a globally renowned cereal company whose vision is deeply rooted in the aspiration to foster a better and more equitable world – one where individuals are not merely fed, but genuinely nourished and satisfied by the food they consume. Throughout its history, Kellogg's has consistently championed the ethos of creating Better Days, advocating for a future in which there is a place at the table for all (Kellogg's Official Website). In addition to this, Kellogg's has steadfastly upheld core values centered around sustainability and healthful eating. In line with these values, the company has long been at the forefront of various initiatives aimed at reducing food waste, including organizing food drives, supporting soup kitchens and donating both snacks and cereals to food banks – efforts that reflect the company's

Figure 31.1 Kellogg's giveaway post on Instagram

Source: Instagram.

active contribution to the alleviation of hunger and its commitment to social responsibility (Kellogg's Official Website).

Building on this vision and the cultural values that have defined the brand, Kellogg's launched the '***Cereals for dinner***' campaign in 2022 in the USA. This initiative emerged amid a period of significant inflation, during which food prices increased by 9.9%.[2] The campaign sought to position Kellogg's cereals as a viable dinner alternative, presenting them as an affordable, practical and convenient option for families struggling with rising food costs. By emphasizing cereals as an economical solution to food insecurity, the campaign appeared to align with the brand's long-standing cultural commitment to addressing hunger and so, socioeconomic challenges. In this sense, the initiative was intended to portray Kellogg's as a brand that stands in solidarity with those facing financial hardship.

The campaign was introduced with a TV advertisement and digital banners featured across various websites, all of which underscored the practicality of choosing cereals for dinner.

These efforts were then further amplified through Instagram, with a dedicated social media campaign centered around an online giveaway. In the giveaway, Kellogg's invited consumers to share a photo of themselves and their families enjoying cereals for dinner, using the hashtag #kelloggcerealfordinnerentry. In response, each week, one winner was selected to receive a $5000 prize along with a year's supply of Kellogg's cereals (see Figure 31.1).

Initially, the campaign gained significant traction, with numerous consumers enthusiastically

[2] US agriculture department's economic research service.

Figure 31.2 Consumers participating in Kellogg's giveaway

Source: Instagram.

sharing family photos of cereal dinners using the branded hashtag (see Figure 31.2).

However, as the campaign progressed, it quickly became a polarizing topic. While some consumers celebrated the campaign's relatability and the great help it could offer, others sharply criticized Kellogg's for promoting cereals – a product typically high in sugar and low in protein and fiber – as a legitimate and nutritious dinner option (see Instagram comments in Figure 31.3). The criticism was particularly pointed, given the brand's stated commitment to healthy eating, as outlined on its official website, which clashed with the promotion of a product widely perceived as an unhealthy choice for one of the three main meals of the day. To counterattack these criticisms and reinforce the activist message, Kellogg's extended the campaign into 2024, maintaining a strong presence on social media by sharing creative, cereal-based dinner recipes and collaborating with popular influencers. Additionally, promotional events were held in supermarkets, allowing consumers to sample these recipes firsthand, cementing the narrative of the brand as addressing inflation and socioeconomic disparities by presenting cereals as an innovative and convenient meal solution.

In February 2024, Kellogg's CEO, Gary Pilnick, made a public appearance on CNBC to further promote the campaign. During the interview, he specifically reiterated that cash-strapped consumers could save money by eating cereals as a meal, stating that a bowl of cereals with milk and fruit costs less than a dollar – making it more affordable than typical dinner options.[3]

Unexpectedly for the company, this interview significantly intensified the campaign's criticism. New audiences, mainly skeptics, began to engage with the campaign on social media, this time mainly accusing the brand of exploiting economic hardship for profit. As illustrated in Figure 31.4, many critics pointed out that cereals were often more expensive than healthier ingredients that can be used to prepare different meal options or more protein-rich foods. Additionally, others noted that Kellogg's prices had risen following the launch of the campaign, which they saw as contradicting both the campaign's message and Kellogg's professed values of fighting food poverty.

Additionally, many consumers accused Gary Pilnick, questioning whether he would personally feed his family cereals for dinner while suggesting it as an option for others. This sentiment led consumers to compare his interview to Marie Antoinette's infamous quote 'Let them eat cake', highlighting what they saw as an extreme disconnect from the financial struggles ordinary people face (see Instagram content in Figure 31.5).

The disconnect, compounded by Kellogg's 'health' stated values and the campaign's messaging, the ambiguity of the campaign message and the price positioning of cereals, as well as the

[3] www.theguardian.com/us-news/2024/feb/27/kelloggs-ceo-cereal-for-dinner

Figure 31.3 Instagram polarized conversation

Source: Instagram.

Figure 31.4 TikTok comments pointing out that cereals are more expensive than healthier options

Source: TikTok.

Figure 31.5 Instagram posts sarcastically comparing Kellogg's and Marie Antoinette's quotes

Source: Instagram.

CEO's personal wealth raised significant concerns among consumers. Many perceived the campaign as a cynical attempt to exploit financial struggles for marketing purposes, leading to accusations of woke washing. This accusation sparked a new wave of intensified criticism on social media, where consumers voiced their discontent through humor, sarcasm, and sharp critiques of the brand. These criticisms gained traction as users creatively amplified their discontent through the use of specific hashtags designed to draw attention to the campaign's perceived flaws. Notable examples included #LetThemEatCereal (>100 posts on Instagram; 30.6 K followers on TikTok), #CerealKillers (18,200 posts on Instagram), #LetThemEatCake (413,000 posts on Instagram) and #EatTheRich (>100 posts on Instagram). The proliferation of these hashtags led to an escalation of critics to the point of reaching a full-scale boycott movement against Kellogg's, fueled by comments, particularly on TikTok, urging others to join the protest: '*Boycotting now*', '*I boycotted Kellogg's in March*', '*Some of us decided to boycott Kellogg's products all our own*' and '*Let's all Boycott this*'. These comments were all shared through hashtags such as #BoycottKelloggs (>100 posts on Instagram and TikTok), #BoycottKellogs (>100 posts on Instagram and TikTok), #BoycottKellogg (100 posts on Instagram) and #KelloggsBoycott (>100 posts on Instagram and TikTok), which became rallying points for consumers expressing dissatisfaction with the brand.

This wave of criticism and boycott is still on even 10 months after the CEO's controversial interview. Social media platforms' algorithms, which prioritize highly engaging content, continue to surface posts associated with the campaign, along with user-generated content linked to these critical hashtags. This fact is so real that users frequently engage in conversations on social media regarding the campaign saying '*it's crazy that this campaign was of 2022 and we are still talking about it*'; '*this campaign is of 2 years ago*'. This persistent visibility ensures that negative narratives dominate the digital conversation surrounding Kellogg's. Today, when users search for Kellogg's online, these critical posts are often among the first results, drawing attention to unfavorable content. Such visibility impacts consumer perception, as these posts are frequently mistaken for the most relevant and up-to-date information. This cycle of engagement amplifies the negative content's reach, further entrenching its position in search rankings and creating a feedback loop that damages the brand's reputation, making it increasingly challenging for Kellogg's to break free from this digital rabbit hole.

Although Kellogg's seemingly created a brand activism campaign aligned with its cultural values, the campaign's ambiguity and contradictions ultimately led to accusations of woke washing, thus creating long-term negative effects for the brand.

DISCUSSION

Brand activism, as an extension of cultural branding, reflects a brand's deliberate engagement with critical social, political, economic or environmental issues, aspiring to contribute to societal progress. This approach offers the brand the potential to deliver meaningful opportunities to consumers while reinforcing its image and reputation. However, engagement in activism decisions and actions simultaneously places brands in a difficult position, compelling them to navigate the complex tension between market imperatives and cultural expectations. Indeed, when brands step into the realm of critical causes, they assume heightened accountability, as consumers increasingly demand sustained and authentic commitments to these topics and so to societal betterment. This expectation transforms activism into a delicate balancing act: brands must maintain profitability while meeting consumers' and stakeholders' demands for transparency, integrity, and authenticity.

As highlighted in the first part of this chapter, navigating successfully this intricate tension requires brands, at least, to ground their activism in causes that align with their core identity and values (Biraghi et al., 2020) and then demonstrate authenticity, consistency, and concreteness in the causes they decide to stand for (Ahmad et al., 2024). Yet, many brands struggle to meet these conditions. Rather than embracing activism as a meaningful, long-term commitment to social progress, brands often reduce it to a superficial strategy aimed at obtaining short-term gains in image and reputation. However, this shallow approach rarely escapes the notice of consumers who are quick to identify inauthenticity. When this happens, brands do not reap the intended benefits; instead, they can face accusations of woke washing, a damaging label that erodes trust in consumers and, ultimately, jeopardizes the brands' legitimacy in the marketplace.

In our digital age, the consequences of brand activism – either positive or negative – are magnified by the unique dynamics of social media. Many brands turn to these platforms for brand activism, but this social network with its affordances and algorithm-driven visibility also acts as an amplifier of both positive and negative consequences. On one hand, social media affordances can extend the reach of both positive and negative feedback to vast audiences, allowing brands to either enhance their reputational standing or face widespread and intense backlash. On the other hand, the algorithmic indexing of interactions – whether supportive or critical – creates a lasting digital footprint that solidifies public perception over time. This enduring narrative can either bolster a brand's image and reputation or reinforce its association with perceived opportunistic activism. As a result, social media not only accelerates the formation of public opinion but also embeds these perceptions into a brand's digital legacy, presenting both opportunities and significant risks in the evolving landscape of brand activism.

Our case study of Kellogg's vividly illustrates the multifaceted challenges inherent in executing credible brand activism, particularly in the age of social media. The company initially appeared to align its activism efforts with its respective brand identity, signaling an ostensibly genuine commitment to the causes it championed. However, as its initiatives unfolded, it was increasingly perceived as ambiguous.

Kellogg's encountered significant missteps in both the design and timing of its campaign. The campaign unfolded in two distinct phases: the first during a 2022 giveaway initiative, which, while aligning with Kellogg's ethos of ensuring food accessibility, failed to address its broader commitment to promoting healthy lifestyles. This perceived inconsistency sowed confusion among consumers and began to erode their trust in the brand's authenticity. The second misstep occurred in 2024 when the controversial interview of the CEO coincided with a price increase in cereal products. This confluence of events further alienated consumers, who came to view the meaning of the company's activism as fake and a veneer for profit-driven motives.

The perceived inauthenticity of the brand fueled polarized public discourse on social media, ultimately culminating in widespread accusations of woke washing. The backlash that occurred after the accusation exemplified a recurring trajectory in brand activism: when companies take a stand on divisive or sensitive issues, they often provoke an oscillation of public opinion. Initially, this begins with polarized reactions that evolve into cyclical waves of support and criticism. Over time, these dynamics tend to crystallize into a dominant sentiment – either positive or negative. For Kellogg's, initial polarizing opinions about the campaign ultimately gave way to a prevailing negative sentiment. Recurring waves of criticism deepened consumer skepticism about the brand's authenticity. The criticism was amplified through the creation of negative hashtags explicitly targeting the brand, which quickly gained significant traction online. The substantial engagement generated by these hashtags further amplified their algorithmic visibility, reinforcing the prevailing negative sentiment surrounding the brands. This heightened visibility entrenched the negative discourse and cemented the woke-washing label for the brand in public perception. Unfortunately, the label persisted for months beyond the initial controversies, leaving an enduring blemish on the reputation of Kellogg's, which the company is still striving to overcome.

This case study underscores the critical need to examine the mechanisms that drive the spread and persistence of woke-washing accusations on social media. It also highlights the importance of refining communication and branding strategies to mitigate reputational risks and proactively distance brands from damaging labels. In response to these challenges, we have outlined a future research agenda designed to serve as a valuable resource for both scholars and practitioners. This agenda provides a robust foundation for deeper investigations into the dynamics of social media in amplifying and sustaining woke-washing accusations, the associated reputational risks and the strategic responses brands must adopt to navigate and safeguard their image and reputation in the digital sphere.

CONCLUSIONS AND FUTURE RESEARCH AGENDA

The case study highlights a critical evolution in brand activism: brands now anchor their campaigns on issues that align with consumers' interests and core identity, often driven by business objectives (Kotler & Sarkar, 2020). However, when this alignment is perceived as strategic rather than genuine, inauthentic intent often unravels through inconsistent actions. As the case demonstrates, consumers quickly detect these discrepancies, resulting in heightened frustration and disillusionment, which leads to widespread critique. Mobilizing against the brand, consumers use the very same digital tools that the brand once leveraged to promote its activism campaign. By exploiting platform-specific affordances and algorithms, consumers generate, sustain and amplify their critique. As evidenced by our case study, they employ hashtags, tagging, and algorithmic visibility to create self-reinforcing cycles of negativity that embed accusations of woke-washing deep into public discourse, further eroding the brand's image and making reputational recovery increasingly problematic.

Despite the profound impact of social media-driven criticism on brand legitimacy – both in the short- and long term, this study represents only a preliminary attempt to illustrate how woke-washing accusations are enacted through platform affordances and algorithms. Future research should delve deeper into the underlying mechanisms that influence the severity and persistence of such accusations in digital environments. In particular, future studies could explore critical questions such as: What consumer mobilization tactics most effectively amplify woke-washing accusations? How do these tactics influence a brand's ability to recover? To what extent do platform-specific dynamics shape the intensity and longevity of woke-washing narratives?

Beyond these challenges – rooted in the inherent functioning and characteristics of social media platforms – the rise of artificial intelligence (AI) as a powerful tool for consumer advocacy and brand critique is further complicating how brands receive and navigate woke-washing accusations on these platforms. Consumers are now utilizing AI to generate symbolic artifacts – ranging from satirical images to manipulated videos and AI-generated memes – that effectively express discontent in ways that are visually compelling and emotionally resonant. These AI-generated artifacts significantly amplify consumer backlash, embedding critiques more deeply into both cultural and digital narratives, making it even more difficult for brands to control their messaging. For instance, Figure 31.6 exemplifies this phenomenon, showing AI-generated images that satirize Kellogg's campaign. The image on the right critiques the perceived hypocrisy of Kellogg's CEO, suggesting that while the company publicly promotes cereal as a viable dinner option, its executives would never serve it to their own families. The left-side image amplifies this critique with explicit calls to action, such as '*Don't buy any Kellogg's brand*' and '*Boycott starts April 1st*', transforming the visual artifact into a direct mobilizing message. This fusion of humor, visual storytelling and clear messaging enhances the virality and persuasive power of the critique, making it more resistant to brand-led counter-narratives. As AI-driven content continues to circulate, it presents an escalating challenge for brands, as its immersive, emotionally potent and visually striking nature makes it particularly effective in shaping consumer sentiment. Given these emerging threats, future research could explore the evolving role of AI in influencing consumer perceptions of brands. How do AI-generated artifacts compare to traditional social media affordances in shaping public discourse surrounding brand activism? To what extent do these digital creations intensify consumer critique and hostility toward brands?

Finally, future avenues of research should focus on brands and their communication and branding strategies for restoring their image, reputation and legitimacy in the market. First, future studies could explore whether brands should respond to woke-washing accusations or remain silent. If they do choose to respond, how can brands craft their

Figure 31.6 Collage of two AI-generated images created by consumers as a form of satirical critique aimed at Kellogg's

Source: Instagram.

messaging in reaction to these criticisms? Which communication formats – such as public apologies, transparent dialogue or engagement with digital communities – are most effective in rebuilding trust? Could brands leverage social media to craft and disseminate their recovery messages, and if so, which affordances should be prioritized, and why?

Ultimately, is it truly possible for brands to fully recover from the lasting effects of woke-washing accusations, or do the dynamics of digital discourse make long-term reputation recovery unfeasible? Under what conditions, if any, could brands restore their legitimacy and regain consumer trust in the wake of such accusations?

REFERENCES

Aßländer, M. S., & Curbach, J. (2014). The corporation as citoyen? Towards a new understanding of corporate citizenship. *Journal of Business Ethics, 120*(4), 541–554. https://doi.org/10.1007/s10551-013-2004-8

Ahmad, F., Guzmán, F., & Al-Emran, M. (2024). Brand activism and the consequence of woke washing. *Journal of Business Research, 170*, 114362. https://doi.org/10.1016/j.jbusres.2023.114362

Allagui, I., & Breslow, H. (2016). Social media for public relations: Lessons from four effective cases. *Public Relations Review, 42*(1), 20–30. https://doi.org/10.1016/j.pubrev.2015.12.001

Angell, R., Gorton, M., Bottomley, P., Marder, B., Bhaskar, S., & White, J. (2019). News you can use! Evaluating the effectiveness of newsjacking based content on social media. *Information Technology and People, 33*(2), 755–773. https://doi.org/10.1108/ITP-04-2019-0177

Askegaard, S. (2006). *Brands as a global ideoscape*. In J. Schroeder, & M. Salzer-Mörling (Eds.), *Brand culture* (pp. 91–102). Routledge.

Biraghi, S., Gambetti, R. C., & Beccanulli, A. A. (2020). Achieving cultural relevance in technomediated platforms: instant cultural branding and controversial clicktivism. *Italian Journal of Marketing*, 1–25. https://doi.org/10.1007/s43039-020-00013-6

Brandão, A., & Popoli, P. (2022). "I'm hatin'it"! Negative consumer–brand relationships in online anti-brand communities. *European Journal of Marketing, 56*(2), 622–650. https://doi.org/10.1108/EJM-03-2020-0214

Breidbach, C. F., & Maglio, P. (2020). Accountable algorithms? The ethical implications of data-driven business models. *Journal of Service Management, 31*(2), 163–185. https://doi.org/10.1108/JOSM-03-2019-0073

Cayla, J., & Eckhardt, G. M. (2008). Asian brands and the shaping of a transnational imagined community. *Journal of Consumer Research*, *35*(2), 216–230. https://doi.org/10.1086/587629

Chernev, A., & Blair, S. (2015). Doing well by doing good: The benevolent halo of corporate social responsibility. *Journal of Consumer Research*, *41*(6), 1412–1425. https://doi.org/10.1086/680089

Dessart, L., Veloutsou, C., & Morgan-Thomas, A. (2020). Brand negativity: A relational perspective on anti-brand community participation. *European Journal of Marketing*, *54*(7), 1761–1785. https://doi.org/10.1108/EJM-06-2018-0423

Dowell, E., & Jackson, M. (2020). Woke washing your company won't cut it. *Harvard Business Review*, *27*, 1–7. https://hranewtoolbox.com/wp-content/uploads/2020/11/1-Leadership-Diversity-Organizational-Culture-Race_Woke-Washing-Your-Company-Wont-Cut-It.pdf

Ferrucci, P., & Schauster, E. E. (2022). Keeping up with the boundaries of advertising: Paradigm repair after pepsi's big mess. *Journal of Communication Inquiry* (ePub), *48*(2), 185–204. https://doi.org/10.1177/01968599221095164

Gambetti, R. (2021). Netnography, digital habitus, and technocultural capital. In R. V. Kozinets, & R. Gambetti (Eds.), *Netnography unlimited* (pp. 293–319). Routledge.

Gambetti, R. C., & Biraghi, S. (2023). Branded activism: Navigating the tension between culture and market in social media. *Futures*, *145*, 103080. https://doi.org/10.1016/j.futures.2022.103080

Gill, R. (2022). Being watched and feeling judged on social media. *Feminist Media Studies*, July, 19–24 2020, *21*(8), 1387–1392. https://doi.org/10.1080/14680777.2021.1996427

Gomez-Mejia, G. (2020). Fail, clickbait, cringe, cancel, woke: Vernacular criticisms of digital advertising in social media platforms. International conference on human-computer interaction (pp. 309–324). Springer.

Holt, D. (2002). Why do brands cause trouble? A dialectical theory of consumer culture and branding. *Journal of Consumer Research*, *29*(1), 70–90. https://doi.org/10.1086/339922

Holt, D. (2004). *How brands become icons: The principles of cultural branding*. Harvard Business Press.

Holt, D. (2016). Branding in the age of social media. *Harvard Business Review*, *94*(3), 40–50.

Kotler, P., & Sarkar, C. (2017). Finally, brand activism. *The Marketing Journal*, 9. www.marketingjournal.org/finally-brand-activism-philip-kotler-and-christian-sarkar/

Kotler, P., & Sarkar, C. (2020). *Bran activism: From purpose to action*. Idea Bite Press.

Kozinets, R. V. (2020). *Netnography: The essential guide to qualitative social media research*. Sage Publications.

Kozinets, R. V. (2022). Algorithmic branding through platform assemblages: core conceptions and research directions for a new era of marketing and service management. *Journal of Service Management*, *33*(3), 437–452. https://doi.org/10.1108/JOSM-07-2021-0263

Lee, J. K., Choi, J., Kim, C., & Kim, Y. (2014). Social media, network heterogeneity, and opinion polarization. *Journal of Communication*, *64*(4), 702–722. https://doi.org/10.1111/jcom.12077

Luo, X., & Bhattacharya, C. B. (2009). The debate over doing good: Corporate social performance, strategic marketing levers, and firm-idiosyncratic risk. *Journal of Marketing*, *73*(6), 198–213. https://doi.org/10.1509/jmkg.73.6.198

Majchrzak, A., Faraj, S., Kane, G. C., & Azad, B. (2013). The contradictory influence of social media affordances on online communal knowledge sharing. *Journal of Computer-Mediated Communication*, *19*(1), 38–55. https://doi.org/10.1111/jcc4.12030

Matten, D., & Crane, A. (2005). Corporate citizenship: Toward an extended theoretical conceptualization. *Academy of Management Review*, *30*(1), 166–179. https://doi.org/10.5465/amr.2005.15281448

Mirzaei, A., Wilkie, D. C., & Siuki, H. (2022). Woke brand activism authenticity or the lack of it. *Journal of Business Research*, *139*, 1–12. https://doi.org/10.1016/j.jbusres.2021.09.044

Moorman, C. (2020). Commentary: Brand activism in a political world. *Journal of Public Policy & Marketing*, *39*(4), 388–392. https://doi.org/10.1177/0743915620945260

Mukherjee, S., & Althuizen, N. (2020). Brand activism: Does courting controversy help or hurt a brand? *International Journal of Research in Marketing*, *37*(4), 772–788. https://doi.org/10.1016/j.ijresmar.2020.02.008

Pimentel, D., Lagarto, S., & Marques-Quinteiro, P. (2024). Examining dark triad traits in formal leaders and their impact on employee workplace stress: A comparative study of family and non-family businesses. *Businesses*, *4*(3), 331–346. https://doi.org/10.3390/businesses4030021

Popp, B., Germelmann, C. C., & Jung, B. (2016). We love to hate them! Social media-based anti-brand communities in professional football. *International Journal of Sports Marketing and Sponsorship*, *17*(4), 349–367. https://doi.org/10.1108/IJSMS-11-2016-018

Raffio, N. (2024). *Trust in voting: USC experts discuss misinformation, threats to democracy ahead of election 2024*. Today.usc. https://today.usc.edu/trust-in-voting-usc-experts-discuss-misinformation-threats-to-democracy-ahead-of-election-2024/

Rodrigues, C., Brandão, A., & Rodrigues, P. (2021). I can't stop hating you: an anti-brand-community perspective on apple brand hate. *Journal of Product & Brand Management*, *30*(8), 1115–1133. https://doi.org/10.1108/JPBM-10-2019-2621

Sarkar, C. (2018). The case for brand activism' – A discussion with Philip Kotler and Christian Sarkar. *The Marketing Journal*. www.marketingjournal.org/the-case-for-brand-activism-a-discussion-with-philipkotler-and-christian-sarkar/

Schroeder, J. E. (2017). Corporate branding in perspective: A typology. *European Journal of Marketing*, *51*(9/10), 1522–1529. https://doi.org/10.1108/EJM-07-2017-0450

Sibai, O., Mimoun, L., & Boukis, A. (2021). Authenticating brand activism: Negotiating the boundaries of free speech to make a change. *Psychology & Marketing*, *38*(10), 1651–1669. https://doi.org/10.1002/mar.21477

Verlegh, P. W. (2024). Perspectives: a research-based guide for brand activism. *International Journal of Advertising*, *43*(2), 388–402. https://doi.org/10.1080/02650487.2023.2228117

Vredenburg, J., Kapitan, S., Spry, A., & Kemper, J. (2020). Brands Taking a Stand: Authentic Brand Activism or Woke Washing? *Journal of Public Policy & Marketing*, *39*(4), 444–460. https://doi.org/10.1177/0743915620947359

Warren, D. E. (2022). "Woke" corporations and the stigmatization of corporate social initiatives. *Business Ethics Quarterly*, *32*(1), 169–198. https://doi.org/10.1017/beq.2021.48

Zhou, X., Lou, C., & Huang, X. (2024). When social media gets political: How message–platform match affects consumer responses to brand activism advertising. *Journal of Advertising*, 1–17. https://doi.org/10.1080/00913367.2024.2347271

32

Branding for Impact in Nonprofit Organizations: Understanding the Strategies

Lara Mendes Christ Bonella Sepulcri and Emerson Wagner Mainardes

INTRODUCTION

Nonprofit organizations (NPOs) operate within increasingly competitive and dynamic markets. With millions of NPOs worldwide supporting a variety of causes, these organizations play essential roles in addressing societal challenges, ranging from poverty alleviation to environmental conservation. Simultaneously, they influence social, economic and political conditions while reflecting the nature and severity of the challenges faced by the communities they serve.

Interdependence theory suggests that nonprofit density is shaped by local areas with greater resource availability and access to government subsidies, highlighting the competitive dynamics among nonprofits competing for limited resources (Dalvi et al., 2024). As the nonprofit landscape grows more saturated, organizations face intensifying pressure to distinguish themselves to secure funding, attract volunteers and build public trust.

In response to these pressures, branding emerges as a critical strategy for achieving these objectives. By effectively communicating their mission, values and societal contributions, nonprofits can create a distinct and compelling identity (Sepulcri et al., 2020a). Beyond differentiation, nonprofit branding works as a strategic asset, fostering trust and encapsulating the organization's essence, values and enduring legacy – often referred to as its corporate heritage.

Historically, marketing has been used to advance social causes, but branding was long considered a concept exclusive to the commercial sector. Today, marketing principles are increasingly embraced by nonprofit professionals, with studies exploring their application to this sector (Bennett & Sargeant, 2005; Gruber & Deschênes, 2024; Hommerová & Severová, 2019; Hou et al., 2018; Wymer & Akbar, 2017). Adapted concepts such as relationship marketing have proven effective in fostering donor loyalty and differentiation (Weir & Hibbert, 2000). While brand communities offer opportunities to build loyalty among donors, attract volunteers and engage supporters (Hassay & Peloza, 2009), brand equity can enhance the authenticity and reputation of NPOs (Romero et al., 2023).

This broader view highlights that branding in the nonprofit sector extends beyond logos and taglines; it involves creating a cohesive identity that resonates with diverse stakeholders, including donors, volunteers, beneficiaries and policymakers. The brand serves as a primary differentiator in both intersectoral and intrasectoral competition, playing a pivotal role in nonprofit success (Harrison, 2023; Mort et al., 2007; Sepulcri & Mainardes, 2025).

One recurring topic in the literature is the influence of branding on donation behavior. Brand personality – attributing human characteristics to a brand – is a concept that can be adapted effectively to nonprofits. For example, the World Wildlife Fund (WWF) is often associated with traits such as caring, trustworthy and nature-loving. In contrast, Greenpeace, though also an environmental organization, projects a more rebellious and dynamic personality. These personalities guide each organization's actions and communications.

Closely related to brand personality is brand image, which encompasses the perceptions, associations and mental impressions stakeholders form about a brand. For nonprofits, brand image is crucial in conveying their mission and values, shaping stakeholder trust and loyalty, and motivating actions such as donations, volunteering and advocacy.

However, despite the strategic potential of branding, managing a nonprofit brand is no simple task. While maintaining traditions and core values is essential, brands must also evolve to remain relevant to emerging audiences. For instance, the United Nations launched the global campaign #ActNow, leveraging digital platforms to promote the Sustainable Development Goals. Similarly, Oxfam International faced significant challenges in rebuilding trust in its brand following crises, underscoring the importance of managing a brand not only externally but also internally. Internal actions must reflect the brand's values to ensure alignment with external stakeholders.

Branding is also a powerful tool for establishing partnerships with the for-profit sector, enhancing awareness of the nonprofit's cause while raising funds. Effective partnerships require strategic alignment to ensure consistency in values and messaging. A notable example is the All Out[1] and the Tamar Project[2] in Brazil, which has leveraged its strong brand identity to secure impactful collaborations with, respectively, Havaianas and Petrobras.

Through its collaboration with Havaianas, All Out receives a part of the revenue from a line of flip-flops called Havaianas Pride. This initiative not only generates direct financial contributions to the project but also raises awareness among a global audience. The flip-flops serve as both a product and a storytelling medium, reinforcing All Out mission to support LGBT+ rights while associating Havaianas with a socially conscious cause.

Similarly, Tamar's long-standing partnership with Petrobras, a state-owned oil company, demonstrates the importance of aligning a nonprofit's brand with a for-profit partner's corporate social responsibility (CSR) goals. Petrobras has supported Tamar since the 1980s until 2021, providing significant funding for conservation efforts and community programs. This partnership is a testament to the shared responsibility of mitigating environmental risks, as Petrobras works with Tamar to address the potential impacts of oil exploration on marine ecosystems. While such collaborations can amplify a nonprofit's mission, they also carry risks, such as perceptions of greenwashing, which could damage the nonprofit's brand image, if not managed carefully.

Ultimately, the foundation of a strong nonprofit brand lies in strategic communication with both internal and external stakeholders. Effective communication establishes a brand identity that resonates with diverse audiences while aligning with the organization's mission and values. In today's digital era, social media has emerged as a powerful and cost-effective tool for nonprofits, offering opportunities to amplify their message, engage audiences and strengthen relationships.

Nonprofit branding and communication strategies – both online and offline – are central to shaping public perception, building stakeholder trust and ensuring financial sustainability (D'Arco et al., 2025; Morgan et al., 2024). When leveraged strategically, tools like social media can significantly enhance these efforts, but their potential must be carefully harnessed to maximize impact. This leads to a marketing strategy that encompasses brand as the center of the decisions of the organization, a so-called brand orientation.

BRAND ORIENTATION IN NONPROFITS

Brand orientation is defined as a strategic approach where the brand becomes the central axis of decision-making. For nonprofits, this involves aligning organizational processes and communication strategies with the brand's core values and mission. Thus, nonprofit brand orientation (NBO) is not merely about creating a brand; it involves implementing a strategic approach to define the brand's essence and determine what it should convey to stakeholders. Studies by Urde (1994, 1999) and Hankinson (2001) highlighted how brand orientation enhances stakeholder engagement and organizational performance. This aligns with the broader shift in strategic marketing orientations toward social value generation, as recent literature has highlighted the growing convergence between market objectives and societal impact (Mazzarolo et al., 2024).

[1] See more at https://campaigns.allout.org/pt/havaianas

[2] See more at http://projetotamar.com.br/noticia1.php?cod=209

It acknowledges the brand as a strategic resource, recognizes its emotional appeal and symbolism and manages internal and external activities to enhance the brand's capacity to generate value (Sepulcri et al., 2020b). Through strategic communication, organizations define how to convey and disseminate the brand strategy, aligning actions to achieve their goals, thereby enhancing stakeholder engagement and improving organizational performance.

Building upon this foundation, NBO serves as a strategic communication framework that integrates the organization's cause, mission, symbols and values to effectively align and disseminate its identity to internal and external stakeholders (Sepulcri et al., 2022; Sepulcri & Mainardes, 2023). Central to this approach is the understanding that communication is not merely an operational tool but a core strategy for building relationships and fostering alignment with the nonprofit brand. A two-way authentic communication process is critical to co-creating meaning and value for donors and fostering engagement with the brand (D'Arco et al., 2025; Harrison, 2023).

The cause, as the reason for the NPO's existence, is foundational to NBO. It reflects the social gap the organization seeks to address and must resonate deeply with stakeholders. Effective communication ensures that the cause is clearly defined and consistently promoted, enabling stakeholders to form emotional connections with the organization. For instance, stakeholders who identify with a cause are more likely to 'hug the cause' and view the nonprofit brand as a representation of that cause, which encompasses the marketing definition of positioning.

Similarly, the mission of an NPO, encompassing its purpose and processes to achieve goals, must be conveyed strategically to demonstrate alignment with the organization's values and beliefs. Communication efforts translate the mission into actionable messages that stakeholders can understand and support. The mission involves fostering long-term engagement by instilling core values. By embedding the mission in its communication strategy, an NPO reinforces its identity and purpose. The use of symbols, such as logos, slogans and uniforms, further strengthens brand communication by creating immediate associations with the organization's cause and mission. Symbols act as visual and emotional touchpoints that enhance stakeholders' comprehension and connection to the brand.

In practice, strategic communication in NBO also involves leveraging diverse platforms and activities to reach and engage stakeholders. Websites, social media, events and branded merchandise serve as effective channels for disseminating the nonprofit brand. Uniforms, for instance, often not only promote the brand externally but also foster a sense of pride. These efforts create a cohesive and recognizable brand identity that strengthens stakeholder relationships and amplifies the organization's impact.

In essence, NBO as a strategic communication approach ensures that every interaction – be it through messaging, visuals or stakeholder engagement – aligns with the nonprofit's core values and objectives, which means it is a reflection of the nonprofit brand. This alignment fosters trust, enhances brand recognition and builds lasting connections with the organization's audience.

ANTENCEDENTS, CONSEQUENCES AND BARRIERS TO NBO

Antecedents

To successfully implement brand-oriented strategies, the antecedents of NBO are influenced by a complex interplay of internal and external factors, as well as the role of community involvement (Sepulcri et al., 2022). These factors shape how nonprofits adopt brand-oriented strategies, which ultimately influence their ability to achieve organizational goals and enhance stakeholder engagement. Therefore, a nuanced understanding of these antecedents is essential for nonprofits seeking to implement or strengthen brand orientation effectively.

Internal factors

Internal factors largely revolve around the organization's culture, leadership and the level of maturity in managing its brand. Key antecedents include:

- Leadership and Managerial Characteristics
  The role of managers in shaping NBO is critical. Their personal vision, skills, level of education and prior experience with branding significantly impact the adoption of brand-oriented strategies (Apaydın, 2011; Ewing & Napoli, 2005; Hankinson, 2001). Managers who view branding as a strategic resource, rather than simply as a logo or unnecessary cost, foster a supportive environment for NBO. For instance, as noted in field observations, certain managers introduced branding efforts to promote their NPO's image, while others neglected branding altogether, resulting in limited communication and brand

development. In emerging economies, where resource constraints are prevalent, brand orientation serves as a critical tool for maximizing impact with limited means. However, the lack of knowledge of brand strategy can limit the actions of these NPOs.

- Organizational Maturity
  Organizational maturity directly influences the understanding and implementation of NBO. As organizations mature, their mission, vision and values become more defined, creating a foundation for a cohesive brand strategy.
- Training and Internal Branding
  Training programs play a crucial role in building an organizational culture aligned with NBO. Proper training helps employees and volunteers understand the brand promises and the importance of living up to them in their daily work. As such, training is essential for creating a supportive environment for brand development.

External factors

External factors include environmental conditions that push nonprofits to adopt brand orientation as a strategic necessity:

- Resource Scarcity and Competition
  Limited financial resources, heightened competition among NPOs, and the need to address public distrust drive nonprofits to adopt NBO. Economic crises can exacerbate these pressures, particularly for NPOs reliant on government funding, which often involves bureaucratic selection processes rather than competitive market-based considerations (Sheth, 2011).
- Sponsoring model
  Different sponsoring models can influence how NPOs perceive their brands and the extent to which they are driven to compete for a specific target audience (Evans et al., 2012). In economies that are more market-driven, NPOs face greater competition and are, consequently, pushed to develop their brands to stand out and attract resources. Unlike government-dependent organizations, which often lack incentives for branding, NPOs operating in market-oriented environments must actively compete for donor support, partnerships and public attention. This competitive pressure encourages these organizations to invest in brand development as a strategic tool for differentiation and to effectively engage with their target audiences.

This characteristic has a particularly distinct impact on NPOs in emerging economies. Sheth (2011) highlights that much of the consumption in these regions involves unbranded products and services, a phenomenon termed 'unbranded competition.' Similarly, the government selection of NPOs often overlooks brand-related factors. As a result, NPOs heavily reliant on government funding lack the incentives to prioritize brand development or adopt a brand-oriented approach. This lack of motivation to invest in branding represents a significant barrier, commonly referred to as 'government barriers'.

Community involvement

Beyond internal and external factors, community involvement plays a unique role, where NPOs are often required to engage with local communities beyond their immediate beneficiaries. Community engagement fosters brand recognition and trust. Such involvement also serves as a motivating factor for public engagement and advocacy.

Community involvement is not merely a supporting factor but can act as a co-creation strategy for brand development. As Vallaster and von Wallpach (2018) argue, brand orientation should not be viewed solely as a managerial activity but as a collaborative effort with external stakeholders. For instance, some NPOs have established visitor centers and organized public events to showcase their work and involve the community. These efforts strengthen the brand by creating opportunities for public interaction and engagement, which is especially vital in emerging economies.

The antecedents of brand orientation in NPOs encompass a range of internal and external factors, as well as the critical role of community involvement. Leadership, organizational maturity and training are pivotal internal drivers, while resource scarcity, competition and government dependency represent significant external pressures. Community involvement emerges as both an antecedent and a strategy for co-creating brand value. By addressing these diverse influences in a coordinated manner, nonprofits can develop a robust brand orientation strategy, enhancing their ability to navigate challenges.

Consequences

As discussed in the previous section, NBO can offer significant benefits to these organizations, influencing their performance across various dimensions. These outcomes range from enhanced staff engagement and improved reputation to stronger partnerships and greater resource acquisition. By aligning their mission, values and actions with a cohesive brand strategy, nonprofits can achieve greater impact and operational effectiveness. Accordingly, outcomes of NBO can be noted internally, enhancing staff relationships, but also externally, increasing partnership reputation and performance indicators (Sepulcri et al., 2022).

Staff engagement and alignment

One of the most notable outcomes of NBO is its positive influence on staff relationships. When employees and volunteers fully understand and internalize the organization's brand values, they are more likely to feel a sense of purpose, commitment and engagement. This alignment fosters a high-quality service delivery that reflects the brand promises (Liu et al., 2015; Piehler et al., 2016). Staff members often describe their work as 'motivating,' 'gratifying' and essential to fulfilling the organization's mission. One of the advantages of nonprofit companies is that they usually are founded with a deep-rooted sense of purpose from the outset, represented by their cause. This purpose helps with engagement but needs to be aligned between different staff.

When brand orientation is embedded in the organization's culture, it reinforces internal cohesion, strengthens trust among team members and promotes engagement with the mission – regardless of resource limitations or contextual challenges. Staff alignment with brand values becomes a strategic asset, contributing not only to motivation and commitment but also to the consistency and credibility of the brand across all interactions with stakeholders (Sepulcri & Mainardes, 2025).

Enhanced reputation

A well-implemented NBO contributes significantly to an organization's reputation, which is closely tied to its values and consistency in delivering its social mission. Stakeholders often associate strong nonprofit brands with credibility, authenticity, trustworthiness and respectability (Apaydın, 2011; Romero & Abril, 2024; Tilley, 1999). For instance, when stakeholders see consistent delivery of promised outcomes, they develop a deeper trust in the organization. Effective communication and consistent feedback to stakeholders reinforce these perceptions, boosting the organization's esteem and reputation over time.

In the specific context of NPOs, reputation emerges as a central dimension of donor-based brand equity (Romero et al., 2023). It reflects the collective perception of the organization's legitimacy, ethical integrity and effectiveness in pursuing its mission. A strong reputation enhances not only trust but also emotional and attitudinal commitment from donors, fostering deeper engagement and long-term loyalty. Moreover, it serves as a key differentiator in an increasingly competitive nonprofit landscape, where donors are more selective and values-driven. NPOs with high reputational capital are also more likely to attract media attention, strategic partnerships and endorsements from authentic influencers – elements that further reinforce their brand strength and social impact.

Strengthened partnerships

Building a strong nonprofit brand facilitates the establishment of mutually beneficial partnerships, particularly with for-profit organizations. These partnerships often involve resource exchanges, such as financial contributions, services or products, in return for the for-profit company's association with the nonprofit's brand. However, successful partnerships require alignment between the nonprofit's brand and the partner's values to ensure mutual benefits and consistency in messaging.

Beyond benefiting nonprofits, these collaborations also offer significant advantages for for-profit organizations by generating social value, which has become a critical element in modern marketing strategies. Social value reflects practices and policies that not only enhance a company's competitiveness but also address societal and environmental challenges, aligning with the concept of shared value as defined by Porter and Kramer (2011). For-profit companies that partner with nonprofits can leverage these relationships to demonstrate their commitment to CSR, improve their reputation and build stronger connections with socially conscious consumers.

Cause-related marketing, for instance, links consumer purchases to corporate philanthropy, creating a win-win scenario where consumers feel empowered to contribute to societal causes while companies benefit from increased sales and enhanced brand perception. Such strategies are not just transactional but form part of a broader narrative where businesses actively contribute to solving social and environmental problems.

Moreover, partnerships with nonprofits enable for-profit organizations to engage in positive marketing and social marketing, focusing on creating value through initiatives that benefit society (Soares Júnior et al., 2024). By collaborating with nonprofits, companies gain insights into community needs, allowing them to align their marketing efforts with genuine societal demands, which enhances brand authenticity and customer loyalty. This alignment can also extend to macrosocial marketing, where partnerships are geared toward addressing systemic social issues, amplifying the impact of both organizations.

A growing dimension within these partnerships is the collaboration with social media influencers engaged in activism. Known as *influencer activism*, this strategy involves partnering with individuals who publicly support sociopolitical causes aligned with the nonprofit's mission. When the influencer's personal values and advocacy efforts are congruent with the nonprofit's brand, the perceived authenticity of the campaign is significantly enhanced. This perceived authenticity positively influences followers' attitudes toward the organization, boosting engagement, donations and long-term support. Therefore, selecting the right influencer partner – one whose values, voice and audience naturally align with the cause – becomes a strategic branding decision for nonprofits (D'Arco et al., 2025).

In this sense, such partnerships not only bring resources and visibility to nonprofits but also help for-profits create a meaningful narrative around their brand. These narratives demonstrate that their business success is intrinsically tied to societal well-being, fostering goodwill among consumers, stakeholders and employees. This synergy between nonprofits and for-profits exemplifies how strategic partnerships, underpinned by strong nonprofit brands, can simultaneously generate social value and drive competitive advantage.

Resource acquisition and financial sustainability

NBO enhances an NPO's ability to attract resources, including financial donations and volunteer support. A strong brand increases donor confidence and encourages public engagement with the cause. 'Because people see (the NPO) work' is a well-known justification to enhance resource mobilization. Brand equity, especially when grounded in values such as authenticity, reputation and emotional connection, significantly influences donor preference and intention to give, which are essential for financial resilience (Romero et al., 2023; Romero & Abril, 2024). Furthermore, by perceiving themselves as brands, nonprofits can diversify their funding sources and move toward self-sustainability. This includes not only traditional fundraising but also more market-oriented strategies, such as branded e-commerce, cause-related products and social enterprises. These initiatives allow supporters to engage with the brand through consumption, blending personal benefit with social contribution (Romero et al., 2023). For example, many nonprofits now have e-commerce platforms selling more than just products – they sell the idea of a cause. When the brand is strong, the perceived value of those products increases, echoing the logic of for-profit markets: strong brands drive higher engagement and purchasing behavior (Romero & Abril, 2024; Sepulcri & Mainardes, 2025). This approach ensures that new funding sources align with the organization's mission and values, reinforcing brand coherence while supporting financial sustainability.

Increased influence and benchmark status

A robust brand can position an NPO as a benchmark in its field, increasing its societal influence and the demand for its services. This benchmark status not only reinforces the brand's visibility but also enhances the organization's ability to mobilize support for its cause. 'Be the first or be the best' is a phrase usually associated with for-profit organizations, but it can also be used in nonprofit ecosystem.

The outcomes of brand orientation demonstrate its transformative potential for NPOs. By fostering staff alignment, building a strong reputation, enabling partnerships, enhancing resource acquisition and positioning as benchmarks in their fields, NBO empowers nonprofits to achieve their missions more effectively. These benefits underscore the strategic importance of adopting and sustaining brand-oriented practices.

Barriers

Despite its benefits, NBO faces significant barriers in these organizations, particularly in emerging economies. These barriers stem from organizational culture, limited resources, communication challenges and external factors, including government bureaucracy and societal attitudes (Sepulcri et al., 2022).

Noncommercial mindset

As branding and marketing practices are still not common among NPOs, especially the small ones, many NPOs and their stakeholders resist branding practices, perceiving them as overly commercial and misaligned with the nonprofit ethos. This mindset discourages branding efforts, with donors often questioning whether funds should be spent on advertisements or other typical communication activities. It is not uncommon to see arguments like the cause 'is not to sell', especially in countries that are less market-oriented and strongly dependent on government funding for NPOs. Other points such as short-term focus, which can also be a cultural characteristic and organizational culture can be barriers to implement NBO.

In this context, branding is sometimes perceived not only as a distraction from the mission but also as a potential threat to the authenticity of the organization, and it can also involve ethical considerations. Depending on the organizational culture, branding can be viewed as a 'dirty word,' associated with commercial exploitation and misaligned with the pro-social values of the sector (Hand et al., 2021). This cultural rejection can lead to superficial brand assimilation rather than genuine integration, ultimately hindering the strategic potential of branding to align stakeholders and amplify the organization's purpose.

Short-term focus

Another internal barrier is the short-term mindset. NPOs frequently prioritize immediate needs over long-term strategies like branding. This short-termism arises from their focus on addressing pressing social issues or responding to emergencies. The love for the cause and the necessity to assist can become traps in terms of management and branding. As a result, resources are allocated to urgent tasks rather than building sustainable brand strategies. This reactive approach limits the ability to implement NBO effectively, as long-term branding requires consistent investment and vision.

Communication challenges

Compounding these issues, effective communication is essential for NBO but remains a persistent challenge. Many NPOs lack dedicated communication teams or strategies, resulting in inconsistent messaging. As organizations grow, aligning communication across multiple stakeholders becomes increasingly complex. Additionally, stakeholders often struggle to understand the organization's mission or even its results, undermining trust and engagement.

Organizational culture

Resistance to change within organizational culture also hinders NBO. This resistance is particularly prevalent among long-standing staff who may view branding initiatives as unnecessary or misaligned with the organization's traditional values. Moreover, the lack of professionalization in management and processes exacerbates this barrier, as many NPOs lack the expertise to develop and implement branding strategies effectively.

Government barriers

Government dependencies and bureaucratic hurdles create additional challenges for NPOs. In many emerging economies, public funding is allocated through political networks or complex bureaucratic processes, which often overlook the importance of branding. This lack of incentive for brand development, coupled with legislative conflicts and tax-related difficulties, further restricts NPOs from adopting long-term branding strategies.

Resource limitations

A pervasive lack of financial and human resources severely limits NPOs' ability to implement NBO. Staff shortages and inadequate funding leave little capacity for strategic planning or branding initiatives. Many NPOs are trapped in a cycle of addressing basic operational needs, neglecting the investments required for long-term branding. This is common, especially in local and small NPOs but similar patterns can also be found in small, family-owned for-profit companies.

In summary, NBO represents a transformative strategy for NPOs, enabling them to enhance internal alignment, reputation, partnerships and resource acquisition while positioning themselves as leaders in their respective fields. However, the adoption of NBO is not without challenges. Barriers such as resource limitations, communication difficulties, cultural resistance and government dependencies must be addressed strategically. By overcoming these obstacles, nonprofits can unlock the full potential of brand orientation, leveraging it not only as a tool for operational success but also as a catalyst for broader social impact. In a competitive and resource-constrained landscape, a well-defined and strategically managed brand can empower NPOs to thrive, expand their reach and deliver lasting change in the communities they serve.

CONTEXT DIFFERENCES: EMERGING AND DEVELOPED ECONOMIES

The nonprofit sector operates under distinct conditions in emerging and developed countries due to differences in political, economic and cultural contexts. While emerging markets face significant challenges, they also foster innovation and adaptability that contrast with the more structured environments of developed economies.

Challenges in Emerging Countries

Emerging economies face numerous obstacles that impact the development of NPOs. These include inadequate infrastructure, unstable regulatory systems, corruption and a lack of skilled employees. Economic instability further complicates operations, requiring NPOs to adopt flexible strategies such as diversifying funding sources, creating contingency plans and investing in scalable digital branding initiatives to mitigate risks.

Additionally, cultural perceptions often frame branding as a commercial practice incompatible with nonprofit missions, creating skepticism among stakeholders. To address this, NPOs can focus on educating stakeholders on the societal benefits of branding, emphasizing transparency in fund utilization and customizing branding strategies to align with the local cultural values.

Innovations and Strengths in Emerging Markets

Despite these challenges, NPOs in emerging markets have developed innovative solutions to fulfill their missions. Limited resources have driven organizations to leverage independent volunteers, forge partnerships with governments and private companies and adapt marketing strategies to local contexts. For instance, Artemisia, a Brazilian NPO, focuses on promoting social businesses that address socio-environmental challenges for economically vulnerable populations, demonstrating how NPOs can create significant impact even in resource-constrained settings. According to the organization, they 'amplifies the positive impact of business and innovation in search of a fairer and more sustainable world' (Artemisia, 2024). Working since 2005, Artemisia was the first organization in Latin America to integrate business logic with positive impact.

The strategic use of branding in these contexts is pivotal. For example, research in emerging economies, such as India and Iran, highlights how branding enhances trust, increases donation intentions, and fosters engagement through digital platforms (Garg et al., 2019; Maleki & Hosseini, 2020). A practical illustration is found in the case of Ifood (one of the biggest FoodTech in Latin America) maintains partnerships with social organizations and enables small donations with each purchase made by its customers. This microdonation strategy also allows funding to come from more donors, as, in these countries, the average income is usually low. These efforts allow NPOs to maintain relevance and sustainability despite economic variability.

Advantages in Developed Countries

In contrast, developed economies provide NPOs with more stable political and economic environments, better infrastructure and greater access to skilled personnel. These advantages enable organizations to focus on long-term goals, strategic growth and advanced branding efforts. Branding strategies in developed countries often emphasize innovation, reputation management and public policy influence, supported by robust regulatory frameworks that ensure transparency and accountability.

Cultural and Economic Factors

While branding is often misunderstood in emerging markets, it is generally well-integrated into the operations of NPOs in developed economies. The skepticism toward branding in emerging economies, rooted in cultural and historical contexts, contrasts with the acceptance and strategic use of branding in developed markets. Similarly, economic variability in emerging markets necessitates flexible branding approaches, whereas NPOs in developed economies benefit from consistent funding and stable operational conditions.

Challenges in Nonprofit Branding

Across both contexts, NPOs face both traditional and contemporary challenges in branding. Traditional constraints such as resource scarcity and the need to balance mission with operational sustainability remain significant in emerging and developed markets alike. Contemporary challenges include aligning communication across diverse stakeholders, managing partnerships while maintaining consistent branding and leveraging digital spaces effectively.

In emerging economies, skepticism toward commercial practices adds an additional layer of complexity, necessitating culturally sensitive branding strategies. Economic instability further exacerbates these challenges, making it essential for NPOs to prioritize flexibility and adaptability in their branding efforts.

STRATEGIES FOR NONPROFIT BRANDING

Strategic imperatives for nonprofit branding focus on addressing challenges, leveraging opportunities and integrating innovative practices to ensure mission alignment and organizational sustainability. In this section, we discuss key imperatives with practical examples to illustrate their application.

Addressing Resource Scarcity

Resource scarcity is a persistent challenge for NPOs, which often rely on donations, grants, and volunteer support. Effective branding plays a vital role in mitigating this challenge through various strategic avenues. One key approach is enhancing fundraising capacity: a compelling brand builds trust and credibility, encouraging donations. For example, the WWF uses its globally recognized panda logo to attract individual and corporate donors, raising substantial funds for conservation projects.

In addition to fundraising, branding is instrumental in attracting talent. Volunteers and employees are more likely to engage with organizations whose brands align with their values. Habitat for Humanity exemplifies this dynamic, as its clear mission of building affordable housing has successfully cultivated a brand that draws in volunteers from around the world.

Finally, strong brand identities also foster partnerships with government bodies and private sector actors. These collaborations not only amplify visibility but also unlock new funding mechanisms such as microdonations. For instance, the pet supply retailer Petz encourages customers to round up their change at checkout, with proceeds directed to animal welfare organizations.[3] Similarly, the food delivery platform iFood allows consumers to donate to Ação da Cidadania[4] when they order. This NPO is a leading advocate against hunger in Brazil and plays a key role in monitoring, inspiring, and influencing public policies related to food security.

Navigating Stakeholder Complexity

NPOs must manage relationships with diverse stakeholders, including donors, beneficiaries, and policymakers. Branding strategies play a critical role in aligning these varied interests and facilitating meaningful engagement. One way to navigate this complexity is by segmenting audiences and tailoring messages to specific groups. Organizations like UNICEF exemplify this by developing targeted campaigns that address the unique motivations and expectations of different donor demographics, ranging from corporate sponsors to individual child sponsors.

Another important strategy is building coherence across communication platforms. Consistent branding fosters recognition and trust among stakeholders. Charity: Water,[5] an organization known for its mission to provide clean water to underserved communities, maintains strong visual and narrative consistency across all of its channels. This includes using compelling data and transparent reporting, which reinforces the organization's credibility and commitment to its mission.

In addition to segmentation and consistency, encouraging stakeholder co-creation has emerged as a powerful branding approach. Involving stakeholders in brand development promotes a sense of ownership and alignment with the organization's values. The World Health Organization (WHO), for example, engages local communities in the co-creation of health communication campaigns, ensuring cultural relevance and stakeholder buy-in (World Health Organization, 2021). This co-creation process yields multiple benefits: it fosters deeper engagement by encouraging active participation, draws on diverse perspectives to generate innovative solutions, and ensures stronger alignment between the brand and its audiences. When branding strategies are developed collaboratively, they tend to resonate more effectively with target public, increasing both impact and long-term support.

Leveraging Digital Platforms

Digital platforms have profoundly transformed nonprofit communication, offering cost-effective and impactful tools to connect with audiences and mobilize support. Beyond reach and visibility, these platforms foster community building and active engagement among diverse stakeholders (Morgan et al., 2024).

One major advantage of digital platforms is their ability to significantly increase visibility. Social media, in particular, has enabled nonprofits to engage broader and more diverse audiences across the globe. A compelling example is Movember, a campaign promoting men's health, which has successfully used social platforms to build global recognition. The campaign's hashtag, #movember, has accumulated over 2.5 million posts on Instagram, illustrating the campaign's capacity to generate mass participation and spark conversations around critical health issues.

Digital tools are also particularly effective in engaging younger demographics. Innovations such as virtual reality and gamified content appeal to younger audiences who seek interactive and immersive experiences. UNICEF has developed virtual reality simulations that depict life in refugee camps, helping to build empathy and drive action. These immersive experiences have not only increased awareness but have also proven effective in motivating donations, demonstrating the potential of emerging technologies in humanitarian storytelling.

[3] See more at https://www.adotepetz.com.br/

[4] See more at https://institucional.ifood.com.br/noticias/acao-da-cidadania-mobiliza-politicas-contra-a-fome/

[5] See more at https://www.charitywater.org/

In addition to reach and immersion, digital platforms offer unique opportunities for organizations to showcase the tangible impact of their work. A widely recognized example is the ALS Ice Bucket Challenge of 2014. This viral campaign mobilized millions of people – including celebrities and public figures – to pour buckets of ice water over their heads, post the videos online, and encourage others to do the same or donate to ALS research. The initiative dramatically raised both awareness and funds for amyotrophic lateral sclerosis, serving as a benchmark for how social media can drive large-scale engagement for charitable causes.

Underlying all of these strategies is the power of storytelling. Especially, for nonprofits with limited resources, storytelling remains an accessible and effective tool for brand building (Keel & Tran, 2023). By sharing authentic and emotionally resonant narratives about the communities and causes they serve, organizations can articulate their mission in ways that foster trust, differentiate their brand, and strengthen emotional connections with supporters. Storytelling not only conveys the essence of a cause – it also invites public participation in shaping and sharing that narrative, transforming audiences from passive observers into active co-creators of meaning and identity. In doing so, storytelling becomes a strategic asset for visibility, legitimacy, and long-term engagement in the digital age.

Adapting and Reinventing Brand Context from For-Profit Sector

As NPOs evolve within an increasingly competitive and media-saturated environment, many have begun to adapt and reinvent branding strategies traditionally associated with the for-profit sector. This adaptation, however, requires a careful balance between staying true to the organization's mission and communicating that mission in ways that resonate with diverse audiences.

A central aspect of this adaptation is the ability to maintain a dual focus on cause and communication. Effective branding in the nonprofit context hinges on the alignment between mission-driven messaging and strategic brand expression. When communication efforts clearly articulate an organization's core purpose, stakeholders are more likely to understand, trust, and support its initiatives. Médecins Sans Frontières (Doctors Without Borders) exemplifies this approach by consistently communicating its commitment to providing urgent medical aid in crisis zones while cultivating a strong and trusted brand identity across international contexts.

In parallel, many nonprofits have also begun to adopt commercial branding techniques to enhance their visibility and stakeholder engagement. These strategies – borrowed from the for-profit world – include sophisticated storytelling, audience segmentation, brand consistency and transparency. Charity: Water is an example in this regard, leveraging emotionally powerful storytelling and radical transparency to reinforce its credibility with donors. Another noteworthy case is SOS Mata Atlântica, a Brazilian organization dedicated to environmental preservation. It not only presents compelling narratives about its reforestation efforts but also integrates robust data reporting into its communication strategy, effectively combining emotional appeal with evidence-based results. By doing so, the organization not only diversifies its donation channels but also strengthens its brand equity and expands its supporter base.

These examples illustrate how NPOs can strategically adapt branding practices from the for-profit sector – without compromising their values – to build stronger, more engaging and more sustainable brands.

RESEARCH AGENDA

Despite the increasing relevance of the third sector in addressing complex societal challenges, research on branding in NPOs remains limited and largely centered on fundraising outcomes, especially donor behavior. However, the evolving dynamics of social organizations – marked by the digitalization of communication, the diversification of stakeholders and the blending of sectors – demand new research lenses capable of capturing the multifaceted roles of nonprofit brands in society.

One promising direction for future research involves understanding how brand co-creation processes influence long-term loyalty and advocacy. As nonprofit stakeholders increasingly expect participatory experiences, scholars could explore how the involvement of donors, volunteers, beneficiaries and staff in shaping brand narratives affects their emotional and behavioral commitment over time. This calls for longitudinal and multi-method approaches to capture not only engagement patterns but also the symbolic power embedded in co-created brand identities.

Another rich avenue concerns the strategic use of digital storytelling in building brand authenticity and emotional resonance. As organizations experiment with new formats – such as video campaigns, immersive platforms and real-time testimonials – there is a need to investigate how different narrative structures and media affect stakeholder perceptions and the perceived credibility of the brand. This also raises questions about the role of storytelling in contexts of low visibility or stigmatized causes, where the brand must work harder to connect with audiences.

Additionally, the growing use of social media influencers in nonprofit campaigns offers fertile ground for inquiry. Future studies could examine the impact of influencers with different levels of reach, cultural alignment and perceived authenticity on brand visibility, trust and donor behavior. This line of inquiry could bridge branding literature with influencer marketing and pro-social behavior, especially in contexts where the cause is politically or socially sensitive.

Equally important is the need to critically assess the ethical implications of adopting commercial branding techniques in mission-driven organizations. Scholars could explore whether the professionalization of nonprofit branding risks diluting the core values of the organization or marginalizing beneficiary voices. This includes reflections on the commodification of suffering, performative activism and the balance between strategic image-building and moral integrity.

Branding strategies also influence how individuals decide to engage with an organization – not only as donors but also as volunteers and beneficiaries. Research could investigate how identity, value congruence and motivational drivers are shaped by brand perception, particularly from a business to volunteer (B2V) perspective (Mitchell & Clark, 2020). This area remains underexplored despite the centrality of volunteers to nonprofit operations.

Furthermore, the alignment of brand identities in cross-sector partnerships presents complex challenges. In collaborations between nonprofits, for-profits, and public organizations, tensions may arise around brand coherence, message control and stakeholder expectations. These tensions are especially pronounced in fragile or emerging democracies, where branding strategies intersect with political discourse, cultural sensitivities and issues of public trust.

Finally, nonprofit branding can – and should – be examined beyond its instrumental role in fundraising. Brands in the third sector increasingly function as vehicles for civic engagement, political advocacy and cultural transformation. Future research could investigate how nonprofit brands mobilize public opinion, influence policy debates and catalyze collective action. In doing so, branding scholarship can contribute not only to more effective organizational strategies but also to broader conversations about democracy, equity and social justice.

CONCLUSION

Strategic branding is essential for NPOs to navigate resource constraints, engage stakeholders and amplify their societal impact. By addressing resource scarcity, managing stakeholder complexity and leveraging digital platforms, NPOs can build resilient and impactful brands. Practical cases – such as the Tamar Project, Movember, and UNICEF – demonstrate how strategic branding enhances visibility, trust and alignment, ensuring long-term success in achieving organizational missions.

Ultimately, nonprofit branding is more than a tool for visibility; it is a strategic imperative for organizational success. By adopting brand orientation, leveraging digital platforms and fostering co-creation, NPOs can overcome challenges and maximize their impact. As the nonprofit sector continues to evolve in complexity and scale, innovative branding strategies will play an essential role in shaping the future of NPOs globally.

ACKNOWLEDGMENT

This research was supported by Brazilian National Council for Scientific and Technological Development (CNPq/Brazil), project 307202/2021-6, by Foundation for Research Support of Espírito Santo (FAPES/Brazil), projects 2022-687ZR (644/2022), 2022-31G9Q (1010/2022), 2024-6GHS8 (335/2024), 2024-C29RR (392/2024), by NECE, also by FCT – Fundação para a Ciência e a Tecnologia, I.P. by project reference UIDB/04630/2020 and DOI:10.54499/UIDP/04630/2020, and by IFTS (Instituto Fucape de Tecnologias Sociais), project 2022–2025.

REFERENCES

Apaydın, F. (2011). A proposed model of antecedents and outcomes of brand orientation for nonprofit sector. *Asian Social Science*, *7*(9), 194–202. https://doi.org/10.5539/ass.v7n9p194

Artemisia. (2024). Quem somos. Retrieved December 24, 2024, from https://artemisia.org.br/quem-somos/

Bennett, R., & Sargeant, A. (2005). The nonprofit marketing landscape: Guest editors' introduction to a special section. *Journal of Business Research*, *58*(6), 797–805. https://doi.org/10.1016/j.jbusres.2003.12.001

Dalvi, R. B., Mainardes, E. W., & Sepulcri, L. M. C. B. (2024). The relationship between nonprofit density and socioeconomic indicators in an emerging country. *Voluntas*, *35*, 1091–1104 (2024). https://doi.org/10.1007/s11266-024-00676-1

D'Arco, M., Branca, G., Marino, V., & Resciniti, R. (2025). Influencer activism: Insights for effective partnership with brands and organizations. *Psychology & Marketing*, *42*(3), 741–766. https://doi.org/10.1002/mar.22149

Evans, J., Bridson, K., & Rentschler, R. (2012). Drivers, impediments and manifestations of brand orientation: An international museum study. *European Journal of Marketing*, *46*(11/12), 1457–1475. https://doi.org/10.1108/03090561211259934

Ewing, M. T., & Napoli, J. (2005). Developing and validating a multidimensional nonprofit brand orientation scale. *Journal of Business Research*, *58*(6), 841–853. https://doi.org/10.1016/j.jbusres.2003.09.012

Garg, E., Swami, S., & Malhotra, S. K. (2019). Branding effectiveness measurement in non-profit environment. *Journal of Advances in Management Research*, *16*(1), 4–22. https://doi.org/10.1108/JAMR-05-2018-0039

Gruber, V., & Deschênes, J. (2024). Managing brand relationship plurality: Insights from the nonprofit sector. *Journal of Marketing*, *88*(6), 24–42. https://doi.org/10.1177/00222429241253193

Hand, K., Murphy, R., MacLachlan, M., & Carr, S. C. (2021). Worlds apart? – The challenges of aligning brand value for NGO's. *International Review on Public and Nonprofit Marketing*, *19*, 575–598 (2022). https://doi.org/10.1007/s12208-021-00312-4

Hankinson, P. (2001). Brand orientation in the charity sector: A framework for discussion and research. *International Journal of Nonprofit and Voluntary Sector Marketing*, *6*(3), 231–242. https://doi.org/10.1002/nvsm.149

Harrison, V. S. (2023). The communicative power of nonprofit actions and values: A pilot study of dialogic stewardship. *Public Relations Review*, *49*(1), 102280. https://doi.org/10.1016/j.pubrev.2022.102280

Hassay, D. N., & Peloza, J. (2009). Building the charity brand community. *Journal of Nonprofit & Public Sector Marketing*, *21*(1), 24–55. https://doi.org/10.1080/10495140802111927

Hommerová, D., & Severová, L. (2019). Fundraising of nonprofit organizations: Specifics and new possibilities. *Journal of Social Service Research*, *45*(2), 181–192. https://doi.org/10.1080/01488376.2018.1479678

Hou, J., Zhang, C., & King, R. A. (2018). Measuring trust damage in nonprofit marketing: The role of cognitive and emotional perceptions. *International Review on Public and Nonprofit Marketing*, *15*(1), 25–47. https://doi.org/10.1007/s12208-017-0189-8

Keel, A. L., & Tran, A. T. (2023). Increasing small nonprofits' influence through strategic storytelling. *Business Horizons*, *66*(3), 359–370. https://doi.org/10.1016/j.bushor.2023.01.004

Liu, G., Chapleo, C., Ko, W. W., & Ngugi, I. K. (2015). The role of internal branding in nonprofit brand management: An empirical investigation. *Nonprofit and Voluntary Sector Quarterly*, *44*(2), 319–339. https://doi.org/10.1177/0899764013511303

Maleki, F., & Hosseini, S. M. (2020). Charity donation intention via m-payment apps: Donor-related, m-payment system-related, or charity brand-related factors, which one is overkill? *International Review on Public and Nonprofit Marketing*, *17*(4), 409–443. https://doi.org/10.1007/s12208-020-00254-3

Mazzarolo, A. H., Mainardes, E. W., Sepulcri, L. M. C. B., & de Oliveira, A. B. S. P. (2024). Strategic marketing orientations for social value generation: Systematic literature review and research agenda. *European Journal of Management and Marketing Studies*, *9*(2), 27–63. https://doi.org/10.46827/ejmms.v9i2.1793

Mitchell, S. L., & Clark, M. (2020). Rethinking nonprofit brands through a volunteer lens: Time for B2V. *Journal of Marketing Management*, *37*(5–6), 464–487. https://doi.org/10.1080/0267257X.2020.1818804

Morgan, K., DeMasters, C., & Wiley, K. (2024). Nonprofits, social media, and mission. *Journal of Nonprofit & Public Sector Marketing*, *37*(2), 163–188. https://doi.org/10.1080/10495142.2024.2372102

Mort, G. S., Weerawardena, J., & Williamson, B. (2007). Branding in the non-profit context: The case of surf life saving Australia. *Australasian Marketing Journal (AMJ)*, *15*(2), 108–119. https://doi.org/10.1016/S1441-3582(07)70047-2

Piehler, R., King, C., Burmann, C., & Xiong, L. (2016). The importance of employee brand understanding, brand identification, and brand commitment in realizing brand citizenship behaviour. *European Journal of Marketing*, *50*(9/10), 1575–1601. https://doi.org/10.1108/EJM-11-2014-0725

Porter, M. E., & Kramer, M. R. (2011). Creating shared value. *Harvard Business Review*, *89*, 62–77. https://hbr.org/2011/01/the-big-idea-creating-shared-value

Romero, M. J. R., & Abril, C. (2024). Exploring the dimensions of NGO donor-based brand equity: A literature review. *Nonprofit Management and Leadership*, *35*(1), 219–235. https://doi.org/10.1002/nml.21601

Romero, M. J. R., Abril, C., & Urquia-Grande, E. (2023). Insights on NGO brand equity: A donor-based brand equity model. *European Journal of*

Management and Business Economics, *32*(4), 452–468. https://doi.org/10.1108/EJMBE-08-2022-0261

Sepulcri, L. M. C. B., & Mainardes, E. W. (2023). Elements that compose the non-profit BRAND orientation in an emerging country. *International Review on Public and Nonprofit Marketing*, *20*(1), 85–123. https://doi.org/10.1007/s12208-022-00333-7

Sepulcri, L. M. C. B., & Mainardes, E. W. (2025). The role of nonprofit brand orientation in the context of an emerging country. *Journal of Marketing Analytics*, 1–19. https://doi.org/10.1057/s41270-025-00378-7

Sepulcri, L. M. C. B., Mainardes, E. W., & Belchior, C. C. (2020a). Nonprofit branding: A bibliometric analysis. *Journal of Product & Brand Management*, *29*(5), 655–673. https://doi.org/10.1108/JPBM-05-2019-2366

Sepulcri, L. M. C. B., Mainardes, E. W., & Marchiori, D. M. (2020b). Brand orientation: A systematic literature review and research agenda. *Spanish Journal of Marketing-ESIC*, *24*(1), 97–114. https://doi.org/10.1108/SJME-06-2019-0035

Sepulcri, L. M. C. B., Mainardes, E. W., & Pascuci, L. (2022). Non-profit brand orientation as a strategic communication approach. *International Journal of Strategic Communication*, *16*(4), 572–598. https://doi.org/10.1080/1553118X.2022.2058948

Sheth, J. N. (2011). Impact of emerging markets on marketing: Rethinking existing perspectives and practices. *Journal of Marketing*, *75*(4), 166–182. https://doi.org/10.1509/jmkg.75.4.166

Soares Júnior, A. P., Espanhol, C. A., Mainardes, E. W., & Sepulcri, L. M. C. B. (2024). Social value of marketing: A bibliometric analysis. *Journal of Nonprofit & Public Sector Marketing*, *37*(1), 133–162. https://doi.org/10.1080/10495142.2024.2353382.

Tilley, C. (1999). Built-in branding: How to engineer a leadership brand. *Journal of Marketing Management*, *15*(1–3), 181–191. https://doi.org/10.1362/026725799784870405

Urde, M. (1994). Brand orientation: A strategy for survival. *Journal of Consumer Marketing*, *11*(3), 18–32. https://doi.org/10.1108/07363769410065445

Urde, M. (1999). Brand orientation: A mindset for building brands into strategic resources. *Journal of Marketing Management*, *15*(1–3), 117–133. https://doi.org/10.1362/026725799784870504

Vallaster, C., & von Wallpach, S. (2018). Brand strategy cocreation in a nonprofit context: A strategy-as-practice approach. *Nonprofit and Voluntary Sector Quarterly*, *47*(5), 984–1006. https://doi.org/10.1177/0899764018776373

Weir, L., & Hibbert, S. (2000). Building donor relationships: An investigation into the use of relationship and database marketing by charity fundraisers. *The Service Industries Journal*, *20*(2), 114–132. https://doi.org/10.1080/02642060000000023

World Health Organization. (2021). *Global strategy on digital health 2020–2025*. World Health Organization. www.who.int/docs/default-source/documents/gs4dhdaa2a9f352b0445bafbc-79ca799dce4d.pdf

Wymer, W., & Akbar, M. M. (2017). Brand authenticity, its conceptualization, and its relevance to nonprofit marketing. *International Review on Public and Nonprofit Marketing*, *14*(3), 359–374. https://doi.org/10.1007/s12208-017-0177-z

33

Brand Happiness as a Promising Brand Asset: Important Empirical Insights

Manfred Bruhn, Stefanie Stilz, and Anja Zimmermann

RELEVANCE OF HAPPINESS RESEARCH IN BRAND MANAGEMENT

The pursuit of happiness is a fundamental human endeavor, often regarded as the highest good that a person can achieve and therefore an integral part of human life, with life satisfaction being one of the highest goals of human existence (Pavot & Diener, 2013; Veenhoven, 2012a). It is, therefore, not surprising that various scientific disciplines such as philosophy, psychology and sociology have been concerned with the question of what happiness is and how it can be achieved.

Individuals seek happiness in different ways, for example, in positive relationships with other people or with living creatures, within entire systems such as families or organizations, or through the fulfillment of tasks and goals they dedicate themselves to in life. This pursuit of happiness is apparently a universal phenomenon, although the perceived level of happiness varies significantly across cultures (Veenhoven, 2012b). Research on happiness has identified different types of happiness, the eudemonic and hedonic happiness, different external circumstances and self-related, internal and social variables determining happiness as well as different happiness-increasing strategies (for an overview of happiness research see, e.g., Clark et al., 2017, 2018; Frawley, 2015; Jain et al., 2019; Tkach & Lyubomirsky, 2006).

In the social and economic sciences, research on happiness and life satisfaction has also become an increasingly important field of study, gaining significant attention in this century. This is evident, among other things, in the establishment of the '*Journal of Happiness Studies*' in 2000 or the annual publishing of the 'World Happiness Report'. Since 2012, this annual survey carried out by the UN Sustainable Development Solutions Network (SDSN) in partnership with Gallup Research and the University of Oxford's Wellbeing Research Center, has ranked more than 150 countries by their happiness levels.

So far, economic happiness research has primarily focused on macroeconomic perspectives, analyzing the happiness levels of entire economies, while on a micro level, individual happiness has been at the center of attention. In business economics, happiness research is a relatively new territory, where the focus has been so far on the happiness of individuals in the context of their work and their well-being at work.

Happiness, in the sense of a short-term affective feeling which can arise through the purchase and consumption of brands, has only been analyzed, and discussed in more detail in recent years (Schnebelen, 2015). The purchase and the consumption of products or service brands have been identified as an effective path to happiness by, among others, Bettingen and Luedicke (2009), Mogilner et al. (2012) and Nicolao et al. (2009). Marketing and consumer research shows that different types of purchases, brand experiences and also certain types of advertising are promising paths to happiness. Based on the initial findings of Van Boven and Gilovich (2003), Nicolao et al. (2009) demonstrated the superior influence of experiential purchases over material purchases on consumer's feelings of happiness. Similarly, Bettingen and Luedicke (2009) hypothesized that happiness is triggered by different types of brand experiences. Other studies have succeeded in showing that happiness is a predictor of satisfaction and loyalty (Gelbrich, 2011), service quality and commitment (Hellén & Sääksjärvi, 2011) as well as charity giving behavior (Chang, 2014). These research findings promote brand happiness as a valuable and promising new branding asset for brand managers.

Furthermore, it could be proven that feelings of happiness that are presented in various forms of advertising (e.g., in TV commercials and print ads) have an impact on consumers, making them feel happier and the feeling of happiness subsequently also affects the evaluation of advertising and the service itself (e.g., Goldberg & Gorn, 1987; Labroo & Rucker, 2010). However, one must take into consideration that the focus of advertising is not necessarily always on triggering feelings of happiness; avoiding negative feelings can also be a reason for consuming advertising and products that address happiness (Becker, 2010).

Considering research findings on happiness, it is not surprising that marketers are increasingly focusing on triggering this desired feeling of happiness through the consumption of products and services. This can be observed, for example, when they explicitly address this in campaigns – for example, McDonalds talks about a 'Happy Meal', and the cosmetics brand 'Bliss' promises a higher state of happiness through the consumption of its cosmetic products and Coca-Cola has launched an entire 'open happiness' campaign that promises happiness and joy through the opening of a can of Coke. However, the mere use of happiness terms in advertising is usually just a tactical way of working with feelings of happiness. The success of such campaigns must therefore be critically scrutinized.

The power of emotions and their ability to effectively position offers in people's perception as such has been recognized in marketing for many years, especially with the increasing convergence of products and services. Emotions, delivered by a brand or by a personal interaction, are much more difficult to copy than product features and they often have a stronger influence on purchasing decisions than rational arguments. In many cases, consumers do not want to buy brands only for fulfilling functional needs – on the contrary, they choose brands for the emotional experiences or the social values that they deliver. Emotional brand values are said to be able to transcend the life cycle of a product in an intangible asset (Li, 2021). Brands, therefore, should associate with values that have a positive impact on consumer happiness as consumers search for intangible emotional values beyond the mere tangible product (Gutiérrez-Villar et al., 2019). Consequently, brand managers are recommended to identify those brand emotions that can be influenced by brand management activities and are of great importance for the behavior of brand buyers. As happiness is an emotion with these characteristics (e.g., Soscia, 2007), it is worth devoting attention to the topic of brand happiness.

The relevance of brand happiness therefore appears to be recognized, at least in different contexts and from different perspectives. It is, therefore, even more astonishing that so far only a little research has been done on brand happiness (Matsubara, 2024; Schnebelen & Bruhn, 2018). Brand happiness as a subject of research has hardly been examined to date, even if research activities have recently been intensified. Particularly, the relationship between happiness and brands is still an understudied area of marketing research (Bettingen & Luedicke, 2009; Bruhn & Schnebelen, 2017; Schnebelen, 2015). Furthermore, current research has paid little attention to the multidimensional nature of this construct (e.g., Mogilner et al., 2012; Nicolao et al., 2009). Schnebelen and Bruhn address these two deficits in their research by bringing together the research fields of brands and happiness in the multidimensional construct of brand happiness. The comprehensive research study conducted has directly investigated the determinants and consequences of brand happiness as well as its relevance as a dominant marketing goal (Bruhn & Schnebelen, 2017; Schnebelen, 2015; Schnebelen & Bruhn, 2016). The research findings suggest that brand happiness is one of the highest goals that a consumer strives for when interacting with brands. Bruhn & Schnebelen provoke with their statement that brand happiness is the highest goal of brand managers, kind of a 'holy grail', worth striving for in order to give a brand infinite vitality (Bruhn & Schnebelen, 2017, p. 464).

CONCEPT AND MEASUREMENT OF BRAND HAPPINESS

In this chapter, a definition and conceptualization of brand happiness will be given. Brand happiness will be defined as understood by the authors against the background of their research elaborated on the concept. Furthermore, brand happiness will be described in more detail based on various characteristics and dimensions. This will also involve distinguishing it from other similar constructs.

Comparatively little research has dealt with brand happiness and its definition and conceptualization to date. Two different reasons could be suspected for this. The first reason for the difficulty in defining brand happiness is that the concept of the brand itself is complex and has been widely and heterogeneously discussed in the literature from different perspectives for many years. As a result, researchers must deal with a multitude of brand definitions without having a common and enforced understanding of the brand concept itself. This results in a wealth of different brand definitions, each of which emphasizes different brand aspects such as brand identification, brand identity or brand image. Furthermore, there are also different brand values such as functional, emotional, or social values among many others (for a literature review on the importance and different meanings of brands, see Maurya & Mishra, 2012).

Brand research consequently also reflects the complexity of brand-related emotions and perceptions. The spectrum of brand-related emotions is very broad and ranges from very positive characteristics such as brand happiness or brand love to the opposite, more negative connotations such as brand hate. Both, almost extreme forms of emotions have gained increasing attention in brand research and shown to have a significant impact on consumer behavior. Therefore, they should be of interest to brand management to enhance desired or avoid unintended effects on brands. Brand love has received increasing conceptual and empirical attention due to its impact on customer engagement, brand advocacy, commitment, and loyalty (Palusuk et al., 2019). Among many other findings, Gumparthi and Patra (2019) found that brand love experienced by satisfied consumers leads to customer loyalty. Research on brand hate, which mainly relates to industrialized nations, shows that there is a need for more robust metrics and research on boundary conditions (for an overview of research on brand hate, see Aziz & Rahman, 2022; Chawla & Chattopadhyay, 2023; Roy et al., 2022; Yadav & Chakrabart, 2023).

A second reason can be assumed in the difficulties in defining happiness in the context of consumption. Previous research on consumer happiness has addressed and developed various concepts such as 'consumer well-being', 'consumer satisfaction' and 'subjective well-being', but has yet to create a clear construct. Dhiman and Kumar (2022) record in their work that evidence of consumer happiness has been found in different research contexts, but with different interpretations of the term and concept. They show that there is no accepted standard definition of consumer happiness, and they define 'consumer happiness' as momentary positive emotions experienced during interactions with marketing activities before, during and after consumption (Dhiman & Kumar, 2022, p. 117). Furthermore, there are only a few studies that deal with consumer happiness in connection with brands. Comparatively little research has dealt with brand happiness to date. Sousa et al. (2023) found in their study of 138 documents retrieved from the Web of Science that the concepts of brand happiness and consumer happiness are often used in research without clearly distinguishing or differentiating the two concepts. Further conceptual research is necessary to clarify these related concepts.

Against the background of the great importance that people attach to happiness and the understanding of happiness in psychology, sociology and marketing, Bruhn and Schnebelen (2017, p. 467) define brand happiness as follows: Brand happiness is a consumer's greatest emotional fulfillment, a momentary experience of pleasant emotions, both high and low arousal, triggered at various points of contact with the brand, such as purchase, consumption or advertising.

Based on this definition, different characteristics can be attributed to the concept. Brand happiness is characterized by the fact that it represents the greatest emotional fulfillment that a brand can offer consumers (fulfillment). It is a moment-based, temporary (duration) positive emotional state (character) that varies in intensity, from high- to low-arousal pleasant emotions (intensity). It encompasses a range of different positive emotional experiences and therefore has a multi-dimensional character (complexity). It is triggered at different points of contact with the brand and is therefore situation-dependent (specificity). It has a strong tendency to trigger actions (activity). This feature is generally characteristic of all concepts of happiness (Veenhoven, 2012b).

Other studies offer related insights. Han et al. (2018) link brand happiness to the alignment between a consumer's ideal self and a brand's image. Kumar et al. (2021) adopt the explicit definition while examining the effects of mass prestige and self-consciousness. Niedermeier et al. (2018), Razmus et al. (2022) and Nobi (2024) emphasize that positive emotional states, customer engagement, co-creation activities and self-concept integration may foster brand happiness. Bettingen and Luedicke (2009) propose a roadmap for research on brand-related happiness, while Fournier et al. (2012) focus on brand love rather than happiness.

Only a few studies explicitly define the concept of brand happiness; others lack a standardized and clear definition or equate brand happiness with other brand-related emotional constructs like brand pride (e.g., Knaur & Verma, 2024) or brand love (e.g., Batra et al., 2012) – constructs that have also been shown to influence consumer–brand relationships but need to be defined and conceptualized differently.

Following the definition of happiness as a short-term emotional state (e.g., Delle Fave et al., 2011), brand happiness is defined as a moment-based consumer experience of pleasant emotions elicited at various brand touch points. To better understand the concept of brand happiness, its definition and measurement, Schnebelen and Bruhn (2016) initiated a scale development process, which consists of six studies carried out in three stages. The process started with exploratory research studies and ended with more focused and confirmatory studies. The qualitative stage identified a broad range of aspects associated by consumers with the experience of happiness created by brands. In Study 1, a total of 65 interviews were conducted with consumers and experts. The purpose of Study 2 as well as Study 3 was to reduce the number of items generated in Study 1. For this purpose, 187 consumers were asked to rate how well the identified items describe a brand that makes them happy (items with low mean scores and low factor loadings were excluded from further analysis) in Study 2. In this stage, mean and variance criteria and additional exploratory factor analysis were used to reduce the initial item pool. In Study 3, unimportant items based on low factor loadings were further reduced by interviewing a further 206 participants. The remaining 12 items were subjected to factor analysis, resulting in a four-factor solution: joy (emotions reflecting consumers' exuberance toward brands), vigor (a high level of activation and vitality), pride (feelings of self-esteem toward the brand), and serenity (emotional harmony and balance toward the brand). Studies 4–6 constitute the confirmatory phase of scale development. In this phase, different samples were used to further evaluate the developed brand happiness scale. Nine different models were tested (e.g., a one-factor model, a three-factor model, and a four-factor model) to uncover the relationship of the four factors to the larger construct of brand happiness. The four-factor correlated model provides the best fit (see Figure 33.1).

To evaluate the nomological validity of the brand happiness scale, the effects of brand happiness on brand behavior were demonstrated. Applying evaluation theories, the proposed hypotheses state that the experience of brand happiness leads to the desire to experience it again (through purchase and word-of-mouth). The results support the hypotheses that brand happiness has a positive impact on purchase intention and word-of-mouth, thus providing evidence of the importance of brand happiness for brand success. Study 5 examines cross-cultural validity, and Study 6 further validates the scale and analyses its discriminant and predictive validity. The empirical evidence for the antecedent and main conditions that support the claim that brand happiness is an autonomous brand goal were assessed. These empirical findings should encourage brand managers to create brands and brand experiences that make consumers happy.

Brand happiness is conceptualized as a short-term emotional state comprising four factors: joy, vigor, pride and serenity (Schnebelen & Bruhn, 2016). It positively influences purchase intention and word-of-mouth behavior, highlighting its importance for brand success. The research findings just presented have been developed on the premise that brand happiness differs conceptually from related constructs, such as affective-relational constructs (emotional brand loyalty, customer enthusiasm, brand love and brand relationship quality) and cognitive-evaluative constructs (brand satisfaction, brand attitude, brand experience and brand involvement) and can, therefore, in the presence of dominant effects on consumption-relevant behavior, take on the claim of a dominant marketing objective in the sense of the 'holy grail'.

At a conceptual level, brand happiness has many references and similarities with other key constructs in connection with brands. For example, there is a similarity to related constructs such as brand satisfaction or emotional brand attachment. A differentiation of brand happiness from these constructs and a clear definition is therefore necessary. If one compares brand happiness as a pleasant emotional experience that varies in intensity between high and low arousal with customer delight, then the latter is only an intense, highly aroused positive emotional reaction that includes joy and surprise (Oliver et al., 1997). Furthermore, emotional brand loyalty differs from brand happiness in its relationship-orientated character. Emotional brand loyalty describes the experience of relational emotions that are moderately positively aroused (affection, passion, connection; Thomson et al., 2005). Brand love and brand relationship quality are partly affective and also capture affective aspects more in terms of the emotional quality of relationships with brands (Batra et al., 2012; Fournier, 1998). They are therefore also less emotional themselves, but rather relational in nature. While brand happiness is a short-term emotional state that can arise unexpectedly at various brand contact points during or immediately after contact with a brand

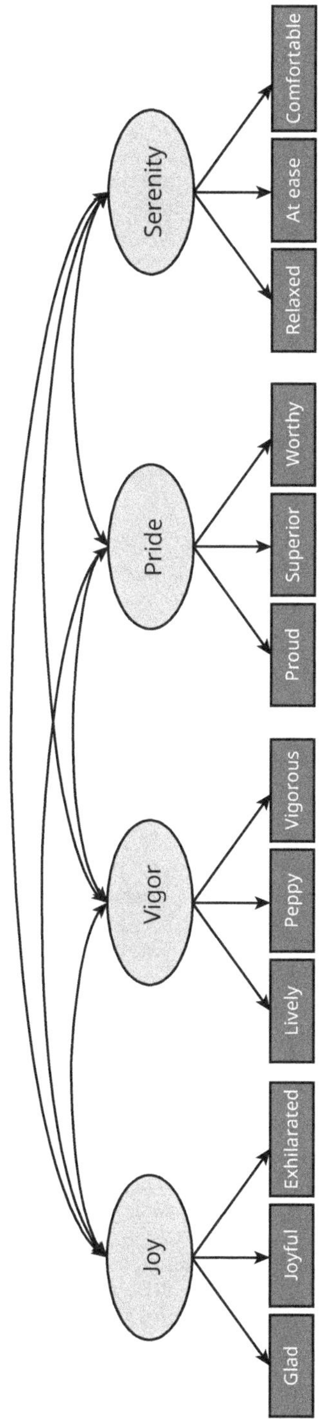

Figure 33.1 Measurement model of brand happiness

Source: Bruhn & Schnebelen, 2017, p. 476.

(e.g., through purchases, consumption or advertising), emotional brand loyalty, brand love and the quality of the brand relationship are constructs that tend to develop over time through experience with the brand (Batra et al., 2012; Fournier, 1998; Palusuk et al., 2019; Thomson et al., 2005). They are therefore characterized as more long-term and less situation-dependent than brand happiness.

DETERMINANTS AND CONSEQUENCES OF BRAND HAPPINESS

To document evidence for the effectiveness of brand happiness and its superior position in brand management and thus provide significant new findings in this field of research, Schnebelen and Bruhn theoretically develop an evaluation framework for the determinants and consequences of brand happiness. This evaluation framework was empirically tested in Germany in four different industries, consumer electronics, groceries, textiles and cosmetics (Schnebelen & Bruhn, 2018).

The authors identified several factors that influence brand happiness. These factors can be divided into two main categories: brand-related appraisal determinants, which relate to the characteristics and perception of the brand itself and situational appraisal determinants, which comprise factors concerning external circumstances or situations in which the consumer interacts with the brand. Brand appraisals were found to be more important predictors of brand happiness than situational appraisals.

At a cross-industry level, four brand-related determinants were identified as being important evaluation determinants of brand happiness:

- Brand relationship quality describes the strengths and intensity between a brand and its consumers. A strong and positive bond leads to higher brand happiness.
- Brand self-relevance characterizes the importance of the brand in a consumer's life. The stronger the alignment of a brand with the personal needs and objectives of a consumer, the greater the brand happiness.
- Brand goal congruence describes the fit between the goals of the brand with those of the consumers. If brand goals align with consumer's goals, brand happiness increases.
- Actual and ideal brand self-congruence describes the match between the consumer's self (how the consumer actually perceives or would like to perceive, him- or herself) and brand personality. When a brand matches the consumer's self-image, a strong positive emotional connection develops.

In addition, three further situational evaluation determinants were identified as important determinants of brand happiness: pleasantness and fairness, showing that pleasant experiences with a brand and the perception of brands as being fair and just, lead to brand happiness; and, finally, certainty as an enhancement factor of brand happiness, resulting from the perception that the brand offering is reliable and thus conveying security to the customer.

The fact that brand happiness can strongly predict five coping strategies concerning brand consumption confirms the behavioral relevance of brand happiness. These five strategies are distinguished by Schnebelen & Bruhn as problem-related and emotional-related strategies.

- Problem-related coping strategies relate to the (re)purchase intention and the willingness to pay a price premium. Consumers who experience brand happiness tend to be more likely to repurchase a brand and accept higher prices as they are emotionally attached to the brand.
- Emotion-related coping strategies refer to the recommendation behavior in the sense of the positive word of mouth, brand evangelism, and brand forgiveness. Consumers who are happy with a brand like to share their positive experiences with others. They often function as 'brand ambassadors', actively promoting the brand, and are more likely to forgive mistakes or disappointments they have experienced with the brand, which, in general, make them happy.

By applying appraisal theory, which assumes that emotions evoke a readiness to act in consumers (Roseman, 2013; Soscia, 2007), and by developing an appraisal framework that identifies internal and external conditions influencing brand happiness, as well as different brand-related behavior patterns arising from brand happiness (see Figure 33.2), the authors significantly expand the understanding of this concept.

The research shows that brand happiness is affected by brand perceptions and situational factors. At an industry-specific level, differences were observed in the influence of certain appraisal determinants on brand happiness, as well as in the influence of situational appraisal determinants on brand happiness across the four industries analyzed.

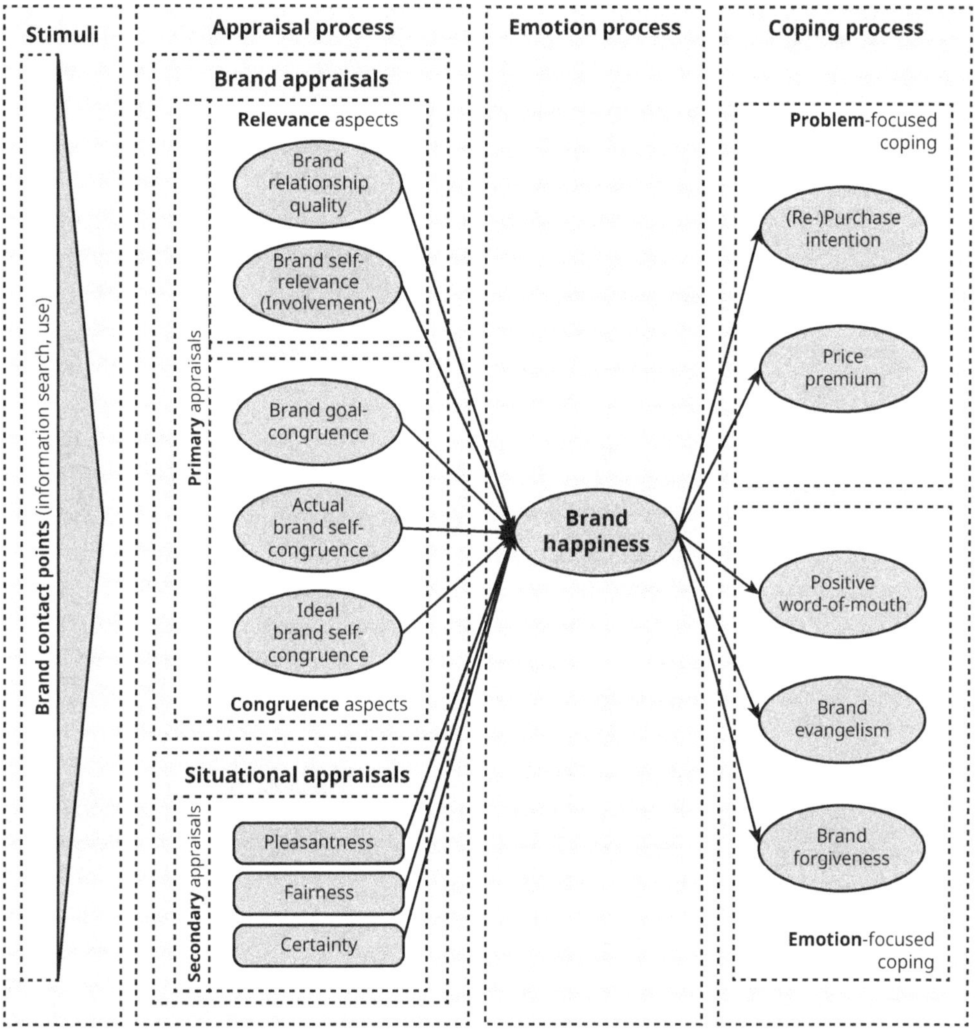

Figure 33.2 Appraisal framework of brand happiness

Source: Schnebelen & Bruhn, 2018, p. 105.

Industry-specific characteristics of brands must be considered when working on brand happiness (Schnebelen & Bruhn, 2018, p. 111). Therefore, it is recommended to conduct further industry-specific research to assist brand management in developing tailored strategies for brand happiness, taking into account the type and context of their brand and, thereby, further substantiating the previous research findings.

In this context, cultural aspects should be taken into consideration as they also influence the way consumers experience and express brand happiness. For example, in collectivist cultures such as China, social harmony and relating to others may play a greater role, while in individualistic cultures, personal happiness and pride are more emphasized. In addition, cultural involvement in different brand types can influence consumers' willingness to pay a price premium, with brand happiness playing a mediating role. This means that cultural differences not only influence the perception of the brand and the experience of brand happiness, but also affect purchase behavior and brand loyalty (Zhou et al., 2024).

RECENT EMPIRICAL FINDINGS ON THE EFFECTS OF BRAND HAPPINESS

Research on happiness in marketing and consumer research has mainly focused on purchase and consumption situations. As scientific research on brand happiness has only been conducted for a few years, there are yet few statements on the industry-specific or long-term effects of brand happiness. In summary, however, existing research studies show that brand happiness is an independent construct that positively influences consumer behavior, particularly regarding purchase intention, willingness to pay and positive word-of-mouth in the sense of brand recommendations.

Since the comprehensive conceptual and empirical work on brand happiness at the University of Basel, research on the topic has intensified considerably. In the following section, various recently conducted empirical studies on brand happiness in product and service contexts will be presented, covering different countries and industries (see Table 33.1).

The table provides an overview of relevant studies on brand happiness that have been conducted recently. It includes 16 different studies and systematically presents various conceptualizations, theoretical foundations, methodological approaches, key findings and implications for both practice and science.

When taking a closer look at the research studies, the concept of masstige consumption turns up – a combination of mass consumption and prestige (Paul, 2018). It becomes apparent that brand happiness has been investigated in recent years often in connection with masstige brands (Fridian & Burhanudin, 2023; Kumar et al., 2021; Mansoor & Paul, 2022; Nobre et al., 2023; Purohit et al., 2024). Mansoor and Paul (2022), for example, examined in their study the role of brand happiness as a mediator. They analyzed the direct and indirect impacts of a brand's mass prestige, brand perception and the propensity to pay a price premium on brand evangelism via brand happiness as a mediator. In two independent studies in the cosmetic and clothing industry, they could show that consumer's self-pleasing experience has a moderating role between mass prestige and brand happiness. Self-pleasing experience is regarded as a catalyst for extending brand happiness in consumers, moderating product beliefs and motivating to evangelize others to buy or use prestigious brands.

An obvious association with the topic of brand happiness arises in relation to the luxury goods industry. The mere ownership of luxury goods can immediately produce a feeling of pleasure and generate hedonic value for the consumer. When working hard for a luxury product or service, a more calculated hedonic benefit through self-gratification is generated, in contrast to a luxury brand that focuses on sustainability (for further insights see Quintal & Cheah, 2024). It is, therefore, not surprising that studies on brand happiness can currently be found in the luxury goods industry. What is surprising, however, is that some of the studies barely conceptualize the construct of brand happiness. The research focuses on the relationship between masstige branding and brand happiness (e.g., Nobre et al., 2023; Purohit et al., 2024).

Further interesting findings can be observed in the context of brand happiness and sustainability (e.g., Gilal et al., 2024; Han et al., 2018; Khandai et al., 2024). The study of Khandai et al. (2024), for example, explores the psychological and behavioral effects of consuming sustainable brands, particularly how such choices influence consumer happiness and lead to brand evangelism. Rooted in the self-perception theory, which suggests individuals infer attitudes based on their behavior, the research examines whether buying eco-friendly products makes people feel happier and more inclined to advocate for the brands. The authors focus on skincare brands in India and use a survey across three generational cohorts (Gen X to Z) in order to analyze patterns. The study proposes that consuming sustainable products evokes a sense of moral satisfaction and emotional well-being – termed 'brand happiness'. The findings indicate that sustainable consumption indeed leads to happiness, which subsequently increases the intent to repurchase and advocate for the brand. The study also highlights generational differences. While all cohorts (Gen X, Y, Z) show some degree of connection between happiness and evangelism, Gen Z demonstrates the strongest correlation. These younger consumers are more emotionally engaged with sustainable brands and more likely to act as passionate promoters, likely due to higher environmental awareness and value alignment.

Matsubara (2024) selected 38 articles for analysis, more than half of these were published within the last 4 years, demonstrating the increasing interest in the relationship between brands and consumer happiness. The variety of purposes, research scopes, contexts and methodological approaches gives hope for further interesting insights into brand happiness. Recent literature reviews show the increasing relevance of brand happiness in the last few years.

RESULTS AND IMPLICATIONS FOR MANAGEMENT

In her conceptual work, which stands up to subsequent empirical testing, Schnebelen (2015) and Bruhn and Schnebelen (2017) conclude that

Table 33.1 Research studies on brand happiness

Source	*Purpose*	*Conceptualization/ Definition of Brand Happiness*	*Theoretical Foundation*	*Context/Sector*	*Methodology*	*Findings*	*Implications*	*Limitations/Further Research*
Banerjee et al. (2024)	To examine how online retail website experience influences brand happiness and consumers' willingness to share personal information	A consumer's emotional and psychological well-being associated with interactions with a brand	Stimulus-Organism-Response - Framework	Online retail	Survey, structural equation modeling	Positive website experiences increase brand happiness, leading to greater willingness to share personal information	Retailers should optimize website design and user experience to enhance brand happiness	Future research could explore different product categories and cultural influences
Gilal et al. (2024)	To explore the impact of relatedness-supportive CSR on brand happiness	Defined through Relationship Motivation Theory as a consumer's sense of well-being derived from brand-related CSR activities	Relationship Motivation Theory	Retail banking	Survey-based study using structural equation modeling	CSR initiatives that support relatedness enhance brand happiness, which in turn strengthens customer loyalty	Firms should design CSR initiatives that foster consumer relationships to boost brand happiness	Study limited to the banking sector; future research should expand to other industries
Khandai et al. (2024)	To investigate the relationship between green consumption choices and brand happiness	Consumer well-being linked to environmentally sustainable brand choices	Self-perception Theory	Sustainable product consumption	Survey-based quantitative research	Consumers who engage in green choices experience increased brand happiness, leading to stronger brand advocacy	Brands should emphasize sustainability and environmental responsibility to enhance consumer happiness	Further exploration needed in different cultural contexts and product categories
Matsubara (2024)	To analyze conceptual issues in brand happiness research and examine antecedents and consequences	An evaluative and affective response towards a brand	A multidisciplinary approach including consumer psychology	General branding context	Conceptual analysis and review of existing studies	Brand happiness is influenced by brand trust, emotional engagement, and perceived value	Firms should integrate emotional branding strategies to enhance consumer happiness	Need for empirical validation across diverse industries

(Continued)

Table 33.1 (Continued)

Source	*Purpose*	*Conceptualization/ Definition of Brand Happiness*	*Theoretical Foundation*	*Context/Sector*	*Methodology*	*Findings*	*Implications*	*Limitations/Further Research*
Nobi (2024)	To explore the role of co-creation in shaping brand happiness from a Korean market perspective	The emotional well-being of consumers engaging in brand co-creation	Co-creation and consumer engagement	Korean consumer market and co-creation branding	Survey-based research with consumer engagement data	Co-creation activities positively impact brand happiness and customer loyalty	Brands should involve consumers in the creative process to strengthen emotional connections	More cross-cultural studies needed to validate findings in other markets
Purohit et al. (2024)	To examine how masstige consumption affects brand happiness and advocacy	The pleasure derived from consuming mass prestige products	Masstige Theory	Luxury and masstige branding	Survey-based research analyzed through structural modeling	Masstige consumption enhances brand happiness, increasing brand advocacy	Brands should balance exclusivity and accessibility to maximize brand happiness	Need to explore long-term effects and cross-cultural validation
Dhiman and Kumar (2023)	To review three decades of research on consumer happiness and propose future research directions	A component of consumer happiness, which involves well-being and satisfaction derived from brand interactions	...	General consumer markets	Systematic literature review	Consumer happiness is segregated across three themes: marketing beyond satisfaction, marketing for health and mind, and digital felicity	Future research should explore how digital interactions shape brand happiness	Limited empirical validation; more longitudinal studies needed
Fridian and Burhanudin (2023)	To analyze how social comparison orientation influences brand happiness and attitudinal loyalty	A consumer's positive affect and satisfaction with a brand	Social Comparison Orientation	Masstige brand consumption	Survey-based empirical study	Social comparison orientation significantly impacts brand happiness and purchase intentions	Masstige brands should leverage social identity elements to enhance brand happiness	Findings may vary by cultural and demographic factors
Nobre et al. (2023)	To examine the relationship between mass prestige brands and consumer happiness	Happiness derived from consuming and associating with mass prestige brands	Masstige Theory	Luxury and mass prestige branding	Quantitative analysis using consumer surveys	The prestige associated with brands induces consumers to formulate relationships with those brands and brands' masstige helps them achieve brand happiness	Brands should align masstige positioning with consumer self-concept	Additional studies needed on emotional branding impact

(Continued)

Table 33.1 (Continued)

Source	*Purpose*	*Conceptualization/ Definition of Brand Happiness*	*Theoretical Foundation*	*Context/Sector*	*Methodology*	*Findings*	*Implications*	*Limitations/Further Research*
Sousa et al. (2023)	To conduct a systematic literature review on masstige and brand happiness	Synthesized from prior studies as the emotional response to masstige brands	…	Masstige branding	Literature review with qualitative synthesis	Identifies key research themes related to brand happiness and masstige: feelings of happiness, luxury and consumption	Encourages integration of hedonic and functional brand values	More empirical studies needed on masstige-brand happiness links
Mansoor and Paul (2022)	To investigate how mass prestige branding influences brand happiness and evangelism	A consumer's response to brand prestige	Masstige Theory	Mass prestige and consumer branding	Empirical study with consumer data	Mass prestige enhances brand happiness, leading to higher brand advocacy	Brands should create accessible prestige elements	More cross-cultural validation needed
Razmus et al. (2022)	To examine the role of brand engagement in self-concept (BESC) in moderating the relationship between purchase type (material vs. experiential) and purchase-related happiness	Purchase-related happiness is influenced by the extent to which consumers integrate brands into their self-concept (BESC)	Social Exchange Theory	Retail and consumer goods	Comparative survey, experiments, structural equation modelling	Consumers with low BESC experience more happiness from experiential than material purchases. Consumers with high BESC derive similar happiness from both purchase types.	Marketers should emphasize brand relationships, especially for material purchases	Future research should examine how brand engagement influences purchase happiness across different brand categories and luxury vs. non-luxury products
Kumar et al. (2021)	To examine whether brands contribute to consumer happiness from a masstige theory perspective	Brand happiness is linked to the joy and satisfaction derived from interacting with masstige brands	Masstige Theory	Retail and consumer goods	Survey-based quantitative research using structural equation modeling	Consumers experience brand happiness when masstige brands balance prestige and accessibility	Brands should optimize their masstige positioning to enhance consumer happiness	Further research needed on long-term brand happiness effects

(*Continued*)

Table 33.1 (Continued)

Source	*Purpose*	*Conceptualization/ Definition of Brand Happiness*	*Theoretical Foundation*	*Context/Sector*	*Methodology*	*Findings*	*Implications*	*Limitations/Further Research*
Li (2021)	To analyze how companies can gain brand advocates by fostering brand happiness	The emotional connection between consumers and brands, influencing loyalty	Consumer–brand relationship theory	General branding and marketing	Conceptual analysis with case examples	Happy consumers are more likely to advocate for brands	Companies should focus on emotional branding strategies	Lack of empirical validation; future research should test hypotheses
Gutiérrez-Villar et al. (2019)	To examine the relationship between happiness indices and consumer perception of brand well-being contributions	Linked to subjective well-being and how consumers perceive brands as contributors to happiness	...	Global consumer perception and branding	Analysis of happiness indices (HPI and WHR) and their relation to brand perception	Brands are often associated with subjective well-being, and consumers evaluate brands based on their contribution to happiness	Marketers should align brand messaging with well-being concepts to enhance consumer perception	No unified measure of happiness currently exists; future studies could develop a more holistic framework
Niedermeier et al. (2018)	To propose a conceptual framework of customer happiness in brand communities and analyze the effect of customer engagement on customer happiness, as well as its impact on word-of-mouth and purchase intentions	A specific form of happiness that consists of customer satisfaction, customer delight, and customer harmony	Flow Theory, Self-Determination Theory, Engagement Theory	Online brand community for a German automotive brand	Survey-based empirical study using structural equation modelling	Both active and passive customer engagement positively influence customer happiness. Customer happiness significantly enhances word-of-mouth and purchase intentions.	Brands should invest in community-building initiatives to increase customer engagement	Further studies across different industries, longitudinal studies, experimental research.

Source: The authors.

brand happiness is a valid and reliable construct, representing a short-term emotional state comprising the factors of joy, vigor, pride and serenity. The developed brand happiness scale, on which the empirical work is based, proves to be stable across different brands and cultures, differs from other related constructs and is superior to them in predicting purchase intention, price premium and word-of-mouth.

Against this background, it is astonishing that the goal of brand happiness still has received relatively little attention in marketing and consumer research to date and that it does not occupy a leading position in the hierarchy of brand goals in brand management. As the 'holy grail' of marketing, it is not only one of the top goals that consumers strive for when dealing with brands but also the ultimate brand goal that marketers should try to achieve in order to ensure a long, eternal life for their brand.

In terms of the practical application of the findings on brand happiness, the following trends are worth discussing for brand managers. A significant trend in brand happiness is the focus on building strong emotional connections with consumers. Brands are increasingly designed as personalized experiences, engaging the consumer as an individual and thus adding a personal relation between the consumer and the brand. Individual brand marketing approaches, utilizing technology and artificial intelligence (AI), as well as experimental brand investments such as events, immersive experiences or interactive campaigns that create memorable and sustainable experiences, are within scope. Furthermore, community building around brands must also be considered, as it fosters a sense of belonging and, consequently, emotional and social bonding. Brands that are authentic and transparent about their values, practices and social as well as environmental impact, are likely to establish stronger emotional bonds with customers. Transparency and authenticity create trust, which is considered a relevant ingredient of happiness. Today, the expectation of transparency also includes, above all, the assumption of social and ecological responsibility within society.

Demonstrating and showing commitment to environmental and social questions aligns with the growing awareness of these global issues, having the potential to strive as a brand in 2025, as mentioned by Baron in January's *Forbes Magazine*. This compact selection of trends highlights strategies that brands can employ to establish deeper and more meaningful connections with their consumers. By staying attuned to these trends, brands can better address the emotional and psychological needs of their consumers, leading to greater loyalty and, consequently, economic success through brand happiness.

FUTURE RESEARCH

Research on the topic of brand happiness is still in its infancy in relation to its potential significance for sustainable brand success. Researchers are therefore faced with numerous open questions relating to the construct of brand happiness itself and its stability in different market and application contexts. The significance of brand happiness in intercultural and generational contexts and in the light of current consumer demands with regard to sustainability are also of interest for further research.

Up until today, no unified measure of brand happiness exists. A central task for future research will be to develop a more universally valid definition and conceptualization of brand happiness based on diverse studies across different contexts, providing a more holistic framework for brand happiness. According to his bibliographical analysis of brand happiness, the inconsistent conceptualization of the brand happiness construct, including its inadequate conceptualization in various studies, was noted (Matsubara, 2024). He refers to the difference between eudaimonic and hedonic happiness and therefore recommends that future research clarify the conceptual scope of happiness in relation to these two different approaches. Research should distinguish between short-term emotional happiness (rather than the hedonic approach) and long-term brand happiness, which relates to psychological well-being (eudaimonic approach). Differences in brand happiness between branded and non-branded, luxury and non-luxury, as well as long- and short-life products can provide valuable insights into the concept of brand happiness, enabling brand management to develop targeted brand-related activities.

Additionally, investigating different types of brands and consumption experiences can enrich the knowledge base. Empirical validation of the concept of brand happiness across diverse industries, involving different cultural and demographic aspects, is needed. Beyond quantitative studies, qualitative approaches such as consumer observations can provide deeper insights into the phenomenon of brand-induced happiness. Furthermore, future research on brand happiness should encompass more specific aspects of the service industry, for example, the impact of personal interaction, cocreation with consumers, the impact and role of employees at the service front on brand happiness, and the potential to personalize services with AI, thereby augmenting brand happiness. How brand happiness interacts in a long-term perspective with brand value and consumer happiness has not yet been adequately explored and clarified. Brand happiness is supposed to extend the life cycle of products and services, thereby contributing to a brand's vitality. However, no research to date has provided evidence of these long-term effects. A closer look at brands with a history of several decades could provide further insight into this question.

Considering that the generational aspect appears to be a promising avenue for research on brand happiness. While younger generations are the focus of research, the economic potential of senior age groups has not yet been sufficiently examined. Further analyzing the determinants of brand happiness, the effects and connected behavior patterns among different generations, taking into consideration different types of touch points [like, e.g., the study of Lyroni & Spais (2024)] did by examining the impact of digital platforms in generations Y and Z, can ensure a better understanding of the differences in the determinants and effects of brand happiness between generations. This knowledge can help develop generation-specific strategies to enhance brand happiness as a strategic goal in brand management. Understanding the use and impact of different digital channels, as Banerjee et al. (2024) found regarding experiences with online retail websites and their effect on sharing personal information with providers, can be very helpful for online businesses.

The research conducted at the University of Basel shows that brand happiness is a valid and reliable construct that is superior to the related brand-related constructs in terms of influencing willingness to buy, acceptance of a price premium, and word-of-mouth communication. The positive short-term effect on brand management, from both the company and consumer perspectives, is thus proven. Whether and how the happiness derived from brand consumption can contribute to general satisfaction and happiness in life still needs to be investigated. In particular, issues related to the consumption of ecologically and/or socially sustainable brands could raise exciting new research questions, especially in light of the global necessity and importance of sustainable development.

So far, research on brand happiness has only emphasized its positive effects on both consumers' and companies' side. Science must also question whether brand happiness can have harmful effects or negative impacts that may arise over time, both on an individual and a societal level. Here, the research so far is one-sided and biased.

REFERENCES

Aziz, R., & Rahman, Z. (2022). Brand hate: A literature review and future research agenda. *European Journal of Marketing*, *56*(7), 2014–2051. https://doi.org/10.1108/EJM-03-2021-0189

Banerjee, S., Shaikh, A., & Sharma, A. (2024). The role of online retail website experience on brand happiness and willingness to share personal information: An SOR perspective. *Marketing Intelligence & Planning*, *42*(3), 553–575. https://doi.org/10.1108/MIP-08-2023-0413

Baron, K. (2025, January 6). How brands can thrive in 2025: 9 trends and strategies for the year ahead (online).

Batra, R., Ahuvia, A., & Bagozzi, R. P. (2012). Brand love. *Journal of Marketing*, *76*(2), 1–16. https://doi.org/10.1509/jm.09.0339

Becker, F. (2010, June). Die Macht der Emotionen. *Harvard Business Manager* (online).

Bettingen, J.-F., & Luedicke, M. K. (2009). Can brands make us happy? A research framework for the study of brands and their effects on happiness. *Advances in Consumer Research*, *36*, 308–315.

Bruhn, M., & Schnebelen, S. (2017). Brand happiness: The searching and finding of the 'Holy Grail' of marketing. *Die Unternehmung*, *71*(4), 464–490. https://doi.org/10.5771/0042-059X-2017-4-464

Chang, C. (2014). Guilt regulation: The relative effects of altruistic versus egoistic appeals for charity advertising. *Journal of Advertising*, *43*(3), 211–227. https://doi.org/10.1080/00913367.2013.853632

Chawla, U., & Chattopadhyay, S. (2023). Brand hatred: A literature review and research agenda. *International Journal of Professional Business Review*, *8*(3), 1–23.

Clark, A. E., Flèche, S., Layard, R., Powdthavee, N., & Ward, G. (2017). The key determinants of happiness and misery. CEP discussion paper 1485, center of economic performance. London School of Economics and Political Science.

Clark, A. E., Flèche, S., Layard, R., Powdthavee, N., & Ward, G. (2018). The origins of happiness. Princeton University Press.

Delle Fave, A., Brdar, I., Freire, T., Vella-Brodrick, D., & Wissing, M. P. (2011). The eudaimonic and hedonic components of happiness: Qualitative and quantitative findings. *Social Indicators Research*, *100*(2), 185–207. https://doi.org/10.1007/s11205-010-9632-5

Dhiman, N., & Kumar, A. (2022). What we know and don't know about consumer happiness: Three-decade review, synthesis, and research propositions. *Journal of Interactive Marketing*, *58*(2/3), 115–135.

Fournier, S. (1998). Consumers and their brands: Developing relationship theory in consumer research. *Journal of Consumer Research*, *24*(4), 343–353. https://doi.org/10.1086/209515

Fournier, S., Breazeale, M., & Fetscherin, M. (2012). *Consumer-brand relationships: Theory and practice*. Routledge.

Frawley, A. (2015). *Happiness research*: A review of critiques. *Sociology Compass*, *9*(1), 62–77. https://doi.org/10.1111/soc4.12236

Fridian, R. T., & Burhanudin, B. (2023). The influence of social comparison orientation on attitudinal loyalty, brand happiness, and willingness to purchase a masstige brand. *Jurnal Manajemen dan Kewirausahaan*, *11*(2), 203–211. https://doi.org/10.26905/jmdk.v11i2.10501

Gelbrich, K. (2011). I have paid less than you! The emotional and behavioral consequences of advantaged price inequality. *Journal of Retailing*, *87*(2), 207–224. https://doi.org/10.1016/j.jretai.2011.03.003

Gilal, F. G., Gilal, N. G., Gilal, R. G., & Yang, Z. (2024). How relatedness-supportive CSR enhances brand happiness: A relationship motivation theory perspective. *International Journal of Bank Marketing*, *42*(2), 226–257. https://doi.org/10.1108/IJBM-06-2022-0225

Goldberg, M. E., & Gorn, G. J. (1987). Happy and sad TV programs: How they affect reactions to commercials. *Journal of Consumer Research*, *14*(3), 387–403. https://doi.org/10.1086/209122

Gumparthi, V. P., & Patra, S. (2019). The phenomenon of brand love: A systematic literature review. *Journal of Relationship Marketing*, *19*(2), 93–132. https://doi.org/10.1080/15332667.2019.1664871

Gutiérrez-Villar, B., Castro-González, P., Melero-Bolaños, R., & Carbonero-Ruz, M. (2019). Branding and the happiness formula. In J. A. Muñiz-Velázquez, & C. M. Pulido (Eds.), *The routledge handbook of positive communication: Contributions of an emerging community of research on communication for happiness and social change* (pp. 192–201). Routledge.

Han, J., Jun, M., Kim, M., & Key, S. (2018). Influence of congruency between ideal self and brand image on sustainable happiness. *Sustainability*, *10*(11), 4076. https://doi.org/10.3390/su10114076

Hellén, K., & Sääksjärvi, M. (2011). Happiness as a predictor of service quality and commitment for utilitarian and hedonic services. *Psychology & Marketing*, *28*(9), 934–957. https://doi.org/10.1002/mar.20420

Jain, M., Sharma, G. D., & Mahendru, M. (2019). Can I sustain my happiness? A review, critique and research agenda for economics of happiness. *Sustainability*, *11*(22), 6375. https://doi.org/10.3390/su11226375

Khandai, S., Kataria, S., Kohli, H. S., Yadav, R., & Mathew, J. (2024). Green choices and brand happiness: A recipe for brand evangelism. *Sustainable Development*, *33*(2), 1–16. https://doi.org/10.1002/sd.3237

Knaur, H., & Verma, H. (2024). Brand pride: Concept and measurement. *Journal of Product and Brand Management*, *33*(6), 668–683. https://doi.org/10.1108/JPBM-06-2023-4555

Kumar, A., Paul, J., & Starčević, S. (2021). Do brands make consumers happy? A masstige theory perspective. *Journal of Retailing and Consumer Services*, *58*, 102318. https://doi.org/10.1016/j.jretconser.2020.102318

Labroo, A. A., & Rucker, D. D. (2010). The orientation-matching hypothesis: An emotion-specificity approach to affect regulation. *Journal of Marketing Research*, *47*(5), 955–966. https://doi.org/10.1509/jmkr.47.5.955

Li, M. (2021). Gain company fans by building brand happiness. *International Journal of Trend in Research and Development*, *8*(6), 30–31.

Lyroni, C., & Spais, G. (2024). Consumer (brand) happiness of premium fashion brands and value consciousness: The case of clothing and footwear for Gen X and Gen Z as shoppers via digital platforms. *Journal of Marketing Analytics*, *8*(14), 1–30.

Mansoor, M., & Paul, J. (2022). Mass prestige, brand happiness and brand evangelism among consumers. *Journal of Business Research*, *144*, 484–496. https://doi.org/10.1016/j.jbusres.2022.02.015

Matsubara, Y. (2024). Happiness and well-being of consumers in brand research. *Japan Marketing Journal*, *44*(1), 68–75 [Japanese article, translated with ChatGPT Pro]. https://doi.org/10.7222/marketing.2024.032

Maurya, U. K., & Mishra, P. (2012). What is a brand? A perspective on brand meaning. *European Journal of Business and Management*, *4*(3), 122–134.

Mogilner, C., Aaker, J., & Kamvar, S. D. (2012). How happiness affects choice. *Journal of Consumer Research*, *39*(2), 429–443. https://doi.org/10.1086/663774

Nicolao, L., Irwin, J. R., & Goodman, J. K. (2009). Happiness for sale: Does experiential purchases make consumers happier than material purchases? *Journal of Consumer Research*, *36*(2), 188–198. https://doi.org/10.1086/597049

Niedermeier, A., Albrecht, L., & Jahn, B. (2018). 'Happy Together': Effects of brand community engagement on customer happiness. *Journal of Relationship Marketing*, *18*(19), 54–76.

Nobi, B. (2024). Co-creation and brand happiness: Insights from a Korean perspective. *Journal of Consumer Marketing*, *41*(5), 540–548. https://doi.org/10.1108/JCM-08-2023-6185

Nobre, H., Kumar, A., Kastanakis, M. N., & Paul, J. (2023). Consumers' relationship with mass prestige brands and happiness. *European Management Review*, *20*(2), 306–325. https://doi.org/10.1111/emre.12538

Oliver, R. L., Rust, R. T., & Varki, S. (1997). Customer delight: Foundations, findings, and managerial insight. *Journal of Retailing*, *73*(3), 311–336. https://doi.org/10.1016/S0022-4359(97)90021-X

Palusuk, N., Koles, B., & Hasan, R. (2019). 'All you need is brand love': A critical review and comprehensive conceptual framework for brand love. *Journal of Marketing Management*, *35*(1–2), 97–129. https://doi.org/10.1080/0267257X.2019.1572025

Paul, J. (2018). Toward a «Masstige» theory and strategy for marketing. *European Journal of International Management*, *12*(5/6), 722–745.

Pavot, W., & Diener, E. (2013). *Happiness experienced*: The science of subjective well-being. In S. A. David, I. Boniwell, & A. C. Ayers (Eds.), *Oxford handbook of happiness* (pp. 134–154). Oxford University Press.

Purohit, S., Arora, V., & Radia, K. N. (2024). Masstige consumption, brand happiness, and brand advocacy: A service perspective. *International Journal of Consumer Studies*, *48*(1), 1–15. https://doi.org/10.1111/ijcs.12944

Quintal, V., & Cheah, I. (2024). Introduction to a special section on branding, buyer choices and the pursuit of happiness in luxury fashion consumption. *Journal of Global Fashion Marketing*, *15*(4), 417–421. https://doi.org/10.1080/20932685.2024.2388040

Razmus, W., Grabner-Kräuter, S., Kostyra, M., & Zawadzka, A. M. (2022). Buying happiness: How brand engagement in self-concept affects purchase happiness. *Psychology & Marketing*, *39*(119), 2096–2109. https://doi.org/10.1002/mar.21714

Roseman, I. J. (2013). Appraisal in the emotion system: Coherence in strategies for coping. *Emotion Review*, *5*(2), 141–149. https://doi.org/10.1177/1754073912469591

Roy, S. K., Sharma, A., Bose, S., & Singh, G. (2022). Consumer - brand relationship: A brand hate perspective. *Journal of Business Research*, *144*, 1293–1304. https://doi.org/10.1016/j.jbusres.2022.02.065

Schnebelen, S. (2015). *Brand happiness – conceptual, theoretical, and empirical investigations of a promising new branding asset* [*Doctoral dissertation*]. University of Basel.

Schnebelen, S., & Bruhn, M. (2016). Brands can make consumers happy! Development of a scale to measure brand happiness. In M. Obal, N. Krey, & C. Bushardt (Eds.), *Let's get engaged! crossing the threshold of marketing's engagement era. Developments in marketing science: Proceedings of the academy of marketing science* (pp. 341–342). Springer.

Schnebelen, S., & Bruhn, M. (2018). An appraisal framework of the determinants and consequences of brand happiness. *Psychology & Marketing*, *35*(2), 101–119. https://doi.org/10.1002/mar.21073

Soscia, I. (2007). Gratitude, delight, or guilt: The role of consumers' emotions in predicting post consumption behaviors. *Psychology & Marketing*, *24*(10), 871–894. https://doi.org/10.1002/mar.20188

Sousa, A., Madeira, C., & Rodrigues, P. (2023, September 27–29). A systematic literature review and research agenda of masstige and brand happiness. In *16th annual conference of the EuroMed academy of business*, Vilnius, Lithuania (p. 1119).

Thomson, M., MacInnis, D. J., & Park, C. W. (2005). The ties that bind: Measuring the strength of consumers' emotional attachments to brands. *Journal of Consumer Psychology*, *15*(1), 77–91. https://doi.org/10.1207/s15327663jcp1501_10

Tkach, C., & Lyubomirsky, S. (2006). How do people pursue happiness? Relating personality, happiness-increasing strategies, and well-being. *Journal of Happiness Studies*, *7*(2), 183–225. https://doi.org/10.1007/s10902-005-4754-1

Van Boven, L., & Gilovich, T. (2003). To do or to have? That is the question. *Journal of Personality and Social Psychology*, *85*(6), 1193–1202. https://doi.org/10.1037/0022-3514.85.6.1193

Veenhoven, R. (2012a). *Happiness*: Also known as 'life satisfaction' and 'subjective well-being'. In K. C. Land, A. C. Michalos, & M. J. Sirgy (Eds.), *Handbook of social indicators and quality of life research* (pp. 63–77). Springer Science & Business Media.

Veenhoven, R. (2012b). Does happiness differ across cultures? In H. Selin, & G. Davey (Eds.), *Happiness across cultures: Views of happiness and quality of life in non-western cultures* (pp. 451–472). Springer Science & Business Media.

Yadav, A., & Chakrabart, S. (2023). Brand hate: A systematic literature review and future research agenda. *International Journal of Consumer Studies*. https://doi.org/10.1111/ijcs.12772

Zhou, Z., He, Y., Xie, Y., & Mehmood, S. (2024). How cultural involvement in different brand types influences willingness to pay premium: The mediating role of brand happiness. *Behavioral Sciences*, *14*(10), 908. https://doi.org/10.3390/bs14100908

34

Technology-Augmented Brand Management

Saleh Bazi

INTRODUCTION

The way companies manage and grow their brands has been completely revolutionized by the digital transformation of business. With more and more consumers turning to digital channels to interact with brands. Statista (2024) reports that 85% of consumers now research online before buying something), organizations are under immense pressure to incorporate technology into how they handle their brands. This has made technology-augmented brand management a necessity, marking a fundamental change in how businesses conceive, execute and evaluate their brand development initiatives. Global spending on digital transformation is projected to reach $4 trillion by 2026 (IDC, 2024), with brand management technology comprising a significant portion of this investment. Organizations are responding to changing consumer expectations, with 76% of consumers expecting consistent interactions across departments and 67% willing to pay more for a great experience (Salesforce, 2024). However, this technological revolution presents significant challenges, particularly regarding bias and discrimination (Goglin, 2023), asserts the ethical complexities of technology adoption. This digital transformation of brand management is not merely an operational upgrade but a strategic necessity for maintaining a competitive advantage in an increasingly digital marketplace.

The convergence of artificial intelligence (AI), big data analytics and digital platforms has created new possibilities for brand management. Organizations now process unprecedented volumes of brand-related data, with leading companies analyzing over 50 million customer touchpoints daily to inform their brand strategies. However, this technological augmentation brings both opportunities and challenges. While 89% of companies compete primarily on customer experience, only 26% have successfully implemented technology-driven brand management systems (McKinsey & Company, 2023).

This chapter addresses three critical objectives. First, it provides a comprehensive framework for understanding technology-augmented brand management, synthesizing insights from both academic research and industry practice. Second, it examines the key technological components and capabilities that enable modern brand management, offering practical guidance for implementation. Third, it explores emerging trends and future directions, helping organizations prepare for the next wave of technological innovation in brand management. The importance of this chapter lies in its

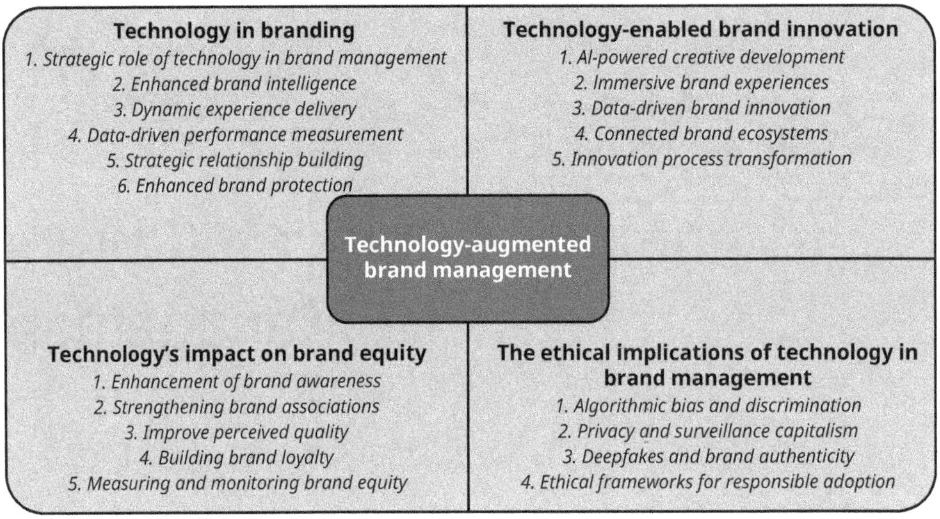

Figure 34.1 Technology-augmented brand management framework

Source: The author.

timely examination of how technology is reshaping brand management practices. Businesses have been pouring resources into digital transformation with budgets accounting for 26.2% of total marketing budgets in 2023 (McKinsey & Company, 2023). Brands are grappling with a critical question: How can they effectively integrate technology into their brand management strategies? This isn't just a position of staying on trend or at the cutting edge. For many organizations, it's a question of survival. The challenge lies in leveraging technology to enhance brand experiences and operations while maintaining the authentic human connection that resonates with customers.

This chapter aims to shed light on this complex issue, serving as a valuable resource for both academics and practitioners seeking to understand the interplay between technology and brand management. Whether you're a seasoned marketing executive, a brand strategist charting a new course, or a researcher exploring this uncharted territory, the insights within these pages will help you navigate this multifaceted landscape.

Through a mix of emerging trend analysis and practical guidance, we'll break down the often intimidating concept of technology-augmented brand management into digestible, actionable pieces. We'll explore how organizations at various stages of technological adoption are grappling with these challenges and share lessons learned from their successes and missteps. This chapter is more than just a retrospective chapter of what's been done. It's a forward-looking guide, a compass for steering your brand through the uncharted waters of the digital age. We'll delve into the latest tools and techniques, from AI-powered chatbots to immersive AR experiences, and examine how they can be harnessed to create more compelling, personalized brand interactions as illustrated in Figure 34.1.

TECHNOLOGY IN BRANDING

Technology has revolutionized the way companies manage and build their brands in today's digital age (Faulds & Raju, 2024). The rise of AI, data analytics and other innovative tools has transformed brand management from a one-way communication strategy to a dynamic, interactive process that puts the customer at the center (Gupta et al., 2020).

Traditionally, brand management relied heavily on broadcasting messages to a wide audience, with limited ability to track their impact. It was like shooting arrows in the dark, hoping to hit the target without knowing where they landed (Batra & Keller, 2016). However, the digital revolution has fundamentally shifted this paradigm. Now, with the power of AI and advanced analytics, brands can gain deep, granular insights into their customers' preferences, behaviors and needs (Faulds & Raju, 2024). It's as if a spotlight has been turned on, illuminating the target and enabling brands to aim their arrows with unprecedented precision.

One of the most significant ways technology is transforming brand management is by enabling personalization at scale (Kumar, 2018). Imagine a world where brands can anticipate your needs and desires before you even articulate them, where every interaction feels tailor-made just for you (Dwivedi et al., 2022). That's the promise of technology-augmented brand management. Technology also enables brands to leverage predictive analytics and recommendation engines to enhance customer engagement (Theodorakopoulos & Theodoropoulou, 2024). Just as Netflix seems to magically know what show you'll want to watch next, or Amazon suggests products that uncannily match your interests, brands can now use machine learning algorithms to make highly educated predictions about your likely preferences and behaviors. These technologies enable brands to create rich, responsive ecosystems that blur the boundaries between the digital and physical realms, creating experiences that feel both automated and highly personal (Mele & Russo-Spena, 2024). Brands are no longer static entities merely pushing products or services; they are living, learning and evolving alongside their customers.

In this new era of brand management, technology serves as a sophisticated navigation system (Huang & Rust, 2021). Just as GPS has replaced paper maps, guiding us to our destinations with real-time updates and alternate routes, technology-augmented brand management helps brands navigate the complexities of today's market. With tools to track shifting consumer preferences, monitor market dynamics and identify emerging trends, brands can adapt their strategies in real-time, ensuring they stay relevant and responsive in an ever-changing landscape (Mohapatra et al., 2025; Rosário & Dias, 2023). However, as brands gain access to ever-more detailed customer data, they must also navigate the delicate balance between personalization and privacy. There's a risk of overstepping boundaries and making customers feel surveilled rather than understood (Merfeld et al., 2025; Scholdra et al., 2023; Wang et al., 2024b).

To build trust and loyalty, brands must use their technological capabilities responsibly, be transparent about data collection and usage, and give customers control over their information (Deryl et al., 2023). Brands must walk the line between being helpful and being intrusive, always respecting their customers' privacy and autonomy (Regenbrecht et al., 2024). As technology continues to advance, the brands that thrive will be those that harness its power while maintaining authentic human connections. They will use technology not to replace human interaction, but to enhance it, creating brands that are not just technologically sophisticated, but emotionally resonant (Shahin et al., 2024). The future of brand management is tech-powered but human-centered.

Strategic Role of Technology in Brand Management

Technology has fundamentally reshaped how organizations approach brand management by enabling more sophisticated, data-driven and dynamic brand-building capabilities (Kumar et al., 2024). The strategic role of technology in brand management manifests across five key dimensions: intelligence gathering, experience delivery, performance measurement, relationship building and brand protection.

Enhanced Brand Intelligence

Technology has revolutionized organizations' ability to understand and track their brand's health through advanced analytics and AI (Chan & Choi, 2025). Natural language processing and machine learning algorithms can now analyze vast amounts of unstructured data from social media, customer reviews, support interactions and other digital touchpoints to provide real-time insights into brand perceptions and sentiment (Shankar & Parsana, 2022). This technological capability enables brand managers to: First, detect and respond to brand-related issues before they escalate into crises (Schau et al., 2024). AI-powered sentiment analysis can identify potential reputation threats in their early stages, allowing for proactive rather than reactive brand management (Basu et al., 2023; Nuortimo et al., 2024). For instance, many global brands now use AI systems to monitor social media conversations 24/7 for early warning signs of emerging brand issues (Hayes et al., 2021). Second, understand nuanced brand associations and perceptions across different customer segments and markets (Rambocas & Pacheco, 2018). Advanced analytics can uncover subtle patterns in how different consumer groups perceive and interact with the brand, enabling more targeted brand-building strategies (Cui et al., 2024). This granular understanding was previously impossible to achieve through traditional market research methods. Third, track competitive brand positioning and market dynamics in real-time. AI systems can continuously monitor competitor activities and consumer responses, providing brand managers with timely insights for strategic decision-making (Rust et al., 2021). This enables more agile and responsive brand management strategies.

Dynamic Experience Delivery

Technology has transformed how brands deliver consistent yet personalized experiences across multiple touchpoints. Through AI-powered content management systems and digital asset management platforms, organizations can maintain brand consistency while adapting messaging and experiences based on individual consumer preferences and behaviors. Machine learning algorithms can optimize content delivery in real-time while ensuring alignment with core brand guidelines. This technological augmentation helps resolve the traditional tension between brand consistency and personalization (Davenport et al., 2020).

Organizations create more immersive and interactive brand experiences through emerging technologies like augmented reality (AR) and (VR). These technologies enable brands to engage consumers in novel ways that strengthen emotional connections and brand relationships (Aluri et al., 2019). However, research indicates that such technology-enabled experiences must be carefully designed to enhance rather than detract from the core brand experience (Cherenkov et al., 2024). Organizations deliver seamless omnichannel brand experiences by coordinating interactions across physical and digital touchpoints. AI systems can integrate data from multiple sources to create coherent customer journeys that reinforce brand positioning consistently across channels (Liu-Thompkins et al., 2022).

Data-Driven Performance Measurement

Technology has revolutionized brand performance measurement through advanced analytics and AI-driven metrics (Schrage et al., 2023). Organizations can now, First, track brand performance across multiple dimensions in real-time, from immediate engagement metrics to long-term brand equity measures (Kumar & Venkatesan, 2021). AI systems can analyze complex relationships between different brand metrics to provide a more comprehensive view of brand health. Second, attribute brand impact more accurately across different marketing activities and touchpoints (Wang et al., 2024a). Machine learning models can untangle the complex web of influences on brand performance, enabling more precise measurement of ROI on brand investments. Third, predict future brand performance through predictive analytics (Yu, 2023). AI models can forecast brand metrics based on historical patterns and current market conditions, enabling more proactive brand management strategies (Ramos et al., 2025).

Strategic Relationship Building

Technology enables more sophisticated approaches to building and maintaining brand relationships. AI-powered personalization creates more relevant and meaningful brand interactions. Machine learning algorithms can analyze customer data to determine optimal engagement strategies for different segments and individuals. Automated yet personalized customer service through chatbots and virtual assistants that maintain brand voice and values (Sidlauskiene et al., 2023). These systems can handle routine interactions while escalating complex issues to human agents, ensuring consistent brand experiences. Community building through digital platforms that facilitate connections between customers around the brand. AI systems can moderate and nurture these communities while gathering valuable insights about brand advocates and influencers (Peltier et al., 2024).

Enhanced Brand Protection

Finally, technology plays a crucial role in protecting brand assets and reputation. Automated monitoring for trademark infringement and brand misuse across digital channels. AI systems can scan the internet for unauthorized brand usage and potential counterfeits. Digital rights management systems that protect branded content and assets (Mahmood & Bashir, 2020). Blockchain technology is emerging as a powerful tool for verifying brand authenticity and protecting intellectual property. Cybersecurity measures protect brand-related data and digital assets from breaches that could damage brand trust (Pigola & de Souza Meirelles, 2024). As brands become increasingly digital, technological protection of brand assets becomes critically important.

TECHNOLOGY-ENABLED BRAND INNOVATION

The integration of advanced technologies has fundamentally transformed how organizations innovate and evolve their brands. This technological revolution extends beyond merely enhancing existing brand management practices to enabling entirely new approaches to brand building, engagement and value creation.

AI-Powered Creative Development

AI has emerged as a powerful tool for brand creative development, though its application requires careful consideration of both capabilities and limitations. Research indicates that AI can effectively support various aspects of brand creative processes (Ameen et al., 2022; Heigl, 2025). AI systems can now assist in fundamental brand design elements, including logo creation, color palette selection and visual identity development (Bertão et al., 2025). However, studies suggest that consumer responses to AI-designed brand elements vary significantly based on product category and brand positioning (Xu & Mehta, 2022). For hedonic products where emotional connections are crucial, consumers may respond less favorably to AI-designed elements, perceiving them as lacking authentic emotional resonance (Xu & Mehta, 2022). AI enables more sophisticated content creation and optimization (Haleem et al., 2022). Natural language processing and generation technologies can produce brand-aligned content at scale while maintaining consistent brand voice and messaging (Buckley et al., 2025). However, successful implementation requires careful human oversight to ensure content quality and authentic brand representation. The most effective approaches typically combine AI's efficiency with human creativity and strategic insight. AI facilitates rapid testing and optimization of brand creative elements (Cui et al., 2024). Machine learning algorithms can analyze consumer responses to different creative variations in real-time, enabling more agile and data-driven creative development processes. This capability allows brands to continuously refine their visual and verbal identity based on actual consumer engagement data.

Immersive Brand Experiences

Emerging technologies have created unprecedented opportunities for immersive brand experiences that blur the lines between physical and digital brand interactions (Kumar, 2018). AR technology enables brands to create interactive experiences that overlay digital brand elements onto the physical world. This capability has proven particularly valuable in retail contexts, where AR can enhance product visualization and trial, leading to increased purchase confidence and brand engagement (Chylinski et al., 2020). VR technology allows brands to create fully immersive brand environments that facilitate deeper emotional connections with consumers (de Regt et al., 2021). These virtual brand spaces can serve multiple purposes, from product demonstrations to brand storytelling, enabling more memorable and impactful brand experiences (Wedel et al., 2020). Third, the emergence of the metaverse presents new opportunities for persistent virtual brand presence and engagement. Brands can create permanent virtual spaces where consumers can interact with the brand and each other, fostering community building and long-term brand relationships (Hadi et al., 2024).

Data-Driven Brand Innovation

Advanced analytics and AI enable more sophisticated approaches to brand innovation through an enhanced understanding of consumer needs and preferences. Predictive analytics can identify emerging brand opportunities before they become apparent through traditional market research methods. Machine learning algorithms can analyze vast amounts of consumer data to detect subtle patterns indicating unmet needs or emerging preferences (Gupta et al., 2020). AI-powered consumer insight platforms can process multiple data streams simultaneously, including social media, search trends and purchase data, to provide a more comprehensive view of brand innovation opportunities (Nikseresht et al., 2024; Yeo et al., 2022). This capability enables brands to identify and respond to changing consumer needs more quickly and effectively (Balducci & Marinova, 2018; Bharadwaj et al., 2022). Real-time testing and optimization capabilities allow brands to experiment with new brand elements and experiences more efficiently. AI systems can rapidly analyze consumer responses to brand innovations, enabling faster iteration and refinement of new brand initiatives (Verganti et al., 2020).

Connected Brand Ecosystems

Technology enables the creation of interconnected brand ecosystems that deliver more comprehensive and consistent brand experiences. Internet of Things (IoT) technology allows brands to create networks of connected products and touchpoints that share data and coordinate experiences. This connectivity enables more personalized and responsive brand interactions based on real-time consumer behavior and preferences (Hoffman & Novak, 2024). Blockchain technology enables new forms of brand authentication and value creation through digital assets and non-fungible tokens (NFTs). These technologies can create unique digital brand experiences and products while ensuring authenticity and scarcity (Colicev, 2023). Application programming interfaces (API)-driven platforms enable brands to integrate their presence and functionality across multiple digital services and platforms, creating more seamless and comprehensive brand experiences. This integration capability allows brands to maintain consistent presence and functionality across an expanding digital ecosystem (Tellis et al., 2019).

Innovation Process Transformation

Technology has also transformed how organizations approach the brand innovation process itself. AI-powered innovation platforms can accelerate the ideation and concept development process by analyzing vast amounts of market and consumer data to identify promising innovation opportunities (Just, 2024). These platforms can also facilitate more efficient evaluation and prioritization of brand innovation initiatives (Cooper, 2024). Digital collaboration tools enable more inclusive and efficient brand innovation processes by facilitating collaboration among diverse stakeholders, including employees, partners and customers (Madanaguli et al., 2023). This collaborative capability can lead to more robust and market-relevant brand innovations. Advanced prototyping and simulation technologies enable faster and more cost-effective testing of brand innovations before full-scale implementation. VR and AR tools can provide realistic simulations of new brand experiences for evaluation and refinement.

TECHNOLOGY'S IMPACT ON BRAND EQUITY

The integration of advanced technologies has fundamentally transformed how organizations build, measure and maintain brand equity in the digital age. Technology affects brand equity through multiple pathways, influencing both the creation of brand value and consumers' perceptions of that value (Swaminathan et al., 2020).

Enhancement of Brand Awareness

Technology has revolutionized organizations' ability to create and maintain brand awareness through several mechanisms. Digital platforms and advanced analytics enable brands to achieve more precise targeting and consistent presence across multiple touchpoints, enhancing brand recognition and recall (Wichmann et al., 2022). AI helps optimize content delivery and media placement, ensuring brand messages reach the right audiences at optimal times. Moreover, technology enables brands to maintain more consistent visibility through automated content distribution and real-time engagement monitoring (Kumar et al., 2024). Machine learning algorithms can identify patterns in consumer attention and engagement, allowing brands to adjust their presence dynamically to maintain optimal awareness levels (Yan et al., 2024). This technological capability is particularly valuable in today's fragmented media landscape, where maintaining consistent brand awareness requires a coordinated presence across numerous channels and platforms.

Strengthening Brand Associations

Technology has enhanced organizations' ability to create and reinforce positive brand associations through more sophisticated and personalized brand experiences (Divakaran & Xiong, 2022). AI-powered systems can analyze individual consumer preferences and behaviors to deliver customized brand interactions that reinforce desired associations while maintaining consistency with core brand values (Cheng & Jiang, 2022). This personalization capability helps brands create stronger and more relevant associations in consumers' minds. Furthermore, advanced analytics enable brands to better understand and influence the network of associations consumers hold about their brands. Natural language processing and sentiment analysis can track how different brand touchpoints and experiences contribute to specific associations, allowing for more precise management of brand meaning (Xu et al., 2024). This technological capability enables brands to build more coherent and compelling brand images across diverse consumer segments.

Improve Perceived Quality

Technology influences perceived quality through multiple pathways. It enables more consistent delivery of brand experiences across touchpoints, helping maintain quality perceptions through standardization and quality control (Sheng et al., 2024). AI-powered systems can monitor service delivery and product performance in real-time, enabling rapid identification and correction of quality issues before they impact brand perceptions (Gama & Magistretti, 2023; Hoffman & Novak, 2024). Technology enables brands to provide more transparent information about product quality and authenticity (Brüns & Meißner, 2024). Blockchain and other verification technologies allow brands to provide verifiable proof of quality claims, enhancing consumer trust (Rapezzi et al., 2024). This transparency capability is particularly valuable in categories where quality verification is traditionally difficult for consumers. Technology-enabled personalization can enhance quality perceptions by better matching product and service delivery to individual consumer preferences and needs (Riegger et al., 2021). Machine learning algorithms can predict consumer preferences and adjust offerings (Wu et al., 2024), which leads to higher perceived quality through better preference matching.

Building Brand Loyalty

Technology has transformed how brands build and maintain customer loyalty (Desveaud et al., 2024). Advanced analytics and AI enable a more sophisticated understanding of loyalty drivers and more effective loyalty program design (Chatterjee et al., 2019). Machine learning algorithms can identify early indicators of customer churn and trigger appropriate interventions to maintain loyalty (Ameen et al., 2024). Moreover, technology enables more personalized loyalty programs that provide relevant rewards and recognition based on individual customer preferences and behaviors. This customization capability can strengthen emotional connections to the brand and increase switching costs, enhancing loyalty (Lin & Lin, 2023; Weidig et al., 2024). Digital platforms also facilitate community building among loyal customers, creating additional social bonds that reinforce brand loyalty.

Measuring and Monitoring Brand Equity

Technology has revolutionized organizations' ability to measure and track brand equity through more sophisticated analytics and real-time monitoring capabilities (Pamuksuz et al., 2021). AI-powered systems can integrate multiple data sources to provide more comprehensive and timely measures of brand equity. Social media listening and sentiment analysis provide real-time tracking of brand perceptions and associations (Swaminathan et al., 2022). Natural language processing can analyze vast amounts of unstructured data to identify subtle shifts in brand equity before they become apparent through traditional measures (Gross & Desveaud, 2024). Machine learning models can untangle complex relationships between different brand-building activities and their effects on various brand equity components (Wang et al., 2022). Predictive analytics can forecast future brand equity trends based on current metrics and market conditions, enabling more proactive brand management (Jamarani et al., 2024). This predictive capability helps organizations identify potential threats to brand equity early and take corrective action.

THE ETHICAL IMPLICATIONS OF TECHNOLOGY IN BRAND MANAGEMENT

The rapid integration of advanced technologies into brand management has created profound ethical challenges that threaten consumer trust and brand integrity (Hari et al., 2025). As companies increasingly rely on AI, data analytics and automation, they must carefully balance innovation with responsibility. Statistics shows that 74% of consumers now consider ethical tech practices when evaluating brands (VentureBeat, 2022), indicating that technology governance has become a competitive differentiator.

Algorithmic Bias and Discrimination

One of the most pressing issues is algorithmic bias in marketing systems. Studies reveal that AI-powered advertising platforms systematically disadvantage minority groups, with one analysis showing 35% lower ad visibility for Black-owned businesses (Raval, 2020). Similar biases emerge in chatbot interactions, where female-voiced assistants are perceived as subservient while male-voiced bots are viewed as authoritative (Cheng & Jiang, 2022). These patterns reflect how unchecked algorithms can amplify societal prejudices, as demonstrated when Amazon abandoned an AI recruiting tool that discriminated against women (Dastin, 2018).

Privacy and Surveillance Capitalism

Modern tracking technologies enable what scholars term 'surveillance branding' (Poyntz & Pedri, 2018), the extensive monitoring of consumer behavior across digital and physical spaces. Research indicates that 78% of consumers unknowingly consent to excessive data collection due to deliberately confusing interface designs known as 'dark patterns' (Luguri & Strahilevitz, 2021). Even more concerning are emerging neuromarketing techniques that use electroencephalography (EEG) headsets and eye-tracking to measure subconscious responses, which 62% of respondents consider psychologically manipulative (Sheng et al., 2024).

Deepfakes and Brand Authenticity

Generative AI introduces additional ethical dilemmas regarding authenticity. The rise of synthetic influencers like Lil Miquela, who earns millions promoting products despite being computer-generated, has led consumers to distrust AI brand representatives (Hagendorff, 2024). Deepfake technology poses even greater risks, increase in fraud complaints related to AI-generated impersonations of company executives (van der Sloot & Wagensveld, 2022). These developments challenge fundamental assumptions about truth in advertising and demand new verification standards.

Ethical Frameworks for Responsible Adoption

To address these issues, leading researchers propose three key solutions. First, mandatory bias audits conducted by third parties could identify and correct discriminatory algorithms (Raji et al., 2020). Second, 'nutrition label' transparency systems would disclose how AI systems make decisions and what data they use (Forbes, 2023). Third, maintaining human oversight, with human involvement in AI-generated content (Xu & Mehta, 2022), preserves ethical judgment that machines lack.

Forward-thinking companies are already implementing these measures. Some have appointed Chief Ethics Officers specifically to oversee technology deployments, while others are adopting co-governance models that let consumers opt out of certain tracking methods (Hermann et al., 2024). Industry groups like the Partnership on AI have also developed responsible marketing guidelines that set benchmarks for ethical tech use.

Ultimately, the brands that succeed in this new era will be those that recognize technology's ethical dimensions are not constraints but opportunities. As Hermann et al. (2024) conclude in an age of algorithmic influence, integrity becomes the ultimate competitive advantage. By aligning innovation with ethical principles, companies can build deeper trust while still harnessing technology's transformative potential. The path forward requires viewing ethics not as an afterthought, but as the foundation of technological brand strategy.

OPPORTUNITIES AND FUTURE RECOMMENDATIONS

As we stand at the crossroads of technological innovation and brand management, the future presents a landscape both exhilarating and complex. The integration of advanced technologies is not merely a trend but a fundamental reimagining of how brands create, communicate and deliver value. From AI and immersive experiences to blockchain and IoT, technological augmentation offers unprecedented opportunities to transform brand strategies, deepen consumer connections and create more dynamic, responsive brand ecosystems. However, this technological evolution demands more than just implementation – it requires a holistic, thoughtful approach that balances technological capabilities with human creativity, ethical considerations and genuine emotional resonance. The organizations that will thrive are those that view technology not as a replacement for human insight, but as a powerful tool to enhance understanding, personalization and meaningful brand experiences. Table 34.1 illustrates the opportunities and proposes questions for scholars to study in the future.

CONCLUSION

Brand management is changing dramatically, and technology is at the heart of this transformation. What used to be a straightforward process of creating marketing messages has become a complex, dynamic ecosystem of interactions, insights and experiences.

Today's brands are working with an incredible array of technological tools that go far beyond traditional marketing. AI, advanced analytics, blockchain and immersive digital platforms are giving companies unprecedented ways to understand and connect with their customers. It's not just about collecting data anymore, it's about truly understanding people's behaviors, preferences and emotional worlds. But here's the crucial part: this isn't about replacing human creativity with algorithms. The most forward-thinking companies see technology as a powerful amplifier of human insight, not a substitute. It's like having a supercharged collaborative partner that helps brands understand and engage with customers in more meaningful, personalized ways.

The strategic potential is enormous. Brands are moving from static, one-size-fits-all approaches to dynamic, adaptive systems that can anticipate customer needs and create deeply personalized experiences. Emerging technologies like emotional AI and blockchain aren't just technical tools, they're strategic instruments for building more authentic, responsive relationships with customers. However, this technological revolution comes with significant responsibilities. Companies must develop

Table 34.1 Opportunities, recommendations and future questions

Opportunities	*Themes*	*Recommendations*	*Future Questions*
Strategic role of technology in brand management	Enhanced brand intelligence	1. Develop more advanced AI-powered sentiment analysis tools that can detect nuanced emotional contexts across cultural and linguistic boundaries. 2. Create integrated intelligence platforms that combine multiple data sources for holistic brand perception mapping. 3. Invest in cross-cultural AI training to improve global brand intelligence capabilities. 4. Develop ethical AI frameworks for sentiment analysis that respect consumer privacy and cultural sensitivities.	1. How might AI sentiment analysis evolve to capture the emotional subtleties that human analysts currently detect? 2. What are the potential risks of over-relying on AI-driven brand intelligence? 3. How can organizations balance technological insights with human intuition in brand management?
	Dynamic experience delivery	1. Explore emerging technologies like brain-computer interfaces for ultra-personalized brand experiences. 2. Develop more sophisticated AI systems that can create truly adaptive brand interactions across multiple touchpoints. 3. Create comprehensive training programs for marketing teams to effectively leverage AI-driven personalization technologies. 4. Develop ethical guidelines for personalization that maintain consumer trust and privacy.	1. At what point does personalization become intrusive rather than helpful? 2. How can brands maintain authenticity while using AI to customize experiences? 3. What are the potential psychological impacts of hyper-personalized brand interactions?
	Data-driven performance measurement	1. Develop more advanced predictive models that can forecast long-term brand equity impacts. 2. Create holistic measurement frameworks that integrate traditional and digital brand metrics. 3. Invest in interdisciplinary teams that combine data science, psychology and marketing expertise. 4. Develop more sophisticated attribution models that account for complex consumer decision-making processes.	1. How can we measure the emotional value of a brand beyond traditional metrics? 2. What are the limitations of AI-driven performance prediction? 3. How might emerging technologies change our understanding of brand value?
	Strategic relationship building	1. Create more advanced AI-powered community management platforms. 2. Develop more sophisticated chatbots that can handle complex emotional interactions. 3. Implement continuous learning systems for AI-powered customer interaction tools. 4. Develop empathy protocols for AI-driven customer interactions.	1. Can AI truly build emotional connections with consumers? 2. What are the ethical considerations of using AI in relationship building? 3. How can brands maintain human touch while leveraging technological capabilities?
	Enhanced brand protection	1. Develop more advanced blockchain-based brand authentication systems. 2. Create AI-powered real-time brand protection monitoring tools. 3. Invest in cross-platform brand protection technologies. 4. Develop global standards for digital brand protection.	1. How can brands protect their digital assets in an increasingly complex online ecosystem? 2. What are the potential long-term implications of technological brand protection? 3. How might emerging technologies like quantum computing impact brand protection?

(Continued)

Table 34.1 (Continued)

Opportunities	*Themes*	*Recommendations*	*Future Questions*
Technology-based brand innovation	AI-powered creative development	1. Develop AI tools that can generate more emotionally nuanced creative content. 2. Create collaborative platforms that optimize human-AI creative interactions. 3. Establish creative AI ethics guidelines. 4. Develop training programs that help creative professionals effectively collaborate with AI.	1. Can AI truly replace human creativity in brand development? 2. How can we ensure that AI-generated creative content maintains brand authenticity? 3. What skills will creative professionals need to thrive in an AI-augmented creative landscape?
	Immersive brand experiences	1. Explore full sensory immersion technologies for brand experiences. 2. Develop more sophisticated AR and VR brand interaction platforms. 3. Invest in cross-platform immersive experience technologies. 4. Create accessibility guidelines for immersive brand experiences.	1. How might immersive technologies fundamentally transform brand interactions? 2. What are the potential psychological impacts of increasingly realistic virtual brand experiences? 3. How can brands ensure inclusive design in immersive technologies?
	Connected brand ecosystems	1. Develop more sophisticated IoT integration strategies. 2. Explore blockchain-based brand experience platforms. 3. Create standardized protocols for cross-platform brand ecosystem integration. 4. Develop robust security frameworks for connected brand technologies.	1. How will the concept of a brand change as technological ecosystems become more interconnected? 2. What are the potential risks of increasingly complex brand ecosystems? 3. How can brands maintain coherence across diverse technological platforms?
	Innovation process transformation	1. Invest in interdisciplinary training programs that help teams leverage AI-driven innovation tools effectively. 2. Develop ethical frameworks for AI-assisted innovation that ensure human creativity remains at the core of the process. 3. Create flexible organizational structures that can rapidly adapt to AI-identified innovation opportunities. 4. Establish continuous learning mechanisms that allow innovation platforms to become more sophisticated over time.	1. How can organizations ensure that AI-driven innovation complements rather than replaces human creativity? 2. What are the potential risks of over-relying on algorithmic approaches to brand innovation? 3. How might AI change the fundamental nature of creative ideation and concept development? 4. Can technology truly democratize the innovation process, or will it create new forms of technological gatekeeping? 5. What skills will innovation professionals need to develop to effectively collaborate with AI-powered tools? 6. How can organizations maintain the serendipity and unexpected insights that often drive breakthrough innovations?

(*Continued*)

Table 34.1 (Continued)

Opportunities	*Themes*	*Recommendations*	*Future Questions*
Technology impact on brand equity	Enhancement of brand awareness	1. Invest in cross-platform awareness integration technologies that can provide unified insights across diverse media ecosystems. 2. Develop advanced machine learning algorithms that can predict emerging awareness opportunities in rapidly changing media landscapes. 3. Create ethical frameworks for hyper-targeted brand awareness strategies that respect consumer privacy and data protection. 4. Establish continuous learning mechanisms that allow brands to rapidly adapt their awareness strategies to changing consumer behaviors.	1. How can brands maintain authenticity while leveraging increasingly sophisticated awareness technologies? 2. At what point does targeted awareness become intrusive or manipulative? 3. How might emerging technologies like augmented reality and metaverse platforms transform traditional concepts of brand awareness? 4. Can AI-driven awareness strategies create meaningful emotional connections, or do they risk becoming sterile and impersonal? 5. What are the potential long-term psychological impacts of hyper-personalized brand awareness technologies? 6. How can organizations balance global brand consistency with localized awareness strategies?
	Strengthening brand associations	1. Invest in cross-cultural AI training to improve global brand association understanding. 2. Develop sophisticated multi-dimensional brand association mapping platforms that integrate diverse data sources. 3. Create ethical frameworks for emotional and cognitive brand association technologies. 4. Establish continuous learning mechanisms that allow brands to adapt their association strategies dynamically. 5. Develop interdisciplinary teams combining data scientists, psychologists and brand strategists to create more nuanced association strategies.	1. How can brands create authentic associations in an increasingly cynical and technology-mediated consumer landscape? 2. What are the ethical boundaries of using advanced technologies to influence brand perceptions? 3. Can AI truly understand the nuanced emotional landscape of brand associations? 4. How might emerging technologies like brain-computer interfaces transform our understanding of brand connections? 5. What are the potential psychological risks of hyper-personalized brand association strategies? 6. How can brands maintain cultural sensitivity while developing global association technologies?

(*Continued*)

Table 34.1 (Continued)

Opportunities	*Themes*	*Recommendations*	*Future Questions*
	Improve perceived quality	1. Invest in integrated quality management platforms that combine AI, IoT and advanced analytics. 2. Develop sophisticated predictive quality maintenance technologies across different industry sectors. 3. Create transparent quality communication strategies that leverage technology to build consumer trust. 4. Establish ethical frameworks for quality verification technologies that prioritize consumer privacy and data protection. 5. Design continuous learning mechanisms that allow quality perception systems to evolve with changing consumer expectations.	1. How can brands use technology to transform quality perception from a passive measurement to an active consumer experience? 2. What are the psychological implications of hyper-transparent quality verification technologies? 3. Can technological quality verification create genuine trust, or will it be perceived as a marketing manipulation? 4. How might emerging technologies like quantum computing revolutionize quality assessment? 5. What are the potential unintended consequences of AI-driven quality management? 6. How can brands balance technological efficiency with human-centric quality experiences?
	Building brand loyalty	1. Invest in holistic loyalty platforms that combine predictive analytics, AI and human-centric design. 2. Create ethical frameworks for personalized loyalty technologies that respect consumer privacy and autonomy. 3. Develop continuous learning mechanisms that allow loyalty strategies to adapt to changing consumer behaviors. 4. Establish interdisciplinary teams combining data scientists, psychologists and brand strategists to design more nuanced loyalty approaches. 5. Implement advanced data integration technologies that provide a 360-degree view of customer loyalty dynamics.	1. How can brands create genuine emotional connections in an increasingly technological loyalty landscape? 2. At what point does personalization become intrusive rather than beneficial? 3. Can AI truly understand and replicate the emotional nuances of brand loyalty? 4. How might emerging technologies like augmented reality transform loyalty experiences? 5. What are the potential psychological impacts of hyper-personalized loyalty strategies? 6. How can brands maintain authenticity while leveraging advanced loyalty technologies?

(*Continued*)

Table 34.1 (Continued)

Opportunities	*Themes*	*Recommendations*	*Future Questions*
	Measuring and monitoring brand equity	1. Invest in comprehensive, interdisciplinary brand equity measurement technologies. 2. Create ethical frameworks for advanced brand equity analytics that protect consumer privacy. 3. Develop continuous learning mechanisms that allow brand equity measurement systems to adapt to changing market dynamics. 4. Establish advanced data integration platforms that can provide 360-degree brand equity insights. 5. Build sophisticated visualization tools that make complex brand equity data accessible and actionable.	1. How can brands measure the emotional and intangible aspects of brand equity beyond traditional metrics? 2. What are the potential limitations of AI-driven brand equity measurement? 3. Can technology truly capture the nuanced, emotional nature of brand value? 4. How might emerging technologies like quantum computing transform brand equity analysis? 5. What are the ethical considerations of advanced brand equity tracking? 6. How can brands ensure their equity measurement approaches remain human-centric?
The ethical implications of technology in brand management	Algorithmic bias and discrimination	1. Conduct quarterly algorithmic fairness assessments using frameworks like AI Fairness 360 (IBM) or Google's What-If Tool. 2. Ensure datasets represent all demographic groups. 3. Use LIME or SHAP models to make algorithmic decisions interpretable. 4. Include sociologists, ethicists and community advocates in AI governance.	1. How do biases in brand algorithms amplify or diminish over time with continuous learning systems? 2. Do Western-centric fairness metrics (e.g., 'equal opportunity') align with non-Western ethical frameworks 3. . Does disclosing bias-remediation efforts increase trust or backfire by highlighting prior discrimination? 4. How can brands quantify compounded discrimination (e.g., race + gender + age) in algorithmic targeting? 5. Do GDPR-style 'right to explanation' laws meaningfully reduce algorithmic harm, or create compliance theater?
	Privacy and surveillance capitalism	1. Avoid manipulative UX designs (e.g., pre-checked consent boxes, hidden opt-outs). 2. Provide **real-time dashboards** showing data collection and usage. 3. Disclose biometric tracking (e.g., eye-tracking, EEG) and offer opt-outs. 4. Advocate for GDPR-style laws in unregulated markets (e.g., US federal privacy law).	1. Under what conditions are consumers willing to trade personal data for hyper-personalized experiences? 2. Do privacy-enhancing technologies (PETs) like federated learning or homomorphic encryption meaningfully protect users without degrading ad performance? 3. How do privacy concerns vary between collectivist (e.g., Japan) vs. individualist (e.g., USA) cultures? 4. Has GDPR actually reduced data exploitation, or just shifted it to unregulated regions? 5. Is it ethical to predict consumer behavior before users are aware? 6. Can decentralized models replace extractive data practices?

(Continued)

Table 34.1 (Continued)

Opportunities	*Themes*	*Recommendations*	*Future Questions*
	Deepfakes and brand authenticity	1. Implement AI-powered tools (e.g., Microsoft Video Authenticator or Deepware Scanner) to identify synthetic media in real time. 2. Use **C2PA (Coalition for Content Provenance and Authenticity) standards** to tag synthetic media. 3. Launch **awareness campaigns** (e.g., TikTok's 'Synthetic Media Labeling' initiative). 4. Create **crisis playbooks** for deepfake scams (e.g., fake CEO fraud). 5. Create **crisis playbooks** for deepfake scams (e.g., fake CEO fraud).	1. At what point does AI-generated content erode brand trust, even when labeled as synthetic? 2. Who is responsible when a deepfake damages a brand: creators, platforms, or AI vendors? 3. Can detection AI keep pace with generative AI advances (e.g., Sora, MidJourney v6)? 4. How do attitudes toward deepfakes vary in collectivist (e.g., China) vs. individualist (e.g., USA) markets? 5. Is it acceptable to use deepfake tech for 'positive' purposes (e.g., reviving historical figures for ads)? 6. Can decentralized authentication work at social media scale, or will costs limit adoption?
	Ethical framework for responsible adoption	1. Create cross-functional teams (legal, marketing, data science, ethics) to review high-risk AI deployments. 2. Disclose training data, accuracy rates and limitations. 3. Require human approval for sensitive AI decisions (e.g., loan denials, medical ad targeting). 4. Use tools like **IBM Fairness 360** or **Google's What-If Tool** to audit models for gender/racial bias. 5. Follow frameworks like **OECD AI Principles** or **EU AI Act** for risk classification.	1. Do ethics disclosures (e.g., 'This ad was AI-generated') increase trust or backfire by highlighting automation? 2. Can Western-centric frameworks (e.g., GDPR) work in markets like China with different privacy norms? 3. Do ethical AI practices actually improve long-term customer lifetime value (LTV), or just add costs? 4. How much accuracy must be sacrificed to make AI decisions interpretable to consumers? 5. Are 'high-risk' AI bans (e.g., EU's emotion recognition) enforceable given rapid technological change? 6. Is it ethical to use AI to augment human influencers (e.g., AI-filtered voices, deepfake aging)?

Source: The author.

robust frameworks that protect consumer privacy, maintain transparency and ensure that technology serves human needs rather than exploiting them. It's a delicate balance of leveraging advanced capabilities while staying true to fundamental human values.

Looking ahead, the most successful brands will be those that view technology not as a fixed solution, but as a continuously evolving journey. They'll create cultures that embrace complexity, encourage experimentation and remain fundamentally committed to understanding human aspirations. This isn't about technology taking over, but about creating a more intelligent, responsive dialogue between brands and consumers. It's an exciting frontier that promises to reshape how we think about connection, communication and value creation in an increasingly digital world.

REFERENCES

Aluri, A., Price, B. S., & McIntyre, N. H. (2019). Using machine learning to cocreate value through dynamic customer engagement in a brand loyalty program. *Journal of Hospitality & Tourism Research*, *43*(1), 78–100. https://doi.org/10.1177/1096348017753521

Ameen, N., Pagani, M., Pantano, E., Cheah, J.-H., Tarba, S., & Xia, S. (2024). The rise of human–machine collaboration: Managers' perceptions of leveraging artificial intelligence for enhanced b2b service recovery. *British Journal of Management*, *36*(1), 91–109. https://doi.org/10.1111/1467-8551.12829

Ameen, N., Sharma, G. D., Tarba, S., Rao, A., & Chopra, R. (2022). Toward advancing theory on creativity in marketing and artificial intelligence. *Psychology & Marketing*, *39*(9), 1802–1825. https://doi.org/10.1002/mar.21699

Balducci, B., & Marinova, D. (2018). Unstructured data in marketing. *Journal of the Academy of Marketing Science*, *46*(4), 557–590. https://doi.org/10.1007/s11747-018-0581-x

Basu, R., Lim, W. M., Kumar, A., & Kumar, S. (2023). Marketing analytics: The bridge between customer psychology and marketing decision-making. *Psychology & Marketing*, *40*(12), 2588–2611. https://doi.org/10.1002/mar.21908

Batra, R., & Keller, K. L. (2016). Integrating marketing communications: New findings, new lessons, and new ideas. *Journal of Marketing*, *80*(6), 122–145. https://doi.org/10.1509/jm.15.0419

Bertão, R. A., Yeoun, M.-H., & Joo, J. (2025). A blind spot in AI-powered logo makers: Visual design principles. *Visual Communication*, *24*(1), 222–250. https://doi.org/10.1177/14703572231155593

Bharadwaj, N., Ballings, M., Naik, P. A., Moore, M., & Arat, M. M. (2022). A new livestream retail analytics framework to assess the sales impact of emotional displays. *Journal of Marketing*, *86*(1), 27–47. https://doi.org/10.1177/00222429211013042

Brüns, J. D., & Meißner, M. (2024). Do you create your content yourself? Using generative artificial intelligence for social media content creation diminishes perceived brand authenticity. *Journal of Retailing and Consumer Services*, *79*, 103790. https://doi.org/10.1016/j.jretconser.2024.103790

Buckley, O., Ashman, R., & Haenlein, M. (2025). Leveraging livestreaming to enrich influencer marketing. *California Management Review*, *67*(2), 111–140. https://doi.org/10.1177/00081256241300730

Chan, H.-L., & Choi, T.-M. (2025). Using generative artificial intelligence (GenAI) in marketing: Development and practices. *Journal of Business Research*, *191*, 115276. https://doi.org/10.1016/j.jbusres.2025.115276

Chatterjee, S., Ghosh, S. K., Chaudhuri, R., & Nguyen, B. (2019). Are CRM systems ready for AI integration? *The Bottom Line*, *32*(2), 144–157. https://doi.org/10.1108/BL-02-2019-0069

Cheng, Y., & Jiang, H. (2022). Customer–brand relationship in the era of artificial intelligence: Understanding the role of chatbot marketing efforts. *Journal of Product & Brand Management*, *31*(2), 252–264. https://doi.org/10.1108/JPBM-05-2020-2907

Cherenkov, E., Benga, V., Lee, M., Nandwani, N., Raguin, K., Sueur, M. C., & Sun, G. (2024). From machine learning algorithms to superior customer experience: Business implications of machine learning-driven data analytics in the hospitality industry. *Journal of Smart Tourism*, *4*(2), 5–14. https://doi.org/10.52255/smarttourism.2024.4.2.2

Chylinski, M., Heller, J., Hilken, T., Keeling, D. I., Mahr, D., & de Ruyter, K. (2020). Augmented reality marketing: A technology-enabled approach to situated customer experience. *Australasian Marketing Journal*, *28*(4), 374–384. https://doi.org/10.1016/j.ausmj.2020.04.004

Colicev, A. (2023). How can non-fungible tokens bring value to brands. *International Journal of Research in Marketing*, *40*(1), 30–37. https://doi.org/10.1016/j.ijresmar.2022.07.003

Cooper, R. G. (2024). The AI transformation of product innovation. *Industrial Marketing Management*, *119*, 62–74. https://doi.org/10.1016/j.indmarman.2024.03.008

Cui, Y., van Esch, P., & Phelan, S. (2024). How to build a competitive advantage for your brand using generative AI. *Business Horizons*, *67*(5), 583–594. https://doi.org/10.1016/j.bushor.2024.05.003

Dastin, J. (2018). *Insight – Amazon scraps secret AI recruiting tool that showed bias against women*. Retrieved March 25, from www.reuters.com/article/us-amazon-com-jobs-automation-insight-idUSKCN1MK08G/

Davenport, T., Guha, A., Grewal, D., & Bressgott, T. (2020). How artificial intelligence will change the future of marketing. *Journal of the Academy of Marketing Science*, *48*(1), 24–42. https://doi.org/10.1007/s11747-019-00696-0

de Regt, A., Plangger, K., & Barnes, S. J. (2021). Virtual reality marketing and customer advocacy: Transforming experiences from story-telling to story-doing. *Journal of Business Research*, 136, 513–522. https://doi.org/10.1016/j.jbusres.2021.08.004

Deryl, M. D., Verma, S., & Srivastava, V. (2023). How does AI drive branding? Towards an integrated theoretical framework for AI-driven branding. *International Journal of Information Management Data Insights*, *3*(2), 100205. https://doi.org/10.1016/j.jjimei.2023.100205

Desveaud, K., Mandler, T., & Eisend, M. (2024). A meta-model of customer brand loyalty and its antecedents. *Journal of Business Research*, *176*, 114589. https://doi.org/10.1016/j.jbusres.2024.114589

Divakaran, P. K. P., & Xiong, J. (2022). Eliciting brand association networks: A new method using online community data. *Technological Forecasting and Social Change*, *181*, 121769. https://doi.org/10.1016/j.techfore.2022.121769

Dwivedi, Y. K., Hughes, L., Baabdullah, A. M., Ribeiro-Navarrete, S., Giannakis, M., Al-Debei, M. M., Dennehy, D., Metri, B., Buhalis, D., Cheung, C. M. K., Conboy, K., Doyle, R., Dubey, R., Dutot, V., Felix, R., Goyal, D. P., Gustafsson, A., Hinsch, C., Jebabli, I., ... Wamba, S. F. (2022). Metaverse beyond the hype: Multidisciplinary perspectives on emerging challenges, opportunities, and agenda for research, practice and policy. *International Journal of Information Management*, *66*, Article 102542. https://doi.org/10.1016/j.ijinfomgt.2022.102542

Faulds, D. J., & Raju, P. S. (2024). Branding strategies in the digital era: An interview with Nick Westergaard. *Business Horizons*. https://doi.org/10.1016/j.bushor.2024.12.005

Forbes. (2023). *It's time for 'nutrition labels' in artificial intelligence*. Retrieved March 25, from www.forbes.com/sites/greglicholai/2023/11/21/its-time-for-nutrition-labels-in-artificial-intelligence/

Gama, F., & Magistretti, S. (2023). Artificial intelligence in innovation management: A review of innovation capabilities and a taxonomy of AI applications. *Journal of Product Innovation Management*, *42*(1), 76–111. https://doi.org/10.1111/jpim.12698

Goglin, C. (2023). The ethics of artificial intelligence: Review of ethical machines: Your concise guide to totally unbiased, transparent, and respectful AI by R. Blackman; ethics of artificial intelligence: Case studies and options for addressing ethical challenges by B.C. Stahl, D. Schroeder, and R. Rodrigues; and AI ethics by M. Coeckelbergh. *Journal of Business Ethics*, *188*(3), 623–627. https://doi.org/10.1007/s10551-023-05538-2

Gross, J., & Desveaud, K. (2024). Navigating computational linguistic in marketing practices: The barriers of natural language processing in social media marketing and a path to future research. *Journal of Marketing Analytics*, 1–11. https://doi.org/10.1057/s41270-024-00337-8

Gupta, S., Leszkiewicz, A., Kumar, V., Bijmolt, T., & Potapov, D. (2020). Digital analytics: Modeling for insights and new methods. *Journal of Interactive Marketing*, *51*(1), 26–43. https://doi.org/10.1016/j.intmar.2020.04.003

Hadi, R., Melumad, S., & Park, E. S. (2024). The metaverse: A new digital frontier for consumer behavior. *Journal of Consumer Psychology*, *34*(1), 142–166. https://doi.org/10.1002/jcpy.1356

Hagendorff, T. (2024). Mapping the ethics of generative ai: A comprehensive scoping review. *Minds and Machines*, *34*(4), 39. https://doi.org/10.1007/s11023-024-09694-w

Haleem, A., Javaid, M., Asim Qadri, M., Pratap Singh, R., & Suman, R. (2022). Artificial intelligence (AI) applications for marketing: A literature-based study. *International Journal of Intelligent Networks*, *3*, 119–132. https://doi.org/10.1016/j.ijin.2022.08.005

Hari, H., Sharma, A., Verma, S., & Chaturvedi, R. (2025). Exploring ethical frontiers of artificial intelligence in marketing. *Journal of Responsible Technology*, *21*, 100103. https://doi.org/10.1016/j.jrt.2024.100103

Hayes, J. L., Britt, B. C., Evans, W., Rush, S. W., Towery, N. A., & Adamson, A. C. (2021). Can social media listening platforms' artificial intelligence be trusted? examining the accuracy of crimson hexagon's (now brandwatch consumer research's) ai-driven analyses. *Journal of Advertising*, *50*(1), 81–91. https://doi.org/10.1080/00913367.2020.1809576

Heigl, R. (2025). Generative artificial intelligence in creative contexts: A systematic review and future research agenda. *Management Review Quarterly*. https://doi.org/10.1007/s11301-025-00494-9

Hermann, E., Williams, G. Y., & Puntoni, S. (2024). Deploying artificial intelligence in services to AID vulnerable consumers. *Journal of the Academy of Marketing Science*, *52*(5), 1431–1451. https://doi.org/10.1007/s11747-023-00986-8

Hoffman, D. L., & Novak, T. P. (2024). The evolving consumer IoT: A novel framework for marketing strategy based on assemblage theory. *Journal of Product Innovation Management*. https://doi.org/10.1111/jpim.12767

Huang, M.-H., & Rust, R. T. (2021). A strategic framework for artificial intelligence in marketing. *Journal of the Academy of Marketing Science*, *49*(1), 30–50. https://doi.org/10.1007/s11747-020-00749-9

IDC. (2024). *Worldwide digital transformation spending guide*. www.idc.com/getdoc.jsp?containerId=IDC_P32575

Jamarani, A., Haddadi, S., Sarvizadeh, R., Haghi Kashani, M., Akbari, M., & Moradi, S. (2024). Big data and predictive analytics: A systematic review of applications. *Artificial Intelligence Review*, *57*(7), 176. https://doi.org/10.1007/s10462-024-10811-5

Just, J. (2024). Natural language processing for innovation search – Reviewing an emerging non-human innovation intermediary. *Technovation*, *129*, 102883. https://doi.org/10.1016/j.technovation.2023.102883

Kumar, V. (2018). Transformative marketing: The next 20 years. *Journal of Marketing*, *82*(4), 1–12. https://doi.org/10.1509/jm.82.41

Kumar, V., Ashraf, A. R., & Nadeem, W. (2024). AI-powered marketing: What, where, and how? *International Journal of Information Management*, *77*, 102783. https://doi.org/10.1016/j.ijinfomgt.2024.102783

Kumar, V., & Venkatesan, R. (2021). Transformation of metrics and analytics in retailing: The way forward. *Journal of Retailing*, *97*(4), 496–506. https://doi.org/10.1016/j.jretai.2021.11.004

Lin, S., & Lin, J. (2023). How organizations leverage digital technology to develop customization and enhance customer relationship performance: An empirical investigation. *Technological Forecasting and Social Change*, *188*, 122254. https://doi.org/10.1016/j.techfore.2022.122254

Liu-Thompkins, Y., Okazaki, S., & Li, H. (2022). Artificial empathy in marketing interactions: Bridging the human-AI gap in affective and social customer experience. *Journal of the Academy of Marketing Science*, *50*(6), 1198–1218. https://doi.org/10.1007/s11747-022-00892-5

Luguri, J., & Strahilevitz, L. J. (2021). Shining a light on dark patterns. *Journal of Legal Analysis*, *13*(1), 43–109. https://doi.org/10.1093/jla/laaa006

Madanaguli, A., Dhir, A., Talwar, S., Clauss, T., Kraus, S., & Kaur, P. (2023). Diving into the uncertainties of open innovation: A systematic review of risks to uncover pertinent typologies and unexplored horizons. *Technovation*, *119*, 102582. https://doi.org/10.1016/j.technovation.2022.102582

Mahmood, A., & Bashir, J. (2020). How does corporate social responsibility transform brand reputation into brand equity? Economic and noneconomic perspectives of CSR. *International Journal of Engineering Business Management*, *12*, 1847979020927547. https://doi.org/10.1177/1847979020927547

McKinsey & Company. (2023). *The future of corporate and business functions: An opportunity to Reset + Reimagine*. Retrieved November 13, 2025, from www.mckinsey.com/~/media/mckinsey/business%20functions/operations/our%20insights/the%20future%20of%20corporate%20and%20business%20functions/the-future-of-corporate-and-business-functions.pdf

Mele, C., & Russo-Spena, T. (2024). Agencement of onlife and phygital: Smart tech–enabled value co-creation practices. *Journal of Service Management*, *36*(2), 217–240. https://doi.org/10.1108/JOSM-03-2023-0113

Merfeld, K., Klein, J. F., de Regt, A., Baltin, A.-S., & Henkel, S. (2025). In-store technology personalization: A typology and research agenda based on type of automation and data collection. *Journal of Business Research*, *191*, 115236. https://doi.org/10.1016/j.jbusres.2025.115236

Mohapatra, A. G., Mohanty, A., Mohanty, S. K., Mahalik, N. P., & Nayak, S. (2025). Personalization and customer experience in the era of data-driven marketing. In S. Dixit, M. Maurya, V. Jain, & G. Subramaniam (Eds.), *Artificial intelligence-enabled businesses* (pp. 467–511). John Wiley & Sons. https://doi.org/10.1002/9781394234028.ch26

Nikseresht, A., Shokouhyar, S., Tirkolaee, E. B., & Pishva, N. (2024). Applications and emerging trends of blockchain technology in marketing to develop Industry 5.0 Businesses: A comprehensive survey and network analysis. *Internet of Things*, *28*, 101401. https://doi.org/10.1016/j.iot.2024.101401

Nuortimo, K., Harkonen, J., & Breznik, K. (2024). Exploring corporate reputation and crisis communication. *Journal of Marketing Analytics*, 1–22. https://doi.org/10.1057/s41270-024-00353-8

Pamuksuz, U., Yun, J. T., & Humphreys, A. (2021). A Brand-new look at you: Predicting brand personality in social media networks with machine learning. *Journal of Interactive Marketing*, *56*(1), 1–15. https://doi.org/10.1016/j.intmar.2021.05.001

Peltier, J. W., Dahl, A. J., Drury, L., & Khan, T. (2024). Cutting-edge research in social media and interactive marketing: A review and research agenda. *Journal of Research in Interactive Marketing*, *18*(5), 900–944. https://doi.org/10.1108/JRIM-02-2024-0074

Pigola, A., & de Souza Meirelles, F. (2024). Unraveling trust management in cybersecurity: Insights from a systematic literature review. *Information Technology and Management*, 1–23. https://doi.org/10.1007/s10799-024-00438-x

Poyntz, S. R., & Pedri, J. (2018). *Youth and media culture*. Oxford University Press.

Raji, I. D., Gebru, T., Mitchell, M., Buolamwini, J., Lee, J., & Denton, E. (2020, February 7–9). Saving face: Investigating the ethical concerns of facial recognition auditing. *Proceedings of the AAAI/ ACM conference on AI, ethics, and society*, New York, NY, USA. https://doi.org/10.1145/3375627.3375820

Rambocas, M., & Pacheco, B. G. (2018). Online sentiment analysis in marketing research: A review. *Journal of Research in Interactive Marketing*, *12*(2), 146–163. https://doi.org/10.1108/JRIM-05-2017-0030

Ramos, F. R., Martinez, L. M., Martinez, L. F., Abreu, R., & Rubio, L. (2025). Mapping e-commerce trends in the USA: A time series and deep learning approach. *Journal of Marketing Analytics*, 1–29. https://doi.org/10.1057/s41270-025-00392-9

Rapezzi, M., Pizzi, G., & Marzocchi, G. L. (2024). What you see is what you get: The impact of blockchain technology transparency on consumers. *Marketing Letters*, *36*(1), 51–64. https://doi.org/10.1007/s11002-024-09723-9

Raval, D. (2020). Whose voice do we hear in the marketplace? Evidence from consumer complaining behavior. *Marketing Science*, *39*(1), 168–187. https://doi.org/10.1287/mksc.2018.1140

Regenbrecht, H., Knott, A., Ferreira, J., & Pantidi, N. (2024). To see and be seen – perceived ethics and acceptability of pervasive augmented reality. *IEEE Access*, *12*, 32618–32636. https://doi.org/10.1109/ACCESS.2024.3366228

Riegger, A.-S., Klein, J. F., Merfeld, K., & Henkel, S. (2021). Technology-enabled personalization in retail stores: Understanding drivers and barriers. *Journal of Business Research*, *123*, 140–155. https://doi.org/10.1016/j.jbusres.2020.09.039

Rosário, A. T., & Dias, J. C. (2023). How has data-driven marketing evolved: Challenges and opportunities with emerging technologies. *International Journal of Information Management Data Insights*, *3*(2), 100203. https://doi.org/10.1016/j.jjimei.2023.100203

Rust, R. T., Rand, W., Huang, M.-H., Stephen, A. T., Brooks, G., & Chabuk, T. (2021). Real-time brand reputation tracking using social media. *Journal of Marketing*, *85*(4), 21–43. https://doi.org/10.1177/0022242921995173

Salesforce. (2024). *What are customer expectations, and how have they changed?* www.salesforce.com/resources/articles/customer-expectations/

Schau, H. J., Luri, I., & Akaka, M. A. (2024). Organizational resiliency through practice innovation: Forced brand evolution in a prolonged exogenous service ecosystem disruption. *Journal of Service Management*, ahead-of-print. https://doi.org/10.1108/JOSM-03-2023-0115

Scholdra, T. P., Wichmann, J. R. K., & Reinartz, W. J. (2023). Reimagining personalization in the physical store. *Journal of Retailing*, *99*(4), 563–579. https://doi.org/10.1016/j.jretai.2023.11.001

Schrage, M., Kiron, D., Candelon, F., Khodabandeh, S., & Chu, M. (2023). AI is helping companies redefine, not just improve, performance. *MIT Sloan Management Review*, *64*(3), 1–7.

Shahin, M., Chen, F. F., & Hosseinzadeh, A. (2024). Harnessing customized AI to create voice of customer via GPT3.5. *Advanced Engineering Informatics*, *61*, 102462. https://doi.org/10.1016/j.aei.2024.102462

Shankar, V., & Parsana, S. (2022). An overview and empirical comparison of natural language processing (NLP) models and an introduction to and empirical application of autoencoder models in marketing. *Journal of the Academy of Marketing Science*, *50*(6), 1324–1350. https://doi.org/10.1007/s11747-022-00840-3

Sheng, M. L., Natalia, N., & Rusfian, E. Z. (2024). AI Chatbot, human, and in-between: Examining the broader spectrum of technology-human interactions in driving customer-brand relationships across experience and credence services. *Psychology & Marketing*, *42*(4), 1051–1071. https://doi.org/10.1002/mar.22165

Sidlauskiene, J., Joye, Y., & Auruskeviciene, V. (2023). AI-based chatbots in conversational commerce and their effects on product and price perceptions. *Electronic Markets*, *33*(1), 24. https://doi.org/10.1007/s12525-023-00633-8

Statista. (2024). *Digital shopping behaviour*. www.statista.com/markets/413/topic/984/digital-shopping-behaviour/#overview

Swaminathan, V., Schwartz, H. A., Menezes, R., & Hill, S. (2022). The language of brands in social media: Using topic modeling on social media conversations to drive brand strategy. *Journal of Interactive Marketing*, *57*(2), 255–277. https://doi.org/10.1177/10949968221088275

Swaminathan, V., Sorescu, A., Steenkamp, J.-B. E. M., O'Guinn, T. C. G., & Schmitt, B. (2020). Branding in a hyperconnected world: Refocusing theories and rethinking boundaries. *Journal of Marketing*, *84*(2), 24–46. https://doi.org/10.1177/0022242919899905

Tellis, G. J., MacInnis, D. J., Tirunillai, S., & Zhang, Y. (2019). What drives virality (sharing) of online digital content? The critical role of information, emotion, and brand prominence. *Journal of Marketing*, *83*(4), 1–20. https://doi.org/10.1177/0022242919841034

Theodorakopoulos, L., & Theodoropoulou, A. (2024). Leveraging big data analytics for understanding consumer behavior in digital marketing: A systematic review. *Human Behavior and Emerging Technologies*, *2024*(1), 3641502. https://doi.org/10.1155/2024/3641502

van der Sloot, B., & Wagensveld, Y. (2022). Deepfakes: Regulatory challenges for the synthetic society. *Computer Law & Security Review*, *46*, 105716. https://doi.org/10.1016/j.clsr.2022.105716

VentureBeat. (2022). *Data privacy truly matters to your customers. It's time to make it a core business value*. Retrieved March 25, from https://venturebeat.com/security/data-privacy-truly-matters-to-your-customers-its-time-to-make-it-a-core-business-value/

Verganti, R., Vendraminelli, L., & Iansiti, M. (2020). Innovation and design in the age of artificial intelligence. *Journal of Product Innovation Management*, *37*(3), 212–227. https://doi.org/10.1111/jpim.12523

Wang, X., Bendle, N., & Pan, Y. (2024a). Beyond text: Marketing strategy in a world turned upside down. *Journal of the Academy of Marketing Science*, *52*(4), 939–954. https://doi.org/10.1007/s11747-023-01000-x

Wang, X., He, J., Curry, D. J., & Ryoo, J. H. (2022). Attribute embedding: Learning hierarchical representations of product attributes from consumer reviews. *Journal of Marketing*, *86*(6), 155–175. https://doi.org/10.1177/00222429211047822

Wang, Y., Zhu, J., Liu, R., & Jiang, Y. (2024b). Enhancing recommendation acceptance: Resolving the personalization–privacy paradox in recommender systems: A privacy calculus perspective. *International Journal of Information Management*, *76*, 102755. https://doi.org/10.1016/j.ijinfomgt.2024.102755

Wedel, M., Bigné, E., & Zhang, J. (2020). Virtual and augmented reality: Advancing research in consumer marketing. *International Journal of Research in Marketing*, *37*(3), 443–465. https://doi.org/10.1016/j.ijresmar.2020.04.004

Weidig, J., Weippert, M., & Kuehnl, C. (2024). Personalized touchpoints and customer experience: A conceptual synthesis. *Journal of Business Research*, *177*, 114641. https://doi.org/10.1016/j.jbusres.2024.114641

Wichmann, J. R. K., Wiegand, N., & Reinartz, W. J. (2022). The platformization of brands. *Journal of Marketing*, *86*(1), 109–131. https://doi.org/10.1177/00222429211054073

Wu, J., Liu, H., Yao, X., & Zhang, L. (2024). Unveiling consumer preferences: A two-stage deep learning approach to enhance accuracy in multi-channel retail sales forecasting. *Expert Systems with Applications*, *257*, 125066. https://doi.org/10.1016/j.eswa.2024.125066

Xu, L., & Mehta, R. (2022). Technology devalues luxury? Exploring consumer responses to AI-designed luxury products. *Journal of the Academy of Marketing Science*, *50*(6), 1135–1152. https://doi.org/10.1007/s11747-022-00854-x

Xu, Z., Kohli, A., Nkhalamba, S., & Gai, L. (2024). Analyzing product attributes and brand sentiment of smartwatches using Twitter/X data from a time series perspective. *Journal of Marketing Analytics*, 1–17. https://doi.org/10.1057/s41270-024-00349-4

Yan, Z., Lv, C., Chen, Q., & Shang, D. (2024). Impact of user engagement on virtual reality behavioral response from the human–computer interaction perspective toward a service context: A hybrid statistics and machine learning approach. *Expert Systems with Applications*, *247*, 123243. https://doi.org/10.1016/j.eswa.2024.123243

Yeo, S. F., Tan, C. L., Kumar, A., Tan, K. H., & Wong, J. K. (2022). Investigating the impact of AI-powered technologies on instagrammers' purchase decisions in digitalization era–A study of the fashion and apparel industry. *Technological Forecasting and Social Change*, *177*, 121551. https://doi.org/10.1016/j.techfore.2022.121551

Yu, B. (2023). Deep learning applications for interactive marketing in the contemporary digital age. In C. L. Wang (Ed.), *The palgrave handbook of interactive marketing* (pp. 705–728). Springer International Publishing. https://doi.org/10.1007/978-3-031-14961-0_31

35

The Influencer Effect: Mapping Influencer Marketing in Brand Management

Martina Quadri and Liselot Hudders

INTRODUCTION

The Stanley Quencher Tumbler has become a highly sought-after accessory among Generation Z. Originally patented in 1913 as the first vacuum-insulated bottle, the Tumbler underwent a significant redesign in 2016 to align with contemporary aesthetics and functionality. Its widespread popularity can be largely attributed to social media, where viral TikTok and Instagram videos showcase influencers seamlessly integrating the tumbler into their daily routines. These videos often depict influencers coordinating the tumbler's accessories with their outfits or incorporating them into various lifestyle activities, such as workouts and shopping. This heightened visibility has led to an unprecedented surge in demand, with over one million individuals joining the company's waiting lists. The Stanley Quencher's success exemplifies influencer marketing's transformative power (Retail Drive, 2023).

Influencer marketing has become a widely used marketing communication tactic in recent years due to its efficiency and cost-effectiveness. Brands leverage the power of influential and highly popular social media users, known as social media influencers, to promote their products or services. These influencers are content creators with a large follower base on social media platforms like Instagram, TikTok or Twitch. They monetize their content and wield significant influence over their followers. In the early years of the internet, influencers were recognized as opinion leaders who primarily communicated with audiences through personal blogs. With the rise of social media, they expanded their reach, demonstrating effectiveness in enhancing brand awareness and fostering purchase intent by producing engaging, brand-aligned content and distributing it to their niche audiences (e.g., Han & Balabanis, 2024).

The success of influencers lies in their ability to create fun, interesting and engaging content by combining their expertise in a particular niche (such as fashion, luxury, fitness or gaming) by providing their followers an authentic insight into their daily lives. Recognizing their substantial influence, brands have increasingly engaged influencers as strategic partners in the advertising process (Borchers & Enke, 2021), evolving into more structured, long-term partnerships (Marketing Charts, 2022). This success has pushed influencer marketing to a professional level, involving a diverse range of stakeholders such as management and marketing agencies, as well as regulators. Consequently, the landscape of influencer marketing has been changing rapidly.

This chapter explores the role of influencers as intermediaries between brands and consumers, providing insights into their historical evolution and their emergence as central figures within the social media landscape. Furthermore, it examines how influencers can serve as a strategic marketing tool to enhance brand engagement and consumer trust. The chapter concludes with a research agenda aimed at advancing scholarly inquiry into the role of influencers in brand management.

THE RISE OF INFLUENCERS IN MODERN MARKETING

In the current digital era, social media influencers have assumed a pivotal role in content creation and online relationship-building, serving as intermediaries between brands and consumers (Delbaere et al., 2021; Schouten et al., 2020). They represent the evolution of bloggers, who originally emerged from traditional opinion leaders. Opinion leaders are individuals who influence others' attitudes and behaviors, particularly regarding purchasing decisions. Traditionally, they acted as intermediaries in the communication process between brands and consumers, leveraging mass media to exert their influence (Grau, 2022).

However, with the advent of digital technologies, opinion leaders increasingly embraced online platforms as tools for social persuasion. By the early 1990s, blogs had become a significant medium for these individuals to disseminate knowledge, establish expertise within specific fields and engage in brand endorsements. They provided both hedonic and utilitarian value by offering entertainment and information to readers. Beyond their subject–matter expertise, these individuals distinguished themselves from the broader public by being perceived as credible and intrinsically motivated to enhance their status (Grau, 2022).

With the dawn of the 21st century, the rise of social media platforms such as Facebook, YouTube and Instagram provided new avenues for online opinion leaders to expand their reach, cultivate their credibility and attain 'micro-celebrity' status, thus evolving into what is now recognized as social media influencers (Abidin, 2015). Notable examples include Mr. Beast, an American YouTuber who began creating content in 2012 and has since become one of the platform's most prominent figures, and Charli D'Amelio, who launched her TikTok career in 2019 with dance videos and became the platform's leading personality, surpassing 100 million followers. In recent years, these influencers have extended their influence beyond social media, gaining recognition in traditional entertainment sectors. For instance, D'Amelio appeared in ABC's television special 'The Disney Family Singalong'. Some influencers have even launched their television programs, such as Ryan Kaji, a renowned YouTube child star whose 'Ryan's Mystery Playdate', a children's television series, was developed based on his highly successful YouTube channel, Ryan's World.

Today, influencers are a pivotal element of modern marketing strategies. They cultivate and maintain a personal brand while fostering an online community through the consistent creation of authentic and distinctive content (Joshi et al., 2023; Kozinets et al., 2023). Their effectiveness lies in their ability to seamlessly integrate branded content into their posts, crafting tailored advertisements and engaging videos that resonate with audiences in ways traditional celebrities often fail to achieve (Abidin, 2015; Shtern & Hill, 2021).

The strategy of engaging influencers to leverage their audience reach and engagement capabilities, widely recognized as Influencer Marketing, has transformed the digital, advertising and marketing industries. The overarching goal is to enhance organizational performance and achieve favorable marketing and public relations outcomes, such as amplifying brand messages or driving product sales. The commercial impact of this strategy has been significant, compelling firms to increase their investments in influencer partnerships (Joshi et al., 2023; Leung et al., 2022). The influencer marketing industry is expected to reach a market size of $32.55 billion in 2025, with the majority of brands and marketing agencies allocating more than 75% of their marketing budgets to influencer marketing as of February 2024 (Influencer Marketing Hub, 2025). This growing trend continues unabated, with the industry projected to grow at a compound annual growth rate of 33.17%, reaching an estimated $71 billion by 2032 (Fortune Business Insights, 2025).

SOCIAL MEDIA INFLUENCERS AND THE CREATOR ECONOMY

Influencers constitute the backbone of the creator economy, a multifaceted network of business relationships that facilitates the commercialization of digital content. This allows stakeholders, such as influencers, brands and platforms, to generate revenue through multiple channels, legitimizing content creation as a proper profession (Kozinets et al., 2023; Peres et al., 2024).

The core activities of influencers encompass content production and distribution, often across multiple platforms, as well as community engagement (Zabel, 2024). Their primary objective is to cultivate strong and positive relationships with their audience, leveraging this influence to collaborate with brands and other stakeholders (Campbell & Farrell, 2020). Companies select influencers either based on internal criteria aligned with their marketing objectives or through external agencies (Peres et al., 2024). Public relations firms, digital marketing agencies and talent agencies serve as intermediaries, connecting brands with suitable influencers and managing commercial agreements (Kozinets et al., 2023).

Social media platforms such as Facebook, Instagram, YouTube and TikTok are the means through which messages and content are produced and disseminated. Each platform enforces distinct guidelines, tools and algorithms that influencers must navigate to optimize content visibility and engagement (Zabel, 2024). Furthermore, platform-specific tools facilitate interactions between influencers and their followers through likes, comments and direct messages. These technologies not only grant access to content but also regulate interactive (e.g., chat functionalities) and commercial (e.g., transaction-based) exchanges between influencers and their audience.

Consequently, influencers are increasingly assuming entrepreneurial roles, employing various monetization strategies to capitalize on their content and community engagement (Peres et al., 2024). Their revenue streams derive from multiple sources, including brand partnerships, platform-generated earnings (e.g., ad revenue, channel subscriptions and virtual tokens), direct sales of their own branded products and crowdfunding initiatives (Goanta, 2021). To maximize earnings, influencers must deeply understand their audience's preferences and spending behaviors (Grau, 2022). For instance, casual fans, who exhibit minimal or no spending behavior, are best targeted through sponsored posts, capitalizing on reach rather than engagement. Conversely, active fans, who frequently engage through participation, interaction and financial contributions, can be encouraged to subscribe to exclusive content, fostering deeper community involvement. The most devoted segment, known as super fans, represents the influencer's inner circle. These individuals consistently engage with content and offer substantial financial support. To maintain their loyalty, influencers must provide tailored experiences, such as exclusive digital goods (e.g., NFTs, eBooks, PDFs, etc.) (Grau, 2022). An influencer's financial success hinges on the effectiveness of their strategy in targeting followers with appropriate content, which reflects the advertiser's goals and suitable brand partnerships.

A COMPREHENSIVE REVIEW OF INFLUENCER MARKETING RESEARCH

Influencer Marketing Research Methodologies

Influencer marketing has garnered significant scholarly attention, with researchers employing various systematic review methods to track its evolution. Vrontis et al. (2021) used a domain-based selection approach, while Ye et al. (2021) applied bibliometric analysis to 387 peer-reviewed articles to provide a comprehensive overview of the existing literature. Hudders et al. (2021a, 2021b) categorized influencer marketing studies using Stern's Revised Communication Model for Advertising, focusing on influencer characteristics, content strategies and audience impact. Similarly, Leung et al. (2022) conducted a scoping review with thematic analysis to identify research gaps.

Recent large-scale reviews have further structured influencer marketing research. For instance, Joshi et al. (2023) systematically reviewed 214 academic articles (2008–2021) to establish a framework for future investigations. Fowler and Thomas (2023) applied a framework-based scoping review to analyze theoretical perspectives, research contexts and methodological approaches, while Tanwar et al. (2024) conducted a bibliometric and content analysis (2011–2020), mapping key theoretical trends.

These reviews show that empirical research in influencer marketing predominantly used quantitative methodologies. Vrontis et al. (2021), for instance, noted that 81% of studies rely on surveys and experimental methods, often examining influencer credibility, attractiveness and consumer behavior (Joshi et al., 2023). Regression analysis and structural equation modeling are frequently used to assess predictive factors of purchase intentions (Tanwar et al., 2024), while computational techniques, such as network analysis, sentiment analysis and algorithm-based modeling, have been applied in 33 studies (Joshi et al., 2023).

Qualitative studies, though less common, provide deeper insights into influencer–follower dynamics, authenticity and content strategies. Existing studies adopt multiple qualitative methods such as in-depth interviews, case studies, focus groups, netnography and content and thematic analysis (Joshi et al., 2023; Tanwar et al., 2024). Since 2018, mixed-method approaches have gained traction, integrating qualitative interviews with quantitative methodologies to better provide an in-depth understanding of such phenomenon. Scholars encourage the adoption of this methodology to facilitate the evolution of the domain (Fowler & Thomas, 2023; Vrontis et al., 2021).

Emerging research methodologies include eye-tracking studies to measure engagement, web scraping, social media analytics to track influencer trends and A/B testing for real-time campaign assessment (Fowler & Thomas, 2023; Tanwar et al., 2024). These advancements signal a growing interest in data-driven insights and experimental methods to enhance influencer marketing research.

Influencer Marketing Research Themes

Since 2011, influencer marketing research has evolved from defining influencers and measuring success through follower count and engagement to examining their distinct impact on brand performance (Fowler & Thomas, 2023; Hudders et al., 2021a, 2021b; Leung et al., 2022). Between 2015 and 2017, scholars focused on self-branding and parasocial interactions, analyzing how influencers build trust, credibility and emotional connections to drive consumer decisions (Hudders et al., 2021a, 2021b; Joshi et al., 2023; Tanwar et al., 2024). From 2017 to 2019, attention shifted to sponsorship transparency, persuasion knowledge and ethics, with studies highlighting the impact of advertising disclosures on consumer trust and the need for standardized regulations (Hudders et al., 2021a, 2021b; Joshi et al., 2023; Leung et al., 2022).

Since 2020, research has increasingly examined platform algorithms, influencer credibility and psychological effects on consumers (Hudders et al., 2021a, 2021b; Tanwar et al., 2024; Vrontis et al., 2021). While current studies focus on branding effectiveness and content creation, only 12% critically analyze influencer marketing's negative consequences, revealing a gap in research on its 'dark side'. Furthermore, only 39% of studies explore specific industries, with beauty, fashion, travel and lifestyle being the most examined sectors, primarily on Instagram, YouTube and Facebook (Tanwar et al., 2024).

Despite the expanding body of influencer marketing literature, key insights into its effectiveness from both commercial and social perspectives remain underexplored. For instance, research on influencer pricing models and cost-effectiveness is limited, as is the study of algorithm-driven influencer selection and predictive analytics for campaign success (Leung et al., 2022). Additionally, growing scholarly interest in the broader societal impact of influencers – including their influence on public opinion, mental health and social behaviors – suggests a need for further research extending beyond the commercial domain of influencer marketing (Hudders et al., 2021a, 2021b).

INFLUENCERS AS A STRATEGIC APPROACH TO BRAND PROMOTION

Influencer marketing effectiveness refers to the extent to which influencers establish a strong, direct and organic connection between brands and consumers. This connection ultimately enhances engagement, shapes consumer attitudes and drives sales performance (Costello & Yesiloglu, 2020; Leung et al., 2022). Influencer marketing is often compared to traditional celebrity endorsements, where companies leverage the perceived credibility, attractiveness and reputation of celebrities to promote brands (Grau, 2022). However, influencers' credibility and popularity stem from their expertise in specific areas – such as travel, beauty or gaming; their ability to offer followers an authentic insight into their private lives and their talent to create unique, platform-specific content and other digital spaces. Moreover, influencers maintain closer and more interactive relationships with their followers, fostering a sense of similarity, relatability and perceived proximity. This enables them to exert greater influence and achieve higher effectiveness (Sammis et al., 2015). Empirical studies demonstrate that influencer-driven marketing strategies are more effective than traditional advertising approaches or conventional celebrity endorsements (Leung et al., 2022; De Jans et al., 2020; Djafarova & Rushworth, 2017).

The effectiveness of influencer marketing can be delineated into two primary outcomes. First, transactional effectiveness pertains to the direct impact on sales and purchase behavior. Scholars have examined how influencers translate engagement into consumer purchasing decisions, making their endorsements transactionally impactful (Pan et al., 2024; Vrontis et al., 2021). Second, non-transactional effectiveness encompasses broader consumer outcomes, such as shaping consumer preferences, attitudes and intentions (Leung et al., 2022; Costello & Yesiloglu, 2020). This dimension includes influencer marketing's impact on brand awareness, attitudes toward advertisements, brand perception, product perception, customer engagement intentions, purchase intentions and engagement behaviors (Spörl-Wang et al., 2025).

The following sections will explore the most widely used theories to explain influencer marketing effectiveness and provide a comprehensive overview of its antecedents.

UNDERLYING MECHANISMS EXPLAINING THE EFFECTIVENESS: THE 4Cs OF INFLUENCERS

In fulfilling their intermediary role between brands and consumers, influencers generate value by providing both community-oriented and commercial content and leveraging personal characteristics. The powerful nature of these attributes can be explained by different psychological and social mechanisms, including source credibility, parasocial interaction, congruity and the persuasion knowledge model, among others (e.g., Han & Balabanis, 2024; Pan et al., 2024). Spörl-Wang et al. (2025) conducted a meta-analytical review synthesizing insights from 93 studies to determine the primary predictors of consumer engagement and purchase intention in influencer marketing. Similarly, Han and Balabanis (2024) undertook a meta-analysis examining the antecedents and theoretical foundations of influencer impact. Pan et al. (2024) further contributed to this body of research by analyzing 251 studies, encompassing 1531 effect sizes, to identify the key drivers of influencer marketing effectiveness. Several theoretical constructs overlap, revealing the deep interconnectedness between factors related to influencer characteristics, audience engagement and the nature of the content created and disseminated on social media (e.g., Spörl-Wang et al., 2025).

By grouping the extant literature, we identified four factors (4Cs) that influence the effectiveness of influencers, namely personal characteristics (Characteristics), the relationships they cultivate (Connections), their alignment with brands and followers (Congruence) and their distinctive communication styles (Communication). Figure 35.1 presents a comprehensive visual representation of this process.

Characteristics of the Source: Credibility and Authenticity

Source Credibility Theory (Hovland & Weiss, 1951) has been identified as a critical determinant of both transactional and non-transactional outcomes, exerting a profound influence on overall influencer marketing effectiveness (Han & Balabanis, 2024). Source credibility refers to the characteristics of communicators that affect the receivers' acceptance of a message, determined by three key dimensions: expertise, trustworthiness and attractiveness (Ohanian, 1990). Expertise pertains to an influencer's perceived knowledge and competence in a specific domain. Trustworthiness relates to an influencer's perceived honesty, reliability and integrity, influencing whether consumers perceive their endorsements as genuine. Attractiveness extends beyond physical appearance to encompass likability, relatability and the influencer's ability to resonate with their audience (Ohanian, 1990). Research indicates that influencers who score highly in these dimensions significantly enhance consumer attitudes and purchase intentions (Pan et al., 2024). Han and Balabanis (2024) further indicate that the impact of source credibility depends on product category choices, with trustworthiness being a stronger predictor for

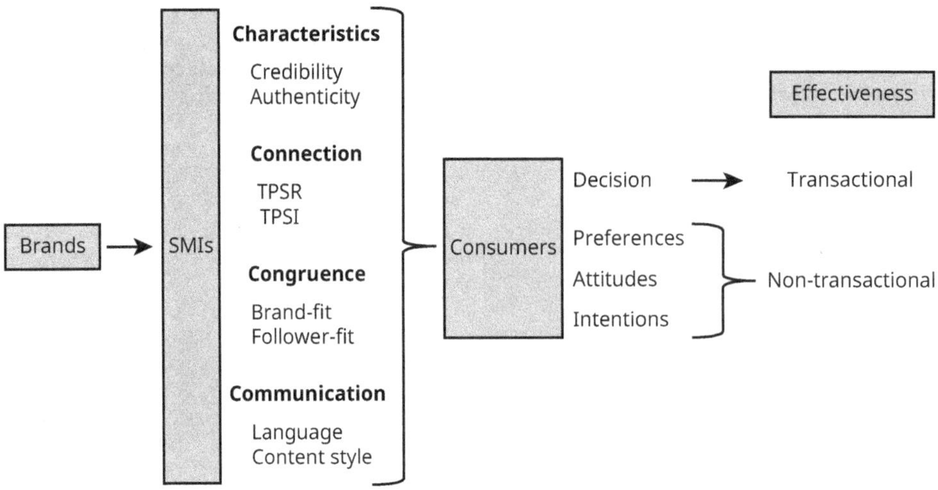

Figure 35.1 4Cs of Influencers Impacting Effectiveness

Source: the authors.

hedonic products, while expertise is more effective for utilitarian products.

The success of social media influencers, however, lies in their talent to combine expertise with authenticity. Although influencers are highly professionalized and become expert in a particular niche, it is their talent to bring content in an authentic way that explains their huge success (Audrezet et al., 2020; Aw and Agnihotri, 2024). Authenticity refers to the perception that an individual behaves by their true self (Moulard et al., 2015). In the context of influencer marketing, it represents the degree to which an influencer appears trustworthy and genuine in their presence and content (Kim & Kim, 2021). Parallels can be drawn with traditional marketing and communication principles, such as personal branding, strategic communication, self-presentation and advertorial campaigns (Joshi et al., 2023). The perception of authenticity is cultivated through a deliberate balancing act, a phenomenon termed 'calibrated amateurism' (Abidin, 2017). Influencers curate a mix of both edited and raw content, enabling them to maintain a professional image while being perceived as genuine and relatable by their audience (Abidin, 2017). This balance extends to self-disclosure and transparency, namely the extent to which influencers share personal information, experiences and opinions with their followers. To enhance relatability, influencers are expected to provide honest opinions, explain personal viewpoints and exhibit intrinsic motivation and passion in their endeavors. Consequently, influencers are often regarded as more authentic than traditional celebrities, as they offer unbiased perspectives and demonstrate a genuine commitment to their niche topics and the personalized experiences of their followers (Audrezet et al., 2020; Pan et al., 2024).

The quantitative attributes of an influencer's account, such as follower count and audience composition, often serve as key indicators of brand engagement and sponsored campaign success. Influencers are categorized based on follower count: celebrity and mega influencers have over one million followers, macro influencers range from 100,000 to one million, micro-influencers from 10,000 to 100,000 and nano influencers have fewer than 10,000 followers (Campbell & Farrell, 2020). Research suggests that as follower count decreases, perceived authenticity and accessibility increase. Micro and nano influencers enable marketers to reach niche audiences, whereas mega and macro influencers are more effective in generating widespread brand awareness. This aligns with previous studies, such as De Vries' (2019) experimental research, which revealed that an excessive follower count may diminish influencer credibility, thereby reducing effectiveness. Similarly, De Veirman et al. (2017) emphasized the necessity of striking an optimal balance in both follower and followee numbers to maintain trustworthiness and endorsement efficacy. Specifically, they suggested that high follower counts coupled with a low number of followers may indicate fake accounts or excessive focus on brand collaborations, ultimately decreasing authenticity.

In essence, an authentic influencer is perceived as more credible, leading to increased influence on consumer behaviors and positive brand outcomes (Audrezet et al., 2020; Han & Balabanis, 2024). Moreover, higher perceived authenticity is strongly correlated with influencer credibility, fostering positive sentiments such as trust, familiarity and friendship, which in turn facilitate the development of parasocial relationships. These relationships enhance followers' sense of closeness and admiration, augmenting influencers' capacity to influence consumer behavior and drive brand loyalty (Mrisha & Xixiang, 2024).

Connection: Transparasocial Relationships and Interaction

Originally conceptualized by Horton and Richard Wohl (1956), parasocial relationship theory described the sense of intimacy audiences developed toward television personalities due to repeated unidirectional exposure. In the social media era, this concept has been adapted to capture the relationships followers develop with influencers. Compared with the one-directional parasocial relationships developed in traditional media, the reciprocal and interactive nature of influencer–follower relationships has led to the emergence of a new concept, namely trans-parasocial relationships (Lou, 2022). Trans-parasocial relationships exhibit three defining characteristics: (1) they are collectively reciprocal, as influencers engage with their audiences as a whole; (2) they are synchronously interactive, depending on the extent to which audiences can provide timely feedback to influence content; and (3) they have a co-creative nature, as influencers and followers collaborate in shaping content, in fact through the reciprocal engagement, followers may perceive themselves as active contributors to an influencer's success, thereby enhancing their participation and loyalty (Abidin, 2015; Leung et al., 2022; Lou, 2022).

Studies have explored how influencers strategically manage these relationships to strengthen their personal brands, underscoring the importance of relationship management in sustaining audience engagement and trust (Joshi et al., 2023). Attractiveness and perceived similarity (homophily) serve as underlying psychological mechanisms reinforcing parasocial relationships. Consequently, brands can leverage influencers' pre-existing rapport and credibility within their target demographics to build deeper consumer relationships. Importantly, parasocial relationships are more effective than opinion leadership in driving purchase intentions, highlighting the pivotal role of the social aspect of influencer marketing (Farivar et al., 2021). Unlike traditional media figures, social media influencers break the 'fourth wall' – the conceptual barrier separating media figures from audiences (Ballantine & Martin, 2005) – by directly engaging with their followers through comments, live interactions and personal disclosures (Abidin, 2015; Kim & Kim, 2021). This interaction fosters a collective sense of community, perceived friendship and similarity (Kowert & Daniel, 2021), leading to increased interest in endorsed products (Yuan & Lou, 2020).

Congruence: Brand and Follower Fit

Influencer congruence refers to the degree of alignment between an influencer and the brand, product and audience (Kim & Kim, 2021). Congruity theory posits that individuals seek cognitive consistency when evaluating messages and opinions (Osgood & Tannenbaum, 1955). The greater the perceived congruence, the more favorable the evaluation. Accordingly, when a person shares a message that resonates with the audience's values and beliefs, it is more likely to be persuasive and well-received. Conversely, an incongruent message may be perceived as less persuasive and evaluated more negatively (Han & Balabanis, 2024). This characteristic is essential for brands seeking to optimize influencer partnerships, as selecting the right influencer hinges on achieving a strategic fit between the product and the intended target audience. For this reason, several distinctions have been made to facilitate the brand-fit process.

Traditionally, influencers have been categorized either by their specialization in a particular niche or by the size of their audience. The former categorization pertains to influencers' expertise in specific fields, which is crucial in assessing the congruence between a sponsored brand and the influencer's identity. Influencers may be classified as vertical (or 'monomorphic') influencers, who focus on a single domain, or horizontal (or 'polymorphic') influencers, who engage across multiple industries. Their expertise may center on a particular product category (e.g., beauty and gaming) or a broader industry (e.g., travel) (Grau, 2022).

Empirical research substantiates the importance of influencer congruence, with either brands and followers, for marketing outcomes. For instance, the survey study by Torres et al. (2019) revealed that influencer-brand congruence can predict brand attitudes, and subsequently, purchase intentions. The study further showed that a higher perceived attractiveness contributed to perceptions of congruity. Additionally, Vrontis et al. (2021) emphasized the critical role of influencer-brand congruence in fostering trust and shaping brand perception, further reinforcing its impact on credibility. To maximize effectiveness, influencers should align their personal brand, values and expertise with the endorsed brand, thereby enhancing perceived authenticity and increasing follower purchase intention (Kim & Kim, 2021).

Beyond influencer-brand alignment, congruence between influencers and their followers is equally vital. Research by Belanche et al. (2021) found that when there is high influencer–consumer congruence, this similarity enhances the congruence between the consumer and the product, leading to higher purchase intentions and recommendations. Such alignment is built on shared values, habits and preferences, fostering a more authentic and meaningful connection with the audience, and highlighting the significance of similarity and homophily (Freberg et al., 2011; Russell, 2020). As a consequence, brands must carefully select influencers whose audience demographics align with their target market. For instance, Cybex©, a brand specializing in baby strollers, carriers and car seats, collaborates with 'momfluencers' and family influencers on Instagram to promote its products. These influencers frequently share images and videos demonstrating how they use Cybex© strollers on walks with their babies or how they install car seats for family trips. Through these partnerships, Cybex© effectively reaches an engaged audience of young mothers and expectant parents who are highly interested in their products.

Communication: Language and Content Style

The communication style of influencers encompasses their interaction strategies, linguistic choices, visual aesthetics and content themes. According to Pan et al. (2024), influencer communication exerts a significant effect on purchase intention due to its unique combination of direct interaction and perceived personal relationships. In particular, followers' sense of closeness and intimacy with influencers plays a crucial role in shaping the impact of content. For example, Farivar et al. (2021) found that storytelling-based posts – where influencers share personal narratives rather than solely promoting products – are more engaging and persuasive for followers compared to purely informational content. Similarly, the visual presence and image of influencers influence marketing effectiveness. Jin et al. (2019) conducted an experimental study demonstrating that followers perceive brands as more credible and develop more favorable attitudes when influencers appear in sponsored posts rather than when only the product is shown. Expanding on this, Spörl-Wang et al. (2025) emphasized that an influencer's language style, specifically their expressive and personalized communication, fosters psychological closeness, thereby enhancing consumer engagement. Their research further highlights that content style also significantly impacts consumer responses: when influencers provide utilitarian content (i.e., informational or functional value), it has a stronger influence on purchase intention, whereas hedonic content (i.e., emotionally engaging or experiential) is more effective in fostering audience interaction and engagement (Spörl-Wang et al., 2025).

Communication can also be a strategic choice to manage authenticity. Audrezet et al. (2020) conducted a qualitative study analyzing influencer–brand partnerships, identifying two key strategies through which influencers communicate their authenticity, namely transparency and passion. Specifically, they argue that influencers demonstrate passionate authenticity when they create content that is inherently enjoyable and hedonic, while transparent authenticity is evident when influencers explicitly disclose sponsorships in informational content. Therefore, in communicating authenticity, influencers need to be intrinsically driven and transparent with their followers, even in disclosing a partnership. Research indicates that when followers recognize an influencer's endorsement as a commercial tactic, they may become skeptical and resistant to persuasion (Ye et al., 2021). The Persuasion Knowledge Model (Friestad & Wright, 1994) has been widely used to explain such responses. For instance, Spörl-Wang et al. (2025) investigated how sponsorship disclosure impacts consumer trust and engagement, finding that explicit disclosure can negatively affect purchase intention. However, if influencers maintain strong authenticity and credibility, the adverse effects of disclosure can be mitigated (Lou, 2022). This aligns with Hughes et al. (2019), who suggest that when consumers perceive value in influencer content, whether through informative utility or hedonic enjoyment, they are less likely to activate persuasion knowledge. In such cases, influencer marketing remains effective as audiences perceive the content as providing useful information and an enjoyable experience (Pan et al., 2024).

The following section explores implications for brands, emphasizing the need for further research into the darker aspects of influencer marketing effectiveness.

FUTURE RESEARCH AGENDA: EXPLORING THE DARK SIDE OF INFLUENCER MARKETING EFFECTIVENESS

Existing research has primarily emphasized the positive aspects of influencer marketing, positioning social media influencers as effective advertising tools (e.g., Campbell & Farrell, 2020). Hudders and Lou (2022) called for further research that explored influencer marketing's dark side by providing a comprehensive overview of potential risks faced by influencers and their audiences, categorizing these risks across influencers, audiences and regulatory concerns. Recently, Ekinci et al. (2025) delineated a research agenda to analyze the deceptive practice and regulatory challenges of influencers which may negatively impact the consumers' well-being. However, previous studies did not account for the implications for brands. This section critically examines the key challenges associated with influencer partnerships and identifies directions for future research from a brand-oriented perspective (see Table 35.1 for an overview of research questions).

Diminishing Authenticity Through Over-Exposure and Excessive Control

One of the most relevant implications of influencer marketing is the overexposure of followers to commercial influencer content. Indeed, by undertaking too many initiatives to sponsor different brands, influencers may see their credibility diminished and lose the trust of followers as they switch from one brand to another (Taylor, 2020). Furthermore, a high frequency of sharing sponsored content decreases the effectiveness of influencers. In particular, if the influencer specializes in product reviews, these reviews exert a greater impact if they are less common (Gerrath & Usrey, 2021). Conversely, brands should consider that engaging too much in partnerships with different influencers may lead to a dilution of brand meaning and a deviation from corporate goals due to the lack of control over different communication channels (Campbell & Farrell, 2020). Although it can increase the reach of a campaign, it can activate persuasion knowledge among followers. For instance, when followers notice that several of the influencers they follow "coincidentally" have spent the weekend in a holiday park, it becomes pretty clear that they all have been sponsored by this theme park. It can diminish the perceived creativity and uniqueness of the content. Moreover, brands should also monitor the parallel advertising they engage in

Table 35.1 Future research avenues

Diminishing authenticity through over-exposure and excessive control	• How does content saturation impact influencer credibility and audience trust? • How do followers perceive brand-scripted content compared to influencer-scripted content? • What is the optimal frequency of sponsored posts to maintain engagement while avoiding overexposure?
Harming brand reputation: spillover effect, disclosure, negative PSR and ethical concerns	• How can brands mitigate the negative spillover effect when partnering with influencers? • How can brands design effective disclosure strategies to maintain credibility while complying with regulations? • What governance strategies can be developed to ensure ethical and legal compliance in influencer-brand collaborations?
Virtual influencers and consumer distrust	• How does consumer perception of virtual influencers compare to human influencers? • Can virtual influencers build the same level of trust and engagement as human influencers? • How does the use of VIs affect consumer-brand relationships over time?
The impact on children	• What are the psychological and emotional effects of influencer marketing on child influencers? • How do audiences perceive the ethical implications of child influencers in brand collaborations? • How do child labor laws differ across regions, and how do they impact influencer marketing practices?

Source: The authors.

with other brands to track and avoid potential cannibalization and competition with other brands' campaigns (Alipour et al., 2025). For instance, when an influencer becomes a brand ambassador for a competitor brand as well.

Moreover, as the industry has evolved with stricter regulations, professionalization and agency involvement, campaign costs have increased. Consequently, brands now seek greater control over content through detailed creative briefs outlining objectives, key messages and deliverables. However, increased brand oversight can conflict with influencers' creative autonomy, potentially diminishing content authenticity (Alipour et al., 2025). Highly prescriptive guidelines may disrupt an influencer's editorial style, making the content feel overly commercial, thereby reducing audience engagement and campaign effectiveness. Striking a balance between brand control and influencer creativity is essential to optimizing outcomes. Brands must recognize the inherent risks of influencer collaborations and acknowledge that some degree of creative freedom is necessary to preserve authenticity and prevent reputational damage (Borchers & Enke, 2021).

Further research should consider the role of content saturation on platforms and the strategies that can be used to avoid reduced authenticity for both brands and influencers while maintaining consumer engagement. Similarly, future studies may consider the different impact of brand- versus influencer-scripted content on followers.

Harming Brand Reputation: Spillover Effect, Disclosure, Negative Parasocial Relationship (PSR) and Ethical Concerns

While much of the research on the influencer spillover effect has focused on its positive implications, particularly in contexts such as co-branding, brand extension, celebrity endorsement and sponsorship (for a review, see Raufeisen et al., 2019), its potential drawbacks should not be overlooked. Influencers with strong reputations can effectively transfer their credibility to endorsed brands, enhancing brand perception and consumer trust (Fowler & Thomas, 2023). This effect is particularly evident when influencers maintain consistency between their organic and sponsored content (Cheng & Zhang, 2024). However, spillover can also have negative consequences. Underperforming influencers may damage a brand's image, and when influencers become embroiled in scandals or engage in ethically questionable behavior, the brands they endorse risk reputational harm (Campbell & Farrell, 2020; Leung et al., 2022). Similarly, if the fit between the influencer's organic content and the espoused content is incongruent, a negative perception may occur and result in the loss of followers for both sides (Belanche et al., 2021). This challenge is becoming increasingly prominent, especially as social media interactions grow more dynamic and unpredictable. The evolving nature of digital engagement means that influencers are not only content creators but also key players in real-time conversations, making it harder for brands to control narratives and anticipate potential crises. This challenge is particularly evident in live streaming, where real-time engagement demands a flexible approach to content creation. Unlike pre-recorded videos, which allow for postproduction editing, live-streaming features extended durations and direct audience interaction (Sjöblom et al., 2019; Tammy Lin et al., 2019). As interactions between influencers and their audiences become more spontaneous and participatory, the risk of reputational spillover intensifies. Research lacks evidence on how brands can mitigate the spillover effect or how they can prevent it when dealing with an influencer. Future studies may explore the implication of the spillover effect in a more interactive environment and what are the implications for brands.

Transparency in advertising and sponsorship is crucial for influencer marketing, yet influencers and brands often struggle to balance financial incentives with maintaining credibility. Influencers should prioritize audience over brand relationships. If followers perceive promotions as self-serving, influencers may disengage from brand awareness efforts like electronic word-of-mouth, suggesting that monetary incentives alone do not ensure partnership success (López et al., 2022). Brands should facilitate authentic engagement through long-term partnerships leveraging influencers' intrinsic motivations, providing product giveaways and exclusive experiences like sponsored trips or events (Gerrath & Usrey, 2021). This issue becomes even more critical given that sponsorship disclosure can also negatively affect consumer attitudes. Disclosing sponsorships can reduce influencer credibility and authenticity (De Veirman & Hudders, 2020), as well as positive reviews of a disclosed–sponsored product. However, if an influencer is intrinsically motivated by product reviews, the negative effect on followers can be mitigated (Gerrath & Usrey, 2021). Moreover, this mechanism relates to the spreading of misinformation including fake endorsement, undisclosed sponsorship and brand alignment discrepancies, which is one of the most prominent dark sides impacting consumer well-being (Ekinci et al., 2025).

Current regulations regarding sponsorship disclosures are becoming stricter. In Belgium, the Content Creator Protocol dictates the use of three types of disclosures for a sponsored post, story or reel: a clear hashtag (e.g., advertising, publicity) at the beginning of the caption, a mention of the sponsoring brand and an indication that the post is sponsored using the platform's disclosure feature (see Vlamsee Regulator Voor De Media, 2025). The regulation does not distinguish between types of sponsorships, so free products must be disclosed similarly to paid collaborations. This causes some resistance among influencers because they fear negative responses from their viewers when disclosing all brand deals as advertising. They argue that there is a strong difference between paid partnerships and gifts, and influencers are now starting to additionally disclose the type of sponsorship to make the distinction. In addition, influencers are hesitant to use the paid partnership label of the platform because they fear punishment by the platform algorithm, which makes the post less visible.

A multicountry study of Instagram content published by influencers in the USA, Brazil, the Netherlands and Germany shows that disclosure practices differ across these countries and align with their respective regulations (Bertaglia et al., 2025). While influencers in the Netherlands and Brazil often use the paid partnership label, influencers in the USA and Germany more frequently use hashtags and keywords in captions to indicate sponsorship. The latter is less clear to users as it can be hidden within the caption content, whereas a paid partnership label is disclosed at the top of the post (Bertaglia et al., 2025). Interestingly, their analysis revealed that sponsored posts have longer captions, nearly double the length of non-sponsored posts. This might indicate that influencers put more effort into storytelling and explaining why they chose to endorse the brand and how it fits their image.

Further research should deepen the knowledge on how brands can deal with sponsorship disclosures and especially, what are the other mechanisms that both influencers and brands can enact to mitigate its negative effects.

Moreover, this aspect is strictly related to law complaints. Ethically and legally, proper disclosure is essential to avoid penalties and contract breaches (Campbell & Farrell, 2020). The Chiara Ferragni–Balocco scandal exemplifies the risks of misleading transparency, where a charity-driven product launch failed to deliver promised donations, causing significant reputational damage and legal scrutiny. This underscores the need for clear disclosure practices to protect both brand integrity and influencer trust. Additionally, the absence of standardized contractual agreements within the influencer marketing industry exacerbates these risks: influencers may violate agreements, either intentionally or due to the informal nature of some brand partnerships (Alipour et al., 2025). Addressing these issues requires further research to develop effective governance strategies, ensuring brand protection while maintaining the benefits of influencer collaboration. In particular, it would be valuable to explore potential ethical dilemmas and examine their impact on brand reputation and consumer loyalty (Ekinci et al., 2025).

Finally, mismanagement of influencer communication can harm audience relationships. Hudders et al. (2021a, 2021b) found that defensive responses to negative comments erode consumer trust, lower product perceptions and damage brand attitudes. Singh et al. (2020) found that the perception of a manipulative attempt from influencers may also undermine the brand's reputation, especially if the brand is facing a crisis. The unpredictability of the influencers' communication is a crucial factor to consider when partnering with them. This may signal a shift in parasocial relationships, though further research is needed to explore the effects of followers' experienced betrayal, deception or mistrust experience on brand reputation.

Virtual Influencers (VIs) and Consumer Distrust

The rise of artificial intelligence (AI) has led to the emergence of VIs – digital personas designed to engage audiences and enhance brand visibility. Unlike human influencers, VIs offer greater control over messaging and branding, making them an increasingly attractive option for companies. A notable example is Lil Miquela, a VI with over three million Instagram followers. Her 2018 collaboration with Prada during Milan Fashion Week – featuring posts and stories with the hashtag #PradaFW18 – demonstrated the power of AI-driven influencers in generating media impact and brand engagement (Launchmetrics, 2018). Despite advantages such as customization, flexibility and automation (Mouritzen et al., 2024), VIs face challenges related to authenticity and consumer perception. Research by Sands et al. (2022) found mixed reactions – while some consumers view them as trustworthy and relatable, others find them artificial and unconvincing.

As influencer marketing evolves, brands must navigate challenges in content control, brand reputation and audience trust. Future research should explore how to balance authenticity with AI-driven marketing and whether VIs can achieve the same consumer engagement as human influencers. Addressing these concerns will be essential for optimizing long-term influencer strategies and maintaining audience credibility.

The Impact on Children

The increasing involvement of children in commercial content has become a major concern in influencer marketing. Parent influencers frequently feature their children to enhance authenticity, attracting brand sponsorships and, in some cases, leading children to manage their own social media accounts. Platforms like TikTok and YouTube have fueled a kidfluencer culture, with young influencers such as Ryan's World, LikeNastya and Vlad and Niki turning into lucrative brands managed by agencies like Pocket Watch (Feller & Burroughs, 2022).

However, the rise of child influencers raises ethical and societal concerns. Clark and Jno-Charles (2025) identify five key risks: lack of consent, public exposure leading to emotional and reputational harm, financial control over earnings, psychological and physical pressures from performance expectations and restricted freedom of expression due to scripted content. These concerns have led to calls for stricter child labor regulations, prompting France, Illinois and California to enact legal protections against child influencer exploitation.

In response to growing awareness, some influencers are adopting privacy-conscious practices. For example, a Belgian influencer ensures her children remain unidentifiable in social media posts by using emojis or other covering techniques. For brands, incorporating child influencers carries ethical risks and may lead to public backlash over commercial exploitation. Therefore, brands must carefully assess these implications and implement responsible guidelines to uphold ethical standards in influencer marketing.

CONCLUSION

In this chapter, we have examined the key themes within the influencer marketing literature and its integration into brand management, highlighting the strategic potential of influencers as a dynamic marketing asset. The parasocial relationships they cultivate over time, reinforced by the trust engendered through perceived authenticity, position influencers as a more impactful alternative to traditional marketing approaches. However, the effectiveness of influencer marketing is contingent upon strategic alignment with brand objectives, audience engagement dynamics, the continuously evolving digital ecosystem and, crucially, the distinctive attributes of influencers themselves. This chapter establishes a conceptual foundation for future scholarly inquiry, encouraging a more nuanced exploration of influencer marketing's long-term impact. Specifically, we advocate for an intensified research focus on the darker facets of influencer marketing, aiming to generate critical insights into crisis scenarios that may pose significant risks to brands, audiences and influencers alike.

REFERENCES

Abidin, C. (2015). Communicative ♥ intimacies: Influencers and perceived interconnectedness. *Ada: A Journal of Gender, New Media, and Technology*, *8*, 1–16. http://dx.doi.org/10.7264/N3MW2FFG

Abidin, C. (2017). #Familygoals: Family influencers, calibrated amateurism, and justifying young digital labor. *Social Media and Society*, *3*(2), 1–15. https://doi-org.unibg.idm.oclc.org/10.1177/2056305117707191

Alipour, S. M., Ghaffari, M., & Zare, H. (2025). Influencer marketing research: A systematic literature review to identify influencer marketing threats. *Management Review Quarterly*, *75*, 1393–1418 https://doi.org/10.1007/s11301-024-00412-5

Audrezet, A., de Kerviler, G., & Guidry Moulard, J. (2020). Authenticity under threat: When social media influencers need to go beyond self-presentation. *Journal of Business Research*, *117*, 557–569. https://doi.org/10.1016/j.jbusres.2018.07.008

Aw, E. C. X., & Agnihotri, R. (2024). Influencer marketing research: Review and future research agenda. *Journal of Marketing Theory and Practice*, *32*(4), 435–448. https://doi.org/10.1080/10696679.2023.2235883

Ballantine, P. W., & Martin, B. A. S. (2005). *Forming parasocial relationships in online communities* (Vol. 32). Association for Consumer Research.

Belanche, D., Casaló, L. V., Flavián, M., & Ibáñez-Sánchez, S. (2021). Understanding influencer marketing: The role of congruence between influencers, products and consumers. *Journal of Business Research*, *132*, 186–195. https://doi.org/10.1016/j.jbusres.2021.03.067

Bertaglia, T., Goanta, C., Spanakis, G., & Iamnitchi, A. (2025). Influencer self-disclosure practices on Instagram: A multi-country longitudinal study. *Online Social Networks and Media*, *45*, 100298. https://doi.org/10.1016/j.osnem.2024.100298

Borchers, N. S., & Enke, N. (2021). Managing strategic influencer communication: A systematic overview on emerging planning, organization, and control routines. *Public Relations Review*, *47*(3), 1–13. https://doi.org/10.1016/j.pubrev.2021.102041

Campbell, C., & Farrell, J. R. (2020). More than meets the eye: The functional components underlying influencer marketing. *Business Horizons*, *63*(4), 469–479. https://doi.org/10.1016/j.bushor.2020.03.003

Cheng, M., & Zhang, S. (2024). Reputation burning: Analyzing the impact of brand sponsorship on social influencers. *Management Science*. *7*, 5910–5932. http://dx.doi.org/10.2139/ssrn.4071188

Clark, D. R., & Jno-Charles, A. B. (2025). The child labor in social media: Kidfluencers, ethics of care, and exploitation. *Journal of Business Ethics*. https://doi.org/10.1007/s10551-025-05953-7

Costello, J., & Yesiloglu, S. (Eds.) (2020). *Influencer marketing: Building brand communities and engagement* (1st ed.). Routledge.

De Jans, S., Van de Sompel, D., De Veirman, M., & Hudders, L. (2020). # Sponsored! How the recognition of sponsoring on Instagram posts affects adolescents' brand evaluations through source evaluations. *Computers in Human Behavior*, *109*, 106342. https://doi.org/10.1016/j.chb.2020.106342

Delbaere, M., Michael, B., & Phillips, B. J. (2021). Social media influencers: A route to brand engagement for their followers. *Psychology and Marketing*, *38*(1), 101–112. https://doi.org/10.1002/mar.21419

De Veirman, M., Cauberghe, V., & Hudders, L. (2017). Marketing through instagram influencers: The impact of number of followers and product divergence on brand attitude. *International Journal of Advertising*, *36*(5), 798–828. https://doi.org/10.1080/02650487.2017.1348035

De Veirman, M., & Hudders, L. (2020). Disclosing sponsored Instagram posts: The role of material connection with the brand and message-sidedness when disclosing covert advertising. *International Journal of Advertising*, *39*(1), 94–130.

De Vries, E. L. E. (2019). When more likes is not better: The consequences of high and low likes-to-followers ratios for perceived account credibility and social media marketing effectiveness. *Marketing Letters*, *30*(3–4), 275–291. https://doi.org/10.1007/s11002-019-09496-6

Djafarova, E., & Rushworth, C. (2017). Exploring the credibility of online celebrities' Instagram profiles in influencing the purchase decisions of young female users. *Computers in Human Behavior*, *68*, 1–7. https://doi.org/10.1016/j.chb.2016.11.009

Ekinci, Y., Dam, S., & Buckle, G. (2025). The dark side of social media influencers: A research agenda for analysing deceptive practices and regulatory challenges. *Psychology & Marketing*, *42*(4), 1201–1214. https://doi.org/10.1002/mar.22173

Farivar, S., Wang, F., & Yuan, Y. (2021). Opinion leadership vs. para-social relationship: Key factors in influencer marketing. *Journal of Retailing and Consumer Services*, *59*, 1–11. https://doi.org/10.1016/j.jretconser.2020.102371

Feller, G., & Burroughs, B. (2022). Branding kidfluencers: Regulating content and advertising on YouTube. *Television & New Media*, *23*(6), 575–592. https://doi.org/10.1177/15274764211052882

Fortune Business Insight. (2025, February 25). Retrieved March 17, 2025, from www.fortunebusinessinsights.com/influencer-marketing-platform-market-108880

Fowler, K., & Thomas, V. L. (2023). Influencer marketing: A scoping review and a look ahead. *Journal of Marketing Management*, *39*(11–12), 933–964. https://doi.org/10.1080/0267257X.2022.2157038

Freberg, K., Graham, K., McGaughey, K., & Freberg, L. A. (2011). Who are the social media influencers? A study of public perceptions of personality. *Public Relations Review*, *37*(1), 90–92. https://doi.org/10.1016/j.pubrev.2010.11.001

Friestad, M., & Wright, P. (1994). The persuasion knowledge model: How people cope with persuasion attempts. *Journal of Consumer Research*, *21*(1), 1–31.

Gerrath, M. H., & Usrey, B. (2021). The impact of influencer motives and commonness perceptions on follower reactions toward incentivized reviews. *International Journal of Research in Marketing*, *38*(3), 531–548. https://doi.org/10.1016/j.ijresmar.2020.09.010

Goanta, C. (2021). *Emerging business models and the crowdfunding regulation: Income crowdfunding on social media by content creators.* Available at SSRN 3885581.

Grau, S. L. (2022). *Celebrity 2.0: The role of social media influencer marketing in building brands.* Business Expert Press.

Han, J., & Balabanis, G. (2024). Meta-analysis of social media influencer impact: Key antecedents and theoretical foundations. *Psychology and Marketing*, *41*(2), 394–426. https://doi.org/10.1002/mar.21927

Horton, D., & Richard Wohl, R. (1956). Mass communication and para-social interaction. *Psychiatry*, *19*(3), 215–229. https://doi.org/10.1080/00332747.1956.11023049

Hovland, C. I., & Weiss, W. (1951). The influence of source credibility on communication effectiveness. *The Public Opinion Quarterly*, *15*(4), 635–650. www.jstor.org/stable/2745952

Hudders, L., De Jans, S., & De Veirman, M. (2021a). The commercialization of social media stars: A literature review and conceptual framework on the strategic use of social media influencers. *International Journal of Advertising*, *40*(3), 327–375. https://doi.org/10.1080/02650487.2020.1836925

Hudders, L., & Lou, C. (2022). The rosy world of influencer marketing? Its bright and dark sides, and future research recommendations. *International Journal of Advertising*, *42*(1), 151–161. https://doi.org/10.1080/02650487.2022.2137318

Hudders, L., Lou, C., & de Brabandere, M. (2021b). Understanding the impact of influencers' responses to negative follower comments on the persuasiveness of sponsored Instagram posts. *International Journal of Advertising*, *41*(1), 178–204. https://doi.org/10.1080/02650487.2021.1963554

Hughes, C., Swaminathan, V., & Brooks, G. (2019). Driving brand engagement through online social influencers: An empirical investigation of sponsored blogging campaigns. *Journal of Marketing*, *83*(5), 78–96. https://doi.org/10.1177/0022242919854374

Influencer Marketing Hub. (2025, January 30). *Influencer marketing benchmark report 2025.* Retrieved March 12, 2025, from https://influencermarketinghub.com/influencer-marketing-benchmark-report/

Jin, S. V., Muqaddam, A., & Ryu, E. (2019). Instafamous and social media influencer marketing. *Marketing Intelligence & Planning*, *37*(5), 567–579. https://doi.org/10.1108/MIP-09-2018-0375

Joshi, Y., Lim, W. M., Jagani, K., & Kumar, S. (2023). Social media influencer marketing: Foundations, trends, and ways forward. *Electronic Commerce Research*, *25*, 1199–1253. https://doi.org/10.1007/s10660-023-09719-z

Kim, D. Y., & Kim, H. Y. (2021). Influencer advertising on social media: The multiple inference model on influencer-product congruence and sponsorship disclosure. *Journal of Business Research*, *130*, 405–415. https://doi.org/10.1016/j.jbusres.2020.02.020

Kowert, R., & Daniel, E. (2021). The one-and-a-half sided parasocial relationship: The curious case of live streaming. *Computers in Human Behavior Reports*, *4*, 1–7. https://doi.org/10.1016/j.chbr.2021.100150

Kozinets, R. V., Gretzel, U., & Gambetti, R. C. (2023). *Influencers and creators: Business, culture and practice*. Sage.

Launchmetrics. (2018, September 19). *Prada FW 18. Analisi di una Sfilata Organicamente Digitale.* Retrieved January 20, 2025, from www.launchmetrics.com/it/risorse/blog/prada-fw18-sfilata-analisi-digitale

Leung, F. F., Gu, F. F., & Palmatier, R. W. (2022). Online influencer marketing. *Journal of the Academy of Marketing Science*, *50*(2), 226–251. https://doi.org/10.1007/s11747-021-00829-4

López, M., Sicilia, M., & Verlegh, P. W. J. (2022). How to motivate opinion leaders to spread e-WoM on social media: Monetary vs non-monetary incentives. *Journal of Research in Interactive Marketing*, *16*(1), 154–171. https://doi.org/10.1108/JRIM-03-2020-0059

Lou, C. (2022). Social media influencers and followers: Theorization of a trans-parasocial relation and explication of its implications for influencer advertising. *Journal of Advertising*, *51*(1), 4–21. https://doi.org/10.1080/00913367.2021.1880345

Marketing Charts. (2022, September 7). *Leading ways in which influencers can become more valuable to brands according to marketers worldwide as of August 2022 [Graph]. In Statista.* Retrieved

January 07, 2025, from www-statista.com.unibg.idm.oclc.org/statistics/1340833/top-ways-influencers-can-become-more-valuable-brands/

Moulard, J. G., Garrity, C. P., & Rice, D. H. (2015). What makes a human brand authentic? Identifying the antecedents of celebrity authenticity. *Psychology & Marketing*, *32*(2), 173–186. https://doi.org/10.1002/mar.20771

Mouritzen, S. L. T., Penttinen, V., & Pedersen, S. (2024). Virtual influencer marketing: The good, the bad and the unreal. *European Journal of Marketing*, *58*(2), 410–440. https://doi.org/10.1108/EJM-12-2022-0915

Mrisha, S. H., & Xixiang, S. (2024). The power of influence: How social media influencers are shaping consumer decision making in the digital age. *Journal of Consumer Behaviour*, *23*(4), 1844–1853. https://doi.org/10.1002/cb.2308

Ohanian, R. (1990). Construction and validation of a scale to measure celebrity endorsers' perceived expertise, trustworthiness, and attractiveness. *Journal of Advertising*, *19*(3), 39–52. https://doi.org/10.1080/00913367.1990.10673191

Osgood, C. E., & Tannenbaum, P. H. (1955). The principle of congruity in the prediction of attitude change. *Psychological Review*, *62*(1), 42.

Pan, M., Blut, M., Ghiassaleh, A., & Lee, Z. W. Y. (2024). Influencer marketing effectiveness: A meta-analytic review. *Journal of the Academy of Marketing Science*, *53*, 52–78. https://doi.org/10.1007/s11747-024-01052-7

Peres, R., Schreier, M., Schweidel, D. A., & Sorescu, A. (2024). The creator economy: An introduction and a call for scholarly research. *International Journal of Research in Marketing*, *41*(3), 403–410. https://doi.org/10.1016/j.ijresmar.2024.07.005

Raufeisen, X., Wulf, L., Köcher, S., Holzmüller, H. H. (2019). Spillover effects in marketing: Integrating core research domains. *AMS Review*, *9*(3–4), 249–267. https://doi.org/10.1007/s13162-019-00143-x

Retail Drive. (2023, November 14). *The rise of the Stanley tumbler: How a 110-year-old brand achieved viral success.* Retrieved February 23, 2025, from www.retaildive.com/news/stanley-quencher-tumblers-viral-success/699416/

Russell, A. (2020). *The influencer code: How to unlock the power of influencer marketing*. Hatherleigh Press.

Sammis, K., Lincoln, C., & Pomponi, S. (2015). *Influencer marketing for dummies*. John Wiley & Sons.

Sands, S., Campbell, C. L., Plangger, K., & Ferraro, C. (2022). Unreal influence: Leveraging AI in influencer marketing. *European Journal of Marketing*, *56*(6), 1721–1747. https://doi.org/10.1108/EJM-12-2019-0949

Schouten, A. P., Janssen, L., & Verspaget, M. (2020). Celebrity vs. influencer endorsements in advertising: The role of identification, credibility, and product-endorser fit. *International Journal of Advertising: The Review of Marketing Communications*, *39*(2), 258–281. https://doi.org/10.1080/02650487.2019.1634898

Shtern, J., & Hill, S. (2021). 13 The political economy of sponsored content and social media entertainment production. In S. Cunningham, & D. Craig (Eds.), *Creator culture: An introduction to global social media entertainment,* (p. 250–270). New York University Press. https://doi.org/10.18574/nyu/9781479890118.003.0017

Singh, J., Crisafulli, B., & Xue, M. T. (2020). 'To trust or not to trust': The impact of social media influencers on the reputation of corporate brands in crisis. *Journal of Business Research*, *119*, 464–480. https://doi.org/10.1016/j.jbusres.2020.03.039

Sjöblom, M., Törhönen, M., Hamari, J., & Macey, J. (2019). The ingredients of Twitch streaming: Affordances of game streams. *Computers in Human Behavior*, *92*, 20–28. https://doi.org/10.1016/j.chb.2018.10.012

Spörl-Wang, K., Krause, F., & Henkel, S. (2025). Predictors of social media influencer marketing effectiveness: A comprehensive literature review and meta-analysis. *Journal of Business Research*, *186*, 1–15. https://doi.org/10.1016/j.jbusres.2024.114991

Tammy Lin, J. H., Bowman, N., Lin, S. F., & Chen, Y. S. (2019). Setting the digital stage: Defining game streaming as an entertainment experience. *Entertainment Computing*, 31. https://doi.org/10.1016/j.entcom.2019.100309

Tanwar, A. S., Chaudhry, H., & Srivastava, M. K. (2024). Social media influencers: Literature review, trends and research agenda. *Journal of Advances in Management Research*, *21*(2), 173–202. https://doi.org/10.1108/JAMR-10-2022-0218

Taylor, C. R. (2020). The urgent need for more research on influencer marketing. *International Journal of Advertising*, *39*(7), 889–891. https://doi.org/10.1080/02650487.2020.1822104

Torres, P., Augusto, M., & Matos, M. (2019). Antecedents and outcomes of digital influencer endorsement: An exploratory study. *Psychology and Marketing*, *36*(12), 1267–1276. https://doi.org/10.1002/mar.21274

Vlamsee Regulator Voor De Media. (2025). *Content creator protocol*. Retrieved March 17, 2025, from www.vlaamseregulatormedia.be/nl/content-creator-protocol

Vrontis, D., Makrides, A., Christofi, M., & Thrassou, A. (2021). Social media influencer marketing: A systematic review, integrative framework and future research agenda. *International Journal of Consumer Studies*, *45*(4), 617–644. https://doi.org/10.1111/ijcs.12647

Ye, G., Hudders, L., De Jans, S., & De Veirman, M. (2021). The value of influencer marketing for business: A bibliometric analysis and managerial implications. *Journal of Advertising*, *50*(2), 160–178. https://doi.org/10.1080/00913367.2020.1857888

Yuan, S., & Lou, C. (2020). How social media influencers foster relationships with followers: The roles of source credibility and fairness in parasocial relationship and product interest. *Journal of Interactive Advertising*, 133–147. https://doi.org/10.1080/15252019.2020.1769514

Zabel, C. (2024). Mapping factors of success: A structured literature review on social media influencers' business models. *Journal of Creative Industries and Cultural Studies – JOCIS*, *11*(2), 84–139. https://doi.org/10.56140/JOCIS-v11-5

36

Play Smart, Win Big: How Game Elements Can Benefit Brands

Laurence Dessart and Lisa Baiwir

INTRODUCTION

Powered by technological advancement and societal forces, brand management is increasingly participative, and brand meaning is co-created (Ramaswamy & Ozcan, 2016). As consumers become empowered in their brand consumption, they seek opportunities to engage with brands in interactive manners, breaking the rule of the traditional one-way brand relationship style (Cambier & Poncin, 2020; Füller et al., 2009). As a result, consumers perform an increasingly active and co-creative role in brand meaning creation, development and sustenance (Merz et al., 2009). Social media have been a critical impulsion in this change of paradigm (Malthouse et al., 2016), shifting how brands are embedded in consumers' lives to a more networked, open and technology-driven approach (Swaminathan et al., 2020), which is in constant mutation.

Additionally, the exponential growth in smartphones and mobile devices has drastically changed how brands interact with their consumers. With 7.4 billion mobile phone owners worldwide (Statista, 2024) and a rapidly growing portable devices market, technologies such as mobile applications (apps) offer a wide array of opportunities for brands to connect with their users in a meaningful way through engaging experiences and a tight embedding in their everyday lives (Mardon & Belk, 2018). Branded apps are means for brands to engage their consumers in daily experiences and activities. Recently, brands have started using apps as flagship platforms mediating versatile interactions between participants around the brand (Wichmann et al., 2022). Branded applications offer a wide range of benefits to users, tapping into motivations such as usefulness, utility or entertainment (Stocchi et al., 2018) and spanning a variety of sectors, from health management to home automation. Further, such platforms create a rich playground for the gamification market (Kunkel et al., 2021).

Gamification is 'the use of game mechanisms in non-game contexts' (Deterding et al., 2011, p. 2). As a result, gamification is the application of gaming principles to change behaviors in non-game situations (Robson et al., 2015) while tapping into the basic human impulses to socialize, achieve, be engaged and be rewarded. Spurred by the rise of mobile technologies and branded apps, as well as managers' eagerness to capitalize on them, gamification is increasingly becoming one of the drivers of technological and behavioral change in many industries. With an estimated market size of 15.43 billion USD in 2024 and an expected 48.72 billion by 2029, gamification is recognized as a key tool to influence consumer behavior, innovation, productivity and engagement (Mordor Intelligence, 2024) and thus shape brand management.

In this interactive landscape, a number of brands have hopped on the gamification bandwagon. Typical examples include branded apps designed to achieve personal goals, such as fitness apps like Nike Run Club or Strava. These branded apps allow users to set training objectives, measure activity that has been personalized to users' needs and connect with a community of like-minded people. L'Occitane en Provence takes a different approach and creates an app that allows users to nurture a seed and grow a plant with limited resources. By doing so, users get educated on sustainable behavior but also unlock rewards, thus supporting benefits based on moral values while enhancing the brand image.

Gamification is often supported by, but not constrained to, mobile environments. For instance, McDonald's has installed touchpads on tables in certain branches, allowing children to play branded games while waiting for their meals. This technique makes a trip to McDonald's more than just a dining-out experience and enhances user engagement with the brand. The variety of game elements adopted by brands is indicative of the power of gamification to support positive brand outcomes, attain a variety of marketing objectives and offer consumer benefits.

To date, research at the intersection of gamification, consumer behavior and brand management has highlighted some of the potential outcomes of gamified experiences for brands, including consumer engagement with the game, which may extend to the brand (Hammedi et al., 2019), increased purchase intention and behavioral or attitudinal loyalty (Stocchi et al., 2018), data collection or ideas for segmentation and innovation purposes (Nobre & Ferreira, 2017). Further, marketing researchers highlight several factors driving the successful use of gamification for marketing purposes, which may pertain to the situational context in which gamification is embedded (e.g., time available to play, Berger et al., 2018), consumer characteristics (e.g., individual goals and competitiveness, Robson et al., 2015) or the type of game technique used (e.g., Eisingerich et al., 2019). Yet, there needs to be a comprehensive overview of the interplay of various factors that may contribute to positive brand outcomes in the context of game elements adoption in a brand strategy. Further, the array of potential brand outcomes has been approached in a scattered manner, with each author focusing on a limited set of brand benefits of gamification separately.

As a result, this chapter aims to address these critical gaps by proposing an integrative framework and related propositions, of the individual factors (consumer-level), contextual and game-related factors that lead to positive brand outcomes when brands adopt game elements as part of their strategy. In this way, we offer a theoretical contribution to the brand management literature, showing that the interplay of game elements and their integration into the brand strategy, alongside contextual and individual factors will influence affective, cognitive and behavioral brand outcomes.

In particular, and based on the extant marketing, branding, services and information technology literature, we conceptualize which game elements might be conducive to specific brand outcomes and under which conditions through a conceptual framework, set of propositions and explanations of specific conditions of application. This contribution is relevant because gamification is a multifaceted technique that can be used in many ways by brand managers and for varying purposes. Building on these conceptual foundations, the chapter offers pragmatic advice for managers who wish to use gamification to support their brand creation or development efforts.

UNDERSTANDING GAMIFICATION

Definition and Characteristics

Gamification links game studies to marketing, bridging the perspectives of game designers and users. It is broadly defined as the application of gaming principles to change behaviors in real-life contexts (Deterding et al., 2011). While the gaming perspective emphasizes the game design elements (e.g., frameworks and rules; Robson et al., 2015), the user perspective acknowledges the importance of the gamified experience for individual users (e.g., fun and enjoyment; Huotari & Hamari, 2017). Gamification is thus characterized by the interaction of two separate entities: (a) the system developed by designers, which contains goals, rules and challenges, and (b) the user who interacts with this system, leading to individual experiences with specific dynamics and affective states (Landers et al., 2019; Robson et al., 2015).

Both games and gamification can be used by brands, yet they differ in their applications and implementations. Gamification shares a foundational relationship with traditional games, drawing on elements that are considered 'characteristic' of games (Deterding et al., 2011, p. 12) to tap into human motivation principles and satisfy basic human needs such as relatedness, competence and escapism (Koivisto & Hamari, 2019; Landers et al., 2019). However, gamification differs from typical game environments as its aims often extend beyond the game itself (Landers et al., 2019). While games are designed to create flow and motivation to achieve in-game objectives, gamification applies gaming principles to real-world activities. For example, 'Red Bull Racers' is a game where users compete to reach the finish line of a racing track as fast as possible by controlling the speed of a customized racing car and driver. Players can click on a button during the race to 'drink a Redbull', giving their racing car a limited speed boost. While fun, entertaining and engaging, the game's goal (winning the race) is constrained to the game context. If the brand were to award loyalty points and exclusive rewards to top players, the game's purpose would extend beyond the game environment, exemplifying gamification. The main distinction is that gamification can produce real-world outcomes, whereas games remain self-contained.

In marketing management, gamification is mainly used to enhance a firm's perceived value by tapping into primary human motivations (Ciuchita et al., 2023). For instance, the famous athletic apparel retailer Lululemon boosts the experience of its consumers through incremental rewards and exclusive benefits following milestone engagement behaviors, with the final aim of fostering brand loyalty and reinforcing connections with the firm and the lifestyle it offers. The brand is then not only seen as a fitness apparel provider but is also linked to fun and enjoyable experiences thanks to its gamified strategy.

Game Elements

Game elements (i.e., the game's goals, rules and general structure) are the building blocks and common characteristics of all games and gamified approaches (Deterding et al., 2011). While there is currently no explicit agreement on what constitutes a game element (Landers et al., 2019), scholars have historically classified game design into three categories (e.g., Ryan et al., 2006; Tobon et al., 2020).

First, gamification designs use achievement elements, which typically focus on the mastery of the game (Ryan et al., 2006). Challenges, badges, rewards and progression metrics are achievement elements that allow users to track their progress toward a specific goal, often set by the gamified system (Tobon et al., 2020). For instance, the language-learning app Duolingo uses badges to trigger users' sense of reward linked to personal growth. These badges can be obtained by accomplishing different tasks in-app, such as gaining experience points, learning in the morning or completing a level, directly fostering engagement with the branded app.

Second, immersion elements such as avatars, narratives and role-playing tap into consumers' intrinsic motivation for escapism and discovery (Ryan et al., 2006; Tobon et al., 2020). They focus on fantasy and creativity, as well as being part of a higher purpose and story (Vega & Camarero, 2024). Nike capitalized on this game technique during a campaign for their winter training gear by implementing an action-live online game. In this game, participants assumed the role of famous Nike athletes training in challenging weather. Through the game, users were helping athletes reach their training objectives in cold weather. This narrative-driven experience also led consumers to discover Nike products.

Third, gamification design is usually embedded in the same functions and principles as those used for social media (Yang & Li, 2021). Indeed, gamification often includes social elements that facilitate user interaction and competition (Ryan et al., 2006; Tobon et al., 2020). These social elements can be used in combination with achievement and/or immersion elements to further engage users. For instance, the LEGO Play app allows users to share their creations and interact with fellow enthusiasts. The app offers regular building challenges (mixing achievement and social elements) and uses AR to bring models to life, creating engaging stories (mixing immersion and social elements). Users can post photos, comment on others' builds, and like their favorite posts, fostering both community and brand engagement (Dessart et al., 2015). LEGO highlights outstanding creations, awards virtual badges and features users' work in official communications. Depending on the game feature used, the community can be based on competition or cooperation, thus fostering positive or negative impacts (Ciuchita et al., 2023).

Typology of Game Elements in Brand Strategy

Gamification research often considers the implementation of game principles as a holistic construct without accounting for the variety of implementation approaches developed by the brands (Koivisto & Hamari, 2019; Sailer et al., 2017). Nevertheless, considering the role of gamification in brand strategy requires understanding both the role of game elements and their level of integration into the overall brand offering. This has important implications going ahead because consumers differ in their experience of game elements (Landers et al., 2019), leading to distinct engagement types and supporting different brand objectives. In other words, one must understand (1) how central to the brand offering are the game elements (i.e., if the game elements are core or peripheral to the offering) and (2) if the game elements constitute a self-contained game versus a gamified system.

Table 36.1 summarizes this typology, considering the integration of the game elements in the brand offering on the horizontal axis and what we call the 'gaming perspective' adopted on the vertical axis.

First, a brand can take what we call a 'low' gaming perspective, meaning that they only integrate gamification features into their offering. In this perspective, various possibilities exist, ranging from gamification representing simple add-ons (a 'low' integration) or a core offering ('high' integration).

At a basic level, gamification features can be approached from a brand activation perspective. Here, the gamified brand activation does not represent a central element of the offering but rather a side offering or punctual addition to its promotion and activation. For instance, contests, sweepstakes and other forms of gamification features added to the brand's communication efforts are known to bring fun and engagement to support the promotion of a product or service (see top left quadrant of Table 36.1). Marketing research has long acknowledged the power of these 'gamified interactions' as part of a firm's promotional strategy (Feinman et al., 1986). Gamified loyalty programs can also bring positive brand outcomes, such as long-term gamified brand activations (Hollebeek et al., 2021).

Integration into the brand offering based on gamification features can also be high (top right quadrant of Table 36.1). Increasing scholarship recognizes now that complete brand offerings can be based on gamification principles, making gamification an inherent and essential part of the brand (e.g., Jang et al., 2018; Whittaker et al., 2021). Brands often create gamified applications to fully activate gamification in a core and long-term aspect of the offering. These applications typically focus on fostering self-improvement and behavior change, such as language learning, sports practice or sustainability habits. Such gamified platforms have grown to be central offerings for newer brands (e.g., Strava) while also becoming new elements in the offering of established firms (e.g., Nike Run Club or Nike +). Gamification in such contexts often leads to enhanced brand experiences (Hsu, 2023) as well as engagement and behavior change (e.g., Liu et al., 2024), particularly when mechanisms are directly tied to user performance of targeted behaviors (Feng et al., 2020).

Second, we now consider the bottom line of Table 36.1, which represents a 'high' gaming perspective, that is, when game elements are used to create a comprehensive, standalone game. This game can either be a side to the brand offering or the brand offering itself.

The bottom left quadrant of Table 36.1 represents brands going further into the integration of game elements into a brand activation, with the use of advergames or in-game advertising. Advergames are custom-made games developed to promote a firm's brand or products (Waiguny et al., 2013). For example, food and beverage companies have introduced packaging with codes redeemable in mobile applications to unlock mini-games, such as KitKat

Table 36.1 Typology of game elements in brand strategy

	Integration Into a Brand Offering	
Gaming Perspective	*Low* *Brand Activation*	*High* *Core Brand Offering*
Low Gamification features	Brand activation with gamification features • *The Body Shop spin-the wheel Christmas promotion* • *Sports Round Quiz by Heineken* • *Starbucks Rewards*	Branded gamified application as part of the core brand offering • *Strava, Nike+* • *Clue* • *Pokemon Go app*
High Game as a full product/ standalone game	Branded game as temporary activation or campaign, in-game advertising or advergame • *Burberry x Snapchat Animal Kingdom* • *Gucci World in Roblox* • *KFC Shrimp Attack* • *Poke Shops in Pokemon Go*	Game as a core offering of the brand • *World of Warcraft* • *Roblox* • *Fortnite* • *League of Legends* • *Etc.*

Source: The authors.

Break. The recently launched KFC Shrimp Attack is another example. Advergames have evolved in technology and can now integrate advanced virtual reality (VR) or artificial intelligence features, offering advanced experiential engagement activities (Berger et al., 2018; Harmeling et al., 2017). A similar output is in-game advertising, placing a product within an existing game (Berger et al., 2018; Schneider et al., 2005). In this case, a non-game brand partners with a game brand to feature its product in the game. For instance, Pokemon Go created value for the Nintendo brand and benefited companies like Starbucks and McDonald's, which owned Poke Shops in the game, leveraging the platform to engage with customers. These campaigns offer several advantages, including gathering consumer data, achieving competitive advantage and enhancing brand engagement and community connections (e.g., Eisingerich et al., 2019; Harmeling et al., 2017; Nobre & Ferreira, 2017). Metaverses like Roblox now also collaborate with brands like Gucci to let them be featured in their massive virtual worlds.

Last, games as a core brand offering are a well-established industry (i.e., the gaming industry, see bottom right quadrant), which has largely inspired the gamification approach in marketing (Landers et al., 2019; Robson et al., 2015). For instance, Nintendo, a significant player in the gaming industry, offers games such as Super Mario Bros® as products. Here, the brand creates value for users through entertainment and escapism, which are critical motivations in gaming. Game brands such as Nintendo incorporate gamification principles into their non-core offerings, such as the My Nintendo Rewards program. Through this program, users earn points for various activities such as purchasing products, playing mobile games or interacting with Nintendo services. These points can be redeemed for tangible rewards such as discounts, digital content and exclusive items, enhancing the consumer experience and creating value (Eisingerich et al., 2019). Other examples of integration of full-fledged games are World of Warcraft, Leagues of Legends or the previously mentioned Roblox.

This matrix's distinctions and granularity have essential implications regarding brand management and consumer perceptions. Different forms of game elements' integration and roles do not support the same brand objectives, partly due to their central or peripheral role in the strategy. Branded gamified applications as core offerings are more likely to foster strong self-brand connections and long-term loyalty because they are more likely fully embedded in the lives of consumers versus a gamified brand activation. On the other hand, brand activations such as advergames can foster brand image, preference and attitudes or generate one-off purchases.

This chapter examines the impact of integrating game elements into brand strategies through gamification features or standalone games, explicitly focusing on brand management and real-world brand outcomes. While we have acknowledged and detailed the distinction between gamification and games, we will use the terms 'gamification' and 'game elements' interchangeably for simplicity. Further, we acknowledge the unique nature of games and the existence of a whole body of literature on gaming and games as standalone offerings (bottom right quadrant of Table 36.1). In this paper, we focus on the integration of gamification in brand offerings (top quadrants) and the usage of games as specific activations (bottom left quadrant).

THE ROLE OF GAME ELEMENTS IN DRIVING BRAND OUTCOMES

The effectiveness of game elements in achieving positive brand outcomes is documented in extensive research, demonstrating that gamified offerings impact brand attitudes and purchase intentions, amongst others (e.g., Berger et al., 2018). However, more information is needed about the comprehensive range of effects that game elements can have on brand outcomes. Studies have addressed this issue in a piecemeal manner, often focusing on a couple of branding outcomes at a time, as depicted in Table 36.2. Furthermore, they often consider 'gamification' as an umbrella term, without specifying the specific game elements under investigation and their deployment in brand strategy.

Interestingly, a literature overview suggests that, to date, a wide range of methods have been used to understand the link between game elements and brand outcomes (see Table 36.2). A number of conceptual studies, some of them including systematic literature reviews, have addressed this link (e.g., Hollebeek et al., 2021; Xu et al., 2017), but often focusing on a limited set of outcomes (e.g., experience, loyalty and engagement in Ciuchita et al., 2023). A number of early studies took an exploratory perspective with qualitative methods such as interviews, focus groups (Nobre & Ferreira, 2017) and netnography (Harwood & Garry, 2015) – laying the groundwork for more deductive approaches recently. Key publications since 2018 include one to several quantitative studies, including experiments and surveys. We can note that a number of these articles focus on panel

Table 36.2 Overview of key studies on gamification and branding

Authors, Year	*Game Elements Studied*	*Impact on Brands*	*Method*
Lucassen and Jansen (2014)	Gamification mechanisms	Brand engagement, loyalty and awareness	Qualitative (interviews with executives)
Harwood and Garry (2015)	Gamification	Brand loyalty and trust	Qualitative (netnography and participant observations)
Nobre and Ferreira (2017)	Goals and challenges, competition, customization, rewards, status	Brand value co-creation, engagement and self-connection	Qualitative (interviews and focus groups)
Xu et al. (2017)	Game elements	Brand awareness	Conceptual
Berger et al. (2018)	(e.g., advergames and in-game ads)	Brand engagement (mediator), and self-brand connection	Quantitative (field study and experiments). Real users
Eisingerich et al. (2019)	Gamification principles (i.e., social interaction, control…)	Brand engagement (mediator), and purchase behavior	Qualitative and Quantitative
Högberg et al. (2019)	Gamification	Brand engagement	Quantitative (experiment)
Xi and Hamari (2020)	Immersion, achievement and social features	Brand engagement (mediator), awareness, and loyalty	Quantitative (survey). Real users
Syrjälä et al. (2020)	Gamification (gamified packaging)	Brand engagement	Qualitative (focus groups)
Hwang and Choi (2020)	Reward type	Participation in branded loyalty programs	Quantitative (experiment). Panel
Hollebeek et al. (2021)	Gamified loyalty program	Brand engagement value	Conceptual
van Berlo et al. (2021)	Virtual reality games	Brand attitude, and purchase intention through consumer learning	Quantitative (lab experiment). Real users
Hsu (2023)	Gamified app as a whole	Brand experience, and repurchase intentions	Quantitative (survey). Real users
Saxena et al. (2023)	Gamification	Brand engagement (mediator), self-brand connection and affective commitment	Quantitative (survey)
Ciuchita et al. (2023)	Gamification	Experience, loyalty and engagement	Conceptual
Kapoor et al. (2024)	Gamified social media content	Brand engagement (mediator), purchase intentions	Quantitative (experiments). Panel
Vega and Camarero (2024)	Gamified storytelling	Brand experience, attitude and word of mouth	Quantitative (experiments). Panel

Source: The authors.

respondents, while a smaller number include real-life consumers having experienced gamification first-hand (e.g., Hsu, 2023 or Xi & Hamari, 2020). Despite the promising evolution and wide array of methods considered, the literature still suffers shortcomings in comprehensively bridging game elements and brand outcomes.

The existing literature regularly considers brand engagement as a key outcome of gamification, also often taking the role of mediator to achieve higher-end brand benefits such as brand loyalty. Brand engagement is defined as '*the level of a customer's motivational, brand-related, and context-dependent state of mind characterized by specific levels of cognitive, emotional, and behavioral activity in brand interactions*' (Hollebeek, 2011, p. 790). Due to the interaction-focused approach to engagement, it is highly relevant for delivering a brand experience which stresses value-laden interactivity (Harmeling et al., 2017; Vega & Camarero, 2024). Further, brand engagement is a multidimensional construct, allowing the capture of a variety of consumer behavior mechanisms, ranging from affective (affect-transfer) to cognitive (telepresence) or mixed mechanisms (flow) (Berger et al., 2018; Kapoor et al., 2024; Saxena et al., 2023) – which can be aligned with different gamification elements. While gamification studies often consider the role of engagement with the game or platform (referred to as 'user engagement', e.g., Bitrián et al., 2021) or general customer engagement (e.g., Leclercq et al., 2018) as mediators to sustain desirable output, engagement with the brand is also inherently and ultimately enhanced through gamified interactions, as the brand is a key constituent of the experience (branded interface, prompts, goods, features, etc.).

As outcomes of brand engagement (e.g., Xi & Hamari, 2020) or studied in isolation (e.g., Harwood & Garry, 2015), other brand benefits can ensue from positive gamified interactions. For instance, gamified mechanisms such as social sharing, leaderboards or gamified monetary incentives (Lucassen & Jansen, 2014) can enhance brand awareness. Users are compelled to share information outside the game, for instance, by sharing their performance on their social networks, which enhances the visibility of the brand to, potentially, non-customers and prospects. Transactional outcomes such as brand purchase behaviors and behavioral loyalty also often result from gamified interaction. When prioritized in the short term, such outcomes are often associated with time-bound gamified campaigns, rather than a full-blown gamified offering.

Further, gamified products or campaigns can exist for the sake of enhancing the consumption experience without a transactional objective. However, the gamified experience is often promoting purchases, at least indirectly. Gamification has indeed extensively been linked to loyalty and increased purchase intentions (e.g., Xi & Hamari, 2020). First, gamification is used extensively to promote loyalty programs and foster their adoption. Gamified loyalty programs are more efficient and experiential than traditional loyalty programs in that they drive more consumer behavioral responses (Hwang & Choi, 2020) and more indirect engagement (Hollebeek et al., 2021). Similarly, gamified applications that represent a standalone brand offering also generate strong behavioral loyalty intentions for the brand in question. This is evidenced by the Nike + app, through enhanced brand engagement (Hsu, 2023), integration into the everyday lives of consumers, and specific features such as the app notifying users when it 'might be a good time to change your shoes because of wear and tear'.

While these insights demonstrate gamification's effectiveness in delivering positive outcomes for brands in specific contexts, they also lead to a fragmented understanding. In particular, the specific game elements and type of brand strategy investigated are often referred to under the umbrella term of 'gamification', without recognizing the diversity of approaches that gamification can represent when it comes to a gamified branded strategy. Furthermore, existing research often fails to consider the complementary role of various forces in successfully integrating game elements into a brand strategy.

As highlighted in Figure 36.1, we propose that four key factors will play a role in the effectiveness of adopting game elements for reaching positive brand outcomes: contextual elements, individual consumer-level elements, aspects related to the game elements used, as well as the level of game integration and role of the game/gamification in the brand offering (i.e., the typology of game elements in brand strategy discussed above). In the following paragraphs, we offer a detailed description of relevant individual and contextual factors and discuss their relative potential in driving certain brand outcomes when coupled with specific game elements and brand strategies. By doing so, we stress the complementary role of a diverse set of factors working together in achieving the most prevalent brand-related consumer responses and offer reflections on the links characterizing the relationships between those brand-related responses and their drivers.

Contextual Factors

A variety of contextual elements impact the implementation and performance of gamification for brand management. First, the type of medium, platform or ecosystem used can influence gamification's effectiveness (Landers et al., 2019; Liu et al., 2024), mainly because distinct game elements need different types of platform affordances. To illustrate, the level of immersion of a gamified offering will likely depend on the interactive and sensory features of the media and platforms used and the quality of the sensory imagery offered. For instance, employing VR in gamification can help brands provide highly experiential and personalized experiences for customers, particularly effective in enhancing affective brand outcomes such as emotional connections and brand attitudes (e.g., van Berlo et al., 2021), but also enhancing memory of brand elements (Kostyk et al., 2024).

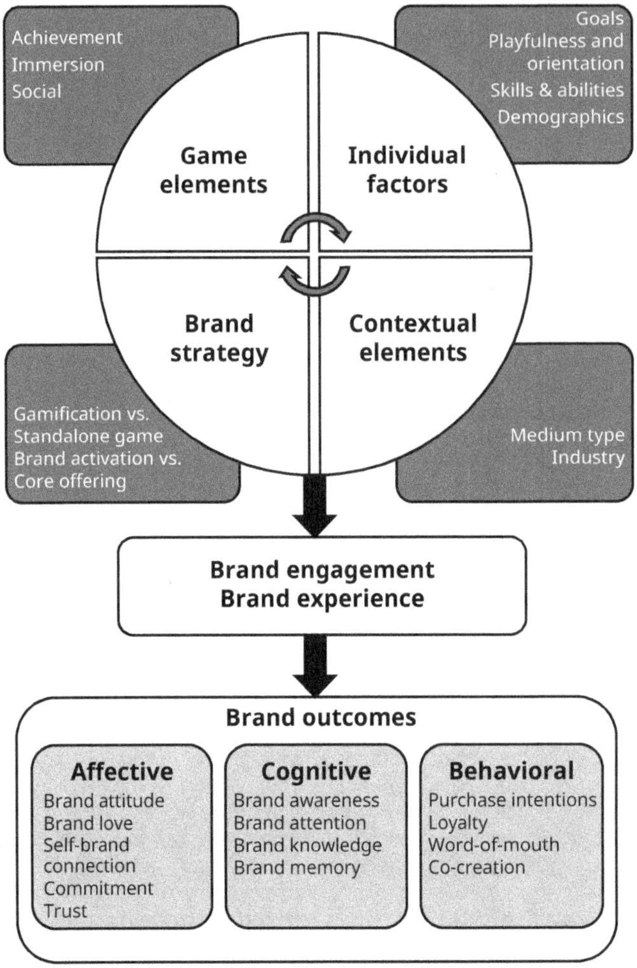

Figure 36.1 Integrative gamification-branding framework

Source: The authors.

For example, Sephora's Beauty Insider program uses VR elements to reward loyal customers with unique experiences. Users can unlock exclusive VR content, like behind-the-scenes footage and virtual makeup tutorials, by earning points through the loyalty program.

Integrating game elements in a brand strategy can also be achieved through third-party platforms. In this case, the adequacy of the medium used will also influence its effectiveness, as congruence with the brand identity and values is considered essential to drive positive outcomes, such as engagement. For instance, Kunkel et al. (2021) show that gamification offered by a third-party platform using game elements related to a brand can enhance attitudinal outcomes for the brand (through heightened engagement with the third-party platform and heightened knowledge of and identity with the brand). Other platforms enabling social network features can indirectly influence brands by creating a stronger community appeal and positive associations. Research shows that gamified advertising from influencers on social media can also enhance brand engagement and intentions (Kapoor et al., 2024), especially when the message delivered and the influencer's characteristics match the perceived brand image.

Second, the industry or sector in which the brand operates is crucial. While gamification was initially thought to have the most impact in high involvement, emotional sectors (e.g., automotive industry), research increasingly shows the relevance of gamification in other B2C sectors and with non-symbolic brands, like toothpaste or shampoo (Nobre & Ferreira, 2017). The narrative style of gamification should align with the product type: action-focused narratives suit utilitarian products, while experience-focused narratives are better for hedonic products (Bekk et al., 2022; Hofacker et al., 2016). In this regard, game elements focused on achievement might be better suited to foster robust engagement with and experience of utilitarian brands, ultimately leading to positive behavioral brand outcomes such as loyalty. On the other hand, game elements focused on immersion are particularly relevant for experiential services and products (Hofacker et al., 2016), such as luxury or destination brands. Indeed, immersive gamification taps into consumers' emotions, providing unique, memorable, and stimulating experiences and enhancing emotional connections (Saxena et al., 2023).

Gamification's transformative potential is also notable in areas requiring long-term commitment, such as health, well-being or learning (Koivisto & Hamari, 2019). Because such contexts involve customer habit creation (and maintenance), they largely benefit from a mix of achievement and social game elements through a core brand offering (e.g., branded gamified applications) to encourage behavioral change. For instance, online challenges improve attitudes toward healthy food content on social media (Charry et al., 2024), while rewards enhance consumer learning and intentions for sustainable offerings (Mulcahy et al., 2021).

Individual Factors

Individuals experience different types of games and gamification in distinct ways (Landers et al., 2019), thus highlighting the importance of individual factors in brand gamification's effectiveness.

Notably, users differ in the goals they hope to achieve when and their motives for interacting with gamified brand offerings (Koivisto & Hamari, 2019). Motivation types for gaming vary, with Bartle's four player types – achievers, explorers, socializers and killers – highlighting diverse player profiles (Tobon et al., 2020). Specifically, achievers are typically motivated by high-performance levels or gaining rewards, socializers like to interact with other players, explorers thrive on the discovery of new aspects of the game and killers enjoy being better than anyone else. These further align with key motivational factors explaining why people play games, including social interaction, escape, competition, skill development or fantasy (Demetrovics et al., 2011). Accordingly, the type of feedback provided by gamified platforms influences user outcomes depending on their personal goals toward the brand and the gamified activity. Put plainly, game elements focused on immersion will particularly resonate with individuals looking for escapism and exploration, while achievement elements foster skill development and rewards. Depending on the brand's industry, its customer base might have a prominent motive for interacting with gamified brand offerings. For instance, immersive gamification might enhance enjoyment and engagement for hedonic products, whereas for utilitarian products, it may act as a distraction due to the dominance of cognitive processes in consumer decision-making (Bekk et al., 2022; Hofacker et al., 2016).

Additionally, player orientation, the preference for competitive versus cooperative experiences, further shapes how users interact with gamification (Robson et al., 2015). Those with a competitive orientation may derive more satisfaction from leaderboards and achievement badges, whereas cooperative players value team-based challenges and collaborative goals. Hence, the platform type further reinforces these differences, as the presence of social affordances might shape how the gamified offering is presented. In summary, users have different motivations for engaging with gamified brand offerings. Accordingly, individuals are drawn to distinct motivational affordances and may encompass multiple motivations within a single player, depending on contextual factors.

Other individual factors play a role in shaping the effectiveness of gamification strategies. Skills, knowledge and abilities act as pivotal resources that moderate consumer engagement with gamified brand experiences (Ciuchita et al., 2023; Landers et al., 2019), influencing discussions on consumer vulnerability within such contexts. Moreover, individual differences in playfulness impact consumers' attraction to game-like interactions and susceptibility to gaming addiction (Hofacker et al., 2016; Landers et al., 2019). Demographic factors, such as age and gender, might further influence the effects of gamification (Ciuchita et al., 2023). Notably, younger users generally exhibit more favorable attitudes toward gamification, likely due to the perceived ease of use of gamified systems (Koivisto & Hamari, 2014) and their inherent interest in gaming activities (Deterding, 2019). Additionally, gender plays a role in shaping the perceived benefits of gamification (Koivisto & Hamari, 2014; Zhang et al., 2021), suggesting that a single gamification approach may vary in effectiveness across different consumer segments.

Game Elements

The type of game elements (i.e., the game's goals, rules and general structure) plays a crucial role in

Table 36.3 Propositions and specific conditions

Propositions	*Specific Conditions*	*Key References*
P1: Contextual factors influence gamification's effectiveness in driving affective, cognitive, and brand outcomes.	I. Highly immersive platforms (e.g., VR) are conducive of affective brand outcomes (e.g., self-brand connections and brand attitudes). II. Game elements focused on achievement are particularly relevant for behavioral brand outcomes in utilitarian contexts, while game elements focused on immersion are particularly relevant for affective brand outcomes in experiential contexts. III. Brands involved in transformative industries (e.g., health, education) will be particularly enhanced in terms of cognitive and behavioral outcomes through achievement and social game elements.	Bekk et al. (2022); Hofacker et al. (2016); Mulcahy et al. (2021); Nobre and Ferreira (2017); van Berlo et al. (2021)
P2: Individual factors influence gamification's effectiveness in driving affective, cognitive, and brand outcomes.	I. Consumers with escapism and exploratory motivations will respond more positively to immersive and social game elements, driving affective brand outcomes (e.g., self-brand connection). II. Consumers with skill development and reward-based motivations will respond more positively to achievement game elements, driving cognitive and behavioral brand outcomes (e.g., loyalty). III. Consumers with higher social orientation and motivations will respond more positively to competition and cooperation game elements, enhancing cognitive and behavioral brand outcomes (e.g., value co-creation, brand knowledge). IV. Consumer skills, abilities and existing knowledge should match the gamified brand offering to provide optimal levels of challenge and flow, driving cognitive brand outcomes (e.g., brand knowledge).	Koivisto and Hamari (2019); Robson et al. (2015); Tobon et al. (2020)
P3: The type of game elements used influence gamification's effectiveness in driving affective, cognitive and brand outcomes.	I. Immersion elements (potentially coupled with social elements) are particularly suited to foster affective brand outcomes (e.g., brand love, self-brand connections). II. Achievement game elements (potentially coupled with social elements) are particularly suited to foster behavioral brand outcomes (e.g., word-of-mouth, loyalty), especially when designed with an optimal level of challenge. III. Interactivity features strengthen gamification's potential in supporting affective, cognitive, and behavioral brand outcomes through heightened brand engagement and experience.	Berger et al. (2018); Bitrián et al. (2021); Hwang and Choi (2020)
P4: The brand strategy in integrating gamification into its offering influence gamification's effectiveness in driving affective, cognitive and brand outcomes.	I. Immersion and interactivity elements are more favorable in the context of core brand offerings as they might direct consumers' attention to other (deeply immersive) game elements rather than the branded elements, which would fail in terms of brand shorter-term activation campaigns. II. Branded games as activation campaigns are best suited to foster affective brand outcomes through enhanced experience (e.g., positive associations around the brand). On the other hand, gamification features are best suited to foster cognitive and behavioral brand outcomes through heightened engagement (e.g., value co-creation, loyalty). III. Compulsory (versus voluntary) play, and the implementation of time pressure, reduce brand engagement and experience, weakening brand outcomes.	Bekk et al. (2022); Berger et al. (2018); Huotari and Hamari (2017)

Source: The authors.

attaining various brand objectives. In designing game elements, companies can typically implement three main types of gamification techniques, namely social, immersion and achievement (Tobon et al., 2020). To date, research shows that social and immersion techniques promote relatedness as a psychological outcome (Bitrián et al., 2021), as well as affective brand outcomes, thus particularly impacting the emotional brand relationship positively (e.g., Berger et al., 2018). Achievement elements, on the other hand, tend to be more efficient at supporting behavioral outcomes such as positive word-of-mouth or brand loyalty (e.g., Hwang & Choi, 2020), tapping into consumer's drive for action, when the challenge level is appropriate and fostering users' sense of competence (Bitrián et al., 2021).

Another key aspect of game elements and features is the level of interactivity of the game or gamified support. While gamification is based on the principle of consumers being active co-creators of their experience, the brand can leave more or less room for interactivity in the game or gamified offering. Interactivity in the game has been recognized to support psychological, emotional and cognitive brand outcomes (e.g., Berger et al., 2018).

Brand Strategy

Branded gamified applications as core offerings are more likely to foster strong self-brand connections and long-term loyalty because they are more likely fully embedded in the lives of consumers versus a gamified brand activation. On the other hand, brand activations such as advergames can be used to foster brand image, preference and attitudes or generate one-off purchases.

While gamification can positively impact consumer enjoyment and experiential brand outcomes, it might reduce cognitive brand outcomes because of its distracting potential, especially when the brand is not easily recognizable (for instance, in a branded game in which the consumer does not understand well the link with the brand or doesn't notice the brand at all) (Bekk et al., 2022). Differently put, positive effects of gamification often arise when affective outcomes (i.e., driven by emotions) are the focus (Bekk et al., 2022).

Last, caution must be applied when integrating game elements into a brand offering. Gamification is generally based on the premise that the consumer is voluntarily involved in value co-creation and game(ful) activities (Huotari & Hamari, 2017). However, gamified branded activities may not always be used voluntarily. Landers et al. (2019) state that a gameful experience only occurs when usage is voluntary. The problem with the implementation of gamification when the consumer wants to avoid using it (e.g., access to a product feature is conditioned to playing a game, or a previously non-gamified offering has been gamified) is that the design system of gamification is there. However, the consumer does not experience the positive effect, which typically results in positive outcomes. For instance, compulsory play weakens emotional brand engagement and time pressure reduces cognitive brand engagement (Berger et al., 2018). To have a gameful experience (and thus, gamification), the consumer must feel free to stop playing if they don't want to anymore, even if it's not true (Landers et al., 2019).

Based on the reviewed literature and overview of the current knowledge at the intersection of gamification and branding, we propose a series of relevant propositions that aggregate key considerations addressing the role and impact of gamification in modern brand management. The propositions address as well as the conditions under which these relationships can occur and develop optimally or not. Specifically, our propositions (first column) consider how each factor influences the way brand outcomes are delivered by games or gamification, but we also suggest specific conditions (second column) for the success of game elements for brands that are based on the interplays between these factors. Table 36.3 summarizes these considerations in the form of propositions and specific conditions.

CONTRIBUTION AND FUTURE RESEARCH

Scientific Contribution

Gamification and, more generally, the introduction of game elements in a branded offering can bring undeniable benefits to brands. This paper offers a comprehensive, yet non-systematic, view of current research combining gamification and branding interests. It develops propositions that guide future scholarship and brand specialists' practical use of gamification. In doing so, this chapter offers important and nuanced insight into the benefits and appropriate use of gamification in various situations.

Specifically, our work shows that the interplay of game elements and their integration into the brand strategy, alongside contextual and individual factors, will influence affective, cognitive and behavioral brand outcomes. In doing so, we first offer a more comprehensive overview of the factors that come into play when applying game elements to a brand strategy, and we also show how their specific integration and interplay can generate brand outcomes.

First, gamification effectiveness is largely conditioned by its integration into the brand offering. In other words, how prominent and central to the brand offering the game elements are bears significant strategic implications. Branded gamified applications as a product are more likely to foster strong self-brand connections. As core brand offerings, these applications (often mobile- or wearable-based) are more likely to be fully embedded in the lives of consumers. Mobile technologies support the close proximity and usability of the gamified platform, and if they are core to the brand offering, usage propensity is increased to fully benefit from the brand experience. On the other hand, gamified brand activations such as advergames can be used to foster brand image, preference and attitudes. Often used in the shorter term or as part of limited campaigns, these tools contribute to the vitality of the brand and generate faster adoption rates and behavioral outcomes.

Second, gamification is a highly personalized and personal matter, building on human motivation principles to appeal to and engage consumers (Koivisto & Hamari, 2019; Landers et al., 2019). Our work stresses the role of individual factors such as consumer personality, motivations and traits, as gamification is often used to support individualistic objectives (such as self-improvement, self-care, and enjoyment). As a result, each individual consumer will respond to a lesser or greater extent to a specific trigger based on their profile. In this regard, it is essential to match the game elements in the gamified brand strategy to the industry the brand operates in and the potential motivations consumers have for interacting with the brand offering. For instance, luxury or experiential brands can capitalize on gamification to tap into the potential need for escapism that consumers showcase in this particular context. On the other hand, different considerations are needed for gamification's implementation for functional brands, which fulfill distinct consumer needs. Furthermore, brands using gamification in their strategy should pay particular attention to the knowledge and skills of their customer base to ensure that the game elements can be used optimally. Suppose brands fail to consider the specific individual factors of their target audience. In that case, they risk missing the mark by developing game elements in their brand strategy that lack relevance and impact.

Third, gamification elements and their combinations can offer various benefits and support varying brand objectives. As a result, managers seeking to implement gamification in their offering should therefore make sure that the gamification or game elements are integrated in their offering in a way that supports their objectives. For instance, any brand seeking to create long-lasting engagement and strong brand relationships could consider the development of a gamified brand offering that is tightly integrated with the current offer in a seamless customer experience. Platform brands (Wichmann et al., 2022) rely on versatile platforms, allowing them to engage with consumers beyond product purchase, thus creating an all-encompassing ecosystem of interactions and touchpoints around the brand. These platforms often capitalize on gamification features to keep consumers engaged and interested.

Managerial Recommendations

The 'specific' conditions that we develop in Table 36.3 offer a number of actionable recommendations for managers, which highlight first that game elements should be tailored to the type of industry in which the brand operates and that the choice of platforms is crucial, as well as the specific features developed.

Beyond the specific type of integration into the brand strategy, which we explore as a key factor of success, managers should always ensure that the brand is highly recognizable, particularly when dealing with third-party integrations. While gamification can positively impact consumer enjoyment and experiential brand outcomes, it might reduce cognitive brand outcomes because of its distracting potential, especially when the brand is not easily recognizable (for instance, in a branded game in which the consumer does not understand well the link with the brand or doesn't notice the brand at all) (Bekk et al., 2022). Positive effects of gamification often arise when affective outcomes (i.e., driven by emotions) are the focus and the brand is identifiable (Bekk et al., 2022). Last, managers should also be aware of the critical amount of consumer data generated by gamified interactions. Such data can serve strategic branding objectives such as consumer profiling and targeting.

Future Research

Our research also sheds light on various underexplored yet topical aspects of gamification, which also concern brand managers. Future research should address several promising questions. First, most game-related affordances studied rely on competitive dynamics (points and leaderboards). Yet, more research is needed to better understand how gamification can support collective behaviors (Koivisto & Hamari, 2019). For instance, gamification can support connection and cooperation within a brand community, rather than competition (Leclercq et al., 2018), which is highly relevant for brand community managers. The collective dimension of gamification outcomes is under-explored in extant research to benefit individual dynamics and brands (Nobre & Ferreira, 2017).

Further, the impact of gamification on cognitive brand-related outcomes has received less attention than affective or behavioral aspects. While we know that gamification often supports consumer learning (e.g., van Berlo et al., 2021) and that immersive interactive environments can enhance memory of brand-related elements (Kostyk et al., 2024), there is a dearth of focus on how gamification supports consumer cognition concerning brands. Studies should elucidate the role of gamification in fostering brand awareness, knowledge, attention and memory.

Next, gamification has frequently been studied not only for high-involvement, hedonic goods (e.g., Xu et al., 2017) but also increasingly for utilitarian products or mass-market offerings (Nobre & Ferreira, 2017). Yet, there is a lack of application in social and sustainable brands. Apart from notable exceptions (e.g., Mulcahy et al., 2021; Whittaker et al., 2021), few studies investigate the potential for brands to use gamification for good and promote sustainable and ethical practices. Given the power of gamification to educate consumers, shape their attitudes, and impact their intentions, brands with sustainable values and missions, along with researchers, should harness this tool and study its impact as a lever of positive societal change.

Finally, while this chapter aimed to present an integrative framework highlighting the brand benefits of incorporating game elements into a brand strategy, an increasing body of research highlights the potential adverse effects of gamification. Accordingly, we encourage future research to investigate the potential detrimental impacts of gamification on both brands and their consumers. For instance, Bekk et al. (2022) evidence that gamification can negatively impact product information recognition. Hammedi et al. (2024) further show that consumer engagement declines when gamification is too frequent. In some cases, gamification may result in disengagement (Hammedi et al., 2021), as well as impede the development of key behavioral brand outcomes, including word-of-mouth (Wolf et al., 2020) and co-creation (Leclercq et al., 2018). The negative impact of gamification and the conditions under which they occur warrant further elucidation to avoid satiation effects and missing brand objectives. To elucidate this aspect of gamification, the involvement of real-life users of game elements is warranted, to have first-hand information, crucial to address such experience-sensitive questions.

Gamification can also result in unintended consequences for users. While brands incorporate game elements into their strategies to enhance engagement (Landers et al., 2019), an emerging body of research questions the assumption that increased engagement necessarily leads to improved outcomes for users (e.g., Baiwir et al., 2024; O'Brien et al., 2022). Gamification can thus backfire for brands. Particularly, heightened interactions with technologies have been linked to negative effects on well-being, including addiction, anxiety and stress (Kumar et al., 2022; McLean et al., 2024). In this context, future research should critically investigate the relationship between gamified brand offerings and negative consumer outcomes, focusing on identifying the conditions under which specific game elements may contribute to well-being and dysfunctional brand engagement. Additionally, given the highly personalized nature of gamification and its dependence on individual factors, future research should examine the role of these factors in driving the negative consequences of gamification. Particularly, identifying the consumer profiles that may be more vulnerable to the adverse effects of gamified brand offerings is warranted to ensure ethical brand practices.

REFERENCES

Baiwir, L., Dessart, L., & Delcourt, C. (2024). Consumer engagement with preventive health technologies: A double-edged sword for consumer wellbeing. *Journal of Consumer Affairs*, *58*(4), 872–904. https://doi.org/10.1111/joca.12603

Bekk, M., Eppmann, R., Klein, K., & Völckner, F. (2022). All that glitters is not gold: An investigation into the undesired effects of gamification and how to mitigate them through gamification design. *International Journal of Research in Marketing*, *39*(4), 1059–1081. https://doi.org/10.1016/j.ijresmar.2022.03.002

Berger, A., Schlager, T., Sprott, D. E., & Herrmann, A. (2018). Gamified interactions: Whether, when, and how games facilitate self–brand connections. *Journal of the Academy of Marketing Science*, *46*(4), 652–673. https://doi.org/10.1007/s11747-017-0530-0

Bitrián, P., Buil, I., & Catalán, S. (2021). Enhancing user engagement: The role of gamification in mobile apps. *Journal of Business Research*, *132*, 170–185. https://doi.org/10.1016/j.jbusres.2021.04.028

Cambier, F., & Poncin, I. (2020). Inferring brand integrity from marketing communications: The effects of brand transparency signals in a consumer empowerment context. *Journal of Business Research*, *109*, 260–270. https://doi.org/10.1016/j.jbusres.2019.11.060

Charry, K., Poncin, I., Kullak, A., & Hollebeek, L. D. (2024). Gamification's role in fostering user engagement with healthy food-based digital content. *Psychology & Marketing*, *41*(1), 69–85. https://doi.org/10.1002/mar.21892

Ciuchita, R., Heller, J., Köcher, S., Köcher, S., Leclercq, T., Sidaoui, K., & Stead, S. (2023). It is really not a game: An integrative review of gamification for service research. *Journal of Service Research*, *26*(1), 3–20. https://doi.org/10.1177/10946705221076272

Demetrovics, Z., Urbán, R., Nagygyörgy, K, Farkas, J., Zilahy, D., Mervó, B., Reindl, A., Ágoston, C., Kertész, A., and Harmath, E. (2011). Why do you play? The development of the motives for online gaming questionnaire (MOGQ). *Behavior Research Methods 43*(3), 814–825. https://doi.org/10.3758/s13428-011-0091-y

Dessart, L., Veloutsou, C., & Morgan-Thomas, A. (2015). Consumer engagement in online brand communities: A social media perspective. *Journal of Product & Brand Management*, *24*(1), 28–42. https://doi.org/10.1108/JPBM-06-2014-0635

Deterding, S. (2019). Gamification in management: Between choice architecture and humanistic design. *Journal of Management Inquiry*, *28*(2). 131–136. https://doi.org/10.1177/1056492618790912

Deterding, S., Dixon, D., Khaled, R., & Nacke, L. (2011). From game design elements to gamefulness: Defining 'gamification'. Proceedings of the 15th international academic MindTrek conference: Envisioning future media environments, September 28. (pp. 9–15).

Eisingerich, A. B., Marchand, A., Fritze, M. P., & Dong, L. (2019). Hook vs. hope: How to enhance customer engagement through gamification. *International Journal of Research in Marketing*, *36*(2), 200–215. https://doi.org/10.1016/j.ijresmar.2019.02.003

Feinman, J., Blashek, R., & McCabe, R. (1986). *Sweepstakes, prize promotions, and contests.* Dow Jones-Irwin.

Feng, W., Tu, R., & Hsieh, P. (2020). Can gamification increases consumers' engagement in fitness apps? The moderating role of commensurability of the game elements. *Journal of Retailing and Consumer Services*, *57*, 102229. https://doi.org/10.1016/j.jretconser.2020.102229

Füller, J., Mühlbacher, H., Matzler, K., & Jawecki, G. (2009). Consumer empowerment through internet-based co-creation. *Journal of Management Information Systems*, *26*(3), 71–102. https://doi.org/10.2753/MIS0742-1222260303

Hammedi, W., Leclercq, T., & Poncin, I. (2019). Customer engagement: The role of gamification. In L. Hollebeek, & D. E. Sprott (Eds.), *Handbook of research on customer engagement* (pp. 164–185). Edward Elgar Publishing.Hammedi, W., Leclercq, T., Poncin, I., & Alkire, L. (2021). Uncovering the dark side of gamification at work: Impacts on engagement and well-being. *Journal of Business Research*, *122*, 256–269. https://doi.org/10.1016/j.jbusres.2020.08.032

Hammedi, W., Leclercq, T., & Steils, N. (2024). Gamification Myopia: Satiation effects in gamified activities. *Journal of Service Research*, *27*(2), 213–230. https://doi.org/10.1177/10946705231190873

Harmeling, C. M., Moffett, J. W., Arnold, M. J., & Carlson, B. D. (2017). Toward a theory of customer engagement marketing. *Journal of the Academy of Marketing Science*, *45*(3), 312–335. https://doi.org/10.1007/s11747-016-0509-2

Harwood, T., & Garry, T. (2015). An investigation into gamification as a customer engagement experience environment. *Journal of Services Marketing*, *29*(6/7), 533–546. https://doi.org/10.1108/JSM-01-2015-0045

Hofacker, C. F., De Ruyter, K., Lurie, N. H., Manchanda, P., & Donaldson, J. (2016). Gamification and mobile marketing effectiveness. *Journal of Interactive Marketing*, *34*(1), 25–36. https://doi.org/10.1016/j.intmar.2016.03.001

Högberg, J., Ramberg, M. O., Gustafsson, A., & Wästlund, E. (2019). Creating brand engagement through in-store gamified customer experiences. *Journal of Retailing and Consumer Services*, *50*, 122–130. https://doi.org/10.1016/j.jretconser.2019.05.006

Hollebeek, L. D. (2011). Demystifying customer brand engagement: Exploring the loyalty nexus. *Journal of Marketing Management*, *27*(7–8), 785–807. https://doi.org/10.1080/0267257X.2010.500132

Hollebeek, L. D., Das, K., & Shukla, Y. (2021). Game on! How gamified loyalty programs boost customer engagement value. *International Journal of Information Management*, *61*, 102308. https://doi.org/10.1016/j.ijinfomgt.2021.102308

Huotari, K., & Hamari, J. (2017). A definition for gamification: Anchoring gamification in the service marketing literature. *Electronic Markets*, *27*(1), 21–31. https://doi.org/10.1007/s12525-015-0212-z

Hsu, C. L. (2023). Enhancing brand love, customer engagement, brand experience, and repurchase intention: Focusing on the role of gamification in mobile apps. *Decision Support Systems*, *174*, 114020. https://doi.org/10.1016/j.dss.2023.114020

Hwang, J., & Choi, L. (2020). Having fun while receiving rewards?: Exploration of gamification in loyalty programs for consumer loyalty. *Journal of Business Research*, *106*, 365–376. https://doi.org/10.1016/j.jbusres.2019.01.031

Jang, S., Kitchen, P. J., & Kim, J. (2018). The effects of gamified customer benefits and characteristics on behavioral engagement and purchase: Evidence from mobile exercise application uses. *Journal of Business Research*, *92*, 250–259. https://doi.org/10.1016/j.jbusres.2018.07.056

Kapoor, P., Balaji, M. S., & Maity, M. (2024). Game on: Enhancing customer engagement through influencers' gamified messages. *Journal of Travel Research*, Online First. https://doi.org/10.1177/00472875241289565

Koivisto, J., & Hamari, J. (2014). Demographic differences in perceived benefits from gamification. *Computers in Human Behavior*, *35*, 179–188. https://doi.org/10.1016/j.chb.2014.03.007

Koivisto, J., & Hamari, J. (2019). The rise of motivational information systems: A review of gamification research. *International Journal of Information Management*, *45*, 191–210. https://doi.org/10.1016/j.ijinfomgt.2018.10.013

Kostyk, A., Cowan, K., Dessart, L., & Schyns, M. (2024). Memories of tourism brands in virtual reality. *Annals of Tourism Research*, *109*, 103824. https://doi.org/10.1016/j.annals.2024.103824

Kumar, V., Rajan, B., Salunkhe, U., & Joag, S. G. (2022). Relating the dark side of new-age technologies and customer technostress. *Psychology & Marketing*, *39*(12), 2240–2259. https://doi.org/10.1002/mar.21738

Kunkel, T., Lock, D., & Doyle, J. P. (2021). Gamification via mobile applications: A longitudinal examination of its impact on attitudinal loyalty and behavior toward a core service. *Psychology and Marketing*, *38*(6), 948–964. https://doi.org/10.1002/mar.21467

Landers, R. N., Tondello, G. F., Kappen, D. L., Collmus, A. B., Mekler, E. D., & Nacke, L. E. (2019). Defining gameful experience as a psychological state caused by gameplay: Replacing the term 'Gamefulness' with three distinct constructs. *International Journal of Human-Computer Studies*, *127*, 81–94. https://doi.org/10.1016/j.ijhcs.2018.08.003

Leclercq, T., Hammedi, W., & Poncin, I. (2018). The boundaries of gamification for engaging customers: Effects of losing a contest in online co-creation communities. *Journal of Interactive Marketing*, *44*(1), 82–101. https://doi.org/10.1016/j.intmar.2018.04.004

Liu, X., Zhou, Z., Yuen, K. F., & Wang, X. (2024). Green and gamified! An investigation of consumer participation in green last-mile from a gamification affordance perspective. *Journal of Retailing and Consumer Services*, *79*, 103808. https://doi.org/10.1016/j.jretconser.2024.103808

Lucassen, G., & Jansen, S. (2014). Gamification in consumer marketing-future or fallacy? *Procedia-Social and Behavioral Sciences*, *148*, 194–202. https://doi.org/10.1016/j.sbspro.2014.07.034

Malthouse, E. C., Calder, B. J., Kim, S. J., & Vandenbosch, M. (2016). Evidence that user-generated content that produces engagement increases purchase behaviours. *Journal of Marketing Management*, *32*(5–6), 427–444. https://doi.org/10.1080/0267257X.2016.1148066

Mardon, R., & Belk, R. (2018). Materializing digital collecting: An extended view of digital materiality. *Marketing Theory*, *18*(4), 543–570. https://doi.org/10.1177/1470593118767725

McLean, G., Krey, N., & Barhorst, J. B. (2024). Revealing the double-edged sword: Introducing the technology and consumer well-being paradox model. *Psychology & Marketing*, *42*(1), 5–20. https://doi.org/10.1002/mar.22110

Merz, M., He, Y., & Vargo, S. (2009). The evolving brand logic: A service-dominant logic perspective. *Journal of the Academy of Marketing Science*, *37*(3), 328–344. https://doi.org/10.1007/s11747-009-0143-3

Mordor Intelligence. (2024). *Gamification market size and share analysis – growth trends and forecasts (2024–2029)*. www.mordorintelligence.com/industry-reports/gamification-market

Mulcahy, R. F., McAndrew, R., Russell-Bennett, R., & Iacobucci, D. (2021). 'Game on!' Pushing consumer buttons to change sustainable behavior: A gamification field study. *European Journal of Marketing*, *55*(10), 2593–2619. https://doi.org/10.1108/EJM-05-2020-0341

Nobre, H., & Ferreira, A. (2017). Gamification as a platform for brand co-creation experiences. *Journal of Brand Management*, *24*(4), 349–361. https://doi.org/10.1057/s41262-017-0055-3

O'Brien, H. L., Roll, I., Kampen, A., & Davoudi, N. (2022). Rethinking (dis)engagement in human-computer interaction. *Computers in Human Behavior*, *128*, 107109. https://doi.org/10.1016/j.chb.2021.107109

Ramaswamy, V., & Ozcan, K. (2016). Brand value co-creation in a digitalized world: An integrative framework and research implications. *International Journal of Research in Marketing*, *33*(1), 93–106. https://doi.org/10.1016/j.ijresmar.2015.07.001

Robson, K., Plangger, K., Kietzmann, J. H., McCarthy, I., & Pitt, L. (2015). Is it all a game? Understanding the principles of gamification. *Business Horizons*, *58*(4), 411–420. https://doi.org/10.1016/j.bushor.2015.03.006

Ryan, R. M., Rigby, C. S., & Przybylski, A. (2006). The motivational pull of video games: A self-determination theory approach. *Motivation and Emotion*, *30*(4), 344–360. https://doi.org/10.1007/s11031-006-9051-8

Sailer, M., Hense, J. U., Mayr, S. K., & Mandl, H. (2017). How gamification motivates: An experimental study of the effects of specific game design elements on psychological need satisfaction. *Computers in Human Behavior*, *69*, 371–380. https://doi.org/10.1016/j.chb.2016.12.033

Saxena, G., Jain, S., & Mishra, S. (2023). Enhancing affective commitment through gamified services of luxury brands: Role of game mechanics and self-congruity. *Journal of Services Marketing*, *37*(8), 1018–1031. https://doi.org/10.1108/JSM-06-2022-0217

Schneider, L. P., Systems, B., & Cornwell, T. B. (2005). Cashing in on crashes via brand placement in computer games: The effects of experience and flow on memory. *International Journal of Advertising*, *24*(3), 321–343. https://doi.org/10.1080/02650487.2005.11072928

Statista. (2024). *Number of global mobile users since 2010*. www.statista.com/statistics/218984/number-of-global-mobile-users-since-2010/

Stocchi, L., Michaelidou, N., Pourazad, N., & Micevski, M. (2018). The rules of engagement: How to motivate consumers to engage with branded mobile apps. *Journal of Marketing Management*, *34*(13–14), 1196–1226. https://doi.org/10.1080/0267257X.2018.1544167

Swaminathan, V., Sorescu, A., Steenkamp, J. B. E., O'Guinn, T. C. G., & Schmitt, B. (2020). Branding in a hyperconnected world: Refocusing theories and rethinking boundaries. *Journal of Marketing*, *84*(2), 24–46. https://doi.org/10.1177/0022242919899905

Syrjälä, H., Kauppinen-Räisänen, H., Luomala, H. T., Joelsson, T. N., Könnölä, K., & Mäkilä, T. (2020). Gamified package: Consumer insights into multidimensional brand engagement. *Journal of Business Research*, *119*, 423–434. https://doi.org/10.1016/j.jbusres.2019.11.089

Tobon, S., Ruiz-Alba, J. L., & García-Madariaga, J. (2020). Gamification and online consumer decisions: Is the game over? *Decision Support Systems*, *128*, 113167. https://doi.org/10.1016/j.dss.2019.113167

van Berlo, Z. M., van Reijmersdal, E. A., Smit, E. G., & van der Laan, L. N. (2021). Brands in virtual reality games: Affective processes within computer-mediated consumer experiences. *Journal of Business Research*, *122*, 458–465. https://doi.org/10.1016/j.jbusres.2020.09.006

Vega, E., & Camarero, C. (2024). Once upon a game: Boosting brand storytelling through gamification. *Journal of Product and Brand Management*, *33*(6), 717–732. https://doi.org/10.1108/JPBM-10-2023-4796

Waiguny, M. K., Nelson, M. R., & Marko, B. (2013). How advergame content influences explicit and implicit brand attitudes: When violence spills over. *Journal of Advertising*, *42*(2–3), 155–169. https://doi.org/10.1080/00913367.2013.774590

Whittaker, L., Mulcahy, R., & Russell-Bennett, R. (2021). 'Go with the flow' for gamification and sustainability marketing. *International Journal of Information Management*, *61*, 102305. https://doi.org/10.1016/j.ijinfomgt.2020.102305

Wichmann, J. R., Wiegand, N., & Reinartz, W. J. (2022). The platformization of brands. *Journal of Marketing*, *86*(1), 109–131. https://doi.org/10.1177/00222429211054073

Wolf, T., Weiger, W. H., & Hammerschmidt, M. (2020). Experiences that matter? The motivational experiences and business outcomes of gamified services. *Journal of Business Research*, *106*, 353–364. https://doi.org/10.1016/j.jbusres.2018.12.058

Xi, N., & Hamari, J. (2020). Does gamification affect brand engagement and equity? A study in online brand communities. *Journal of Business Research*, *109*, 449–460. https://doi.org/10.1016/j.jbusres.2019.11.058

Xu, F., Buhalis, D., & Weber, J. (2017). Serious games and the gamification of tourism. *Tourism Management*, *60*, 244–256. https://doi.org/10.1016/j.tourman.2016.11.020

Yang, H., & Li, D. (2021). Understanding the dark side of gamification health management: A stress perspective. *Information Processing & Management*, *58*(5), 102649. https://doi.org/10.1016/j.ipm.2021.102649

Zhang, L., Shao, Z., Li, X., & Feng, Y. (2021). Gamification and online impulse buying: The moderating effect of gender and age. *International Journal of Information Management*, *61*, 102267. https://doi.org/10.1016/j.ijinfomgt.2020.102267

PART 6
Future Directions in Brand Management

37

Augmenting Brands: Harnessing Artificial Intelligence for Brand Management

Yang Cheng, Mengge Yang, and Chen Lin

INTRODUCTION

Research into artificial intelligence (AI) dates back to 1950, when Turing (1950) posed the question, 'Can machines think?' Later, McCarthy et al. (1955) formally introduced AI in their proposal for the Dartmouth Summer Research Project on AI, suggesting that machines could simulate the aspects of human intelligence, such as learning, language use, problem-solving and self-improvement. As machine learning, deep learning and natural language processing (NLP) have evolved (Tang, 2023), AI has expanded into diverse domains, particularly within business and management, where it has been widely applied in service industries (Bornet et al., 2021; Wirtz et al., 2018), supply chain management, human resources and, more recently, marketing and brand management (Harrison et al., 2022; Mariani et al., 2023; Mariani & Baggio, 2022).

AI's growing integration into everyday life has transformed brand management, enabling brands to engage with their audiences in innovative ways. This shift has the potential to enhance customer experiences and foster stronger brand loyalty (Kumar et al., 2023). Key applications of AI, such as voice assistants, chatbots, personalized product recommendations and predictive analytics, are reshaping how brands interact with consumers. AI-powered chatbots, for instance, enhance customer service by offering instant, accurate and personalized responses, thereby improving customer satisfaction and strengthening brand trust (Kumar et al., 2023). Predictive analytics helps brands anticipate consumer behaviors, optimize marketing strategies and refine pricing models, which in turn improves customer acquisition and retention (Murray & Wardley, 2014; Power, 2016). Furthermore, AI neural networks, including multilayer perceptron, convolutional neural networks and recurrent neural networks (De Bruyn et al., 2020), play a pivotal role in identifying patterns that predict customer churn, assess brand loyalty and forecast branding outcomes, providing actionable insights to enhance market positioning (Ansari & Riasi, 2016; De Bruyn et al., 2020; Ismail et al., 2015).

AI enhances brand communication and customer relationship management (CRM). Table 37.1 highlights AI-driven tools optimizing brand communication across various modalities and platforms, addressing needs from customer service to project management. Salesforce Einstein and Zendesk Answer Bot illustrate AI's role in improving brand–customer interactions. Salesforce Einstein

Table 37.1 AI tools for brand management

AI Tools	*Application*	*Modality*	*Platform*
Salesforce Einstein	Customer relationship management (CRM)	Cloud-based	Web and Mobile app
Zendesk Answer Bot	Customer service	AI Chatbot	Web and Mobile app
IBM Watson	Business intelligence	AI Platform	Web and Cloud Service
Google Ads AI	Marketing and advertising	AI Algorithms	Web
Adobe Sensei	Creative and design	AI Tools	Web and Desktop app
Asana Automation	Project management	Automation	Web and Mobile app
Tableau CRM	Analytics and data visualization	AI Analytics	Web and Mobile app
Hootsuite Insights	Social media management	AI Analytics	Web and Mobile app
Mailchimp AI	Email marketing	AI Tools	Web and Mobile app
HubSpot	Inbound marketing, sales and service	AI Platform	Web and Mobile app

Source: The authors.

(2024) predicts customer behavior, enabling personalized experiences at scale. Zendesk Answer Bot integrates AI-powered chatbots, enhancing customer service and enabling data-driven decisions. In business intelligence, IBM Watson (2024) transforms data analysis by offering customizable models while ensuring regulatory compliance. In marketing, AI tools like Google (2024a) optimize ad bidding, personalize campaigns and refine messaging. Adobe Sensei (2024) automates design tasks and provides real-time insights. Project management tools like Asana Automation (2024) boost team productivity by automating repetitive tasks. For data analysis, Tableau CRM (2024) and Hootsuite Insights (2024) convert complex data into actionable insights, empowering informed decision-making.

AI also drives marketing automation through Mailchimp AI (2024) and HubSpot (2024), enhancing personalized interactions and streamlining operations to foster brand loyalty. In conclusion, AI is a strategic asset, enabling personalized communication, improving responsiveness and driving brand performance. The synergy between AI and human creativity shapes data-driven strategies aligned with consumer preferences, ensuring brands remain competitive in a dynamic marketplace.

This chapter explores both the opportunities and challenges of AI in brand management, with a focus on its theoretical foundations and practical applications. Drawing on the framework established by Deryl et al. (2023), the chapter examines the antecedents, mediators and outcomes of AI in branding. It also extends this framework by incorporating the three distinct types of AI capabilities described by Huang and Rust (2020): Mechanical AI for data acquisition, Thinking AI for market evaluation and Feeling AI for understanding consumer sentiment. The chapter concludes with a discussion on emerging trends and the future potential of AI to reshape consumer relationships and drive sustainable growth.

TOWARD AN INTEGRATED FRAMEWORK OF AI IN BRAND MANAGEMENT

Recent literature explores AI's role in brand management, showing its impact on brand performance through eco-innovation (Larbi-Siaw et al., 2022) and competitive advantage (Goralski & Tan, 2020). AI enhances brand personality, fostering consumer relationships through human-like traits (Machado et al., 2019; Torres & Augusto, 2019). It also improves brand elements such as logos and designs, increasing visibility and loyalty (Capatina et al., 2020; Dew et al., 2022). AI-powered conversational agents personalize interactions, strengthening trust and engagement (Jham et al., 2023; Lin & Wu, 2023). Despite benefits for sustainable business, AI poses challenges, including cybersecurity risks and impact assessment difficulties (Nishant et al., 2020). Interestingly, Kirkby et al. (2023) found that disclosing AI-generated marketing text does not harm brand authenticity, suggesting transparency in AI use is viable.

Building on empirical studies, theoretical perspectives on AI-driven branding have evolved. Deryl et al. (2023) present an integrated framework analyzing AI's role in branding. This chapter extends their work by incorporating Huang and Rust's (2020) AI typology: Mechanical AI for data, Thinking AI for market evaluation and Feeling AI for sentiment analysis. Figure 37.1 illustrates this extended framework, guiding brands in leveraging AI for sustainable transformation and consumer engagement.

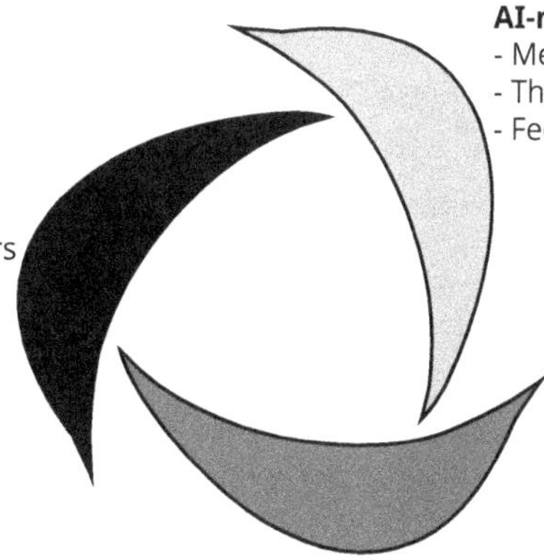

Figure 37.1 The framework of AI in brand management

Source: The authors.

Drivers of AI Integration in Branding

The application of AI technologies in brand development is primarily driven by three factors: social psychology, marketing and information science. Together, these factors shape consumer perceptions, behavioral patterns and the acceptance of new technologies in branding.

Social psychology drivers

From a social psychology perspective, subjective norms, self-efficacy and behavioral attitudes are core elements influencing the consumer adoption of AI technologies. Subjective norms refer to the perceived social pressure an individual faces, stemming from the expectations and influences of significant others such as family members, friends or industry leaders on their behavior. According to the Theory of Planned Behavior proposed by Ajzen (1991), subjective norms shape an individual's behavioral intentions through social influence. Dwivedi et al. (2021) applied this theoretical framework to demonstrate the role of subjective norms in eliciting positive responses to AI-driven branding. Based on the technology acceptance model (TAM), Cantallops and Salvi (2014) employed subjective norms to explain users' acceptance of AI in brand interactions. Therefore, before deciding to implement AI, brands need to recognize and proactively assess the significant impact of subjective norms on consumer acceptance. Self-efficacy, originating from Social Cognitive Theory (Bandura, 1986), refers to an individual's confidence in their ability to use technology successfully. From the perspective of AI-driven branding, judgments about one's ability to perform tasks and the expected outcomes of those tasks are crucial for brand evaluation (Deryl et al., 2023). Consumers' positive responses to AI-driven brand interactions contribute to building a strong brand image and positive brand associations, and self-efficacy largely influences consumers' reactions and attitudes toward advanced AI-driven brands (Deryl et al., 2023). Behavioral attitudes involve an individual's positive or negative evaluations of using technology. Fishbein and Ajzen's (1975) theory posits that attitudes are determined by an individual's beliefs about the consequences of the behavior. Therefore, consumers' behavioral attitudes are also a crucial factor in understanding their responses to AI-driven brands. Subjective norms, self-efficacy and behavioral attitudes collectively shape consumers' acceptance of AI technology. The Theory of Cognitive Dissonance (TCD) (Festinger et al., 1959) explains the psychological discomfort consumers may experience when AI interactions, such as those with chatbots, virtual assistants or automated systems, deviate from their expectations. This discomfort can result from factors such as incorrect responses (Binns et al., 2018), lack of personalization (Xu & Liao, 2013) or the system's inability to address specific concerns effectively (Shneiderman, 2020).

These negative experiences can alter consumers' perception of the brand, highlighting the importance of considering psychological discomfort and building emotional connections when integrating AI into branding. For example, Chicecream, a premium ice cream brand founded in Shanghai in 2018, demonstrates how social psychology drivers, particularly subjective norms and self-efficacy, can shape AI integration in branding. The brand leverages AI to personalize consumer experiences and appeal to youth-oriented trends, especially targeting Generation Z's affinity for innovation and individuality (Zhou, 2023). By aligning with the subjective norms of this demographic, such as a preference for unique, cutting-edge products, Chicecream effectively taps into the cultural and societal influences that drive consumer behavior. AI tools allow the brand to customize interactions, ensuring that its persona resonates emotionally with consumers and fosters a sense of belonging, which in turn enhances brand loyalty and trust. Moreover, Chicecream supports self-efficacy, the belief in one's ability to achieve desired outcomes, by using AI to offer tailored recommendations and assistance that empower consumers to make confident, personalized choices. This proactive approach not only prevents psychological discomfort by meeting consumer expectations but also reinforces the brand's commitment to responsiveness, ultimately strengthening the emotional bond between Chicecream and its audience. Through the strategic integration of subjective norms and self-efficacy, brands can build a deeper connection with consumers, creating a positive feedback loop that supports sustained engagement (Zhang & Mao, 2022).

Marketing drivers

Marketing drivers focus on deepening consumer–brand relationships through personalization (Huang & Rust, 2022; Zhang et al., 2023), emotional connections (Huang & Rust, 2022; Kim & Park, 2023) and sociocultural integration (Lee et al., 2023; Nguyen & Belk, 2022), which are increasingly facilitated by AI technologies. By offering tailored experiences, AI helps brands build trust and loyalty by aligning with shared values, a core element of emotional connections (Morgan & Hunt, 1994). For instance, AI enables brands to offer individualized content and interactions, fostering a stronger emotional bond with consumers. The Consumer Culture Theory further highlights how AI reshapes branding by influencing consumer identity (Zhou et al., 2024) and the culture surrounding the marketplace (Liang, 2024). Brands can use AI to integrate cultural elements and values into their identity, enhancing their relevance to specific consumer groups.

Brand personality, which includes traits like competence and sophistication, plays a pivotal role in creating meaningful interactions and enhancing affinity with consumers (Aaker, 1997; Dickinger & Lalicic, 2016). AI tools, such as chatbots and virtual assistants, leverage these traits to craft personalized experiences that engage consumers on a deeper level. These tools help brands deliver experiences that feel more human and relatable, fostering trust and long-term engagement. For example, Chicecream, a premium ice cream brand based in Shanghai, utilizes AI to create personalized consumer experiences, which strengthens its emotional connections with consumers. By tapping into Generation Z's desire for innovation and individuality (Zhou, 2023), Chicecream has used AI-powered sentiment analysis to track shifts in consumer preferences and adjust its branding strategies accordingly, further enhancing consumer engagement and loyalty.

Additionally, AI helps brands optimize marketing strategies and decision-making by predicting market trends and consumer behavior. For Chicecream, AI technologies like Baidu's Ernie Bot were used to anticipate key market factors, including consumer price sensitivity and competitive dynamics (Zhang, 2023). This enabled the brand to tailor its marketing strategies more effectively, ensuring that its product offerings resonated with the target demographic. In particular, AI played a crucial role in refining the pricing strategy for Chicecream's new product, Sa'Saa, ensuring that it appealed to the right consumer group while maintaining affordability without sacrificing value. As a result, Chicecream experienced increased brand visibility and engagement, particularly on social media platforms such as Weibo, where AI tools helped the brand better understand and interact with its audience (Miao, 2023). Through these examples, we can see how AI-driven marketing strategies can foster stronger consumer–brand relationships and drive long-term brand success.

Information science drivers

Finally, information science drivers focus on technology adoption and the diffusion of innovation. According to the TAM, consumers' perceptions of the usefulness and ease of use of AI tools are key to their adoption (Davis et al., 1989). As a result, online vendors are increasingly using virtual salespersons, or 'recommendation agents', to minimize search efforts and support more efficient decision-making (Rust & Kannan, 2003). These AI-driven tools, such as user-friendly recommendation engines, improve the efficiency of interactions between brands and consumers, seamlessly integrating AI into the decision-making process. In the example of Chicecream, the role of AI in information science drivers is particularly evident in its ability to analyze large volumes of consumer data and optimize product offerings. AI-driven insights guided the naming and flavor selection for Chicecream's Sa'Saa ice cream, ensuring that it resonated with market trends and consumer preferences. Additionally, AI-powered predictive analytics enabled Chicecream to forecast seasonal demand, adjust inventory levels and strategically position products to enhance consumer convenience. Together, these information science drivers, through their impact on data analysis, consumer insights and AI integration, play a pivotal role in shaping branding strategies (Dsouza Deryl et al., 2023). They provide valuable support in building sustainable relationships between brands and consumers, driving the widespread adoption of AI in branding.

AI-Mediated Brand Communication and Three AI Capacities

Past literature (Huang et al., 2019; Huang & Rust, 2018) categorizes AI capacities into three distinct types, reflecting different aspects of human capabilities that AI simulates: Mechanical AI, which facilitates data acquisition; Thinking AI, conducting market evaluations; and Feeling AI, enhancing comprehension of consumer sentiments (Huang & Rust, 2020). Mechanical AI automates repetitive tasks, such as machine translation and classification; Thinking AI analyzes unstructured data for conclusions or decisions, encompassing text mining and speech recognition; and Feeling AI involves human interaction and analyzes emotions, including sentiment analysis and anthropomorphic chatbots (Huang & Rust, 2020). These three categories simulate different human capabilities and can enhance various aspects of brand communication, especially in brand personalization, efficiency, consistency and emotional connection.

Mechanical AI for brand efficiency and consistency

Mechanical AI enhances operational efficiency and consistency by automating repetitive tasks and streamlining production processes (Huang & Rust, 2020). It is particularly valuable in industries such as manufacturing, logistics and payment systems, where it improves tasks such as inventory management, logistics and payments (Mende et al., 2019; van Doorn et al., 2017). This reduces human error and ensures a seamless experience for both consumers and businesses. One notable example is the consumer electronics industry, where robotic automation is used to assemble delicate components like cameras and sensors in smartphones. This not only enhances production efficiency but also ensures consistency in product quality (Davenport & Ronanki, 2018). Companies like IBM Watson (2024) leverage Mechanical AI to analyze data from production lines, optimizing manufacturing processes and improving overall operational efficiency. This allows brands to reduce costs, speed up production and maintain consistent quality across large-scale manufacturing operations. The standardization that Mechanical AI brings to the production process helps companies scale more efficiently while minimizing errors and maintaining high-quality standards. By utilizing AI tools like sentiment analysis and machine learning algorithms, Chicecream can quickly interpret consumer feedback and adjust messaging accordingly (Zhou, 2023). For example, the creation of the Sa'Saa brand name was influenced by AI, ensuring that it evoked the desired fun, adventurous spirit while aligning with consumer expectations.

In addition, Mechanical AI plays a critical role in pricing and payment automation. For instance, platforms such as Google Pay, Amazon Payments and Square use Mechanical AI to streamline payment processes and provide automated payment solutions, enhancing both the efficiency and security of transactions (Huang & Rust, 2020). AI also aids in strategic pricing decisions (Huang & Rust, 2020), such as setting Sa'Saa's price at 3.5 yuan and determining optimal store locations in high-traffic areas to enhance brand visibility.

Finally, Mechanical AI improves brand communication efficiency by streamlining content creation. Tools such as Midjourney, Stable Diffusion and Ultron Light Year help Chicecream create visually appealing and cost-effective promotional materials, including posters and videos (Zhou, 2023). These tools ensure that the brand's visual identity stays fresh and engaging, while enabling rapid adjustments based on real-time customer insights. During the launch of Sa'Saa, AI-driven adaptations of promotional content helped address the needs of different consumer segments, reinforcing a consistent and positive brand perception. This blend of efficiency and responsiveness strengthens Chicecream's dynamic brand strategy and solidifies its emotional connection with consumers.

Thinking AI for Brand Personalization

The application of Thinking AI exerts a substantial influence on the customization of products, services and marketing endeavors. By analyzing large datasets, including consumer preferences and behaviors, Thinking AI helps brands deliver tailored experiences that resonate deeply with individual consumers. Machine learning algorithms and NLP technologies enable AI systems to predict consumer preferences, recommend products and customize interactions in real time (Kumar et al., 2019).

This level of personalization enhances customer satisfaction, builds loyalty and drives engagement. For instance, e-commerce giant TrendHub uses AI-powered chatbots to deliver personalized product recommendations, leading to enhanced conversion rates and improved customer engagement (Kumar et al., 2019). Furthermore, AI systems like those at JD.com analyze consumer behavior, browsing patterns and geographical information to customize pricing and discounts based on individual needs (Yu, 2017). These tailored offerings ensure that consumers receive what they want, when they want it and at a price that suits them, improving the overall shopping experience.

Thinking AI has the pivotal function in shaping and refining a brand's identity by enabling personalized experiences and targeted marketing strategies (Huang & Rust, 2020). By analyzing vast amounts of consumer data, including preferences, behaviors and emerging trends, Thinking AI empowers brands to gain deeper insights into their customers and create tailored interactions (Dekimpe, 2020). This personalization not only enhances customer satisfaction and loyalty but also builds a deeper connection with consumers, reinforcing a brand's unique identity.

Machine learning techniques, a core component of Thinking AI, help brands identify and target the most promising consumer segments (Ascarza, 2018; Neumann et al., 2019; Simester et al., 2020). By analyzing patterns in consumer behavior, AI systems can predict shifts in preferences and refine segmentation strategies. For instance, brands can use AI to deliver personalized product recommendations, pricing, offers and communication that resonate more effectively with individual consumers. This refined targeting leads to stronger consumer connections, influencing purchasing decisions and ultimately improving long-term customer relationships (Simester et al., 2020). An example of Thinking AI shaping a brand's identity is Chicecream, which uses AI tools like Baidu's Ernie Bot to analyze consumer data and identify emerging trends, particularly among Generation Z. This insight allows Chicecream to tailor its products and marketing strategies to align with the values and tastes of its target audience. For instance, Chicecream's Sa'Saa ice cream line was developed using sentiment analysis, influencing decisions on product name, flavor and packaging. The result was a product that resonated with younger, trend-conscious consumers seeking novelty and individuality (Zhou, 2023). In this way, Thinking AI supports Chicecream's brand identity by aligning customer experiences with consumer expectations. By quickly adapting to preferences and incorporating AI-driven insights into product development and marketing, Chicecream strengthens its identity and fosters emotional connections with its audience. This dynamic use of Thinking AI ensures the brand identity continues to evolve in line with the values of its target demographic.

Feeling AI for Brand Emotional Connection

Feeling AI focuses on building emotional connections between brands and consumers by understanding and responding to emotional cues. This AI technology is designed to recognize, interpret and react to the emotions of consumers, creating more personalized and engaging experiences (Huang & Rust, 2021). Through emotional intelligence, Feeling AI can adjust interactions to better suit consumer needs, making the customer experience feel more genuine and meaningful (Huang & Rust, 2021).

The anthropomorphic qualities of Feeling AI, such as simulating human-like emotions and conversational interactions, are particularly effective in customer service and relationship-building. Research by Youn and Jin (2021) highlights how AI chatbots can create a sense of virtual friendship, fostering positive interactions that deepen consumer trust and engagement. Spotify (2024) uses Feeling AI to analyze users' music preferences and emotional states, personalizing music recommendations based on inferred emotional profiles. This not only elevates the music experience but also deepens the emotional bond between the brand and its users.

Furthermore, Feeling AI enhances price negotiations and customer service by responding to emotional cues. For example, Mint Personal Finance App (2024) leverages Feeling AI to understand users' financial habits and goals, providing personalized financial management advice that resonates emotionally. By tailoring services to meet emotional and personal needs, brands using Feeling AI can enhance customer satisfaction and foster customer loyalty, improving long-term relationships. Chicecream, for instance, uses AI-driven insights to craft emotionally resonant brand narratives that speak directly to its target demographic – young, trend-conscious consumers. Through tools like sentiment analysis and AI-powered video content creation, the brand tailors its messaging to elicit targeted emotional responses.

In the context of promotional strategies, Feeling AI can track real-time emotional reactions to marketing campaigns, allowing brands to adjust their messages and tactics to improve engagement and responsiveness (Hartmann et al., 2019; Lee et al., 2018). During the launch of Sa'Saa, Chicecream, for instance, leveraged Feeling AI to create emotion-driven campaigns that resonated with the values and preferences of its consumers, fostering a sense of belonging and connection with the brand. This emotional engagement not only strengthens customer loyalty but also drives positive brand associations, ensuring long-term brand affinity. By recognizing and responding to consumers' emotional states, Feeling AI transforms how brands interact with their customers, enhancing customer experiences and the overall effectiveness of marketing, customer service and promotional strategies. This emotional intelligence enables brands to establish more profound connections with their audience, ensuring more meaningful and enduring relationships. Google (2024b) is another example of how Feeling AI can understand user emotions and search intentions, offering tailored content that enhances the user experience. This real-time adaptability helps brands connect with their audience on a deeper emotional level, ensuring more effective communication and fostering stronger customer–brand relationships.

In summary, Thinking AI, Mechanical AI and Feeling AI each contribute uniquely to enhancing brand value and customer experience. Thinking AI focuses on personalizing interactions, Mechanical AI ensures efficiency and consistency, and Feeling AI builds emotional connections, creating a comprehensive approach to understanding and engaging customers across all touchpoints.

Outcomes of AI-Driven Branding

AI-driven branding significantly impacts brand trust, loyalty and consumer relationships through personalization, predictive analytics and dynamic engagement strategies. These outcomes are central to the success of modern brands, particularly in the digital age, where consumers expect tailored, timely experiences.

Building brand trust and loyalty

Trust is a cornerstone of consumer–brand relationships, and AI enhances it through tools like sentiment analysis, which enables real-time monitoring of consumer feedback (Ching & De Dios Bulos, 2019). For example, Chicecream leverages AI to understand customer sentiment and quickly address any negative feedback. This proactive approach helps to maintain transparency and reliability, which in turn reinforces the emotional bond between the brand and its consumers (Sansome et al., 2023). In this way, AI helps build trust by ensuring that customer concerns are addressed swiftly, leading to stronger brand loyalty. Additionally, AI-powered tools like chatbots or virtual assistants offer personalized, consistent and authentic interactions. Chicecream uses AI to engage with consumers through these tools, ensuring that each interaction feels timely and thoughtful, which further bolsters consumer trust (Lin & Wu, 2023).

Personalization and micro-targeting

AI's ability to analyze vast amounts of consumer data allows brands to deliver highly personalized experiences, a key factor in building deeper emotional connections and fostering loyalty. For instance, Chicecream uses AI to segment its customer base, understanding preferences and behaviors of different groups, especially trend-conscious Generation Z. This personalized approach enables the brand to offer tailored products like Sa'Saa, which was designed based on consumer sentiment analysis to align with the values and tastes of its target audience (Zhou, 2023). By doing so, Chicecream creates a personalized brand experience that resonates with its consumers on a deeper level, reinforcing their emotional connection and ensuring long-term loyalty. The ability to adapt messaging and offerings to specific cultural and regional contexts enhances the brand's relevance, allowing it to connect meaningfully with diverse consumer identities (Arnould & Thompson, 2005).

Enhanced consumer engagement

AI's predictive capabilities play a crucial role in anticipating consumer needs, further enhancing trust and engagement. Chicecream utilizes predictive analytics to forecast customer preferences and market trends, ensuring that its product offerings remain aligned with consumer demand. For example, AI allows the company to adjust pricing strategies and product placements based on real-time data, ensuring that Sa'Saa is available in high-demand areas during peak seasons (Zhou, 2023). This predictive approach not only increases convenience for customers but also improves satisfaction by anticipating their needs, leading to a stronger bond with the brand. Personalized recommendations, like those made by Amazon's recommendation engine or Netflix's content suggestions, show how predictive analytics can keep consumers engaged by offering relevant and timely experiences (Dwivedi et al., 2023).

AI also integrates with augmented reality (AR) and gamification, creating immersive brand experiences that deepen emotional connections with consumers. Chicecream has embraced AI-powered tools such as Midjourney, Stable Diffusion and Ultron Light Year to produce eye-catching promotional content, which strengthens its market presence and appeals to consumers in creative, interactive ways (Zhang, 2023). These tools allow the brand to engage consumers through dynamic content that resonates emotionally and keeps them engaged over time. Similar to how IKEA's AR application enables consumers to digitally superimpose furniture within their living spaces, thereby facilitating a virtual preview of product placement, Chicecream uses AI to enhance the way its products are presented, providing a more immersive and personalized shopping experience. Such experiences not only drive consumer satisfaction but also encourage long-term advocacy for the brand (Kaplan & Haenlein, 2019).

EMERGING TRENDS AND FUTURE DIRECTIONS

The remarkable advancement of AI technologies has the potential to significantly reshape brand management practices, offering increased intelligence, adaptability and precision. AI is transforming brand management by enhancing the ability to understand consumer behavior, personalize marketing strategies and optimize brand positioning with greater accuracy. However, while the integration of AI technologies offers numerous benefits, several challenges remain, presenting both opportunities and research gaps for future exploration.

Current Trends of AI's Role in Brand Management

Recent studies underscore the transformative potential of AI in brand management. AI technologies, such as NLP, sentiment analysis and machine learning, are pivotal in facilitating personalized marketing campaigns, understanding consumer behavior and refining brand positioning strategies (Huang & Rust, 2020). For example, AI enables brands to analyze large datasets to understand consumer preferences and behaviors with unprecedented accuracy, which aids in precise target market identification and segmentation. Companies such as PTC Frustum have leveraged AI-driven solutions to innovate manufacturing processes and introduce new design concepts, illustrating AI's capacity to influence product and service innovation (PTC, 2020).

Furthermore, AI-powered tools enhance customer relationship management (CRM) by streamlining various aspects, including customer acquisition, loyalty enhancement and retention (Kumar et al., 2019). The growing use of AI for predictive analytics has allowed companies to forecast consumer demand and behavior, thereby optimizing marketing strategies (Stephen & Ahmad, 2017). For instance, AI's ability to predict consumer behavior has revolutionized personalized recommendations and service delivery, enhancing consumer experiences and driving brand loyalty (Loureiro et al., 2021). These advances lead to the enhanced comprehension of consumer preferences, which facilitates the creation of highly tailored marketing campaigns and experiences.

However, while the implementation of AI technologies in brand management has been widely acknowledged, the current literature highlights several critical research gaps. For instance, most studies focus on specific AI applications in brand management, such as sentiment analysis or consumer behavior prediction (Madanchian, 2024; Singh et al., 2024), but few explore how different AI technologies can be integrated holistically to enhance brand management strategies. Additionally, there is a lack of comprehensive studies on the long-term impacts of AI on consumer trust and brand loyalty, especially in industries where customer data privacy is a significant concern. The integration of AI in brand management presents numerous opportunities, but several research gaps remain that require further exploration. These gaps range from the integration of different AI technologies to ethical considerations and data privacy concerns. Below, three key areas for future research are outlined, combining the current gaps with potential directions for further investigation.

Research Gaps and Future Directions

Mechanical AI

Demystifying AI for Consumers and Brands. Current literature on Mechanical AI highlights its potential in demystifying the complexities of AI, making these technologies more accessible to a wider audience. Studies such as those by Loureiro et al. (2021) highlight the critical need for simplifying AI language to ensure that both consumers and businesses can navigate AI-driven brand interactions with ease. This simplification is crucial as AI becomes increasingly integrated into consumer experiences. While much of the research focuses on technical advancements and the potential applications of AI, there is a growing recognition that making AI more understandable to the general public is essential for its widespread acceptance and trust (Lahusen et al., 2024). Through clearer communication, brands can empower consumers to make informed decisions, thus reducing potential anxieties or misunderstandings surrounding AI technologies.

Despite the progress in simplifying AI for consumer understanding, gaps remain in how effectively these simplified models translate into tangible trust and engagement in real-world applications. While accessibility is a key focus (Wang, 2024), much of the existing research tends to prioritize the development of AI algorithms and models rather than the practical aspects of how these innovations are communicated to and perceived by the public. There is a need for more in-depth studies on the psychological and sociocultural factors that influence consumer perceptions of AI. Research could explore how different consumer segments (e.g., age, education and culture) respond to various levels of AI complexity and the role transparency plays in their trust-building processes (Afroogh et al., 2024). Additionally, while Mechanical AI has been recognized as a useful tool in making AI more approachable, there is limited exploration into the specific methods or frameworks that are most effective in fostering this understanding.

Further academic inquiry in this field ought to delve deeper into how education and awareness initiatives can enhance trust and acceptance of AI-powered brand interactions. For instance, exploring the role of interactive learning experiences, user-friendly interfaces and even gamification in communicating AI concepts to consumers could provide valuable insights. Furthermore, research could investigate how brands can create transparent and effective communication strategies that resonate with diverse consumer groups. Longitudinal studies on the impact of these efforts could help determine the long-term effects of increased AI literacy on consumer loyalty and engagement. As Mechanical AI continues to evolve, understanding the relationship between accessibility, trust and consumer behavior will be pivotal for shaping the future of AI-integrated brand experiences.

Thinking AI: Enhancing transparency and ethical decision-making

The latest research on Thinking AI stresses the critical significance of not only ensuring the accuracy of AI algorithms but also ensuring their transparency and fairness. These two factors are essential for fostering consumer trust, especially when AI is used for sensitive aspects such as personalized marketing and dynamic pricing strategies. Rai (2020) underscores the need for AI systems that engage with consumers in a manner that is both transparent and unbiased. However, current research primarily focuses on AI's technical capabilities and its ability to improve efficiency in decision-making. There is a gap in understanding how AI systems can be developed to be both ethically responsible and effective in the long term. This gap presents an opportunity for future research to explore how Thinking AI can be refined to create personalized marketing algorithms that are transparent, fair and responsible (Huang & Rust, 2020). Such research could offer valuable insights into how brands can ensure that their AI-driven marketing efforts do not perpetuate biases, ultimately improving both brand reputation and consumer trust.

A major challenge in the current research is the opacity and biases embedded in many AI algorithms, particularly when used for consumer decision-making, such as in pricing and personalized marketing (Rudin, 2019). These algorithmic biases may result in detrimental consequences for the brand, such as loss of consumer trust and damage to brand reputation. Despite advancements in AI, concerns about fairness and transparency remain critical, highlighting the need for more research focused on minimizing biases. Future research should delve into developing more transparent, accountable AI systems that mitigate biases by using diverse datasets, ensuring robust data collection practices and incorporating ethical frameworks that align with societal norms (Gross et al., 2017; Tang, 2023). In addition, involving diverse teams in algorithm development and cleansing AI training data to eliminate biases are crucial next steps for achieving fairness and accuracy in AI-driven brand management strategies.

Another critical issue is the growing concern around data privacy, security and consumer trust as AI systems increasingly collect and analyze sensitive consumer data. While AI-driven personalization offers brands the ability to create tailored experiences for consumers, it also raises significant privacy concerns. The trade-off between offering personalized marketing and protecting consumer data has become a pressing challenge. Future research must explore how brands can balance these competing interests by investigating privacy-preserving AI techniques and their impact on consumer trust. Additionally, developing robust data protection measures and ensuring transparency in data usage policies will be crucial for safeguarding sensitive consumer information (Green, 2018). The role of AI in ensuring consumer privacy, while still providing valuable personalization, is a key area of focus for future research in brand management.

In summary, while current research on Thinking AI has highlighted its potential to enhance the transparency, fairness and accuracy of brand-driven AI systems, there are significant gaps in understanding how these systems can be refined to avoid biases and ensure consumer trust. Future research should focus on how to improve the transparency and ethical responsibility of AI algorithms, particularly in sensitive areas like personalized marketing and pricing strategies. Additionally, exploring ways to safeguard data privacy and security will be critical for building lasting consumer relationships and ensuring that AI technologies are used responsibly. By addressing these gaps, researchers can guide brands in deploying AI technologies that are both effective and aligned with consumer expectations of fairness, transparency and privacy.

Feeling AI: Leveraging long-term impact of emotional intelligence

Current research on AI in brand management has primarily focused on the short-term effects of AI technologies, particularly in terms of enhancing customer engagement and streamlining operational efficiencies (V. Kumar et al., 2019). AI systems have been widely studied for their ability to deliver personalized experiences, improve customer service and increase brand visibility through tools such as chatbots, recommendation engines and targeted advertisements (Cheng & Jiang, 2022). These technologies enable brands to tailor their offerings to individual preferences, leading to more relevant interactions and increased consumer satisfaction. For instance, AI-driven personalization has been shown to enhance brand loyalty by providing customers with customized recommendations and content that resonate with their interests (Dwivedi et al., 2023).

However, while these research studies have yielded significant understanding of the immediate benefits of AI in brand management, there exists a material gap in understanding the long-term impact of AI technologies on consumer behavior and brand loyalty (Verhoef et al., 2021). Most research has yet to explore how sustained interactions with AI systems influence consumer perceptions and their ongoing relationship with brands over time. While AI can effectively engage consumers in the short run, the long-term effects on brand equity, customer retention and shifts in consumer preferences have not been thoroughly examined. There is a need for longitudinal studies that track consumer interactions with AI over extended periods, which would help uncover how AI-driven personalization evolves and continues to affect customer loyalty. Addressing this gap in the literature is critical for developing sustainable AI strategies that build lasting relationships with consumers (Kumar et al., 2019; Loureiro et al., 2021).

Looking forward, there are several important future research agendas to consider. First, researchers should focus on understanding the long-term effect of AI on customer behavior patterns and brand loyalty. Investigating how AI systems influence consumer trust and satisfaction over time will be essential in refining AI-driven branding strategies. Longitudinal studies can also reveal how AI interacts with changing consumer preferences and market trends, providing valuable insights into the ways brands can adapt and stay relevant. Additionally, research should explore how AI systems can be designed to foster emotional engagement with consumers, particularly through the development of Feeling AI – a system that integrates emotional intelligence into AI interactions. As brands increasingly look to AI to strengthen emotional connections with consumers, it will be crucial to understand how these emotionally resonant experiences impact customer loyalty and brand equity in the long term.

The concept of Feeling AI itself represents a promising frontier in AI research, particularly in its application to brand management. By leveraging principles from neuroscience, brands can design AI systems that recognize, interpret and respond to emotional cues, creating personalized experiences that resonate emotionally with consumers. Huang and Rust (2020) argue that this type of emotional engagement is crucial for enhancing customer loyalty, as it fosters deeper emotional connections between consumers and brands. Future research should investigate how AI systems can be further developed to not only recognize consumer emotions but also respond in ways that feel authentic and human-like. This will ensure that AI interactions are not only functional but also emotionally impactful, leading to stronger customer–brand relationships.

As we look ahead, there are broader societal challenges related to AI that also need to be addressed. Pueyo (2018) highlights the promise of an increasingly intelligent society, built on the integration of AI agents and technologically enhanced individuals. However, this future also presents complex ecological and communal challenges, such as the potential risks of AI system safety, transparency issues, biases in algorithmic decision-making and growing human dependence on these technologies. These concerns must be addressed to guarantee the ethical and responsible implementation of AI technologies. Green (2018) raises alarms about the potential for biases in AI-driven systems that could result in inequitable treatment of certain groups, which could erode consumer trust and damage brand loyalty. Therefore, future research must also focus on developing frameworks that address these risks and guarantee that AI technologies are architected with safety, transparency and fairness as integral design imperatives.

As Table 37.2 demonstrated and summarized, mechanical AI aims to demystify AI jargon for the layperson (Loureiro et al., 2021), while Thinking

Table 37.2 AI's challenges and potential strategies

Category of AI	*Challenges*	*Potential Strategies*
Mechanical AI	• Non-contextual data • Machine-to-machine interactions	• Translate AI terminology for average comprehension (Loureiro et al., 2021).
Thinking AI	• Opaque AI • AI biases	• Advance AI to clarify and ensure fairness in marketing decisions (Rai, 2020). • Create personalized marketing algorithms using diverse customer data (Huang & Rust, 2020). • Focus on ethical AI development through initiatives like 'AI for Humanity' (Nebeker et al., 2019).
Feeling AI	• Technology unreadiness • Customer unreadiness	• Use neuroscience to study consumer emotions towards sentient AI (Huang & Rust, 2020).

Source: The authors.

AI focuses on creating transparent and unbiased decision-making processes (Rai, 2020) and algorithms that enhance customer engagement through personalized experiences (Huang & Rust, 2020). For Feeling AI, adopting neuroscience to better understand consumer emotional reactions to AI is proposed (Huang & Rust, 2020). Across all AI facets, there is a concerted effort to align AI advancements with humanistic values and ethics (Nebeker et al., 2019), ensuring AI development remains beneficial and ethically grounded. Enterprises thus could develop transparent data collection systems, minimizing data collection to what is necessary for service provision and informing users about the collected data and its use. Additionally, they should enhance the detection and cleansing of AI algorithm training data to mitigate biases, employing diverse datasets and teams to improve fairness and accuracy (Tang, 2023).

The future of AI in brand management presents exciting opportunities to foster deeper consumer connections through emotional engagement, transparency and ethical practices. By exploring and refining the three AI paradigms, Mechanical AI, Thinking AI and Feeling AI, brands can enhance consumer trust, loyalty and engagement. Integrating emotional intelligence into AI systems and ensuring that AI technologies are accessible, transparent and ethical will be key to creating a positive and lasting impact on brand management strategies. Future research in these areas will be crucial for shaping the next generation of AI-powered brand experiences.

CONCLUSION

Throughout this chapter, scholars have delved into the multifaceted role of AI in brand management. Key insights and findings emerged from our exploration of various AI-driven communication channels, theoretical foundations and emerging trends and future research agendas in AI-powered brand management.

AI-driven communication channels offer brands unprecedented opportunities to engage with their audiences in personalized and meaningful ways. Through intelligent customer service, predictive analytics and neural network technologies, brands can enhance customer satisfaction, optimize marketing strategies and predict consumer behavior more accurately than ever before. Real-world case studies, such as the Sa'Saa ice cream brand crisis, provide significant perspectives into the strategic use of AI in rebranding efforts and consumer engagement.

However, the implementation of AI in brand management also brings unique challenges. Maintaining brand authenticity and consistency across AI-driven touchpoints, addressing algorithmic bias and ensuring data privacy are critical considerations for brand managers. Proactive strategies, including transparent data collection systems and efforts to address algorithmic bias, are essential to mitigate risks and leverage the transformative potential of AI effectively.

Looking ahead, the future of AI in brand management is promising. Emerging trends such as AI-driven market analysis, personalized service provision and ethical AI development present new growth opportunities for brands. By staying abreast of AI technology trends and addressing ethical considerations, brands can foster deeper connections with consumers and drive sustainable growth in an increasingly digitalized marketplace.

As AI continues to evolve, it will undoubtedly reshape the landscape of brand management. By embracing AI technologies and navigating the challenges they present, brands can thereby establish themselves as pioneers in innovation and generate enduring value for both consumers and other stakeholders.

Call to Action for Practitioners and Scholars

The era of AI-powered branding has arrived, calling for a strategic shift in how brands are managed and communicated. Practitioners and scholars must not only embrace this transformation but also approach it with a balanced perspective. For practitioners, the call to action involves adopting AI-powered branding strategies to thrive in the digital age. By harnessing the capabilities of AI, enterprises can thereby acquire a competitive advantage, optimize customer experiences and foster sustainable development. Success requires investment in AI technologies, development of implementation expertise, and a commitment to continuous innovation. At the same time, it is essential to recognize that AI should complement, not replace, core brand strategies. While AI can enhance personalization, efficiency, and engagement, it must not override the brand's foundational identity or values. Strong marketing positioning remains the foundation of effective branding. In this context, AI should be seen as an enabling tool: one that supports and strengthens brand integrity and authenticity, rather than redefining them.

Simultaneously, scholars are called to delve deeper into AI's role in branding, exploring topics such as ethics, algorithmic bias and societal implications. By advancing understanding of AI's transformative potential, scholars can inform best practices, shape industry standards and contribute to the evolution of brand management in the digital era. Through rigorous research and critical analysis, scholars can guide practitioners in navigating the ethical and strategic complexities of AI-powered branding.

In conclusion, the integration of AI into brand management represents a watershed moment in marketing history. By embracing AI-powered strategies while preserving brand identity and values, practitioners and scholars can unlock new possibilities, drive innovation and create meaningful experiences that resonate with consumers in the digital age. Collaboration between these two groups is fundamental for realizing the full potential of AI in brand management and ensuring its responsible and ethical use.

REFERENCES

Aaker, J. L. (1997). Dimensions of brand personality. *Journal of Marketing Research*, *34*(3), 347–356. https://doi.org/10.1177/002224379703400304

Adobe. (2024). *Gen studio*. Retrieved May 16, 2024, from https://business.adobe.com/products/genstudio.html

Afroogh, S., Akbari, A., & Alambeigi, H. (2024). Trust in AI: Progress, challenges, and future directions. *Humanities and Social Sciences Communications*, *11*(1), 1568. https://doi.org/10.1057/s41599-024-04044-8

Ajzen, I. (1991). The theory of planned behavior. *Organizational Behavior and Human Decision Processes*, *50*(2), 179–211. https://doi.org/10.1016/0749-5978(91)90020-T

Arnould, E. J., & Thompson, C. J. (2005). Consumer culture theory (CCT): Twenty years of research. *Journal of Consumer Research*, *31*(4), 868–882. https://doi.org/10.1086/426626

Ansari, A., & Riasi, A. (2016). Modelling and evaluating customer loyalty using neural networks: Evidence from startup insurance companies. *Future Business Journal*, *2*(1), 15–30. https://doi.org/10.1016/j.fbj.2016.04.001

Asana. (2024). *Introducing AI studio: A new era of intelligent workflows*. Retrieved October 15, 2024, from https://asana.com/inside-asana/introducing-ai-studio

Ascarza, E. (2018). Retention futility: Targeting high-risk customers might be ineffective. *Journal of Marketing Research*, *55*(1), 80–98. https://doi.org/10.1509/jmr.16.0163

Bandura, A. (1986). The explanatory and predictive scope of self-efficacy theory. *Journal of Social and Clinical Psychology*, *4*(3), 359–373. https://doi.org/10.1521/jscp.1986.4.3.359

Binns, R., Van Kleek, M., Veale, M., Lyngs, U., Zhao, J., & Shadbolt, N. (2018). 'It's reducing a human being to a percentage': Perceptions of justice in algorithmic decisions. Proceedings of the 2018 CHI conference on human factors in computing systems, April 21–26,2018 (pp. 1–14).

Bornet, P., Barkin, I., & Wirtz, J. (2021). *Intelligent automation: Welcome to the world of hyperautomation*. Shroff Publishers.

Cantallops, A. S., & Salvi, F. (2014). New consumer behavior: A review of research on eWOM and hotels. *International Journal of Hospitality Management*, *36*, 41–51. https://doi.org/10.1016/j.ijhm.2013.08.007

Capatina, A., Kachour, M., Lichy, J., Micu, A., Micu, A. E., & Codignola, F. (2020). Matching the future capabilities of an artificial intelligence-based software for social media marketing with potential users' expectations. *Technological Forecasting and Social Change*, *151*, 119794. https://doi.org/10.1016/j.techfore.2019.119794

Cheng, Y., & Jiang, H. (2022). Customer–brand relationship in the era of artificial intelligence: Understanding the role of chatbot marketing efforts. *Journal of Product & Brand Management*, *31*(2), 252–264. https://doi.org/10.1108/JPBM-05-2020-2907

Ching, M. R. D., & De Dios Bulos, R. (2019). Improving restaurants' business performance using Yelp data sets through sentiment analysis. Proceedings of the 2019 3rd international conference on E-commerce, E-business and E-government – ICEEG 2019, June 17–19, 2019 (pp. 62–67). https://doi.org/10.1145/3340017.3340018

Davenport, T. H., & Ronanki, R. (2018). Artificial intelligence for the real world. *Harvard Business Review*, *96*(1), 108–116. https://doi.org/10.1080/15332861.2024.2350326

Davis, F. D., Bagozzi, R. P., & Warshaw, P. R. (1989). User acceptance of computer technology: A comparison of two theoretical models. *Management Science*, *35*(8), 982–1003. https://doi.org/10.1287/mnsc.35.8.982

De Bruyn, A., Viswanathan, V., Beh, Y. S., Brock, J. K.-U., & von Wangenheim, F. (2020). Artificial intelligence and marketing: Pitfalls and opportunities. *Journal of Interactive Marketing*, *51*(1), 91–105. https://doi.org/10.1016/j.intmar.2020.04.007

Dekimpe, M. G. (2020). Retailing and retailing research in the age of big data analytics. *International Journal of Research in Marketing*, *37*(1), 3–14. https://doi.org/10.1016/j.ijresmar.2019.09.001

Deryl, M., Verma, S., & Srivastava, V. (2023). How does AI drive branding? Towards an integrated theoretical framework for AI-driven branding. *International Journal of Information Management Data Insights*, *3*(2), 100205. https://doi.org/10.1016/j.jjimei.2023.100205

Dew, R., Ansari, A., & Toubia, O. (2022). Letting logos speak: Leveraging multiview representation learning for data-driven branding and logo design. *Marketing Science*, *41*(2), 401–425. https://doi.org/10.1287/mksc.2021.1326

Dickinger, A., & Lalicic, L. (2016). An analysis of destination brand personality and emotions: A comparison study. *Information Technology & Tourism*, *15*(4), 317–340. https://doi.org/10.1007/s40558-015-0044-x

Dsouza Deryl, M., Verma, S., & Srivastava, V. (2023). How does AI drive branding? Towards an integrated theoretical framework for AI-driven branding. *International Journal of Information Management Data Insights*, *3*, 100205. https://doi.org/10.1016/j.jjimei.2023.100205

Dwivedi, R., Nerur, S., & Balijepally, V. (2023). Exploring artificial intelligence and big data scholarship in information systems: A citation, bibliographic coupling, and coword analysis. *International Journal of Information Management Data Insights*, *3*(2), 100185. https://doi.org/10.1016/j.jjimei.2023.100185

Dwivedi, Y. K., Hughes, L., Ismagilova, E., Aarts, G., Coombs, C., Crick, T., Duan, Y., Dwivedi, R., Edwards, J., Eirug, A., Galanos, V., Vigneswara Ilavarasan, P., Janssen, M., Jones, P., Kar, A. K., Kizgin, H., Kronemann, B., Lal, B., Lucini, B., … Williams, M. D. (2021). Artificial intelligence (AI): Multidisciplinary perspectives on emerging challenges, opportunities, and agenda for research, practice and policy. *International Journal of Information Management*, *57*, 101994. https://doi.org/10.1016/j.ijinfomgt.2019.08.002

Festinger, L., & Carlsmith, J. M. (1959). Cognitive consequences of forced compliance. *Journal of Abnormal and Social Psychology*, *58*(2), 203–210. https://doi.org/10.1037/h0041593

Fishbein, M., & Ajzen, I. (1975). Belief, attitude, intention and behavior: An introduction to theory and research. *Addison-Wesley Publishing Company*.

Google. (2024a). *Artificial intelligence*. Retrieved May 16, 2024, from https://blog.google/technology/ai/

Google. (2024b). *Increase full funnel conversions*. Retrieved May 16, 2024, from www.thinkwithgoogle.com/consumer-insights/consumer-trends/increase-full-funnel-conversions/

Goralski, M. A., & Tan, T. K. (2020). Artificial intelligence and sustainable development. *The International Journal of Management Education*, *18*(1), 100330. https://doi.org/10.1016/j.ijme.2019.100330

Green, B. P. (2018). Ethical reflections on artificial intelligence. *Scientia et Fides*, *6*(2), 9–31. https://doi.org/10.12775/SetF.2018.015

Gross, S. R., Possley, M., & Stephens, K. (2017). Race and wrongful convictions in the United States. National Registry of Exonerations. www.law.umich.edu/special/exoneration/Documents/Race_and_Wrongful_Convictions.pdf

Harrison, R., Xiao, Y., Jasti, N., & Larner, J. (2022). Artificial intelligence empowered conversational agents: A systematic literature review and research agenda. *Journal of Business Research*, *161*, 113838. https://doi.org/10.1016/j.jbusres.2023.113838

Hartmann, J., Huppertz, J., Schamp, C. P., & Heitmann, M. (2019). Comparing automated text classification methods. *International Journal of Research in Marketing*, *36*(1), 20–38. https://doi.org/10.1016/j.ijresmar.2018.09.009

Hootsuite. (2024). *Home – Hootsuite*. Retrieved May 16, 2024, from www.hootsuite.com/

Huang, M. H., & Rust, R. T. (2018). Artificial intelligence in service. *Journal of Service Management*, *29*(1), 9–27. https://doi.org/10.1177/1094670517752459

Huang, M. H., & Rust, R. T. (2020). A strategic framework for artificial intelligence in marketing. *Journal of the Academy of Marketing Science*, *49*(1), 30–50. https://doi.org/10.1007/s11747-020-00749-9

Huang, M.-H., & Rust, R. T. (2021). A strategic framework for artificial intelligence in marketing.

Journal of Service Research, *24*(1), 30–50. https://doi.org/10.1177/1094670520964106

Huang, M. H., & Rust, R. T. (2022). AI-Enabled customer relationship management: From data to empathy. *Journal of the Academy of Marketing Science*, *50*(3), 432–450. https://doi.org/10.1007/s11747-021-00827-6

Huang, M. H., Rust, R. T., & Maksimovic, V. (2019). The feeling economy: Managing in the next generation of artificial intelligence (AI). *California Management Review*, *61*(4), 43–65. https://doi.org/10.1177/0008125619863436

HubSpot. (2024). *Software, tools, resources for your business*. Retrieved May 16, 2024, from www.hubspot.com/

IBM. (2024). IBM Watsonx – AI and data platform for enterprises. Retrieved May 16, 2024, from www.ibm.com/your-specific-page-url

Ismail, M. R., Awang, M. K., Rahman, M. N. A., & Makhtar, M. (2015). A multi-layer perceptron approach for customer churn prediction. *International Journal of Multimedia and Ubiquitous Engineering*, *10*(7), 213–222. https://doi.org/10.14257/ijmue.2015.10.7.22

Jham, V., Malhotra, G., & Sehgal, N. (2023). Consumer-brand relationships with AI anthropomorphic assistant: Role of product usage barrier, psychological distance and trust. *The International Review of Retail, Distribution and Consumer Research*, *33*(2), 117–133. https://doi.org/10.1080/09593969.2023.2178023

Kaplan, A., & Haenlein, M. (2019). Siri, Siri, in my hand: Who's the fairest in the land? On the interpretations, illustrations, and implications of artificial intelligence. *Business Horizons*, *62*(1), 15–25. https://doi.org/10.1016/j.bushor.2018.08.004

Kim, S., & Park, J. (2023). Sentiment-driven AI in brand communication: A neuroscientific perspective. *Computers in Human Behavior*, *142*, 107623. https://doi.org/10.1016/j.chb.2022.107623

Kirkby, A., Baumgarth, C., & Henseler, J. (2023). To disclose or not disclose, is no longer the question – effect of AI-disclosed brand voice on brand authenticity and attitude. *Journal of Product & Brand Management*, *32*(7), 1108–1122. https://doi.org/10.1108/JPBM-02-2022-3864

Kumar, A., Bapat, G., Kumar, A., Hota, S. L., Abishek, G. D., & Vaz, S. (2023). Unlocking brand excellence: Harnessing AI tools for enhanced customer engagement and innovation. *RAiSE*, *2023*, 204. https://doi.org/10.3390/engproc2023059204

Kumar, V., Rajan, B., Venkatesan, R., & Lecinski, J. (2019). Understanding the role of artificial intelligence in personalized engagement marketing. *California Management Review*, *61*(4), 135–155. https://doi.org/10.1177/0008125619859317

Lahusen, C., Maggetti, M., & Slavković, M. (2024). Trust, trustworthiness and AI governance. *Scientific Reports*, *14*(1), 20752. https://doi.org/10.1038/s41598-024-71761-0

Larbi-Siaw, O., Xuhua, H., Owusu, E., Owusu-Agyeman, A., Fulgence, B. E., & Frimpong, S. A. (2022). Eco-innovation, sustainable business performance and market turbulence moderation in emerging economies. *Technology in Society*, *68*, 101899. https://doi.org/10.1016/j.techsoc.2022.101899

Lee, D., Hosanagar, K., & Nair, H. S. (2018). Advertising content and consumer engagement on social media: Evidence from Facebook. *Management Science*, *64*(11), 5105–5131. https://doi.org/10.1287/mnsc.2017.2902

Lee, H., Chen, Y., & Kumar, V. (2023). AI and cultural adaptation: Bridging global brands with local communities. *International Journal of Research in Marketing*, *40*(1), 89–105. https://doi.org/10.1016/j.ijresmar.2022.11.003

Liang, J. (2024). The application of artificial intelligence-assisted technology in cultural and creative product design. *Scientific Reports*, *14*(1), 31069. https://doi.org/10.1038/s41598-024-82281-2

Lin, J. S. E., & Wu, L. (2023). Examining the psychological process of developing consumer-brand relationships through strategic use of social media brand chatbots. *Computers in Human Behavior*, *140*, 107488. https://doi.org/10.1016/j.chb.2022.107488

Loureiro, S. M. C., Guerreiro, J., & Tussyadiah, I. (2021). Artificial intelligence in business: State of the art and future research agenda. *Journal of Business Research*, *129*, 911–926. https://doi.org/10.1016/j.jbusres.2020.11.001

Machado, J. C., Vacas-de-Carvalho, L., Azar, S. L., Andŕe, A. R., & Dos Santos, B. P. (2019). Brand gender and consumer-based brand equity on Facebook: The mediating role of consumer-brand engagement and brand love. *Journal of Business Research*, *96*, 376–385. https://doi.org/10.1016/j.jbusres.2018.07.016

Madanchian, M. (2024). Generative AI for consumer behavior prediction: Techniques and applications. *Sustainability*, *16*(22), Article 22. https://doi.org/10.3390/su16229963

Mailchimp. (2024). *Turn emails into revenue*. Retrieved May 16, 2024, from https://mailchimp.com/

Mariani, M., & Baggio, R. (2022). Big data and analytics in hospitality and tourism: A systematic literature review. *International Journal of Contemporary Hospitality Management*, *34*(1), 231–278. https://doi.org/10.1108/IJCHM-03-2021-0301

Mariani, M. M., Hashemi, N., & Wirtz, J. (2023). Artificial intelligence empowered conversational agents: A systematic literature review and research agenda. *Journal of Business Research*, *161*, 113838. https://doi.org/10.1016/j.jbusres.2023.113838

McCarthy, J., Minsky, M. L., Rochester, N., & Shannon, C. E. (1955). A proposal for the Dartmouth

summer research project on artificial intelligence, August 31, 1955. *AI Magazine*, *27*(4), 12. https://doi.org/10.1609/aimag.v27i4.1904
Mende, M., Scott, M. L., van Doorn, J., Grewal, D., & Shanks, I. (2019). Service robots rising: How humanoid robots influence service experiences and elicit compensatory consumer responses. *Journal of Marketing Research*, *56*(4), 535–556. https://doi.org/10.1177/0022243718822827
Miao, Z. Q. (2023). *Can AI 'find' the tongues of young people? Zhong Xuegao gave it a try*. Retrieved June 19, 2023, from https://mp.weixin.qq.com/s/o3cg_KMFw7OK8kh4MsdY_A
Mint. (2024). *ZDNet*. Retrieved May 16, 2024, from www.zdnet.com/finance/mint-brings-financial-literacy-to-consumers-and-underserved-communities-to-help-build-healthy-financial-habits/
Morgan, R. M., & Hunt, S. D. (1994). The commitment-trust theory of relationship marketing. *Journal of Marketing*, *58*(3), 20–38. https://doi.org/10.1177/002224299405800302
Murray, G., & Wardley, M. (2014). The math of modern marketing: How predictive analytics makes marketing more effective. IDC white paper.
Nebeker, C., Torous, J., & Bartlett Ellis, R. J. (2019). Building the case for actionable ethics in digital health research supported by artificial intelligence. *BMC Medicine*, *17*(1), 137. https://doi.org/10.1186/s12916-019-1377-7
Neumann, N., Tucker, C. E., & Whitfield, T. (2019). Frontiers: How effective is third-party consumer profiling? Evidence from field studies. *Marketing Science*, *38*(6), 918–926. https://doi.org/10.1287/mksc.2019.1193
Nguyen, T. H., & Belk, R. W. (2022). AI as a cultural mediator: Algorithmic localization in global marketing. *Journal of Consumer Psychology*, *32*(4), 567–582. https://doi.org/10.1002/jcpy.1321
Nishant, R., Kennedy, M., & Corbett, J. (2020). Artificial intelligence for sustainability: Challenges, opportunities, and a research agenda. *International Journal of Information Management*, *53*, Article 102104. https://doi.org/10.1016/j.ijinfomgt.2020.102104
Power, D. J. (2016). 'Big brother' can watch us. *Journal of Decision Systems*, *25*(1, Suppl.), 578–588. https://doi.org/10.1080/12460125.2016.1187420
PTC. (2020). Retrieved April 22, from www.ptc.com/en/about/frustum
Pueyo, S. (2018). Growth, degrowth, and the challenge of artificial superintelligence. *Journal of Cleaner Production*, *197*(2), 1731–1736. https://doi.org/10.1016/j.jclepro.2016.12.138
Rai, A. (2020). Explainable AI: From black box to glass box. *Journal of the Academy of Marketing Science*, *48*(1), 137–141. https://doi.org/10.1007/s11747-019-00710-5
Rudin, C. (2019). Stop explaining black box machine learning models for high-stakes decisions and use interpretable models instead. *Nature Machine Intelligence*, *1*(5), 206–215. https://doi.org/10.1038/s42256-019-0048-x
Rust, R. T., & Kannan, P. K. (2003). E-service: A new paradigm for business in the electronic environment. *Communications of the ACM*, *46*(6), 36–42. https://doi.org/10.1145/777313.777336
Salesforce. (2024). Salesforce Einstein overview. *Salesforce*. Retrieved May 16, 2024, from www.salesforce.com/cn/products/einstein/overview/
Sansome, K., Wilkie, D., & Conduit, J. (2023). Beyond information availability: Specifying dimensions of consumer-perceived brand transparency. *Journal of Business Research*, *144*, 114358. https://doi.org/10.1016/j.jbusres.2022.114358
Shneiderman, B. (2020). Human-centered artificial intelligence: Reliable, safe & trustworthy. *International Journal of Human-Computer Interaction*, *36*(6), 495–504. https://doi.org/10.1080/10447318.2020.1741118
Simester, D., Timoshenko, A., & Zoumpoulis, S. I. (2020). Targeting prospective customers: Robustness of machine-learning methods to typical data challenges. *Management Science*, *66*(6), 2495–2522. https://doi.org/10.1287/mnsc.2019.3308
Singh, C., Dash, M. K., Sahu, R., & Kumar, A. (2024). Artificial intelligence in customer retention: A bibliometric analysis and future research framework. *Kybernetes*, *53*(11), 4863–4888. https://doi.org/10.1108/K-02-2023-0245
Spotify. (2024). *Home – Spotify*. Retrieved May 16, from www.spotify.com/
Stephen, A., & Ahmad, Y. (2017). Recreating intimacy with connected consumers. *GfK Marketing Intelligence Review*, *9*(2), 48–53. https://doi.org/10.1515/gfkmir-2017-00018
Tableau. (2024). *Tableau desktop*. Retrieved May 16, 2024, from www.tableau.com/zh-cn/products/desktop#content-434551
Tang, Y. J. (2023). Overview of the application of artificial intelligence technology in e-commerce. *Modern Business*, *10*, 35–38. https://doi.org/10.14097/j.cnki.5392/2023.10.037
Torres, P., & Augusto, M. (2019). Building resilience to negative information and increasing purchase intentions in a digital environment. *Journal of Business Research*, *101*, 528–535. https://doi.org/10.1016/j.jbusres.2018.11.045
Turing, A. M. (1950). *Computing machinery and intelligence* (pp. 23–65). Springer Netherlands.
van Doorn, J., Mende, M., Noble, S., Hulland, J., Ostrom, A., Grewal, D., & Petersen, A. (2017). Domo arigato Mr. Roboto: Emergence of automated social presence in organizational frontlines and customers' service experiences. *Journal of Service Research*, *20*(1), 43–58. https://doi.org/10.1177/1094670516679272

Verhoef, P. C., Broekhuizen, T., Bart, Y., Bhattacharya, A., Dong, J. Q., Fabian, N., & Haenlein, M. (2021). Digital transformation: A multidisciplinary reflection and research agenda. *Journal of Business Research*, *122*, 113342. https://doi.org/10.1016/j.jbusres.2019.09.022

Wang, X. (2024). How to build a trustworthy AI system. *Digital China Construction Summit Official Website*. Retrieved from http://szzg.gov.cn,

Wirtz, J., Patterson, P. G., Kunz, W. H., Gruber, T., Lu, V. N., Paluch, S., & Martins, A. (2018). Brave new world: Service robots in the frontline. *Journal of Service Management*, *29*(5), 907–931. https://doi.org/10.1108/JOSM-04-2018-0119

Xu, D. J., & Liao, S. S. (2013). Integrating perceived playfulness into expectation-confirmation model for web portal context. *Information & Management*, *50*(1), 31–43. https://doi.org/10.1016/j.im.2012.10.004

Youn, S., & Jin, S. V. (2021). 'In A.I. we trust?': The effects of parasocial interaction and technopian versus luddite ideological views on chatbot-based customer relationship management in the emerging 'feeling economy'. *Computers in Human Behavior*, *119*, 106721. https://doi.org/10.1016/j.chb.2021.106721

Yu, Y. (2017). Intelligent supply chain + intelligent logistics: JD.com enhances retail efficiency comprehensively. *WeChat*. Retrieved May 13, from https://mp.weixin.qq.com/s/VvQUNL4Z3afIvdsUHh_FZA

Zhang, F. (2023). How AI drives billions in traffic and saves millions annually: How brands like Zhongxuegao are doing it. Brand Dialogue. *Operation Society*. Retrieved April 28, 2023, from https://mp.weixin.qq.com/s/SgwBHmj0ZNtYtLD36e38uQ

Zhang, J., & Mao, E. (2022). How social norms and self-efficacy drive sustainable consumer behavior: A meta-analysis. *Journal of Business Research*, *145*, 1–12. https://doi.org/10.1016/j.jbusres.2022.02.067

Zhang, Y., Li, X., & Huang, M. H. (2023). Generative AI in personalized marketing: A human-centered approach. *Journal of Marketing*, *87*(2), 45–63.

Zhou, B. (2023). *Can AI accurately gauge the taste of young people's tongues? Chicecream gives it a try*. Hu Xiu. Retrieved May 12, 2024, from https://mp.weixin.qq.com/s/o3cg_KMFw7OK8kh4MsdY_A

Zhou, Y. Y., Zhu, H., & Xiao, C. Q. (2024). The tension of self-identity: Defining and reshaping the relationship between artificial intelligence and consumers. *Jiangsu Social Sciences*, *2024*(3), 187–194. https://doi.org/10.13858/j.cnki.cn32-1312/c.20240515.003

38

Branding and Ageing Consumers: Breaking the Stereotype

Carolyn Wilson-Nash

SEGMENTATION BY AGE AND GENERATIONAL COHORTS

Segmenting consumers by age is a long-standing tradition in marketing. It dates to the early 20th century when businesses began recognising that consumers' needs and values varied significantly across life stages. In the 1920s and 1930s, brands used age groups to target products like baby formula or retirement savings, reflecting the distinct needs of younger and older demographics. For example, in 1928, Gerber launched baby food and targeted parents of infants and young children. The brand's advertisements used the iconic 'Gerber Baby' to emphasise the nutritional value of the baby food and consequently appeal to families with young children. Ovaltine used a similar approach and promoted itself as a healthy drink to support children's growth and development. Similarly, Coca-Cola realised that it appealed to young adults and teens and started promoting the drink as a modern and youthful lifestyle choice. At the other end of the age spectrum, brands like Metropolitan Life Insurance targeted older consumers with retirement and end-of-life planning products. Their campaigns focused on the financial security of ageing individuals and their families.

In 1956, Wendell Smith formally introduced market segmentation in his pivotal article 'Product Differentiation and Market Segmentation as Alternative Marketing Strategies'. He argued that markets can be divided into distinct segments, with each segment sharing characteristics. This breakthrough enabled brands to target specific groups more effectively. Although this market segmentation approach did not explicitly focus on age, age naturally emerged as one of the most significant dimensions. This is because, at the time, age was seen to have a clear influence on consumer behaviour as products aligned with various life stages such as childhood, adolescence, adulthood and retirement (Smith, 1956). The segmentation model, therefore, encouraged organisations to identify age-related patterns in product usage and preferences and continue the work instigated in the 1920s and 1930s.

In the 1980s and 1990s, age segmentation evolved into generational marketing as organisations and researchers began recognising the value of tailoring strategies, not just to life stages but to generational cohorts. The concept gained traction after historian-sociologists Strauss and Howe (1991) developed their generational theory, where they defined generational cohorts such as baby boomers, Generation X, millennials (initially labeled the next generation), and later Generation Z, by linking birth years to formative events and societal changes (Strauss & Howe, 1991). It was not long before marketing professionals adopted these generational cohorts, applying them to market segmentation (Schewe & Meredith, 2004; Schewe & Noble, 2000).

For instance, baby boomers (born 1946–1964) were targeted with brands, products and services that aligned with their post-war optimism, economic prosperity and focus on family and homeownership. On the other hand, Generation X (1965–1980) emerged as a pragmatic, self-reliant group, often marketed to with technology, finance and convenience-driven brands. Millennials (1981–1996), shaped by the digital revolution, economic challenges and environmental concerns became a primary focus for brands emphasising technology, experiences and social responsibility. More recently, Generation Z (1997–2012) has captured marketers' attention with their digital fluency, inclusivity and demand for authenticity.

There are, however, criticisms over marketers' dependency on segmentation using age and generational cohorts (Noble & Schewe, 2003). First, the generational cohorts themselves were developed by historians and sociologists and, therefore, are not necessarily related to consumer behaviour. The generations share experiences of formative events and societal changes, which will have some effect on purchasing preferences. Still, this approach does not account for shared values and behaviours across groups or the variation within groups (Cheah & Phua, 2024). For example, only 45% of consumers can be correctly classified into their generational cohort (Noble & Schewe, 2003). Furthermore, the generational cohorts are developed from the history of the USA and, therefore, are more applicable to consumers in America than other countries worldwide. For instance, in South Africa, there are few significant differences between baby boomers and Generation X, cautioning against applying generational theory in marketing in this context (Knipe & Du Plessis, 2005). Moreover, in Malaysia there are five distinct cohorts that differ from US classifications, demonstrating the importance of context-specific cohort identification in emerging markets (Ting & De Run, 2015).

Further criticisms of generational cohorts stem from research into younger generations but are equally applicable to all. For example, a consumer possesses a biological age (e.g., real age) but in reality, they might also have a subjective age, which is how old they perceive themselves to be (Batat, 2021). In younger people, somebody who is aged 10 might perceive themselves to be older and associate with teenager-related consumption. Whereas, in older consumers, somebody might perceive themselves to be younger so that they engage in 'younger' pursuits (e.g., graffiti or break dancing). Equally, they might perceive themselves to be older due to ageism and internalised stereotypes (Dionigi, 2015). This perception can, therefore, blur the boundaries of age- or generation-based segmentation.

Moreover, the theory and practice of market segmentation are critiqued, especially age-based segmentation, by demonstrating that consumers in liminal states (e.g., moving from child to teenager) are between two conditions and do not belong to either constructed boundary (Cody, 2012). Thus, the realities of how age is viewed, experienced and performed do not relate to the parameters of age-segmented groups. This is equally true for anyone in a liminal time, space, position and body, irrespective of age (Darveau & Cheikh-Ammar, 2021). Liminality can occur at all stages of life, such as when people move into care homes, face retirement, go through menopause, change jobs, try to have children and graduate from university.

When it comes to older consumers, using age- and generation-based segmentation not only excludes certain people from marketing messages but can also generate harm for older people. For instance, younger consumers receive more attention in marketing practice and literature because they are perceived as open to new technologies, lifestyles and brand engagement strategies. They are believed to drive innovation, making them a focal point for businesses aiming to stay relevant and competitive (Anesbury et al., 2022). With scholarship and understanding, it becomes too easy for marketers to place older consumers into one generational cohort (e.g., baby boomers), which can lead to oversimplifications and stereotypes, such as assuming all older individuals are tech-averse or uninterested in new trends. This approach can risk overlooking the diversity of older consumers, perpetuate ageism in marketing messages and harm older people through internalised stereotyping.

STEREOTYPING OF OLDER CONSUMERS

Extant marketing literature traditionally categorises older consumers as a powerful purchasing group and an important market segment to target because they have more affluence and time than other consumers (Mertz & Stephens, 1986; Schewe, 1991; Tynan, 1990). Later research, however, reveals that 'baby boomers' are no more a distinctive or strategic generation than younger consumers, except for older women who shop more for clothes and cosmetics and regularly attend hairdressers (Twigg & Majima, 2014). Consequently, assumptions about ageing consumers have existed throughout the marketing literature for decades and have impacted academia, practice and older consumers' views of themselves (Nelson, 2005).

Interestingly, in the early 1990s, scholars called for the stereotyping of ageing consumers to cease (Leventhal, 1990; Wolfe, 1992); however, it still occurs today. Frequent assumptions are made about older consumers and technology, such as that they struggle to use it or are uninterested in learning (Franco, 2023). Further assumptions are made about older consumers and their innovativeness or so-called lack of it, with many believing they are resistant to change or innovation, preferring traditional products and routines (Bae et al., 2020). Another stereotype is that older consumers are universally frail, dependent on others and experience declining health (Dionigi, 2015). Consequently, policymakers and marketers often take a single-minded approach to issues of ageing consumer welfare and do not consider the needs of the whole group (Perry & Wolburg, 2011). This consistent stereotyping has pervasive implications for older consumers' well-being and the success of brands, products and services.

For example, in the technology market, there is an urgent need for research and practice to reassess stereotypes surrounding older consumers and technology. Older consumers are often viewed as being incompetent in technology use, unwilling to learn new technologies or socially isolated with poor health, which impacts the adoption process (Birkland, 2024; Franco, 2023). When in fact the baby boomer demographic exhibits low anxiety and high internet usage, contradicting these common assumptions (Niemelä-Nyrhinen, 2007). Unfortunately, many older consumers internalise these stereotypes and actually reduce their technology consumption because they are worried about appearing incompetent and consequently confirming the negative assumption (Birkland, 2024; Mariano et al., 2022). Marketing literature is also a culprit for perpetuating age-related stereotypes and requires further reflexivity to reimagine older consumers as both capable and discerning technology users (Franco, 2023).

Unfortunately, these assumptions move beyond the technology market and transcend into every market, as older consumers are stereotyped as resistant to innovation and change (Laukkanen et al., 2007; Leventhal, 1997). Contrary to traditional perceptions, older consumers may be more willing to try new products and pay premium prices for innovations (Leek et al., 2001). However, awareness of age-related stereotypes can decrease innovativeness among older consumers. This is because, similar to technology adoption, older consumers who feel as if they are being negatively perceived as 'older people' tend to reduce their innovativeness so that they do not appear incompetent to others (Bae et al., 2020). The result is that brands, products and services are not designed and marketed for older people because marketers believe that the younger generations are the early adopters, and older consumers are merely the laggards.

Furthermore, stereotypes about older people's health and social situations can have detrimental effects on their well-being and behaviour (Dionigi, 2015). Assumptions about older consumers being frail, dependent and unhealthy are an unjustified distortion of the true picture (Freer, 1988), yet they occur in many consumption settings such as service interactions between older consumers and frontline employees (Westberg et al., 2020). Older people are stereotyped as dependent, regardless of who is helping them (Adams-Price & Morse, 2009). As older consumers begin to internalise these stereotypes, it often creates further dependency as they reduce their risk-taking, subjective health and extraversion, increasing their loneliness and help-seeking behaviour (Coudin & Alexopoulos, 2010). Furthermore, if older people begin to think they are frail and unwell, it can affect their health and well-being and actually enhance frailty and ill-health (Dionigi, 2015; Warmoth et al., 2016).

The impact of these stereotypes on marketing communications is extensive, with both positive and negative portrayals of older people. For example, research in Brazil reveals that of 104 advertisements, 19 contain stereotypes, with 12 depicting positive traits like accumulated experience and 7 showing negative characteristics such as technology difficulties (Monteiro Machado & Pedro Sousa, 2019). In the advertising industry, even though ageing consumers respond to advertisements that include aspirational older celebrities rather than traditional negative stereotyping (Powell & Yoon, 2011), older people remain invisible, under-represented or caricatured (Carrigan & Szmigin, 2000; Rosenthal et al., 2021). For example, in the 2015 'You're Not You When You're Hungry' Snickers advert, Betty White (an American actress and comedian), who was 93 at the time, was involved in an American Football Game. She was depicted as fumbling, weak and without her head in the game. Once given a Snickers, she transforms into a young, athletic male player, suggesting that hunger can affect sporting performance, but also inadvertently implying that older people are physically incapable, frail and out of place in sporting environments.

This often feeds into stigmatisation, especially within the anti-ageing industry, where ageing is a negative state that should be avoided by using anti-ageing products and services (Levy, 2017). For instance, Olay's 'Erase 7 Years in 7 Days' campaign advertised a product that could erase the signs of ageing, explicitly targeting wrinkles, fine lines and other features typically associated with older skin. The imagery and language of the advertisement focused heavily on the idea that ageing is undesirable, it should be erased, and women should attempt to reverse its effects. Older consumers, therefore, tend to reject stereotypical portrayals in advertising, even when positive, preferring to distance themselves from social images of old age (Eisend, 2022; Rosenthal et al., 2021).

As older people internalise stereotypes that harm their confidence, well-being and health, research and understanding are needed to counteract these stereotypes so that fewer assumptions are integrated and communicated through marketing scholarship and practice. Furthermore, knowing more about the ageing market would help brands tailor their products and services to older consumers. The following section will discuss what we know about older consumers and where future research should focus.

WHAT WE KNOW ABOUT OLDER CONSUMERS

As ageing stereotypes are so embedded within marketing scholarship and practice, even within our own perceptions and biases, it is difficult to decipher what we know about older consumers. Instead of perceiving older consumers as frail, dependent, wise and loyal, who possess a high disposable income but cannot use technology and are uninterested in novelty and innovation, the key is to perceive them as heterogeneous. Similar to younger generations, all older people have cultural, generational and individual differences that shape their preferences and behaviours. Their characteristics are not necessarily tied to chronological age (Ahmad, 2002). This complexity calls for more nuanced approaches to market segmentation, targeting and positioning.

For example, it is easy for marketers to segment older consumers as homogeneous and target them as a powerful purchasing group because they have more time and money than other consumers (Mertz & Stephens, 1986; Schewe, 1991; Tynan, 1990). However, older consumers exhibit varied spending habits based on their economic situations. Some have significant discretionary income, particularly in developed countries, whereas others rely on fixed incomes from pensions or retirement savings. Making assumptions about older consumers' spending power could marginalise those in less affluent situations, making people feel inadequate, invisible and uncatered for, especially within essential services and products such as healthcare, energy providers and household appliances.

Relating to social life, older consumers are often perceived to be isolated, lonely and dependent on their friends and relatives (Adams-Price & Morse, 2009). While situations and health conditions can cause loneliness and isolation, other older people are increasingly active and engaged, defying traditional signs of ageing. For example, many engage in travel, education, wellness and hobbies, such as the 'Graffiti Grannies' of Lisbon, who learn about creating urban art in workshops organised by LATA 65. The aim is to break stereotypes about graffiti and ageing and demonstrate that urban art is not just for the younger generations (Lorenz, 2015). This is now becoming a trend across Europe, and Irmela Mensah-Schramm (born 1945) is a 'Graffiti Grandma' in Eisenach, Germany, who is covering up Neo-Nazi graffiti with signs of peace and love (Wighton, 2019). She says: 'People tell me I am intolerant, that I don't respect the far-right's freedom of speech. But I say: Freedom of speech has limits. It ends where hatred and contempt for humanity begins' (Payton, 2016). Marketers should therefore understand and cater to the diversity in older consumers' social interactions, hobbies and leisure pursuits (Wilson-Nash et al., 2023).

Equally, when understanding older people and technology, instead of perceiving all older consumers to be incapable and uninterested, marketers should realise that there is a mix of factors that affect technology adoption. Some older consumers are skilled technology-seekers who are capable, innovative and interested whilst others choose to be non-adopters for non-technophobic reasons (Franco, 2023). Whether a person adopts technology or not has less to do with age and more to do with factors such as value, usability, affordability, support, emotion, independence, experience and confidence (Lee & Coughlin, 2015). Technology itself does not help adoption as it is often designed by younger people for younger people (Rosales & Fernández-Ardèvol, 2020). It can consequently cause functional (e.g., efficiency/inefficiency), social (e.g., assimilation/isolation) and psychological (e.g., competence/incompetence) technology paradoxes, which create stress and anxiety for consumers (Wilson-Nash & Tinson, 2022). Consequently, technology developers need to better understand the requirements of older consumers to avoid technology paradoxes.

There is, therefore, a current gap in knowledge surrounding older people's consumer behaviour. This includes a lack of understanding of ageing consumers' need recognition, information search behaviours and online purchasing habits (Hettich et al., 2018). To address these gaps, future research should take a holistic approach by further considering older consumers in the context of time and life circumstances, factors influencing their brand preferences and purchase decisions (Ahmad, 2002; Moschis, 2012). As longevity increases, businesses and policymakers must understand and cater to the evolving needs of older consumers to effectively serve this dynamic population.

THE CONTRADICTIONS OF BRANDING AND AGE

When branding and age intersect in the literature, multiple contradictions emerge, possibly stemming from the deeply embedded biases and assumptions identified earlier in the chapter. Some studies outline that older consumers vary from younger generations, for instance, with differing cognition, affect and goals, which impact brand choices (Cole et al., 2008). A study on radio stations states that older consumers tend to prefer long-established brands and have smaller consideration sets (Lambert-Pandraud et al., 2017). Whereas alternative literature demonstrates similarities in brand choice between older and younger consumers (Yang et al., 2005). For example, a study in Japan discovered that in the fast-moving consumer goods (FMCG) industry, there are more similarities than differences between younger and older consumers' choice of brand (Singh et al., 2012). This indicates that understanding older consumers' brand choices must go beyond chronological age towards understanding variations in individuals, cultures and product/service categories.

In the brand equity literature, older consumers are homogenised and seen to have higher brand equity (brand loyalty, awareness, association and perceived quality) than younger consumers (Chen & Green, 2012). In the literature, they are perceived to prefer established brands and maintain longer brand relationships (Lambert-Pandraud & Laurent, 2010) due to their decreased tolerance for ambiguity and desire for low cognitive-affective complexity (Sikkel, 2013). Brand love emerges as a significant predictor of brand equity, with older consumers more likely to transform brand love into equity compared with younger consumers (Nawaz et al., 2020). For instance, in the banking sector, the constructs for older consumers' brand equity include a 'loyalty and brand friendliness' metric that has not been discovered in prior research (López-Rodríguez & Sandoval-Escobar, 2023). These findings suggest that older consumers are attractive targets for established brands, as they are likely to remain attached to a brand for longer periods, presenting opportunities for long-term customer relationships (Lambert-Pandraud & Laurent, 2010; Sikkel, 2013).

As a result, it is often thought that older consumers love their brands and have a stronger brand relationship because of it (Sikkel, 2013). Interestingly, however, this conventional wisdom that older adults prefer emotional appeals is challenged as recent findings indicate a clear preference for rational advertising (Sudbury-Riley & Edgar, 2016). For instance, for age-denial (e.g., sports gyms) and age-adaptive (e.g., hospital services) brands, the functional benefit is the most important factor, whereas emotional benefits are only important for age-denial brands (Huang, 2021). This research, therefore, implies that whether consumers possess brand love and consequently increased brand equity very much depends on the product or service category. As such we should make fewer assumptions that 'all older people love established brands' but instead investigate in which product or service category this phenomenon occurs.

Moreover, the intersection of age with brand loyalty is better understood when researchers move beyond chronological age. It appears that the brand loyalty and ageing literature is embedded with stereotypes that older consumers are 'stuck in their ways' and, therefore more likely to be brand loyal than other consumers (Thompson & Thompson, 2009). Whereas, in reality, behavioural research demonstrates that age-related brand loyalty is minimal and easily disguised by confounding factors (Mecredy et al., 2022). For instance, older consumers' brand loyalty is more likely to be influenced by affection towards the brand, the perceived ethicality of the brand, accumulated experience, development of purchase habits and declining category purchase rates than it is to be influenced by chronological age (Eryandra et al., 2018; Kaur et al., 2018; Mecredy et al., 2024).

These factors, especially the perceived ethicality of the brand, challenge current assumptions that older generations are indifferent to environmental and ethical concerns. It is often believed that younger generations, such as millennials, are more concerned with the environment, social responsibility and the ethicality of products, whilst older generations, such as baby boomers, are less concerned because they are associated with past environmental degradation. However, recent research contradicts this notion by indicating that older consumers from Indonesia are more likely to remain loyal to brands that prioritise ethical practices (Eryandra et al., 2018). In fact, ethicality influences their loyalty more strongly than brand affection, which is traditionally considered a key driver of brand loyalty among this group (Kaur et al., 2018). Brands should, therefore, avoid stereotyping older consumers as being ethically disengaged but instead demonstrate ethicality to this consumer group, especially if they wish to encourage brand loyalty.

The stereotype that older consumers are 'stuck in their ways' and lack innovativeness also transcends into the brand-switching literature. Similarly to the brand loyalty and brand equity literature, older consumers are perceived to be more likely to stay with their older brand than switch to a newer one due to lower innovativeness (Helm & Landschulze, 2013; Karani & Fraccastoro, 2010; Lambert-Pandraud & Laurent, 2010). However, recent behavioural research challenges this assumption. By analyzing 88,000 purchases of 60 FMCG brands within six product categories, older consumers are found to purchase newer brands just as much as the preferred older brands (Phua et al., 2020). In summation, consumers of all ages buy all types of brands, old or new. Brands are thus competing for all consumers, regardless of age.

It is thought that one of the reasons older consumers have a smaller consideration set and are consequently less likely to switch brands is because they are more socially isolated and, therefore, receive less social influence through word-of-mouth (WOM; East et al., 2014). This social isolation can influence older consumers' brand decisions (East et al., 2014). Yet, we need to acknowledge that this is not the case for all older consumers as levels of social isolation vary within the consumer group. Furthermore, even when older consumers are socially isolated, they can use online platforms to generate electronic word-of-mouth (eWOM), which enhances their social well-being and feelings of belonging (Wilson-Nash & Pavlopoulou, 2024).

The key to avoiding stereotypes biasing the branding research and literature is to acknowledge the complexity and diversity of situations. Older consumers in one country, buying within a specific product category and with certain individual characteristics, might prefer certain brands, possess brand love and be brand loyal. Whereas older consumers in a different situation, with a different culture and characteristics, and purchasing in a different product or service category might be more variety-seeking, search for functionality and be less loyal. For example, there seem to be fewer age-related differences in the FMCG industry compared with other higher-involvement industries, which would be an interesting avenue for future research to explore.

THE SKEW FOR MARKETERS TO DEVELOP NEW PRODUCTS FOR YOUNGER CONSUMERS

Growing, stable and declining brands appeal equally to consumers of all ages. However, there is still a skew for marketers to direct new brands and products to younger consumers (Anesbury et al., 2022; Silvers, 1997). This is because younger consumers spend more time on social media, which makes them easy and important targets for brand engagement strategies (Florenthal, 2019). Whereas older consumers are perceived to be less of an attractive market because they are less likely to respond to (e)WOM, other social media marketing strategies, and adopt new innovations. However, recent research has discovered that older consumers are mentally, socially and digitally active and, therefore, more open to trying new products than initially thought (Taylor et al., 2021). As a result, brands that skew to younger consumers are more likely to risk failure, so they should launch new products and market existing products to consumers of all ages (Anesbury et al., 2022).

This skew and resultant failure has been happening for decades. One example is Pepsi, which has long positioned itself as a brand for the younger generation. This is evident in their 1963 campaign, 'Pepsi Generation', which evolved to 'The Choice of a New Generation' in 1984. Moreover, they tend to use celebrity endorsements from pop icons such as Michael Jackson and Britney Spears, making them appear trendy and youthful. As a result, this approach has alienated older consumers and allowed competitors, such as Coca-Cola, to position themselves to a broader demographic. For instance, Coca-Cola's 1993 campaign 'Always Coca-Cola' highlighted universal and timeless themes, creating a broader emotional connection. Consequently, in 2004 Coca-Cola's market share in the USA was 17%, whilst Pepsi's dropped to 10%.

A more recent example is in the fashion industry. Abercrombie & Fitch built its brand identity around exclusivity and youth culture, targeting teenagers and college-aged consumers. The brand's advertising featured young and attractive models in minuscule materials whilst the stores had a nightclub atmosphere with low lighting, loud music and strong fragrances. The brand ignored older consumers and anyone outside its ideal youthful demographic. The former CEO, Mike Jeffries, stated that the brand only wanted "cool, good-looking people" to wear their clothes. This not only alienated larger body types, but also older shoppers, creating a backlash and boycott from older millennials and parents of teenagers. Older consumers and socially conscious younger consumers shopped elsewhere and chose competitors with more inclusive sizing, styles and lower prices (e.g., H&M, Zara and American Eagle). Abercrombie & Fitch's sales dropped, stores closed and the brand's reputation suffered, resulting in an eventual rebrand and adoption of more inclusive marketing.

There is also a skew towards brands designing products and services for younger consumers within the technology industry. Digital platforms, for instance, demonstrate homophilic patterns as young people often design them for young people (Rosales & Fernández-Ardèvol, 2020). One example of how this led to brand failure is Myspace. Myspace was one of the first major social networking platforms, dominating the market from 2003 to 2008. It positioned itself as a youthful space for self-expression, creativity and music discovery by allowing users to customise their profiles with themes and music, often creating a chaotic and unprofessional appearance. It also lacked moderation, leading to concerns about inappropriate content. This alienated older users looking for a more straightforward, safer and polished social networking experience. When Facebook entered the market in 2004 with a cleaner and more professional design, it not only attracted its target audience of university students but also successfully attracted older users and professionals. Its minimalistic design and user-friendly interface appealed to all age groups, creating a more inclusive platform. In 2008, Facebook overtook Myspace in user numbers as Myspace struggled to retain its relevance.

Considering that one of the most effective actions a brand could do is to create a relationship with ageing consumers (Leventhal, 1997; Sikkel, 2013), marketers need to interact more with this age group. This should involve avoiding campaigns that neglect and exclude older audiences as this can limit sales and reduce market share. It should also involve conducting research, including qualitative and quantitative data collection, to understand the needs, wants and desires of older consumers as well as using co-creation practices. As a result, brands should develop inclusive and versatile products and services that cater to multiple demographics. The concluding sections will demonstrate how brands can engage with ageing consumers and what tools they can use to understand this diverse demographic further.

RECONCEPTUALISING AGEING CONSUMERS' INTERACTIONS WITH BRANDS: RECOMMENDATIONS FOR FUTURE RESEARCH

This penultimate section provides a comprehensive summary of the chapter's key arguments, highlighting the insights gained regarding ageing consumers and their engagement with brands. Additionally, it outlines recommendations for future research, suggesting ways to reconceptualise ageing consumers' brand engagement beyond traditional assumptions. It encourages scholars to consider older consumers' heterogeneity and examine the evolving factors that influence their consumption and brand experiences. By doing so, future research can contribute to a more nuanced understanding of this consumer group and help brands develop more inclusive marketing strategies.

The chapter demonstrates how traditional segmentation by age and generational cohorts can oversimplify diverse behaviours, especially among older consumers. It can lead to age-based stereotypes and ageing, including perceptions that older people are resistant to technology or innovation (Franco, 2023). The effects of this may harm the self-perception, confidence and well-being of older consumers as they internalise the external stereotypes (Dionigi, 2015; Mariano et al., 2022). Therefore, future research should adopt nuanced approaches that recognise the heterogeneity of older consumers, challenge stereotypes and address gaps in understanding their behaviours and needs. This research should explore the potential of inclusive marketing strategies and make recommendations on how brands can cater to older consumers with varied individual characteristics, situations and cultures.

By reviewing the literature on how age intersects with branding, this chapter reveals complex contradictions as older consumers are often stereotyped as being brand loyal and resistant to change (Thompson & Thompson, 2009). Some research suggests that older consumers prefer established brands and possess a higher brand equity (Chen & Green, 2012; López-Rodríguez & Sandoval-Escobar, 2023) but other research indicates significant variability based on individual, cultural and product-specific factors (Phua et al., 2020). Contrary to assumptions, older consumers can exhibit brand-switching behaviours and may value functionality over emotional appeals in certain product/service categories (Huang, 2021; Phua et al., 2020; Sudbury-Riley & Edgar, 2016).

Despite this, there is still a bias in marketing towards positioning brands as being for younger consumers, leading to the alienation of older consumers and consequent drop in market share or even new product failure (Anesbury et al., 2022). Future research needs to explore these contradictions further by investigating older consumers' brand choice, equity, loyalty and switching in different contexts, for instance, across product/service categories, in varying countries and cultures, and most importantly, by focusing on older consumers with differing characteristics. This research needs to establish how marketers and brand managers can challenge stereotypes, conduct deeper market research and co-create versatile offerings that resonate across demographics.

Consequently, when researching older consumers and their brand experiences, a useful approach to take is intersectionality (see Figure 38.1). Intersectionality considers social categories such as age, disability, race, gender, wealth and sexuality to develop overlapping systems of discrimination or privilege (Crenshaw, 1994), which interrelate with theoretical constructs and marketing outcomes (Uduehi et al., 2024). For example, ageing consumers belonging to multiple marginalised groups (e.g., black, female and LGBTQ+) would face further complexity and different experiences to consumers not subject to marginalisation. Intersectionality can, therefore, provide insights into unequal ageing and health inequalities and where and how these occur (Holman & Walker, 2021). Rather than assuming that all older consumers are unwell and frail, this approach could identify situations where this is the case and situations where it is not, helping develop recommendations for brands to tailor products, services and messages effectively.

Intersectionality is particularly relevant for marketing scholars as it offers a theoretical lens to understand understudied consumers further and develop inclusive approaches (Uduehi et al., 2024).

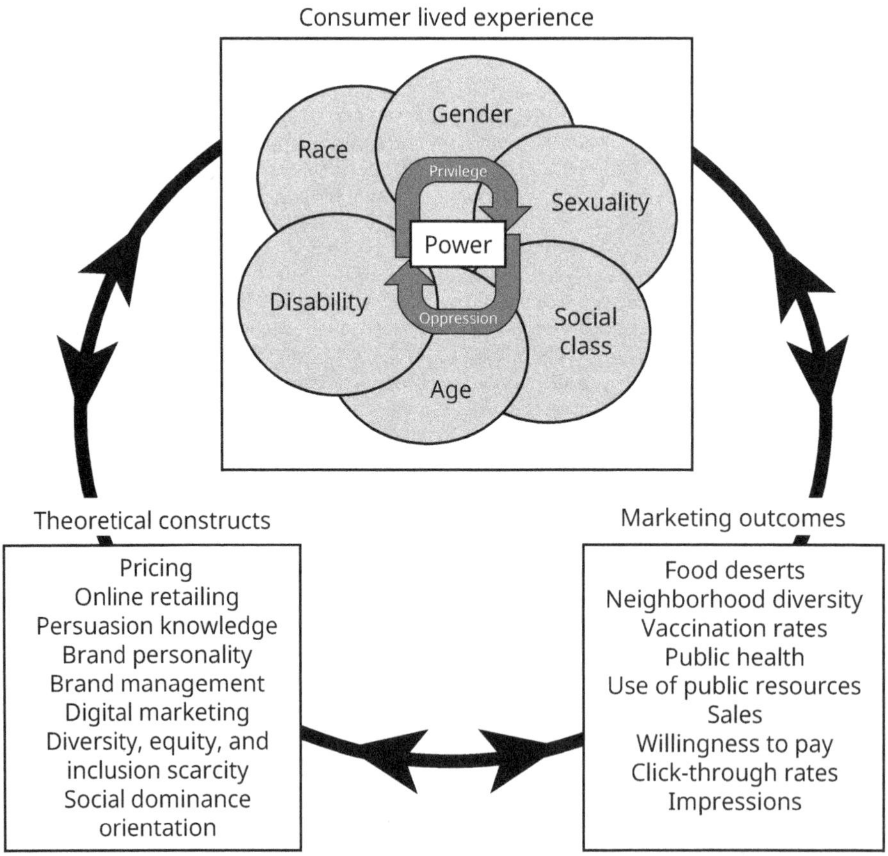

Figure 38.1 Intersectional marketing paradigm

Source: Uduehi et al. (2024).

For branding literature (e.g., brand management and brand personality), focusing on older consumers, understanding the intersectionality of these consumers and subsequent individual experiences is imperative to avoid homogenisation and further deepening of stereotypes (Huang, 2021; Melović et al., 2021). For example, a group of older female influencers use social media platforms like Instagram to challenge agist and sexist norms in the fashion and beauty markets (Veresiu & Parmentier, 2021). Researching the brand choices, brand equity and experiences of these influencers and their followers would provide nuanced insights beyond the stereotypical assumptions embedded within current marketing literature.

In summary, this chapter highlights several contradictions within the literature on ageing and branding, which are due to the ingrained ageing stereotypes that are embedded within marketing. To understand why these contradictions occur and how to fill the missing gaps in the literature, branding scholars should move away from making assumptions about ageing consumers and treating them as one homogeneous group. Intersectionality provides a theoretical lens to this by understanding that consumers' lived experiences can affect power dynamics, which influences current theoretical constructs and marketing outcomes (see Figure 38.1).

UNDERSTANDING HOW AGEING CONSUMERS ENGAGE WITH BRANDS: RECOMMENDATIONS FOR PRACTICE

The final section offers valuable insights for marketers and brand managers to recognise the diversity among older consumers and the importance of treating them as a heterogeneous group. It emphasises the need to develop inclusive products and services that cater to the varied preferences, lifestyles and needs of ageing consumers. Additionally, the section explores key approaches and practical frameworks, such as the customer journey model (e.g., Huang, 2021), which can help practitioners gain a deeper understanding of how older consumers engage with brands at different touchpoints. By applying these approaches, businesses can create more meaningful and accessible experiences that foster long-term customer relationships.

In general, marketers and brand managers should avoid skewing their products and services towards younger consumers as this can risk alienating older consumers and result in product/service failure (Anesbury et al., 2022). There are several marketing theories and frameworks that can help improve understanding of the heterogeneity of older consumers and tailoring products and services for them. The first, as mentioned in the previous section, is to understand older consumers and their interactions with brands through the lens of intersectionality, which encourages a more detailed exploration of marginalisation and how it can affect consumption within varying social categories (Crenshaw, 1994; Uduehi et al., 2024). The second is the customer journey, which is a useful framework and methodology to identify how individual older consumers engage with brands through various stages and touchpoints (Lemon & Verhoef, 2016).

The customer journey can further investigate older consumers' interactions with brands at an individual level. Customer journeys map the evolving processes through which customers' expectations, behaviours and goals shape their experiences with a brand (Sultan, 2018). These journeys are made up of various stages and touchpoints that influence customer decision-making and interactions with the brand (see Figure 38.2; Lemon & Verhoef, 2016). While there is debate over the precise number of stages in a customer journey, the most widely accepted framework divides it into three phases: pre-purchase, purchase and post-purchase (Lemon & Verhoef, 2016). Within these stages, touchpoints play an important role, which are interactions between the customer and the firm across various mediums, such as human, spatial, communicative and digital (Dhebar, 2013). Although the categorisation of touchpoints evolves, most studies group them into brand-, partner-, customer-owned and social/external categories (Lemon & Verhoef, 2016).

Marketers and brand managers could, therefore, use the customer journey model and associated methods (e.g., interviews, surveys, observations, blueprinting, photo diaries, etc.) to further understand the experiences of older consumers in certain contexts. Brand-owned touchpoints could explicitly be explored alongside other touchpoints to garner information on older consumers' interactions with the brand, shopping habits, social and cultural interactions, and online activity. What brand managers would aim to achieve is a seamless customer journey that fosters meaningful engagement and enhances brand loyalty by creating cohesive and consistent interactions across all touchpoints and messages (Cocco & Demoulin, 2022; Siebert et al., 2020).

A recent study provides an excellent example of how the customer journey and the brand resonance pyramid can be leveraged to explore ageing consumers' interactions with brands (Huang, 2021). Through in-depth qualitative research (e.g.

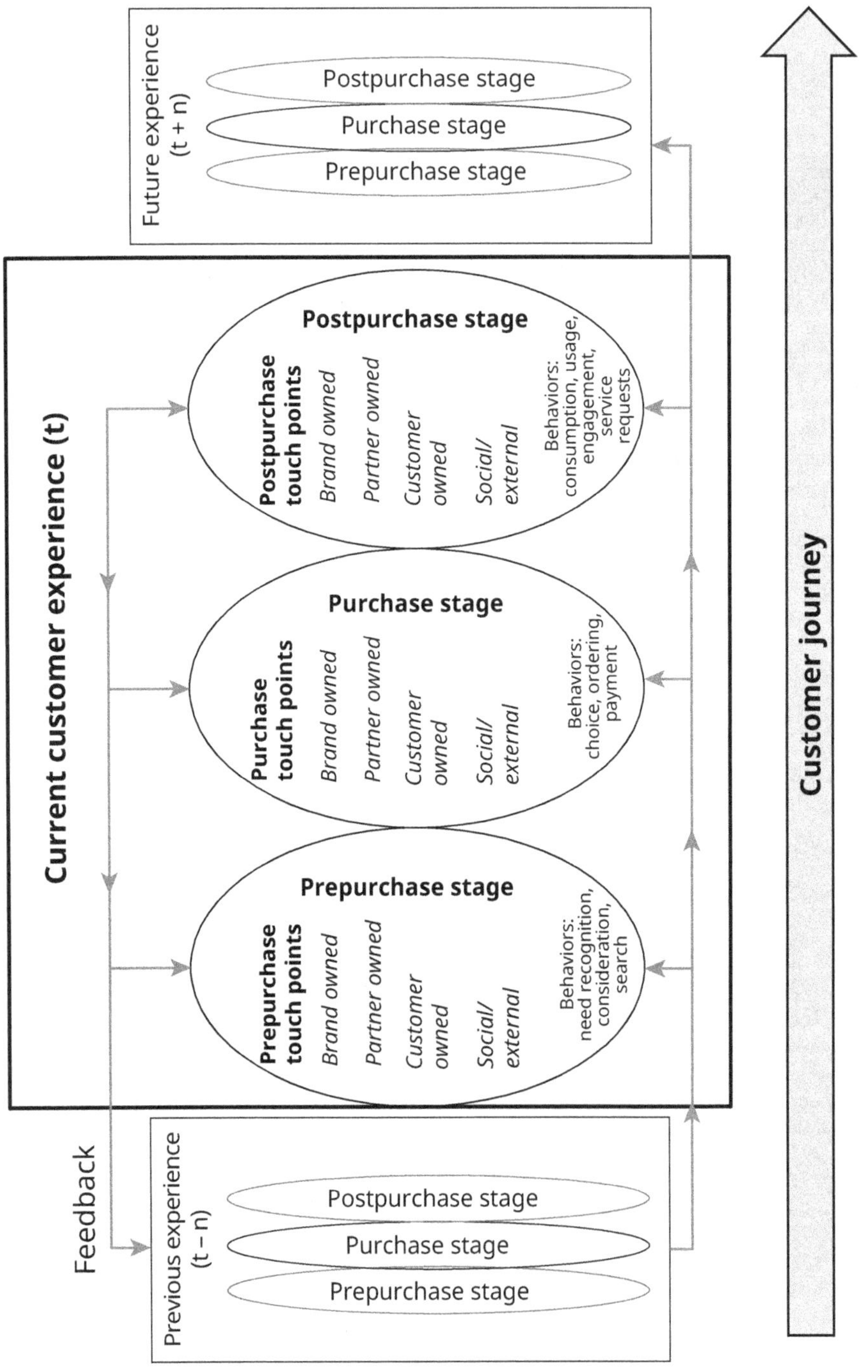

Figure 38.2 Process model for customer journey and experience

Source: Lemon and Verhoef (2016).

long interviews), the study reveals that older consumers interact differently with age-denial brands (e.g., fitness gyms) than they do with age-adaptive brands (e.g., healthcare). Functional benefits are essential for both types of brands, whilst enhancing social, behavioural and intellectual experiences is important for age-denial brands, and improving the emotional connection is imperative for age-adaptive brands. The findings suggest that age-denial brands should focus on functional attributes, social experiences and diversified offerings. In contrast, age-adaptive brands should enhance the skills of frontline employees, improve service provider–user relationships and ensure high service quality. These insights are extremely beneficial to brand managers and demonstrate the potential for the customer journey to be used in practical settings.

In conclusion, understanding how ageing consumers engage with brands requires a nuanced and inclusive approach that acknowledges their diverse needs, preferences and behaviours. By leveraging frameworks such as the customer journey, marketers and brand managers can gain deeper insights into how older consumers interact with products and services across different touchpoints. Ultimately, businesses that prioritise inclusivity and adaptability in their marketing strategies will be better positioned to serve the ageing population effectively, ensuring that their offerings remain relevant and appealing in an increasingly diverse consumer landscape.

REFERENCES

Adams-Price, C. E., & Morse, L. W. (2009). Dependency stereotypes and aging: The implications for getting and giving help in later life. *Journal of Applied Social Psychology*, *39*(12), 2967–2984. https://doi.org/10.1111/j.1559-1816.2009.00557.x

Ahmad, R. (2002). The older or ageing consumers in the UK: Are they really that different? *International Journal of Market Research*, *44*(3), 337–360.

Anesbury, Z. W., Bellman, S., Driesener, C., Page, B., & Sharp, B. (2022). Ageism kills brands. *Australasian Marketing Journal*, *30*(4), 364–370. https://doi.org/10.1177/18393349211017316

Bae, H., Jo, S. H., & Lee, E. (2020). Why do older consumers avoid innovative products and services? *Journal of Services Marketing*, *35*(1), 41–53. https://doi.org/10.1108/JSM-10-2019-0408

Batat, W. (2021). Chapter 1: Why youth culture beats age segmentation when it comes to marketing to young consumers. *Youth Marketing to Digital Natives*. Edward Elgar Publishing. www.elgaronline.com/monochap/9781839109294.00009.xml

Birkland, J. L. (2024). How older adult information and communication technology users are impacted by aging stereotypes: A multigenerational perspective. *New Media & Society*, *26*(7), 3967–3988. https://doi.org/10.1177/14614448221108959

Carrigan, M., & Szmigin, I. (2000). Advertising in an ageing society. *Ageing & Society*, *20*(2), 217–233. https://doi.org/10.1017/S0144686X99007709

Cheah, I., & Phua, P. (2024). Generational advertising: Literature review and practitioner insights on key pitfalls and implications. *International Journal of Advertising*, *44*(2), 286–312. https://doi.org/10.1080/02650487.2024.2429904

Chen, H.-C., & Green, R. D. (2012). Developing marketing strategies to increase brand equity: The differences between age groups. *International Business & Economics Research Journal (IBER)*, *11*(2), 241. https://doi.org/10.19030/iber.v11i2.6779

Cocco, H., & Demoulin, N. T. M. (2022). Designing a seamless shopping journey through omnichannel retailer integration. *Journal of Business Research*, *150*, 461–475. https://doi.org/10.1016/j.jbusres.2022.06.031

Cody, K. (2012). 'Between two worlds': Critically exploring marketing segmentation and liminal consumers. *Young Consumers*, *13*(3), 284–302. https://doi.org/10.1108/17473611211264068

Cole, C., Laurent, G., Drolet, A., Ebert, J., Gutchess, A., Lambert-Pandraud, R., Mullet, E., Norton, M. I., & Peters, E. (2008). Decision making and brand choice by older consumers. *Marketing Letters*, *19*(3), 355–365. https://doi.org/10.1007/s11002-008-9058-x

Coudin, G., & Alexopoulos, T. (2010). 'Help me! I'm old!' How negative aging stereotypes create dependency among older adults. *Aging & Mental Health*, *14*(5), 516–523. https://doi.org/10.1080/13607861003713182

Crenshaw, K. W. (1994). Mapping the margins: Intersectionality, identity politics, and violence against women of color. In M. A. Fineman, (Ed.), *The public nature of private violence* (pp. 93–118). Routledge.

Darveau, J., & Cheikh-Ammar, M. (2021). The interplay between liminality and consumption: A systematic literature review with a future research agenda. *International Journal of Consumer Studies*, *45*(4), 867–888. https://doi.org/10.1111/ijcs.12678

Dhebar, A. (2013). Toward a compelling customer touchpoint architecture. *Business Horizons*, *56*(2), 199–205. https://doi.org/10.1016/j.bushor.2012.11.004

Dionigi, R. A. (2015). Stereotypes of AGING: Their effects on the health of older adults. *Journal of Geriatrics*, *2015*(1), 954027. https://doi.org/10.1155/2015/954027

East, R., Uncles, M. D., & Lomax, W. (2014). Hear nothing, do nothing: The role of word of mouth in the decision-making of older consumers. *Journal of Marketing Management*, *30*(7–8), 786–801. https://doi.org/10.1080/0267257X.2013.841275

Eisend, M. (2022). Older PEOPLE IN ADVErtising. *Journal of Advertising*, *51*(3), 308–322. https://doi.org/10.1080/00913367.2022.2027300

Eryandra, A., Sjabadhyni, B., & Mustika, M. D. (2018). How older consumers' perceived ethicality influences brand loyalty. *Sage Open*, *8*(2), 2158244018778105. https://doi.org/10.1177/2158244018778105

Florenthal, B. (2019). Young consumers' motivational drivers of brand engagement behavior on social media sites: A synthesized U&G and TAM framework. *Journal of Research in Interactive Marketing*, *13*(3), 351–391. https://doi.org/10.1108/JRIM-05-2018-0064

Franco, P. (2023). Older consumers and technology: A critical systematic literature review. *AMS Review*, *13*(1), 92–121. https://doi.org/10.1007/s13162-023-00256-4

Freer, C. (1988). Old myths: Frequent misconceptions about the elderly. In N. Wells, & C. Freer (Eds.), *The ageing population: Burden or challenge?* (pp. 3–15). Macmillan Education UK. https://doi.org/10.1007/978-1-349-19093-5_1

Helm, R., & Landschulze, S. (2013). How does consumer age affect the desire for new products and brands? A multi-group causal analysis. *Review of Managerial Science*, *7*(1), 29–59. https://doi.org/10.1007/s11846-011-0072-7

Hettich, D., Hattula, S., & Bornemann, T. (2018). Consumer decision-making of older people: A 45-year review. *The Gerontologist*, *58*(6), e349–e368. https://doi.org/10.1093/geront/gnx007

Holman, D., & Walker, A. (2021). Understanding unequal ageing: Towards a synthesis of intersectionality and life course analyses. *European Journal of Ageing*, *18*(2), 239–255. https://doi.org/10.1007/s10433-020-00582-7

Huang, C.-C. (2021). Aging consumers and their brands: The customer journey perspective. *Asia Pacific Journal of Marketing and Logistics*, *34*(1), 31–59. https://doi.org/10.1108/APJML-10-2021-0733

Karani, K. G., & Fraccastoro, K. (2010). Resistance to brand switching: The elderly consumer. *Journal of Business & Economics Research*, *8*(12), 77–84.

Kaur, D., Mustika, M. D., & Sjabadhyni, B. (2018). Affect or cognition: Which is more influencing older adult consumers' loyalty? *Heliyon*, *4*(4), 1–15. https://doi.org/10.1016/j.heliyon.2018.e00610

Knipe, S., & Du Plessis, P. (2005). Generational cohort segmentation: Magic or myth? *International Retail and Marketing Review*, *1*(1), 28–43. https://doi.org/doi/abs/10.10520/EJC47022

Lambert-Pandraud, R., & Laurent, G. (2010). Why do older consumers buy older brands? The role of attachment and declining innovativeness. *Journal of Marketing*, *74*(5), 104–121. https://doi.org/10.1509/jmkg.74.5.104

Lambert-Pandraud, R., Laurent, G., Mullet, E., & Yoon, C. (2017). Impact of age on brand awareness sets: A turning point in consumers' early 60s. *Marketing Letters*, *28*(2), 205–218. https://doi.org/10.1007/s11002-016-9407-0

Laukkanen, T., Sinkkonen, S., Kivijärvi, M., & Laukkanen, P. (2007). Innovation resistance among mature consumers. *Journal of Consumer Marketing*, *24*(7), 419–427. https://doi.org/10.1108/07363760710834834

Lee, C., & Coughlin, J. F. (2015). PERSPECTIVE: Older adults' adoption of technology: An integrated approach to identifying determinants and barriers. *Journal of Product Innovation Management*, *32*(5), 747–759. https://doi.org/10.1111/jpim.12176

Leek, S., Szmigin, I., & Carrigan, M. (2001). Older consumers and food innovation. *Journal of International Food & Agribusiness Marketing*, *12*(1), 71–89. https://doi.org/10.1300/J047v12n01_04

Lemon, K. N., & Verhoef, P. C. (2016). Understanding customer experience throughout the customer journey. *Journal of Marketing* *80*(6), 69–96. https://doi.org/10.1509/jm.15.0420

Leventhal, R. C. (1990). The aging consumer: What's all the fuss about anyway? *Journal of Services Marketing*, *4*(3), 39–44. https://doi.org/10.1108/EUM0000000002517

Leventhal, R. C. (1997). Aging consumers and their effects on the marketplace. *Journal of Consumer Marketing*, *14*(4), 276–281. https://doi.org/10.1108/07363769710188527

Levy, B. R. (2017). Age-stereotype paradox: Opportunity for social change. *The Gerontologist*, *57*(suppl_2), S118–S126. https://doi.org/10.1093/geront/gnx059

Lorenz, T. (2015, September 13). Meet the 'graffiti grannies' of Lisbon. *The Guardian*. www.theguardian.com/artanddesign/shortcuts/2015/sep/13/the-graffiti-grannies-of-lisbon

López-Rodríguez, C. E., & Sandoval-Escobar, M. (2023). Dimensions of brand equity for the banking sector: A study in the elderly segment. *Journal of International Studies*, *16*(4), 205–219.

Mariano, J., Marques, S., Ramos, M. R., Gerardo, F., Cunha, C. L. d., Girenko, A., Alexandersson, J., Stree, B., Lamanna, M., Lorenzatto, M., Mikkelsen, L. P., Bundgård-Jørgensen, U., Rêgo, S., & de Vries, H. (2022). Too old for technology? Stereotype threat and technology use by older adults. *Behaviour & Information Technology*, *41*(7), 1503–1514. https://doi.org/10.1080/0144929X.2021.1882577

Mecredy, P., Wright, M., Feetham, P., & Stern, P. (2022). Re-examining age-related loyalty for low-involvement purchasing. *European Journal of Marketing*, *56*(7), 1773–1798. https://doi.org/10.1108/EJM-06-2021-0440

Mecredy, P., Wright, M., Feetham, P., & Stern, P. (2024). Remembering less, or needing less? Age-related differences in the purchase funnel. *Marketing Letters*, *35*(2), 171–186. https://doi.org/10.1007/s11002-023-09681-8

Melović, B., Ćirović, D., Vukčević, M., & Stojanović, A. J. (2021). Behavior of older consumers in the digital age and creating marketing strategies: Mature population as part of customer 4.0. In Y. Bayer (Ed.), *Handbook of research on economic and social impacts of population aging* (pp. 17–38). IGI Global Scientific Publishing. https://doi.org/10.4018/978-1-7998-7327-3.ch002

Mertz, B., & Stephens, N. (1986). Marketing to older American consumers. *The International Journal of Aging and Human Development*, *23*(1), 47–58. https://doi.org/10.2190/T972-YEXD-DRVF-APAV

Monteiro Machado, C., & Pedro Sousa, J. (2019). Stereotypes of old age: Views on the elderly in Brazilian advertising. *Medijske Studije*, *10*(20), 69–88. https://doi.org/10.20901/ms.10.20.4

Moschis, G. P. (2012). Consumer behavior in later life: Current knowledge, issues, and new directions for research. *Psychology & Marketing*, *29*(2), 57–75. https://doi.org/10.1002/mar.20504

Nawaz, S., Jiang, Y., Alam, F., & Nawaz, M. Z. (2020). Role of brand love and consumers' demographics in building consumer–brand relationship. *SAGE Open*, *10*(4), 2158244020983005. https://doi.org/10.1177/2158244020983005

Nelson, T. D. (2005). Ageism: Prejudice against our feared future self. *Journal of Social Issues*, *61*(2), 207–221. https://doi.org/10.1111/j.1540-4560.2005.00402.x

Niemelä-Nyrhinen, J. (2007). Baby boom consumers and technology: Shooting down stereotypes. *Journal of Consumer Marketing*, *24*(5), 305–312. https://doi.org/10.1108/07363760710773120

Noble, S. M., & Schewe, C. D. (2003). Cohort segmentation: An exploration of its validity. *Journal of Business Research*, *56*(12), 979–987. https://doi.org/10.1016/S0148-2963(02)00268-0

Payton, M. (2016, December 19). Grandmother covers up neo-Nazi hate messages with graffiti hearts. *The Independent*. www.independent.co.uk/news/world/europe/berlin-neo-nazi-graffiti-cover-up-70-grandmother-irmela-schramm-a7483136.html

Perry, V. G., & Wolburg, J. M. (2011). Aging gracefully: Emerging issues for public policy and consumer welfare. *Journal of Consumer Affairs*, *45*(3), 365–371. https://doi.org/10.1111/j.1745-6606.2011.01208.x

Phua, P., Kennedy, R., Trinh, G., Page, B., & Hartnett, N. (2020). Examining older consumers' loyalty towards older brands in grocery retailing. *Journal of Retailing and Consumer Services*, *52*, 101893. https://doi.org/10.1016/j.jretconser.2019.101893

Powell, H., & Yoon, H. (2011). Older consumers and celebrity advertising. *Ageing and Society*, *32*(8), Article 8. https://doi.org/10.2017/S0144686X1100095X

Rosales, A., & Fernández-Ardèvol, M. (2020). Ageism in the era of digital platforms. *Convergence*, *26*(5–6), 1074–1087. https://doi.org/10.1177/1354856520930905

Rosenthal, B., Cardoso, F., & Abdalla, C. (2021). (Mis) Representations of older consumers in advertising: Stigma and inadequacy in ageing societies. *Journal of Marketing Management*, *37*(5–6), 569–593. https://doi.org/10.1080/0267257X.2020.1850511

Schewe, C. D. (1991). Strategically positioning your way into the aging marketplace. *Business Horizons*, *34*(3), 59–67.

Schewe, C. D., & Meredith, G. (2004). Segmenting global markets by generational cohorts: Determining motivations by age. *Journal of Consumer Behaviour*, *4*(1), 51–63. https://doi.org/10.1002/cb.157

Schewe, C. D., & Noble, S. M. (2000). Market segmentation by cohorts: The value and validity of cohorts in America and abroad. *Journal of Marketing Management*, *16*(1–3), 129–142. https://doi.org/10.1362/026725700785100479

Siebert, A., Gopaldas, A., Lindridge, A., & Simões, C. (2020). Customer experience journeys: Loyalty loops versus involvement spirals. *Journal of Marketing*, *84*(4), 45–66. https://doi.org/10.1177/0022242920920262

Sikkel, D. (2013). Brand relations and life course: Why old consumers love their brands. *Journal of Marketing Analytics*, *1*(2), 71–80. https://doi.org/10.1057/jma.2013.5

Silvers, C. (1997). Smashing old stereotypes of 50-plus America. *Journal of Consumer Marketing*, *14*(4), 303–309. https://doi.org/10.1108/07363769710188554

Singh, J., Riley, F. D., Hand, C., & Maeda, M. (2012). Measuring brand choice in the older customer segment in Japan. *International Journal of Market Research*, *54*(3), 347–368. https://doi.org/10.2501/ijmr-54-3-347-368

Smith, W. R. (1956). Product differentiation and market segmentation as alternative marketing strategies. *Journal of Marketing*, *21*(1), 3–8. https://doi.org/10.1177/002224295602100102

Strauss, W., & Howe, N. (1991). Generations: The history of America's future, 1584 to 2069. *Harper Perennial*. https://cir.nii.ac.jp/crid/1130000797332460288

Sudbury-Riley, L., & Edgar, L. (2016). Why older adults show preference for rational over emotional advertising appeals: A U.K. brand study challenges the applicability of socioemotional selectivity theory to advertising. *Journal of Advertising Research*, *56*(4), 441–455. https://doi.org/10.2501/JAR-2016-048

Sultan, A. J. (2018). Orchestrating service brand touchpoints and the effects on relational outcomes. *Journal of Services Marketing*, *32*(6), 777–788. https://doi.org/10.1108/JSM-12-2016-0413

Taylor, L., Raisborough, J., Harrison, K., & Dulson, S. (2021). 'It's like going to the regular class but without being there': A qualitative analysis of older people's experiences of exercise in the home during covid-19 lockdown in England. *International Journal of the Sociology of Leisure*, *4*(3), 177–192. https://doi.org/10.1007/s41978-020-00078-9

Thompson, N. J., & Thompson, K. E. (2009). Can marketing practice keep up with Europe's ageing population? *European Journal of Marketing*, *43*(11/12), 1281–1288. https://doi.org/10.1108/03090560910989885

Ting, H., & De Run, E. C. (2015). A qualitative inquiry into the formation of generational cohorts: A case of an emerging market. *Journal of Economics and Business Research*, *21*(1), 126–143.

Twigg, J., & Majima, S. (2014). Consumption and the constitution of age: Expenditure patterns on clothing, hair and cosmetics among post-war 'baby boomers'. *Journal of Aging Studies*, *30*, 23–32. https://doi.org/10.1016/j.jaging.2014.03.003

Tynan, C. (1990). Marketing to the older consumer: A qualitative perspective. *Management Decision*, *28*(6), 34–41. https://doi.org/10.1108/00251749010000696

Uduehi, E., Clair, J. K. S., & Crabbe, R. (2024). Intersectionality in marketing: A paradigm for understanding understudied consumers. *Journal of Marketing*. 00222429241258493 https://doi.org/10.1177/00222429241258493

Veresiu, E., & Parmentier, M.-A. (2021). Advanced style influencers: Confronting gendered ageism in fashion and beauty markets. *Journal of the Association for Consumer Research*, *6*(2), 263–273. https://doi.org/10.1086/712609

Warmoth, K., Tarrant, M., Abraham, C., & Lang, I. A. (2016). Older adults' perceptions of ageing and their health and functioning: A systematic review of observational studies. *Psychology, Health & Medicine*, *21*(5), 531–550. https://doi.org/10.1080/13548506.2015.1096946

Westberg, K., Reid, M., & Kopanidis, F. (2020). Age identity, stereotypes and older consumers' service experiences. *Journal of Services Marketing*, *35*(1), 54–64. https://doi.org/10.1108/JSM-10-2019-0386

Wighton, D. (2019, October 13). 'Graffiti Grandma' fined €300 for painting over swastikas. *The Telegraph*. www.telegraph.co.uk/news/2019/10/13/graffiti-grandma-fined300-painting-swastikas/

Wilson-Nash, C., & Pavlopoulou, I. (2024). Nostalgia and negotiation: The electronic word-of-mouth and social well-being of older consumers. *Psychology & Marketing*, *41*(3), 532–546. https://doi.org/10.1002/mar.21933

Wilson-Nash, C., Pavlopoulou, I., & Wang, Z. (2023). Selecting, optimizing, and compensating during lockdown: How older consumers use social networking services to improve social well-being. *Journal of Interactive Marketing*, *58*(2–3), 301–320. https://doi.org/10.1177/10949968231155156

Wilson-Nash, C., & Tinson, J. (2022). 'I am the master of my fate': Digital technology paradoxes and the coping strategies of older consumers. *Journal of Marketing Management*, *38*(3–4), 248–278. https://doi.org/10.1080/0267257X.2021.1945662

Wolfe, D. B. (1992). The key to marketing to older consumers. *Journal of Business Strategy*, *13*(6), 14–18. https://doi.org/10.1108/eb039522

Yang, Z., Zhou, N., & Chen, J. (2005). Brand choice of older Chinese consumers. *Journal of International Consumer Marketing*, *17*(4), 65–81. https://doi.org/10.1300/J046v17n04_04

39

Becoming Conscientious: How Brands Can Shape a Better World

Nicholas Ind, Michela Mingione, and Oriol Iglesias

INTRODUCTION

Looking forward, in 2049, it is predicted that climate change will cost the global economy $38 trillion a year (in 2005 international dollars).[1] If the mid-21st century seems distant, damages due to climate change are already considerably larger than mitigation costs (Kotz et al., 2024). Also, climate change and the impact of population growth have led to a precipitous decline in global biodiversity – down by 73% according to the Living Planet Index (2024). Yet, it is also worth noting that over half the world's economic value creation – $44 trillion – is moderately or highly dependent on nature (World Economic Forum, 2020) and that there are significant business opportunities in such areas as solar energy, hydrogen, new materials and carbon capture (DNV ETO, 2024). Yet, we might ask what is the role of brands in mitigating impacts and seizing these opportunities? If we take the view that brands are purely commercial – there only to maximize market share and profitability – then their role is constrained. They are less likely to contribute significantly to environmental or social challenges and indeed are more likely to have a negative effect by either ignoring or working around externalities. By contrast, if we take the view that brands are part of the world we live in, by virtue of the people they employ, the partners and suppliers they use and the consumers they provide value to, then they ought to be attentive to generating well-being for all their stakeholders – including the planet. To limit risk and realize opportunities, brand owners will need to develop new collaborative business models, reduce external impacts and work to change the behavior of consumers and business partners. This means they will need a belief system rooted in a recognition of their broader responsibilities that guides their actions, consistently. This is the thinking behind the construct of conscientious brands.

In this chapter, we will outline the driving forces that have led some brands to discard corporate social responsibility (CSR) activities and embrace a more conscientious approach that recognizes their responsibility to current and future stakeholders. We will then show how the construct of conscientious brands has developed and the key attributes that have emerged through research before considering the barriers to adoption. Finally, we will look at the future of conscientious brands and how they can influence others to adopt a new way of doing business.

---

[1] Kotz et al. (2024) used this measure of value, which is a hypothetical unit of currency that has the same purchasing power parity as a US dollar at a specific date (in this case 2005).

BRANDS BECOMING CONSCIENTIOUS

There has been a long-held view that morality has no place in business (Ladd, 1970) and that the over-arching requirement for a company is simply to deliver value to shareholders. If this means ignoring morally demeaning practices, such as employing slave labor (still common in cocoa production) or despoiling the environment (still typical in fast fashion), this is acceptable, unless the law mandates otherwise or there are corporate reputation risks (Friedman, 1970). This idea of shareholder primacy has exerted a powerful influence over organizations and the brands they own, such that it has become an article of faith. However, as Stout (2013) points out, according to US law, company managers have a significant degree of latitude in determining how they run a business. In the UK, the law mandates the delivery of long-term shareholder value, alongside a need to be attentive to the needs of different stakeholders, while in Germany the stakeholder requirement is rooted in the responsibility of directors to the company as a legal person. Nonetheless, even if shareholder primacy is tempered by other requirements, it is still the case that investors can exert significant influence over the way a business is run. To meet societal expectations and still maintain shareholder primacy, businesses have adopted CSR policies, which allow good deeds to be done, without the commitment to address business model failings. As a result, CSR and its related models 'do not aim to alter the fundamental direction of the organization as a profit maximizer, but rather try to ameliorate some of the negative consequences of actions' (Ind & Iglesias, 2023, p. 216). Increasingly CSR has come to be seen as a palliative practice that lacks the substance to effect real change.

To address the perceived failings of CSR, the construct of conscientious business (and more recently, conscientious brands) has emerged, which argues for an approach that places responsibility at the core. This re-orientation has been driven by business opportunity and risk, societal pressure, legal requirements and moral belief (Figure 39.1).

First, business opportunity and risk: Consumers have become increasingly demanding of the brands they choose. While there is variability in consumers' engagement with sustainability, it is estimated that 77% of people in Europe and North America take sustainability into account in their buying decisions (von der Gathen et al., 2024). Even if, companies seem to underestimate the power of sustainability to motivate consumers, it is notable that, in the USA, sustainably marketed packaged goods grew seven times faster than conventional products between 2015 and 2020 (Kronthal-Sacco & Whelan, 2021). In spite of the lack of clarity as to what constitutes sustainable goods, the business opportunity is notable because sustainability has the potential to create a relevant point of difference for brands (Ford & Stohl, 2019; White et al., 2019) especially for those consumers who are open to change and willing to adopt trustworthy sustainable options (von der Gathen et al., 2024).

Alongside changing consumer expectations, business-to-business (B2B) relationships increasingly demand that partners and suppliers meet certain environmental and social standards if they want to be part of business ecosystems. This concerns both realizing business opportunities and managing risk. Unilever, for example, has clearly stated requirements of its suppliers that are defined in its codes of practice in such areas as business ethics, employment and human rights policies and sustainability (Iglesias et al., 2023; Ind & Iglesias,

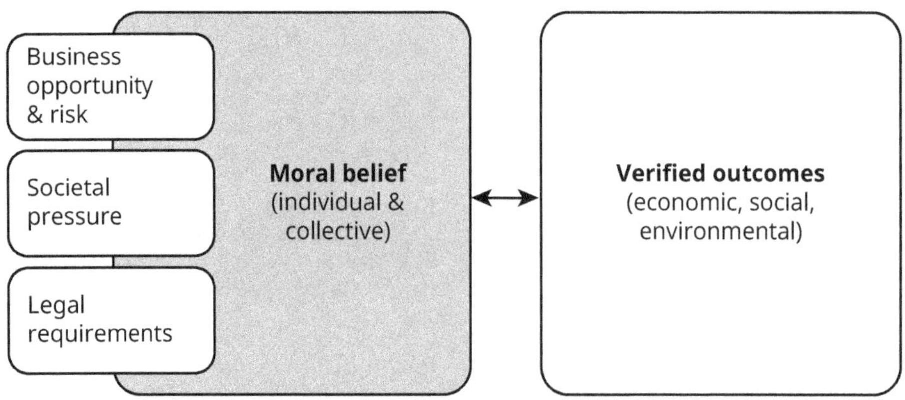

Figure 39.1 Internal and external drivers of conscientious brands

2022). Similarly, retailers such as Walmart and Tesco demand that suppliers work to reduce environmental impacts by shifting to renewable practices in agriculture and developing new packaging formats. Within supply chains, brands increasingly use verification processes, including such methods as blockchain, sensors and satellite monitors, to help ensure that ecosystems are accountable, which in turn reduces the reputational and business risks associated with practices that might run counter to a brand's belief system and public commitments (Duan et al., 2024; Ind & Iglesias, 2021). The concern as to risk and possible legal consequences encourages brands to help enhance the way partners work and to develop robust systems to monitor practices (Iglesias et al., 2023; Longoni & Luzzini, 2016). Failure to meet supply chain standards means that partner relationships can be terminated and brands delisted. On the positive side, partners and suppliers that have adopted and validated their practices are in an advantageous position when it comes to competing for and maintaining contracts.

Second, societal pressure: This emanates from citizens, the media and influential bodies. When businesses act unethically and ignore their responsibilities to stakeholders, people and communities become critical. In some cases, media attention follows – even in the form of investigative films, such as Dupont (use of a carcinogenic chemical), Purdue Pharma (promotion of Opioids) and Boeing (737 Max disasters).[2] Notably, each of these companies had extensive CSR programmes, which might suggest a broader responsibility, but this seemed to have no significant impact on corporate behavior in core business activities (Ind & Iglesias, 2022). Goodpaster argues that such problems are the result of teleopathy – the unbalanced pursuit of objectives that encourages myopia, in which 'the natural and social environments tend to be seen as resources or playing fields' (Goodpaster, 2007, p. 29).

Alongside, but linked to the growing influence of consumers, various influential bodies are pushing businesses to change. This has long been the case with NGOs, such as Greenpeace, WWF and the Ellen MacArthur Foundation, but it is notable that rather than sitting on the outside and criticizing, increasingly NGOs are willing to work together in partnership to help deliver change. This is further aided by such coalitions as the Science Based Targets initiative (SBTi), which is funded by various Foundations and Funds, to help companies set measurable targets in reducing impacts and by providing a credible framework and tools for companies to set and implement transition plans, and the Business Roundtable, which represents most of the largest 200 companies in the USA and now advocates for a stakeholder-based approach. Also, of particular note here is the UN, which adopted the issue of sustainable development in 1992. This was followed by the launch of the Global Compact in 2000 to promote the importance of environmental, social and governance factors in business performance. Most recently, in 2015, the UN launched the Sustainable Development Goals, which was based on the recognition that while business has contributed to many environmental and social ills, it also has the knowledge, inventiveness and influence, to effect positive change (Scheyvens et al., 2016). As a result, the monitoring of data related to the SDGs has improved considerably. However, the goals in such areas as education, environment, poverty and health have not been met. Only 17% of the SDG targets are on track and progress on over one third has stalled or regressed (United Nations, 2024).

Third, legal requirements: A legislative framework has emerged and is still emerging. Different countries and territories have developed regulatory environments that require companies to adhere to separate standards, but there is a growing coalition around the International Sustainability Standards Board's (ISSB) framework for sustainability reporting - even if there are concerns about legitimacy, investor prioritization and a lack of alignment with the SDGs (de Villiers et al., 2024). The ISSB framework requires companies to disclose financial risks and opportunities associated with sustainability. This means that investors, regulators and other stakeholders should have a common perspective on the environmental and social factors that influence value creation and capture.

Within the EU, the Corporate Sustainability Reporting Directive (CSRD) requires companies that meet a specified threshold, and that are based in the EU or do business there, to report on sustainability impact, risks and opportunities. This is a double materiality approach in that companies must disclose both how sustainability issues affect them and how they affect the environment and society in such areas as environmental protection, human rights, diversity and anti-corruption. The CSRD is part of the European Green Deal, which aims to reduce greenhouse gas emissions by at least 55% by 2030 from 1990 levels and make the EU climate neutral by 2050. In recognition of the impact of operations on business ecosystems, the Corporate Sustainability Due Diligence Directive (CSDDD) also puts the onus on companies to ensure that their partners and supply chains adhere to human rights and social and environmental requirements (European Union, 2024; European Commission,

[2] The documentary films are Dark Waters, The Crime of the Century and Downfall: the case against Boeing.

2024). Overall, the legal requirements should not only lead to the delivery of better data on sustainability to the benefit of stakeholders, but also greater insight for companies to develop business strategies and practices that enhance sustainability performance (Mezzanotte, 2023). The challenge is that double materiality requires considerable depth of analysis and increased stakeholder engagement. For example, there are over 1000 possible data points linked to the material impacts, risks and opportunities in CSRD reporting. Not surprisingly, regulatory complexity is a major concern for managers, alongside the belief that climate-friendly investments deliver lower returns – a perception that research suggests is misplaced (de Lange & Jackson-Moore, 2024).

Fourth, moral belief: The three drivers listed above provide business reasons as to why companies should be attentive to social and environmental issues. The drivers influence managerial decisions and actions in delivering effective outcomes. However, as we will see later, many businesses are adept at ignoring or circumventing some of these external factors in favor of business as usual, and by themselves, they do not drive the new business models that can transform industries (Damsté et al., 2024). By contrast, conscientious businesses and brands are internally motivated by individual and collective moral beliefs to effect positive change in the world. In this sense, they are driven by intentions that influence how they address the external drivers and deliver relevant verifiable outcomes. This experience of enacting conscientious choices then provides the opportunity for reflection on the outcomes and insight into the belief system and its meaning. As Vincent Stanley, Head of Patagonia Philosophy notes, 'when I look at real instances in which people have made changes it really comes down to moral commitment' (Ind & Iglesias, 2022, p. 29).

WHAT DOES A CONSCIENTIOUS BRAND THINK AND DO?

Individual conscience has a long history within the fields of philosophy and theology (Sorabji, 2014). One element of conscience that has endured is the idea of the split individual. This is the notion that conscience requires stepping outside of oneself and trying to observe objectively what is going on. Adam Smith in *The Theory of Moral Sentiments* (2009) likens this to having an independent observer sitting on one's shoulder, while Immanuel Kant in *The Metaphysics of Morals* (2017) writes about conscience as an inner court of judgment, in which a case is argued backward and forward: 'Consciousness of an *internal court in the human being* ('before which his thoughts accuse or excuse one another') is **conscience**' (Kant, 2017, p. 203). The philosopher, Thomas Nagel (1986) also adopts this idea of the split individual as a means to step outside ourselves and to compare alternatives, but he also observes that while it is valuable, in practice the ability to do so is problematic because we are still often wedded to existing views and find it difficult to shed our opinions. The second aspect of conscience is that while it is concerned with a belief system born of experience, it also concerns the actions that result from those beliefs and the impacts they have on others (Fuss, 1964; Korsgaard, 2009). Thus, it looks to the future as we imagine making choices and causes us to reflect back on decisions made which enables us to improve as active moral characters (Dierksmeier, 2013; Kant, 2017).

Even if we can define conscience from an individual viewpoint, the question emerges as to whether it *can be applied to the context of business and brands*. Goodpaster and Matthews (1982) made the argument that the traits of rationality and responsibility that we can find in individual agents can also be seen in businesses and that they have sufficient unity to act with moral agency. For this to happen, there needs to be sufficient clarity of purpose to meld together the diversity inherent in organizational life and to create cultures that support the adoption and use of specific moral beliefs (Bernacchio, 2019; Ind & Iglesias, 2022; Sulmasy, 2008). The idea that corporate brands and product brands could also demonstrate unity based on purpose, internally and externally, has spurred research into the attributes that define a conscientious brand (Fernandes et al., 2024; Hutchinson et al., 2013; Rindell et al., 2011). Conscience itself is ineffable and irreducible, but by synthesizing these studies, we put forward the argument that conscientious brands (and businesses) are stakeholder-oriented and typically possess a transformative purpose, a belief in fairness and openness, and a balanced temporal perspective (Iglesias et al., 2023; Iglesias & Ind, 2016). Further, together with their ecosystems, they are committed to enacting decisions in line with these attributes.

A **purpose** represents the *raison d'être* of a brand and is typically defined in a statement, which together with principles or values, articulates the essence of the brand and what it will and will not do. A purpose is derived from experience over time and consciousness of the world. Such statements can be goal-based and focused on a business opportunity or they can be duty-based and concerned with creating economic, social and/or environmental value for different stakeholders (George et al., 2023; Williams et al., 2022). However, what makes purpose explicitly conscientious is the way it draws on brand identity to develop a transformative ambition that changes business practices and delivers a positive impact on the world (Guzmán et al., 2024; Spry et al., 2021). For example, Spanish energy and infrastructure brand, Acciona, defines its purpose as 'Business as unusual: to make a positive contribution to society and the planet, providing sustainable solutions to the most urgent issues such as global warming and water scarcity' (Acciona, 2024). The statement articulates a clear and distinctive purpose, but it goes on to state a specific transformative ambition, 'we want to lead, accelerate and complete the transition towards a decarbonized economic model' (Acciona, 2024). Similarly, Dutch chocolate brand, Tony's Chocolonely is not only driven by making its own chocolate slave-free, but a transformative quest to make all chocolate production globally, slave-free (Horlings, 2016; Ind & Iglesias, 2022).

Fairness describes the requirement of brands to consider seriously different interests when making decisions. In the shareholder primacy model, there was no such explicit need as the priority was always the shareholder, but stakeholders possess needs that can be mutual, but can also be at odds (Aguilera, 2023). Porter and Kramer (2011) argue the case for shared value, which posits the idea that economic value is reconcilable with social and environmental benefits. Yet, as Berkey (2022) observes, this is a kind of wishful thinking. The implication is that for a brand to be conscientious, it must assess and try to balance competing claims in a reasonable way, especially on behalf of those stakeholders who are passive, or lack influence, while recognizing that there may be tensions and moral costs involved in reaching the best possible solution (Keränen et al., 2023).

Openness reflects the point that brands exist within the world and are built on ecosystems comprising diverse stakeholders. Brands can adopt a transactional perspective that objectifies others or they can build relationships that provide opportunities to co-create value. Conscientious brands do the latter by opening up the boundaries of the organization and encouraging participation. Typically, they share knowledge and promote transparency, so that ideas and influences flow outward and inward. This democratization enables brands to become better connected with stakeholders and innovative due to the opportunities of co-creating with them. The change from a closed to an open approach transforms stakeholders from passive beneficiaries of managerial decisions to active agents in defining meaning (Dierksmeier, 2013).

A balanced temporal perspective concerns the challenge for conscientious brands of delivering benefits in the present while being cognizant of the possible impacts on future generations. Often brands make long-term commitments to achieve certain environmental targets in twenty or thirty years, but without explicit measures to underpin them, these ambitions will remain fuzzy (Ind & Iglesias, 2021). There is also an implicit tension here because the shorter-term demands of quarterly reporting and the pressures from activist investors encourage a focus on the here and now. This can lead to longer-term aspects, particularly on the environment and biodiversity, being kicked down the road. Also, within this temporal framework is the increasing challenge of intergenerational justice that derives from the need to address the well-being of those who will occupy the world in the later 21st and 22nd centuries (Berkey, 2014; Kapitan et al., 2022). As Derek Parfit notes (1982, p. 114), after reminding of the special obligations we owe to our contemporaries, 'But our concern about future people should not be less simply when, and simply because, they will live later. If other things are equal, we ought to have as much concern about the predictable effects of our acts whether these will occur in 200 or 400 years'.

MAJOR ISSUES: VALIDITY, VALUE AND PRACTICE

Even though there is an emergent consensus as to the important attributes of conscience and its application to business and brands, there are question marks over its validity, its value and its practice. Since Goodpaster & Matthews's, 1982 article, there have been a significant number of articles that have developed the idea that 'conscience' can be used beyond individuals. Most of the early articles look at businesses, rather than brands, and they often draw on philosophical sources to make the case that an organization can have moral agency (Gray & Clarke, 2005; Primeaux, 1992; Rasberry, 2000). The supposition is that there is sufficient coherence in an organization for it to act in a unified way because individuals are defined by the structure, culture and processes they encounter in their working environments. In turn, they too project their beliefs and practices in their working lives. This argues that even if organizations are organic and always evolving, they also have identities that are distinctive and, to some degree, enduring (Iglesias et al., 2020a). The counterpoint of view is articulated by Köllen (2016) who, drawing on Schopenhauer's ethics, argues for an atomic point of view, as opposed to an organic one. The argument is that it is the individuals in organizations that have moral agency, not the organization, as such: '…from a Schopenhauerian standpoint, there is no evidence for attaching moral agency to organizations themselves, because they are not capable of developing incentives for their actions that are valid for moral considerations' (Köllen, 2016, p. 222). This Schopenhauerian view though can be contested if we resist the idea that organizations are simply objects. As Mota and Morrison argue, if we see organizations as having a corporate mind and as subjects that act, then they do have moral agency and can be held accountable for their actions (Morrison & Mota, 2023; Mota & Morrison, 2024). From this perspective, we can argue that the corporate mind possesses a conscience in the way that it creates a framework for thought and action. This does not mean that all actions are derived from a corporate conscience. Individual actors can, for good and bad, make choices that challenge the framework or its enactment. In these contexts, what matters from a conscientious perspective is how an organization responds.

As well as the steady stream of literature on conscientious business, since 2011, there have been a number of books, articles and book chapters on conscientious brands (see boxed section below). Most of the research has focused on corporate brands, although product brands are also cited as references, and there has been a bias toward business-to-business contexts. To date, the conscientious brand strand has been less philosophical and more concerned with understanding the specific attributes of conscience as seen from a managerial perspective. As described above, there is some consensus as to the core attributes, but as the area of study evolves and more empirical studies are conducted, new attributes and models may gain acceptance. As with the conscientious business literature, there is some skepticism toward the notion that conscientious brands can have moral agency, yet managers also note that the construct resonates if the brand is transparent about its motivations and actions (Ind & Iglesias, 2022).

THE EVOLUTION OF CONSCIENTIOUS BRAND RESEARCH

2011–2013 Initial articulation of the construct

Since the mid-2000s, a think tank called the Medinge Group has been developing the link between conscience and brands. Building on this work, in 2011, two members of the group edited a special issue of the *Journal of Brand Management* on Conscientious Brands. Ind and Ryder's (2011) editorial defined some key elements of the construct: the potential benefits of a stakeholder-based approach (relative to shareholder primacy); the need to go beyond CSR practices to embed conscience into the core; a longer-term perspective to balance short-term goals; and the advocacy of a human-centric approach. Interestingly the companies cited (Unilever, Patagonia, Danone, Grameen and HP) are still the reference points for conscientious brands.

As the construct was still quite ill defined, the contributors explored diverse themes. Wilson and Morgan (2011) focused on the way conscience nurtures brand communities and the way brand meaning develops. Olsen and Peretz's (2011), case study of a conscientious sport clothing brand, discussed the value of altruism in the delivery of positive social and environmental impacts while Rindell et al.'s model (2011) based on Nordic conscientious corporate brands (CCBs) showed managers' willingness to use aspects of CCBs in their business-to.business relationships. This model was then taken up by Hutchinson et al. (2013) in a quantitative study of 150 Canadian companies which endorsed the role of conscience in relationships. Interestingly, in this phase, the idea that conscience could be applied to brands was largely taken for granted and there was very little reflection on the construct as such.

2016–2022 Challenges to CSR and the emergence of conscientious brand attributes

From 2016 onwards, researchers began to be more critical of CSR. Questioning voices had already challenged its underlying basis because of its adherence to shareholder primacy (Freeman & Liedtka, 1991), but writers now noted its inauthenticity (Alhouti et al., 2016; Song & Dong, 2022) and its tangentiality (Last, 2021; Markovic et al., 2018). The failings of CSR led to the view that conscience could be a more effective construct. In 2020, Iglesias and Ind's conceptual paper again challenged the relevance of CSR and argued in favor of conscience as the means to steer a brand's commitments to responsible and sustainable actions. This approach was then developed by Vallaster and Lechner (2022), who argued for the importance of incorporating a multiple-stakeholder approach and the use of co-creation. In the 2022 book *In Good Conscience*, Ind and Iglesias reflected on some of the philosophical underpinnings of the idea of conscience as applied to business and brands and identified some specific attributes that had been latent: the centrality of purpose, a balanced stakeholder approach, a balanced temporal perspective and the importance of openness. In a book chapter in 2022, Biedenbach and Biedenbach adopted an inside-out perspective and argued that conscientious brands co-create value by engaging and empowering employees.

2023–2024 Empirical validation of the construct with a specific focus on B2B corporate brands

In 2023, Markovic, Iglesias and Ind edited a special issue of *Industrial Marketing Management* on Conscientious Corporate Brands. Not surprisingly with an explicit business-to-business focus, there was an emphasis on relationships. Beitelspacher and Getchell and Iglesias et al. noted the key role played by business partners and the importance of strategically aligning and encouraging partners to embrace balanced multistakeholder and temporal perspectives. Keränen et al. and Vallaster et al., both highlighted the key role of identity in fostering a conscientious approach. In Vallaster et al.'s quantitative study on 413 European organizations, the researchers found that conscientious organizations search for mutual relationships with different, but complementary, corporate brand identities in order to strengthen their meaningful impact on society. Finally, Kapitan et al. used in-depth interviews with B2B marketers to investigate conscientious purpose for social impact.

In addition to the special issue, Abratt and Kleyn (2023) produced a literature review and developed a framework to operationalize conscientious brands, while Guzmán et al. (2024) researched business-to-business brands and noted the importance of aligning brand values and ensuring that actions were consonant with a brand promise. Fernandes et al. (2024) conducted a study of young adults and their perceptions of brands which provided insights into the way conscientious purpose-driven branding can be effective.

The second issue that confronts the construct of conscientious brands is the question mark over its value. There is a strong orientation in business thinking that encourages a focus on measurable outcomes. In a shareholder primacy perspective, the focus is on delivering the best outcome for shareholders and the only point of debate is whether the outcome should be toward the short- or long-term. In the short-term, negative externalities such as pollution and over-production/consumption can be ignored in pursuit of gains, but if all the participants in an industry pursue such policies, the long-term benefits can diminish for all. Take aquaculture, which is the fastest-growing food supply sector – from 1990 to 2020, annual output expanded by 600%. While aquaculture generates healthy profits, the externalities have been significant. In Norway (the biggest producer), 62.5 million salmon and 2.5 million trout died in the sea phase of production in 2023 – a mortality rate of around 17% (Veterinærinstituttet, 2024). The fish are beset by parasites and aquaculture generates pollutants in coastal waters. The high level of escaped salmon also impacts the wild Atlantic salmon, such that the number returning to the coast of Norway is less than half of that recorded in the 1980s. Apart from fish welfare and damage to the environment, commentators and politicians have become critical and there has been a loss of consumer trust (Browning, 2023), which raises question marks over the industry's longer-term social license to operate (Mather & Fanning, 2019).

In a stakeholder perspective, the bigger challenge is not only the issue of temporality but the assessment of the needs of stakeholders. As Aguilera notes, this concerns 'how the value created by the corporation is going to be appropriated and subsequently shared among its different stakeholders' (Aguilera, 2023, p. 2). Making such judgments requires understanding the motivations of stakeholders and their interdependencies in the context of value creation and value capture. Businesses have to weigh up the claims from different stakeholders and match them against their purpose and operating principles (Freeman & Elms, 2023). For example, a clothing brand might want to reduce prices to compete more effectively and make its product more accessible. This has an obvious benefit for consumers, but if the brand is to maintain profitability and deliver results to its owners, it will have to sell more and/or find ways to cut costs. Cutting costs could be realized by more efficient processes, but it can also lead to reducing payments to ecosystem partners (and impacting their profitability and wages paid to employees) or a reduction in quality, leading to foreshortening of product life. As a side effect of selling more, there is also an environmental impact in terms of the raw material used in production, consumer usage and end-of-life processes (King & Pucker, 2021). For a conscientious business that is committed to environmental stewardship and paying fair wages in its supply chain, this scenario is unacceptable and means thinking anew about the inter-dependencies between its stakeholders and innovating a new way of making its brand more affordable - such as that adopted by Patagonia and the development of its Worn Wear business.

The third problem with conscience relates to its practice. Businesses easily embrace the rhetoric of stakeholderism but often fail to match words with actions. Of course, we should not expect perfection from businesses. There will be failings in supply chains, compromises will be made and future commitments will be deferred. Yet, if the intention of the brand is genuine, these failings should be rarities and dealt with in an open and honest way. There are many instances when this is not the case, which suggests the intention is often weak. For example, take the Business Roundtable manifesto (2019), which having praised the virtues of the US free-market system in Friedman-like language then states, ‘while each of our individual companies serves its own corporate purpose, we share a fundamental commitment to all our stakeholders’. It then goes on to list those stakeholders: customers, employees, suppliers, communities and (finally) shareholders. It is notable then that in a study of the 181 companies who signed, they subsequently incurred higher rates of environmental and labor-related compliance violations than within-industry peer firms (Raghunandan & Rajgopal, 2024). Similarly, in spite of the interest in corporate and brand purpose, researchers note that purpose is all too easily sacrificed to the needs of shareholders (Davis, 2021; Fisch & Solomon, 2020; Kaplan, 2023) and that businesses try to shape the legal framework to their advantage through lobbying and the promotion of environmental skepticism (Klimecki & Parker, 2024; Lyon et al., 2018).

Given the legal framework and the drive of self-interest, the emphasis on shareholders is not surprising, but if the purpose of a brand aims to effect an environmental or social transformation, then there must be a willingness to consider other stakeholders and to sometimes accept the economic costs (especially in the short-term) in pursuit of moral gains (Henderson & Steen, 2015). To achieve this, businesses have looked beyond the constraints of the traditional shareholder model to different structures. Thus, we see such conscientious brands as Tony’s Chocolonely, Patagonia, Ecoalf and Auping (Ind & Iglesias, 2022) having B Corps certification (of which there are 8254, as of February 2024), which requires a purpose-driven stakeholder culture that is evaluated in terms of its contribution to community, customers, environment, workers and governance. Similarly in France, the 2019 law, which established the new corporate form of *société* à *mission*, was designed, as described in the letter of intent, (as translated by Segrestin, Hatchuel and Levillain), to give ‘an enterprise a purpose that is not exclusively guided by short-term considerations, thus promoting a vision of capitalism that is more respectful of the general interest and that of future generations’. The law allows a business to pursue goals other than profit maximization and to incorporate social and environmental opportunities (Segrestin et al., 2021).

NEW DIRECTIONS

The previous section might raise doubts in the mind of the reader as to the viability of the construct of conscientious brands. Is a conscientious brand even possible in a capitalistic world? Or is conscience the preserve of a few idealist brands that are B Corps or *sociétés* à *mission*? It would certainly seem that removing the pressure of delivering short-term returns to shareholders enables a longer-term, more stakeholder-oriented perspective. However, to see the construct as an end state would be a mistake. Becoming conscientious is a process driven by the intentionality that is captured in a purpose. It concerns thinking and acting in such a way that a brand evolves toward ever more conscientious practices that benefit it as an entity while meeting the needs and desires of diverse stakeholders (Dierksmeier, 2013; Ind & Iglesias, 2022). Publicly traded companies such as UK retailer Tesco, Spanish bank BBVA, HP and Unilever (Iglesias et al., 2023; Ind & Iglesias, 2022) all demonstrate some of the attributes of conscientious brands. Even if the progress toward being consistently conscientious is uneven, there is a clear intent from leaders to develop the competencies and practices necessary to deliver positive social and environmental impacts.

Even if we reject the idea of shared value as a norm, there are instances where conscientious brands find a confluence between business performance and social and environmental factors. By using their belief system, they are able to develop new business models, tackle dilemmas with probity and foster conscientious innovation. For example, the Maldivian luxury hospitality brand, Soneva constantly seeks new ways of working. This is in part driven by the recognition that in the low-lying Maldives, rising sea levels present an existential challenge, but also by the knowledge that the seemingly unspoilt beauty of the islands would disappear with an extractive mindset. To counter this, the brand has done perhaps obvious things, like creating solar energy systems, but also the less obvious, such as a Waste to Wealth initiative which aims to reuse waste such as packaging materials in building construction, making charcoal and composting some 20,000 kilograms of organic material each month that is then used to grow vegetables and herbs for the restaurants. Additionally, to avoid the practice of dumping ground-up glass bottles in the sea, which incurs costs, Soneva started a glass-blowing studio using recycled glass, where visitors can take courses on glass blowing and where glass artists come and create glass art that is then sold. This turns a cost into a revenue stream. Bruce Bromley, CFO and Head of Sustainability says,

'This idea that your waste streams are an asset not a liability, that's a mindset shift that everyone can make ... in almost every single example I could give, the sustainable way of doing business creates more value for the business top line, bottom line than anything else' (Ind & Iglesias, 2022, p. 31). Notably, Soneva has a Guardian of the Conscience and every resort has a Conscience Manager, who is responsible for social and environmental initiatives. These positions reflect the perspective that embedding conscience into the practices of the organization is a continuous process of identifying challenges and dilemmas, seeking equitable solutions, measuring the benefits and impacts and then learning from the outcomes. Making sound judgments on issues requires clarity about the belief system itself. Its articulation must be sufficiently specific to determine the right actions and practices (Korsgaard, 2019). Yet, at the same time that it provides clarity and continuity, the underlying ideas should be challenged (Nagel, 1986). A key element of conscience is a willingness to think critically and to question assumptions about the existing ways of doing things, with the end aim of ensuring alignment between the belief system and the resulting actions (Ind & Iglesias, 2022). This reinforces the view that brands have to consider both intentions and outcomes. Drawing on Kantian ethics, Dierksmeier (2013, p. 605) notes, 'The deontological criterion is only the necessary condition for sound moral action, whereas the teleological dimension functions as its satisfying condition'.

A further point about intentions and outcomes is that these cannot simply be understood from within the boundary of the company. When Unilever set out its purpose in 2009 'To make sustainable living commonplace', it had the ambition to double the size of the business and halve its environmental impacts over a 10-year period. However, at the mid-way point of the plan, environmental impacts were going up, not down (Bartlett, 2015). The issue was not one of a failure to improve internal processes but an under-estimation as to the scale of impacts from suppliers and partners within Unilever's ecosystem (59,000 suppliers and 1.5 million farmers) and the impacts from consumer usage (its brands are used 2 billion times a day), which accounted for 70% of emissions. The implications for a conscientious brand are twofold. First, it has to use its belief system to set standards, influence its supply chain and verify its actions – ideally using independent verifiers. In practice, this means ensuring that contractual arrangements are rooted in the purpose and principles and in supporting partners to change processes, so that they better align with the brand's ambitions, while also being open to the opportunities of co-creating initiatives that derive from within the ecosystem (Ind & Iglesias, 2021). Second, it means recognizing that a brand's responsibility extends beyond the point of sale into ongoing usage and disposal. Brands can do this by using in-depth research methods to uncover consumer motivations and the specific role that sustainability plays and then use communications to nudge consumers into new, less impactful behaviors (White et al., 2019). The ability to realize change requires then a willingness to be open; to learn, to share and to co-create.

To illustrate this approach, take the Swedish fashion brand, Asket – note the name is the Swedish word for ascetic. It has an over-arching approach called, The Pursuit of Less, which has three underlying ideas: buy less, buy better; know your garment; and wear each item longer. The range of clothes is designed to be a permanent collection of classics (e.g., jeans, t-shirts and sweaters) rather than items that change with fashion seasons. The cut of the clothes is based on consumer insights and items are tested before production. To ensure that the clothes are then made to high standards and in line with the brand's beliefs, the brand works with RiSE (Research Institute of Sweden) as a verifier. The materials and where they come from are then detailed precisely on the product labels – online you can also see the costs of each stage, including the margin that Asket is making. When someone buys a product, they get an impact receipt, which details the CO_2 equivalents of each stage in the process of making and shipping. The receipt also details the number of wears one should get from the product. To help ensure the longevity of the garment, Asket provides the buyer with advice on washing products (and the impacts of high-temperature washing relative to washing at 30 degrees) and how to repair tears and tackle stains. Finally, the brand offers the customer the opportunity to bring their product back when they have finished with it, for resale or recycling. The attentiveness to quality and the commitment to full transparency are central to the brand in that they create a point of difference, but they also engender trust by enabling consumers to see behind the façade of the brand and to share in the narrative of the clothes they buy and use. Asket argues that storytelling makes consumers feel closer to the brand and more appreciative of the clothes, which in turn helps them to live with less (Ind & Iglesias, 2022).

Consumers and business-to-business customers are not necessarily driven by environmental or societal factors when making decisions. Issues concerned with quality, reliability or design may be to the fore, but, for example, when a brand makes a commitment to tackling biodiversity loss or promoting social equality it creates a point of distinction. As long as the brand then enacts its commitment and communicates it effectively, it has the potential to enhance its reputation internally and externally. This indicates the importance of a participative approach inside the organization, which empowers individuals and encourages the active use of conscience in making decisions (Biedenbach & Biedenbach, 2022). Embedding conscience provides the structures and processes that help leaders and employees to consider the specifics of a context and work through critically the potential negatives and positives in making a choice (Arendt, 2003).

CONCLUSION

The construct of conscientious brands has emerged as a way to describe those brands that have embraced the opportunity to engage with urgent environmental and societal challenges. This goes beyond the practice of corporate social responsibility, which has come to be seen as inadequate and tangential. As outlined in this chapter, the distinctive point about conscience is that it is rooted in brand identity and provides a way of thinking and acting that underpins sustainability strategies. The extant research indicates that conscientious brands have certain attributes, namely, a transformative purpose, a balanced stakeholder and balanced temporal perspective and commitment to openness, which they embed into their operations. Olsen and Peretz, 2011, also make the claim that conscientious brands are altruistic. However, we argue that while the construct is concerned with compassion for others, overall, it aims to marry the need to generate economic and social value (Carney, 2021). In other words, when brands work to solve societal and environmental problems, they can also realize economic benefits (de Lange & Jackson-Moore, 2024). Yet, there will also be tensions and dilemmas as stakeholder needs and temporal horizons clash. When this happens, a conscientious brand does not simply do the expedient thing, but instead thinks critically about how best to meet these challenges in a fair, open and responsible way. This does not mean that conscientious brands always make the most ethical choices. As noted, there are pressures from investors, business partners and other stakeholders, alongside legal requirements that sometimes result in compromise and inconsistency. Even, seemingly, exemplary brands also have blind spots on issues. We should perhaps instead think of conscience as a process that, internally, drives self-awareness and integrity and, externally, the well-being of stakeholders. This raises an important final point. If conscientious brands are to make a truly positive impact, they need to influence the way business works and overcome the question marks as to their validity, value and practice. In other words, they need to become role models by demonstrating that becoming conscientious leads to better outcomes for all stakeholders. Brands, such as Patagonia, Asket, Soneva, HP, Acciona and BBVA already use their soft power to influence others and to form coalitions of change. As Gabriela Ramos, who sits on the Mission Committee of Danone (a Société à Mission business) notes:

> The world is stuck on the old way of doing things, despite knowing that it is not sustainable. Danone pursuing the 'Société à Mission' model is sending the right message that change is possible. We, as mission committee members, have a great responsibility to accompany Danone in delivering this, and therefore we need to be demanding. It is not about us, it is about charting the path towards a more inclusive and sustainable growth model. If we achieve our objectives, others will move too, and many are watching. There is no room to fail. (Danone Mission Committee Report, 2021)

Looking ahead, the conscientious brand construct needs further work. In spite of the research that has already been conducted, there are still many unanswered questions and areas for exploration.

First, as noted at the beginning of this chapter, as well as external drivers of change, conscientious brands are driven by internal moral belief. However, we know relatively little about how moral belief inter-relates with the other drivers. To gain a clearer understanding, more in-depth studies are needed to explore how conscientious brands make and enact decisions.

Second, since decision-making in a stakeholder-driven environment often involves navigating complex dilemmas, it is also essential to conduct case studies that investigate how conscientious brands tackle such dilemmas and innovate new business models. In particular, it would be valuable to understand how brands draw on their identities as they practice critical thinking and overcome barriers to change in enacting new ways of working.

Third, intentions play a crucial role for conscientious brands, as they provide a framework for making judgments and enabling reflection. Hence, it would be valuable to investigate how managers of conscientious brands weigh intentions and outcomes.

Fourth, the attributes of conscientious brands that have been established by research need further development. For example, what are the processes employed to define and then embed a transformational purpose; how do brands balance short-term objectives and longer-term ambitions; and how do brands work with their ecosystems to deliver change?

Fifth, some managers believe that conscience has the potential to create benefits in terms of brand differentiation and reputation. However, this belief ought to be validated by conducting research into the attitudes and behavior of consumers and other external stakeholders.

Sixth, much of the research to date has focused primarily on managers and, in a couple of studies, on consumers. However, some important questions about other stakeholders remain. For instance, how do investors see conscience? Does conscience matter to potential and current employees?

Finally, the range of studies into conscientious brands is still too limited and, as noted, many of the cited examples reappear. We still need to better understand how the conscientious brands' construct applies in hard to transition industries, the public sector, cultural entities and places. There has also been a focus on US and Western European examples. More work needs to be done to understand the interpretation of the construct in other cultures and its acceptability and applicability in different business contexts.

REFERENCES

Abratt, R., & Kleyn, N. (2023). The conscientious corporate brand: Definition, operationalization and application in a B2B context. *Journal of Business & Industrial Marketing*, *38*(10), 2122–2133. https://doi.org/10.1108/JBIM-10-2021-0468

Acciona. (2024). www.acciona.com/our-purpose/

Aguilera, R. V. (2023). Corporate purpose in comparative perspective: The role of governance. *Strategy Science*, *8*(2), 193–201. https://doi.org/10.10.1287/stsc.2023.0198

Alhouti, S., Johnson, C.M., & Holloway, B.B. (2016). Corporate social responsibility authenticity: Investigating its antecedents and outcomes. *Journal of Business Research*, *69*(3), 1242–1249. https://doi.org/10.1016/j.jbusres.2015.09.007

Arendt, H. (2003). *Responsibility and judgment*. Schocken Books.

Bartlett, C. A. (2015). Unilever's new global strategy: Competing through sustainability. *Harvard Business School Case 916–414*, November 2015. (Revised August 2016).

Berkey, B. (2014). Climate change, moral intuitions, and moral demandingness. *Philosophy and Public Issues*, *4*(2), 157–189.

Berkey, B. (2022). Facing up to conflicts between ethics and profits: Against wishful thinking. In N. Ind, & O. Iglesias (Eds.), *In good conscience: Do the right thing while building a profitable business* (pp. 43–47). Palgrave Macmillan.

Bernacchio, C. (2019). Pope Francis on conscience, gradualness, and discernment: Adapting Amoris Laetitia for business ethics. *Business Ethics Quarterly*, *29*(4), 437–460. https://doi.org/10.10.1017/beq.2019.15

Biedenbach, G., & Biedenbach, T. (2022). Co-creating conscientious corporate brands inside-out through values-driven branding. In O. Iglesias, N. Ind, & M. Schultz (Eds.), *The Routledge companion to corporate branding* (pp. 480–495). Routledge.

Browning, H. (2023). Improving welfare assessment in aquaculture. *Frontiers in Veterinary Science*, *10*, 1060720. https://doi.org/10.10.3389/fvets.2023.1060720

Business Roundtable (2019). Business Roundtable redefines the purpose of a corporation to promote 'An economy that serves all Americans'. www.businessroundtable.org/business-roundtable-redefines-the-purpose-of-a-corporation-to-promote-an-economy-that-serves-all-americans

Carney, M. (2021). *Values: Building a better world for all*. Signal.

Damsté, C. B., Kinghorn, R., Kuo, I., & Murphy, B. (2024). How the EU's Green Deal is driving business reinvention. *Strategy+Business*. www.pwc.com/gx/en/issues/esg/eu-green-deal-reinvention.html

Davis, G. F. (2021). Corporate purpose needs democracy. *Journal of Management Studies*, *58*(3), 902–913. https://doi.org/10.10.1111/joms.12659

De George, R. (1993). *Competing with integrity in international business*. Oxford University Press.

de Lange, R., & Jackson-Moore, W. (2024). From trade-offs to payoffs: CEOs on creating value with climate action. *Strategy+Business*. www.pwc.com/gx/en/issues/esg/ceos-creating-value-climate-action.html

de Villiers, C., Dimes, R., La Torre, M., & Molinari, M. (2024). The International Sustainability Standards Board's (ISSB) past, present, and future: critical reflections and a research agenda. *Pacific Accounting Review*, *36*(2), 255–273. https://doi.org/10.1108/PAR-02-2024-0038

Dierksmeier, C. (2013). Kant on virtue. *Journal of Business Ethics*, *113*(4), 597–609. https://doi.org/10.10.1007/s10551-013-1683-5

DNV ETO. (2024). *Energy transition outlook*. www.dnv.com/energy-transition-outlook/

Duan, K., Pang, G., & Lin, Y. (2024). Exploring the current status and future opportunities of blockchain technology adoption and application in supply chain management. *Journal of Digital*

Economy 2, 244–288. https://doi.org/10.1016/j.jdec.2024.01.005

European Commission (2024). Corporate sustainability due diligence. https://commission.europa.eu/business-economy-euro/doing-business-eu/sustainability-due-diligence-responsible-business/corporate-sustainability-due-diligence_en

European Union. (2024). *CSRD directive*. https://eur-lex.europa.eu/legal-content/EN/TXT/?uri=CELEX:32022L2464

Fernandes, T., Guzman, F., & Mota, M. (2024). Purpose is the new branding: Understanding conscientious purpose-driven marketing and its impact on brand outcomes. *Journal of Product & Brand Management*, *33*(6), 761–782. https://doi.org/10.1108/JPBM-08-2023-4667

Fisch, J. E., & Solomon, S. D. (2020). Should corporations have a purpose? *Texas Law Review*, *99*, 1309–1346.

Ford, B. R., & Stohl, C. (2019). Does CSR matter? A longitudinal analysis of product reviews for CSR-associated brands. *Journal of Brand Management*, *26*(1), 60–70. https://doi.org/10.10.1057/s41262-018-0108-2

Freeman, R. E., & Liedtka, J. (1991). Corporate social responsibility: A critical approach. *Business Horizons*, *34*(4), 92–99.

Freeman, R. E., & Elms, H. (2023). The social responsibility of business is to create value for stakeholders. In S. D. Dmytriyev, & R. E. Freeman (Eds.), *R. Edward Freeman's selected works on stakeholder theory and business ethics* (pp. 807–810). Springer International Publishing.

Friedman, M. (1970, September 13). The social responsibility of business is to increase its profits. *The New York Times Magazine*.

Fuss, P. (1964). Conscience. *Ethics*, *74*(2), 111–120. https://doi.org/10.10.1086/291483

George, G., Haas, M. R., McGahan, A. M., Schillebeeckx, S. J., & Tracey, P. (2023). Purpose in the for-profit firm: A review and framework for management research. *Journal of Management*, *49*(6), 1841–1869. https://doi.org/10.10.1177/01492063211006450

Goodpaster, K. E. (2007). *Conscience and corporate culture*. Blackwell Publishing.

Goodpaster, K. E., & Matthews, Jr., J. B. (1982). Can a corporation have a conscience? *Harvard Business Review*. https://hbr.org/1982/01/can-a-corporation-have-a-conscience

Gray, D., & Clarke, P. (2005). Meeting Goodpaster's challenge: A Smithian approach to Goodpaster's paradox. *Business Ethics: A European Review*, *14*(2), 119–126. https://doi.org/10.10.1111/j.1467-8608.2005.00396.x

Guzmán, F., Ahmad, F., & Johnson, R. W. (2024). What drives business-to-business brands to be conscientious? *Journal of Product & Brand Management*, *33*(1), 138–161. https://doi.org/10.10.1108/JPBM-07-2023-4595

Henderson, R., & Steen, E. V. D. (2015). Why do firms have 'purpose'? The firm's role as a carrier of identity and reputation. *American Economic Review*, *105*(5), 326–330. https://doi.org/10.10.1257/aer.p20151072

Horlings, S. (2016). Crazy about chocolate, serious about people. In N. Ind, & S. Horlings (Eds.), *Brands with a conscience: How to build a successful and responsible brand* (pp. 85–101). Kogan Page Publishers.

Hutchinson, D., Singh, J., Svensson, G., & Mysen, T. (2013). Towards a model of conscientious corporate brands: A Canadian study. *Journal of Business & Industrial Marketing*, *28*(8), 687–695. https://doi.org/10.10.1108/JBIM-05-2012-0085

Iglesias, O., & Ind, N. (2016). How to be a brand with a conscience. In N. Ind, & S. Horlings (Eds.), *Brands with a conscience: How to build a successful and responsible brand* (pp. 203–211). Kogan Page Publishers.

Iglesias, O., & Ind, N. (2020). Towards a theory of conscientious corporate brand co-creation: The next key challenge in brand management. *Journal of Brand Management*, *27*(6), 710–720. https://doi.org/10.10.1057/s41262-020-00205-7.

Iglesias, O., Landgraf, P., Ind, N., Markovic, S., & Koporcic, N. (2020a). Corporate brand identity co-creation in business-to-business contexts. *Industrial Marketing Management*, *85*, 32–43. https://doi.org/10.10.1016/j.indmarman.2019.09.008

Iglesias, O., Mingione, M., Ind, N., & Markovic, S. (2023). How to build a conscientious corporate brand together with business partners: A case study of Unilever. *Industrial Marketing Management*, *109*, 1–13. https://doi.org/10.10.1016/j.indmarman.2022.12.008

Ind, N., & Iglesias, O. (2021). Promises, promises: How to showcase the authenticity of sustainability claims through digitalization. In S. Markovic, C. Sancha, & A. Lindgreen (Eds.), *Handbook of sustainability-driven business strategies in practice* (pp. 94–107). Edward Elgar Publishing.

Ind, N., & Iglesias, O. (2022). *In good conscience: Do the right thing while building a profitable business*. Palgrave Macmillan.

Ind, N., & Iglesias, O. (2023). Why the practice of CSR needs a conscience. In S. Markovic, A. Lindgreen, N. Koporcic, & M. Micevski (Eds.), *Approaches to corporate social responsibility* (pp. 215–230). Routledge.

Ind, N., & Ryder, I. (2011). Conscientious brands editorial. *Journal of Brand Management*, *18*(9), 635–638. https://doi.org/10.10.1057/bm.2011.16

Kant, I. (2017). *The metaphysics of morals*. Cambridge University Press.

Kapitan, S., Kemper, J. A., Vredenburg, J., & Spry, A. (2022). Strategic B2B brand activism: Building conscientious purpose for social impact. *Industrial Marketing Management*, *107*, 14–28. https://doi.org/10.10.1016/j.indmarman.2022.09.015

Kaplan, S. (2023). The promises and perils of corporate purpose. *Strategy Science*, *8*(2), 288–301. https://doi.org/10.1287/stsc.2023.0187

Keränen, A., Malmi, K., Nätti, S., & Ulkuniemi, P. (2023). Developing identity of conscientious business-to-business organizations through integrative leadership. *Industrial Marketing Management*, *109*, 188–203. https://doi.org/10.10.1016/j.indmarman.2023.01.007

King, A. A., & Pucker, K. P. (2021). The dangerous allure of win–win strategies. *Stanford Social Innovation Review*, *19*(1), 34–39.https://doi.org/10.48558/jdxh-qh17

Klimecki, R., & Parker, M. (2024). Business ethics, law and zemiology: The criminology of social and environmental harm. *Business Ethics, the Environment & Responsibility*. 1–11. https://doi.org/10.1111/beer.12742

Korsgaard, C. M. (2009). *Self constitution: Agency, identity and integrity*. Oxford University Press.

Korsgaard, C. M. (2019). Constitutivism and the Virtues. *Philosophical Explorations*, *22*(2), 98–116. https://doi.org/10.10.1080/13869795.2019.1599050

Kotz, M., Levermann, A., & Wenz, L. (2024). The economic commitment of climate change. *Nature*, *628*(8008), 551–557. https://doi.org/10.10.1038/s41586-024-07219-0

Köllen, T. (2016). Acting out of compassion, egoism, and malice: A Schopenhauerian view on the moral worth of CSR and diversity management practices. *Journal of Business Ethics*, *138*(2), 215–229. https://doi.org/10.10.1007/s10551-015-2599-z

Kronthal-Sacco, R., & Whelan, T. (2021). *Sustainable market share index*. Center for Sustainable Business. New York University Stern. www.stern.nyu.edu/experience-stern/about/departments-centers-initiatives/centers-of-research/center-sustainable-business/research/research-initiatives/csb-sustainable-market-share-index.

Ladd, J. (1970). Morality and the Ideal of rationality in formal organizations. *The Monist*.

Last, A. (2021). *Business on a mission: How to build a sustainable brand*. (2nd ed.). Routledge. https://doi.org/10.4324/9781003176817

Living Planet Index. (2024). *Living planet report: A system in peril*. www.livingplanetindex.org

Longoni, A., & Luzzini, D. (2016). Building social capital into the disrupted green coffee supply chain: Illy's journey to quality and sustainability. *Organizing Supply Chain Processes for Sustainable Innovation in the Agri-Food Industry*, *5*, 83–108. https://doi.org/10.1108/S2045-060520160000005012

Lyon, T. P., Delmas, M. A., Maxwell, J. W., Bansal, P., Chiroleu-Assouline, M., Crifo, P., Durand, R., Gond, J.-P., King, A., Lenox, M., Toffel, M., Vogel, D., & Wijen, F. (2018). CSR needs CPR: Corporate sustainability and politics. *California Management Review*, *60*(4), 5–24. https://doi.org/10.10.1177/0008125618778854

Markovic, S., Iglesias, O., Singh, J.J., & Sierra, V. (2018). How does the perceived ethicality of corporate services brands influence loyalty and positive word-of-mouth? Analyzing the roles of empathy, affective commitment, and perceived quality. *Journal of Business Ethics*, *148*, 721–740. https://doi.org/10.1007/s10551-015-2985-6

Mather, C., & Fanning, L. (2019). Social licence and aquaculture: Towards a research agenda. *Marine Policy*, *99*, 275–282. https://doi.org/10.10.1016/j.marpol.2018.10.049

Mezzanotte, F. E. (2023). Corporate sustainability reporting: Double materiality, impacts, and legal risk. *Journal of Corporate Law Studies*, *23*(2), 633–663. https://doi.org/10.1080/14735970.2024.2319058

Morrison, A. D., & Mota, R. (2023). A theory of organizational purpose. *Academy of Management Review*, *48*(2), 203–219. https://doi.org/10.10.5465/amr.2019.0307

Mota, R., & Morrison, A. D. (2024). Mapping the contours of blame: An account of the moral boundaries of organizations. *Journal of Business Ethics*, *196*, 523–537. https://doi.org/10.1007/s10551-024-05708-w

Nagel, T. (1986). *The view from nowhere*. Oxford University Press.

Olsen, L. E., & Peretz, A. (2011). Conscientious brand criteria: A framework and a case example from the clothing industry. *Journal of Brand Management*, *18*(9), 639–649. https://doi.org/10.10.1057/bm.2011.30

Parfit, D. (1982). Future generations: Further problems. *Philosophy & Public Affairs*, *11*(2), 113–172.

Porter, M. E., & Kramer, M. R. (2011, January–February). Creating shared value. *Harvard Business Review*, *89*(1–2), 62–77.

Primeaux, P. (1992). Experiential ethics: A blueprint for personal and corporate ethics. *Journal of Business Ethics*, *11*(10), 779–788. https://doi.org/10.10.1007/BF00872310

Raghunandan, A., & Rajgopal, S. (2024). Do socially responsible firms walk the talk? *Journal of Law and Economics*, *67*(4), 767–810. https://doi.org/10.1086/728855

Rasberry, R. W. (2000). The conscience of an organization: The ethics office. *Strategy & Leadership*, *28*(3), 17–21. https://doi.org/10.10.1108/10878570010348558

Rindell, A., Svensson, G., Mysen, T., Billström, A., & Wilén, K. (2011). Towards a conceptual foundation of 'Conscientious Corporate Brands'. *Journal of Brand Management, 18*(9), 709–719. https://doi.org/10.10.1057/bm.2011.38

Scheyvens, R., Banks, G., & Hughes, E. (2016). The private sector and the SDGs: The need to move beyond 'business as usual'. *Sustainable Development, 24*(6), 371–382. https://doi.org/10.10.1002/sd.1623

Schmidt, H. J., Ind, N., Guzmán, F., & Kennedy, E. (2021). Sociopolitical activist brands. *Journal of Product & Brand Management, 31*(1), 40–55. https://doi.org/10.10.1108/JPBM-03-2020-2805

Segrestin, B., Hatchuel, A., & Levillain, K. (2021). When the law distinguishes between the enterprise and the corporation: The case of the new French law on corporate purpose. *Journal of Business Ethics, 171*(1), 1–13. https://doi.org/10.10.1007/s10551-020-04439-y

Smith, A. (2009). *The theory of moral sentiments*. Penguin Classics.

Song, B., & Dong, C. (2022). What do we know about CSR authenticity? A systematic review from 2007 to 2021. *Social Responsibility Journal, 19*(3), 525–548. https://doi.org/10.1108/SRJ-07-2021-0276

Sorabji, B. (2014). *Moral conscience through the ages: Fifth century BCE to the present*. University of Chicago Press.

Spry, A., Figueiredo, B., Gurrieri, L., Kemper, J. A., & Vredenburg, J. (2021). Transformative branding: A dynamic capability to challenge the dominant social paradigm. *Journal of Macromarketing, 41*(4), 531–546. https://doi.org/10.10.1177/02761467211043074

Stout, L. A. (2013). The toxic side effects of shareholder primacy. *University of Pennsylvania Law Review, 161*(7), 2003–2023.

Sulmasy, D. P. (2008). What is conscience and why is respect for it so important? *Theoretical Medicine and Bioethics, 29*(3), 135–149. https://doi.org/10.10.1007/s11017-008-9072-2

United Nations. (2024). *The sustainable development goals report*. https://unstats.un.org/sdgs/report/2024/The-Sustainable-Development-Goals-Report-2024.pdf

Vallaster, C., Cesinger, B., Niemand, T., Huis, C., & Lienbacher, E. (2023). Conscientious enterprises: The role of decision makers' social identity and the preference to engage in B2B relationships. *Industrial Marketing Management, 111*, 216–228. https://doi.org/10.10.1016/j.indmarman.2023.04.006

Vallaster, C., & Lechner, P. (2022). Co-creation of conscientious corporate brands-facilitating societal change towards sustainability: A structured literature analysis. In S. Markovic, R. Jones, S. von Wallpach, & A. Lindgreen (Eds.), *Research handbook on brand co-creation* (pp. 256–273). Edward Elgar Publishing.

Veterinærinstituttet. (2024). *Norwegian fish health report 2023*. Report 8b/2024. www.vetinst.no/rapporter-og-publikasjoner/rapporter/2024/fishhealthreport-2023

von der Gathen, A., Eckert, N. B., & Kastbjerg, C. (2024). The myth of the sustainable consumer. *MIT Sloan Management Review, 66*(2), 56–61.

Vredenburg, J., Kapitan, S., Spry, A., & Kemper, J. A. (2020). Brands taking a stand: Authentic brand activism or woke washing? *Journal of Public Policy & Marketing, 39*(4), 444–460. https://doi.org/10.10.1177/0743915620947359

White, K., Habib, R., & Hardisty, D. J. (2019). How to SHIFT consumer behaviors to be more sustainable: A literature review and guiding framework. *Journal of Marketing, 83*(3), 22–49. https://doi.org/10.10.1177/0022242919825649

Williams, P., Escalas, J. E., & Morningstar, A. (2022). Conceptualizing brand purpose and considering its implications for consumer eudaimonic well-being. *Journal of Consumer Psychology, 32*(4), 699–723. https://doi.org/10.10.1002/jcpy.1324

Wilson, J. A., & Morgan, J. E. (2011). Friends or free-loaders? Encouraging brand conscience and introducing the concept of emotion-based consumer loss mitigation. *Journal of Brand Management, 18*(9), 659–676. https://doi.org/10.10.1057/bm.2011.4

World Economic Forum. (2020). *Nature risk rising: Why the crisis engulfing nature matters for business and the economy*. www3.weforum.org/docs/WEF_New_Nature_Economy_Report_2020.pdf

Index

Note: Page numbers followed by "f" indicate figure, "t" indicates table in the text

Aaker, D. A., 146, 148–149, 151–155, 162, 186–187, 207, 212, 430, 488
Aaker, J. L., 119, 121, 124
Aaron, D., 72
Abrar, M., 397
Abratt, R., 23, 625
Abundant rarity, 280
Academic(s), 135, 137, 139
evolution of academic research on brand equity, 148–151
inquiry, 597
research, 239
Accessibility, 235–236, 597
Accidental crises, 260, 263, 265
Accountability, 8, 262, 265
pressure, 7–9
Achievement elements, 573, 581
ACID test, 34, 183
AC[4]ID test, 181
of corporate brand management, 183–185
Acquisition, 197–198, 297
Actor-network, 376
Adaptability, 295
Adjusted Corporate Brand Identity, 109
Advanced analytical methods, 419
Advergames, 574–575, 581–582
Advertising industry, 25, 607
Advocacy, 315–316, 438–439
Affective engagement, 357, 361
Age, 579, 612
age-adaptive brands, 615
age-denial brands, 615
age-related stereotypes, 607
contradictions of, 609–610
segmentation by, 605–606
Ageing consumers, 607
contradictions of branding and age, 609–610
intersectional marketing paradigm, 612*f*
older consumers, 608–609
process model for customer journey and experience, 614*f*
reconceptualising ageing consumers' interactions with brands, 611–613
segmentation by age and generational cohorts, 605–606
skew for marketers to develop new products for younger consumers, 610–611
stereotyping of older consumers, 606–608
understanding ageing consumers engage with brands, 613–615
Aggarwal, P., 236
Aguilera, R. V., 625
Ahmad, F., 495
Ahn, J., 234
Ahuvia, A. C., 309, 315
Aided awareness, 432
Ajzen, I., 591
Akbar, M. M., 135
Akman, H., 379
Albert, A., 42
Algorithm-based modeling, 558
Algorithmic bias, 543, 597
Algorithmic mechanisms, 497–498
Algorithms, 9, 498
Alhashem, M., 380
Allgemeine Elektricitäts-Gesellschaft (AEG), 23
Alphanumeric brand names (ABNs), 213–214
Altaras, S., 52
American Express (AmEx), 76
American multinational corporations, 122
Amos, C., 455
Analytical AI, 9
Anantachart, S., 157
Angulo-Ruiz, F., 421
Anthropology, 133, 346
Anthropomorphism, 119, 124, 455
Anti-ageing industry, 607
Anti-brand communities, 332
Anticipated separation distress, 324–325
Anti-DEI campaigns, 488
Anti-laws of luxury, 276
Antoinette, M., 500
Application programming interfaces (API), 541
Appraisal theories, 328, 526
and cognitive perspectives, 329–330
Apps, 118, 122, 571
Arnould, E. J., 375
Arora, S. V., 216, 218
Arsel, Z., 483
Artificial intelligence (AI), 9, 61, 78, 89–91, 122, 138–139, 141, 169, 182, 259, 264, 283, 297, 318, 420, 504, 533, 537, 566, 589
AI-driven branding, 595
AI-driven crisis communication strategies, 269

AI-driven sentiment analysis tools, 383
AI-mediated brand communication and three AI capacities, 593
AI-powered creative development, 540–541
AI-thenticity, 138
building brand trust and loyalty, 595
EBBE future in context of, 169
enhanced consumer engagement, 595–596
features, 575
feeling AI for brand emotional connection, 594–595
framework in brand management, 591*f*
integration drivers in branding, 591–593
mechanical AI for brand efficiency and consistency, 593
personalization and micro-targeting, 595
practical integration in crisis management, 264–266
role current trends in brand management, 596
thinking AI for brand personalization, 593–594
toward integrated framework of AI in brand management, 590
transparency, 269
Artistic Consultant, 23
Arvidsson, A., 376
Assemblage theories, 376
Assessment criteria, 204–205
Associative network theory, 234–235
Attachment theory, 310, 327–329
Attitude accessibility theory, 234–235
Attractiveness, 558, 560–561
Attribution theory, 234, 236
Audience-centric messaging, 263
Audrezet, A., 563
Augmented reality (AR), 121, 124, 156, 283, 312, 318, 339, 342–343, 355, 399, 540, 595
Augusto, M., 120
Authentic advertisement, 136
Authentic brands, 138, 317
Authentic communication process, 510
Authentic inclusion, 484, 488
Authentic influencer, 561
Authenticity, 133–134, 136, 141–142, 155, 452, 533, 560–561

Babić R. A., 439
Baby boomers, 606, 609
Bairrada, C. M., 314
Balabanis, G., 560
Balachander, S., 235
Balanced temporal perspective, 623, 628
Balance theory, 234
Balmer, J. M. T., 37–38, 186–187, 190
AC³ID Test of corporate brand management, 183–185
corporate brand architecture, 187
Bandyopadhyay, A., 152
Banerjee, S., 534
Banking sector, 609
Bapat, D., 156
Bar, R. N., 411
Barros, D., 390–391
Baršytė, J., 57
Bartsch, F., 57
Baruah, L., 104–105
Batra, R., 249, 309
Baxter, S., 223
Béal, M., 123
Behavioral constructs, 311
brand engagement, 312
brand heroes, 312
brand loyalty, 311–312
brand resurrection movements, 312–313
Behavioral data, 342, 345
Behavioural experiences, 615
Behrens, P., 23
Bekk, M., 583
Belanche, D., 562
Bendle, N. T., 412, 430
Beneficence, 452
Benevolence, 452, 459
Berkey, B., 623
Betjamin, J., 36
Bettingen, J.-F., 522–523
Bettman, J. R., 313
Beukeboom, C. J., 121
Beverland, M. B., 135
Bhattacharya, A., 434
Bianchi, C., 157
Bibliographical analysis, 533
Bibliometric analysis, 558
Bickerton, D., 38
Bidar, R., 381
Big data, 9, 264
analysis, 4, 9
analytics, 537
empower brands, 338
Big Five, 121
personality traits, 330
structure, 119
Biglione, S., 69
Binet, L., 430
Biometric tools, 91
Bitman, N., 486
Black box,
algorithms, 266
opacity, 267
Blackston, M., 246
Blasco-Arcas, L., 361
Blended brand names (BBNs), 216
Blockchain, 283, 339, 542, 544
technology, 540–541
Bonet, E., 10
Bootstrapping, 299
Borges-Tiago, M. T., 123
Borkovsky, R. N., 411

Boston Consulting Group (BCG), 206–207, 433
Bottomley, P. A., 85
Boukis, A., 165, 169
Boundary spanning interactions, 110
Bourdin, D., 59
Bouten, L. M., 234
#BoycottKelloggs, 502
Bradshaw, A., 377
Brand Advocacy Index (BAI), 439
Brand approaches, 21–22
community approach, 27
consumer-based approach, 24–25
cultural approach, 27–28
economic approach, 22–23
identity approach, 23–24
personality approach, 25–26
relational approach, 26–27
sensory approach, 28
Brand architecture, 197–199
approaches, 186–187
eight-step brand audit framework combining brand portfolio and, 201–208
frameworks, 199–201, 201*t*
strategy, 208
Brand Asset Valuator (BAV), 474
Brand audit, 207, 430
brand architecture frameworks, 199–201, 201*t*
brand portfolio frameworks, 199
DouroAzul brand portfolio at time of, 202*t*
eight-step brand audit framework combining brand portfolio and brand architecture, 201–208
methodologies, 199
scorecard, 203*f*
theoretical framework, 202*f*
Brand authenticity, 134, 137–138, 142, 314, 472
definitions, 135–136, 136*t*
dimensions, 135–136
evolution, 136–139, 137*f*
future research agenda, 139–141, 140*t*
implications, 142
theoretical foundations, 134–135, 134*f*
Brand engagement, 312, 355–356, 358, 366–367, 576–577
definitions and dimensions of, 356–358
differentiating brand engagement from brand-related concepts, 358
engagement considered in branding literature, 357*t*
future research agenda, 366–367
importance of adopting customer-centric approach to design brand experiences for, 364–365
and individual traits, 358–359
interplay between online brand communities and, 365
key drivers of, 359–360
main outcomes of, 360–361
measuring brand engagement, 361
methods to capture, 363–364
power of content marketing and influencer marketing in shaping, 365–366
quantitative scales, 361–363, 362*t*–363*t*
scale items, 312*t*
strategies to enhance brand engagement, 364
theoretical foundations of, 356
Brand engagement in self-concept (BESC), 359, 359*t*
Brand equity, xxii, 29, 146–147, 150, 162–163, 206, 263, 290–291, 299, 384, 397, 409, 412, 513
articles by citations in WoS and Scopus, 149*t*
authors by number of indexed articles, 151*t*
CBBE modelling and measurement, 151–154
challenges in measuring, 154–155
conceptual framework, 147–148
contextual factors and impact on, 155–156
evolution in number of scientific articles about, 149*f*
evolution of academic research on, 148–151
index, 418
integrated marketing communication and impact on, 157–158
journals by number of articles, 150*t*
literature, 609
in luxury tourism, 157
new contexts for research, 156
research challenges and opportunities in, 154
ten scale, 148, 151
tourism and hospitality applications, 156–157
Brand experience, 358, 364
customized brand experiences, 338–339
designing brand experience through customer journey map, 340
digital transformation challenges in, 351
dynamic experiences, 339–340
engaging experiences, 339
and impact of digital transformation, 338, 339*f*
importance of adopting customer-centric approach to design, 364–365
omnichannel experiences, 339
Brand happiness, xxiii, 522–524, 526, 528, 533–534
appraisal framework of, 527*f*
concept and measurement of, 522–526
determinants and consequences of, 526–527
future research, 533–534
measurement model of, 525*f*
recent empirical findings on effects of, 528
relevance of happiness research in brand management, 521–522
research studies on, 529*t*–532*t*
results and implications for management, 528–533
Brand identity, xxii, 23, 83–84, 91, 99, 104
B2B brand architecture, 102–103
co-creation of, 107–114
Coleman et al. brand identity model, 101–102
de Chernatony's brand identity model, 99
Kapferer's brand prism, 99–101
Rode and Vallaster's corporate identity model, 101
supply-and demand-side advantages and disadvantages, 103*t*

Brand image, 105, 153
co-creation of, 107–114
and reputation role in B2B buying, 105–107
Brand management, xxi–xxiv, 3–4, 18, 21–22, 37, 87–88, 91, 119, 146, 163, 268, 290, 294, 429, 484, 534, 538, 544, 596
AI tools for, 590*t*
AI's challenges and potential strategies, 599*t*
algorithmic bias and discrimination, 543
benefits of becoming global brand, 69
call to action for practitioners and scholars, 600
challenges facing B2B entrepreneurs, 294–299
company/sender focus, 28
context, 24
core that counts, 74–75
cultural/context focus, 29
current trends of AI's role in, 596
deepfakes and brand authenticity, 544
eight brand approaches, 21–28
emerging trends and future directions, 596
ethical frameworks for responsible adoption, 544
ethical implications of technology in, 543
exporting AmEx brand to South Africa, 76
feeling AI, 598–599
four periods of time, 28
history of, 18–19
human/receiver focus, 28–29
key international issues to explore, 69–72
key mistakes marketers make, 72–73
let us get smart on marketing AI for global brand management, 78–79
location, location, location, 73–74
MarTech enabling brand's global consistency, 77–78
mechanical AI, 596–597
privacy and surveillance capitalism, 543
research gaps and future directions, 596
sensory/biological perspective, 29
strategic role of technology in, 539
strategy, 229
taxonomy of, 19–21, 20*f*
thinking AI, 597–598
toward integrated framework of AI in, 590–593
two brand management paradigms, 29–30
Brand management system, 3–4
accountability pressure, 7
adaptation to digitalization and datafication, 9–12
category management, 8–9
development of, 4*f*
early forms of, 4–5
extension and standardization of, 6–7
globalization of brands, 7–8
golden age, 6
infancy, 4
McElroy memo, 5
official birth of, 5
origin and development of, 4
professionalization of consumer knowledge and market research, 6
slow spread of, 5–6
threat to, 8–9
Brand manager(s), 4, 10–11, 85, 232, 522, 613, 615
dual expertise of, 10–11
role, 8
Brand metrics, 429
advocacy, 438–439
after purchase, 437
along customer journey, 432*f*
before purchase, 432
brand advocacy index, 439
brand awareness, 432–433
brand consideration, 433
brand purchase intention, 433
components of market share, 434–437
consumer-mindset and customer-behaviour metrics, 431–432
customer satisfaction index, 437
evidence-based marketing, 430–431
limitations and suggestions for future research, 440–441
loyalty, 438
managerial implications, 439–440
net promoter score, 437
performance measurement, 429–430
purchase and market share, 433–434
repeat purchase rate, 437–738
retention rate, 438
satisfaction, 437
within brand value chain, 430*f*
Brand morality, 447, 449
antecedents and consequences of, 455–459, 456*t*
apply in crisis contexts, 460
business-focused brand morality, 450–451
challenges will brand morality study face, 459–460
consequentialist perspective, 452
consumer-focused brand morality, 449–450
consumer-focused morality, 450*t*
deontological perspective, 451–452
dimensions of, 453–455, 454*t*, 459
distinction between morality and ethics in branding, 448*t*
ethics, 448
future research agenda, 458
integrated multidimensional perspective, 453
moral as cooperation perspective, 453
moral foundations perspective, 452–453
morality, 447–448
multiple research frameworks, 455
multiple theoretical perspectives, 451, 451*t*
necessary to differentiate brand morality from ethics, 458
significance of brand morality in business and society, 448–449
theoretical perspective to apply, 459
theoretical perspectives of morality, 448*t*
virtue ethics perspective, 452

Brand name/naming, 212–213, 216, 220, 222
attributes, 220
classification frameworks, 217–220, 217*t*
creative brand-naming strategies and future directions, 222–223
foreign branding and COO effects, 220
historical development of, 213
influence of words forming, 214
language translation and transliteration, 220–221
letters in, 213
line and brand extensions, 221–222
modified Arora–Kalro–Sharma framework for, 219*f*
numbers in, 213–214
sound symbolism in brand names, 214–217, 215*t*
Brand orientation, 289–292
entrepreneurial orientation *vs.*, 294*t*
in nonprofits, 509–510
Brand performance indicators (BPIs), 403
consumer-market level BPIs, 404–409
emerging BPIs at resource-market level, 413
financial-market level BPIs, 411–413
product-market level BPIs, 409–411
Brand performance measurement,
designing brand performance tracking system based on brand value chain, 415–417
Harris Interactive's EquiTrend, 418
Interbrand, 418–419
Kantar BrandZ, 419
measuring brand performance across borders, 420–421
with new data, methods and technologies, 419–420
products, 417
revised brand value chain and brand performance indicators, 415*f*
stakeholder relevance matrix for brand performance indicator categories, 416*t*
tools of trade, 417
unpacking layers of, 404–413
updated brand value chain, 413–415
YouGov's BrandIndex, 418
Young & Rubicam's brand asset valuator, 417
Brand personality, 25–26, 101, 119–120, 122, 125, 154, 237, 314, 471, 509, 592
B2C and B2B brand personality, 119
digital-based methods to study brand personality, 124–126
future of digital brand personality research, 126–127
research across digital contexts, 121–124
theories and characteristics of digital brand personality, 119–121
theory and research, xxii, 119
Brand portfolio(s), 197
audit, 206
eight-step brand audit framework combining brand architecture and, 201–208
frameworks, 199, 200*t*
management, 198
Brand-related moderators, 317
brand innovativeness, 317
brand reputation, 317
Brand relationships, 245–246
basis, 248
out of commonly expected forms, 250
comprehensive insights, 246
having mixed feelings towards brand, 251
looking into future, 252–253
metaphors, 246–247
moving from one relationship type to another, 250
passion intensity, 247
research, 252
sentiment/valance, 247
simultaneous opposing passionate feelings to different consumer groups, 251–252
spectrum, 208
studies, 252
theory, 26
types based on level of passion and sentiment, 248–250
Brand(s), xxiii, 60, 98, 146, 197, 216–217, 245, 247, 313, 318, 342, 364, 374, 467, 518, 522, 533, 537, 556, 562–563, 574, 598, 621–623, 627–628
like, 249–250
activations, 575, 581
activism, 490, 495–496, 503
adapting and reinventing brand context from for-profit sector, 517
advantage, 405
advocacy, 361, 380
alliance strategies, 230
ambivalence, 251
anthropomorphism, 471
associations, 153, 405
attachment, 310–311, 311*t*, 358
avoidance, 319, 328
awareness, 154, 204, 206, 295, 384, 404–405
becoming conscientious, 620–622
brand-as-a-personality model, 121
brand-focused morality, 449
brand-owned touchpoints, 613
brand-related factors, 314–315
brand-related schadenfreude, 326
brand–consumer exchange, 25
building brand loyalty, 543
building brand trust and loyalty, 595
citizenship behaviours, 396
climate, 393
commitment, 396
community, 27, 315, 364–265, 375, 508, 582
confidence, 164
conscientious brand, 622–623
consideration, 405
consistency, 291
consumers participating in Kellogg's giveaway, 500*f*

contextual factors, 577–579
contribution dimension, 206
coolness, 237
cultural branding and brand activism, 495–496
differentiation, 204
dislike, 249–250, 325
embarrassment, 325, 331
enhancement of brand awareness, 542
evangelism, 528
as experienced through our senses, 28
extensions, 136–138, 141, 221–222, 239
favorability, 384
feeling AI for brand emotional connection, 594–595
formation, 39
future research agenda, 504–505
game elements, 579–581
globalness, 51, 56
hate, 248–249, 325–326
heroes, 312, 312*t*
honesty, 457
house of brands modality, 187
as human-like character, 25–26
identification, 396
improve perceived quality, 542–543
individual factors, 579
industry, 579
influencers as strategic approach to brand promotion, 559
Instagram polarized conversation, 501*f*
integrative gamification-branding framework, 578*f*
interactivity, 360
internal and external drivers of conscientious brands, 620*f*
involvement, 358–360
issues, 623–626
Kellogg's cereal for dinner case study, 498–503
Kellogg's giveaway post on Instagram, 499*f*
key studies on gamification and branding, 576*t*
leadership, 394
legitimacy, 504
as linked to corporate identity, 23–24
as linked with consumer associations, 24–25
longitudinal studies of brand resilience post-crisis, 269
love, 248–249, 309, 310*t*, 313, 329, 358
loyalty, 153, 204, 311–313, 312*t*, 360, 396, 409, 576
marketers, 74
masculinity, 216
measuring and monitoring brand equity, 543
mechanical AI for brand efficiency and consistency, 593
new directions, 626–628
nostalgia, 326
ownership, 69
paradigm, 29
as part of broader cultural fabric, 27–28
as part of traditional marketing mix, 22–23
participation, 359
passion, 251, 309–310, 310*t*, 313
perspective, 19
as pivotal point of social interaction, 27
polarization, 251–252
police, 77
posts sarcastically comparing Kellogg's and Marie Antoinette's quotes, 502*f*
preference, 409, 421
propositions and specific conditions, 580*t*
publics, 376
reconceptualising ageing consumers' interactions with, 611–613
relevance, 204
reputation, 104, 204, 457
resurrection movements, 312–313, 313*t*
retaliation, 332
role of game elements in driving brand outcomes, 575–577
sales, 409
satisfaction, 154, 457
scope and application to, 468
self-connection, 473
self-introduction, 223
sensitivity, 296
social media and polarizations, 497–498
specialists, 112
SR, 468–469
storytelling, 311
strategies, 299
strategy, 581
strengthening brand associations, 542
technology's impact on brand equity, 542
thinking AI for brand personalization, 593–594
TikTok comments pointing out cereals expensive healthier options, 501*f*
transgression, 330
trust, 154, 360, 457
two AI-generated images created by consumers, 505*f*
typologies of brand crises, 259
typology of game elements in brand strategy, 573–575, 574*t*
understanding ageing consumers engage with, 613–615
validation across brand types, 318
as viable relationship partner, 26–27
visual identity, 89, 91
voice, 139
websites, 122
woke washing, 496–497

Brand social responsibility, 468, 471
corporate brand SR, 473–475
product brand SR, 470–473
reciprocal effects of corporate and product brand SR, 476
SR, 468–470

Brand-to-volunteer (B2V), 518
Brand valuation,
  firms, 384
  tools, 417
Brand value, 290–291, 523
  chain, 430
  creation, 25
Brand Visual Elicitation Platform, 126
Brandão, A., 197, 201–203, 206
BrandAsset Valuator (BAV), 417
Branded approach, 187
Branded apps, 122, 571
Branded gamified applications, 582
Branded house, 187
Branded websites, 122
Branding, 3, 35, 37, 483, 509
  conceptualising DEI in branding research, 483
  data-driven performance measurement, 540
  drivers of AI integration in, 591
  dynamic experience delivery, 540
  enhanced brand intelligence, 539
  enhanced brand protection, 540
  information science drivers, 592–593
  integrating inclusivity into branding research, 488–490
  literature, 613
  marketing drivers, 592
  pool, 110, 112
  practices, 162
  research, 119
  social psychology drivers, 591–592
  strategic relationship building, 540
  strategic role of technology in brand management, 539
  technology in, 538–539
  theory and research, 123
  training programs, 393
Branding consumers,
  contradictions of branding and age, 609–610
  intersectional marketing paradigm, 612*f*
  older consumers, 608–609
  process model for customer journey and experience, 614*f*
  reconceptualising ageing consumers' interactions with brands, 611–613
  segmentation by age and generational cohorts, 605–606
  skew for marketers to develop new products for younger consumers, 610–611
  stereotyping of older consumers, 606–608
  understanding ageing consumers engage with brands, 613–615
Bravo, R., 394
Brexendorf, T. O., 10
Broad branding territory, 37
Broader cultural fabric, brand as part of, 27–28
Brown, S., 455
Broyles, S. A., 154, 421
Bruhn, M., 135, 315, 523–524, 526
Brüns, J. D., 139
Buhalis, D., 381
Bui, H. T., 138
Building, 499
  brand awareness and reputation, 294–295
  brand loyalty, 543
Burgess, A., 484
Burghausen, M., 190
Burke, 6, 390
Burmann, C., 396
Business(es), 449, 537, 625
  brand relationships, 252
  business-centric antecedent, 457
  business-focused brand morality, 450–451
  business-focused ethics, 450
  business-focused frameworks, 455
  categories, 374
  economics, 521
  intelligence, 590
  managers, 146
  opportunity, 620
  practice, 363
  process, 351
  significance of brand morality in, 448–449
Business landscapes, 453
  adaptation to new digital media platforms, 89–91
  logos in evolving, 89
Business-to-business (B2B), 73, 98, 118, 166, 190, 245, 289–290, 373, 620
  brand architecture, 102–103
  brand identity, 99–103, 102*f*
  brand image, 105–114
  brand image and reputation role in, 105–107
  brand personality, 119
  branding, 98
  companies, 98
  context, 105–106, 472, 475
  customers, 627
  development of corporate brand identity in, 108*f*
  marketing, 98
  markets, 433
  network actors' participation in SME, 111*f*
  network of actors in, 109*f*
  reputation, 104–105
Business-to-business (B2B) brand management, 290
  brand management challenges facing B2B entrepreneurs, 294
  and brand orientation, 290–292
  building brand awareness and reputation, 294–295
  customer acquisition and retention, 297
  employee recruitment and retention, 298
  entrepreneurship and entrepreneurial orientation, 292–294
  insights from, 295–299
  insights from entrepreneurship literature, 295–299
  literature review, 290
  long sales cycles, 296

motivation, 289–290
principles and key literature, 291*t*
questions for future research, 295–299
research agenda, 299–301, 300*t*
scalability and managing growth, 298–299
Business-to-consumer (B2C), 118, 373, 433
brand personality, 119
Butt, M. N., 412
Buzzell, R. D., 433

Caliandro, A., 376
Calibration, 181
California Consumer Privacy Act (CCPA), 367
Campagna, C. L., 135
Campbell, C., 361
Cantallops, A. S., 591
Capitalism, 626
Carlson, J., 361
Carnevale, M., 222
Carroll, B. A., 309, 315
Carroll, D., 375
Cash flow, 147, 411
Categorization theory, 59, 234, 236
Category-level characteristics, 58
Celebrity endorsements, 75, 315
Celhay, F., 85
Celsi, R. L., 375
Centralized DAM system, 77
Centralized style guide, 77
Chailan, C., 198
Chakraborty, S., 156
Chang, Y., 290
Characteristics, Connections, Congruence, Communication (4Cs), 560
Charismatic influencers, 7
Chatbots, 592, 595
ChatGPT, 11, 78
Checks and validations, automation of, 77
Chen, T., 379
Chicecream, 592, 595
Chief Customer Officer (CCO), 10
Chief marketing officer (CMO), 3
Chief Marketing Technologist (CMT), 11
Child influencers, 566
Children, impact on, 566
Chinese gooseberry, 71
Christian theology and law, 38
Christodoulides, G., 165, 169
Chua, B.-L., 141
Churn rate, 383
Circular consumption models, 282
Circularity, rise of, 284
Cisco, 98, 213
Clarified Corporate Vision and Values, 107
Clark, D. R., 566
Climate change, 458, 619
Close/strong/deep brand relationship, 247
Co-branded product or service, 233
Co-branding authenticity, 136, 138
Co-branding strategy, 229–230, 240
among other brand alliance strategies, 231*t*
co-branding *vs.* other brand alliance strategies, 230
contemporary co-branding practices, 230–232, 230*t*
future research agenda, 240*t*
key success factors for, 237–238
managerial implications and future research agenda, 238–240
motivations for adopting, 232–234
theoretical underpinnings of, 234–236, 235*t*
Coca-Cola, 50, 177–178, 208, 355
Co-creating value, 297
Co-creation, 127
brand identity/image and corporate reputation, 107–114
in CCs, 378–381
corporate brands, 188–189
partners' roles in co-creating corporate brand image, 112*f*
perspective, 189
Co-destruction in CCs, 378–381
Cognitive-affective theories, 327
Cognitive alignment, 236
Cognitive appraisal theories, 328
Cognitive-based theories, 54
Cognitive constructs, 310
brand attachment, 310–311
brand storytelling, 311
Cognitive fluency, 236
Cohen, E., 137
Cohort management strategy, 10
Co-innovator, 112
Coleman, D., 99–100, 102
B2B service brand identity network, 102*f*
brand identity model, 101–102
Collaboration, 11, 516, 518, 600
Collaborative innovation, 379
Collective interviews, 345–346
Collectivist cultures, 317, 527
Collins, M., 137
Co-marketer, 112
Communicating brand identity, role of logo elements in, 83–87
Communication, 517, 562–563
challenges, 514
metrics, 418
process, 557
strategies, 509
Communitarian perspective, 447
Community, 375, 377, 381
administrators, 365
approach, 21, 27, 29
building, 533, 540
community-based SR, 474
conceptualizations of, 378

criticism, 376
engagement, 315, 318, 380
influences, 315
involvement, 511
managers, 381
members, 384
participation, 316
Company brands, 37
Comparability, 282
Compelling storytelling, 485
Competitive aggressiveness, 293
Complex crises, 262
Complex morality, 450
Compound annual growth rate (CAGR), 205
Comprehensive style guide, 77
Computer, 24–25
computer-owned agents, 268
technology, 9
Conglomerates, 283
Congruity theory, 562
Connected brand ecosystems, 541–542
Connection, 561–562
Conscience, 622–623, 627, 629
Conscientious brands, 620*f*, 622–625, 628
Conscientious business, 622, 624–625
Conscientious corporate brands (CCBs), 624
Consequences, 455–458, 511–512
Consistency, 488, 490
Conspicuous consumption, 274, 360
Conspicuousness, 279, 282
Constant brands marketers, 74
Constructive authenticity, 134
Consumer-based brand equity (CBBE), 147–148, 153, 155–157, 162
Aaker's model, 151
integrating EBBE with, 169
Keller's model, 151–152
key components of perceptual brand equity, 153–154
modelling and measurement, 151
Yoo and Donthu model, 152–153
Consumer culture theory, 375, 592
Consumer-market level BPIs, 404
brand advantage, 405
brand associations, 405
brand awareness, 404–405
brand consideration, 405
brand equity, 409
brand loyalty, 409
brand preference, 409
consumer-market level brand performance measures, 406*t*–408*t*
purchase intention, 405
Consumer-Mindset Metrics (CMMs), 431–432, 439
Consumer packaged goods (CPG), 434
Consumer(s), 23–26, 52, 73, 121, 236, 239, 252, 284, 314–316, 324, 328, 331–332, 355, 359, 367, 385, 451, 469, 484, 495–496, 504, 571, 581, 620, 627
animosity, 327
awareness, 455
behavior, 147, 596
brand as linked with consumer associations, 24–25
computer, 25
consumer- and customer-centric organizations, 9–10
consumer-based approach, 24–25
consumer-based perspective, 429
consumer-based study, 475
consumer–brand attachment theories, 328, 330–331
consumer–brand interactions online, 121
consumer–brand relationships theory, 120, 248, 249*f*, 252, 326
consumer-focused brand morality, 449–450
consumer-focused morality, 451
consumer-market indicators, 403, 415
consumer-related characteristics, 238
culture, 385
data, 6, 582
dispositions, 57–58, 57*t*
distrust, 566
electronics industry, 593
empowerment, 485
engagement, xxiii
experience research, 348
focused morality, 449
happiness, 523
involvement, 359
logo execution across consumer touchpoints, 88–89
negative emotions towards brands, 323
observations, 533
participation, 360, 364
perspectives, 19
prefer global brands, 53–54
professionalization of consumer knowledge, 6
research, 25, 522
researchers, 375
satisfaction, 523
understanding ageing consumers engage with brands, 613–615
well-being, 63, 523
Consumption communities (CCs), 373–374
brief history from theoretical perspective, 375–378
co-creation and co-destruction in, 378–381
future research, 385
measurement, 381–385
in practice, 374–375
sources of value co-creation in, 379*t*–380*t*
synthesis and takeaways, 385–386
tentative chronology of, 378*t*
value co-creation and value co-destruction measurement, 382*t*
Contemporary conspicuous luxury, 280–281

Contemporary crisis, 260
Contemporary inconspicuous luxury, 282
Content analysis, 169, 364, 558
Content-based approaches, 126
Content-based studies, 125
Content marketing, 296, 365
  in shaping brand engagement, 365–366
Content Style, 562–563
Contextual elements, 577
Contextual factors, 577–579
Contextual moderators, 317
  economic conditions, 317
  individualism–collectivism, 317
Contractual agreements, 565
Conventional banking, 164
Convergent validity, 471
Conversational AI, 78
Coombs' model, 260
Cooperation perspective, moral as, 453
Core brand values, 456–457, 542
Corporate branding, 33, 35, 290, 295
  idea of, 24
Corporate brand management, xxii, 180–181, 190
  Balmer's AC^{3}ID Test/AC^{4}ID Test of, 183–185
  benchmarks, 181–182
Corporate brand orientation, 179
  corporate brand identification provides foundation for, 179–180
  importance of, 178–179
Corporate brand(s), 33–34, 37–39, 177–178, 189–190, 290, 468
  architecture, 186–187
  building, 299
  canon, 38
  co-creation of, 188–189
  corporate brand-scape, 34
  corporate identity, 42–43
  corporate image and corporate reputation, 43–44
  covenant, 179, 38–39
  differences between corporate and product brands, 40*t*–41*t*
  emergence of, 44–45
  evangelists, 44
  formation,
  formation and significance of corporate identity, total corporate brand communication and corporate brand image, 39–42, 42*f*
  historical origins, 35–37
  identification provides foundation for corporate brand orientation, 179–180
  identity, 105, 108*f*, 109
  management, 34
  as organization's lodestar, 183–186
  partnerships, 263, 265
  and product brands differences, 39
  scholarship, 37
  terrorists, 44
  total corporate communications, 43
  valuations, 178, 474
  through vector of corporate brand communication, 182–183
  weaknesses and strengths, 190
Corporate brands alignment, 183
  corporate marketing/multi-disciplinary approach, 183–185
  management/organisational behaviour approach of Hatch & Schultz, 185–186
  model by Balmer, 184*f*–185*f*
Corporate brand SR, 473
  brand social responsibility, 475*f*
  and corporate brand valuation, 474
  and customer-based brand equity, 475
  reciprocal effects of, 476
Corporate communication, 101
Corporate culture, 101, 184
Corporate identity, 38, 42–44, 101, 105, 199, 290
  alignment, 183
  brand as linked to, 23–24
  corporate brand formation and significance of, 39–44
  traits, 44
Corporate image, 43–44
Corporate marketing orientation, 178–179
  corporate brand identification provides foundation for corporate brand orientation, 179–180
  importance of, 178–179
Corporate reputation, 43–44, 104
  co-creation of, 107–114
Corporate social responsibility (CSR), 28, 104, 156, 159, 263, 448, 467–468, 496, 509, 619, 628
Corporate social responsibility orientation (CSRO), 456*t*, 457
Corporate Sustainability Due Diligence Directive (CSDDD), 621
Corporate Sustainability Reporting Directive (CSRD), 621
Corporate trademarks, use of, 36
Corporate visual identity, 89
Corporate wrongdoing, 330
Cortez, M., 123
Cost–benefit analysis, 251
Cost-effectiveness, 419, 559
Costello, J. P., 222
Country of origin (COO), 59, 220
  foreign branding and COO effects, 220
Country stereotypes, compensatory strategies based on, 59–60
Cova, B., 375–376
Covenant, 38, 44
COVID-19, 451, 459
  pandemic, 63, 156
Crane, A., 495
Creative brand-naming strategies and future directions, 222–223
Creator economy, 557–558
Credibility, 181, 560–561

Crisis, 261, 265
AI as crisis oracle, 266–267
mitigating digital misinformation during, 268
Crisis communication, 259, 266
AI as crisis oracle, 266–267
DRT, 260–261
ethical AI paradigm, 267
evolving challenges, 261–262
integrated crisis management strategies, 262–264
practical integration of AI in crisis management, 264–266
recommendations for future research, 268–269
research implications and future trajectories, 267–268
SCCT, 260
theories in principle and practice, 260
Crisis management, 259
ethics in, 269
practical integration of AI in, 264–266
Cristini, H., 275
Criticism, 4, 497, 500
Cross-cultural and industry applications of EBBE, 164–165
Cross-cultural crisis response analysis, 269
Cross-cultural research, 61
Cross-cultural studies, 168
Cross-industry co-branding, 233
Cross-industry crisis response analysis, 269
Cross-referencing metrics, 386
Crystallisation, 44
Culotta, A., 419
Cultural approach, 21, 27–28
Cultural aspects, 527
Cultural branding, 495–496
Cultural changes, 29
Cultural contexts, expanding EBBE across, 168
Cultural destigmatisation of disability on social media, 486–487
Cultural differences, 69
Cultural factors, 515
Cultural iconicity, 52
Cultural integration, 75
Cultural involvement, 527
Culturally mixed symbolic products (CMPSs), 58
Cultural orientation, 317–318
Cultural perceptions, 515
Cultural sensitivity, 263
Cultural values, 317
Curry, O. S., 453
Custodianship, 181
Customer acquisition cost (CAC), 384
Customer-based brand equity (CBBE), 25, 232, 397, 475
Customer-Behaviour Metrics (CBMs), 431–432, 439
Customer brand,
bonds, 245
engagement, 356
identification, 360
relationships, 359–360
Customer journey, 342, 344, 364, 431, 613, 615
designing brand experience through, 340
model, 613
Customer lifetime value (CLV), 383
Customer relationship management (CRM), 9, 299, 589, 596
Customer(s), 33, 39
acquisition and retention, 297
customer-based strategy, 350
customer-centric approach, 364–365
customer-centric branding, 297
customer-corporate identification, 473
customer–stakeholders relationships, 38
data privacy, 596
delight, 360
engagement, 356, 361
research methodologies to understand customers throughout journey, 340, 341*t*
trust, 43
Customer Satisfaction Index (CSI), 437
Customized brand experiences, 338–339
Cutler, J., 419
Cybersecurity, 540
Cybex©, 562

Daecke, N., 10
Dastidar, G., 123
Data, 341
analysis, 346, 347, 590
collection, 29, 204, 344, 347, 599
data-driven brand innovation, 541
data-driven performance measurement, 540
experts, 10–11
rise of, 9
Datafication,
adaptation of brand management system to, 9
consumer- and customer-centric organizations, 9–10
facilitators and data experts, 10–11
prospective outlook on GenAI, 11–12
rise of data and data analytics, 9
transformations brought by, 9
Datta, H., 410
Davis, J. A., 438
Davis, S. M., 430
Davvetas, V., 54, 56, 58
Decision-making process, 290, 599, 628
de Chernatony, L., 99–102
brand identity model, 99, 99*f*
Dedoose tool, 384
Deepfakes, 544
Deep learning, 589
De Gauquier, L., 124
Deglobalization, 50
Democratization, 275, 277
Demographic factors, 579
De Mooij, M., 421
Deontological criterion, 627

Deontological ethics perspectives, 453
Deontological perspective, 447, 451–452, 457
Deryl, M., 590
Descriptive names, 217–218
De Swaan A. M., 10
De Veirman, M., 561
De Vries, E. L. E., 561
Dew, R., 90
Dhiman, N., 523
Diagnosticity multiplier, 60
Dialogic communication, 262
Dialogue-based approach, 26
Diamantopoulos, A., 54, 57–58
Dierksmeier, C., 627
Differentiation, 292
Digital age, 377, 503
Digital Asset Management (DAM), 77
Digital assets, 541
Digital-based measurement techniques, 126
Digital-based methods to study brand personality, 124–126
Digital-based research, 126
Digital brand personality, 121–122, 126
 different perspectives and angles taken to conceptualize, 120*t*
 future of, 126–127
 research, 124–125
 theories and characteristics of, 119–121
Digital brand presence, 318
Digital collaboration tools, 542
Digital communication, 166
Digital communities, 505
Digital consumer, 118
 behavior, 409
Digital contexts, 122, 126
 brand personality research across, 121–122
 new technologies, 123–124
 social media platforms, 122–123
 websites, e-stores and apps, 122
Digital conversation, 502
Digital corporate communication, 182
Digital ecosystem, 566
Digital engagement, 564
Digital environments, 318
Digital era, 339, 376, 509, 557
Digital experiences, 350
Digital-first approach, 280
Digital footprint, 503
Digital innovations, 90
Digitalization, 156
 adaptation of brand management system to, 9
 consumer- and customer-centric organizations, 9–10
 facilitators and data experts, 10–11
 prospective outlook on GenAI, 11–12
 rise of data and data analytics, 9
 transformations brought by, 9
Digital landscape, 497
Digital marketing, 76
 agencies, 558
Digital media, 121
Digital media platforms, 89
 adaptation to new, 89–91
Digital metrics, 419
Digital platforms, 89, 377, 517, 534, 537, 542, 611
 leveraging, 516–517
Digital revolution, 538
Digital rights management systems, 540
Digital spaces, 497
Digital storytelling, 486, 517
Digital technology, xxiii, 9, 124, 127, 297, 338, 419, 557
Digital tools, 297, 338, 516
Digital touchpoints, 88, 122
Digital transformation, 338–339, 350–351, 537
 brand experience and impact of, 338–340, 339*f*
 challenges in brand experience, 351
 consumption step, 345
 designing brand experience through customer journey map, 340
 ethnographic and netnography analyses, 346
 experimental design, 350
 funding, 351
 future directions, 350–351
 individual and collective interviews, 345–346
 IoT and AR, 342–343
 metaverse, 344–345
 mistery shopping, 343
 multisensory analysis, 348
 personal introspection, 348–349
 photo-elicitation, 346–347
 post-consumption step, 348
 pre-purchase step, 340–341
 purchase step, 343
 research methodologies to understand customers throughout journey, 340, 341*t*
 surveys, 349–350
 text mining, 341–342
 website analysis, 343–344
 ZMET, 347–348
Digital world, 118, 126–127
Direct-to-consumer (D2C), 212
Disability, 483, 612
 inclusion, 484–485
 Lolo Spencer and cultural destigmatisation of disability on social media, 486–487
Disability representation, 490
 on social media, 485–486
Discourse of renewal theory (DRT), 259
Discrimination, 543
Disidentification theory, 330
Disney, 487–488
Distant/weak/shallow brand relationship, 247
Diversity, 483, 487–488
Diversity, equity and inclusion (DEI), 482, 490
 conceptualising DEI in branding research, 483

disney and diversity, 487–488
future research agenda, 489*t*
future research directions, 488–490
key strategies for inclusive branding, 484–487
social identity theory & stigma theory, 483–484
theoretical perspectives, 483
Diversity and inclusion (D&I), 484
Donthu, N., 148–149, 151–152, 154–155, 162, 312
Door-to-door interviewers, 6
Double-jeopardy law, 436
Douro Azul, 201, 204–205, 207
brand portfolio at time of brand audit, 202*t*
Dow Jones Sustainability Index, 474
Doyle, J. R., 85
Dubin, J. A., 411
Duffy, S., 69, 71
Dwivedi, A., 135
Dwivedi, Y. K., 591
Dynamic concept, 274
Dynamic experience delivery, 540
Dynamic interactions, longitudinal studies on, 318
Dynasty, S., 35
Dyson, P., 148
Dzyabura, D., 126

Echeverri, P., 381
E-commerce, 212, 279, 594
platforms, 384
Economic approach, 22–23, 28
Economic consumer, 22
Economic environments, 515
Economic factors, 515
Economic happiness research, 521
Economic Impact Research (EIR), 73
Economic instability, 514–515
Economic man, 22
Economic sciences, 521
Edeling, A., 433
Effective brand identity communication, logo execution for, 87–89
Effective branding, 517
Effective communication, 509–510, 514
Effective customer experiences, 340
Effective internal communication, 394
Effective logos, 83
Effective partnerships, 509
Effective storytelling, 485
Eigenraam, A. W., 123
Ekinci, Y., 151, 563
Elaborateness, 85–86
El-Adly, M. I., 156
Electroencephalogram, 91
Electroencephalography (EEG), 543
Electronic word-of-mouth (eWOM), 331, 610
Elkanova, E., 199
ELSamen, A. A., 156
Elusive construct, 162
Emergent Corporate Brand Identity, 107
Emerging technologies, 346
role of, 318–319
Emotional AI, 544
Emotional brand, 524
values, 522
Emotional constructs, 309
brand love, 309
brand passion, 309–310
Emotional data, 342, 345
Emotional engagement, 485, 595
Emotional intelligence, 594–595, 598–599
leveraging long-term impact of, 598–599
Emotional ownership, 34
Emotional states, 357
Emotional values, 523
Emotional well-being, 528
Emotion analysis, 383
Emotions, 522
Empathy, 452
Employee-based brand equity (EBBE), 163, 397
conceptualizations and implications, 163
with consumer-based and FBBE, 169
cross-cultural and industry applications of, 164–165
across cultural and industry contexts, 168
directions for future research, 168
employee-generated content on social media, 167–168
expanding, 165
future in context of AI, 169
implications in organizational branding, 164
key conceptualizations, 172*t*
leveraging qualitative approaches and social media data for, 168–169
new frameworks and perspectives, 165
on social media, 166–167
use, 172*t*–173*t*
Employee(s), 163–168, 207, 292, 390, 394
employee-generated content on social media, 167–168
engagement, 390
influencers, 167
perspectives, 262
recruitment and retention, 298
Employer branding, 164, 298
Employment-based SR, 474
Employment relationship, 168
Endorsed approach, 187
Engagement levels, 382
Engagement metrics, 382, 386
Enhanced consumer engagement, 595–596
Enhancing transparency, 597–598
Enterprises, 599
Enthusiasm, 7, 357, 360
Entitativity, 223
Entrepreneurial approach, 294
Entrepreneurial evolution, 377
Entrepreneurial focus, 292

Entrepreneurial mindset, 292, 296
Entrepreneurial orientation, 289, 292–294
brand orientation vs., 294*f*
Entrepreneurial resourcefulness, 299
Entrepreneurial transformation, 377
Entrepreneurs, 289, 292–293, 295–297, 299
Entrepreneurship, 289, 292–294, 293*t*
Entrepreneurship literature, 293
insights from, 295–299
Environmental, Social and Governance (ESG), 467
Environmental transformation, 626
Ephemeralization, 338
Equity, 483
Escalas, J. E., 313
E-stores, 122
Ethical AI, 267–268
Ethical commitments, 262
Ethical communication, 260
Ethical considerations, 262
Ethical decision-making, 597–598
Ethical growth and renewal, 260
Ethical implications, 265
Ethicality, 610
Ethics, 448
necessary to differentiate brand morality from, 458
Ethnographic analyses, 346
Eudaimonic happiness, 533
Eudemonic happiness, 521
Events and experiences strategies in South Africa, 76
Evidence-based marketing, 430–431
Evidence-based reality, 134
Exclusive digital goods, 558
Existential authenticity, 134–135
Existentialism, 26
Expectation theory, 331
Experiential value, 276–277
Experimental design, 350
Experimental research, 350
Expertise, 295
Explicable AI, 267
Exploratory techniques, 345
Extended reality, 122
technologies, 124
External actors, 112
External branding initiatives, 397
External factors, 511
External interactions, 110
Externally facing, 186
External values, 456
Eye tracking, 91

Facebook, 166, 284, 339, 349, 366, 377, 557–558, 611
Facial expression recognition, 91
Fairness, 449, 452, 453
Fajer, M. T., 246
Fang, Y. H., 122
Farivar, S., 562
Farrelly, F. J., 135
Fashion, luxury and premium strategies, blurring boundaries between, 277–279, 278*f*
Fast fashion brands, 278, 467
Fast-moving consumer goods (FMCG), 4–5, 37, 205, 609
Fay, B., 440
Fazili, A. I., 157
Fear of missing out (FOMO), 280
Feeling AI, 11, 593, 595, 598–599
for brand emotional connection, 594–595
Feminine brand personality, 216
Femininity, 85–86, 216
Ferjani, M., 411
Fernandes, T., 625
Ferreira, P., 168–169, 397
Fetscherin, M., 250
Field, P., 430
Financial resources, 413
Financial sustainability, 513
Financial Times (newspaper), 7
Financial-based brand equity (FBBE), 169, 397
integrating EBBE with, 169
Financial-market indicators, 413
Financial-market level BPIs, 411–413
Financial-market metrics, 403
Fine, G. A., 135
Firm value, 403, 412
Fishbein, M., 591
Fitness industry, 374
Five-factor model, 121
Flavor innovation, 75
Floyd, K., 439
Focus groups, 345, 558
Follower Fit, 562
Fombrun, C. J., 104–105
Food brands, 218
For-profit sector, adapting and reinventing brand context from, 517
Ford, H., 3
Foroudi, P., 89
Forward-looking change, 260
Fosso Wamba, S., 11
Fostering emotional engagement, 165
Fournier, S., 26, 246, 328, 523
Fowler, K., 558
France, C., 361
Freberg, K., 167
Freire, J. R., 198
Frías-Jamilena, D. M., 152, 155
Fritz, K., 133, 135
Fullerton, R. A., 6–7
Functional associations, 105
Functional brand relationship, 248
Functional diffuse optical tomography (fDOT), 348
Functional magnetic resonance imaging (fMRI), 91, 348, 405
Functional value, 54, 276, 523

Gallup, 6, 521
Galvanic skin response, 91
Gambetti, R. C., 380
Game elements, 573, 578–581
    contribution and future research, 581
    future research, 582–583
    managerial recommendations, 582
    role of game elements in driving brand outcomes, 575–581
    scientific contribution, 581–582
    typology of game elements in brand strategy, 573–575, 574*t*
    understanding gamification, 572–575
Games, 572, 575
    technique, 573
Gamification, 312, 360, 571–572, 577, 581–583, 595
    definition and characteristics, 572–573
    designs, 573
    effectiveness, 582
    elements, 582
    game elements, 573
    typology of game elements in brand strategy, 573–575, 574*t*
    understanding, 572
Gamified brand activations, 582
Garcia, E., 390
Gardner, B., 212
Gender, 579, 612
General Data Protection Regulation (GDPR), 367
Generational cohorts, 606
    segmentation by, 605–606
Generation technologies, 541
Generation X, 606
Generative artificial intelligence (GenAI), 4, 78, 90, 139, 265, 404, 419, 544
    applications, 127
    for communication, 264
    prospective outlook on, 11–12
Gen Z, 53, 367
Geuens, M., 121, 124
Ghose, S., 235
Gilal, F. G., 313
Gilmore, J. H., 133
Gilovich, T., 522
Global brand cultural capital (GBCC), 52
Global brand cultural iconicity (GBCI), 52–53
Global branding, 50
    literature, 52, 57
    MarTech in, 77
Global brand management, xxii
    let us get smart on marketing AI for, 78–79
Global brand(s), 8, 50–51, 53, 59, 63, 73
    advantage still strong, 54–57
    benefits of, 69
    boundary conditions, 57
    category social signaling, 58–59
    compensatory strategies based on country stereotypes, 59–60
    consumer dispositions, 57–58, 57*t*
    consumers prefer global brands, 53–54
    cultivate cultural iconicity, 61
    definition and conceptualization of, 51–53
    functional and psychological benefits of, 53*f*
    future research agenda, 61–63, 62*t*
    halo effect, 54
    hybrid/hybridization strategies, 60–61
    methodological approaches used in global branding literature, 61
    origin-based strategies, 59
    pathways to global brand preference, 53–54
    preference framework, 51*f*
    product-/category-level characteristics, 58
    strategies employed by, 59
    theoretical foundations of global brand preference, 54
    theories used in global branding literature, 55*t*
Global consumer culture (GCC), 50
Global consumer culture positioning (GCCP), 53
Global consumers, 482
Global developments, 70
Global equals better, 54–56
Globalization, 50, 53–54
    of brands, 7–8
Global warming, 623
Glocalization, 74, 76
Glocalized brand campaign examples, 74–75
Goillart, F., 188
Goldfarb, A., 411
Goldstein, E., 485
Good hunters, 297
Goodpaster, K. E., 622
Google, 9, 590, 595
Government barriers, 514
Goyard, 281
Grace, D., 163–165, 397
Graffigna, G., 380
Graham, J., 452
Grayson, K., 134–135, 137
Great Western Railway (GWR), 36
Green, B. P., 598
Green brand authenticity, 139
Greenhouse gas emissions, 621
Greenpeace, 509, 621
Grégoire, Y., 123
Gretzel, U., 122
Greyser, S. A., 37
Grohs, R., 394
Guest-Based Hotel Equity (GBHE), 156
Guided techniques, 345–346
Guido, G., 89
Guo, X., 58, 60–61
Gupta, V., 9
Gürhan-Canli, Z., 60
Guzmán, F., 625
Gyrd-Jones, R. I., 107, 108*f*, 109–110

Haidt, J., 452
Halinen, A., 110, 111*f*
Halkias, G., 59
Hallucinations, 78
Hammedi, W., 583
Han, J., 523, 560
Handelman, J. M., 376
Hankinson, P., 509
Hanssens, D. M., 411
Hao, J., 61
Happiness, 521–522
  relevance of happiness research in brand management, 521–522
  research, 521
Hardcastle, K., 381
Harlow, W., 485
Harris Interactive's EquiTrend, 418
Hart, L., 487
Harvard Business Review (magazine), 7
Hasni, M. J. S., 396–397
Hatch, M. J., 23, 38, 185–186
  management/organisational behaviour approach of, 185–186
Havaianas Pride, 509
Haviv, A., 411
Haws, K. L., 222
Healy, J. C., 380
Heavy usage index, 434
Hedonic happiness, 521, 533
Hedonic pricing models, 410
Hedonic products, 541
Heinberg, M., 314
Helm, S., 317
Helmig, B., 236
Henderson, C. M., 483
Heritage-driven conspicuous luxury, 281
Heritage-driven inconspicuous luxury, 281–282
Hermann, E., 544
Hermeneutic of continuity, 188–189
Hermeneutic of disruption, 188–189
Hesse, A., 166
Heterosexual consumer, 484
Hill, T., 377
Himme, A., 433
Hofer, K. M., 394
Hofstede, G., 317, 421
Hogan, R., 125
Högberg, J., 361
Holbrook, M. B., 347
Holistic crisis communication models, 262
Hollebeek, L. D., 156, 234, 312, 361
Holt, D. B., 27
Homburg, C., 9
Homophily, 484
Honesty, 452, 457
Hoppe, D., 396
Horizontal co-branding, 232
Horton, D., 561
Hospitality applications, 156–157
Howe, N., 605
Hsieh, M. H., 52, 421
Hu, J., 124
Hu, M., 60
Huang, M. H., 590, 598
Huang, Y., 381
Hudders, L., 558, 563, 566
Hughes, C., 366, 563
Human influencers, 566
Human intelligence, 589
Humanitarian organizations, 460
Humanity, 453
Human-like character, brand as, 25–26
Human personality model, 121, 470
Human resources, 101, 413, 415, 589
Hutchinson, D., 624
Hybrid contexts, 376
Hybrid economies, 376
Hybrid strategies, 60–61
Hybridization strategies, 60–61
Hypodermic Needle Theory, 72

Iconic authenticity, 134–135
Iconic brand, 27
Identity, 24
  approach, 23–24, 28
  currency, 54
  identity-based models, 186
  type, 33
Ideological discourse, 27
Iglesias, O., 10, 390
Ilicic, J., 138, 455
Im, H. H., 155
Image, 153
  incongruence, 251
Immersion elements, 573
Immersive brand experiences, 541
Immersive experiences, 516
Immersive gamification, 579
Immersive interactive environments, 583
Implicit association test (IAT), 348
Inauthentic inclusion, 488
In-branch promotions, 76
Inclusive branding,
  disability representation and storytelling on social media, 485–487
  key strategies for, 484
  storytelling and disability inclusion, 484–485
  strategies, 484
Inclusive brands, 482
Inclusive storytelling, 490
Inclusivity, 485
  integrating inclusivity into branding research, 488–490
Inconspicuousness, 279, 282
Ind, N., 624
In-depth interviews, 345

In-depth qualitative research, 613
Indexical authenticity, 134
Individual factors, 579
Individual-level moderators, 316
need for uniqueness, 316–317
self-brand connection strength, 316
Individual interviews, 345–346
Individualism–collectivism cultural orientation, 317
Industrial Marketing Management, 625
Industry contexts, expanding EBBE across, 168
Influencer effect,
4Cs of influencers impacting effectiveness, 560*f*
characteristics of source, 560–561
communication, 562–563
comprehensive review of influencer marketing research, 558
congruence, 562
connection, 561–562
diminishing authenticity through over-exposure and excessive control, 563–564
future research agenda, 563
future research avenues, 564*t*
harming brand reputation, 564–566
impact on children, 566
influencer marketing research methodologies, 558–559
influencer marketing research themes, 559
influencers as strategic approach to brand promotion, 559
rise of influencers in modern marketing, 557
social media influencers and creator economy, 557–558
underlying mechanisms explaining effectiveness, 560
virtual influencers and consumer distrust, 566
Influencer marketing, 364–365, 556–557
exploring dark side of influencer marketing effectiveness, 563
industry, 557
in shaping brand engagement, 365–366
Influencer(s), 167, 556–558, 561–562
4Cs of, 560
activism, 513
congruence, 562
Information integration theory, 234
Information science drivers, 592–593
Information velocity, 261
Informativeness, 221
Ingredient branding, 232
Innovation process transformation, 542
Innovative brand image, 86
Innovativeness, 293
Inspiration porn, 485
Instagram, 165, 284, 339, 349, 366, 377, 499, 557–558, 613
Institutional economics, 61
Integrated approach, 262
Integrated communication, 263
Integrated crisis,
comparative effectiveness of, 268
management strategies, 262–264
Integrated marketing communications (IMCs), 136, 157, 263
and impact on brand equity, 157–158
Integrated Retailer Brand Equity (IRBE), 165
Integrity, 452
Intellectual experiences, 615
Intelligent society, 598
Intensity, 497
Intentionality, 457
Interactions, 110
data, 342
interactive network branding's three types of, 111*f*
Interactivity, 581
Interbrand data, 418–419
Interdependence theory, 508
Internal actions, 509
Internal brand communications, 394
Internal branding, 292, 298, 390, 399, 511
current status of, 391–392
dimensions of internal branding, 395*f*
expected outcomes of internal branding and guidelines for measurement, 394–394
final reflections and future research agenda, 397–399
guide to implementing internal branding based on dimensions, 392–394
measure outcomes of, 395*t*
process, 392
program, 397
Internal factors, 510–511
Internal interactions, 110
Internally facing, 186
Internal marketing approach, 390
Internal values, 456
International brand, 69
International Hotel Group, 177
International Sustainability Standards Board (ISSB), 621
Internet industry, 222
Internet of things (IoT), 122, 341–343, 514
Interpersonal relationships, 247, 484
Intersectional crises, 262
Intersectional identities, 490
Intersectionality, 612
Intrapersonal authenticity, 135
Investor appeal, 299
Invisible hand, 22
Inward articulation, 222
Inward names, 222
Irrelevant names, 218
Islamic banking, 164
Isomorphism, 61

Jackson, F. H., 138
Jackson, M., 610
Jacobson, J., 167

James, D., 235
Jeffery, M., 430
Jeffries, M., 610
Jiang, H., 379
Jiang, Z., 156
Jiménez, F. R., 311
Jin, S. V., 124, 563
Jno-Charles, A. B., 566
Joachimsthaler, E., 186–187, 207
John Lewis Partnership, 449, 457
Jordan, M., 315
Joshi, Y., 558
Jun, S., 138

Kachersky, L., 222
Kaji, R., 557
Kalafatis, S. P., 235
Kalra, A., 483
Kannan, P. K., 419
Kant, I., 622
Kantar BrandZ, 419
Kapferer, J. N., 38, 99–102, 148
  brand prism, 99–101, 100*f*
Kaplan, R. S., 429
Katsikeas, C. S., 403, 431
Keiningham, T. L., 437
Keith, R., 7
Keller, K. L., 24–25, 102, 146, 148–149, 151–156, 162, 295, 403–404, 413, 430
Kelley, H., 236
Kellogg's cereal for dinner case study, 498–503
#KelloggsBoycott, 502
Key readings, 19
Khan, U., 483
Kim, J., 121
Kimpakorn, N., 396
Kinder, Lydenberg and Domini (KLD) Research, 474
King, C., 163–166, 168, 397
King, S., 37
Kirkby, A., 590
Kirmani, A., 455
Kleyn, N., 625
Klink, R. R., 214, 216, 218
Knox, S., 38
Köllen, T., 623
Koporcic, N., 110, 111*f*
Kotler, P., 495
Kozinets, R. V., 376, 377
Kraft, 75
Kramer, M. R., 512, 623
Kuehnl, C., 220
Kuhn, T., 19, 29
Kumar, A., 523
Kumar, J., 360
Kumar, V., 361
Kunkel, T., 578
Kwon, Y., 165

Labrecque, L. I., 85
Lafferty, B., 236
Laforet, S., 198
Landers, R. N., 581
Language, 562–563
  and pronunciation differences, 70
  translation and transliteration, 220–221
Lanseng, E. J., 234
Large language models (LLMs), 11, 420
Latent Corporate Brand Identity, 107
Leadership, 293, 510–511
Lechner, P., 624
Lee, D., 123
Lee, Z., 484
Legal ownership, 34
Legal requirements, 621–622
Lehmann, D. R., 162, 295, 403–405, 413, 430
Lehtonen, M. J., 381
Leigh, T. W., 134
Lemon, K. N., 441
Letters in brand names, 213
Leung, F. F., 558
Levy, S., 212
Lewis, J., 453
Li, M., 381
Li, X., 90
Lin, Y. T., 312
Lindblom, A., 8
Lindgreen, A., 291
Line extensions, 221–222
Lingua franca, 178
Linguistic analysis, 126
LinkedIn, 165–166
Little general manager, 7
Liu, H., 52
Living Planet Index, 619
Local communities, 381
Local culture, icon of, 53
Local iconness, 53, 60
Local Interpretable Model-agnostic Explanations (LIME), 267
Localized brand performance, 70
Logo execution, 87
  across consumer touchpoints, 88–89
  for effective brand identity communication, 87
  processing fluency theory, 87–88
Logo(s), 83, 88
  color, 84–85
  conceptual framework in, 84*f*
  elements role in communicating brand identity, 83–84
  in evolving business landscapes, 89–91
  frame, 86
  future research directions, 91–92, 92*t*
  interplay among logo elements, 87
  shape, 85–86
  typeface, 86
Lomauto, 216

London Stock Exchange Group (LSEG), 199
Longer names, 217
Long sales cycles, 296
Long-term value creation, 297
Lopez, A., 455
Lou, C., 563
Louis Vuitton, 281
Loureiro, S. M. C., 135–137, 141, 596
Lowe, M. L., 222
Lowrey, T., 223
Loyalty, 27, 315–316, 438
    value creation, 297
Luedicke, M. K., 522–523
Luffarelli, J., 85
Lusch, R. F., 155
Luxury, 274–275
    brand equity in luxury tourism, 157
    branding, 485
    fashion brand, 314, 485
    pricing, 71
    sector, 157
Luxury branding strategy, 280
    blurring boundaries between luxury, fashion and premium strategies, 277–279, 278*f*
    contemporary conspicuous luxury, 280–281
    contemporary inconspicuous luxury, 282
    defining meaning(s) of luxury, 274–276
    emerging challenges in, 283
    exploring, 276–277
    heritage-driven conspicuous luxury, 281
    heritage-driven inconspicuous luxury, 281–282
    introducing framework for evolving, 279–280, 280*f*
    key aspects of, 276*f*
    key concepts in current, 283*f*
    key insights from framework, 282–283
    rise of new technologies, 283–284
    rise of sustainability and circularity, 284
Luxury brands, 275, 277, 280–282, 284, 318, 374
    core elements of, 275*t*
Lv, L., 139
Lyu, J., 156

Machine learning, 91, 339, 589
    algorithms, 539–542, 593
    models, 543
    techniques, 594
Macro influencers, 561
Madhavaram, S., 157
Magic-bullet marketers, 72
Magic bullet theory, 72–73
Malär, L., 313, 316
Mäläskä, M., 107, 109–110, 109*f*, 111*f*, 112–113
Mamali, E., 376–377
Management behaviour approach of Hatch & Schultz, 185
Managerial characteristics, 510
Managerial keywords, 19
Mancuso, J., 311
Mandler, T., 52, 56, 58–60
Mangold, G., 163
Mantau, A., 220
Market,
    dynamics, 411
    leaders, 438
    segmentation, 605–606
    uncertainty, 105
Marketers, 607–608, 613, 615
    skew for marketers to develop new products for younger consumers, 610–611
Marketing, 22, 76, 393, 508
    activities, 430
    drivers, 592
    investments, 415
    let us get smart on marketing AI for global brand management, 78–79
    literature, 137, 391, 468
    management, 573
    managers, 394
    organizations, 8
    research, 522, 574
    researchers, 375
    revolution, 7
Market research, 6
    professionalization of, 6
Market share, 409, 411, 433–434
    components of m, 434
    heavy usage index, 434
    impact, 384
    penetration rate, 434–435
    premium, 409–410
    price index, 434
    share-in-shops handling, 436–437
    SOW, 435–436
    trial rate, 435
    weighted distribution, 436
Marr, B., 430
MarTech enabling brand's global consistency, 77–78
Martinec, R., 134–135, 137
Masiello, B., 123
Materialism, 360
Matson-Barkat, S., 484
Matsubara, Y., 528
Matten, D., 495
Matthews, J. B., 622
Mazodier, M., 234
McAlexander, J. H., 375
McCarthy, J., 589
McCormick, K., 487
McDonagh, P., 380
McDonald, R., 135
McElroy, N. H., 3–4
    memo, 5, 15–17
Mechanical AI, 9, 11, 593, 595, 596–597
    for brand efficiency and consistency, 593
Mecredy, P., 433

Media,
channels, 110
metrics, 418
Mediator, product brand SR as, 473
Medinge Group, 624
Meißner, M., 139
Mena, T., 487
Mende, M., 484
Menon, G., 216
Mensah-Schramm, I., 608
Mental health studies, 346
Mercer, J., 36
Merunka, D., 137, 234
Meta-analysis, 238
Metaphors, 246, 347
Metaverse, 344–345
Metrics for qualitative interpretation, 364
Microeconomics, 22
Micro-influencers, 561
Microsoft, 50, 98, 374
Micro-targeting, 595
Miles, S. J., 163
Millennials, 606, 609
Milne, G. R., 85
Minimal logo design, 90
Minsky, L., 72
Mint Personal Finance App, 594
Miquela, L., 566
Misinformation, 262, 268
management, 264
Mistery shopping, 343
Mixed reality (MR), 124
Mixed symbolic products (CMSPs), 60
Mobile technologies, 582
Model T, 3
Moderate incongruity, 236
Moderator, product brand SR as, 473
Modernism, 279, 282
Modern luxury, 275
brands, 281
Modern marketing, 72
rise of influencers in, 557
Modern organizations, 261
Modern simplicity, 90
Modern technologies, 348
Mogilner, C., 522
Mokhtar, S. S., 168
Momfluencers, 562
Monolithic approach, 187
Moon, H., 141
Moorman, C., 488
Moral as cooperation perspective, 453
Moral belief, 622
Moral branding, 449
Moral cooperation (MaC), 449
Moral foundation,
perspective, 452–453
theory, 453
Moral identity, 450
Moralistic brand endeavors, 453
Moralistic communication, 449
Moralituition, 267
Morality, 447–448
Moral satisfaction, 528
Moral stewardship, 267
Morgan, J. E., 624
Morgan, N. A., 433
Morhart, F., 135, 314
Motameni, R., 148
Moulard, J. G., 134
Mukherjee, A., 190
Multinational corporations (MNCs), 122
Multiplicity, 453
Multisensory analysis, 348
Multisensory sculpting (MSS) method, 348
Multi-stakeholder engagement frameworks, 269
Muñiz, A. M. J., 375
Murdoch, R., 8
Musk, E., 69
Myspace, 611
Mystery shopping, 343

Nagel, T., 622
Naidoo, V., 234
Nam, H., 419
Nano influencers, 561
Napoli, J., 135
National Biscuit Company, 74
National Brand Equity model, 421
Natural language processing (NLP), 539, 541–543, 589, 594
Natural tendency, 359
Nayak, J. K., 360
Negative appraisals, 329
Negative brand,
emotions, 329
nostalgic emotions, 326–327
relationship, 247
Negative emotions towards brands, 323, 323*t*
anticipated separation distress, 324–325
appraisal theories and cognitive perspectives, 329–330
brand dislike, 325
brand embarrassment, 325
brand hate, 325–326
brand jealousy, 326
brand-related schadenfreude, 326
consumer–brand attachment, 330–331
first quadrant, 328
fourth quadrant, 329
negative brand nostalgic emotions, 326–327
second quadrant, 328–329
social identity theory, 332
social influence theory, 331–332
theoretical frameworks and research agenda, 329
theoretical grid on, 328*t*

theoretical perspectives on, 327–328
third quadrant, 329
types of, 323–324
Negative sentiment ratio, 383
Negative word of mouth (NWoM), 247
Neslin, S. A., 441
Netflix, 338, 374
Netnography analyses, 346
Net Promoter Score (NPS), 283, 437
Networking, 11
Network(s), 295
analysis, 558
network-based methods, 240
Netzer, O., 419
Neurodiversity, 490
Neuroimaging,
data, 419
techniques, 348, 419
Neuroscience, 347
New technologies, 121, 123–124
rise of, 283–284
Nicolao, L., 522
Niedermeier, A., 523
Nielsen, 6
Nobi, B., 523
Noncommercial mindset, 513–514
Non-fungible tokens (NFTs), 283, 541
Non-product-related factors, 477
Nonprofit brand orientation (NBO), 509
antecedents, 510
antencedents, consequences and barriers to, 510
barriers, 513
communication challenges, 514
community involvement, 511
consequences, 511–512
enhanced reputation, 512
external factors, 511
government barriers, 514
increased influence and benchmark status, 513
internal factors, 510–511
noncommercial mindset, 513–514
organizational culture, 514
resource acquisition and financial sustainability, 513
resource limitations, 514
short-term focus, 514
staff engagement and alignment, 512
strengthened partnerships, 512–513
Nonprofit branding, 509, 518
adapting and reinventing brand context from for-profit sector, 517
addressing resource scarcity, 515–516
challenges in, 515
leveraging digital platforms, 516–517
navigating stakeholder complexity, 516
strategies for, 515
Nonprofit companies, 512
Nonprofit landscape, 508
Nonprofit organizations (NPOs), 508
advantages in developed countries, 515
antencedents, consequences and barriers to NBO, 510–514
brand orientation in nonprofits, 509–510
challenges in emerging countries, 514–515
challenges in nonprofit branding, 515
context differences, 514
cultural and economic factors, 515
innovations and strengths in emerging markets, 515
research agenda, 517–518
strategies for nonprofit branding, 515–517
Nonprofit sector, 514, 518
Nonprofit stakeholders, 517
Non-transactional effectiveness, 559
Non-transactional outcomes, 560
Norton, D. P., 429
Numbers in brand names, 213–214
Nunes, J. C., 135
NVivo tool, 384

Objective authenticity, 134–135
Offline contexts, 361
O'Guinn, T. C., 375
Okazaki, S., 122
Older consumers, 606–610
stereotyping of, 606–608
Older people, 607
Olins, W., 186–187
Oliver, R. L., 312
Olkkonen, R., 8
Olsen, L. E., 234, 624, 628
OneBiz, 201
Online,
collaboration tools, 77
communities, 346, 361
contexts, 361
firestorms, 332
Online brand community, 364
contexts, 360
interplay between online brand communities and brand engagement, 365
OpenAI, 11
Open-ended techniques, 345–346
Openness, 456, 623
Open-source communities, 379
Opinion leaders, 557
Opportunism, 246
Opportunity recognition, 293
Optimism, 260, 266
Oreo cookie, 75, 232
Organisational behaviour approach of Hatch & Schultz, 185
Organisational identity, 186
Organisational members, 179
Organization, 169, 186, 259, 263, 378, 381, 392, 394, 477, 508, 510, 514–517, 537, 540, 544, 623, 627
corporate brand as organization's lodestar, 183–186
Organizational branding, implications of EBBE in, 164

Organizational buying process, 297
Organizational culture, 514
Organizational introspection, 260
Organizational learning, 260
Organizational maturity, 511
Organizational performance, 397
Organizational structure, 394
Origin-based strategies, 59
Outward articulation, 222
Overall brand equity (OBE), 152
Özer, L., 152
Özsomer, A., 52, 56, 58, 60

Package size, 75
Packaging design, 87
Pan, M., 560, 562
Panda, N. M., 104–105
Panel regression study, 474
Pansari, A., 361
Parasocial relationship (PSR), 562, 564, 566
Parfit, D., 623
Park, C. W., 311
Participation rate, 382
Particular emphasis, 146
Partners, 167
Partnerships, 76, 512
  strengthened, 512–513
Passion,
  brand relationships types based on level of, 248–250, 249*f*
  high passion, 248–249
  lack of passion, 250
  low passion, 249–250
Pauwels, K., 409, 421
Peer-to-peer platforms, 381
Penetration rate, 434–435
Perceived Brand Globalness (PBG), 51
Perceived inauthenticity, 503
Perceived quality, 153
Perceived value, 154, 314–315
Perception related crisis, 259
Perceptual brand equity,
  brand associations, 153
  brand awareness, 154
  brand loyalty, 153
  key components of, 153
  perceived quality, 153
  perceived value, 154
Perceptual fluency, 87
Peres, R., 126
Peretz, A., 624, 628
Perfect information, 22
Performance related crisis, 259
Pergelova, A., 421
Perren, R., 377
Person-based names, 217
Personal branding, 293, 295
Personal introspection, 348–349
Personal values, 449, 455–456
Personality,
  approach, 25–26
  traits, 119
Personalization, 595
Persuasion Knowledge Model, 563
Persuasive brand management, 10
Pew Research Center, 495
Phau, I., 313
Phenomenological interviews, 346
Philanthropy, 477
Phonosemanticn translation, 220
Photo-elicitation, 346–347
Phygital marketing, 157
Physical brand presence, 318
Physical co-branding, 232
Physiological data, 345
Piehler, R., 393–396
Pilnick, G., 500
Pine, B. J., 133
Pink, C., 138
Pitt, C. S., 166
Plotkina, D., 124
Plummer, J., 26
Plural brand names, 223
Polarization, 251, 497–498
Policies, 168
Policy-makers, 378, 607
Political environments, 515
Popular brand, 105
Porter, M. E., 433, 512, 623
Positive brand relationship, 247, 252
Positive brand-related constructs, 309, 315
  antecedents of, 313
  behavioral constructs, 311–313
  behavioral outcomes, 315–316
  brand-related factors, 314–315
  brand-related moderators, 317
  cognitive constructs, 310–311
  contextual moderators, 317
  cultural differences, 318
  digital *vs.* physical brand presence, 318
  emotional constructs, 309–310
  emotional outcomes, 315
  future research directions, 318
  incorporating negative constructs, 319
  individual-level moderators, 316–317
  interaction between constructs, 318
  longitudinal studies on dynamic interactions, 318
  moderators of, 316
  needs satisfaction, 313–314
  psychological drivers, 313
  relational outcomes, 316
  role of emerging technologies, 318–319
  self-congruence, 313
  social and community influences, 315
  theoretical framework, 314*f*
  validation across brand types, 318

Positive emotions, 315
Positive reputation, 104
Positive sentiment ratio, 383
Positivity, 486
Positron emission tomography (PET), 348
Post-crisis analysis, 263
Postmodern perspective, 448
Posts, 167
Practice, 623–626
Practitioners, 600
Predictive AI, 78
Predictive analytics, 541, 543, 589
Predictive crisis analytics, 264
Preference data, 342
Premium, 275
    blurring boundaries between luxury and fashion and premium strategies, 278–279, 278*f*
Preventable crises, 260, 263, 265
Price, L. L., 375
Price index, 434
Price premium, 411
Pricing, 71, 469, 471
Primary communication, 43, 182
Primary experimental designs, 350
Print advertising, 76
Prism, 38, 100
Privacy, 265
    capitalism, 543
Proactive approach, 294
Processing fluency theory, 87–88
Procter & Gamble (P&G), 3–6, 208
Product brand SR, 470, 476
    antecedents and outcomes of product brand SR, 471–473
    brand social responsibility, 472*t*
    definition, conceptualization and measurement, 470–471
    product brand SR as mediator and moderator, 473
    reciprocal effects of, 476
Product branding, 24, 290
Product brands, 39, 290, 470
Product education, 71
Product-level characteristics, 58
Product management system, 5
Product manager, 5
Product-market indicators, 403
Product-market level BPIs, 409–411
Product-related factors, 477
Product SR, 469–470
Promissory communication, 182
Prompted awareness, 432
Pronunciation and language differences, 70
Prosumer, 21
Proto-corporate brands, 35
Proximity, 74
Pseudohomophone brand names, 218
Psychological perspective, 28, 447
Public criticism, 449
Public movements, 497
Public relations (PR), 264, 558
Pueyo, S., 598
Punjaisri, K., 396
Purchase intentions, 316, 405
Purchase share, 433–434
Purpose, 622

Quach, S., 381
Qualitative approaches for EBBE research, 168–169
Qualitative data collection, 611
Qualitative methods, 575
Qualitative research, 240, 430
    methodologies, 300
Qualitative stage, 524
Qualitative studies, 558
Quantitative data, 28
    collection, 611
Quantitative research, 430
    methodologies, 300
Quantitative scales, 361–363
Quantitative techniques, 346
Quantity premium, 410
Quasi-experiments, 350
Quaternary communication, 43, 182
Quinton, S., 10

Race, 612
Rahman, M. S., 157
Rai, A., 597
Rajavi, K., 152
Ramaswamy, V., 188
Ranfagni, S., 125
Rapidity, 497
Razmus, W., 523
Real brand value, 21
Real-time adaptability, 595
Red Bull Racers, 573
Regional sensitivity, 263
Rego, L. L., 433, 437
Regression analysis, 558
Regret theory, 332
Regulatory complexity, 622
Reilly, M. D., 375
Reimagined packaging, 75
Relational approach, 26–27, 30
Relational resources, 413
Relationship(s), 99
    building, 292
    quality, 292
    violations, 250
Relative market share, 434
Reliability, 457
Repeat purchase rate, 437–438
Republic of China (ROC), 70
Reputation, 104–105
    role in B2B buying, 105–107

Reputational resources, 413
Research,
methodologies, 61
new contexts for, 156
Research Institute of Sweden (RiSE), 627
Resource acquisition, 513
Resourcefulness, 299
Resource-market indicators, 404, 415
Resource-market level, emerging BPIs at, 413
Response latency techniques, 348
Responsibility, 453
Responsory communication, 182–183
Retailers, 621
Retention, 297
rate, 384, 438
Return-on-assets (ROA), 412
Return-on-equity (ROE), 412
Reveal, Examine, Diagnose, Select, Strategy ($REDS^2$), 185
Revenue premium, 410
Richard Wohl, R., 561
Riefler, P., 138
Rindell, A., 624
Risk, 412, 620
Risk-taking, 293
Robust brand equity, 155
Rode, V., 99–102
corporate identity model, 101
holistic approach to corporate branding, 101*f*
Rodrigues, C., 315
Rodrigues, P., 315
Rodriguez, R., 455
Role of brand index (RBI), 418
Romani, S., 455
Romantic brand jealousy, 326
Rosado-Pinto, F., 135–137, 141
Rossi, S., 363
Roy, S. K., 156, 361
Rubicam's brand asset valuator, 417
Rudkowski, J., 165, 169
Rust, R. T., 441, 590, 598
Ryder, I., 624

Sahaf, T. M., 157
Saleem, F. Z., 390
Sales decline from negative campaigns, 384
Salvi, F., 591
Sama, R., 315
Samu, S., 235
Sands, S., 566
Sankaran, R., 156
Sapir, E., 214
Saraniemi, S., 112–113, 112*f*
Sarkar, C., 495
Sarwar, M., 151
Sayin, E., 56, 58
Scalability, 419
and managing growth, 298–299
Schema congruity theory, 234, 236
Schloss, I., 213
Schmidt-Devlin, E., 60
Schnebelen, S., 528, 315, 523–524, 526
Schouten, J. W., 246, 375
Schultz, M., 23, 38, 185–186
management/organisational behaviour approach of, 185–186
Schulz, S. A., 396
Science Based Targets initiative (SBTi), 621
Scientific tradition, 19
Scopus, 149, 149*t*
Secondary communication, 43, 182
Segmentation by age and generational cohorts, 605–606
Segmentation model, 605
Segmenting consumers, 605
Self-brand connection, 316, 457
Self-brand integration, 249
Self-categorisation theory, 179–180
Self-congruence, 154, 313
Self-congruity theory, 120
Self-efficacy, 591–592
Self-pleasing experience, 528
Semantic names, 218
Senechal, S., 234
Sensory approach, 28–29
Sentiment,
analysis, 364, 542–543, 558, 596
brand relationships types based on level of, 248–250, 249*f*
Seraj, M., 380
Service brand names, 217
Service-dominant logic (SDL), 147, 356
Sexual orientations, 483
Sexuality, 612
Shahrokhi, M., 148
SHapley Additive exPlanations (SHAP), 267
Share in handlers, 436
Share-in-shops handling (SISH), 436–437
Share-of-requirements, 435–436
Share-of-wallet (SOW), 431, 435–436
Shareholder primacy, 620
model, 623
perspective, 625
Shareholders, 626
Sharp, B., 440
Shee, P. S. B., 23
Sheth, J. N., 511
Shimul, A. S., 311, 313
Shobeiri, S., 122
Siddiqui, D. A., 151
Signalling theory, 54, 127, 234, 483
Simple logo design, 90
Singh, J., 566
Situational crisis communication theory (SCCT), 259–260
Skålén, P., 380–381
Skepticism, 495, 515

Small and medium-sized enterprises (SMEs), 4, 109–110, 293
network actors' participation in SME B2B branding, 111*f*
Smart marketer, 72
Smith, A., 22, 622
Smith, D., 166–167
Smith, W., 605
Social anxiety, 325
Social Cognitive Theory, 591
Social comparison theory, 331
Social connectedness, 380
Social elements, 573
Social experiences, 615
Social identity, 179–180, 331
Social Identity Theory (STI), 329, 332, 483–484, 490
Social impact, 452
Social inequality, 458
Social influences, 315
theory, 329, 331–332
Social interaction, brand as pivotal point of, 27
Social isolation, 610
Social media, 121, 127, 165–166, 261, 295, 346, 355–356, 360, 375, 497–498, 509, 516, 556, 571, 578
algorithms, 4
analytics platforms, 283
case example, 486–487
channel selection, 262
communication, 123
context, 364
crises, 260
crisis communication in, 268
data for EBBE research, 168–169
disability representation and storytelling on, 485–486
dynamics, 259
EBBE on, 166–167
employee-generated content on, 167–168
engagement, 75
era, 561
influencers, 166–167, 312, 366, 518, 557–558, 561–562
listening, 543
Lolo Spencer and cultural destigmatisation of disability on, 486–487, 487*f*
marketing strategies, 610
platforms, 9, 122–123, 485, 497, 504, 557–558, 592, 613
Social-mediated crisis communication (SMCC), 261
Social network, 578
mining methods, 405
Social organizations, 517
Social psychology drivers, 591–592
Social responsibility (SR), 449, 455, 467–468
brand SR, 468–469
corporate, brand and product, 470*t*
corporate SR, 468
product SR, 469–470
Social sciences, 521
Social signaling, category, 58–59
Social tags, 419
Social theory, 377
Social transformation, 626
Social value, 512, 523
Societal pressure, 621
Society, significance of brand morality in, 448–449
Socio-cultural artefacts, 485
Socio-cultural contexts, 496
Socio-cultural issues, xxiii
Soft skills, 11
Solar energy systems, 626
Sole brand users (SBUs), 438
Soleimani, M., 396
Sound symbolism in brand names, 214–217
Source Credibility Theory, 560
Sousa, A., 523
Sousa, B., 168–169, 397
South Africa, exporting AmEx brand to, 76
Spears, B., 610
Spencer, L., 486–487
Spielmann, N., 60
Spiggle, S., 138
Sponsoring model, 511
Spontaneous awareness, 432
Spörl-Wang, K., 560, 563
Spotify, 232, 594
Srinivasan, S., 411, 431
Srinivasan, V., 411
Srivastava, A., 138
Staff engagement and alignment, 512
Stakeholder(s), 33, 39, 179, 260–261, 266, 327, 496, 510, 512, 514, 556–557, 619, 621
alignment, 263
expectations, 262
mapping, 263
navigating stakeholder complexity, 516
perspective, 625
and speed, 261
trust, 43, 177
Stanley, V., 622
Status consumption, 360
Steenkamp, J. B. E., 51–52
Stereotype, 607, 610
Stereotype Content Model (SCM), 59
Stereotyping of older consumers, 606–608
Stigma theory, 483–484, 490
Stock returns, 412
Storytelling, 484–485, 517
on social media, 485–486
Strategic branding, 518
Strategic communication, 510
Strauss, W., 605
Strizhakova, Y., 54, 58
Strong brands, 245, 290
relationships, 248
Strong positive relationships, 248

Strongly agree, 312–313
Strongly disagree, 312–313
Study brand personality,
digital-based methods to, 124–126
survey-based and content-based research approaches to, 125*t*
Stuth, K., 311
Sub-brands, 187
Subjective well-being, 523
Substantial purchases, 433
Suggestive names, 218
Sullivan, Y., 11
Super Mario Bros®, 575
Supermarket partnerships, 456
Supply chains, 621
management, 589
Supporting theories, 19
Surveillance capitalism, 543
Survey-based approaches, 126
Survey data, 341
Surveys, 349–350
Sustainability, 156, 284, 452, 458, 620
Sustainable business, 590
Sustainable Development Goals, 482, 621
Sustainable practices, 284
Swoboda, B., 60
Symbolic brand relationship, 248
Symbolic co-branding, 232
Symbolic value, 276–277
Synesthetic names, 218
Systematic risk, 412
Szymanski, D. M., 433

Takamatsu, S., 316
Tanwar, A. S., 558
Tarnovskaya, V., 39
Tasci, A. D. A., 148
Tavassoli, N. T., 164, 169
Tax, S. S., 149
Technological advancements, 349
Technological augmentation, 537
Technological changes, 29
Technology, 114, 338, 381, 539, 542, 608
market, 607
strategic role of technology in brand management, 539
Technology acceptance model (TAM), 591
Technology-augmented brand management,
AI-powered creative development, 540–541
connected brand ecosystems, 541–542
data-driven brand innovation, 541
ethical implications of technology in brand management, 543–544
frame work, 538*f*
immersive brand experiences, 541
innovation process transformation, 542
opportunities, recommendations and future questions, 545*t*–550*t*
opportunities and future recommendations, 544
technology in branding, 538–540
technology-enabled brand innovation, 540
technology's impact on brand equity, 542–543
Tedlow, R. S., 6
Television, 76
programs, 557
Template libraries, 77
Tertiary communication, 182
Tesco, 621
Text mining, 341–342
Thaichon, P., 381
Theory of Cognitive Dissonance (TCD), 591
Theory of Planned Behavior, 591
Thinking AI, 9, 11, 593–595, 597–598
for brand personalization, 593–594
Thomas, V. L., 558
Thomson, M., 311
Tian, K. T., 316
TikTok, 165–167, 284, 377, 558
Tocquer, G., 396
Top-of-the-mind awareness (TOMA), 432
Torelli, C. J., 58
Törmälä, M., 107, 108*f*, 109–110, 112–113, 112*f*
Torres, P., 120, 562
Total Corporate Brand Communications, 182
corporate brand formation and significance of, 39–44
Total corporate communications, 43
Tourism, 156–157
context, 139
Townsend, J. D., 8
Traditionalism, 279, 282
Traditional marketing, 178–179
brand as part of, 22–23
Traditional media figures, 562
Traditional shareholder model, 626
Traditional survey-based measurement approaches, 126
Training branding, 511
Transaction uncertainty, 105
Transactional effectiveness, 559
Transactional outcomes, 560
Transparency, 263, 265, 467, 533, 565
capability, 542
Transparent authenticity, 563
Transparent data collection systems, 599
Trans-parasocial relationships, 561
Trial rate, 435
Tripartite brand architecture approach, 187
Trivedi, J., 315
Trump, D., 495
Trunfio, M., 363
Trust, 295
building, 292
Trusted crisis leadership, pathway to, 267
Trustworthiness, 560

Tsai, C. T. S., 315
Turing, A. M., 589
Tuunanen, T., 381
Twitter, 349, 366

Uhling, C. C., 5
Unaided awareness, 432
Unethical labor practices, 458
Uniqueness moderates, need for, 316–317
Unpredictability, 566
UN Sustainable Development Solutions Network (SDSN), 521
Unsystematic risk, 412
Urde, M., 509
User-generated content (UGC), 156, 373, 382
Utilitarian perspective, 447

Vaidyanathan, R., 236
Validity, 623–626
Vallaster, C., 99–102, 511, 624
 corporate identity model, 101
 holistic approach to corporate branding, 101*f*
Vallerand, R. J., 309
Value, 623–626
 co-creation, 373–374, 386
 co-destruction, 386
 related crisis, 259
Van Boven, L., 522
Vanden Bergh, B., 213–214
Van Ewijk, B., 409
Vargo, S. L., 155
Verhoef, P. C., 441
Verma, P., 316
Vertical co-branding, 232
Viable relationship partner, brand as, 26–27
Victim crises, 260
Victim related crisis, 259
Victim-type crisis, 260
Virtual assistants, 592, 595
Virtual brand spaces, 541
Virtual crisis training and simulation, 265
Virtual influencers (VIs), 566
Virtual Private Network (VPN), 68
Virtual reality (VR), 124, 156, 283, 318, 339, 399, 516, 540, 575
Virtue ethics perspectives, 452–453
Vision-driven leadership, 298
Visual brand identity, 90–91
Visual data, 419
Von Wallpach, S., 511
Voss, K. E., 311
Vowel-less brand names, 218
Vrontis, D., 558, 562

Wallendorf, M., 375
Walmart, 621
Walsh, G., 421
Wang, M., 90
Wang, N., 135, 137
Wang, Y. C., 315
Wartick, S. L., 105
Washburn, J. H., 234
Water scarcity, 623
Wealth, 612
Web 2.0, 156
Web of Science (WoS), 149, 149*t*, 523
Websites, 122
 analysis, 343–344
Weibo, 592
Weighted distribution, 436
Weighted Satisfaction Index (WSI), 437
Weiner, B., 236
Weiss, M., 137
Whetten, D. A., 42
Williams, S., 315
Wilson, A., 396
Wilson, J. A., 624
Winit, W., 60
Winning through focus, 75
Woke washing, 483, 496–497
#womensupportingwomen, 487
Word-based names, 218
Word-of-mouth (WOM), 310, 610
 intentions and referrals, 361
Wordmark logos, 86
World Health Organization (WHO), 516
World Travel & Tourism Council (WTTC), 73
World War II, 5–6
World Wide Web, 9
World Wildlife Fund (WWF), 509, 621
Wu, J. F., 124, 156
Wu, L., 216
Wymer, W., 135
Wynstra, F., 291

Xie, L., 157
Xie, Y., 54
Xu, H., 394

Yağız, K., 152
Yang, C., 124
Yang, D. Y. J., 61
Yang, J., 138
Ye, G., 558
Yi, J., 138
Yoo, B., 148–149, 151–152, 154–155, 162, 312
 model, 152–153
Yorkston, E., 216
You, Y., 439
Youn, S., 124
Young brand asset valuator, 417
Younger consumers, 606, 610
 skew for marketers to develop new products for, 610–611
Younger people, 606
YouTube, 557, 558

Zaltman, G., 347
Zaltman Metaphor-Elicitation Technique (ZMET), 347–348
Zarantonello, L., 153
Zebal, M. A., 138
Zelenskaya, E., 199
Zeplin, S., 396
Zero-tolerance mindset, 262
Zhang, H., 394
Zhang, M., 137
Zhou, F., 315
Zhu, T., 379
Zwick, D., 377